Global Burden of Disease and Risk Factors

Global Burden of Disease and Risk Factors

Editors

Alan D. Lopez

Colin D. Mathers

Majid Ezzati

Dean T. Jamison

Christopher J. L. Murray

A copublication of Oxford University Press and The World Bank

©2006 The International Bank for Reconstruction and Development / The World Bank
1818 H Street NW
Washington DC 20433
Telephone: 202-473-1000
Internet: www.worldbank.org
E-mail: feedback@worldbank.org

1 2 3 4 09 08 07 06

A copublication of The World Bank and Oxford University Press.

Oxford University Press
165 Madison Avenue
New York NY 10016

This volume was funded in part by a grant from the Bill & Melinda Gates Foundation and is a product of the staff of the International Bank for Reconstruction and Development / The World Bank, the World Health Organization, and the Fogarty International Center of the National Institutes of Health. The findings, interpretations, and conclusions expressed in this volume do not necessarily reflect the views of the executive directors of The World Bank or the governments they represent, the World Health Organization, or the Fogarty International Center of the National Institutes of Health.

ISBN-10: 0-8213-6262-3
ISBN-13: 978-0-8213-6262-4
eISBN: 0-8213-6263-1
DOI: 10.1596/978-0-8213-6262-4

Library of Congress Cataloguing-in-Publication Data has been applied for.

This book is dedicated to the memory of Sir Richard Doll, Fellow of the Royal Society (born Hampton, United Kingdom, October 28, 1912; died Oxford, United Kingdom, July 24, 2005). It is entirely fitting that an assessment of world health at the end of the 20th century should be dedicated to the memory of a man whose work did so much to improve it.

Contents

List of Tables

Foreword

"Every observer of human misery among the poor reports that disease plays the leading role." Irving Fisher (1909, p. 124)[1]

Before 1990, the global disease landscape was perceived "through a glass darkly." Mortality conditions by cause of death were known with some precision only for the relatively small minority of the world's population residing in countries with adequate vital statistics. Nowhere were estimates of disease incidence, prevalence, survival, and disabling sequelae consistently combined into population-level profiles of morbidity and mortality.

Publication of the *Global Burden of Disease* (1990) was a watershed event in the assessment of health and disease. Through careful synthesis of disease conditions revealed in thousands of piecemeal studies and data systems, it constructed a comprehensive portrait of diseases, injuries, and causes of death. It dealt creatively and carefully with the hundreds of issues that had to be addressed to develop useful, broadly gauged indicators of health. These included establishing terms of trade among disabling conditions, among age groups and generations, and between the living and the dead. At all points that offered tempting shortcuts, the authors decided in favor of comprehensiveness.

Like the microscope, the *Global Burden of Disease* (1990) brought diseases into much sharper focus. Like national income accounts, it connected parts to a whole and measured the whole with unprecedented precision. As a sophisticated measuring device, it could not be ignored by any serious student of epidemiology or development. One might have experimented with its calibrations, but the device itself was irreplaceable.

However, the value of a measuring device lies in its measurements, not in its abstract qualities on the shelf. The world

has changed dramatically since 1990, and we must be grateful for the fresh assessment of disease conditions presented in this volume. The picture that it paints is not only updated; it is also more precise. Better data have become available through expanded vital statistics systems, improved surveys, and more extensive population surveillance systems. The measurement instrument has also been improved. Most notably, a critical new layer of physical risk factors and their distribution has been added, providing valuable new tools for policy makers.

This second application of the global burden of disease framework permits an analysis of trends observed since the first application. The intervening period was clearly one of slow progress, impeded by the HIV/AIDS epidemic and setbacks in Eastern Europe. The volume is appropriately cautious in drawing inferences about disease-specific trends because of changes in data sources and, in some instances, improvements in approaches to measurement.

The volume also contains a valuable and admirably frank chapter on the sensitivity of estimates to various sources of uncertainty in methods and data. Some estimates are found to have wide bands of uncertainty. While this outcome is disappointing, uncertainty about the burden of disease in all its dimensions—including the degree of uncertainty itself—would be much greater without the heroic efforts reflected in this volume.

My congratulations to the authors and the sponsoring agencies.

Samuel H. Preston, *Fredrick J. Warren Professor of Demography, University of Pennsylvania*

---

[1]Irving Fisher. 1909. *Report on National Vitality, Its Wastes and Conservation.* Prepared for the National Conservation Commission. Washington, DC: Government Printing Office.

Preface

This book emerges from two separate, but intersecting, strands of work that began in the late 1980s, when the World Bank initiated a review of priorities for the control of specific diseases. The review generated findings about the comparative cost-effectiveness of interventions for most diseases important in developing countries. The purpose of the cost-effectiveness analysis (CEA) was to inform decision making within the health sectors of highly resource-constrained countries. This process resulted in the publication of the first edition of *Disease Control Priorities in Developing Countries* (Jamison and others 1993). Also important for informing policy is a consistent, quantitative assessment of the relative magnitudes of diseases, injuries, and their risk factors. The first edition of *Disease Control Priorities in Developing Countries* included an initial assessment of health status for low- and middle-income countries as measured by deaths from specific causes; importantly, the numbers of cause-specific deaths for each age-sex group were constrained by the total number of deaths as estimated by demographers. This consistency constraint led to downward revision of the estimates of deaths from many diseases.

These two strands of work—CEA and burden of disease—were further developed during preparation of the *World Development Report 1993: Investing in Health* (World Bank 1993). This report drew on both the CEA work in the first edition of *Disease Control Priorities in Developing Countries* and on a growing academic literature on CEA. In addition, the World Bank invested in generating improved estimates of deaths and the disease burden by age, cause, and region for 1990. Results of this initial assessment of the global burden of disease appeared both in the *World Development Report 1993* and widely in the academic literature (see, for example, Murray and Lopez 1996a, 1996b; Murray, Lopez, and Jamison 1994). Over the past six years, the World Health Organization has undertaken a new assessment of the global burden of disease for 2000–2, with consecutive revisions and updates published annually in its *World Health Reports*. The World Health Organization has also invested in improving the conceptual, methodological, and empirical basis of burden of disease assessments and the assessment of the disease and injury burden from major risk factors (Ezzati and others 2004; Murray and others 2002; World Health Organization 2002).

In 2002, a number of organizations—the Fogarty International Center of the U.S. National Institutes of Health, the World Bank, the World Health Organization, and the Bill & Melinda Gates Foundation—initiated the Disease Control Priorities Project (DCPP), located at the Fogarty International Center. The DCPP's purpose has been to review, generate, and disseminate information that contributes to the scientific evidence base for improving population health in developing countries. A major product is the second edition of *Disease Control Priorities in Developing Countries* (DCP2) (Jamison and others 2006), which updates and extends available CEA relevant to developing countries and explores the institutional, organizational, financial, and research capabilities essential for health systems to be able to select and deliver the appropriate interventions.

DCP2 was to have included two major chapters on burden, one dealing with deaths and the disease burden by cause and the other with the burden from major risk factors. Two points quickly became clear. First, even though *DCP2* had allocated substantial space for these chapters, much valuable background, methodology, and results still had to be relegated to a separate document on the Web. Second, this material would generate substantial interest independently of its tie to *DCP2*, because health system activities, including the choice of interventions, depend partly on the magnitude of health problems, and because assessment of the burden of diseases, injuries, and risk factors includes important methodological and empirical dimensions. The sponsors of the DCPP therefore decided to publish this volume, which includes a full account of methods, the complete results of recent work, and an assessment of trends for total mortality and for major causes of death among children under five along with two chapters that cover sensitivity and uncertainty analyses in relation to a broad range of potentially important parameters.

During 1999–2004, the authors of this volume and many collaborators from around the world worked intensively to assemble an updated, comprehensive assessment of the global burden of disease and its causes. This book provides the definitive, scientific account of that effort and of the health conditions of the world's population at the beginning of the 21st century.

Both *DCP2* and this book are available on the DCPP Web site (http://www.dcp2.org), as well as through the National Library of Medicine's PubMedCentral. From the DCPP Web site, users can download individual chapters or create an ad hoc group of chapters formatted for printing booklets or course packets. We encourage users to construct variants of the book most suited to their work or their teaching. The DCPP Web site also allows access to Excel versions of all global burden of disease tables so that users can freely reanalyze the data to meet their own needs.

REFERENCES

Ezzati, M., A. D. Lopez, A. Rodgers, and C. J. L. Murray. 2004. *Comparative Quantification of Health Risks: The Global and Regional Burden of Disease Attributable to Selected Major Risk Factors.* Geneva: World Health Organization.

Jamison, D. T., J. G. Breman, A. R. Measham, G. Alleyne, M. Claeson, D. B. Evans, P. Jha, A. Mills, and P. Musgrove, eds. 2006. *Disease Control Priorities in Developing Countries,* 2nd ed. New York: Oxford University Press.

Jamison, D. T., W. H. Mosley, A. R. Measham and J. L. Bobadilla, eds. 1993. *Disease Control Priorities in Developing Countries.* New York: Oxford University Press.

Murray, C. J. L,. and A. D. Lopez, eds. 1996a. *The Global Burden of Disease.* Cambridge, MA: Harvard University Press.

———. 1996b. *Global Health Statistics: A Compendium of Incidence. Prevalence, and Mortality Estimates for over 200 Conditions* Cambridge, MA: Harvard University Press.

Murray, C. J. L., A. D. Lopez, and D. T. Jamison. 1994. The Global Burden of Disease in 1990: Summary Results, Sensitivity Analysis, and Future Directions." In *Global Comparative Assessments in the Health Sector: Disease Burden, Expenditures, and Intervention Packages,* eds. C. J. L. Murray and A. D. Lopez, 97–138. Geneva: World Health Organization.

Murray, C. J. L, J. A. Salomon, C. D. Mathers, and A. D. Lopez. 2002. *Summary Measures of Population Health: Concepts, Ethics, Measurement, and Applications.* Geneva: World Health Organization.

World Bank. 1993. *World Development Report 1993: Investing in Health.* New York: Oxford University Press.

World Health Organization. 2002. *Reducing Risks: Promoting Healthy Life. World Health Report 2002.* Geneva: World Health Organization.

Editors

Alan D. Lopez is professor of medical statistics and population health and Head of the School of Population Health at the University of Queensland, Australia. Prior to joining the university in January 2003, he worked for 22 years at the World Health Organization in Geneva, where he held a series of technical and senior managerial posts, including chief epidemiologist in the Tobacco Control Program (1992–5), manager of the Program on Substance Abuse (1996–8), director of the Epidemiology and Burden of Disease Unit (1999–2001), and senior science adviser to the director-general (2002).

Professor Lopez has published widely on mortality analysis and causes of death, including the impact of the global tobacco epidemic, and on the global descriptive epidemiology of major diseases, injuries, and risk factors. He is the coauthor of the seminal *Global Burden of Disease Study* (1996), which has greatly influenced debates about priority setting and resource allocation in health. He has been awarded major research grants in epidemiology, health services research, and population health; chairs the Health and Medical Research Council of Queensland; and is a member of Australia's Medical Services Advisory Committee.

Professor Lopez graduated with an honors degree in mathematics from the University of Western Australia in 1973 and a master of science degree in statistics from Purdue University in the United States. He was awarded a Ph.D. in medical demography from the Australian National University in 1979. His principal research interests are analysis of mortality data; burden of disease methods and applications; and quantification of the health effects of tobacco, particularly in developing countries. He has collaborated extensively with leading researchers throughout the world on these issues, particularly at Harvard and Oxford universities, and he holds an adjunct appointment at Harvard University as professor of population and international health.

Colin D. Mathers is a senior scientist in the Evidence and Information for Policy Cluster at the World Health Organization in Geneva. From 2002 to 2005, he managed the World Health Organization's Epidemiology and Burden of Disease Unit. Prior to joining the World Health Organization in 2000, he worked for the Australian Institute of Health and Welfare for 13 years in technical and senior managerial posts.

Dr. Mathers has published widely on population health and mortality analysis; on inequalities in health, health expectancies, and burden of disease; and on health system costs and performance. He developed the first set of Australian health accounts mapping health expenditures by age, sex, and disease and injury causes (1998) and carried out an influential national burden of disease and risk factors study (1999). At the World Health Organization, he played a key role in the development of comparable estimates of healthy life expectancy for 192 countries, in the reassessment of the global burden of disease for the years 2000–2, and in the development of software tools to support burden of disease analysis at the country level. He recently completed new projections of global, regional, and country mortality and burden of disease from 2002 to 2030.

Dr. Mathers graduated with an honors degree and university medal in physics from the University of Sydney in 1975 and was awarded a Ph.D. in theoretical physics from the University of Sydney in 1979. His principal research interests are the measurement and reporting of population health and its determinants, burden of disease methods and applications, measurement of health state prevalences, and cross-population comparability. He has collaborated with leading researchers throughout the world on issues relating to the development and applications of summary measures of population health.

Majid Ezzati is an assistant professor of international health at the Harvard School of Public Health. He holds bachelor's and master's degrees in engineering from McMaster and McGill Universities and a Ph.D. in science, technology, and environmental policy from Princeton University. Dr. Ezzati's research interests center around understanding the causal determinants of health and disease, especially as they change in the process of social and economic development and as a result of technological innovation and technology management.

His current research focuses on two main areas. The first area is the relationship among energy, air pollution, and health in developing countries, on which he conducts field research projects in Asia and sub-Saharan Africa. This research has led to the identification and design of technological interventions for reducing exposure to indoor air pollution from household energy use. His second area of research is major health risk factors and their role in the current and future disease burden globally and in specific countries and regions. His research on risk factors focuses on environmental risks, smoking, and nutritional risks. He was the lead scientist for the World Health Organization's Comparative Risk Assessment Project, which was reported in the *World Health Report 2002: Reducing Health, Promoting Healthy Life*. He is currently studying the role of major risk factors in health inequalities.

Dean T. Jamison is a professor of health economics in the School of Medicine at the University of California, San Francisco (UCSF), and an affiliate of UCSF Global Health Sciences. Dr. Jamison concurrently serves as an Adjunct Professor in both the Peking University Guanghua School of Management and in the University of Queensland School of Population Health.

Before joining UCSF, Dr. Jamison was on the faculty of the University of California, Los Angeles, and also spent a number of years at the World Bank, where he was a senior economist in the research department, division chief for education policy, and division chief for population, health, and nutrition. In 1992–93 he temporarily rejoined the World Bank to serve as Director of the World Development Report Office and as lead author for the Bank's 1993 *World Development Report: Investing in Health*. His publications are in the areas of economic theory, public health and education. Dr. Jamison studied at Stanford (B.A., Philosophy; M.S., Engineering Sciences) and at Harvard (Ph.D., Economics, under K.J. Arrow). In 1994 he was elected to membership in the Institute of Medicine of the U.S. National Academy of Sciences.

Christopher J. L. Murray is the Richard Saltonstall professor of public policy, professor of social medicine, and director of the Harvard Initiative for Global Health. Prior to his return to the university, for five years he led the World Health Organization's Evidence and Information for Policy Cluster, which was dedicated to building the evidence base and fostering a culture of evidence to inform health decision making. The cluster was responsible for work on epidemiology and the burden of disease, the World Health Survey, cost-effectiveness analysis, national health accounts, catastrophic health spending, responsiveness, health financing policy, human resources for health systems, coverage of health interventions, quality of care and patient safety, stewardship of health systems, assessment of health system performance, health research policy, and a range of efforts to manage and disseminate information through print and the Web.

A physician and health economist, Dr. Murray's early work focused on tuberculosis control and the development with Alan D. Lopez of global burden of disease methods and applications. During the course of this work, they developed a new metric for comparing deaths and disabilities caused by various diseases and the contribution of risk factors to the overall burden of disease in developing and developed countries. This pioneering effort has been hailed as a major landmark in public health and an important foundation for policy formulation and priority setting. Recently, Dr. Murray has contributed to the development of a range of new methods and empirical studies for strengthening the basis for population health measurement and cost-effectiveness analysis. A main thrust of his work has been the conceptualization, measurement, and application of approaches to understanding the inputs, organization, outputs, and outcomes of health systems. He has authored or edited eight books, many book chapters, and more than 90 journal articles in internationally peer-reviewed publications.

Dr. Murray holds a B.A. from Harvard College, a D. Phil. from Oxford University, and an M.D. from Harvard Medical School.

Advisory Committee to the Editors

J. R. Aluoch
Professor, Nairobi Women's Hospital, Nairobi, Kenya

Jacques Baudouy
Director, Health, Nutrition, and Population, World Bank, Washington, DC, United States

Fred Binka
Executive Director, INDEPTH Network, Accra, Ghana

Mayra Buvinić
Director, Gender and Development, World Bank, Washington, DC, United States

David Challoner, Co-chair
Foreign Secretary, Institute of Medicine, U.S. National Academies, Gainesville, Florida, United States

Guy de Thé, Co-chair
Research Director and Professor Emeritus, Institut Pasteur, Paris, France

Timothy Evans
Assistant Director General, Evidence and Information for Policy, World Health Organization, Geneva, Switzerland

Richard Horton
Editor, *The Lancet*, London, United Kingdom

Sharon Hrynkow
Acting Director, Fogarty International Center, National Institutes of Health, Bethesda, Maryland, United States

Gerald Keusch
Provost and Dean for Global Health, Boston University School of Public Health, Boston, Massachusetts, United States

Kiyoshi Kurokawa
President, Science Council of Japan, Kanawaga, Japan

Peter Lachmann
Past President, U.K. Academy of Medical Sciences, Cambridge, United Kingdom

Mary Ann Lansang
Executive Director, INCLEN Trust International, Inc., Manila, Philippines

Christopher Lovelace
Director, Kyrgyz Republic Country Office and Central Asia Human Development, World Bank, Bishkek, Kyrgyz Republic

Anthony Mbewu
Executive Director, Medical Research Council of South Africa, Tygerberg, South Africa

Rajiv Misra
Former Secretary of Health, Government of India, Haryana, India

Perla Santos Ocampo
President, National Academy of Science and Technology, San Juan, Philippines

G. B. A. Okelo
Secretary General and Executive Director, African Academy of Sciences, Nairobi, Kenya

Sevket Ruacan
General Director, MESA Hospital, Ankara, Turkey

Pramilla Senanayake
Chairman, Foundation Council of the Global Forum for Health Research, Colombo, Sri Lanka

Jaime Sepúlveda, Chair
Director, National Institutes of Health of Mexico, Mexico City, Mexico

Chitr Sitthi-amorn
Director, Institute of Health Research, Dean, Chulalongkorn University, College of Public Health, Bangkok, Thailand

Sally Stansfield
Associate Director, Global Health Strategies, Bill & Melinda Gates Foundation, Seattle, Washington, United States

Misael Uribe
President, National Academy of Medicine of Mexico, Mexico City, Mexico

Zhengguo Wang
Professor, Chinese Academy of Engineering, Daping, China

Witold Zatonski
Professor, Health Promotion Foundation, Warsaw, Poland

Contributors

Stephen J. Begg
University of Queensland

Eduard R. Bos
World Bank

Goodarz Danaei
Harvard School of Public Health; Harvard University
Initiative for Global Health

Majid Ezzati
Harvard School of Public Health; Harvard University
Initiative for Global Health

Dean T. Jamison
University of California, San Francisco; Disease Control
Priorities Project

Julian Jamison
University of California, Berkeley

Joy E. Lawn
Save the Children-USA, Institute of Child Health, London

Alan D. Lopez
University of Queensland; Harvard School of Public Health

Colin D. Mathers
World Health Organization

Christopher J. L. Murray
Harvard University Initiative for Global Health; Harvard
School of Public Health

Anthony Rodgers
University of Auckland

Joshua Salomon
Harvard School of Public Health

Sonbol A. Shahid-Salles
Population Reference Bureau; Disease Control Priorities
Project

Stephen Robert Vander Hoorn
University of Auckland

Jelka Zupan
World Health Organization

Disease Control Priorities Project Partners

The Disease Control Priorities Project is a joint enterprise of the Fogarty International Center of the National Institutes of Health, the World Health Organization, the World Bank, and the Population Reference Bureau.

The Fogarty International Center is the international component of the National Institutes of Health. It addresses global health challenges through innovative and collaborative research and training programs and supports and advances the mission of the National Institutes of Health through international partnerships.

The World Health Organization is the United Nations' specialized agency for health. Its objective, as set out in its constitution, is the attainment by all peoples of the highest possible level of health, with health defined as a state of complete physical, mental, and social well-being and not merely the absence of disease or infirmity.

The World Bank Group is one of the world's largest sources of development assistance. The Bank, which provides US$18 billion to $22 billion each year in loans to its client countries, provided $1.27 billion for health, nutrition, and population in 2004. The World Bank is working in more than 100 developing economies, bringing a mix of analytical work, policy dialogue, and lending to improve living standards—including health and education—and reduce poverty.

The Population Reference Bureau informs people around the world about health, population, and the environment and empowers them to use that information to advance the well-being of current and future generations. For 75 years, the bureau has analyzed complex data and research results to provide objective and timely information in a format easily understood by advocates, journalists, and decision makers; conducted workshops around the world to give key audiences the tools they need to understand and communicate effectively about relevant issues; and worked to ensure that developing country policy makers base policy decisions on sound evidence.

Acknowledgments

This volume brings together results of the work of many institutions and individuals spanning a period of more than 15 years. Several contributions to this process should be acknowledged. The Disease Control Priorities Project (DCPP) provided sponsorship for the specific work leading to this volume and for its publication. The DCPP itself resulted from collaboration among the following four institutions and benefited from the contributions of those institutions and the efforts of the responsible individuals within them:

- *The Fogarty International Center of the U.S. National Institutes of Health.* The FIC supported both the senior editor and one of the co-managing editors of this project, as well as support staff. FIC also provided office space for the secretariat and other administrative support. Gerald Keusch, former director of the FIC, initiated and facilitated this effort, and FIC's acting director, Sharon Hrynkow, continued to provide support and counsel.
- *The World Bank.* Successive directors of the World Bank's Health, Nutrition, and Population Department, Christopher Lovelace and Jacques Baudouy, provided support, guidance, and critical reactions and facilitated the involvement of Bank staff as coauthors and reviewers.
- *The World Health Organization.* Successive leaders of the Evidence and Information for Policy Cluster, Christopher Murray and Timothy Evans, coordinated the involvement of the World Health Organization. For much of the past eight years, the Evidence and Information for Policy Cluster has sponsored research and analysis central to this volume and we are particularly grateful for that support.
- *The Bill & Melinda Gates Foundation.* Richard Klausner, Sally Stansfield, and Beth Peterman arranged for the foundation to provide major financial support to the DCPP.

The DCPP was guided by a group of editors for its publication of the second edition of *Disease Control Priorities in Developing Countries.* The editors of this volume wish to thank the following for their inclusion of this book within the DCPP effort: George A. O. Alleyne, Joel G. Breman, Mariam Claeson, David B. Evans, Prabhat Jha, Anne Mills, Philip Musgrove, and, in particular, Anthony R. Measham.

We are grateful to the National Institute on Aging of the U.S. National Institutes of Health, which provided grant support for much of the research reported in this book under PO1–AG17625. Richard Suzman of the National Institute on Aging provided invaluable support and critical reactions.

We benefited from the strong collaboration with the InterAcademy Medical Panel (IAMP), an association of the medical academies or medical divisions of the scientific academies of 44 countries. David Challoner and Guy de Thé co-chaired the Steering Committee of the IAMP and invested much time and effort into facilitating the collaboration. The IAMP sponsored the peer review process for the chapters in this volume. The IAMP's second global meeting in Beijing in April 2006 included the launch of this volume, which was hosted by the Chinese Academies of Engineering and Science. The Institute of Medicine of the U.S. National Academy of Sciences, the U.S. member of the IAMP, played a critical role in facilitating all aspects of the IAMP's collaboration. Patrick Kelley and Dianne Stare of the Institute of Medicine managed this effort and provided critical, substantive inputs.

The Office of the Publisher at the World Bank provided outstanding assistance, enthusiastic advice, and support during every phase of production of this volume and helped coordinate publicity and initial distribution. We particularly wish to thank Dirk H. Koehler, the publisher, and Carlos Rossel, Mary Fisk, Randi Park, Santiago Pombo-Bejarano, Nancy Lammers, Alice Faintich, Nita Congress, Valentina Kalk, and Andrés Meneses for their timely, high-quality professionalism.

Donald Lindberg, director, and Julia Royall, chief, International Programs, of the National Library of Medicine of the U.S. National Institutes of Health, graciously offered the competent services of the Information Engineering Branch of the National Center for Biotechnology Information to convert the text into an electronic product available to all visitors to the National Library of Medicine's PubMed Web site. We would like to extend our gratitude to the National Center for Biotechnology Information team members—David Lipman, Jo McEntyre, Mohammad Al-Ubaydli, and Belinda Beck—for their technical expertise and commitment.

The Harvard Initiative for Global Health and the University of Queensland School of Population Health assisted with the production of chapters and hosted meetings in support of this effort, and we are grateful for their contributions and hospitality. We would like to thank Teri McGuane at Harvard University and Trish Sharkey and Kim Wicks at the University of Queensland for their valuable assistance.

Finally, we would like to acknowledge the critical role that Sonbol A. Shahid-Salles played in the creation of this book. She participated in all the meetings of the editors; she coordinated the peer review process, reacted critically to chapter content and presentation, and reviewed drafts and proofs; she interacted with the World Bank's Office of the Publisher on all aspects of production; and she kept the effort on its extremely tight time line in an environment where editors and authors were dispersed worldwide. The book simply could not have been completed without her efforts and we are very grateful indeed.

The Editors

Abbreviations and Acronyms

ALP	acquisition of life potential	HALE	health-adjusted life expectancy
CHERG	Child Health Epidemiology Reference Group	ICD	international classification of diseases
CRA	comparative risk assessment	IHD	ischemic heart disease
CVD	cardiovascular disease	PAF	population attributable fraction
DALY	disability-adjusted life year	TB	tuberculosis
DCP2	*Disease Control Priorities in Developing Countries,* second edition	UN	United Nations
		WHO	World Health Organization
DCPP	Disease Control Priorities Project	YLD	years of life lost due to disability
GBD	global burden of disease	YLL	years of life lost due to premature mortality
GDP	gross domestic product		

All dollar amounts are U.S. dollars unless otherwise indicated.

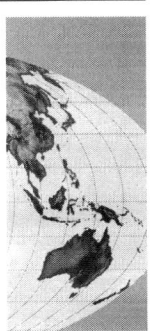

Chapter 1

Measuring the Global Burden of Disease and Risk Factors, 1990–2001

Alan D. Lopez, Colin D. Mathers, Majid Ezzati, Dean T. Jamison, and Christopher J. L. Murray

In an era when most societies must cope with increasing demand for health resources, they will inevitably have to make choices about the provision of health services, even if those choices are, by default, to continue current practices. Strategic health planning can accelerate health development and the attainment of health goals or reduce the cost of reaching such goals. Such planning must take into account the needs that the health system must address; that is, policy makers must be aware of the comparative burden of diseases and injuries and the risk factors that cause them, and how this burden is likely to change with the adoption of various policies and interventions. Needs are, of course, not the only factors determining service provision, but should be a critical component of the decision-making and planning processes.

The issue then becomes how to assess the comparative importance of risks to health and their outcomes in different demographic groups of the population. What is needed is a framework for integrating, validating, analyzing, and disseminating the fragmentary, and at times contradictory, information that is available on a population's health, along with some understanding of how that population's health is

changing, so that the information is more relevant for health policy and planning purposes. The Global Burden of Disease (GBD) framework is the principal, if not the only, attempt to do so. Features of the GBD framework include the incorporation of data on nonfatal health outcomes into summary measures of population health, the development of methods for assessing the reliability of data and imputing missing data, and the use of a common metric to summarize the disease burden from diagnostic categories of the International Classification of Diseases and the major risk factors that cause those health outcomes. Figure 1.1 presents a simplified version of this framework and indicates the causal chain of events that matter for health outcomes, identifying the key components and determinants of health status that require quantification.

Many countries and health development agencies have adopted the GBD approach as the standard for health accounting and for guiding the determination of health research priorities, for example, Australia (Mathers, Vos, and Stevenson 1999); the state of Andra Pradesh, India (Mahapatra 2002); Mauritius (Vos and others 1995); Mexico (Lozano and others 1995); South Africa (Bradshaw and

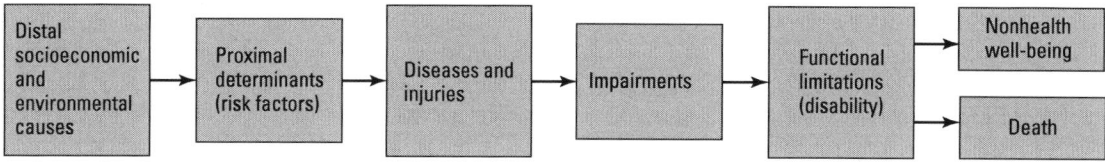

Source: Mathers and others 2002.

Note: This presentation is intended as a broad schema: for example, some exposures, such as environmental factors, can be proximate causes of disease, and injuries can lead directly to death.

Figure 1.1 Overview of Burden of Disease Framework

others 2003); Thailand (Bundhamcharoen and others 2002); Turkey (Baskent University 2005); the United States (McKenna and others 2005); and the World Health Organization (WHO 1996).

This chapter begins with a brief history of the work on burden of disease, including a discussion of the nature and origins of the disability-adjusted life year (DALY) as a measure of disease burden. Next it discusses applications of burden of disease analysis to the formulation of health policy. The chapter then summarizes the methods and findings of the 2001 GBD study, reported in more detail in chapters 3 and 4 of this volume. A concluding section takes stock of the work on disease burden since the early 1990s and suggests some key areas for further work.

Following this introductory and summarizing chapter, chapter 2 describes the demographic underpinnings for the epidemiological assessments that follow and provides context by briefly reviewing recent changes (from 1990 to 2001) in key demographic parameters. The chapter also assesses changes in the cause distribution of mortality among children under five between 1990 and 2001 and the difficulties of reliably assessing trends in mortality. Chapters 3 and 4 provide the definitive methods and results of the 2001 GBD study. Chapter 3 reports on deaths and the disease and injury burden by age, sex, and 136 disease and injury categories. Chapter 4 reports on the disease and injury burden resulting from 19 risk factors, specifically for a number of important conditions. Both chapters present results using the World Bank's classification of low- and middle-income countries into six regional groups. Chapter 5 then explores the robustness of the major findings to uncertainties in the data and to alternative assumptions concerning construction of the DALY. Chapter 6 examines the implications of including stillbirths in a global burden of disease assessment. Their inclusion is potentially significant, both because the numbers are large (3.3 million in 2001), and because including stillbirths raises major questions about how to assess the DALY loss associated with deaths near the time of birth.

HISTORY OF BURDEN OF DISEASE STUDIES

In 1992, the World Bank commissioned the initial GBD study to provide a comprehensive assessment of the disease burden in 1990. The study was undertaken for the world as a whole and for 8 regions (Lopez and Murray 1998; Murray and Lopez 1996a,d; Murray, Lopez, and Jamison 1994; World Bank 1993). In order to recommend intervention packages for countries at different stages of development, the estimates were combined with analyses of the cost-effectiveness of interventions in different populations (World Bank 1993; Jamison and Jardel 1994). Whereas earlier attempts to quantify global cause of death patterns (Hakulinen and others 1986; Lopez 1993) were valuable initial contributions to building the evidence base for policy, they were largely restricted to broad cause of death groups, for example, all infections and parasitic diseases combined, and did not address nonfatal health outcomes.

The methods and findings of the 1990 GBD study have been widely published and, as noted earlier, have spawned multiple disease burden exercises (Murray and Lopez 1996c,d; 1997a,b,c). One of the basic principles guiding a burden of disease assessment is that almost all sources of health data are likely to contain useful information provided they are carefully screened for validity and completeness. With appropriate methods, investigator commitment, and expert judgment, obtaining internally consistent estimates of the global descriptive epidemiology of major conditions is possible. To prepare internally consistent estimates of incidence, prevalence, duration, and mortality for almost 500 sequelae of the diseases and injuries under consideration, a mathematical model, DisMod, was developed for the 1990 GBD study to convert partial, often nonspecific, data on disease and injury occurrence into a consistent description of the basic epidemiological parameters in each region by age group (Barendregt and others 2003; Murray and Lopez 1996b).

Many diseases, for example, neuropsychiatric conditions and hearing loss, and injuries may cause considerable ill health but no or few direct deaths. Therefore separate

Disability-Adjusted Life Years

The DALY is a health gap measure that extends the concept of potential years of life lost due to premature death to include equivalent years of healthy life lost by virtue of individuals being in states of poor health or disability (Murray 1996). One DALY can be thought of as one lost year of healthy life and the burden of disease as a measure of the gap between current health status and an ideal situation where everyone lives into old age free from disease and disability. This conceptualization of DALYs as a measure of health, and not of lost utility, is analogous to the principles of measuring gross domestic product as summarized by Eisner (1989, p. 7): "Our focus . . . is on measures of all economic activity related to welfare [for example, gross domestic product], but not of welfare itself." Information on calculating DALYs, on time discounting, and on age weights is provided in chapter 3.

DALYs for a disease or health condition are calculated as the sum of YLL in the population and YLD for incident cases of the health condition. YLL is calculated from the number of deaths at each age multiplied by a global standard life expectancy for the age at which death occurs. To estimate YLD for a particular cause for a particular time period, the number of incident cases in that period is multiplied by the average duration of the disease and a weight factor that reflects the severity of the disease on a scale from 0 (perfect health) to 1 (dead). The weights used in the 2001 GBD study are listed in detail elsewhere (see annex tables 3A.6 to 3A.8 in chapter 3).

In addition, in calculating DALYs, the GBD study used 3 percent time discounting and non-uniform age weights which give less weight to years lived at young and older ages. For the results reported in this volume and used in the *Disease Control Priorities in Developing Countries*, second edition (DCP2) 3 percent time discounting was applied but not non-uniform age weights. A death in infancy then corresponds to 30 DALYs, and deaths at age 20 to around 28 DALYs. Thus a disease burden of 3,000 DALYs in a population would be the equivalent of around 100 infant deaths or to approximately 5,000 persons aged 50 years living one year with blindness (disability weight 0.6).

measures of survival and of health status among survivors, while useful inputs when formulating health policy, need to be combined in some fashion to provide a single, holistic measure of overall population health. To assess the burden of disease, the 1990 GBD study used a time-based metric that measures both premature mortality (years of life lost because of premature mortality or YLL) and disability (years of healthy life lost as a result of disability or YLD, weighted by the severity of the disability). The sum of the two components, namely, DALYs, provides a measure of the future stream of healthy life (years expected to be lived in full health) lost as a result of the incidence of specific diseases and injuries in 1990 (box 1.1). The effect of fatal cases (of disease or injury) is captured by years of life lost, while YLD captures the future health consequences in terms of sequelae of diseases or injuries of incident cases in 1990 that were not fatal. (For a more complete account of the DALY measure and the philosophy underlying parameter choices, see Murray 1996; Murray, Salomon, and others 2002).

DALYs are not unique to the GBD study. The World Bank used a variant of DALYs in its seminal review of health sector priorities (Jamison and others 1993), and they are derived from earlier work to develop time-based measures that better reflect the public health impact of death or illness at young ages (Dempsey 1947; Ghana Health Assessment Project Team 1981).

Much of the comment on, and criticism of, the GBD study focused on the construction of DALYs (Anand and Hanson 1998; Hyder, Rotllant, and Morrow 1998; Williams 1999), particularly the social choices pertaining to age weights and severity scores for disabilities. Relatively little criticism was directed at the vast uncertainty of the basic descriptive epidemiology for some populations, especially in Sub-Saharan Africa (see chapter 5 in this volume), which is likely to be far more consequential for setting health priorities (Cooper and others 1998).

The results of the 1990 GBD study confirmed what many health workers had suspected for some time, namely, that noncommunicable diseases and injuries were a significant cause of health burden in all regions, and in some rapidly industrializing regions such as East Asia and Pacific, were already by far the leading cause of death and disability. Neuropsychiatric disorders and injuries in particular were major causes of lost years of healthy life as measured by DALYs, and were vastly underappreciated when measured by mortality alone. The original GBD study estimated that noncommunicable diseases, including neuropsychiatric disorders, caused 41 percent of the global burden of disease in 1990, only slightly less than communicable, maternal, perinatal, and nutritional conditions combined (44 percent), and that 15 percent of the burden was due to injuries. Earlier assessments of global health priorities based on mortality data attributed no deaths to mental health disorders and less than half (7 percent) of that suggested by DALYs to injuries (Lopez 1993).

Estimates of the disease and injury burden caused by exposure to major risk factors are likely to be a much more useful guide to policies and priorities for prevention than a "league table" of the disease and injury burden. In recent decades, researchers have attempted to quantify the effects of specific exposures, for instance, tobacco smoking, on mortality from major diseases such as cancers (Doll and Peto 1981; Parkin and others 1994) or from multiple diseases (Peto and others 1992; United States Department of Health and Human Services 1992), either in individual countries or across groups of countries using comparable methods.

Specific country studies have examined the impact of several leading risk factors (Holman and others 1988; McGinnis and Foege 1993), but prior to the 1990 GBD study, no global assessments of the fatal and nonfatal burden of disease and injury resulting from exposure to multiple major health risks had been attempted. The 1990 study quantified 10 risk factors based on information about causation, prevalence, exposure, and disease and injury outcomes available at the time. The study attributed almost 16 percent of the entire global burden of disease and injury to malnutrition; another 7 percent to poor water and sanitation; and 2 to 3 percent to such risks as unsafe sex, tobacco, alcohol, and occupational exposures (Lopez and Murray 1998; Murray and Lopez 1996a; Murray and Lopez 1997a; Murray, Lopez, and Jamison 1994; World Bank 1993).

APPLICATIONS OF BURDEN OF DISEASE ANALYSIS

Burden of disease analyses are useful for informing health policy in at least five major ways as outlined in this section. Estimates of deaths by cause or years of life lost serve these same purposes, but for some uses, less well.

Assessing Performance

The burden of disease provides an indicator that can be used to judge progress over time within a single country or region or relative performance across countries and regions. In this application, burden of disease may be considered analogous to national income and product accounts, developed by

Simon Kuznets and others in the 1930s and culminating in 1939 with a complete national income and product account for the United Kingdom prepared at the request of the treasury. In subsequent decades, national income and product accounts have transformed the empirical underpinnings of economic policy analysis. As one leading scholar put it, "The national income and product accounts for the United States . . . , and kindred accounts in other nations, have been among the major contributions to economic knowledge over the past half century . . . Several generations of economists and practitioners have now been able to tie theoretical constructs of income, output, investment, consumption, and savings to the actual numbers of these remarkable accounts with all their fine detail and soundly meshed interrelations" (Eisner 1989, p. 1).

Generating Forums for Informed Debate of Values and Priorities

In practice, assessing the disease burden involves participation by a broad range of disease specialists, epidemiologists, and often, policy makers. Debating the appropriate values for, say, disability weights or for years of life lost at different ages helps clarify values and objectives for national health policy. Discussing the relationships between diseases and their risk factors in the light of local conditions sharpens consideration of priorities and of programs to address them.

Identifying National Control Priorities

Many countries now identify a relatively short list of interventions whose full implementation becomes an explicit priority for national political and administrative attention. Examples include interventions to control tuberculosis, poliomyelitis, HIV/AIDS, smoking, and specific micronutrient deficiencies. Because political attention and high-level administrative capacity are in relatively fixed and short supply, the benefits from using those resources will be maximized if they are directed toward interventions that are both cost-effective and aimed at problems associated with a high disease burden. National assessments of disease burden are one input into the process of establishing a shortlist of disease control priorities.

Creating Knowledge

Medical schools offer a fixed number of instructional hours, and training programs for other levels and types of health workers are similarly limited. A major instrument for implementing health policy priorities is to allocate this fixed time resource well. This implies allocating time to training for interventions where the disease burden is high and cost-effective interventions exist.

Information on the disease or risk factor burden is also a vital input for informing resource allocation for research and development. In particular, whenever a fixed effort will have a benefit proportional not only to the size of that effort, but also to the size of the problem being addressed, estimates of the disease burden become essential for formulating and implementing research and development priorities. For example, developing a vaccine for a broad range of viral pneumonias would have perhaps hundreds of times the impact of a vaccine against hantavirus infection.

Allocating Resources across Health Interventions

A key task for priority-setting analyses in health is to create the evidence base to stimulate the reallocation of resources to interventions that, at the margin, will generate the greatest reduction in health loss. When there are major fixed costs in mounting an intervention, as is the case with political and managerial attention for national control priorities, burden estimates are required to improve resource allocation. Similarly, major fixed costs may be associated with the universalization (or major expansion) of an intervention and, if so, the cost-effectiveness of the expansion will depend in part on the size of the burden.

IMPROVING THE COMPARATIVE QUANTIFICATION OF DISEASES, INJURIES, AND RISK FACTORS: THE 2001 GBD STUDY

The 1990 GBD study represented a major advance in the quantification of the impact of diseases, injuries, and risk factors on population health globally and by region. Government and nongovernmental agencies alike have used its results to argue for more strategic allocations of health resources to disease prevention and control programs that are likely to yield the greatest gains in terms of population health. The results have also greatly increased understanding of the basic descriptive epidemiology of diseases and injuries worldwide.

Following publication of the initial results of the GBD study, several national applications of the methods it used have led to substantially more data on the descriptive epidemiology of diseases and injuries becoming available, as well as to improvements in analytical methods and mortality data in a number of countries. By emphasizing substan-

tially more sophisticated approaches than in the past to the interpretation and presentation of population health data to policy makers, national burden of disease studies have stimulated efforts to improve and extend the collection of the health information data that are the basis for such analyses. A good example is the Islamic Republic of Iran where, over the last five years, the government has implemented a system of death registration with medical information on the cause of death that has been extended from four provinces initially to include 26, or almost all of the country's provinces. Another example is the government of Thailand's extensive verbal autopsy study aimed at addressing major coding deficiencies in Thailand's national mortality data (Choprapawon and others 2005).

Critiques of the original study's approach, particularly of the methods used to assess the severity weightings for disabling health states, have led to fundamental changes in the way that investigators incorporate health state valuations, that is, the use of population-based rather than expert opinion as used in the 1990 study, and to substantially better methods for improving the cross-national comparability of survey data on health status (Murray, Tandon, and others 2002; Salomon and Murray 2004). Better methods for modeling the relationship between the level of mortality and the broad cause of death structure in populations that are based on proportions rather than rates have led to greater confidence in cause of death estimates for developing countries (Salomon and Murray 2002). In addition, improved population surveillance for some major diseases such as HIV/AIDS, and the wider availability of data from verbal autopsy methods, particularly in Sub-Saharan Africa, have lessened the dependence on models for cause of death estimates, although substantial uncertainty in the use of such data persists. For more details on these and other methodological advances, see chapter 3 in this volume.

Perhaps the major methodological progress since the 1990 GBD study has been with respect to the quantification of the disease burden from risk factors. The initial study quantified the population health effects of 10 risk factors, but serious concerns exist about the comparability of the methods and estimates used. Different risk factors have different epidemiological traditions, particularly with regard to the definitions of hazardous exposure, the strength of the evidence on causality, and the availability of epidemiological research on exposure and hazard. As a result, comparability across estimates of the disease burden caused by different risk factors has been difficult to establish. In particular, much of classical risk factor research has treated exposures as dichotomous, with individuals either exposed or not exposed, with exposure defined according to an often arbitrary threshold value, for example, systolic blood pressure of 140 millimeters of mercury as the threshold for hypertension. Recent evidence for such continuous exposures as cholesterol, blood pressure, and body mass index suggests that such arbitrarily defined thresholds are inappropriate, because the hazards for these risks decline continuously across the entire range of measured exposure levels, with no obvious threshold (Eastern Stroke and Coronary Heart Disease Collaborative Research Group 1998; Ezzati and others 2004; Rose 1985; WHO 2002).

For the 2001 GBD study, a new framework for risk factor assessment was defined that examines changes in the disease burden that would be expected under alternative population distributions of exposure to a risk factor or groups of risk factors (Murray and Lopez 1999). Attributable fractions of disease due to a risk factor were then calculated based on a comparison of the disease burden expected under the current estimated distribution of exposure by age, sex, and region with that expected under a counterfactual distribution of exposure. One such counterfactual distribution was defined for each risk factor as the population distribution of exposure that would lead to the lowest levels of disease burden. Thus, for example, in the case of tobacco, this theoretical-minimum-risk counterfactual exposure would be 100 percent of the population being never-smokers, for overweight and obesity it would be a narrow distribution of body mass index centered around an optimal level of 21 kg/m^2 and so on. The distributions of the theoretical-minimum-risk exposure for the risk factors quantified in the World Health Organization's study of comparative risk assessment (the methodological and empirical basis for the 2001 GBD study) were developed by expert groups for each risk factor based on available scientific knowledge of risk factor hazard. The study also used systematic reviews and analyses of extant sources on risk factor exposure and hazard in an iterative process that increased comparability across risk factors (Ezzati and others 2002, 2004). These methods and results are described in more detail in chapter 4 in this volume.

Risk factors may affect disease and injury outcomes through other intermediate factors. For instance, some of the effects of diet and physical activity on cardiovascular diseases are mediated through changes in such intermediate factors as weight, blood pressure, and cholesterol. Risk factors may also affect disease and injury outcomes in combination with one another. For example, people who smoke and have elevated blood pressure and cholesterol have substantially higher probabilities of cardiovascular events. Finally, some risks have common social and behavioral determinants. For instance, members of poor households in rural areas are the most likely to be undernourished, use unsafe water sources, and be exposed to indoor smoke from solid fuels. Because of these epidemiological and social characteristics of risk factor exposure and hazard, policy-relevant analysis should include an assessment of the health benefits of simultaneous reductions in multiple risks. Multicausality also means that a range of interventions can be used for disease prevention, with the specific choices determined by such factors as costs, technology availability, infrastructure, and preferences. A novel aspect of the analysis of risk factors in the 2001 GBD study is the development and application of methods for estimating the disease burden attributable to the combined hazards of multiple risk factors (Ezzati and others 2003).

The basic units of analysis in the 1990 GBD study were the eight World Bank regions defined for the World Bank's (1993) *World Development Report 1993*. Designed to be geographically contiguous, these regions were nonetheless extremely heterogeneous with respect to health development, for example, the region referred to as Other Asia and Islands included countries with such diverse epidemiological profiles as Myanmar and Singapore. This seriously limited the applicability of these regions to comparative epidemiological assessments. Thus the 2001 GBD study followed a more refined approach. Estimates of overall mortality were first developed for World Health Organization member states using different methods for countries at different stages of health development. The choice of methods was largely determined by the availability of data (Lopez and others 2002). Age- and sex-specific death rates for countries were essentially determined using one of three standard approaches: the use of routine life table methods for countries with complete vital registration; the application of standard demographic methods to correct for underregistration of deaths; or the application of model life tables where no vital registration or survey data on adult mortality were available (Lopez and others 2002; Murray and others 2003).

The detailed methodological approaches adopted for estimating cause-specific mortality for countries and the descriptive epidemiology of nonfatal conditions for countries or subregions are described elsewhere (Mathers and others 2002; chapter 3 in this volume). This focus on individual countries as the unit of analysis, as well as the systematic application of standardized approaches for all countries in any given category of data availability, has vastly improved the cross-population comparability of disease and injury quantification.

A final major advance of the 2001 GBD study has been the systematic attempts to quantify some of the uncertainty in both national and global assessments of the disease burden (see chapter 5 in this volume). This uncertainty must be taken into account when making cross-national comparisons and needs to be carefully communicated to and interpreted by epidemiologists and policy makers alike.

MAJOR FINDINGS OF THE 2001 GBD STUDY

This section, and tables 1.1 and 1.2, summarize the principle findings of the 2001 GBD study. More detailed findings are reported in chapters 3 and 4.

Global and Regional Mortality

Slightly more than 56 million people died in 2001, 10.5 million (or nearly 20 percent) of whom were children younger than five years of age. Almost 4 million children died before 1 month of age, with an additional 3.3 million stillbirths (see chapter 6). Of these child deaths, 99 percent occurred in low- and middle-income countries. Low- and middle-income countries also account for a comparatively large number of deaths at young and middle adult ages: 30 percent of all deaths occur at ages 15 to 59, compared with 15 percent in high-income countries. The causes of death at these ages, as well as in childhood, are thus important for assessing public health priorities.

Worldwide, one death in every three is from what the GBD study terms Group I causes (communicable diseases, maternal and perinatal conditions, and nutritional deficiencies) (see table 1.1). This proportion remains almost unchanged from 1990, with one major difference. Whereas HIV/AIDS accounted for only 2 percent of Group I deaths in 1990, it accounted for 14 percent in 2001. Excluding HIV/AIDS, Group I deaths fell from one-third of total deaths in 1990 to less than one-fifth in 2001. Virtually all Group I deaths are in low- and middle-income countries.

In low- and middle-countries, Group II causes (noncommunicable diseases) are now responsible for more than 50 percent of deaths in adults ages 15 to 59 in all regions except South Asia and Sub-Saharan Africa, where Group I causes, including HIV/AIDS, remain responsible for one-third and two-thirds of deaths, respectively. Outside these two regions, developing countries are now facing a triple burden of disease from communicable diseases, noncommunicable diseases, and injuries (Group III causes). Among low- and middle-income countries as a group, the three leading causes of death in 2001 included ischemic heart disease and cerebrovascular disease, which together accounted for almost one-fifth of all deaths. In other words, the epidemiological transition from infectious to chronic noncommunicable diseases in this group of countries is already well established and is of major relevance to health planning.

Leading Causes of Disability

The 1990 GBD study brought the previously largely ignored burden of nonfatal illnesses, particularly neuropsychiatric disorders, to the attention of health policy makers. The findings of the 2001 GBD study, based on updated data and analyses, confirm that disability and states of less than full health caused by diseases and injuries play a central role in determining the overall health status of populations in all regions of the world. Neuropsychiatric conditions, vision disorders, hearing loss, and alcohol use disorders dominate the overall burden of nonfatal disabling conditions.

In all regions, neuropsychiatric conditions are the most important causes of disability, accounting for more than 37 percent of YLD among adults aged 15 years and older worldwide. The disabling burden of neuropsychiatric conditions is almost the same for males and females, but the major contributing causes are different. While depression is the leading cause of disability for both males and females, the burden of depression is 50 percent higher for females than males, and females also have higher burdens from anxiety disorders, migraine, and senile dementia. In contrast, the male burden for alcohol and drug use disorders is nearly six times higher than that for females and accounts for a quarter of the male neuropsychiatric burden.

More than 85 percent of disease burden from nonfatal health outcomes occurs in low- and middle-income countries, and South Asia and Sub-Saharan Africa account for 40 percent of all YLD. Even though the prevalence of disabling conditions such as dementia and musculoskeletal disease is higher in countries with long life expectancies, this is offset by lower contributions to disability from conditions such as cardiovascular disease, chronic respiratory diseases, and long-term sequelae of communicable diseases and nutritional deficiencies. In other words, people living in developing countries not only face shorter life expectancies than those in developed countries, but also live a higher proportion of their lives in poor health.

Burden of Disease and Injuries

The results of the 2001 GBD study reinforce some of the conclusions of the 1990 GBD study about the importance of including nonfatal outcomes in a comprehensive assessment

Table 1.1 Deaths and Burden of Disease by Cause—Low- and Middle-Income Countries, High-Income Countries, and World, 2001

	Low- and middle-income		High-income		World	
	Deaths	**DALYs(3,0)**[a]	**Deaths**	**DALYs(3,0)**[a]	**Deaths**	**DALYs(3,0)**[a]
All causes						
Total number (thousands)	48,351	1,386,709	7,891	149,161	56,242	1,535 871
Rate per 1,000 population	9.3	265.7	8.5	160.6	9.1	249.8
Age-standardized rate per 1,000[b]	11.4	281.7	5.0	128.2	10.0	256.5
Selected cause groups:			*Number in thousands (percent)*			
I. COMMUNICABLE DISEASES, MATERNAL AND PERINATAL CONDITIONS AND NUTRITIONAL DEFICIENCIES	**17,613 (36.4)**	**552,376 (39.8)**	**552 (7.0)**	**8,561 (5.7)**	**18,166 (32.3)**	**560,937 (36.5)**
Tuberculosis	1,590 (3.3)	35,874 (2.6)	16 (0.2)	219 (0.1)	1,606 (2.9)	36,093 (2.3)
HIV/AIDS	2,552 (5.3)	70,796 (5.1)	22 (0.3)	665 (0.4)	2,574 (4.6)	71,461 (4.7)
Diarrheal diseases	1,777 (3.7)	58,697 (4.2)	6 (<.1)	444 (0.3)	1,783 (3.2)	59,141 (3.9)
Measles	762 (1.6)	23,091 (1.7)	1 (<.1)	23 (<.1)	763 (1.4)	23,113 (1.5)
Malaria	1,207 (2.5)	39,961 (2.9)	0 (0.0)	9 (<.1)	1,208 (2.1)	39,970 (2.6)
Lower respiratory infections	3,408 (7.0)	83,606 (6.0)	345 (4.4)	2,314 (1.6)	3,753 (6.7)	85,920 (5.6)
Perinatal conditions	2,489 (5.1)	89,068 (6.4)	32 (0.4)	1,408 (0.9)	2,522 (4.5)	90,477 (5.9)
Protein-energy malnutrition	241 (0.5)	15,449 (1.1)	9 (0.1)	130 (<.1)	250 (0.4)	15,578 (1.0)
II. NONCOMMUNICABLE CONDITIONS	**26,023 (53.8)**	**678,483 (48.9)**	**6,868 (87.0)**	**129,356 (86.7)**	**32,891 (58.5)**	**807,839 (52.6)**
Stomach cancers	696 (1.4)	9,616 (0.7)	146 (1.9)	1,628 (1.1)	842 (1.5)	11,244 (0.7)
Colon and rectum cancers	357 (0.7)	5,060 (0.4)	257 (3.3)	3,175 (2.1)	614 (1.1)	8,236 (0.5)
Liver cancer	505 (1.0)	7,945 (0.6)	102 (1.3)	1,223 (0.8)	607 (1.1)	9,169 (0.6)
Trachea, bronchus, and lung cancers	771 (1.6)	10,701 (0.8)	456 (5.8)	5,397 (3.6)	1,227 (2.2)	16,099 (1.0)
Diabetes mellitus	757 (1.6)	15,804 (1.1)	202 (2.6)	4,192 (2.8)	960 (1.7)	19,997 (1.3)
Unipolar depressive disorders	10 (<.1)	43,427 (3.1)	3 (<.1)	8,408 (5.6)	13 (<.1)	51,835 (3.4)
Alcohol use disorders	62 (0.1)	11,007 (0.8)	23 (0.3)	4,171 (2.8)	84 (0.2)	15,178 (1.0)
Cataracts	0 (0.0)	28,150 (2.0)	0 (0.0)	493 (0.3)	0 (0.0)	28,643 (1.9)
Vision disorders, age-related	0 (0.0)	15,364 (1.1)	0 (0.0)	1,525 (1.0)	0 (0.0)	16,889 (1.1)
Hearing loss, adult onset	0 (0.0)	24,607 (1.8)	0 (0.0)	5,387 (3.6)	0 (0.0)	29,994 (2.0)
Hypertensive heart disease	760 (1.6)	9,969 (0.7)	129 (1.6)	1,209 (0.8)	889 (1.6)	11,178 (0.7)
Ischemic heart disease	5,699 (11.8)	71,882 (5.2)	1,364 (17.3)	12,390 (8.3)	7,063 (12.6)	84,273 (5.5)
Cerebrovascular disease	4,608 (9.5)	62,669 (4.5)	781 (9.9)	9,354 (6.3)	5,390 (9.6)	72,024 (4.7)
Chronic obstructive pulmonary disease	2,378 (4.9)	33,453 (2.4)	297 (3.8)	5,282 (3.5)	2,676 (4.8)	38,736 (2.5)
Cirrhosis of the liver	654 (1.4)	13,633 (1.0)	118 (1.5)	2,146 (1.4)	771 (1.4)	15,778 (1.0)
Nephritis and nephrosis	552 (1.1)	9,076 (0.7)	111 (1.4)	929 (0.6)	663 (1.2)	10,005 (0.7)
Osteoarthritis	2 (<.1)	13,666 (1.0)	3 (<.1)	3,786 (2.5)	5 (<.1)	17,452 (1.1)
Congenital anomalies	477 (1.0)	23,533 (1.7)	30 (0.4)	1,420 (1.0)	507 (0.9)	24,952 (1.6)
Alzheimer and other dementias	173 (0.4)	9,640 (0.7)	207 (2.6)	7,468 (5.0)	380 (0.7)	17,108 (1.1)
III. INJURIES	**4,715 (9.8)**	**155,850 (11.2)**	**471 (6.0)**	**11,244 (7.5)**	**5,186 (9.2)**	**167,094 (10.9)**
Road traffic accidents	1,069 (2.2)	32,017 (2.3)	121 (1.5)	3,045 (2.0)	1,189 (2.1)	35,063 (2.3)
Falls	316 (0.7)	13,582 (1.0)	71 (0.9)	1,459 (1.0)	387 (0.7)	15,041 (1.0)
Self-inflicted injuries	749 (1.5)	17,674 (1.3)	126 (1.6)	2,581 (1.7)	875 (1.6)	20,255 (1.3)
Violence	532 (1.1)	18,132 (1.3)	24 (0.3)	765 (0.5)	556 (1.0)	18,897 (1.2)

Source: Chapter 3.

Notes: Numbers in parentheses indicate percentage of column total.

Broad group totals in bold are additive but should not be summed with all other conditions listed in table.

a. DALYs (3,0) refer to the version of the DALY based on a 3% annual discount rate and uniform age weights.

b. Age-standardized using the WHO World Standard Population.

c. Includes only causes responsible for more than 1% of global deaths or DALYs in 2001.

of global population health. They also confirm the growing importance of noncommunicable diseases in low- and middle-income countries and highlight important changes in population health in some regions since 1990.

HIV/AIDS is now the fourth leading cause of the burden of disease globally and the leading cause in Sub-Saharan Africa, where it is followed by malaria in second place. Seven other Group I causes also appear in the top 10 causes for this region. The epidemiological transition in low- and middle-income countries has resulted in a 20 percent reduction in the per capita disease burden due to Group I causes since 1990. Without the HIV/AIDS epidemic and the associated lack of decline in the burden of tuberculosis, this reduction would have been closer to 30 percent.

The per capita disease burden in Europe and Central Asia has increased by nearly 40 percent since 1990, and population health in this region is now worse than all other regions except South Asia and Sub-Saharan Africa. This reflects the sharp increase in adult male mortality and disability in the 1990s, leading to the highest male-female differential in the disease burden in the world. A significant factor in this increase is probably the high level of harmful alcohol consumption among men, which has led to high rates of accidents, violence, and cardiovascular disease. From 1991 to 1994, the risk of premature adult (15 to 59 years) death increased by 50 percent for Russian males. It improved somewhat between 1994 and 1998, but subsequently increased.

The burden of noncommunicable diseases is increasing, accounting for nearly half the total global burden of disease, a 10 percent increase from estimated levels in 1990. Almost 50 percent of the adult disease burden in low- and middle income countries is now attributable to noncommunicable diseases. The implementation of effective interventions for Group I diseases, coupled with population aging and the spread of risks for noncommunicable disease in many low- and middle-income countries, are the likely causes of this shift. Ischemic heart disease and stroke dominate the burden of disease in Europe and Central Asia and together account for more than a quarter of the total disease burden. In contrast, in Latin America and the Caribbean these diseases account for 8 percent of the disease burden, but this region also has high levels of diabetes and endocrine disorders compared with other regions. Violence is the fourth leading cause of the disease and injury burden in Latin America and the Caribbean. Violence does not appear among the top 10 causes of burden in any other region, but is nonetheless significant.

Injuries primarily affect young adults and often result in severe, disabling sequelae. All forms of injury accounted for 16 percent of the adult burden in 2001. In parts of Europe and Central Asia, Latin America and the Caribbean, and the Middle East and North Africa, more than 30 percent of the entire disease and injury burden among male adults aged 15 to 44 is attributable to injuries. Road traffic accidents, violence, and self-inflicted injuries are all among the top 10 leading causes of burden in these regions. The former Soviet Union and other high-mortality (among adults) countries of Eastern Europe have rates of injury death and disability among males that are similar to those in Sub-Saharan Africa.

Burden of Disease Attributable to Risk Factors

As described earlier, a major advance of the 2001 GBD study has been in creating a unified framework for quantifying the burden of disease and injury attributable to major risk factors and in applying this framework to exposure and hazard data for selected major risk factors based on comprehensive and systematic reviews of published literature and other sources. Notwithstanding the inherent uncertainties in assessing the population-level health effects of risk factors, the quantification of the burden of disease attributable to the individual and joint hazards of selected risks suggests that the leading causes of mortality and disease burden include risk factors for Group I conditions (for example, undernutrition; indoor smoke from household use of solid fuels; poor water, sanitation, and hygiene; and unsafe sex), whose burden is primarily concentrated in South Asia and Sub-Saharan Africa, and risk factors for Group II conditions (especially, smoking, alcohol, high blood pressure and cholesterol, and overweight and obesity), which are widespread globally (see table 1.2). In low- and middle-income countries, the leading causes of disease burden included risk factors prevalent among the poor and associated with Group I conditions (for example, childhood underweight [8.7 percent of the disease burden in these regions]; unsafe water, sanitation, and hygiene [3.7 percent]; and indoor smoke from household use of solid fuels [3.0 percent]), unsafe sex (5.8 percent), and risk factors for noncommunicable diseases (for example, high blood pressure [5.6 percent], smoking [3.9 percent], and alcohol use [3.6 percent]). Across high-income countries, risk factors associated with Group II and Group III conditions were the leading causes of loss of healthy life (smoking [12.7 percent], high blood pressure [9.3 percent], overweight and obesity [7.2 percent], high cholesterol [6.3 percent], and alcohol use [4.4 percent]).

An estimated 45 percent of global mortality and 36 percent of the global burden of disease were attributable to the joint hazards of the 19 selected global risk factors. The joint hazards were even larger in regions where a relatively small number of diseases and their risk factors were responsible for large losses of life (HIV/AIDS and risk factors for child mortality in Sub-Saharan Africa; cardiovascular risks, including smoking and alcohol use in Europe and Central Asia). Globally, large fractions of major diseases such as diarrhea, lower respiratory infections, HIV/AIDS, lung cancer,

Table 1.2 Deaths and Burden of Disease Attributable to Risk Factors—Low- and Middle-Income Countries, High-Income Countries, and World, 2001

	Low- and middle-income		High-income		World	
	Deaths	DALYs(3,0)[a]	Deaths	DALYs(3,0)[a]	Deaths	DALYs(3,0)[a]
Total number (thousands)	**48,351**	**1,386 709**	**7,891**	**149,161**	**56,242**	**1,535 871**
Rate per 1,000 population	**9.3**	**265.7**	**8.5**	**160.6**	**9.1**	**249.8**
Age-standardized rate per 1,000[b]	**11.4**	**281.7**	**5.0**	**128.2**	**10.0**	**256.5**
Risk factor	*Number in thousands (percent)*					
Childhood and maternal undernutrition						
Childhood underweight	3,630 (7.5)	120,579 (8.7)	0 (0.0)	67 (<0.1)	3,630 (6.5)	120,647 (7.9)
Iron-deficiency anemia	613 (1.3)	23,933 (1.7)	8 (0.1)	789 (0.5)	621 (1.1)	24,722 (1.6)
Vitamin A deficiency	800 (1.7)	24,686 (1.8)	0 (0.0)	0 (0.0)	800 (1.4)	24,686 (1.6)
Zinc deficiency	849 (1.8)	27,631 (2.0)	0 (0.0)	5 (<0.1)	849 (1.5)	27,636 (1.8)
Other nutrition-related risk factors and physical activity						
High blood pressure	6,223 (12.9)	78,063 (5.6)	1,392 (17.6)	13,887 (9.3)	7,615 (13.5)	91,950 (6.0)
High cholesterol	3,038 (6.3)	42,815 (3.1)	842 (10.7)	9,431 (6.3)	3,880 (6.9)	52,246 (3.4)
Overweight and obesity	1,747 (3.6)	31,515 (2.3)	614 (7.8)	10,733 (7.2)	2,361 (4.2)	42,248 (2.8)
Low fruit and vegetable intake	2,308 (4.8)	32,836 (2.4)	333 (4.2)	3,982 (2.7)	2,641 (4.7)	36,819 (2.4)
Physical inactivity	1,559 (3.2)	22,679 (1.6)	376 (4.8)	4,732 (3.2)	1,935 (3.4)	27,411 (1.8)
Addictive substances						
Smoking	3,340 (6.9)	54,019 (3.9)	1,462 (18.5)	18,900 (12.7)	4,802 (8.5)	72,919 (4.7)
Alcohol use	1,869 (3.9)	49,449 (3.6)	24 (0.3)	6,580 (4.4)	1,893 (3.4)	56,029 (3.6)
Illicit drug use	189 (0.4)	7,890 (0.6)	37 (0.5)	2,024 (1.4)	226 (0.4)	9,914 (0.6)
Sexual and reproductive health						
Unsafe sex	2,819 (5.8)	80,270 (5.8)	32 (0.4)	909 (0.6)	2,851 (5.1)	81,179 (5.3)
Non-use and use of ineffective methods of contraception	162 (0.3)	7,411 (0.5)	0 (0.0)	23 (<0.1)	162 (0.3)	7,434 (0.5)
Environmental risks						
Unsafe water, sanitation, and hygiene	1,563 (3.2)	51,622 (3.7)	4 (<0.1)	289 (0.2)	1,567 (2.8)	51,911 (3.4)
Urban air pollution	735 (1.5)	8,707 (0.6)	76 (1.0)	664 (0.4)	811 (1.4)	9,371 (0.6)
Indoor smoke from household use of solid fuels	1,791 (3.7)	41,731 (3.0)	0 (0.0)	2 (<0.1)	1,791 (3.2)	41,734 (2.7)
Other selected risks						
Contaminated injections in health care setting	407 (0.8)	8,974 (0.6)	4 (<0.1)	76 (<0.1)	412 (0.7)	9,050 (0.6)
Child sexual abuse	65 (0.1)	5,381 (0.4)	6 (<0.1)	699 (0.5)	71 (0.1)	6,079 (0.4)
All selected risk factors together	22,014 (45.6)	500,066 (36.1)	3,473 (44.0)	51,092 (34.3)	25,488 (45.3)	551,158 (35.9)

Source: Chapter 4. Note that mortality and disease burden attributable to individual risk factors cannot be added due to multi-causality. See Chapter 4 for details.

a. (some footnote as Table 1.1)

b. Age-standardized using the WHO World Standard Population

chronic obstructive pulmonary disease, ischemic heart disease, and stroke were attributable to the joint effects of the risk factors considered in this volume. The joint hazards of these 19 risks for a number of other important diseases and injuries, such as perinatal and maternal conditions, selected other cancers, and intentional and unintentional injuries, which have more diverse risk factors, were smaller, but nonnegligible. The relatively small number of risk factors that account for a large fraction of the disease burden underscores the need for policies, programs, and scientific research to take advantage of interventions for multiple major risks to health (Ezzati and others 2003).

CONCLUSIONS

The substantial scientific and policy interest in the methods and findings of the 1990 GBD study, the widespread application of the methods by countries at all levels of health development, and the adoption of the framework as the preferred method for health accounting by international health agencies such as the World Health Organization attest to the critical need for objective and systematic assessments of the disease burden for priority setting in health. The vast and comprehensive effort to quantify the disease burden worldwide dramatically changed views about the importance of some conditions, particularly psychiatric disorders, and drew global public health attention to the unrecognized burden of injuries. The methodological developments over the past decade, a more systematic approach to collecting key data and research findings on the health of populations, and the results of numerous national and subnational burden of disease studies have dramatically improved the methodological armamentarium and the empirical base for disease burden assessment, in particular, the comparability of the estimated contributions of diseases, injuries, and risk factors to this burden.

As reported in this volume, the 2001 GBD study provides a comprehensive update of the comparative importance of diseases, injuries, and risk factors for global health. The study incorporates a range of new data sources to develop internally consistent estimates of incidence, prevalence, severity and duration, and mortality for 136 major causes by sex and by eight age groups. Estimates of deaths by cause, age, and sex were carried out separately for 226 countries and territories, drawing on a total of 770 country-years of death registration data, 535 additional sources of information on levels of child and adult mortality, and more than 2,600 data sets providing information on specific causes of death in regions not well covered by death registration systems. Together with the more than 8,500 data sources (epidemiological studies, disease registers, notifications systems, and so on) used to estimate incidence, prevalence, and YLD by cause, the 2001 GBD study has incorporated information from more than 10,000 datasets relating to population health and mortality (see chapter 3). This represents one of the largest syntheses of global information on population health carried out to date.

Much of the research on the burden of disease undertaken over the past decade or so has relied on the methodological and empirical efforts that defined the 1990 GBD study as a major advance in global public health statistics. Progress in updating the epidemiological basis for assessing the disease burden from the various diseases and injuries of interest has been uneven, although improvements in the data and methods available for assessing global and regional mortality by cause have been substantial, and some advances have been made in the data for, and epidemiological understanding of some major causes of ill health such as HIV/AIDS and diabetes mellitus. Nevertheless, making more reliable estimates of global, regional, and national disease burdens still faces many methodological and empirical challenges. The substantive agenda, mapped out over a decade ago (Murray, Lopez and Jamison, 1994) remains

equally valid today and needs to be addressed more systematically if the burden of disease framework is to gain greater acceptance as *the* international tool for health accounting.

Assessing and documenting in detail the state of the world's health at the beginning of the millennium is a useful undertaking. This volume will provide scholars today and in the future with a definitive historical record of the leading causes of the burden of disease for major regions of the world at the start of the 21st century. An account of global health at the beginning of the 20th century, or earlier, would no doubt have been of more than just historical interest, but given the methods of scientific interchange and the state of scientific and methodological knowledge at the time, this was impossible.

In presenting the comprehensive findings of the 2001 GBD study, this volume is, in many respects, a culmination of the effort launched in 1990 and represents the end of the beginning of global disease burden assessments. The widespread use of disease burden concepts by national and international bodies since the first results were published and the heightened interest in improving the basic descriptive epidemiology of diseases, injuries, and risk factors by both countries and agencies has laid the foundations for future population health assessments. As programs and policies to improve health worldwide become more widespread, so too will the need for more comprehensible, credible, and comparable assessments to periodically monitor world health and the success, or otherwise, of measures to promote health and reduce the burden of disease. New initiatives, and perhaps new global institutions, are required to measure the burden of disease worldwide and how it is changing, more reliably than hitherto. This book provides the baseline against which such progress with global health development will be measured.

REFERENCES

Anand, S., and K. Hanson. 1998. "DALYs: Efficiency Versus Equity." *World Development* 26 (2): 307–10.

Barendregt, J. J., G. J. van Oortmarssen, T. Vos, and C. J. L. Murray. 2003. "A Generic Model for the Assessment of Disease Epidemiology: The Computational Basis of DisMod II." *Population Health Metrics* 1 (1): e4.

Baskent University. 2005. *Burden of Disease Final Report*. Ankara, Turkey: Baskent University and the School of Public Health, Refik Saydam Hygiene Center, Ministry of Health.

Bradshaw, D., P. Groenewald, R. Laubscher, N. Nannan, B. Nojilana, R. Norman, D. Pieterse, M. Schneider, D. E. Bourne, I. M. Timaeus, R. Dorrington, and L. Johnson. 2003. *Initial Burden of Disease Estimates for South Africa, 2000*. Cape Town: South African Medical Research Council. http://www.mrc.ac.za/bod/bod.htm.

Bundhamcharoen, K., Y. Teerawatananon, T. Vos, and S. Begg. 2002. *Burden of Disease and Injuries in Thailand: Priority Setting for Policy.* Bangkok: Ministry of Public Health.

Choprapawon, C., Y. Porapakkham, O. Sablon, R. Panjajaru and B. Jhantharatat. 2005. "Thailand's National Death Registration Reform: Verifying the Causes of Death between July 1997 and December 1999." *Asia-Pacific Journal of Public Health* 17 (2): 110–116.

Cooper, R. S., B. Osotimehin, J. S. Kaufman, and T. Forrester. 1998. "Disease Burden in Sub-Saharan Africa: What Should We Conclude in the Absence of Data?" *Lancet* 351 (9087): 208–10.

Dempsey, M. 1947. "Decline in Tuberculosis: The Death Rate Fails to Tell the Entire Story." *American Review of Tuberculosis* 56 (2): 157–64.

Doll, R., and R. Peto. 1981. *The Causes of Cancer.* Oxford, U.K.: Oxford University Press.

Eastern Stroke and Coronary Heart Disease Collaborative Research Group. 1998. "Blood Pressure, Cholesterol, and Stroke in Eastern Asia." *Lancet* 352 (9143): 1801–7.

Eisner, R. 1989. *The Total Incomes System of Account.* Chicago and London: University of Chicago Press.

Ezzati, M., A. D. Lopez, A. Rodgers, and C. J. L. Murray. 2004. *Comparative Quantification of Health Risks: The Global and Regional Burden of Disease Attributable to Selected Major Risk Factors.* Geneva: World Health Organization.

Ezzati, M., A. D. Lopez, A. Rodgers, S. Vander Hoorn, C. J. L. Murray, and the Comparative Risk Assessment Collaborating Group. 2002. "Selected Major Risk Factors and Global and Regional Burden of Disease." *Lancet* 360 (9343): 1347–60.

Ezzati, M., S. Vander Hoorn, A. Rodgers, A. D. Lopez, C. D. Mathers, C. J. L. Murray, and the Comparative Risk Assessment Collaborating Group. 2003. "Estimates of Global and Regional Potential Health Gains from Reducing Multiple Major Risk Factors." *Lancet* 362 (9380): 271–80.

Ghana Health Assessment Project Team. 1981. "Quantitative Method of Assessing the Health Impact of Different Diseases in Less Developed Countries." *International Journal of Epidemiology* 10 (1): 73–80.

Hakulinen, T., H. Hansluwka, A. D. Lopez, and T. Nakada. 1986. "Global and Regional Mortality Patterns by Cause of Death in 1980." *International Journal of Epidemiology* 15 (2): 226–33.

Holman, C. D. J., B. K. Armstrong, L. N. Arias, C. A. Martin, W. M. Hatton, L. D. Hayward, M. A. Salmon, R. E. Shean, V. P. Waddell. 1990. *The Quantification of Drug Caused Morbidity and Mortality in Australia 1988.* Canberra: Commonwealth Department of Community Services and Health.

Hyder, A. A., G. Rotllant, and R. Morrow. 1998. "Measuring the Burden of Disease: Healthy Life Years." *American Journal of Public Health* 88 (2): 196–202.

Jamison, D. T., and J.-P. Jardel. 1994. "Comparative Health Data and Analyses." In *Global Comparative Assessments in the Health Sector: Disease Burden, Expenditures, and Intervention Packages,* ed. C. J. L. Murray and A. D. Lopez, v–vii. Geneva: World Health Organization.

Jamison, D. T., W. H. Mosely, A. R. Measham, and J. L. Bobadilla, eds. 1993. *Disease Control Priorities in Developing Countries.* New York: Oxford University.

Lopez, A. D. 1993. "Causes of Death in the Industrialized and Developing Countries: Estimates for 1985–1990." In *Disease Control Priorities in Developing Countries,* ed. Dean Jamison, W. Henry Mosely, A. R. Measham, and J. L. Bobadilla, 15–30. New York: Oxford University Press.

Lopez, A. D., and C. J. L. Murray. 1998. "The Global Burden of Disease, 1990–2020." *Nature Medicine* 4 (11): 1241–43.

Lopez, A. D., O. B. Ahmad, M. Guillot, B. D. Ferguson, J. A. Salomon, C. J. L. Murray, and K. Hill. 2002. *World Mortality in 2000: Life Tables for 191 Countries.* Geneva: World Health Organization.

Lozano, R., C. J. L. Murray, J. Frenk, and J. Bobadilla. 1995. "Burden of Disease Assessment and Health System Reform: Results of a Study in Mexico." *Journal for International Development* 7 (3): 555–64.

Mahapatra, P. 2002. *Estimating National Burden of Disease: The Burden of Disease in Andhra Pradesh, 1990s.* Hyderabad, India: Institute of Health Systems.

Mathers, C. D., T. Vos, and C. Stevenson. 1999. *The Burden of Disease and Injury in Australia.* Canberra: Australian Institute of Health and Welfare. http://www.aihw.gov.au/publications/index.cfm/title/5180.

Mathers, C. D., C. Stein, M. Ma Fat, C. Rao, M. Inoue, K. Shibuya, N. Tomijima, C. Bernard, and H. Xu. 2002. *The Global Burden of Disease 2000 Study (version 2): Methods and Results.* Discussion Paper 50. Geneva: Global Program on Evidence for Health Policy, World Health Organization. http://www.who.int/evidence.

McGinnis, J. M., and W. H. Foege. 1993. "Actual Causes of Death in the United States." *Journal of the American Medical Association* 270 (18): 2207–12.

McKenna, M. T., C. M. Michaud, C. J. L. Murray, and J. S. Marks. 2005. "Assessing the Burden of Disease in the United States Using Disability-Adjusted Life Years." *American Journal of Preventive Medicine* 28 (5): 415–23.

Murray, C. J. L. 1996. "Rethinking DALYs." In *The Global Burden of Disease,* ed. C. J. L. Murray and A. D. Lopez, 1–89. Cambridge, MA: Harvard University Press .

Murray, C. J. L., and A. D. Lopez. 1996a. "Evidence-Based Health Policy: Lessons from the Global Burden of Disease Study." *Science* 274 (5288): 740–43.

———. 1996b. "Global and Regional Descriptive Epidemiology of Disability: Incidence, Prevalence, Health Expectancies, and Years Lived with Disability." In *The Global Burden of Disease,* ed. C. J. L. Murray and A. D. Lopez, 201–46. Cambridge, MA: Harvard University Press.

———. 1996c. *Global Health Statistics: A Compendium of Incidence, Prevalence, and Mortality Estimates for over 200 Conditions.* Cambridge, MA: Harvard University Press.

———, eds. 1996d. *The Global Burden of Disease,* vol. 1. Cambridge, MA: Harvard University Press.

———. 1997a. "Global Mortality, Disability, and the Contribution of Risk Factors: Global Burden of Disease Study." *Lancet* 349 (9063): 1436–42.

———. 1997b. "Mortality by Cause for Eight Regions of the World: Global Burden of Disease Study." *Lancet* 349 (9061): 1269–76.

———. 1997c. "Regional Patterns of Disability-Free Life Expectancy and Disability-Adjusted Life Expectancy: Global Burden of Disease Study." *Lancet* 349 (9062): 1347–52.

———. 1999. "On the Comparable Quantification of Health Risks: Lessons from the Global Burden of Disease Study." *Epidemiology* 10 (5): 594–605.

Murray, C. J. L., A. D. Lopez, and D. T. Jamison. 1994. "The Global Burden of Disease in 1990: Summary Results, Sensitivity Analyses, and Future Directions." *Bulletin of the World Health Organization* 72 (3): 495–508.

Murray, C. J. L., J. A. Salomon, C. D. Mathers, and A. D. Lopez. 2002. *Summary Measures of Population Health: Concepts, Ethics, Measurement, and Applications.* Geneva: World Health Organization.

Murray, C. J. L., A. Tandon, J. A. Salomon, C. D. Mathers, and R. Sadana. 2002. "New Approaches to Enhance Cross-Population Comparability of Survey Results". In *Summary Measures of Population Health: Concepts, Ethics, Measurement, and Applications,* ed. C. J. L. Murray, J. A. Salomon, C. D. Mathers, and A. D. Lopez, 421–32. Geneva: World Health Organization.

Murray, C. J. L., B. D. Ferguson, A. D. Lopez, M. Guillot, J. A. Salomon, and O.B. Ahmad. 2003. "Modified Logit Life Table System: Principles, Empirical Validation, and Application." *Population Studies* 57 (2): 165–82.

Parkin, D. M., P. Pisani, A. D. Lopez, and E. Masuyer. 1994. "At Least One in Seven Cases of Cancer Is Caused by Smoking: Global Estimates for 1985." *International Journal of Cancer* 59 (4): 494–504.

Peto, R., A. D. Lopez, J. Boreham, M. Thun, and C. Heath. 1992. "Mortality from Tobacco in Developed Countries: Indirect Estimates from National Vital Statistics." *Lancet* 339 (8804): 1268–78.

Rose, G. 1985. "Sick Individuals and Sick Populations." *International Journal of Epidemiology* 14 (1): 32–38.

Salomon, J. A., and C. J. L. Murray. 2002. "The Epidemiologic Transition Revisited: Compositional Models for Causes of Death by Age and Sex." *Population and Development Review* 28 (2): 205–28.

————. 2004. "A Multimethod Approach to Measuring Health State Valuations." *Health Economics* 13: 281–90.

United States Department of Health and Human Services. 1992. *Smoking and Health in the Americas. Report of the Surgeon General, in Collaboration with the Pan-American Health Organization,* Department of Health and Human Services publication (CDC) 92-8419. Washington, DC: Office on Smoking and Health.

Vos, T., M. Tobias, H. Gareeboo, F. Roussety, S. Huttley, and C. J. L. Murray. 1995. *Mauritius Health Sector Reform, National Burden of Disease Study, Final Report of Consultancy.* Port Louis, Mauritius: Ministry of Health and Ministry of Economic Planning and Development.

Williams, A. 1999. "Calculating the Global Burden of Disease: Time for a Strategic Appraisal?" *Health Economics* 8 (1): 1–8.

World Bank. 1993. *Investing in Health: World Development Report 1993.* New York: Oxford University Press.

WHO (World Health Organization). 1996. *Investing in Health Research and Development. Report of the Ad Hoc Committee on Health Research Relating to Future Intervention Options.* Geneva: WHO.

————. 2002. *Reducing Risks: Promoting Healthy Life. World Health Report 2002.* Geneva: WHO.

Part **I**

Global Burden of Disease and Risk Factors

Chapter **2**

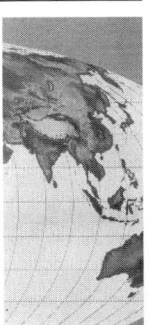

Demographic and Epidemiological Characteristics of Major Regions, 1990–2001

Alan D. Lopez, Stephen Begg, and Ed Bos

Health status is both a determinant of population change, largely through population aging, and a consequence of population growth, with smaller family size associated with lower mortality, and of economic and social development. Studies of the interrelationship between demographic trends and health have typically focused on health as the independent or determining variable. Indeed, a population's health status influences all components of population change. In addition to the obvious direct effect of individual health status on mortality and morbidity, it has a direct impact on fertility, largely through improved child survival, but also through the biological capability of a sick woman to bear children. Processes such as screening potential migrants for disease are also mechanisms whereby health status exerts a direct impact on population change, and thus on population size and composition.

In contrast, demographic variables influence health through two interrelated phenomena. First, a population's size, composition by age and sex, and geographical distribution have a direct influence on overall health status. Age has a particularly marked effect on the pattern and extent of ill-health in populations because of the strong relationship

between age and mortality and morbidity. Second, each of the dynamic processes influencing population size and growth, structure, and distribution, namely, fertility, mortality, and migration, will also affect health status. Thus, any discussion of disease control priorities and of the health system for delivering interventions requires an understanding of the demographic context and how it is changing.

This chapter begins by providing an overview of global population trends in each major region of the world and the current size and composition of the population. Given this volume's focus on the descriptive epidemiology of diseases, injuries, and risk factors, we then examine trends in mortality over the past decade in more detail as background against which the current assessment of the disease burden might be more usefully interpreted. This includes both an assessment of trends in age-specific mortality and summary measures of the age schedule of mortality, such as life expectancy and the probability of dying within certain age ranges, as well as a specific discussion of trends in the main causes of child mortality. The focus on child mortality is entirely appropriate because (a) the fact that at the end of the 20th century, we remained woefully ignorant of its levels, let alone its causes, is highlighted; (b) the reduction of child mortality should remain a priority for global health development efforts, and the moral imperative to do so remains as relevant today as it was 30 years ago, when efforts to improve child survival became increasingly organized and focused; and (c) the resulting emphasis by the global public health community on reducing child mortality has yielded vastly more epidemiological information that can be used to assess trends in levels and causes. Nevertheless, we argue later in the chapter that large and unacceptable uncertainties about trends in cause-specific child mortality rates persist, with important implications for program planning and evaluation.

REGIONAL DEMOGRAPHIC CHARACTERISTICS

The key characteristics of regional demography of concern for health services provision include the size, age structure, and sex structure of the population and its rate of growth and comparative measures of fertility and mortality.

Sources of Population Data and Methodology

The population and mortality estimates for various regions summarized here are based on different data sources and methods, and thus are not strictly comparable. This primarily concerns the impact of different estimates of deaths by age and sex on population size and structure. Because the effect of mortality on population size and structure is generally modest, such differences have little impact on the findings reported in this chapter. The population estimates are based on data the United Nations (UN) Population Division compiled and analyzed for its biennial assessment of global population trends and regional demographic patterns (United Nations 2003). The UN Population Division estimates population size and vital rates (births and deaths) from censuses, vital registration, and demographic and health surveys and evaluates the data for completeness, accuracy, and consistency. Where necessary, it adjusts the data to achieve internal consistency and cross-country comparability. The baseline from which the UN projections are made is mid-2003. Because the 2002 revision was produced without complete data for 2001 for all countries, the baseline estimates are also projections, and the population figures in this chapter are therefore a mixture of both observed and projected data.[1]

The UN Population Division assesses a number of demographic parameters to produce country projections. In addition to total population, the baseline assessment includes a breakdown of population by sex and age (in five-year aggregates). Fertility is specified as age-specific fertility rates for females and mortality rates are based on survival probabilities from life tables. Age-specific patterns of migration are also incorporated for countries in which migration flows are observed or are thought to occur. When these inputs are not available from any of the sources listed earlier, the UN uses demographic models, such as model life tables or indirect mortality estimation techniques, to generate the information. Additional modeling is applied to estimate mortality patterns in countries with significant HIV/AIDS prevalence levels.

The UN Population Division provides a limited amount of information about the data in its reports, including the dates of censuses, the adjustment factors applied to total census populations, and the type and year of the latest surveys that contained mortality and fertility estimates. It does not provide information about the adjustments made to reported fertility rates, age and sex structures, or mortality rates. Basic information on population size and composition is available for most countries for 1990, and with the exception of Sub-Saharan Africa, for 2000 (or thereabouts) as well (table 2.1). Around both dates, censuses covered more than 90 percent of populations in all the regions except Sub-Saharan Africa. Thus, the basic population estimates developed by the UN Population Division and summarized in this chapter have a reasonable evidence base.

The UN projections of population size and vital rates are based on assumptions about levels and trends in vital rates. Fertility is assumed to follow a path modeled on the experience of countries with declining fertility, except when a country's recent fertility trend deviates considerably from

Table 2.1 Percentage of Regional Population Covered by Censuses, circa 1990 and 2000

Region	1990	2000
East Asia and Pacific	95.7	96.2
Europe and Central Asia	100.0	93.9
Latin America and the Caribbean	95.2	91.9
Middle East and North Africa	96.9	98.6
South Asia	87.0	98.1
Sub-Saharan Africa	81.6	53.4
High-income countries	90.2	99.0

Source: U.S. Census Bureau, Population Division, International Programs Center (July 7, 2004).

the model pattern, in which case the country-specific pattern is followed (United Nations 2003).

Our 2001 estimates and future projections are generated on the basis of the cohort component methodology. This approach applies estimated trends in birth and death rates and migration by age and sex to a baseline age and sex structure. Population growth rates are determined by the levels of age-specific fertility and mortality rates and migration and the size of the initial age groups (base year population) against which these levels are applied. We constructed demographic estimates for the aggregate regional and income groupings used for the second edition of *Disease Control Priorities in Developing Countries* (Jamison and others 2006) from the UN Population Division country-level estimates by aggregating populations in specific age and sex groups and age-specific fertility rates. The aggregates are thus weighted by the different population sizes of individual countries.

The mortality estimates presented in this chapter are developed from other sources using methods different than those the UN employed, as described later. As a result, the age and sex structures reported here, as well as any indicators derived from them (such as crude birth and death rates) are not strictly internally consistent. In particular, the mortality rates estimated for this chapter would, in some cases, have produced different age and sex population structures than those estimated by the UN, as well as different numbers of births and deaths. These differences are unlikely to be large, however, as the estimated age-specific mortality rates reported later in this chapter agree quite closely with those of the UN, except for Sub-Saharan Africa.

Population Size and Growth

Between 1990 and 2001, global population increased from about 5.3 billion to 6.1 billion people, an average rate of increase of 1.4 percent per year, equivalent to about 220,000 people per day (table 2.2). During the decade, the growth rate in developing regions ranged from 0.2 percent in Europe and Central Asia to 2.6 percent in Sub-Saharan Africa.

Estimates at the global level conceal large differences in population growth among regions, which in turn consist of countries that may have quite different demographic trends. For example, Europe and Central Asia added just 1 million people per year between 1990 and 2001, whereas South Asia added 25 million people each year.

The World Bank regions (see map 1 inside the front cover of this volume) vary substantially in terms of population size, with East Asia and the Pacific accounting for about 30 percent of the global population and South Asia for roughly another 20 percent. Thus, about half the world's population live in the low- and middle-income countries of these two regions. The smallest region in terms of population size is the Middle East and North Africa, with just 5 percent of the world's population. Just over 10 percent of the world's population live in Sub-Saharan Africa. Another 15 percent live in high-income countries, a proportion that is declining.

Distribution by Age, Sex, and Location

How populations are distributed by age matters a great deal for public health, because many aspects of risk behavior, as well as disease and injury outcomes, are strongly associated with age. While many other factors contribute to mortality and fertility levels, the age distribution of a population is an important factor in explaining differences in demographic and epidemiological indicators. Regions differ significantly in how their populations are distributed across age groups, with almost 45 percent of the population of Sub-Saharan Africa being younger than 15, compared with 20 percent of the population in high-income countries, where fertility has been low for decades. Nevertheless, the trends during 1990–2001 show a great deal of similarity: in all regions the proportion of the population in the youngest age groups was lower in 2001 than in 1990, with most of the increase occurring in the 15 through 69 age group. As a result, the median age of the population has increased in all regions. At the same time, the population aged 70 and older has been increasing in most regions as mortality has declined, and this age group now represents more than 10 percent of the population in the high-income countries.

These changes in the relative age distribution of populations since 1990 reflect changes in the growth rates of different age groups (figure 2.1). In three of the six regions (East Asia and Pacific, Europe and Central Asia, and the Middle East and North Africa), as well as the world as a whole, the number of children under five was smaller in absolute terms in 2001 than in 1990. The highest growth rates during this period were in the 40- through 55-year-old age group and among those over 70. The irregularities in growth rates of different age groups reflect past trends in the initial size of each cohort and its subsequent mortality and migration experiences. This is particularly evident for Europe and Central Asia, where the impact of the regional conflicts in the early 1990s on demographic structure is particularly evident.

Table 2.2 Population Size and Composition, Fertility, and GNP, by World Bank Region, 1990 and 2001

Population Characteristic	Low- and middle-income countries		East Asia and Pacific		Europe and Central Asia		Latin America and the Caribbean	
	1990	2001	1990	2001	1990	2001	1990	2001
Size								
Total population (thousands)	4,398,401	5,216,587	1,625,868	1,848,388	467,797	477,116	439,709	525,864
Proportion of world population (%)	83.6	84.9	30.9	30.1	8.9	7.8	8.4	8.6
Annual average growth rate, 1990–2001 (%)	1.6		1.2		0.2		1.6	
Composition (%)								
Age								
0–14	34.8	31.8	30.2	26.5	26.5	21.8	36.2	31.5
15–59	57.6	59.8	61.8	64.1	59.5	62.6	56.8	60.4
60–69	4.7	5.0	4.9	5.6	8.3	8.5	4.2	4.5
70+	2.9	3.4	3.0	3.8	5.6	7.2	2.9	3.6
Urban	36.9	41.6	28.8	37.0	63.2	63.5	71.1	75.4
Female	49.4	49.5	48.9	49.0	51.9	51.9	50.3	50.5
Fertility								
Total fertility rate	3.5	2.9	2.6	2.1	2.3	1.6	3.2	2.6
Total no. of births (thousands)	123,400	122,400	36,200	31,500	8,300	6,300	11,700	11,600
Crude birth rate per 1,000	28.2	23.4	22.3	17.0	16.7	12.7	26.6	22.0
GNP (exchange rate dollars)								
GNP per capita	870	1,170	420	890	39,737	54,933	2,260	3,570

Source: UN Population Division 2002 revision estimates.
Note: GNP = gross national product.

Along with the progressive aging of the population, the relentless trend toward increasing urbanization has continued, with consequences for health in terms of both health service provision, which, in principle, is better with urbanization, and risk of exposure to chronic disease, which is, on balance, worse (Ezzati and others 2005). Almost half the world's population lived in urban areas in 2001, up 4 percentage points from 1990. The increase in urbanization was particularly marked in East Asia and the Pacific (increase from 29 to 37 percent of the population) and in Sub-Saharan Africa (from 28 to 34 percent). Overall, 42 percent of the population in low- and middle-income countries now live in urban areas.

In general, more boys than girls are born, with sex ratios at birth of between 1.03 and 1.06 in most countries, though in some Asian countries, sex-selective abortions have skewed this ratio to more than 1.10. Differential mortality and, to a limited extent, migration, shape the sex ratio at other ages (figure 2.2). In South Asia, higher mortality for girls and for women during their childbearing years leads at first to an increasing and then to a constant sex ratio to about age 45, after which male mortality is higher. Excess mortality of adult males in Europe and Central Asia explains the particularly low sex ratio observed there (Lopez and others 2002). In all regions, the higher mortality of males

relative to females accounts for the sharp decline in the population sex ratio after age 50 or thereabouts.

The overall effects of the age-specific mortality differences between the sexes are relatively minor in terms of total population sex ratios. All regions have roughly equal numbers of males and females in the population, with the proportion of males being slightly higher in Europe and Central Asia and in the high-income regions (51 to 52 percent) than in East Asia and the Pacific and South Asia (49 percent).

Fertility

Table 2.2 shows recent trends in fertility, as indicated by the total fertility rate for the period, that is, the average number of children a woman could expect to have if she were subject indefinitely to current age-specific fertility rates. Even though fertility levels vary a good deal among regions, all low- and middle-income regions witnessed large declines in fertility levels during the 1990s. Overall fertility levels in low- and middle-income countries fell by almost 20 percent over the decade, a remarkable decline, with levels falling by as much as 33 percent in the Middle East and North Africa, and even by 10 percent in Sub-Saharan Africa. However, fertility rates in Sub-Saharan Africa remain high, with the total fertility rate of 5.6 being about twice as high as that for any other region.

Table 2.2 Continued

Middle East and North Africa		South Asia		Sub-Saharan Africa		High-income		World	
1990	2001	1990	2001	1990	2001	1990	2001	1990	2001
243,973	309,762	1,117,887	1,387,873	503,166	667,583	862,342	928,110	5,260,742	6,144,696
4.6	5.0	21.2	22.6	9.6	10.9	16.4	15.1	100.0	100.0
2.2		2.0		2.6		0.7		1.4	
43.1	36.4	37.8	35.3	45.7	44.3	20.0	18.5	32.4	29.8
51.5	57.7	55.7	57.6	49.7	51.0	62.5	62.2	58.4	60.2
3.5	3.6	4.2	4.4	3.0	3.0	9.0	9.1	5.4	5.6
1.9	2.4	2.3	2.7	1.6	1.7	8.5	10.2	3.8	4.5
53.5	57.5	25.0	27.4	27.9	34.0	74.4	77.1	43.0	46.9
49.0	49.3	48.4	48.5	50.4	50.4	51.0	50.8	49.6	49.7
5.0	3.6	4.3	3.4	6.3	5.6	1.7	1.7	3.2	2.7
9,300	9,400	36,500	37,300	21,400	26,300	11,300	10,800	134,700	133,200
34.8	27.3	32.7	26.7	44.6	40.8	13.4	11.9	25.7	21.6
1,770	3,570	380	450	470	550	19,760	26,760	4,060	5,180

Few low- and middle-income countries experienced increasing fertility during 1990–2001,[2] though a few high-income countries have seen small upturns from previously low levels. Fertility is below replacement levels (about two children) in all but five high-income countries (Brunei Darussalam, Israel, Kuwait, Qatar, and the United Arab Emirates), as well as in most countries in Europe and Central Asia. When fertility drops to below replacement levels, population growth often continues for several decades, as the number of births exceeds the number of deaths because of the high proportion of women of childbearing age.

CHANGES IN MORTALITY, 1990–2001

Change in patterns of mortality is a major determinant of the demography of populations and underlies important population differentials. For example, the differences in mortality by sex across regions contribute to the variable pattern of population sex ratios described earlier. The theory of demographic transition suggests that the rapid declines in fertility observed during the 1990s in most regions would be preceded, and perhaps accompanied, by a similarly rapid decline in child mortality. To help interpret the broad regional demographic patterns described earlier, a review of trends in mortality and the causes underlying such trends is useful.

Estimating Mortality

Various methods are available to estimate age patterns and levels of mortality in populations. These fall into three broad categories depending on the available data: direct estimation from complete vital registration, estimates from vital registration corrected for undercounting, and estimates derived from models based on child mortality levels. Mathers and others (2005) review the availability and quality of mortality data and group the 192 member states of the World Health Organization into broad categories according to criteria pertaining to the coverage, completeness, and quality of cause of death data. Their findings indicate that only about 33 percent (64) of World Health Organization member states, mostly high-income countries, have complete mortality data and that another 26 percent (50 countries) have data that can be used for mortality estimation purposes. The approximately 40 percent of remaining countries either have no recent data or no data at all that can be used to estimate causes of death or the level of adult mortality directly.

The situation is somewhat different for levels of child mortality, where decades of interest in monitoring child survival by the global public health community have yielded either direct or indirect estimates of child mortality for all but a handful of countries (Hill and others 1999; Lopez and others 2002). Based on a careful review of the time trend of

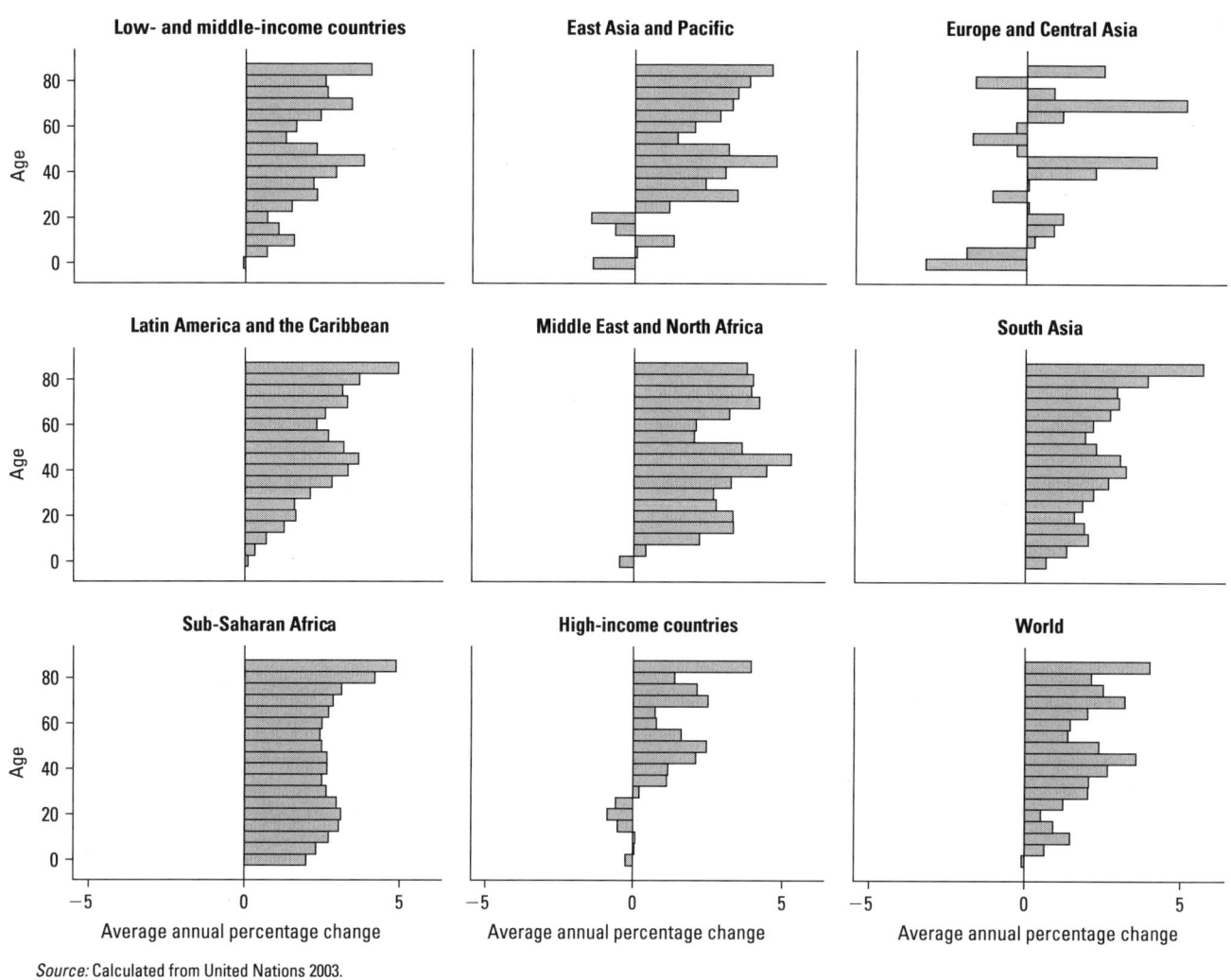

Figure 2.1 Changes in Population Age Distribution, 1990–2001

Source: Calculated from United Nations 2003.

these estimates of child deaths, which come primarily from censuses and surveys, estimating child mortality levels in 1990 and 2001 is possible for virtually all countries with an acceptable level of uncertainty. Levels of child mortality are unavailable for only about 10 countries that together account for about 2 percent of child deaths (Lopez and others 2002). Formal curve-fitting procedures to estimate time trends in child mortality can be applied to all the data, but given the subjective assessments that are required to judge which data points are plausible and which are not, simple averaging of all plausible observations at any given point in time is likely to be sufficient, and this was the procedure used to estimate child mortality levels for this chapter.

For those countries with complete vital registration data, age-specific and cause-specific death rates are easily derived directly from the registration data and from population censuses. For those countries where registration data are incomplete, demographers have developed indirect demographic methods to correct for underreporting of deaths before estimating age-specific mortality (Bennett and Horiuchi 1984; Hill 1987). These countries include China and India, where application of such methods suggest that data from the disease surveillance points system in China and the sample registration system in India are 85 to 90 percent complete (Mari Bhat 2002; Rao and others 2005).

For countries with no usable data on adult mortality levels, age-specific death rates were predicted from the modified logit life table system (Murray and others 2003). The median level of adult mortality was predicted based on a modeled relationship between adult and child mortality as determined from a historical data set of more than 1,800 life tables judged to be reasonably complete. Uncertainty about these predicted mean values of adult mortality is considerable given the few observations with comparatively

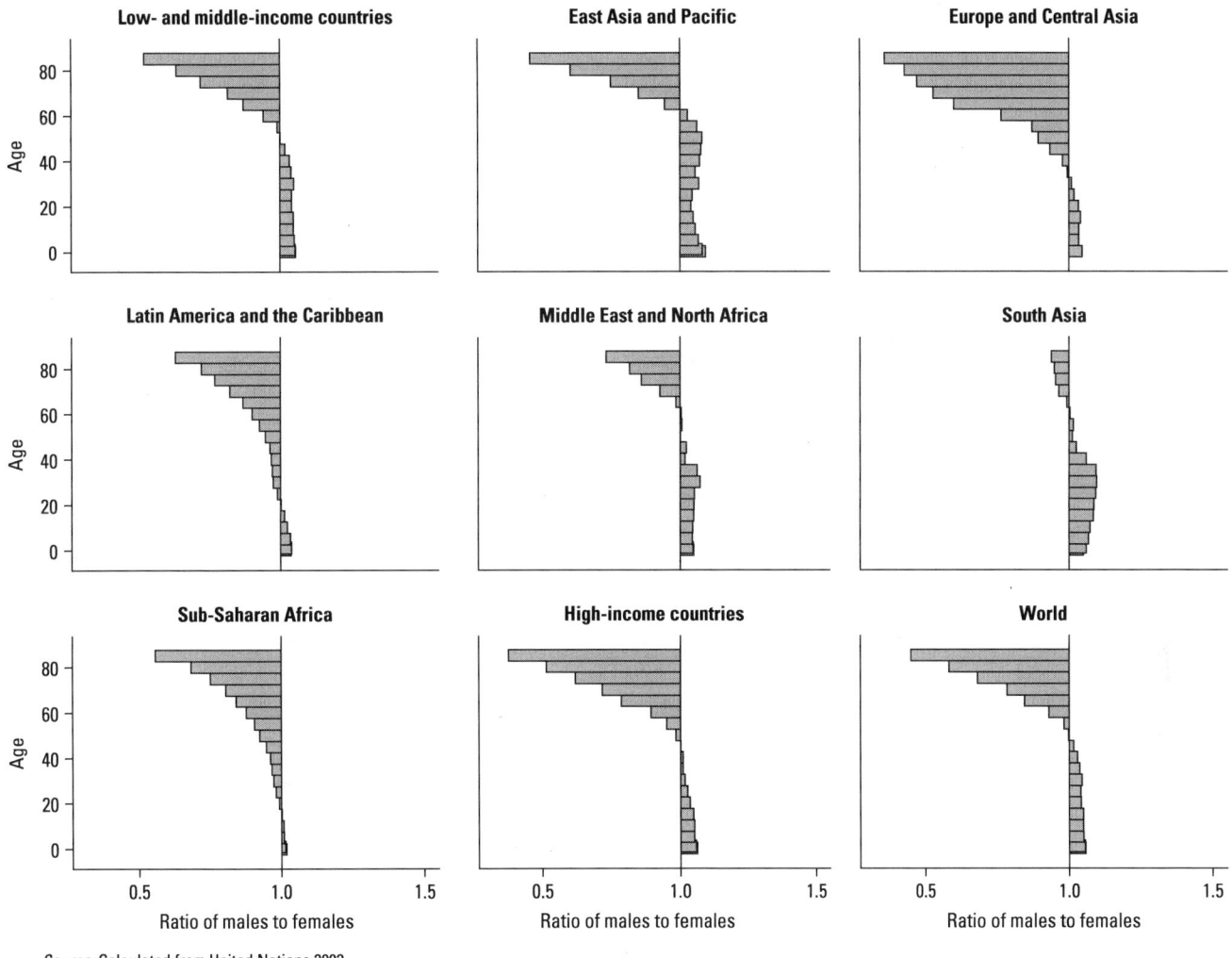

Figure 2.2 Population Sex Ratios at Different Ages, 2001

Source: Calculated from United Nations 2003.

high levels of child and adult mortality. The estimated and predicted levels of child and adult mortality, respectively, were then applied to the modified life table system by selecting the best match from among 50,000 life tables to estimate a complete, smoothed set of age-specific death rates (Murray and others 2003). This method was applied for all but about 70 countries.

Obvious uncertainties are associated with this procedure. Hence, the life tables for East Asia and the Pacific, the Middle East and North Africa, and Sub-Saharan Africa (where HIV/AIDS mortality was added to the predicted adult mortality rates) in particular need to be viewed with caution, because the rates for many countries in these regions have been modeled using these methods.

Identical methods were applied to estimate national age-specific mortality rates for both 1990 and 2001; thus, the two sets of estimates are, in principle at least, comparable.

Annex 2A provides detailed estimates of summary measures of mortality by country for the two years based on these methods. The annex also shows the percentage decline in child mortality during the period.

Whether these methods correctly describe levels and patterns of mortality is difficult to ascertain given the substantial uncertainties in the data, particularly for adult mortality. The only other systematic attempt to estimate national and global death rates in 1990 is that of the UN Population Division (United Nations 2003). Figure 2.3 presents estimated mortality parameters for 1990 by region. For a comparison of mortality estimates for 2001, see Lopez and others (2002).

Despite the UN's different model life table approach for estimating age-specific death rates based on child mortality, the two sets of estimates shown in figure 2.3 are remarkably congruent. Regional estimates of child mortality $_5q_0$ (the

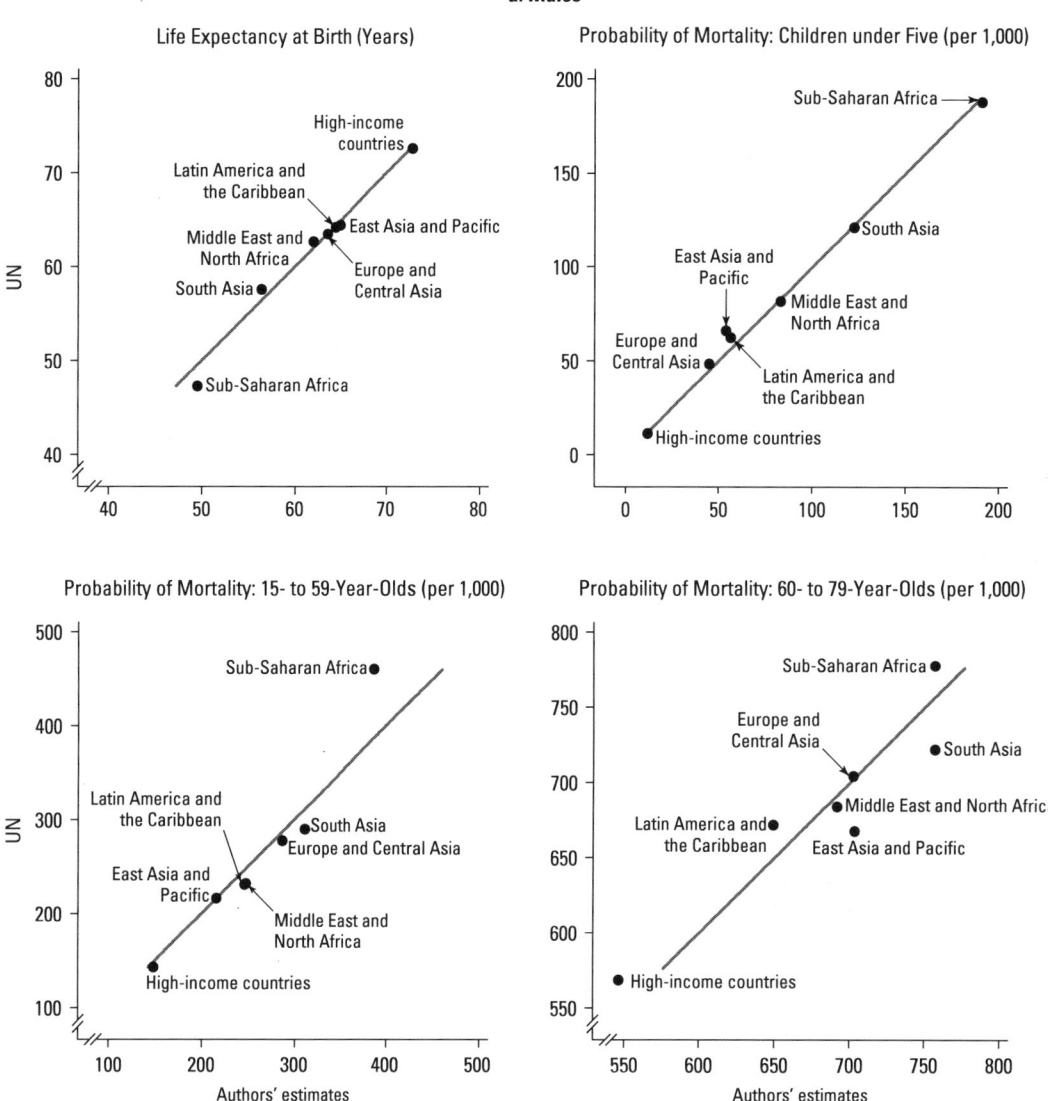

a. Males

Figure 2.3 UN's versus Authors' Life Table Parameters, 1990

mortality risk for children under five years of age) are virtually identical, with a possible exception being the UN's slightly higher levels of child mortality for East Asia and the Pacific (which is dominated by China). This congruence is not unexpected given the intense collaborative efforts of the past five years or so by the World Health Organization, the United Nations Children's Fund, the United Nations, and the World Bank to agree upon a common interpretation of the extensive data available on trends in child mortality in low- and middle-income countries.

Somewhat surprisingly given the quite different methodological approaches, regional estimates of adult mortality $_{45}q_{15}$ (the mortality risk for adults between the ages of 15 and 60) are remarkably similar, with our estimates tending to be slightly higher in the Middle East and North Africa and South Asia for males and slightly lower in the same regions for females. That is, we have estimated larger sex mortality differentials among adults than the UN on the basis of observed patterns of mortality where data were available (as in the Arab Republic of Egypt and India), and where not, on the basis of observed differences in child mortality for boys and girls. Some investigators expect male excess mortality to increase with social development and economic growth (Bhatia 1983), but whether this is better reflected in our estimates or those of the UN is not clear. In any case, the differences are minor. Significantly more disagreement is apparent for Sub-Saharan Africa, with the UN estimates of adult mortality in 1990 being one-quarter to one-third higher than ours. This is obviously

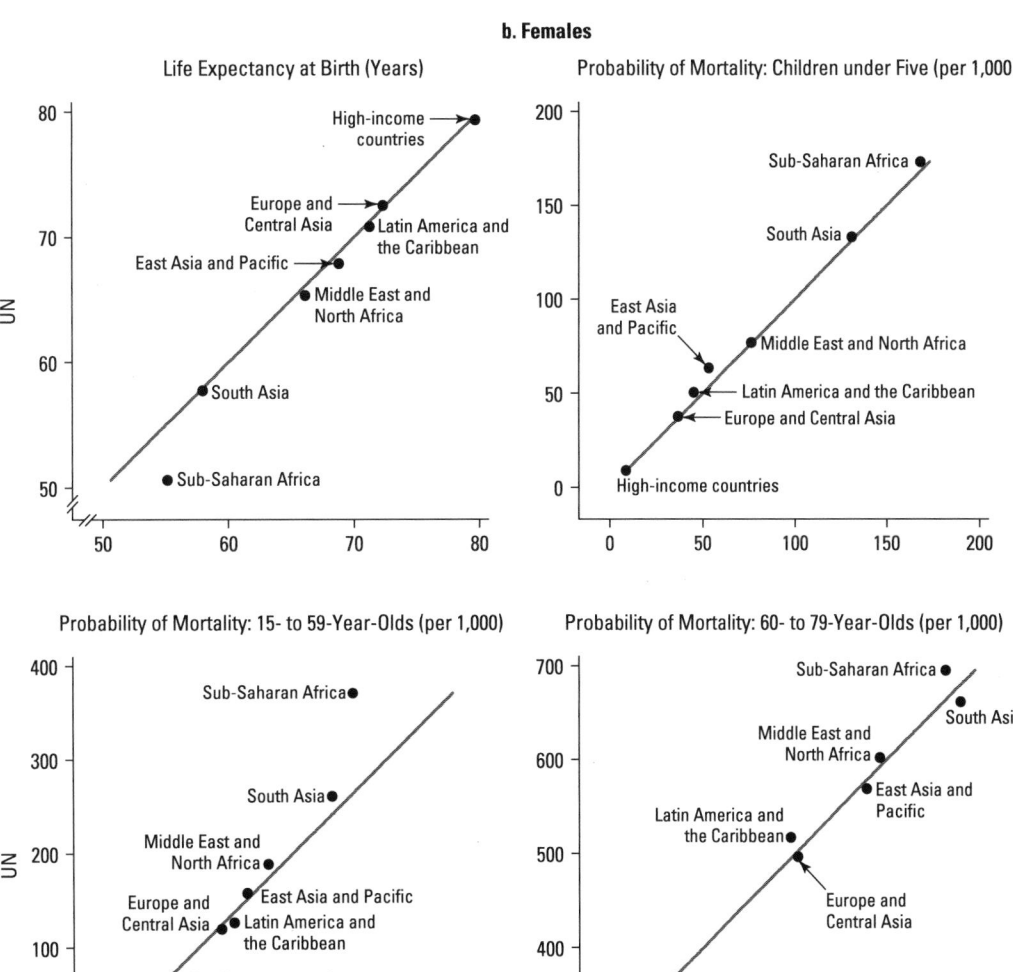

b. Females

Life Expectancy at Birth (Years)

Probability of Mortality: Children under Five (per 1,000)

Probability of Mortality: 15- to 59-Year-Olds (per 1,000)

Probability of Mortality: 60- to 79-Year-Olds (per 1,000)

Sources: UN parameters are from United Nations 2005b; authors' estimates are from this chapter.

Figure 2.3 Continued

uncertain given the sparse data available on adult mortality in the region and the fact that the HIV epidemic in Sub-Saharan Africa was well established by then, and hence a higher estimate may be justified. Recent evidence, however, has suggested that basing mortality estimates on prenatal clinic data may well lead to an overestimation of death rates due to HIV.

Differences in methodology and adjustment criteria appear to have the greatest effect at older ages, especially for males. The UN estimates indicate significantly higher mortality in high-income countries at ages 60 to 79 even though complete vital registration data are available for virtually all the countries except some of the small Gulf states. Differences in estimated mortality for the Sub-Saharan

Africa region are not unexpected given the differences reported for younger adults, and are less extreme than at ages 15 to 59, as one might expect given that HIV/AIDS mortality is not of major consequence for older ages. Otherwise, estimates for females at older ages agree quite closely, but the UN's are significantly higher than ours for Latin America and the Caribbean and significantly lower for East Asia and the Pacific and South Asia. These differences arise because the model life table methods used by the UN tend to shift deaths from younger to older adult ages at lower levels of child mortality (Latin America and the Caribbean) and the converse at higher levels of child death rates (East Asia and the Pacific and South Asia).

Table 2.3 Selected Mortality Characteristics by Sex and World Bank Region, 1990 and 2001

| | | | | % of deaths | | Probability of dying per 1,000 | | | | Expectation of life at |
Sex and region	Year	Deaths (millions)	Crude death rate per 1,000	Under age 5	Over age 60	Ages 0–5[a]	Ages 15–60	Ages 0–60	Ages 60–80	birth (years)
Low- and middle-	1990	22.5	10.1	27.9	39.5	98	269	351	712	59.9
income countries	2001	25.5	9.7	21.2	42.2	86	269	341	667	61.2
East Asia and Pacific	1990	6.6	8.0	16.3	50.6	54	215	265	699	64.9
	2001	6.9	7.4	10.2	56.2	41	189	228	623	67.8
Europe and Central Asia	1990	2.5	11.1	7.9	55.9	45	286	323	696	63.6
	2001	3.0	13.0	3.2	59.6	32	328	353	711	63.0
Latin America and	1990	1.7	7.8	19.5	44.7	56	245	294	640	64.5
the Caribbean	2001	1.8	7.0	12.4	49.1	38	218	252	572	67.6
Middle East and	1990	1.0	8.2	34.9	34.2	83	247	318	688	62.0
North Africa	2001	1.1	6.8	21.6	45.2	56	216	267	674	65.2
South Asia	1990	6.8	11.7	32.4	35.0	122	310	407	754	56.4
	2001	7.1	9.9	25.1	39.2	94	285	362	710	59.9
Sub-Saharan Africa	1990	3.9	15.6	54.1	17.0	191	386	517	758	49.6
	2001	5.6	16.9	42.2	16.9	178	518	616	760	46.0
High-income countries	1990	3.9	9.1	1.7	76.2	12	148	160	542	72.9
	2001	4.0	8.8	1.0	78.7	7	124	132	469	75.5
World	1990	26.4	10.0	24.0	44.8	91	245	323	667	61.7
	2001	29.5	9.6	18.5	47.2	80	243	312	618	63.1

Sources: Estimates for 1990 are authors' calculations, based on country-level life tables (see annex 2A). Estimates for 2001 are derived from Lopez and others 2002.
a. Estimates of child mortality are rounded to the nearest whole number.

Overall, as figure 2.3 demonstrates, the age patterns are largely compensatory, with the result that estimates of life expectancy at birth for the two series are remarkably similar for both males and females, with the notable exception being Sub-Saharan Africa, where the higher adult mortality assumptions favored by the UN result in life expectancies at birth that are about 2.5 years lower than ours for males and 5.0 years lower for females.

Trends in Mortality Levels

The 1990s were characterized by significant economic gains in most regions, with growth in gross national product per capita ranging from 18 percent in South Asia and Sub-Saharan Africa to more than 100 percent in East Asia and the Pacific and the Middle East and North Africa (table 2.2). Overall, gross national product per capita grew by about 35 percent in low- and middle-income countries during the decade. One would expect this to have led to a significant improvement in life expectancy, and this indeed occurred in most regions with the notable exception of Europe and Central Asia and, in particular, Sub-Saharan Africa (table 2.3). In the former region, life expectancy was largely

unchanged over the decade, primarily because of the massive rise in adult mortality in countries such as the Russian Federation and its neighbors during the first part of the decade, which negated the declines in child mortality. Much of this extraordinary increase in adult mortality, which rose by about 50 percent between 1987 and 1994, has been attributed to alcohol abuse, particularly among men (Leon and others 1997; Shkolnikov, McKee, and Leon 2001).

Economic development and better coverage of the population with essential child health services have ensured continued declines in levels of child mortality, as measured by the risk of death from birth to age five, in all regions. The notable exception is Sub-Saharan Africa, where child mortality among girls remained unchanged at around 165 per 1,000, with only a modest decline (5 percent) in the risk of death for boys. The absence of significant declines in child mortality in the 1990s in Sub-Saharan Africa is most likely largely due to the impact of HIV/AIDS. Overall, the risk of child death declined from 90 per 1,000 in 1990 to 80 per 1,000 in 2001, with the risk being remarkably similar for males and females (table 2.3); however, the differential in child mortality between the world's richest and poorest populations is stark, with a newborn in Sub-Saharan Africa

Table 2.3 Continued

		Female						
Deaths (millions)	Crude death rate per 1,000	% of deaths		Probability of dying per 1,000				Expectation of life at birth (years)
		Under age 5	Over age 60	Ages 0–5[a]	Ages 15–60	Ages 0–60	Ages 60–80	
19.4	8.9	29.7	44.6	95	182	270	585	64.2
22.8	8.8	22.5	48.3	86	191	271	554	64.9
5.5	7.0	17.8	56.2	53	152	204	577	68.8
6.1	6.8	11.4	64.6	44	127	171	519	71.3
2.4	9.9	6.4	77.5	37	125	162	503	72.3
2.7	10.8	2.9	81.5	26	133	159	511	72.8
1.3	5.7	20.1	53.9	45	138	182	493	71.3
1.4	5.4	12.5	61.3	32	124	155	434	73.9
0.8	6.9	37.7	36.1	76	174	245	593	66.1
0.8	5.5	23.5	49.7	51	144	193	562	69.5
6.1	11.2	37.0	33.7	131	243	357	680	57.9
6.5	9.6	28.3	40.2	101	226	317	645	61.5
3.3	12.9	54.8	19.6	168	265	403	664	55.1
5.2	15.5	40.9	18.3	166	437	545	680	48.9
3.6	8.2	1.3	87.3	9	74	83	346	79.7
3.9	8.2	0.8	88.3	6	65	73	297	81.6
23.0	8.8	25.2	51.3	88	161	244	516	66.6
26.7	8.7	19.3	54.1	80	168	244	487	67.3

facing 25 times the risk of death before the age of five than a newborn in a high-income country.

Despite the much greater uncertainty in relation to levels of adult mortality compared with those for children, the estimates shown in table 2.3 nonetheless indicate substantially different trends in adult mortality across different regions between 1990 and 2001. For most regions, the risk of death between ages 15 and 60 fell by about 10 to 17 percent over the decade. This was not the case in Europe and Central Asia, where policy shifts, particularly in relation to alcohol, together with broader social change, have largely been responsible for the 15 percent rise in adult male mortality and the 6 percent increase in the risk of death for women. Note that these estimates mask the large cyclical fluctuations in adult mortality in Russia, in particular, that characterized the region's mortality trends in the 1990s.

Table 2.3 also reveals the large increase in adult mortality in Sub-Saharan Africa, which was due primarily to the unfolding of the HIV/AIDS epidemic in southern Africa. Notwithstanding the substantial uncertainty surrounding these estimates, the epidemic appears to have been of proportionately greater consequence for women, with the rise in their risk of death (67 percent) being twice that of males, among whom other causes of death such as violence were more common. If these estimates are correct, then

52.0 percent of African males reaching age 15 and 44.0 percent of females will die before their 60th birthdays, compared with, for instance, 6.5 percent of women in high-income countries, who despite their already low risk enjoyed a further 11 percent decline in mortality during the 1990s. These reversals in mortality decline have effectively negated gains elsewhere, with the result that the global risk of adult death has remained essentially unchanged for males, and may even have risen slightly for females.

Taken together, the probability of death up to the age of five and between the ages of 15 and 60 are a better reflection of the risk of premature death than either alone, although both have particular public health implications. One might argue that health policy should be equally concerned with keeping adults alive into old age as it is with keeping children alive into adulthood. A convenient metric in this regard is the risk of death between birth and age 60 (table 2.3). In high-income countries, given 2001 mortality rates, only about 7 percent of females and 13 percent of males would be dead by age 60, compared with 55 percent of females and 62 percent of males in Sub-Saharan Africa. Significant improvements in this summary measure of premature death can be observed in all regions except Europe and Central Asia and Sub-Saharan Africa. Worldwide, the index appears to have improved slightly for males and not at all for females.

Other features of global mortality summarized in table 2.3 are worth highlighting. First is the impressive evidence of a continued decline in mortality among older age groups in high-income countries that began in the early 1970s. The risk of a 60-year-old dying before age 80 declined by about 15 percent for both men and women in high-income countries so that at 2001 rates, less than 30 percent of women who reach age 60 will be dead by age 80, as will less than 50 percent of men. Second, crude death rates in East Asia and the Pacific, Latin America and the Caribbean, and the Middle East and North Africa are lower than in high-income countries, reflecting the impact of the older age structure of rich countries, and are particularly low in Latin America and the Caribbean. Third, the proportion of deaths that occur below age five, while declining in all regions, varies enormously across them, from just over 1 percent in high-income countries to just over 40 percent in Sub-Saharan Africa. In some low- and middle-income regions, particularly East Asia and the Pacific, Europe and Central Asia, and Latin America and the Caribbean, the proportion is well below 20 percent. The net effect of these changes in age-specific mortality since 1990 has been to increase global life expectancy at birth by 0.7 years for females and by about twice this for males: a modest scorecard.

TRENDS IN CAUSES OF CHILD DEATH, 1990–2001

The estimation of cause of death patterns for world regions will, for the foreseeable future, be substantially uncertain given the paucity of data on medically certified deaths in many low- and middle-income countries (Mathers and others 2005; Sibai 2004). Verbal autopsies, that is, structured interviews with relatives of the deceased about symptoms experienced prior to death, will not yield the diagnostic accuracy achievable with medical certification based on good clinical case histories and medical records. This is not to deny that verbal autopsies can meet broad policy needs for information about causes of death, particularly with clinical input into the coding of interviewees' responses, but their reliability for diagnosing leading causes of child death is questionable (Snow and others 1992). Thus, estimates of child mortality derived from proportionate mortality models that are based largely on verbal autopsies need to be viewed with caution (Lopez 2003; Morris, Black, and Tomaskovic 2003).

Yet, despite these concerns about the quality of cause of death data, investigators can more confidently assess the comparative magnitude of causes of death for children than for adults. The fact that the demographic "envelope" of child deaths is reasonably well understood in all regions limits excessive claims about deaths due to individual causes, a constraint that is not a feature of adult mortality given the relative ignorance of age-specific death rates in many countries. In addition, the need for data on cause-specific outcomes to assess and monitor the impact of various child survival programs in recent decades has led to a reasonably substantial epidemiological literature that might permit cause-specific estimation, but under an unacceptably large number of assumptions (Black, Morris, and Bryce 2003).

A critical feature of any estimation exercise is a rigorous assessment of data sets for biases, study methods, and generalizability of results. Investigators have undertaken a number of efforts to estimate the causes of child mortality over the past decade or so (Bryce and others 2005; Lopez 1993; Morris, Black, and Tomaskovic 2004; Williams and others 2002), but undoubtedly the most comprehensive was the study by Murray and Lopez (1996) and its 2001 revision (chapter 3 in this volume). Both the latter Global Burden of Disease (GBD) studies apply methods to force epidemiological consistency according to the evidence available for each region, and inevitably the constraint of demography has meant that the GBD estimates of cause-specific mortality will differ from those developed largely independently of other causes. That is, the GBD estimates of specific causes of death are constrained to sum to the number of deaths derived from demographic analyses, whereas cause-specific estimates that are derived in the absence of such demographic constraints are unbounded and tend to be inclusive at the margin rather than exclusive. Differences in regional estimates between 1990 and 2001 arise in part because the countries included in the regions differed and, more important, because of better information for more recent periods. Yet, despite improved information, the true level of child death rates from major causes such as malaria and perinatal conditions (birth trauma, birth asphyxia, sepsis, and prematurity) remains largely unknown.

Notwithstanding methodological differences and uncertainties, deriving implied estimates of trends in the leading causes of child mortality is possible by comparing results from the two GBD studies, and these are summarized in table 2.4. These estimates have been simply obtained as the difference between the regional estimates for 1990 and 2001, but the implied pattern of change is interesting nonetheless. The conversion of the 1990 regional GBD estimates (Murray and Lopez 1996) to the regions used for the 2001 assessment

Table 2.4 Mortality in Children Under Five by Cause, 1990 and 2001

Disease and indicator	Low- and middle-income countries 1990	2001	East Asia and Pacific 1990	2001	Europe and Central Asia 1990	2001	Latin America and the Caribbean 1990	2001	Middle East and North Africa 1990	2001	South Asia 1990	2001	Sub-Saharan Africa 1990	2001	High-income countries 1990	2001	World 1990	2001
Acute respiratory infections																		
Deaths (thousands)	2,521	1,943	492	197	68	36	83	44	138	76	1,027	833	713	757	13	2	2,533	1,944
% of childhood deaths	21.0	18.4	23.8	14.0	19.5	20.6	14.1	10.9	20.6	17.7	23.2	23.1	18.3	16.8	11.1	2.3	20.9	18.3
Probability of dying before age 5 per 1,000 live births	20	16	13	6	8	6	7	4	16	9	29	22	33	29	1	0	19	15
Congenital anomalies																		
Deaths (thousands)	421	421	118	115	25	24	30	41	22	41	186	142	41	58	19	18	440	439
% of childhood deaths	3.5	4.0	5.7	8.2	7.1	13.5	5.1	10.1	3.3	9.5	4.2	3.9	1.0	1.3	16.3	24.6	3.6	4.1
Probability of dying before age 5 per 1,000 live births	3	3	3	4	3	4	3	4	3	5	5	4	2	2	2	2	3	3
Diarrheal diseases																		
Deaths (thousands)	2,362	1,599	274	201	61	12	108	46	144	66	991	631	784	643	11	0	2,374	1,600
% of childhood deaths	19.7	15.2	13.2	14.3	17.4	6.9	18.3	11.4	21.6	15.3	22.4	17.5	20.1	14.3	9.9	0.6	19.6	15.1
Probability of dying before age 5 per 1,000 live births	19	13	7	6	7	2	9	4	17	8	28	17	36	25	1	0	17	12
HIV/AIDS																		
Deaths (thousands)	62	340	—	5	—	0	2	6	0	1	—	14	60	313	0	0	62	340
% of childhood deaths	0.5	3.2	0.0	0.4	0.0	0.2	0.3	1.4	0.0	0.1	0.0	0.4	1.5	7.0	0.0	0.1	0.5	3.2
Probability of dying before age 5 per 1,000 live births	0	3	0	0	0	0	0	1	0	0	0	0	3	12	0	0	0	3
Injuries																		
Deaths (thousands)	647	302	206	82	25	11	28	19	32	24	188	79	169	87	9	7	656	309
% of childhood deaths	5.4	2.9	9.9	5.8	7.0	6.6	4.7	4.6	4.8	5.6	4.2	2.2	4.3	1.9	7.8	9.8	5.4	2.9
Probability of dying before age 5 per 1,000 live births	5	2	5	2	3	2	2	2	4	3	5	2	8	3	1	1	5	2
Malaria																		
Deaths (thousands)	588	1,086	7	27	0	0	2	1	1	17	9	57	570	984	0	0	588	1,086
% of childhood deaths	4.9	10.3	0.3	1.9	0.1	0.0	0.3	0.3	0.1	3.9	0.2	1.6	14.6	21.8	0.2	0.1	4.8	10.2
Probability of dying before age 5 per 1,000 live births	5	9	0	1	0	0	0	0	0	2	0	2	26	38	0	0	4	8

(Continues on the following page.)

Table 2.4 Continued

Disease and indicator	Low- and middle-income countries		East Asia and Pacific		Europe and Central Asia		Latin America and the Caribbean		Middle East and North Africa		South Asia		Sub-Saharan Africa		High-income countries		World	
	1990	2001	1990	2001	1990	2001	1990	2001	1990	2001	1990	2001	1990	2001	1990	2001	1990	2001
Measles																		
Deaths (thousands)	869	556	75	45	12	5	38	—	30	10	239	145	474	351	3	0	872	556
% of childhood deaths	7.2	5.3	3.6	3.2	3.5	2.9	6.5	0.0	4.5	2.3	5.4	4.0	12.2	7.8	2.5	0.1	7.2	5.2
Probability of dying before age 5 per 1,000 live births	7	5	2	1	1	1	3	0	4	1	7	4	22	13	0	0	6	4
Perinatal conditions																		
Deaths (thousands)	2,261	2,492	480	506	83	57	162	164	141	106	906	1,086	487	573	38	32	2,298	2,524
% of childhood deaths	18.8	23.7	23.2	36.0	23.6	32.9	27.6	40.3	21.2	24.7	20.4	30.1	12.5	12.7	33.0	44.5	18.9	23.8
Probability of dying before age 5 per 1,000 live births	18	20	12	15	10	10	14	14	17	13	26	29	22	22	3	3	17	19
Other causes																		
Deaths (thousands)	2,288	1,792	420	228	77	28	137	85	159	90	888	625	607	737	22	13	2,309	1,805
% of childhood deaths	19.0	17.0	20.3	16.2	21.9	16.3	23.2	21.0	23.8	20.9	20.0	17.3	15.5	16.4	19.1	17.9	19.0	17.0
Probability of dying before age 5 per 1,000 live births	18	15	11	7	9	5	12	7	19	11	25	17	28	28	2	1	17	14
Total																		
Deaths (thousands)	12,019	10,532	2,072	1,407	352	174	588	407	668	429	4,434	3,612	3,904	4,504	115	73	12,134	10,605
% of childhood deaths	100.0	100.0	100.0	100.0	100.0	100.0	100.0	100.0	100.0	100.0	100.0	100.0	100.0	100.0	100.0	100.0	100.0	100.0
Probability of dying before age 5 per 1,000 live births	97	86	54	43	41	29	51	35	80	53	127	97	180	172	10	7	89	80

Sources: Estimates for 1990 are based on Murray and Lopez 1996, weighted to World Bank regions using population under five years old. Estimates for 2001 are from chapter 3 in this volume.

Note: — = not available or not applicable. Estimates of child mortality are rounded to the nearest whole number.

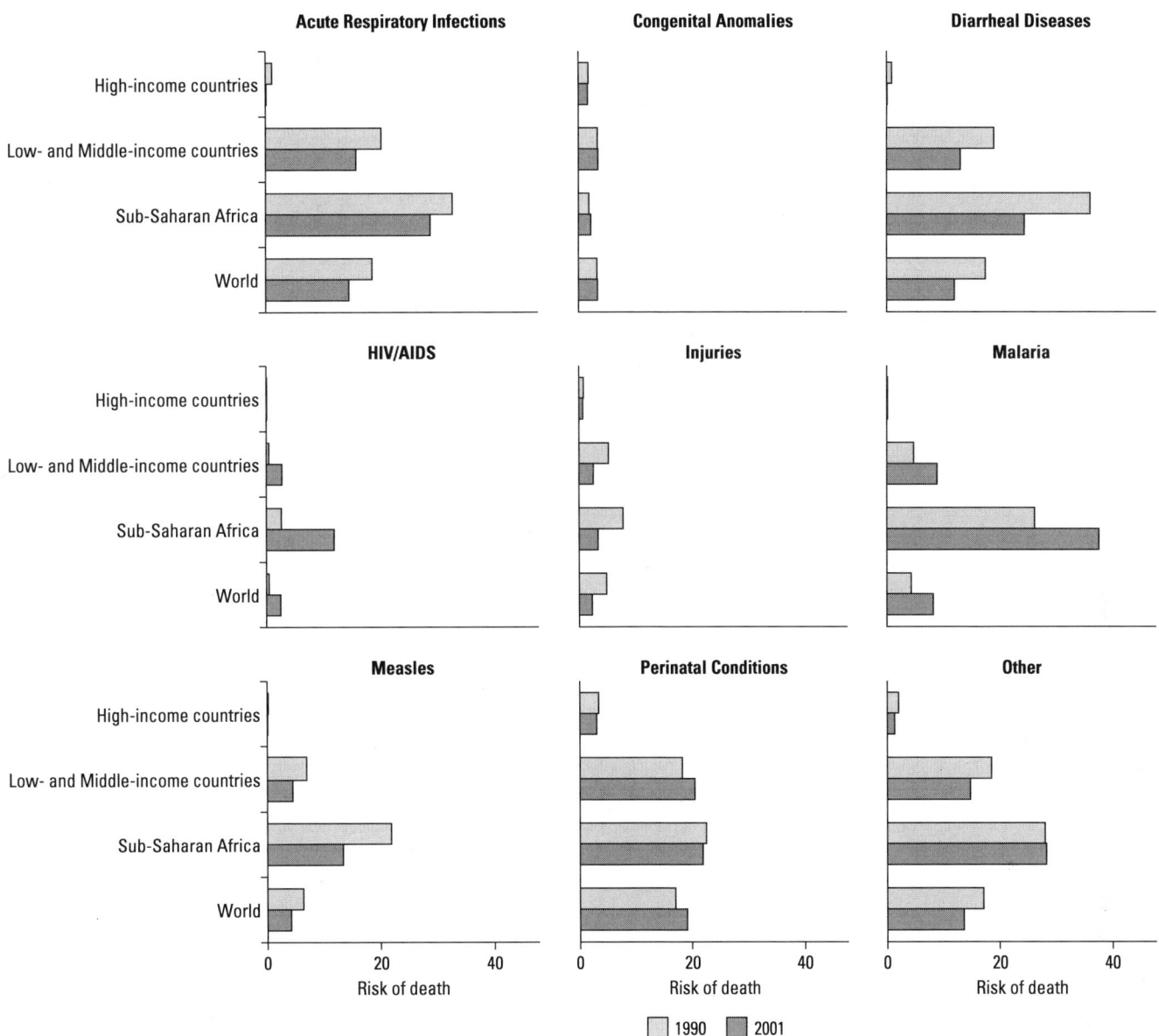

Acute Respiratory Infections   **Congenital Anomalies**   **Diarrheal Diseases**

HIV/AIDS   **Injuries**   **Malaria**

Measles   **Perinatal Conditions**   **Other**

Risk of death   Risk of death   Risk of death

☐ 1990   ▨ 2001

Sources: Estimates for 1990 are from Murray and Lopez 1996; estimates for 2001 are from chapter 3 in this volume.

Figure 2.4 Change in Risk of Death for Children Under Five by Cause (probability of mortality per 1,000 live births), 1990–2001

was done simply by population weighting, a very approximate procedure. By contrast, the 2001 estimates were prepared as regional aggregates of country-specific estimates (see chapter 3,) and this has undoubtedly affected comparisons further.

Global mortality from malaria increased by 0.5 million during the 1990s, with 80 percent of the deaths occurring in Sub-Saharan Africa. The proportion of all child deaths due to malaria doubled from 5 percent in 1990 to 10 percent in 2001 worldwide and increased from 15 percent in 1990 to

22 percent in 2001 in Sub-Saharan Africa. The only other causes that appear to have increased are HIV/AIDS in Africa, a reasonable conclusion given female prevalence levels, and the category of perinatal conditions, which are strongly dependent on the quality and availability of prenatal services. Causes that appear to have declined substantially include acute respiratory infections (2.5 million to 1.9 million deaths or 15 percent of all child deaths), diarrheal diseases (2.4 million to 1.6 million deaths or 13 percent of child deaths), measles (0.8 million to 0.5 million

deaths or 5 percent of child deaths), and injuries (0.6 million to 0.3 million deaths or 2 percent of child deaths).

The implied pattern of change in the risk of child death varies across regions for all major conditions listed in table 2.4, particularly with regard to the magnitude of change. This can be seen more clearly from figure 2.4, which summarizes these trends for broad regional aggregates and for Sub-Saharan Africa. In general, the absolute change in risk of death has been greater in Sub-Saharan Africa than elsewhere, both for causes with increased risk (HIV/AIDS, malaria) and where risk has declined (diarrheal diseases, measles).

While these changes may be in accord with what is known about regional health development and economic growth, they need to be confirmed. Some of the suggested changes warrant further investigation, for example, death rates from perinatal causes appear to have risen in both East Asia and the Pacific and South Asia and remained unchanged in Latin America and the Caribbean, which may or may not be in line with what is known about developments in prenatal care and safe motherhood initiatives. Similarly, measles appears to have disappeared as a cause of child death in Latin America and the Caribbean. The risk of child death from congenital anomalies appears to have risen in both Latin America and the Caribbean and the Middle East and North Africa, but why is unclear. Similarly, the large suggested declines in the risk of child deaths because of injury in South Asia and Sub-Saharan Africa appear unlikely and may largely reflect better data and methods for measuring injury deaths.

DISCUSSION

Understanding the demographic context of health status assessments such as the GBD studies is essential if policy directions and program delivery are to be focused appropriately. Knowledge about the size and composition of populations and how they are changing is critical for health planning and priority setting. Demographers and demographic institutions such as the UN Population Division have applied the demographic ethos that available data permit making estimates and reasonable predictions of population change provided the data are interpreted and used appropriately.

Such estimates and projections have been useful for social and economic development for countries, regions, and the world as a whole. They suggest that health and social policies

need to pay increasing attention to the key demographic trends observed in the 1990s, namely, rapidly falling fertility virtually everywhere, rapidly aging populations, and unprecedented reversals of the long-term path of mortality decline in Europe and Central Asia and Sub-Saharan Africa The causes of these so-called mortality shocks are reasonably well understood, but the lessons for health policy cannot be overemphasized. Globally, the mortality reversals caused by inadequate preventive programs, social disintegration, and failure to understand the gravity of rapidly expanding epidemics have meant that the 1990s were a lost decade for further improvements in adults' survival prospects. Thus, despite the substantial and continued declines in mortality from major vascular diseases in high-income countries, worldwide the risk of death in adulthood did not change in the 1990s, although some gains in reducing mortality in the elderly were achieved, particularly in rich countries.

The trend in child mortality during the 1990s was only marginally more satisfactory. While most regions achieved significant gains in child survival, progress was modest in Sub-Saharan Africa, and as a result, the global decline in child mortality slowed to an annual average of about 1 percent over the decade.

Decades of intensive data collection on child mortality in many low- and middle-income countries by dedicated international survey programs and the efforts of agencies such as the United Nations Children's Fund mean that trends in overall child mortality, and the numbers of child deaths they imply, can be established with reasonable certainty. The trends in the leading causes of child mortality are, however, much more difficult to establish (Rudan and others 2005). Much debate in the literature has centered on whether the risk of malaria infection in Sub-Saharan Africa increased in the 1990s, and thus whether the massive increase in malaria deaths suggested in table 2.4 is real (Korenromp and others 2003; Snow, Trape, and Marsh 2001; Trape 2001). Most malaria mortality in Sub-Saharan Africa is diagnosed via verbal autopsies, which, where studied, have been shown to be a poor diagnostic tool for malaria (Snow and others 1992). While some evidence from demographic surveillance sites using verbal autopsies indicates that malaria mortality rates have increased in eastern and southern Africa (summarized in Korenromp and others 2003) and that the spread of chloroquine resistance may have been the primary reason (Snow and others 1999; Trape 2001), whether this is sufficiently widespread to account for the implied rise of almost 50 percent in malaria mortality rates over the decade (figure 2.4) is unclear. Other factors, such as a general deterioration in clinical care and a decline in the efficacy of chloroquine therapy, may also have contributed (Snow and others 2001), but how much of the rise is real and how much is due to different interpretations of available data in 1990 and 2001 remains unknown.

Similarly, the substantial implied declines in the risk of child death from acute respiratory infections and diarrheal diseases need to be understood in the context of likely contributing factors. One of these is no doubt malnutrition, because it is a major risk factor for both conditions (Black, Morris, and Bryce 2003; Pelletier, Frongillo, and Habicht 1993; Rice and others 2000; Tupasi and others 1988). In the 1990s, malnutrition, as assessed by childhood stunting, declined in all regions except Sub-Saharan Africa (de Onis, Frongillo, and Blossner 2000), which is consistent with the modest declines in mortality from respiratory infections among children in the region. Increased use of oral rehydration therapy and improved access to safe water and sanitation in the 1990s would suggest some decline in mortality from diarrheal disease, but whether they were sufficient to account for the one-third decline in risk, including in Sub-Saharan Africa, is also unclear (Victora and others 2000). The large absolute decline in childhood diarrheal deaths from 2.4 million in 1990 to 1.6 million in 2001 is surprising, and suggests that the 2001 estimate may be an undercount. Some other studies (Morris, Black, and Tomaskovic 2003; UNICEF 2003) suggest a figure about 20 percent higher for 2001.

Malnutrition is also a leading risk factor for measles mortality, and hence changes in the proportion and distribution of underweight children should be broadly consistent with mortality trends from the disease (Fishman and others 2004). Effective vaccination coverage is a primary determinant of mortality from measles, and further increases in vaccination coverage in the 1990s should have led to lower mortality. This is certainly apparent from the estimates reported here, but the extent of that decline is subject to some controversy, depending on the methods used to estimate current mortality. Using proportionate mortality models largely derived from verbal autopsy data, Morris, Black, and Tomaskovic (2003) estimate that measles deaths account for only about 2.2 percent of all child deaths in South Asia and Sub-Saharan Africa, significantly less than Stein and others' (2003) estimates of 4 to 8 percent for the same period using data on vaccination coverage and assumptions about efficacy and case fatality rates. This implies a global estimate of measles deaths that is about half the 556,000 estimated for 2001 in chapter 3, and thus a much faster rate of decline in the measles mortality rate during the 1990s than the one-third reduction suggested by the GBD estimates. The truth may well lie somewhere in between and requires urgent resolution if measles control efforts are to be appropriately guided.

While the confirmation of mother to child transmission of HIV infection implies that mortality from the disease will increase with increasing prevalence among women, the extent of the impact on child mortality continues to be debated. The GBD estimates suggest that HIV/AIDS led to an increase in child mortality of, on average, 10 per 1,000 in Sub-Saharan Africa between 1990 and 2001. Recent research suggesting a potential overestimation of HIV/AIDS mortality may lead to lower estimates of child mortality from the disease, which may attenuate this trend estimate. What is clear is that HIV/AIDS has not been the only cause of recent reversals in the decline in child mortality in Sub-Saharan Africa (Walker, Schwartzlander, and Bryce 2002) and that its effect on child survival in the 1990s may not have been as great as initially thought (Adetunji 2000).

Perinatal conditions that cover specific risks for the newborn, primarily birth asphyxia, birth trauma, prematurity, and sepsis, are undoubtedly a major cause of death among children, but until recently did not receive sufficient attention in the epidemiological literature, perhaps because interventions are largely related to the delivery of prenatal care and the intrapartum period. Virtually all children born alive who die from these causes do so in the first few days of life (Lawn, Cousens, and Zupan 2005). Hence some constraint on the probable demographic envelope of mortality from these causes can be derived by estimating the neonatal mortality rate in different regions as was done for the 1990 GBD study (Murray and Lopez 1996) and repeated for the 2001 estimates (chapter 3 in this volume). This has undoubtedly removed a major source of uncertainty about mortality from these conditions, but substantial uncertainty remains about their relative importance as a cause of neonatal death when considering other conditions such as tetanus (classified under infectious diseases in the 1990 and 2001 GBD studies), neonatal diarrhea, congenital anomalies, and injuries. As a result, the global estimate of deaths from perinatal causes is influenced by the availability and reliability of data on the causes of neonatal mortality, particularly in countries with the largest number of neonatal deaths: China, India, Nigeria, and Pakistan account for half of all neonatal deaths, and with the possible exception of China, none has reliable, nationally representative systems for cause of death reporting.

Given this context, judging whether mortality from perinatal causes indeed rose by 10 percent during the 1990s as suggested by figure 2.4 is difficult. If improvements in survival from these causes are largely related to better and more comprehensive service provision for pregnant women, which in turn is dependent on substantial infrastructure investments to improve health services, then modest declines in risk should be expected given economic growth in the 1990s. This was indeed the case in all regions except East Asia and the Pacific and South Asia, where the risk appears to have risen. Without compelling evidence that health service provision deteriorated in these regions during the 1990s, this increase in the risk of death from perinatal causes is probably a statistical artifact of data availability and different interpretation criteria used for 1990 and 2001. Privatization of the rural health care system in China during the 1990s may have led to a deterioration of prenatal care, but this remains to be established.

Finally, note the 50 percent reduction in the risk of child death from injuries implied by the GBD studies, which is primarily due to large reductions suggested for East Asia and the Pacific, South Asia, and Sub-Saharan Africa. Some decline in injury mortality is to be expected with economic and social development and the introduction of injury control programs and legislation, but the massive declines estimated for these regions may well be attributable to methodological differences in estimation procedures between the two dates (see chapter 3 in this volume). The descriptive epidemiology of injuries remains a major neglected area of the information base for policy to improve child health. For example, Rudan and others' (2005) review of information gaps in relation to assessing the burden of illness in children fails to even mention childhood injuries, even though burns, falls, and drownings are likely to be significant causes of child death (Etebu and Ekere 2004; Gali, Madziga, and Naaya 2004; Istre and others 2003; Mock and others 2004; Shen, Sanno-Duanda, and Bickler 2003). Thus, establishing the extent of changes in these risks, whose levels are based on essentially anecdotal evidence, remains difficult. Evidence of major declines in injury death rates therefore need to be viewed with great caution and may well be largely artifactual.

The global public health community's increasing interest in gaining a better understanding of the successes of, and challenges facing programs and policies to improve child survival has led to alternative assessments of the leading causes of child death. With the substantial data gaps and data quality issues pertaining to the estimation of child mortality, varying estimates of the leading causes of child death because of different estimation principles and variable interpretation of the data are hardly surprising. Scientific debate is to be encouraged insofar as it will guide data collection strategies to reduce unacceptable uncertainty, but the existence of alternative estimates of child mortality for 2001 makes the interpretation of changes over the past decade even more complex. The World Health Organization's Child Health Epidemiology Reference Group (CHERG), for example, working within the same total number of child deaths (10.5 million), has recently published quite different estimates of the causes of child mortality (Bryce and others 2005). According to CHERG's estimates, in 2001 perinatal causes were responsible for 3.9 million child deaths, that is, 37 percent of all child deaths and 55 percent more than the GBD figure (see chapter 3). Conversely, CHERG estimated lower levels of malaria mortality in children (853,000 deaths compared with 1,110,000 in the GBD study) and much lower measles mortality (395,000 versus 562,000 deaths). CHERG's implied rise in perinatal causes of child death is even more extreme than that suggested by the GBD study, whereas the rise in malaria deaths is less extreme. CHERG's estimates also imply far greater success of vaccination programs to reduce measles mortality than does the GBD figure. Note also that CHERG, which does not include any experts in noncommunicable diseases, including congenital anomalies, estimated only about half the number of noncommunicable disease deaths among children than estimated in the GBD study.

Public policy to accelerate the decline in child mortality would be well served through greater scientific collaboration to better understand the descriptive epidemiology of the leading causes of child death over the past decade or so and how this has changed. Notwithstanding the legitimate role of scientific discourse and the issue of comorbidity among the leading causes of child death, particularly diarrhea and pneumonia (Fenn, Morris, and Black 2005), the lack of clarity about the extent of the decline (or rise) in child deaths from specific causes or groups of causes, particularly those that have been the focus of massive programmatic efforts, hinders policy making. Having said this, it should also be borne in mind that for the GBD estimates at least, which have followed a consistent methodology and estimation framework, uncertainty in the rate of change of mortality for any given condition may well be less than period uncertainty around estimates for 1990 and 2001 because of the high likelihood of correlation of uncertainty of estimates for the two periods.

CONCLUSIONS

Priority setting in health, as in other sectors concerned with social development, will increasingly depend on the availability of reliable, timely, representative, and relevant information on the comparative importance of diseases, injuries, and risk factors for the health of populations and how these are changing. Population scientists, particularly epidemiologists, have provided important insights into the descriptive epidemiology of some segments of some populations and on the causes of disease and injuries in those populations. Administrative requirements have resulted in most countries undertaking routine data collection efforts, but these are highly variable in terms of both quality and of what is being measured. As a result, we have substantial partial data collections on many aspects of population health status, but no country has complete data on all aspects of health relevant for policy, and in many parts of the world, health status is largely unknown. Efforts to bring these fragmentary pieces of data together to develop comprehensive estimates of the disease and injury burden and its causes are likely to be extremely valuable for policy making, particularly if the analytical methods and frameworks employed are understandable, transparent, and rigorously argued. Demographers were the first to attempt global, regional, and national efforts to estimate population size, structure, and determinants of change in a coherent fashion, and despite scientific differences of opinion about some of the methods and assumptions, the results have been enormously influential for guiding social development policies and programs.

The two GBD studies for 1990 (Murray and Lopez 1996) and 2001 (chapter 3 in this volume) attempted something similar for mortality and the burden of disease. Scholars and global health development agencies alike have repeatedly emphasized the interrelationship between demographic change and the health conditions of populations. This chapter has summarized the key quantitative findings about global demography and epidemiology that are relevant for disease control and public health development, leading to the following three broad conclusions:

- Despite significant investments in disease control in low- and middle-income countries over the past 50 years and the considerable success in reducing mortality, commensurate investments have not been made in the health intelligence base needed to monitor and evaluate changes in population health. As a result, uncertainty about the causes of child mortality in many countries and how these have changed over the last decade or so because of intervention programs is considerable. Moreover, data collection pertaining to health conditions among adults has been almost totally neglected, with the result that virtually nothing is known reliably about levels, let alone causes, of adult death in much of the developing world. HIV/AIDS has highlighted this neglect, but continued ignorance of the leading causes of adult mortality will continue to hinder policy action to reduce the large, avoidable causes of adult mortality that can be addressed through targeted prevention and treatment programs.

- Demographic change is often poorly understood, and thus potentially underappreciated in relation to health and social development policies. The evidence summarized in this chapter suggests that population aging is likely to become rapidly more pronounced in low- and middle-income countries than is currently appreciated, in part because swift fertility declines are under way in much of the developing world. The little evidence that is available about mortality trends among adults in developing countries suggests different paths of mortality change among regions, but indicates that globally, little progress was achieved in the 1990s. At older ages, the impressive and widely unappreciated declines in mortality that began in the high-income countries in the 1970s continued through the 1990s and show little sign of deceleration. In large part, these declines reflect progress in the control of major vascular diseases and point to continued steady gains in life expectancy in high-income countries.

- Despite at least two decades of intensive efforts by the global public health community to implement intervention programs and reorganize health services to reduce child mortality, knowledge about the major causes of death among children is insufficiently precise to resolve uncertainties about global progress with specific disease control strategies, and thus to be of maximum benefit for global policy action to reduce the more than 10 million child deaths that still occur each year. Results from the two GBD studies, while suggesting trends that are broadly consistent with public health knowledge, are equivocal about trends in specific conditions in some regions. Policy action to rapidly and substantially reduce this enormous burden of premature mortality will be better served if policy makers can be more appropriately informed about the causes of child death, including hitherto neglected areas such as perinatal conditions and injuries.

Annex 2A Key Demographic Indicators, by Country/Territory, 1990 and 2001

Country/Territory	World Bank region	1990 Population (thousands)	1990 Life expectancy at birth (years) Males	Females	1990 Probability of dying per 1,000 Under age 5 Males	Females	Ages 15-59 Males	Females	2001 Population (thousands)	2001 Life expectancy at birth (years) Males	Females	2001 Probability of dying per 1,000 Under age 5 Males	Females	Ages 15-59 Males	Females	Annual change in probability of dying under age 5, 1990–2001 (%) Males	Females
Afghanistan	South Asia	13,799	43.8	47.8	267	253	421	295	22,083	41.4	43.3	257	255	510	419	−0.3	0.1
Albania	Europe and Central Asia	3,289	64.1	71.2	52	38	253	140	3,122	67.0	73.4	28	23	171	97	−5.6	−4.4
Algeria	Middle East and North Africa	25,017	65.4	67.8	70	68	188	153	30,746	67.4	71.0	55	44	172	129	−2.3	−3.9
American Samoa	East Asia and Pacific	—	—	—	—	—	—	—	59	59.9	36.4	86	79	295	229	—	—
Andorra	High-income countries	—	—	—	—	—	—	—	68	76.6	83.7	5	4	113	45	—	—
Angola	Sub-Saharan Africa	9,340	42.7	49.0	280	239	427	288	12,768	37.5	42.3	277	246	605	475	−0.1	0.2
Anguilla	Not included	—	—	—	—	—	—	—	11	68.0	72.8	34	27	216	116	—	—
Antigua and Barbuda	Latin America and the Caribbean	—	—	—	—	—	—	—	72	68.9	73.7	22	18	197	128	—	—
Argentina	Latin America and the Caribbean	32,527	68.9	75.8	32	26	196	103	37,529	70.9	78.5	20	17	177	91	−4.2	−4.0
Armenia	Europe and Central Asia	3,545	61.9	69.0	68	52	276	158	3,088	67.0	72.9	38	34	208	99	−5.3	−3.8
Aruba	High-income countries	—	—	—	—	—	—	—	92	66.9	72.8	36	28	230	116	—	—
Australia	High-income countries	16,888	74.1	80.4	10	8	124	66	19,352	77.6	83.0	7	5	94	54	−4.2	−4.1
Austria	High-income countries	7,729	72.4	79.0	10	9	153	74	8,106	76.1	82.2	6	5	121	61	−5.1	−5.6
Azerbaijan	Europe and Central Asia	7,192	56.4	63.6	119	93	327	199	8,226	62.5	68.2	77	68	247	129	−3.9	−2.8
Bahamas, The	High-income countries	255	66.6	74.2	35	23	224	115	307	68.8	75.2	14	11	249	152	−8.5	−6.4
Bahrain	High-income countries	490	71.7	73.6	25	26	124	104	693	72.4	74.3	14	10	112	82	−5.6	−8.6
Bangladesh	South Asia	109,403	53.8	58.1	145	143	348	236	140,880	62.3	62.2	76	78	251	258	−5.9	−5.5
Barbados	Latin America and the Caribbean	257	69.2	76.4	21	14	193	96	268	70.5	77.7	18	17	187	103	−1.6	1.7
Belarus	Europe and Central Asia	10,266	66.2	75.8	17	12	282	107	9,986	63.0	74.5	14	11	361	129	−1.5	−1.0
Belgium	High-income countries	9,967	72.7	79.5	11	8	139	75	10,273	74.9	81.4	6	5	128	67	−5.2	−4.5
Belize	Latin America and the Caribbean	186	64.4	69.5	50	48	250	154	245	67.2	72.2	45	34	191	124	−0.9	−3.2
Benin	Sub-Saharan Africa	4,650	49.0	55.5	201	168	385	251	6,387	50.4	52.8	165	157	415	351	−1.8	−0.6
Bermuda	High-income countries	—	—	—	—	—	—	—	80	68.0	72.8	34	27	216	116	—	—
Bhutan	South Asia	1,696	53.8	59.5	145	129	349	227	2,125	60.0	62.1	95	94	275	228	−3.8	−2.9
Bolivia	Latin America and the Caribbean	6,669	55.3	61.1	129	114	336	216	8,481	61.6	64.4	80	75	261	211	−4.4	−3.8
Bosnia and Herzegovina	Europe and Central Asia	4,308	68.3	75.3	26	18	204	105	4,067	69.1	76.3	21	16	193	91	−2.0	−1.3
Botswana	Sub-Saharan Africa	1,354	62.4	69.0	64	52	271	158	1,750	41.5	42.2	99	97	762	718	4.0	5.7
Brazil	Latin America and the Caribbean	148,809	61.9	69.0	68	51	276	158	174,029	65.5	72.1	44	36	247	135	−4.0	−3.3
British Virgin Islands	Not included	—	—	—	—	—	—	—	20	68.0	72.8	34	27	215	116	—	—
Brunei Darussalam	High-income countries	257	70.0	77.7	18	11	182	85	342	74.7	77.4	15	13	115	87	−1.9	1.6
Bulgaria	Europe and Central Asia	8,718	68.2	74.9	20	15	216	97	8,033	68.6	75.2	18	15	221	97	−1.2	−0.1
Burkina Faso	Sub-Saharan Africa	8,921	47.1	52.9	224	196	398	267	12,259	40.6	42.7	232	217	596	520	0.3	0.9
Burundi	Sub-Saharan Africa	5,609	49.2	55.4	198	169	384	252	6,412	39.0	42.7	192	180	680	565	−0.3	0.5
Cambodia	East Asia and Pacific	9,744	55.7	62.4	126	103	334	207	13,478	52.3	57.5	147	123	392	290	1.4	1.6
Cameroon	Sub-Saharan Africa	11,661	54.1	60.2	142	123	346	222	15,429	48.0	50.0	160	155	498	434	1.1	2.1

Canada	High-income countries	27,701	74.0	80.7	9	7	132	71	31,025	77.0	82.5	6	5	98	59	-3.5	-3.
Cape Verde	Sub-Saharan Africa	349	61.6	69.4	71	49	279	155	445	66.4	72.7	44	32	209	121	-4.3	-4.1
Cayman Islands	High-income countries	—	—	—	—	—	—	—	38	68.0	72.8	34	27	216	116	-0.6	—
Central African Republic	Sub-Saharan Africa	2,943	49.0	56.5	200	159	385	246	3,770	42.6	44.1	187	173	607	556	—	0.1
Chad	Sub-Saharan Africa	5,822	47.5	53.7	218	187	395	262	8,103	45.7	49.2	203	181	485	401	-0.7	-0.
Channel Islands	High-income countries	142	—	—	—	—	—	—	145	75.5	81.6	6	5	120	60	—	-2.1
Chile	Latin America and the Caribbean	13,100	69.8	76.6	21	17	191	97	15,419	73.1	79.9	17	14	137	68	-1.9	-0.
China	East Asia and Pacific	1,161,382	66.9	69.6	38	46	190	145	1,292,586	69.5	72.6	32	42	166	104	-1.7	-4.
Colombia	Latin America and the Caribbean	34,970	65.8	72.4	40	31	234	130	42,826	67.5	76.3	27	19	235	102	-3.7	-3.
Comoros	Sub-Saharan Africa	527	55.0	61.9	132	107	339	210	726	60.9	64.5	84	75	273	210	-4.2	0.
Congo, Democratic Republic of	Sub-Saharan Africa	37,370	47.4	53.6	221	189	397	263	49,785	41.1	46.1	222	198	583	449	0.0	-3.1
Congo, Republic of	Sub-Saharan Africa	2,494	55.9	63.2	123	96	331	202	3,542	52.2	54.5	109	101	460	409	-1.1	0.
Cook Islands	Not included	—	—	—	—	—	—	—	18	68.9	74.1	23	19	176	112	—	0.1
Costa Rica	Latin America and the Caribbean	3,076	73.0	77.7	19	15	129	79	4,013	74.4	79.3	12	10	128	75	-3.6	-3.1
Côte d'Ivoire	Sub-Saharan Africa	12,505	51.7	58.0	169	144	365	237	16,098	43.5	48.1	192	143	567	498	1.2	-0.
Croatia	Europe and Central Asia	4,842	68.6	76.3	14	10	223	89	4,445	70.9	78.5	9	8	180	73	-4.3	-2.
Cuba	Latin America and the Caribbean	10,628	72.8	76.7	15	11	155	111	11,238	75.2	80.0	9	7	139	90	-4.4	-4.
Cyprus	High-income countries	681	71.7	77.3	12	12	161	88	789	75.0	78.8	8	8	105	53	-3.8	-3.
Czech Republic	Europe and Central Asia	10,306	68.0	75.5	14	10	220	95	10,257	72.1	79.0	5	4	168	74	-8.7	-8.1
Denmark	High-income countries	5,140	72.1	77.9	10	8	152	99	5,338	74.7	79.6	6	5	124	77	-4.5	-3.1
Djibouti	Middle East and North Africa	528	46.4	49.8	188	161	487	417	681	49.5	51.9	157	144	455	400	-1.7	-1.
Dominica	Latin America and the Caribbean	—	—	—	—	—	—	—	78	71.1	75.7	13	14	204	121	—	—
Dominican Republic	Latin America and the Caribbean	7,058	61.2	68.5	74	55	283	162	8,485	64.8	71.4	38	32	256	151	-6.0	-5.1
Ecuador	Latin America and the Caribbean	10,264	62.5	69.2	63	50	270	156	12,616	67.5	73.1	36	32	219	135	-5.2	-4.
Egypt, Arab Republic of	Middle East and North Africa	55,768	57.8	62.4	109	99	307	215	69,124	65.0	68.7	42	42	240	158	-8.7	-7.1
El Salvador	Latin America and the Caribbean	5,110	62.2	68.7	66	54	273	160	6,313	66.2	72.6	37	34	265	145	-5.2	-4.1
Equatorial Guinea	Sub-Saharan Africa	354	47.3	53.5	222	190	397	263	468	51.8	54.7	160	147	382	317	-3.0	-2.
Eritrea	Sub-Saharan Africa	3,103	52.9	58.6	156	138	356	232	3,847	42.9	57.3	118	103	659	334	-2.5	-2.
Estonia	Europe and Central Asia	1,584	64.8	74.9	18	14	298	107	1,353	65.1	76.7	12	8	319	116	-4.3	-5.1
Ethiopia	Sub-Saharan Africa	48,856	47.5	53.6	219	189	395	263	67,266	46.2	49.5	186	169	500	417	-1.5	-1.
Faeroe Islands	High-income countries	—	—	—	—	—	—	—	46	75.5	81.6	6	5	120	60	—	—
Falkland Islands	Not included	—	—	—	—	—	—	—	3	68.0	72.7	34	27	216	117	—	—
Fiji	East Asia and Pacific	724	67.2	72.6	32	30	217	128	822	64.4	70.2	30	27	287	180	-0.6	-1.
Finland	High-income countries	4,986	70.9	78.9	7	7	183	70	5,188	74.5	81.5	5	3	139	61	-3.6	-6.
France	High-income countries	56,735	73.3	81.7	10	8	162	67	59,564	75.7	83.7	6	5	136	60	-5.0	-4.
French Guiana	Not included	—	—	—	—	—	—	—	169	68.1	72.8	33	27	216	116	—	—
French Polynesia	High-income countries	195	—	—	—	—	—	—	237	59.8	36.6	88	81	295	230	-0.2	—
Gabon	Sub-Saharan Africa	953	58.0	64.1	103	89	313	196	1,283	57.2	61.3	101	80	342	281	-0.2	-1.1

(Continues on the following page.)

Annex 2A Continued

Country/Territory	World Bank region	1990 Population (thousands)	1990 Life expectancy at birth (years) Males	Females	1990 Under age 5 Males	Females	1990 Ages 15-59 Males	Females	2001 Population (thousands)	2001 Life expectancy at birth (years) Males	Females	2001 Under age 5 Males	Females	2001 Ages 15-59 Males	Females	Annual change in probability of dying under age 5, 1990–2001 (%) Males	Females
Gambia, The	Sub-Saharan Africa	936	52.0	58.1	165	143	362	235	1,351	55.3	58.8	134	119	330	264	−1.9	−1.6
Georgia	Europe and Central Asia	5,460	67.9	74.9	28	20	210	109	5,224	68.3	74.3	26	20	216	89	−0.7	−0.1
Germany	High-income countries	79,433	72.0	78.5	10	8	157	77	82,349	75.4	81.6	6	4	121	62	−5.3	−4.9
Ghana	Sub-Saharan Africa	15,277	54.9	61.0	134	115	340	217	20,028	56.3	58.8	107	100	355	303	−2.1	−.3
Gibraltar	Not included	—	—	—	—	—	—	—	27	75.5	81.6	6	5	120	60	—	—
Greece	High-income countries	10,161	74.7	79.5	11	10	117	56	10,947	75.5	80.9	7	6	118	49	−3.8	−6.7
Greenland	High-income countries	—	—	—	—	—	—	—	56	75.5	81.6	6	5	120	60	—	—
Grenada	Latin America and the Caribbean	—	—	—	—	—	—	—	81	65.8	68.7	25	21	263	224	—	—
Guadeloupe	Not included	—	—	—	—	—	—	—	432	68.0	72.8	34	27	216	116	—	—
Guam	High-income countries	134	—	—	—	—	—	—	158	59.9	36.5	86	80	295	229	—	—
Guatemala	Latin America and the Caribbean	8,749	59.5	65.8	89	75	299	183	11,728	62.9	68.7	58	51	285	167	−3.8	−3.5
Guinea	Sub-Saharan Africa	6,122	45.2	49.7	248	232	411	285	8,242	50.5	53.5	166	155	408	333	−3.7	−3.6
Guinea-Bissau	Sub-Saharan Africa	1,016	43.3	49.6	273	232	424	285	1,407	45.4	48.4	219	201	464	384	−2.0	−1.3
Guyana	Latin America and the Caribbean	731	57.9	65.7	104	76	314	184	762	61.3	66.7	62	51	302	206	−4.6	−3.5
Haiti	Latin America and the Caribbean	6,914	52.7	58.2	157	142	357	235	8,111	48.8	50.8	140	130	497	444	−1.0	−0.8
Holy See (Vatican City)	Not included	—	—	—	—	—	—	—	1	75.5	81.6	6	5	120	60	—	—
Honduras	Latin America and the Caribbean	4,868	61.9	68.7	68	54	276	160	6,619	64.4	70.4	45	42	263	148	−3.8	−2.1
Hungary	Europe and Central Asia	10,365	65.1	73.8	19	15	305	133	9,968	68.0	76.7	11	9	264	113	−5.0	−4.6
Iceland	High-income countries	255	75.5	80.7	9	5	116	77	285	78.1	81.7	4	3	88	56	−8.0	−5.5
India	South Asia	846,418	57.3	58.0	113	126	301	246	1,033,395	60.0	61.8	89	98	291	222	−2.2	−2.3
Indonesia	East Asia and Pacific	182,117	58.3	64.9	100	82	310	189	214,356	64.4	67.4	50	40	246	213	−6.2	−6.4
Iran, Islamic Republic of	Middle East and North Africa	56,703	62.5	66.5	73	71	253	173	67,245	65.8	71.1	45	38	225	140	−4.4	−5.8
Iraq	Middle East and North Africa	17,341	63.5	68.3	79	71	215	138	23,860	58.7	62.8	122	112	258	180	3.9	4.2
Ireland	High-income countries	3,515	71.9	77.6	11	9	133	81	3,865	74.1	79.5	8	6	117	68	−3.0	−3.6
Isle of Man	Europe and Central Asia	—	—	—	—	—	—	—	74	75.5	81.6	6	5	120	60	—	—
Israel	High-income countries	4,514	75.0	78.4	13	11	107	71	6,174	77.1	81.2	7	6	100	54	−5.0	−5.7
Italy	High-income countries	56,719	73.7	80.4	10	8	129	60	57,521	76.6	82.6	6	5	99	50	−5.5	−4.6
Jamaica	Latin America and the Caribbean	2,369	69.0	75.5	22	17	195	103	2,603	71.0	74.4	16	14	164	123	−3.0	−1.7
Japan	High-income countries	123,537	76.1	82.4	7	6	109	53	127,271	78.2	85.8	5	4	97	47	−3.9	−3.3
Jordan	Middle East and North Africa	3,254	66.5	71.0	44	42	209	137	5,183	68.5	73.1	29	27	193	122	−3.9	−4.0
Kazakhstan	Europe and Central Asia	16,809	63.2	69.9	58	46	262	151	15,533	58.4	68.9	40	30	420	192	−3.4	−3.9
Kenya	Sub-Saharan Africa	23,585	57.6	64.2	106	87	316	194	31,065	50.4	52.6	117	112	496	434	0.9	2.3
Kiribati	East Asia and Pacific	—	—	—	—	—	—	—	85	61.8	66.5	82	69	288	194	—	—

Korea, Democratic People's Republic of	East Asia and Pacific	19,956	63.6	68.5	55	55	259	162	22,409	64.4	67.1	56	54	236	191	0.1	-0.2
Korea, Republic of	High-income countries	42,869	69.5	78.2	20	9	189	81	47,142	71.5	79.1	8	7	173	65	-8.5	-2.8
Kuwait	High-income countries	2,143	72.7	75.6	20	16	118	81	2,353	75.6	76.5	14	10	84	62	-3.5	-3.8
Kyrgyz Republic	Europe and Central Asia	4,395	59.0	66.1	93	73	304	181	4,995	60.1	68.4	65	57	346	165	-3.2	-2.3
Lao People's Democratic Republic	East Asia and Pacific	4,132	51.4	57.1	173	153	368	242	5,403	53.8	55.9	149	133	340	308	-1.4	-1.3
Latvia	Europe and Central Asia	2,713	64.2	74.5	20	15	311	118	2,351	64.8	75.8	15	12	323	117	-2.7	-2.0
Lebanon	Middle East and North Africa	2,712	66.7	71.6	42	32	210	143	3,537	67.4	71.9	36	29	205	140	-1.3	-0.9
Lesotho	Sub-Saharan Africa	1,570	52.6	59.1	159	134	358	229	1,794	34.6	40.1	159	153	871	705	0.0	1.2
Liberia	Sub-Saharan Africa	2,135	45.0	50.8	251	219	412	278	3,099	40.5	43.9	244	223	569	463	-0.3	0.2
Libya	Middle East and North Africa	4,306	67.0	72.1	44	40	199	121	5,340	70.2	75.4	20	19	174	100	-7.4	-6.9
Liechtenstein	High-income countries	—	—	—	—	—	—	—	33	75.5	81.6	6	5	120	60	—	—
Lithuania	Europe and Central Asia	3,739	66.5	76.3	15	12	286	107	3,484	66.5	77.7	11	10	297	102	-2.5	-1.9
Luxembourg	High-income countries	378	72.1	78.5	10	8	151	86	441	75.6	81.8	5	5	120	66	-5.9	-4.6
Macedonia, FYR	Europe and Central Asia	1,909	69.1	73.9	37	32	167	94	2,035	69.0	75.0	19	16	195	90	-6.3	-6.4
Madagascar	Sub-Saharan Africa	11,956	50.9	56.6	178	158	371	245	16,439	54.2	58.2	147	127	335	264	-1.7	-2.0
Malawi	Sub-Saharan Africa	9,456	45.1	49.7	250	232	412	285	11,627	40.0	40.9	199	192	648	601	-2.1	-1.7
Malaysia	East Asia and Pacific	17,845	68.7	75.3	24	18	199	105	23,492	69.6	74.8	10	9	193	107	-7.5	-6.7
Maldives	South Asia	216	58.0	59.7	103	127	314	225	300	66.3	65.4	42	49	211	207	-8.1	-8.7
Mali	Sub-Saharan Africa	9,046	44.1	49.1	262	238	418	288	12,256	43.7	45.5	235	226	489	418	-1.0	-0.5
Malta	Middle East and North Africa	360	73.8	78.4	13	9	101	62	391	75.9	79.8	8	6	89	54	-4.5	-2.7
Marshall Islands	East Asia and Pacific	—	—	—	—	—	—	—	52	60.7	64.3	47	37	347	292	—	—
Martinique	Not included	—	—	—	—	—	—	—	388	68.0	72.8	34	27	215	116	—	-0.7
Mauritania	Sub-Saharan Africa	2,030	49.3	55.5	197	169	383	251	2,724	49.7	54.4	187	156	394	305	-0.5	-3.5
Mauritius	Sub-Saharan Africa	1,057	65.5	73.3	27	20	263	121	1,198	68.1	75.4	21	14	222	119	-2.4	-4.9
Mexico	Latin America and the Caribbean	83,225	64.4	70.5	50	42	250	146	100,456	71.8	77.1	31	25	175	99	-4.3	—
Micronesia, Federated States of	East Asia and Pacific	96	—	—	—	—	—	—	107	64.6	67.8	65	53	214	179	—	—
Moldova	Europe and Central Asia	4,364	66.9	73.3	33	27	221	123	4,276	63.8	71.4	32	24	301	149	-0.4	-1.1
Monaco	High-income countries	—	—	—	—	—	—	—	34	77.3	84.3	5	4	113	49	—	—
Mongolia	East Asia and Pacific	2,216	57.0	62.6	112	101	322	206	2,528	59.8	66.0	80	70	320	209	-3.1	-3.3
Montserrat	Not included	—	—	—	—	—	—	—	4	68.9	73.6	32	26	205	110	—	—
Morocco	Middle East and North Africa	24,564	63.1	67.4	90	80	206	141	29,585	68.6	72.6	45	43	161	104	-6.3	-5.6
Mozambique	Sub-Saharan Africa	13,465	44.7	50.3	255	225	415	281	18,204	41.7	44.4	211	201	596	503	-1.7	-1.0
Myanmar	East Asia and Pacific	40,506	53.8	61.2	146	114	349	215	48,205	56.2	61.8	118	95	332	236	-1.9	-1.7
Namibia	Sub-Saharan Africa	1,409	59.0	65.3	93	78	304	186	1,930	49.7	52.2	92	88	572	496	-0.2	1.1
Nauru	Not included	—	—	—	—	—	—	—	12	59.3	66.2	19	14	456	308	—	—
Nepal	South Asia	18,625	54.4	57.7	139	147	344	238	24,060	59.6	59.6	87	93	300	292	-4.3	-4.2
Netherlands	High-income countries	14,952	73.8	80.2	10	8	116	67	15,982	75.8	80.9	7	6	97	66	-3.7	-3.1
Netherlands Antilles	High-income countries	188	—	—	—	—	—	—	217	68.1	72.8	33	27	216	116	—	—
New Caledonia	High-income countries	171	—	—	—	—	—	—	220	59.8	36.5	87	80	295	230	—	—

(Continues on the following page.)

Annex 2A Continued

Country/Territory	World Bank region	1990 Population (thousands)	1990 Life expectancy at birth (years) Males	Females	1990 Probability of dying per 1,000 Under age 5 Males	Females	Ages 15–59 Males	Females	2001 Population (thousands)	2001 Life expectancy at birth (years) Males	Females	2001 Probability of dying per 1,000 Under age 5 Males	Females	Ages 15–59 Males	Females	Annual change in probability of dying under age 5, 1990–2001 (%) Males	Females
New Zealand	High-income countries	3,360	72.5	78.5	13	9	143	93	3,815	76.5	81.6	8	6	101	65	−4.8	−3.1
Nicaragua	Latin America and the Caribbean	3,824	61.3	68.0	73	58	282	166	5,204	67.7	72.3	39	34	213	146	−5.7	−5.0
Niger	Sub-Saharan Africa	7,650	39.2	42.9	329	311	449	320	11,134	42.6	42.6	251	257	496	442	−2.5	1.7
Nigeria	Sub-Saharan Africa	86,018	49.8	54.7	191	177	379	256	117,823	48.1	49.8	184	181	448	387	−0.3	0.2
Niue	Not included	—	—	—	—	—	—	—	2	67.9	73.1	34	26	193	132	—	—
Northern Mariana Islands	High-income countries	—	—	—	—	—	—	—	73	65.3	36.4	86	80	295	229	—	—
Norway	High-income countries	4,241	73.4	79.9	10	7	128	65	4,494	76.1	81.7	5	4	103	61	−6.1	−5.3
West Bank and Gaza	Middle East and North Africa	2,154	—	—	—	—	—	—	3,310	68.4	72.0	27	29	200	140	—	—
Oman	Middle East and North Africa	1,845	68.6	74.3	33	27	184	106	2,688	70.8	76.1	17	16	168	95	−6.1	−4.8
Pakistan	South Asia	110,901	54.6	58.4	137	140	342	233	146,277	61.1	61.5	105	115	228	203	−2.4	−1.7
Palau	East Asia and Pacific	—	—	—	—	—	—	—	20	66.3	71.4	24	22	241	194	—	—
Panama	Latin America and the Caribbean	2,411	66.0	72.9	39	29	232	126	3,007	73.1	78.4	26	22	143	85	−3.6	−2.4
Papua New Guinea	East Asia and Pacific	4,114	58.1	62.8	102	100	312	205	5,460	58.3	61.4	99	92	310	250	−0.2	−0.7
Paraguay	Latin America and the Caribbean	4,219	65.6	72.2	42	32	237	131	5,604	68.7	74.2	37	27	170	123	−1.0	−1.6
Peru	Latin America and the Caribbean	21,753	59.5	66.3	88	71	299	179	26,362	67.1	71.6	41	37	206	145	−6.9	−6.0
Philippines	East Asia and Pacific	61,104	62.2	69.3	65	50	272	156	77,151	64.9	71.4	41	35	260	136	−4.2	−3.3
Pitcairn	Not included	0	—	—	—	—	—	—	0	59.9	36.4	86	80	295	230	—	—
Poland	Europe and Central Asia	38,111	66.5	75.6	20	16	263	102	38,651	70.2	78.5	9	8	209	84	−6.9	−6.2
Portugal	High-income countries	9,899	70.4	77.3	16	12	178	80	10,033	73.2	80.5	7	6	155	66	−7.2	−6.7
Puerto Rico	Latin America and the Caribbean	3,528	68.7	77.6	17	13	237	90	3,838	70.5	78.4	13	11	217	93	−2.1	−1.2
Qatar	High-income countries	467	67.7	74.6	29	21	211	111	591	75.2	74.3	15	13	93	82	−5.7	−4.3
Romania	Europe and Central Asia	23,207	66.8	73.2	34	27	239	114	22,437	67.9	74.9	24	20	235	107	−3.1	−3.0
Russian Federation	Europe and Central Asia	148,292	63.8	74.4	24	18	318	117	144,877	58.6	72.1	22	17	453	163	−0.8	−0.6
Rwanda	Sub-Saharan Africa	6,775	50.6	55.9	181	165	373	249	8,066	41.6	46.3	189	173	608	483	0.4	0.5
Réunion	Not included	734	—	—	—	—	—	—	734	49.4	52.0	176	168	422	352	—	—
Samoa	East Asia and Pacific	160	65.0	71.1	45	39	243	141	175	66.7	69.6	28	22	235	203	−4.4	−5.1
San Marino	High-income countries	—	—	—	—	—	—	—	27	77.2	84.0	6	3	85	32	—	—
São Tomé and Principe	Sub-Saharan Africa	116	—	—	—	—	—	—	153	61.1	63.1	85	86	262	220	—	—
Saudi Arabia	Middle East and North Africa	16,554	66.3	71.6	47	41	208	128	22,829	68.4	73.8	31	26	192	113	−3.9	−4.2
Senegal	Sub-Saharan Africa	7,345	52.6	58.7	158	138	358	232	9,621	54.2	57.1	140	131	350	285	−1.1	−0.5
Serbia and Montenegro	Europe and Central Asia	10,156	66.8	74.0	34	24	223	116	10,545	69.7	74.8	17	13	187	98	−6.2	−5.1

(Continues on the following page.)

Economy	Region																
Seychelles	Sub-Saharan Africa	—	—	—	—	—	—	—	80	66.7	77.7	15	10	248	113	—	—
Sierra Leone	Sub-Saharan Africa	4,054	39.5	45.6	324	279	447	306	4,573	31.2	35.8	330	301	718	567	0.2	0.7
Singapore	High-income countries	3,016	72.8	77.8	10	8	152	93	4,105	76.8	81.7	4	3	93	54	-8.3	-7.4
Slovak Republic	Europe and Central Asia	5,256	70.3	76.9	17	13	179	92	5,394	69.5	78.0	10	8	210	79	-4.4	-4.8
Slovenia	High-income countries	1,918	69.9	77.9	12	8	207	81	1,988	72.5	80.2	6	4	165	72	-6.6	-5.2
Solomon Islands	East Asia and Pacific	319	—	—	—	—	—	—	450	63.5	67.3	86	75	202	149	—	—
Somalia	Sub-Saharan Africa	7,163	45.8	51.6	240	210	407	274	9,088	43.7	46.1	217	223	516	407	-0.9	0.6
South Africa	Sub-Saharan Africa	36,848	61.9	69.0	68	52	275	158	44,416	50.4	54.5	80	75	566	448	1.5	3.4
Spain	High-income countries	39,303	73.3	80.4	10	8	146	60	40,875	76.1	83.2	6	5	121	48	-5.3	-5.1
Sri Lanka	South Asia	16,830	67.2	74.9	32	20	218	109	18,752	66.1	74.2	21	17	260	125	-3.8	-1.6
St. Helena	Not included	—	—	—	—	—	—	—	5	49.5	52.0	176	168	422	352	—	—
St. Kitts and Nevis	Latin America and the Caribbean	—	—	—	—	—	—	—	42	68.4	72.1	21	24	210	150	—	—
St. Lucia	Latin America and the Caribbean	131	66.9	72.3	22	17	246	158	147	69.5	74.9	14	14	217	138	-4.2	-1.7
St. Pierre et Miquelon	Not included	—	—	—	—	—	—	—	6	74.7	80.0	9	7	139	81	—	—
St. Vincent and the Grenadines	High-income countries	110	—	—	—	—	—	—	118	68.0	72.2	24	20	235	180	—	—
Sudan	Sub-Saharan Africa	24,927	55.5	61.4	128	112	335	214	32,151	55.4	59.6	112	106	364	269	-1.2	-0.4
Suriname	Latin America and the Caribbean	402	65.8	72.9	40	29	233	126	429	64.2	70.6	34	28	282	166	-1.4	-0.3
Swaziland	Sub-Saharan Africa	847	56.1	63.0	122	98	330	203	1,058	38.5	42.1	145	137	784	673	1.6	3.0
Sweden	High-income countries	8,559	74.8	80.5	8	6	114	66	8,860	77.8	82.5	4	3	85	54	-5.9	-6.3
Switzerland	High-income countries	6,834	73.9	80.9	9	8	126	62	7,173	77.4	83.2	6	5	95	53	-3.7	-4.0
Syrian Arab Republic	Middle East and North Africa	12,717	66.1	70.7	48	40	211	147	16,968	68.6	73.4	28	21	192	128	-4.8	-5.6
Tajikistan	Europe and Central Asia	5,303	60.1	66.8	83	67	293	175	6,144	60.7	66.0	69	58	290	182	-1.7	-1.4
Tanzania	Sub-Saharan Africa	26,068	51.6	56.8	170	156	366	244	35,565	45.4	47.5	164	145	559	510	-0.3	-0.7
Thailand	East Asia and Pacific	54,389	64.6	72.4	48	31	248	130	61,555	66.1	72.6	33	27	276	156	-3.4	-1.5
Timor-Leste	East Asia and Pacific	740	—	—	—	—	—	—	711	55.2	60.9	139	106	323	237	—	—
Togo	Sub-Saharan Africa	3,455	52.1	58.5	165	139	362	233	4,686	50.1	53.5	150	128	454	388	-0.8	-0.7
Tokelau	Not included	—	—	—	—	—	—	—	2	59.9	36.4	86	80	295	230	—	—
Tonga	East Asia and Pacific	99	—	—	—	—	—	—	102	69.2	71.7	23	15	190	175	—	—
Trinidad and Tobago	Latin America and the Caribbean	1,215	67.5	75.4	30	18	214	105	1,294	67.3	72.8	24	18	243	153	-2.0	-0.1
Tunisia	Middle East and North Africa	8,207	66.4	70.1	55	49	194	141	9,624	69.3	73.8	32	25	171	116	-5.0	-6.3
Turkey	Europe and Central Asia	57,593	60.3	65.9	82	74	292	182	69,303	67.8	72.1	44	42	180	113	-5.7	-5.2
Turkmenistan	Europe and Central Asia	3,668	57.4	64.3	108	87	318	194	4,720	58.7	66.8	65	49	365	192	-4.7	-5.3
Turks and Caicos Islands	Not included	—	—	—	—	—	—	—	19	68.0	72.8	34	27	216	116	—	—
Tuvalu	Not included	—	—	—	—	—	—	—	10	60.3	61.4	73	57	293	279	—	—
Uganda	Sub-Saharan Africa	17,359	51.4	57.6	172	148	367	239	24,225	47.2	50.0	150	138	518	449	-1.2	-0.6
Ukraine	Europe and Central Asia	51,891	65.6	74.9	19	14	287	112	49,290	61.8	73.1	23	17	376	137	1.8	1.9
United Arab Emirates	High-income countries	2,035	68.5	75.7	25	17	201	102	2,879	71.3	75.1	10	10	170	123	-7.9	-5.0
United Kingdom	High-income countries	56,761	72.9	78.6	11	8	129	78	58,881	75.2	80.0	7	6	111	70	-3.6	-3.0
United States	High-income countries	255,712	71.9	79.0	13	10	172	91	288,025	74.5	79.7	9	7	144	83	-3.2	-2.9
U.S. Virgin Islands	High-income countries	101	—	—	—	—	—	—	110	68.0	72.8	34	27	216	116	—	—

Annex 2A Continued

Country/Territory	World Bank region	1990							2001							Annual change in probability of dying under age 5, 1990–2001 (%)	
		Population (thousands)	Life expectancy at birth (years)		Probability of dying per 1,000				Population (thousands)	Life expectancy at birth (years)		Probability of dying per 1,000					
					Under age 5		Ages 15–59					Under age 5		Ages 15–59			
			Males	Females	Males	Females	Males	Females		Males	Females	Males	Females	Males	Females	Males	Females
Uruguay	Latin America and the Caribbean	3,106	69.0	76.5	27	23	196	98	3,366	71.1	79.5	18	13	181	89	-3.6	-5.2
Uzbekistan	Europe and Central Asia	20,515	62.3	69.0	65	52	272	158	25,313	65.2	70.7	39	28	246	150	-4.5	-5.7
Vanuatu	East Asia and Pacific	149	61.9	66.1	68	72	276	180	202	66.2	68.9	43	42	219	177	-4.3	-5.0
Venezuela, República Bolivariana de	Latin America and the Caribbean	19,502	69.1	74.4	35	29	181	107	24,752	70.9	77.0	24	20	185	98	-3.4	-3.5
Vietnam	East Asia and Pacific	66,074	63.1	69.8	59	47	264	152	79,197	67.1	72.0	42	33	200	132	-3.2	-3.1
Wallis and Futuna Islands	Not included	—	—	—	—	—	—	—	15	59.9	36.4	86	80	295	230	—	—
Western Sahara	Not included	—	—	—	—	—	—	—	293	63.2	49.7	72	67	233	159	—	—
Yemen, Republic of	Middle East and North Africa	11,944	54.5	57.1	147	137	327	271	18,651	58.2	61.7	111	98	292	232	-2.5	-3.0
Zambia	Sub-Saharan Africa	8,200	48.7	54.9	204	175	387	255	10,570	39.3	40.5	192	177	692	646	-0.5	-0.1
Zimbabwe	Sub-Saharan Africa	10,467	59.7	66.0	87	73	297	181	12,756	38.5	38.8	114	105	805	775	2.5	3.3

Sources: Population data are from United Nations 2003. Mortality estimates for 1990 are authors' calculations; estimates for 2001 are from chapter 3 in this volume.

Note: — = not available or not applicable. Estimates of child mortality are rounded to the nearest whole number.

ACKNOWLEDGMENTS

We are grateful to Colin Mathers for his input into the estimation of child mortality levels in 1990 reported in this chapter.

NOTES

1. While it would have been much more informative to base this assessment of demographic change on the 2004 Revision of *World Population Prospects* (United Nations 2005a), the results were released too late to be incorporated into the estimates reported in this and subsequent chapters. The differences between the two revisions, at least for regional aggregates, are unlikely to be substantial.

2. An exception is Timor-Leste, where fertility increased following independence in 2002 and is currently higher than in any other country.

REFERENCES

Adetunji, J. 2000. "Trends in under-5 Mortality Rates and the HIV/AIDS Epidemic." *Bulletin of the World Health Organization* 78 (10): 1200–6.

Bennett, N. G., and S. Horiuchi. 1984. "Mortality Estimation from Registered Deaths in Less Developed Countries." *Demography* 21 (2): 217–33.

Bhatia, S. 1983. "Traditional Practices Affecting Female Health and Survival: Evidence from Countries of South Asia." In *Sex Differentials in Mortality*, ed. A. D. Lopez and L. T. Ruzicka, 165–77. Canberra: Australian National University Press.

Black, R. E., S. S. Morris, and J. Bryce. 2003. "Where and Why Are 10 Million Children Dying Every Year?" *Lancet* 361 (9376): 2226–34.

Bryce, J., C. Boschi-Pinto, K. Shibuya, R. E. Black, and the WHO Child Health Epidemiology Reference Group. 2005. "WHO Estimates of the Causes of Death in Children." *Lancet* 365 (9465): 1147–52.

de Onis, M., E. A. Frongillo, and M. Blossner. 2000. "Is Malnutrition Declining? An Analysis of Changes in Levels of Child Malnutrition since 1980." *Bulletin of the World Health Organization* 78 (10): 1222–33.

Etebu, E. N., and A. U. Ekere. 2004. "Paediatric Accidental Deaths in Port Harcourt, Nigeria: A 10-Year Retrospective Study." *Nigerian Journal of Medicine* 13 (2): 140–3.

Ezzati, M., S. Vander Hoorn, C. M. M. Lawes, R. Leach, W. P. T. James, A. D. Lopez, A. Rodgers, and C. J. L. Murray. 2005. "Rethinking the 'Diseases of Affluence' Paradigm: Global Patterns of Nutritional Risks in Relation to Economic Development." *PLoS Medicine* 2: e133.

Fenn, B., S. S. Morris, and R. F. Black. 2005. "Comorbidity in Childhood in Northern Ghana: Magnitude, Associated Factors, and Impact on Mortality." *International Journal of Epidemiology* 34 (2): 368–74.

Fishman, S., L. E. Caulfield, M. de Onis M, M. Blossner, A. A. Hyder, L. Mullany, and R. E. Black. 2004. "Childhood and Maternal Underweight." In *Comparative Quantification of Health Risks: Global and Regional Burden of Disease Attributable to Selected Major Risk Factors*, ed. M. Ezzati, A. D. Lopez, A. Rodgers, and C. J. L. Murray, 39–61. Geneva: World Health Organization.

Gali, B. M., A. G. Madziga, and H. U. Naaya. 2004. "Epidemiology of Childhood Burns in Maiduguri, Northeastern Nigeria." *Nigerian Journal of Medicine* 13 (2): 144–7.

Hill, K. 1987. "Estimating Census and Death Registration Completeness." *Asian and Pacific Population Forum* 1 (3): 8–24.

Hill, K., R. Pande, M. Mahy, and G. Jones. 1999. *Trends in Child Mortality in the Developing World: 1960–1996*. New York: United Nations Children's Fund.

Istre, G. R., M. A. McCoy, M. Stowe, K. Davies, D. Zane, R. J. Anderson, and R. Wieber. 2003. "Childhood Injuries Due to Falls from Apartment Balconies and Windows." *Injury Prevention* 9 (4): 349–52.

Jamison, D. T., G. Alleyne, J. G. Breman, M. Claeson, D. B. Evans, P. Jha, and others. 2006. *Disease Control Priorities in Developing Countries*, 2nd ed. New York: Oxford University Press.

Korenromp, E. L., B. G. Williams, E. Gouws, C. Dye, and R. W. Snow. 2003. "Measurement of Trends in Childhood Malaria Mortality in Africa: An Assessment of Progress toward Targets Based on Verbal Autopsy." *Lancet Journal of Infectious Diseases* 3 (6): 349–58.

Lawn, J. E., S. Cousens, and J. Zupan. 2005. "Four Million Neonatal Deaths: When? Where? Why?" *Lancet* 363 (9462): 9–18.

Leon, D., A. Chenet, V. Shkolnikov, S. Zakharov, J. Shapiro, G. Rakhmanova, S. Vassin, and M. McKee. 1997. "Huge Variation in Russian Mortality Rates, 1984–1994: Artefact, Alcohol, or What?" *Lancet* 350 (9075): 383–8.

Lopez, A. D. 1993. "Causes of Death in Industrial and Developing Countries: Estimates for 1985." In *Disease Control Priorities in Developing Countries*, ed. D. Jamison, H. Mosely, A. Measham, and J. L. Bobodilla, 35–50. New York: Oxford University Press.

Lopez, A. D. 2003. "Estimating the Causes of Child Deaths." *International Journal of Epidemiology* 32 (6): 1052–3.

Lopez, A. D, O. B. Ahmad, M. Guillot, M. Inoue, B. Fergusson, J. Salomon, C. J. L. Murray, and K. Hill. 2002. *World Mortality in 2000: Life Tables for 191 Countries*. Geneva: World Health Organization.

Mari Bhat, P. N. 2002. "Completeness of India's Sample Registration System: An Assessment Using the General Growth Balance Method." *Population Studies* 56 (2): 119–34.

Mathers, C. D., D. Mafat, M. Inoue, C. Rao, and A. D. Lopez. 2005. "Counting the Dead and What They Died from: An Assessment of the Global Status of Cause of Death Data." *Bulletin of the World Health Organization* 83 (3): 171–7.

Mock, C., R. Quansah, R. Krishnan, C. Arreola-Risa, and F. Rivara. 2004. "Strengthening the Prevention and Care of Injuries Worldwide." *Lancet* 363 (9427): 2172–9.

Morris, S. S., R. E. Black, and L. Tomaskovic. 2003. "Predicting the Distribution of Under-Five Deaths by Cause in Countries without Adequate Vital Registration Systems." *International Journal of Epidemiology* 32 (6): 1041–51.

Murray, C. J. L., B. D. Ferguson, A. D. Lopez, M. Guillot, J. A. Salomon, and O. B. Ahmad. 2003. "Modified Logit Life Table System: Principles, Empirical Validation, and Application." *Population Studies* 57 (2): 165–82.

Murray, C. J. L., and A. D. Lopez, eds. 1996. *The Global Burden of Disease*, vol. 1. Cambridge, MA: Harvard University Press.

Pelletier, D. L., E. A. Frongillo, and J. P. Habicht. 1993. "Epidemiologic Evidence for a Potentiating Effect of Malnutrition on Child Mortality." *American Journal of Public Health* 83 (8): 1130–3.

Rao, C., A. D. Lopez, G. Yang, S. Begg, and J. Ma. 2005. "Evaluating National Cause of Death Statistics: Principles and Application to the Case of China." *Bulletin of the World Health Organization* 83 (8): 618–25.

Rice, A. L., L. Sacco, A. Hyder, and R. E. Black. 2000. "Malnutrition as an Underlying Cause of Childhood Deaths Associated with Infectious Diseases in Developing Countries." *Bulletin of the World Health Organization* 78 (10): 1207–21.

Rudan, I., J. Lawn, S. Cousens, A. K. Rowe, C. Boschi-Pinto, L. Tomaskovic, W. Mendoza, C. F. Lanata, A. Roca-Feltrer, I. Carneira, J. A. Schellenberg, O. Polasek, M. Weber, J. Bryce, S. S. Morris, R. E. Black, and H. Campbell. 2005. "Gaps in Policy-Relevant Information on Burden of Disease in Children: A Systematic Review." *Lancet* 365 (9476): 2031–40.

Shen, C., B. Sanno-Duanda, and S. W. Bickler. 2003. "Paediatric Trauma at a Government Referral Hospital in The Gambia." *West African Journal of Medicine* 22 (4): 287–90.

Shkolnikov, V., M. McKee, and D. A. Leon. 2001. "Changes in Life Expectancy in Russia in the Mid-1990s." *Lancet* 357 (9260): 917–21.

Sibai, A. M. 2004. "Mortality Certification and Cause of Death Reporting in Developing Countries." *Bulletin of the World Health Organization* 82 (2): 83.

Snow, R. W., M. T. Winstanley, V. M. Marsh, C. R. C. J. Newton, C. Waruiru, I. Mwangi, P. A. Winstanley, and K. Marsh. 1992. "Childhood Deaths in Africa: Uses and Limitations of Verbal Autopsies." *Lancet* 340 (8815): 351–5.

Snow, R. W., M. Craig, U. Deichmann, and K. W. Marsh. 1999. "Estimating Mortality, Morbidity, and Disability Due to Malaria among Africa's Non-pregnant Population." *Bulletin of the World Health Organization* 77 (8): 624–40.

Snow, R. W., J.-F. Trape, and K. Marsh. 2001. "The Past, Present, and Future of Childhood Malaria Mortality in Africa." *Trends in Parasitology* 17 (12): 593–7.

Stein, C. E., M. Birmingham, M. Kurian, P. Duclos, and P. Strebel. 2003. "The Global Burden of Measles in the Year 2000: A Model That Uses Country-Specific Indicators." *Journal of Infectious Diseases* 187 (Suppl1): S8–S14.

Trape, J.-F. 2001. "The Public Health Impact of Chloroquine Resistance in Africa." *American Journal of Tropical Medicine and Hygiene* 64 (1–2): 12–17.

Tupasi, T. E., M. A. Velmonte, M. E. G. Sanvitores, L. Abraham, L. E. De Leon, S. A. Tan, C. A. Miquel, and M. C. Saniel. 1988. "Determinants of Morbidity and Mortality Due to Acute Respiratory Infections: Implications for Intervention." *Journal of Infectious Diseases* 157 (4): 615–23.

UNICEF (United Nations Children's Fund). 2003. *State of the World's Children 2003.* New York: UNICEF.

United Nations. 2003. *World Population Prospects: The 2002 Assessment.* ST/ESA/SER.A/222. New York: United Nations.

———. 2005a. *World Population Prospects: The 2004 Assessment.* New York: United Nations.

———. 2005b. *World Population Prospects: The 2002 Revision and World Urbanization Prospects: The 2001 Revision.* New York: United Nations, Department of Economic and Social Affairs, Population Division. http://esa.un.org/unpp.

Victora, C. G., J. Bryce, O. Fontaine, and R. Monash. 2000. "Reducing Deaths from Diarrhea through Oral Rehydration Therapy." *Bulletin of the World Health Organization* 78 (10): 1246–55.

Walker, N., B. Schwartlander, and J. Bryce. 2002. "Meeting International Goals in Child Survival and HIV/AIDS." *Lancet* 360 (9329): 284–9.

Williams, B. G., E. Gouws, C. Boshi-Pinto, C. Bryce, and C. Dye. 2002. "Estimates of Worldwide Distribution of Child Deaths from Acute Respiratory Infections." *Lancet Journal of Infectious Diseases* 2 (1): 25–32.

Chapter 3

The Burden of Disease and Mortality by Condition: Data, Methods, and Results for 2001

Colin D. Mathers, Alan D. Lopez, and Christopher J. L. Murray

In 1993 the World Bank, in collaboration with the World Health Organization (WHO) and the Harvard School of Public Health, sponsored a study to assess the global burden of disease in 1990 (Murray, Lopez, and Jamison 1994; World Bank 1993). As well as generating the first comprehensive and consistent set of estimates of mortality and morbidity by age, sex, and region for the world, the Global Burden of Disease (GBD) study also introduced a new metric, the disability-adjusted life year (DALY), to quantify the burden of disease (Murray and Lopez 1996c, 1996d). The DALY is a summary measure of population health that combines years of life lost from premature death and years of life lived in less than full health and is described in more detail later. Thus, burden of disease analysis provides a unique perspective on health that integrates fatal and nonfatal outcomes, yet allows the two classes of outcomes to be examined separately as well.

The original (1990) GBD study analyzed and synthesized a large volume of data on population health to produce comprehensive and comparable information on the causes of loss of health globally and regionally, including low- and middle-income countries with considerable limitations in data availability and comparability. In addition, the GBD study made estimates even for diseases and conditions for which data were limited and involved considerable uncertainty to ensure that causes of the disease burden for which information was sparse were not implicitly considered to impose no burden and hence be ignored by health policy makers (Murray, Mathers, and Salomon 2003).

Under the leadership of Chris Murray, WHO's executive director of the Evidence and Information for Policy Cluster from 1998 to 2003, WHO undertook a new assessment of the global burden of disease for 2000 to 2002, with consecutive revisions and updates published annually in WHO's world health reports. Version 1 estimates for 2000 were published in the *World Health Report 2001* (WHO 2001d), and Version 3 estimates for 2002, with consistent back revision of the 2000 estimates, were published in the *World Health Report 2003* (WHO 2003b).

The editors of the second edition of *Disease Control Priorities in Developing Countries* (DCP2) (Jamison and others 2006) decided to use the Version 3 GBD estimates for

2001 to provide a common framework for assessing the causes of burden of disease in low- and middle-income countries and in analyzing priorities for interventions. We refer to these estimates as the GBD 2001. DCP2 measured the burden of disease in DALYs using a 3 percent discount rate, but without the nonuniform age weights used in the 1990 GBD study and in the results WHO published for 2000 to 2002.

This chapter documents the data sources and methods used to prepare the GBD 2001 estimates for DCP2 and provides an overview of the global and regional results for causes of disease and injury. The results presented here are those DCP2 used as a starting point for disease-specific economic and intervention analyses. The GBD 2001 incorporates a range of new data sources for developing internally consistent estimates of incidence, health state prevalence, severity, duration, and mortality for 136 major causes by sex and by eight age groups. It estimates deaths by cause, age, and sex for 226 countries and territories drawing on a total of 770 country-years of death registration data, as well as 535 additional sources of information on levels of child and adult mortality and in excess of 2,700 data sets providing information on specific causes of death in regions not well covered by death registration systems. Estimates of incidence, prevalence, severity, duration, and DALYs by cause, age, and sex drew on more than 8,500 data sources, including epidemiological studies, disease registers, and notification systems.

The results are presented here in terms of the World Bank's income and regional groupings of countries, which DCP2 used to facilitate matching causes of death and disease burden data with the economic and social data compilation in the *World Development Report 2003* (World Bank 2003). Countries are divided into seven groups: the high-income countries constitute one group and the low- and middle-income countries are divided into six geographical regions: East Asia and the Pacific, Europe and Central Asia, Latin America and the Caribbean, the Middle East and North Africa, South Asia, and Sub-Saharan Africa (see annex table 3A.1 and map 1 inside the front cover). Annex 3A includes tables documenting definitions of cause and sequela categories and regional categories and summarizing country-specific sources of information on mortality and causes of death and the disability weights used for each cause-sequela category. The tables in annexes 3B and 3C include results for the low- and middle-income countries as a whole as well as for the six regional groups.

QUANTIFYING THE GLOBAL BURDEN OF DISEASE

We first give an overview of the GBD approach toward summarizing the health of populations and the disease and injury causes of loss of health through the use of a particular form of summary measure, the DALY, and discuss the value choices incorporated in the DALY.

The GBD Study

The simplest and most widely used method for producing population health statistics is to aggregate data on individuals to generate estimates of quantities, for example, the proportion of the population (or of a particular grouping by age or sex) suffering from a particular health problem, being in a particular health state, or dying from a specific cause in a defined time period. This approach rapidly becomes unwieldy when a number of problems are being monitored and the intent is to make comparisons over time, across population groups, or before and after specific health interventions, as in cost-effectiveness analyses. Policy makers then face an explosion in the number of statistics they must compare and difficulties in comparing indicators relating to different health states, mortality risks, or disease events. Such statistics on the health status of populations also suffer from several other limitations that reduce their practical value for policy makers:

- Health statistics are partial and fragmented. In many countries, basic information on causes of death is not available for all important causes, and even where mortality data are available, they fail to capture the impact of nonfatal outcomes of disease and injury, such as mental disorders, musculoskeletal disorders, blindness, or deafness, on population health.
- Analyses of incidence, prevalence, or mortality for single causes often result in overestimates, even when carried out by well-intentioned epidemiologists, if not constrained to fit within demographically plausible limits and to be internally consistent and consistent with information on other causes. These problems are compounded when estimates are carried out by groups in competition for scarce resources that are acting as advocates for affected populations or by groups carrying out program evaluation that are also responsible for program implementation (Murray, Lopez, and Wibulpolprasert 2004).
- Health statistics based on a compilation of separate measures of mortality and of incidence and prevalence

rates for a large number of conditions do not allow analysts or policy makers to evaluate outcomes of policies or to compare the relative cost-effectiveness of different interventions.

The 1990 GBD study developed a comprehensive framework for integrating, validating, analyzing, and disseminating fragmented information on the health of populations so that it is truly useful for health policy and planning (Murray and Lopez 1996b, 1996c, 1997a, 1997b). Features of this framework included the incorporation of data on nonfatal health outcomes into summary measures of population health (described in the next subsection), the development of methods and approaches to estimate missing data and to assess the reliability of data, and the use of a common metric to summarize the disease burden both from diagnostic categories of the International Classification of Diseases (ICD) and the major risk factors that cause those disease and injury outcomes.

The basic philosophy guiding the burden of disease approach is that almost all sources of health data are likely to have information content provided that they are carefully screened for plausibility and completeness and that internally consistent estimates of the global descriptive epidemiology of major conditions are possible with appropriate tools, investigator commitment, and expert opinion. This philosophy remains central to the 2001 GBD study, which has expanded the framework of the 1990 GBD study to

- quantify the burden of premature mortality and disability by age, sex, and region for 136 causes;
- develop internally consistent estimates of incidence, prevalence, duration, and case fatality rates for more than 500 sequelae resulting from the foregoing causes;
- analyze the contribution to this burden of major physiological, behavioral, and social risk factors by age, sex, and region.

Summary Measures of Population Health and the DALY

To address the problems described above and to provide an outcome measure for cost-effectiveness analyses and priority-setting exercises, a common metric is required for mortality and for loss of health that can be disaggregated into disease and injury causes and risk factors. Since the mid-20th century, analysts have generally agreed that time is the most appropriate metric: time in years lived or lost because of mortality and years lived in various health states.

Investigators have developed a wide range of such time-based summary measures of population health, many of them generalizations of life expectancy, such as disability-free life expectancy or variants of the so-called quality-adjusted life year (QALY). For assessing the health of populations, summary measures of population health provide a simple and useful digest of the vast array of components of population health (Murray, Salomon, and Mathers 2000; Wolfson 1999). Summary measures of population health do not replace the more detailed reporting of data for specific aspects of health and mortality or for specific causes of health problems; rather, they supplement these data by providing a metric that can be used to monitor trends and compare health across populations or for measuring health outcomes in cost-effectiveness analyses. The last two decades have seen a marked increase in interest in the development, calculation, and use of summary measures (Field and Gold 1998; Murray, Salomon, and others 2002a; Robine and others 2003).

Two classes of summary measures of population health have been developed: health expectancies, for example, disability-free life expectancy; active life expectancy, and healthy life expectancy; and health gaps, such as DALYs and healthy life years (figure 3.1). Health expectancies extend the concept of life expectancy to refer to expectations of various states of health or of the overall expectation of years of equivalent full health, not just of life per se. Health gaps are a complementary class of indicators that measure lost years

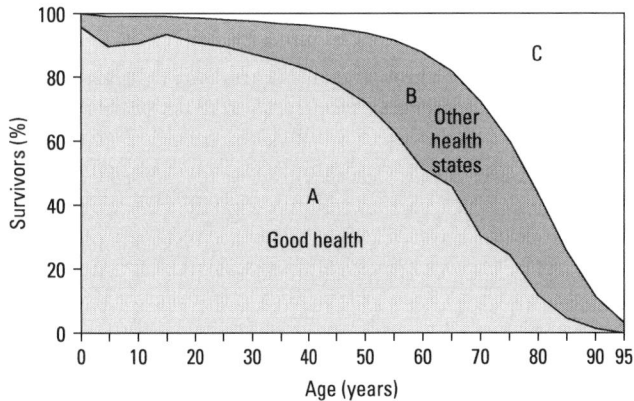

Source: Murray, Salomon, and Mathers 2000.

Note: The health gap is area C + f(B) where f(B) is a function of B in the range 0 to area B representing the lost equivalent years of full health lived in states B. The health expectancy is the area A + g(B), where g(B) = B − f(B) represents the equivalent years of full health lived in states B.

Figure 3.1 Relationship between Health Expectancies and Health Gaps in a Stationary Population

of full health against some normative ideal. Measures of potential years of life lost due to premature mortality have been used for many years to measure the mortality burden of various causes of death. These all measure the gap in years between age at death and some arbitrary standard age before which death is considered premature (typically 65 or 75). The DALY, developed for the GBD study, is an example of a health gap indicator that extends the notion of mortality gaps to include time lived in states other than excellent health.

One of the fundamental goals in choosing a summary measure of population health for quantifying the global burden of disease was to be able to identify the relative magnitude of different health problems, including diseases, injuries, and risk factors. A health gap measure was chosen because it permits categorical attribution of the fatal and nonfatal burden of diseases and injuries to an exhaustive and mutually exclusive set of disease and injury causes (Mathers, Ezzati, and others 2002; Murray, Salomon, and Mathers 2000). The lost years of health (or DALYs) are additive across such a set of disease or injury categories. By contrast, health expectancy measures do not naturally lend themselves to disaggregation by categorically defined causes. Instead, counterfactual methods such as disease elimination are required to quantify the contribution of disease causes to overall health expectancy measures, as well as for dealing with risk factors. Health gap measures also generally require counterfactual analysis to attribute the burden of disease to health determinants and risk factors, as discussed in chapter 4.

DALYs for a specific cause are calculated as the sum of the years of life lost due to premature mortality (YLL) from that cause and the years of healthy life lost as a result of disability (YLD) for incident cases of the health condition as follows:

$$DALY = YLL + YLD.$$

The YLL are essentially calculated as the number of cause-specific deaths multiplied by a loss function specifying the years lost as a function of the age at which death occurs. Ignoring for the moment other social preferences discussed later, the basic formula for YLL for a given cause c, age a, and sex s is as follows:

$$YLL(c,a,s) = N(c,a,s) \times L(a,s),$$

where $N(c,a,s)$ is the number of deaths due to cause c for given age a and sex s and $L(a,s)$ is the standard loss function in years for age a and sex s.

The 1990 GBD study did not use an arbitrary age cutoff such as 70 for the loss function used to calculate YLL, but instead specified the loss function in terms of the life expectancies at various ages in standard life tables, with life expectancy at birth fixed at 82.5 years for females and 80.0 years for males (Coale and Demeny West Model Levels 26 and 25, respectively, see Murray 1996), the highest observed life expectancies in the mid-1990s. The sex difference in the loss function was based on evidence of an intrinsic biological difference in life expectancy for males and females, but one that it is much less than the approximately five to seven years observed in developed countries (Murray 1996). Chapter 5 presents a more detailed specification of the loss function used in the standard DALY calculation.

Because YLL measure the incident stream of lost years of life due to deaths, an incidence perspective is also taken for the calculation of YLD. To estimate YLD for a particular cause during a particular time period, the number of incident cases in that period is multiplied by the average duration of the disease and a weight factor that reflects the severity of the resulting health states on a scale from 0 (perfect health) to 1 (dead). Again without yet considering other social preferences, the basic formula for YLD is as follows:

$$YLD(c,a,s) = I(c,a,s) \times DW(c,a,s) \times L(c,a,s),$$

where $I(c,a,s)$ is the number of incident cases for cause c, age a, and sex s; $DW(c,a,s)$ is the disability weight for cause c, age a, and sex s; and $L(c,a,s)$ is the average duration in years of the case until remission or death.

The valuation of time lived in nonfatal health states formalizes and quantifies social preferences for different states of health as disability weights. Depending on how these weights are derived, they are variously referred to as disability weights, QALY weights, health state valuations, or health state preferences. Because the DALY is measuring loss of health (unlike the QALY, which measures equivalent healthy years lived), the disability weights for DALYs are inverted, running from 0 (ideal health) to 1 (state comparable to death). Health state valuations are discussed in more detail later.

DALYs are not unique to the GBD study. The World Bank used a variant of DALYs in its seminal study of health sector priorities (Jamison and others 1993), which was derived from earlier work to develop time-based measures that reflected the public health impact of death or illness at different ages better than mortality or prevalence counts or rates (Dempsey 1947; Ghana Health Assessment Project Team 1981). As noted, DALYs are an inverse form of the more general concept of QALYs, proposed by Zeckhauser and Shepard (1976) and widely used in economic evaluations. DCP2 (Jamison and others 2006) and WHO's generalized cost-effectiveness analyses for more than 170 health interventions (Tan-Torres Edejer and others 2003) use DALYs as the health outcome measure for their economic analyses.

Countries and health development agencies alike have widely adopted the burden of disease approach as the standard for health accounting, as well as for guiding the determination of health research priorities (Baskent University 2005; Bradshaw and others 2003; Bundhamcharoen and others 2002; Lozano and others 1995; Mahapatra 2002; Mathers and de Francisco 2004; Mathers, Vos, and Stevenson 1999; McKenna and others 2005; Vos and others 1995; WHO 1996).

Making Social Value Choices Explicit

In developing the DALY indicator, Murray (1996) identified three additional value choices that he argued should be made explicit in the formulation of the summary measure:

- How long "should" people in good health expect to live? This choice determines the loss function $L(a,s)$ for age a and sex s. Should the loss function be determined at the national level or globally? The DALY uses a global loss function that is the same for all people of a given age and sex, irrespective of other characteristics such as race, socioeconomic status, or occupation.
- Is a year of healthy life gained now worth more to society than a year of healthy life gained in 20 years' time? In other words, should time discounting be applied to the stream of incident lost healthy years represented by the DALY?
- Are lost years of healthy life valued more at some ages than others? Is a year of life at young adult ages valued more than in old age or infancy? In other words, should unequal age weights be applied to years of healthy life lost at different ages?

Much of the comment on and criticism of the GBD study focused on the explicit social value choices incorporated in the DALY (Anand and Hanson 1997, 1998; Hyder, Rotllanat, and Morrow 1998; Williams 1997, 1999), particularly the social choices pertaining to age weights and severity scores for disabilities, rather than on the uncertainty of the basic descriptive epidemiology. The latter, particularly in the least developed regions, is likely to be far more consequential for setting health priorities (see chapter 5). See Murray and Acharya (1997) and Murray and Lopez (2000) for responses to the criticisms of the value choices made for the 1990 GBD study.

Murray (1996) argues on equity grounds for use of the same life expectancy "ideal" standard for specifying years of life lost for a death in all population subgroups, whether or not their current life expectancy was lower than that of other groups. In addition, he argues that the same disability weight should be used for people of the same age in the same health state.

The DALY measures the future stream of healthy years of life lost due to each incident case of disease or injury and for each death. It is thus an incidence-based rather than a prevalence-based measure. The GBD study applied a 3 percent time discount rate to years of life lost in the future to estimate the net present value of years of life lost. With this discount rate, a year of healthy life gained in 10 years' time is worth 24 percent less than one gained now. Discounting future benefits is standard practice in economic analysis and the following specific arguments can be made for applying discounting to the DALY when measuring population health (Murray and Acharya 1997):

- to be consistent with the measurement of health outcomes in cost-effectiveness analyses;
- to prevent giving excessive weight to deaths at younger ages;
- to address the disease eradication and research paradox, that is, assuming that investment in research or disease eradication has a nonzero chance of succeeding, then without discounting, all current expenditure should be shifted to such investment because the future stream of benefits is infinite.

Chapter 5 examines the sensitivity of the burden of disease results to the choice of discount rate.

In addition to 3 percent time discounting, the 1990 GBD study (Murray 1996) and the GBD results reported in recent world health reports (WHO 2000, 2002d, 2004b) used nonuniform age weights that give less weight to years lived at younger and older ages in calculating DALYs. The inclusion of nonuniform age weights was based on human capital arguments and on a number of studies that suggest the existence of a broad social preference to value a year lived by a young adult more highly than a year lived by a young child or an older person (Murray 1996). At its extreme, age preference manifests as a lack of policy interest in any deaths at ages where the death is not considered premature.

The particular age weights used in the GBD study result in greater weight being given to all deaths below age 39 compared with deaths at older ages. Age weights have perhaps been the most contentious social value incorporated into the DALY (Anand and Hanson 1997; Murray and Acharya 1997), and some national burden of disease studies have chosen not to use them (Mathers, Vos, and Stevenson 1999). The editors of DCP2 decided that uniform age weights should be used. Chapter 5 examines the sensitivity of the burden of disease results to different age weighting choices.

To denote different choices for discounting and age weights, we use the notation DALYs(r,K), where r is the discount rate in percent (not a fraction as in the GBD 1990) and K is the age-weighting modulation factor. The age weights used in the GBD are denoted by $K = 1$ and the nonuse of age weights (that is, uniform age weighting) is denoted by $K = 0$. Thus DALYs(3,0) denotes the DALY with 3 percent discounting and uniform age weights as used in DCP2 and DALYs(3,1) denotes the 3 percent discounting and varying age weights as used in the GBD study. Using DALYs(3,0), an infant death represents the loss of 30.3 DALYs(3,0) for males and 30.5 DALYs(3,0) for females, compared with 26.0 and 26.6 DALYs(3,0) at age 30 for males and females, respectively. A death at age 60 represents 16.0 DALYs(3,0) for males and 17.5 for females.

Comparing Time Lived in Different States of Health

To use time as a common currency for nonfatal health states and for years of life lost due to mortality, we must define, measure, and numerically value time lived in nonfatal health states. The valuation of time lived in nonfatal health states formalizes and quantifies social preferences for different states of health as health state weights. While death is not difficult to define, nonfatal health states are. They involve multiple domains of health that relate to different functions, capacities, or aspects of living. During the last three decades, there has been general acceptance of an approach to describing individuals' health states in terms of multiple domains of health and to developing self-reporting instruments that seek information on a core set of these domains, typically no more than five to eight, that capture most of the important variations in health states across individuals (McDowell and Newell 1996; Sadana 2002).

One common approach is to describe health as a profile of levels on a series of domains. The Medical Outcomes Study (MOS) Short Form 36 is an example of such an instrument, with eight domains covering self-perceived health, vitality, bodily pain, mental health, physical functioning, social functioning, physical role limitations, and social role limitations (Ware and Sherbourne 1992). MOS Short Form 36 domains are scored on continuous scales from 0 to 100, resulting in a large number of potential health states. Health state profiles intended for use with health state valuations tend to use a more limited number of levels in each domain.

Murray and colleagues argue that health state valuations should be conceptualized and operationalized as judgments about the overall level of health associated with a multidimensional description of an individual's health state, not about overall levels of well-being, quality of life, or utility (Murray, Salomon, and others. 2002b; Salomon, Mathers, and others 2003). In this conceptualization, health state valuations formalize the intuitive notion that health levels lie on a continuum and that we may characterize one individual as being more or less healthy than another individual at a particular moment in time. Health state valuations quantify departures from perfect health, that is, the reductions in health associated with particular health states. Note that these weights do not measure the quality of life of people with disabilities and do not measure the value of people to society.

By assigning a single number to an individual's health state with reference to ideal health, health state valuations permit aggregating individual health levels over time and comparing health across individuals, and thereby provide the critical link that allows individuals' nonfatal health experience to be combined with information about mortality in summary measures of population health. Researchers have developed a number of choice-based methods to measure preferences for health states (Salomon and Murray 2004).

The 1990 GBD used two forms of the person trade-off method and asked participants in weighting exercises to make a composite judgment about the severity distribution of the condition and the preference for time spent in each severity level (Murray 1996). This was largely necessitated by the lack of population information on the severity distribution of most conditions at the global and regional levels. The disability weights used in the GBD 2001 are still based in large part on the GBD 1990 disability weights (Murray 1996). Disability weights may vary by age, sex, and region, reflecting variations in the severity distributions of health states and the proportions of cases treated. A common global valuation function is assumed for the underlying health state valuations for specific health states. Despite the assertion by some commentators that valuations for certain health states are likely to be extremely heterogeneous across individuals and populations, empirical evidence suggests otherwise. Valuation studies carried out with deliberative small groups from a wide range of countries have found surprising consistency in valuations across cultures (Salomon and Murray 2002b). More recently, valuation studies carried out as part of the WHO multicountry survey study have also found reasonable consistency in health state valuations for most health states (Salomon, Murray, and others 2003).

Following the GBD terminology, the term disability is used here broadly to refer to departures from optimal health in any of the important domains of health, including mobility, self-care, participation in usual activities, pain and discomfort, anxiety and depression, and cognition and social participation. We thus refer to disability weights and healthy years lost due to disability as shorthand terms for health state preferences and years of healthy life lost because of time lived in states other than the reference state of optimal health, respectively. Note that with this usage, disability, that is, states other than ideal health, may be short term or long term: a day with a common cold is a day with disability.

ESTIMATING DEATHS BY CAUSE: METHODS AND DATA

Complete death registration data cover only one-third of the world's population. Some information on another third is available through the urban death registration systems and national sample registration systems of China and India. For the remaining one-third of the world's population, including most countries in Sub-Saharan Africa, only partial information is available from epidemiological studies, disease registers, and surveillance systems.

The original (1990) GBD study was the first attempt to estimate the global and regional numbers of deaths resulting from a comprehensive set of causes while ensuring consistency with death totals provided by death registration and demographic methods (Murray and Lopez 1996c). Ensuring this consistency was a major advance and is an essential first step in measuring the disease burden. Estimates of numbers of deaths carried out separately for individual causes that are not constrained to sum to a demographically derived total often result in substantial overestimates of deaths from each cause (Jamison 1996). In part, this occurs because in carrying out analysis for a single cause, researchers may easily be overinclusive in counting the deaths attributable to the cause of interest, even without any intent to maximize the size of the specific problem.

Thus, the first analytical step in estimating deaths by cause was to estimate age-specific total death rates by sex. The importance of this step cannot be overemphasized. The number of deaths by age and sex provided an essential "envelope" that constrained individual disease and injury estimates of deaths. Competing claims for the magnitude of deaths from various causes must then be reconciled within this envelope.

Next, to estimate the number of deaths by cause we drew on the following four broad sources of data:

- *Death registration systems.* Complete or incomplete death registration systems provide information about causes of death for almost all high-income countries and for many countries in Europe (Eastern) and Central Asia and in Latin America and the Caribbean. Some vital registration (VR) information is also available in all other regions.
- *Sample death registration systems.* In China and India, sample registration systems for rural areas supplement urban death registration systems. Information systems now provide data on causes of death for several other large countries for which information was not available at the time of the original GBD study.
- *Epidemiological assessments.* Epidemiologists have estimated deaths for specific causes, such as HIV/AIDS, malaria, and tuberculosis (TB), for most countries in the regions most affected. These estimates usually combine information from surveys on the incidence or prevalence of the disease with data on case fatality rates.
- *Cause of death models.* The cause of death models used in the original GBD study (Murray and Lopez 1996a) were substantially revised and enhanced for estimating deaths by broad cause group in regions with limited information on mortality. The CodMod software developed for this study and described later drew on a data set of 1,613 country-years of observation of cause of death distributions from 58 countries between 1950 and 2001.

All-Cause Mortality for 192 Countries

According to data provided by 112 WHO member states, only about one-third of the estimated 56 million deaths occurring annually are recorded in death registration systems. If the sample registration systems of China and India are considered to provide information on their entire populations, then information is available for around 72 percent of the global population. In recent years, considerable priority has also been given to obtaining data on child and maternal mortality through such instruments as the Demographic and Health Survey (DHS) program funded by the U.S. Agency for International Development and the Multiple Indicator Cluster Survey program carried out by the United Nations Children's Fund. Table 3.1 summarizes sources of information on levels of child and adult all-cause

Table 3.1 Availability of Data for Estimation of All-Cause Mortality Rates by Age and Sex

Type of data	East Asia and Pacific	Europe and Central Asia	Latin America and the Caribbean	Middle East and North Africa	South Asia	Sub-Saharan Africa	High-income countries	Total
Number of countries with all-cause mortality data								
Death registration data for 2001								
Complete	1	11	2	1	0	1	25	41
Incomplete[a]	1	6	5	0	1	0	2	15
Death registration data for years prior to 2001[b]								
Complete	1	0	3	0	0	0	5	9
Incomplete[a]	3	9	13	1	1	2	2	31
Data for levels of child and adult mortality	12	1	6	9	4	2	3	37
Data for levels of child mortality only	4	0	3	4	2	42	0	55
Number of data collections								
Country-years of death registration data								
2001 available	4	17	7	1	1	1	28	59
2001 not available[c]	89	132	279	45	23	29	114	711
Other sources of information on child and adult mortality	70	22	122	67	48	190	16	535
Total data sets used	163	171	408	113	72	220	158	1,305

Source: Authors' compilation.

a. Completeness of death registration data was assessed using standard demographic methods (see text).

b. Includes countries where death registration data for years prior to 2001 were used to project levels of child and adult mortality to construct a life table based on a country standard derived from the last available year of death registration data.

c. Also includes countries where death registration data were used to project levels of child and adult mortality as inputs to the WHO logit life table system using a global standard.

mortality used to construct life tables for 192 WHO member states by region and by type of data.

For countries with death registration data, demographic techniques (Preston-Coale, Brass growth-balance, generalized growth-balance, and Bennett-Horiuchi methods) were first applied, as appropriate, to assess the extent of completeness of the recorded mortality data for adults. If the data coverage estimates were high enough to be meaningful, death rates for those aged five years and over were then adjusted accordingly. The completeness of death registration for children was assessed separately using other available sources of information on child mortality. For countries without usable VR data, other available sources of adult mortality such as surveys and censuses were used to estimate the level of adult mortality as measured by $_{45}q_{15}$ (the probability of dying between exact ages 15 and 60). For child mortality under five, again, all available survey, census, and VR data were assessed, adjusted, and averaged to estimate the probable trend in child mortality ($_5q_0$) in recent decades.

The population estimates used for all countries were those prepared by the United Nations Population Division (2003). Note that these estimates refer to de facto populations, that is, they include residents such as guest workers and refugees, rather than de jure populations, meaning citizens, and in some countries, permanent residents. Member states that report death registration data to WHO also routinely report population data for the population the death registration system covers, which in some cases is a subset of the national population. Death registration data may cover less than 100 percent of the population not only because some geographical areas may be excluded, but also because registration may be restricted to a subset of the resident population, such as citizens, and may thus exclude deaths among groups such as guest workers or refugees.

For the GBD 2001 study, age- and sex-specific death rates were calculated from the death and population data provided by countries, with adjustments made for completeness of the registration data where needed, and then total deaths by age and sex were calculated for each country by applying these rates to the United Nations Population Division estimates of de facto populations for 2001.

Four methods were used to construct life tables for each country depending on the type of data available (Lopez and others 2002):

- *Countries with death registration data for 2001.* Such data were used directly to construct life tables for 56 countries after adjusting for incomplete registration if necessary.
- *Countries with a time series of death registration data.* Where the latest year of death registration data available was prior to 2001, a time series of annual life tables (adjusted if the registration level was incomplete) between 1985 and the latest available year was used to project levels of child and adult mortality for 2001. For small countries with populations of less than 500,000, moving averages were used to smooth the time series. Projected values of child and adult mortality were then applied to a modified logit life table model (Murray, Ferguson, and others 2003), using the most recent national data as the standard, to predict the full life table for 2001, and HIV/AIDS and war deaths were added to total mortality rates for 2001 where necessary. This method was applied for 40 countries using a total of 711 country-years of death registration data.
- *Countries with other information on levels of child and adult mortality.* For 37 countries, estimated levels of child and adult mortality were applied to a modified logit life table model (Murray, Ferguson, and others 2003), using a global standard, to estimate the full life table for 2001, and HIV/AIDS deaths and war deaths were added to total mortality rates as necessary. For most of these countries, data on levels of adult mortality were obtained from death registration data, official life tables, or mortality information derived from other sources such as censuses and surveys. The all-cause mortality envelope for China was derived from a time series analysis of deaths for every household in China reported in the 1982, 1990, and 2000 censuses. The extent of underreporting of deaths in the 2000 census was estimated at about 11.3 percent for males and 18.1 percent for females (Bannister and Hill 2004). The all-cause mortality envelope for India was derived from a time series analysis of age-specific death rates from the Sample Registration System after correction for underregistration (88 percent completeness) (Mari Bhat 2002).
- *Countries with information on levels of child mortality only.* For 55 countries, 42 of them in Sub-Saharan Africa, no information was available on levels of adult mortality.

Based on the predicted level of child mortality in 2001, the most likely corresponding level of adult mortality (excluding HIV/AIDS deaths where necessary) was selected, along with uncertainty ranges, based on regression models of child versus adult mortality as observed in a set of almost 2,000 life tables judged to be of good quality (Lopez and others 2002; Murray, Ferguson, and others 2003). These estimated levels of child and adult mortality were then applied to a modified logit life table model, using a global standard, to estimate the full life table in 2001, and HIV/AIDS deaths and war deaths were added to total mortality rates as necessary. Evidence on adult mortality in Sub-Saharan African countries remains limited, even in areas with successful child and maternal mortality surveys.

Classification of Causes of Disease and Injury

Disease and injury causes of death and of burden of disease were classified using the same tree structure as in the original GBD study (Murray and Lopez 1996c). The first level of disaggregation comprises the following three broad cause groups:

- Group I: communicable, maternal, perinatal, and nutritional conditions
- Group II: noncommunicable diseases
- Group III: injuries.

Each group was then divided into major cause subcategories, for example, cardiovascular disease (CVD) and malignant neoplasms (cancers) are two major cause subcategories of Group II. Beyond this level, two further disaggregation levels were used, resulting in a complete cause list of 136 categories of specific diseases and injuries. Annex table 3A.2 lists the GBD 2001 cause categories and their ICD codes in terms of the ICD 9th revision (ICD-9) and 10th revision (ICD-10) (WHO 1977, 1992).

Group I causes of death consist of the cluster of conditions that typically decline at a faster pace than all-cause mortality during the epidemiological transition. In high-mortality populations, Group I dominates the cause of death pattern, whereas in low-mortality populations, Group I accounts for only a small proportion of deaths. The major cause subcategories are closely based on the ICD chapters with a few significant differences. Whereas the ICD classifies chronic respiratory diseases and acute respiratory infections into the same chapter, the GBD cause classification includes acute respiratory infections in Group I and chronic respiratory diseases in Group II. Note also that the Group I subcategory of "causes arising in the perinatal period" relates to the causes included in the corresponding ICD chapter, principally low birthweight, prematurity, birth asphyxia, and birth trauma, but does not include all causes of deaths occurring during the perinatal period, such as infections, congenital malformations, and injuries. In addition, the GBD includes only deaths among children born alive and does not estimate stillbirths (see chapter 6).

The development and successive revisions of the ICD have facilitated the comparability of cause of death data within and across countries. Although each revision has produced some discontinuities in cause of death data, the revision from ICD-9 to ICD-10 resulted in more substantial changes than previous revisions. ICD-10 is considerably more detailed than ICD-9, with almost twice the number of codes, and includes both conceptual and classification revisions as well as changes in the coding rules used to select the underlying cause of death. Additional problems in comparing data on causes of death across countries arise from variations in the accuracy of diagnoses of causes of death.

In most developed countries, medical practitioners certify the underlying cause of death even though they may not always have had prior contact with the deceased or access to relevant medical records. In developing countries, a significant proportion of deaths may occur without medical attention and such deaths may be registered without a medical opinion about the cause of death. At the same time, selecting a single underlying cause of death is often problematic for the elderly, who have often had several chronic diseases that concurrently led to their death. This results in higher levels of uncertainty about cause of death distributions in the oldest age group. Finally, in both developing and developed countries, legal, societal, and other reasons may lead to the underreporting of causes of death of a sensitive nature, such as suicide or HIV/AIDS. For this reason, other sources of information for specific causes such as HIV/AIDS, illicit drug use, and war have been used where necessary to modify cause-specific estimates based on death registration data.

The GBD classification system does not include the ICD category "symptoms, signs, and ill-defined conditions" as one of the major causes of deaths. The GBD classification scheme has reassigned deaths assigned to this ICD category, as well as some other codes used for ill-defined conditions, to specific causes of death. This is important from the perspective of generating useful information to compare cause of death patterns or to inform health policy making, because it allows unbiased comparisons of cause of death patterns across countries or regions.

Deaths are categorically attributed to one underlying cause using ICD rules and conventions. In some cases where the ICD rules are ambiguous, the GBD 2001 follows the conventions used by the GBD 1990 study (Murray and Lopez 1996a). Note also that a number of causes of death act as risk factors for other diseases. Total mortality attributable to such causes may be substantially larger than the mortality estimates for the cause in terms of ICD rules for underlying causes. For example, the GBD 2001 estimates that 960,000 deaths were due to diabetes mellitus as an underlying cause, but when deaths from CVD and renal failure attributable to diabetes are included, the global total of attributable deaths rises to almost 3 million (Roglic and others 2005). Other causes for which important components of attributable mortality are included elsewhere in the GBD cause list include hepatitis B or C (mortality attributable to liver cancer and renal failure), unipolar or bipolar depressive disorders and schizophrenia (mortality attributable to suicide), and blindness (mortality attributable to blindness whether from infectious or noninfectious causes).

Countries with Complete or Incomplete Death Registration Data

In the last decade, computerization of death registration data at the country level and electronic transmission to WHO have considerably improved the timeliness of information. In addition, the number of countries submitting their underlying cause of death data to WHO using ICD-10 increased from 4 in 1995 to 75 in 2003. Some 50 countries are still reporting data using ICD-9 and only 1 country is still using ICD-8 (Mathers and others 2005).

Several new features and changes from ICD-9 to ICD-10 have a major impact on the interpretation of statistical data, and the implications of these changes have been taken into account to a limited extent when making trend comparisons and estimations for causes of death. ICD-10 is more detailed, with about 10,000 codes compared with around 5,100 in ICD-9, and the rules for selecting the underlying cause of death have been reevaluated and sometimes changed. For example, ICD-10 considers pneumonia to be a consequence of a much wider range of conditions than ICD-9, and it therefore would be less likely to be selected as the underlying cause. Modification of the death certificate with the inclusion of an additional line in part 1 of the certificate (for diseases related to the chain of events leading directly to death) as recommended by WHO may also have had an impact on the selection of the underlying cause of death.

Accuracy in diagnosing causes of death still varies substantially across countries with death registration systems. In addition, even in countries where medically qualified staff assign causes of death, some degree of misattribution or miscoding occurs during the process of coding underlying causes of death, mainly because of incorrect or systematic biases in diagnoses, incorrect or incomplete death certificates, misinterpretation of ICD rules for selecting underlying causes, and variations in the use of categories for unknown and ill-defined causes (Mathers and others 2005).

Death registration data containing usable information on cause of death distributions were available for 107 countries, mostly in the high-income group, Europe and Central Asia, and Latin America and the Caribbean (table 3.2, annex table 3A.3). Where the latest available year was earlier than 2001, death registration data from 1980 through the latest available year were analyzed as a basis for projecting recent trends for specific causes, and these trend estimates were used to project the cause distribution for 2001. When estimating cause of death distributions for very small countries, an average of the three last years of data was used to minimize stochastic variation.

In the case of the few countries still reporting data using the condensed ICD-9 Basic Tabulation List, algorithms based on data from countries with more detailed coding were applied to estimate deaths due to asthma as no Basic Tabulation List code for asthma is available. Also, China and some of the newly independent states of the former Soviet

Table 3.2 Availability of Data for Estimation of Causes of Death by Age and Sex

Type of data	East Asia and Pacific	Europe and Central Asia	Latin America and the Caribbean	Middle East and North Africa	South Asia	Sub-Saharan Africa	High-income countries	Total
Number of countries								
Death registration data (coverage of 85% or more)[a]	1	11	5	1	0	1	29	48
Death registration data (coverage <85%) – adjusted using cause-of-death models	5	16	25	3	1	3	5	58
Sample registration and surveillance[b]	2	0	0	1	1	1	0	5
No data–cause-of-death models used with detailed cause patterns based on regional data	14	0	2	10	6	42	3	77
Epidemiological estimates for mortality due to specific causes used where applicable	c	d	c	c	c	c	e	c
Percent of population								
Death registration data (coverage of 85% or more)[a]	0.0	52.7	13.0	0.1	0.0	0.2	94.4	19.5
Death registration data (coverage <85%) — adjusted using cause-of-death models	5.6	47.3	84.2	50.0	1.4	8.6	5.3	17.1
Sample registration and surveillance[b]	73.3	0.0	0.0	1.7	74.5	1.4	0.0	39.1
No data–cause-of-death models used with detailed cause patterns based on regional data	21.1	0.0	2.9	48.1	24.2	89.8	0.3	24.3
Total	100.0	100.0	100.0	100.0	100.0	100.0	100.0	100.0

Source: Authors' compilation.
a. The threshold of coverage of 85 percent used for causes of death differs from that used for registration of deaths (95 percent) because the biases from underreporting of the fact of death are more serious for assessing levels of all-cause mortality than for assessing the distribution of causes.
b. Includes countries with death registration or surveillance systems relying heavily on verbal autopsy methods for ascertaining causes of death.
c. HIV/AIDS, tuberculosis, measles, pertussis, poliomyelitis, tetanus, acute lower respiratory infections, Chagas' disease, maternal conditions, perinatal conditions, cancers, drug use disorders, rheumathoid arthritis, and war. See table 3.5 for details.
d. AIDS, drug use disorders, and war. See table 3.5 for details.
e. Drug use disorders and war. See table 3.5 for details.

Union still use some special condensed ICD-9 cause of death classifications, which were then mapped to the GBD cause list. Missing values for some GBD conditions were estimated with the use of algorithms. Similarly, algorithms were also applied for countries reporting data using the condensed ICD-10 Mortality Tabulation List 1.

Deaths resulting from war are not systematically included in the cause of death data. For example, in the United States, the Department of Defense records deaths resulting from war, and for security reasons they are not included in the death registration system. Some death registration data undercount deaths due to HIV/AIDS and drug use partly because of miscoding and partly because of reluctance to record these diagnoses. In some cases, adjustments for deaths due to war, HIV/AIDS, and drug use have been made using other sources of information as described later.

Cause of death data were carefully analyzed to take incomplete coverage of VR into account and the likely differences in cause of death patterns among the uncovered and often poorer subpopulations. When the coverage of death registration data was assessed as less than 85 percent, cause of death modeling was used to adjust the proportions of deaths occurring in Groups I, II, and III by age and sex. Table 3.2 shows the regional distribution of the 58 countries for which such adjustments were carried out. In total, useful information on cause of death distributions was available for 37 percent of the world's population, or 76 percent if China and India's sample registration and mortality surveillance systems were included. Usable death registration information was available for only four Sub-Saharan African countries: Mauritius, the Seychelles, South Africa, and Zimbabwe. Death registration data are available for several other Sub-Saharan African countries, but are largely restricted to deaths in urban hospitals, with overall coverage being too low to provide useful population-level information on cause of death distributions (Rao, Bradshaw, and Mathers 2004).

Annex table 3A.3 summarizes the years of death registration data with information on underlying cause available for each country, together with information on the methods used to estimate cause of death distributions. As shown in table 3.1, a total of 770 country-years of death registration data were used in the analysis of causes of death for the GBD 2001.

Redistribution of Ill-Defined Causes and "Garbage Codes"

Even in countries where medically qualified staff assign causes there is substantial use of coding categories for unknown and ill-defined causes. In addition to the ICD codes for "symptoms, signs, and ill-defined conditions" (ICD-9 codes 780–799 and ICD-10 codes R00–R99), a number of other ICD codes do not represent useful underlying causes from a policy perspective and their inappropriate overuse compromises the usefulness of information on causes of death. These garbage codes or ill-defined codes include deaths from injuries where the intent was not determined (ICD-9 codes E980–989 and ICD-10 codes Y10–Y34 and Y872); CVD categories lacking diagnostic meaning, such as cardiac arrest and heart failure (ICD-9 codes 427.1, 427.4, 427.5, 428, 429.0, 429.1, 429.2, 429.9, and 440.9; and ICD-10 codes I47.2, I49.0, I46, I50, I51.4, I51.5, I51.6, I51.9, and I70.9); and cancer deaths coded to categories for secondary or unspecified sites (ICD-9 codes 195 and 199 and ICD-10 codes C76, C80, and C97). The percentage of deaths coded as ill-defined causes varies from 4 percent in New Zealand to more than 40 percent in Sri Lanka and Thailand.

Table 3.3 shows the distribution of deaths assigned to ill-defined codes for the 105 WHO member states reporting data on death registrations since 1990 with at least 50 percent completeness or coverage. The median percentage of deaths coded to ill-defined causes was 12 percent; the median percentage of symptoms, signs, and ill-defined conditions was 4.0 percent; and the median of ill-defined cardiovascular causes was 5.3 percent. In more than 15 high-income countries, more than 10 percent of deaths were coded to these ill-defined conditions, not so much because of overuse of codes for symptoms, signs, and ill-defined conditions, but because of excessive use of garbage codes for CVD, cancers, and injuries (Mathers and others 2005).

To produce unbiased estimates of cause-specific death rates, and to maximize comparability across member states, deaths coded to general ill-defined categories (ICD-9, chapter XVI; ICD-10, chapter XVIII) were redistributed pro rata across all Group I and Group II causes, that is, all causes excluding injuries. Correction algorithms were also applied to resolve problems of miscoding for the cardiovascular, cancer, and injury garbage codes.

Ill-Defined Cardiovascular Codes. Physicians may use a number of cardiovascular codes in ICD-9 and ICD-10 to assign deaths that are actually due to ischemic heart disease (IHD). They may assign IHD deaths to ill-defined cardiovascular codes because of insufficient clinical information at the time of death, local medical diagnostic practices, or simply by error. These include codes for heart failure, ventricular dysrhythmias, generalized atherosclerosis, and ill-defined descriptions and complications of heart disease.

Table 3.3 Distribution of Percentage of Total Deaths Assigned to Ill-Defined Codes for 105 WHO Member States, Most Recent Available Year

Ill-defined code group	Percentage of deaths assigned to ill-defined codes			
	Median	25th percentile	75th percentile	Maximum
Symptoms	4.0	2.1	8.7	44.0
Injury	0.5	0.2	1.3	5.1[a]
Cancer	1.0	0.5	1.5	2.7
Cardiovascular disease	5.3	2.7	7.7	23.4
Total ill-defined	12.0	7.0	17.2	48.8

Source: Mathers and others 2005.

Note: Table includes those countries supplying data on death registration for most recent year since 1990 and with at least 50 percent completeness or coverage.

a. These data exclude South Africa, where 93 percent of deaths from external causes were coded to ill-defined injuries.

Figure 3.2 illustrates the enormous variation across countries in coding practice with respect to these ill-defined cardiovascular codes. For each country, the fraction of cardiovascular deaths (excluding stroke) assigned to the ill-defined cardiovascular codes is plotted against the fraction of cardiovascular deaths (excluding stroke) assigned to IHD (ICD-9 codes 410–414 or ICD-10 codes I20–I25). The strong negative relationship between IHD mortality and that from the ill-defined CVD codes ($r^2 = 0.90$) strongly supports the hypothesis that the quality of CVD death certification varies substantially across countries. The upper left portion of figure 3.2 shows countries where doctors certified, on average, more ill-defined CVD than IHD deaths, and these include France, Japan, Portugal, and Spain. The bottom right corner of the figure shows those countries where doctors assign, on average, a small proportion of ill-defined CVD deaths. This second group includes Australia, Canada, Finland, New Zealand, Norway, and the United Kingdom (Scotland). We refer to these two groups of countries as the high ill-defined coding and low ill-defined coding groups.

To correct for the likely underregistration of IHD in countries such as France, Japan, and Spain in the original GBD study, Murray and Lopez (1996a) developed an algorithm based on the assumption that the cluster of countries comprising Canada, Finland, New Zealand, and Norway, where ill-defined coding was low, would define the standard coding practice. For all other countries, the percentage of cardiovascular deaths (excluding stroke) assigned to these codes in excess of this standard percentage was then assumed to be largely miscertified IHD. For the GBD 2001, Lozano and others (2001) developed a revised method to estimate the fraction of IHD deaths assigned to ill-defined cardiovascular codes. This involved estimating age- and sex-specific regression equations predicting observed IHD death

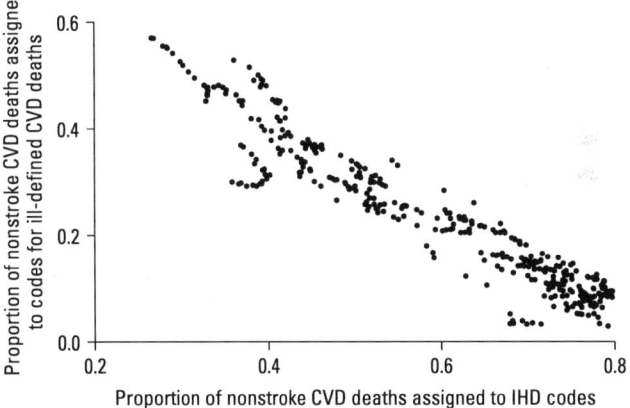

Source: Lozano and others 2001.

Figure 3.2 Variation across Selected Countries in Coding for Ill-Defined CVD Causes, 1979–98

rates in terms of the ill-defined CVD death rates and the smoking impact ratio for a cross-national data set of 372 country-years of death registration data for 26 countries between 1979 and 1998. The smoking impact ratio, estimated from lung cancer mortality rates using the Peto-Lopez method (Peto and others 1992), is a measure of the cumulative effects of tobacco exposure as a risk factor for IHD.

Table 3.4 shows the resulting correction factors, that is, the proportion of ill-defined CVD deaths reassigned to IHD. As expected, the extent of miscoding at every age, for both males and females, was systematically higher in high ill-defined coding countries, where the results suggest that 50 to 95 percent of ill-defined CVD codes should be reassigned to IHD.

With correction, the age standardized death rates increased in all countries, but most notably in Japan (26 percent for males and 24 percent for females), France (27 percent

Table 3.4 Correction Factors Giving Proportion of Ill-Defined CVD Deaths to Be Reassigned to IHD, by Age and Sex

Age group	Males		Females	
	Low ill-defined coding countries	High ill-defined coding countries	Low ill-defined coding countries	High ill-defined coding countries
35–39	0.000	0.000	0.000	0.000
40–44	0.107	0.107	0.000	0.000
45–49	0.039	0.273	0.000	0.041
50–54	0.040	0.696	0.101	0.446
55–59	0.203	0.941	0.139	0.689
60–64	0.160	0.754	0.119	0.660
65–69	0.253	0.827	0.251	0.615
70–74	0.264	0.732	0.202	0.469
75–79	0.233	0.576	0.170	0.358
80+	0.030	0.242	0.060	0.198

Source: Lozano and others 2001.

for males and 35 percent for females), and Greece (32 percent for males and 47 percent for females). Smaller increases were apparent for Belgium, the Czech Republic, Hungary, Italy, Portugal, and Spain (12 to 25 percent on average for males and females), and only small changes were observed for Austria, Germany, the Netherlands, and the United States (about 5 percent). In other countries, including Australia, Canada, Finland, Ireland, New Zealand, Norway, and the United Kingdom (Northern Ireland and Scotland), no corrections were suggested by this analysis.

Corrections for miscertification narrow the range in death rates across countries from a fivefold to a fourfold variation and also change the relative rankings of countries. The analysis of IHD miscertification is supported by the dramatic increase of more than 25 percent in recorded IHD mortality rates in Japan between 1994 and 1995 with the change from ICD-9 to ICD-10, whereby physicians were encouraged not to use heart failure as an underlying cause of death. Prior to the introduction of ICD-10, corrected rates were more than 80 percent higher in males and around 70 percent greater in females compared with what was recorded in vital statistics.

Lozano and others (2001) compare the miscertification levels estimated using their regression approach with those observed in the WHO Monitoring Cardiovascular Disease (MONICA) study sites. They find general agreement in relation to the existence of significant miscertification in each country, but less clear agreement on specific levels of miscertification. This latter finding is difficult to interpret given some difficulties in mapping the MONICA "possible IHD category" to ICD categories and the fact that the study sites may not be representative of national populations.

While the empirical results of applying the recoding model are encouraging, and the GBD 2001 has used it to reassign ill-defined CVD codes, two points are noteworthy. First, the fraction of ill-defined cardiovascular deaths that are due to IHD is assumed to be constant across countries within each of the low and high ill-defined code groups. Statistical models can only go so far in extracting truth from poorly coded deaths data, and more precise country-specific analyses really require recoding studies for samples of relevant deaths, ideally involving autopsy or other clinical diagnostic information. Second, due to the nonstandard disease classification used in Russia and other newly independent states (175 categories based on ICD-9), the method cannot be applied without further evidence from autopsies as to the true cause of cardiovascular deaths. The single most important cause of cardiovascular death in these countries is "coronary atherosclerosis" (093 in the Soviet classification of diseases), which in part reflects a disease process different than what the term implies elsewhere (Chenet and others 1998; Zatonski 1998). The use of the code "sudden death" to describe mortality often associated with binge drinking in Russia and neighboring countries may also conceal cases of IHD (Kauhanen and others 1997).

Ill-Defined Cancer Codes. In the GBD 1990 study, deaths coded to ICD-9 195–199 (malignant neoplasm of other and unspecified sites, including those whose point of origin cannot be determined, secondary and unspecified neoplasm) were redistributed pro rata across all malignant neoplasm categories within each age and sex group, so that the category "other malignant neoplasms" included only malignant neoplasms of other specified sites (Murray and Lopez 1996a).

For the GBD 2001, the survival model developed for estimating cancer deaths by site from cancer incidence data (Mathers, Shibuya, and others 2002) was used to compare predicted deaths from the survival model for the United States with those reported in U.S. vital statistics. This comparison identified four sites that did not appear to have any significant coding of cancer deaths to the garbage codes ICD-9 195–199. The redistribution algorithm for cancer garbage codes was therefore revised for the GBD 2001 to redistribute cancer garbage code deaths pro rata across all cancer sites except liver; pancreas; ovary; and trachea, bronchus, and lung.

Intent of Injuries Undetermined. Deaths assigned to codes for injuries undetermined whether accidentally or purposefully inflicted (ICD-9 codes E980–989 and ICD-10 codes Y10–Y34 and Y872) are those where the person certifying the cause of death has not determined whether the injuries were unintentional or intentional, for example, an outcome of self-inflicted injury or assault. While there will remain a residue of deaths for which insufficient information is available to determine intent, this should be a small fraction of injury deaths if appropriate forensic and coronial investigations are carried out. Excluding South Africa, the proportion of injury deaths assigned to these codes varies from less than 0.5 percent in most developed countries to just over 5 percent (table 3.3). To reduce bias in estimating deaths due to unintentional and intentional injuries, deaths coded as undetermined intent were redistributed pro rata by age and sex to the GBD categories for intentional and unintentional injury.

Data Sources and Methods for Some Specific Countries

In some cases, either because of large population size, and hence implications for global mortality estimates, or because of recent national burden of disease research involving one or more of the authors, more detailed methods to estimate mortality patterns were applied, as summarized in the following subsections.

China. Cause-specific mortality data for China are available from two sources: the sample VR system administered by the Ministry of Health and the Disease Surveillance Point (DSP) system established by the Chinese Center for Disease Control (see Yang and others 2005 for an overview of the design and operational characteristics of these systems). The VR system covers a population of 120 million people at 137 sample sites and captures around 700,000 deaths per year. The DSP system has 145 surveillance points, covers a population of around 11 million, and collects information on around 50,000 deaths per year.

The Ministry of Health classifies sample sites for the DSP system into an urban stratum and four socioeconomic strata for rural areas, based on an analysis of nine indicators for rural counties from the 1990 national census. These indicators include birth and mortality rates, dependency ratios, literacy rates, and proportions of agricultural versus industrial occupations in the overall workforce. The VR system's sample sites are classified into one urban and three rural socioeconomic strata. Because the sample sites for the DSP system are considered to be nationally representative, the fraction of the national population in each socioeconomic stratum was assumed to follow the same population distribution as the DSP sites.

Data from the VR system for 2000 and a three-year average for the DSP system from 1997–9 were separately appraised for their usability in estimating national-level, cause-specific mortality for China. From the two systems, a comparison of age-standardized mortality rates for specific conditions was carried out for each socioeconomic stratum, as shown in figure 3.3.

We found that the mortality rates of the DSP system reflected the broad cause, group-specific mortality distribution more accurately, especially in rural areas. Also, the sampling distribution of sites in the DSP system was more nationally representative than that of the VR system. Thus, the proportional distribution of broad cause group mortality

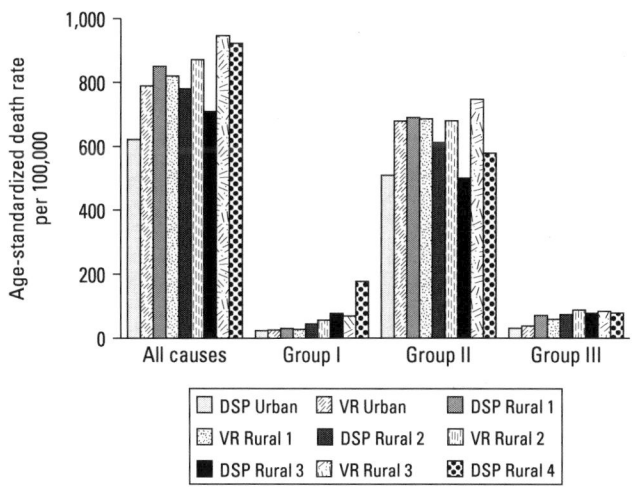

Source: Authors' calculations.

Note: Mortality rates are age standardized using the WHO world standard population.

Figure 3.3 Mortality Rates for Socioeconomic Strata, by Cause Group, from China's Two Mortality Data Systems

for each stratum from the DSP data was applied to each stratum-specific mortality envelope to derive the broad cause group mortality in absolute numbers of deaths by age and sex.

The VR system's data captured mortality at the level of subgroup and specific cause more accurately, and because it was based on a significantly larger sample of deaths, it showed more plausible age patterns for specific causes. Hence, the specific cause-proportionate mortality distributions from the VR system's data were used for distributions within broad cause groups.

Finally, we summed the mortality estimates by cause, age, and sex from each stratum to obtain a national estimate of cause-specific mortality that had not been corrected for underregistration. We then inflated this cause-specific mortality to the national all-cause mortality envelope from the life table analysis to obtain the final national estimate of cause-specific mortality for 2001. We adjusted these estimates with information from WHO technical programs on maternal, perinatal, and childhood-cluster conditions and from epidemiological estimates for TB, HIV/AIDS, illicit drug dependence and problem use, rheumatoid arthritis, and war deaths.

India. For India, separate mortality recording systems for rural and urban areas were used to estimate all-cause death rates by age and sex for rural and urban areas and these were added to obtain national all-cause death rates to construct a national life table. The all-cause mortality envelope was derived from a time series analysis of age-specific death rates from the Sample Registration System after correcting them for underregistration (88 percent completeness) (Mari Bhat 2002).

Cause patterns of mortality were based on the Medical Certification of Cause of Death Database for urban areas of India and the Annual Survey of Causes of Death for rural areas of India. The all-cause mortality envelope was split into separate envelopes for urban and rural populations using a 70:30 ratio. Data on cause-specific mortality from separate sources for rural and urban areas were used with these mortality envelopes to build up independent estimates for urban and rural areas, which were summed to obtain national cause-specific mortality estimates.

For rural areas, the Andhra Pradesh burden of disease study (Mahapatra 2002) analyzed data from the Annual Survey of Causes of Death for 1996–8. The analysis included the redistribution of ill-defined deaths to specific causes based on a verbal autopsy retest survey conducted as part of the field studies for the project. For urban areas, data from

the Medical Certification of Cause of Death system for 1996 were used. This system provides data on about 400,000 deaths annually coded to a national list of ICD-9 causes groups that approximates the ICD-9 Basic Tabulation List. These data were mapped onto the GBD classification and inflated to the urban mortality envelope. The proportion of urban deaths due to injuries was adjusted based on results from a large-scale verbal autopsy study in the city of Chennai, which detected that about 2.5 percent of deaths certified as due to ill-defined medical causes were actually due to injuries (Gajalakshmi and others 2002).

The summed national-level, cause-specific mortality estimates were adjusted with information from WHO technical programs on maternal, perinatal, and childhood-cluster conditions, as well as epidemiological estimates for TB, HIV/AIDS, illicit drug dependence and problem use, rheumatoid arthritis, and war deaths.

Egypt. Even though Lopez and others (2002) assessed Egyptian death registration data for 2000 to be almost complete, these data contained high proportions of deaths coded to symptoms and ill-defined conditions, as well as to conditions such as heart failure and cardiac arrest that were not underlying causes of death. Hence, a model-based prediction of the broad cause proportionate distribution by age and sex was used and applied to the cause-specific mortality structure from the country data after excluding a major proportion of the ill-defined deaths.

Turkey. The national life table for Turkey was estimated from separate urban and rural life tables. To estimate the urban life table, reported deaths during 1991–9 in the 81 provincial and distinct urban centers were evaluated for completeness using established demographic methods. These methods suggested that for more recent years, adult deaths were about 80 percent complete for males and 78 percent complete for females. These correction factors were used to estimate the level of adult mortality $(_{45}q_{15})$ in 1999 and the rate was then projected forward to 2000. The resulting estimates (0.190 for males and 0.106 for females) were similar to the levels estimated from the 2002–3 nationally representative mortality survey carried out by the Ministry of Health and Başkent University (Baskent University 2005). Together with estimated child mortality values from the 1998 DHS projected to 2000, a full life table was estimated for urban Turkey, which is equivalent to about two-thirds of the national population. Death rates were projected to 2001 assuming an annual rate of mortality decline of 1.25 percent. For rural areas, child mortality was first estimated from the DHS in the same way as for urban areas. Adult mortality ($_{45}q_{15}$) was estimated from the WHO modified logit life table system (0.235 for males, 0.189 for females), values that were broadly similar to national mortality survey data, although the relatively small number of rural deaths in the survey, about 300, gave rise to substantial uncertainty about the true levels of adult mortality in rural areas. The urban and rural death rates were then weighted by population size to obtain estimated national death rates, and hence the life table.

Data on causes of death were only available for urban areas of Turkey. These data were systematically reviewed for cause miscoding and adjusted based on clinical opinion and evidence on a sample of deaths from urban hospitals in Ismir and Ankara. In particular, most of the large proportion of deaths coded to "other heart disease" were reassigned to specific vascular pathologies based on this clinical evidence. For rural areas, causes of death were estimated using CodMod as described later. Adjusted proportions of Group I, II, and III deaths by age and sex were first estimated, and then the same proportionate distribution of deaths by cause as observed for urban areas was applied, after adjustment, to estimate the detailed pattern of causes of death.

Islamic Republic of Iran. Data from the VR system in Iran were compiled for 18 of the country's 26 provinces for 2001. The data were coded to a condensed list of 150 cause categories using ICD-10. Because the registration system only covered part of the national population, a model-based prediction was used to estimate the broad cause proportionate mortality for the whole country. The results are shown in figure 3.4. The model predicted a higher proportion of Group I causes for both males and females in childhood and a higher proportion of Group I causes for females ages 15 to 44, reflecting higher maternal mortality among the nonregistered population than among the registered population. The predicted distributions for the broad cause groups were then applied to the specific-cause proportionate mortality from the reported data and adjusted to the national mortality envelope derived from the life table analysis.

Thailand. VR data were available for 2000 with an estimated coverage of about 80 percent (Lopez and others 2002). However, the proportion of ill-defined conditions was nearly 50 percent, because many deaths in Thailand occur at home and the cause of death is often reported by lay persons. To improve the usability of data from the VR system, the Ministry of Public Health conducted a retest survey on a

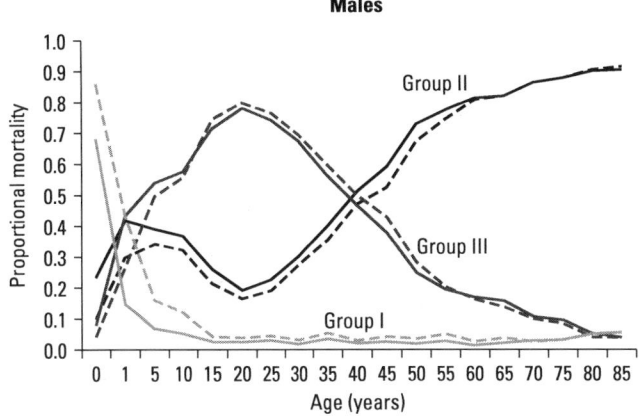

Males

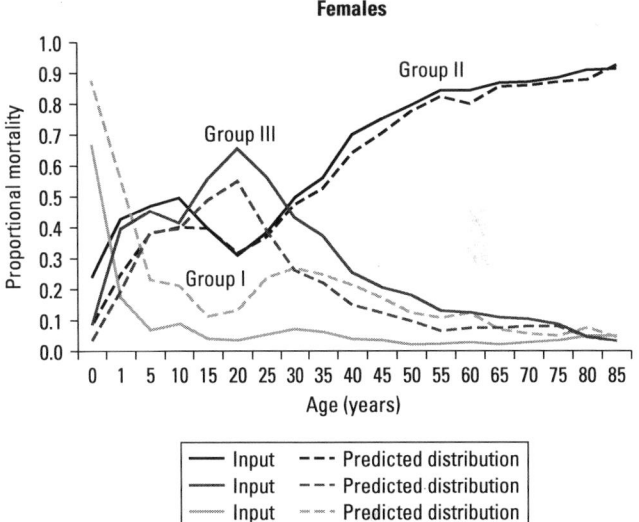

Females

	Input	---	Predicted distribution
	Input	---	Predicted distribution
	Input	---	Predicted distribution

Source: Authors' calculations.

Figure 3.4 CodMod Estimation of Major Cause Group Proportional Mortality for Islamic Republic of Iran, 2001

sample of about 33,000 deaths, using verbal autopsy methods, to ascertain the true cause of death (Ministry of Public Health 2002). This included a sample of 12,000 deaths with ill-defined causes. The study reallocated about 66 percent of deaths with ill-defined causes to specific causes, including reclassifying many deaths as caused by HIV/AIDS. The reallocation algorithm for ill-defined causes from the verbal autopsy study was used to correct the high proportion of ill-defined deaths from the VR data, and then the resultant cause-specific proportionate mortality was inflated to the national mortality envelope derived from the life table analysis.

Epidemiological Estimates of Mortality for Specific Causes

As outlined in table 3.2, specific epidemiological estimates for some causes were also taken into account in analyzing

Table 3.5 Numbers of Data Sets Contributing to Epidemiologically Based Estimates of Deaths Due to Specific Causes

Cause	East Asia and Pacific	Europe and Central Asia	Latin America and the Caribbean	Middle East and North Africa	South Asia	Sub-Saharan Africa	High-income countries	Total
Tuberculosis[a]	24	27	34	16	8	39	31	179
HIV/AIDS[a]	14	26	27	13	5	37	29	150
Diarrheal diseases		0	15	8	21	24	0	73
Childhood-cluster diseases								
Pertussis	14	33	64	14	8	45	124	302
Poliomyelitis	22	27	32	15	8	47	37	192
Diphtheria	12	25	2	14	8	46	8	115
Measles	22	18	32	12	8	47	22	127
Tetanus	48	23	27	40	32	79	34	289
Meningitis	23	18	30	12	4	27	43	157
Hepatitis B and C	40	27	47	43	18	67	113	355
Malaria	9	0	2	1	7	142	0	161
Tropical-cluster diseases								
Trypanosomiasis	0	0	0	0	0	36	0	36
Chagas' disease	0	0	31	0	0	0	0	31
Schistosomiasis	6	0	3	8	0	37	1	55
Lower respiratory infections	2	0	18	0	9	18	2	49
Maternal conditions (all causes)	6	0	9	5	4	20	1	45
Unsafe abortion	14	32	27	11	13	49	10	156
Perinatal causes	7	0	7	11	19	12	0	56
Malignant neoplasms	14	12	12	10	3	14	40	105
Drug use disorders	11	11	18	10	6	15	43	114
War	3	1	1	0	0	6	7	18
Total	296	280	438	243	181	807	545	2,765

Source: Authors' calculations.

Note: The data sources include population-based epidemiological studies, disease registers, and surveillance and notification systems. Where possible, regional and global totals refer to numbers of separate studies, or country-years of reported data from surveillance or notification systems. Refer to text for more information on data sources for specific causes.

a. Totals refer to numbers of countries for which data were available, not to total data sets or country-years.

causes of death for countries. Table 3.5 summarizes the numbers of studies (population-based epidemiological studies, disease registers, and notification systems) that contributed to the estimation of mortality due to 21 specific causes of death, including HIV/AIDS, malaria, and TB. As the table shows, more than 2,700 data sets contributed to the estimates for these 21 causes of death, with almost one-third of these relating to Sub-Saharan Africa.

Tuberculosis. In 1997, WHO began a study to develop country estimates of incidence, prevalence, and mortality from TB (for a detailed description of data sources and methods see Dye and others 1999). The study derived estimates of incidence from case notifications adjusted by estimated case detection rates, prevalence data on active disease combined with estimates of average case durations, or estimates of infection risk multiplied by a scalar factor relating the incidence of smear-positive pulmonary TB to annual risks of infection.

Since the original estimates for 1997 were completed, revised and updated estimates have been prepared. Most countries reporting to WHO have provided notification data with interpretable trends and with no other evidence for any significant change in the case detection rate. Trends in notification rates were assumed to represent trends in incidence rates for most countries except those with evidence of changes in case detection rates. China carried out a countrywide disease prevalence survey during 2000, and the results were used to reevaluate incidence for 1999. For other countries with evidence of changes in case detection rates, the trend for one of eight groups of epidemiologically similar countries was assumed to apply (Corbett and others 2003). Annual reports on TB control have included further details on surveillance methods, case notifications, and incidence estimates by country (WHO 2003a).

Deaths due to all forms of TB (excluding HIV-infected persons) were estimated for 2001. For countries with VR data, these estimates were based on the most recently available VR data. For other countries, estimates were based on the estimated TB incidence rates (excluding HIV-infected persons) multiplied by the estimated case fatality rates and weighted for the proportion of cases treated and the proportion smear-positive.

HIV/AIDS. The Joint United Nations Programme on HIVAIDS and WHO have developed country-specific estimates of HIV/AIDS mortality and revise them periodically to account for new data and improved methods (Schwartlander and others 1999; Walker and others 2003). For the most recent round of estimates, they used two different types of models depending on the nature of the epidemic in a particular country. For generalized epidemics, in which infection is spread primarily through heterosexual contact, they used a simple epidemiological model to estimate epidemic curves based on sentinel surveillance data on HIV seroprevalence (UNAIDS Reference Group on Estimates Model and Projections 2002). For countries with epidemics concentrated in high-risk groups, they used prevalence estimates derived from the estimated population size and prevalence surveillance data in each high-risk category, and then employed simple models to back-calculate incidence and mortality based on these estimated prevalence trends (Stover and others 2002).

For countries with death registration data, HIV/AIDS mortality estimates were generally based on the most recently available VR data except where miscoding of HIV/AIDS deaths was evident. In such cases, a time series analysis of causes was carried out to identify and reassign miscoded HIV/AIDS deaths. For other countries, estimates were based on the Joint United Nations Programme on HIV/AIDS and WHO estimates of HIV/AIDS mortality for 2001, or in some cases where these were not available, on the estimated prevalence of HIV/AIDS in 2001 multiplied by the average subregional mortality to prevalence ratio.

Diarrheal Diseases. For countries with usable death registration data, deaths due to diarrheal diseases were estimated directly from that data. For other countries, a regression model was used to estimate proportional mortality from diarrhea for children under five (Boschi-Pinto and others forthcoming). The regression model included the logit of the proportional mortality from diarrheal diseases in children from birth through four as a dependent variable and gross domestic product (GDP) per capita in international dollars, time, and region indicator variables as explanatory variables. The regression data were drawn from more than 60 community-based studies carried out

since 1980 with study durations of multiples of 12 months. This model was validated and supplemented with vital statistics from developing countries where coverage was high.

Vaccine-Preventable Childhood Diseases. Mortality for measles was estimated using two approaches. In countries where routine vaccine coverage was low (less than 80 percent), incidence data were derived from a natural history model using country-specific vaccine coverage and attack rates from population-based studies (Crowcroft and others 2003). For countries with higher routine coverage and in the elimination phase, case notification and country-specific correction factors were used to estimate incidence. To obtain mortality in countries where VR data were not available, age- and region-specific case fatality rates from community-based and outbreak studies were applied to incidence estimates derived from both approaches.

Pertussis cases and deaths were based on a natural history model using vaccine coverage and age-specific case fatality rates from community based studies, where available (Crowcroft and others 2003). The model is a revision of Galezka and Robertson's (2004) approach.

The incidence estimates for polio and diphtheria (Stein 2002b; Stein and Robertson 2002) were based on country-specific reported cases of acute flaccid paralysis with adjustments for underreporting and on country-specific notifications of diphtheria cases with an assumed notification efficiency of 20 percent, respectively. A case fatality rate of 10 percent was assumed for diphtheria in countries without high death registration coverage.

Acute Respiratory Infections. Community-based studies with durations of one year or longer, published since 1980, were used to estimate the proportional mortality from acute respiratory infections in children under five in developing countries (Williams and others 2002). The results confirmed earlier findings that the proportion of deaths attributable to acute respiratory infections diminishes as general mortality diminishes. Much of the variability across studies in the proportion of child deaths attributed to acute respiratory infections was due to the use of verbal autopsies to determine the cause of death. Data from seven studies that compared verbal autopsies with hospital-based diagnoses indicated that the percentage of deaths due to acute respiratory infections could be underestimated by up to 4 percent. The modeled estimates were supplemented with vital statistics from developing countries where coverage was high to develop regional and global estimates.

Malaria. Malaria mortality estimates for all regions except Sub-Saharan Africa were derived from the cause of death data sources described earlier. For Sub-Saharan Africa, country-specific estimates of malaria mortality were based on analyses by Snow and others (1999) and updated using the most recent geographical distributions of risks from the Mapping Malaria Risks in Africa International Collaboration. Subsequent adjustments were made to the estimated country-specific malaria deaths to ensure that total mortality for Group I causes, particularly in the 0–4 year age group, and including estimates for other specific causes such as TB, HIV/AIDS, and measles, added to the total all-cause mortality envelopes for the relevant countries. Work is currently under way to refine and revise these country-specific estimates of malaria mortality in collaboration with other WHO programs and external expert groups (Korenromp and others 2003; Rowe and others 2004).

Chagas' Disease. Chagas' disease estimates were obtained from recent intensive surveillance activities in the Southern Cone American countries and community-based studies (Moncayo 2003; Moncayo, Guhl, and Stein 2002). These estimates were supplemented with and validated against vital statistics from Latin American countries where coverage was high.

Maternal Mortality. Mortality from maternal conditions was estimated following a similar approach to earlier analyses (Abdallah and Zehani 2000; Hill, AbouZahr, and Wardlaw 2001), using the most recently available mortality data for developing countries, together with improved estimates of the impact of HIV/AIDS as a competing cause of mortality (WHO, UNICEF, and UNFPA 2003). Depending on the availability and quality of data on detailed causes of maternal deaths, the methods used to estimate the proportion of deaths of women of reproductive age that is due to maternal causes (PMDF) varied and included vital records, DHSs and other surveys, Reproductive Age Mortality Study surveys, and epidemiological models. For countries without death registration data, both nationally reported data and specific criteria for a regression model were used to estimate maternal mortality. The dependent variable in this model was the logit of the PMDF after subtracting HIV/AIDS deaths and the explanatory variables were the proportion of deliveries with skilled birth attendance, the GDP per capita in international dollars, and the general fertility rate plus region dummy variables. The total number of deaths from maternal causes for each country was estimated by multi-plying the PMDF by the overall mortality envelope for women aged 15 to 49 after subtracting HIV/AIDS deaths.

Abortion-related mortality occurs mainly as a result of unsafe induced abortion. It has been estimated using published and unpublished reports for 131 countries together with other information on legal and social contexts and summed to give regional totals (WHO 2004a).

Perinatal Causes. The cause category "perinatal causes" refers to the ICD cause group "conditions arising in the perinatal period" (ICD chapter 16, P-codes). Deaths from these causes, primarily low birthweight, prematurity, and birth trauma or asphyxia, may occur at any age, and can include some maternal or placental causes, such as multiple pregnancy. Deaths from these causes should not be confused with deaths that occur during the perinatal period, which include stillbirths and neonatal deaths from other causes such as tetanus and congenital malformations. However, acknowledging that nearly all deaths due to perinatal causes occur during the neonatal period, we first estimated the envelope of neonatal mortality for every country (for details of the method see Murray and Lopez 1998). The analysis has been updated using recent death registration data and DHS data. Work is currently under way in collaboration with other WHO programs and external expert groups to refine and revise these country-specific estimates of mortality due to perinatal causes (Lawn, Cousens, and Zupan 2005).

Cancer. For countries without good VR data to estimate the site-specific distribution of cancer mortality, a site-specific model for relative interval survival was developed and applied to cancer incidence estimates by site (Mathers, Shibuya, and others 2002; Shibuya and others 2002). This age-period-cohort model of cancer survival was based on data from the Surveillance, Epidemiology, and End Results program of the National Cancer Institute (Ries and others 2002). The model was further adjusted by site for each country based on observed correlations in regional and country survival probabilities and level of economic development (GDP per capita in international dollars) (Mathers, Shibuya, and others 2002). Combined with available incidence data from the International Agency for Research on Cancer (Ferlay and others 2001), cancer death distributions were estimated and the model estimates were validated against available VR data from countries other than the United States.

Drug Use Disorders. This category includes dependence on and nondependent problem use of both licit and illicit drugs, excluding tobacco and alcohol (see table 3A.2). Estimating mortality directly attributable to drug use disorders, such as death from overdose, is difficult because of variations in the quality and quantity of mortality data. For some regions with a substantial prevalence of illicit drug use, available data sources do not record any deaths as due to drug dependence. As a result, it is necessary to make indirect estimates based on estimates of the prevalence of illicit drug use and of case fatality rates, on the assumption that almost all mortality directly attributable to drug use disorders is associated with illicit drugs. However, making even indirect estimates is difficult because the use of these drugs is illegal, stigmatized, and hidden.

The comparative risk assessment work carried out for the *World Health Report 2002* (WHO 2002d) included estimating the prevalence of illicit drug dependence and direct mortality based on available data (Degenhardt and others 2003; Ezzati and others 2002). Data on the prevalence of problematic illicit drug use were derived from a range of sources, including a formal literature search of all studies that estimated the prevalence of problematic drug use, the United Nations Drug Control Program, and the European Monitoring Centre for Drugs and Drug Addiction (2002).

A search was also conducted for cohort studies of drug users that had estimated mortality due to individual causes of death (overdose, suicide, and trauma) and to all causes of death (updating previous systematic reviews). Data on the number of years of follow up were extracted from each study and a weighted average annual mortality rate was calculated for each cause of death and for their sum.

The total regional deaths due directly to illicit drug use were then distributed among countries in each region in proportion to estimated prevalences of drug dependence and problem use. For developed countries with good VR data, evidence suggests that deaths due to drug use disorders are underrecorded (European Monitoring Centre for Drugs and Drug Addiction 2002; Single and others 2002). For these countries, mortality figures were adjusted for age groups in which the estimated deaths derived from the comparative risk assessment analysis exceeded the number of deaths recorded on the assumption that these additional deaths were originally miscoded as due to accidental poisoning or ill-defined causes.

War Deaths. Country-specific estimates of war deaths and corresponding uncertainty ranges were obtained from a variety of published and unpublished databases. The *Armed Conflict Report* (Project Ploughshares 2001, 2002), a report

that supplies several databases with mortality estimates (see, for example, Center for Research on the Epidemiology of Disasters 2001), was the primary source used for time trend and mortality estimates. This report was a preferred source of information, because it includes war deaths by country and year, a departure from the typical practice of supplying estimates by conflict and across years. The report's data were checked against historical and current estimates by other research groups, such as those of the Uppsala Conflict Data Project (Gleditsch and others 2002) and the Center for International Development and Conflict Management at the University of Maryland (Marshall and Gurr 2003).

These data sets rely on press reports of eyewitness accounts and official announcements of combatants, which are, unfortunately, the main and often only possible method of estimating casualties in armed conflicts. Murray, King, and others (2002) summarize the issues involved in estimating war deaths and emphasize the considerable uncertainty in the GBD 2000 and GBD 2001 estimates. Many of the available data sources on conflict deaths only count deaths in conflicts that involve the armed forces of at least one state or one or more armed factions seeking to gain control of all or part of the state, and in which more than a certain number of people have been killed, for instance, more than 1,000 total or more than 25 per year. Some sources count only battlefield deaths and deaths that occur concurrently with conflict.

In contrast, the GBD 2001 estimated deaths occurring in 2001 in which the underlying cause (following ICD conventions) was an injury due to operations of war or civil insurrection, whether or not that injury occurred during the time of war or following the cessation of hostilities, which in some cases occurred many years earlier than 2001. The GBD 2001 estimates included injury deaths resulting from all civil insurrection, whether or not the state was involved. They also included deaths due to terrorism carried out by organized groups. The GBD 2001 estimates of war deaths did not include deaths from other causes, such as starvation, infectious disease epidemics, or lack of medical intervention for chronic diseases, that may be counterfactually attributable to war or civil conflict.

Deaths due to landmines and unexploded ordnance were estimated separately by country. The primary sources for these data were the *Landmine Monitor Report* of the International Campaign to Ban Landmines (Human Rights Watch 2001) and Handicap International's annual report on landmine victims (Handicap International 2001).

Whereas total injury deaths for most countries were derived either from death registration data or from cause of death models, war deaths were treated as "outside the enve-lope," and for countries for which life tables were estimated from data for earlier years not affected by war, war deaths were added to the total deaths estimated from the life tables.

Cause of Death Modeling for Countries with Poor Data

Although epidemiological studies and other data sources described in the previous section allow the estimation of deaths due to certain causes in populations without death registration data, they do not cover many important causes of death in these populations, such as CVD or injuries. To address these information gaps, models for estimating broad cause of death patterns can serve as the starting point for indirect methods of estimating attributable mortality for a comprehensive list of causes.

Preston (1976) was the first to develop indirect methods for estimating cause of death structure. Preston modeled the relationship between total mortality and cause-specific mortality for 12 broad groups of causes using historical VR data for the industrial countries and a few developing countries. In particular, Preston postulated that cause-specific mortality was a linear function of total mortality. The GBD 1990 study (Murray and Lopez 1996a) used cause of death models to estimate mortality for the three major cause groups (Groups I, II, III) as a function of mortality from all causes, based on regression analysis of observations on recent mortality patterns from 67 countries. The log of cause-specific mortality was postulated to be a linear function of the log of total mortality, and poorly coded deaths were redistributed before estimating the regression equations.

The cause of death model used in the GBD 1990 has been substantially revised and enhanced for estimating deaths by broad cause group in regions with limited information on mortality. The statistical model has been improved by adapting models for compositional data that were previously developed in other areas, and a substantially larger data set of 1,613 country-years of observations was used for analysis. Income per capita has been added to the model as an explanatory variable in addition to the level of all-cause mortality (Salomon and Murray 2002a).

This section provides an overview of the new model, CodMod, developed by Salomon and Murray for the GBD 2001, and describes its application for estimating (a) broad cause patterns for populations where no cause of death information is available, and (b) broad cause of death patterns when incomplete death registration data are available. The estimation of broad cause of death patterns is critical to avoid overemphasizing or underemphasizing specific causes

due to biases in the data sets available to estimate national mortality patterns, for example, if data are derived from urban hospital statistics.

Statistical Methods and Data. The statistical basis for cause of death models has also been enhanced by the adaptation of models for compositional data that were previously developed in other areas (Katz and King 1999). These models take account of the key features of this type of data, namely, that the fraction of deaths attributable to each cause is bounded by 0 and 1 and that all the fractions must sum to unity. Violations of both constraints were possible with the regression models used in the GBD 1990; an additional normalization step was undertaken to impose these constraints. The new model explicitly ensures both these constraints using a seemingly unrelated regression model (for a full description of this model and its application to analysis of the epidemiological transition, see Salomon and Murray 2002a).

In addition to revising the statistical model used in the previous study, Salomon and Murray also considered additional covariates beyond all-cause mortality. The objective was to identify variables likely to have a strong relationship to cause-specific mortality, but also variables for which estimates would be available in all countries, because one of the goals of the exercise was to use the model to predict broad patterns of mortality for countries without VR data. The variables that were selected based on these criteria were all-cause mortality, as before, plus income per capita in international dollars. Both variables were included in logged form, because this formulation tended to provide a better fit than the linear form.

Perhaps most important, the new cause of death model incorporated a more extensive database on mortality by age, sex, and cause than previous efforts, with substantially more representation of middle-income countries. Increasing the range of observed cause of death patterns should improve the validity of extrapolations from countries with registration systems to data-poor settings.

Separate models were estimated for each sex and the following age groups: younger than 1 month, 1–11 months, 1–4 years, 5–9 years, 10–14 years, and so on by five-year age groups up to 80–84 years and 85 years and older. For the two youngest age groups, a smaller number of observations were available because some countries for some periods reported only on the age range from birth to 11 months. A total of 586 country-years of observations were available for the first two age groups and 1,613 country-years of observations for each of the other 18 age groups. The regression results provided insights into the relationships between cause of death patterns, all-cause mortality levels, and increases in income per capita (Salomon and Murray 2002a).

Salomon and Murray also used Monte Carlo simulation techniques to estimate the probability distributions of the predicted cause of death components given a particular set of values for all-cause mortality and GDP per capita (Salomon and Murray 2001a). The results from this approach were useful in estimating cause of death patterns for residual areas in countries where VR covers only part of the population and in defining regional cause of death patterns.

Application of CodMod for Countries without Good Registration Data. As with the GBD 1990, one of the useful applications of cause of death models is to examine patterns of deviation from the expected cause composition across countries or regions based on the probability distribution for a predicted cause of death pattern. In other words, the models permit comparison of the observed pattern with the pattern that would be predicted conditional on the levels of all-cause mortality and income per capita associated with that observation.

Given some assumptions about the stability of this pattern of deviation over short time intervals within a country or across countries in the same mortality stratum, it is possible to use the observed cause of death pattern in a reference population to estimate the cause of death pattern for some other population while taking into account differences in the explanatory variables. Some examples of applications would be

- estimating the cause of death pattern in nonregistration areas for a country in which part of the population is covered by a VR system,
- forecasting the cause of death pattern for a country where the most recent VR data are for several years in the past, and
- estimating the cause of death pattern for a country for which information is not available but is available for other countries in the same region.

All these applications are based on the assumption that patterns of deviation from the cause compositions predicted by the model will have some stability across time and place, for example, if young adults in Canada tend to have a low proportion of Group I deaths and a high proportion of Group II deaths in one year given the levels of all-cause mortality and income in that year, a reasonable assumption would be that the next year's composition will be similarly low in Group I and high in Group II given that year's total income and mortality. This hypothesis builds on the notion that all-cause mortality and income per capita explain only some of the variation in cause of death patterns, while the other sources of this variation are unmeasured but are assumed to be relatively stable. In other words, the cause of death pattern in Canada differs from what we would predict based only on total mortality and income because other factors influence the pattern. We assume that these other factors will change gradually over time, which would imply that the deviation from the prediction should also move gradually.

Using similar arguments, Salomon and Murray (2001a) suggested that it may be possible to use patterns of deviation from one country to predict cause of death patterns in another country in the same demographic region. They demonstrated an example of this for mortality data from Chile and Mexico for women aged 35 to 39 for 1965–94. They estimated the percentiles at which the observed cause fractions for the two countries fell in the probability distribution of predicted fractions produced by the Monte Carlo simulations conditional on the mortality and income levels in those years for each country and found similarities in the deviation patterns. Overall, this example suggested that deviation patterns in groups of similar countries may be similar, allowing predictions of cause of death patterns in countries where registration data are not available but for which neighboring countries do have data.

The application of this method has been formalized in a simple spreadsheet program called CodMod (Salomon and Murray 2001a). The program incorporates the regression models described earlier and uses Monte Carlo simulation methods to generate probability distributions around predicted cause of death patterns conditional on values for all-cause mortality and income per capita. CodMod allows two main operations: (a) analysis of deviations in observed cause of death patterns given levels of mortality and income, and (b) predictions of cause of death patterns conditional on a reference pattern of deviation and levels of mortality and income.

Thus, for example, if the VR system covers only one region in a country, CodMod may be used to examine the pattern of deviation in that region from the predicted cause of death pattern at local income and total mortality levels. We assume that a similar pattern of deviation will hold in the nonregistration areas of the country, then we can use information on total mortality levels and income in the nonregistration areas to predict cause of death patterns in these areas. The GBD 2001 used CodMod for countries with incomplete death registration data to adjust for biases in cause composition. Annex table 3A.3 lists countries for which such adjustments were carried out.

CodMod was also used to develop regional patterns of deviation from predicted cause compositions, which were then used to estimate mortality by broad causes for countries for which no registration data were available. Annex table 3A.3 summarizes details of these regional models. In the case of the Sub-Saharan Africa region, where good VR data were available for only three countries, a regional pattern of specific causes of deaths was based on VR data from urban and rural South Africa. For the Middle East and North Africa, a similar pattern was built for the Gulf states based on the four latest years of data from Bahrain and Kuwait. For other countries in that region, regional models were based on weighted death rates using Egyptian and Iranian VR data. The weights used were determined by the income levels of the individual countries and overall death rates. For the Pacific islands, a regional pattern was based on data available from islands reporting death registration data.

Whereas the original GBD study used a more detailed cause of death model for 12 causes of death to estimate deaths below the broad group level for countries without death registration data, the increased availability of death registration data in most regions has enabled us to use detailed proportional cause distributions within Groups I, II, and III based on death registration data from within each region (see annex table 3A.3 for more details). Specific causes were further adjusted on the basis of epidemiological evidence from registries, verbal autopsy studies, disease surveillance systems, and analyses from WHO technical programs as described earlier.

This section provides an overview of global and regional causes of death in 2001. Note that as described earlier, the results reported here are tabulated by underlying disease cause or external cause of injury. Total attributable deaths for some diseases that increase the risk of other diseases or injuries will be substantially larger than the estimates of direct deaths given here. Chapter 4 estimates deaths attributable to 26 global risk factors. The tables in annex 3B provide detailed tabulations of deaths by cause and sex for regions, for low- and middle-income countries, for high-income countries, and for the world.

Distribution of Deaths by Major Cause Group

Worldwide, one death in every three is from a Group I cause. This proportion remains almost unchanged from 1990 with one big difference: whereas HIV/AIDS accounted for only 2 percent of Group I deaths in 1990, it accounted for 44 percent of Group I deaths in 2001. Excluding HIV/AIDS, Group I deaths fell from 33 percent of total deaths in 1990 to less than 20 percent in 2001. Virtually all the Group I deaths are in low- and middle-income countries. Just under 10 percent are from Group III causes (injuries) and almost 60 percent of deaths are from Group II causes (noncommunicable diseases). Figure 3.5 shows the proportional distribution of these major cause groups for low- and middle-income countries and high-income countries.

Group I causes remain the leading cause of child deaths in all regions, although they are now responsible for fewer child deaths than Group II and Group III combined in high-income countries (figure 3.6). In contrast, Group II causes are now responsible for more than 50 percent of deaths in adults ages 15 to 59 in all regions except South Asia and

GLOBAL AND REGIONAL MORTALITY IN 2001

Slightly more than 56 million people died in 2001, 10.5 million, or nearly 20 percent, of whom were children younger than five. Of these child deaths, 99 percent occurred in low- and middle-income countries. Those age 70 and over accounted for 70 percent of deaths in high-income countries, compared with 30 percent in other countries. Thus, a key point is the comparatively large number of deaths among the young and the middle-aged in low- and middle-income countries. In these countries, 30 percent of all deaths occur at ages 15 to 59, compared with 15 percent in high-income countries. The causes of death at these ages, as well as in childhood, are thus important in assessing public health priorities.

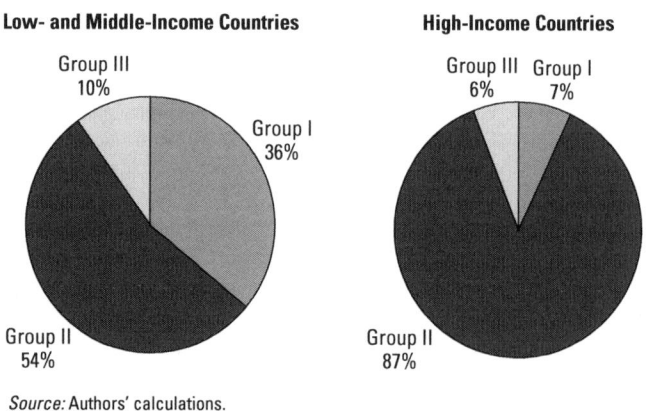

Source: Authors' calculations.

Figure 3.5 Proportional Distribution of Total Deaths by Broad Cause Group, 2001

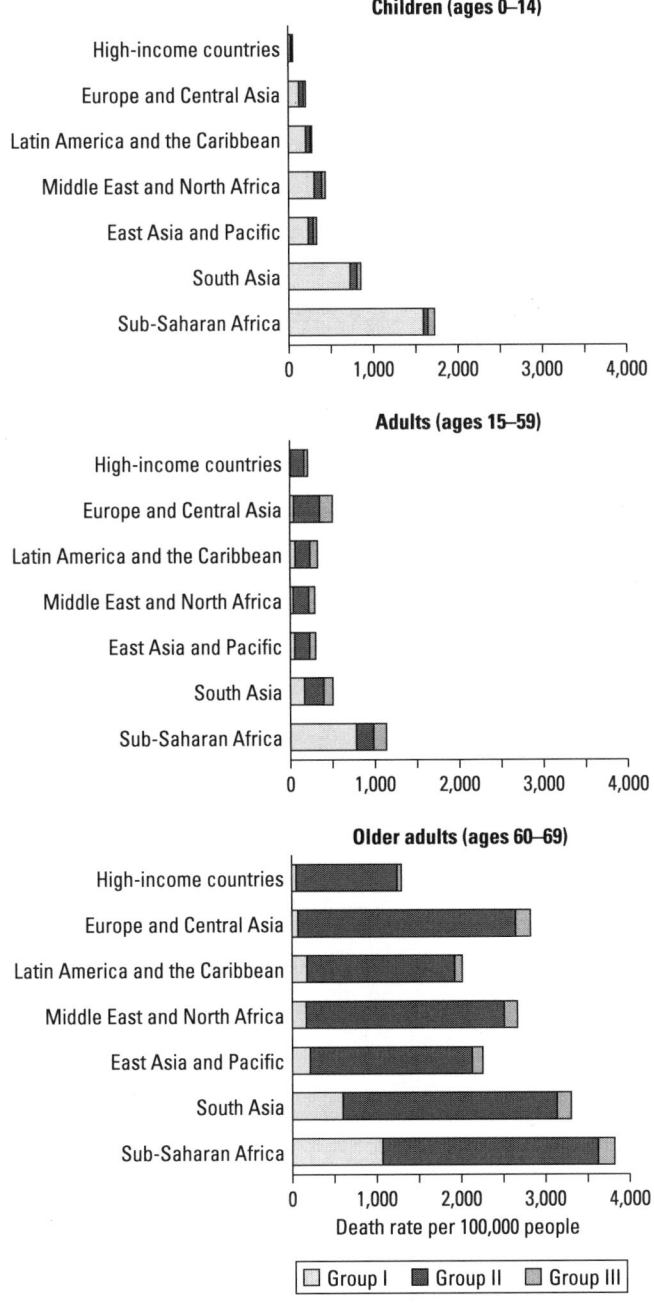

Children (ages 0–14)

(horizontal bar chart, Death rate per 100,000 people, axis 0 to 4,000)

- High-income countries
- Europe and Central Asia
- Latin America and the Caribbean
- Middle East and North Africa
- East Asia and Pacific
- South Asia
- Sub-Saharan Africa

Adults (ages 15–59)

(horizontal bar chart, axis 0 to 4,000)

- High-income countries
- Europe and Central Asia
- Latin America and the Caribbean
- Middle East and North Africa
- East Asia and Pacific
- South Asia
- Sub-Saharan Africa

Older adults (ages 60–69)

(horizontal bar chart, axis 0 to 4,000)

- High-income countries
- Europe and Central Asia
- Latin America and the Caribbean
- Middle East and North Africa
- East Asia and Pacific
- South Asia
- Sub-Saharan Africa

Death rate per 100,000 people

☐ Group I ■ Group II ☐ Group III

Source: Authors' calculations.

Figure 3.6 Death Rates by Broad Cause Group, Region, and Broad Age Group, 2001

Sub-Saharan Africa, where Group I causes, including HIV/AIDS, remain responsible for 33 and 67 percent of deaths, respectively. For adults ages 15 to 59, death rates from Group II causes are higher for all low- and middle-income regions than for high-income countries, and in Europe and Central Asia are almost double the rate for the high-income countries. These results show that premature mortality from noncommunicable diseases is higher in pop-ulations with high mortality and low incomes than in the high-income countries.

Leading Causes of Death

Table 3.6 shows the top 10 disease and injury causes of death in 2001 for low- and middle-income countries and for high-income countries. IHD and cerebrovascular disease (stroke) were the leading causes of death in both groups of countries in 2001, responsible for 12 million deaths globally, or almost one-quarter of the global total. Only 1.4 million of the 7.1 million who died of IHD were in the high-income coun-tries. Stroke killed 5.4 million, of whom less than 1.0 million were in high-income countries.

Whereas lung cancer, predominantly due to tobacco smoking, remains the third leading cause of death in high-income countries, reflecting high levels of smoking in previ-ous years, the increasing prevalence of smoking in low- and middle-income countries has not yet driven lung cancer into the top 10 causes of death for these countries. HIV/AIDS is the fourth leading cause of death in low- and middle-income countries, and HIV/AIDS death rates are projected to contin-ue to rise, albeit at a slower pace, despite recent increased efforts to improve access to antiretroviral drugs.

Lower respiratory infections, conditions arising during the perinatal period, and diarrheal diseases remain among the top 10 causes of death in low- and middle-income coun-tries. In 2001, these three causes of death together account-ed for nearly 60 percent of child deaths globally.

Table 3.7 shows the 10 leading causes of death in low- and middle-income countries by sex in 2001. Leading causes of death are generally similar for males and females, although road traffic accidents appear in the top 10 only for males and diabetes appears only for females.

Leading Causes of Death in Children. Infectious and par-asitic diseases remain the major killers of children in the developing world. Although notable success has been achieved in certain areas, for example, polio, communicable diseases still account for 7 out of the top 10 causes and are responsible for about 60 percent of all child deaths. Overall, the 10 leading causes in low- and middle-income countries represent 80 percent of all child deaths in those countries, and also worldwide (table 3.8).

Many Latin American and some Asian and Middle Eastern countries have shifted somewhat toward the cause of death pattern observed in developed countries. In these countries, conditions arising during the perinatal period, including birth asphyxia, birth trauma, and low birthweight,

Table 3.6 The 10 Leading Causes of Death, by Broad Income Group, 2001

	Low- and middle-income countries				High-income countries		
	Cause	Deaths (millions)	Percentage of total deaths		Cause	Deaths (millions)	Percentage of total deaths
1	Ischemic heart disease	5.70	11.8	1	Ischemic heart disease	1.36	17.3
2	Cerebrovascular disease	4.61	9.5	2	Cerebrovascular disease	0.78	9.9
3	Lower respiratory infections	3.41	7.0	3	Trachea, bronchus, and lung cancers	0.46	5.8
4	HIV/AIDS	2.55	5.3	4	Lower respiratory infections	0.34	4.4
5	Perinatal conditions	2.49	5.1	5	Chronic obstructive pulmonary disease	0.30	3.8
6	Chronic obstructive pulmonary disease	2.38	4.9	6	Colon and rectal cancers	0.26	3.3
7	Diarrheal diseases	1.78	3.7	7	Alzheimer's and other dementias	0.21	2.6
8	Tuberculosis	1.59	3.3	8	Diabetes mellitus	0.20	2.6
9	Malaria	1.21	2.5	9	Breast cancer	0.16	2.0
10	Road traffic accidents	1.07	2.2	10	Stomach cancer	0.15	1.9

Source: Authors' calculations.

Table 3.7 The 10 Leading Causes of Death, by Sex, in Low- and Middle-Income Countries, 2001

	Males				Females		
	Cause	Deaths (millions)	Percentage of total deaths		Cause	Deaths (millions)	Percentage of total deaths
1	Ischemic heart disease	3.01	11.8	1	Ischemic heart disease	2.69	11.8
2	Cerebrovascular disease	2.17	8.5	2	Cerebrovascular disease	2.44	10.7
3	Lower respiratory infections	1.72	6.7	3	Lower respiratory infections	1.68	7.4
4	Perinatal conditions	1.38	5.4	4	HIV/AIDS	1.18	5.2
5	HIV/AIDS	1.38	5.4	5	Chronic obstructive pulmonary disease	1.17	5.1
6	Chronic obstructive pulmonary disease	1.21	4.7	6	Perinatal conditions	1.11	4.9
7	Tuberculosis	1.04	4.1	7	Diarrheal diseases	0.85	3.7
8	Diarrheal diseases	0.93	3.6	8	Malaria	0.63	2.8
9	Road traffic accidents	0.78	3.1	9	Tuberculosis	0.55	2.4
10	Malaria	0.58	2.3	10	Diabetes mellitus	0.42	1.8

Source: Authors' calculations.

Table 3.8 The 10 Leading Causes of Death in Children Ages 0–14, by Broad Income Group, 2001

	Low- and middle-income countries				High-income countries		
	Cause	Deaths (millions)	Percentage of total deaths		Cause	Deaths (millions)	Percentage of total deaths
1	Perinatal conditions	2.49	20.7	1	Perinatal conditions	0.03	33.9
2	Lower respiratory infections	2.04	17.0	2	Congenital anomalies	0.02	20.0
3	Diarrheal diseases	1.61	13.4	3	Road traffic accidents	0.01	5.9
4	Malaria	1.10	9.2	4	Lower respiratory infections	0.00	2.5
5	Measles	0.74	6.2	5	Endocrine disorders	0.00	2.4
6	HIV/AIDS	0.44	3.7	6	Drownings	0.00	2.4
7	Congenital anomalies	0.44	3.7	7	Leukemia	0.00	1.9
8	Whooping cough	0.30	2.5	8	Violence	0.00	1.8
9	Tetanus	0.22	1.9	9	Fires	0.00	1.2
10	Road traffic accidents	0.18	1.5	10	Meningitis	0.00	1.2

Source: Authors' calculations.

have replaced infectious diseases as the leading cause of death and are now responsible for 21 to 34 percent of deaths. Such a shift in the cause of death pattern has not occurred in Sub-Saharan Africa, where perinatal conditions rank in fourth place and malaria, lower respiratory infections, and diarrheal diseases continue to be the leading causes of death in children, accounting for 53 percent of all deaths.

About 90 percent of all HIV/AIDS and malaria deaths in children in developing countries occur in Sub-Saharan Africa, which accounts for 23 percent of the world's births and 42 percent of the world's child deaths. The immense surge of HIV/AIDS mortality in children in recent years means that HIV/AIDS is now responsible for 332,000 child deaths annually in Sub-Saharan Africa and nearly 8 percent of all child deaths in the region.

Some progress has been made against diarrheal diseases and measles in low- and middle-income countries. While the incidence of diarrheal diseases is thought to have remained stable, mortality from diarrheal diseases has fallen from 2.5 million deaths in 1990 to about 1.6 million deaths in 2001, and now accounts for 13 percent of all deaths of children under age 15. Deaths from measles have declined modestly, although more than half a million children under five still died from this disease in 2001. Malaria causes more than a million child deaths per year or nearly 11 percent of all deaths of children under five.

Leading Causes of Death in Adults

Table 3.9 shows the leading causes of deaths among adults ages 15 to 59 worldwide in 2001. Despite a global trend of declining communicable disease burden in adults, HIV/AIDS has become the leading cause of mortality and the single most important contributor to the burden of disease among adults in this age group.

Nearly 80 percent of the 2.1 million adult deaths from HIV/AIDS in 2001 occurred in Sub-Saharan Africa. In this region, HIV/AIDS is the leading cause of death, resulting in more than 6,000 deaths every day and accounting for almost one in five deaths for all ages and one in two deaths of adults ages 15 to 59. HIV/AIDS has reversed mortality trends among adults in the region, and in many countries, life expectancies have declined since 1990.

The 4.5 million adult injury deaths in 2001 were heavily concentrated among young adults, particularly men. In the 15 to 59 age group, road traffic accidents and suicide were among the 10 leading causes of death in high-income and low- and middle-income countries, and violence (homicide) was also among the 10 leading causes in low- and middle-income countries. Among adults ages 15 to 44 worldwide, road traffic accidents were the leading cause of death for men after HIV/AIDS, followed by TB and violence. Suicide was the third leading cause of death for women in this age group, after HIV/AIDS and TB, with road traffic accidents in fifth place.

The risk of death rises rapidly with age among adults age 60 and over in all regions. Globally, 60-year-olds have a 55 percent chance of dying before their 70th birthday. Regional variations in the risk of death are smaller at older ages than at younger ages, ranging from around 40 percent in the developed countries of Western Europe to 60 percent in most developing regions and 70 percent in Sub-Saharan Africa. Historical data from countries such as Australia and Sweden show that life expectancy at age 60 changed slowly during the first six to seven decades of the 20th century, but started to increase substantially since around 1970. Life

Table 3.9 The 10 Leading Causes of Death in Adults Ages 15–59, by Broad Income Group, 2001

Low- and middle-income countries			High-income countries		
Cause	Deaths (millions)	Percentage of total deaths	Cause	Deaths (millions)	Percentage of total deaths
1 HIV/AIDS	2.05	14.1	1 Ischemic heart disease	0.13	10.8
2 Ischemic heart disease	1.18	8.1	2 Self-inflicted injuries	0.09	7.2
3 Tuberculosis	1.03	7.1	3 Road traffic accidents	0.08	6.9
4 Road traffic accidents	0.73	5.0	4 Trachea, bronchus, and lung cancers	0.08	6.8
5 Cerebrovascular disease	0.71	4.9	5 Cerebrovascular disease	0.05	4.4
6 Self-inflicted injuries	0.58	4.0	6 Cirrhosis of the liver	0.05	4.4
7 Violence	0.45	3.1	7 Breast cancer	0.05	4.0
8 Lower respiratory infections	0.33	2.3	8 Colon and rectal cancers	0.04	3.1
9 Cirrhosis of the liver	0.32	2.2	9 Diabetes mellitus	0.03	2.1
10 Chronic obstructive pulmonary disease	0.32	2.2	10 Stomach cancer	0.02	2.0

Source: Authors' calculations.

Table 3.10 The 10 Leading Causes of Death in Low- and Middle-Income Countries, by Region, 2001

East Asia and Pacific	Percentage of total deaths	Europe and Central Asia	Percentage of total deaths
1 Cerebrovascular disease	14.6	1 Ischemic heart disease	29.7
2 Chronic obstructive pulmonary disease	10.8	2 Cerebrovascular disease	18.2
3 Ischemic heart disease	8.8	3 Trachea, bronchus, and lung cancers	2.9
4 Lower respiratory infections	4.2	4 Chronic obstructive pulmonary disease	2.3
5 Tuberculosis	4.1	5 Self-inflicted injuries	2.1
6 Perinatal conditions	3.8	6 Hypertensive heart disease	1.9
7 Stomach cancer	3.4	7 Poisonings	1.9
8 Trachea, bronchus, and lung cancers	3.0	8 Lower respiratory infections	1.8
9 Liver cancer	2.9	9 Cirrhosis of the liver	1.8
10 Road traffic accidents	2.8	10 Stomach cancer	1.8

Latin America and the Caribbean	Percentage of total deaths	Middle East and North Africa	Percentage of total deaths
1 Ischemic heart disease	10.9	1 Ischemic heart disease	16.9
2 Cerebrovascular disease	8.2	2 Cerebrovascular disease	6.8
3 Perinatal conditions	5.0	3 Lower respiratory infections	5.6
4 Diabetes mellitus	5.0	4 Perinatal conditions	5.5
5 Lower respiratory infections	4.8	5 Road traffic accidents	5.1
6 Violence	4.0	6 Hypertensive heart disease	3.9
7 Chronic obstructive pulmonary disease	3.0	7 Diarrheal diseases	3.9
8 Road traffic accidents	2.7	8 Congenital anomalies	2.4
9 Hypertensive heart disease	2.7	9 Nephritis and nephrosis	2.2
10 HIV/AIDS	2.5	10 Chronic obstructive pulmonary disease	2.1

South Asia	Percentage of total deaths	Sub-Saharan Africa	Percentage of total deaths
1 Ischemic heart disease	13.6	1 HIV/AIDS	19.0
2 Lower respiratory infections	10.4	2 Malaria	10.1
3 Perinatal conditions	8.0	3 Lower respiratory infections	10.0
4 Cerebrovascular disease	6.8	4 Diarrheal diseases	6.6
5 Diarrheal diseases	5.1	5 Perinatal conditions	5.3
6 Tuberculosis	4.5	6 Measles	4.1
7 Chronic obstructive pulmonary disease	4.3	7 Cerebrovascular disease	3.3
8 HIV/AIDS	2.0	8 Ischemic heart disease	3.2
9 Road traffic accidents	1.8	9 Tuberculosis	2.9
10 Self-inflicted injuries	1.7	10 Road traffic accidents	1.8

Source: Authors' calculations.

expectancy at age 60 has now reached 25 years in Japan. In Eastern Europe from 1990 onward, Hungary and Poland started to experience similar improvements in mortality for older people, but Russia has not, and is actually experiencing a worsening trend.

Regional Variations in Causes of Death

The tables in annex 3B show total deaths by age, sex, and cause for each of the regions and the world. The 10 leading causes of mortality differ greatly among low-income and middle-income countries (table 3.10) and between them and high-income countries (table 3.6). IHD and cerebrovascular disease are among the top four causes of death in all

low- and middle-income regions except Sub-Saharan Africa, where they are eighth and seventh, respectively. Cerebrovascular disease is the leading cause of death in East Asia and the Pacific, unlike in most other regions, where IHD causes more deaths than cerebrovascular disease. In Sub-Saharan Africa, 6 of the top 10 causes are communicable diseases, with HIV/AIDS being the leading cause of death, followed by malaria and lower respiratory infections.

South Asia (mainly India) and Latin America and the Caribbean are the only two other low- and middle-income regions where HIV/AIDS is one of the top 10 causes of death. Lower respiratory infections, primarily pneumonia, are the third leading cause of death, especially among children under five, who account for 60 percent of these

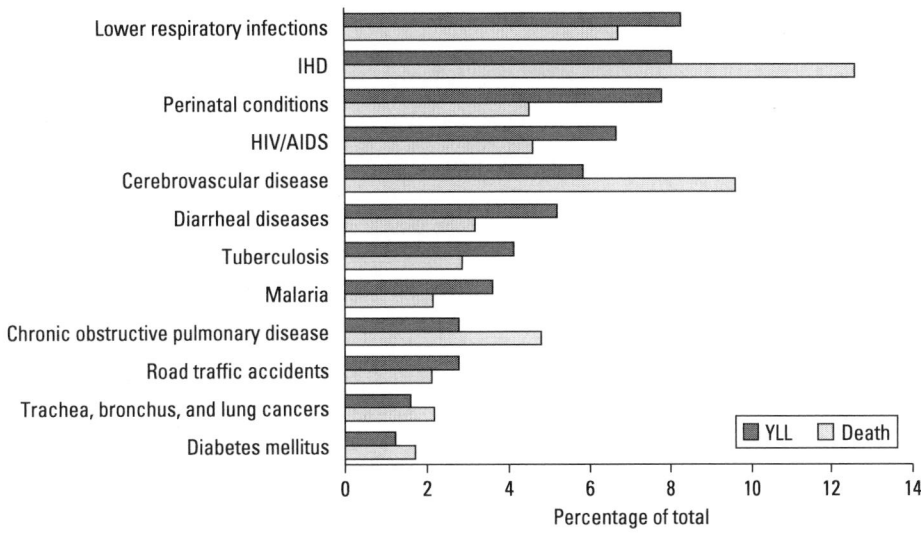

Source: Authors' calculations.

Figure 3.7 Leading Causes of Premature Death (YLL) and of Deaths, Worldwide, 2001

deaths. Chronic obstructive pulmonary disease kills more people (1.4 million) in the East Asia and Pacific region, primarily China, than anywhere else in the world, with 50 percent of global mortality from the disease occurring there.

Europe and Central Asia differs from all other low- and middle-income regions in the size of the CVD epidemic (with almost 50 percent of deaths due to CVD), followed by trachea, bronchus, and lung cancers in third place. Self-inflicted injuries (suicide) are the fifth leading cause of death in this region. South Asia is the only other region where suicide is in the top 10 causes of death. Latin America and the Caribbean is distinguished as the only region where violence falls in the top 10 causes of death, responsible for 1 in 25 deaths. In all low- and middle-income regions apart from Europe and Central Asia, road traffic accidents are included among the top 10 causes of death, reaching fifth position in the Middle East and North Africa, where they are responsible for 1 in 20 deaths.

Years of Life Lost Due to Premature Death

In contrast to crude numbers of deaths, a time-based measure such as YLL allows us to identify those causes that account for premature deaths by giving greater weight to deaths at younger ages. Thus, while noncommunicable diseases accounted for nearly 60 percent of deaths globally in 2001, they accounted for only 40 percent of YLL, whereas injuries accounted for 12 percent of YLL and 9 percent of deaths.

Figure 3.7 compares the 10 leading causes of YLL and 10 leading causes of death for 2001. YLL give relatively greater importance to HIV/AIDS, perinatal conditions, and diarrheal diseases, whereas counts of deaths give relatively greater importance to IHD, stroke, and chronic obstructive pulmonary disease.

ESTIMATING INCIDENCE, PREVALENCE, AND YLD: METHODS AND DATA

This section provides an overview of the methods, software tools, and data sources used to calculate YLD for the GBD 2001 together with a short description of the disease models, assumptions, and data sources for important cause groups. Estimating YLD is the most complex and time-consuming component of burden of disease analysis, because it requires systematic assessments of the available evidence on incidence, prevalence, duration, and severity of a wide range of conditions. The GBD study has developed various methods to reconcile often fragmented and partial estimates available from different studies. A specific software tool, DisMod, described later, has been developed to assist in the analysis of epidemiological data and the preparation of internally consistent estimates.

Assessing YLD

YLD are essentially calculated as follows (ignoring the complications of discounting):

$$YLD = I \times D \times L,$$

where I is the number of incident cases in the reference period, D is the disability weight (in the range 0 to 1), and L is the average duration of disability measured in years. With discounting at rate r, the formula for calculating YLD becomes

$$YLD = I \times D \times [1-\exp(-rL)]/r.$$

To prepare consistent and unbiased estimates of YLD by cause, it is important to ensure that the disability weight and the population incidence and prevalence data relate to the same case definitions. The data required to estimate YLD are incidence, disability duration, age of onset, and distribution by severity class, all of which must be disaggregated by age and sex. These in turn require estimates of incidence, remission, and case fatality rates or relative risks by age and sex.

For some conditions, numbers of incident cases were available directly from disease registers or epidemiological studies, but for most conditions, only prevalence data were available. In these cases, the DisMod II software program was used to model incidence and duration from estimates of prevalence, remission, case fatality rates, and background mortality.

The sources of data and methods used for each of the major disease and injury groups are summarized in later subsections. Given the large number of categories analyzed and the paucity of epidemiological information for many of them, many of the disease models were necessarily simple and approximate. For most disease and injury groups, relevant experts were consulted during the development and revision of YLD estimates.

The disability weights used for the GBD 2001 are still largely based on the GBD 1990 disability weights and are summarized in annex tables 3A.6 to 3A.8. For certain conditions for which weights were not available from the original GBD study, provisional weights were used from Mathers, Vos, and Stevenson (1999) and Stouthard and others (1997).

As discussed earlier, the disability weights used in DALY calculations quantify societal preferences for different health states. These weights do not represent the lived experience of any disability or health state or imply any societal value of the person in a disability or health state. Thus, for example, disability weights of 0.57 for paraplegia and 0.43 for blindness quantify a social judgment that a year with blindness represents less loss of health than a year with paraplegia. It also means that, on average, a person who lives three years with paraplegia followed by death is considered to experience more equivalent healthy years than a person who has one year of good health followed by death (3 years $\times$ [1 − 0.57] = 1.3 "healthy" years is greater than 1 year of good health).

Ensuring Internal Consistency Using DisMod

Estimating prevalence and incidence is usually much harder than estimating mortality. Data collection, when done, is often limited in terms of both time and geographical area and problems of case definition abound. Not surprisingly, data are frequently incomplete, and when available, their validity may be in doubt. In particular, given differences in the way the data for incidence, prevalence, and mortality are collected, it is almost inevitable that observations are internally inconsistent. For example, when a cohort study misses more incident cases than deaths, the observed incidence will be too small to account for the observed mortality.

To address such issues, the GBD studies have exploited two kinds of knowledge. First, disease characteristics, such as remission, case fatality rates, and duration, may be relatively constant across countries and known from studies in some populations, from clinical studies, or from expert knowledge. Supplementing observed data with expert knowledge may help to overcome a lack of data. Second, because the various epidemiological variables are causally linked by a disease process, a disease model that explicitly describes these causal pathways allows us to infer missing data if existing data are sufficient to do so.

DisMod was developed for the original GBD study to help model the parameters needed for YLD calculations, to incorporate expert knowledge, and to check the consistency of different epidemiological estimates and ensure that the estimates used were internally consistent. Figure 3.8 shows the underlying model used by DisMod.

Based on experience with the DisMod software tool in the original GBD study, a new version, DisMod II, was developed with a number of additional features (Barendregt and others 2003). Unlike DisMod I, which used finite difference methods to "solve" the disease model, DisMod II implements an exact solution to the underlying differential equations. As well as calculating solutions when the three

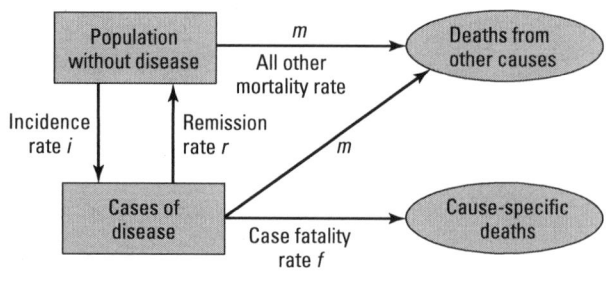

Source: Barendregt and others 2003.

Figure 3.8 Disease Model Underlying DisMod

hazard rates (for incidence, remission, and mortality) are provided as inputs, DisMod II allows other combinations of inputs, such as prevalence, remission, and case fatality rates. In these cases, DisMod uses a goal-seeking algorithm to fit hazards such that the model reproduces the available input variables. DisMod II also has a range of advanced features, including the ability to undertake sensitivity analysis and uncertainty analysis, to give different weights to the various inputs, and to smooth inputs and specify age patterns for outputs. (The software may be downloaded from the WHO Web site at http://www.who.int/evidence/dismod.)

DisMod II was extensively used in the analyses for the GBD 2001 for four main purposes:

- to estimate a set of incidence rates by age from observed prevalences for a condition, given estimates of remission rates and cause-specific mortality risk derived from population data or epidemiological studies;
- to check whether available data for a condition are consistent with each other, for example, when separate estimates of incidence and prevalence were available for a condition;
- to calculate the average duration of incident cases, needed to calculate YLD for a condition;
- to extrapolate estimates in GBD age categories from epidemiological data for different age categories.

Whereas different assumptions regarding remission and case fatality rates affect the age distribution of incident cases and YLD estimates, total YLD are relatively insensitive to these assumptions if matched to a fixed prevalence distribution. This is because YLD estimates are proportional to incidence multiplied by duration, which approximately equals the prevalence of the condition. In other words, for most conditions the combination of incidence, case fatality, and remission rates (and thus derived durations) used in the YLD calculations makes relatively little difference to total YLD across age groups assuming the same prevalence figures are used as the basis. The effect of discounting complicates this, however, with low incidence and long duration conditions being more discounted than high incidence but short duration conditions.

Figure 3.9 illustrates the use of DisMod II to calculate the incidence of diabetes mellitus in males in Sub-Saharan Africa given estimates of the age-specific prevalence of cases, the relative risk of mortality for those with diabetes compared with those without diabetes (Roglic and others 2005), and the assumption that remission rates are zero.

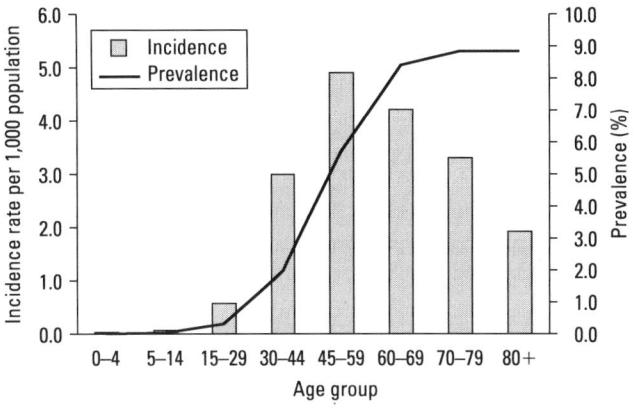

Figure 3.9 Input Prevalences and Incidence Rates Estimated Using DisMod II, for Diabetes Mellitus Cases in Males, Sub-Saharan Africa

YLD Estimates for Regions in 2001

The GBD 2001 estimated incidence, prevalence, and YLD for 17 epidemiological regions based on the 6 WHO regions subdivided by 5 mortality strata. The five mortality strata were defined in terms of quintiles of the distribution of child and adult mortality for males in 1999 (WHO 2002d, pp. 233–5). These regions are defined in annex table 3A.4.

The Disease Control Priorities Project followed the World Bank approach in treating all high-income countries as one region even though they are not geographically contiguous, and then dividing the rest of the world into six geographic regions that together are referred to as low- and middle-income countries. These regions are defined in annex table 3A.1.

To estimate YLD by cause, age, sex, and region for 2001, incidence and prevalence rates were imputed from the 17 epidemiological subregions to the country level using cause-specific methods documented by Mathers, Murray, and Salomon (2003). Absolute incidence and prevalence numbers by age and sex were then added for all countries in each region to provide regional estimates for 2001. Because Version 3 estimates for 2000 had been prepared so that they were consistent with those for 2002, estimates for 2001 were imputed by averaging the Version 3 estimated cause-, age-, sex-, and country-specific rates for mortality, incidence, and prevalence for 2000 and 2002 and applying them to population data for 2001.

Overview of Data Sources

A wide range of data sources were used to analyze incidence, prevalence, and YLD for the GBD 2001. These included

- *Disease registers.* Disease registers record new cases of disease based on reports by physicians and laboratories.

Registers are common for infectious diseases, for instance, TB; cancer; congenital anomalies; for some relatively rare diseases, such as cystic fibrosis or thallassaemia; and sometimes for conditions such as diabetes, schizophrenia, and epilepsy.

- *Population surveys.* Interview surveys, such as the National Health Interview Survey in the United States, can provide self-reported information on disabilities, impairments, and diseases; however, self-reported data are generally not comparable across countries (Murray, Tandon, and others 2002; Sadana and others 2002). In addition, attributing impairment to the underlying causes is often difficult and frequently considerable differences are apparent between lay self-reporting of disease causes and actual underlying disease causes in terms of defined GBD disease categories. In general, the results of health examination surveys have contributed more to YLD calculations than self-reported interview surveys. The Composite International Diagnostic Interview (CIDI) and Diagnostic Interview Schedule (DIS) questionnaires used for mental health surveys are examples of standard questionnaires based on self-reporting that have undergone validity testing and have been used in assessing YLD for mental disorders for the GBD 2001.

- *Epidemiological studies.* Some of the most useful sources of information for the GBD 2001 were population-based epidemiological studies. In particular, longitudinal studies of the natural history of a disease have provided a wealth of information about incidence, average duration, levels of severity, remission, and case fatality rates. Such studies are rare because they are costly to undertake. In addition, as they are often conducted in a particular region or town, judgment is needed when extrapolating results to the entire population.

- *Health facility data.* In most cases, routine data on consultations by diagnosis were not found to be a great deal of use in estimating YLD. Unless coverage of the health system is virtually total, facilities-based data will be based on biased samples that do not reflect the prevalence or severity distributions of conditions in the community. Likewise, hospital deaths are unlikely to be useful because of the same problems of selection bias. Examples of conditions that were estimated from hospital data with national or quasi-national population coverage include perinatal and maternal conditions, meningitis, stroke, myocardial infarction, some sequelae identifiable from data on surgical interventions, and injuries.

The following sections provide an overview of data sources and methods for various specific causes and references to more detailed documentation. For some conditions, WHO programs maintain up-to-date databases based on diseases registers, population surveys, and epidemiological studies. These have been used where available. Many of the epidemiological reviews underlying the GBD 2001 estimates of YLD have been documented and published in draft form on the WHO Web site (http://www.who.int/evidence/bod) and in peer-reviewed publications.

While it is difficult to quantify the exact numbers of data sources used for the YLD estimates for the GBD 2001, table 3.11 provides an approximate count by region. This table counts the number of data sources (registers, notifications, health facility and other official data sets, and epidemiological studies) for each of the causes included in the GBD 2001. For some causes, the only counts available were of the number of countries in each region for which country-specific data were used. In some cases, an exact recount of studies by region was not feasible, and an approximate regional breakdown was estimated from prior counts according to 17 subdivisions of the 6 WHO regions used in WHO documentation of GBD analyses and data sources (Mathers, Lopez, and others 2003). In addition, it was not always possible to be consistent in the counting of studies carried out across multiple countries or multiple years. Finally, note that there is huge variability in the information content across studies or data sets, and that small epidemiological studies are counted equally in table 3.11 with national hospital inpatient data on injuries for an entire population-year. Thus the counts in table 3.11 should be treated as reasonably indicative of the empirical bases underlying the GBD 2001 without overinterpreting differences between causes or regions.

That said, it is striking that of the more than 8,000 data sets estimated to have been used for the GBD 2001 estimation of YLD, nearly 6,600 relate to Group I causes and only 18 to Group III causes. Furthermore, one-quarter of the data sets relate to populations in Sub-Saharan Africa and around one-fifth to populations in high-income countries. While this predominance of data relating to Group I conditions and to Sub-Saharan Africa is not entirely surprising, the paucity of data for some of the leading noncommunicable diseases is more surprising. For example, for several of the leading causes of burden among mental disorders, one or no usable population-based studies were found for some regions, and for IHD, few studies of the incidence or prevalence of angina pectoris or acute myocardial infarction were found outside high-income countries.

Table 3.11 Numbers of Country Data Sources Contributing to the Estimation of YLD, by Region and Cause

GBD cause category	East Asia and Pacific	Europe and Central Asia	Latin America and the Caribbean	Middle East and North Africa	South Asia	Sub-Saharan Africa	High-income countries	Total[a]
I. Communicable, maternal, perinatal, and nutritional conditions								
Tuberculosis[b]	24	27	34	16	8	39	31	179
Sexually transmitted diseases excluding HIV/AIDS[c]	143	318	148	45	99	406	297	1,456
HIV/AIDS[b]	14	26	27	13	5	37	29	150
Diarrheal diseases	155	0	27	55	29	91	0	357
Childhood-cluster diseases[d]								
Pertussis	14	33	64	14	8	45	124	302
Poliomyelitis	22	27	32	15	8	47	37	192
Diphtheria	12	25	2	14	8	46	8	115
Measles	22	18	32	12	8	47	22	127
Tetanus	48	23	27	40	32	79	34	289
Meningitis	23	18	30	12	4	27	43	157
Hepatitis B	4	4	6	6	10	11	28	69
Hepatitis C[e]	36	23	41	37	8	56	85	286
Malaria	9	0	2	1	7	98	0	117
Tropical-cluster diseases								
Trypanosomiasis[b]	0	0	0	0	0	36	0	36
Chagas' disease	0	0	31	0	0	0	0	31
Schistosomiasis	6	0	3	8	0	37	1	55
Leishmaniasis[f]	3	7	15	13	4	20	4	66
Lymphatic filariasis[b]	29	0	8	5	5	40	2	89
Onchocerciasis	0	0	6	0	0	26	0	32
Leprosy[b]	32	10	8	14	8	45	3	120
Dengue[g]	91	0	170	0	4	2	15	282
Japanese encephalitis[b]	10	1	0	0	3	0	4	18
Trachoma	11	0	4	5	4	19	0	43
Intestinal nematode infections	29	0	23	13	10	53	6	134
Lower respiratory infections	15	0	15	12	30	18	5	95
Otitis media	4	0	0	2	2	7	9	24
Maternal conditions								
Maternal hemorrhage	3	0	2	0	1	13	9	28
Maternal sepsis	2	0	3	0	1	14	11	31
Hypertensive disorders of pregnancy	1	0	1	0	2	12	2	18
Obstructed labor	2	0	2	0	1	14	2	21
Abortion	32	10	11	13	49	156	27	32
Perinatal conditions								
Low birthweight[h]	28	27	33	15	7	41	33	184
Birth asphyxia and birth trauma	7	0	7	11	19	12	0	56
Nutritional deficiencies								
Protein-energy malnutrition[i]	61	28	116	37	30	132	15	419
Iodine deficiency	17	13	13	17	12	44	20	136
Vitamin A deficiency	10	2	12	4	4	29	8	67
Iron-deficiency anemia	14	1	1	15	5	33	0	69
II. Noncommunicable diseases								
Malignant neoplasms								
Incidence	11	8	11	10	2	14	25	81
Survival	3	4	1	0	1	0	15	24

(Continues on the following page.)

Table 3.11 Continued

GBD cause category	East Asia and Pacific	Europe and Central Asia	Latin America and the Caribbean	Middle East and North Africa	South Asia	Sub-Saharan Africa	High-income countries	Total[a]
Diabetes mellitus – type 1[j]	22	12	17	5	1	2	41	100
Diabetes mellitus – type 2	6	4	5	8	3	6	8	40
Neuropsychiatric conditions								
Unipolar depressive disorders	5	5	6	3	4	6	27	56
Bipolar affective disorder	2	1	1	1	2	0	14	21
Schizophrenia	4	3	3	1	3	6	25	45
Epilepsy[k]	1	1	6	1	4	8	7	28
Alcohol use disorders	24	43	39	13	5	34	56	214
Alzheimer's and other dementias	10	3	3	0	4	3	87	110
Parkinson's disease[k]	2	1	1	0	1	1	7	13
Multiple sclerosis	4	24	3	5	1	1	116	154
Drug use disorders	11	11	18	10	6	15	43	114
Post-traumatic stress disorder	1	0	1	0	0	0	6	6
Obsessive-compulsive disorder	2	0	3	0	1	0	14	20
Panic disorder	2	0	3	1	0	2	22	30
Insomnia (primary)	2	2	5	1	1	1	9	21
Migraine	6	2	5	2	0	1	11	43
Mental retardation attributable to lead exposure	10	12	21	4	14	9	23	93
Sense organ diseases								
Vision disorders[b]	11	3	4	5	4	19	9	55
Hearing loss, adult onset	5	0	1	1	5	1	12	25
Cardiovascular diseases	0	0	0	0	0	0	0	0
Rheumatic heart disease	15	0	12	9	15	26	7	84
Ischemic heart disease	3	11	0	2	4	1	58	79
Cerebrovascular disease	4	8	1	5	0	6	28	52
Other cardiovascular diseases	0	0	0	0	0	0	5	5
Respiratory diseases								
Chronic obstructive pulmonary disease	24	10	10	4	16	8	32	104
Asthma	17	14	20	12	6	7	74	149
Musculoskeletal diseases								
Rheumatoid arthritis	4	1	4	4	2	5	9	29
Osteoarthritis	1	1	1	0	2	1	9	15
Congenital malformations	3	42	29	6	9	6	5	100
Oral conditions[f]	22	24	32	15	7	35	27	162
III. Injuries	**3**	**1**	**1**	**0**	**0**	**6**	**7**	**18**
Total[l]	**1,155**	**914**	**1,239**	**590**	**522**	**1,955**	**1,735**	**8,096**

Source: Authors' compilation.

Note: The data sources include population-based epidemiological studies, disease registers, and surveillance and notification systems, but exclude death registration data (see tables 3.1 and 3.2). Where possible, regional and global totals refer to numbers of separate studies, or country-years of reported data from surveillance or notification systems. For some causes, regional subtotals for the Disease Control Priorities Project regions were estimated from subtotals for WHO regions and subregions. See text for more information on data sources for specific causes.

a. Global totals may include global review studies not counted in regional subtotals.

b. Totals refer to numbers of countries for which data were available, not to total data sets or country-years.

c. Regional subtotals were estimated from the current distribution of studies in the WHO sexually transmitted infection (STI) surveillance database.

d. Regional subtotals were estimated from numbers of studies by WHO region, rather than by re-accessing original databases.

e. Country-years of data available for 133 countries.

f. Approximate estimate from current WHO database; original extraction from surveillance data sources is not available.

g. Country-years of surveillance reports (approximate, minimum estimate for Latin America and the Caribbean).

h. Estimate based on final published literature review.

i. Regional distribution of the 419 national studies used is assumed to be similar to that of the current 442 national studies in the WHO malnutrition database.

j. Total of 100 population-based registries in 50 countries.

k. Approximate minimum estimate. Several global reviews were used; studies were not separately counted.

l. Actual numbers of studies used exceed the minimums shown here, based on summed table entries for specific causes regardless of whether counts were of data sets or of countries.

Assuming that for causes in table 3.11 where the counts relate to countries rather than to data sets there are, on average, two data sets per country; then overall, approximately 8,700 data sets contributed to the estimation of YLD. Not counting again studies that also contributed to the estimation of cause-specific mortality rates, an additional 1,370 data sets were used to estimate YLL. In total, the GBD 2001 has drawn on more than 10,000 data sets or studies, making it almost certainly the largest synthesis and analysis of global population health data carried out to date.

Communicable Diseases and Maternal, Perinatal, and Nutritional Conditions

This section gives an overview of data sources and methods for specific Group I causes and references to more detailed documentation.

Tuberculosis. Estimates of incidence and deaths due to TB (excluding HIV-infected persons) for countries in 2001 formed the basis of estimates of TB prevalence in 2001. The methods and data used to estimate incidence and mortality for each country were described earlier. For countries with VR data for TB deaths, incidence estimates have been revised to be consistent with estimated deaths, estimated case fatality rates for treated and untreated cases, and proportion of incident cases treated.

Estimated prevalence of all forms of TB (excluding HIV-infected persons) for 2001 was calculated by multiplying estimated incidence by estimated duration. Country-specific estimates of duration were weighted for the proportion of cases treated and that were smear-positive.

Sexually Transmitted Infections Other Than HIV/AIDS. More than 300 community-based and prenatal care-based prevalence and incidence studies of pregnant women were used to generate region-specific estimates of the prevalence of syphilis, chlamydia, and gonorrhea. The methodology is described in detail elsewhere (Gerbase and others 1998; WHO 2001c) and was used to update estimates to 2001.

HIV/AIDS. The Joint United Nations Programme on HIV/AIDS and WHO have developed country-specific estimates of HIV/AIDS for most countries and revise them periodically to account for new data and improved methods (Salomon and Murray 2001b; Schwartlander and others 1999; Walker and others 2003). For the most recent round of estimates, they used two different types of models, one for generalized epidemics and one for epidemics concentrated in high-risk groups.

For a few countries where prevalence estimates for HIV seropositive cases were not directly available, they were derived by scaling regional prevalence estimates according to the ratio of country-specific HIV/AIDS mortality to regional HIV/AIDS mortality. Because different countries may be in different phases of the epidemic, the relationship between prevalence and mortality may vary across countries.

Diarrheal Diseases. To estimate the incidence of diarrheal diseases in children under five in developing and developed countries, 357 community-based studies and population surveys were used (Bern 2004; Murray and Lopez 1996d). Point prevalences were estimated assuming an average duration of six days per episode. Work is currently in progress to update these estimates with more recent evidence from community-based studies.

Vaccine-Preventable Childhood Diseases and Meningitis. The methods used to estimate incidence for childhood-cluster diseases were summarized earlier. The incidence of meningitis due to *Haemophilus influenzae* type b together with the incidence of meningitis due to *Streptococcus pneumoniae* and *Neisseria meningitides*, was updated from the 1990 estimates using information from the WHO Vaccines and Biologicals Program derived from country notifications of cases and deaths, from WHO surveillance centers and, where relevant, from immunization coverage data (WHO 2001b).

Hepatitis B and C. Available data on the prevalence of chronic hepatitis B and hepatitis C infection were used together with disease models to estimate regional incidence and mortality rates (Global Burden of Hepatitis C Working Group 2004; Lavanchy 2004; WHO 2002a, 2002b).

Malaria. Malaria prevalence was based on regional prevalence rates for acute symptomatic episodes estimated by Murray and Lopez (1996d). Country-specific estimates of malaria prevalence were derived by adjusting subregional prevalence by the ratio of country to subregional malaria mortality. Work is currently under way in collaboration with other WHO programs and external expert groups to refine and revise these country-specific estimates of malaria prevalence (Korenromp 2005).

Schistosomiasis. The *CEGET/WHO Atlas of the Global Distribution of Schistosomiasis* (Doumenge and others 1987) and population-based prevalence studies were used to estimate country-specific prevalence rates. Prevalence estimates were based on regional prevalence rates for schistosomiasis infection (Murray and Lopez 1996d) applied to updated estimates of country-specific populations at risk in 2001 (van der Werf and de Vlas 2001).

Lymphatic Filariasis. Estimates for lymphatic filariasis were developed for six of the eight regions defined for the GBD 1990 study (Murray and Lopez 1996d). The established market economies and formerly socialist economies of Europe were excluded, because infection was not considered to be endemic in these countries. The prevalence data were obtained from community-based surveys and complemented with reports by the Information and Reference Service of the Parasitic Diseases Program, WHO. Prevalence estimates were based on regional prevalence rates for cases of hydrocele or lymphodaema caused by infection with filariae. These estimates were updated using estimates of country-specific populations at risk in 2001 provided by the WHO Lymphatic Filiariasis Elimination Program.

Onchocerciasis. In the early 1990s, WHO estimated the prevalence of blindness due to onchocerciasis from surveys and national reports (WHO 1995). Following the continued success of the Onchocerciasis Control Program in western African countries and the introduction of population-wide administration of ivermectin in other endemic areas, the prevalence of onchocerciasis and its disabling sequelae has been dramatically reduced in all 36 endemic countries in Latin America and the Caribbean and Sub-Saharan Africa (Richards and others 2001). Therefore, the prevalence of blindness from onchocerciasis was reestimated by taking into account the declining trends in prevalence and the coverage and duration of onchocerciasis control programs (Alley and others 2001).

Reliable sources of information on the prevalence of blindness due to onchocerciasis are available from several population-based studies, usually as part of an overall blindness survey. However, prevalence studies of onchocerciasis-specific blindness are often carried out in hyperendemic areas and/or in local communities, and thus the estimated prevalence may not be generalizable to the country as a whole. For this reason, the current prevalence of blindness due to onchocerciasis was estimated by nationally reported data, if available, and extrapolation from 1993 estimates using trend analysis of onchocerciasis control programs in each endemic country (Shibuya and Ezzati 2003).

Leprosy. Regional incidence and prevalence rates for leprosy were based on case reporting and surveillance by 120 WHO member states (Stein 2002a; WHO 2002c).

Dengue and Dengue Hemorrhagic Fever. Regional incidence and prevalence rates for dengue and dengue hemorrhagic fever were based on a review of nearly 300 population-based studies, but data were sparse for regions apart from East Asia and the Pacific and Latin America and the Caribbean (LeDuc, Esteves, and Gratz 2004).

Trachoma. The baseline regional and subregional prevalence of blinding trachoma was first estimated as described elsewhere (Frick and others 2003; Ranson and Evans 1995) and then updated using several recent population-based studies in the Middle East and North Africa and Sub-Saharan Africa. As the prevalence of blinding trachoma declines with socioeconomic development even in the absence of a specific trachoma control program (Dolin and others 1997), the extrapolation from regional prevalence estimates made in the 1980s would overestimate current prevalence. For this reason, both nationally reported data and specific criteria for a regression model of time-series data were used to estimate the prevalence of blinding trachoma. The model estimates were then applied to countries that have reported cases of blinding trachoma (Shibuya and Mathers 2003).

Intestinal Nematode Infections. Updated estimates of the prevalence of intestinal nematode infections were based on WHO's new global databank on schistosomiasis and soil-transmitted helminths, which contains data derived from community-based, cross-sectional surveys for subnational administrative regions (Brooker and others 2000; de Silva and others 2003). In areas without comprehensive data, predictions of the distribution of soil-transmitted helminths were developed using environmental data derived from satellite remote sensing (Brooker and others 2002). Incidence rates and YLD for disabling sequelae of helminth infections were modeled using a mathematical model developed by Chan and others (Bundy and others 2004; Chan 1997).

Lower Respiratory Infections. Prevalence and incidence estimates for lower respiratory infections were based on an analysis of published data on the incidence of clinical pneumonia from 95 community-based studies published since 1961 (Rudan and others 2004). Most of the studies were longitudinal and conducted over long enough periods to account for seasonal variation. Studies over short periods of time were excluded.

Maternal Conditions. Incidence rates for maternal conditions and disabling sequelae were derived from reviews of published population-based studies supplemented by studies of hospital-based deliveries adjusted for the proportion of deliveries occurring in hospitals (Dolea and AbouZahr 2003a, 2003b; Dolea, AbouZahr, and Stein 2003; Dolea and Stein 2003). The incidence of unsafe induced abortion was estimated at the country level using 156 published and unpublished reports for 131 countries together with information on legal and social contexts (Ahman, Dolea, and Shah 2003; WHO 2004a).

Perinatal Conditions. Incidence rates for low birthweight, birth asphyxia and trauma, and disabling sequelae were derived from health service–based data and national birth registration systems in high-income countries and from mothers participating in nationally representative household surveys (such as the U.S. Agency for International Development–funded DHSs and the Multiple Indicator Cluster Surveys carried out by the United Nations Children's Fund), supplemented by reviews of published population-based and hospital-based studies (UNICEF and WHO 2005).

Protein-Energy Malnutrition. More than 400 recent nationally representative studies from WHO's global database on child growth and malnutrition (http://www.who.int/nutgrowthdb/) were used to estimate the prevalence of child stunting and wasting in every country (de Onis and Blossner 2003; de Onis, Frongillo, and Blossner 2000; de Onis and others 2004). Where country estimates were not available from the database, the regional average calculated from the available studies or data from other countries with similar epidemiological characteristics were used (Stein 2002c).

Iodine Deficiency and Vitamin A Deficiency. Country-specific estimates for goiter rates were obtained and used to calculate regional estimates for total goiter rates. The primary data source was the WHO Nutrition and Health for Development Program, which is developing and refining a comprehensive database of country-specific estimates of both clinical and subclinical iodine deficiency disorders from national level and subnational nutrition surveys (Rastogi and Mathers 2002a; WHO 2001a; WHO Nutrition Program 2005).

Country-specific estimates were obtained and used to calculate regional estimates for both xerophthalmia and corneal scars resulting from vitamin A deficiency (Rastogi and Mathers 2002c). Again, the primary data source was the WHO Nutrition and Health for Development Program, which is also developing and refining a comprehensive

database of country-specific estimates of both clinical and subclinical vitamin A deficiency from national-level and subnational nutrition surveys (WHO Nutrition Program 2002b). The database compiles information for all population groups, especially preschool-age children and women of childbearing age, and includes information on the prevalence of xerophthalmia, including night blindness and serum retinol distributions.

Iron Deficiency Anemia. Country-specific prevalence estimates of iron deficiency anemia were obtained from 69 studies and used to estimate regional age- and sex-specific prevalence rates for mild, moderate, and severe anemia. The primary data source was the WHO Nutrition and Health for Development Program. The program is currently preparing a comprehensive database of country-specific prevalence estimates of both clinical and subclinical iron deficiency anemia from national-level and subnational nutrition surveys (WHO Nutrition Program 2002a).

All prevalence estimates were reviewed, with priority being given to the most recent national-level estimates (most were obtained from studies conducted in the last 10 years). For countries for which no studies were available, the regional average was applied (Rastogi and Mathers 2002b).

Noncommunicable Diseases

This section gives an overview of data sources and methods for specific Group II causes and references to more detailed documentation.

Malignant Neoplasms. Regional survival models were developed for each cancer site and used to estimate numbers of incident cases from estimated deaths by site for each country (Mathers, Shibuya, and others 2002; Shibuya and others 2002). The same models were used to estimate numbers of prevalent cases, defined as cases of malignant neoplasms causing death within 15 years, and cases of nonfatal malignant neoplasms (where the person is likely to survive 15 years or more) diagnosed within the last five years.

Diabetes Mellitus. Diabetes prevalence estimates for those age 20 and older were based on an analysis of 41 representative population-based studies that used oral glucose tolerance tests and either 1980 WHO criteria to define diabetes cases or similar criteria that produced comparable prevalences (Wild and others 2004). For countries for which eligible data were not available, data from a proxy country believed to have similar diabetes prevalence were used. Most studies of diabetes prevalence did not indicate the type of diabetes, and consequently the estimates refer to all diabetes. The prevalence of diabetes among people under 20 years of age was estimated from incidence data derived from 100 published studies (Karvonen and others 2000).

Depressive Disorders. Point prevalence estimates for episodes of unipolar major depression were derived from a systematic review of available published and nonpublished population studies on depressive disorders, which identified 56 studies from all World Bank regions (Ustun and others 2005). Variations in the prevalence of unipolar depressive disorders in some European countries, Australia, Japan, and New Zealand were estimated directly from relevant population studies (Ayuso-Mateos and others 2001). For other high-income European countries, country-specific prevalences were estimated using a regression model of available prevalence data on suicide rates (for ages 15 to 59, both sexes combined). For other regions, prevalence estimates were based on regional prevalence rates applied to country-specific population estimates for 2002. Unlike the original GBD study, survey data on the severity of unipolar depressive disorders (mild, moderate, or severe) were used together with disability weights for these three severity classes from Stouthard and others (1997). This resulted in an overall disability weight for unipolar depressive disorders across regions from 0.30 to 0.46. This compares reasonably well with a more recent analysis of the distribution of depression by severity and disability weights for a Dutch community, which resulted in an overall disability weight of 0.41 (Kruijshaar and others 2005). YLD due to dysthymia not associated with major depressive episodes were estimated separately using the disability weight for mild depressive disorders.

Subregional prevalence rates for bipolar disorder were derived from a systematic review of all available published and unpublished population studies using case definitions that met the diagnostic criteria of the fourth edition of the *Diagnostic and Statistical Manual of Mental Disorders* (DSM-IV) of the American Psychiatric Association (1994) or of ICD-10 (Ayuso-Mateos 2002a).

Anxiety Disorders and Schizophrenia. Subregional prevalence rates for panic disorder, obsessive-compulsive disorder, and post-traumatic stress disorder were also derived from systematic reviews of all available published and unpublished population studies using case definitions that met ICD-10 or DSM-IV criteria (Ayuso-Mateos 2002b, 2002c, 2002d; Ustun and Chisholm 2001). Those with comorbid depressive disorder or alcohol or drug use disorders

were excluded from prevalence estimates. For data sources and methods for schizophrenia see Ayuso-Mateos (2002d).

Alcohol and Drug Use Disorders. The case definition for alcohol use disorders is based on ICD-10 criteria for alcohol dependence and harmful use, excluding cases with comorbid depressive episode. DSM-IV alcohol abuse is included in the case definition. All available population-based surveys using diagnostic criteria that could be mapped to this case definition were identified. Population estimates of the point prevalence of alcohol use disorders were obtained from 55 studies (Mathers and Ayuso-Mateos 2003).

Published data on alcohol production, trade, and sales, adjusted for estimates of illegally produced alcohol, were used to estimate country averages of the volume of alcohol consumed. These preliminary estimates were then further adjusted on the basis of survey data on alcohol consumption to estimate the prevalence of alcohol use disorders for countries where recent population-based survey data were not available (Rehm and others 2004).

Estimating the prevalence of illicit drug use is difficult, because the use of these drugs is illegal, stigmatized, and hidden. In addition, definitions differ from country to country, as does the quality of data collected. The definition used for the GBD 2001 was based on ICD-10 criteria for opioid dependence and harmful use or cocaine dependence and harmful use, excluding cases with comorbid depressive episodes. Data on the prevalence of problematic illicit drug use were derived from a range of sources (Degenhardt and others 2003). A literature search was conducted of all studies that estimated the prevalence of problematic drug use and more than 100 studies were identified. Other data sources included the United Nations Drug Control Program and the European Monitoring Centre for Drugs and Drug Addiction.

Insomnia (Primary). Subregional prevalence rates for primary insomnia were derived from systematic reviews of all available published and unpublished population studies using case definitions that met ICD-10 or DSM-IV criteria, where the insomnia causes problems with usual activity and is not secondary to other diseases. Persons with comorbid depressive disorder or alcohol or drug use disorders were excluded from the prevalence estimates.

Epilepsy and Multiple Sclerosis. Subregional prevalence rates for epilepsy, excluding epilepsy or seizure disorder secondary to other diseases or injury, were derived from systematic reviews of available published and unpublished population studies. Subregional prevalence rates for multiple sclerosis, derived for the GBD 1990, were updated using recent epidemiological studies (Warren and Warren 2001).

Alzheimer's Disease and Other Dementias. Subregional prevalence rates, incidence rates, and durations for Alzheimer's disease and other dementias were estimated based on 110 available population studies and assumed to apply to countries within each subregion (Mathers and Leonardi 2003).

Parkinson's Disease. Regional incidence to mortality rates for Parkinson's disease estimated by Murray and Lopez (1996d) were used to derive country-specific estimates for incidence from the estimated country-specific mortality rates.

Migraine. Regional prevalence rates for people who experience migraine were estimated from 43 available population studies and assumed to apply to countries within each subregion (Leonardi and Mathers 2003). Migraine has been treated as a chronic disease lasting from 15 years to around 45 years with sporadic episodes. The case definition was taken from the International Headache Society's definition of migraine. Available population studies using this definition provided prevalence estimates that were quite similar across most regions.

Mental Retardation. An attempt was made to assess the prevalence of all forms of mental retardation, but due to difficulties with data comparability, we decided to assess only the burden resulting from childhood exposure to environmental lead, plus mental retardation estimated as sequelae to diseases or injuries or associated with specific congenital malformations. The YLD associated with mental retardation as a sequela of diseases and injuries or as a component of a syndrome are included in the estimation of total YLD for such causes in the tables presented in annex 3C. In addition, YLD were estimated separately for mental retardation as a consequence of environmental lead exposure, because this was required for the assessment of the total attributable burden of environmental lead exposure. For details of methods and data sources see Fewtrell and others (2004) and Pruss-Ustun and others (2004).

Low Vision and Blindness. Both regional and subregional prevalences for blindness and low vision were updated using all available data gathered since 1980 (Resnikoff and others 2004; Thylefors and others 1995). Subregional prevalences were estimated from more than 50 cross-sectional, population-based surveys of blindness and low vision, both published and unpublished. For countries for which no data were available, prevalences were extrapolated from available data for neighboring subregions or countries with a similar epidemiological and socioeconomic environment. The DisMod software was then used to obtain internally consistent age- and sex-specific estimates of incidence, prevalence, remission, and relative risks of mortality. Ratios of blindness to low vision for each region were used to estimate the prevalence of low vision and DisMod analyses were then carried out to ensure internal consistency among parameters.

Hearing Loss. Despite the number of published studies on hearing loss, many of them use different criteria and relate to subnational or nonrepresentative populations. Data from 25 representative population surveys of measured hearing loss (19 surveys for adults and 14 surveys for children) were used to estimate subregional prevalences of moderate or greater hearing loss according to the WHO definition (hearing threshold level in the better ear is 41 decibels or greater averaged over 0.5, 1.0, 2.0, and 4.0 kilohertz) and of severe or greater hearing loss (hearing threshold level in the better ear is 61 decibels or greater averaged over 0.5, 1.0, 2.0, and 4.0 kilohertz) (Mathers, Smith, and Concha 2003). Regional estimates of the prevalence of hearing aid use were used in the calculation of average disability weights for moderate, severe, and profound hearing loss in each region, and thus to calculate YLD associated with hearing loss.

Congestive Heart Failure. The incidence of congestive heart failure following acute myocardial infarction was estimated using a model for IHD based on available population data on incidence and case fatality rates for acute myocardial infarction and on the proportion of acute myocardial infarction patients who go on to develop congestive heart failure (Mathers, Truelson, and others 2004). The incidence of congestive heart failure as a sequela to rheumatic heart disease, hypertensive heart disease, and inflammatory heart diseases was estimated using incidence to mortality ratios from the GBD 1990 (Murray and Lopez 1996d).

Angina Pectoris. The GBD 2001 study developed a model for IHD based on available population data on the incidence and case fatality rates for acute myocardial infarction and on the prevalence and case fatality rates for angina pectoris (Mathers, Truelson, and others 2004). Observed correlations between the prevalence of acute myocardial infarction survivors and the prevalence of angina pectoris (whether incident before or after acute myocardial infarction) were used to estimate the prevalence of angina pectoris from the modeled prevalences of acute myocardial infarction survivors. The latter were estimated from country-specific IHD mortality estimates together with estimated regional case fatality rates for acute myocardial infarction.

Stroke. The GBD 2001 study developed a model for stroke based on available population data on case fatality rates within 28 days for incident cases of first-ever stroke and on long-term survival in cases surviving this initial period, in which the risk of mortality is highest (Truelsen and others 2002). A consistent relationship between incidence, prevalence, and mortality was established using U.S. data. The resulting age- and sex-specific 28-day and long-term case fatality rates were used as the basis for estimating subregional case fatality rates after adjusting for the observed relationship between GDP per capita and overall 28-day case fatality rates in published studies from various countries. Consistent epidemiological models for the prevalence of stroke survivors in each subregion were then estimated using these case fatality rates and observed mortality after adjustment to account for the fact that deaths recorded as resulting from stroke in vital statistics do not fully reflect the true excess risk of mortality among survivors.

Chronic Obstructive Pulmonary Disease. Chronic obstructive pulmonary disease is characterized by airway obstruction with lung function levels of forced expiratory volume in one second (FEV_1) to forced vital capacity ratio of less than 70 percent and the presence of a postbronchodilator FEV_1 of less than 80 percent of the predicted value that is not fully reversible. Because accurate prevalence data based on spirometry are not available in many regions, an alternative approach was used to infer disease occurrence from regional estimates of mortality due to chronic obstructive pulmonary disease that made use of the constraints imposed by the consistent epidemiological relationships among prevalence to incidence, remission, case fatality, and mortality rates. The relative risk of mortality due to chronic obstructive pulmonary disease across subregions was estimated as a function of its two leading risk factors—tobacco smoking and indoor air pollution from solid fuel used for cooking—along with regional fixed effects (Lopez and others forthcoming). Data on risk factors were derived from the comparative risk assessment carried out for the *World Health Report 2002* (Ezzati and others 2002; WHO 2002d). The estimated relative risks were validated by comparing estimated regional prevalence with data from available population studies. For regions where surveys of representative populations based on spirometry were available, both direct estimation and model estimation were used.

Asthma. Asthma prevalence estimates were based on a case definition requiring a positive airway hyper-responsiveness test in addition to symptoms in the last 12 months. Specifically, the prevalence estimates related to cases defined in terms of reported wheeze in the last 12 months plus current bronchial hyper-responsiveness, defined as a mean provocation concentration of histamine required to produce a 20 percent fall in FEV_1 of 8 milligrams per milliliter or less.

While epidemiological studies commonly use a broader definition of asthma based on symptom reporting, the 2001 GBD study used a narrower definition in order to identify cases experiencing a significant loss of health. The disability threshold for inclusion in the prevalence estimates is mild asthma, defined as occasional wheeze that does not affect usual activities, but which, if untreated, may result in occasional episodes that cause sleep disturbance and/or speech limitations.

A review of published literature identified studies using the foregoing definition, but also many studies using self-reported symptoms only, self-reported current asthma (asthma attack in the last 12 months or currently in treatment), or physician diagnosis of current asthma in the last 12 months. Based on study populations for which prevalence data were available according to one of these alternative definitions, as well as the foregoing stricter definition, we calculated adjustment factors to estimate asthma prevalence from community surveys using other definitions of asthma.

A total of 149 population-based studies were used to derive estimates of asthma prevalence for a wide range of countries for children, teenagers, and adults. In particular, extensive use was made of two multicountry studies: the International Study of Asthma and Allergies in Childhood using self-reported symptoms in children ages 6 to 7 and 13 to 14 (ISAAC Steering Committee 1998a, 1998b), and the European Community Respiratory Health Survey of adults ages 20 to 44 using self-reported symptoms and bronchial hyper-responsiveness (Chinn and others 1997; Pearce and others 2000). Estimates from the population-based studies were then used to derive subregional average prevalence rates, which were assumed to apply in countries without specific population studies.

Rheumatoid Arthritis. Subregional prevalence rates for rheumatoid arthritis were derived from available published population studies using case definitions for definite or classical rheumatoid arthritis (Symmons, Mathers, and Pfleger 2002b).

Osteoarthritis. Subregional prevalence rates for osteoarthritis were derived from available published population studies that provided prevalence data for symptomatic osteoarthritis of the hip or knee, radiologically confirmed as Kellgren-Lawrence grade 2 or greater (Symmons, Mathers, and Pfleger 2002a).

Edentulism. Prevalence numbers were based on regional prevalence rates for edentulism estimated by Murray and Lopez (1996d). New data from the 2002–4 WHO World Health Survey will enable revision of these estimates in the future.

Injuries

An incident episode of a nonfatal injury is defined as an episode that is severe enough for the person to be hospitalized or that requires emergency room care (if such care is available). Begg and others (2002) describe methods used to estimate injury-related prevalences and prevalence YLD. In brief, the incidence of nonfatal injuries by external cause category, age, and sex was estimated by applying regional and country-specific death to incidence ratios to the injury deaths estimated for each country in 2002.

Age- and sex-specific ratios were based on new analyses of health facility data provided by 18 countries in five World Bank regions. For most cause categories, extrapolations from observed death to incidence ratios were derived for all countries at a regional level, with final adjustments using mortality and per capita GDP as predictors of expected variability in case fatality rates.

Prevalences for disabling injuries were estimated from the proportions of cases by injury type estimated to result in long-term disability, together with estimates of short- and long-term disability durations. The latter were based on analyses of excess mortality risks from epidemiological studies (Begg and others 2002).

BURDEN OF DISABILITY AND POOR HEALTH IN 2001

As defined earlier, YLD measure the equivalent years of healthy life lost through time spent in states of less than full health. The original GBD study brought the previously largely ignored burden of nonfatal illnesses, particularly mental disorders, to the attention of health policy makers.

The findings of the GBD 2001, based on updated data and analyses, confirm that disability and states of less than full health caused by diseases and injuries play an important role in determining the overall health status of populations in all regions of the world.

Leading Causes of YLD in 2001

Tables 3.12 and 3.13 show the 10 leading causes of YLD(3,0) by broad income group and by sex. A relatively short list of causes dominates the overall burden of nonfatal disabling conditions. In both income regions, neuropsychiatric conditions are the most important causes of disability, accounting for more than 37 percent of YLDs(3,0) among adults ages 15 and over. The disabling burden of neuropsychiatric conditions is almost the same for males and females, but the major contributing causes are different. While depression is the leading cause for both males and females, the burden of depression is 50 percent higher for females than for males, and females also have a higher burden from anxiety disorders, migraine, and senile dementias. In contrast, the male burden for alcohol and drug use disorders is nearly six times higher than that for females and accounts for one-quarter of the male neuropsychiatric burden.

Globally, cataracts and age-related vision disorders together account for more than 9 percent of total YLD(3,0), and adult-onset hearing loss accounts for another 5.2 percent. Adult-onset hearing loss is extremely prevalent, with more than 27 percent of men and 24 percent of women aged 45 and over experiencing mild hearing loss or greater. The GBD 2001 has estimated only the burden of moderate or greater hearing loss. Childhood-onset hearing loss is not included in this cause category, as most childhood hearing loss is due to congenital causes, infectious diseases, or other diseases or injuries, and is included as sequelae for such causes in the estimation of the burden of disease.

In both low- and middle-income countries and high-income countries, alcohol use disorders are among the 10 leading causes of YLD(3,0). This includes only the direct burden of alcohol dependence and problem use. The total attributable burden of disability due to alcohol use is much larger (see chapter 4).

More than 80 percent of global nonfatal health outcomes occur in developing countries, and high-mortality developing countries account for nearly half of all YLD. Although the prevalences of disabling conditions such as dementia and musculoskeletal disease are higher in countries with long life expectancies, this is offset by lower contributions to disability from conditions such as CVD, chronic respiratory

Table 3.12 The 10 Leading Causes of YLD by Broad Income Group, 2001

	Low- and middle-income countries			High-income countries		
Cause	YLD (millions of years)	Percentage of total YLD		Cause	YLD (millions of years)	Percentage of total YLD
1 Unipolar depressive disorders	43.22	9.1		1 Unipolar depressive disorders	8.39	11.8
2 Cataracts	28.15	5.9		2 Alzheimer's and other dementias	6.33	8.9
3 Hearing loss, adult onset	24.61	5.2		3 Hearing loss, adult onset	5.39	7.6
4 Vision disorders, age-related	15.36	3.2		4 Alcohol use disorders	3.77	5.3
5 Osteoarthritis	13.65	2.9		5 Osteoarthritis	3.77	5.3
6 Perinatal conditions	13.52	2.8		6 Cerebrovascular disease	3.46	4.9
7 Cerebrovascular disease	11.10	2.3		7 Chronic obstructive pulmonary disease	2.86	4.0
8 Schizophrenia	10.15	2.1		8 Diabetes mellitus	2.25	3.2
9 Alcohol use disorders	9.81	2.1		9 Endocrine disorders	1.68	2.4
10 Protein-energy malnutrition	9.34	2.0		10 Vision disorders, age-related	1.53	2.1

Source: Authors' calculations.

Table 3.13 The 10 Leading Causes of YLD by Sex, Worldwide, 2001

	Males			Females		
Cause	YLD (millions of years)	Percentage of total YLD		Cause	YLD (millions of years)	Percentage of total YLD
1 Unipolar depressive disorders	20.35	7.7		1 Unipolar depressive disorders	31.26	11.0
2 Hearing loss, adult onset	14.96	5.6		2 Cataracts	16.49	5.8
3 Cataracts	12.16	4.6		3 Hearing loss, adult onset	15.03	5.3
4 Alcohol use disorders	11.50	4.3		4 Osteoarthritis	10.83	3.8
5 Cerebrovascular disease	7.58	2.9		5 Vision disorders, age-related	9.66	3.4
6 Vision disorders, age-related	7.23	2.7		6 Alzheimer's and other dementias	9.46	3.3
7 Perinatal conditions	7.03	2.7		7 Cerebrovascular disease	6.98	2.5
8 Osteoarthritis	6.59	2.5		8 Perinatal conditions	6.91	2.4
9 Chronic obstructive pulmonary disease	6.55	2.5		9 Schizophrenia	5.58	2.0
10 Schizophrenia	5.66	2.1		10 Bipolar disorder	4.82	1.7

Source: Authors' calculations.

diseases, and long-term sequelae of communicable diseases and nutritional deficiencies. In other words, people living in developing countries not only face shorter life expectancies than those in developed countries, but also live a larger proportion of their lives in poor health.

Regional Variations in Healthy Life Expectancy

In the original GBD study, Murray and Lopez (1996c) computed a form of health expectancy referred to as disability-adjusted life expectancy using age- and sex-specific YLD rates and regional life tables to compute the expected equivalent years of healthy life in each region. Their results clearly demonstrated that populations with higher mortality also had higher prevalences of disability and lower health expectancies.

WHO has used a similar indicator, referred to as healthy life expectancy (HALE), to report on the average levels of population health for its 192 member countries (WHO 2004b). We calculated HALE at birth for regions in 2001 (figure 3.10) using the GBD 2001 estimates for YLD by region, age, and sex, together with information on health state prevalences and valuations from the WHO Multicountry Survey Study on Health and Responsiveness carried out in 2000 and 2001 (Ustun, Chatterji, Villanueva, and others 2003). For a description of the methods used to calculate HALE see Mathers, Salomon, and others (2003). Regional variations in HALE have also been discussed in more detail elsewhere, as have estimates of regional variations in increases in HALE associated with the elimination of selected health risks (Ezzati and others 2003; Mathers, Murray, and others 2003).

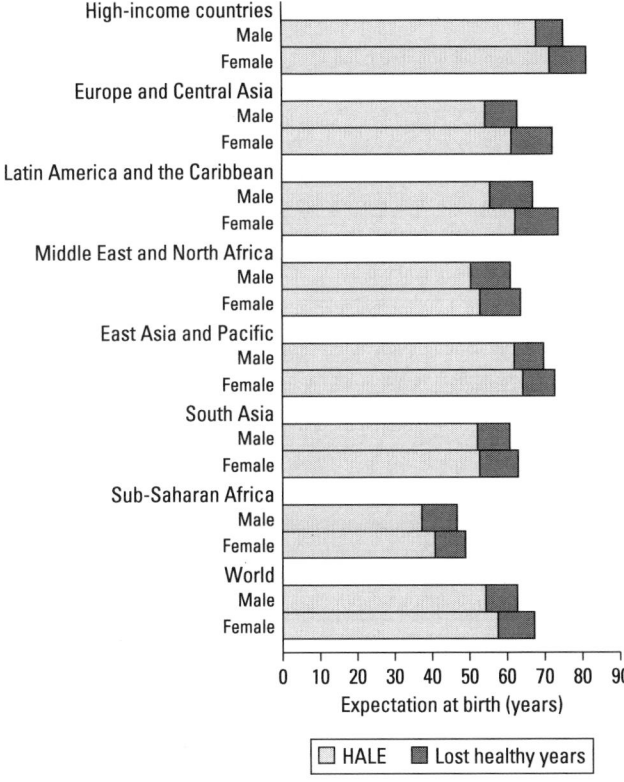

Source: Authors' calculations.

Figure 3.10 Life Expectancy, HALE, and Lost Healthy Years by Region and Sex, 2001

Overall, global HALE at birth in 2001 for males and females combined was 57.4 years, 7.5 years lower than total life expectancy at birth (figure 3.10). In other words, on average, poor health resulted in a loss of nearly eight years of healthy life globally. Global HALE at birth for females was only 2.7 years greater than that for males. In comparison, female life expectancy at birth was 4.2 years higher than that for males. Global HALE at age 60 was 12.7 years and 14.7 years for males and females, respectively, 4.3 years lower than total life expectancy at age 60 for males and 5.3 years lower for females.

HALE at birth ranged from a low of 40 years for males in Sub-Saharan Africa to more than 70 years for females in high-income countries. This reflects an almost twofold difference in HALE between major regional populations (figure 3.10). The equivalent "lost" healthy years (total life expectancy minus HALE) ranged from 15 percent of total life expectancy at birth in Sub-Saharan Africa to 8 percent in high-income countries. The sex gap was highest for Europe and Central Asia and lowest in the Middle East and North Africa.

GLOBAL BURDEN OF DISEASE IN 2001

This section provides an overview of the global and regional burden of disease in 2001 as measured in DALYs, more specifically, in DALYs(3,0). As defined earlier, DALYs(3,0) do not apply nonuniform age weights, but incorporate a 3 percent discount rate and should be distinguished from the DALYs(3,1) used in the GBD results reported by WHO in recent world health reports. In 2001, the global average burden of disease across all regions was 250 DALYs(3,0) per 1,000 population, of which almost two-thirds were due to premature death.

YLL varied dramatically across regions, with YLL rates nearly five times higher in Sub-Saharan Africa than in high-income countries (figure 3.11). In contrast, YLD rates were less varied, with Sub-Saharan Africa having 50 percent higher rates than high-income countries. South Asia and Sub-Saharan Africa together bore 45 percent of the total GBD in 2001, even though they account for only one-third of the world's population. East Asia and the Pacific is the "healthiest" of the low- and middle-income regions, with countries such as China now having life expectancies similar to those of many Latin American countries and higher than those in some European countries (see chapter 2).

Europe and Central Asia now experiences a higher burden of disease than all other low- and middle-income regions except South Asia and Sub-Saharan Africa. This reflects the sharp increase in adult male mortality and disability in the 1990s. A significant factor in this increase was the high incidence of male alcohol abuse, which led to high rates of accidents, violence, and CVD. From 1991 to 1994, the risk of premature death increased by 50 percent for Russian males (Gavrilova and others 2000; Semenova and

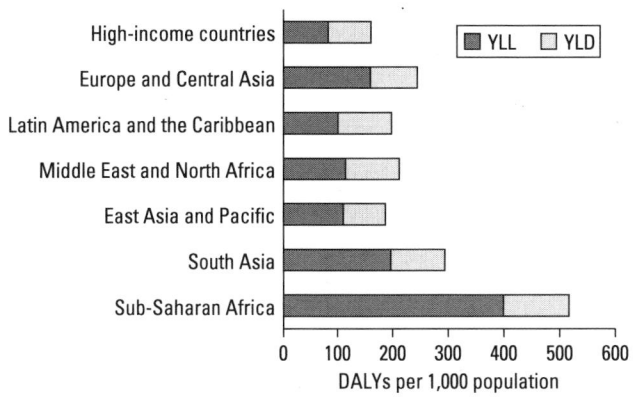

Source: Authors' calculations.

Figure 3.11 YLL, YLD, and DALYs by Region, 2001

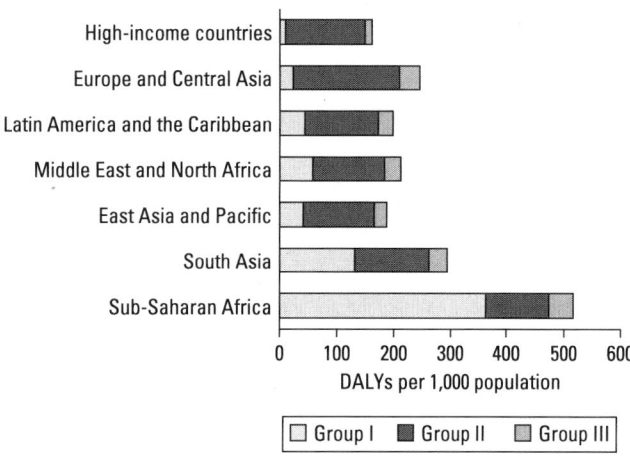

Figure 3.12 Burden of Disease by Broad Cause Group and Region, 2001

Source: Authors' calculations.

others 2000; Shkolnikov, McKee, and Leon 2001). Between 1994 and 1998, life expectancy for males improved, but declined again significantly between 1998 and 2001 (Men and others 2003).

While countries in Europe and Central Asia have a substantially higher burden of noncommunicable disease than high-income countries (figure 3.12), they also have a higher burden due to Group I causes and Group III causes. Indeed, countries in Europe and Central Asia have the highest proportion of the burden due to injuries of all the regions, 14 percent, followed by the Middle East and North Africa.

Leading Causes of the Burden of Disease in 2001

The 20 leading causes of burden of disease for both sexes together are shown in table 3.14. While the two leading causes of death, IHD and cerebrovascular disease, remain among the top four causes of the burden of disease, four nonfatal condi-

tions are also among the top 20 causes of burden: unipolar depressive disorders, adult-onset hearing loss, cataracts, and osteoarthritis. This once again illustrates the importance of taking nonfatal conditions into account, as well as deaths, when assessing the causes of loss of health in populations.

In 2001, the leading causes of the burden of disease in low- and middle-income countries were broadly similar to those for the world as a whole (table 3.15), and included six Group I causes among the top 10, but the leading causes in high- income countries consisted entirely of Group II conditions, including three (unipolar depressive disorders, adult-onset hearing loss, and alcohol use disorders) for which direct mortality is low.

Age and Sex Differences in the Burden of Disease

Measured in DALYs(3,0), children younger than 15 accounted for 36 percent of the world's total burden of disease and injury in 2001 and adults ages 15 to 59 accounted for almost 50 percent. Low- and middle-income countries accounted for the vast majority of the disease burden for children (figure 3.13). While the proportion of the total burden of disease borne by adults ages 15 to 59 was the same in both groups of countries, adults older than 60 accounted for a significantly larger share of the disease burden in high-income countries.

Although injuries become more important for boys beyond infancy, the causes of the burden of disease are broadly similar for boys and girls. However, striking gender differences emerge in adulthood. In low- and middle-income countries, 5 of the 10 leading causes of DALYs(3,0) for men ages 15 to 44 are injuries. Indeed, after HIV/AIDS, road traffic accidents were the second leading cause of the burden of disease for men in this age group. Other unintentional injuries and violence were the third and fourth

Table 3.14 The 20 Leading Causes of Global Burden of Disease, DALYs(3,0), 2001

Cause	DALYs (millions of years)	Percentage of total DALYs (3,0)	Cause	DALYs (millions of years)	Percentage of total DALYs (3,0)
1 Perinatal conditions	90.48	5.9	11 Road traffic accidents	35.06	2.3
2 Lower respiratory infections	85.92	5.6	12 Hearing loss, adult onset	29.99	2.0
3 Ischemic heart disease	84.27	5.5	13 Cataracts	28.64	1.9
4 Cerebrovascular disease	72.02	4.7	14 Congenital anomalies	24.95	1.6
5 HIV/AIDS	71.46	4.7	15 Measles	23.11	1.5
6 Diarrheal diseases	59.14	3.9	16 Self-inflicted injuries	20.26	1.3
7 Unipolar depressive disorders	51.84	3.4	17 Diabetes mellitus	20.00	1.3
8 Malaria	39.97	2.6	18 Violence	18.90	1.2
9 Chronic obstructive pulmonary disease	38.74	2.5	19 Osteoarthritis	17.45	1.1
10 Tuberculosis	36.09	2.3	20 Alzheimer's and other dementias	17.11	1.1

Source: Authors' calculations.

Table 3.15 The 10 Leading Causes of Burden of Disease, by Broad Income Group, 2001

Low- and middle-income countries			High-income countries		
Cause	DALYs (millions of years)	Percentage of total DALYs(3,0)	Cause	DALYs (millions of years)	Percentage of total DALYs(3,0)
1 Perinatal conditions	89.07	6.4	1 Ischemic heart disease	12.39	8.3
2 Lower respiratory infections	83.61	6.0	2 Cerebrovascular disease	9.35	6.3
3 Ischemic heart disease	71.88	5.2	3 Unipolar depressive disorders	8.41	5.6
4 HIV/AIDS	70.80	5.1	4 Alzheimer's and other dementias	7.47	5.0
5 Cerebrovascular disease	62.67	4.5	5 Trachea, bronchus, and lung cancers	5.40	3.6
6 Diarrheal diseases	58.70	4.2	6 Hearing loss, adult onset	5.39	3.6
7 Unipolar depressive disorders	43.43	3.1	7 Chronic obstructive pulmonary disease	5.28	3.5
8 Malaria	39.96	2.9	8 Diabetes mellitus	4.19	2.8
9 Tuberculosis	35.87	2.6	9 Alcohol use disorders	4.17	2.8
10 Chronic obstructive pulmonary disease	33.45	2.4	10 Osteoarthritis	3.79	2.5

Source: Authors' calculations.

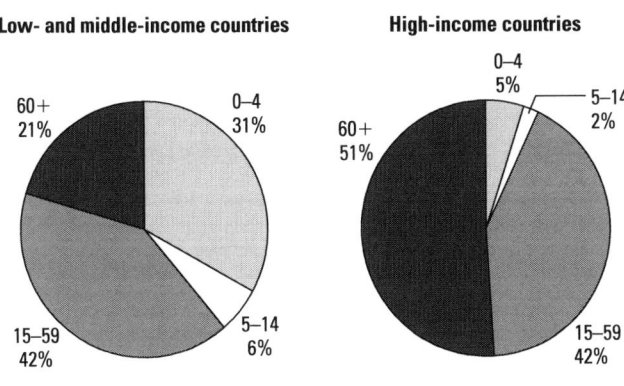

Source: Authors' calculations.

Note: The disease burden is measured in DALYs.

Figure 3.13 Age Distribution of Burden of Disease by Income Group, 2001

leading causes, with self-inflicted injuries and war also appearing in the top 10 causes. Injuries were also important for women ages 15 to 44, although road traffic accidents were the 10th leading cause, preceded by other unintentional injuries in 4th place and self-inflicted injuries in 6th place. Unipolar depressive disorders were the second leading cause of the burden for women in this age group, after HIV/AIDS.

The Growing Burden of Noncommunicable Diseases

The burden of noncommunicable diseases is increasing, accounting for nearly half the global burden of disease for all ages, a 10 percent increase from estimated levels in 1990. While the proportion of the burden from noncommunicable disease in high-income countries has remained stable at

around 85 percent in adults ages 15 and older, the proportion in middle-income countries has already exceeded 70 percent. Surprisingly, almost 50 percent of the adult disease burden in low- and middle-income countries is now attributable to noncommunicable disease. Population aging and changes in the distribution of risk factors have accelerated the epidemic of noncommunicable disease in many developing countries.

CVD accounted for 13 percent of the disease burden among adults ages 15 and older in 2001. IHD and cerebrovascular disease (stroke) were the two leading causes of mortality and the disease burden among adults ages 60 and older and were also among the top 10 causes of the disease burden in adults ages 15 to 59. In low- and middle income countries, IHD and cerebrovascular disease (stroke) were together responsible for 15 percent of the disease burden in those ages 15 and older, and DALYs(3,0) rates were higher for men than for women.

The proportion of the burden among adults ages 15 and older attributable to cancer was 6 percent in low- and middle income countries and 14 percent in high-income countries in 2001. Of the 7.1 million cancer deaths estimated to have occurred in that year, 17 percent, or 1.2 million, were attributable to lung cancer alone, and of these, three-quarters occurred among men. The number of cases of lung cancer increased nearly 30 percent since 1990, largely reflecting the emergence of the tobacco epidemic in low- and middle-income countries.

Stomach cancer, which until recently was the leading site of cancer mortality worldwide, has been declining in all parts of the world where trends can be reliably assessed, and in 2001 caused 842,000 deaths, or about two-thirds as many as lung cancer. Liver cancer was the third leading site, with

607,000 deaths in 2001, more than 60 percent of them in the East Asia and Pacific region. Among women, the leading cause of cancer deaths was breast cancer. Breast cancer survival rates have been improving during the past decade, but the chance of survival varies according to the coverage of and access to secondary prevention. Globally, neuropsychiatric conditions accounted for 19 percent of the disease burden among adults, primarily from nonfatal health outcomes.

Injuries: The Hidden Epidemic

Injuries, both unintentional and intentional, primarily affect young adults, and often result in severe, disabling sequelae. In 2001, injuries accounted for 16 percent of the adult burden of ill-health and premature death worldwide. In parts of Europe and Central Asia, Latin America and the Caribbean, and the Middle East and North Africa, more than 30 percent of the entire disease and injury burden among male adults ages 15 to 44 was attributable to injuries, and road traffic accidents, violence, and self-inflicted injuries were all among the top 10 leading causes of the burden of disease. Globally, road traffic accidents were the third leading cause of burden in the same age and sex group, preceded only by HIV/AIDS and unipolar depression. The burden of road traffic accidents has been increasing, especially in the developing countries of Sub-Saharan Africa and South and Southeast Asia, and particularly affects males.

Intentional injuries, which include self-inflicted injuries and suicide, violence, and war, accounted for an increasing share of the burden, especially among economically productive young adults. In developed countries, suicides accounted for the largest share of the intentional injury burden, whereas in developing regions, violence and war were the major sources. The former Soviet Union and other high-mortality countries of Eastern Europe have rates of death and disability resulting from injury among males that are similar to those in Sub-Saharan Africa.

Regional Variations in the Burden of Disease

The tables in annex 3C show estimated total DALYs(3,0) by age, sex, and cause in 2001 for each region and for the world as a whole. Table 3.16 summarizes the 10 leading causes of burden for each of the low- and middle-income regions.

In 2001, IHD and stroke dominated the burden of disease in Europe and Central Asia, and together accounted for more than a quarter of the total disease burden. In contrast, in Latin America and the Caribbean, these diseases accounted for 8 percent of disease burden. However, this region also had high levels of diabetes and endocrine disorders compared with other regions. Violence was the third leading cause of burden in Latin America and Caribbean countries, but did not reach the top 10 in any other region.

HIV/AIDS was the leading cause of the burden of disease in Sub-Saharan Africa, followed by malaria. Seven other Group I causes also appear in the top 10 causes for this region, with road traffic accidents being the only non-Group I cause.

Group I, II, and III causes all appear among the top 10 causes of the disease burden for the Middle East and North Africa. Of particular note, road traffic accidents were the third leading cause and congenital anomalies were the seventh leading cause.

Group I causes of the disease burden remained dominant in South Asia, and this burden fell particularly on children, but noncommunicable diseases such as IHD, stroke, and chronic obstructive pulmonary disease also featured in the list of top 10 causes.

In East Asia and the Pacific, stroke was the leading cause of disease burden in 2001, with IHD in fourth place, although Group I causes such as conditions arising during the perinatal period, TB, lower respiratory infections, and diarrheal diseases remained important.

DISCUSSION AND CONCLUSIONS

The analysis presented in this chapter has confirmed some of the conclusions of the original GBD study about the importance of including nonfatal outcomes in a comprehensive assessment of global population health, and has also confirmed the growing importance of noncommunicable diseases in low- and middle-income countries. However, it has also documented dramatic changes in population health in some regions since 1990. The key findings include the following:

- HIV/AIDS is now the fourth leading cause of the burden of disease globally and the leading cause in Sub-Saharan Africa.
- In low- and middle-income countries, the epidemiological transition has resulted in a 20 percent reduction in the per capita disease burden due to Group I causes since 1990. Without the HIV/AIDS epidemic, this reduction would have been closer to 30 percent. Several of the "traditional" infectious diseases, such as TB and malaria, have not declined, in part because of weak public health services and the increased numbers of people with immune systems weakened by HIV/AIDS.

Table 3.16 The 10 Leading Causes of the Burden of Disease in Low- and Middle-Income Countries, by Region, 2001

East Asia and Pacific	Percentage of total DALYs(3,0)	Europe and Central Asia	Percentage of total DALYs(3,0)
1 Cerebrovascular disease	7.5	1 Ischemic heart disease	15.9
2 Perinatal conditions	5.4	2 Cerebrovascular disease	10.8
3 Chronic obstructive pulmonary disease	5.0	3 Unipolar depressive disorders	3.7
4 Ischemic heart disease	4.1	4 Self-inflicted injuries	2.3
5 Unipolar depressive disorders	4.1	5 Hearing loss, adult onset	2.2
6 Tuberculosis	3.1	6 Chronic obstructive pulmonary disease	2.0
7 Lower respiratory infections	3.1	7 Trachea, bronchus, and lung cancers	2.0
8 Road traffic accidents	3.0	8 Osteoarthritis	2.0
9 Cataracts	2.8	9 Road traffic accidents	1.9
10 Diarrheal diseases	2.5	10 Poisonings	1.9

Latin America and the Caribbean	Percentage of total DALYs(3,0)	Middle East and North Africa	Percentage of total DALYs(3,0)
1 Perinatal conditions	6.0	1 Ischemic heart disease	6.6
2 Unipolar depressive disorders	5.0	2 Perinatal conditions	6.3
3 Violence	4.9	3 Road traffic accidents	4.6
4 Ischemic heart disease	4.2	4 Lower respiratory infections	4.5
5 Cerebrovascular disease	3.8	5 Diarrheal diseases	3.9
6 Endocrine disorders	3.0	6 Unipolar depressive disorders	3.1
7 Lower respiratory infections	2.9	7 Congenital anomalies	3.1
8 Alcohol use disorders	2.8	8 Cerebrovascular disease	3.0
9 Diabetes mellitus	2.7	9 Vision disorders, age-related	2.7
10 Road traffic accidents	2.6	10 Cataracts	2.3

South Asia	Percentage of total DALYs(3,0)	Sub-Saharan Africa	Percentage of total DALYs(3,0)
1 Perinatal conditions	9.2	1 HIV/AIDS	16.5
2 Lower respiratory infections	8.4	2 Malaria	10.3
3 Ischemic heart disease	6.3	3 Lower respiratory infections	8.8
4 Diarrheal diseases	5.4	4 Diarrheal diseases	6.4
5 Unipolar depressive disorders	3.6	5 Perinatal conditions	5.8
6 Tuberculosis	3.4	6 Measles	3.9
7 Cerebrovascular disease	3.2	7 Tuberculosis	2.3
8 Cataracts	2.3	8 Road traffic accidents	1.8
9 Chronic obstructive pulmonary disease	2.3	9 Pertussis	1.8
10 Hearing loss, adult onset	2.0	10 Protein-energy malnutrition	1.5

Source: Authors' calculations.

- The per capita disease burden in Europe and Central Asia increased by nearly 40 percent during 1990–2001, meaning that this region now has worse health than all other regions except South Asia and Sub-Saharan Africa. The unexpected increase in the disease burden, and the concomitant reduction in life expectancy, in countries of this region appear to be related to such factors as alcohol abuse, suicide, and violence, which seem to be associated with societies facing dramatic social and economic changes. The rapidity of these declines has dramatically changed our perceptions of the time frames within which substantial changes in the burden of chronic disease can occur and of the potential for such adverse health trends to occur elsewhere.

- Adults under the age of 70 in low- and middle-income countries face a greater risk of death from noncommunicable diseases than adults of the same age in high-income countries.

- In Europe and Central Asia, Latin America and the Caribbean, and the Middle East and North Africa, more than 30 percent of the entire disease burden among male adults ages 15 to 44 is attributable to injuries, including road traffic accidents, violence, and self-inflicted injuries. In addition, injury deaths are noticeably higher for women in some parts of Asia and the Middle East and North Africa than in other regions, partly because of high levels of suicide and violence. Combined with higher rates of infant and child mortality for girls, this results in a narrower differential between male and female healthy life expectancy than in any other region.

- Sense organ disorders, principally hearing and sight loss, contribute significantly to disability in all regions of the world.
- Levels of nonfatal health loss are proportionately greater in low- and middle-income countries than in high-income countries, contrary to the perception that disability is associated with older populations. The gap between healthy life expectancy and total life expectancy is proportionately highest for the low-income countries.

The analysis presented in this chapter has aimed to produce a comprehensive and detailed assessment of the global burden of disease, based on all available relevant data. It has attempted to maximize the use of high-quality, population-based data, and for regions and causes for which data are sparse has used the available evidence and the best available methods to make inferences and to assess the uncertainty in resulting estimates (see chapter 5). The need for internal consistency between estimates of incidence, prevalence, case fatality rates, and mortality rates for a given disease and for consistency across diseases and injuries with known total levels of mortality are crucial strategies for making the best use of multiple sources of uncertain and potentially biased data.

The data inputs used for the GBD 2001 estimation of global and regional causes of death have been summarized in tables 3.1, 3.2, and 3.5. In excess of 770 country-years of death registration data and more than 3,000 additional sources of information on levels of child and adult mortality and on specific causes of death were used to estimate global and regional patterns of mortality. Together with the more than 8,500 data sources used for the estimation of YLD, the GBD 2001 has incorporated information from more than 10,000 data sets relating to population health and mortality. This represents the largest synthesis of global information on population health carried out to date.

Despite the perceptions of some critics that the GBD study is inadequately empirically based for some regions, particularly Sub-Saharan Africa (Cooper and others 1998), it is notable that fully one-third of the more than 10,000 data sources used relate to Sub-Saharan African populations, albeit with the serious limitations on the information available on mortality noted earlier. We believe that the GBD studies have demonstrated the importance of including assessments of all causes of the disease and injury burden, even in the face of limited or missing data, to ensure that a comprehensive overview is provided to gain a better understanding of the importance of specific diseases and risk factors in causing loss of health. Otherwise, limitations in the evidence base for certain causes or regions might lead to their omission, and hence to the conclusion that they cause no burden, thereby presenting health decision makers with a misleading picture.

Nevertheless, the fact that estimates are possible does not obviate the need to put a higher priority on addressing the serious lack of information on levels of adult mortality and causes of death in some regions, particularly Sub-Saharan Africa. The key need for countries is to establish a system that registers the most common causes of death for the entire population without serious biases (such as an emphasis on urban mortality), in which there is reasonable confidence, and which yields timely data. Complete VR with annual population updates is the ideal system to generate this information, but it is not essential. Recent experience in countries such as China, India, and Tanzania suggests that sample registration based on a representative set of surveillance sites, and with appropriate controls and reporting procedures, can yield extremely useful information about levels, patterns, and causes of mortality for large populations (Setel and others 2005; Yang and others 2005). Low- and middle-income countries can benefit from the advantages of death registration without implementing a system of complete population coverage and medical certification (Rao, Bradshaw, and Mathers 2004). To support such systems, priority needs to be given to developing a standardized reporting form for verbal autopsies and to implementing validation studies to assess the reliability and accuracy of verbal autopsy methods.

Improved verbal autopsy methods will also contribute to improving the accuracy of estimates of the causes of child deaths under five, the majority of which occur in countries without useable death registration data. As discussed in chapters 5 and 6, new data and syntheses for major causes of child death may result in future revisions to the estimates of child deaths for certain causes.

There is also a lack of good population-based epidemiological data for developing regions, particularly for noncommunicable diseases. For example, even though IHD and stroke are among the leading causes of the burden of disease in most regions, few recent and reliable sources of information on the prevalence and severity distribution of chronic cardiovascular conditions and long-term disability following stroke are available outside the high-income countries. Similarly, even in high-income countries, few population-based studies of the prevalence of chronic lung disease or musculoskeletal conditions have been carried out.

Cross-national surveys, such as WHO's World Health Survey conducted during 2002 and 2003 in 73 countries, will fill some information gaps for some chronic diseases and mental disorders (Ustun, Chatterji, Mechbal, and others 2003). However, there remain significant issues that will need to be addressed relating to the comparability of prevalence data derived from self-reported survey data on symptoms of mental disorders, angina, and other chronic diseases.

Lack of information has resulted in limitations in the disease models used to estimate the burden of disease for some causes. Future iterations of burden of disease analysis will need to review disease models and sequelae chosen for estimating YLD to ensure that the best available estimates of the disease burden for each cause continue to remain based on current knowledge and data.

A particular difficulty is how to measure and characterize the average health states associated with sequelae. This is partly an issue of valuation of health states for the construction of disability weights, and partly an issue of lack of information on the population-level distribution of outcomes and the severity of health states. To a large extent, the disability weights used here derive from the original GBD study (Murray 1996), where typically an average disability weight was estimated for disease sequelae averaged across the distribution of outcomes, in some cases separately for treated and untreated cases. Stouthard and others (1997) have gone further in assessing disability weights for a range of severity levels of outcomes for a particular sequela, thereby allowing the overall final disability weight for a sequela to take account of regional variations in the severity distribution of outcomes.

The 2001 WHO Multicountry Survey Study collected health state valuation data on more than 500,000 health states from respondents in 71 countries, which Salomon and Murray (2004) used to construct a health state valuation function. The World Health Survey also included a health state valuation module, and analysis of the resulting data is under way (Salomon, Murray, and others 2003). In the next iteration of burden of disease analysis, it should be feasible to use health state valuations based on such survey data, together with descriptions of outcomes associated with disease sequelae, to produce updated disability weights that take into account not only the available information on health state distributions for disease sequelae, but also the health state preferences of people from all regions. A particular issue is the measurement of disability weights for low severity but highly prevalent conditions, such as anemia and hearing loss, where the current disability weights are small but quite uncertain and are multiplied by large prevalences (see chapter 5).

Burden of disease analysis provides a comprehensive, comparative overview of the state of population health and the factors affecting the health of populations. The 2001 GBD study is an expanded effort compared with the original 1990 study, with the incorporation of much new data and a greater understanding of the limitations of routinely available data sets. Nevertheless, substantial uncertainty remains about the comparative burden of diseases and injuries in many parts of the world that has significantly greater consequences for policy than the inclusion or otherwise of social choices such as age weighting in the basic burden of disease metric. We can conclude with some certainty that major causes of death and disability, such as tobacco and HIV/AIDS, are global pandemics and are likely to become more widespread unless control programs are more widely implemented. However, we remain substantially uncertain about the true levels of the disease burden from chronic lung disease, heart disease, stroke, mental disorders, various forms of injury, and a number of other key health concerns. International health agencies such as WHO and public health and epidemiological researchers need to make a concerted effort to improve data collection, and hence knowledge, about the true extent of the disease burden worldwide. Even efforts that substantially reduce uncertainty will be a major advance toward this goal.

With rising pressure on resources for health in all countries, priority setting in the health sector will increasingly depend on comprehensive, comparative information about the impact of diseases, injuries, and risk factors on population health. The burden of disease framework, with 15 years of development and application in numerous countries across the globe, offers the best, indeed the only, approach to comprehensively assess the impact of conditions and exposures that health systems need to deal with if population health is to improve rapidly. Yet to be even more useful for setting and monitoring global health priorities, a more concerted effort is needed to obtain and critically assess data sets on the health of populations in all countries. This must be a key focus of future efforts to assess the burden of disease. With WHO now giving greater emphasis to working with countries on capacity building and on specific organizational intervention priorities, new global partners such as the Ellison Institute for Global Health (Horton 2005) are urgently required to provide stewardship and guarantee that the evidence base for health policy and priority setting will develop at a pace commensurate with need.

ANNEX 3A: Definitions, Mortality Data Sources, and Disability Weights

Table 3A.1 Regional Reporting Categories for the Disease Control Priorities Project

Region	Countries included
East Asia and Pacific	American Samoa, Cambodia, China, Fiji, Indonesia, Kiribati, Democratic People's Republic of Korea, Lao People's Democratic Republic, Malaysia, Marshall Islands, Federated States of Micronesia, Mongolia, Myanmar, Palau, Papua New Guinea, Philippines, Samoa, Solomon Islands, Thailand, Timor-Leste, Tonga, Vanuatu, Vietnam
Europe and Central Asia	Albania, Armenia, Azerbaijan, Belarus, Bosnia and Herzegovina, Bulgaria, Croatia, Czech Republic, Estonia, Georgia, Hungary, Isle of Man, Kazakhstan, Kyrgyz Republic, Latvia, Lithuania, the former Yugoslav Republic of Macedonia, Moldova, Poland, Romania, Russian Federation, Serbia and Montenegro, Slovak Republic, Tajikistan, Turkey, Turkmenistan, Ukraine, Uzbekistan
High-income countries	Andorra, Aruba, Australia, Austria, The Bahamas, Bahrain, Belgium, Bermuda, Brunei Darussalam, Canada, Cayman Islands, Channel Islands, Cyprus, Denmark, Faeroe Islands, Finland, France, French Polynesia, Germany, Greece, Greenland, Guam, Iceland, Ireland, Israel, Italy, Japan, Kuwait, Liechtenstein, Luxembourg, Monaco, the Netherlands, Netherlands Antilles, New Caledonia, New Zealand, Northern Mariana Islands, Norway, Portugal, Qatar, Republic of Korea, San Marino, Singapore, Slovenia, Spain, Sweden, Switzerland, United Arab Emirates, United Kingdom, United States, U.S. Virgin Islands
Latin America and the Caribbean	Antigua and Barbuda, Argentina, Barbados, Belize, Bolivia, Brazil, Chile, Colombia, Costa Rica, Cuba, Dominica, Dominican Republic, Ecuador, El Salvador, Grenada, Guatemala, Guyana, Haiti, Honduras, Jamaica, Mexico, Nicaragua, Panama, Paraguay, Peru, Puerto Rico, St. Kitts and Nevis, St. Lucia, St. Vincent and the Grenadines, Suriname, Trinidad and Tobago, Uruguay, República Bolivariana de Venezuela
Middle East and North Africa	Algeria, Djibouti, Arab Republic of Egypt, Islamic Republic of Iran, Iraq, Jordan, Lebanon, Libya, Malta, Morocco, Oman, Saudi Arabia, Syrian Arab Republic, Tunisia, West Bank and Gaza, Republic of Yemen
South Asia	Afghanistan, Bangladesh, Bhutan, India, Maldives, Nepal, Pakistan, Sri Lanka
Sub-Saharan Africa	Angola, Benin, Botswana, Burkina Faso, Burundi, Cameroon, Cape Verde, Central African Republic, Chad, Comoros, Democratic Republic of Congo, Republic of Congo, Côte d'Ivoire, Equatorial Guinea, Eritrea, Ethiopia, Gabon, Gambia, Ghana, Guinea, Guinea-Bissau, Kenya, Lesotho, Liberia, Madagascar, Malawi, Mali, Mauritania, Mauritius, Mozambique, Namibia, Niger, Nigeria, Rwanda, São Tomé and Principe, Senegal, Seychelles, Sierra Leone, Somalia, South Africa, Sudan, Swaziland, Tanzania, Togo, Uganda, Zambia, Zimbabwe
Other	Anguilla, British Virgin Islands, Cook Islands, Falkland Islands, French Guiana, Gibraltar, Guadeloupe, Holy See (Vatican City), Martinique, Montserrat, Nauru, Niue, Pitcairn, Réunion, St. Helena, St. Pierre et Miquelon, Tokelau, Turks and Caicos Islands, Tuvalu, Wallis and Futuna Islands, Western Sahara

Source: Jamison and others 2006.

Table 3A.2 GBD Cause Categories and ICD Codes

Code	GBD cause name	ICD-9 code	ICD-10 code
U000	**All causes**		
U001	**I. Communicable, maternal, perinatal, and nutritional conditions**[a]	001–139, 243, 260– 269,*279.5,* 280–281, 285.9, 320–323, 381–382,460–465, 466, 480–487, 614–616, 630–676, 760–779	A00–B99, G00–G04, N70–N73, J00–J06, J10–J18, J20–J22, H65–H66, O00–O99, P00–P96, E00–E02, E40–E46, E50, D50–D53, D64.9, E51–64
U002	**A. Infectious and parasitic diseases**	001–139, *279.5,* 320–323, 614–616, 771.3	A00–B99, G00, G03–G04, N70–N73
U003	1. **Tuberculosis**	010–018, 137	A15–A19, B90
U004	2. **Sexually transmitted diseases excluding HIV/AIDS**	090–099, 614–616	A50–A64, N70–N73
U005	a. Syphilis	090–097	A50–A53
U006	b. Chlamydia	—	A55–A56
U007	c. Gonorrhea	098	A54
U008	d. Other sexually transmitted diseases	099, 614–616	A57–A64, N70–N73
U009	3. **HIV/AIDS**	279.5 (=042–044)	B20–B24
U010	4. **Diarrheal diseases**	001, 002, 004, 006–009	A00, A01, A03, A04, A06–A09
U011	5. **Childhood-cluster diseases**	032, 033, 037, 045, 055, 138, 771.3	A33–A37, A80, B05, B91
U012	a. Pertussis	033	A37
U013	b. Poliomyelitis	045, 138	A80, B91
U014	c. Diphtheria	032	A36
U015	d. Measles	055	B05
U016	e. Tetanus	037, 771.3	A33–A35
U017	6. **Meningitis**	036, 320–322	A39, G00, G03
U018	7. **Hepatitis B**	070.2–070.9	B16–B19 (minus B17.1, B18.2)
U019	**Hepatitis C**	—	B17.1, B18.2
U020	8. **Malaria**	084	B50–B54
U021	9. **Tropical-cluster diseases**	085, 086, 120, 125.0, 125.1, 125.3	B55–B57, B65, B73, B74.0–B74.2
U022	a. Trypanosomiasis	086.3, 086.4, 086.5,	B56
U023	b. Chagas' disease	086.0, 086.1, 086.2, 086.9	B57
U024	c. Schistosomiasis	120	B65
U025	d. Leishmaniasis	085	B55
U026	e. Lymphatic filariasis	125.0, 125.1	B74.0–B74.2
U027	f. Onchocerciasis	125.3	B73
U028	10. **Leprosy**	030	A30
U029	11. **Dengue**	061	A90–A91
U030	12. **Japanese encephalitis**	062.0	A83.0
U031	13. **Trachoma**	076	A71
U032	14. **Intestinal nematode infections**	126–129	B76–B81
U033	a. Ascariasis	127.0	B77
U034	b. Trichuriasis	127.3	B79
U035	c. Hookworm disease (Ancylostomiasis and necatoriasis)	126	B76
U036	Other intestinal infections	127.1, 127.2, 127.4–127.9, 128, 129	B78, B80, B81

(Continues on the following page.)

Table 3A.2 Continued

Code	GBD cause name	ICD-9 code	ICD-10 code
U037	Other infectious diseases	003, 005, 020–027, 031, 034, 035, 038–041, 046–049, 050–054, 056–057, 060, 062.1–066, 070.0–070.1, 071–075, 077–079, 080–083, 087–088, 100–104, 110–118, 121–124, 125.2, 125.4, 125.5, 125.6, 125.7, 125.9, 130–136, 139, 323	A02, A05, A20–A28, A31, A32, A38, A40–A49, A65–A70, A74–A79, A81, A82, A83.1–A83.9, A84–A89, A92–A99, B00–B04, B06–B15, B25–B49, B58–B60, B64, B66–B72, B74.3–B74.9, B75, B82–B89, B92–B99, G04
U038	**B. Respiratory infections**	460–466, 480–487, 381–382	J00–J06, J10–J18, J20–J22, H65–H66
U039	1. Lower respiratory infections	466, 480–487	J10–J18, J20–J22
U040	2. Upper respiratory infections	460–465	J00–J06
U041	3. Otitis media	381–382	H65–H66
U042	**C. Maternal conditions**	630–676	O00–O99
U043	1. Maternal hemorrhage	640, 641, 666	O44–O46, O67, O72
U044	2. Maternal sepsis	670	O85–O86
U045	3. Hypertensive disorders of pregnancy	642	O10–O16
U046	4. Obstructed labor	660	O64–O66
U047	5. Abortion	630–639	O00–O07
U048	Other maternal conditions	643–659, 661–665, 667–669, 671–676	O20–O043, O47–O063, O68–O071, O73–O075, O87–O99
U049	**D. Conditions arising during the perinatal period**	760–779 (minus 771.3)	P00–P96
U050	1. Low birthweight	764–765	P05–P07
U051	2. Birth asphyxia and birth trauma	767–770	P03, P10–P15, P20–P29
U052	Other perinatal conditions	760–763, 766, 771 (minus 771.3), 772–779	P00–P02, P04, P08, P35–P96
U053	**E. Nutritional deficiencies**	243, 260–269, 280–281, 285.9	E00–E02, E40–E46, E50, D50–D53, D64.9, E51–E64
U054	1. Protein-energy malnutrition	260–263	E40–E46
U055	2. Iodine deficiency	243	E00–E02
U056	3. Vitamin A deficiency	264	E50
U057	4. Iron-deficiency anemia	280, 285.9	D50, D64.9
U058	Other nutritional disorders	265–269, 281	D51–D53, E51–E64
U059	**II. Noncommunicable diseases**[a]	140–242, 244–259, 270–279 (minus 279.5), 282–285 (minus 285.9), 286–319, 324–380, 383–459, 470–478, 490–611, 617–629, 680–759	C00–C97, D00–D48, D55–D64 (minus D 64.9) D65–D89, E03–E07, E10–E16, E20–E34, E65–E88, F01–F99, G06–G98, H00–H61, H68–H93, I00–I99, J30–J98, K00–K92, N00–N64, N75–N98, L00–L98, M00–M99, Q00–Q99
U060	**A. Malignant neoplasms**	140–208	C00–C97
U061	1. Mouth and oropharynx cancers[b]	140–149	C00–C14
U062	2. Esophageal cancer[b]	150	C15
U063	3. Stomach cancer[b]	151	C16
U064	4. Colon and rectal cancers[b]	153–154	C18–C21
U065	5. Liver cancer	155	C22
U066	6. Pancreas cancer	157	C25
U067	7. Trachea, bronchus, and lung cancers	162	C33–C34
U068	8. Melanoma and other skin cancers[b]	172–173	C43–C44
U069	9. Breast cancer[b]	174–175	C50
U070	10. Cervix uteri cancer[b]	180	C53

Table 3A.2 Continued

Code	GBD cause name	ICD-9 code	ICD-10 code
U071	11. Corpus uteri cancer[b]	179, 182	C54–C55
U072	12. Ovarian cancer	183	C56
U073	13. Prostate cancer[b]	185	C61
U074	14. Bladder cancer[b]	188	C67
U075	15. Lymphomas and multiple myeloma[b]	200–203	C81–C90, C96
U076	16. Leukemia[b]	204–208	C91–C95
U077	Other malignant neoplasms[b]	152, 156, 158–161, 163–171, 181, 184, 186–187, 189–199	C17, C23, C24, C26–C32, C37–C41, C45–C49, C51, C52, C57–C60, C62–C66, C68–C80, C97
U078	**B. Other neoplasms**	210–239	D00–D48
U079	**C. Diabetes mellitus**	250	E10–E14
U080	**D. Endocrine disorders**	240–242, 244–246, 251–259, 270–279 (minus 274, 279.5), 282–285 (minus 285.9), 286–289	D55–D64 (minus D64.9), D65–D89, E03–E07, E15–E16, E20–E34, E65–E88
U081	**E. Neuropsychiatric conditions**	290–319, 324–359	F01–F99, G06–G98
U082	1. Unipolar depressive disorders	296.1, 311	F32–F33
U083	2. Bipolar affective disorder	296 (minus 296.1)	F30–F31
U084	3. Schizophrenia	295	F20–F29
U085	4. Epilepsy	345	G40–G41
U086	5. Alcohol use disorders	291, 303, 305.0	F10
U087	6. Alzheimer's disease and other dementias	290, 330, 331	F01, F03, G30–G31
U088	7. Parkinson's disease	332	G20–G21
U089	8. Multiple sclerosis	340	G35
U090	9. Drug use disorders	304, 305.2–305.9	F11–F16, F18–F19
U091	10. Post-traumatic stress disorder	308–309	F43.1
U092	11. Obsessive-compulsive disorder	300.3	F42
U093	12. Panic disorder	300.2	F40.0, F41.0
U094	13. Insomnia (primary)	307.4	F51
U095	14. Migraine	346	G43
U096	15. Mental retardation, lead-caused	317–319	F70–F79
U097	Other neuropsychiatric disorders	292–294, 297–300.1, 300.4–302, 305.1, 306–307 (minus 307.4), 310, 312–316, 324–326, 333–337, 341–344, 347–349, 350–359	F04–F09, F17, F34–F39, F401–F409, F411–F419, F43 (minus F43.1), F44–F50, F52–F69, F80–F99, G06–G12, G23–G25, G36, G37, G44–G98
U098	**F. Sense organ diseases**	360–380, 383–389	H00–H61, H68–H93
U099	1. Glaucoma	365	H40
U100	2. Cataracts	366	H25–H26
U101	3. Vision disorders, age-related	367.4	H524
U102	4. Hearing loss, adult onset	389	H90–H91
U103	Other sense organ disorders	360–364, 367–380 (minus 367.4), 383–388	H00–H21, H27–H35, H43–H61 (minus H524), H68–H83, H92–H93
U104	**G. Cardiovascular diseases**	390–459	I00–I99
U105	1. Rheumatic heart disease	390–398	I01–I09
U106	2. Hypertensive heart disease	401–405	I10–I13
U107	3. Ischemic heart disease[c]	410–414	I20–I25
U108	4. Cerebrovascular disease	430–438	I60–I69
U109	5. Inflammatory heart diseases	420, 421, 422, 425	I30–I33, I38, I40, I42

(Continues on the following page.)

Table 3A.2 Continued

Code	GBD cause name	ICD-9 code	ICD-10 code
U110	Other cardiovascular diseases[c]	415–417, 423–424, 426–429, 440–448, 451–459	I00, I26–I28, I34–I37, I44–I51, I70–I99
U111	**H. Respiratory diseases**	470–478, 490–519	J30–J98
U112	1. Chronic obstructive pulmonary disease	490–492, 495–496	J40–J44
U113	2. Asthma	493	J45–J46
U114	Other respiratory diseases	470–478, 494, 500–508, 510–519	J30–J39, J47–J98
U115	**I. Digestive diseases**	530–579	K20–*K92*
U116	1. Peptic ulcer disease	531–533	K25–K27
U117	2. Cirrhosis of the liver	571	K70, K74
U118	3. Appendicitis	540–543	K35–K37
U119	Other digestive diseases	530, 534–537, 550–553, 555–558, 560–570, 572–579	K20–K22, K28–K31, K38, K40–K66, K71–K73, K75–K92
U120	**J. Genitourinary diseases**	580–611, 617–629	N00–N64, N75–N98
U121	1. Nephritis and nephrosis	580–589	N00–N19
U122	2. Benign prostatic hypertrophy	600	N40
U123	Other genitourinary system diseases	590–599, 601–611, 617–629	N20–N39, N41–N64, N75–N98
U124	**K. Skin diseases**	680–709	L00–L98
U125	**L. Musculoskeletal diseases**	710–739, 274	M00–M99
U126	1. Rheumatoid arthritis	714	M05–M06
U127	2. Osteoarthritis	715	M15–M19
U128	3. Gout	274	M10
U129	4. Low back pain	720–724 (minus 721.1, 722.0, 722.4)	M45–M48, M54 (minus M54.2)
U130	Other musculoskeletal disorders	710–713, 716–719, 721.1, 722.0, 722.4, 723, 725–739	M00–M02, M08, M11–M13, M20–M43, M50–M53, M54.2, M55–M99
U131	**M. Congenital anomalies**	740–759	Q00–Q99
U132	1. Abdominal wall defect	756.7	Q79.2–Q79.5
U133	2. Anencephaly	740.0	Q00
U134	3. Anorectal atresia	751.2	Q42
U135	4. Cleft lip	749.1	Q36
U136	5. Cleft palate	749.0	Q35, Q37
U137	6. Esophageal atresia	750.3	Q39.0–Q39.1
U138	7. Renal agenesis	753.0	Q60
U139	8. Down syndrome	758.0	Q90
U140	9. Congenital heart anomalies	745–747	Q20–Q28
U141	10. Spina bifida	741	Q05
U142	Other congenital anomalies	740.1, 740.2, 742–744, 748, 749.2, 750.0, 750.1, 750.2, 750.4–751.1, 751.3–751.9, 752, 753.1–753.9, 754, 755, 756.0–756.6, 756.8, 756.9, 757, 758.1–758.9, 759	Q01–Q04, Q06–Q18, Q30–Q34, Q38, Q392–Q399, Q40–Q41, Q43–Q56, Q61–Q78, Q790, Q791, Q796, Q798, Q799, Q80–Q89, Q91–Q99
U143	**N. Oral conditions**	520–529	K00–K14
U144	1. Dental caries	521.0	K02
U145	2. Periodontal disease	523	K05
U146	3. Edentulism	—	—
U147	Other oral diseases	520, 521.1–521.9, 522, 524–529	K00, K01, K03, K04, K06–K14

Code	GBD Cause Name	ICD-9 code	ICD-10 code
U148	**III. Injuries**	E800–999	V01–Y89
U149	**A. Unintentional injuries**[d]	E800–949	V01–X59, Y40–Y86, Y88, Y89
U150	1. Road traffic accidents	E810–819, E826–829, E929.0	[e]
U151	2. Poisonings	E850–869	X40–X49
U152	3. Falls	E880–888	W00–W19
U153	4. Fires	E890–899	X00–X09
U154	5. Drownings	E910	W65–W74
U155	6. Other unintentional injuries	E800–E807, E820–E848, E870–E879, E900–E909, E911–E949	Rest of V, W20–W64, W75–W99, X10–X39, X50–X59, Y40–Y86, Y88, Y89
U156	**B. Intentional injuries**[d]	E950–978, 990–999	X60–Y09, Y35–Y36, Y870, Y871
U157	1. Self-inflicted injuries	E950–959	X60–X84, Y870
U158	2. Violence	E960–969	X85–Y09, Y871
U159	3. War	E990–999	Y36
U160	Other intentional injuries	E970–E978	Y35

Source: Mathers, Lopez and others 2004.

a. Deaths coded to "Symptoms, signs and ill-defined conditions" (780–799 in ICD-9 and R00–R99 in ICD-10) are distributed proportionately to all causes within Group I and Group II.

b. Cancer deaths coded to ICD categories for malignant neoplasms of other and unspecified sites including those whose point of origin cannot be determined, and secondary and unspecified neoplasms (ICD-10 C76, C80, C97 or ICD-9 195, 199) were redistributed pro rata across the footnoted malignant neoplasm categories within each age-sex group, so that the category "Other malignant neoplasms" includes only malignant neoplasms of other specified sites.

c. Ischemic heart disease deaths may be miscoded to a number of so-called cardiovascular "garbage" codes. These include heart failure, ventricular dysrhythmias, generalized atherosclerosis, and ill-defined descriptions and complications of heart disease. Proportions of deaths coded to these causes were redistributed to ischemic heart disease as described by Lozano and others (2001). Relevant ICD-9 codes are 427.1, 427.4, 427.5, 428, 429.0, 429.1, 429.2, 429.9, 440.9; relevant ICD-10 codes are I47.2, I49.0, I46, I50, I51.4, I51.5, I51.6, I51.9, I70.9.

d. Injury deaths where the intent is not determined (E980–989 of ICD-9 and Y10–Y34, Y872 in ICD-10) are distributed proportionately to all causes below the group level for injuries.

e. For countries with three-digit ICD-10 data, use: V01–V04, V06, V09–V80, V87, V89, V99. For countries with four-digit ICD-10 data, use: V01.1–V01.9, V02.1–V02.9, V03.1–V03.9, V04.1–V04.9, V06.1–V06.9, V09.2, V09.3, V10.4–V10.9, V11.4–V11.9, V12.3–V12.9, V13.3–V13.9, V14.3–V14.9, V15.4–V15.9, V16.4–V16.9, V17.4–V17.9, V18.4–V18.9, V19.4–V19.6, V20.3–V20.9, V21.3–V21.9, V22.3–V22.9, V23.3–V23.9, V24.3–V24.9, V25.3–V25.9, V26.3–V26.9, V27.3–V27.9, V28.3–V28.9, V29.4–V29.9, V30.4.V30.9, V31.4–V31.9, V32.4–V32.9, V33.4–V33.9, V34.4–V34.9, V35.4–V35.9, V36.4–V36.9, V37.4–V37.9, V38.4–V38.9, V39.4–V39.9, V40.4–V40.9, V41.4–V41.9, V42.4–V42.9, V43.4–V43.9, V44.4–V44.9, V45.4–V45.9, V46.4–V46.9, V47.4–V47.9, V48.4–V48.9, V49.4–V49.9, V50.4–V50.9, V51.4–V51.9, V52.4–V52.9, V53.4–V53.9, V54.4–V54.9, V55.4–V55.9, V56.4–V56.9, V57.4–V57.9, V58.4–V58.9, V59.4–V59.9, V60.4–V60.9, V61.4–V61.9, V62.4–V62.9, V63.4–V63.9, V64.4–V64.9, V65.4–V65.9, V66.4–V66.9, V67.4–V67.9, V68.4–V68.9, V69.4–V69.9, V70.4–V70.9, V71.4–V71.9, V72.4–V72.9, V73.4–V73.9, V74.4–V74.9, V75.4–V75.9, V76.4–V76.9, V77.4–V77.9, V78.4–V78.9, V79.4–V79.9, V80.3–V80.5, V81.1, V82.1, V83.0–V83.3, V84.0–V84.3, V85.0–V85.3, V86.0–V86.3, V87.0–V87.8, V89.2, V89.9, V99, Y850.

Table 3A.3 Data Sources and Methods for Estimation of Mortality by Cause, Age, and Sex

Country	Vital registration data	Year used	Other sources of information	Method	Cause of death distribution pattern used
Afghanistan			a	CodMod	Arab Rep. of Egypt 2000, Islamic Rep. of Iran 2001
Albania	1987–9, 1992–2000	2000	a	CodMod	2000
Algeria			a	CodMod	South Africa 1996
Andorra			b	Based on 2000 data from Aragon, Navarra, and Cataluna provinces of Spain	
Angola			a	CodMod	South Africa 1996
Antigua and Barbuda	1961–4, 1966, 1969–78, 1983, 1985–95	1993–5	c	Vital registration	Vital registration
Argentina	1966–70, 1977–2001	2001	b	Vital registration	Vital registration
Armenia	1981–2, 1985–2001	2001	a	CodMod	2001
Australia	1950–2000	2000	b	Vital registration	Vital registration
Austria	1955–2001	2001	b	Vital registration	Vital registration
Azerbaijan	1981–2, 1985–2001	2001	a	CodMod	2001
Bahamas, The	1969, 1971–2, 1974–7, 1979–81, 1983–5, 1987, 1993–8	1996–8	c	Vital registration	Vital registration
Bahrain	1985, 1987–8, 1997–2001	2000–1	b	Vital registration	Vital registration
Bangladesh			a	CodMod	India, Philippines
Barbados	1955–95	1993–5	Preliminary vital registration data for 2000c	Vital registration	Vital registration
Belarus	1981–2, 1985–2001	2001	c	Vital registration	Vital registration
Belgium	1954–97	1997	b	Vital registration	Vital registration
Belize	1964–84, 1986–7, 1989–91, 1993–8	1997–8	c	Vital registration	Vital registration
Benin			a	CodMod	South Africa 1996
Bhutan			a	CodMod	India
Bolivia			a	CodMod	Peru 2000
Bosnia and Herzegovina	1985–91, 1999	1999	c	Vital registration	Vital registration
Botswana	1995–8		a	CodMod	South Africa 1996
Brazil	1977–2000	2000	a	CodMod	2000
Brunei Darussalam	1996–2000	1998–2000	b	Vital registration	Vital registration
Bulgaria	1964–2001	2001	c	Vital registration	Vital registration
Burkina Faso			a	CodMod	South Africa 1996
Burundi			a	CodMod	South Africa 1996
Cambodia			a	CodMod	Philippines, Thailand
Cameroon			a	CodMod	South Africa 1996
Canada	1950–2000	2000	b	Vital registration	Vital registration
Cape Verde	1980		a	CodMod	South Africa 1996
Central African Republic			a	CodMod	South Africa 1996
Chad			a	CodMod	South Africa 1996
Chile	1954–99	1999	Preliminary vital registration data for 2000b	Vital registration	Vital registration

Table 3A.3 Continued

Country	Vital registration data	Year used	Other sources of information	Method	Cause of death distribution pattern used
China	1987–2000	2000	DSP[a]	Vital registration	Vital registration
Colombia	1953–70, 1972, 1974–7, 1979, 1981, 1984–99	1999	[a]	CodMod	1999
Comoros			[a]	CodMod	South Africa 1996
Congo, Dem. Rep. of			[a]	CodMod	South Africa 1996
Congo, Rep. of			[a]	CodMod	South Africa 1996
Cook Islands	1995–2001	1999–2001	[a]	Vital registration	Vital registration
Costa Rica	1956–2002	2002	[b]	Vital registration	Vital registration
Côte d'Ivoire			Abidjan, 1973–92: deaths assessed by medical personnel in city hospitals. Source: ENSEA, Abidjan[a]	CodMod	South Africa 1996
Croatia	1985–2001	2001	[b]	Vital registration	Vital registration
Cuba	1959, 1964–5, 1968–2001	2001	[b]	Vital registration	Vital registration
Cyprus	1996–9	1997–9	[a]	CodMod	1997–9
Czech Republic	1985–2001	2001	[b]	Vital registration	Vital registration
Denmark	1951–99	1999	[b]	Vital registration	Vital registration
Djibouti			[a]	CodMod	Arab Rep. of Egypt 2000, Islamic Rep. of Iran 2000
Dominica	1961–2, 1967–94	1992–4	[c]	Vital registration	Vital registration
Dominican Republic	1956–63, 1965–92, 1994–8	1998	[a]	CodMod	1998
Ecuador	1961, 1963–75, 1977–2000	2000	[a]	CodMod	2000
Egypt, Arab Rep. of	1954–67, 1970–80, 1987, 1991–2, 1996–2000	2000	[a]	CodMod	2000
El Salvador	1950–74, 1981–4, 1990–3, 1995–9	1999	[a]	CodMod	1999
Equatorial Guinea			[a]	CodMod	South Africa 1996
Eritrea	1998–9		[a]	CodMod	South Africa 1996
Estonia	1981–2, 1985–2001	2001	[b]	Vital registration	Vital registration
Ethiopia			[a]	CodMod	South Africa 1996
Fiji	1978, 1992–7, 1999–2000	2000	[a]	Vital registration	Vital registration
Finland	1952–2001	2001	[b]	Vital registration	Vital registration
France	1950–99	1999	[b]	Vital registration	Vital registration
Gabon			[a]	CodMod	South Africa 1996
Gambia, The			[a]	CodMod	South Africa 1996
Georgia	1981–2, 1985–92, 1994–2000	2000	[a]	CodMod	2000
Germany	1969–2000	2000	[b]	Vital registration	Vital registration
Ghana			Hospital mortality data for Eastern Region, 1990–2000[a]	CodMod	South Africa 1996
Greece	1956–99	1999	[b]	Vital registration	Vital registration
Grenada	1974–8, 1984, 1988, 1994–6	1994–6	[c]	Vital registration	Vital registration

(Continues on the following page.)

Table 3A.3 Continued

Country	Vital registration data	Year used	Other sources of information	Method	Cause of death distribution pattern used
Guatemala	1958–71, 1974–81, 1984	1996	Preliminary vital registration data for 1996[a]	CodMod	1996
Guinea			[a]	CodMod	South Africa 1996
Guinea-Bissau			[a]	CodMod	South Africa 1996
Guyana	1975–7, 1979, 1984, 1988, 1990, 1993–6	1994–6	[c]	Vital registration	Vital registration
Haiti	1980–1, 1983, 1997, 1999	1999	[a]	CodMod	1999
Honduras	1966, 1968–83		[a]	CodMod	Nicaragua, El Salvador, Guatemala
Hungary	1955–2001	2001	[b]	Vital registration	Vital registration
Iceland	1951–99	1997–9	[b]	Vital registration	Vital registration
India	Survey of Cause of Death (Rural)	1996–8	Urban Medical Certification of Cause of Death System, 1995[a]	Proportionate mortality for urban and rural summed up to national estimate	Cause of death information from urban and rural data sources
Indonesia			[a]	CodMod	Singapore, India, Thailand, Philippines
Iran, Islamic Rep. of	1999–2001	2001	[a]	CodMod	2001 (18 provinces' mortality data)
Iraq			[a]	CodMod	Arab Rep. of Egypt 2000, Islamic Rep. of Iran 2001
Ireland	1950–2000	2000	[c]	Vital registration	Vital registration
Israel	1975–98	1998	[b]	Vital registration	Vital registration
Italy	1951–99	1999	[b]	Vital registration	Vital registration
Jamaica	1960–1, 1964–5, 1967–71, 1975, 1977, 1980–91	1991	[a]	CodMod	1991
Japan	1950–2000	2000	[b]	Vital registration	Vital registration
Jordan	1959–60, 1962–6, 1968, 1970–5, 1978–9		Mortality and causes of death in Jordan 1995–6: assessment by verbal autopsy. Source: S.A. Khoury, D. Massad, and T. Fardous, *Bulletin of the World Health Organization* 77(8)[a]	Verbal autopsy data	Verbal autopsy data
Kazakhstan	1981–2, 1985–2001	2001	[a]	CodMod	2001
Kenya			Ministry of Health, hospital data, 1996, 1998–2000[a]	CodMod	South Africa 1996
Kiribati	1999–2002	2000–2	Ministry of Health, Family Planning and Social Welfare, Third National Health, Family Planning and Social Welfare Plan 1992–5[a]	Vital registration	2000–2
Korea, Democratic People's Rep. of			[a]	CodMod	Philippines, India
Korea, Rep. of	1985–2001	2001	[b]	Vital registration	Vital registration
Kuwait	1972, 1975–87, 1993–2001	1999–2001	[b]	Vital registration	Vital registration
Kyrgyz Republic	1981–2, 1985–2001	2001	[a]	CodMod	2001
Lao PDR			[a]	CodMod	Philippines, Thailand

Table 3A.3 Continued

Country	Vital registration data	Year used	Other sources of information	Method	Cause of death distribution pattern used
Latvia	1980–2001	2001	b	Vital registration	Vital registration
Lebanon	1997–9		a	CodMod	Arab Rep. of Egypt 2000, Islamic Rep. of Iran 2001
Lesotho			a	CodMod	South Africa 1996
Liberia			a	CodMod	South Africa 1996
Libya			a	CodMod	Arab Rep. of Egypt 2000, Islamic Rep. of Iran 2001
Lithuania	1981–2, 1985–2001	2001	b	Vital registration	Vital registration
Luxembourg	1955–62, 1965–2001	1999–2001	b	Vital registration	Vital registration
Macedonia, FYR	1991–2000	2000	c	Vital registration	Vital registration
Madagascar			Antananarivo, 1976–95: deaths certified by medical personnel. Source: CEPED, Paris[a]	CodMod	South Africa 1996
Malawi			a	CodMod	South Africa 1996
Malaysia	1986, 1990–8		a	CodMod	Singapore, China, Thailand
Maldives			a	CodMod	India, Philippines
Mali			a	CodMod	South Africa 1996
Malta	1955–2001	1999–2001	b	Vital registration	Vital registration
Marshall Islands			a		Cook Islands, Marshall Islands, Niue, Samoa, Tonga, Tuvalu, Vanuatu, Kiribati, Nauru, Fiji
Mauritania			a	CodMod	South Africa 1996
Mauritius	1957–2000	1998–2000	c	Vital registration	Vital registration
Mexico	1955–2001	2001	b	Vital registration	Vital registration
Micronesia, Federated States of			1999 Federated States of Micronesia Statistical Yearbook[a]		Cook Islands, Marshall Islands, Niue, Samoa, Tonga, Tuvalu, Vanuatu, Kiribati, Nauru, Fiji
Moldova	1981–2, 1985–2001	2001	b	Vital registration	Vital registration
Monaco			b		Based on 1998 data from Provence Alpes Côte d'Azur, Department of France
Mongolia	1990–2000	2000	a	CodMod	2000
Morocco	1990–7		a	CodMod	Arab Rep. of Egypt 2000, Islamic Rep. of Iran 2001
Mozambique			a	CodMod	Zimbabwe 1995, South Africa 1996
Myanmar	1977–8		a	CodMod	Philippines, India
Namibia			a	CodMod	South Africa 1996
Nauru	1994–6	1994–6	Mortality decline in Nauru. Source: R. Taylor and K. Thoma, unpublished 1998[a]	Vital registration	1994–6
Nepal			a	CodMod	Philippines, India
Netherlands	1950–2000	2000	b	Vital registration	Vital registration

(Continues on the following page.)

Table 3A.3 Continued

Country	Vital registration data	Year used	Other sources of information	Method	Cause of death distribution pattern used
New Zealand	1950–99	1999	[b]	Vital registration	Vital registration
Nicaragua	1959, 1961–5, 1968–9, 1973–8, 1988–94, 1996–2000	2000	[a]	CodMod	2000
Niger			[a]	CodMod	South Africa 1996
Nigeria			[a]	CodMod	South Africa 1996
Niue	1995–2000	1998–2000	[a]	Vital registration	Vital registration
Norway	1951–2000	2000	[b]	Vital registration	Vital registration
Oman	1997		[a]	CodMod	Bahrain, Kuwait, 1997–2001
Pakistan			[a]	CodMod	India
Palau			[a]		Cook Islands, Marshall Islands, Niue, Samoa, Tonga, Tuvalu, Vanuatu, Kiribati, Nauru, Fiji
Panama	1954–89, 1996–2000	2000	[a]	CodMod	2000
Papua New Guinea	1977, 1980		[a]	CodMod	Philippines, India
Paraguay	1961–3, 1965–91, 1994, 1996–2000	2000	[a]	CodMod	2000
Peru	1966–73, 1977–8, 1980–3, 1986–92, 1994–2000	2000	[a]	CodMod	2000
Philippines	1963–78, 1981, 1992–8	1998	[a]	CodMod	1998
Poland	1959–2001	2001	[b]	Vital registration	Vital registration
Portugal	1955–2000	2000	[b]	Vital registration	Vital registration
Qatar	1995, 2000–1	2001	[a]	CodMod	2001
Romania	1959–2001	2001	[b]	Vital registration	Vital registration
Russian Federation	1980–2001	2001	[c]	Vital registration	Vital registration
Rwanda			[a]	CodMod	South Africa 1996
St. Kitts and Nevis	1961–3, 1965–7, 1969–95	1993–5	[c]	Vital registration	Vital registration
St. Lucia	1968–81, 1983, 1986–95	1993–5	[c]	Vital registration	Vital registration
St. Vincent and the Grenadines	1970–2, 1974, 1977, 1979, 1982–7, 1995–9	1997–9	[c]	Vital registration	Vital registration
Samoa			Department of Health Statistics, Demographic and Health Survey, 1999 and 2000[a]		Cook Islands, Marshall Islands, Niue, Samoa, Tonga, Tuvalu, Vanuatu, Kiribati, Nauru, Fiji
San Marino	1995–2000	1998–2000	[b]	Vital registration	Vital registration
São Tomé and Principe	1984–5, 1987		[a]	CodMod	South Africa 1996
Saudi Arabia			[a]	CodMod	Bahrain, Kuwait, 1997–2001
Senegal			Niakhar 1983–90: deaths assessed by verbal autopsy. Source: CEPED, Paris[a]	CodMod	South Africa 1996

Country	Vital registration data	Year used	Other sources of information	Method	Cause of death distribution pattern used
Serbia and Montenegro	2000	2000	b	Vital registration	Vital registration
Seychelles	1981–2, 1985–7, 1997–2000	1998–2000	b	Vital registration	Vital registration
Sierra Leone			a	CodMod	South Africa 1996
Singapore	1955–2001	2001	c	Vital registration	Vital registration
Slovak Republic	1992–2001	2001	b	Vital registration	Vital registration
Slovenia	1985–2001	2001	b	Vital registration	Vital registration
Solomon Islands			a		Cook Islands, Marshall Islands, Niue, Samoa, Tonga, Tuvalu, Vanuatu, Kiribati, Nauru, Fiji
Somalia			a	CodMod	Arab Rep. of Egypt 2000, South Africa 1996
South Africa	1993–6	1996	National Injury Mortality Surveillance System. Summary Report 2000; K. Kahn, S. M. Tollman, M. Garenne, and J. S. Gear, "Causes of Death in a Rural Area of South Africa: An International Perspective, Journal of Tropical Pediatrics, 46 (June)[c]; and Violence and Injury Surveillance Consortium, Rapid Assessment of Trauma Facilities at State Hospitals in South Africa, 2000[a]	CodMod	South Africa 1996
Spain	1951–2000	2000	b	Vital registration	Vital registration
Sri Lanka	1950–68, 1977, 1980–9, 1991–2, 1995–6	1996	a	CodMod	1996
Sudan			a	CodMod	Arab Rep. of Egypt 2000, South Africa 1996
Suriname	1963–6, 1971–3, 1975–82, 1984–92	1990–2	a	Vital registration	Vital registration
Swaziland			a	CodMod	South Africa 1996
Sweden	1951–2000	2000	b	Vital registration	Vital registration
Switzerland	1951–99	1999	b	Vital registration	Vital registration
Syrian Arab Republic	1973–8, 1980–1, 1984–5, 2000–1	2001	a	CodMod	2001
Tajikistan	1981–2, 1985–95, 1999	1999	a	CodMod	1999
Tanzania			a	CodMod	Zimbabwe 1995, South Africa 1996
Thailand	1955–87, 1990–2000	2000	Ministry of Health, verbal autopsy study[a]	Vital registration corrected by verbal autopsy study	
Timor-Leste			a	CodMod	India, Philippines
Togo			a	CodMod	South Africa 1996

(Continues on the following page.)

Table 3A.3 Continued

Country	Vital registration data	Year used	Other sources of information	Method	Cause of death distribution pattern used
Tonga	1998	1998	Report of the Minister of Health for 1994	Vital registration	Vital registration
Trinidad and Tobago	1951–98	1996–8	b	Vital registration	Vital registration
Tunisia			a	CodMod	Arab Rep. of Egypt 2000, Islamic Rep. of Iran 2001
Turkey	1987–98	1998	a	CodMod	1998
Turkmenistan	1981–2, 1985–98	1998	a	CodMod	1998
Tuvalu			a		Cook Islands, Marshall Islands, Niue, Samoa, Tonga, Tuvalu, Vanuatu, Kiribati, Nauru, Fiji
Uganda			a	CodMod	South Africa 1996
Ukraine	1981–2, 1985–2000	2000	c	Vital registration	Vital registration
United Arab Emirates			a	CodMod	Bahrain and Kuwait, 1997–2001
United Kingdom	1950–2000	2000	b	Vital registration	Vital registration
United States	1950–2000	2000	b	Vital registration	Vital registration
Uruguay	1955–60, 1963–78, 1980–91, 1993–2000	2000	b	Vital registration	Vital registration
Uzbekistan	1981–2, 1985–2000	2000	a	CodMod	2000
Vanuatu			Ministry of Health, hospital data, 2001a		Cook Islands, Marshall Islands, Niue, Samoa, Tonga, Tuvalu, Vanuatu, Kiribati, Nauru and Fiji
Venezuela (R.B. de)	1955–83, 1985–90, 1992–2000	2000	b	Vital registration	Vital registration
Vietnam			a	CodMod	China, India, and Thailand
Yemen, Republic of			a	CodMod	Arab Rep. of Egypt 2000, Islamic Rep. of Iran 2001
Zambia	1999–2000		a	CodMod	South Africa 1996
Zimbabwe	1990, 1994–5		a	CodMod	Zimbabwe 1995, South Africa 1996

Source: Mathers, Lopez, and others 2004.

Note: CEPED = Centre Population et Développement; ENSEA = l'Ecole Nationale Supérieure de Statistiques et d'Economie Appliquée.

a. Epidemiological estimates obtained from studies, WHO technical programs, and UNAIDS for the following conditions: HIV/AIDS, tuberculosis, measles, pertussis, poliomyelitis, tetanus, lower respiratory infections, Chagas' disease, maternal conditions, perinatal conditions, cancers, drug use disorders, rheumatoid arthritis, and war.

b. Epidemiological estimates obtained from studies, WHO technical programs, and UNAIDS for the following conditions: drug use disorders and war.

c. Epidemiological estimates obtained from studies, WHO technical programs, and UNAIDS for the following conditions: HIV/AIDS, drug use disorders, and war.

Table 3A.4 GBD Regional Epidemiological Analysis Categories

GBD region	Mortality stratum	Region code	WHO member states	WHO region
AFRO	D[a]	1	Algeria, Angola, Benin, Burkina Faso, Cameroon, Cape Verde, Chad, Comoros, Equatorial Guinea, Gabon, The Gambia, Ghana, Guinea, Guinea-Bissau, Liberia, Madagascar, Mali, Mauritania, Mauritius, Niger, Nigeria, São Tomé and Principe, Senegal, Seychelles, Sierra Leone, Togo	AFRO
			Djibouti, Somalia, Sudan	EMRO
AFRO	E	2	Botswana, Burundi, Central African Republic, Democratic Republic of Congo, Republic of Congo, Côte d'Ivoire, Eritrea, Ethiopia, Kenya, Lesotho, Malawi, Mozambique, Namibia, Rwanda, South Africa, Swaziland, Tanzania, Uganda, Zambia, Zimbabwe	AFRO
AMRO	A[b]	3	Canada, United States of America	AMRO
AMRO	B[c]	4	Antigua and Barbuda, Argentina, The Bahamas, Barbados, Belize, Brazil, Chile, Colombia, Costa Rica, Cuba, Dominica, Dominican Republic, El Salvador, Grenada, Guyana, Honduras, Jamaica, Mexico, Panama, Paraguay, St. Kitts and Nevis, St. Lucia, St. Vincent and the Grenadines, Suriname, Trinidad and Tobago, Uruguay, República Bolivariana de Venezuela	AMRO
AMRO	D	5	Bolivia, Ecuador, Guatemala, Haiti, Nicaragua, Peru	AMRO
EMRO	B	6	Bahrain, Islamic Republic of Iran, Jordan, Kuwait, Lebanon, Libya, Oman, Qatar, Saudi Arabia, Syrian Arab Republic, Tunisia, United Arab Emirates	EMRO
			Cyprus	EURO
EMRO	D[d]	7	Arab Republic of Egypt, Iraq, Morocco, Republic of Yemen	EMRO
EURO	A[e]	8	Andorra, Austria, Belgium, Croatia, Czech Republic, Denmark, Finland, France, Germany, Greece, Iceland, Ireland, Israel, Italy, Luxembourg, Malta, Monaco, Netherlands, Norway, Portugal, San Marino, Slovenia, Spain, Sweden, Switzerland, United Kingdom	EURO
EURO	B1	9	Albania, Bosnia and Herzegovina, Bulgaria, Georgia, Former Yugoslav Republic of Macedonia, Poland, Romania, Serbia and Montenegro, Slovak Republic, Turkey	EURO
EURO	B2	10	Armenia, Azerbaijan, Republic of Kyrgyz, Tajikistan, Turkmenistan, Uzbekistan	EURO
EURO	C	11	Belarus, Estonia, Hungary, Kazakhstan, Latvia, Lithuania, Moldova, Russian Federation, Ukraine	EURO
SEARO	B	12	Indonesia, Sri Lanka, Thailand	SEARO
			Brunei Darussalam, Malaysia, the Philippines, Singapore	WPRO
SEARO	D	13	Bangladesh, Bhutan, India, Maldives, Nepal, Timor-Leste	SEARO
			Afghanistan, Pakistan	EMRO
WPRO	A	14	Australia, Japan, New Zealand	WPRO
WPRO	B1	15	China, Mongolia, Republic of Korea	WPRO
			Democratic People's Republic of Korea	SEARO
WPRO	B2	16	Cambodia, Lao People's Democratic Republic, Vietnam	WPRO
			Myanmar	SEARO
WPRO	B3[f]	17	Cook Islands, Fiji, Kiribati, Marshall Islands, Federated States of Micronesia, Nauru, Niue, Palau, Papua New Guinea, Samoa, Solomon Islands, Tonga, Tuvalu, Vanuatu	WPRO

Source: Authors' compilation.

a. Réunion and St. Helena are assumed to have the same burden of disease rates as the WHO member states shown.

b. St. Pierre et Miquelon is assumed to have the same burden of disease rates as the WHO member states shown.

c. Anguilla, Aruba, Bermuda, British Virgin Islands, Caymen Islands, Falkland Islands, French Guiana, Guadeloupe, Martinique, Montserrat, Netherlands Antilles, Puerto Rico, Turks and Caicos Islands, and U.S. Virgin Islands are assumed to have the same burden of disease rates as the WHO member states shown.

d. Western Sahara is assumed to have the same burden of disease rates as the WHO member states shown. Burden of disease rates for the West Bank and Gaza were estimated using death registration data and separate estimates of war deaths.

e. Channel Islands, Faeroe Islands, Isle of Man, Gibraltar, Greenland, Holy See (Vatican City), and Liechtenstein are assumed to have the same burden of disease rates as the WHO member states shown.

f. Samoa, French Polynesia, Guam, New Caledonia, Northern Mariana Islands, Pitcairn, Tokelau, and Wallis and Futuna Islands are assumed to have the same burden of disease rates as the WHO member states shown.

Table 3A.5 GBD Cause Categories, Sequelae, and Case Definitions

GBD cause/sequela	Case definition	Version[a]
I. Communicable, maternal, perinatal, and nutritional conditions		
A1. Tuberculosis	Cases refer to individuals with clinical tuberculosis, normally pulmonary sputum culture positives and extra-pulmonary cases	2
HIV sero-negative cases	HIV sero-negative cases	
HIV sero-positive cases	HIV sero-positive cases	
A2a. Syphilis	Acute and chronic infection with *Treponema pallidum*	2
Congenital syphilis	Syphilis in the newborn due to maternal-fetal transmission in utero	
Low birthweight	Birthweight of less than 2,500 g	
Primary	Initial infection in adults resulting in primary chancre at site of inoculation	
Secondary	Disseminated disease, which appears 2–8 weeks after the primary stage and is usually marked by a rash	
Tertiary—neurologic	Late stage of disease with varied neurological manifestations	
A2b. Chlamydia	Bacterial infection transmitted vaginally, anally, or perinatally with *Chlamydia trachomatis* (excludes ocular trachoma)	2
Cervicitis	Inflammation of the cervix uteri due to *Chlamydia trachomatis*	
Neonatal pneumonia	Pneumonia in infants due to infection with Chlamydia	
Ophthalmia neonatorum	Purulent conjunctivitis in infants less than 30 days, acquired during passage through an infected birth canal	
Low birthweight	Birthweight of less than 2,500 g	
Pelvic inflammatory disease	Inflammation of the adnexa of the uterus (includes endometritis)	
Ectopic pregnancy	Pregnancy located outside the uterus	
Tubo-ovarian abscess	Abscess located in the fallopian tubes or ovaries	
Chronic pelvic pain	Chronic pelvic pain following reproductive tract infection with Chlamydia	
Infertility	Total infertility due to Chlamydia-related pelvic inflammatory disease and ectopic pregnancy in women and epididymitis in men.	
Symptomatic urethritis	Inflammation of the urethra causing symptoms including dysuria and/or hematuria	
Epididymitis	Inflammation of the sperm ducts	
A2c. Gonorrhea	Bacterial infection transmitted vaginally, anally, or perinatally with *Neisseria gonorrhea*	2
Ophthalmia neonatorum	Purulent conjunctivitis in infants less than 30 days, acquired during passage through an infected birth canal	
Low birthweight	Birthweight of less than 2,500 g	
Corneal scar—blindness	Permanent corneal scar resulting from corneal ulceration due to infection with Neisseria gonorrhea and leading to blindness	
Corneal scar—low vision	Permanent corneal scar resulting from corneal ulceration due to infection with *Neisseria gonorrhea* and leading to low vision	
Cervicitis	Inflammation of the cervix uteri due to *Neisseria gonorrhea*	
Pelvic inflammatory disease	Includes both acute and recurrent pelvic inflammatory disease due to gonorrhea	
Ectopic pregnancy	Pregnancy located outside the uterus	
Tubo-ovarian abscess	Abscess located in the fallopian tubes or ovaries	
Chronic pelvic pain	Chronic pelvic pain following reproductive tract infection with *Neisseria gonorrhea*	
Infertility	Total infertility due to gonorrhea-related pelvic inflammatory disease and ectopic pregnancy in women and epididymitis in men	
Symptomatic urethritis	Inflammation of the urethra causing symptoms including dysuria and/or hematuria	
Epididymitis	Inflammation of the sperm ducts	
Stricture	Narrowing of the urethra due to urethritis	

Table 3A.5 Continued

GBD cause/sequela	Case definition	Version[a]
A3. HIV/AIDS		2
HIV cases	HIV sero-positive, not yet progressed to AIDS	
AIDS cases	HIV sero-positive and progressed to AIDS	
A4. Diarrheal diseases—episodes	Episodes of diarrhea including acute watery diarrhea, persistent diarrhea, and dysentery; deaths of children with both measles and diarrhea or both lower respiratory infection and diarrhea are not included in estimates of diarrhea mortality	2
A5a. Pertussis	Acute bacterial infection of the respiratory tract with *Bordetella pertussis* or *parapertussis*	2
Episodes	Acute bacterial infection of the respiratory tract with *Bordetella pertussis* or *parapertussis,* characterized by paroxysmal, violent coughs followed by high-pitched inspiratory whoop	
Encephalopathy	Degenerative disease of the brain, which in pertussis is usually a result of hypoxia, leading to mental retardation	
A5b. Poliomyelitis—lameness	Viral infection characterized by acute flaccid paralysis and proven by isolation of polio virus from stool	2
A5c. Diphtheria	Acute disease caused by toxin-producing *Corynebacterium diphtheriae*	2
Episodes	Acute bacterial disease involving primarily tonsils, pharynx, larynx, nose, and other sites, characterized by grayish plaques or membranes with surrounding tissue inflammation	
Neurological complications	Polyneuritis involving both cranial and peripheral nerve palsies, which are largely reversible	
Myocarditis	Inflammation of the heart muscle leading to electrocardiographic aberrations and sometimes permanent damage with congestive heart failure, which may be fatal	
A5d. Measles—episodes	Acute and highly contagious infection with measles virus characterized by red, blotchy rash, fever, cough, coryza, and conjunctivitis	2
A5e. Tetanus—episodes	Neonatal: infection with *Clostridium tetani* in infants less than 30 days with progressive difficulty and inability to feed because of trismus, generalized stiffness, spasms, and opisthotonus	2
	Non-neonatal: infection with *Clostridium tetani* in non-neonates with initial localized spasms lead to general rigidity, opisthotonus, and risus sardonicus	
A6. Meningitis	Acute bacterial disease with sudden onset and fever, intense headache, nausea, vomiting, neck stiffness, and—in meningococcal disease—petechial rash with pink macules; must be accompanied by laboratory evidence (in cerebrospinal fluid or blood) of *Neisseria meningitidis, Strep pneumoniae,* or *Haemophilus influenzae type B*	2
Streptococcus pneumoniae—episodes	Acute bacterial disease with sudden onset and fever, intense headache, nausea, vomiting, and neck stiffness; must be accompanied by laboratory evidence (in cerebrospinal fluid or blood) of *Strep pneumoniae*	
Haemophilus influenzae—episodes	Acute bacterial disease with sudden onset and fever, intense headache, nausea, vomiting, and neck stiffness; must be accompanied by laboratory evidence (in cerebrospinal fluid or blood) of *Haemophilus influenza type B*	
Neisseria meningitidis—episodes	Acute bacterial disease with sudden onset and fever, intense headache, nausea, vomiting, and neck stiffness; must be accompanied by laboratory evidence (in cerebrospinal fluid or blood) of *Neisseria meningitidis*	
Meningococcaemia without meningitis—episodes	Invasion of the bloodstream with *Neisseria meningitidis.*	
Deafness	At least *moderate* impairment, where person is able to hear and repeat words using raised voice at 1 meter, resulting from meningitis	
Seizure disorder	Seizures of any type that were present at least six months after hospitalization, resulting from meningitis	

(Continues on the following page.)

Table 3A.5 Continued

GBD cause/sequela	Case definition	Version[a]
Motor deficit	Spasticity or paresis of one or more limbs resulting from meningitis	
Mental retardation	IQ of 70 or below	
A7a. Hepatitis B—episodes	Inflammation of the liver due to Hepatitis B virus	1
A7b. Hepatitis C—episodes	Inflammation of the liver due to Hepatitis C virus	1
A8. Malaria	Infectious disease caused by protozoa of the genus *Plasmodium*	1
Episodes	Attacks of chills, fever, and sweating due to *Plasmodium* infection	
Anemia	Defined using WHO criteria for mild to very severe anemia	
Neurological sequelae	Includes hemiplegia, aphasia, ataxia, and cortical blindness	
A9a. Trypanosomiasis—episodes	Infection with protozoa of the genus *Trypanosoma*, excluding *T. cruzi*	1
A9b. Chagas' disease	Infection with *Trypanosoma cruzi*	2
Infection	Episode of infection with *Trypanosoma cruzi*	
Cardiomyopathy without congestive heart failure	Disorder of the heart muscle resulting from infection with *T. cruzi* without congestive heart failure	
Cardiomyopathy with congestive heart failure	Disorder of the heart muscle resulting from infection with *T. cruzi* with congestive heart failure	
Megaviscera	Dilation of interior organ in the abdominal cavity, particularly of esophagus and colon, due to *T. cruzi*	
A9c. Schistosomiasis—infection	Infection and associated direct mortality from schistosomiasis; does not include estimates of mortality from bladder cancer, cirrhosis, or colon cancer that may be related to schistosomiasis	1
A9d. Leishmaniasis	Infection with flagellate protozoa of the genus *Leishmania*	1
Visceral	Generalized involvement of the reticulo-endothelial system due to infection with *Leishmania*	
Cutaneous	Presence of skin lesions (which may ulcerate) due to infection with *Leishmania*	
A9e. Lymphatic filariasis	Infection with filariae (*Wucheria bancrofti* and *Brugia malayi*)	1
Hydrocele > 15cm	Circumscribed collection of fluid in testicle or along the spermatic cord due to filariasis	
Bancroftian lymphoedema	Swelling of subcutaneous tissues due to the presence of excessive lymph fluid as a result of infection with *Wucheria bancrofti*	
Brugian lymphedema	Swelling of subcutaneous tissues due to the presence of excessive lymph fluid as a result of infection with *Brugia malaye*	
A9f. Onchocerciasis	Infection with worms of the genus *Onchocerca*	2
Blindness	Inability to distinguish the fingers of a hand at a distance of 3 meters, or less than 5 percent of remaining vision as compared to a normally sighted individual, as a result of infection with *Onchocerca volvulus*	
Itching	Itchy dermatitis as a result of infection with *Onchocerca volvulus*	
Low vision	Corrected visual acuity in the better eye of less than 6/18 but better than or equal to 3/60 due to infection with *Onchocerca volvulus*	
A10. Leprosy	Chronic disease resulting from infection with *Mycobacterium leprae*	2
Cases	WHO case definition: Person showing clinical signs of leprosy, with or without bacteriological confirmation of the diagnosis, and requiring chemotherapy	
Disabling leprosy	Grade 1 and 2 of WHO grades of disability for leprosy	
A11. Dengue	Mosquito-born disease caused by viruses of the family *Flaviviridae*	0
Dengue hemorrhagic fever	Severe manifestation of dengue infection characterized by multiple hemorrhages and potentially followed by circulatory failure, neurological manifestations, and shock	

GBD cause/sequela	Case definition	Version[a]
A12. Japanese encephalitis	Mosquito-born encephalitis caused by Japanese encephalitis virus	0
Episodes	Episode of Japanese encephalitis infection	
Cognitive impairment	Reduced cognitive function resulting from encephalitis due to Japanese encephalitis virus	
Neurological sequelae	Neurological deficits resulting from encephalitis due to Japanese encephalitis virus	
A13. Trachoma	Cases of follicular or inflammatory trachoma	2
Blindness	Corrected visual acuity in the better eye of less than 3/60	
Low vision	Corrected visual acuity in the better eye of less than 6/18 but better than or equal to 3/60	
A14a. Ascariasis	Infection with roundworms of the genus *Ascaris*	1
High-intensity infection	Infection resulting in at least 20–40 worms per stool load	
Contemporaneous cognitive deficit	Reduction in cognitive ability in school-age children, which occurs only while infection persists	
Cognitive impairment	Delayed psychomotor development and impaired performance in language skills, motor skills, and coordination equivalent to a 5- to 10-point deficit in IQ	
Intestinal obstruction	Blockage of the intestines due to worm mass	
A14b. Trichuriasis	Infection with the whipworm *Trichuris trichiura*	1
High-intensity infection	Infection resulting in at least 250–500 worms per stool load	
Contemporaneous cognitive deficit	Reduction in cognitive ability in school-age children, which occurs only while infection persists	
Massive dysentery syndrome	Rectal prolapse and/or tenesmus and/or bloody mucoid stools due to carpeting of intestinal mucosa by worms	
Cognitive impairment	Delayed psychomotor development and impaired performance in language skills, motor skills, and coordination equivalent to a 5- to 10-point deficit in IQ	
A14c. Hookworm disease	Infection with hookworms of the genus *Ancylostomiasis* and *Necatoriasis*	1
High-intensity infection	Infection resulting in at least 80–160 worms per stool load	
Anemia	Anemia due to hookworm infection	
Cognitive impairment	Delayed psychomotor development and impaired performance in language skills, motor skills, and coordination equivalent to a 5- to 10-point deficit in IQ	
B1. Lower respiratory infections		2
Episodes	Episode of lower respiratory infection	
Chronic sequelae	Includes bronchiectasis and impaired lung function as measured by a decrease in forced expiratory volume	
B2. Upper respiratory infections		2
Episodes	Episode of upper respiratory infection	
Pharyngitis	Inflammation of the pharynx	
B3. Otitis media	Inflammation of the middle ear	0
Episodes	Episodes of acute otitis media	
Deafness	At least moderate impairment, where person is able to hear and repeat words using raised voice at 1 meter, resulting from otitis media	
C1. Maternal hemorrhage		2
Episodes	All episodes of antepartum and postpartum hemorrhage	
Severe anemia	Blood hemoglobin level < 10 mg/dl following postpartum hemorrhage	

(Continues on the following page.)

GBD cause/sequela	Case definition	Version[a]
C2. Maternal sepsis		2
Episodes	Major puerperal infection, excluding infection following abortion, minor genital tract infection following delivery, and urinary tract infections following delivery	
Infertility	Failure to conceive again after a previous conception (secondary infertility), caused by maternal sepsis	
C3. Hypertensive disorders of pregnancy—episodes	Includes pre-eclampsia and eclampsia	2
C4. Obstructed labor		2
Episodes	Labor with no advance of the presenting part of the fetus despite strong uterine contractions	
Cesarean section for obstructed labor	Cases of obstructed labor for which cesarean section has been performed	
Stress incontinence	Cases with leaking of urine during coughing or sneezing	
Rectovaginal fistula	Cases with a communication between the vaginal wall and the bladder/rectum resulting from obstructed labor	
C5. Abortion		2
Episodes	Episodes of unsafe abortion (termination of an unwanted pregnancy either by persons lacking the necessary skills or in an environment lacking the necessary standards or both)	
Infertility	Failure to conceive following unsafe abortion	
Reproductive tract infection	Cases of reproductive tract infection resulting from unsafe abortion	
D1. Low birthweight—all sequelae	Birthweight below 2,500 g, including small-for-gestational-age infants and premature infants (all developmental sequelae due to low birthweight have been clustered into one outcome, which includes cerebral palsy, mental retardation, epilepsy, hearing loss, and vision loss)	2
D2. Birth asphyxia and birth trauma—all sequelae	All developmental sequelae due to birth asphyxia and birth trauma have been clustered into one outcome, which includes cerebral palsy, mental retardation, epilepsy, hearing loss, and vision loss	2
E1. Protein-energy malnutrition		2
Wasting	Observed weight for height at least 2 standard deviations below the mean for children ages 0–5	
Stunting	Observed height for age at least 2 standard deviations below the mean for children ages 0–5	
Developmental disability	Limited physical and mental ability to perform most activities in *all* of the following areas: recreation, education, procreation, or occupation	
E2. Iodine deficiency		2
Goiter grades 1 and 2	Cases of goiter grade 1 (a mass in the neck consistent with an enlarged thyroid—grade 1: palpable but not visible) and grade 2 (a mass in the neck consistent with an enlarged thyroid—grade 2: palpable and visible in neutral neck position)	
Mild developmental disability	Any of the following due to iodine deficiency: Bilateral hearing loss, delay of walking ability, mild intellectual impairment	
Cretinoidism	Hypothyroid cretinism: Hypothyroidism and stunting as a result of iodine deficiency. Neurological cretinism: Mental deficiency (IQ below 70), deaf-mutism, and spastic paralysis as a result of iodine deficiency	
Cretinism	Some but not all features of full cretinism as a result of iodine deficiency	
E3. Vitamin A deficiency		2
Xerophthalmia	All ocular manifestations of vitamin A deficiency: night blindness, Bitot's spots, corneal xerosis, corneal ulceration, and corneal scarring	
Corneal scar	Permanent corneal scar resulting from corneal ulceration due to vitamin A deficiency and potentially leading to blindness	

Table 3A.5 Continued

GBD cause/sequela	Case definition	Version[a]
E4. Iron-deficiency anemia		2
Mild	Hemoglobin of 100–109 g/l in pregnant women, 110–119 g/l in children and adult women, and 120–129 g/l in adult men	
Moderate	Hemoglobin of 70–99 g/l in pregnant women, 80–109 g/l in children and adult women, and 90–119 g/l in adult men	
Severe	Hemoglobin of 40–69 g/l in pregnant women, 50–79 g/l in children and adult women, and 60–89 g/l in adult men	
Cognitive impairment	Delayed psychomotor development and impaired performance in language skills, motor skills, and coordination equivalent to a 5- to 10-point deficit in IQ	
II. Noncommunicable diseases		
A. Malignant neoplasms sequelae		2
Diagnosis and primary therapy	Chemotherapy, radiotherapy, surgery	
Control	Clinical observation during control/remission phase	
Preterminal (metastasis)	Metastatic dissemination of the disease	
Terminal	Terminal stage prior to death	
Mastectomy	Mastectomy in five-year breast cancer survivor	
Infertility	Infertility in five-year survivor of cervical, uterine, or ovarian cancer	
Incontinence or impotence	Incontinence or impotence in five-year survivor of prostate cancer	
Stoma	Stoma in five-year survivor of digestive system cancer	
C. Diabetes mellitus		2
Cases	Venous plasma concentration of μ 11.1 mmol/l 2 h after a 75 g oral glucose challenge	
Diabetic foot	Chronic or recurring diabetic foot ulcers	
Neuropathy	Loss of reflexes and vibration; damage and dysfunction of sensory, motor, or autonomic nerves attributable to diabetes	
Retinopathy—blindness	Retinopathy: Microaneurysms or worse lesions in at least one eye; progressive damage of the small blood vessels of the retina	
	Blindness: Unable to distinguish the fingers of a hand at the distance of 3 meters, or has less than 5 percent of remaining vision as compared to a normally sighted individual; visual acuity of less than 3/60 or corresponding visual field loss in the better eye with best possible correction	
Amputation	Surgical elimination of the lower extremity or part of it due to gangrene	
E1. Unipolar depressive disorders		2
Mild episode	Mild major depressive episode (ICD-10 codes F 32.0 and F 33.0)	
Moderate episode	Moderate major depressive episode (ICD-10 codes F 32.1 and F 33.1)	
Severe episode	Severe major depressive episode (ICD-10 codes F 32.2 , F 32.3, F 33.2 and F 33.3)	
Dysthymia	Dysthymia case with no concurrent major depressive episode	
E2. Bipolar affective disorder—cases	Cases meeting ICD-10 criteria	2
E3. Schizophrenia—cases	Cases meeting ICD-10 criteria	2
E4. Epilepsy—cases	Cases meeting ILAE definition	1
	Cases meeting ICD-10 criteria for alcohol dependence and harmful use (F10.1 and F 10.2), excluding cases with comorbid depressive episode	
E6. Alzheimer's and other dementias—cases	Mild, moderate, and severe Alzheimer's disease; senility; and other dementias	2
E7. Parkinson's disease—cases	Cases meeting clinical criteria for Parkinson's disease	1
E8. Multiple sclerosis—cases	Cases of chronic or intermittent relapsing multiple sclerosis	1

(Continues on the following page.)

Table 3A.5 Continued

GBD cause/sequela	Case definition	Version[a]
E9. Drug use disorders	Cases meeting ICD-10 criteria for opioid dependence and harmful use (F 11.1 F 11.2) or cocaine dependence and harmful use (F 14.1 and F 14.2), excluding cases with comorbid depressive episode	2
E10. Post-traumatic stress disorder—cases	Cases meeting DSM IV criteria[b] for post-traumatic stress disorder, excluding cases with comorbid depressive episode or alcohol and drug use (harmful and/or dependence)	2
E11. Obsessive-compulsive disorder—cases	Cases meeting ICD-10 criteria (F 42), excluding cases with comorbid depressive episode	2
E12. Panic disorder—cases	Cases meeting ICD-10 criteria for panic disorder (F 41.0) or agoraphobia with panic disorder (F 40.01), excluding cases with comorbid depressive episode.	2
E13. Insomnia (primary)	Cases meeting DSM IV criteria for primary insomnia (307.42) where the insomnia causes problems with usual activities; excludes cases with comorbid depressive episode or alcohol and drug use (harmful and/or dependence)	2
E14. Migraine	Cases meeting IHS definition for migraine	2
E15. Mild mental retardation attributable to lead exposure	IQ in the range of 50–69 attributable to childhood lead exposure	2
F1. Glaucoma	Cases of primary angle closure glaucoma and primary open angle glaucoma	2
Low vision	Corrected visual acuity in the better eye of less than 6/18 but better than or equal to 3/60	
Blindness	Corrected visual acuity in the better eye of less than 3/60	
F2. Cataracts	Cases of senile cataract causing progressive visual impairment	2
Low vision	Corrected visual acuity in the better eye of less than 6/18 but better than or equal to 3/60	
Blindness	Corrected visual acuity in the better eye of less than 3/60	
F3. Vision disorders, age-related	Low vision or blindness due to macular degeneration, refractive errors, or other age-related causes; excludes sight loss due to congenital causes, other diseases, or injury	2
Low vision	Corrected visual acuity in the better eye of less than 6/18 but better than or equal to 3/60	
Blindness	Corrected visual acuity in the better eye of less than 3/60	
F4. Hearing loss, adult onset	Cases of adult onset hearing loss due to aging or noise exposure; excludes hearing loss due to congenital causes, infectious diseases, other diseases, or injury	2
Mild hearing loss, untreated	Hearing threshold level in the better ear is 41–60 dBHTL (averaged over 0.5, 1, 2, 4kHz) (some difficulty understanding or actively participating in a conversation with one person, great difficulty with more than one person); person does not use a hearing aid	
Moderate hearing loss, treated	Hearing threshold level in the better ear is 41–60 dBHTL (averaged over 0.5, 1, 2, 4kHz) (some difficulty understanding or actively participating in a conversation with one person, great difficulty with more than one person); person uses a hearing aid	
Severe or profound hearing loss, untreated	Hearing threshold level in the better ear is 61 dBHTL or more (averaged over 0.5, 1, 2, 4kHz) (great difficulty or unable to understand or participate in a conversation with one other person); person does not use a hearing aid	
Severe or profound hearing loss, treated	Hearing threshold level in the better ear is 61 dBHTL or more (averaged over 0.5, 1, 2, 4kHz) (great difficulty or unable to understand or participate in a conversation with one other person); person uses a hearing aid	
G1. Rheumatic heart disease	Symptomatic cases of congestive heart failure due to rheumatic heart disease	0
G2. Hypertensive heart disease	Symptomatic cases of congestive heart failure due to hypertensive heart disease	0

GBD cause/sequela	Case definition	Version[a]
G3. Ischemic heart disease		2
Acute myocardial infarction	Definite and possible episodes of acute myocardial infarction according to MONICA study criteria	
Angina pectoris	Cases of clinically diagnosed angina pectoris or definite angina pectoris according to Rose questionnaire	
Congestive heart failure	Mild and greater (Killip scale k2–k4)	
G4. Cerebrovascular disease		2
First-ever stroke cases	First-ever stroke according to WHO definition; includes subarachnoid hemorrhage, but excludes transient ischemic attacks, subdural hematoma, and hemorrhage or infarction due to infection or tumor	
Long-term stroke survivors	Persons who survive more than 28 days after first-ever stroke	
G5. Inflammatory heart diseases		0
Myocarditis	Symptomatic cases of congestive heart failure due to myocarditis	
Pericarditis	Symptomatic cases of congestive heart failure due to pericarditis	
Endocarditis	Symptomatic cases of congestive heart failure due to endocarditis	
Cardiomyopathy	Symptomatic cases of congestive heart failure due to cardiomyopathy	
H1. Chronic obstructive pulmonary disease—symptomatic cases	Chronic (stable) airways obstruction with $FEV_1 < 1$ liter (corresponding to symptomatic disability)	2
H2. Asthma—cases	Reported wheeze in the last 12 months plus current bronchial hyperresponsiveness, defined as a 20 percent fall in FEV_1 with a provoking concentration of histamine (PC20) at 8 mg/ml or less	1
I1. Peptic ulcer disease	Individuals with peptic ulcers, most of whom have recurrent intermittent symptoms	0
Cases with antibiotic treatment	Active gastric or peptic duodenal ulcer receiving appropriate antibiotic treatment	
Cases not treated with antibiotic	Other active gastric or peptic duodenal ulcer; includes untreated cases and cases receiving symptomatic treatment	
I2. Cirrhosis of the liver—symptomatic cases	Individuals with symptomatic cirrhosis	0
I3. Appendicitis—episodes	Episodes of acute appendicitis (treated or untreated)	0
J1. Nephritis and nephrosis		0
Acute glomerulonephritis	Acute episode of glomerulonephritis	
End-stage renal disease	End-stage renal failure with or without dialysis, excluding diabetic nephropathy and nephropathy due to cancers, congenital conditions, and injury	
J2. Benign prostatic hypertrophy—symptomatic cases	Individuals with some, albeit intermittent, symptoms from benign prostatic hypertrophy	0
L1. Rheumatoid arthritis—cases	Definite or classical rheumatoid arthritis by 1958 ARA or 1987 ACR criteria	2
L2. Osteoarthritis		2
Hip	Symptomatic osteoarthritis of the hip, radiologically confirmed as Kellgren-Lawrence grade 2–4	
Knee	Symptomatic osteoarthritis of the knee, radiologically confirmed as Kellgren-Lawrence grade 2–4	
L3. Gout	Cases of gout (ARA 1977 survey criteria; at least 6 of 11 symptoms)	1
L4. Low back pain		1
Episode of limiting low back pain	Acute episode of low back pain resulting in moderate or greater limitations to mobility and usual activities; excludes low back pain due to intervertebral disc displacement or herniation, and low back pain that does not result in some limitations to mobility and usual activities	

(Continues on the following page.)

Table 3A.5 Continued

GBD cause/sequela	Case definition	Version[a]
Acute intervertebral disc disorder	Episode of intervertebral disc displacement or herniation	
Chronic intervertebral disc disorder	Disorder of intervertebral disc resulting in pain and disability that does not resolve within six weeks following treatment (medical or surgical)	
M1. Abdominal wall defect—cases	Live-born cases with exomphalos or gastroschisis	0
M2. Anencephaly—cases	Live-born cases with anencephaly	0
M3. Anorectal atresia—cases	Live-born cases with anorectal atresia	0
M4. Cleft lip—cases	Live-born cases, includes individuals who have had surgical correction	0
M5. Cleft palate—cases	Live-born cases, includes individuals who have had surgical correction	0
M6. Esophageal atresia—cases	Live-born cases with esophageal atresia	0
M7. Renal agenesis—cases	Live-born cases with renal agenesis	0
M8. Down syndrome—cases	Live-born cases with Down syndrome	0
M9. Congenital heart anomalies—cases	Live-born cases with major congenital malformations of the heart	0
M10. Spina bifida—cases	Live-born cases with spina bifida aperta (low, medium, or high level)	0
N1. Dental caries—episodes	Episodes per person, not per tooth, quadrant, or sextant	0
N2. Periodontal disease—cases	Pockets greater than 6 mm deep	0
N3. Edentulism—cases	Cases of treated and untreated edentulism (absence of all teeth)	0

III. Injuries

External cause categories	Includes injury severe enough to warrant medical attention or that leads immediately to death. In other words, injuries that are severe enough that if an individual had access to a medical facility he or she would seek attention[c]	
A1. Road traffic accidents	Includes crashes and pedestrian injuries due to motor vehicles	2
A2. Poisonings	Only one outcome is included for poisonings	2
A3. Falls	Includes falls resulting from osteoporotic fractures	2
A4. Fires	Most of the sequelae of fires are due to burns; some individuals, however, jump from buildings or are otherwise injured because of fires	2
A5. Drownings	Other than drowning and near-drowning rates, the only other major disabling sequelae from near-drowning included is quadriplegia	2
A6. Other unintentional injuries	This is not a residual category, but includes injuries due to environmental factors, machinery and electrical equipment, cutting and piercing implements, and various other external causes of unintentional injury	2
B1. Self-inflicted injuries	Suicide attempts, whether or not resulting in death	2
B2. Violence	Interpersonal violence, including assault and homicide	2
B3. War	Injuries directly attributable to war or organized civil conflict in combatants and noncombatants	2
Type of injury—sequelae	For each of the external cause categories, injury sequelae defined in terms of type of injury were analyzed. The type of injury sequelae were defined in terms of ICD-9 and ICD-10 nature of injury codes (N-codes) as follows:	
	ICD-9 Code *ICD-10 Code*	

Table 3A.5 Continued

GBD cause/sequela	ICD-9 code	ICD-10 code
1. Fractures		
Skull—short-term[d]	800 to 801	S02.0/1/7/9, T90.2
Skull—long-term[d]	800 to 801	S02.0/1/7/9, T90.2
Face bones[d]	802	S02.2/6/8
Vertebral column	805	S12, S22.0/1, S32.0/7, T91.1
Rib or sternum[e]	807	S22.2-9
Pelvis[e]	808	S32.1-5/8, T91.2
Clavicle, scapula or humerus[f]	810–812	S42, S49.7
Radius or ulna[f]	813	S52, S59.7, T10, T92.1
Hand bones[f]	814–817	S62, S69.7, T92.2
Femur—short-term[g]	820–821	S72, S79.7
Femur—long-term[g]	820–821	S72, S79.7
Patella, tibia, or fibula[g]	822–823	S82.0-4, S82.7/9, S89.7, T12
Ankle[g]	824	S82.5-6/8
Foot bones[g]	825–826	S92, S99.7
2. Injured spinal cord	806 and 952	S14, S24, S34, T06.0/1, T08, T91.3
3. Dislocations		
Shoulder, elbow, or hip	831, 832, 835	S43, S73
Other dislocation	830, 833–834, 836–839	S03.0-3, S13, S23, S33, S53, S63.0/1, S83.1-3, S93.1-3, T03, T11.2, T13.2, T14.3, T92.3, T93.3
	840–848	S03.4/5, S16, S29.0, S39.0, S46, S56, S63.5-7, S66, S76, S83.4/7, S86, S93.4/6, S96, T06.4, T11.5, T13.5, T14.6, T92.5, T93.5
4. Sprains		
5. Intracranial injuries		
Short-term	850–854	S06, T90.5
Long-term	850–854	S06, T90.5
6. Internal injuries	860–869	S25-S27, S35-S37, S39.6, T06.4, T91.4/5
7. Open wound	870, 872–884, 890–894	S01, S08, S11, S15, S21, S31, S41, S45, S51, S55, S61, S65, S71, S75, S81, S85, S91, S95, T01, T11.1/4, T13.5, T14.6, T90.1, T92.5, T93.5
8. Injury to eyes		
Short-term	871, 950	S05, T90.4
Long-term	871, 950	S05, T90.4
9. Amputations		
Thumb	885	S68.0
Finger	886	S68.1/2
Arm	887	S48, S58, S68.3-9, T05.0/2, T11.6
Toe[h]	895	S98.1/2
Foot[h]	896, 897.0–1	S98.0/3/4, T05.3
Leg[h]	897.2–3	S78, S88, T05.4/6, T13.6
10. Crushing	925–929	S07, S17, S28, S38, S47, S57, S67, S77, S87, S97, T04, T14.7, T92.6, T93.6
11. Burns		
Less than 20%—short-term[i]	940-947, 948.0–1	T31.0/1
Less than 20%—long-term[i]	940-947, 948.0–1	T31.0/1
20 to 60%—short-term[i]	948.2–5	T331.2/5

(Continues on the following page.)

Table 3A.5 Continued

GBD cause/sequela	ICD-9 code	ICD-10 code
20 to 60%—long-term[i]	948.2–5	T331.2/5
Greater than 60%—short-term[i]	948.6–9	T31.6/9
Greater than 60%—long-term[i]	948.6–9	T31.6/9
12. Injured nerves		
Short-term	951, 953–957	S04, S44, S54, S64, S74, S84, S94, T06.2, T11.3, T13.3, T14.4
Long-term	951, 953–957	S04, S44, S54, S64, S74, S84, S94, T06.2, T11.3, T13.3, T14.4
13. Poisoning	960–979, 980–989	T36–T65, T96–T97

Source: Authors' compilation.

a. Version 0 estimates for YLD are based on epidemiological reviews and disease models from the GBD 1990, adjusted for time trends and internal consistency with 2001 population estimates, and cause-specific and background mortality for 2001. Version 1 estimates for YLD are provisional revised estimates based on new epidemiological reviews and disease models for 2001. These estimates may change with further revisions. Version 2 estimates for YLD are final estimates based on new epidemiological reviews and disease models for 2001. YLL for all causes are based on complete analysis of available mortality data for years up to and including 2002.

b. DSM IV is the *Diagnostic and Statistical Manual of Mental Disorders—Fourth Edition* (Washington, DC: American Psychiatric Association, C., 1994).

c. See table 3A.2 for ICD-9 and ICD-10 definitions.

d. The N-codes 803 and 804 were assigned to fractured skull following the distribution of N-codes 801 and 802.

e. The N-code 809 was assigned to fractured rib, sternum, and pelvis following the distribution of N-codes 807 and 808.

f. The N-codes 818 and 819 were assigned to fractured clavicle, scapula, humerus, radius, ulna, and hand bones following the distribution of N-codes 810–817.

g. The N-codes 827 and 828 were assigned to fractured patella, tibia, fibula, ankle, and foot bones following the distribution of N-codes 822–826.

h. The N-codes 897.4–897.7 were assigned to amputated toe, foot, and leg following the distribution of N-codes 895, 896, and 897.0–897.3.

i. The N-code 949 was assigned to bums following the N-codes 940–948. In ICD-10, burns are classified by site (T20–T30) and/or proportion of body surface affected (T31).

Table 3A.6 Disability Weights for Diseases and Conditions (Except Cancers and Injuries)

Sequela	Average disability weight[a]	Range[b]	Source
Tuberculosis—cases	0.271	0.264–0.294	GBD 1990[c], varies with age
Syphilis			
Congenital syphilis	0.315		GBD 1990
Primary	0.015	0.014–0.015	GBD 1990[c], varies with age
Secondary	0.048	0.044–0.048	GBD 1990[c], varies with age
Tertiary—neurologic	0.283		GBD 1990
Chlamydia			
Cervicitis	0.049		GBD 1990
Neonatal pneumonia	0.280		GBD 1990
Ophthalmia neonatorum	0.180		GBD 1990
Pelvic inflammatory disease	0.327	0.194–0.382	GBD 1990[c]: untreated 0.420, treated 0.169
Ectopic pregnancy	0.549		GBD 1990
Tubo-ovarian abscess	0.548		GBD 1990
Chronic pelvic pain	0.122		GBD 1990
Infertility	0.180		GBD 1990
Symptomatic urethritis	0.067		GBD 1990
Epididymitis	0.167		GBD 1990
Gonorrhea			
Cervicitis	0.049		GBD 1990
Corneal scar—blindness	0.600		GBD 1990
Ophthalmia neonatorum	0.180		GBD 1990
Pelvic inflammatory disease	0.169		GBD 1990
Ectopic pregnancy	0.549		GBD 1990
Tubo-ovarian abscess	0.548		GBD 1990
Chronic pelvic pain	0.122		GBD 1990
Infertility	0.180		GBD 1990
Symptomatic urethritis	0.067		GBD 1990
Epididymitis	0.167		GBD 1990
Corneal scar—low vision	0.233	0.233–0.245	GBD 1990[c], varies with age
Stricture	0.151		GBD 1990
HIV/AIDS			
HIV cases	0.135	0.123–0.136	GBD 1990[c], varies with age
AIDS cases	0.505		GBD 1990
Diarrheal diseases—episodes	0.105	0.086–0.119	GBD 1990[c], varies with age
Pertussis			
Episodes	0.129	0.016–0.160	GBD 1990
Encephalopathy	0.450	0.402–0.484	GBD 1990[c], varies with age and treatment
Poliomyelitis—cases—lameness	0.369		GBD 1990
Diphtheria			
Episodes	0.231		GBD 1990
Neurological complications	0.078		GBD 1990
Myocarditis	0.323		GBD 1990
Measles—episodes	0.152		GBD 1990
Tetanus—episodes	0.633	0.604–0.640	GBD 1990[c], varies with age
Meningitis			
Streptococcus pneumoniae—episodes	0.615	0.613–0.616	GBD 1990[c], varies with age
Haemophilus influenzae—episodes	0.616	0.613–0.616	GBD 1990[c], varies with age
Neisseria meningitidis—episodes	0.615	0.613–0.616	GBD 1990[c], varies with age
Meningococcaemia without meningitis—episodes	0.152		GBD 1990
Deafness	0.229	0.213–0.233	GBD 1990[c], varies with age and treatment
Mental retardation	0.456	0.402–0.484	GBD 1990[c], varies with age and treatment
Motor deficit	0.380	0.339–0.460	GBD 1990[c], varies with age and treatment
Seizure disorder	0.097	0.046–0.142	GBD 1990[c], varies with age and treatment
Hepatitis B—episodes	0.211	0.170–0.212	GBD 1990[c], varies with age
Hepatitis C—episodes	0.211	0.170–0.212	GBD 1990[c], varies with age

(Continues on the following page.)

Table 3A.6 Continued

Sequela	Average disability weight[a]	Range[b]	Source
Malaria			
Episodes	0.191	0.172–0.211	GBD 1990[c], varies with age and treatment
Neurological sequelae	0.471	0.443–0.471	GBD 1990[c], varies with age and treatment
Anemia	0.012	0.012–0.013	GBD 1990[c], varies with age
Trypanosomiasis—episodes	0.350		GBD 1990
Chagas' disease			
Infection	0.000		GBD 1990
Cardiomyopathy without congestive heart failure	0.062		GBD 1990
Cardiomyopathy with congestive heart failure	0.270	0.186–0.308	GBD 1990[c]: untreated 0.323, treated 0.171
Megaviscera	0.240		GBD 1990
Schistosomiasis—infection	0.006	0.005–0.006	GBD 1990[c], varies with age
Leishmaniasis			
Visceral	0.243		GBD 1990
Cutaneous	0.023		GBD 1990
Lymphatic filariasis			
Hydrocele > 15 cm	0.073	0.066–0.075	GBD 1990[c], varies with age
Bancroftian lymphedema	0.106	0.067–0.128	GBD 1990[c], varies with age
Brugian lymphedema	0.116	0.064–0.128	GBD 1990[c], varies with age
Onchocerciasis			
Blindness	0.600		GBD 1990
Itching	0.068		GBD 1990
Low vision	0.260		GBD 1990[d]
Leprosy			
Cases	0.000		GBD 1990
Disabling leprosy	0.152		GBD 1990
Dengue—dengue hemorrhagic fever	0.210	0.195–0.211	GBD 1990[c], varies with age
Japanese encephalitis			
Episodes	0.616	0.613–0.616	GBD 1990[c], varies with age
Cognitive impairment	0.468	0.402–0.484	GBD 1990[c], varies with age and treatment
Neurological sequelae	0.380	0.339–0.460	GBD 1990[c], varies with age and treatment
Trachoma			
Blindness	0.600		GBD 1990
Low vision	0.278	0.227–0.282	GBD 1990[d]: untreated 0.282, treated 0.227
Ascariasis			
High-intensity infection	0.000		GBD 1990
Contemporaneous cognitive deficit	0.006		GBD 1990
Cognitive impairment	0.463		GBD 1990
Intestinal obstruction	0.024		GBD 1990
Trichuriasis			
High-intensity infection	0.000		GBD 1990
Contemporaneous cognitive deficit	0.006		GBD 1990
Massive dysentery syndrome	0.116	0.114–0.138	GBD 1990[c], varies with age
Cognitive impairment	0.024		GBD 1990
Hookworm disease (ancylostomiasis and necatoriasis)			
High-intensity infection	0.000		GBD 1990
Anemia	0.024		GBD 1990
Cognitive impairment	0.024		GBD 1990
Lower respiratory infections			
Episodes	0.279		GBD 1990
Chronic sequelae	0.099		GBD 1990
Upper respiratory infections			
Episodes	0.000		GBD 1990
Pharyngitis	0.070		GBD 1990
Otitis media			
Episodes	0.023		GBD 1990
Deafness	0.229	0.213–0.233	GBD 1990[c], varies with age and treatment

Sequela	Average disability weight[a]	Range[b]	Source
Maternal hemorrhage			
Episodes	0.000		GBD 1990
Severe anemia	0.093	0.087–0.093	GBD 1990[c], varies with age
Maternal sepsis			
Episodes	0.000		GBD 1990
Infertility	0.180		GBD 1990
Hypertensive disorders of pregnancy— episodes	0.000		GBD 1990
Obstructed labor			
Episodes	0.000		GBD 1990
Cesarean section for obstructed labor	0.349		GBD 1990
Stress incontinence	0.025		GBD 1990
Rectovaginal fistula	0.430		GBD 1990
Abortion			
Episodes	0.000		GBD 1990
Infertility	0.180		GBD 1990
Reproductive tract infection	0.067		GBD 1990
Other maternal conditions			
Stress incontinence	0.025		GBD 1990
Low birthweight—all sequelae	0.106		GBD 1990
Birth asphyxia and birth trauma— all sequelae	0.372	0.343–0.379	GBD 1990[c]: untreated 0.381, treated 0.334
Protein-energy malnutrition			
Wasting	0.053		GBD 1990
Stunting	0.002		GBD 1990
Developmental disability	0.024		GBD 1990
Iodine deficiency			
Goiter grades 1 and 2	0.000		GBD 1990
Mild developmental disability	0.006		GBD 1990
Cretinoidism	0.255		GBD 1990
Cretinism	0.804		GBD 1990
Vitamin A deficiency			
Xerophthalmia	0.000		GBD 1990
Corneal scar	0.276	0.274–0.282	GBD 1990[c], varies with age
Iron-deficiency anemia			
Mild	0.000		GBD 1990
Moderate	0.011	0.011–0.012	GBD 1990[c], varies with age
Severe	0.090	0.087–0.093	GBD 1990[c], varies with age
Cognitive impairment	0.024		GBD 1990
Diabetes mellitus			
Cases	0.015	0.012–0.018	GBD 1990[c]: untreated 0.012, treated 0.033
Diabetic foot	0.133	0.130–0.136	GBD 1990[c]: untreated 0.137, treated 0.129
Neuropathy	0.072	0.066–0.076	GBD 1990[c]: untreated 0.078, treated 0.064
Retinopathy—blindness	0.550	0.511–0.595	GBD 1990[c]: untreated 0.600, treated 0.493
Amputation	0.102	0.086–0.151	GBD 1990[c]: untreated 0.155, treated 0.068
Unipolar depressive disorders			
Mild episode	0.140		Netherlands study[e]
Moderate episode	0.350		Netherlands study[e]
Severe episode	0.760		Netherlands study[e]
Dysthymia	0.140		Netherlands study[e]
Bipolar affective disorder—cases	0.367	0.309–0.387	Untreated 0.400, treated 0.140
Schizophrenia—cases	0.528	0.406–0.572	GBD 1990[c], varies with age and treatment
Epilepsy—cases	0.113	0.052–0.142	GBD 1990[c], varies with age and treatment
Alcohol use disorders—cases	0.155		[d]
Alzheimer's disease and other dementias—cases	0.666	0.627–0.667	GBD 1990[c], varies with age

(Continues on the following page.)

Table 3A.6 Continued

Sequela	Average disability weight[a]	Range[b]	Source
Parkinson's disease—cases	0.351	0.324–0.395	GBD 1990[c], varies with age and treatment
Multiple sclerosis—cases	0.411	0.410–0.437	GBD 1990[c], varies with age
Drug use disorders—cases	0.252		GBD 1990
Post-traumatic stress disorder—cases	0.105		GBD 1990
Obsessive-compulsive disorder—cases	0.127	0.122–0.129	GBD 1990[c]: untreated 0.129, treated 0.080
Panic disorder—cases	0.165	0.153–0.171	GBD 1990[c]: untreated 0.173, treated 0.091
Insomnia (primary)—cases	0.100		[f]
Migraine—cases	0.029	0.025–0.030	[f]
Mild mental retardation, lead-caused—cases	0.361		Netherlands study[e]
Glaucoma			
Low vision	0.247	0.227–0.282	GBD 1990[d]: untreated 0.282, treated 0.227
Blindness	0.600		GBD 1990
Cataracts			
Low vision	0.271	0.234–0.280	GBD 1990[d]: untreated 0.282, treated 0.227
Blindness	0.568	0.511–0.595	GBD 1990[c]: untreated 0.600, treated 0.488
Vision disorders, age-related and other			
Low vision	0.263	0.227–0.282	GBD 1990[d]: untreated 0.282, treated 0.227
Blindness	0.600		GBD 1990
Hearing loss, adult onset			
Mild	0.000		Assumed to have no disability for GBD
Moderate, treated	0.040		Assumed similar to mild hearing loss[f]
Moderate, untreated	0.120		Netherlands study[e]
Severe or profound, treated	0.120		Assumed similar to moderate loss[f]
Severe or profound, untreated	0.333		GBD 1990 deafness weight[c]
Rheumatic heart disease—cases	0.253	0.186–0.300	GBD 1990[c]: untreated 0.323, treated 0.171
Hypertensive heart disease—cases	0.243	0.201–0.300	[f]: untreated 0.323, treated 0.171
Ischemic heart disease			
Acute myocardial infarction	0.437	0.405–0.477	GBD 1990[c]: untreated 0.491, treated 0.395
Angina pectoris	0.137	0.108–0.207	GBD 1990[c]: untreated 0.227, treated 0.095
Congestive heart failure	0.234	0.186–0.300	GBD 1990[c]: untreated 0.323, treated 0.171
Cerebrovascular disease			
First-ever stroke cases	0.920		[f]
Long-term stroke survivors	0.270	0.228–0.295	[d], varies with age and treatment
Inflammatory heart disease—all sequelae	0.252	0.201–0.300	GBD 1990[c]: untreated 0.323, treated 0.171
Chronic obstructive pulmonary disease			
Mild and moderate symptomatic cases	0.170		Netherlands study[e]
Severe symptomatic cases	0.530		Netherlands study[e]
Asthma—cases	0.043	0.036–0.050	[f]: untreated 0.054, treated 0.043
Peptic ulcer disease			[f]
Cases with antibiotic treatment	0.003		GBD 1990
Cases not treated with antibiotic	0.115		GBD 1990
Cirrhosis of the liver—symptomatic cases	0.330		GBD 1990
Appendicitis—episodes	0.463		GBD 1990
Nephritis and nephrosis			
Acute glomerulonephritis	0.091	0.082–0.104	GBD 1990[c], varies with age and treatment
End-stage renal disease	0.098	0.087–0.107	GBD 1990[c], varies with age and treatment
Benign prostatic hypertrophy—symptomatic cases	0.038		GBD 1990
Skin diseases—cases	0.056		[f]
Rheumatoid arthritis—cases	0.199	0.185–0.221	GBD 1990[c]: untreated 0.233, treated 0.174
Osteoarthritis			
Hip	0.126	0.118–0.147	GBD 1990[c]: untreated 0.156, treated 0.108
Knee	0.129	0.118–0.147	GBD 1990[c]: untreated 0.156, treated 0.108
Gout—cases	0.132	0.061–0.189	[f]

Table 3A.6 Continued

Sequela	Average disability weight[a]	Range[b]	Source
Low back pain			
Episode of limiting low back pain	0.061		[e]
Acute intervertebral disc disorder	0.061		[f]
Chronic intervertebral disc disorder	0.121	0.103–0.125	[f]
Abdominal wall defect—cases	0.850		GBD 1990
Anencephaly—cases	0.850		GBD 1990
Anorectal atresia—cases	0.850		GBD 1990
Cleft lip—cases	0.049	0.002–0.082	GBD 1990[c]: untreated 0.016, treated 0.098
Cleft palate—cases	0.101	0.036–0.187	GBD 1990[c]: untreated 0.015, treated 0.231
Esophageal atresia—cases	0.850		GBD 1990
Renal agenesis—cases	0.850		GBD 1990
Down syndrome—cases	0.593		GBD 1990
Congenital heart anomalies—cases	0.323		GBD 1990
Spina bifida—cases	0.593		GBD 1990
Dental caries—episodes	0.081		GBD 1990
Periodontal disease—cases	0.001		GBD 1990
Edentulism—cases	0.020	0.007–0.052	GBD 1990[c]: untreated 0.062, treated 0.001

Source: Authors' compilation.

a. Global average disability weight.

b. Minimum and maximum disability weights if there is variation across age-sex-region categories. For disability weights based on the GBD 1990 study, further details of age-sex variation, treated and untreated weights, are given in annex tables 3 and 4 of Murray and Lopez 1996a.

c. Disability weights from GBD 1990 (Murray and Lopez 1996a).

d. Disability weights based on GBD 1990 (Murray and Lopez 1996a) with some revisions.

e. Disability weights drawn from Netherlands disability weights study (Stouthard and others 1997).

f. Provisional disability weights based on GBD 1990 or Netherlands weights for comparable health states.

Table 3A.7 Disability Weights for Malignant Neoplasms and Their Long-Term Sequelae

Site	Stage Diagnosis/ therapy	Stage Control	Long-term sequela	Mortality stratum (for WHO subregions) A	B	C	D/E
Mouth and oropharynx	0.09	0.09					
Esophagus	0.20	0.20					
Stomach	0.20	0.20					
Colon and rectum	0.20	0.20	Stoma	0.09	0.09	0.06	0.02
Liver	0.20	0.20					
Pancreas	0.20	0.20					
Trachea, bronchus, and lung	0.15	0.15					
Melanoma and other skin	0.05	0.05					
Breast	0.09	0.09	Mastectomy	0.03	0.05	0.06	0.08
Cervix uteri	0.08	0.08	Infertility/incontinence	0.04	0.11	0.13	0.17
Corpus uteri	0.10	0.10	Infertility/incontinence	0.18	0.18	0.18	0.18
Ovary	0.10	0.10	Infertility/incontinence	0.18	0.18	0.18	0.18
Prostate	0.13	0.13	Impotence/incontinence	0.06	0.06	0.06	0.06
Bladder	0.09	0.09					
Non-Hodgkin's lymphoma	0.06	0.06					
Hodgkin's lymphoma	0.06	0.06					
Leukemia	0.09	0.09					
Other	0.09	0.09					

Sources: Mathers, Vos, and Stevenson 1999; Stouthard and others 1997.

Note: For all cancer sites, the disability weight is 0.75 for the preterminal metastasis stage, and 0.81 in the terminal stage. For definitions of the mortality strata, see WHO 2002e.

Table 3A.8 Disability Weights for Injuries

Injury category	Short-term weight		Long-term weight	
	Treated	**Untreated**	**Treated**	**Untreated**
Fractured skull	0.431	0.431		
Ages 0–44			0.350	0.410
Ages 45–59			0.350	0.419
Ages 60+			0.404	0.471
Intracranial injuries	0.359	0.359		
Ages 0–44			0.350	0.410
Ages 45–59			0.350	0.419
Ages 60+			0.404	0.471
Fracture				
Face bones	0.223	0.223		
Vertebral column	0.266	0.266		
Rib or sternum	0.199	0.199		
Pelvis	0.247	0.247		
Clavicle, scapula, or humerus	0.153	0.153		
Ulna or radius	0.180	0.180		
Hand bones	0.100	0.100		
Femur	0.372	0.372	0.272	0.272
Patella, tibia, or fibula	0.271	0.271		
Ankle	0.196	0.196		
Foot bones	0.077	0.077		
Injured spinal cord			0.725	0.725
Dislocation of shoulder, elbow, or hip	0.074	0.074		
Other dislocation	0.074	0.074		
Sprains	0.064	0.064		
Amputation				
Thumb			0.165	0.165
Finger			0.102	0.102
Arm			0.257	0.308
Toe			0.102	0.102
Foot			0.300	0.300
Leg			0.300	0.300
Internal injuries	0.208	0.208		
Open wound	0.108	0.108		
Injury to eyes	0.108	0.108	0.300	0.354
Crushing	0.218	0.218		
Burns				
< 20%	0.158	0.156	0.001	0.002
> 20% and < 60%	0.441	0.469	0.255	0.255
> 60%	0.441	0.469	0.255	0.255
Injured nerves	0.064	0.078	0.064	0.078
Poisoning				
Ages 0–14	0.611	0.611		
Ages 14+	0.608	0.608		

Source: Murray and Lopez 1996a.

Table 3B.1 Deaths by Cause, Sex, and Age in Low- and Middle-Income Countries, 2001
(thousands)

Cause	Total	Male								Total
		0–4	5–14	15–29	30–44	45–59	60–69	70–79	80+	
Population (millions)	*5,219*	*288*	*563*	*712*	*545*	*326*	*124*	*61*	*15*	*2,636*
All causes	**48,351**	**5,407**	**733**	**1,835**	**2,786**	**3,998**	**4,069**	**4,376**	**2,349**	**25,554**
I. Communicable, maternal, perinatal, and nutritional conditions	*17,613*	*4,837*	*375*	*585*	*1,150*	*853*	*529*	*469*	*268*	*9,068*
A. Infectious and parasitic diseases	**10,686**	**2,360**	**295**	**539**	**1,085**	**734**	**348**	**249**	**111**	**5,724**
1. **Tuberculosis**	**1,590**	**22**	**16**	**138**	**256**	**281**	**184**	**115**	**31**	**1,043**
2. **Sexually transmitted diseases excluding HIV/AIDS**	**176**	**31**	**0**	**2**	**11**	**26**	**10**	**6**	**3**	**89**
a. Syphilis	155	30	0	1	10	23	10	6	3	83
b. Chlamydia	9	—	—	—	—	—	—	—	—	—
c. Gonorrhea	1	—	0	0	0	0	0	0	0	0
d. Other sexually transmitted diseases	12	1	0	0	1	4	0	0	0	6
3. **HIV/AIDS**	**2,552**	**173**	**52**	**258**	**640**	**221**	**29**	**4**	**0**	**1,377**
4. **Diarrheal diseases**	**1,777**	**837**	**3**	**6**	**11**	**15**	**15**	**19**	**23**	**930**
5. **Childhood-cluster diseases**	**1,362**	**524**	**109**	**24**	**11**	**6**	**3**	**1**	**1**	**679**
a. Pertussis	301	150	0	—	—	—	0	—	—	150
b. Poliomyelitis[a]	0	0	0	0	0	0	0	0	0	0
c. Diphtheria	6	3	0	0	0	0	0	0	0	3
d. Measles	762	277	91	11	0	0	0	—	—	379
e. Tetanus	293	94	18	13	11	6	3	1	1	147
6. **Meningitis**	**169**	**29**	**14**	**11**	**9**	**10**	**5**	**6**	**3**	**87**
7. **Hepatitis B**[b]	**95**	**3**	**4**	**8**	**16**	**22**	**7**	**4**	**2**	**66**
Hepatitis C[b]	**39**	**1**	**1**	**3**	**7**	**9**	**3**	**2**	**1**	**27**
8. **Malaria**	**1,207**	**521**	**7**	**10**	**11**	**11**	**7**	**7**	**4**	**579**
9. **Tropical-cluster diseases**	**128**	**4**	**21**	**15**	**13**	**13**	**7**	**4**	**1**	**78**
a. Trypanosomiasis	48	2	11	6	6	5	1	0	0	31
b. Chagas' disease	14	0	0	0	1	2	2	1	1	8
c. Schistosomiasis	14	0	0	0	1	3	3	2	0	9
d. Leishmaniasis	51	2	10	8	5	3	1	1	0	30
e. Lymphatic filariasis	0	0	0	0	0	0	0	0	0	0
f. Onchocerciasis	0	0	—	—	—	—	—	—	—	0
10. **Leprosy**	**6**	**0**	**0**	**0**	**1**	**1**	**1**	**1**	**0**	**4**
11. **Dengue**	**19**	**2**	**5**	**0**	**0**	**0**	**0**	**0**	**0**	**9**
12. **Japanese encephalitis**	**14**	**2**	**0**	**1**	**2**	**0**	**0**	**0**	**0**	**7**
13. **Trachoma**	**0**	**0**	**0**	**0**	**—**	**0**	**—**	**0**	**—**	**0**
14. **Intestinal nematode infections**	**12**	**1**	**3**	**0**	**0**	**1**	**0**	**0**	**0**	**6**
a. Ascariasis	3	0	1	0	0	0	0	0	0	1
b. Trichuriasis	3	0	1	0	0	0	0	0	0	2
c. Hookworm disease	3	0	0	0	0	0	0	0	0	2
Other intestinal infections	2	1	0	0	0	0	0	0	0	1
Other infectious diseases	1,540	210	59	62	97	117	76	80	42	744
B. Respiratory infections	**3,481**	**1,003**	**58**	**37**	**54**	**94**	**168**	**203**	**145**	**1,761**
1. Lower respiratory infections	3,408	989	55	35	51	90	163	198	141	1,724
2. Upper respiratory infections	69	14	2	2	2	4	5	5	3	35
3. Otitis media	3	0	1	0	0	0	0	0	0	2
C. Maternal conditions	**507**	**—**	**—**	**—**	**—**	**—**	**—**	**—**	**—**	**—**
1. Maternal hemorrhage	141	—	—	—	—	—	—	—	—	—
2. Maternal sepsis	75	—	—	—	—	—	—	—	—	—
3. Hypertensive disorders of pregnancy	71	—	—	—	—	—	—	—	—	—
4. Obstructed labor	43	—	—	—	—	—	—	—	—	—
5. Abortion	66	—	—	—	—	—	—	—	—	—
Other maternal conditions	111	—	—	—	—	—	—	—	—	—
D. Perinatal conditions[c]	**2,489**	**1,381**	**0**	**0**	**0**	**0**	**0**	**0**	**—**	**1,381**
1. Low birthweight	1,291	704	0	—	0	—	0	—	—	704
2. Birth asphyxia and birth trauma	728	426	0	0	0	0	—	—	—	426
Other perinatal conditions	470	251	0	0	0	0	—	0	—	251
E. Nutritional deficiencies	**450**	**93**	**22**	**9**	**10**	**25**	**13**	**16**	**13**	**201**
1. Protein-energy malnutrition	241	70	15	4	3	6	7	8	7	121
2. Iodine deficiency	7	2	1	0	0	0	0	0	0	3
3. Vitamin A deficiency	23	7	2	0	0	1	0	0	0	11
4. Iron-deficiency anemia	126	9	3	4	6	15	2	2	2	43
Other nutritional disorders	54	5	1	1	1	3	3	6	3	23

Table 3B.1 Continued

	Female								
	0–4	5–14	15–29	30–44	45–59	60–69	70–79	80+	Total
274	*533*	*682*	*530*	*326*	*136*	*78*	*25*	*2,583*
5,123	**738**	**1,576**	**1,831**	**2,521**	**2,960**	**4,319**	**3,729**	**22,797**
4,555	*451*	*950*	*959*	*512*	*358*	*408*	*353*	*8,546*
2,406	**347**	**628**	**666**	**400**	**205**	**191**	**118**	**4,962**
18	**16**	**106**	**135**	**117**	**79**	**56**	**19**	**547**
37	**0**	**13**	**10**	**14**	**7**	**4**	**1**	**87**
37	0	12	8	6	4	4	1	72
—	—	0	1	6	1	0	0	9
0	—	0	0	0	0	0	0	1
0	0	0	1	2	1	0	0	6
166	**51**	**384**	**423**	**128**	**20**	**4**	**0**	**1,175**
762	**3**	**3**	**5**	**10**	**14**	**20**	**30**	**847**
525	**111**	**24**	**11**	**6**	**3**	**1**	**1**	**682**
151	0	0	—	0	0	—	—	151
0	0	0	0	0	0	0	0	0
2	1	0	0	0	0	0	0	3
279	93	11	—	0	0	—	—	383
93	18	13	11	6	3	1	1	146
35	**18**	**9**	**5**	**5**	**4**	**4**	**2**	**82**
5	**2**	**5**	**4**	**6**	**3**	**2**	**2**	**29**
2	**1**	**2**	**2**	**3**	**1**	**1**	**1**	**12**
566	**8**	**12**	**12**	**13**	**8**	**7**	**4**	**629**
4	**15**	**10**	**6**	**7**	**4**	**3**	**2**	**50**
1	6	4	3	3	0	0	—	17
0	0	0	1	2	1	1	1	7
0	0	0	0	1	1	2	1	5
3	8	5	1	1	1	0	0	21
0	0	0	0	0	0	0	0	0
—	—	0	—	—	0	—	—	0
0	**0**	**0**	**0**	**0**	**0**	**0**	**0**	**2**
2	**6**	**1**	**0**	**0**	**0**	**0**	**0**	**10**
4	**2**	**1**	**1**	**0**	**0**	**0**	**0**	**7**
—	—	—	—	—	—	—	—	
2	**3**	**0**	**0**	**0**	**0**	**0**	**0**	**6**
1	1	0	0	0	0	0	0	2
0	1	0	0	0	0	0	0	1
—	0	0	0	0	0	0	0	1
1	0	0	0	0	0	0	0	1
277	113	59	53	90	62	87	55	796
939	**78**	**57**	**44**	**57**	**131**	**197**	**215**	**1,719**
924	73	56	44	57	128	194	209	1,684
15	5	1	1	1	3	3	6	34
0	0	0	0	0	0	0	0	1
0	**0**	**257**	**232**	**18**	**0**	**0**	**0**	**507**
0	0	63	71	7	—	—	—	141
—	0	37	35	4	—	—	—	75
—	0	41	28	2	—	—	0	71
—	—	26	17	0	—	—	—	43
—	0	44	22	0	—	—	—	66
—	0	46	59	5	0	0	0	111
1,109	**0**	**0**	**0**	**0**	**0**	**0**	**0**	**1,109**
587	0	—	—	—	—	—	—	587
302	0	0	—	0	—	0	0	302
219	0	0	0	0	0	0	0	219
101	**25**	**8**	**16**	**37**	**22**	**20**	**20**	**249**
69	17	2	3	5	7	7	10	119
3	0	0	0	0	0	0	0	3
9	2	0	0	0	0	0	0	12
11	5	5	13	30	12	4	4	83
9	1	0	0	2	3	8	6	31

(Continues on the following page.)

Table 3B.1 Continued

Cause	Total	Male 0–4	5–14	15–29	30–44	45–59	60–69	70–79	80+	Total
II. Noncommunicable diseases	*26,023*	*416*	*116*	*339*	*834*	*2,575*	*3,290*	*3,743*	*2,006*	*13,317*
A. Malignant neoplasms	**4,955**	**18**	**25**	**68**	**186**	**671**	**834**	**708**	**250**	**2,762**
1. Mouth and oropharynx cancers	271	0	0	4	16	54	62	37	13	187
2. Esophageal cancer	380	0	0	1	13	59	84	62	17	235
3. Stomach cancer	696	0	0	4	25	110	131	117	42	429
4. Colon and rectal cancers	357	0	0	4	15	39	53	52	22	185
5. Liver cancer	505	1	0	8	38	122	97	69	16	350
6. Pancreas cancer	117	0	0	0	4	18	19	16	6	64
7. Trachea, bronchus, and lung cancers	771	0	0	2	24	138	205	160	39	569
8. Melanoma and other skin cancers	35	0	0	1	2	4	4	4	2	17
9. Breast cancer	317	0	0	0	0	0	0	0	0	1
10. Cervix uteri cancer	218	—	—	—	—	—	—	—	—	—
11. Corpus uteri cancer	44	—	—	—	—	—	—	—	—	—
12. Ovarian cancer	86	—	—	—	—	—	—	—	—	—
13. Prostate cancer	145	0	0	0	0	9	35	65	35	145
14. Bladder cancer	117	0	0	0	2	12	24	30	14	81
15. Lymphomas and multiple myeloma	216	2	7	11	15	22	23	19	8	107
16. Leukemia	190	7	12	23	12	16	16	14	6	105
Other malignant neoplasms	490	8	5	9	22	69	80	64	29	285
B. Other neoplasms	**89**	**2**	**2**	**5**	**5**	**10**	**9**	**9**	**4**	**45**
C. Diabetes mellitus	**757**	**1**	**1**	**7**	**18**	**75**	**92**	**94**	**47**	**337**
D. Endocrine disorders	**170**	**21**	**4**	**6**	**8**	**11**	**9**	**10**	**8**	**76**
E. Neuropsychiatric conditions	**701**	**24**	**16**	**42**	**76**	**69**	**36**	**82**	**53**	**398**
1. Unipolar depressive disorders	10	0	0	0	2	2	1	0	0	5
2. Bipolar affective disorder	0	0	0	0	0	0	0	0	0	0
3. Schizophrenia	21	0	0	0	3	4	1	1	0	10
4. Epilepsy	116	12	7	14	14	9	4	3	2	65
5. Alcohol use disorders	62	0	0	5	16	19	9	4	1	54
6. Alzheimer's and other dementias	173	1	0	0	1	3	4	39	28	77
7. Parkinson's disease	51	0	0	0	1	1	3	12	8	25
8. Multiple sclerosis	8	0	0	0	1	1	1	0	0	4
9. Drug use disorders	73	0	0	11	28	19	2	0	0	60
10. Post-traumatic stress disorder	0	0	0	0	0	0	0	0	0	0
11. Obsessive-compulsive disorder	—	—	—	—	—	—	—	—	—	—
12. Panic disorder	—	—	—	—	—	—	—	—	—	—
13. Insomnia (primary)	—	—	—	—	—	—	—	—	—	—
14. Migraine	—	—	—	—	—	—	—	—	—	—
15. Mental retardation, lead-caused	5	1	1	1	0	0	0	0	0	3
Other neuropsychiatric disorders	183	11	8	10	9	12	12	23	13	97
F. Sense organ diseases	**3**	**0**	**0**	**0**	**0**	**0**	**0**	**0**	**0**	**1**
1. Glaucoma	0	0	—	0	0	0	0	0	0	0
2. Cataracts	—	—	—	—	—	—	—	—	—	—
3. Vision disorders, age-related	—	—	—	—	—	—	—	—	—	—
4. Hearing loss, adult onset	—	—	—	—	—	—	—	—	—	—
Other sense organ disorders	3	0	0	0	0	0	0	0	0	1
G. Cardiovascular diseases	**13,354**	**38**	**24**	**103**	**320**	**1,170**	**1,670**	**2,047**	**1,168**	**6,541**
1. Rheumatic heart disease	307	7	5	18	17	28	24	22	10	131
2. Hypertensive heart disease	760	1	1	4	17	65	97	113	64	361
3. Ischemic heart disease	5,699	3	3	26	144	620	818	928	467	3,010
4. Cerebrovascular disease	4,608	7	5	21	68	328	575	758	410	2,171
5. Inflammatory heart diseases	319	7	2	9	18	31	31	38	27	163
Other cardiovascular diseases	1,661	12	7	26	56	98	126	189	191	704
H. Respiratory diseases	**3,125**	**33**	**9**	**23**	**55**	**236**	**368**	**537**	**342**	**1,604**
1. Chronic obstructive pulmonary disease	2,378	2	0	2	16	167	297	449	275	1,209
2. Asthma	205	2	4	10	18	29	19	17	7	106
Other respiratory diseases	542	29	5	11	20	40	52	71	60	289

			Female					
0–4	5–14	15–29	30–44	45–59	60–69	70–79	80+	Total
419	*123*	*285*	*584*	*1,760*	*2,466*	*3,779*	*3,289*	*12,705*
19	**22**	**54**	**194**	**524**	**537**	**550**	**293**	**2,193**
0	0	1	5	20	22	21	14	84
0	0	1	5	33	41	42	22	144
0	0	3	21	52	61	80	50	266
0	0	2	13	32	42	50	34	172
1	1	5	15	36	39	41	16	154
0	0	0	3	10	14	17	9	53
0	1	1	11	46	58	64	21	203
0	0	0	2	3	4	5	3	18
0	0	2	44	108	74	57	31	316
0	0	11	19	68	59	44	17	218
0	0	0	3	10	12	12	6	44
0	1	3	9	24	22	19	8	86
—	—	—	—	—	—	—	—	—
1	0	0	3	5	8	10	8	35
3	6	8	12	19	23	25	14	109
8	9	12	12	14	12	12	7	85
6	4	5	17	42	46	51	34	204
2	**2**	**3**	**5**	**11**	**8**	**8**	**5**	**44**
2	**2**	**6**	**14**	**76**	**121**	**133**	**67**	**421**
22	**3**	**7**	**10**	**11**	**12**	**14**	**14**	**94**
19	**15**	**23**	**27**	**34**	**25**	**81**	**78**	**303**
0	0	0	1	3	1	0	0	5
0	0	0	0	0	0	0	0	0
0	0	0	2	4	2	2	1	10
9	8	12	8	6	3	3	2	51
0	0	0	2	3	2	1	0	8
1	0	1	1	2	5	40	47	96
0	0	0	0	1	2	11	11	26
0	0	0	1	2	1	1	0	5
—	0	2	6	4	0	0	0	13
0	0	0	0	0	0	0	0	0
—	—	—	—	—	—	—	—	—
—	—	—	—	—	—	—	—	—
—	—	—	—	—	—	—	—	—
—	—	—	—	—	—	—	—	—
0	1	1	0	0	0	0	0	2
8	6	7	6	9	10	24	16	86
0	**0**	**0**	**0**	**0**	**0**	**0**	**0**	**1**
—	—	—	0	0	0	0	0	0
—	—	—	—	—	—	—	—	—
—	—	—	—	—	—	—	—	—
—	—	—	—	—	—	—	—	—
0	0	0	0	0	0	0	0	1
45	**26**	**91**	**192**	**723**	**1,312**	**2,274**	**2,150**	**6,814**
8	8	19	21	35	31	35	18	175
1	1	3	12	52	85	132	114	399
2	2	27	68	290	581	911	808	2,689
5	5	13	45	238	463	869	799	2,437
6	3	6	9	20	24	43	45	156
23	8	24	36	88	127	284	366	957
30	**9**	**22**	**44**	**173**	**249**	**483**	**512**	**1,521**
2	0	1	13	122	199	411	421	1,169
2	4	12	19	26	14	13	10	99
26	5	9	12	25	36	58	81	252

(Continues on the following page.)

Table 3B.1 Continued

Cause	Total	0–4	5–14	15–29	30–44	45–59	60–69	70–79	80+	Total
					Male					
I. Digestive diseases	**1,600**	**47**	**16**	**48**	**123**	**252**	**183**	**156**	**74**	**899**
1. Peptic ulcer disease	234	3	2	7	18	40	29	28	14	140
2. Cirrhosis of the liver	654	8	4	16	63	143	94	65	21	413
3. Appendicitis	19	0	1	1	1	3	2	2	1	11
Other digestive diseases	694	37	10	23	41	66	58	61	38	335
J. Genitourinary diseases	**676**	**11**	**7**	**21**	**35**	**70**	**79**	**87**	**53**	**363**
1. Nephritis and nephrosis	552	9	6	19	31	58	61	64	37	285
2. Benign prostatic hypertrophy	29	—	—	0	0	5	6	10	7	29
Other genitourinary system diseases	96	2	1	2	4	8	11	13	8	50
K. Skin diseases	**53**	**1**	**0**	**1**	**3**	**4**	**3**	**5**	**4**	**21**
L. Musculoskeletal diseases	**60**	**1**	**1**	**2**	**2**	**4**	**4**	**6**	**4**	**24**
1. Rheumatoid arthritis	15	0	0	0	0	1	1	1	1	5
2. Osteoarthritis	2	0	0	0	0	0	0	0	0	1
3. Gout	1	0	0	0	0	0	0	0	0	1
4. Low back pain	1	0	0	0	0	0	0	0	0	1
Other musculoskeletal disorders	41	1	1	2	1	3	3	4	3	16
M. Congenital anomalies	**477**	**217**	**10**	**12**	**3**	**2**	**1**	**1**	**0**	**246**
1. Abdominal wall defect	4	2	0	0	0	0	0	0	0	2
2. Anencephaly	18	9	0	0	0	0	0	0	0	9
3. Anorectal atresia	1	1	0	0	0	0	0	0	0	1
4. Cleft lip	0	0	0	0	0	0	0	0	0	0
5. Cleft palate	1	1	0	0	0	0	0	0	0	1
6. Esophageal atresia	1	1	0	0	0	0	0	0	0	1
7. Renal agenesis	2	1	0	0	0	0	0	0	0	1
8. Down syndrome	22	8	1	2	0	0	0	0	0	11
9. Congenital heart anomalies	257	112	6	7	2	1	0	0	0	128
10. Spina bifida	24	11	0	0	0	0	0	0	0	12
Other congenital anomalies	148	73	3	3	1	1	0	0	0	82
N. Oral conditions	**1**	**0**	**0**	**0**	**0**	**0**	**0**	**0**	**0**	**1**
1. Dental caries	0	—	—	—	—	—	—	0	0	0
2. Periodontal disease	0	—	—	0	0	0	0	0	0	0
3. Edentulism	—	—	—	—	—	—	—	—	—	—
Other oral diseases	1	0	0	0	0	0	0	0	0	1
III. Injuries	***4,715***	***154***	***242***	***911***	***802***	***571***	***250***	***164***	***75***	***3,169***
A. Unintentional injuries	**3,214**	**147**	**222**	**511**	**478**	**386**	**174**	**119**	**56**	**2,095**
1. Road traffic accidents	1,069	28	82	217	204	143	58	37	13	781
2. Poisonings	328	9	11	35	52	65	26	10	3	211
3. Falls	316	9	13	28	33	38	26	30	21	199
4. Fires	300	17	16	23	24	15	8	6	3	113
5. Drownings	368	33	57	66	44	30	11	7	3	252
6. Other unintentional injuries	832	50	43	141	121	95	45	29	14	539
B. Intentional injuries	**1,501**	**7**	**20**	**400**	**324**	**184**	**76**	**45**	**18**	**1,074**
1. Self-inflicted injuries	749	0	8	137	124	94	47	31	11	453
2. Violence	532	6	9	179	131	66	19	10	5	425
3. War	207	0	2	80	66	24	10	3	2	187
Other intentional injuries	12	1	0	3	3	1	1	1	0	10

Table 3B.1 Continued

	Female							
0–4	**5–14**	**15–29**	**30–44**	**45–59**	**60–69**	**70–79**	**80+**	**Total**
67	**26**	**47**	**62**	**132**	**123**	**143**	**102**	**702**
3	1	4	9	18	18	22	18	94
17	8	15	24	61	50	46	20	240
0	0	1	1	2	2	2	2	9
47	17	27	28	52	53	72	63	359
9	**7**	**16**	**26**	**61**	**67**	**75**	**52**	**313**
7	6	14	22	54	58	64	43	267
—	—	—	—	—	—	—	—	—
1	1	3	4	8	9	12	9	46
1	**0**	**1**	**3**	**5**	**6**	**8**	**8**	**32**
1	**1**	**4**	**5**	**6**	**5**	**8**	**7**	**37**
0	0	0	1	2	2	4	1	10
0	0	0	0	0	0	0	0	1
0	0	0	0	0	0	0	0	0
0	0	0	0	0	0	0	0	0
1	1	4	4	4	3	4	5	25
204	**10**	**10**	**3**	**2**	**1**	**1**	**0**	**231**
2	0	0	0	0	0	0	0	2
9	0	0	0	0	0	0	0	9
0	0	0	0	0	0	0	0	0
0	0	0	0	0	0	0	0	0
1	0	0	0	0	0	0	0	1
1	0	0	0	0	0	0	0	1
1	0	0	0	0	0	0	0	1
7	1	2	0	0	0	0	0	11
112	6	6	2	1	0	0	0	128
12	0	0	0	0	0	0	0	12
60	3	1	1	1	0	0	0	66
0	**0**	**0**	**0**	**0**	**0**	**0**	**0**	**1**
—	—	—	—	0	—	—	0	0
—	0	0	0	0	0	0	0	0
—	—	—	—	—	—	—	—	—
0	0	0	0	0	0	0	0	1
148	*164*	*342*	*288*	*249*	*136*	*132*	*87*	*1,546*
142	**148**	**212**	**179**	**166**	**99**	**101**	**73**	**1,119**
22	48	52	57	54	25	20	9	288
7	10	16	21	26	22	10	5	117
7	8	9	9	15	13	29	28	117
23	18	66	38	19	9	10	6	187
25	31	21	13	10	6	6	4	116
59	34	48	40	41	23	26	22	293
6	**16**	**130**	**109**	**83**	**37**	**31**	**14**	**427**
0	6	98	75	57	25	23	11	296
6	9	28	28	20	9	6	2	108
0	1	4	5	5	3	1	1	20
0	0	1	0	1	0	0	0	3

Source: Authors' compilation.

Note: — = an estimate of zero; the number zero in a cell indicates a non-zero estimate of less than 500.

a. For East Asia and Pacific, Europe and Central Asia, and Latin America and the Caribbean regions, these figures include late effects of polio cases with onset prior to regional certification of polio eradication in 1994, 2000, and 2002, respectively.

b. Does not include liver cancer and cirrhosis deaths resulting from chronic hepatitis virus infection.

c. This cause category includes "Causes arising in the perinatal period" as defined in the International Classification of Diseases, principally low birthweight, prematurity, birth asphyxia, and birth trauma, and does not include all causes of deaths occurring in the perinatal period.

Table 3B.2 Deaths by Cause, Sex, and Age in the East Asia and Pacific Region, 2001

Cause	Total	Male 0–4	5–14	15–29	30–44	45–59	60–69	70–79	80+	Total
Population (millions)	1,849	80	175	244	224	136	51	25	6	942
All causes	**13,070**	**701**	**121**	**416**	**624**	**1,182**	**1,388**	**1,619**	**895**	**6,945**
I. Communicable, maternal, perinatal, and nutritional conditions	***2,470***	***535***	***35***	***83***	***153***	***160***	***137***	***135***	***86***	***1,324***
A. Infectious and parasitic diseases	1,299	196	25	70	139	132	102	88	37	790
1. **Tuberculosis**	534	2	3	29	64	82	82	65	19	347
2. **Sexually transmitted diseases excluding HIV/AIDS**	9	1	0	0	0	1	1	1	1	4
a. Syphilis	5	1	0	0	0	0	1	1	0	4
b. Chlamydia	1	—	—	—	—	—	—	—	—	—
c. Gonorrhea	0	—	—	0	0	—	—	—	—	0
d. Other sexually transmitted diseases	3	0	—	0	0	0	0	—	0	1
3. **HIV/AIDS**	106	3	0	15	43	16	1	0	0	79
4. **Diarrheal diseases**	226	105	1	1	2	2	2	2	3	118
5. **Childhood-cluster diseases**	107	32	14	5	1	1	0	0	0	54
a. Pertussis	3	2	—	—	—	—	—	—	—	2
b. Poliomyelitis[a]	0	0	0	—	—	—	—	—	—	0
c. Diphtheria	1	0	0	0	0	0	0	—	0	0
d. Measles	76	22	12	3	—	—	—	—	—	38
e. Tetanus	27	8	2	1	1	1	0	0	0	14
6. **Meningitis**	33	7	1	3	2	2	1	1	1	16
7. **Hepatitis B[b]**	32	1	0	3	7	11	3	1	1	26
Hepatitis C[b]	13	0	0	1	3	5	1	0	0	11
8. **Malaria**	30	18	0	0	0	0	0	0	0	20
9. **Tropical-cluster diseases**	5	0	0	0	0	1	1	0	0	4
a. Trypanosomiasis	—	—	—	—	—	—	—	—	—	—
b. Chagas' disease	0	—	—	—	—	—	—	—	—	—
c. Schistosomiasis	3	—	0	0	0	1	1	0	0	3
d. Leishmaniasis	2	0	0	0	0	0	0	0	—	1
e. Lymphatic filariasis	0	0	—	0	0	0	0	—	0	0
f. Onchocerciasis	—	—	—	—	—	—	—	—	—	—
10. **Leprosy**	2	0	0	0	0	0	1	1	0	2
11. **Dengue**	8	1	2	0	0	0	0	0	0	3
12. **Japanese encephalitis**	4	1	0	0	0	0	0	0	0	2
13. **Trachoma**	0	0	—	0	—	0	—	0	—	0
14. **Intestinal nematode infections**	2	1	0	0	0	0	0	0	0	1
a. Ascariasis	1	0	0	—	—	0	—	0	—	0
b. Trichuriasis	0	0	0	—	—	—	—	—	—	0
c. Hookworm disease	0	—	—	0	0	0	0	0	0	0
Other intestinal infections	1	0	0	0	0	0	0	0	0	0
Other infectious diseases	190	24	3	13	16	11	8	15	12	102
B. Respiratory infections	571	68	8	10	11	25	33	45	48	248
1. Lower respiratory infections	544	63	8	9	10	22	32	44	46	233
2. Upper respiratory infections	27	6	0	1	1	2	2	1	2	14
3. Otitis media	1	0	0	0	0	0	0	0	0	1
C. Maternal conditions	37	—	—	—	—	—	—	—	—	—
1. Maternal hemorrhage	12	—	—	—	—	—	—	—	—	—
2. Maternal sepsis	3	—	—	—	—	—	—	—	—	—
3. Hypertensive disorders of pregnancy	5	—	—	—	—	—	—	—	—	—
4. Obstructed labor	2	—	—	—	—	—	—	—	—	—
5. Abortion	5	—	—	—	—	—	—	—	—	—
Other maternal conditions	10	—	—	—	—	—	—	—	—	—
D. Perinatal conditions[c]	502	262	0	—	—	—	—	—	—	262
1. Low birthweight	193	100	—	—	—	—	—	—	—	100
2. Birth asphyxia and birth trauma	158	83	—	—	—	—	—	—	—	83
Other perinatal conditions	152	78	0	—	—	—	—	—	—	78
E. Nutritional deficiencies	61	9	1	3	2	3	2	2	2	24
1. Protein-energy malnutrition	27	7	1	1	1	1	1	1	1	14
2. Iodine deficiency	0	0	0	—	0	—	—	—	0	0
3. Vitamin A deficiency	0	0	0	—	0	0	—	—	—	0
4. Iron-deficiency anemia	25	1	0	1	1	2	0	0	0	6
Other nutritional disorders	9	1	0	0	0	0	0	1	1	3

Table 3B.2 Continued

	Female								
0–4	**5–14**	**15–29**	**30–44**	**45–59**	**60–69**	**70–79**	**80+**	**Total**
74	*161*	*232*	*217*	*131*	*52*	*30*	*10*	*907*
697	**97**	**220**	**408**	**747**	**936**	**1,530**	**1,491**	**6,124**
542	*34*	*67*	*100*	*85*	*80*	*106*	*130*	*1,145*
168	**25**	**44**	**69**	**67**	**52**	**53**	**32**	**509**
2	**3**	**22**	**39**	**42**	**36**	**31**	**12**	**187**
0	**—**	**0**	**1**	**2**	**1**	**1**	**0**	**4**
0	—	0	0	0	0	0	0	1
—	—	—	0	1	0	—	—	1
0	—	0	0	0	—	—	—	0
0	—	0	0	1	0	0	0	2
2	**0**	**5**	**9**	**8**	**2**	**1**	**0**	**27**
95	**1**	**1**	**1**	**1**	**2**	**3**	**4**	**107**
32	**14**	**5**	**1**	**1**	**0**	**0**	**0**	**53**
2	—	—	—	—	—	—	—	2
0	—	—	—	0	—	—	—	0
0	0	0	0	0	—	—	—	0
23	12	3	—	—	—	—	—	38
7	2	1	1	1	0	0	0	13
6	**1**	**3**	**3**	**2**	**1**	**1**	**0**	**17**
1	**0**	**1**	**2**	**1**	**1**	**0**	**1**	**6**
0	**0**	**0**	**1**	**0**	**0**	**0**	**0**	**2**
8	**0**	**0**	**0**	**0**	**0**	**0**	**0**	**9**
0	**0**	**0**	**0**	**0**	**0**	**0**	**0**	**1**
—	—	—	0	—	—	—	—	0
—	0	0	0	0	0	0	0	1
0	0	0	0	0	0	0	—	1
—	—	—	—	0	—	0	0	0
0	**0**	**0**	**0**	**0**	**0**	**0**	**0**	**0**
1	**2**	**0**	**0**	**0**	**0**	**0**	**0**	**5**
1	**0**	**0**	**0**	**0**	**0**	**0**	**0**	**2**
1	**0**	**0**	**0**	**0**	**0**	**0**	**0**	**1**
0	0	0	0	—	0	—	—	0
—	0	—	—	—	—	—	—	0
—	—	0	0	0	0	0	0	0
0	0	0	0	—	0	0	0	0
18	3	7	12	8	9	17	13	87
127	**8**	**5**	**6**	**10**	**24**	**49**	**93**	**323**
122	8	5	5	10	24	48	89	311
6	0	0	0	0	0	1	5	12
0	0	0	0	0	0	—	0	0
—	0	16	20	0	—	—	—	37
—	—	5	6	0	—	—	—	12
—	—	2	2	0	—	—	—	3
—	0	2	2	0	—	—	—	5
—	—	1	1	0	—	—	—	2
—	—	3	2	0	—	—	—	5
—	—	3	6	0	—	—	—	10
241	**0**	**—**	**—**	**—**	**—**	**—**	**—**	**241**
92	0	—	—	—	—	—	—	92
74	—	—	—	—	—	—	—	74
74	—	—	—	—	—	—	—	74
6	**1**	**2**	**6**	**8**	**5**	**4**	**5**	**37**
5	1	0	1	1	1	1	2	12
0	0	—	0	—	0	—	—	0
0	0	—	—	—	—	—	—	0
1	0	2	5	7	3	1	1	19
0	0	0	0	0	1	2	2	6

(Continues on the following page.)

Table 3B.2 Continued

Cause	Total	Male 0–4	5–14	15–29	30–44	45–59	60–69	70–79	80+	Total
II. Noncommunicable diseases	**9,221**	*125*	*26*	*96*	*254*	*860*	*1,168*	*1,429*	*783*	*4,741*
A. Malignant neoplasms	**2,143**	6	8	26	90	346	382	316	91	1,264
1. Mouth and oropharynx cancers	66	0	0	1	5	16	12	8	2	45
2. Esophageal cancer	234	—	—	1	8	36	52	41	9	147
3. Stomach cancer	442	0	0	3	16	76	84	75	25	278
4. Colon and rectal cancers	159	0	0	2	7	20	24	22	9	83
5. Liver cancer	373	0	0	5	29	99	74	51	11	269
6. Pancreas cancer	37	0	0	0	2	7	6	5	2	22
7. Trachea, bronchus, and lung cancers	387	0	0	1	12	60	94	77	18	262
8. Melanoma and other skin cancers	5	0	0	0	0	1	1	1	0	2
9. Breast cancer	93	—	—	—	0	0	0	0	0	0
10. Cervix uteri cancer	47	—	—	—	—	—	—	—	—	—
11. Corpus uteri cancer	8	—	—	—	—	—	—	—	—	—
12. Ovarian cancer	25	—	—	—	—	—	—	—	—	—
13. Prostate cancer	16	0	0	0	0	1	4	8	3	16
14. Bladder cancer	30	0	0	0	0	2	6	9	4	21
15. Lymphomas and multiple myeloma	42	0	1	2	4	6	5	3	1	24
16. Leukemia	76	3	5	10	4	7	6	5	2	42
Other malignant neoplasms	104	2	1	1	3	15	15	12	5	54
B. Other neoplasms	**21**	1	1	1	1	3	2	2	1	9
C. Diabetes mellitus	**233**	0	0	1	5	20	29	29	12	97
D. Endocrine disorders	**61**	9	1	2	2	3	2	3	3	25
E. Neuropsychiatric conditions	**186**	3	2	8	15	14	11	21	18	91
1. Unipolar depressive disorders	1	0	0	0	0	0	0	0	0	1
2. Bipolar affective disorder	0	0	0	0	0	0	0	0	0	0
3. Schizophrenia	6	0	0	0	1	1	0	0	0	3
4. Epilepsy	24	2	1	3	4	2	1	0	0	13
5. Alcohol use disorders	12	0	0	1	3	4	2	1	0	11
6. Alzheimer's and other dementias	58	0	0	0	1	1	2	8	9	21
7. Parkinson's disease	26	0	0	0	1	0	1	5	4	11
8. Multiple sclerosis	1	0	0	0	0	0	0	0	0	0
9. Drug use disorders	7	0	0	1	3	2	0	0	0	6
10. Post-traumatic stress disorder	0	0	0	0	0	0	0	0	0	0
11. Obsessive-compulsive disorder	—	—	—	—	—	—	—	—	—	—
12. Panic disorder	—									—
13. Insomnia (primary)	—									—
14. Migraine	—									—
15. Mental retardation, lead-caused	0	0	0	0	0	0	0	0	0	0
Other neuropsychiatric disorders	50	1	1	2	2	4	5	7	4	26
F. Sense organ diseases	**0**	0	0	0	0	0	0	0	0	0
1. Glaucoma	0	0	—	0	0	0	0	—	—	0
2. Cataracts	—	—	—	—	—	—	—	—	—	—
3. Vision disorders, age-related	—	—	—	—	—	—	—	—	—	—
4. Hearing loss, adult onset	—	—	—	—	—	—	—	—	—	—
Other sense organ disorders	0	0	0	0	0	0	0	0	0	0
G. Cardiovascular diseases	**4,003**	7	4	27	81	310	493	664	389	1,976
1. Rheumatic heart disease	121	1	1	5	6	11	10	10	4	47
2. Hypertensive heart disease	333	0	0	1	7	28	47	54	29	166
3. Ischemic heart disease	1,151	1	1	8	31	104	149	189	109	591
4. Cerebrovascular disease	1,902	2	1	6	25	139	249	351	188	959
5. Inflammatory heart diseases	81	1	0	1	2	5	7	11	10	36
Other cardiovascular diseases	415	3	2	6	10	25	33	50	49	177
H. Respiratory diseases	**1,660**	7	1	5	11	62	158	308	225	775
1. Chronic obstructive pulmonary disease	1,415	0	0	0	2	46	136	275	191	651
2. Asthma	56	1	1	3	5	8	5	5	2	28
Other respiratory diseases	189	5	1	2	3	8	16	27	32	96

			Female					
0–4	5–14	15–29	30–44	45–59	60–69	70–79	80+	Total
115	*25*	*67*	*195*	*571*	*808*	*1,375*	*1,324*	*4,479*
6	**6**	**15**	**79**	**217**	**211**	**229**	**114**	**879**
0	0	0	1	6	5	6	3	22
0	0	0	2	20	25	27	12	87
0	0	2	13	33	36	49	31	164
0	0	1	7	16	19	20	14	76
1	0	2	10	25	28	27	10	104
0	0	0	1	3	4	5	2	16
0	0	0	6	27	36	42	12	125
0	0	0	0	0	0	1	0	2
0	0	1	16	38	19	13	7	93
0	0	2	3	14	13	11	4	47
0	0	0	1	2	2	2	1	8
0	0	1	4	8	6	5	2	25
—	—	—	—	—	—	—	—	—
0	0	0	0	1	2	3	2	8
0	1	1	3	4	3	4	2	18
3	4	4	6	7	4	4	2	35
2	1	1	5	12	10	11	8	50
1	**0**	**0**	**1**	**3**	**2**	**2**	**1**	**11**
0	**0**	**1**	**5**	**23**	**39**	**46**	**22**	**136**
9	**1**	**4**	**6**	**3**	**3**	**4**	**6**	**36**
2	**2**	**5**	**7**	**9**	**9**	**24**	**38**	**95**
—	—	0	0	0	0	0	0	1
0	—	0	0	0	0	0	0	0
0	0	0	1	1	0	0	0	3
1	1	3	3	1	0	0	0	11
—	—	0	1	1	0	0	0	2
0	0	0	1	1	2	9	24	37
0	—	0	0	0	1	6	7	15
0	0	0	0	0	0	0	0	1
—	—	0	1	0	0	0	0	1
—	—	—	—	0	0	0	0	0
—	—	—	—	—	—	—	—	—
—	—	—	—	—	—	—	—	—
—	—	—	—	—	—	—	—	—
—	—	—	—	—	—	—	—	—
0	0	0	0	0	0	0	0	0
0	1	1	1	3	4	8	7	25
0	**0**	**0**	**0**	**0**	**0**	**0**	**0**	**0**
—	—	—	—	—	—	—	—	—
—	—	—	—	—	—	—	—	—
—	—	—	—	—	—	—	—	—
—	—	—	—	—	—	—	—	—
0	0	0	0	0	0	0	0	0
5	**4**	**19**	**54**	**209**	**355**	**684**	**695**	**2,027**
1	1	5	8	16	14	18	10	74
0	0	1	4	20	34	57	51	167
0	0	6	16	58	111	181	186	560
1	1	3	15	90	158	343	332	943
1	0	1	1	4	6	14	20	46
2	1	4	9	22	32	71	96	237
5	**1**	**4**	**11**	**48**	**126**	**307**	**382**	**884**
0	0	0	3	35	109	282	333	763
1	1	3	6	8	5	3	2	28
4	1	1	2	5	11	21	47	93

(Continues on the following page.)

Table 3B.2 Continued

Cause	Total	Male								Total
		0–4	5–14	15–29	30–44	45–59	60–69	70–79	80+	
I. Digestive diseases	**514**	**28**	**3**	**13**	**35**	**76**	**60**	**53**	**27**	**294**
1. Peptic ulcer disease	94	1	0	2	5	14	13	13	6	54
2. Cirrhosis of the liver	193	1	0	4	19	44	28	21	7	126
3. Appendicitis	6	0	0	0	0	1	0	1	0	3
Other digestive diseases	220	26	2	6	10	16	18	19	13	111
J. Genitourinary diseases	**233**	**2**	**2**	**8**	**13**	**24**	**29**	**29**	**17**	**124**
1. Nephritis and nephrosis	186	1	2	8	11	20	22	20	11	94
2. Benign prostatic hypertrophy	8	—	—	—	0	1	2	3	3	8
Other genitourinary system diseases	39	1	0	1	2	3	6	5	3	21
K. Skin diseases	**9**	**0**	**0**	**0**	**0**	**0**	**1**	**1**	**1**	**4**
L. Musculoskeletal diseases	**23**	**0**	**0**	**0**	**0**	**2**	**2**	**2**	**1**	**9**
1. Rheumatoid arthritis	6	0	0	0	0	0	1	1	0	2
2. Osteoarthritis	1	0	0	0	0	0	0	0	0	0
3. Gout	1	0	0	0	0	0	0	0	0	1
4. Low back pain	0	0	0	0	0	0	0	0	0	0
Other musculoskeletal disorders	15	0	0	0	0	1	1	1	1	5
M. Congenital anomalies	**136**	**61**	**4**	**5**	**1**	**1**	**0**	**0**	**0**	**72**
1. Abdominal wall defect	0	0	—	—	0	—	—	—	0	0
2. Anencephaly	2	1	0	—	—	—	—	—	0	1
3. Anorectal atresia	—	—	—	—	—	—	—	—	—	—
4. Cleft lip	—	—	—	—	—	—	—	—	—	—
5. Cleft palate	0	0	0	0	0	—	—	—	—	0
6. Esophageal atresia	—	—	—	—	—	—	—	—	—	—
7. Renal agenesis	0	0	—	—	0	—	—	—	—	0
8. Down syndrome	1	0	0	0	0	—	—	—	—	1
9. Congenital heart anomalies	78	33	2	3	1	0	0	0	0	39
10. Spina bifida	1	1	0	—	—	0	0	—	—	1
Other congenital anomalies	52	26	1	1	0	0	0	0	0	30
N. Oral conditions	**0**	**0**	**0**	**0**	**0**	**0**	**0**	**0**	**0**	**0**
1. Dental caries	—	—	—	—	—	—	—	—	—	—
2. Periodontal disease	0	—	—	—	—	—	—	—	—	—
3. Edentulism	—	—	—	—	—	—	—	—	—	—
Other oral diseases	0	0	0	0	0	0	0	0	0	0
III. Injuries	*1,379*	*41*	*60*	*237*	*217*	*162*	*82*	*55*	*25*	*880*
A. Unintentional injuries	**936**	**40**	**56**	**160**	**142**	**111**	**53**	**37**	**19**	**616**
1. Road traffic accidents	361	4	13	85	72	51	22	13	4	263
2. Poisonings	83	2	3	8	11	13	8	4	1	51
3. Falls	122	2	4	12	14	16	10	10	8	76
4. Fires	36	2	1	3	3	1	2	2	1	15
5. Drownings	144	17	28	22	9	7	4	3	2	92
6. Other unintentional injuries	189	12	8	29	32	22	8	5	3	119
B. Intentional injuries	**443**	**1**	**4**	**77**	**75**	**51**	**30**	**18**	**7**	**263**
1. Self-inflicted injuries	323	—	2	40	40	34	25	16	6	164
2. Violence	103	1	2	30	30	15	4	2	1	84
3. War	14	0	0	5	4	2	1	0	0	13
Other intentional injuries	3	0	0	1	1	0	0	0	0	2

Table 3B.2 Continued

0–4	5–14	15–29	30–44	45–59	60–69	70–79	80+	Total
				Female				
31	**3**	**7**	**16**	**34**	**37**	**49**	**43**	**219**
1	0	1	4	7	8	10	9	40
2	1	2	7	17	15	16	8	68
0	0	0	0	1	0	1	1	3
28	2	4	5	10	13	22	25	109
1	**2**	**6**	**11**	**21**	**24**	**26**	**18**	**109**
1	2	5	10	18	20	21	15	91
—	—	—	—	—	—	—	—	—
0	0	1	2	3	3	5	3	18
0	**0**	**0**	**0**	**1**	**1**	**1**	**1**	**5**
0	**0**	**1**	**2**	**2**	**2**	**3**	**3**	**14**
0	0	0	0	1	1	1	0	4
0	0	0	0	0	0	0	0	0
0	0	0	0	0	0	0	0	0
0	0	0	0	0	0	0	0	0
0	0	1	2	1	1	1	2	9
53	**4**	**3**	**2**	**1**	**0**	**0**	**0**	**64**
0	—	—	—	—	—	0	—	0
1	0	0	0	0	—	—	—	1
—	—	—	—	—	—	—	—	—
—	—	—	—	—	—	—	—	—
0	0	0	0	0	—	—	—	0
—	—	—	—	—	—	—	—	—
0	—	—	—	—	—	—	—	0
0	0	0	0	0	—	—	—	1
30	3	3	1	0	0	0	0	39
1	0	0	0	0	—	0	0	1
21	1	0	0	0	0	0	0	23
0	**0**	**0**	**0**	**0**	**0**	**0**	**0**	**0**
—	—	—	—	—	—	—	—	—
—	0	0	0	0	—	—	—	0
—	—	—	—	—	—	—	—	—
0	0	0	0	0	0	0	0	0
40	*38*	*86*	*113*	*91*	*47*	*48*	*36*	*499*
40	35	45	61	52	27	31	28	319
3	8	16	28	24	9	7	3	98
3	3	4	7	6	4	3	2	32
2	1	3	4	6	5	10	14	46
2	2	7	5	2	1	1	1	22
11	16	6	6	4	3	3	2	53
20	4	8	11	9	5	5	6	69
1	**3**	**40**	**52**	**39**	**20**	**17**	**8**	**180**
—	2	35	45	35	18	16	7	159
1	1	5	6	4	2	1	0	19
0	0	0	0	0	0	0	0	1
0	0	0	0	0	0	0	0	1

Source: Authors' compilation.

Note: — = an estimate of zero; the number zero in a cell indicates a non-zero estimate of less than 500.

a. These figures include late effects of polio cases with onset prior to regional certification of polio eradication in 1994.

b. Does not include liver cancer and cirrhosis deaths resulting from chronic hepatitis virus infection.

c. This cause category includes "Causes arising in the perinatal period" as defined in the International Classification of Diseases, principally low birthweight, prematurity, birth asphyxia, and birth trauma, and does not include all causes of deaths occurring in the perinatal period.

Table 3B.3 Deaths by Cause, Sex, and Age in the Europe and Central Asia Region, 2001
(thousands)

Cause	Total	Male								Total
		0–4	5–14	15–29	30–44	45–59	60–69	70–79	80+	
Population (millions)	*477*	*15*	*38*	*59*	*51*	*37*	*17*	*9*	*2*	*230*
All causes	5,669	97	21	148	323	619	707	720	348	2,985
I. **Communicable, maternal, perinatal, and nutritional conditions**	*326*	*70*	*4*	*15*	*40*	*42*	*21*	*13*	*7*	*211*
A. **Infectious and parasitic diseases**	152	17	2	13	36	29	10	4	1	112
1. **Tuberculosis**	66	0	0	5	19	20	7	2	0	55
2. **Sexually transmitted diseases excluding HIV/AIDS**	1	0	0	0	0	0	0	0	0	0
a. Syphilis	0	0	0	0	0	0	0	0	0	0
b. Chlamydia	—	—	—	—	—	—	—	—	—	—
c. Gonorrhea	0	—	—	0	0	0	—	0	—	0
d. Other sexually transmitted diseases	0	0	—	0	0	0	0	0	—	0
3. **HIV/AIDS**	28	0	0	5	13	5	1	0	0	24
4. **Diarrheal diseases**	15	6	0	0	0	0	0	0	0	8
5. **Childhood-cluster diseases**	8	3	1	0	0	0	0	0	0	4
a. Pertussis	0	0	0	—	—	—	—	—	—	0
b. Poliomyelitis[a]	0	0	0	0	0	0	0	0	0	0
c. Diphtheria	0	0	0	0	0	0	0	0	0	0
d. Measles	8	3	1	0	0	0	0	—	—	4
e. Tetanus	0	0	0	0	0	0	0	0	0	0
6. **Meningitis**	14	5	0	1	1	1	0	0	0	8
7. **Hepatitis B**[b]	3	0	0	1	0	0	0	0	0	2
Hepatitis C[b]	1	0	0	0	0	0	0	0	0	1
8. **Malaria**	0	0	0	0	0	0	0	0	0	0
9. **Tropical-cluster diseases**	0	0	—	0	0	0	0	0	0	0
a. Trypanosomiasis	0	—	—	—	—	—	—	—	—	—
b. Chagas' disease	—	—	—	—	—	—	—	—	—	—
c. Schistosomiasis	0	0	—	0	—	0	0	0	—	0
d. Leishmaniasis	0	0	—	—	0	0	0	0	0	0
e. Lymphatic filariasis	0	0	—	0	0	—	0	—	—	0
f. Onchocerciasis	—	—	—	—	—	—	—	—	—	—
10. **Leprosy**	0	—	—	—	0	0	0	0	0	0
11. **Dengue**	0	—	—	—	—	0	—	—	—	0
12. **Japanese encephalitis**	—	—	—	—	—	—	—	—	—	—
13. **Trachoma**	—	—	—	—	—	—	—	—	—	—
14. **Intestinal nematode infections**	0	0	—	0	—	0	0	0	0	0
a. Ascariasis	0	—	—	—	—	—	—	—	0	0
b. Trichuriasis	—	—	—	—	—	—	—	—	—	—
c. Hookworm disease	0	—	—	—	—	0	0	0	0	0
Other intestinal infections	0	0	—	0	—	—	—	—	0	0
Other infectious diseases	15	2	0	1	2	1	1	1	0	9
B. **Respiratory infections**	109	19	2	2	4	13	11	8	5	64
1. Lower respiratory infections	104	18	1	1	3	13	11	8	5	61
2. Upper respiratory infections	4	1	0	0	0	0	0	0	0	3
3. Otitis media	0	0	0	0	0	0	0	0	0	0
C. **Maternal conditions**	3	—	—	—	—	—	—	—	—	—
1. Maternal hemorrhage	1	—	—	—	—	—	—	—	—	—
2. Maternal sepsis	0	—	—	—	—	—	—	—	—	—
3. Hypertensive disorders of pregnancy	0	—	—	—	—	—	—	—	—	—
4. Obstructed labor	0	—	—	—	—	—	—	—	—	—
5. Abortion	0	—	—	—	—	—	—	—	—	—
Other maternal conditions	1	—	—	—	—	—	—	—	—	—
D. **Perinatal conditions**[c]	57	33	0	0	0	0	0	0	—	33
1. Low birthweight	24	13	—	—	—	—	0	—	—	13
2. Birth asphyxia and birth trauma	17	10	0	0	—	0	—	—	—	10
Other perinatal conditions	16	10	0	0	0	0	—	0	—	10
E. **Nutritional deficiencies**	5	0	0	0	0	0	0	0	0	3
1. Protein-energy malnutrition	2	0	0	0	0	0	0	0	0	1
2. Iodine deficiency	0	0	0	0	0	0	0	0	0	0
3. Vitamin A deficiency	0	—	—	—	—	—	—	—	0	0
4. Iron-deficiency anemia	3	0	0	0	0	0	0	0	0	2
Other nutritional disorders	0	0	0	0	0	0	0	0	0	0

			Female					
0–4	**5–14**	**15–29**	**30–44**	**45–59**	**60–69**	**70–79**	**80+**	**Total**
14	*36*	*58*	*52*	*41*	*23*	*17*	*6*	*248*
77	**13**	**46**	**105**	**257**	**434**	**845**	**907**	**2,685**
56	*3*	*7*	*9*	*9*	*7*	*11*	*12*	*115*
15	**2**	**4**	**7**	**5**	**3**	**3**	**2**	**41**
0	**0**	**1**	**4**	**3**	**1**	**1**	**1**	**11**
0	**0**	**0**	**0**	**0**	**0**	**0**	**0**	**0**
0	—	0	0	0	0	0	0	0
—	—	—	—	—	—	—	—	—
0	—	—	—	0	0	—	—	0
0	0	0	0	0	0	0	0	0
0	**0**	**1**	**1**	**1**	**0**	**0**	**0**	**4**
6	**0**	**0**	**0**	**0**	**0**	**0**	**0**	**7**
3	**1**	**0**	**0**	**0**	**0**	**0**	**0**	**4**
0	—	—	—	0	0	—	—	0
0	0	0	0	0	0	0	0	0
0	0	0	0	0	0	0	0	0
2	1	0	—	0	0	—	—	4
0	—	0	0	0	0	0	0	0
4	**0**	**0**	**0**	**0**	**0**	**0**	**0**	**6**
0	**0**	**0**	**0**	**0**	**0**	**0**	**0**	**1**
0	**0**	**0**	**0**	**0**	**0**	**0**	**0**	**0**
0	**0**	**0**	**0**	**0**	**0**	**0**	**0**	**0**
—	**0**	**0**	**0**	**0**	**0**	**0**	**0**	**0**
—	—	—	0	—	0	—	—	0
—	—	—	—	—	—	—	—	—
—	—	—	—	0	0	—	—	0
—	—	0	0	—	0	0	0	0
—	0	—	—	—	—	—	—	0
—	—	—	—	—	—	—	—	—
—	—	—	—	—	**0**	—	**0**	**0**
—	—	—	—	—	—	—	—	—
—	—	—	—	—	—	—	—	—
—	—	—	—	—	—	—	—	—
0	—	—	**0**	**0**	—	**0**	**0**	**0**
0	—	—	—	—	—	—	—	0
—	—	—	—	—	—	—	—	—
—	—	—	0	—	—	—	—	0
0	—	—	—	0	—	0	0	0
2	0	1	1	1	1	1	1	6
16	**1**	**1**	**2**	**4**	**4**	**7**	**9**	**45**
15	1	1	2	4	4	7	9	43
1	0	0	0	0	0	0	0	2
0	0	0	0	0	0	0	0	0
—	**0**	**2**	**1**	**0**	**0**	—	—	**3**
—	—	0	0	0	—	—	—	1
—	—	0	0	0	—	—	—	0
—	—	0	0	0	—	—	—	0
—	—	0	0	0	—	—	—	0
—	0	0	0	0	0	—	—	0
—	—	1	0	0	0	—	—	1
24	**0**	**0**	**0**	**0**	**0**	—	—	**24**
11	—	—	—	—	—	—	—	11
7	0	0	—	—	—	—	—	7
6	0	0	0	0	0	—	—	6
0	**0**	**0**	**0**	**0**	**0**	**1**	**0**	**3**
0	0	0	0	0	0	0	0	1
0	0	0	0	0	0	0	0	0
0	0	0	0	0	0	0	0	0
0	0	0	0	0	0	0	0	2
0	0	0	0	0	0	0	0	0

(Continues on the following page.)

Table 3B.3 Continued

Cause	Total	Male 0–4	5–14	15–29	30–44	45–59	60–69	70–79	80+	Total
II. Noncommunicable diseases	*4,736*	*20*	*7*	*34*	*143*	*445*	*633*	*685*	*336*	*2,304*
A. Malignant neoplasms	**825**	**1**	**2**	**7**	**24**	**113**	**158**	**129**	**32**	**465**
1. Mouth and oropharynx cancers	27	0	0	0	1	9	7	3	1	22
2. Esophageal cancer	21	0	0	0	0	5	6	4	1	15
3. Stomach cancer	101	0	0	0	3	14	21	18	4	60
4. Colon and rectal cancers	96	0	0	0	2	8	15	17	5	47
5. Liver cancer	28	0	0	0	1	4	6	5	1	17
6. Pancreas cancer	35	0	0	0	1	5	6	5	1	19
7. Trachea, bronchus, and lung cancers	165	0	0	0	5	36	53	37	6	137
8. Melanoma and other skin cancers	11	0	0	0	1	1	1	1	1	5
9. Breast cancer	63	—	0	0	0	0	0	0	0	1
10. Cervix uteri cancer	19	—	—	—	—	—	—	—	—	—
11. Corpus uteri cancer	17	—	—	—	—	—	—	—	—	—
12. Ovarian cancer	21	—	—	—	—	—	—	—	—	—
13. Prostate cancer	25	0	0	0	0	2	7	11	5	25
14. Bladder cancer	24	0	0	0	0	3	6	7	2	19
15. Lymphomas and multiple myeloma	23	0	0	1	2	3	3	2	1	12
16. Leukemia	27	0	1	2	2	3	3	3	1	15
Other malignant neoplasms	123	0	1	3	6	20	22	15	4	71
B. Other neoplasms	**8**	**0**	**0**	**0**	**0**	**1**	**1**	**1**	**0**	**4**
C. Diabetes mellitus	**51**	**0**	**0**	**1**	**2**	**4**	**6**	**6**	**2**	**21**
D. Endocrine disorders	**6**	**0**	**0**	**0**	**0**	**1**	**0**	**0**	**0**	**3**
E. Neuropsychiatric conditions	**66**	**2**	**2**	**5**	**10**	**12**	**6**	**4**	**2**	**41**
1. Unipolar depressive disorders	0	0	0	0	0	0	0	0	0	0
2. Bipolar affective disorder	0	—	—	—	0	0	0	0	0	0
3. Schizophrenia	1	0	0	0	0	0	0	0	0	1
4. Epilepsy	9	0	0	1	2	1	0	0	0	6
5. Alcohol use disorders	10	0	0	0	2	3	2	1	0	8
6. Alzheimer's and other dementias	10	0	0	0	0	1	1	1	1	4
7. Parkinson's disease	4	0	0	0	0	0	0	1	0	2
8. Multiple sclerosis	4	0	0	0	0	1	0	0	0	2
9. Drug use disorders	11	0	0	2	4	3	1	0	0	9
10. Post-traumatic stress disorder	0	0	0	0	0	0	0	0	0	0
11. Obsessive-compulsive disorder	—	—	—	—	—	—	—	—	—	—
12. Panic disorder	—	—	—	—	—	—	—	—	—	—
13. Insomnia (primary)	—	—	—	—	—	—	—	—	—	—
14. Migraine	—	—	—	—	—	—	—	—	—	—
15. Mental retardation, lead-caused	1	0	0	0	0	0	0	0	0	0
Other neuropsychiatric disorders	17	1	1	2	1	2	1	1	0	10
F. Sense organ diseases	**0**	**0**	**0**	**0**	**0**	**0**	**0**	**0**	**0**	**0**
1. Glaucoma	0	—	—	—	—	0	0	0	0	0
2. Cataracts	—	—	—	—	—	—	—	—	—	—
3. Vision disorders, age-related	—	—	—	—	—	—	—	—	—	—
4. Hearing loss, adult onset	—	—	—	—	—	—	—	—	—	—
Other sense organ disorders	0	0	0	0	0	0	0	0	0	0
G. Cardiovascular diseases	**3,295**	**1**	**1**	**12**	**75**	**250**	**389**	**477**	**274**	**1,480**
1. Rheumatic heart disease	22	0	0	0	2	3	2	1	0	9
2. Hypertensive heart disease	109	0	0	0	2	9	13	15	7	47
3. Ischemic heart disease	1,685	0	0	3	38	153	226	266	131	817
4. Cerebrovascular disease	1,029	0	1	3	13	54	109	144	80	405
5. Inflammatory heart diseases	67	0	0	2	7	11	8	7	5	40
Other cardiovascular diseases	383	1	0	4	14	20	30	44	50	162
H. Respiratory diseases	**190**	**1**	**0**	**2**	**5**	**17**	**37**	**41**	**17**	**121**
1. Chronic obstructive pulmonary disease	130	0	0	0	2	10	25	32	13	84
2. Asthma	27	0	0	0	1	3	6	5	2	17
Other respiratory diseases	33	1	0	1	3	4	5	4	2	21

				Female				
0–4	5–14	15–29	30–44	45–59	60–69	70–79	80+	Total
17	*5*	*19*	*68*	*214*	*407*	*818*	*884*	*2,432*
1	**2**	**5**	**25**	**73**	**94**	**113**	**48**	**360**
0	0	0	0	1	1	1	1	5
0	—	0	0	1	1	2	1	6
0	0	0	2	6	11	15	6	41
0	0	0	2	7	13	18	9	49
0	0	0	0	2	3	4	2	11
0	0	0	0	2	5	6	3	16
0	0	0	1	6	8	10	3	29
0	0	0	1	1	1	1	1	6
0	0	0	6	19	16	15	7	63
—	0	0	3	6	4	4	2	19
0	0	0	1	3	5	5	2	17
0	0	0	2	6	6	5	2	21
—	—	—	—	—	—	—	—	—
0	0	0	0	0	1	2	1	5
0	0	1	1	2	3	3	1	10
0	1	1	1	2	3	3	1	12
0	1	1	4	10	13	16	7	52
0	**0**	**0**	**0**	**1**	**1**	**1**	**1**	**4**
0	**0**	**1**	**1**	**4**	**9**	**12**	**4**	**31**
0	**0**	**0**	**0**	**1**	**1**	**1**	**0**	**3**
1	**1**	**2**	**4**	**5**	**3**	**4**	**4**	**25**
0	0	0	0	0	0	0	0	0
0	0	0	0	0	0	0	0	0
0	0	0	0	0	0	0	0	1
0	0	1	1	1	0	0	0	3
0	0	0	0	1	0	0	0	2
0	0	0	0	0	1	2	2	6
0	0	0	0	0	0	1	0	2
0	0	0	1	1	0	0	0	2
—	0	0	1	1	0	0	0	2
0	0	0	0	0	0	0	0	0
—	—	—	—	—	—	—	—	—
—	—	—	—	—	—	—	—	—
—	—	—	—	—	—	—	—	—
—	—	—	—	—	—	—	—	—
0	0	0	0	0	0	0	0	0
1	1	1	1	1	1	1	1	7
0	**0**	**0**	**0**	**0**	**0**	**0**	**0**	**0**
—	—	—	—	0	0	0	0	0
—	—	—	—	—	—	—	—	—
—	—	—	—	—	—	—	—	—
—	—	—	—	—	—	—	—	—
0	0	0	0	0	0	0	0	0
1	**1**	**5**	**24**	**101**	**262**	**634**	**788**	**1,815**
0	0	0	1	3	4	3	1	13
0	0	0	1	6	13	23	19	62
0	0	1	7	44	129	314	374	868
0	0	2	7	35	92	224	264	624
0	0	1	2	3	4	8	9	27
0	0	1	5	10	20	62	122	221
1	**0**	**1**	**2**	**6**	**12**	**24**	**23**	**69**
0	0	0	1	3	7	17	18	46
0	0	0	1	1	3	3	3	11
1	0	1	1	1	2	3	3	12

(Continues on the following page.)

Table 3B.3 Continued

Cause	Total	Male 0–4	5–14	15–29	30–44	45–59	60–69	70–79	80+	Total
I. Digestive diseases	**205**	**1**	**1**	**4**	**21**	**40**	**30**	**20**	**6**	**122**
1. Peptic ulcer disease	23	0	0	1	2	4	4	3	1	16
2. Cirrhosis of the liver	103	0	0	2	12	24	17	9	1	65
3. Appendicitis	1	0	0	0	0	0	0	0	0	1
Other digestive diseases	77	1	0	2	7	10	9	8	3	41
J. Genitourinary diseases	**53**	**0**	**0**	**2**	**3**	**6**	**6**	**7**	**3**	**28**
1. Nephritis and nephrosis	36	0	0	1	3	4	4	4	2	18
2. Benign prostatic hypertrophy	3	—	—	0	0	0	1	1	1	3
Other genitourinary system diseases	14	0	0	0	1	1	2	2	1	7
K. Skin diseases	**3**	**0**	**0**	**0**	**0**	**0**	**0**	**0**	**0**	**2**
L. Musculoskeletal diseases	**6**	**0**	**0**	**0**	**0**	**1**	**0**	**0**	**0**	**2**
1. Rheumatoid arthritis	2	0	0	0	0	0	0	0	0	0
2. Osteoarthritis	0	0	0	0	0	0	0	0	0	0
3. Gout	0	0	0	0	0	0	0	0	0	0
4. Low back pain	0	0	0	0	0	0	0	0	0	0
Other musculoskeletal disorders	3	0	0	0	0	0	0	0	0	1
M. Congenital anomalies	**28**	**13**	**1**	**1**	**0**	**0**	**0**	**0**	**0**	**16**
1. Abdominal wall defect	0	0	0	0	0	0	0	0	0	0
2. Anencephaly	0	0	0	0	0	0	0	0	0	0
3. Anorectal atresia	0	0	0	0	0	0	0	0	0	0
4. Cleft lip	0	0	0	0	0	0	0	0	—	0
5. Cleft palate	0	0	0	0	0	0	0	0	—	0
6. Esophageal atresia	0	0	0	0	0	0	0	0	0	0
7. Renal agenesis	0	0	0	0	0	0	0	0	0	0
8. Down syndrome	1	0	0	0	0	0	0	0	0	0
9. Congenital heart anomalies	13	6	0	0	0	0	0	0	0	7
10. Spina bifida	1	1	0	0	0	0	0	0	0	1
Other congenital anomalies	12	6	0	0	0	0	0	0	0	7
N. Oral conditions	**0**	**0**	**—**	**0**	**0**	**0**	**0**	**0**	**0**	**0**
1. Dental caries	0	—	—	—	—	—	—	—	—	—
2. Periodontal disease	0	—	—	—	0	—	—	—	—	0
3. Edentulism	—	—	—	—	—	—	—	—	—	—
Other oral diseases	0	0	—	0	0	0	0	0	0	0
III. Injuries	***607***	***6***	***10***	***99***	***140***	***132***	***53***	***22***	***6***	***470***
A. Unintentional injuries	**401**	**6**	**8**	**59**	**87**	**89**	**37**	**14**	**4**	**304**
1. Road traffic accidents	83	1	2	18	18	13	6	3	1	62
2. Poisonings	106	1	0	12	26	30	11	2	0	82
3. Falls	35	0	0	3	5	7	4	3	2	24
4. Fires	20	1	0	2	4	4	2	1	0	14
5. Drownings	35	1	2	7	9	6	3	1	0	29
6. Other unintentional injuries	121	3	3	18	25	28	12	4	1	93
B. Intentional injuries	**207**	**0**	**2**	**40**	**53**	**43**	**16**	**8**	**2**	**165**
1. Self-inflicted injuries	121	0	1	22	29	27	11	6	2	99
2. Violence	68	0	0	11	18	14	4	1	0	50
3. War	17	0	0	7	6	2	1	0	0	16
Other intentional injuries	1	0	0	0	0	0	0	—	0	0

Table 3B.3 Continued

| | Female | | | | | | | |
0–4	5–14	15–29	30–44	45–59	60–69	70–79	80+	Total
1	0	2	8	18	19	22	13	83
0	0	0	0	1	1	2	2	7
0	0	1	4	12	11	8	3	39
0	0	0	0	0	0	0	0	1
1	0	1	3	5	7	11	8	36
0	0	1	3	4	6	6	4	24
0	0	1	2	3	4	5	3	18
—	—	—	—	—	—	—	—	—
0	0	0	1	1	2	2	1	7
0	0	0	0	0	0	0	0	2
0	0	0	0	1	1	1	0	4
0	0	0	0	0	1	1	0	2
0	0	0	0	0	0	0	0	0
0	0	0	0	0	0	0	0	0
0	0	0	0	0	0	0	0	0
0	0	0	0	1	0	0	0	2
10	1	0	0	0	0	0	0	13
0	0	0	0	0	0	0	0	0
0	0	0	0	0	0	0	0	0
0	0	0	0	0	0	0	—	0
0	0	0	0	0	0	0	0	0
0	0	0	0	0	0	0	0	0
0	0	0	0	0	0	0	0	0
0	0	0	0	0	0	0	0	0
5	0	0	0	0	0	0	0	6
1	0	0	0	0	0	0	0	1
4	0	0	0	0	0	0	0	5
0	—	0	0	0	0	0	0	0
—	—	—	—	0	—	—	0	0
—	—	—	—	—	—	—	0	0
—	—	—	—	—	—	—	—	—
0	—	0	0	0	0	0	0	0
5	5	20	27	34	20	17	11	138
5	4	12	17	24	14	12	9	96
1	1	5	4	4	3	3	1	21
0	0	3	6	9	4	2	1	24
0	0	1	1	1	1	3	4	12
1	0	0	1	1	1	1	1	5
1	1	1	1	1	1	1	0	6
2	1	3	5	7	4	3	2	27
0	1	8	10	10	5	5	3	42
—	1	4	4	5	3	3	2	22
0	0	3	5	4	2	2	1	18
0	0	0	0	0	0	0	0	2
0	0	0	0	0	0	0	0	0

Source: Authors' compilation.

Note: — = an estimate of zero; the number zero in a cell indicates a non-zero estimate of less than 500.

a. These figures include late effects of polio cases with onset prior to regional certification of polio eradication in 2000.

b. Does not include liver cancer and cirrhosis deaths resulting from chronic hepatitis virus infection.

c. This cause category includes "Causes arising in the perinatal period" as defined in the International Classification of Diseases, principally low birthweight, prematurity, birth asphyxia, and birth trauma, and does not include all causes of deaths occurring in the perinatal period.

Table 3B.4 Deaths by Cause, Sex, and Age in the Latin America and the Caribbean Region, 2001 (thousands)

Cause	Total	Male									
		0–4	5–14	15–29	30–44	45–59	60–69	70–79	80+	Total
Population (millions)	526	28	56	74	52	31	11	6	2	260
All causes	3,277	226	30	178	211	288	276	336	288	1,833
I. Communicable, maternal, perinatal, and nutritional conditions	716	177	8	26	50	37	24	31	38	390
A. Infectious and parasitic diseases	324	52	5	22	44	27	14	14	11	189
1. **Tuberculosis**	45	1	0	4	6	7	5	4	2	29
2. **Sexually transmitted diseases excluding HIV/AIDS**	2	1	0	0	0	0	0	0	0	1
a. Syphilis	1	1	0	0	0	0	0	0	0	1
b. Chlamydia	0	—	—	—	—	—	—	—	—	—
c. Gonorrhea	0	—	0	0	—	—	—	0	0	0
d. Other sexually transmitted diseases	1	0	—	—	0	0	—	0	0	0
3. **HIV/AIDS**	83	3	1	11	27	9	1	0	0	54
4. **Diarrheal diseases**	55	24	0	0	0	1	1	1	1	29
5. **Childhood-cluster diseases**	7	4	0	0	0	0	0	0	0	4
a. Pertussis	6	3	—	—	—	—	0	—	—	3
b. Poliomyelitis[a]	0	0	0	0	0	0	0	—	0	0
c. Diphtheria	0	0	—	—	0	—	—	—	0	0
d. Measles	—	—	—	—	—	—	—	—	—	—
e. Tetanus	1	0	0	0	0	0	0	0	0	0
6. **Meningitis**	17	5	1	1	1	1	0	0	0	10
7. **Hepatitis B**[b]	4	0	0	1	1	1	0	0	0	3
Hepatitis C[b]	2	0	0	0	0	0	0	0	0	1
8. **Malaria**	2	1	0	0	0	0	0	0	0	1
9. **Tropical-cluster diseases**	15	0	0	0	1	3	2	1	1	8
a. Trypanosomiasis	0	—	—	—	—	—	0	—	—	0
b. Chagas' disease	14	0	0	0	1	2	2	1	1	8
c. Schistosomiasis	1	0	0	0	0	0	0	0	0	0
d. Leishmaniasis	0	0	0	0	0	0	0	0	0	0
e. Lymphatic filariasis	0	—	—	—	0	—	0	0	—	0
f. Onchocerciasis	0	0	—	—	—	—	—	—	—	0
10. **Leprosy**	1	—	—	0	0	0	0	0	0	0
11. **Dengue**	2	0	1	0	0	0	0	0	0	1
12. **Japanese encephalitis**	—	—	—	—	—	—	—	—	—	—
13. **Trachoma**	0	0	0	—	—	—	—	—	—	0
14. **Intestinal nematode infections**	2	0	0	0	0	0	0	0	0	1
a. Ascariasis	0	0	0	0	0	0	0	0	0	0
b. Trichuriasis	0	—	—	—	0	—	—	—	—	0
c. Hookworm disease	0	—	0	—	0	0	—	—	—	0
Other intestinal infections	1	0	0	0	0	0	0	0	0	1
Other infectious diseases	87	13	2	4	6	6	5	6	6	48
B. Respiratory infections	160	24	2	3	5	7	8	13	21	82
1. Lower respiratory infections	157	23	2	3	5	7	8	13	20	81
2. Upper respiratory infections	3	1	0	0	0	0	0	0	0	1
3. Otitis media	0	0	0	0	0	0	0	0	0	0
C. Maternal conditions	16	—	—	—	—	—	—	—	—	—
1. Maternal hemorrhage	4	—	—	—	—	—	—	—	—	—
2. Maternal sepsis	1	—	—	—	—	—	—	—	—	—
3. Hypertensive disorders of pregnancy	4	—	—	—	—	—	—	—	—	—
4. Obstructed labor	0	—	—	—	—	—	—	—	—	—
5. Abortion	2	—	—	—	—	—	—	—	—	—
Other maternal conditions	5	—	—	—	—	—	—	—	—	—
D. Perinatal conditions[c]	164	93	0	0	0	0	—	—	—	93
1. Low birthweight	20	11	—	—	—	—	—	—	—	11
2. Birth asphyxia and birth trauma	89	51	0	0	0	0	—	—	—	51
Other perinatal conditions	54	31	0	0	—	—	—	—	—	31
E. Nutritional deficiencies	52	8	1	1	2	2	2	4	6	26
1. Protein-energy malnutrition	37	7	1	1	1	1	1	3	4	19
2. Iodine deficiency	0	0	—	—	—	0	0	0	0	0
3. Vitamin A deficiency	0	0	—	—	—	—	0	—	0	0
4. Iron-deficiency anemia	13	1	0	1	1	1	1	1	1	6
Other nutritional disorders	3	0	0	0	0	0	0	0	0	2

	Female							
0–4	5–14	15–29	30–44	45–59	60–69	70–79	80+	Total
27	*54*	*73*	*55*	*33*	*13*	*8*	*3*	*266*
181	**23**	**66**	**104**	**185**	**206**	**294**	**386**	**1,444**
140	*8*	*26*	*31*	*21*	*18*	*28*	*52*	*326*
42	**5**	**15**	**20**	**15**	**10**	**12**	**15**	**135**
0	**0**	**3**	**3**	**3**	**2**	**2**	**1**	**16**
0	**0**	**0**	**0**	**0**	**0**	**0**	**0**	**1**
0	—	0	0	0	0	0	0	0
—	—	—	—	—	0	0	0	0
0	—	—	—	0	—	—	—	0
0	0	0	0	0	0	0	0	1
3	**1**	**9**	**13**	**3**	**0**	**0**	**0**	**30**
22	**0**	**0**	**0**	**0**	**1**	**1**	**2**	**26**
3	**0**	**0**	**0**	**0**	**0**	**0**	**0**	**4**
3	0	0	—	—	—	—	—	3
0	0	0	0	0	0	—	0	0
0	0	—	—	0	—	—	—	0
—	—	—	—	—	—	—	—	—
0	0	0	0	0	0	0	0	0
4	**1**	**0**	**0**	**1**	**0**	**0**	**0**	**7**
0	**0**	**0**	**0**	**0**	**0**	**0**	**0**	**2**
0	**0**	**0**	**0**	**0**	**0**	**0**	**0**	**1**
1	**0**	**0**	**0**	**0**	**0**	**0**	**0**	**1**
0	**0**	**0**	**1**	**2**	**2**	**1**	**1**	**7**
—	0	—	—	—	—	—	—	0
0	0	0	1	2	1	1	1	7
0	0	0	0	0	0	0	0	0
0.	0	0	0	0	0	0	0	0
—	—	—	0	0	0	—	0	0
—	—	0	—	—	0	—	—	0
—	0	0	0	0	0	0	0	**0**
0	**1**	**0**	**0**	**0**	**0**	**0**	**0**	**1**
—	—	—	—	—	—	—	—	—
0	**0**	**0**	**0**	**0**	**0**	**0**	**0**	**1**
0	0	0	0	0	0	0	0	0
0	0	—	—	0	—	—	—	0
—	—	—	—	—	0	—	—	0
0	0	0	0	0	0	0	0	1
8	2	2	2	5	5	7	10	39
20	**2**	**2**	**3**	**4**	**6**	**12**	**29**	**78**
20	2	2	3	4	6	12	29	76
1	0	0	0	0	0	0	0	1
0	0	0	0	0	0	0	0	0
0	**0**	**9**	**7**	**0**	—	**0**	**0**	**16**
0	0	2	2	0	—	—	—	4
—	0	1	0	0	—	—	—	1
—	0	2	2	0	—	—	0	4
—	—	0	0	—	—	—	—	0
—	0	2	1	0	—	—	—	2
—	0	2	2	0	—	0	0	5
71	**0**	—	**0**	—	—	—	**0**	**71**
9	—	—	—	—	—	—	—	9
38	0	—	—	—	—	—	0	38
24	0	—	0	—	—	—	0	24
7	**1**	**1**	**1**	**2**	**2**	**4**	**9**	**26**
6	1	0	0	1	1	3	7	18
0	0	0	0	0	0	0	0	0
0	—	—	0	0	—	—	0	0
1	0	0	0	1	0	1	2	6
0	0	0	0	0	0	0	1	1

(Continues on the following page.)

Table 3B.4 Continued

Cause	Total	Male 0–4	5–14	15–29	30–44	45–59	60–69	70–79	80+	Total
II. Noncommunicable diseases	*2,187*	*38*	*10*	*32*	*81*	*206*	*235*	*293*	*243*	*1,138*
A. **Malignant neoplasms**	**484**	**2**	**3**	**7**	**14**	**47**	**60**	**70**	**44**	**247**
1. Mouth and oropharynx cancers	14	0	0	0	1	3	3	2	1	10
2. Esophageal cancer	16	—	0	0	1	3	3	3	2	12
3. Stomach cancer	57	0	0	0	2	7	9	10	6	34
4. Colon and rectal cancers	37	0	0	0	1	3	4	5	3	18
5. Liver cancer	21	0	0	0	1	2	3	3	2	11
6. Pancreas cancer	20	0	0	0	0	2	3	3	2	10
7. Trachea, bronchus, and lung cancers	55	0	0	0	1	8	12	12	5	38
8. Melanoma and other skin cancers	7	0	0	0	0	1	1	1	1	4
9. Breast cancer	37	0	—	0	0	0	0	0	0	0
10. Cervix uteri cancer	26	—	—	—	—	—	—	—	—	—
11. Corpus uteri cancer	12	—	—	—	—	—	—	—	—	—
12. Ovarian cancer	9	—	—	—	—	—	—	—	—	—
13. Prostate cancer	37	0	0	0	0	2	7	15	13	37
14. Bladder cancer	9	0	0	0	0	1	1	2	2	6
15. Lymphomas and multiple myeloma	24	0	1	1	2	3	3	3	1	13
16. Leukemia	22	1	2	2	1	2	1	2	1	12
Other malignant neoplasms	82	1	1	2	4	10	10	9	5	43
B. **Other neoplasms**	**13**	**0**	**0**	**0**	**1**	**1**	**1**	**1**	**1**	**6**
C. **Diabetes mellitus**	**163**	**0**	**0**	**1**	**4**	**15**	**19**	**20**	**11**	**70**
D. **Endocrine disorders**	**30**	**2**	**1**	**1**	**1**	**2**	**2**	**2**	**3**	**14**
E. **Neuropsychiatric conditions**	**70**	**2**	**1**	**5**	**9**	**10**	**5**	**6**	**6**	**44**
1. Unipolar depressive disorders	0	0	0	0	0	0	0	0	0	0
2. Bipolar affective disorder	0	0	0	0	0	0	0	0	0	0
3. Schizophrenia	0	0	0	0	0	0	0	0	0	0
4. Epilepsy	8	0	0	1	1	1	0	0	0	5
5. Alcohol use disorders	17	0	0	1	5	6	2	1	0	15
6. Alzheimer's and other dementias	14	0	0	0	0	0	1	2	3	5
7. Parkinson's disease	5	0	0	0	0	0	0	1	1	3
8. Multiple sclerosis	1	—	—	0	0	0	0	0	0	0
9. Drug use disorders	2	—	—	0	1	1	0	0	0	2
10. Post-traumatic stress disorder	0	0	0	0	0	0	0	0	0	0
11. Obsessive-compulsive disorder	—	—	—	—	—	—	—	—	—	—
12. Panic disorder	—	—	—	—	—	—	—	—	—	—
13. Insomnia (primary)	—	—	—	—	—	—	—	—	—	—
14. Migraine	—	—	—	—	—	—	—	—	—	—
15. Mental retardation, lead-caused	0	0	0	0	0	0	0	0	0	0
Other neuropsychiatric disorders	23	2	1	2	2	2	2	2	1	13
F. **Sense organ diseases**	**0**	**0**	**0**	**0**	**0**	**0**	**0**	**0**	**0**	**0**
1. Glaucoma	0	—	—	0	—	—	0	0	0	0
2. Cataracts	—	—	—	—	—	—	—	—	—	—
3. Vision disorders, age-related	—	—	—	—	—	—	—	—	—	—
4. Hearing loss, adult onset	—	—	—	—	—	—	—	—	—	—
Other sense organ disorders	0	0	0	0	0	0	0	0	0	0
G. **Cardiovascular diseases**	**910**	**2**	**1**	**7**	**25**	**79**	**97**	**130**	**120**	**462**
1. Rheumatic heart disease	6	0	0	0	0	1	0	0	0	2
2. Hypertensive heart disease	87	0	0	0	2	7	8	11	11	39
3. Ischemic heart disease	358	0	0	2	9	39	48	59	44	202
4. Cerebrovascular disease	267	0	0	2	7	22	27	38	33	129
5. Inflammatory heart diseases	31	0	0	1	2	4	4	4	3	18
Other cardiovascular diseases	160	1	0	2	5	8	9	17	28	72
H. **Respiratory diseases**	**195**	**5**	**1**	**3**	**5**	**11**	**19**	**32**	**32**	**107**
1. Chronic obstructive pulmonary disease	99	0	0	0	1	5	11	20	20	58
2. Asthma	12	1	0	0	0	1	1	1	1	5
Other respiratory diseases	84	4	1	2	4	6	7	10	11	44

			Female					
0–4	5–14	15–29	30–44	45–59	60–69	70–79	80+	Total
33	*9*	*23*	*61*	*155*	*183*	*260*	*325*	*1,049*
2	**2**	**6**	**23**	**55**	**51**	**56**	**42**	**237**
0	0	0	0	1	1	1	1	4
—	0	0	0	1	1	1	1	4
0	0	0	2	4	5	6	6	23
0	0	0	1	3	4	5	5	19
0	0	0	1	2	2	3	2	10
0	0	0	0	2	2	3	2	10
0	0	0	1	4	5	5	3	17
0	0	0	0	1	1	1	1	3
0	0	0	5	12	8	7	5	37
—	0	1	4	9	5	5	2	26
0	—	0	1	3	3	3	2	12
0	0	0	1	3	2	2	1	9
—	—	—	—	—	—	—	—	—
0	0	0	0	0	0	1	1	3
0	0	1	1	2	2	3	2	11
1	1	1	1	2	1	2	1	10
1	1	1	3	8	9	10	7	40
0	**0**	**0**	**1**	**1**	**1**	**1**	**1**	**6**
0	**0**	**1**	**3**	**16**	**24**	**28**	**21**	**93**
1	**1**	**1**	**1**	**2**	**2**	**3**	**4**	**16**
2	**1**	**2**	**3**	**3**	**2**	**5**	**8**	**26**
0	0	0	0	0	0	0	0	0
0	0	0	0	0	0	0	0	0
0	0	0	0	0	0	0	0	0
0	0	1	1	0	0	0	0	3
0	0	0	0	0	0	0	0	1
0	0	0	0	0	1	2	6	8
0	0	0	0	0	0	1	1	2
—	0	0	0	0	0	0	0	1
—	—	0	0	0	0	0	0	0
0	0	0	0	0	0	0	0	0
—	—	—	—	—	—	—	—	—
—	—	—	—	—	—	—	—	—
—	—	—	—	—	—	—	—	—
0	0	0	0	0	0	0	0	0
1	1	1	1	1	1	1	2	10
0	**0**	**0**	**0**	**0**	**0**	**0**	**0**	**0**
—	—	—	—	—	—	—	0	0
—	—	—	—	—	—	—	—	—
—	—	—	—	—	—	—	—	—
0	0	0	0	0	0	0	0	0
2	**1**	**5**	**18**	**52**	**71**	**119**	**180**	**448**
0	0	0	1	1	1	1	0	4
0	0	0	2	6	8	13	18	48
0	0	1	4	18	29	45	60	156
0	0	2	7	18	22	37	52	138
0	0	0	1	2	2	3	4	14
1	1	2	4	7	9	20	46	88
5	**1**	**2**	**3**	**8**	**13**	**22**	**35**	**88**
1	0	0	1	3	7	12	17	42
0	0	0	1	1	1	1	2	6
3	1	1	2	4	5	9	16	40

(Continues on the following page.)

Table 3B.4 Continued

Cause	Total	Male								Total
		0–4	5–14	15–29	30–44	45–59	60–69	70–79	80+	
I. Digestive diseases	**185**	**2**	**1**	**4**	**19**	**33**	**23**	**21**	**14**	**117**
1. Peptic ulcer disease	14	0	0	0	1	2	2	2	2	8
2. Cirrhosis of the liver	74	0	0	2	12	21	12	7	3	57
3. Appendicitis	3	0	0	0	0	0	0	0	0	2
Other digestive diseases	94	2	1	2	6	11	9	11	9	51
J. Genitourinary diseases	**70**	**1**	**0**	**2**	**3**	**5**	**7**	**10**	**11**	**38**
1. Nephritis and nephrosis	55	1	0	1	2	5	6	7	7	30
2. Benign prostatic hypertrophy	2	—	—	0	0	0	0	1	1	2
Other genitourinary system diseases	13	0	0	0	0	1	1	2	2	6
K. Skin diseases	**8**	**0**	**0**	**0**	**0**	**0**	**0**	**1**	**1**	**3**
L. Musculoskeletal diseases	**12**	**0**	**0**	**0**	**0**	**1**	**1**	**1**	**1**	**4**
1. Rheumatoid arthritis	3	—	0	0	0	0	0	0	0	1
2. Osteoarthritis	1	0	—	0	0	0	0	0	0	0
3. Gout	0	—	—	0	0	0	0	0	0	0
4. Low back pain	0	—	—	0	0	0	0	0	0	0
Other musculoskeletal disorders	8	0	0	0	0	0	0	1	1	3
M. Congenital anomalies	**47**	**22**	**1**	**1**	**0**	**0**	**0**	**0**	**0**	**25**
1. Abdominal wall defect	1	1	0	0	0	—	0	0	0	1
2. Anencephaly	2	1	0	0	0	—	0	0	0	1
3. Anorectal atresia	0	0	0	0	0	—	0	0	0	0
4. Cleft lip	0	0	0	0	0	—	0	0	0	0
5. Cleft palate	0	0	0	0	0	—	0	0	0	0
6. Esophageal atresia	1	0	0	0	0	—	0	0	0	0
7. Renal agenesis	0	0	0	0	0	0	0	0	0	0
8. Down syndrome	2	1	0	0	0	0	0	0	0	1
9. Congenital heart anomalies	20	9	1	1	0	0	0	0	0	11
10. Spina bifida	1	1	0	0	0	0	0	0	0	1
Other congenital anomalies	19	9	0	0	0	0	0	0	0	10
N. Oral conditions	**0**	**0**	**0**	**0**	**0**	**0**	**0**	**0**	**0**	**0**
1. Dental caries	—	—	—	—	—	—	—	—	—	—
2. Periodontal disease	0	—	—	0	0	0	0	0	0	0
3. Edentulism	—	—	—	—	—	—	—	—	—	—
Other oral diseases	0	0	0	0	0	0	0	0	0	0
III. Injuries	*374*	*11*	*12*	*120*	*80*	*45*	*18*	*12*	*8*	*305*
A. Unintentional injuries	**207**	**10**	**10**	**46**	**37**	**26**	**12**	**9**	**6**	**157**
1. Road traffic accidents	88	2	4	23	19	12	5	3	1	69
2. Poisonings	3	0	0	1	1	0	0	0	0	2
3. Falls	15	0	0	1	2	2	1	1	1	10
4. Fires	5	1	0	0	1	0	0	0	0	3
5. Drownings	19	2	2	6	3	2	1	0	0	15
6. Other unintentional injuries	78	6	3	14	12	9	5	4	3	57
B. Intentional injuries	**167**	**1**	**2**	**74**	**43**	**19**	**6**	**3**	**1**	**148**
1. Self-inflicted injuries	30	0	0	8	6	4	2	1	1	23
2. Violence	130	1	1	63	34	14	3	1	1	119
3. War	6	0	0	2	2	1	0	0	0	6
Other intentional injuries	1	0	0	1	0	0	0	0	0	1

Table 3B.4 Continued

				Female				
0–4	5–14	15–29	30–44	45–59	60–69	70–79	80+	Total
1	1	2	5	12	12	16	18	68
0	0	0	0	1	1	2	2	6
0	0	0	2	5	4	4	2	18
0	0	0	0	0	0	0	0	1
1	0	1	3	6	7	11	13	43
1	0	1	2	4	5	7	11	32
0	0	1	2	4	4	6	8	25
—	—	—	—	—	—	—	—	—
0	0	0	0	1	1	1	3	7
0	0	0	0	0	0	1	2	5
0	0	1	1	1	1	1	2	8
—	0	0	0	0	0	1	1	2
—	0	0	0	0	0	0	0	0
0	0	0	0	0	0	0	0	0
0	0	0	0	0	0	0	0	0
0	0	1	1	1	1	1	1	6
19	1	1	0	0	0	0	0	22
0	0	0	0	—	—	0	0	0
1	0	0	0	0	—	0	—	1
0	0	0	0	0	0	0	—	0
0	0	0	0	—	—	0	—	0
0	0	0	0	—	—	0	—	0
0	0	0	0	0	—	0	0	0
0	0	0	0	0	0	0	0	0
1	0	0	0	0	0	0	0	1
8	0	0	0	0	0	0	0	9
1	0	0	0	0	—	—	—	1
8	0	0	0	0	0	0	0	9
0	0	0	0	0	0	0	0	0
—	—	—	—	—	—	—	—	—
—	—	0	0	0	0	0	0	0
—	—	—	—	—	—	—	—	—
0	0	0	0	0	0	0	0	0
8	6	17	11	8	5	6	8	69
7	5	9	7	6	4	5	8	50
1	2	5	4	3	2	1	1	18
0	0	0	0	0	0	0	0	1
0	0	0	0	0	0	1	3	5
0	0	0	0	0	0	0	0	2
1	1	1	0	0	0	0	0	3
5	2	3	2	2	2	2	4	21
0	1	8	5	3	1	1	0	19
0	0	3	1	1	0	0	0	6
0	1	5	3	1	0	0	0	12
0	0	0	0	0	0	0	0	1
0	—	0	0	—	0	0	0	0

Source: Authors' compilation.

Note: — = an estimate of zero; the number zero in a cell indicates a non-zero estimate of less than 500.

a. These figures include late effects of polio cases with onset prior to regional certification of polio eradication in 2002.

b. Does not include liver cancer and cirrhosis deaths resulting from chronic hepatitis virus infection.

c. This cause category includes "Causes arising in the perinatal period" as defined in the International Classification of Diseases, principally low birthweight, prematurity, birth asphyxia, and birth trauma, and does not include all causes of deaths occurring in the perinatal period.

Table 3B.5 Deaths by Cause, Sex, and Age in the Middle East and North Africa Region, 2001
(thousands)

Cause	Total	Male								
		0–4	5–14	15–29	30–44	45–59	60–69	70–79	80+	Total
Population (millions)	*310*	*19*	*39*	*47*	*29*	*15*	*5*	*3*	*1*	*157*
All causes	**1,914**	**231**	**33**	**78**	**85**	**158**	**173**	**206**	**103**	**1,068**
I. Communicable, maternal, perinatal, and nutritional conditions	*464*	*178*	*7*	*5*	*8*	*12*	*11*	*14*	*8*	*243*
A. Infectious and parasitic diseases	216	69	5	4	6	10	8	8	4	113
1. Tuberculosis	23	1	0	1	2	3	2	2	1	13
2. Sexually transmitted diseases excluding HIV/AIDS	4	0	0	0	0	1	0	0	0	2
a. Syphilis	3	0	0	0	0	1	0	0	0	1
b. Chlamydia	0	—	—	—	—	—	—	—	—	—
c. Gonorrhea	0	—	—	0	0	0	0	—	—	0
d. Other sexually transmitted diseases	1	0	0	0	0	0	0	0	0	1
3. HIV/AIDS	4	0	0	1	1	0	0	0	0	2
4. Diarrheal diseases	74	34	0	0	1	1	1	1	1	39
5. Childhood-cluster diseases	27	10	3	0	0	0	0	0	0	13
a. Pertussis	8	4	—	—	—	—	—	—	—	4
b. Poliomyelitis	0	0	—	—	—	—	—	—	—	0
c. Diphtheria	0	0	—	0	—	—	—	0	—	0
d. Measles	15	5	2	0	—	—	—	—	—	8
e. Tetanus	4	2	0	0	0	0	0	0	0	2
6. Meningitis	10	3	0	0	0	0	0	0	0	4
7. Hepatitis B[a]	6	0	0	0	0	1	1	0	0	3
Hepatitis C[a]	3	0	0	0	0	0	0	0	0	2
8. Malaria	19	8	0	0	0	0	0	0	0	9
9. Tropical-cluster diseases	9	0	0	0	0	2	1	1	0	6
a. Trypanosomiasis	1	0	0	0	0	0	0	0	—	0
b. Chagas' disease	—	—	—	—	—	—	—	—	—	—
c. Schistosomiasis	8	0	0	0	0	1	1	1	0	5
d. Leishmaniasis	1	0	0	0	0	0	0	0	0	0
e. Lymphatic filariasis	0	—	—	—	0	—	—	—	—	0
f. Onchocerciasis	—	—	—	—	—	—	—	—	—	—
10. Leprosy	0	—	—	—	—	0	0	0	—	0
11. Dengue	0	0	0	0	0	0	0	0	0	0
12. Japanese encephalitis	—	—	—	—	—	—	—	—	—	—
13. Trachoma	—	—	—	—	—	—	—	—	—	—
14. Intestinal nematode infections	0	0	0	0	0	0	0	0	0	0
a. Ascariasis	0	—	0	0	0	—	—	—	—	0
b. Trichuriasis	0	—	0	—	—	—	—	—	—	0
c. Hookworm disease	0	0	—	0	0	0	0	0	0	0
Other intestinal infections	0	—	0	0	0	0	0	0	0	0
Other infectious diseases	37	11	0	0	1	1	2	2	1	19
B. Respiratory infections	110	40	2	1	1	2	3	5	4	58
1. Lower respiratory infections	108	39	2	1	1	2	3	5	4	57
2. Upper respiratory infections	2	1	0	0	0	0	0	0	0	1
3. Otitis media	0	0	0	0	0	—	0	—	0	0
C. Maternal conditions	15	—	—	—	—	—	—	—	—	—
1. Maternal hemorrhage	4	—	—	—	—	—	—	—	—	—
2. Maternal sepsis	1	—	—	—	—	—	—	—	—	—
3. Hypertensive disorders of pregnancy	2	—	—	—	—	—	—	—	—	—
4. Obstructed labor	0	—	—	—	—	—	—	—	—	—
5. Abortion	1	—	—	—	—	—	—	—	—	—
Other maternal conditions	6	—	—	—	—	—	—	—	—	—
D. Perinatal conditions[b]	106	64	—	—	—	—	—	—	—	64
1. Low birthweight	54	32	—	—	—	—	—	—	—	32
2. Birth asphyxia and birth trauma	30	19	—	—	—	—	—	—	—	19
Other perinatal conditions	21	13	—	—	—	—	—	—	—	13
E. Nutritional deficiencies	16	5	0	0	0	0	0	1	0	7
1. Protein-energy malnutrition	8	3	0	0	0	0	0	0	0	4
2. Iodine deficiency	0	0	0	0	0	0	0	0	0	0
3. Vitamin A deficiency	0	0	0	0	0	0	0	0	0	0
4. Iron-deficiency anemia	6	1	0	0	0	0	0	0	0	2
Other nutritional disorders	2	1	0	0	0	0	0	0	0	1

Table 3B.5 Continued

	Female								
0–4	**5–14**	**15–29**	**30–44**	**45–59**	**60–69**	**70–79**	**80+**	**Total**
18	*37*	*45*	*28*	*15*	*6*	*3*	*1*	*153*
199	**25**	**44**	**56**	**102**	**122**	**175**	**123**	**846**
151	*8*	*12*	*14*	*8*	*7*	*11*	*10*	*221*
68	**5**	**4**	**5**	**6**	**5**	**6**	**5**	**103**
1	0	2	2	2	1	1	0	10
0	0	0	0	1	1	0	—	2
0	0	0	0	0	0	0	—	1
—	—	0	0	0	0	—	—	0
0	—	0	0	0	0	—	—	0
0	0	0	0	0	0	0	—	0
0	**0**	**0**	**0**	**0**	**0**	**0**	**0**	**1**
32	0	0	0	0	1	1	1	35
10	2	0	0	0	0	0	0	13
4	—	—	—	—	—	—	—	4
0	—	—	—	—	—	—	—	0
0	0	—	—	—	—	—	0	0
5	2	0	—	—	—	—	—	8
2	0	0	0	0	0	0	0	2
5	**0**	**0**	**0**	**0**	**0**	**0**	**0**	**6**
0	**0**	**0**	**0**	**1**	**1**	**1**	**0**	**3**
0	**0**	**0**	**0**	**0**	**0**	**0**	**0**	**1**
9	**0**	**0**	**0**	**0**	**0**	**0**	**0**	**10**
0	**0**	**0**	**0**	**1**	**1**	**1**	**1**	**4**
0	0	0	0	0	0	0	—	0
0	0	0	0	0	1	1	1	3
0	0	0	0	0	0	0	—	0
—	—	—	—	0	—	—	0	0
—	—	—	—	—	—	—	—	—
0	—	—	—	—	**0**	**0**	**0**	**0**
0	**0**	**0**	**0**	**0**	**0**	**0**	**0**	**0**
—	—	—	—	—	—	—	—	—
—	—	—	—	—	—	—	—	—
—	0	0	0	0	0	0	0	0
—	0	—	—	—	—	—	—	0
—	0	—	—	—	—	—	—	0
—	0	0	0	0	0	0	0	0
—	0	0	0	0	0	0	0	0
10	1	1	1	1	1	2	2	18
36	**2**	**1**	**1**	**1**	**2**	**4**	**4**	**52**
35	2	1	1	1	2	3	4	51
1	0	0	0	0	0	0	0	1
0	—	0	—	0	—	—	0	0
—	**0**	**7**	**8**	**0**	—	—	—	**15**
—	0	2	2	0	—	—	—	4
—	0	0	0	0	—	—	—	1
—	0	1	1	0	—	—	—	2
—	—	0	0	0	—	—	—	0
—	—	1	1	—	—	—	—	1
—	0	3	3	0	—	—	—	6
42	—	—	—	—	—	—	—	**42**
22	—	—	—	—	—	—	—	22
11	—	—	—	—	—	—	—	11
9	—	—	—	—	—	—	—	9
5	**1**	**0**	**0**	**0**	**0**	**1**	**1**	**9**
4	0	0	0	0	0	0	0	5
0	0	0	0	0	0	0	0	0
0	0	0	0	0	0	0	0	0
1	1	0	0	0	0	1	1	3
1	0	0	0	0	0	0	0	1

(Continues on the following page.)

Cause	Total	Male 0–4	5–14	15–29	30–44	45–59	60–69	70–79	80+	Total
II. Noncommunicable diseases	**1,235**	**38**	**11**	**26**	**49**	**123**	**149**	**183**	**91**	**671**
A. Malignant neoplasms	165	2	2	5	8	20	24	24	9	95
1. Mouth and oropharynx cancers	5	0	0	0	0	1	1	1	0	3
2. Esophageal cancer	5	0	0	0	0	1	1	1	0	3
3. Stomach cancer	18	0	0	0	1	2	3	4	1	11
4. Colon and rectal cancers	10	0	0	0	1	1	1	1	1	6
5. Liver cancer	9	0	0	0	0	1	2	2	0	6
6. Pancreas cancer	4	0	0	0	0	1	1	1	0	2
7. Trachea, bronchus, and lung cancers	20	0	0	0	1	4	5	4	1	15
8. Melanoma and other skin cancers	1	0	0	0	0	0	0	0	0	1
9. Breast cancer	14	—	—	—	0	0	0	—	—	0
10. Cervix uteri cancer	5	—	—	—	—	—	—	—	—	—
11. Corpus uteri cancer	1	—	—	—	—	—	—	—	—	—
12. Ovarian cancer	2	—	—	—	—	—	—	—	—	—
13. Prostate cancer	6	0	0	0	0	1	1	3	1	6
14. Bladder cancer	15	0	0	0	1	3	3	3	1	12
15. Lymphomas and multiple myeloma	12	0	1	1	1	1	1	1	0	7
16. Leukemia	14	1	1	2	1	1	1	1	0	8
Other malignant neoplasms	26	1	1	1	2	3	4	3	1	15
B. Other neoplasms	**19**	**0**	**0**	**1**	**1**	**2**	**3**	**3**	**1**	**11**
C. Diabetes mellitus	**31**	**0**	**0**	**0**	**1**	**3**	**4**	**5**	**2**	**14**
D. Endocrine disorders	**20**	**1**	**0**	**1**	**1**	**2**	**2**	**2**	**1**	**9**
E. Neuropsychiatric conditions	**51**	**2**	**1**	**6**	**10**	**7**	**3**	**3**	**2**	**34**
1. Unipolar depressive disorders	0	0	0	0	0	0	0	0	0	0
2. Bipolar affective disorder	0	0	0	0	0	0	0	0	0	0
3. Schizophrenia	0	—	0	0	0	0	0	0	0	0
4. Epilepsy	5	0	0	1	1	0	0	0	0	3
5. Alcohol use disorders	3	—	0	1	1	1	0	0	0	3
6. Alzheimer's and other dementias	3	0	0	0	0	0	0	1	1	2
7. Parkinson's disease	3	0	0	0	0	0	0	0	0	1
8. Multiple sclerosis	1	—	0	0	0	0	0	0	0	0
9. Drug use disorders	19	—	0	3	7	5	0	0	0	16
10. Post-traumatic stress disorder	0	0	0	0	0	0	0	0	0	0
11. Obsessive-compulsive disorder	—	—	—	—	—	—	—	—	—	—
12. Panic disorder	—	—	—	—	—	—	—	—	—	—
13. Insomnia (primary)	—	—	—	—	—	—	—	—	—	—
14. Migraine	—	—	—	—	—	—	—	—	—	—
15. Mental retardation, lead-caused	3	0	0	1	0	0	0	0	0	2
Other neuropsychiatric disorders	14	1	0	1	1	1	1	2	1	8
F. Sense organ diseases	**1**	**0**	**0**	**—**	**0**	**0**	**0**	**0**	**0**	**0**
1. Glaucoma	0	—	—	—	—	—	—	—	0	0
2. Cataracts	—	—	—	—	—	—	—	—	—	—
3. Vision disorders, age-related	—	—	—	—	—	—	—	—	—	—
4. Hearing loss, adult onset	—	—	—	—	—	—	—	—	—	—
Other sense organ disorders	1	0	0		0	0	0	0	0	0
g. Cardiovascular diseases	**671**	**5**	**3**	**8**	**20**	**65**	**84**	**111**	**60**	**356**
1. Rheumatic heart disease	10	0	0	1	1	1	0	0	0	5
2. Hypertensive heart disease	74	0	0	0	1	6	10	13	7	38
3. Ischemic heart disease	323	0	0	2	11	41	49	59	26	188
4. Cerebrovascular disease	130	2	1	3	3	9	14	22	13	66
5. Inflammatory heart diseases	26	1	0	1	1	2	3	4	3	14
Other cardiovascular diseases	108	2	1	2	3	6	8	13	11	46
H. Respiratory diseases	**80**	**4**	**1**	**1**	**3**	**6**	**10**	**14**	**8**	**46**
1. Chronic obstructive pulmonary disease	41	0	0	0	1	3	6	9	5	23
2. Asthma	7	0	0	1	2	1	0	0	0	4
Other respiratory diseases	33	3	0	1	1	2	4	5	3	18

Table 3B.5 Continued

	Female							
0–4	5–14	15–29	30–44	45–59	60–69	70–79	80+	Total
39	*9*	*16*	*34*	*87*	*110*	*158*	*111*	*564*
1	**2**	**4**	**11**	**19**	**14**	**14**	**6**	**70**
0	0	0	0	0	0	0	0	1
0	0	0	0	0	1	1	0	2
0	0	0	1	1	1	2	1	7
0	0	0	1	1	1	1	1	4
0	0	0	0	1	1	1	0	3
0	0	0	0	0	0	0	0	2
0	0	0	1	1	1	1	0	4
0	0	0	0	0	0	0	0	1
0	0	0	3	5	2	2	1	14
0	0	0	1	2	1	1	0	5
0	0	0	0	0	0	0	0	1
0	0	0	0	1	0	0	0	2
—	—	—	—	—	—	—	—	—
0	0	0	0	1	1	1	0	3
0	0	1	1	1	1	1	0	5
1	1	1	1	1	1	1	0	6
1	0	1	2	2	2	2	1	11
0	**0**	**0**	**1**	**3**	**2**	**2**	**1**	**9**
0	**0**	**0**	**1**	**3**	**5**	**6**	**3**	**17**
1	**0**	**0**	**1**	**1**	**2**	**3**	**1**	**10**
1	**1**	**2**	**3**	**2**	**2**	**3**	**2**	**17**
0	0	0	0	0	0	0	0	0
0	0	0	0	0	0	0	0	0
—	—	0	0	0	0	0	0	0
0	0	1	0	0	0	0	0	2
—	—	0	0	0	0	0	—	0
0	0	0	0	0	0	1	1	2
0	0	0	0	0	0	0	0	1
—	0	0	0	0	0	0	0	0
—	—	1	2	1	0	0	0	3
0	0	0	0	0	0	0	0	0
—	—	—	—	—	—	—	—	—
—	—	—	—	—	—	—	—	—
—	—	—	—	—	—	—	—	—
0	1	0	0	0	0	0	0	2
1	0	0	0	1	1	1	1	6
0	**0**	**0**	**0**	**0**	**0**	**0**	**0**	**0**
—	—	—	—	—	—	0	0	0
—	—	—	—	—	—	—	—	—
—	—	—	—	—	—	—	—	—
0	0	0	0	0	0	0	0	0
10	**3**	**5**	**11**	**40**	**63**	**103**	**79**	**314**
0	0	1	1	1	0	1	0	5
0	0	0	1	4	8	13	9	36
0	0	1	4	19	32	47	31	135
1	1	1	2	7	13	22	17	64
0	0	0	1	1	2	4	3	12
8	1	1	2	6	8	17	18	62
3	**0**	**1**	**3**	**4**	**6**	**10**	**7**	**34**
0	0	0	1	2	4	6	4	17
0	0	0	1	1	0	0	0	3
3	0	0	1	2	2	4	3	14

(Continues on the following page.)

Table 3B.5 Continued

Cause	Total	Male								Total
		0–4	5–14	15–29	30–44	45–59	60–69	70–79	80+	
I. Digestive diseases	**88**	**2**	**1**	**2**	**2**	**12**	**12**	**11**	**4**	**46**
1. Peptic ulcer disease	5	0	0	0	0	1	1	1	0	3
2. Cirrhosis of the liver	37	0	0	1	1	6	6	5	2	21
3. Appendicitis	0	0	0	0	0	0	0	0	0	0
Other digestive diseases	45	1	0	1	1	6	5	5	2	22
J. Genitourinary diseases	**57**	**1**	**1**	**1**	**2**	**6**	**8**	**9**	**5**	**31**
1. Nephritis and nephrosis	42	0	0	1	1	5	6	6	3	23
2. Benign prostatic hypertrophy	2	—	—	—	—	0	0	1	1	2
Other genitourinary system diseases	14	0	0	0	1	1	1	2	1	7
K. Skin diseases	**4**	**0**	**0**	**0**	**0**	**0**	**0**	**1**	**0**	**1**
L. Musculoskeletal diseases	**2**	**0**	**0**	**0**	**0**	**0**	**0**	**0**	**0**	**1**
1. Rheumatoid arthritis	0	0	0	0	0	0	0	0	0	0
2. Osteoarthritis	0	0	—	0	0	0	0	0	0	0
3. Gout	0	0	—	0	0	0	0	0	0	0
4. Low back pain	0	0	—	0	0	0	0	0	0	0
Other musculoskeletal disorders	1	0	0	0	0	0	0	0	0	1
M. Congenital anomalies	**46**	**22**	**1**	**1**	**0**	**0**	**0**	**0**	**0**	**24**
1. Abdominal wall defect	0	0	0	0	0	0	0	0	0	0
2. Anencephaly	2	1	0	0	0	0	0	0	0	1
3. Anorectal atresia	0	0	0	0	0	0	0	0	0	0
4. Cleft lip	0	0	0	0	0	0	0	0	0	0
5. Cleft palate	0	0	0	0	0	0	0	0	0	0
6. Esophageal atresia	0	0	0	0	0	0	0	0	0	0
7. Renal agenesis	0	0	0	0	0	0	0	0	0	0
8. Down syndrome	1	1	0	0	0	0	0	0	0	1
9. Congenital heart anomalies	20	10	0	0	0	0	0	0	0	11
10. Spina bifida	3	1	0	0	0	0	0	0	—	1
Other congenital anomalies	18	9	0	0	0	0	0	0	0	10
N. Oral conditions	**0**	**0**	**0**	**0**	**0**	**0**	**0**	**—**	**0**	**0**
1. Dental caries	—	—	—	—	—	—	—	—	—	—
2. Periodontal disease	—	—	—	—	—	—	—	—	—	—
3. Edentulism	—	—	—	—	—	—	—	—	—	—
Other oral diseases	0	0	0	0	0	0	0	—	0	0
III. Injuries	***216***	***15***	***16***	***47***	***28***	***23***	***13***	***10***	***3***	***154***
A. Unintentional injuries	**181**	**14**	**16**	**36**	**21**	**20**	**11**	**9**	**3**	**129**
1. Road traffic accidents	99	5	8	20	14	12	7	5	1	74
2. Poisonings	7	1	0	1	1	2	0	0	0	5
3. Falls	12	1	1	1	2	2	1	1	0	9
4. Fires	13	1	1	2	1	1	0	0	0	6
5. Drownings	14	2	2	5	1	1	0	0	0	11
6. Other unintentional injuries	36	4	3	7	3	3	2	2	1	25
B. Intentional injuries	**35**	**0**	**1**	**11**	**7**	**4**	**2**	**1**	**0**	**25**
1. Self-inflicted injuries	14	0	0	4	2	1	1	0	0	9
2. Violence	10	0	0	4	2	1	1	0	0	8
3. War	8	0	0	3	3	1	0	0	0	7
Other intentional injuries	2	0	0	1	0	0	0	0	0	1

Table 3B.5 Continued

	Female							
0–4	5–14	15–29	30–44	45–59	60–69	70–79	80+	Total
1	1	1	2	9	10	11	6	42
0	0	0	0	0	0	1	0	2
0	0	0	1	4	4	4	2	16
0	0	0	0	0	0	0	0	0
1	0	0	1	4	6	7	4	24
1	1	1	2	5	6	7	4	26
0	0	1	1	4	4	5	3	19
—	—	—	—	—	—	—	—	—
0	0	0	1	1	1	2	1	7
0	0	0	0	0	1	1	0	2
0	0	0	0	0	0	0	0	1
0	0	0	0	0	0	0	0	0
0	0	0	0	0	0	0	0	0
0	0	0	0	0	0	0	0	0
0	0	0	0	0	0	0	0	0
0	0	0	0	0	0	0	0	1
19	1	1	0	0	0	0	0	21
0	0	0	0	0	0	—	0	0
1	0	0	0	0	0	—	0	1
0	0	0	0	0	0	—	0	0
0	0	0	0	0	0	—	0	0
0	0	0	0	0	0	—	0	0
0	0	0	0	0	0	—	0	0
0	0	0	0	0	0	—	0	0
1	0	0	0	0	0	—	0	1
8	0	0	0	0	0	0	0	9
1	0	0	0	—	0	0	—	1
7	0	0	0	0	0	0	0	8
0	—	—	—	—	0	0	0	0
—	—	—	—	—	—	—	—	—
—	—	—	—	—	—	—	—	—
—	—	—	—	—	—	—	—	—
0	—	—	—	—	0	0	0	0
10	8	16	9	7	5	6	3	61
9	8	11	7	5	4	5	2	52
3	4	5	4	3	2	2	1	25
0	0	1	0	0	0	0	0	2
1	0	0	0	0	0	1	0	3
1	1	3	1	1	0	1	0	8
1	1	1	0	0	0	0	0	3
3	2	2	1	1	1	1	1	11
0	0	4	2	1	1	0	0	9
0	0	3	1	1	0	0	0	6
0	0	1	1	0	0	0	0	2
0	0	0	0	0	0	0	0	1
0	0	0	0	0	0	0	0	0

Source: Authors' compilation.
Note: — = an estimate of zero; the number zero in a cell indicates a non-zero estimate of less than 500.
a. Does not include liver cancer and cirrhosis deaths resulting from chronic hepatitis virus infection.
b. This cause category includes "Causes arising in the perinatal period" as defined in the International Classification of Diseases, principally low birthweight, prematurity, birth asphyxia and birth trauma, and does not include all causes of deaths occurring in the perinatal period.

Table 3B.6 Deaths by Cause, Sex, and Age in the South Asia Region, 2001
(thousands)

Cause	Total	Male 0–4	5–14	15–29	30–44	45–59	60–69	70–79	80+	Total
Population (millions)	1,388	88	164	195	139	81	30	14	4	715
All causes	13,557	1,782	246	485	688	1,117	1,111	1,127	543	7,099
I. Communicable, maternal, perinatal, and nutritional conditions	5,882	1,623	142	167	296	270	201	204	103	3,007
A. Infectious and parasitic diseases	2,987	597	107	153	279	239	115	92	42	1,624
1. Tuberculosis	604	5	6	49	97	118	69	32	5	381
2. Sexually transmitted diseases excluding HIV/AIDS	71	12	0	0	1	7	6	5	2	33
a. Syphilis	59	12	0	0	0	5	6	5	2	30
b. Chlamydia	6	—	—	—	—	—	—	—	—	—
c. Gonorrhea	0	—	—	0	0	—	0	—	—	0
d. Other sexually transmitted diseases	5	0	0	0	1	3	0	0	0	3
3. HIV/AIDS	272	7	2	42	114	41	3	1	0	210
4. Diarrheal diseases	695	329	1	2	4	5	5	7	9	363
5. Childhood-cluster diseases	467	167	41	11	6	3	1	1	1	231
a. Pertussis	108	54	—	—	—	—	—	—	—	54
b. Poliomyelitis	0	0	—	—	—	—	—	—	—	0
c. Diphtheria	3	1	0	0	0	0	0	0	—	1
d. Measles	216	71	31	4	—	—	—	—	—	106
e. Tetanus	140	41	10	7	6	3	1	1	1	70
6. Meningitis	71	4	9	6	4	5	3	4	2	36
7. Hepatitis B[a]	28	0	0	3	4	7	2	2	1	19
Hepatitis C[a]	11	0	0	1	2	3	1	1	0	7
8. Malaria	63	27	0	1	1	0	0	0	0	30
9. Tropical-cluster diseases	41	1	8	6	3	3	1	0	0	22
a. Trypanosomiasis	0	—	—	—	0	—	—	—	—	0
b. Chagas' disease	0	—	—	—	—	—	—	—	0	0
c. Schistosomiasis	0	—	0	0	0	0	0	0	0	0
d. Leishmaniasis	40	1	8	6	3	2	1	0	—	22
e. Lymphatic filariasis	0	0	—	0	0	0	0	—	0	0
f. Onchocerciasis	—	—	—	—	—	—	—	—	—	—
10. Leprosy	3	0	0	0	0	0	0	0	0	2
11. Dengue	9	1	2	0	0	0	0	0	0	4
12. Japanese encephalitis	10	0	0	1	2	0	0	0	0	5
13. Trachoma	0	0	—	0	—	0	—	—	—	0
14. Intestinal nematode infections	4	0	2	0	0	0	0	0	0	2
a. Ascariasis	2	0	1	0	0	0	—	0	—	1
b. Trichuriasis	2	0	1	—	—	—	—	—	—	1
c. Hookworm disease	0	0	—	—	0	—	—	0	0	0
Other intestinal infections	1	0	0	0	0	0	0	0	0	0
Other infectious diseases	638	43	35	32	41	46	22	39	21	278
B. Respiratory infections	1,435	412	19	9	11	16	84	108	58	718
1. Lower respiratory infections	1,414	411	19	9	11	15	82	105	57	708
2. Upper respiratory infections	20	2	0	0	0	1	2	3	1	9
3. Otitis media	1	0	0	0	0	0	0	0	0	0
C. Maternal conditions	199	—	—	—	—	—	—	—	—	—
1. Maternal hemorrhage	61	—	—	—	—	—	—	—	—	—
2. Maternal sepsis	27	—	—	—	—	—	—	—	—	—
3. Hypertensive disorders of pregnancy	28	—	—	—	—	—	—	—	—	—
4. Obstructed labor	19	—	—	—	—	—	—	—	—	—
5. Abortion	28	—	—	—	—	—	—	—	—	—
Other maternal conditions	36	—	—	—	—	—	—	—	—	—
D. Perinatal conditions[b]	1,086	597	—	—	—	—	—	—	—	597
1. Low birthweight	757	406	—	—	—	—	—	—	—	406
2. Birth asphyxia and birth trauma	192	122	—	—	—	—	—	—	—	122
Other perinatal conditions	137	68	—	—	—	—	—	—	—	68
E. Nutritional deficiencies	175	17	16	5	5	15	2	5	3	67
1. Protein-energy malnutrition	67	13	11	2	0	1	0	0	0	29
2. Iodine deficiency	3	1	1	—	0	0	0	0	0	1
3. Vitamin A deficiency	4	0	1	0	—	0	—	—	—	2
4. Iron-deficiency anemia	61	0	2	2	4	11	0	0	0	19
Other nutritional disorders	39	2	1	1	1	3	2	4	2	16

			Female					
0–4	**5–14**	**15–29**	**30–44**	**45–59**	**60–69**	**70–79**	**80+**	**Total**
_83_	_154_	_180_	_128_	_77_	_31_	_16_	_4_	_673_
1,830	**289**	**502**	**480**	**763**	**911**	**1,089**	**594**	**6,458**
_1,619_	_176_	_221_	_231_	_157_	_165_	_190_	_117_	_2,875_
676	**134**	**112**	**119**	**119**	**79**	**79**	**46**	**1,363**
4	**7**	**48**	**61**	**54**	**30**	**17**	**4**	**224**
25	**0**	**0**	**1**	**6**	**4**	**2**	**1**	**38**
25	0	0	0	0	2	2	1	29
—	—	0	1	5	1	—	—	6
0	—	0	0	0	0	—	—	0
0	0	0	0	1	1	0	0	2
7	**2**	**20**	**25**	**8**	**1**	**0**	**0**	**62**
302	**1**	**1**	**2**	**4**	**5**	**7**	**12**	**332**
171	**42**	**11**	**6**	**3**	**1**	**1**	**1**	**236**
54	—	—	—	—	—	—	—	54
0	—	—	—	—	—	—	—	0
1	0	0	0	—	—	—	0	2
74	31	4	—	—	—	—	—	110
42	10	7	6	3	1	1	1	70
13	**11**	**4**	**1**	**1**	**2**	**2**	**1**	**35**
0	**1**	**2**	**1**	**2**	**1**	**1**	**0**	**9**
0	**0**	**1**	**1**	**1**	**0**	**0**	**0**	**4**
30	**0**	**1**	**1**	**1**	**0**	**0**	**0**	**33**
3	**8**	**4**	**1**	**1**	**1**	**0**	**0**	**18**
—	—	—	—	0	—	—	—	0
—	0	0	0	0	0	0	0	0
3	8	4	1	1	1	0	—	18
—	—	—	0	0	—	0	0	0
0	**0**	**0**	**0**	**0**	**0**	**0**	**0**	**1**
1	**3**	**0**	**0**	**0**	**0**	**0**	**0**	**5**
2	**1**	**1**	**0**	**0**	**0**	**0**	**0**	**5**
1	**2**	**0**	**0**	**0**	**0**	**0**	**0**	**2**
0	1	0	0	—	0	—	—	1
—	1	—	—	—	—	0	—	1
—	0	0	—	—	—	—	—	0
0	0	0	0	0	0	0	0	0
117	57	20	19	37	34	48	27	360
420	**25**	**8**	**5**	**11**	**76**	**105**	**67**	**717**
415	24	8	4	11	74	103	66	706
5	0	0	0	0	2	2	1	11
0	0	0	0	0	0	—	0	0
—	—	98	99	2	—	—	—	199
—	—	27	32	1	—	—	—	61
—	—	14	12	0	—	—	—	27
—	—	16	11	0	—	—	—	28
—	—	10	9	0	—	—	—	19
—	—	17	12	—	—	—	—	28
—	—	13	23	1	—	—	—	36
490	—	—	—	—	—	—	—	**490**
351	—	—	—	—	—	—	—	351
70	—	—	—	—	—	—	—	70
68	—	—	—	—	—	—	—	68
33	**17**	**3**	**8**	**25**	**10**	**7**	**4**	**107**
20	14	1	1	2	1	0	0	38
2	0	0	0	0	0	0	0	2
1	1	—	—	0	—	0	0	2
2	1	2	7	21	7	0	0	42
8	1	0	0	1	2	6	3	23

(Continues on the following page.)

Table 3B.6 Continued

Cause	Total	Male 0–4	5–14	15–29	30–44	45–59	60–69	70–79	80+	Total
II. Noncommunicable diseases	*6,346*	*129*	*44*	*107*	*203*	*714*	*854*	*872*	*412*	*3,335*
A. Malignant neoplasms	**927**	**6**	**7**	**18**	**34**	**94**	**154**	**112**	**51**	**476**
1. Mouth and oropharynx cancers	140	0	0	2	7	21	35	20	8	94
2. Esophageal cancer	80	0	0	0	3	9	18	10	4	· 44
3. Stomach cancer	45	0	0	1	2	6	9	7	3	28
4. Colon and rectal cancers	35	0	0	1	3	4	6	5	3	20
5. Liver cancer	27	0	0	1	2	4	5	3	1	17
6. Pancreas cancer	13	0	0	0	1	2	3	2	1	7
7. Trachea, bronchus, and lung cancers	129	0	0	1	5	26	38	28	9	106
8. Melanoma and other skin cancers	3	0	0	0	0	0	0	0	0	1
9. Breast cancer	76	—	—	0	0	0	0	0	0	0
10. Cervix uteri cancer	83	—	—	—	—	—	—	—	—	—
11. Corpus uteri cancer	4	—	—	—	—	—	—	—	—	—
12. Ovarian cancer	21	—	—	—	—	—	—	—	—	—
13. Prostate cancer	21	0	0	0	0	1	6	9	5	21
14. Bladder cancer	30	0	0	0	0	1	5	6	4	16
15. Lymphomas and multiple myeloma	82	1	2	3	4	4	7	5	3	29
16. Leukemia	38	2	3	6	3	2	3	2	1	22
Other malignant neoplasms	99	3	2	2	5	13	20	16	10	71
B. Other neoplasms	**18**	**1**	**1**	**2**	**1**	**2**	**1**	**1**	**1**	**9**
C. Diabetes mellitus	**196**	**1**	**1**	**3**	**5**	**25**	**26**	**27**	**17**	**104**
D. Endocrine disorders	**26**	**5**	**1**	**1**	**1**	**1**	**1**	**1**	**1**	**12**
E. Neuropsychiatric conditions	**234**	**8**	**5**	**10**	**21**	**17**	**6**	**43**	**23**	**132**
1. Unipolar depressive disorders	9	—	—	—	2	2	1	—	—	4
2. Bipolar affective disorder	0	0	0	0	0	0	0	—	—	0
3. Schizophrenia	13	—	0	0	2	3	1	1	0	7
4. Epilepsy	32	7	3	2	1	1	0	1	0	15
5. Alcohol use disorders	13	—	0	2	3	4	2	1	0	12
6. Alzheimer's and other dementias	81	0	0	0	0	0	0	27	14	41
7. Parkinson's disease	9	0	0	0	0	0	0	3	2	5
8. Multiple sclerosis	1	0	0	0	0	0	0	0	0	1
9. Drug use disorders	29	—	0	4	12	7	1	0	0	24
10. Post-traumatic stress disorder	0	—	—	—	0	0	—	—	0	0
11. Obsessive-compulsive disorder	—	—	—	—	—	—	—	—	—	—
12. Panic disorder	—	—	—	—	—	—	—	—	—	—
13. Insomnia (primary)	—	—	—	—	—	—	—	—	—	—
14. Migraine	—	—	—	—	—	—	—	—	—	—
15. Mental retardation, lead-caused	0	0	0	0	0	0	0	0	0	0
Other neuropsychiatric disorders	46	1	2	1	1	1	1	11	6	23
F. Sense organ diseases	**1**	**0**	**0**	**0**	**0**	**0**	**0**	**0**	**0**	**0**
1. Glaucoma	0	0	—	0	0	0	0	—	—	0
2. Cataracts	—	—	—	—	—	—	—	—	—	—
3. Vision disorders, age-related	—	—	—	—	—	—	—	—	—	—
4. Hearing loss, adult onset	—	—	—	—	—	—	—	—	—	—
Other sense organ disorders	1	0	0	0	0	0	0	0	0	0
G. Cardiovascular diseases	**3,421**	**18**	**11**	**36**	**84**	**374**	**495**	**527**	**250**	**1,795**
1. Rheumatic heart disease	128	6	3	9	7	12	10	10	5	61
2. Hypertensive heart disease	90	0	0	1	3	10	12	13	6	47
3. Ischemic heart disease	1,838	2	3	10	49	244	293	297	135	1,032
4. Cerebrovascular disease	923	3	1	4	10	76	140	159	74	467
5. Inflammatory heart diseases	71	2	1	2	4	6	7	8	4	34
Other cardiovascular diseases	372	4	4	9	12	26	32	41	27	154
H. Respiratory diseases	**746**	**8**	**4**	**8**	**19**	**111**	**110**	**103**	**41**	**405**
1. Chronic obstructive pulmonary disease	577	0	0	0	7	91	99	88	34	318
2. Asthma	78	0	2	6	9	14	3	3	1	39
Other respiratory diseases	91	7	2	2	3	7	8	12	6	48

Table 3B.6 Continued

	Female							
0–4	5–14	15–29	30–44	45–59	60–69	70–79	80+	Total
163	*57*	*117*	*153*	*521*	*697*	*852*	*452*	*3,011*
7	**6**	**18**	**37**	**108**	**119**	**91**	**64**	**451**
0	0	1	2	11	14	11	8	47
0	0	0	2	8	11	8	6	36
0	0	0	1	4	4	4	4	17
0	0	0	1	3	4	3	3	15
0	0	2	1	3	2	2	1	11
—	—	0	0	1	1	1	1	5
0	0	0	2	7	7	6	2	23
0	0	0	0	0	0	0	0	1
0	0	1	10	23	20	13	9	76
0	0	6	5	26	26	14	7	83
0	0	0	0	1	1	1	1	4
0	0	1	2	5	6	5	3	21
—	—	—	—	—	—	—	—	—
1	0	0	2	2	3	3	3	14
2	3	4	5	9	12	11	7	53
3	2	3	2	2	2	1	1	16
1	1	0	2	5	6	6	7	28
0	**0**	**1**	**2**	**2**	**1**	**1**	**1**	**9**
1	**1**	**2**	**3**	**19**	**29**	**26**	**11**	**91**
5	**1**	**1**	**1**	**1**	**2**	**2**	**1**	**13**
6	**6**	**6**	**6**	**10**	**5**	**41**	**22**	**103**
—	—	0	1	3	1	0	0	5
0	—	0	0	0	0	0	0	0
0	0	0	1	3	1	1	1	6
6	4	3	1	2	1	1	0	18
—	—	0	0	0	0	0	0	1
0	0	0	0	0	0	26	14	40
0	—	0	0	0	0	3	1	4
0	0	0	0	0	0	0	0	0
—	—	1	2	2	0	0	0	5
—	—	—	—	0	0	—	—	0
—	—	—	—	—	—	—	—	—
—	—	—	—	—	—	—	—	—
—	—	—	—	—	—	—	—	—
—	—	—	—	—	—	—	—	—
0	0	0	0	0	0	0	0	0
0	2	1	1	1	2	11	6	24
0	**0**	**0**	**0**	**0**	**0**	**0**	**0**	**1**
—	—	—	0	—	—	—	—	0
—	—	—	—	—	—	—	—	—
—	—	—	—	—	—	—	—	—
—	—	—	—	—	—	—	—	—
0	0	0	0	0	0	0	0	1
21	**13**	**42**	**58**	**229**	**427**	**553**	**281**	**1,626**
7	4	8	7	12	10	12	6	66
0	1	1	2	9	12	12	7	43
2	1	18	33	125	233	269	125	806
2	1	2	6	51	126	175	93	456
2	1	2	2	5	7	11	6	37
9	4	10	9	27	40	75	44	217
9	**4**	**9**	**18**	**91**	**71**	**91**	**47**	**340**
0	0	0	7	72	62	78	40	259
0	2	7	10	13	2	2	1	39
9	2	2	2	5	7	10	6	42

(Continues on the following page.)

Cause	Total	Male 0–4	5–14	15–29	30–44	45–59	60–69	70–79	80+	Total
I. Digestive diseases	**444**	**11**	**9**	**18**	**27**	**65**	**40**	**35**	**18**	**222**
1. Peptic ulcer disease	82	2	1	3	8	17	8	7	3	50
2. Cirrhosis of the liver	185	6	3	7	13	35	22	16	6	107
3. Appendicitis	7	0	0	0	0	1	1	1	1	4
Other digestive diseases	169	4	5	7	6	12	10	10	8	62
J. Genitourinary diseases	**156**	**5**	**3**	**6**	**10**	**23**	**19**	**19**	**9**	**93**
1. Nephritis and nephrosis	132	4	3	5	9	17	15	15	7	74
2. Benign prostatic hypertrophy	12	—	—	—	0	4	3	3	1	12
Other genitourinary system diseases	13	0	0	1	1	1	1	1	1	7
K. Skin diseases	**10**	**0**	**0**	**0**	**0**	**1**	**1**	**1**	**1**	**5**
L. Musculoskeletal diseases	**11**	**0**	**0**	**1**	**0**	**1**	**1**	**1**	**1**	**5**
1. Rheumatoid arthritis	3	0	0	0	0	0	0	0	0	1
2. Osteoarthritis	0	—	—	—	0	0	0	0	0	0
3. Gout	0	—	—	—	0	0	0	0	0	0
4. Low back pain	0	—	—	—	—	—	0	0	0	0
Other musculoskeletal disorders	8	0	0	1	0	1	1	1	1	4
M. Congenital anomalies	**157**	**67**	**2**	**5**	**0**	**0**	**0**	**0**	**0**	**75**
1. Abdominal wall defect	1	0	—	—	—	—	—	—	—	0
2. Anencephaly	11	5	—	—	—	—	—	—	—	5
3. Anorectal atresia	0	0	—	—	—	—	—	—	—	0
4. Cleft lip	0	0	—	—	—	—	—	—	—	0
5. Cleft palate	0	0	—	0	0	—	—	—	—	0
6. Esophageal atresia	—	—	—	—	—	—	—	—	—	—
7. Renal agenesis	1	0	0	—	—	—	0	—	—	0
8. Down syndrome	12	3	1	2	—	—	—	—	—	5
9. Congenital heart anomalies	105	45	1	3	0	0	0	0	0	49
10. Spina bifida	13	6	0	0	0	0	0	0	—	6
Other congenital anomalies	15	7	0	0	0	0	0	0	0	8
N. Oral conditions	**1**	**0**	**0**	**0**	**0**	**0**	**0**	**0**	**0**	**0**
1. Dental caries	—	—	—	—	—	—	—	—	—	—
2. Periodontal disease	0	—	—	—	—	—	—	—	—	—
3. Edentulism	—	—	—	—	—	—	—	—	—	—
Other oral diseases	0	0	0	0	0	0	0	0	0	0
III. Injuries	***1,329***	***30***	***60***	***212***	***189***	***132***	***56***	***51***	***28***	***758***
A. Unintentional injuries	**994**	**28**	**55**	**131**	**126**	**100**	**45**	**41**	**22**	**548**
1. Road traffic accidents	238	4	14	45	53	36	11	9	4	176
2. Poisonings	90	1	3	8	8	17	6	3	1	47
3. Falls	112	4	4	8	8	9	9	14	9	67
4. Fires	183	5	4	15	15	7	3	2	1	52
5. Drownings	90	5	12	16	9	6	3	3	1	55
6. Other unintentional injuries	280	10	18	38	33	24	13	11	5	152
B. Intentional injuries	**335**	**2**	**5**	**81**	**63**	**32**	**11**	**10**	**6**	**210**
1. Self-inflicted injuries	224	—	3	53	39	20	6	6	3	130
2. Violence	79	1	2	17	15	9	3	3	3	52
3. War	26	0	0	10	8	3	1	0	0	23
Other intentional injuries	6	0	0	1	1	1	1	0	0	5

	Female							
0–4	**5–14**	**15–29**	**30–44**	**45–59**	**60–69**	**70–79**	**80+**	**Total**
31	**19**	**29**	**23**	**45**	**29**	**30**	**16**	**221**
2	1	2	4	8	5	6	3	32
14	6	10	8	17	10	10	4	79
0	0	0	0	1	1	1	1	3
15	12	16	11	19	13	13	8	107
4	**2**	**5**	**5**	**14**	**13**	**13**	**7**	**63**
4	2	4	4	13	12	12	6	57
—	—	—	—	—	—	—	—	—
0	0	1	1	1	1	1	0	6
0	**0**	**0**	**0**	**1**	**1**	**1**	**1**	**5**
1	**0**	**0**	**0**	**1**	**1**	**1**	**1**	**6**
0	0	0	0	0	0	1	0	2
0	—	—	0	0	0	0	0	0
—	—	—	—	0	0	0	0	0
0	0	0	—	0	0	—	0	0
1	0	0	0	0	0	1	1	4
75	**3**	**4**	**0**	**0**	**0**	**0**	**0**	**83**
0	—	—	—	—	—	—	—	0
6	—	—	—	—	0	—	—	6
0	—	—	—	—	—	—	—	0
0	—	—	—	—	—	—	—	0
0	—	—	—	0	—	—	—	0
—	—	—	—	—	—	—	—	—
0	0	—	—	—	0	—	—	0
4	1	2	—	—	—	—	—	6
52	2	2	0	0	0	0	0	56
7	0	0	0	0	—	0	0	7
6	0	0	0	0	0	0	0	7
0	**0**	**0**	**0**	**0**	**0**	**0**	**0**	**0**
—	—	—	—	—	—	—	—	—
—	0	0	0	0	—	—	—	0
—	—	—	—	—	—	—	—	—
0	0	0	0	0	0	0	0	0
49	*56*	*164*	*95*	*86*	*48*	*47*	*25*	*571*
47	52	109	68	64	41	41	23	445
7	8	11	10	14	5	5	2	62
1	4	5	6	9	12	4	2	43
4	4	4	3	6	5	13	6	45
9	10	54	30	13	6	6	3	131
6	9	8	4	3	2	2	1	36
20	16	27	16	18	11	12	8	128
2	**5**	**55**	**27**	**21**	**7**	**6**	**2**	**125**
0	3	49	21	14	3	3	2	95
2	1	6	6	6	4	2	0	27
0	0	0	1	1	0	0	0	3
0	0	0	0	0	0	0	0	1

Source: Authors' compilation.

Note: — = an estimate of zero; the number zero in a cell indicates a non-zero estimate of less than 500.

a. Does not include liver cancer and cirrhosis deaths resulting from chronic hepatitis virus infection.

b. This cause category includes "Causes arising in the perinatal period" as defined in the International Classification of Diseases, principally low birthweight, prematurity, birth asphyxia, and birth trauma, and does not include all causes of deaths occurring in the perinatal period.

Table 3B.7 Deaths by Cause, Sex, and Age in the Sub-Saharan Africa Region, 2001
(thousands)

		Male								
Cause	Total	0–4	5–14	15–29	30–44	45–59	60–69	70–79	80+	Total
Population (millions)	*668*	*57*	*92*	*93*	*49*	*26*	*9*	*4*	*1*	*331*
All causes	**10,837**	**2,367**	**281**	**529**	**852**	**632**	**412**	**366**	**170**	**5,611**
I. Communicable, maternal, perinatal, and nutritional conditions	***7,747***	***2,252***	***179***	***289***	***603***	***331***	***135***	***73***	***26***	***3,888***
A. Infectious and parasitic diseases	**5,702**	**1,428**	**150**	**277**	**580**	**297**	**100**	**45**	**•16**	**2,893**
1. **Tuberculosis**	**317**	**12**	**7**	**49**	**68**	**51**	**19**	**9**	**3**	**218**
2. **Sexually transmitted diseases excluding HIV/AIDS**	**90**	**17**	**0**	**1**	**10**	**17**	**3**	**0**	**0**	**48**
a. Syphilis	87	17	0	1	9	17	3	0	0	47
b. Chlamydia	1	—	—	—	—	—	—	—	—	—
c. Gonorrhea	1	—	—	0	0	0	0	—	—	0
d. Other sexually transmitted diseases	2	0	0	0	0	0	0	0	0	1
3. **HIV/AIDS**	**2,058**	**159**	**48**	**185**	**440**	**148**	**23**	**3**	**0**	**1,007**
4. **Diarrheal diseases**	**712**	**337**	**1**	**2**	**4**	**6**	**6**	**8**	**8**	**373**
5. **Childhood-cluster diseases**	**745**	**308**	**50**	**8**	**4**	**2**	**1**	**0**	**0**	**373**
a. Pertussis	176	88	—	—	—	—	—	—	—	88
b. Poliomyelitis	0	0	—	—	—	—	—	—	—	0
c. Diphtheria	1	1	—	0	—	—	—	—	—	1
d. Measles	447	177	44	3	—	—	—	—	—	224
e. Tetanus	121	43	6	5	4	2	1	0	0	60
6. **Meningitis**	**23**	**5**	**2**	**1**	**2**	**2**	**1**	**0**	**0**	**12**
7. **Hepatitis B**[a]	**21**	**1**	**3**	**1**	**3**	**2**	**1**	**0**	**0**	**12**
Hepatitis C[a]	**8**	**1**	**1**	**0**	**1**	**1**	**0**	**0**	**0**	**5**
8. **Malaria**	**1,093**	**467**	**7**	**9**	**10**	**10**	**7**	**6**	**3**	**518**
9. **Tropical-cluster diseases**	**58**	**3**	**12**	**8**	**7**	**5**	**1**	**1**	**0**	**38**
a. Trypanosomiasis	48	2	11	6	6	5	1	0	0	31
b. Chagas' disease	—	—	—	—	—	—	—	—	—	—
c. Schistosomiasis	2	0	0	0	0	0	1	0	0	1
d. Leishmaniasis	8	1	2	2	1	0	0	0	—	6
e. Lymphatic filariasis	0	0	0	0	0	0	0	0	—	0
f. Onchocerciasis	—	—	—	—	—	—	—	—	—	—
10. **Leprosy**	**1**	—	—	—	**0**	**0**	**0**	**0**	—	**0**
11. **Dengue**	**0**	**0**	**0**	**0**	**0**	**0**	**0**	**0**	**0**	**0**
12. **Japanese encephalitis**	—	—	—	—	—	—	—	—	—	—
13. **Trachoma**	—	—	—	—	—	—	—	—	—	—
14. **Intestinal nematode infections**	**4**	**0**	**0**	**0**	**0**	**0**	**0**	**0**	**0**	**2**
a. Ascariasis	1	0	0	0	0	—	—	—	—	0
b. Trichuriasis	1	—	0	0	0	0	0	0	0	0
c. Hookworm disease	2	0	0	0	0	0	0	0	0	1
Other intestinal infections	0	—	0	0	0	0	0	0	0	0
Other infectious diseases	572	117	18	12	31	52	38	17	1	287
B. Respiratory infections	**1,094**	**439**	**26**	**12**	**22**	**31**	**29**	**23**	**9**	**590**
1. Lower respiratory infections	1,080	435	24	11	21	31	28	23	9	583
2. Upper respiratory infections	13	3	1	0	0	0	1	0	0	6
3. Otitis media	1	0	1	0	0	—	0	—	—	1
C. Maternal conditions	**237**	—	—	—	—	—	—	—	—	—
1. Maternal hemorrhage	60	—	—	—	—	—	—	—	—	—
2. Maternal sepsis	44	—	—	—	—	—	—	—	—	—
3. Hypertensive disorders of pregnancy	32	—	—	—	—	—	—	—	—	—
4. Obstructed labor	22	—	—	—	—	—	—	—	—	—
5. Abortion	28	—	—	—	—	—	—	—	—	—
Other maternal conditions	52	—	—	—	—	—	—	—	—	—
D. Perinatal conditions[b]	**573**	**332**	—	—	—	—	—	—	—	**332**
1. Low birthweight	243	141	—	—	—	—	—	—	—	141
2. Birth asphyxia and birth trauma	240	139	—	—	—	—	—	—	—	139
Other perinatal conditions	90	52	—	—	—	—	—	—	—	52
E. Nutritional deficiencies	**140**	**53**	**3**	**0**	**1**	**4**	**5**	**4**	**2**	**73**
1. Protein-energy malnutrition	99	40	2	0	0	2	4	4	2	55
2. Iodine deficiency	3	1	0	0	0	0	0	0	0	1
3. Vitamin A deficiency	18	7	1	0	0	0	0	0	0	8
4. Iron-deficiency anemia	18	5	1	0	0	1	1	0	0	8
Other nutritional disorders	2	1	0	0	0	0	0	0	0	1

Table 3B.7 Continued

	Female							
0–4	5–14	15–29	30–44	45–59	60–69	70–79	80+	Total
56	*91*	*93*	*51*	*28*	*11*	*5*	*1*	*336*
2,137	**289**	**698**	**678**	**466**	**350**	**384**	**225**	**5,227**
2,046	*221*	*616*	*573*	*231*	*79*	*62*	*31*	*3,859*
1,436	**176**	**449**	**447**	**188**	**57**	**37**	**18**	**2,809**
11	**6**	**30**	**26**	**13**	**9**	**4**	**1**	**99**
12	**0**	**12**	**8**	**6**	**2**	**1**	**0**	**42**
11	0	12	8	6	2	1	0	40
—	—	0	0	0	0	—	—	1
—	—	0	0	0	0	—	—	0
0	0	0	0	0	0	0	0	1
154	**47**	**349**	**374**	**108**	**17**	**4**	**0**	**1,051**
306	**1**	**1**	**2**	**4**	**6**	**8**	**11**	**339**
305	**52**	**8**	**4**	**2**	**1**	**0**	**0**	**372**
88	—	—	—	—	—	—	—	88
0	—	—	—	—	—	—	—	0
1	0	—	—	—	—	—	—	1
175	45	3	—	—	—	—	—	223
42	6	5	4	2	1	0	0	60
4	**4**	**2**	**0**	**1**	**0**	**0**	**0**	**11**
4	**1**	**1**	**1**	**1**	**0**	**0**	**0**	**9**
2	**0**	**1**	**0**	**1**	**0**	**0**	**0**	**3**
518	**7**	**11**	**11**	**12**	**7**	**6**	**4**	**575**
1	**7**	**5**	**3**	**3**	**0**	**0**	**0**	**20**
1	6	4	3	2	0	0	—	17
—	—	—	—	—	—	—	—	—
0	0	0	0	0	0	0	0	1
0	1	1	0	0	0	0	—	2
0	0	0	0	0	0	0	0	0
—	—	—	—	—	—	—	—	—
0	—	—	—	**0**	**0**	**0**	**0**	**0**
0	**0**	**0**	**0**	**0**	**0**	**0**	**0**	**0**
—	—	—	—	—	—	—	—	—
—	—	—	—	—	—	—	—	—
0	**1**	**0**	**0**	**0**	**0**	**0**	**0**	**2**
0	0	—	—	—	—	—	—	0
—	0	0	0	0	0	0	0	0
—	0	0	0	0	0	0	0	1
—	0	0	0	0	0	0	0	0
121	51	29	18	38	14	12	2	285
318	**40**	**39**	**29**	**26**	**19**	**21**	**12**	**504**
317	36	39	28	26	19	21	12	497
2	4	0	0	0	0	0	0	6
0	—	0	—	0	—	—	—	0
—	**0**	**126**	**97**	**14**	—	—	—	**237**
—	—	26	28	5	—	—	—	60
—	—	20	20	4	—	—	—	44
—	0	19	11	1	—	—	—	32
—	—	14	7	0	—	—	—	22
—	—	22	7	—	—	—	—	28
—	—	24	24	4	—	—	—	52
241	—	—	—	—	—	—	—	**241**
102	—	—	—	—	—	—	—	102
101	—	—	—	—	—	—	—	101
38	—	—	—	—	—	—	—	38
50	**5**	**1**	**1**	**2**	**4**	**3**	**1**	**67**
34	1	1	1	1	4	3	1	45
1	0	0	0	0	0	0	0	1
8	1	0	0	0	0	0	0	10
7	2	0	0	1	0	0	0	11
1	0	0	0	0	0	0	0	1

(Continues on the following page.)

Table 3B.7 Continued

Cause	Total	| Male								Total
		0–4	5–14	15–29	30–44	45–59	60–69	70–79	80+	
II. Noncommunicable diseases	*2,283*	*65*	*18*	*45*	*102*	*225*	*249*	*279*	*140*	*1,122*
A. Malignant neoplasms	**409**	**2**	**3**	**6**	**16**	**51**	**57**	**57**	**23**	**214**
1. Mouth and oropharynx cancers	19	0	0	0	1	4	4	3	1	13
2. Esophageal cancer	24	0	0	0	1	5	5	3	1	15
3. Stomach cancer	33	0	0	0	1	5	5	4	2	18
4. Colon and rectal cancers	20	0	0	0	1	3	3	3	1	11
5. Liver cancer	46	0	0	1	4	11	8	5	1	31
6. Pancreas cancer	8	0	0	0	0	1	1	1	0	4
7. Trachea, bronchus, and lung cancers	15	0	0	0	1	4	4	2	1	11
8. Melanoma and other skin cancers	8	0	0	0	0	1	1	1	0	4
9. Breast cancer	34	—	—	—	0	0	0	0	0	0
10. Cervix uteri cancer	38	—	—	—	—	—	—	—	—	—
11. Corpus uteri cancer	3	—	—	—	—	—	—	—	—	—
12. Ovarian cancer	9	—	—	—	—	—	—	—	—	—
13. Prostate cancer	40	0	0	0	0	3	11	18	8	40
14. Bladder cancer	10	0	0	0	0	1	2	2	1	7
15. Lymphomas and multiple myeloma	34	1	2	2	3	4	4	4	2	21
16. Leukemia	14	0	0	1	1	1	1	1	1	7
Other malignant neoplasms	55	1	1	1	2	8	9	8	4	32
B. Other neoplasms	**10**	**1**	**0**	**1**	**1**	**1**	**1**	**1**	**0**	**5**
C. Diabetes mellitus	**82**	**0**	**0**	**1**	**3**	**7**	**8**	**8**	**3**	**30**
D. Endocrine disorders	**28**	**3**	**1**	**1**	**2**	**2**	**1**	**1**	**1**	**12**
E. Neuropsychiatric conditions	**93**	**8**	**5**	**9**	**10**	**9**	**6**	**6**	**3**	**56**
1. Unipolar depressive disorders	0	—	—	—	0	0	—	—	—	0
2. Bipolar affective disorder	—	—	—	—	—	—	—	—	—	—
3. Schizophrenia	0	—	0	—	0	—	0	0	—	0
4. Epilepsy	38	2	2	6	5	4	2	1	1	23
5. Alcohol use disorders	7	—	—	0	2	2	1	1	0	5
6. Alzheimer's and other dementias	7	0	0	0	0	0	0	1	1	4
7. Parkinson's disease	5	0	0	—	0	0	1	1	1	3
8. Multiple sclerosis	0	—	0	0	0	0	0	0	0	0
9. Drug use disorders	4	—	—	1	1	1	0	0	0	3
10. Post-traumatic stress disorder	—	—	—	—	—	—	—	—	—	—
11. Obsessive-compulsive disorder	—	—	—	—	—	—	—	—	—	—
12. Panic disorder	—	—	—	—	—	—	—	—	—	—
13. Insomnia (primary)	—	—	—	—	—	—	—	—	—	—
14. Migraine	—	—	—	—	—	—	—	—	—	—
15. Mental retardation, lead-caused	0	0	0	0	0	0	0	—	—	0
Other neuropsychiatric disorders	32	5	3	2	2	2	2	1	0	18
F. Sense organ diseases	**0**	**0**	**0**	**0**	**0**	**0**	**0**	**0**	**0**	**0**
1. Glaucoma	0	—	—	—	0	—	—	—	—	0
2. Cataracts	—	—	—	—	—	—	—	—	—	—
3. Vision disorders, age-related	—	—	—	—	—	—	—	—	—	—
4. Hearing loss, adult onset	—	—	—	—	—	—	—	—	—	—
Other sense organ disorders	0	0	0	0	0	0	0	0	0	0
G. Cardiovascular diseases	**1,048**	**4**	**3**	**12**	**35**	**91**	**112**	**137**	**76**	**469**
1. Rheumatic heart disease	19	0	1	2	1	1	0	0	0	6
2. Hypertensive heart disease	66	0	0	0	2	5	6	7	4	24
3. Ischemic heart disease	343	0	0	1	7	39	52	58	22	179
4. Cerebrovascular disease	355	0	1	4	11	28	36	44	22	145
5. Inflammatory heart diseases	43	2	1	2	3	4	3	4	2	22
Other cardiovascular diseases	223	1	1	4	11	13	15	24	25	93
H. Respiratory diseases	**253**	**9**	**2**	**5**	**12**	**28**	**35**	**39**	**19**	**149**
1. Chronic obstructive pulmonary disease	116	0	0	1	3	13	20	25	12	74
2. Asthma	26	1	0	1	2	3	3	3	1	13
Other respiratory diseases	112	8	1	4	7	12	12	12	6	62

Table 3B.7 Continued

	Female							
0–4	5–14	15–29	30–44	45–59	60–69	70–79	80+	Total
54	*18*	*43*	*72*	*211*	*259*	*314*	*190*	*1,161*
2	**3**	**5**	**18**	**53**	**48**	**47**	**19**	**194**
0	0	0	0	1	2	2	1	6
0	0	0	1	2	2	2	1	9
0	0	0	1	4	4	4	2	15
0	0	0	1	2	2	2	1	9
0	0	1	2	4	3	4	1	15
0	0	0	0	1	1	1	0	4
0	0	0	0	1	1	1	0	4
0	0	0	0	1	1	2	1	5
0	0	0	4	11	9	7	3	34
0	0	1	2	12	10	9	2	38
0	0	0	0	1	1	1	0	3
0	0	0	1	3	2	2	1	9
—	—	—	—	—	—	—	—	—
0	0	0	0	1	1	1	0	3
1	2	1	1	2	2	3	1	13
0	0	1	1	2	1	1	1	6
1	1	0	2	5	5	6	3	23
0	**1**	**0**	**0**	**1**	**1**	**1**	**0**	**5**
0	**0**	**1**	**2**	**12**	**16**	**15**	**5**	**52**
4	**0**	**1**	**1**	**3**	**3**	**2**	**1**	**16**
7	**4**	**6**	**4**	**5**	**4**	**5**	**3**	**37**
—	—	0	—	—	—	—	—	0
—	—	—	—	—	—	—	—	—
—	—	—	—	0	0	0	—	0
2	2	4	2	2	1	1	1	15
—	—	0	1	1	0	0	—	2
0	0	0	0	0	1	1	1	3
0	—	0	0	0	0	1	1	2
—	—	—	0	0	0	0	0	0
—	—	0	0	0	0	0	0	1
—	—	—	—	—	—	—	—	—
—	—	—	—	—	—	—	—	—
—	—	—	—	—	—	—	—	—
—	—	—	—	—	—	—	—	—
—	—	—	—	—	—	—	—	—
0	0	0	0	0	—	—	—	0
5	2	2	1	2	1	1	0	14
0	**0**	**0**	**0**	**0**	**0**	**0**	**0**	**0**
—	—	—	—	—	—	—	—	—
—	—	—	—	—	—	—	—	—
—	—	—	—	—	—	—	—	—
—	—	—	—	—	—	—	—	—
0	0	0	0	0	0	0	0	0
5	4	14	26	91	133	180	125	579
0	1	3	2	3	1	1	0	13
0	0	0	2	7	10	14	9	42
0	0	1	3	26	46	55	31	163
0	1	3	8	37	53	67	41	209
2	1	2	2	4	4	4	3	21
2	1	6	8	15	19	38	41	130
7	**1**	**5**	**7**	**16**	**22**	**29**	**17**	**104**
0	0	0	1	6	10	15	9	42
0	0	1	1	2	3	3	2	12
6	1	4	5	7	9	11	7	50

(Continues on the following page.)

Cause	Total	Male 0–4	5–14	15–29	30–44	45–59	60–69	70–79	80+	Total
I. Digestive diseases	**164**	**3**	**2**	**7**	**18**	**26**	**18**	**16**	**5**	**95**
1. Peptic ulcer disease	15	0	0	1	2	2	2	1	1	8
2. Cirrhosis of the liver	59	0	0	1	6	13	9	7	2	38
3. Appendicitis	2	0	0	0	0	0	0	0	0	1
Other digestive diseases	88	3	2	5	11	11	8	7	3	48
J. Genitourinary diseases	**107**	**3**	**1**	**3**	**4**	**7**	**10**	**13**	**8**	**48**
1. Nephritis and nephrosis	101	2	1	3	4	7	10	11	7	45
2. Benign prostatic hypertrophy	2	—	—	—	—	0	0	1	1	2
Other genitourinary system diseases	4	0	0	0	0	0	0	1	0	2
K. Skin diseases	**20**	**0**	**0**	**0**	**1**	**1**	**1**	**1**	**1**	**6**
L. Musculoskeletal diseases	**7**	**0**	**0**	**0**	**0**	**0**	**0**	**1**	**0**	**3**
1. Rheumatoid arthritis	1	—	—	0	0	0	0	0	0	0
2. Osteoarthritis	0	—	—	—	—	0	—	0	0	0
3. Gout	0	—	—	—	—	—	—	0	—	0
4. Low back pain	0	—	—	—	0	0	0	0	—	0
Other musculoskeletal disorders	5	0	0	0	0	0	0	1	0	2
M. Congenital anomalies	**63**	**32**	**2**	**1**	**0**	**0**	**0**	**0**	**0**	**35**
1. Abdominal wall defect	1	1	—	—	—	—	—	—	—	1
2. Anencephaly	2	1	0	—	—	—	—	—	—	1
3. Anorectal atresia	0	0	0	—	—	—	—	—	—	0
4. Cleft lip	0	0	—	—	—	—	—	—	—	0
5. Cleft palate	0	0	—	—	—	—	—	—	—	0
6. Esophageal atresia	0	0	0	—	—	—	—	—	—	0
7. Renal agenesis	0	0	—	—	—	—	0	—	—	0
8. Down syndrome	5	3	0	0	0	0	—	—	—	3
9. Congenital heart anomalies	20	10	1	0	0	0	0	0	0	11
10.Spina bifida	4	2	0	0	—	—	—	—	—	2
Other congenital anomalies	31	15	1	0	0	0	0	0	0	17
N. Oral conditions	**0**	**0**	**0**	**0**	**0**	**0**	**0**	**0**	**—**	**0**
1. Dental caries	—	—	—	—	—	—	—	—	—	—
2. Periodontal disease	—	—	—	—	—	—	—	—	—	—
3. Edentulism	—	—	—	—	—	—	—	—	—	—
Other oral diseases	0	0	0	0	0	0	0	0	—	0
III. Injuries	**807**	**51**	**84**	**196**	**147**	**76**	**29**	**14**	**4**	**600**
A. Unintentional injuries	**494**	**48**	**77**	**80**	**65**	**41**	**16**	**9**	**3**	**339**
1. Road traffic accidents	200	12	41	27	28	18	7	4	1	137
2. Poisonings	37	5	4	5	6	3	1	—	—	23
3. Falls	20	1	3	2	2	2	1	1	0	14
4. Fires	44	8	11	1	1	1	1	1	0	24
5. Drownings	66	7	11	11	13	8	1	0	0	50
6. Other unintentional injuries	127	15	8	35	16	9	5	3	1	92
B. Intentional injuries	**313**	**3**	**7**	**116**	**82**	**35**	**12**	**5**	**2**	**261**
1. Self-inflicted injuries	36	—	2	9	7	6	2	1	0	28
2. Violence	141	3	4	53	32	13	4	2	0	111
3. War	136	0	1	53	43	16	7	2	1	123
Other intentional injuries	0	0	0	0	0	0	0	0	0	0

				Female				
0–4	5–14	15–29	30–44	45–59	60–69	70–79	80+	Total
1	2	6	8	15	15	14	7	69
0	0	0	1	1	1	2	1	7
0	0	1	2	6	6	4	1	22
—	0	0	0	0	0	0	0	1
1	1	5	5	7	8	8	5	40
2	1	2	3	12	14	16	9	59
1	1	2	3	11	14	15	8	56
—	—	—	—	—	—	—	—	—
0	0	0	0	0	0	1	1	2
0	0	0	1	3	3	3	3	13
0	0	1	1	1	1	1	0	4
—	0	—	0	0	0	0	0	1
—	—	—	—	0	0	0	0	0
—	—	—	—	—	0	—	—	0
—	0	0	—	0	0	—	0	0
0	0	1	1	1	0	0	0	3
26	1	0	0	0	0	0	0	28
1	—	0	—	—	—	—	—	1
1	—	0	—	—	0	—	—	1
0	—	—	—	—	—	—	—	0
0	—	—	—	—	—	—	—	0
0	—	—	—	—	—	—	—	0
—	—	—	—	—	—	—	—	—
0	—	0	—	—	0	—	—	0
1	0	0	—	0	—	—	—	2
8	0	0	0	0	0	0	0	9
2	0	0	0	—	—	—	—	2
13	1	0	0	0	0	0	0	14
0	—	—	—	—	0	0	0	0
—	—	—	—	—	—	—	—	—
—	—	—	—	—	—	—	—	—
—	—	—	—	—	—	—	—	—
0	—	—	—	—	0	0	0	0
37	51	39	32	23	11	8	4	207
34	45	25	19	15	8	6	3	155
7	25	11	8	7	4	2	1	63
2	2	3	3	2	2	1	0	15
1	2	0	0	1	1	1	1	6
10	4	2	2	1	1	1	0	20
4	3	4	1	2	1	0	0	15
11	8	5	5	3	1	1	1	36
3	6	15	13	9	3	2	1	52
0	0	3	2	2	1	0	0	8
3	5	9	7	4	1	1	0	30
0	1	2	4	4	2	1	1	13
0	0	0	0	0	0	—	0	0

Source: Authors' compilation.

Note: — = an estimate of zero; the number zero in a cell indicates a non-zero estimate of less than 500.

a. Does not include liver cancer and cirrhosis deaths resulting from chronic hepatitis virus infection.

b. This cause category includes "Causes arising in the perinatal period" as defined in the International Classification of Diseases, principally low birthweight, prematurity, birth asphyxia, and birth trauma, and does not include all causes of deaths occurring in the perinatal period.

Table 3B.8 Deaths by Cause, Sex, and Age in High-Income Countries, 2001
(thousands)

Cause	Total	Male 0–4	5–14	15–29	30–44	45–59	60–69	70–79	80+	Total
Population (millions)	*929*	*28*	*60*	*96*	*107*	*88*	*40*	*27*	*10*	*457*
All causes	**7,891**	**41**	**11**	**90**	**192**	**520**	**698**	**1,170**	**1,281**	**4,002**
*I. **Communicable, maternal, perinatal,***	***552***	***21***	***1***	***3***	***16***	***24***	***26***	***60***	***117***	***268***
and nutritional conditions										
A. **Infectious and parasitic diseases**	**152**	**2**	**0**	**2**	**13**	**16**	**12**	**18**	**18**	**81**
1. **Tuberculosis**	**16**	**0**	**0**	**0**	**1**	**2**	**2**	**3**	**3**	**10**
2. **Sexually transmitted diseases**	**1**	**0**	**0**	**0**	**0**	**0**	**0**	**0**	**0**	**0**
excluding HIV/AIDS										
a. Syphilis	0	0	0	0	0	0	0	0	0	0
b. Chlamydia	0	—	—	—	—	—	—	—	—	—
c. Gonorrhea	0	—	0	0	0	—	0	0	0	0
d. Other sexually transmitted diseases	0	0	—	—	0	0	0	0	0	0
3. **HIV/AIDS**	**22**	**0**	**0**	**1**	**9**	**5**	**1**	**0**	**0**	**17**
4. **Diarrheal diseases**	**6**	**0**	**0**	**0**	**0**	**0**	**0**	**1**	**1**	**2**
5. **Childhood-cluster diseases**	**2**	**0**	**0**	**0**	**0**	**0**	**0**	**0**	**0**	**0**
a. Pertussis	0	0	0	—	—	—	0	—	—	0
b. Poliomyelitis	1	0	0	0	0	0	0	0	0	0
c. Diphtheria	0	0	—	—	0	—	—	0	0	0
d. Measles	1	0	0	0	0	0	—	0	—	0
e. Tetanus	0	0	0	0	0	0	0	0	0	0
6. **Meningitis**	**4**	**0**	**0**	**0**	**0**	**0**	**0**	**0**	**0**	**2**
7. **Hepatitis B**[a]	**5**	**0**	**0**	**0**	**0**	**1**	**1**	**1**	**0**	**3**
Hepatitis C[a]	**12**	**0**	**0**	**0**	**1**	**2**	**1**	**1**	**1**	**7**
8. **Malaria**	**0**	**0**	**0**	**0**	**0**	**0**	**0**	**0**	**0**	**0**
9. **Tropical-cluster diseases**	**0**	**0**	**0**	**0**	**0**	**0**	**0**	**0**	**0**	**0**
a. Trypanosomiasis	0	—	—	—	—	—	0	—	—	0
b. Chagas' disease	0	0	0	0	0	0	0	0	0	0
c. Schistosomiasis	0	0	0	0	0	0	0	0	0	0
d. Leishmaniasis	0	0	0	0	0	0	0	0	0	0
e. Lymphatic filariasis	0	0	—	0	0	0	0	0	0	0
f. Onchocerciasis	0	0	—	—	—	—	—	—	—	0
10. **Leprosy**	**0**	**0**	**0**	**0**	**0**	**0**	**0**	**0**	**0**	**0**
11. **Dengue**	**0**	**0**	**0**	**0**	**0**	**0**	**0**	**0**	**0**	**0**
12. **Japanese encephalitis**	**0**	**0**	**0**	**0**	**0**	**0**	**0**	**0**	**0**	**0**
13. **Trachoma**	**0**	**0**	**0**	**0**	**—**	**0**	**—**	**—**	**—**	**0**
14. **Intestinal nematode infections**	**0**	**0**	**0**	**0**	**0**	**0**	**0**	**0**	**0**	**0**
a. Ascariasis	0	0	0	0	0	0	0	0	0	0
b. Trichuriasis	0	—	0	—	—	—	—	—	—	0
c. Hookworm disease	0	—	0	—	0	0	—	0	0	0
Other intestinal infections	0	0	0	0	0	0	0	0	0	0
Other infectious diseases	84	1	0	1	2	5	6	11	13	39
B. **Respiratory infections**	**349**	**1**	**0**	**1**	**2**	**7**	**14**	**41**	**96**	**162**
1. Lower respiratory infections	345	1	0	1	2	7	14	41	95	160
2. Upper respiratory infections	4	0	0	0	0	0	0	0	1	2
3. Otitis media	0	0	0	0	0	0	0	0	0	0
C. **Maternal conditions**	**1**	**—**	**—**	**—**	**—**	**—**	**—**	**—**	**—**	**—**
1. Maternal hemorrhage	0	—	—	—	—	—	—	—	—	—
2. Maternal sepsis	0	—	—	—	—	—	—	—	—	—
3. Hypertensive disorders of pregnancy	0	—	—	—	—	—	—	—	—	—
4. Obstructed labor	0	—	—	—	—	—	—	—	—	—
5. Abortion	0	—	—	—	—	—	—	—	—	—
Other maternal conditions	1	—	—	—	—	—	—	—	—	—
D. **Perinatal conditions**[b]	**32**	**18**	**0**	**0**	**0**	**0**	**0**	**—**	**—**	**18**
1. Low birthweight	10	5	0	—	0	—	0	—	—	5
2. Birth asphyxia and birth trauma	11	6	0	0	0	0	—	—	—	6
Other perinatal conditions	12	7	0	0	0	0	—	—	—	7
E. **Nutritional deficiencies**	**18**	**0**	**0**	**0**	**0**	**0**	**1**	**1**	**4**	**6**
1. Protein-energy malnutrition	9	0	0	0	0	0	0	1	2	3
2. Iodine deficiency	0	0	0	—	0	0	0	0	0	0
3. Vitamin A deficiency	0	0	0	—	—	—	0	—	0	0
4. Iron-deficiency anemia	7	0	0	0	0	0	0	0	1	2
Other nutritional disorders	2	0	0	0	0	0	0	0	0	1

Table 3B.8 Continued

	Female								
	0–4	5–14	15–29	30–44	45–59	60–69	70–79	80+	Total
27	*57*	*92*	*105*	*90*	*44*	*36*	*21*	*472*	
32	**12**	**33**	**98**	**280**	**398**	**923**	**2,114**	**3,890**	
16	*3*	*2*	*7*	*11*	*16*	*47*	*182*	*285*	
1	**2**	**1**	**5**	**7**	**8**	**16**	**29**	**71**	
0	**0**	**0**	**0**	**0**	**1**	**2**	**2**	**6**	
0	**0**	**0**	**0**	**0**	**0**	**0**	**0**	**0**	
0	—	0	0	0	0	0	0	0	
—	—	—	0	0	0	—	0	0	
0	—	0	0	0	—	0	0	0	
0	0	0	0	0	0	0	0	0	
0	**0**	**1**	**3**	**1**	**0**	**0**	**0**	**5**	
0	**0**	**0**	**0**	**0**	**0**	**1**	**2**	**4**	
0	**1**	**0**	**0**	**0**	**0**	**0**	**0**	**1**	
0	0	0	—	0	—	—	—	0	
0	0	0	0	0	0	0	0	0	
0	0	—	—	0	—	—	—	0	
0	1	0	0	0	—	—	0	1	
0	0	0	0	0	0	0	0	0	
0	**0**	**0**	**0**	**0**	**0**	**0**	**0**	**2**	
0	**0**	**0**	**0**	**0**	**0**	**1**	**0**	**2**	
0	**0**	**0**	**0**	**1**	**1**	**2**	**1**	**5**	
0	**0**	**0**	**0**	**0**	**0**	**0**	**0**	**0**	
0	**0**	**0**	**0**	**0**	**0**	**0**	**0**	**0**	
—	0	—	0	—	—	—	—	0	
0	0	0	0	0	0	0	0	0	
0	0	0	0	0	0	0	0	0	
0	0	0	0	0	0	0	0	0	
—	—	—	0	0	0	0	0	0	
—	—	0	—	—	0	—	—	0	
0	**0**	**0**	**0**	**0**	**0**	**0**	**0**	**0**	
0	**0**	**0**	**0**	**0**	**0**	**0**	**0**	**0**	
0	**0**	**0**	**0**	**0**	**0**	**0**	**0**	**0**	
—	—	—	—	—	—	—	—	—	
0	**0**	**0**	**0**	**0**	**0**	**0**	**0**	**0**	
0	0	0	0	0	0	0	0	0	
0	0	—	0	—	—	—	—	0	
—	—	0	—	—	0	—	—	0	
0	0	0	0	0	0	0	0	0	
1	1	0	1	3	5	11	22	45	
1	**1**	**0**	**1**	**4**	**7**	**29**	**144**	**187**	
1	1	0	1	4	7	29	142	185	
0	0	0	0	0	0	0	2	2	
0	0	0	0	0	0	0	0	0	
0	**0**	**0**	**1**	**0**	—	**0**	**0**	**1**	
0	0	0	0	0	—	—	—	0	
—	0	0	0	0	—	—	—	0	
—	0	0	0	0	—	—	0	0	
—	—	0	0	0	—	—	—	0	
—	0	0	0	0	—	0	0	1	
14	**0**	**0**	**0**	**0**	**0**	**0**	**0**	**14**	
4	0	—	—	—	—	—	—	4	
5	0	0	—	0	—	0	0	5	
5	0	0	0	0	0	0	0	5	
0	**0**	**0**	**0**	**0**	**0**	**2**	**9**	**12**	
0	0	0	0	0	0	1	4	6	
0	0	0	0	0	0	0	0	0	
0	0	—	—	—	—	0	0	0	
0	0	0	0	0	0	1	4	5	
0	0	0	0	0	0	0	1	1	

(Continues on the following page.)

Cause	Total	Male 0–4	5–14	15–29	30–44	45–59	60–69	70–79	80+	Total
II. Noncommunicable diseases	*6,868*	*15*	*5*	*24*	*106*	*431*	*638*	*1,074*	*1,127*	*3,420*
A. Malignant neoplasms	**2,066**	**1**	**2**	**7**	**31**	**180**	**284**	**393**	**258**	**1,155**
1. Mouth and oropharynx cancers	41	0	0	0	2	10	8	7	3	30
2. Esophageal cancer	58	0	0	0	1	10	13	13	6	44
3. Stomach cancer	146	0	0	0	2	14	23	30	20	89
4. Colon and rectal cancers	257	0	0	0	3	18	32	46	33	133
5. Liver cancer	102	0	0	0	2	14	21	22	9	69
6. Pancreas cancer	110	0	0	0	1	10	15	19	11	56
7. Trachea, bronchus, and lung cancers	456	0	0	0	5	50	86	115	53	311
8. Melanoma and other skin cancers	30	0	0	0	1	4	4	5	4	18
9. Breast cancer	155	0	—	0	0	0	0	1	0	2
10. Cervix uteri cancer	17	—	—	—	—	—	—	—	—	—
11. Corpus uteri cancer	27	—	—	—	—	—	—	—	—	—
12. Ovarian cancer	46	—	—	—	—	—	—	—	—	—
13. Prostate cancer	119	0	0	0	0	4	16	44	56	119
14. Bladder cancer	59	0	0	0	0	3	8	16	14	42
15. Lymphomas, and multiple myeloma	115	0	0	1	3	9	14	20	13	60
16. Leukemia	73	0	1	2	2	5	8	13	9	41
Other malignant neoplasms	257	0	1	3	7	28	36	43	25	143
B. Other neoplasms	**57**	**0**	**0**	**0**	**1**	**3**	**5**	**9**	**10**	**28**
C. Diabetes mellitus	**202**	**0**	**0**	**0**	**3**	**12**	**19**	**30**	**26**	**91**
D. Endocrine disorders	**70**	**1**	**0**	**1**	**2**	**5**	**5**	**7**	**9**	**31**
E. Neuropsychiatric conditions	**378**	**1**	**1**	**6**	**13**	**19**	**17**	**38**	**65**	**160**
1. Unipolar depressive disorders	3	0	0	0	0	0	0	0	1	1
2. Bipolar affective disorder	0	0	0	0	0	0	0	0	0	0
3. Schizophrenia	2	0	0	0	0	0	0	0	0	1
4. Epilepsy	9	0	0	1	1	1	1	1	1	5
5. Alcohol use disorders	23	0	0	0	4	8	4	2	1	18
6. Alzheimer's and other dementias	207	0	0	0	0	1	3	17	42	64
7. Parkinson's disease	45	0	0	0	0	0	2	9	13	24
8. Multiple sclerosis	8	0	0	0	0	1	1	0	0	3
9. Drug use disorders	13	0	0	3	5	2	0	0	0	10
10. Post-traumatic stress disorder	0	0	0	0	0	0	0	0	0	0
11. Obsessive-compulsive disorder	—	—	—	—	—	—	—	—	—	—
12. Panic disorder	—	—	—	—	—	—	—	—	—	—
13. Insomnia (primary)	—	—	—	—	—	—	—	—	—	—
14. Migraine	—	—	—	—	—	—	—	—	—	—
15. Mental retardation, lead-caused	1	0	0	0	0	0	0	0	0	1
Other neuropsychiatric disorders	68	1	1	2	2	5	6	9	8	33
F. Sense organ diseases	**0**	**0**	**0**	**0**	**0**	**0**	**0**	**0**	**0**	**0**
1. Glaucoma	0	0	—	0	0	0	0	0	0	0
2. Cataracts	—	—	—	—	—	—	—	—	—	—
3. Vision disorders, age-related	—	—	—	—	—	—	—	—	—	—
4. Hearing loss, adult onset	—	—	—	—	—	—	—	—	—	—
Other sense organ disorders	0	0	0	0	0	0	0	0	0	0
G. Cardiovascular diseases	**3,039**	**1**	**1**	**5**	**35**	**148**	**224**	**434**	**564**	**1,412**
1. Rheumatic heart disease	17	0	0	0	0	1	1	2	2	5
2. Hypertensive heart disease	129	0	0	0	2	6	7	14	19	48
3. Ischemic heart disease	1,364	0	0	1	16	88	130	231	250	716
4. Cerebrovascular disease	781	0	0	1	6	25	44	101	145	323
5. Inflammatory heart diseases	72	0	0	1	3	7	8	11	10	41
Other cardiovascular diseases	676	1	0	2	8	21	34	74	139	279
H. Respiratory diseases	**477**	**1**	**0**	**1**	**3**	**14**	**37**	**94**	**112**	**262**
1. Chronic obstructive pulmonary disease	297	0	0	0	1	8	24	65	73	171
2. Asthma	28	0	0	0	1	1	2	4	4	12
Other respiratory diseases	152	0	0	1	2	5	11	25	35	79

				Female				
0–4	5–14	15–29	30–44	45–59	60–69	70–79	80+	Total
13	*5*	*14*	*69*	*248*	*368*	*851*	*1,880*	*3,448*
1	**2**	**5**	**34**	**136**	**172**	**275**	**287**	**911**
0	0	0	0	2	2	3	4	11
0	0	0	0	2	2	4	5	13
0	0	0	2	6	9	17	23	57
0	0	0	2	13	20	37	52	124
0	0	0	1	3	7	12	10	33
0	0	0	1	6	10	19	19	54
0	0	0	4	23	34	50	35	145
0	0	0	1	2	2	3	4	13
0	0	0	11	37	30	37	38	154
0	0	0	3	5	3	3	3	17
—	0	0	1	4	6	8	8	27
0	0	0	2	9	11	14	10	46
—	—	—	—	—	—	—	—	—
0	0	0	0	1	2	5	9	17
0	0	1	2	6	10	18	18	55
0	1	1	2	4	5	9	11	32
0	1	1	4	14	21	35	37	114
0	**0**	**0**	**1**	**2**	**3**	**8**	**14**	**29**
0	**0**	**0**	**2**	**7**	**14**	**34**	**54**	**112**
1	**0**	**1**	**2**	**3**	**4**	**8**	**21**	**40**
1	**1**	**2**	**5**	**10**	**11**	**40**	**148**	**218**
0	0	0	0	0	0	0	1	2
0	0	0	0	0	0	0	0	0
0	0	0	0	0	0	0	0	1
0	0	0	1	1	0	1	1	4
0	0	0	1	2	1	1	0	4
0	0	0	0	1	3	23	117	143
0	0	0	0	0	1	6	13	21
0	0	0	1	2	1	1	0	5
0	0	1	1	1	0	0	0	2
0	0	0	0	0	0	0	0	0
—	—	—	—	—	—	—	—	—
—	—	—	—	—	—	—	—	—
—	—	—	—	—	—	—	—	—
—	—	—	—	—	—	—	—	—
0	0	0	0	0	0	0	0	0
1	1	1	2	4	5	8	14	34
0	**0**	**0**	**0**	**0**	**0**	**0**	**0**	**0**
—	—	—	—	0	0	0	0	0
—	—	—	—	—	—	—	—	—
—	—	—	—	—	—	—	—	—
0	0	0	0	0	0	0	0	0
1	**1**	**3**	**15**	**56**	**111**	**358**	**1,082**	**1,627**
0	0	0	0	1	2	4	5	12
0	0	0	1	3	5	17	54	80
0	0	0	4	23	52	158	412	648
0	0	1	4	16	28	101	307	458
0	0	0	1	3	4	8	15	31
0	0	1	4	11	20	71	289	397
0	**0**	**1**	**2**	**10**	**23**	**62**	**118**	**215**
0	0	0	0	5	15	41	64	127
0	0	0	1	2	2	4	7	15
0	0	0	1	3	6	16	46	73

(Continues on the following page.)

Cause	Total	Male								
		0–4	5–14	15–29	30–44	45–59	60–69	70–79	80+	Total
I. Digestive diseases	**335**	**1**	**0**	**1**	**14**	**42**	**37**	**42**	**40**	**177**
1. Peptic ulcer disease	27	0	0	0	0	2	2	4	5	13
2. Cirrhosis of the liver	118	0	0	0	10	30	21	14	5	80
3. Appendicitis	1	0	0	0	0	0	0	0	0	1
Other digestive diseases	189	1	0	1	4	11	13	24	30	83
J. Genitourinary diseases	**153**	**0**	**0**	**0**	**1**	**5**	**8**	**20**	**35**	**70**
1. Nephritis and nephrosis	111	0	0	0	1	4	7	16	25	53
2. Benign prostatic hypertrophy	2	—	—	0	0	0	0	0	1	2
Other genitourinary system diseases	40	0	0	0	0	1	1	4	9	15
K. Skin diseases	**15**	**0**	**0**	**0**	**0**	**0**	**0**	**1**	**2**	**5**
L. Musculoskeletal diseases	**44**	**0**	**0**	**0**	**1**	**1**	**2**	**4**	**5**	**13**
1. Rheumatoid arthritis	9	0	0	0	0	0	0	1	1	2
2. Osteoarthritis	3	0	0	0	0	0	0	0	0	1
3. Gout	0	—	0	0	0	0	0	0	0	0
4. Low back pain	2	0	0	0	0	0	0	0	0	1
Other musculoskeletal disorders	30	0	0	0	0	1	1	3	4	9
M. Congenital anomalies	**30**	**10**	**1**	**1**	**1**	**1**	**1**	**1**	**1**	**16**
1. Abdominal wall defect	0	0	0	0	0	0	0	0	0	0
2. Anencephaly	1	0	0	0	0	0	0	0	0	0
3. Anorectal atresia	0	0	0	0	0	0	0	0	0	0
4. Cleft lip	0	0	0	0	0	0	0	0	0	0
5. Cleft palate	0	0	0	0	0	0	0	0	0	0
6. Esophageal atresia	0	0	0	0	0	0	0	0	0	0
7. Renal agenesis	1	0	0	0	0	0	0	0	0	0
8. Down syndrome	2	0	0	0	0	0	0	0	0	1
9. Congenital heart anomalies	13	4	0	1	1	1	0	0	0	7
10. Spina bifida	0	0	0	0	0	0	0	0	0	0
Other congenital anomalies	13	5	0	0	0	0	0	0	0	7
N. Oral conditions	**0**	**0**	**0**	**0**	**0**	**0**	**0**	**0**	**0**	**0**
1. Dental caries	0	—	—	—	—	0	—	0	0	0
2. Periodontal disease	0	—	—	0	0	0	0	0	0	0
3. Edentulism	—	—	—	—	—	—	—	—	—	—
Other oral diseases	0	0	0	0	0	0	0	0	0	0
III. Injuries	***471***	***4***	***5***	***63***	***70***	***65***	***34***	***35***	***36***	***314***
A. Unintentional injuries	**321**	**4**	**4**	**40**	**39**	**36**	**22**	**26**	**31**	**202**
1. Road traffic accidents	121	1	2	28	20	15	8	7	4	86
2. Poisonings	21	0	0	3	7	4	1	0	0	15
3. Falls	71	0	0	1	3	5	4	7	13	34
4. Fires	9	0	0	1	1	1	1	1	1	6
5. Drownings	16	1	1	2	2	2	1	1	1	11
6. Other unintentional injuries	82	1	1	5	7	9	7	9	11	49
B. Intentional injuries	**151**	**1**	**1**	**23**	**31**	**29**	**12**	**9**	**6**	**112**
1. Self-inflicted injuries	126	0	0	16	25	27	12	9	6	94
2. Violence	24	1	0	7	5	3	1	0	0	17
3. War	0	0	0	0	0	0	0	0	0	0
Other intentional injuries	0	0	0	0	0	0	0	0	0	0

Table 3B.8 Continued

	Female							
0–4	**5–14**	**15–29**	**30–44**	**45–59**	**60–69**	**70–79**	**80+**	**Total**
0	**0**	**1**	**6**	**16**	**18**	**38**	**79**	**158**
0	0	0	0	1	1	3	9	14
0	0	0	3	10	8	10	6	37
0	0	0	0	0	0	0	0	1
0	0	0	2	6	9	25	64	106
0	**0**	**0**	**1**	**3**	**7**	**19**	**53**	**83**
0	0	0	1	3	5	14	35	58
—	—	—	—	—	—	—	—	—
0	0	0	0	1	1	5	18	25
0	**0**	**0**	**0**	**0**	**1**	**2**	**7**	**10**
0	**0**	**0**	**1**	**2**	**3**	**8**	**16**	**31**
0	0	0	0	0	1	3	3	7
0	0	0	0	0	0	0	2	2
0	0	0	0	0	0	0	0	0
0	0	0	0	0	0	0	0	1
0	0	0	1	2	2	4	11	21
8	**1**	**1**	**1**	**1**	**1**	**1**	**1**	**14**
0	0	0	0	0	0	0	0	0
0	0	0	0	0	0	0	0	0
0	0	0	0	0	0	0	0	0
0	0	0	0	0	0	0	0	0
0	0	0	0	0	0	0	0	0
0	0	0	0	0	0	0	0	0
0	0	0	0	0	0	0	0	0
0	0	0	0	0	0	0	0	1
3	0	0	1	0	0	0	0	6
0	0	0	0	0	0	0	0	0
4	0	0	0	0	0	0	0	6
0	**0**	**0**	**0**	**0**	**0**	**0**	**0**	**0**
—	—	—	—	0	—	—	0	0
—	0	0	0	0	0	0	0	0
—	—	—	—	—	—	—	—	—
0	0	0	0	0	0	0	0	0
3	*4*	*17*	*21*	*22*	*14*	*24*	*52*	*157*
2	*3*	*11*	*11*	*12*	*10*	*20*	*49*	*119*
1	2	8	6	6	4	5	3	35
0	0	1	2	2	0	0	1	6
0	0	0	1	1	2	6	26	37
0	0	0	0	1	0	1	1	4
0	0	0	0	1	1	1	1	5
1	1	1	1	3	3	6	17	32
0	**0**	**6**	**10**	**10**	**5**	**4**	**3**	**38**
0	0	4	7	8	4	4	3	32
0	0	2	2	1	0	0	0	7
0	0	0	0	0	0	0	0	0
0	0	0	0	0	0	0	0	0

Source: Authors' compilation.

Note: — = an estimate of zero; the number zero in a cell indicates a non-zero estimate of less than 500.

a. Does not include liver cancer and cirrhosis deaths resulting from chronic hepatitis virus infection.

b. This cause category includes "Causes arising in the perinatal period" as defined in the International Classification of Diseases, principally low birthweight, prematurity, birth asphyxia, and birth trauma, and does not include all causes of deaths occurring in the perinatal period.

Table 3B.9 Deaths by Cause, Sex, and Age in the World, 2001
(thousands)

Cause	Total	Male 0–4	5–14	15–29	30–44	45–59	60–69	70–79	80+	Total[a]
Population (millions)	*6,148*	*317*	*623*	*808*	*653*	*415*	*164*	*88*	*25*	*3,093*
All causes	**56,242**	**5,448**	**744**	**1,925**	**2,978**	**4,518**	**4,767**	**5,546**	**3,630**	**29,555**
I. Communicable, maternal, perinatal, and nutritional conditions	***18,166***	***4,858***	***376***	***588***	***1,166***	***877***	***555***	***529***	***386***	***9,335***
A. Infectious and parasitic diseases	**10,838**	**2,362**	**296**	**541**	**1,099**	**750**	**360**	**267**	**129**	**5,805**
1. **Tuberculosis**	**1,606**	**22**	**16**	**138**	**257**	**282**	**186**	**118**	**34**	**1,053**
2. **Sexually transmitted diseases excluding HIV/AIDS**	**177**	**31**	**0**	**2**	**11**	**26**	**10**	**6**	**3**	**89**
a. Syphilis	155	30	0	1	10	23	10	6	3	83
b. Chlamydia	9	—	—	—	—	—	—	—	—	—
c. Gonorrhea	1	—	0	0	0	0	0	0	0	0
d. Other sexually transmitted diseases	12	1	0	0	1	4	0	0	0	6
3. **HIV/AIDS**	**2,574**	**173**	**52**	**260**	**649**	**226**	**30**	**4**	**0**	**1,394**
4. **Diarrheal diseases**	**1,783**	**837**	**3**	**6**	**12**	**15**	**15**	**20**	**24**	**932**
5. **Childhood-cluster diseases**	**1,363**	**524**	**110**	**24**	**11**	**6**	**3**	**1**	**1**	**680**
a. Pertussis	301	150	0	—	—	—	0	—	—	150
b. Poliomyelitis[b]	1	0	0	0	0	0	0	0	0	0
c. Diphtheria	6	3	0	0	0	0	0	0	0	3
d. Measles	763	277	91	11	0	0	0	0	—	379
e. Tetanus	293	94	18	13	11	6	3	1	1	147
6. **Meningitis**	**173**	**30**	**14**	**12**	**10**	**10**	**5**	**6**	**3**	**89**
7. **Hepatitis B**[c]	**100**	**3**	**4**	**8**	**17**	**23**	**8**	**5**	**2**	**69**
Hepatitis C[c]	**51**	**1**	**1**	**3**	**7**	**12**	**5**	**3**	**1**	**33**
8. **Malaria**	**1,208**	**521**	**7**	**10**	**11**	**11**	**7**	**7**	**4**	**579**
9. **Tropical-cluster diseases**	**128**	**4**	**21**	**15**	**13**	**13**	**7**	**4**	**1**	**78**
a. Trypanosomiasis	48	2	11	6	6	5	1	0	0	31
b. Chagas' disease	14	0	0	0	1	2	2	1	1	8
c. Schistosomiasis	14	0	0	0	1	3	3	2	0	9
d. Leishmaniasis	51	2	10	8	5	3	1	1	0	30
e. Lymphatic filariasis	0	0	0	0	0	0	0	0	0	0
f. Onchocerciasis	0	0	—	—	—	—	—	—	—	0
10. **Leprosy**	**6**	**0**	**0**	**0**	**1**	**1**	**1**	**1**	**0**	**4**
11. **Dengue**	**19**	**2**	**5**	**0**	**0**	**0**	**0**	**0**	**0**	**9**
12. **Japanese encephalitis**	**14**	**2**	**0**	**1**	**2**	**0**	**0**	**0**	**0**	**7**
13. **Trachoma**	**0**	**0**	**0**	**0**	**—**	**0**	**—**	**0**	**—**	**0**
14. **Intestinal nematode infections**	**12**	**1**	**3**	**0**	**0**	**1**	**0**	**0**	**0**	**6**
a. Ascariasis	3	0	1	0	0	0	0	0	0	1
b. Trichuriasis	3	0	1	0	0	0	0	0	0	2
c. Hookworm disease	3	0	0	0	0	0	0	0	0	2
Other intestinal infections	2	1	0	0	0	0	0	0	0	1
Other infectious diseases	1,624	211	59	63	99	122	82	91	54	783
B. Respiratory infections	**3,830**	**1,004**	**58**	**37**	**56**	**101**	**182**	**244**	**240**	**1,923**
1. Lower respiratory infections	3,753	990	55	35	54	97	177	239	236	1,884
2. Upper respiratory infections	73	14	2	2	2	4	5	5	4	37
3. Otitis media	4	0	1	0	0	0	0	0	0	2
C. Maternal conditions	**508**	**—**	**—**	**—**	**—**	**—**	**—**	**—**	**—**	**—**
1. Maternal hemorrhage	141	—	—	—	—	—	—	—	—	—
2. Maternal sepsis	75	—	—	—	—	—	—	—	—	—
3. Hypertensive disorders of pregnancy	71	—	—	—	—	—	—	—	—	—
4. Obstructed labor	43	—	—	—	—	—	—	—	—	—
5. Abortion	66	—	—	—	—	—	—	—	—	—
Other maternal conditions	111	—	—	—	—	—	—	—	—	—
D. Perinatal conditions[d]	**2,522**	**1,399**	**0**	**0**	**0**	**0**	**0**	**0**	**—**	**1,399**
1. Low birthweight	1,301	709	0	—	0	—	0	—	—	709
2. Birth asphyxia and birth trauma	739	432	0	0	0	0	—	—	—	432
Other perinatal conditions	482	258	0	0	0	0	—	0	—	258
E. Nutritional deficiencies	**468**	**93**	**22**	**10**	**11**	**26**	**13**	**18**	**16**	**208**
1. Protein-energy malnutrition	250	70	15	4	3	7	8	9	9	125
2. Iodine deficiency	7	2	1	0	0	0	0	0	0	3
3. Vitamin A deficiency	23	7	2	0	0	1	0	0	0	11
4. Iron-deficiency anemia	133	9	3	4	6	15	2	3	3	46
Other nutritional disorders	56	5	1	1	1	3	3	6	4	24

Table 3B.9 Continued

	0–4	5–14	15–29	30–44	45–59	60–69	70–79	80+	Total
	301	*589*	*774*	*635*	*415*	*180*	*115*	*47*	*3,055*
	5,155	**750**	**1,610**	**1,928**	**2,802**	**3,358**	**5,242**	**5,843**	**26,687**
	4,571	*454*	*952*	*966*	*523*	*373*	*455*	*535*	*8,830*
	2,407	**350**	**630**	**672**	**406**	**213**	**207**	**147**	**5,033**
	18	**17**	**106**	**135**	**117**	**80**	**58**	**22**	**552**
	37	**0**	**13**	**10**	**14**	**7**	**4**	**1**	**88**
	37	0	12	8	6	4	4	1	72
	—	—	0	1	6	1	0	0	9
	0	—	0	0	0	0	0	0	1
	0	0	0	1	2	1	1	0	6
	166	**51**	**385**	**426**	**129**	**20**	**4**	**0**	**1,180**
	763	**3**	**3**	**5**	**10**	**14**	**21**	**33**	**851**
	525	**112**	**24**	**11**	**6**	**3**	**2**	**1**	**684**
	151	0	0	—	0	0	—	—	151
	0	0	0	0	0	0	0	0	0
	2	1	0	0	0	0	0	0	3
	279	93	11	0	0	0	—	0	383
	93	18	13	11	6	3	1	1	146
	35	**18**	**9**	**6**	**5**	**4**	**4**	**2**	**84**
	5	**2**	**5**	**4**	**6**	**3**	**3**	**2**	**31**
	2	**1**	**2**	**2**	**3**	**3**	**3**	**2**	**17**
	566	**8**	**12**	**12**	**13**	**8**	**7**	**4**	**629**
	4	**15**	**10**	**6**	**7**	**4**	**3**	**2**	**50**
	1	6	4	3	3	0	0	—	17
	0	0	0	1	2	1	1	1	7
	0	0	0	0	1	1	2	1	5
	3	9	5	2	1	1	0	0	21
	0	0	0	0	0	0	0	0	0
	—	—	0	—	—	0	—	—	0
	0	**0**	**0**	**0**	**0**	**0**	**0**	**0**	**2**
	2	**6**	**1**	**0**	**0**	**0**	**0**	**0**	**10**
	4	**2**	**1**	**1**	**0**	**0**	**0**	**0**	**7**
	—	—	—	—	—	—	—	—	—
	2	**3**	**0**	**0**	**0**	**0**	**0**	**0**	**6**
	1	1	0	0	0	0	0	0	2
	0	1	0	0	0	0	0	0	1
	—	0	0	0	0	0	0	0	1
	1	0	0	0	0	0	0	0	1
	277	115	59	54	94	67	98	77	841
	940	**79**	**57**	**46**	**61**	**138**	**226**	**359**	**1,906**
	925	74	56	45	60	135	223	351	1,869
	15	5	1	1	1	3	3	8	36
	0	0	0	0	0	0	0	0	1
	0	**0**	**257**	**233**	**18**	**0**	**0**	**0**	**508**
	0	0	63	72	7	—	—	—	141
	—	0	37	35	4	—	—	—	75
	—	0	41	28	2	—	—	0	71
	—	—	26	17	0	—	—	—	43
	—	0	44	22	0	—	—	—	66
	—	0	47	60	5	0	0	0	111
	1,122	**0**	**0**	**0**	**0**	**0**	**0**	**0**	**1,123**
	591	0	—	—	—	—	—	—	591
	307	0	0	—	0	—	0	0	307
	225	0	0	0	0	0	0	0	225
	101	**25**	**8**	**16**	**37**	**22**	**21**	**29**	**261**
	69	17	2	3	5	7	8	14	125
	3	0	0	0	0	0	0	0	3
	9	2	0	0	0	0	0	0	12
	11	5	5	13	30	12	5	7	88
	9	1	0	0	2	3	9	7	33

(Continues on the following page.)

Cause	Total	Male								
		0–4	5–14	15–29	30–44	45–59	60–69	70–79	80+	Total
II. Noncommunicable diseases	*32,891*	*431*	*121*	*363*	*939*	*3,005*	*3,927*	*4,817*	*3,134*	*16,737*
A. Malignant neoplasms	**7,021**	**19**	**27**	**75**	**217**	**851**	**1,118**	**1,102**	**508**	**3,917**
1. Mouth and oropharynx cancers	312	0	0	4	17	64	71	44	16	217
2. Esophageal cancer	438	0	0	1	14	69	97	75	23	280
3. Stomach cancer	842	0	0	5	27	124	153	147	62	519
4. Colon and rectal cancers	614	0	0	4	18	57	85	98	55	318
5. Liver cancer	607	1	1	8	40	136	118	91	26	420
6. Pancreas cancer	227	0	0	0	5	28	34	35	16	119
7. Trachea, bronchus, and lung cancers	1,227	0	0	2	29	188	291	275	93	879
8. Melanoma and other skin cancers	65	0	0	1	3	8	8	9	6	35
9. Breast cancer	473	0	0	0	0	1	1	1	1	3
10. Cervix uteri cancer	235	—	—	—	—	—	·	—	—	—
11. Corpus uteri cancer	71	—	—	—	—	—	—	—	—	—
12. Ovarian cancer	132	—	—	—	—	—	—	—	—	—
13. Prostate cancer	264	0	0	0	1	12	51	108	91	264
14. Bladder cancer	175	0	0	0	2	15	32	45	29	123
15. Lymphomas and multiple myeloma	331	2	7	12	18	32	37	39	21	167
16. Leukemia	263	8	12	24	14	21	24	27	15	146
Other malignant neoplasms	746	8	6	12	29	97	116	107	54	428
B. Other neoplasms	**146**	**2**	**2**	**5**	**6**	**13**	**14**	**18**	**13**	**73**
C. Diabetes mellitus	**960**	**1**	**1**	**8**	**21**	**88**	**111**	**124**	**73**	**428**
D. Endocrine disorders	**240**	**21**	**4**	**7**	**10**	**15**	**13**	**18**	**18**	**107**
E. Neuropsychiatric conditions	**1,079**	**26**	**16**	**48**	**89**	**88**	**53**	**121**	**117**	**558**
1. Unipolar depressive disorders	13	0	0	0	2	2	1	0	1	6
2. Bipolar affective disorder	1	0	0	0	0	0	0	0	0	0
3. Schizophrenia	23	0	0	0	4	4	1	1	1	11
4. Epilepsy	125	12	7	15	15	10	5	4	2	70
5. Alcohol use disorders	84	0	0	5	20	27	13	6	2	72
6. Alzheimer's and other dementias	380	1	0	0	1	3	8	56	71	141
7. Parkinson's disease	95	0	0	0	1	1	4	20	21	49
8. Multiple sclerosis	16	0	0	0	1	2	1	1	0	6
9. Drug use disorders	86	0	0	13	33	21	2	0	0	70
10. Post-traumatic stress disorder	0	0	0	0	0	0	0	0	0	0
11. Obsessive-compulsive disorder	—	—	—	—	—	—	—	—	—	—
12. Panic disorder	—	—	—	—	—	—	—	—	—	—
13. Insomnia (primary)	—	—	—	—	—	—	—	—	—	—
14. Migraine	—	—	—	—	—	—	—	—	—	—
15. Mental retardation, lead-caused	6	1	1	1	0	0	0	0	0	3
Other neuropsychiatric disorders	251	12	8	12	11	17	18	32	20	130
F. Sense organ diseases	**3**	**0**	**0**	**0**	**0**	**0**	**0**	**0**	**0**	**2**
1. Glaucoma	0	0	—	0	0	0	0	0	0	0
2. Cataracts	—	—	—	—	—	—	—	—	—	—
3. Vision disorders, age-related	—	—	—	—	—	—	—	—	—	—
4. Hearing loss, adult onset	—	—	—	—	—	—	—	—	—	—
Other sense organ disorders	3	0	0	0	0	0	0	0	0	2
G. Cardiovascular diseases	**16,394**	**39**	**24**	**109**	**355**	**1,318**	**1,894**	**2,481**	**1,733**	**7,953**
1. Rheumatic heart disease	324	7	5	18	17	29	25	24	11	136
2. Hypertensive heart disease	889	1	1	4	19	71	104	126	83	409
3. Ischemic heart disease	7,063	3	3	27	160	707	947	1,160	717	3,726
4. Cerebrovascular disease	5,390	7	5	22	74	353	619	859	555	2,494
5. Inflammatory heart diseases	391	7	2	10	21	39	39	49	37	204
Other cardiovascular diseases	2,337	13	8	28	64	119	160	263	330	983
H. Respiratory diseases	**3,603**	**34**	**9**	**24**	**58**	**250**	**405**	**632**	**454**	**1,866**
1. Chronic obstructive pulmonary disease	2,676	2	0	2	17	175	322	515	348	1,380
2. Asthma	233	2	4	11	19	30	21	20	11	119
Other respiratory diseases	694	30	5	12	22	45	62	97	95	368

			Female					
0–4	**5–14**	**15–29**	**30–44**	**45–59**	**60–69**	**70–79**	**80+**	**Total**
432	*128*	*299*	*653*	*2,008*	*2,834*	*4,630*	*5,169*	*16,153*
19	**23**	**59**	**228**	**660**	**709**	**825**	**580**	**3,104**
0	0	1	5	22	24	24	18	95
0	0	1	5	34	44	46	27	158
0	0	4	23	58	70	96	72	323
0	0	2	15	45	62	87	85	296
1	1	5	15	40	46	53	26	187
0	0	0	4	16	24	35	28	108
0	1	1	15	69	92	114	55	347
0	0	1	3	6	6	8	8	30
0	0	2	55	145	104	94	69 、	470
0	0	11	22	73	62	47	20	235
0	0	0	4	14	17	21	15	71
0	1	3	11	34	33	33	19	132
—	—	—	—	—	—	—	—	—
1	0	0	3	6	10	16	17	53
3	6	8	13	25	33	43	32	164
8	10	13	14	18	16	21	18	117
6	5	6	22	56	66	85	71	318
2	**2**	**3**	**6**	**13**	**11**	**16**	**20**	**73**
2	**2**	**6**	**16**	**84**	**135**	**167**	**121**	**532**
22	**3**	**8**	**12**	**15**	**16**	**22**	**35**	**133**
20	**16**	**26**	**32**	**44**	**36**	**121**	**226**	**520**
0	0	0	1	3	1	0	1	7
0	0	0	0	0	0	0	0	1
0	0	0	2	4	2	2	1	11
9	8	13	8	7	3	3	3	55
0	0	0	3	5	2	2	0	12
1	0	1	1	3	8	63	164	240
0	0	0	0	1	3	17	25	46
0	0	0	2	3	2	2	1	9
0	0	3	7	5	0	0	0	15
0	0	0	0	0	0	0	0	0
—	—	—	—	—	—	—	—	—
—	—	—	—	—	—	—	—	—
—	—	—	—	—	—	—	—	—
—	—	—	—	—	—	—	—	—
0	1	1	0	0	0	0	0	3
9	7	8	7	13	15	32	30	120
0	**0**	**0**	**0**	**0**	**0**	**0**	**0**	**2**
—	—	—	0	0	0	0	0	0
—	—	—	—	—	—	—	—	—
—	—	—	—	—	—	—	—	—
—	—	—	—	—	—	—	—	—
0	0	0	0	0	0	0	0	2
45	27	94	206	779	1,424	2,633	3,233	8,441
8	8	19	21	36	33	39	24	188
1	1	3	13	55	91	149	168	480
2	2	27	72	312	633	1,069	1,220	3,338
5	5	13	50	254	492	970	1,106	2,896
6	3	7	10	23	28	51	60	187
23	8	25	41	99	147	355	655	1,354
30	**9**	**22**	**46**	**183**	**272**	**545**	**629**	**1,736**
2	0	1	13	127	214	453	485	1,296
2	4	12	20	28	16	17	17	115
26	5	9	13	28	42	74	127	325

(Continues on the following page.)

Cause	Male									
	Total	0–4	5–14	15–29	30–44	45–59	60–69	70–79	80+	Total
I. Digestive diseases	**1,935**	**48**	**17**	**49**	**137**	**294**	**219**	**198**	**114**	**1,075**
1. Peptic ulcer disease	261	3	2	7	18	42	31	32	19	153
2. Cirrhosis of the liver	771	8	4	17	72	173	115	80	25	493
3. Appendicitis	21	0	1	1	1	3	2	2	1	11
Other digestive diseases	883	37	11	24	45	77	71	85	68	418
J. Genitourinary diseases	**830**	**11**	**7**	**22**	**37**	**75**	**87**	**107**	**87**	**433**
1. Nephritis and nephrosis	663	9	6	19	32	62	68	80	62	338
2. Benign prostatic hypertrophy	31	—	—	0	1	5	6	10	9	31
Other genitourinary system diseases	136	2	1	2	4	9	13	17	17	65
K. Skin diseases	**67**	**1**	**0**	**1**	**3**	**4**	**4**	**6**	**6**	**26**
L. Musculoskeletal diseases	**105**	**1**	**1**	**2**	**3**	**6**	**6**	**10**	**9**	**37**
1. Rheumatoid arthritis	25	0	0	0	0	1	2	2	1	7
2. Osteoarthritis	5	0	0	0	0	0	0	1	1	2
3. Gout	1	0	0	0	0	0	0	0	0	1
4. Low back pain	3	0	0	0	0	0	0	0	0	2
Other musculoskeletal disorders	71	1	1	2	2	4	4	6	6	25
M. Congenital anomalies	**507**	**227**	**11**	**13**	**4**	**3**	**2**	**1**	**1**	**262**
1. Abdominal wall defect	4	2	0	0	0	0	0	0	0	2
2. Anencephaly	19	9	0	0	0	0	0	0	0	9
3. Anorectal atresia	1	1	0	0	0	0	0	0	0	1
4. Cleft lip	0	0	0	0	0	0	0	0	0	0
5. Cleft palate	1	1	0	0	0	0	0	0	0	1
6. Esophageal atresia	1	1	0	0	0	0	0	0	0	1
7. Renal agenesis	2	1	0	0	0	0	0	0	0	1
8. Down syndrome	24	8	1	2	0	1	0	0	0	12
9. Congenital heart anomalies	269	116	6	8	2	1	1	1	0	135
10. Spina bifida	24	11	0	0	0	0	0	0	0	12
Other congenital anomalies	161	78	4	3	1	1	1	1	0	88
N. Oral conditions	**2**	**0**	**0**	**0**	**0**	**0**	**0**	**0**	**0**	**1**
1. Dental caries	0	—	—	—	—	0	—	0	0	0
2. Periodontal disease	0	—	—	0	0	0	0	0	0	0
3. Edentulism	—	—	—	—	—	—	—	—	—	—
Other oral diseases	2	0	0	0	0	0	0	0	0	1
III. Injuries	***5,186***	***158***	***247***	***974***	***872***	***636***	***284***	***200***	***111***	***3,483***
A. Unintentional injuries	**3,535**	**151**	**227**	**551**	**518**	**422**	**196**	**145**	**87**	**2,296**
1. Road traffic accidents	1,189	29	84	246	224	158	65	44	17	867
2. Poisonings	349	9	11	38	59	68	27	10	4	226
3. Falls	387	10	13	29	36	43	31	37	34	234
4. Fires	310	18	17	24	25	16	8	7	3	119
5. Drownings	385	34	58	68	45	32	12	8	4	263
6. Other unintentional injuries	914	51	44	146	128	104	52	39	25	588
B. Intentional injuries	**1,651**	**8**	**21**	**423**	**355**	**213**	**89**	**54**	**24**	**1,187**
1. Self-inflicted injuries	875	0	9	153	149	120	59	40	17	547
2. Violence	556	7	10	186	136	68	20	10	5	442
3. War	208	0	2	80	66	24	10	3	2	187
Other intentional injuries	13	1	0	3	3	1	1	1	0	10

				Female				
0–4	5–14	15–29	30–44	45–59	60–69	70–79	80+	Total
68	**27**	**48**	**67**	**148**	**141**	**181**	**181**	**860**
3	1	4	9	19	19	25	27	108
17	8	15	27	70	58	56	26	278
0	0	1	1	2	2	2	2	9
48	17	27	30	57	62	97	127	465
9	**7**	**17**	**27**	**65**	**73**	**94**	**105**	**396**
7	6	14	22	56	63	77	78	325
—	—	—	—	—	—	—	—	—
1	1	3	5	8	10	17	27	71
1	**1**	**1**	**3**	**5**	**7**	**10**	**15**	**42**
1	**1**	**4**	**6**	**9**	**9**	**15**	**23**	**68**
0	0	0	1	3	3	6	4	17
0	0	0	0	0	0	1	2	3
0	0	0	0	0	0	0	0	0
0	0	0	0	0	0	0	1	1
1	1	4	5	6	5	8	16	46
212	**11**	**10**	**4**	**3**	**1**	**2**	**1**	**245**
2	0	0	0	0	0	0	0	2
10	0	0	0	0	0	0	0	10
0	0	0	0	0	0	0	0	0
0	0	0	0	0	0	0	0	0
1	0	0	0	0	0	0	0	1
1	0	0	0	0	0	0	0	1
1	0	0	0	0	0	0	0	1
7	1	2	0	1	0	0	0	12
115	7	7	3	1	1	1	1	134
12	0	0	0	0	0	0	0	12
64	3	2	1	1	1	1	1	73
0	**0**	**0**	**0**	**0**	**0**	**0**	**0**	**1**
—	—	—	—	0	—	—	0	0
—	0	0	0	0	0	0	0	0
—	—	—	—	—	—	—	—	—
0	0	0	0	0	0	0	0	1
151	*168*	*359*	*309*	*271*	*150*	*156*	*139*	*1,703*
145	151	223	190	178	108	121	122	1,238
23	50	61	63	60	28	25	12	323
7	10	17	24	28	23	10	5	124
7	8	9	9	16	15	35	54	154
23	18	66	39	19	9	10	7	191
25	31	21	13	11	7	7	5	122
60	35	49	42	44	26	32	38	326
7	**16**	**136**	**118**	**92**	**42**	**36**	**17**	**465**
0	6	102	83	66	30	27	14	328
6	9	30	30	21	9	7	2	114
0	1	4	5	5	3	1	1	20
0	0	1	0	1	0	0	0	3

Source: Authors' compilation.

Note: — = an estimate of zero; the number zero in a cell indicates a non-zero estimate of less than 500.

a. World totals for males and females include residual populations not included in the World Bank regions.

b. For East Asia and Pacific, Europe and Central Asia, and Latin America and the Caribbean regions, these figures include late effects of polio cases with onset prior to regional certification of polio eradication in 1994, 2000, and 2002, respectively.

c. Does not include liver cancer and cirrhosis deaths resulting from chronic hepatitis virus infection.

d. This cause category includes "Causes arising in the perinatal period" as defined in the International Classification of Diseases, principally low birthweight, prematurity, birth asphyxia, and birth trauma, and does not include all causes of deaths occurring in the perinatal period.

Table 3C.1 DALYs(3,0) by Cause, Sex, and Age in Low- and Middle-Income Countries, 2001
(thousands)

Cause	Total	Male 0–4	5–14	15–29	30–44	45–59	60–69	70–79	80+	Total
Population (millions)	*5,219*	*288*	*563*	*712*	*545*	*326*	*124*	*61*	*15*	*2,636*
All causes	**1,386,709**	**217,652**	**42,491**	**97,880**	**106,062**	**114,028**	**74,490**	**49,024**	**14,065**	**715,692**
I. Communicable, maternal, perinatal, and nutritional conditions	*552,376*	*169,032*	*16,353*	*22,553*	*32,261*	*18,503*	*7,975*	*4,567*	*1,387*	*272,631*
A. Infectious and parasitic diseases	320,663	78,874	12,391	20,370	30,127	15,899	5,391	2,551	623	166,227
1. **Tuberculosis**	35,874	730	615	4,394	6,966	5,933	2,771	1,162	188	22,760
2. **Sexually transmitted diseases excluding HIV/AIDS**	9,338	1,502	19	703	537	505	145	55	16	3,483
a. Syphilis	4,122	1,004	2	105	267	428	140	52	15	2,014
b. Chlamydia	2,438	34	5	154	32	1	0	—	—	227
c. Gonorrhea	2,550	448	12	441	216	7	1	0	0	1,125
d. Other sexually transmitted diseases	228	15	0	3	22	69	4	2	1	117
3. **HIV/AIDS**	70,796	5,322	1,570	8,834	16,592	4,497	424	40	1	37,280
4. **Diarrheal diseases**	58,697	27,757	691	528	564	463	270	203	115	30,592
5. **Childhood-cluster diseases**	43,131	16,976	3,305	684	278	126	35	12	6	21,422
a. Pertussis	11,403	5,623	49	—	—	—	0	—	—	5,672
b. Poliomyelitis[a]	136	15	8	25	17	4	0	0	0	69
c. Diphtheria	164	76	6	1	1	1	0	0	0	86
d. Measles	23,091	8,432	2,716	302	0	0	0	—	—	11,450
e. Tetanus	8,336	2,831	526	356	260	121	34	12	5	4,145
6. **Meningitis**	5,475	1,308	472	352	244	206	73	54	14	2,723
7. **Hepatitis B**[b]	2,082	92	108	225	398	430	111	38	9	1,411
Hepatitis C[b]	844	31	44	82	163	182	47	17	4	570
8. **Malaria**	39,961	17,344	497	455	384	276	125	70	20	19,172
9. **Tropical-cluster diseases**	10,094	358	1,918	2,175	1,300	695	160	62	13	6,680
a. Trypanosomiasis	1,333	67	322	189	149	104	9	3	0	844
b. Chagas' disease	584	0	0	125	62	67	32	12	4	303
c. Schistosomiasis	1,525	88	279	208	143	113	58	25	5	920
d. Leishmaniasis	1,757	88	382	306	171	66	19	6	0	1,038
e. Lymphatic filariasis	4,455	106	914	1,310	704	261	17	5	1	3,319
f. Onchocerciasis	439	7	20	37	71	84	25	10	3	257
10. **Leprosy**	191	7	19	16	23	29	11	8	1	115
11. **Dengue**	529	61	143	12	9	6	3	2	1	238
12. **Japanese encephalitis**	598	90	67	46	65	11	3	2	1	285
13. **Trachoma**	2,620	2	2	23	152	211	150	88	21	649
14. **Intestinal nematode infections**	2,339	228	910	12	8	10	6	3	1	1,178
a. Ascariasis	1,153	112	462	1	0	0	0	0	0	574
b. Trichuriasis	489	45	205	1	1	1	1	0	0	253
c. Hookworm disease	634	56	237	10	6	8	5	2	1	323
Other intestinal infections	63	16	6	1	1	2	1	0	0	27
Other infectious diseases	38,095	7,065	2,010	1,829	2,442	2,318	1,058	735	213	17,669
B. Respiratory infections	**86,710**	**32,320**	**2,475**	**1,080**	**1,356**	**1,878**	**2,299**	**1,829**	**698**	**43,936**
1. Lower respiratory infections	83,606	31,654	1,930	1,006	1,274	1,799	2,227	1,786	681	42,357
2. Upper respiratory infections	1,680	425	67	64	71	76	71	43	17	833
3. Otitis media	1,424	241	478	11	11	3	2	0	0	747
C. Maternal conditions	**26,383**	—	—	—	—	—	—	—	—	—
1. Maternal hemorrhage	3,922	—	—	—	—	—	—	—	—	—
2. Maternal sepsis	5,267	—	—	—	—	—	—	—	—	—
3. Hypertensive disorders of pregnancy	1,889	—	—	—	—	—	—	—	—	—
4. Obstructed labor	2,495	—	—	—	—	—	—	—	—	—
5. Abortion	3,502	—	—	—	—	—	—	—	—	—
Other maternal conditions	9,308	—	—	—	—	—	—	—	—	—
D. Perinatal conditions[c]	**89,068**	**48,595**	**0**	**0**	**0**	**0**	**0**	**0**	—	**48,596**
1. Low birthweight	42,597	22,984	0	—	0	—	0	—	—	22,984
2. Birth asphyxia and birth trauma	31,429	17,646	0	0	0	0	—	—	—	17,646
Other perinatal conditions	15,043	7,965	0	0	0	0	—	0	—	7,966

Table 3C.1 Continued

			Female					
0–4	5–14	15–29	30–44	45–59	60–69	70–79	80+	Total
274	*533*	*682*	*530*	*326*	*136*	*78*	*25*	*2,583*
206,246	**41,746**	**97,168**	**85,867**	**89,704**	**67,948**	**58,445**	**23,893**	**671,017**
160,933	*18,395*	*43,617*	*30,916*	*12,740*	*6,393*	*4,809*	*1,944*	*279,745*
80,661	**13,212**	**23,628**	**19,916**	**9,880**	**3,908**	**2,474**	**758**	**154,436**
654	**659**	**3,386**	**3,752**	**2,596**	**1,307**	**639**	**121**	**13,114**
1,692	**69**	**2,742**	**887**	**304**	**108**	**47**	**5**	**5,855**
1,215	3	407	244	127	65	42	4	2,107
33	49	1,674	307	127	21	0	0	2,211
433	17	651	315	7	2	0	0	1,426
10	0	10	22	43	19	5	1	111
5,142	**1,543**	**12,402**	**11,328**	**2,738**	**312**	**49**	**1**	**33,516**
25,568	**654**	**424**	**398**	**378**	**281**	**244**	**159**	**28,105**
17,133	**3,391**	**708**	**285**	**133**	**39**	**14**	**6**	**21,709**
5,682	49	0	—	0	0	—	—	5,731
15	7	24	17	4	0	0	0	68
61	16	0	0	0	0	0	0	78
8,544	2,781	315	—	0	0	—	—	11,641
2,830	538	368	268	129	38	14	6	4,191
1,474	**591**	**289**	**157**	**120**	**68**	**41**	**12**	**2,752**
163	**50**	**145**	**106**	**122**	**48**	**26**	**10**	**670**
62	**19**	**57**	**44**	**53**	**22**	**13**	**4**	**273**
18,795	**500**	**516**	**399**	**321**	**145**	**87**	**26**	**20,789**
295	**952**	**939**	**497**	**548**	**108**	**58**	**17**	**3,414**
37	187	121	79	57	6	2	0	490
0	0	138	46	56	24	13	5	282
59	190	151	92	57	23	24	9	606
115	298	192	58	34	17	4	0	719
77	256	305	171	295	22	8	1	1,136
7	20	32	51	49	15	7	2	183
9	**18**	**13**	**15**	**10**	**7**	**4**	**1**	**76**
70	**176**	**19**	**11**	**7**	**4**	**3**	**1**	**291**
144	**100**	**32**	**24**	**8**	**4**	**2**	**0**	**313**
2	**5**	**50**	**441**	**598**	**470**	**313**	**93**	**1,971**
243	**886**	**10**	**5**	**7**	**5**	**2**	**1**	**1,161**
125	453	0	0	0	0	0	0	579
39	195	1	0	1	0	0	0	236
54	231	8	5	6	4	2	0	310
25	7	1	0	1	1	0	0	35
9,215	3,599	1,894	1,568	1,935	980	934	301	20,426
30,485	**3,044**	**1,669**	**1,154**	**1,268**	**2,012**	**2,064**	**1,077**	**42,774**
29,776	2,450	1,621	1,121	1,243	1,963	2,031	1,045	41,249
478	160	40	32	24	48	33	32	847
231	434	8	1	1	1	0	0	678
0	**158**	**17,028**	**8,748**	**448**	**0**	**0**	**0**	**26,383**
0	0	1,913	1,857	152	—	—	—	3,922
—	0	3,767	1,417	83	—	—	—	5,267
—	1	1,145	698	46	—	—	0	1,889
—	—	1,744	737	14	—	—	—	2,495
—	155	2,699	646	2	—	—	—	3,502
—	2	5,760	3,393	153	0	0	0	9,308
40,473	**0**	**0**	**0**	**0**	**0**	**0**	**0**	**40,473**
19,613	0	—	—	—	—	—	—	19,613
13,782	0	0	—	0	—	0	0	13,782
7,077	0	0	0	0	0	0	0	7,077

(Continues on the following page.)

Table 3C.1 Continued

| Cause | Total | \multicolumn{8}{c}{Male} | | | | | | | |
		0–4	5–14	15–29	30–44	45–59	60–69	70–79	80+	Total
E. **Nutritional deficiencies**	**29,552**	**9,242**	**1,486**	**1,102**	**779**	**726**	**285**	**186**	**66**	**13,872**
1. Protein-energy malnutrition	15,449	6,891	433	123	66	120	101	73	34	7,842
2. Iodine deficiency	2,873	1,074	352	0	1	2	1	0	0	1,430
3. Vitamin A deficiency	711	233	70	3	6	10	5	2	0	328
4. Iron-deficiency anemia	9,487	879	598	953	672	530	139	60	15	3,847
Other nutritional disorders	1,032	165	33	23	33	65	38	51	16	424
II. Noncommunicable diseases	*678,483*	*40,662*	*12,508*	*39,898*	*48,592*	*82,245*	*62,479*	*42,709*	*12,241*	*341,334*
A. **Malignant neoplasms**	**74,753**	**560**	**757**	**1,898**	**4,465**	**12,873**	**11,531**	**6,552**	**1,296**	**39,933**
1. Mouth and oropharynx cancers	4,078	5	12	115	382	1,050	866	347	69	2,846
2. Esophageal cancer	5,252	1	2	29	302	1,108	1,146	571	87	3,245
3. Stomach cancer	9,616	3	8	121	597	2,095	1,801	1,073	214	5,913
4. Colon and rectal cancers	5,060	1	4	109	358	773	758	488	114	2,605
5. Liver cancer	7,945	20	15	216	893	2,337	1,327	633	85	5,525
6. Pancreas cancer	1,621	0	2	5	99	340	267	150	29	892
7. Trachea, bronchus, and lung cancers	10,701	3	7	64	564	2,600	2,811	1,481	208	7,738
8. Melanoma and other skin cancers	501	1	2	14	38	83	62	38	11	249
9. Breast cancer	5,527	0	0	0	2	5	4	3	1	15
10. Cervix uteri cancer	3,799	—	—	—	—	—	—	—	—	—
11. Corpus uteri cancer	908	—	—	—	—	—	—	—	—	—
12. Ovarian cancer	1,488	—	—	—	—	—	—	—	—	—
13. Prostate cancer	1,479	1	1	3	12	173	503	601	185	1,479
14. Bladder cancer	1,504	2	2	8	46	237	343	282	77	997
15. Lymphomas and multiple myeloma	3,770	66	196	313	369	432	321	171	41	1,909
16. Leukemia	3,965	224	347	636	290	311	214	132	30	2,184
Other malignant neoplasms	7,538	235	162	261	514	1,330	1,106	582	145	4,335
B. **Other neoplasms**	**1,540**	**69**	**66**	**126**	**116**	**185**	**117**	**77**	**18**	**774**
C. **Diabetes mellitus**	**15,804**	**42**	**70**	**446**	**1,228**	**2,315**	**1,622**	**1,011**	**269**	**7,002**
D. **Endocrine disorders**	**10,943**	**3,663**	**216**	**305**	**297**	**411**	**193**	**138**	**55**	**5,278**
E. **Neuropsychiatric conditions**	**137,074**	**10,291**	**5,938**	**23,898**	**13,022**	**7,037**	**2,731**	**2,323**	**949**	**66,189**
1. Unipolar depressive disorders	43,427	0	2,452	5,692	4,992	3,076	906	180	33	17,331
2. Bipolar affective disorder	8,678	0	247	3,653	454	14	4	0	0	4,372
3. Schizophrenia	10,528	0	781	3,731	568	157	32	14	3	5,287
4. Epilepsy	5,759	501	636	861	591	294	105	48	12	3,049
5. Alcohol use disorders	11,007	2	101	4,029	3,427	1,621	289	62	8	9,540
6. Alzheimer's and other dementias	9,640	181	76	85	68	255	788	1,513	742	3,707
7. Parkinson's disease	1,239	5	3	10	66	150	139	156	49	578
8. Multiple sclerosis	916	1	43	165	126	40	11	4	1	391
9. Drug use disorders	4,405	1	68	1,765	1,170	455	27	4	1	3,491
10. Post-traumatic stress disorder	2,013	0	23	269	177	89	2	1	0	562
11. Obsessive-compulsive disorder	3,136	—	158	698	347	103	20	8	1	1,336
12. Panic disorder	4,015	—	70	1,209	16	56	7	4	0	1,362
13. Insomnia (primary)	2,219	—	29	278	297	188	95	32	6	925
14. Migraine	4,851	44	511	670	80	6	0	0	0	1,311
15. Mental retardation, lead-caused	8,599	4,319	17	22	7	4	1	0	0	4,370
Other neuropsychiatric disorders	16,644	5,236	724	762	637	527	303	296	92	8,577
F. **Sense organ diseases**	**72,275**	**30**	**165**	**1,621**	**8,069**	**12,018**	**7,042**	**3,113**	**604**	**32,662**
1. Glaucoma	4,112	7	30	128	346	649	381	191	45	1,776
2. Cataracts	28,150	17	100	606	2,450	4,569	2,674	1,259	281	11,955
3. Vision disorders, age-related	15,364	3	34	305	1,263	2,465	1,599	774	175	6,617
4. Hearing loss, adult onset	24,607	—	—	581	4,007	4,331	2,387	887	101	12,293
Other sense organ disorders	42	3	2	2	2	4	2	4	1	20
G. **Cardiovascular diseases**	**178,929**	**1,417**	**870**	**3,522**	**8,988**	**24,986**	**25,652**	**20,136**	**6,079**	**91,650**
1. Rheumatic heart disease	6,151	230	170	553	453	603	344	204	50	2,607
2. Hypertensive heart disease	9,969	27	21	110	434	1,294	1,408	1,141	405	4,840
3. Ischemic heart disease	71,882	103	217	1,033	3,782	12,275	11,574	8,509	2,270	39,761
4. Cerebrovascular disease	62,669	215	146	563	2,055	7,924	9,867	8,000	2,202	30,972
5. Inflammatory heart diseases	5,811	260	80	389	615	756	549	420	153	3,222
Other cardiovascular diseases	22,446	582	237	875	1,648	2,134	1,910	1,862	998	10,248

			Female					
0–4	5–14	15–29	30–44	45–59	60–69	70–79	80+	Total
9,314	**1,980**	**1,292**	**1,097**	**1,143**	**474**	**271**	**108**	**15,680**
6,674	489	54	68	97	105	75	45	7,607
1,100	338	1	1	2	1	1	0	1,443
288	69	9	4	8	3	2	0	382
945	1,039	1,210	1,006	989	316	106	30	5,640
308	45	19	19	46	49	88	33	607
38,101	*13,010*	*38,561*	*44,802*	*70,363*	*58,972*	*51,956*	*21,385*	*337,149*
587	669	1,602	5,079	11,048	8,382	5,836	1,618	34,820
9	5	32	123	415	346	224	78	1,232
1	2	21	127	665	632	442	118	2,007
1	4	97	512	1,061	930	832	266	3,704
1	3	47	328	685	672	537	182	2,456
32	19	145	363	740	602	426	91	2,420
0	1	9	70	212	211	176	50	729
6	29	29	280	935	883	682	120	2,963
1	3	12	38	69	59	52	17	251
1	2	62	1,169	2,297	1,180	624	178	5,512
0	2	341	517	1,448	923	470	99	3,799
2	2	18	162	318	226	143	36	908
2	18	90	258	523	348	203	46	1,488
—	—	—	—	—	—	—	—	—
21	7	13	78	109	124	112	44	507
88	171	216	293	398	360	258	77	1,861
238	272	333	303	298	178	121	37	1,781
184	129	136	457	876	708	534	179	3,203
50	**51**	**70**	**132**	**227**	**121**	**88**	**28**	**766**
60	**78**	**400**	**1,231**	**2,623**	**2,313**	**1,660**	**438**	**8,802**
3,354	**213**	**433**	**454**	**526**	**333**	**241**	**111**	**5,665**
9,880	**6,118**	**23,919**	**13,362**	**8,016**	**3,919**	**3,487**	**2,185**	**70,885**
0	2,313	7,821	8,164	5,445	1,815	432	105	26,096
0	212	3,609	462	17	5	1	0	4,306
1	191	3,922	800	241	49	29	6	5,241
415	642	793	437	257	92	57	16	2,710
0	41	661	460	244	44	15	2	1,467
163	72	89	74	281	1,150	2,282	1,821	5,933
6	4	7	56	159	165	189	74	661
1	56	213	174	57	15	6	2	525
—	42	453	295	114	7	2	1	913
0	16	724	491	200	11	6	2	1,450
—	304	769	504	168	37	15	3	1,800
—	71	2,416	25	114	15	11	1	2,653
—	28	304	412	300	168	65	16	1,293
132	1,567	1,421	416	4	0	0	0	3,540
4,182	19	16	8	4	1	1	0	4,229
4,980	539	700	585	411	342	376	135	8,067
30	**114**	**1,268**	**8,483**	**14,213**	**9,493**	**4,835**	**1,176**	**39,613**
4	26	141	401	812	547	309	95	2,336
14	62	560	2,826	6,114	4,023	2,055	542	16,195
9	24	225	1,417	3,092	2,238	1,358	384	8,746
—	—	338	3,838	4,192	2,684	1,109	153	12,314
3	2	3	2	3	2	4	2	22
1,614	**931**	**3,134**	**5,748**	**16,720**	**22,339**	**25,431**	**11,362**	**87,279**
246	247	589	587	809	556	398	113	3,544
23	25	79	308	1,100	1,371	1,502	720	5,129
74	166	1,003	1,893	6,198	9,196	9,592	3,998	32,121
156	139	349	1,480	6,136	8,728	10,344	4,366	31,697
203	84	256	322	488	453	520	262	2,589
912	269	857	1,157	1,989	2,035	3,076	1,903	12,199

(Continues on the following page.)

Table 3C.1 Continued

Cause	Total	Male								Total
		0–4	5–14	15–29	30–44	45–59	60–69	70–79	80+	
H. Respiratory diseases	**58,086**	**3,254**	**1,699**	**2,368**	**2,918**	**7,262**	**6,468**	**5,466**	**1,889**	**31,324**
1. Chronic obstructive pulmonary disease	33,453	48	15	120	1,307	5,359	5,162	4,466	1,499	17,977
2. Asthma	11,514	1,013	1,348	1,783	829	714	285	156	36	6,165
Other respiratory diseases	13,119	2,193	336	464	781	1,188	1,021	845	354	7,182
I. Digestive diseases	**52,402**	**7,366**	**859**	**2,588**	**4,573**	**7,021**	**3,436**	**1,998**	**571**	**28,411**
1. Peptic ulcer disease	4,801	91	67	394	667	967	454	269	74	2,983
2. Cirrhosis of the liver	13,633	256	152	621	1,835	3,171	1,447	674	121	8,278
3. Appendicitis	377	7	28	36	38	55	24	19	6	213
Other digestive diseases	33,591	7,012	612	1,536	2,033	2,829	1,510	1,036	370	16,938
J. Genitourinary diseases	**16,381**	**975**	**345**	**725**	**1,000**	**3,616**	**1,389**	**983**	**320**	**9,352**
1. Nephritis and nephrosis	9,076	327	283	583	777	1,104	837	578	180	4,669
2. Benign prostatic hypertrophy	2,613	—	—	0	12	2,118	255	173	55	2,613
Other genitourinary system diseases	4,691	648	62	142	211	395	296	233	84	2,070
K. Skin diseases	**3,696**	**498**	**225**	**302**	**287**	**256**	**130**	**95**	**36**	**1,828**
L. Musculoskeletal diseases	**25,693**	**202**	**432**	**1,293**	**3,307**	**3,561**	**1,589**	**689**	**137**	**11,210**
1. Rheumatoid arthritis	3,645	11	75	171	246	308	150	71	14	1,046
2. Osteoarthritis	13,666	0	3	367	1,348	1,970	1,060	403	52	5,203
3. Gout	2,785	0	0	123	1,307	854	147	39	6	2,476
4. Low back pain	1,692	69	167	184	212	184	55	23	4	899
Other musculoskeletal disorders	3,905	122	187	448	195	245	178	153	60	1,587
M. Congenital anomalies	**23,533**	**11,352**	**302**	**339**	**67**	**35**	**12**	**6**	**1**	**12,115**
1. Abdominal wall defect	110	59	0	0	0	0	0	0	0	60
2. Anencephaly	545	258	0	0	0	0	0	0	0	259
3. Anorectal atresia	31	20	0	0	0	0	0	0	0	20
4. Cleft lip	117	61	0	0	0	0	0	0	0	61
5. Cleft palate	131	67	0	0	0	0	0	0	0	67
6. Esophageal atresia	46	23	0	0	0	0	0	0	0	23
7. Renal agenesis	53	30	0	1	0	0	0	0	0	31
8. Down syndrome	3,416	1,736	28	57	3	3	0	0	0	1,827
9. Congenital heart anomalies	13,191	6,198	164	202	42	15	5	3	1	6,629
10. Spina bifida	1,488	706	10	4	0	1	0	0	0	721
Other congenital anomalies	4,405	2,196	98	74	21	17	6	3	1	2,417
N. Oral conditions	**7,375**	**942**	**564**	**467**	**256**	**670**	**569**	**121**	**18**	**3,607**
1. Dental caries	4,752	919	558	341	144	250	123	60	15	2,409
2. Periodontal disease	207	—	—	26	47	20	7	4	1	103
3. Edentulism	2,293	—	—	95	59	397	438	57	2	1,047
Other oral diseases	123	24	5	6	6	3	1	1	0	47
III. Injuries	**155,850**	**7,959**	**13,630**	**35,429**	**25,209**	**13,279**	**4,036**	**1,747**	**437**	**101,727**
A. Unintentional injuries	**113,235**	**7,608**	**12,447**	**21,335**	**15,467**	**9,335**	**2,931**	**1,311**	**338**	**70,773**
1. Road traffic accidents	32,017	1,186	3,267	7,571	5,925	3,203	860	362	67	22,441
2. Poisonings	7,115	286	320	962	1,267	1,273	368	91	16	4,583
3. Falls	13,582	983	1,670	2,159	1,384	1,002	468	360	130	8,157
4. Fires	10,080	923	865	884	738	375	112	55	14	3,967
5. Drownings	9,391	1,010	1,680	1,835	1,057	583	151	62	17	6,395
6. Other unintentional injuries	41,050	3,219	4,644	7,923	5,096	2,899	972	381	95	25,229
B. Intentional injuries	**42,615**	**351**	**1,183**	**14,094**	**9,742**	**3,944**	**1,105**	**436**	**99**	**30,954**
1. Self-inflicted injuries	17,674	3	338	3,938	3,054	1,849	646	294	58	10,181
2. Violence	18,132	240	760	7,424	4,360	1,506	291	102	28	14,711
3. War	6,492	91	71	2,628	2,254	563	157	35	12	5,809
Other intentional injuries	317	17	15	104	74	26	11	5	2	253

Table 3C.1 Continued

	Female							
0–4	5–14	15–29	30–44	45–59	60–69	70–79	80+	Total
2,709	**1,790**	**1,938**	**2,405**	**4,997**	**4,615**	**5,539**	**2,770**	**26,762**
63	21	129	1,269	3,543	3,578	4,618	2,255	15,476
740	1,521	1,349	604	658	264	159	54	5,349
1,907	247	459	533	795	772	762	461	5,937
7,072	**1,164**	**2,371**	**2,749**	**4,630**	**2,867**	**2,261**	**878**	**23,990**
98	56	194	332	500	299	244	96	1,819
597	299	501	804	1,523	914	581	136	5,355
6	21	28	20	35	24	22	8	164
6,371	788	1,648	1,592	2,573	1,629	1,413	638	16,653
626	**333**	**720**	**1,015**	**1,685**	**1,280**	**999**	**371**	**7,028**
266	275	436	564	1,095	883	663	224	4,407
—	—	—	—	—	—	—	—	—
360	58	284	452	589	396	336	147	2,621
348	**158**	**284**	**295**	**311**	**200**	**180**	**93**	**1,868**
187	544	1,685	3,504	4,619	2,437	1,186	322	14,483
21	183	476	616	759	338	165	41	2,599
0	4	632	2,133	3,133	1,719	724	120	8,463
0	0	21	146	84	34	20	4	309
35	201	125	199	155	51	22	5	794
131	156	430	410	488	295	256	151	2,318
10,700	**306**	**269**	**78**	**41**	**13**	**9**	**2**	**11,418**
50	0	0	0	0	0	0	0	50
284	1	1	0	0	0	0	0	286
11	0	0	0	0	0	0	0	11
56	0	0	0	0	0	0	0	56
63	0	0	0	0	0	0	0	64
22	0	0	0	0	0	0	0	23
20	0	0	0	0	0	0	0	22
1,497	30	53	3	4	0	0	0	1,588
6,115	187	174	53	21	6	5	1	6,562
755	8	3	1	1	0	0	0	768
1,826	79	37	21	15	6	3	1	1,988
883	**541**	**470**	**266**	**709**	**662**	**205**	**32**	**3,768**
860	534	327	141	251	135	73	22	2,343
—	0	25	45	20	8	4	1	103
—	—	97	63	434	517	126	8	1,246
23	7	20	17	4	2	1	0	76
7,212	**10,342**	**14,990**	**10,149**	**6,602**	**2,583**	**1,680**	**564**	**54,123**
7,006	9,322	10,464	7,096	4,763	1,995	1,334	481	42,462
1,088	2,342	2,178	1,880	1,374	426	237	52	9,576
205	293	472	537	549	345	105	26	2,532
953	1,422	997	569	503	330	446	205	5,424
1,079	1,075	2,066	1,139	472	144	105	33	6,113
762	922	585	328	215	99	64	22	2,995
2,919	3,269	4,167	2,643	1,651	652	378	143	15,821
206	**1,019**	**4,526**	**3,053**	**1,839**	**587**	**347**	**83**	**11,661**
1	409	3,181	1,974	1,213	394	257	64	7,493
187	412	1,205	920	464	146	73	14	3,421
6	190	126	148	151	43	14	5	683
12	7	15	11	12	4	2	1	64

Source: Authors' compilation.

Note: — = an estimate of zero; the number zero in a cell indicates a non-zero estimate of less than 500.

a. For East Asia and Pacific, Europe and Central Asia, and Latin America and the Caribbean regions, these figures include late effects of polio cases with onset prior to regional certification of polio eradication in 1994, 2000, and 2002, respectively.

b. Does not include liver cancer and cirrhosis DALYs(3,0) resulting from chronic hepatitis virus infection.

c. This cause category includes "Causes arising in the perinatal period" as defined in the International Classification of Diseases, principally low birthweight, prematurity, birth asphyxia, and birth trauma, and does not include all causes of DALYs(3,0) occurring in the perinatal period.

Table 3C.2 DALYs(3,0) by Cause, Sex, and Age in the East Asia and Pacific Region, 2001
(thousands)

Cause	Total	Male									
		0–4	5–14	15–29	30–44	45–59	60–69	70–79	80+	Total
Population (millions)	*1,849*	*80*	*175*	*244*	*224*	*136*	*51*	*25*	*6*	*942*
All causes	346,225	32,713	8,127	24,304	27,851	37,655	26,822	18,363	5,448	181,284
I. **Communicable, maternal, perinatal, and nutritional conditions**	*76,710*	*20,685*	*2,069*	*3,489*	*4,693*	*3,712*	*2,155*	*1,345*	*456*	*38,605*
A. **Infectious and parasitic diseases**	36,941	7,035	1,394	2,822	4,207	3,032	1,626	909	214	21,238
1. **Tuberculosis**	10,878	74	110	997	1,812	1,817	1,256	660	117	6,842
2. **Sexually transmitted diseases excluding HIV/AIDS**	848	78	2	86	46	19	11	7	3	252
a. Syphilis	129	37	0	9	7	9	10	7	2	82
b. Chlamydia	409	4	1	27	6	0	0	—	—	38
c. Gonorrhea	263	36	1	49	31	1	0	—	—	118
d. Other sexually transmitted diseases	48	0	—	1	2	9	0	—	1	14
3. **HIV/AIDS**	3,087	94	12	657	1,204	337	21	2	0	2,328
4. **Diarrheal diseases**	8,782	3,661	174	224	228	156	73	44	19	4,579
5. **Childhood-cluster diseases**	3,707	1,201	447	138	40	16	5	2	1	1,849
a. Pertussis	579	276	12	—	—	—	—	—	—	288
b. Poliomyelitis[a]	49	1	3	10	8	2	—	—	—	24
c. Diphtheria	18	12	1	0	1	0	0	—	0	13
d. Measles	2,303	680	370	90	—	—	—	—	—	1,140
e. Tetanus	758	233	61	37	30	13	5	2	1	383
6. **Meningitis**	1,067	295	47	78	49	34	12	10	3	528
7. **Hepatitis B**[b]	673	17	2	70	179	218	52	10	3	551
Hepatitis C[b]	275	4	0	29	76	91	21	4	1	228
8. **Malaria**	1,090	596	43	27	22	14	6	3	1	711
9. **Tropical-cluster diseases**	483	8	51	118	76	63	17	3	1	336
a. Trypanosomiasis	—	—	—	—	—	—	—	—	—	—
b. Chagas' disease	0	—	—	—	—	—	—	—	—	—
c. Schistosomiasis	64	0	2	5	7	22	13	1	0	51
d. Leishmaniasis	48	2	8	10	5	2	1	0	0	28
e. Lymphatic filariasis	371	6	41	103	63	39	4	1	0	257
f. Onchocerciasis	—	—	—	—	—	—	—	—	—	—
10. **Leprosy**	34	0	1	2	4	6	8	4	0	25
11. **Dengue**	217	28	48	7	3	2	1	1	0	90
12. **Japanese encephalitis**	301	74	48	17	12	3	1	1	0	155
13. **Trachoma**	500	0	0	1	22	38	29	20	5	115
14. **Intestinal nematode infections**	680	79	263	1	1	1	1	0	0	347
a. Ascariasis	301	34	117	—	—	0	—	0	—	151
b. Trichuriasis	197	24	79	—	—	—	—	—	—	103
c. Hookworm disease	168	16	65	1	1	1	1	0	0	86
Other intestinal infections	14	5	2	0	0	0	0	0	0	7
Other infectious diseases	4,318	825	146	371	433	217	114	138	60	2,302
B. **Respiratory infections**	11,800	2,414	434	310	300	492	459	402	230	5,044
1. Lower respiratory infections	10,786	2,171	282	274	262	442	435	394	222	4,482
2. Upper respiratory infections	598	177	8	31	36	49	23	8	8	341
3. Otitis media	416	67	143	5	3	1	1	0	0	221
C. **Maternal conditions**	3,475	—	—	—	—	—	—	—	—	—
1. Maternal hemorrhage	322	—	—	—	—	—	—	—	—	—
2. Maternal sepsis	881	—	—	—	—	—	—	—	—	—
3. Hypertensive disorders of pregnancy	128	—	—	—	—	—	—	—	—	—
4. Obstructed labor	239	—	—	—	—	—	—	—	—	—
5. Abortion	191	—	—	—	—	—	—	—	—	—
Other maternal conditions	1,714	—	—	—	—	—	—	—	—	—
D. **Perinatal conditions**[c]	18,696	9,697	0	—	—	—	—	—	—	9,697
1. Low birthweight	6,226	3,233	—	—	—	—	—	—	—	3,233
2. Birth asphyxia and birth trauma	7,737	4,044	—	—	—	—	—	—	—	4,044
Other perinatal conditions	4,734	2,420	0	—	—	—	—	—	—	2,420

Table 3C.2 Continued

	0–4	5–14	15–29	30–44	45–59	60–69	70–79	80+	Total
	Female								
	74	*161*	*232*	*217*	*131*	*52*	*30*	*10*	*907*
	32,207	**7,531**	**20,001**	**22,375**	**29,536**	**22,927**	**20,849**	**9,516**	**164,941**
	20,993	*2,310*	*5,035*	*3,961*	*2,359*	*1,490*	*1,253*	*703*	*38,104*
	6,177	**1,331**	**2,122**	**2,392**	**1,773**	**1,000**	**692**	**215**	**15,702**
	68	**116**	**749**	**1,104**	**963**	**602**	**357**	**77**	**4,036**
	58	**9**	**360**	**115**	**34**	**12**	**6**	**1**	**596**
	19	0	11	7	0	4	3	1	46
	4	7	278	59	20	3	—	—	371
	35	2	69	39	0	0	—	—	145
	0	—	2	9	13	6	3	1	34
	73	**11**	**210**	**259**	**171**	**29**	**6**	**0**	**759**
	3,356	**159**	**199**	**198**	**138**	**73**	**52**	**28**	**4,203**
	1,201	**450**	**143**	**40**	**17**	**5**	**2**	**1**	**1,859**
	280	12	—	—	—	—	—	—	292
	1	3	10	8	2	—	—	—	24
	4	1	0	0	0	—	—	—	5
	698	372	94	—	—	—	—	—	1,163
	219	62	39	32	14	5	2	1	375
	263	**37**	**83**	**80**	**46**	**17**	**9**	**2**	**539**
	16	**2**	**22**	**39**	**25**	**11**	**4**	**3**	**122**
	6	**0**	**9**	**17**	**9**	**4**	**2**	**1**	**48**
	287	**36**	**20**	**17**	**11**	**5**	**3**	**1**	**379**
	6	**16**	**48**	**32**	**37**	**4**	**1**	**2**	**146**
	—	—	—	—	—	—	—	—	—
	—	—	—	0	—	—	—	—	0
	0	1	2	3	3	2	0	2	12
	2	5	7	4	1	0	0	0	20
	4	11	39	25	32	2	1	0	114
	0	**1**	**1**	**3**	**2**	**1**	**0**	**0**	**8**
	40	**60**	**14**	**6**	**4**	**2**	**1**	**1**	**127**
	67	**47**	**14**	**13**	**3**	**1**	**0**	**0**	**146**
	0	**0**	**4**	**76**	**116**	**94**	**70**	**24**	**385**
	76	**252**	**2**	**1**	**1**	**1**	**0**	**0**	**333**
	37	112	0	0	—	0	—	—	149
	18	76	—	—	—	—	—	—	94
	15	62	2	1	1	1	0	0	82
	6	1	0	0	—	0	0	0	8
	659	136	245	392	197	137	177	73	2,016
	4,412	**450**	**172**	**159**	**235**	**373**	**498**	**458**	**6,756**
	4,176	305	157	147	227	365	492	434	6,304
	175	12	14	12	7	8	6	24	258
	62	133	0	0	0	0	—	0	195
	—	**6**	**2,342**	**1,116**	**12**	—	—	—	**3,475**
	—	—	155	165	2	—	—	—	322
	—	—	721	159	1	—	—	—	881
	—	0	66	61	1	—	—	—	128
	—	—	177	62	0	—	—	—	239
	—	6	123	61	2	—	—	—	191
	—	—	1,100	608	6	—	—	—	1,714
	8,999	**0**	—	—	—	—	—	—	**8,999**
	2,993	0	—	—	—	—	—	—	2,993
	3,693	—	—	—	—	—	—	—	3,693
	2,313	—	—	—	—	—	—	—	2,313

(Continues on the following page.)

Table 3C.2 Continued

Cause	Total	Male 0–4	5–14	15–29	30–44	45–59	60–69	70–79	80+	Total
E. Nutritional deficiencies	**5,797**	**1,539**	**241**	**357**	**186**	**188**	**69**	**34**	**12**	**2,626**
1. Protein-energy malnutrition	2,725	1,303	27	29	22	24	13	8	5	1,431
2. Iodine deficiency	251	92	32	0	0	0	0	0	0	125
3. Vitamin A deficiency	10	2	3	—	1	0	—	—	—	7
4. Iron-deficiency anemia	2,695	124	176	325	160	157	50	17	3	1,013
Other nutritional disorders	116	18	2	3	3	7	6	9	3	51
II. Noncommunicable diseases	***228,073***	***10,262***	***3,138***	***12,214***	***16,524***	***30,234***	***23,387***	***16,449***	***4,848***	***117,055***
A. Malignant neoplasms	**32,341**	**181**	**247**	**718**	**2,158**	**6,608**	**5,244**	**2,915**	**482**	**18,553**
1. Mouth and oropharynx cancers	1,064	0	1	33	133	313	170	72	12	736
2. Esophageal cancer	3,217	0	0	16	189	678	703	377	50	2,013
3. Stomach cancer	6,134	1	2	74	375	1,437	1,155	686	131	3,861
4. Colon and rectal cancers	2,330	0	0	49	173	394	339	201	46	1,202
5. Liver cancer	5,923	7	6	145	689	1,905	1,009	472	57	4,290
6. Pancreas cancer	544	0	1	2	39	137	82	47	8	317
7. Trachea, bronchus, and lung cancers	5,333	2	3	25	276	1,124	1,281	709	98	3,518
8. Melanoma and other skin cancers	66	0	0	1	3	12	10	5	1	32
9. Breast cancer	1,730	—	—	—	0	0	0	0	0	1
10. Cervix uteri cancer	805	—	—	—	—	—	—	—	—	—
11. Corpus uteri cancer	175	—	—	—	—	—	—	—	—	—
12. Ovarian cancer	464	—	—	—	—	—	—	—	—	—
13. Prostate cancer	164	0	0	0	1	18	55	73	17	164
14. Bladder cancer	348	0	0	1	6	50	84	85	21	248
15. Lymphomas and multiple myeloma	753	15	44	69	92	121	70	32	7	451
16. Leukemia	1,652	98	156	269	109	136	77	45	9	900
Other malignant neoplasms	1,640	57	33	34	72	282	207	111	25	820
B. Other neoplasms	**354**	**15**	**16**	**17**	**18**	**53**	**24**	**16**	**3**	**163**
C. Diabetes mellitus	**4,918**	**5**	**14**	**116**	**391**	**702**	**514**	**313**	**72**	**2,126**
D. Endocrine disorders	**2,560**	**585**	**57**	**71**	**75**	**93**	**42**	**33**	**18**	**975**
E. Neuropsychiatric conditions	**42,926**	**2,395**	**1,636**	**7,643**	**4,601**	**2,490**	**1,083**	**847**	**354**	**21,050**
1. Unipolar depressive disorders	14,037	0	746	1,902	1,720	1,221	351	68	11	6,019
2. Bipolar affective disorder	3,115	0	64	1,271	201	6	2	0	0	1,544
3. Schizophrenia	3,930	0	362	1,331	284	60	11	3	1	2,051
4. Epilepsy	1,303	80	126	199	178	71	25	11	3	693
5. Alcohol use disorders	4,303	0	33	1,475	1,510	657	100	18	3	3,796
6. Alzheimer's and other dementias	4,110	65	28	35	39	123	437	598	287	1,613
7. Parkinson's disease	435	1	0	3	21	48	46	61	23	202
8. Multiple sclerosis	317	0	14	58	46	11	2	1	0	131
9. Drug use disorders	425	0	17	172	109	40	2	0	0	340
10. Post-traumatic stress disorder	748	0	8	84	75	38	1	1	0	207
11. Obsessive-compulsive disorder	667	—	10	134	94	29	3	1	0	270
12. Panic disorder	1,400	—	26	411	6	25	3	2	0	472
13. Insomnia (primary)	596	—	12	46	51	39	18	11	2	179
14. Migraine	1,691	7	89	295	28	2	0	0	0	421
15. Mental retardation, lead-caused	2,598	1,335	1	0	0	0	0	0	0	1,336
Other neuropsychiatric disorders	3,255	907	100	227	241	120	82	73	24	1,775
F. Sense organ diseases	**27,758**	**1**	**26**	**453**	**2,895**	**5,007**	**3,116**	**1,244**	**223**	**12,964**
1. Glaucoma	1,703	0	2	13	97	336	200	85	19	753
2. Cataracts	9,727	0	1	42	609	1,766	1,214	519	95	4,246
3. Vision disorders, age-related	7,608	0	23	166	617	1,323	828	345	80	3,383
4. Hearing loss, adult onset	8,712	—	—	231	1,571	1,580	873	294	29	4,578
Other sense organ disorders	8	0	0	1	1	1	0	0	0	4
G. Cardiovascular diseases	**52,872**	**249**	**182**	**951**	**2,381**	**6,987**	**7,874**	**6,652**	**2,090**	**27,365**
1. Rheumatic heart disease	2,244	24	32	160	159	228	150	90	21	864
2. Hypertensive heart disease	4,234	6	3	30	170	558	676	545	191	2,180
3. Ischemic heart disease	14,242	26	65	328	807	2,071	2,097	1,725	541	7,661
4. Cerebrovascular disease	25,832	49	20	157	830	3,509	4,377	3,714	1,037	13,692
5. Inflammatory heart diseases	1,147	25	11	52	71	121	123	118	56	577
Other cardiovascular diseases	5,173	119	50	224	345	500	449	461	244	2,392

Table 3C.2 Continued

			Female					
0–4	**5–14**	**15–29**	**30–44**	**45–59**	**60–69**	**70–79**	**80+**	**Total**
1,405	**523**	**399**	**294**	**340**	**117**	**63**	**30**	**3,171**
1,183	22	6	17	20	20	15	11	1,294
94	33	0	0	0	0	0	0	127
2	2	—	—	—	—	—	—	3
116	465	391	275	311	86	29	8	1,682
10	2	1	3	9	11	19	11	65
9,423	*2,874*	*11,115*	*14,652*	*24,822*	*20,560*	*18,988*	*8,584*	*111,018*
196	**207**	**453**	**2,065**	**4,548**	**3,266**	**2,415**	**637**	**13,788**
1	1	6	38	126	79	59	17	329
0	0	5	53	407	384	288	67	1,204
0	0	53	329	670	543	509	169	2,273
0	0	19	172	345	303	211	77	1,128
19	7	69	254	517	424	285	58	1,633
0	1	3	31	70	59	49	14	227
4	24	10	156	559	541	446	74	1,814
0	0	1	5	10	8	7	2	34
0	0	16	423	805	304	143	39	1,730
0	0	65	93	308	196	120	22	805
0	0	2	39	72	38	19	5	175
1	5	28	104	175	91	50	11	464
—	—	—	—	—	—	—	—	—
0	0	1	7	17	29	34	12	100
7	15	31	65	80	49	42	12	303
101	123	123	155	136	62	39	13	753
62	30	21	142	250	158	114	44	819
17	**6**	**13**	**29**	**67**	**30**	**22**	**7**	**191**
7	**15**	**106**	**399**	**830**	**734**	**559**	**142**	**2,792**
884	**52**	**162**	**207**	**112**	**75**	**56**	**36**	**1,585**
2,053	**1,405**	**7,489**	**4,191**	**3,047**	**1,465**	**1,301**	**925**	**21,877**
—	688	1,767	2,472	2,214	671	163	43	8,017
0	83	1,277	201	8	2	0	0	1,571
0	88	1,389	275	98	17	10	2	1,879
55	113	187	145	66	25	14	4	609
—	17	217	190	75	7	2	0	507
54	26	38	42	131	522	900	783	2,496
0	—	3	10	42	55	81	42	233
0	24	75	67	16	3	1	0	186
—	9	38	27	10	0	0	0	85
—	5	241	212	75	4	2	1	540
—	4	200	144	42	4	1	0	396
—	20	840	10	47	6	4	1	927
—	10	81	142	97	59	22	6	417
19	258	945	47	1	0	0	0	1,270
1,261	0	0	0	0	0	0	0	1,261
663	60	192	206	126	90	100	43	1,480
1	**4**	**273**	**2,661**	**5,620**	**3,964**	**1,841**	**431**	**14,794**
—	2	13	99	404	269	125	37	949
0	1	18	529	2,175	1,756	817	185	5,481
0	0	98	784	1,645	1,030	514	154	4,225
—	—	143	1,248	1,395	908	384	55	4,134
1	1	1	0	1	0	0	0	4
206	**165**	**706**	**1,647**	**5,019**	**6,227**	**7,757**	**3,780**	**25,507**
24	38	166	232	355	285	212	67	1,380
4	3	18	104	416	546	638	324	2,054
14	44	245	452	1,246	1,756	1,890	935	6,582
37	24	82	532	2,430	3,057	4,121	1,858	12,140
19	9	32	44	93	102	158	112	570
108	47	163	282	479	481	738	484	2,781

(Continues on the following page.)

Cause	Total	0–4	5–14	15–29	30–44	45–59	60–69	70–79	80+	Total
					Male					
H. Respiratory diseases	**23,551**	**660**	**391**	**613**	**729**	**2,813**	**2,854**	**3,065**	**1,227**	**12,353**
1. Chronic obstructive pulmonary disease	17,181	7	2	13	308	2,346	2,476	2,724	1,049	8,924
2. Asthma	3,203	254	335	513	267	209	77	46	9	1,709
Other respiratory diseases	3,167	399	54	88	154	258	302	296	169	1,720
I. Digestive diseases	**15,419**	**2,427**	**129**	**667**	**1,378**	**2,162**	**1,091**	**687**	**210**	**8,750**
1. Peptic ulcer disease	1,800	32	11	104	229	365	202	119	34	1,096
2. Cirrhosis of the liver	3,882	39	17	163	579	994	437	217	41	2,487
3. Appendicitis	122	2	6	12	14	23	7	5	2	70
Other digestive diseases	9,615	2,354	96	388	556	780	445	346	133	5,097
J. Genitourinary diseases	**5,388**	**185**	**90**	**271**	**347**	**1,328**	**509**	**326**	**99**	**3,154**
1. Nephritis and nephrosis	3,041	52	69	230	287	384	294	186	53	1,555
2. Benign prostatic hypertrophy	997	—	—	—	5	820	91	62	20	997
Other genitourinary system diseases	1,350	132	21	41	55	124	125	78	26	602
K. Skin diseases	**960**	**92**	**58**	**86**	**71**	**70**	**34**	**23**	**8**	**442**
L. Musculoskeletal diseases	**10,389**	**45**	**119**	**382**	**1,372**	**1,666**	**774**	**287**	**57**	**4,702**
1. Rheumatoid arthritis	1,225	1	11	29	86	141	70	31	6	375
2. Osteoarthritis	5,724	0	1	105	475	909	514	146	15	2,166
3. Gout	1,414	0	0	52	667	444	76	20	3	1,262
4. Low back pain	633	20	54	64	82	79	24	10	2	335
Other musculoskeletal disorders	1,394	24	52	131	63	93	90	80	32	565
M. Congenital anomalies	**6,208**	**2,992**	**103**	**128**	**28**	**13**	**4**	**2**	**1**	**3,272**
1. Abdominal wall defect	6	4	—	—	0	—	—	—	0	4
2. Anencephaly	49	28	0	—	—	—	—	—	0	29
3. Anorectal atresia	1	1	—	—	—	—	—	—	—	1
4. Cleft lip	56	29	—	—	—	—	—	—	—	29
5. Cleft palate	35	22	0	0	0	—	—	—	—	22
6. Esophageal atresia	1	0	—	—	—	—	—	—	—	0
7. Renal agenesis	2	1	—	—	0	—	—	—	—	1
8. Down syndrome	447	244	3	5	0	—	—	—	—	252
9. Congenital heart anomalies	3,848	1,781	65	84	21	7	2	1	0	1,960
10. Spina bifida	208	102	0	—	—	0	0	—	—	102
Other congenital anomalies	1,555	779	36	39	7	7	2	1	0	872
N. Oral conditions	**2,429**	**430**	**69**	**97**	**80**	**243**	**223**	**40**	**4**	**1,187**
1. Dental caries	1,400	424	66	54	43	83	31	15	4	720
2. Periodontal disease	48	—	—	6	12	4	1	1	0	24
3. Edentulism	935	—	—	36	22	155	190	24	1	428
Other oral diseases	45	7	3	2	2	1	0	0	0	15
III. Injuries	**41,442**	**1,765**	**2,921**	**8,601**	**6,634**	**3,709**	**1,281**	**569**	**144**	**25,624**
A. Unintentional injuries	**30,638**	**1,718**	**2,701**	**6,138**	**4,545**	**2,666**	**866**	**394**	**108**	**19,136**
1. Road traffic accidents	10,243	207	543	2,812	2,065	1,129	322	122	20	7,221
2. Poisonings	1,793	76	78	235	276	256	105	40	7	1,072
3. Falls	4,675	245	420	832	574	413	172	117	47	2,821
4. Fires	1,135	69	52	111	99	43	22	16	4	416
5. Drownings	3,740	521	817	614	224	138	51	26	9	2,399
6. Other unintentional injuries	9,052	599	792	1,535	1,307	688	193	71	21	5,207
B. Intentional injuries	**10,804**	**47**	**219**	**2,462**	**2,089**	**1,043**	**415**	**175**	**36**	**6,487**
1. Self-inflicted injuries	7,074	—	98	1,135	992	673	338	154	31	3,421
2. Violence	3,118	39	113	1,105	882	315	63	18	4	2,539
3. War	532	7	6	195	190	47	12	3	1	461
Other intentional injuries	79	1	2	28	24	7	2	1	0	65

Table 3C.2 Continued

	Female							
0–4	5–14	15–29	30–44	45–59	60–69	70–79	80+	Total
534	**425**	**439**	**671**	**1,355**	**2,300**	**3,452**	**2,022**	**11,199**
5	0	15	364	967	1,978	3,156	1,772	8,257
204	388	349	200	202	95	41	13	1,494
325	36	75	106	187	227	255	237	1,448
2,268	**139**	**407**	**716**	**1,243**	**805**	**751**	**340**	**6,669**
36	11	54	111	201	137	106	48	704
56	27	82	249	442	278	204	56	1,395
2	4	6	9	12	7	8	3	52
2,173	96	265	348	588	383	432	233	4,518
78	**83**	**214**	**388**	**570**	**441**	**341**	**117**	**2,234**
46	71	149	248	372	305	219	76	1,486
—	—	—	—	—	—	—	—	—
32	13	65	140	199	135	122	41	748
78	**54**	**98**	**102**	**88**	**46**	**35**	**18**	**518**
51	135	559	1,445	2,053	949	378	117	5,687
2	26	72	175	338	157	63	17	850
0	1	303	962	1,435	638	191	28	3,558
0	0	8	76	41	16	9	2	152
10	64	44	84	65	20	9	2	298
38	44	133	148	173	118	106	68	829
2,660	**120**	**89**	**43**	**15**	**4**	**3**	**1**	**2,936**
2	—	—	—	—	—	0	—	2
20	0	0	0	0	—	—	—	20
0	—	—	—	—	—	—	—	0
27	—	—	—	—	—	—	—	27
13	0	0	0	0	—	—	—	13
0	—	—	—	—	—	—	—	0
1	—	—	—	—	—	—	—	1
186	3	6	0	0	—	—	—	195
1,671	94	73	35	10	3	2	1	1,888
106	0	0	0	0	—	0	0	106
633	23	10	8	5	2	1	0	683
390	**64**	**105**	**88**	**254**	**254**	**76**	**10**	**1,242**
385	62	52	43	83	33	18	6	681
—	0	6	12	4	1	1	0	24
—	—	37	24	166	218	57	4	506
6	2	10	10	2	0	0	0	30
1,792	**2,347**	**3,851**	**3,761**	**2,354**	**877**	**608**	**229**	**15,819**
1,773	2,108	2,586	2,366	1,503	567	415	184	11,502
189	396	728	865	584	158	83	18	3,022
82	94	128	176	136	61	35	9	722
266	372	377	250	205	127	161	96	1,854
88	125	250	149	62	19	17	8	718
345	482	178	159	91	40	31	13	1,341
802	639	925	766	424	161	88	40	3,845
19	**239**	**1,265**	**1,395**	**851**	**310**	**193**	**45**	**4,317**
—	153	1,064	1,188	743	281	180	43	3,653
18	59	185	190	89	25	12	1	579
0	25	11	12	17	3	1	0	71
1	1	4	4	3	1	0	0	14

Source: Authors' compilation.

Note: — = an estimate of zero; the number zero in a cell indicates a non-zero estimate of less than 500.

a. These figures include late effects of polio cases with onset prior to regional certification of polio eradication in 1994.

b. Does not include liver cancer and cirrhosis DALYs(3,0) resulting from chronic hepatitis virus infection.

c. This cause category includes "Causes arising in the perinatal period" as defined in the International Classification of Diseases, principally low birthweight, prematurity, birth asphyxia, and birth trauma, and does not include all causes of DALYs(3,0) occurring in the perinatal period.

Table 3C.3 DALYs(3,0) by Cause, Sex, and Age in the Europe and Central Asia Region, 2001
(thousands)

Cause	Total	Male								Total
		0–4	5–14	15–29	30–44	45–59	60–69	70–79	80+	
Population (millions)	*477*	*15*	*38*	*59*	*51*	*37*	*17*	*9*	*2*	*230*
All causes	**116,502**	**5,211**	**1,902**	**8,184**	**11,371**	**15,315**	**11,968**	**8,004**	**1,950**	**63,904**
I. Communicable, maternal, perinatal,	*10,908*	*2,829*	*284*	*631*	*1,135*	*905*	*329*	*128*	*32*	*6,274*
and nutritional conditions										
A. **Infectious and parasitic diseases**	**4,760**	**676**	**102**	**554**	**1,021**	**624**	**153**	**45**	**8**	**3,183**
1. **Tuberculosis**	**1,536**	**4**	**4**	**174**	**498**	**431**	**110**	**27**	**3**	**1,251**
2. **Sexually transmitted diseases**	**200**	**8**	**0**	**20**	**13**	**1**	**0**	**0**	**0**	**43**
excluding HIV/AIDS										
a. Syphilis	12	4	0	1	1	0	0	0	0	6
b. Chlamydia	122	1	0	6	3	0	0	—	—	10
c. Gonorrhea	59	1	0	13	10	0	0	0	—	24
d. Other sexually transmitted	8	2	—	0	0	0	0	0	—	3
diseases										
3. **HIV/AIDS**	**982**	**6**	**7**	**254**	**403**	**121**	**10**	**1**	**0**	**802**
4. **Diarrheal diseases**	**657**	**278**	**13**	**15**	**15**	**10**	**5**	**3**	**1**	**341**
5. **Childhood-cluster diseases**	**323**	**121**	**36**	**5**	**0**	**1**	**0**	**0**	**0**	**164**
a. Pertussis	81	39	1	—	—	—	—	—	—	40
b. Poliomyelitis[a]	2	0	0	0	0	0	0	0	0	1
c. Diphtheria	2	0	0	0	0	0	0	0	0	1
d. Measles	236	82	34	4	0	0	0	—	—	121
e. Tetanus	2	0	0	0	0	0	0	0	0	1
6. **Meningitis**	**403**	**149**	**10**	**18**	**20**	**19**	**7**	**2**	**1**	**225**
7. **Hepatitis B**[b]	**79**	**7**	**2**	**18**	**12**	**5**	**2**	**1**	**0**	**48**
Hepatitis C[b]	**31**	**3**	**1**	**7**	**5**	**2**	**1**	**0**	**0**	**20**
8. **Malaria**	**18**	**3**	**3**	**1**	**1**	**0**	**0**	**0**	**0**	**9**
9. **Tropical-cluster diseases**	**7**	**2**	**1**	**1**	**0**	**0**	**0**	**0**	**0**	**5**
a. Trypanosomiasis	0	—	—	—	—	—	—	—	—	—
b. Chagas' disease	—	—	—	—	—	—	—	—	—	—
c. Schistosomiasis	1	0	—	0	—	0	0	0	—	1
d. Leishmaniasis	6	1	1	0	0	0	0	0	0	4
e. Lymphatic filariasis	1	1	—	0	0	—	0	—	—	1
f. Onchocerciasis	—	—	—	—	—	—	—	—	—	—
10. **Leprosy**	**0**	**—**	**—**	**0**	**0**	**0**	**0**	**0**	**0**	**0**
11. **Dengue**	**0**	**—**	**—**	**—**	**—**	**0**	**—**	**—**	**—**	**0**
12. **Japanese encephalitis**	**—**	**—**	**—**	**—**	**—**	**—**	**—**	**—**	**—**	**—**
13. **Trachoma**	**—**	**—**	**—**	**—**	**—**	**—**	**—**	**—**	**—**	**—**
14. **Intestinal nematode infections**	**1**	**0**	**0**	**0**	**—**	**0**	**0**	**0**	**0**	**0**
a. Ascariasis	0	0	0	—	—	—	—	—	0	0
b. Trichuriasis	0	0	0	—	—	—	—	—	—	0
c. Hookworm disease	0	—	—	—	—	0	0	0	0	0
Other intestinal infections	0	0	—	0	—	—	—	—	0	0
Other infectious diseases	522	94	23	40	54	34	16	9	2	273
B. **Respiratory infections**	**2,305**	**626**	**78**	**48**	**87**	**260**	**152**	**76**	**23**	**1,350**
1. Lower respiratory infections	2,111	573	49	44	81	254	148	74	23	1,245
2. Upper respiratory infections	129	44	7	4	5	6	4	2	0	72
3. Otitis media	65	9	22	0	0	0	0	0	0	33
C. **Maternal conditions**	**486**	**—**	**—**	**—**	**—**	**—**	**—**	**—**	**—**	**—**
1. Maternal hemorrhage	17	—	—	—	—	—	—	—	—	—
2. Maternal sepsis	124	—	—	—	—	—	—	—	—	—
3. Hypertensive disorders	11	—	—	—	—	—	—	—	—	—
of pregnancy										
4. Obstructed labor	2	—	—	—	—	—	—	—	—	—
5. Abortion	17	—	—	—	—	—	—	—	—	—
Other maternal conditions	315	—	—	—	—	—	—	—	—	—
D. **Perinatal conditions**[c]	**2,125**	**1,203**	**0**	**0**	**0**	**0**	**0**	**0**	**—**	**1,203**
1. Low birthweight	822	448	—	—	—	—	0	—	—	448
2. Birth asphyxia and birth trauma	779	444	0	0	—	0	—	—	—	444
Other perinatal conditions	524	311	0	0	0	0	—	0	—	311

Table 3C.3 Continued

	Female							
0–4	5–14	15–29	30–44	45–59	60–69	70–79	80+	Total
14	*36*	*58*	*52*	*41*	*23*	*17*	*6*	*248*
4,372	**1,425**	**5,019**	**6,106**	**9,168**	**9,818**	**11,359**	**5,333**	**52,598**
2,414	*297*	*854*	*485*	*254*	*142*	*129*	*59*	*4,634*
621	**97**	**330**	**272**	**138**	**62**	**43**	**13**	**1,577**
4	**6**	**59**	**107**	**64**	**26**	**15**	**3**	**284**
8	**2**	**111**	**34**	**2**	**0**	**1**	**0**	**158**
4	0	1	1	0	0	0	0	6
1	2	89	19	1	0	—	—	112
1	0	20	13	0	0	—	—	35
2	0	1	1	1	0	0	0	5
6	**6**	**90**	**60**	**16**	**2**	**0**	**0**	**180**
254	**13**	**13**	**12**	**10**	**6**	**6**	**2**	**315**
115	**37**	**5**	**0**	**1**	**1**	**0**	**0**	**159**
39	1	—	—	0	0	—	—	41
0	0	0	0	0	0	0	0	1
0	0	0	0	0	0	0	0	1
75	35	5	—	0	0	—	—	115
0	0	0	0	0	0	0	0	1
136	**8**	**7**	**7**	**9**	**6**	**3**	**1**	**178**
5	**2**	**8**	**7**	**6**	**2**	**1**	**0**	**31**
2	**1**	**3**	**2**	**2**	**1**	**0**	**0**	**11**
3	**3**	**1**	**1**	**0**	**0**	**0**	**0**	**9**
0	**1**	**0**	**0**	**0**	**0**	**0**	**0**	**2**
—	—	—	0	—	0	—	—	0
—	—	—	—	—	—	—	—	—
—	—	—	—	0	0	—	—	0
0	1	0	0	0	0	0	0	2
—	0	—	—	—	—	—	—	0
—	—	—	—	—	—	—	—	—
—	**—**	**0**	**0**	**0**	**0**	**—**	**0**	**0**
—	—	—	—	—	—	—	—	—
—	—	—	—	—	—	—	—	—
—	—	—	—	—	—	—	—	—
0	**0**	**—**	**0**	**0**	**—**	**0**	**0**	**0**
0	0	—	—	—	—	—	—	0
0	0	—	—	—	—	—	—	0
—	—	—	0	—	—	—	—	0
0	—	—	—	0	—	0	0	0
89	19	32	40	28	19	16	6	249
537	**70**	**36**	**44**	**85**	**65**	**75**	**43**	**954**
490	43	32	41	81	62	73	42	865
38	5	3	3	3	2	2	1	57
9	22	0	0	0	0	0	0	32
—	**1**	**357**	**127**	**1**	**0**	**—**	**—**	**486**
—	—	12	5	0	—	—	—	17
—	—	107	16	0	—	—	—	124
—	—	8	3	0	—	—	—	11
—	—	1	0	0	—	—	—	2
—	1	12	4	0	—	—	—	17
—	—	216	99	1	0	—	—	315
923	**0**	**0**	**0**	**0**	**0**	**—**	**—**	**923**
374	—	—	—	—	—	—	—	374
336	0	0	—	—	—	—	—	336
213	0	0	0	0	0	—	—	213

(Continues on the following page.)

Cause	Total	Male 0–4	5–14	15–29	30–44	45–59	60–69	70–79	80+	Total
E. Nutritional deficiencies	**1,232**	**325**	**104**	**28**	**27**	**21**	**24**	**8**	**1**	**538**
1. Protein-energy malnutrition	173	75	1	2	3	4	2	1	0	88
2. Iodine deficiency	566	198	73	0	0	0	0	0	0	272
3. Vitamin A deficiency	1	0	0	—	—	—	—	—	0	0
4. Iron-deficiency anemia	421	34	25	24	22	16	21	7	1	150
Other nutritional disorders	72	18	5	2	1	1	1	0	0	29
II. Noncommunicable diseases	***88,969***	***1,998***	***868***	***3,869***	***6,195***	***11,529***	***10,810***	***7,624***	***1,877***	***44,768***
A. Malignant neoplasms	**12,159**	**32**	**63**	**186**	**573**	**2,195**	**2,211**	**1,217**	**162**	**6,638**
1. Mouth and oropharynx cancers	426	0	1	4	34	179	101	33	4	357
2. Esophageal cancer	288	0	0	1	11	88	78	34	4	216
3. Stomach cancer	1,376	0	0	8	74	266	289	165	20	824
4. Colon and rectal cancers	1,290	0	0	8	47	170	224	159	26	633
5. Liver cancer	379	1	1	4	20	75	80	44	5	230
6. Pancreas cancer	481	0	0	1	28	100	87	46	6	270
7. Trachea, bronchus, and lung cancers	2,323	0	1	8	110	684	736	347	29	1,917
8. Melanoma and other skin cancers	160	0	0	4	15	29	18	11	3	80
9. Breast cancer	1,058	—	0	0	1	3	3	2	0	10
10. Cervix uteri cancer	356	—	—	—	—	—	—	—	—	—
11. Corpus uteri cancer	349	—	—	—	—	—	—	—	—	—
12. Ovarian cancer	350	—	—	—	—	—	—	—	—	—
13. Prostate cancer	283	0	0	1	3	37	105	111	26	283
14. Bladder cancer	300	0	0	1	9	58	91	68	13	240
15. Lymphomas and multiple myeloma	375	3	10	26	39	58	46	23	3	208
16. Leukemia	462	12	25	47	39	52	48	30	5	256
Other malignant neoplasms	1,901	15	24	71	143	395	305	142	18	1,114
B. Other neoplasms	**126**	**2**	**2**	**5**	**9**	**18**	**14**	**9**	**2**	**61**
C. Diabetes mellitus	**1,375**	**1**	**4**	**34**	**109**	**183**	**137**	**78**	**13**	**560**
D. Endocrine disorders	**534**	**131**	**14**	**27**	**28**	**24**	**9**	**5**	**1**	**239**
E. Neuropsychiatric conditions	**14,106**	**595**	**520**	**2,346**	**1,554**	**936**	**374**	**297**	**113**	**6,735**
1. Unipolar depressive disorders	4,268	0	170	488	446	316	110	27	4	1,561
2. Bipolar affective disorder	668	—	17	279	36	1	0	0	0	334
3. Schizophrenia	778	0	76	277	20	6	4	2	0	386
4. Epilepsy	354	9	24	56	60	38	11	4	1	202
5. Alcohol use disorders	1,849	2	14	620	561	294	56	10	1	1,557
6. Alzheimer's and other dementias	1,612	13	7	10	12	37	99	199	97	474
7. Parkinson's disease	228	1	1	1	8	21	33	23	4	93
8. Multiple sclerosis	143	0	3	16	21	14	4	2	0	60
9. Drug use disorders	559	1	5	188	154	73	8	1	0	430
10. Post-traumatic stress disorder	192	0	0	25	17	10	0	0	0	52
11. Obsessive-compulsive disorder	419	—	29	73	62	11	2	4	0	181
12. Panic disorder	340	—	5	100	1	6	1	1	0	114
13. Insomnia (primary)	255	—	2	24	28	24	13	7	1	99
14. Migraine	414	4	62	50	10	1	0	0	0	128
15. Mental retardation, lead-caused	312	148	1	3	2	1	0	0	0	156
Other neuropsychiatric disorders	1,716	417	103	136	116	84	31	16	4	907
F. Sense organ diseases	**5,091**	**1**	**2**	**73**	**304**	**596**	**659**	**390**	**62**	**2,086**
1. Glaucoma	280	0	1	5	10	26	37	27	6	112
2. Cataracts	455	0	0	3	16	44	63	46	10	182
3. Vision disorders, age-related	1,787	0	1	14	27	181	257	168	33	680
4. Hearing loss, adult onset	2,564	—	—	51	250	345	301	149	13	1,109
Other sense organ disorders	5	0	0	1	1	1	0	0	0	3
G. Cardiovascular diseases	**38,281**	**49**	**39**	**390**	**1,993**	**5,225**	**5,843**	**4,694**	**1,335**	**19,569**
1. Rheumatic heart disease	408	1	2	15	45	68	33	12	2	177
2. Hypertensive heart disease	1,346	1	1	8	53	173	192	143	39	611
3. Ischemic heart disease	18,510	0	5	98	944	3,016	3,174	2,444	603	10,286
4. Cerebrovascular disease	12,616	13	15	80	371	1,283	1,852	1,562	405	5,581
5. Inflammatory heart diseases	1,166	15	5	75	202	252	130	79	25	783
Other cardiovascular diseases	4,234	20	10	114	378	432	461	454	261	2,131

			Female					
0–4	5–14	15–29	30–44	45–59	60–69	70–79	80+	Total
334	129	131	41	30	15	11	3	694
74	1	2	3	3	2	2	1	85
211	82	0	0	0	0	0	0	294
0	0	0	0	0	0	0	0	1
32	40	122	31	24	12	8	2	271
17	5	7	7	3	1	1	1	43
1,737	813	3,291	4,738	8,091	9,320	11,010	5,201	44,200
27	46	157	688	1,611	1,504	1,227	261	5,521
0	0	2	8	22	17	15	5	69
0	—	1	5	16	23	22	6	72
0	0	10	59	124	164	162	34	552
0	0	6	44	150	205	203	49	657
1	1	3	10	35	47	44	8	149
0	0	1	10	49	71	66	14	212
0	1	4	33	120	123	106	18	406
0	0	4	15	23	17	15	6	80
0	0	7	164	410	263	167	37	1,049
—	0	15	93	128	64	46	9	356
0	0	6	48	115	103	66	11	349
0	2	11	47	125	97	60	9	350
—	—	—	—	—	—	—	—	—
0	0	0	3	11	18	21	7	60
2	5	20	26	37	41	31	5	167
10	16	26	30	40	43	34	6	206
13	21	42	94	203	208	170	36	787
2	2	4	11	19	14	11	3	65
1	4	37	115	217	222	178	41	815
134	13	33	35	45	17	14	5	294
528	478	2,124	1,504	991	661	647	438	7,371
0	165	649	875	622	288	88	20	2,707
0	14	279	39	2	1	0	0	334
0	36	283	61	6	4	1	0	392
9	21	42	38	23	11	7	2	151
0	4	110	100	61	12	3	0	292
13	8	12	11	41	218	447	387	1,138
1	1	1	10	28	45	40	8	135
0	4	20	28	19	7	3	1	83
—	5	59	42	20	3	1	0	129
0	2	69	47	18	2	2	0	140
—	47	83	78	15	8	6	1	238
—	5	199	2	14	2	2	0	226
—	2	29	41	42	23	15	4	156
6	87	172	21	0	0	0	0	286
147	1	3	2	1	0	0	0	155
351	77	114	109	77	37	32	13	809
1	0	43	298	724	977	772	190	3,005
0	0	1	5	26	59	58	19	168
0	0	0	8	58	84	92	31	273
0	0	1	26	200	396	373	110	1,107
—	—	41	258	440	438	249	30	1,455
1	0	0	0	0	0	0	0	2
41	26	178	735	2,364	4,485	7,007	3,876	18,712
0	2	14	36	80	61	32	5	231
1	0	5	30	129	208	254	108	735
0	4	33	201	933	2,040	3,262	1,751	8,224
13	8	47	244	916	1,783	2,678	1,347	7,035
11	4	22	55	76	74	91	49	383
16	7	56	169	230	320	689	616	2,104

(Continues on the following page.)

Cause	Total	Male 0–4	5–14	15–29	30–44	45–59	60–69	70–79	80+	Total
H. Respiratory diseases	**4,284**	**173**	**81**	**151**	**288**	**533**	**653**	**481**	**103**	**2,462**
1. Chronic obstructive pulmonary disease	2,362	2	2	31	147	312	430	350	74	1,349
2. Asthma	688	36	49	74	39	61	89	45	8	400
Other respiratory diseases	1,234	136	30	45	102	160	133	86	22	713
I. Digestive diseases	**5,675**	**267**	**34**	**301**	**749**	**1,058**	**510**	**240**	**43**	**3,202**
1. Peptic ulcer disease	442	0	3	30	81	102	61	30	5	313
2. Cirrhosis of the liver	2,084	2	7	64	336	540	255	87	8	1,301
3. Appendicitis	31	1	2	4	4	4	3	2	0	18
Other digestive diseases	3,119	263	22	203	329	412	191	121	29	1,570
J. Genitourinary diseases	**1,417**	**42**	**13**	**67**	**109**	**234**	**145**	**101**	**25**	**737**
1. Nephritis and nephrosis	585	5	8	38	68	82	56	37	9	303
2. Benign prostatic hypertrophy	176	—	—	0	0	87	48	33	8	176
Other genitourinary system diseases	656	37	5	29	40	66	42	31	8	258
K. Skin diseases	**237**	**8**	**6**	**20**	**28**	**29**	**13**	**6**	**1**	**112**
L. Musculoskeletal diseases	**3,726**	**10**	**38**	**188**	**400**	**408**	**205**	**95**	**15**	**1,361**
1. Rheumatoid arthritis	578	1	11	32	32	33	21	11	2	141
2. Osteoarthritis	2,281	0	0	63	256	278	153	68	9	827
3. Gout	137	0	0	6	52	45	8	3	1	115
4. Low back pain	143	3	9	14	24	17	6	3	0	76
Other musculoskeletal disorders	587	7	18	74	35	35	17	11	4	201
M. Congenital anomalies	**1,285**	**638**	**19**	**19**	**11**	**8**	**2**	**1**	**0**	**699**
1. Abdominal wall defect	7	4	0	0	0	0	0	0	0	5
2. Anencephaly	8	3	0	0	0	0	0	0	0	3
3. Anorectal atresia	2	2	0	0	0	0	0	0	0	2
4. Cleft lip	3	1	0	0	0	0	0	0	—	1
5. Cleft palate	3	1	0	0	0	0	0	0	—	1
6. Esophageal atresia	6	3	0	0	0	0	0	0	0	3
7. Renal agenesis	6	4	0	0	0	0	0	0	0	4
8. Down syndrome	180	99	1	1	1	1	0	0	0	102
9. Congenital heart anomalies	670	327	9	12	7	3	1	0	0	358
10. Spina bifida	49	23	1	0	0	0	0	0	0	25
Other congenital anomalies	351	171	9	6	3	4	1	1	0	195
N. Oral conditions	**672**	**47**	**33**	**61**	**38**	**82**	**34**	**11**	**2**	**308**
1. Dental caries	375	47	33	35	15	29	14	8	2	181
2. Periodontal disease	19	—	—	2	5	1	1	0	0	9
3. Edentulism	276	—	—	24	18	52	19	3	0	116
Other oral diseases	3	0	0	0	0	0	0	0	0	1
III. Injuries	**16,626**	**384**	**750**	**3,684**	**4,042**	**2,881**	**829**	**252**	**41**	**12,862**
A. Unintentional injuries	**11,366**	**369**	**665**	**2,312**	**2,512**	**1,975**	**597**	**175**	**30**	**8,635**
1. Road traffic accidents	2,264	29	101	608	509	289	81	29	4	1,650
2. Poisonings	2,251	17	15	318	626	594	148	23	2	1,742
3. Falls	1,372	64	127	265	225	186	76	43	13	998
4. Fires	571	49	38	83	119	101	32	10	1	433
5. Drownings	806	32	65	186	209	125	35	8	1	661
6. Other unintentional injuries	4,103	179	320	853	823	679	225	62	9	3,151
B. Intentional injuries	**5,259**	**14**	**85**	**1,372**	**1,530**	**906**	**232**	**77**	**11**	**4,227**
1. Self-inflicted injuries	2,625	0	49	631	719	543	156	58	8	2,165
2. Violence	2,030	9	29	504	591	308	62	16	2	1,520
3. War	585	5	6	233	214	53	14	3	1	530
Other intentional injuries	19	0	0	4	6	3	0	0	0	12

Table 3C.3 Continued

			Female					
0–4	5–14	15–29	30–44	45–59	60–69	70–79	80+	Total
155	**91**	**136**	**292**	**358**	**319**	**331**	**140**	**1,822**
1	13	41	214	244	194	214	93	1,013
30	60	51	21	34	44	35	13	288
124	18	44	57	80	81	82	35	521
222	**25**	**184**	**360**	**717**	**463**	**377**	**125**	**2,474**
0	1	11	21	33	26	28	9	129
2	5	33	149	293	184	99	18	783
0	1	2	2	2	2	2	0	13
220	17	138	188	389	251	248	98	1,549
28	**16**	**81**	**120**	**153**	**130**	**111**	**40**	**680**
5	10	27	51	66	61	48	14	282
—	—	—	—	—	—	—	—	—
23	7	54	69	87	69	63	26	398
9	**6**	**20**	**24**	**28**	**19**	**12**	**8**	**126**
9	**57**	**218**	**505**	**754**	**456**	**297**	**67**	**2,365**
2	30	107	108	97	51	33	9	437
0	0	30	304	538	341	211	29	1,453
0	0	1	6	6	4	3	1	22
1	10	9	17	17	8	4	1	67
6	16	72	71	96	51	46	28	386
536	**15**	**13**	**9**	**9**	**3**	**1**	**0**	**586**
3	0	0	0	0	0	0	0	3
5	0	0	0	0	0	0	0	6
1	0	0	0	0	0	0	0	1
1	0	0	0	0	0	0	—	1
1	0	0	0	0	0	0	0	1
3	0	0	0	0	0	0	0	3
2	0	0	0	0	0	0	0	2
74	0	1	1	1	0	0	0	78
286	7	8	5	4	1	0	0	311
23	1	0	0	0	0	0	0	24
136	7	4	3	4	1	1	0	156
45	**32**	**63**	**42**	**102**	**51**	**25**	**6**	**365**
45	32	34	15	32	19	14	5	194
—	—	2	5	1	1	1	0	10
—	—	26	21	69	31	11	1	160
0	0	0	0	0	0	0	0	1
221	**316**	**873**	**884**	**823**	**355**	**220**	**73**	**3,764**
211	**262**	**592**	**584**	**593**	**266**	**164**	**58**	**2,731**
27	66	195	137	103	48	32	6	614
15	11	73	137	185	66	19	3	508
35	43	75	55	49	36	50	31	374
25	12	20	26	29	13	10	3	138
19	24	32	29	23	10	6	1	145
90	105	198	200	204	93	47	13	952
10	**54**	**281**	**299**	**229**	**89**	**56**	**15**	**1,032**
—	23	123	117	105	49	34	9	460
8	19	147	166	107	36	21	5	510
0	11	10	14	14	4	1	0	55
1	0	0	2	3	0	0	0	7

Source: Authors' compilation.

Note: — = an estimate of zero; the number zero in a cell indicates a non-zero estimate of less than 500.

a. These figures include late effects of polio cases with onset prior to regional certification of polio eradication in 2000.

b. Does not include liver cancer and cirrhosis DALYs(3,0) resulting from chronic hepatitis virus infection.

c. This cause category includes "Causes arising in the perinatal period" as defined in the International Classification of Diseases, principally low birthweight, prematurity, birth asphyxia, and birth trauma, and does not include all causes of DALYs(3,0) occurring in the perinatal period.

Table 3C.4 DALYs(3,0) by Cause, Sex, and Age in the Latin America and the Caribbean Region, 2001
(thousands)

Cause	Total	Male 0–4	5–14	15–29	30–44	45–59	60–69	70–79	80+	Total
Population (millions)	*526*	*28*	*56*	*74*	*52*	*31*	*11*	*6*	*2*	*260*
All causes	**104,287**	**12,782**	**3,168**	**11,429**	**9,087**	**8,940**	**5,505**	**4,078**	**1,730**	**56,718**
I. Communicable, maternal, perinatal, and nutritional conditions	*22,741*	*6,922*	*548*	*1,126*	*1,436*	*806*	*365*	*287*	*176*	*11,666*
A. Infectious and parasitic diseases	10,288	2,057	371	965	1,268	614	223	136	57	5,694
1. Tuberculosis	966	24	20	115	169	150	70	39	11	599
2. Sexually transmitted diseases excluding HIV/AIDS	430	44	1	49	28	1	0	0	0	123
a. Syphilis	77	30	0	9	6	0	0	0	0	46
b. Chlamydia	183	2	0	10	4	0	0	—	—	16
c. Gonorrhea	157	11	1	30	18	0	0	0	0	60
d. Other sexually transmitted diseases	12	0	—	—	0	0	—	0	0	0
3. HIV/AIDS	2,354	91	41	430	735	194	16	2	0	1,510
4. Diarrheal diseases	2,362	983	113	39	34	25	13	10	6	1,224
5. Childhood-cluster diseases	397	191	5	2	1	1	0	0	0	200
a. Pertussis	366	179	3	—	—	—	0	—	—	182
b. Poliomyelitis[a]	6	0	1	1	1	0	0	0	0	3
c. Diphtheria	8	6	0	—	0	—	—	—	0	6
d. Measles	0	0	0	—	—	—	—	—	—	0
e. Tetanus	17	6	1	0	0	1	0	0	0	9
6. Meningitis	591	214	31	35	27	17	6	4	1	335
7. Hepatitis B[b]	95	10	3	17	14	11	4	2	0	61
Hepatitis C[b]	37	0	0	1	6	9	3	1	0	20
8. Malaria	111	34	10	6	5	3	1	1	0	60
9. Tropical-cluster diseases	696	7	12	145	80	76	34	14	4	372
a. Trypanosomiasis	0	—	—	—	—	—	0	—	—	0
b. Chagas' disease	583	0	0	125	62	67	32	12	4	302
c. Schistosomiasis	66	2	6	9	9	6	2	1	0	34
d. Leishmaniasis	37	5	4	8	7	2	0	0	0	28
e. Lymphatic filariasis	9	0	2	2	1	1	0	0	0	7
f. Onchocerciasis	2	0	0	0	0	0	0	0	0	1
10. Leprosy	18	0	2	2	2	2	1	1	0	10
11. Dengue	59	7	19	1	1	1	0	0	0	29
12. Japanese encephalitis	—	—	—	—	—	—	—	—	—	—
13. Trachoma	191	0	0	1	11	16	11	6	2	47
14. Intestinal nematode infections	139	22	43	0	1	1	1	0	0	69
a. Ascariasis	46	6	16	0	0	0	0	0	0	23
b. Trichuriasis	50	5	20	0	0	0	0	0	0	25
c. Hookworm disease	12	1	5	0	0	0	0	0	0	6
Other intestinal infections	31	9	2	0	1	0	1	0	0	14
Other infectious diseases	1,842	429	71	122	154	109	63	56	31	1,035
B. Respiratory infections	3,271	933	125	93	119	147	107	117	93	1,733
1. Lower respiratory infections	3,043	886	75	88	116	144	105	115	92	1,621
2. Upper respiratory infections	80	22	3	4	3	2	1	1	1	38
3. Otitis media	147	26	46	1	1	1	0	0	0	74
C. Maternal conditions	1,329	—	—	—	—	—	—	—	—	—
1. Maternal hemorrhage	98	—	—	—	—	—	—	—	—	—
2. Maternal sepsis	337	—	—	—	—	—	—	—	—	—
3. Hypertensive disorders of pregnancy	112	—	—	—	—	—	—	—	—	—
4. Obstructed labor	52	—	—	—	—	—	—	—	—	—
5. Abortion	117	—	—	—	—	—	—	—	—	—
Other maternal conditions	613	—	—	—	—	—	—	—	—	—
D. Perinatal conditions[c]	6,296	3,473	0	0	0	0	—	—	—	3,473
1. Low birthweight	795	432	—	—	—	—	—	—	—	432
2. Birth asphyxia and birth trauma	3,765	2,072	0	0	0	0	—	—	—	2,072
Other perinatal conditions	1,736	969	0	0	—	—	—	—	—	969
E. Nutritional deficiencies	1,558	459	51	68	48	44	35	34	26	766
1. Protein-energy malnutrition	916	345	15	18	20	23	20	23	19	482
2. Iodine deficiency	110	41	13	0	0	0	0	0	0	54
3. Vitamin A deficiency	1	0	—	—	—	—	0	—	0	0
4. Iron-deficiency anemia	477	62	22	48	25	18	12	9	5	201
Other nutritional disorders	55	11	1	2	4	3	3	3	1	29

	Female							
0–4	5–14	15–29	30–44	45–59	60–69	70–79	80+	Total
27	*54*	*73*	*55*	*33*	*13*	*8*	*3*	*266*
10,831	**2,754**	**7,464**	**6,602**	**7,321**	**5,402**	**4,615**	**2,580**	**47,569**
5,816	*566*	*1,938*	*1,298*	*568*	*319*	*321*	*250*	*11,075*
1,754	**368**	**887**	**733**	**416**	**200**	**155**	**82**	**4,594**
18	**22**	**96**	**95**	**71**	**36**	**22**	**8**	**367**
27	**5**	**205**	**64**	**4**	**1**	**1**	**0**	**306**
14	0	10	7	0	0	0	0	31
2	3	137	23	1	0	0	0	167
11	1	55	30	0	0	—	—	97
0	0	3	3	3	1	1	0	11
88	**40**	**299**	**338**	**72**	**5**	**1**	**0**	**844**
905	**108**	**36**	**30**	**23**	**15**	**13**	**9**	**1,139**
187	**7**	**2**	**1**	**0**	**0**	**0**	**0**	**197**
181	3	0	—	—	—	—	—	184
0	1	1	1	0	0	0	0	3
0	2	—	—	0	—	—	—	2
0	0	—	—	—	—	—	—	0
6	1	0	0	0	0	0	0	8
164	**33**	**18**	**12**	**13**	**8**	**5**	**1**	**256**
6	**3**	**4**	**6**	**7**	**4**	**2**	**2**	**34**
0	**0**	**0**	**2**	**7**	**5**	**2**	**0**	**17**
26	**10**	**6**	**4**	**3**	**1**	**1**	**0**	**51**
4	**8**	**148**	**55**	**62**	**27**	**14**	**5**	**324**
—	0	—	—	—	—	—	—	0
0	0	138	46	56	24	13	5	281
2	6	7	7	5	2	1	1	31
2	1	2	2	1	0	0	0	9
0	0	1	0	1	0	0	0	2
0	0	0	0	0	0	0	0	1
0	**2**	**2**	**2**	**1**	**0**	**0**	**0**	**8**
5	**20**	**1**	**1**	**1**	**0**	**0**	**0**	**29**
—	—	—	—	—	—	—	—	
0	**1**	**5**	**34**	**52**	**27**	**18**	**7**	**144**
25	**43**	**0**	**0**	**0**	**0**	**0**	**0**	**71**
6	15	0	0	0	0	0	0	22
5	20	0	0	0	0	0	0	25
1	5	0	0	0	0	0	0	6
12	4	0	0	0	0	0	0	17
296	65	66	88	99	70	75	48	807
830	**121**	**71**	**75**	**99**	**89**	**124**	**128**	**1,537**
780	72	67	70	96	87	122	127	1,422
26	4	2	3	2	2	2	1	43
24	45	2	1	1	0	0	0	73
0	**6**	**891**	**426**	**6**	—	**0**	**0**	**1,329**
0	0	46	51	1	—	—	—	98
—	0	277	60	0	—	—	—	337
—	1	65	43	2	—	—	0	112
—	—	38	13	0	—	—	—	52
—	3	90	23	0	—	—	—	117
—	2	374	234	3	—	0	0	613
2,823	**0**	—	**0**	—	—	—	**0**	**2,823**
363	—	—	—	—	—	—	—	363
1,693	0	—	—	—	—	—	0	1,693
767	0	—	0	—	—	—	0	767
408	**71**	**89**	**65**	**47**	**29**	**43**	**39**	**792**
311	16	11	11	16	16	26	28	435
42	14	0	0	0	0	0	0	56
0	—	—	0	0	—	—	0	0
47	40	75	51	28	11	15	9	276
8	1	3	3	3	2	2	3	25

(Continues on the following page.)

Cause	Total	0–4	5–14	15–29	30–44	45–59	60–69	70–79	80+	Total
II. Noncommunicable diseases	**67,815**	**5,265**	**1,686**	**5,194**	**4,811**	**6,982**	**4,831**	**3,653**	**1,508**	**33,930**
A. Malignant neoplasms	**7,060**	**56**	**94**	**205**	**338**	**905**	**835**	**639**	**218**	**3,289**
1. Mouth and oropharynx cancers	204	0	0	3	18	67	40	19	5	153
2. Esophageal cancer	215	—	0	1	13	64	48	28	8	160
3. Stomach cancer	735	0	1	10	45	133	121	88	29	427
4. Colon and rectal cancers	485	0	0	9	28	66	60	48	17	229
5. Liver cancer	277	2	1	4	15	43	39	27	8	139
6. Pancreas cancer	248	0	0	1	10	37	37	26	8	120
7. Trachea, bronchus, and lung cancers	728	0	1	5	31	157	160	107	25	486
8. Melanoma and other skin cancers	97	0	0	3	10	16	12	9	4	53
9. Breast cancer	642	0	—	0	1	2	1	1	0	4
10. Cervix uteri cancer	494	—	—	—	—	—	—	—	—	—
11. Corpus uteri cancer	254	—	—	—	—	—	—	—	—	—
12. Ovarian cancer	152	—	—	—	—	—	—	—	—	—
13. Prostate cancer	340	0	0	1	2	34	98	137	67	340
14. Bladder cancer	100	0	0	1	3	15	20	21	9	68
15. Lymphomas and multiple myeloma	383	5	16	33	37	53	40	26	7	217
16. Leukemia	444	24	45	66	36	30	20	16	6	242
Other malignant neoplasms	1,263	23	29	67	90	190	141	86	25	651
B. Other neoplasms	**196**	**9**	**7**	**12**	**13**	**22**	**17**	**13**	**5**	**97**
C. Diabetes mellitus	**2,775**	**2**	**3**	**35**	**152**	**386**	**305**	**203**	**61**	**1,149**
D. Endocrine disorders	**3,150**	**1,221**	**64**	**81**	**71**	**92**	**47**	**37**	**19**	**1,632**
E. Neuropsychiatric conditions	**18,781**	**1,522**	**758**	**3,667**	**1,717**	**951**	**355**	**248**	**144**	**9,362**
1. Unipolar depressive disorders	5,219	0	266	621	591	320	94	20	5	1,917
2. Bipolar affective disorder	883	0	23	362	41	1	0	0	0	428
3. Schizophrenia	1,078	0	77	383	43	9	2	1	0	516
4. Epilepsy	737	33	85	121	85	43	13	7	2	388
5. Alcohol use disorders	2,883	1	30	1,271	590	371	72	18	2	2,355
6. Alzheimer's and other dementias	1,215	20	9	10	7	28	104	165	119	463
7. Parkinson's disease	90	0	0	0	4	12	11	12	6	46
8. Multiple sclerosis	97	—	4	18	12	4	1	1	0	41
9. Drug use disorders	746	—	7	370	152	28	1	0	0	559
10. Post-traumatic stress disorder	177	0	2	29	17	8	0	0	0	58
11. Obsessive-compulsive disorder	480	—	4	121	59	30	8	2	0	225
12. Panic disorder	409	—	3	123	1	5	1	0	0	134
13. Insomnia (primary)	312	—	4	39	45	29	15	3	1	136
14. Migraine	736	6	68	114	5	0	0	0	0	193
15. Mental retardation, lead-caused	1,500	753	0	1	0	0	0	0	0	755
Other neuropsychiatric disorders	2,217	710	177	83	64	61	29	19	8	1,150
F. Sense organ diseases	**5,465**	**6**	**18**	**82**	**484**	**801**	**589**	**384**	**91**	**2,453**
1. Glaucoma	304	1	2	5	24	37	27	22	7	124
2. Cataracts	1,813	3	11	42	122	248	166	103	35	731
3. Vision disorders, age-related	1,639	1	5	34	140	222	143	107	25	677
4. Hearing loss, adult onset	1,706	—	—	1	198	293	253	152	23	920
Other sense organ disorders	3	0	0	0	0	0	0	0	0	2
G. Cardiovascular diseases	**11,827**	**84**	**45**	**243**	**710**	**1,733**	**1,531**	**1,285**	**606**	**6,237**
1. Rheumatic heart disease	133	0	3	12	10	12	6	3	1	49
2. Hypertensive heart disease	1,052	1	1	12	46	128	122	112	62	484
3. Ischemic heart disease	4,328	1	10	70	245	781	696	541	206	2,550
4. Cerebrovascular disease	3,936	11	10	47	214	561	501	419	176	1,939
5. Inflammatory heart diseases	557	15	5	33	62	87	63	44	17	326
Other cardiovascular diseases	1,821	56	15	69	133	164	142	164	144	889
H. Respiratory diseases	**5,198**	**427**	**252**	**352**	**312**	**495**	**398**	**347**	**172**	**2,754**
1. Chronic obstructive pulmonary disease	2,037	14	2	18	126	304	262	224	107	1,057
2. Asthma	1,547	189	216	262	73	39	16	12	6	812
Other respiratory diseases	1,614	224	33	73	113	152	121	111	59	885

			Female					
0–4	5–14	15–29	30–44	45–59	60–69	70–79	80+	Total
4,644	*1,770*	*4,680*	*4,819*	*6,496*	*4,981*	*4,215*	*2,280*	*33,885*
49	**74**	**178**	**641**	**1,194**	**812**	**602**	**222**	**3,771**
0	0	2	6	14	13	12	5	52
—	0	0	4	15	16	13	5	54
0	1	9	46	82	72	67	29	307
0	0	6	34	70	62	57	27	256
2	1	4	13	40	38	31	11	139
0	0	1	9	35	38	33	13	128
0	0	3	27	77	71	49	15	242
0	0	2	8	12	8	8	5	44
0	0	8	144	262	123	73	27	638
—	0	33	124	191	84	49	13	494
0	0	7	58	95	52	32	10	254
0	1	10	26	55	33	21	5	152
—	—	—	—	—	—	—	—	—
0	0	0	2	8	8	9	5	32
3	9	15	23	43	36	29	9	166
22	35	38	34	31	19	16	6	201
21	26	37	84	163	139	103	38	611
6	**6**	**10**	**16**	**23**	**16**	**14**	**6**	**98**
3	**5**	**37**	**160**	**492**	**450**	**349**	**130**	**1,625**
980	**60**	**99**	**96**	**127**	**64**	**56**	**36**	**1,518**
1,420	**813**	**3,207**	**1,936**	**951**	**419**	**355**	**317**	**9,418**
0	256	1,110	1,091	602	186	44	14	3,303
0	23	383	47	2	1	0	0	455
0	10	430	108	10	2	2	0	562
30	79	107	72	38	14	7	2	350
0	8	296	129	77	15	3	1	528
20	9	11	8	33	136	256	281	753
0	0	0	4	12	10	11	6	44
—	5	25	18	6	1	1	0	56
—	7	122	50	9	1	0	0	188
0	1	54	47	15	1	1	0	119
—	2	146	54	42	6	4	1	255
—	8	251	2	11	1	1	0	275
—	3	51	52	38	24	6	2	176
20	241	115	166	0	0	0	0	543
743	0	1	1	0	0	0	0	745
607	163	107	88	54	21	18	9	1,067
2	**8**	**48**	**298**	**978**	**899**	**606**	**172**	**3,012**
0	1	4	25	42	48	45	16	180
1	5	18	83	384	314	200	78	1,082
0	1	25	56	283	297	239	60	962
—	—	1	134	269	240	122	19	785
0	0	0	0	0	0	0	0	2
67	**48**	**180**	**546**	**1,251**	**1,244**	**1,337**	**916**	**5,590**
0	4	13	20	24	12	8	3	84
1	1	12	45	125	130	146	108	568
1	12	38	114	392	469	471	282	1,778
8	9	44	238	510	451	457	280	1,997
13	5	21	31	51	45	41	23	231
43	17	52	98	149	136	214	222	933
384	**300**	**290**	**361**	**366**	**284**	**277**	**181**	**2,444**
36	5	50	254	223	165	155	91	980
158	270	180	33	40	26	19	8	735
190	25	59	74	103	93	103	82	729

(Continues on the following page.)

Cause	Total	Male 0–4	5–14	15–29	30–44	45–59	60–69	70–79	80+	Total
I. Digestive diseases	**5,091**	**510**	**78**	**231**	**606**	**833**	**414**	**251**	**96**	**3,020**
1. Peptic ulcer disease	212	1	2	14	24	37	25	19	9	132
2. Cirrhosis of the liver	1,513	3	3	67	355	461	181	76	16	1,162
3. Appendicitis	55	2	5	8	6	5	3	2	1	33
Other digestive diseases	3,311	505	68	142	220	330	205	153	70	1,693
J. Genitourinary diseases	**1,667**	**99**	**33**	**54**	**79**	**395**	**114**	**110**	**61**	**946**
1. Nephritis and nephrosis	789	25	25	41	56	91	76	65	33	412
2. Benign prostatic hypertrophy diseases	299	—	—	0	0	266	14	12	7	299
Other genitourinary system	580	74	8	13	23	38	24	34	21	235
K. Skin diseases	**410**	**28**	**18**	**33**	**28**	**28**	**18**	**17**	**10**	**181**
L. Musculoskeletal diseases	**2,728**	**18**	**49**	**113**	**266**	**303**	**159**	**110**	**25**	**1,044**
1. Rheumatoid arthritis	555	2	12	25	31	30	11	7	2	120
2. Osteoarthritis	1,283	0	0	15	104	175	117	85	14	510
3. Gout	176	—	—	7	82	54	9	2	1	154
4. Low back pain	148	5	13	18	24	14	4	2	1	80
Other musculoskeletal disorders	566	12	24	49	26	30	18	15	7	180
M. Congenital anomalies	**2,460**	**1,195**	**29**	**25**	**11**	**6**	**2**	**1**	**0**	**1,269**
1. Abdominal wall defect	29	15	0	0	0	—	0	0	0	15
2. Anencephaly	73	31	0	0	0	—	0	0	0	31
3. Anorectal atresia	8	4	0	0	0	—	0	0	0	5
4. Cleft lip	17	9	0	0	0	—	0	0	0	9
5. Cleft palate	15	7	0	0	0	—	0	0	0	7
6. Esophageal atresia	25	14	0	0	0	—	0	0	0	14
7. Renal agenesis	11	6	0	1	0	0	0	0	0	7
8. Down syndrome	309	152	2	3	2	1	0	0	0	160
9. Congenital heart anomalies	1,172	566	15	15	5	2	1	0	0	605
10. Spina bifida	245	112	1	1	0	0	0	0	0	114
Other congenital anomalies	557	278	10	6	3	3	1	1	0	302
N. Oral conditions	**1,005**	**87**	**239**	**60**	**23**	**31**	**45**	**9**	**1**	**495**
1. Dental caries	826	84	238	58	21	10	4	2	1	417
2. Periodontal disease	24	—	—	1	2	5	2	1	0	11
3. Edentulism	141	—	—	—	—	15	39	6	0	60
Other oral diseases	15	3	1	1	1	1	0	0	0	7
III. Injuries	**13,731**	**594**	**934**	**5,109**	**2,840**	**1,152**	**310**	**137**	**45**	**11,122**
A. Unintentional injuries	**7,656**	**570**	**778**	**1,998**	**1,309**	**704**	**221**	**106**	**38**	**5,723**
1. Road traffic accidents	2,686	77	171	816	574	285	72	31	7	2,034
2. Poisonings	87	7	3	18	17	9	3	1	0	58
3. Falls	729	58	79	150	94	59	26	18	10	494
4. Fires	163	28	15	22	17	13	3	2	1	101
5. Drownings	485	48	60	160	76	34	9	4	1	392
6. Other unintentional injuries	3,506	352	450	832	531	303	107	50	18	2,644
B. Intentional injuries	**6,076**	**24**	**156**	**3,112**	**1,531**	**448**	**89**	**31**	**8**	**5,399**
1. Self-inflicted injuries	711	0	17	228	156	88	28	13	3	534
2. Violence	5,154	24	137	2,788	1,302	343	56	17	4	4,670
3. War	189	1	2	80	69	16	5	1	0	173
Other intentional injuries	22	0	0	16	4	1	0	0	0	21

Table 3C.4 Continued

	Female							
0–4	5–14	15–29	30–44	45–59	60–69	70–79	80+	Total
401	**59**	**188**	**270**	**459**	**301**	**258**	**136**	**2,071**
1	1	8	12	18	15	17	11	81
3	2	15	70	121	77	48	13	351
2	4	5	4	4	2	2	1	22
396	52	160	184	317	207	192	111	1,618
82	**43**	**89**	**96**	**140**	**103**	**98**	**71**	**722**
24	30	38	47	78	65	58	36	377
—	—	—	—	—	—	—	—	—
58	13	51	49	62	38	39	34	345
35	**17**	**38**	**38**	**36**	**22**	**23**	**20**	**230**
13	**79**	**235**	**323**	**438**	**308**	**219**	**69**	**1,685**
3	43	132	114	85	33	19	7	435
—	0	5	94	245	228	163	38	774
0	0	1	11	6	2	2	0	22
2	15	12	18	14	4	2	1	67
8	22	85	87	87	41	33	23	387
1,117	**27**	**22**	**12**	**8**	**3**	**2**	**0**	**1,191**
14	0	0	0	—	—	0	0	14
41	0	0	0	0	—	0	—	41
3	0	0	0	0	0	0	—	3
8	0	0	0	—	—	0	—	8
7	0	0	0	—	—	0	—	7
10	0	0	0	0	—	0	0	10
3	0	0	0	0	0	0	0	4
142	2	2	2	2	0	0	0	149
527	15	13	6	4	1	1	0	566
129	1	1	0	0	—	—	—	132
232	8	6	4	3	1	1	0	255
84	**231**	**60**	**24**	**34**	**56**	**18**	**3**	**510**
81	230	58	22	11	4	3	1	409
—	—	1	2	6	2	1	1	13
—	—	—	—	17	49	14	1	81
3	1	1	1	0	0	0	0	8
371	**418**	**846**	**485**	**258**	**103**	**79**	**50**	**2,609**
355	**358**	**514**	**308**	**192**	**87**	**71**	**48**	**1,932**
64	111	217	134	77	28	17	5	651
6	4	8	6	3	1	1	0	29
47	50	43	21	17	15	22	20	235
22	11	11	7	6	2	2	1	63
31	27	20	8	4	2	1	0	93
185	156	214	132	85	39	29	21	862
16	**59**	**332**	**177**	**66**	**16**	**8**	**2**	**677**
0	16	90	38	22	6	3	1	177
16	42	239	134	40	8	4	1	484
0	2	3	4	4	1	0	0	16
0	—	0	0	0	0	0	0	1

Source: Authors' compilation.

Note: — = an estimate of zero; the number zero in a cell indicates a non-zero estimate of less than 500.

a. These figures include late effects of polio cases with onset prior to regional certification of polio eradication in 2002.

b. Does not include liver cancer and cirrhosis DALYs(3,0) resulting from chronic hepatitis virus infection.

c. This cause category includes "Causes arising in the perinatal period" as defined in the International Classification of Diseases, principally low birthweight, prematurity, birth asphyxia, and birth trauma, and does not include all causes of DALYs(3,0) occurring in the perinatal period.

Table 3C.5 DALYs(3,0) by Cause, Sex, and Age in the Middle East and North Africa Region, 2001
(thousands)

Cause	Total	Male 0–4	5–14	15–29	30–44	45–59	60–69	70–79	80+	Total
Population (millions)	*310*	*19*	*39*	*47*	*29*	*15*	*5*	*3*	*1*	*157*
All causes	**65,570**	**11,155**	**2,606**	**5,127**	**4,351**	**5,113**	**3,267**	**2,310**	**630**	**34,559**
I. Communicable, maternal, perinatal,	*17,739*	*6,784*	*503*	*309*	*298*	*286*	*187*	*139*	*45*	*8,552*
and nutritional conditions										
A. **Infectious and parasitic diseases**	**7,320**	**2,424**	**275**	**219**	**235**	**228**	**131**	**84**	**23**	**3,619**
1. **Tuberculosis**	**522**	**37**	**12**	**42**	**67**	**57**	**35**	**21**	**5**	**275**
2. **Sexually transmitted diseases**	**342**	**16**	**1**	**33**	**19**	**17**	**7**	**3**	**1**	**97**
excluding HIV/AIDS										
a. Syphilis	64	3	0	4	6	12	4	1	0	30
b. Chlamydia	166	2	0	11	3	0	0	—	—	16
c. Gonorrhea	97	10	0	18	9	0	0	—	—	39
d. Other sexually transmitted diseases	15	0	0	0	1	5	3	2	0	11
3. **HIV/AIDS**	**105**	**9**	**1**	**22**	**25**	**7**	**0**	**0**	**0**	**64**
4. **Diarrheal diseases**	**2,571**	**1,207**	**47**	**23**	**22**	**18**	**10**	**8**	**5**	**1,339**
5. **Childhood-cluster diseases**	**915**	**357**	**81**	**15**	**2**	**1**	**0**	**0**	**0**	**457**
a. Pertussis	326	161	2	—	—	—	—	—	—	164
b. Poliomyelitis	8	0	1	2	1	0	0	0	0	4
c. Diphtheria	1	0	0	0	—	—	—	0	—	0
d. Measles	470	148	74	12	—	—	—	—	—	234
e. Tetanus	110	48	4	1	1	1	0	0	0	55
6. **Meningitis**	**328**	**113**	**13**	**10**	**4**	**3**	**2**	**1**	**0**	**146**
7. **Hepatitis B**[a]	**111**	**14**	**3**	**4**	**9**	**18**	**9**	**5**	**0**	**63**
Hepatitis C[a]	**55**	**6**	**1**	**2**	**4**	**9**	**5**	**2**	**0**	**30**
8. **Malaria**	**668**	**265**	**21**	**14**	**10**	**7**	**2**	**1**	**1**	**322**
9. **Tropical-cluster diseases**	**281**	**13**	**33**	**29**	**27**	**37**	**22**	**13**	**2**	**176**
a. Trypanosomiasis	22	1	4	4	2	2	0	0	0	13
b. Chagas' disease	—	—	—	—	—	—	—	—	—	—
c. Schistosomiasis	207	4	18	18	20	34	21	12	2	129
d. Leishmaniasis	48	8	11	6	4	2	0	0	0	31
e. Lymphatic filariasis	4	0	0	1	1	0	0	0	0	2
f. Onchocerciasis	0	0	0	0	0	0	0	0	0	0
10. **Leprosy**	**2**	**0**	**0**	**0**	**0**	**0**	**0**	**0**	**—**	**1**
11. **Dengue**	**8**	**1**	**3**	**0**	**0**	**0**	**0**	**0**	**0**	**5**
12. **Japanese encephalitis**	**—**	**—**	**—**	**—**	**—**	**—**	**—**	**—**	**—**	**—**
13. **Trachoma**	**273**	**0**	**0**	**3**	**22**	**23**	**15**	**9**	**2**	**74**
14. **Intestinal nematode infections**	**64**	**5**	**27**	**0**	**0**	**0**	**0**	**0**	**0**	**33**
a. Ascariasis	47	4	20	0	0	—	—	—	—	24
b. Trichuriasis	0	—	0	—	—	—	—	—	—	0
c. Hookworm disease	17	1	7	0	0	0	0	0	0	9
Other intestinal infections	0	—	0	0	0	0	0	0	0	0
Other infectious diseases	1,073	381	31	22	24	30	24	21	7	539
B. **Respiratory infections**	**3,141**	**1,323**	**92**	**33**	**31**	**38**	**44**	**47**	**20**	**1,629**
1. Lower respiratory infections	2,974	1,283	57	31	29	37	43	46	19	1,545
2. Upper respiratory infections	72	24	3	2	1	1	2	2	0	36
3. Otitis media	95	16	32	0	0	—	0	—	—	48
C. **Maternal conditions**	**1,266**	**—**	**—**	**—**	**—**	**—**	**—**	**—**	**—**	**—**
1. Maternal hemorrhage	121	—	—	—	—	—	—	—	—	—
2. Maternal sepsis	222	—	—	—	—	—	—	—	—	—
3. Hypertensive disorders of pregnancy	54	—	—	—	—	—	—	—	—	—
4. Obstructed labor	96	—	—	—	—	—	—	—	—	—
5. Abortion	152	—	—	—	—	—	—	—	—	—
Other maternal conditions	620	—	—	—	—	—	—	—	—	—
D. **Perinatal conditions**[b]	**4,155**	**2,415**	**—**	**—**	**—**	**—**	**—**	**—**	**—**	**2,415**
1. Low birthweight	1,839	1,072	—	—	—	—	—	—	—	1,072
2. Birth asphyxia and birth trauma	1,595	928	—	—	—	—	—	—	—	928
Other perinatal conditions	722	414	—	—	—	—	—	—	—	414
E. **Nutritional deficiencies**	**1,857**	**622**	**136**	**57**	**32**	**19**	**11**	**8**	**2**	**889**
1. Protein-energy malnutrition	712	351	3	0	0	1	1	1	1	358
2. Iodine deficiency	506	192	62	0	0	0	0	0	0	254
3. Vitamin A deficiency	5	1	0	0	0	0	0	0	0	3
4. Iron-deficiency anemia	587	56	70	57	32	17	10	7	2	249
Other nutritional disorders	47	23	1	0	0	0	0	0	0	25

Table 3C.5 Continued

	Female								
0–4	5–14	15–29	30–44	45–59	60–69	70–79	80+	Total
18	*37*	*45*	*28*	*15*	*6*	*3*	*1*	*153*
9,810	**2,313**	**4,666**	**3,887**	**4,214**	**2,904**	**2,368**	**849**	**31,011**
5,945	*595*	*1,244*	*755*	*272*	*166*	*148*	*62*	*9,187*
2,388	**262**	**344**	**246**	**203**	**123**	**99**	**35**	**3,701**
31	**14**	**59**	**65**	**46**	**21**	**10**	**3**	**248**
17	**5**	**161**	**39**	**11**	**9**	**3**	—	**245**
5	0	8	7	6	4	3	—	34
2	3	122	17	2	2	—	—	149
10	1	31	14	2	2	—	—	58
0	0	0	0	2	2	0	—	4
9	**1**	**15**	**12**	**3**	**0**	**0**	**0**	**41**
1,127	**39**	**16**	**13**	**12**	**10**	**9**	**7**	**1,232**
364	**76**	**15**	**2**	**1**	**0**	**0**	**0**	**458**
160	2	—	—	—	—	—	—	163
0	1	2	1	0	0	0	0	4
0	0	—	—	—	—	—	0	0
155	69	12	—	—	—	—	—	236
48	4	1	1	1	0	0	0	55
152	**13**	**6**	**4**	**3**	**2**	**2**	**0**	**182**
10	**4**	**2**	**4**	**11**	**9**	**7**	**2**	**49**
4	**2**	**1**	**3**	**6**	**4**	**4**	**1**	**25**
294	**19**	**12**	**9**	**6**	**3**	**2**	**1**	**346**
7	**22**	**19**	**13**	**16**	**10**	**15**	**4**	**105**
1	3	2	1	1	0	0	0	9
—	—							
3	12	12	9	13	10	14	4	78
3	7	4	2	2	0	0	0	18
0	0	0	0	0	0	0	0	1
0	0	0	0	0	0	0	0	0
0	**0**	**0**	**0**	**0**	**0**	**0**	**0**	**1**
1	**2**	**0**	**0**	**0**	**0**	**0**	**0**	**3**
—								
0	**1**	**8**	**57**	**60**	**38**	**28**	**8**	**199**
5	**26**	**0**	**0**	**0**	**0**	**0**	**0**	**32**
4	19	—	—	—	—	—	—	23
—	0	—	—	—	—	—	—	0
1	7	0	0	0	0	0	0	8
—	0	0	0	0	0	0	0	0
368	37	30	26	27	17	20	10	534
1,214	**109**	**39**	**31**	**29**	**30**	**37**	**22**	**1,512**
1,173	75	37	30	28	28	36	22	1,429
26	4	2	1	1	2	1	0	36
16	31	0	—	0	—	—	0	46
—	**9**	**801**	**443**	**12**	—	—	—	**1,266**
—	0	54	63	4	—	—	—	121
—	0	170	52	1	—	—	—	222
—	0	24	26	4	—	—	—	54
—	—	68	28	0	—	—	—	96
—	9	122	21	0	—	—	—	152
—	0	363	254	3	—	—	—	620
1,740	—	—	—	—	—	—	—	**1,740**
766	—	—	—	—	—	—	—	766
667	—	—	—	—	—	—	—	667
307	—	—	—	—	—	—	—	307
602	**214**	**60**	**35**	**28**	**12**	**12**	**5**	**968**
341	6	1	1	0	2	2	0	354
189	62	0	0	0	0	0	0	252
1	0	0	0	0	0	0	0	2
53	144	58	33	27	10	9	4	338
18	2	0	0	0	1	1	0	23

(Continues on the following page.)

Table 3C.5 Continued

Cause	Total	Male 0–4	5–14	15–29	30–44	45–59	60–69	70–79	80+	Total
II. Noncommunicable diseases	*38,860*	*3,650*	*1,005*	*2,643*	*2,949*	*4,212*	*2,871*	*2,069*	*565*	*19,964*
A. Malignant neoplasms	**2,747**	**54**	**71**	**128**	**206**	**390**	**334**	**226**	**48**	**1,456**
1. Mouth and oropharynx cancers	78	1	1	4	12	17	12	6	1	54
2. Esophageal cancer	72	0	0	1	5	14	12	8	1	41
3. Stomach cancer	252	1	2	5	18	42	43	32	6	149
4. Colon and rectal cancers	164	0	1	8	20	27	19	12	3	90
5. Liver cancer	138	1	1	3	11	26	23	14	2	82
6. Pancreas cancer	55	0	0	0	4	11	9	6	1	31
7. Trachea, bronchus, and lung cancers	283	1	1	5	23	68	66	41	7	211
8. Melanoma and other skin cancers	19	0	0	1	1	2	2	2	1	9
9. Breast cancer	273	—	—	—	0	0	0	—	—	0
10. Cervix uteri cancer	93	—	—	—	—	—	—	—	—	—
11. Corpus uteri cancer	22	—	—	—	—	—	—	—	—	—
12. Ovarian cancer	42	—	—	—	—	—	—	—	—	—
13. Prostate cancer	64	0	0	1	2	12	19	24	6	64
14. Bladder cancer	214	0	0	3	18	61	50	33	8	174
15. Lymphomas and multiple myeloma	232	7	20	27	30	27	16	9	2	138
16. Leukemia	307	21	30	51	24	21	14	9	2	173
Other malignant neoplasms	440	22	15	19	37	65	48	28	7	241
B. Other neoplasms	**324**	**6**	**10**	**20**	**34**	**41**	**34**	**23**	**4**	**172**
C. Diabetes mellitus	**843**	**3**	**4**	**31**	**83**	**111**	**78**	**52**	**11**	**372**
D. Endocrine disorders	**1,152**	**392**	**27**	**30**	**28**	**50**	**31**	**23**	**5**	**586**
E. Neuropsychiatric conditions	**8,310**	**1,096**	**426**	**1,408**	**727**	**351**	**116**	**87**	**32**	**4,244**
1. Unipolar depressive disorders	2,027	0	130	256	267	131	37	8	1	831
2. Bipolar affective disorder	567	0	17	246	24	1	0	0	0	288
3. Schizophrenia	696	—	30	292	29	1	1	0	0	353
4. Epilepsy	248	16	28	46	25	12	4	2	1	134
5. Alcohol use disorders	79	—	0	23	34	13	2	1	0	73
6. Alzheimer's and other dementias	292	11	5	5	3	10	26	48	22	130
7. Parkinson's disease	81	3	2	5	9	12	8	5	1	44
8. Multiple sclerosis	55	—	3	12	7	1	1	0	0	24
9. Drug use disorders	786	—	6	278	241	117	6	1	0	649
10. Post-traumatic stress disorder	124	0	1	20	9	4	0	0	0	34
11. Obsessive-compulsive disorder	300	—	45	56	26	4	1	0	0	132
12. Panic disorder	264	—	3	84	1	2	0	0	0	90
13. Insomnia (primary)	74	—	1	6	9	5	4	1	0	26
14. Migraine	227	6	54	7	2	0	0	0	0	69
15. Mental retardation, lead-caused	725	336	13	15	3	1	0	0	0	369
Other neuropsychiatric disorders	1,764	725	88	57	40	36	26	20	5	997
F. Sense organ diseases	**5,380**	**3**	**37**	**239**	**681**	**886**	**433**	**171**	**35**	**2,485**
1. Glaucoma	681	1	10	48	78	82	42	20	4	286
2. Cataracts	1,491	2	26	120	179	189	92	49	11	667
3. Vision disorders, age-related	1,801	0	1	58	233	296	159	58	14	819
4. Hearing loss, adult onset	1,398	—	—	13	191	319	138	43	4	708
Other sense organ disorders	8	0	0	—	0	0	1	2	1	4
G. Cardiovascular diseases	**9,528**	**169**	**105**	**267**	**550**	**1,353**	**1,246**	**1,063**	**318**	**5,071**
1. Rheumatic heart disease	250	6	17	35	32	18	5	4	1	118
2. Hypertensive heart disease	933	6	3	10	36	120	134	126	41	474
3. Ischemic heart disease	4,315	7	10	90	281	810	696	535	132	2,561
4. Cerebrovascular disease	1,948	49	43	69	83	215	247	233	69	1,008
5. Inflammatory heart diseases	401	24	9	17	26	48	42	42	14	222
Other cardiovascular diseases	1,680	77	23	46	91	142	122	123	62	687
H. Respiratory diseases	**2,285**	**260**	**107**	**156**	**252**	**218**	**168**	**143**	**42**	**1,346**
1. Chronic obstructive pulmonary disease	816	9	2	26	163	127	96	85	24	532
2. Asthma	553	47	79	102	56	20	4	2	1	311
Other respiratory diseases	916	204	26	28	33	71	68	56	17	502

0–4	5–14	15–29	30–44	45–59	60–69	70–79	80+	Total
				Female				
3,355	*1,009*	*2,544*	*2,720*	*3,713*	*2,640*	*2,147*	*768*	*18,897*
41	**56**	**116**	**284**	**394**	**218**	**147**	**33**	**1,290**
0	0	2	5	8	5	3	1	24
0	0	1	4	10	8	7	1	31
0	1	7	20	30	23	18	4	103
0	1	5	18	21	15	11	3	74
1	1	4	8	20	12	8	2	56
0	0	1	3	8	6	5	1	23
0	1	3	13	24	16	11	2	72
0	0	1	2	3	2	1	0	9
0	0	6	85	117	40	20	4	272
0	0	12	14	38	19	9	1	93
0	0	2	5	8	4	3	1	22
0	1	5	11	14	6	4	1	42
—	—	—	—	—	—	—	—	—
0	0	1	7	12	9	8	2	40
4	11	16	19	19	13	9	2	94
16	22	37	24	20	9	6	1	135
19	15	15	45	43	31	24	7	199
5	**7**	**13**	**26**	**54**	**26**	**17**	**4**	**152**
2	**5**	**37**	**99**	**136**	**99**	**75**	**18**	**471**
360	**25**	**29**	**28**	**46**	**39**	**31**	**9**	**566**
903	**426**	**1,411**	**682**	**351**	**144**	**99**	**50**	**4,066**
0	124	388	402	202	62	14	3	1,196
0	15	238	25	1	0	0	0	279
—	16	273	37	15	2	0	0	343
13	27	36	22	11	3	2	1	114
—	0	1	2	2	0	0	0	5
10	4	5	2	11	38	55	36	162
4	3	3	6	9	6	4	2	37
—	3	16	8	2	1	1	0	31
—	5	55	50	25	1	0	0	137
0	1	53	27	8	0	0	0	90
—	47	75	34	8	4	0	0	168
—	6	161	1	5	1	0	0	174
—	2	6	12	21	6	2	0	48
8	107	36	7	0	0	0	0	158
323	15	10	5	2	0	0	0	355
544	51	56	40	29	21	19	7	767
20	**78**	**277**	**752**	**1,002**	**501**	**213**	**51**	**2,895**
3	20	70	104	111	57	24	7	395
9	39	137	193	236	125	67	19	824
8	20	54	268	365	172	76	20	982
—	—	16	188	290	145	45	6	690
0	0	0	0	0	1	2	1	4
366	**93**	**178**	**315**	**889**	**1,038**	**1,129**	**449**	**4,456**
7	18	37	33	21	8	6	2	132
4	3	9	22	93	123	144	59	458
8	8	54	110	411	500	493	171	1,754
31	25	29	66	191	238	259	100	940
16	7	12	20	30	33	42	19	179
300	33	37	64	142	136	185	98	993
208	**105**	**105**	**122**	**130**	**112**	**114**	**42**	**939**
6	2	6	55	65	60	65	24	284
33	86	70	31	16	5	2	1	242
169	17	29	36	50	47	46	18	413

(Continues on the following page.)

Table 3C.5 Continued

Cause	Total	Male 0–4	5–14	15–29	30–44	45–59	60–69	70–79	80+	Total
I. Digestive diseases	**2,948**	**425**	**65**	**132**	**119**	**342**	**226**	**149**	**34**	**1,492**
1. Peptic ulcer disease	100	1	1	9	11	17	10	9	3	61
2. Cirrhosis of the liver	686	17	10	24	26	134	95	52	10	368
3. Appendicitis	11	0	1	2	1	1	0	1	0	6
Other digestive diseases	2,152	406	52	97	81	190	121	87	22	1,057
J. Genitourinary diseases	**1,283**	**91**	**24**	**46**	**55**	**258**	**119**	**94**	**29**	**717**
1. Nephritis and nephrosis	634	15	17	31	33	86	82	57	15	335
2. Benign prostatic hypertrophy	156	—	—	—	—	134	10	8	4	156
Other genitourinary system diseases	493	76	7	16	22	39	28	28	11	226
K. Skin diseases	**234**	**36**	**15**	**18**	**13**	**10**	**7**	**7**	**2**	**109**
L. Musculoskeletal diseases	**1,080**	**16**	**29**	**76**	**164**	**129**	**45**	**21**	**4**	**484**
1. Rheumatoid arthritis	185	1	6	14	12	13	6	3	1	55
2. Osteoarthritis	517	0	0	16	73	64	26	12	2	193
3. Gout	122	0	0	7	60	34	5	2	0	108
4. Low back pain	101	5	12	12	11	9	3	1	0	53
Other musculoskeletal disorders	155	10	11	26	9	9	5	4	1	75
M. Congenital anomalies	**2,026**	**1,006**	**32**	**19**	**6**	**3**	**2**	**1**	**0**	**1,068**
1. Abdominal wall defect	14	7	0	0	0	0	0	0	0	7
2. Anencephaly	47	20	0	0	0	0	0	0	0	21
3. Anorectal atresia	5	3	0	0	0	0	0	0	0	3
4. Cleft lip	5	3	0	0	0	0	0	0	0	3
5. Cleft palate	9	5	0	0	0	0	0	0	0	5
6. Esophageal atresia	6	1	0	0	0	0	0	0	0	1
7. Renal agenesis	13	8	0	0	0	0	0	0	0	8
8. Down syndrome	306	157	1	1	0	0	0	0	0	160
9. Congenital heart anomalies	964	477	14	9	3	1	1	1	0	506
10. Spina bifida	104	45	4	2	0	0	0	0	—	51
Other congenital anomalies	551	281	12	6	2	1	1	0	0	302
N. Oral conditions	**721**	**91**	**54**	**73**	**32**	**69**	**31**	**9**	**1**	**361**
1. Dental caries	463	90	54	38	11	23	11	6	1	235
2. Periodontal disease	9	—	—	2	2	0	0	0	0	4
3. Edentulism	241	—	—	34	18	45	20	3	0	119
Other oral diseases	7	1	0	0	0	0	0	0	0	3
III. Injuries	***8,971***	***721***	***1,098***	***2,175***	***1,104***	***615***	***209***	***102***	***20***	***6,044***
A. Unintentional injuries	**7,854**	**704**	**1,062**	**1,752**	**864**	**531**	**185**	**95**	**18**	**5,211**
1. Road traffic accidents	3,002	183	348	744	455	277	97	51	8	2,162
2. Poisonings	184	20	5	42	20	32	5	2	0	125
3. Falls	915	86	140	156	68	44	16	12	3	525
4. Fires	564	64	43	71	33	19	5	3	1	238
5. Drownings	378	55	67	126	27	15	4	2	0	296
6. Other unintentional injuries	2,810	296	460	613	262	144	59	26	6	1,865
B. Intentional injuries	**1,117**	**17**	**36**	**423**	**240**	**84**	**25**	**7**	**2**	**833**
1. Self-inflicted injuries	364	3	8	107	57	26	9	3	1	213
2. Violence	440	8	23	194	86	31	8	2	1	353
3. War	272	5	4	106	87	23	6	1	1	233
Other intentional injuries	41	2	2	15	11	4	1	0	0	35

Table 3C.5 Continued

			Female					
0–4	5–14	15–29	30–44	45–59	60–69	70–79	80+	Total
364	**53**	**129**	**131**	**324**	**229**	**174**	**54**	**1,456**
0	1	5	7	9	7	7	3	39
15	8	16	26	112	76	51	13	317
0	1	1	1	0	0	0	0	5
348	43	106	98	202	145	115	37	1,095
58	**25**	**51**	**64**	**140**	**106**	**89**	**34**	**566**
11	16	23	30	85	66	52	16	299
—	—	—	—	—	—	—	—	—
47	9	28	34	55	40	37	17	267
24	**10**	**18**	**15**	**16**	**13**	**13**	**16**	**125**
19	**41**	**94**	**163**	**159**	**81**	**34**	**6**	**596**
7	16	27	31	30	11	5	1	130
0	1	38	100	104	58	21	3	325
0	0	1	7	3	1	1	0	13
3	15	9	11	8	2	1	0	48
9	9	18	14	14	8	6	2	80
898	**33**	**15**	**7**	**2**	**1**	**1**	**0**	**958**
6	0	0	0	0	0	—	0	7
24	1	1	0	0	0	—	0	26
2	0	0	0	0	0	—	0	2
2	0	0	0	0	0	—	0	3
4	0	0	0	0	0	—	0	4
5	0	0	0	0	0	—	0	5
5	0	0	0	0	0	—	0	5
144	2	0	0	0	0	—	0	146
429	14	8	4	1	1	1	0	458
48	3	2	0	—	0	0	—	53
228	12	5	2	1	1	0	0	249
87	**52**	**72**	**31**	**70**	**34**	**11**	**2**	**359**
86	52	36	11	23	12	6	2	228
—	—	2	2	0	0	0	0	4
—	—	33	17	46	22	4	0	122
1	0	1	1	0	0	0	0	5
510	*709*	*878*	*412*	*229*	*98*	*72*	*19*	*2,928*
503	673	733	356	203	89	68	18	2,643
140	223	196	129	82	37	27	5	840
11	4	21	13	5	3	2	1	59
96	130	89	29	19	10	13	5	390
57	56	128	43	27	6	7	2	326
35	19	18	6	3	2	1	0	83
165	241	282	136	68	31	19	5	946
7	**35**	**145**	**57**	**26**	**9**	**4**	**1**	**284**
0	8	96	30	11	4	2	0	151
5	8	40	20	8	3	1	1	88
0	19	6	6	7	2	1	0	40
1	1	2	1	0	0	0	0	5

Source: Authors' compilation.

Note: — = an estimate of zero; the number zero in a cell indicates a non-zero estimate of less than 500.

a. Does not include liver cancer and cirrhosis DALYs(3,0) resulting from chronic hepatitis virus infection.

b. This cause category includes "Causes arising in the perinatal period" as defined in the International Classification of Diseases, principally low birthweight, prematurity, birth asphyxia, and birth trauma, and does not include all causes of DALYs(3,0) occurring in the perinatal period.

Table 3C.6 DALYs(3,0) by Cause, Sex, and Age in the South Asia Region, 2001
(thousands)

Cause	Total	Male 0–4	5–14	15–29	30–44	45–59	60–69	70–79	80+	Total
Population (millions)	*1,388*	*88*	*164*	*195*	*139*	*81*	*30*	*14*	*4*	*715*
All causes	**408,655**	**71,133**	**13,630**	**25,697**	**27,281**	**30,913**	**19,697**	**12,168**	**3,233**	**203,753**
I. **Communicable, maternal, perinatal, and nutritional conditions**	*181,180*	*56,837*	*5,771*	*6,612*	*8,602*	*5,776*	*2,890*	*1,913*	*523*	*88,924*
A. **Infectious and parasitic diseases**	**87,705**	**20,242**	**4,416**	**5,937**	**7,938**	**5,060**	**1,692**	**882**	**221**	**46,388**
1. **Tuberculosis**	**13,875**	**194**	**228**	**1,575**	**2,626**	**2,439**	**1,014**	**324**	**34**	**8,435**
2. **Sexually transmitted diseases excluding HIV/AIDS**	**3,670**	**581**	**8**	**276**	**146**	**131**	**89**	**43**	**12**	**1,286**
a. Syphilis	1,490	369	0	20	12	79	89	43	12	625
b. Chlamydia	997	12	2	67	12	0	0	—	—	94
c. Gonorrhea	1,079	199	5	190	108	2	0	—	—	504
d. Other sexually transmitted diseases	105	0	0	0	14	49	0	0	0	64
3. **HIV/AIDS**	**7,413**	**226**	**56**	**1,422**	**2,953**	**840**	**50**	**6**	**0**	**5,553**
4. **Diarrheal diseases**	**22,257**	**10,821**	**184**	**134**	**139**	**124**	**80**	**67**	**44**	**11,592**
5. **Childhood-cluster diseases**	**14,566**	**5,389**	**1,233**	**311**	**149**	**67**	**18**	**6**	**3**	**7,175**
a. Pertussis	3,930	1,934	15	—	—	—	—	—	—	1,949
b. Poliomyelitis	55	6	3	11	7	1	—	—	—	28
c. Diphtheria	90	32	6	1	0	1	0	0	—	40
d. Measles	6,527	2,163	924	110	—	—	—	—	—	3,197
e. Tetanus	3,965	1,254	286	189	142	65	18	6	3	1,961
6. **Meningitis**	**2,142**	**274**	**285**	**177**	**101**	**100**	**39**	**34**	**9**	**1,019**
7. **Hepatitis B**[a]	**585**	**2**	**2**	**90**	**107**	**137**	**27**	**18**	**5**	**387**
Hepatitis C[a]	**228**	**1**	**1**	**34**	**41**	**54**	**11**	**7**	**2**	**149**
8. **Malaria**	**2,603**	**950**	**132**	**68**	**52**	**32**	**13**	**7**	**3**	**1,258**
9. **Tropical-cluster diseases**	**3,721**	**112**	**801**	**877**	**521**	**167**	**22**	**7**	**1**	**2,509**
a. Trypanosomiasis	0	—	—	—	0	—	—	—	—	0
b. Chagas' disease	0	—	—	—	—	—	—	—	0	0
c. Schistosomiasis	3	—	0	1	1	0	0	0	0	2
d. Leishmaniasis	1,306	43	273	211	123	54	15	4	0	724
e. Lymphatic filariasis	2,412	69	528	666	397	113	7	2	0	1,782
f. Onchocerciasis	—	—	—	—	—	—	—	—	—	—
10. **Leprosy**	**113**	**6**	**14**	**10**	**16**	**13**	**3**	**2**	**1**	**64**
11. **Dengue**	**240**	**25**	**73**	**4**	**4**	**3**	**1**	**1**	**0**	**111**
12. **Japanese encephalitis**	**298**	**16**	**19**	**30**	**53**	**8**	**2**	**2**	**0**	**130**
13. **Trachoma**	**197**	**1**	**0**	**3**	**13**	**18**	**13**	**6**	**2**	**55**
14. **Intestinal nematode infections**	**548**	**41**	**233**	**1**	**0**	**1**	**0**	**0**	**0**	**277**
a. Ascariasis	283	22	118	0	0	0	—	0	—	140
b. Trichuriasis	122	6	60	—	—	—	—	—	—	66
c. Hookworm disease	127	12	53	—	0	—	—	0	0	65
Other intestinal infections	16	2	2	0	0	1	0	0	0	6
Other infectious diseases	15,249	1,601	1,147	926	1,020	927	310	352	105	6,388
B. **Respiratory infections**	**35,044**	**13,238**	**774**	**274**	**285**	**348**	**1,136**	**975**	**285**	**17,316**
1. Lower respiratory infections	34,196	13,112	621	259	270	334	1,107	949	278	16,929
2. Upper respiratory infections	428	53	16	14	14	14	29	26	7	173
3. Otitis media	421	73	137	2	1	1	0	0	0	214
C. **Maternal conditions**	**10,069**	—	—	—	—	—	—	—	—	—
1. Maternal hemorrhage	1,718	—	—	—	—	—	—	—	—	—
2. Maternal sepsis	1,857	—	—	—	—	—	—	—	—	—
3. Hypertensive disorders of pregnancy	742	—	—	—	—	—	—	—	—	—
4. Obstructed labor	1,185	—	—	—	—	—	—	—	—	—
5. Abortion	1,467	—	—	—	—	—	—	—	—	—
Other maternal conditions	3,100	—	—	—	—	—	—	—	—	—
D. **Perinatal conditions**[b]	**37,721**	**20,442**	—	—	—	—	—	—	—	**20,442**
1. Low birthweight	25,015	13,292	—	—	—	—	—	—	—	13,292
2. Birth asphyxia and birth trauma	8,283	4,957	—	—	—	—	—	—	—	4,957
Other perinatal conditions	4,423	2,193	—	—	—	—	—	—	—	2,193
E. **Nutritional deficiencies**	**10,640**	**2,915**	**580**	**400**	**380**	**368**	**62**	**56**	**16**	**4,777**
1. Protein-energy malnutrition	5,695	2,319	334	66	10	22	3	3	1	2,759
2. Iodine deficiency	490	168	71	0	0	0	0	0	0	239
3. Vitamin A deficiency	146	23	46	0	—	0	—	—	—	70
4. Iron-deficiency anemia	3,616	330	106	318	346	294	31	15	4	1,443
Other nutritional disorders	693	75	22	16	24	52	28	38	11	267

Table 3C.6 Continued

	0–4	5–14	15–29	30–44	45–59	60–69	70–79	80+	Total
	\-	\-	\-	Female	\-	\-	\-	\-	\-
83	*154*	*180*	*128*	*77*	*31*	*16*	*4*	*673*
72,151	**15,087**	**30,361**	**24,094**	**25,792**	**19,349**	**14,059**	**4,009**	**204,902**
56,809	*6,543*	*11,886*	*7,825*	*3,777*	*2,688*	*2,088*	*638*	*92,256*
22,702	**4,846**	**4,800**	**3,721**	**2,812**	**1,301**	**878**	**257**	**41,317**
175	**268**	**1,479**	**1,664**	**1,161**	**480**	**191**	**23**	**5,440**
979	**26**	**904**	**275**	**124**	**53**	**19**	**4**	**2,384**
778	1	22	14	0	27	19	3	865
12	19	631	127	98	15	—	—	903
189	7	249	128	2	0	—	—	575
0	0	1	6	23	10	0	0	41
217	**54**	**719**	**686**	**174**	**10**	**1**	**0**	**1,860**
10,007	**174**	**98**	**77**	**93**	**85**	**75**	**56**	**10,665**
5,557	**1,259**	**323**	**153**	**70**	**20**	**7**	**3**	**7,391**
1,966	15	—	—	—	—	—	—	1,981
6	3	10	7	1	—	—	—	27
37	13	0	0	—	—	—	0	50
2,276	938	116	—	—	—	—	—	3,330
1,272	290	196	146	69	20	7	3	2,004
527	**348**	**122**	**38**	**32**	**31**	**19**	**6**	**1,123**
4	**16**	**67**	**36**	**47**	**16**	**10**	**3**	**198**
2	**7**	**27**	**14**	**19**	**6**	**4**	**1**	**79**
1,042	**127**	**66**	**50**	**34**	**15**	**8**	**3**	**1,345**
127	**416**	**302**	**129**	**203**	**27**	**8**	**1**	**1,212**
—	—	—	—	0	—	—	—	0
—	0	0	0	0	0	0	0	1
97	249	151	38	28	16	3	0	581
30	167	151	92	174	11	4	1	630
—	—	—	—	—	—	—	—	—
9	**13**	**9**	**8**	**7**	**2**	**2**	**0**	**49**
23	**92**	**4**	**4**	**3**	**1**	**1**	**0**	**129**
77	**52**	**19**	**11**	**5**	**3**	**1**	**0**	**168**
0	**1**	**7**	**37**	**40**	**32**	**20**	**5**	**142**
57	**212**	**1**	**0**	**0**	**0**	**0**	**0**	**271**
34	109	0	0	—	0	—	—	143
6	50	—	—	—	—	0	—	56
11	50	0	—	—	—	—	—	62
7	2	0	0	0	0	0	0	10
3,899	1,782	655	539	801	522	513	150	8,861
13,535	**937**	**241**	**124**	**270**	**1,160**	**1,106**	**356**	**17,728**
13,307	787	231	116	260	1,130	1,086	350	17,267
153	19	10	8	10	29	20	6	255
75	131	0	0	0	1	—	0	206
—	67	**6,461**	**3,474**	67	—	—	—	**10,069**
—	—	847	839	32	—	—	—	1,718
—	—	1,360	497	1	—	—	—	1,857
—	—	451	284	7	—	—	—	742
—	—	803	381	2	—	—	—	1,185
—	67	1,070	330	0	—	—	—	1,467
—	—	1,931	1,144	26	—	—	—	3,100
17,279	—	—	—	—	—	—	—	**17,279**
11,723	—	—	—	—	—	—	—	11,723
3,326	—	—	—	—	—	—	—	3,326
2,230	—	—	—	—	—	—	—	2,230
3,293	**693**	**384**	**507**	**628**	**228**	**104**	**25**	**5,863**
2,441	403	15	23	40	12	3	1	2,937
198	52	0	0	0	0	0	0	251
46	30	—	—	0	—	0	0	77
374	175	363	479	558	182	36	6	2,172
234	32	6	6	31	34	64	19	426

(Continues on the following page.)

Cause	Total	Male 0–4	5–14	15–29	30–44	45–59	60–69	70–79	80+	Total
II. Noncommunicable diseases	*181,339*	*12,192*	*3,875*	*10,614*	*12,752*	*22,030*	*15,881*	*9,726*	*2,553*	*89,623*
A. Malignant neoplasms	**14,127**	**185**	**196**	**487**	**811**	**1,797**	**2,123**	**1,028**	**261**	**6,887**
1. Mouth and oropharynx cancers	2,020	2	7	63	161	400	489	189	42	1,353
2. Esophageal cancer	1,116	1	1	9	63	174	242	93	19	602
3. Stomach cancer	629	0	2	16	53	114	131	60	17	393
4. Colon and rectal cancers	499	0	1	26	61	69	81	41	14	292
5. Liver cancer	464	5	3	30	52	83	65	28	6	272
6. Pancreas cancer	176	0	0	1	12	32	36	16	4	102
7. Trachea, bronchus, and lung cancers	1,807	0	1	19	110	494	515	256	45	1,441
8. Melanoma and other skin cancers	41	1	1	3	3	5	5	3	1	21
9. Breast cancer	1,246	—	—	0	0	0	0	0	0	0
10. Cervix uteri cancer	1,423	—	—	—	—	—	—	—	—	—
11. Corpus uteri cancer	66	—	—	—	—	—	—	—	—	—
12. Ovarian cancer	327	—	—	—	—	—	—	—	—	—
13. Prostate cancer	210	0	0	0	2	20	79	85	24	210
14. Bladder cancer	408	0	0	1	6	28	72	52	19	178
15. Lymphomas and multiple myeloma	1,401	19	55	96	101	87	91	46	13	507
16. Leukemia	851	62	80	171	66	44	38	18	5	484
Other malignant neoplasms	1,444	94	46	52	123	248	280	141	50	1,033
B. Other neoplasms	**350**	**19**	**18**	**56**	**29**	**33**	**16**	**10**	**4**	**185**
C. Diabetes mellitus	**4,433**	**26**	**37**	**190**	**392**	**750**	**464**	**290**	**94**	**2,243**
D. Endocrine disorders	**828**	**257**	**21**	**35**	**31**	**34**	**20**	**13**	**4**	**415**
E. Neuropsychiatric conditions	**37,734**	**2,909**	**1,794**	**5,854**	**3,294**	**1,746**	**603**	**713**	**260**	**17,173**
1. Unipolar depressive disorders	14,582	—	834	1,997	1,633	918	266	49	10	5,706
2. Bipolar affective disorder	2,237	0	78	970	110	3	1	—	—	1,163
3. Schizophrenia	2,896	—	208	954	158	80	14	7	2	1,423
4. Epilepsy	1,741	257	229	211	88	40	16	11	3	854
5. Alcohol use disorders	1,202	—	15	363	533	189	43	9	2	1,153
6. Alzheimer's and other dementias	1,955	43	17	17	2	41	85	437	185	828
7. Parkinson's disease	303	0	0	0	19	43	26	39	10	138
8. Multiple sclerosis	227	0	14	48	30	8	3	1	0	105
9. Drug use disorders	957	—	23	285	347	148	7	1	0	812
10. Post-traumatic stress disorder	548	—	7	76	45	21	0	0	0	149
11. Obsessive-compulsive disorder	649	—	11	168	75	15	3	1	0	273
12. Panic disorder	1,081	—	21	336	4	13	2	1	0	377
13. Insomnia (primary)	747	—	8	105	125	68	35	7	2	349
14. Migraine	1,452	3	196	183	25	2	0	0	0	408
15. Mental retardation, lead-caused	1,955	992	1	2	1	0	0	0	0	997
Other neuropsychiatric disorders	5,202	1,614	133	137	100	157	101	149	46	2,437
F. Sense organ diseases	**19,602**	**4**	**11**	**278**	**2,430**	**3,489**	**1,673**	**655**	**135**	**8,675**
1. Glaucoma	203	3	5	7	12	27	19	8	2	84
2. Cataracts	9,478	0	4	143	900	1,574	810	375	91	3,898
3. Vision disorders, age-related	1,600	0	0	14	128	281	151	67	16	657
4. Hearing loss, adult onset	8,305	—	—	113	1,388	1,606	693	203	26	4,030
Other sense organ disorders	16	1	1	1	1	1	1	1	0	7
G. Cardiovascular diseases	**51,264**	**704**	**392**	**1,288**	**2,434**	**7,821**	**7,517**	**5,149**	**1,325**	**26,629**
1. Rheumatic heart disease	2,635	179	79	276	182	259	144	91	23	1,233
2. Hypertensive heart disease	1,460	11	10	41	87	210	195	147	47	749
3. Ischemic heart disease	25,877	66	114	405	1,314	4,819	4,172	2,723	674	14,287
4. Cerebrovascular disease	13,184	80	35	110	284	1,764	2,346	1,648	397	6,663
5. Inflammatory heart diseases	1,591	102	31	142	150	149	129	94	25	822
Other cardiovascular diseases	6,517	266	122	315	417	620	531	446	158	2,875
H. Respiratory diseases	**16,590**	**968**	**517**	**687**	**943**	**2,568**	**1,858**	**1,054**	**241**	**8,836**
1. Chronic obstructive pulmonary disease	9,416	2	1	2	449	1,972	1,589	848	182	5,045
2. Asthma	3,593	200	383	569	314	304	52	27	6	1,855
Other respiratory diseases	3,581	766	133	116	180	291	217	179	54	1,936

Table 3C.6 Continued

	Female							
0–4	5–14	15–29	30–44	45–59	60–69	70–79	80+	Total
12,653	*4,468*	*11,756*	*12,784*	*19,735*	*15,734*	*11,378*	*3,207*	*91,715*
218	**193**	**540**	**947**	**2,214**	**1,837**	**938**	**353**	**7,239**
6	3	18	56	214	209	115	46	667
1	1	12	49	169	164	85	33	515
0	0	11	28	71	69	38	19	236
0	1	8	36	54	57	33	18	207
7	7	43	28	51	32	19	6	192
0	0	2	10	24	20	13	6	74
0	1	8	44	131	113	59	9	366
1	1	1	2	5	6	3	1	20
0	0	18	247	472	315	139	54	1,246
0	1	175	129	534	397	148	40	1,423
2	2	1	7	16	19	13	6	66
1	6	26	44	99	87	49	16	327
—	—	—	—	—	—	—	—	—
20	6	10	54	49	46	30	15	230
55	82	105	128	179	187	116	41	893
83	63	92	46	36	25	14	7	367
43	18	10	38	109	92	64	37	410
15	**14**	**22**	**38**	**40**	**19**	**13**	**6**	**165**
44	**40**	**141**	**358**	**657**	**545**	**331**	**73**	**2,190**
248	**22**	**25**	**23**	**39**	**30**	**20**	**6**	**414**
3,267	2,059	6,882	3,947	2,113	991	925	376	20,561
—	778	3,194	2,753	1,502	521	106	23	8,876
0	64	902	104	3	1	0	0	1,075
1	34	1,076	215	107	23	14	4	1,473
210	255	240	83	61	21	14	3	887
—	6	13	12	10	6	2	1	49
40	17	17	6	48	185	538	276	1,127
0	—	0	22	54	37	42	10	165
1	13	59	37	9	2	1	0	121
—	7	37	65	33	2	1	0	145
—	5	209	119	61	2	1	0	398
—	7	171	137	51	8	2	0	376
—	19	647	6	26	3	2	0	703
—	7	115	128	82	45	18	2	398
70	752	57	163	3	0	0	0	1,044
953	2	2	0	0	0	0	0	957
1,993	93	145	96	62	136	183	57	2,765
2	**2**	**200**	**2,950**	**4,221**	**2,321**	**1,002**	**230**	**10,926**
—	0	5	23	42	30	15	4	119
0	1	157	1,208	2,242	1,207	606	159	5,580
0	0	18	153	379	253	112	28	943
—	—	18	1,565	1,558	829	267	39	4,275
1	1	2	1	1	1	2	0	9
769	**447**	**1,433**	**1,762**	**5,206**	**7,157**	**6,238**	**1,623**	**24,635**
199	139	261	198	274	169	127	35	1,402
12	16	26	54	188	197	159	59	712
49	77	610	922	2,670	3,690	2,887	684	11,590
59	44	65	178	1,261	2,301	2,072	540	6,521
90	36	107	97	138	126	135	40	769
359	136	364	312	676	674	857	265	3,642
890	**528**	**603**	**749**	**2,414**	**1,239**	**1,052**	**279**	**7,755**
3	0	2	348	1,904	1,022	870	223	4,372
163	427	480	278	306	48	28	8	1,737
725	101	121	124	204	169	154	49	1,646

(Continues on the following page.)

Cause	Total	Male 0–4	5–14	15–29	30–44	45–59	60–69	70–79	80+	Total
I. Digestive diseases	**16,010**	**2,597**	**389**	**838**	**1,126**	**1,809**	**778**	**426**	**133**	**8,096**
1. Peptic ulcer disease	1,901	54	48	196	270	389	129	76	19	1,182
2. Cirrhosis of the liver	4,249	192	110	239	364	761	339	165	35	2,205
3. Appendicitis	113	1	4	8	7	19	10	8	3	60
Other digestive diseases	9,747	2,349	227	396	484	640	300	176	76	4,649
J. Genitourinary diseases	**3,991**	**328**	**114**	**186**	**285**	**946**	**326**	**210**	**56**	**2,452**
1. Nephritis and nephrosis	2,387	133	106	165	236	331	199	132	34	1,334
2. Benign prostatic hypertrophy	692	—	—	—	7	546	80	47	12	692
Other genitourinary system diseases	913	195	9	21	43	69	47	32	11	426
K. Skin diseases	**896**	**199**	**78**	**73**	**53**	**55**	**24**	**15**	**5**	**502**
L. Musculoskeletal diseases	**5,586**	**77**	**129**	**373**	**850**	**778**	**289**	**117**	**26**	**2,639**
1. Rheumatoid arthritis	848	5	27	56	54	69	31	15	3	261
2. Osteoarthritis	2,577	—	0	111	297	349	164	52	8	981
3. Gout	841	—	—	42	405	254	40	10	1	752
4. Low back pain	453	22	51	51	51	46	14	5	1	241
Other musculoskeletal disorders	868	49	51	112	44	60	40	34	13	403
M. Congenital anomalies	**8,101**	**3,771**	**73**	**128**	**7**	**3**	**1**	**1**	**0**	**3,984**
1. Abdominal wall defect	18	8	—	—	—	—	—	—	—	8
2. Anencephaly	322	153	—	—	—	—	—	—	—	153
3. Anorectal atresia	2	1	—	—	—	—	—	—	—	1
4. Cleft lip	24	13	—	—	—	—	—	—	—	13
5. Cleft palate	41	20	—	0	0	—	—	—	—	21
6. Esophageal atresia	7	3	—	—	—	—	—	—	—	3
7. Renal agenesis	18	9	0	—	—	—	0	—	—	9
8. Down syndrome	1,753	838	21	46	—	—	—	—	—	905
9. Congenital heart anomalies	4,881	2,223	43	76	4	1	1	1	0	2,348
10. Spina bifida	588	281	1	0	0	0	0	0	—	283
Other congenital anomalies	449	222	8	6	3	2	1	1	0	241
N. Oral conditions	**1,824**	**149**	**107**	**141**	**68**	**200**	**187**	**46**	**8**	**907**
1. Dental caries	1,189	144	107	126	46	93	58	27	7	607
2. Periodontal disease	84	—	—	11	20	8	3	1	0	43
3. Edentulism	518	—	—	1	1	99	126	16	1	244
Other oral diseases	32	6	1	3	2	1	0	1	0	12
III. Injuries	*46,136*	*2,103*	*3,984*	*8,472*	*5,926*	*3,107*	*926*	*529*	*157*	*25,205*
A. Unintentional injuries	**36,774**	**2,003**	**3,717**	**5,865**	**4,192**	**2,432**	**772**	**438**	**127**	**19,545**
1. Road traffic accidents	7,424	266	691	1,624	1,511	796	174	91	23	5,176
2. Poisonings	1,844	24	100	224	182	331	92	25	6	985
3. Falls	4,907	421	680	644	358	238	152	152	54	2,697
4. Fires	5,905	272	264	528	433	162	38	19	5	1,722
5. Drownings	2,256	149	349	456	215	117	36	23	6	1,351
6. Other unintentional injuries	14,439	872	1,633	2,389	1,492	788	280	127	33	7,613
B. Intentional injuries	**9,362**	**100**	**267**	**2,607**	**1,734**	**674**	**154**	**92**	**31**	**5,660**
1. Self-inflicted injuries	6,015	—	109	1,564	956	404	86	53	13	3,183
2. Violence	2,376	44	140	665	474	195	43	31	15	1,607
3. War	819	43	8	337	275	65	19	4	1	754
Other intentional injuries	152	13	10	41	29	11	7	4	1	116

				Female				
0–4	**5–14**	**15–29**	**30–44**	**45–59**	**60–69**	**70–79**	**80+**	**Total**
2,717	**682**	**1,081**	**923**	**1,305**	**638**	**424**	**143**	**7,914**
60	36	93	148	205	90	68	18	719
513	247	319	241	397	179	120	27	2,043
1	4	5	4	14	12	10	3	53
2,143	395	664	529	690	357	226	94	5,098
224	**94**	**151**	**217**	**372**	**256**	**175**	**51**	**1,539**
118	88	131	110	263	181	128	34	1,053
—	—	—	—	—	—	—	—	—
106	7	19	107	109	74	47	17	486
132	**47**	**58**	**55**	**48**	**28**	**20**	**7**	**395**
68	**163**	**371**	**747**	**907**	**467**	**175**	**48**	**2,946**
3	57	116	145	165	66	31	5	587
0	1	138	446	597	318	82	13	1,595
—	—	6	45	24	9	5	1	89
11	61	34	50	38	12	4	1	212
54	45	77	62	83	62	53	28	464
3,917	**75**	**116**	**4**	**4**	**1**	**1**	**0**	**4,118**
9	—	—	—	—	—	—	—	9
169	—	—	—	—	0	—	—	169
1	—	—	—	—	—	—	—	1
11	—	—	—	—	—	—	—	11
20	—	—	—	0	—	—	—	20
3	—	—	—	—	—	—	—	3
9	0	—	—	—	0	—	—	9
784	21	43	—	—	—	—	—	848
2,417	45	67	2	1	1	1	0	2,533
303	1	0	0	0	—	0	0	305
190	8	6	2	2	0	0	0	208
141	**101**	**134**	**65**	**195**	**205**	**65**	**11**	**917**
136	100	117	42	89	61	30	8	582
—	0	10	18	8	3	2	0	41
—	—	1	1	98	140	33	2	274
5	2	6	4	1	1	0	0	20
2,689	*4,076*	*6,718*	*3,484*	*2,280*	*928*	*592*	*163*	*20,931*
2,624	**3,770**	**4,782**	**2,733**	**1,824**	**819**	**527**	**150**	**17,229**
331	586	456	353	358	94	55	15	2,248
30	111	152	139	189	189	39	11	858
427	677	374	190	191	124	181	46	2,209
538	693	1,595	868	316	95	60	17	4,182
194	266	224	98	59	33	24	7	905
1,104	1,438	1,982	1,084	711	285	168	55	6,826
65	**306**	**1,937**	**751**	**455**	**109**	**65**	**13**	**3,702**
0	196	1,697	549	300	45	35	10	2,832
55	96	218	181	133	56	28	2	769
1	8	14	18	17	5	2	1	65
9	6	7	4	5	3	1	0	36

Source: Authors' compilation.

Note: — = an estimate of zero; the number zero in a cell indicates a non-zero estimate of less than 500.

a. Does not include liver cancer and cirrhosis DALYs(3,0) resulting from chronic hepatitis virus infection.

b. This cause category includes "Causes arising in the perinatal period" as defined in the International Classification of Diseases, principally low birthweight, prematurity, birth asphyxia, and birth trauma, and does not include all causes of DALYs(3,0) occurring in the perinatal period.

Table 3C.7 DALYs(3,0) by Cause, Sex, and Age in the Sub-Saharan Africa Region, 2001 (*thousands*)

Cause	Total	Male 0–4	5–14	15–29	30–44	45–59	60–69	70–79	80+	Total
Population (millions)	*668*	*57*	*92*	*93*	*49*	*26*	*9*	*4*	*1*	*331*
All causes	**344,754**	**84,575**	**13,040**	**23,098**	**26,058**	**16,033**	**7,197**	**4,076**	**1,064**	**175,141**
I. **Communicable, maternal, perinatal, and nutritional conditions**	*242,837*	*74,911*	*7,172*	*10,377*	*16,077*	*7,005*	*2,046*	*752*	*154*	*118,494*
A. **Infectious and parasitic diseases**	**173,484**	**46,407**	**5,827**	**9,866**	**15,439**	**6,331**	**1,563**	**495**	**99**	**86,027**
1. **Tuberculosis**	**8,084**	**397**	**241**	**1,489**	**1,792**	**1,038**	**285**	**91**	**18**	**5,350**
2. **Sexually transmitted diseases excluding HIV/AIDS**	**3,842**	**775**	**6**	**238**	**285**	**336**	**38**	**0**	**0**	**1,679**
a. Syphilis	2,347	560	1	63	235	327	37	0	0	1,223
b. Chlamydia	559	12	1	34	5	0	0	—	—	52
c. Gonorrhea	894	191	4	141	40	3	0	—	—	379
d. Other sexually transmitted diseases	41	12	0	1	5	6	1	0	0	24
3. **HIV/AIDS**	**56,820**	**4,894**	**1,452**	**6,047**	**11,262**	**2,995**	**325**	**29**	**0**	**27,005**
4. **Diarrheal diseases**	**22,046**	**10,797**	**160**	**93**	**127**	**130**	**88**	**71**	**39**	**11,506**
5. **Childhood-cluster diseases**	**23,198**	**9,709**	**1,502**	**213**	**86**	**41**	**11**	**4**	**1**	**11,568**
a. Pertussis	6,116	3,031	15	—	—	—	—	—	—	3,047
b. Poliomyelitis	17	8	—	—	—	—	—	—	—	8
c. Diphtheria	45	26	0	0	—	—	—	—	—	26
d. Measles	13,539	5,354	1,312	85	—	—	—	—	—	6,752
e. Tetanus	3,481	1,289	174	128	86	41	11	4	1	1,735
6. **Meningitis**	**941**	**261**	**85**	**35**	**43**	**32**	**8**	**3**	**0**	**469**
7. **Hepatitis B[a]**	**536**	**43**	**95**	**25**	**77**	**41**	**16**	**3**	**0**	**301**
Hepatitis C[a]	**217**	**17**	**40**	**10**	**32**	**17**	**7**	**1**	**0**	**124**
8. **Malaria**	**35,447**	**15,487**	**287**	**338**	**294**	**220**	**102**	**58**	**15**	**16,801**
9. **Tropical-cluster diseases**	**4,897**	**215**	**1,019**	**1,003**	**594**	**350**	**64**	**26**	**5**	**3,277**
a. Trypanosomiasis	1,310	66	318	185	146	102	9	3	0	830
b. Chagas' disease	—	—	—	—	—	—	—	—	—	—
c. Schistosomiasis	1,184	82	253	175	106	51	22	10	2	701
d. Leishmaniasis	312	29	85	70	31	5	2	1	0	223
e. Lymphatic filariasis	1,656	31	343	537	241	108	6	2	0	1,269
f. Onchocerciasis	436	7	20	36	70	83	25	10	3	255
10. **Leprosy**	**24**	**0**	**2**	**1**	**1**	**9**	**0**	**1**	**—**	**14**
11. **Dengue**	**4**	**0**	**1**	**0**	**0**	**0**	**0**	**0**	**0**	**2**
12. **Japanese encephalitis**	**—**	**—**	**—**	**—**	**—**	**—**	**—**	**—**	**—**	**—**
13. **Trachoma**	**1,455**	**0**	**1**	**15**	**84**	**116**	**83**	**48**	**11**	**357**
14. **Intestinal nematode infections**	**905**	**80**	**343**	**10**	**5**	**7**	**4**	**2**	**0**	**452**
a. Ascariasis	476	45	191	0	0	0	0	0	0	235
b. Trichuriasis	119	10	45	1	1	1	1	0	0	58
c. Hookworm disease	309	26	107	8	5	6	4	1	0	158
Other intestinal infections	1	0	0	0	0	0	0	0	0	1
Other infectious diseases	15,068	3,731	592	348	756	1,000	530	158	7	7,123
B. **Respiratory infections**	**31,107**	**13,774**	**971**	**320**	**533**	**590**	**399**	**212**	**46**	**16,846**
1. Lower respiratory infections	30,455	13,619	845	310	514	586	389	208	46	16,517
2. Upper respiratory infections	371	105	31	8	11	4	11	4	0	173
3. Otitis media	281	50	96	3	7	—	0	—	—	156
C. **Maternal conditions**	**9,743**	**—**	**—**	**—**	**—**	**—**	**—**	**—**	**—**	**—**
1. Maternal hemorrhage	1,643	—	—	—	—	—	—	—	—	—
2. Maternal sepsis	1,843	—	—	—	—	—	—	—	—	—
3. Hypertensive disorders of pregnancy	842	—	—	—	—	—	—	—	—	—
4. Obstructed labor	919	—	—	—	—	—	—	—	—	—
5. Abortion	1,557	—	—	—	—	—	—	—	—	—
Other maternal conditions	2,940	—	—	—	—	—	—	—	—	—
D. **Perinatal conditions[b]**	**20,047**	**11,351**	**—**	**—**	**—**	**—**	**—**	**—**	**—**	**11,351**
1. Low birthweight	7,891	4,501	—	—	—	—	—	—	—	4,501
2. Birth asphyxia and birth trauma	9,256	5,195	—	—	—	—	—	—	—	5,195
Other perinatal conditions	2,899	1,655	—	—	—	—	—	—	—	1,655
E. **Nutritional deficiencies**	**8,455**	**3,378**	**373**	**191**	**105**	**84**	**84**	**46**	**9**	**4,271**
1. Protein-energy malnutrition	5,220	2,496	53	8	11	46	62	38	8	2,722
2. Iodine deficiency	951	383	100	0	1	1	1	0	0	487
3. Vitamin A deficiency	548	206	20	2	5	9	5	1	0	249
4. Iron-deficiency anemia	1,688	273	199	180	88	27	16	6	1	789
Other nutritional disorders	49	20	1	0	0	1	1	0	0	24

Table 3C.7 Continued

	Female								
	0–4	5–14	15–29	30–44	45–59	60–69	70–79	80+	Total
	56	*91*	*93*	*51*	*28*	*11*	*5*	*1*	*336*
	76,795	**12,562**	**29,616**	**22,752**	**13,624**	**7,514**	**5,165**	**1,585**	**169,613**
	68,898	*8,056*	*22,639*	*16,570*	*5,500*	*1,586*	*866*	*228*	*124,343*
	46,986	**6,290**	**15,133**	**12,539**	**4,531**	**1,219**	**605**	**154**	**87,458**
	358	**233**	**945**	**715**	**290**	**142**	**45**	**7**	**2,734**
	602	**21**	**1,001**	**359**	**130**	**32**	**17**	**0**	**2,163**
	394	1	355	207	121	30	16	0	1,124
	12	14	415	60	5	1	—	—	507
	188	7	227	90	2	0	—	—	515
	8	0	3	2	2	1	1	0	17
	4,748	**1,432**	**11,064**	**9,966**	**2,299**	**266**	**41**	**0**	**29,815**
	9,910	**160**	**63**	**69**	**100**	**93**	**89**	**56**	**10,540**
	9,702	**1,558**	**220**	**88**	**44**	**13**	**5**	**2**	**11,630**
	3,054	15	—	—	—	—	—	—	3,069
	9	—	—	—	—	—	—	—	9
	19	0	—	—	—	—	—	—	19
	5,336	1,363	89	—	—	—	—	—	6,787
	1,284	180	131	88	44	13	5	2	1,746
	231	**150**	**53**	**15**	**17**	**4**	**2**	**0**	**473**
	123	**22**	**42**	**14**	**26**	**6**	**2**	**0**	**235**
	48	**9**	**16**	**6**	**10**	**3**	**1**	**0**	**93**
	17,133	304	409	317	267	121	73	21	18,646
	151	487	422	267	230	39	20	5	1,620
	37	184	119	77	55	6	2	0	480
	—	—	—	—	—	—	—	—	—
	55	170	129	74	36	10	8	2	483
	10	36	28	12	2	1	0	0	89
	42	78	114	54	88	8	2	0	387
	7	20	32	50	49	15	7	2	181
	0	**2**	**1**	**1**	**1**	**3**	**1**	**0**	**9**
	0	**2**	**0**	**0**	**0**	**0**	**0**	**0**	**3**
	—	—	—	—	—	—	—	—	—
	1	**2**	**27**	**236**	**330**	**278**	**175**	**48**	**1,097**
	79	**352**	**7**	**4**	**5**	**4**	**1**	**0**	**453**
	44	196	0	0	0	0	0	0	241
	10	49	1	0	1	0	0	0	61
	25	107	6	3	5	3	1	0	151
	—	0	0	0	0	0	0	0	1
	3,900	1,556	864	481	781	215	133	13	7,945
	9,948	**1,349**	**1,108**	**720**	**550**	**294**	**222**	**69**	**14,261**
	9,841	1,159	1,094	716	549	289	221	69	13,938
	60	117	9	4	1	5	2	0	198
	46	74	5	0	—	—	—	—	125
	—	69	6,169	3,156	350	—	—	—	9,743
	—	—	797	734	112	—	—	—	1,643
	—	—	1,131	632	80	—	—	—	1,843
	—	0	530	280	32	—	—	—	842
	—	—	655	253	11	—	—	—	919
	—	69	1,281	207	0	—	—	—	1,557
	—	0	1,774	1,051	114	—	—	—	2,940
	8,696	—	—	—	—	—	—	—	**8,696**
	3,391	—	—	—	—	—	—	—	3,391
	4,062	—	—	—	—	—	—	—	4,062
	1,244	—	—	—	—	—	—	—	1,244
	3,269	**347**	**229**	**154**	**70**	**72**	**38**	**5**	**4,184**
	2,322	40	18	13	19	54	28	4	2,498
	365	95	1	0	1	0	0	0	464
	238	37	8	4	8	3	1	0	299
	323	173	200	137	41	15	8	1	899
	20	2	1	0	1	0	0	0	25

(Continues on the following page.)

Table 3C.7 Continued

Cause	Total	Male 0–4	5–14	15–29	30–44	45–59	60–69	70–79	80+	Total
II. Noncommunicable diseases	**73,069**	**7,276**	**1,930**	**5,350**	**5,335**	**7,218**	**4,673**	**3,166**	**880**	**35,829**
A. Malignant neoplasms	**6,281**	**53**	**87**	**174**	**377**	**972**	**780**	**524**	**125**	**3,092**
1. Mouth and oropharynx cancers	284	0	2	8	24	73	54	27	5	193
2. Esophageal cancer	343	0	0	2	21	90	62	31	6	212
3. Stomach cancer	487	1	2	8	32	102	63	41	10	258
4. Colon and rectal cancers	291	0	1	9	29	48	35	27	8	158
5. Liver cancer	762	3	3	29	107	204	112	47	7	512
6. Pancreas cancer	117	0	0	0	5	23	15	7	2	52
7. Trachea, bronchus, and lung cancers	225	0	0	1	13	72	52	19	3	162
8. Melanoma and other skin cancers	118	0	0	3	6	19	15	7	2	53
9. Breast cancer	574	—	—	—	0	0	0	0	0	1
10. Cervix uteri cancer	627	—	—	—	—	—	—	—	—	—
11. Corpus uteri cancer	41	—	—	—	—	—	—	—	—	—
12. Ovarian cancer	152	—	—	—	—	—	—	—	—	—
13. Prostate cancer	416	0	0	1	2	53	146	170	44	416
14. Bladder cancer	133	0	0	1	5	25	26	23	7	88
15. Lymphomas and multiple myeloma	622	17	51	61	69	85	58	36	9	386
16. Leukemia	245	7	12	32	16	28	16	14	3	128
Other malignant neoplasms	844	24	15	19	48	149	124	73	19	472
B. Other neoplasms	**188**	**16**	**13**	**16**	**12**	**19**	**12**	**6**	**1**	**95**
C. Diabetes mellitus	**1,448**	**4**	**8**	**39**	**100**	**181**	**122**	**75**	**18**	**547**
D. Endocrine disorders	**2,706**	**1,074**	**34**	**61**	**64**	**117**	**42**	**26**	**8**	**1,425**
E. Neuropsychiatric conditions	**15,151**	**1,768**	**802**	**2,970**	**1,122**	**558**	**199**	**129**	**45**	**7,593**
1. Unipolar depressive disorders	3,275	—	306	426	334	169	46	8	1	1,291
2. Bipolar affective disorder	1,204	—	48	524	41	1	0	—	—	615
3. Schizophrenia	1,146	—	28	492	34	2	0	0	0	556
4. Epilepsy	1,373	107	145	228	155	89	36	12	4	777
5. Alcohol use disorders	685	—	10	274	197	97	15	6	1	600
6. Alzheimer's and other dementias	450	29	9	6	5	16	36	65	30	197
7. Parkinson's disease	100	0	0	—	5	15	15	15	4	54
8. Multiple sclerosis	77	—	4	13	9	1	0	0	0	29
9. Drug use disorders	929	—	11	472	165	49	2	0	0	699
10. Post-traumatic stress disorder	224	—	4	35	14	8	0	0	0	61
11. Obsessive-compulsive disorder	619	—	59	145	32	14	3	0	0	254
12. Panic disorder	519	—	11	155	2	5	1	0	0	174
13. Insomnia (primary)	234	—	1	58	41	23	10	3	0	136
14. Migraine	329	18	42	21	10	0	0	0	0	92
15. Mental retardation, lead-caused	1,505	753	0	0	0	0	0	—	—	753
Other neuropsychiatric disorders	2,481	861	122	120	77	68	34	19	4	1,306
F. Sense organ diseases	**8,939**	**15**	**71**	**495**	**1,270**	**1,233**	**569**	**268**	**58**	**3,980**
1. Glaucoma	937	3	10	49	124	140	55	28	7	416
2. Cataracts	5,169	11	57	254	623	746	327	167	39	2,224
3. Vision disorders, age-related	920	1	4	20	116	161	60	28	7	397
4. Hearing loss, adult onset	1,912	—	—	171	407	187	126	46	5	942
Other sense organ disorders	2	0	0	0	0	0	0	0	0	1
G. Cardiovascular diseases	**15,069**	**160**	**108**	**382**	**916**	**1,856**	**1,630**	**1,286**	**401**	**6,738**
1. Rheumatic heart disease	479	20	37	54	24	18	4	5	2	165
2. Hypertensive heart disease	937	1	2	9	42	103	88	68	24	338
3. Ischemic heart disease	4,579	2	13	42	188	772	733	537	112	2,399
4. Cerebrovascular disease	5,125	14	22	100	272	590	541	422	118	2,077
5. Inflammatory heart diseases	945	79	18	71	105	100	59	43	15	490
Other cardiovascular diseases	3,004	43	16	107	284	273	204	212	129	1,268
H. Respiratory diseases	**6,150**	**764**	**351**	**407**	**393**	**633**	**535**	**374**	**102**	**3,559**
1. Chronic obstructive pulmonary disease	1,631	14	6	30	113	296	308	234	62	1,065
2. Asthma	1,925	286	285	263	81	80	47	25	6	1,074
Other respiratory diseases	2,595	464	59	114	199	256	180	115	33	1,420

Table 3C.7 Continued

			Female					
0–4	5–14	15–29	30–44	45–59	60–69	70–79	80+	Total
6,272	*2,049*	*5,159*	*5,064*	*7,469*	*5,708*	*4,191*	*1,327*	*37,240*
55	**90**	**158**	**450**	**1,081**	**740**	**504**	**110**	**3,189**
1	1	2	10	30	23	20	4	91
0	0	2	12	48	38	26	6	131
0	2	7	29	82	59	39	11	229
0	1	4	24	45	30	22	7	133
3	2	22	51	77	49	39	7	250
0	0	1	8	26	17	10	2	64
0	1	1	7	22	18	11	2	63
0	0	2	7	15	19	18	3	64
0	1	7	104	229	133	81	18	574
0	0	41	64	247	162	98	14	627
0	0	1	6	12	10	10	2	41
0	3	10	26	55	34	20	4	152
—	—	—	—	—	—	—	—	—
0	0	1	5	13	15	9	3	45
17	48	29	31	39	34	30	7	236
7	12	17	13	35	19	12	3	118
26	18	11	54	107	79	59	18	372
5	**17**	**7**	**12**	**24**	**16**	**10**	**2**	**93**
2	**7**	**41**	**100**	**290**	**261**	**168**	**33**	**901**
745	**38**	**84**	**66**	**156**	**107**	**64**	**20**	**1,281**
1,704	**932**	**2,797**	**1,095**	**560**	**236**	**158**	**75**	**7,558**
—	301	711	567	300	87	16	3	1,985
—	14	529	45	2	0	—	—	590
—	8	469	103	5	2	1	0	590
98	147	180	77	58	19	13	4	596
—	6	25	26	19	4	5	0	85
26	8	7	5	18	51	84	55	253
0	—	0	4	14	12	10	6	46
—	7	20	15	5	1	0	0	48
—	9	143	62	16	1	0	0	230
—	3	97	40	22	1	0	0	162
—	197	94	56	10	7	2	0	365
—	13	317	4	10	1	1	0	346
—	5	22	37	20	11	2	1	98
9	121	97	10	0	0	0	0	237
752	0	0	0	0	—	—	—	752
820	94	87	46	61	37	23	5	1,174
5	**22**	**428**	**1,519**	**1,661**	**828**	**398**	**100**	**4,959**
1	3	49	144	187	82	42	12	522
3	17	230	804	1,015	534	271	69	2,944
0	2	29	128	219	89	43	13	522
—	—	119	443	239	122	41	5	970
0	0	0	0	0	0	0	0	1
165	**145**	**458**	**739**	**1,983**	**2,180**	**1,953**	**710**	**8,331**
15	45	96	68	54	22	12	2	314
1	1	9	52	148	166	160	62	599
2	21	23	93	545	738	586	173	2,180
8	27	82	221	825	894	752	239	3,048
53	22	62	74	100	72	53	19	455
86	28	186	231	312	288	391	216	1,736
537	**338**	**365**	**208**	**372**	**358**	**311**	**103**	**2,592**
12	0	15	32	141	157	157	52	566
152	289	218	41	61	47	33	10	851
374	48	132	135	170	154	121	41	1,175

(Continues on the following page.)

Cause	Total	Male 0–4	5–14	15–29	30–44	45–59	60–69	70–79	80+	Total
I. Digestive diseases	**7,226**	**1,139**	**163**	**419**	**592**	**812**	**413**	**244**	**54**	**3,836**
1. Peptic ulcer disease	345	2	2	42	51	57	26	14	5	199
2. Cirrhosis of the liver	1,212	3	4	64	173	278	139	78	12	750
3. Appendicitis	44	0	10	4	5	3	2	1	0	25
Other digestive diseases	5,626	1,134	147	309	363	474	246	151	38	2,863
J. Genitourinary diseases	**2,623**	**230**	**70**	**100**	**124**	**452**	**174**	**142**	**50**	**1,341**
1. Nephritis and nephrosis	1,633	96	59	79	96	129	131	101	35	727
2. Benign prostatic hypertrophy	292	—	—	—	—	263	13	11	5	292
Other genitourinary system diseases	697	134	11	21	28	59	30	30	9	322
K. Skin diseases	**956**	**135**	**51**	**71**	**93**	**63**	**34**	**26**	**9**	**482**
L. Musculoskeletal diseases	**2,171**	**36**	**67**	**160**	**253**	**275**	**116**	**59**	**9**	**975**
1. Rheumatoid arthritis	252	2	7	15	31	23	11	4	1	94
2. Osteoarthritis	1,278	—	1	57	143	194	84	40	5	523
3. Gout	94	—	0	8	41	23	7	3	1	83
4. Low back pain	214	14	28	25	20	18	4	2	0	113
Other musculoskeletal disorders	333	20	31	55	18	18	8	9	3	162
M. Congenital anomalies	**3,441**	**1,746**	**46**	**21**	**5**	**2**	**0**	**0**	**0**	**1,819**
1. Abdominal wall defect	36	20	—	—	—	—	—	—	—	20
2. Anencephaly	47	23	0	—	—	—	—	—	—	23
3. Anorectal atresia	14	9	0	—	—	—	—	—	—	9
4. Cleft lip	12	6	—	—	—	—	—	—	—	6
5. Cleft palate	28	11	—	—	—	—	—	—	—	11
6. Esophageal atresia	2	1	0	—	—	—	—	—	—	1
7. Renal agenesis	2	2	—	—	—	—	0	—	—	2
8. Down syndrome	419	244	1	2	0	0	—	—	—	248
9. Congenital heart anomalies	1,651	821	18	7	2	1	0	0	0	849
10. Spina bifida	293	142	3	1	—	—	—	—	—	146
Other congenital anomalies	938	465	23	11	3	1	0	0	0	504
N. Oral conditions	**720**	**137**	**60**	**35**	**14**	**45**	**48**	**7**	**1**	**347**
1. Dental caries	496	130	60	30	8	13	5	2	0	248
2. Periodontal disease	23	—	—	4	5	1	0	0	0	11
3. Edentulism	181	—	—	—	—	31	43	5	0	80
Other oral diseases	21	6	1	0	0	0	0	0	0	8
III. Injuries	***28,848***	***2,388***	***3,937***	***7,371***	***4,647***	***1,809***	***479***	***157***	***29***	***20,819***
A. Unintentional injuries	**18,876**	**2,241**	**3,518**	**3,262**	**2,036**	**1,023**	**290**	**104**	**18**	**12,491**
1. Road traffic accidents	6,374	424	1,412	964	807	425	113	37	5	4,186
2. Poisonings	954	143	120	126	145	51	15	0	0	599
3. Falls	976	109	224	113	65	60	27	17	4	619
4. Fires	1,739	441	453	69	37	38	12	5	1	1,057
5. Drownings	1,720	204	322	293	305	153	15	0	0	1,294
6. Other unintentional injuries	7,112	919	988	1,698	677	296	108	44	7	4,736
B. Intentional injuries	**9,972**	**148**	**419**	**4,109**	**2,611**	**787**	**189**	**54**	**12**	**8,328**
1. Self-inflicted injuries	882	—	57	272	174	115	29	13	2	663
2. Violence	4,996	116	318	2,161	1,019	314	59	18	2	4,007
3. War	4,090	31	44	1,675	1,418	357	101	22	7	3,655
Other intentional injuries	3	1	0	1	0	0	0	0	0	2

Table 3C.7 Continued

			Female					
0–4	5–14	15–29	30–44	45–59	60–69	70–79	80+	Total
1,097	**204**	**381**	**347**	**578**	**428**	**275**	**79**	**3,390**
0	5	24	34	35	24	18	6	146
7	9	35	69	157	119	58	9	462
0	7	8	0	2	1	1	0	19
1,090	184	314	244	384	285	198	64	2,763
155	**69**	**133**	**130**	**308**	**243**	**184**	**58**	**1,281**
62	60	68	78	230	204	158	47	907
—	—	—	—	—	—	—	—	—
93	10	66	53	78	39	26	10	375
71	**25**	**51**	**61**	**94**	**73**	**75**	**24**	**473**
27	**68**	**206**	**319**	**306**	**175**	**81**	**14**	**1,196**
3	11	21	45	43	20	13	2	158
—	1	118	225	213	134	55	9	755
—	0	3	1	3	2	1	0	11
8	36	18	20	14	4	1	0	101
16	20	46	29	33	14	11	3	172
1,569	**33**	**13**	**2**	**2**	**1**	**1**	**0**	**1,622**
16	—	0	—	—	—	—	—	16
24	—	0	—	—	0	—	—	24
4	—	—	—	—	—	—	—	4
6	—	—	—	—	—	—	—	6
17	—	—	—	—	—	—	—	17
1	—	—	—	—	—	—	—	1
0	—	0	—	—	0	—	—	0
166	3	2	—	1	—	—	—	171
782	11	5	2	1	0	1	0	802
146	0	1	0	—	—	—	—	147
407	19	6	1	1	1	0	0	434
135	**61**	**37**	**15**	**53**	**62**	**10**	**1**	**373**
128	59	30	8	14	5	3	1	248
—	—	4	6	1	0	0	0	12
—	—	—	—	37	56	7	0	101
7	2	2	1	0	0	0	0	13
1,625	**2,457**	**1,817**	**1,117**	**655**	**221**	**108**	**29**	**8,030**
1,536	**2,132**	**1,252**	**745**	**445**	**167**	**87**	**22**	**6,385**
336	950	384	261	169	62	22	4	2,188
60	70	90	65	31	25	10	2	355
82	148	39	23	23	17	19	6	357
348	177	62	46	30	8	9	2	682
137	103	113	28	34	12	0	0	426
572	685	564	322	158	43	26	8	2,377
89	**325**	**565**	**373**	**210**	**54**	**21**	**7**	**1,645**
0	13	110	52	32	8	4	1	220
85	187	375	227	86	18	8	3	989
4	125	81	93	92	27	9	3	435
0	0	0	0	0	0	—	0	1

Source: Authors' compilation.

Note: — = an estimate of zero; the number zero in a cell indicates a non-zero estimate of less than 500.

a. Does not include liver cancer and cirrhosis DALYs(3,0) resulting from chronic hepatitis virus infection.

b. This cause category includes "Causes arising in the perinatal period" as defined in the International Classification of Diseases, principally low birthweight prematurity, birth asphyxia, and birth trauma, and does not include all causes of DALYs(3,0) occurring in the perinatal period.

Table 3C.8 DALYs(3,0) by Cause, Sex, and Age in High-Income Countries, 2001
(thousands)

Cause	Total	Male 0–4	5–14	15–29	30–44	45–59	60–69	70–79	80+	Total
Population (millions)	*929*	*28*	*60*	*96*	*107*	*88*	*40*	*27*	*10*	*457*
All causes	**149,161**	**3,641**	**1,706**	**8,093**	**10,396**	**16,700**	**14,284**	**14,522**	**7,444**	**76,786**
I. ***Communicable, maternal, perinatal, and nutritional conditions***	*8,561*	*1,170*	*126*	*365*	*601*	*561*	*411*	*573*	*503*	*4,310*
A. **Infectious and parasitic diseases**	**3,375**	**288**	**68**	**228**	**506**	**375**	**182**	**176**	**86**	**1,909**
1. **Tuberculosis**	**219**	**1**	**1**	**8**	**23**	**36**	**28**	**33**	**15**	**146**
2. **Sexually transmitted diseases excluding HIV/AIDS**	**145**	**7**	**0**	**9**	**9**	**1**	**0**	**0**	**0**	**26**
a. Syphilis	13	5	0	0	0	0	0	0	0	7
b. Chlamydia	100	1	0	4	4	0	0	—	—	9
c. Gonorrhea	27	0	0	5	5	0	0	0	0	10
d. Other sexually transmitted diseases	4	0	—	0	0	0	0	0	0	0
3. **HIV/AIDS**	**665**	**2**	**1**	**84**	**288**	**119**	**14**	**3**	**0**	**510**
4. **Diarrheal diseases**	**444**	**121**	**13**	**20**	**22**	**19**	**11**	**9**	**6**	**222**
5. **Childhood-cluster diseases**	**175**	**70**	**2**	**1**	**1**	**1**	**1**	**1**	**0**	**76**
a. Pertussis	139	68	1	—	—	—	0	—	—	69
b. Poliomyelitis	8	0	0	0	0	1	1	1	0	4
c. Diphtheria	0	0	0	—	0	—	—	0	0	0
d. Measles	23	1	1	0	0	0	—	0	—	3
e. Tetanus	5	0	0	0	0	0	0	0	0	1
6. **Meningitis**	**131**	**27**	**5**	**7**	**7**	**9**	**5**	**4**	**1**	**65**
7. **Hepatitis B**[a]	**86**	**0**	**0**	**2**	**12**	**23**	**10**	**6**	**2**	**55**
Hepatitis C[a]	**185**	**0**	**0**	**1**	**19**	**53**	**22**	**15**	**3**	**113**
8. **Malaria**	**9**	**1**	**0**	**0**	**1**	**2**	**0**	**0**	**0**	**6**
9. **Tropical-cluster diseases**	**219**	**4**	**22**	**75**	**65**	**11**	**2**	**1**	**0**	**180**
a. Trypanosomiasis	0	—	—	—	—	—	0	—	—	0
b. Chagas' disease	1	0	0	0	0	0	0	0	0	0
c. Schistosomiasis	1	0	0	0	0	0	0	0	0	1
d. Leishmaniasis	5	0	0	0	0	0	0	0	0	1
e. Lymphatic filariasis	212	4	21	75	64	11	2	1	0	178
f. Onchocerciasis	0	0	0	0	0	0	0	0	0	0
10. **Leprosy**	**1**	**0**	**0**	**0**	**0**	**0**	**0**	**0**	**0**	**0**
11. **Dengue**	**0**	**0**	**0**	**0**	**0**	**0**	**0**	**0**	**0**	**0**
12. **Japanese encephalitis**	**6**	**1**	**1**	**0**	**0**	**0**	**0**	**0**	**0**	**3**
13. **Trachoma**	**10**	**0**	**0**	**0**	**3**	**2**	**0**	**0**	**0**	**5**
14. **Intestinal nematode infections**	**11**	**1**	**4**	**0**	**0**	**0**	**0**	**0**	**0**	**5**
a. Ascariasis	5	0	2	0	0	0	0	0	0	2
b. Trichuriasis	3	0	1	—	—	—	—	—	—	1
c. Hookworm disease	2	0	1	—	0	0	—	0	0	1
Other intestinal infections	1	0	0	0	0	0	0	0	0	0
Other infectious diseases	1,070	53	18	21	56	101	87	104	58	497
B. **Respiratory infections**	**2,474**	**52**	**46**	**24**	**61**	**141**	**188**	**356**	**396**	**1,264**
1. Lower respiratory infections	2,314	33	10	21	57	137	184	351	391	1,183
2. Upper respiratory infections	60	3	2	3	4	4	4	5	4	30
3. Otitis media	100	17	34	0	0	0	0	0	0	51
C. **Maternal conditions**	**391**	**—**	**—**	**—**	**—**	**—**	**—**	**—**	**—**	**—**
1. Maternal hemorrhage	4	—	—	—	—	—	—	—	—	—
2. Maternal sepsis	78	—	—	—	—	—	—	—	—	—
3. Hypertensive disorders of pregnancy	4	—	—	—	—	—	—	—	—	—
4. Obstructed labor	9	—	—	—	—	—	—	—	—	—
5. Abortion	4	—	—	—	—	—	—	—	—	—
Other maternal conditions	292	—	—	—	—	—	—	—	—	—
D. **Perinatal conditions**[b]	**1,408**	**773**	**1**	**1**	**0**	**0**	**0**	**—**	**—**	**775**
1. Low birthweight	467	252	0	—	0	—	0	—	—	252
2. Birth asphyxia and birth trauma	530	291	1	0	0	0	—	—	—	292
Other perinatal conditions	412	229	0	1	0	0	—	—	—	230
E. **Nutritional deficiencies**	**912**	**57**	**12**	**112**	**33**	**44**	**41**	**41**	**21**	**362**
1. Protein-energy malnutrition	130	35	0	1	2	6	5	6	7	61
2. Iodine deficiency	2	1	0	0	0	0	0	0	0	1
3. Vitamin A deficiency	1	0	0	—	—	—	0	—	0	0
4. Iron-deficiency anemia	758	20	11	111	31	37	35	33	13	291
Other nutritional disorders	21	1	0	0	1	2	1	1	2	9

Table 3C.8 Continued

	Female								
	0–4	5–14	15–29	30–44	45–59	60–69	70–79	80+	Total
	27	*57*	*92*	*105*	*90*	*44*	*36*	*21*	*472*
	3,163	**1,636**	**6,661**	**8,187**	**12,971**	**11,408**	**15,017**	**13,333**	**72,375**
	1,007	*206*	*626*	*532*	*350*	*290*	*511*	*729*	*4,251*
	275	**113**	**192**	**252**	**174**	**140**	**184**	**136**	**1,466**
	1	**4**	**7**	**9**	**10**	**11**	**20**	**12**	**73**
	6	**2**	**79**	**27**	**2**	**1**	**1**	**1**	**119**
	5	0	0	0	0	0	0	0	6
	1	2	69	18	1	0	—	0	91
	0	0	9	8	0	0	0	0	18
	0	0	0	1	1	1	1	1	4
	2	**2**	**32**	**88**	**28**	**3**	**1**	**0**	**155**
	114	**13**	**19**	**22**	**18**	**11**	**13**	**13**	**222**
	71	**22**	**1**	**1**	**1**	**1**	**1**	**1**	**99**
	70	1	0	—	0	—	—	—	70
	0	0	0	0	1	1	1	0	4
	0	0	—	—	0	—	—	—	0
	2	18	0	0	0	—	—	0	20
	0	3	0	0	0	0	0	0	4
	23	**12**	**7**	**6**	**7**	**5**	**5**	**2**	**66**
	0	**0**	**1**	**4**	**8**	**8**	**7**	**2**	**30**
	0	**0**	**1**	**7**	**18**	**20**	**20**	**6**	**72**
	1	**1**	**0**	**0**	**0**	**0**	**0**	**0**	**4**
	1	**7**	**15**	**13**	**2**	**0**	**0**	**0**	**38**
	—	0	—	0	—	—	—	—	0
	0	0	0	0	0	0	0	0	0
	0	0	0	0	0	0	0	0	0
	0	4	0	0	0	0	0	0	4
	1	3	14	13	1	0	0	0	34
	—	0	0	0	0	0	0	0	0
	0	**0**	**0**	**0**	**0**	**0**	**0**	**0**	**0**
	0	**0**	**0**	**0**	**0**	**0**	**0**	**0**	**0**
	1	**2**	**0**	**0**	**0**	**0**	**0**	**0**	**3**
	0	**0**	**0**	**2**	**1**	**0**	**0**	**0**	**5**
	1	**4**	**0**	**0**	**0**	**0**	**0**	**0**	**5**
	0	2	0	0	0	0	0	0	2
	0	1	—	0	—	—	—	—	2
	0	1	0	—	—	0	—	—	1
	0	0	0	0	0	0	0	0	0
	53	44	31	74	79	78	115	99	573
	46	**59**	**19**	**41**	**86**	**113**	**291**	**555**	**1,210**
	28	25	15	37	82	110	286	548	1,131
	2	2	4	4	3	3	6	7	31
	16	32	0	0	0	0	0	0	49
	0	**0**	**241**	**150**	**1**	**—**	**0**	**0**	**391**
	0	0	1	2	0	—	—	—	4
	—	0	56	22	0	—	—	—	78
	—	0	2	2	0	—	—	0	4
	—	—	6	3	0	—	—	—	9
	—	0	3	1	0	—	—	—	4
	—	0	172	119	0	—	0	0	292
	632	**1**	**0**	**0**	**0**	**0**	**0**	**0**	**634**
	215	0	—	—	—	—	—	—	215
	237	0	0	—	0	—	0	0	237
	181	0	0	0	0	0	0	0	182
	54	**33**	**174**	**89**	**89**	**37**	**35**	**38**	**550**
	33	3	1	2	3	4	8	16	69
	1	0	0	0	0	0	0	0	1
	0	0	—	—	—	—	0	0	1
	20	28	173	85	85	33	25	18	467
	1	1	1	2	1	1	2	4	12

(Continues on the following page.)

Table 3C.8 Continued

Cause	Total	Male								Total
		0–4	5–14	15–29	30–44	45–59	60–69	70–79	80+	
II. Noncommunicable diseases	*129,356*	*2,238*	*1,189*	*5,421*	*7,675*	*14,623*	*13,311*	*13,573*	*6,756*	*64,784*
A. Malignant neoplasms	**25,888**	**30**	**55**	**189**	**764**	**3,587**	**4,150**	**3,840**	**1,334**	**13,949**
1. Mouth and oropharynx cancers	576	0	0	4	38	193	120	65	17	437
2. Esophageal cancer	702	0	0	1	25	195	184	124	32	561
3. Stomach cancer	1,628	0	0	6	59	258	313	282	99	1,017
4. Colon and rectal cancers	3,175	0	0	9	79	422	519	484	179	1,692
5. Liver cancer	1,223	1	1	6	49	265	291	204	46	863
6. Pancreas cancer	1,232	0	0	1	30	191	207	172	53	654
7. Trachea, bronchus, and lung cancers	5,397	0	0	4	125	945	1,193	1,066	271	3,606
8. Melanoma and other skin cancers	409	0	0	7	36	80	55	46	19	244
9. Breast cancer	2,509	0	—	0	2	5	4	4	2	17
10. Cervix uteri cancer	319	—	—	—	—	—	—	—	—	—
11. Corpus uteri cancer	586	—	—	—	—	—	—	—	—	—
12. Ovarian cancer	651	—	—	—	—	—	—	—	—	—
13. Prostate cancer	1,212	0	0	0	4	104	309	500	295	1,212
14. Bladder cancer	670	0	0	2	12	94	137	172	80	497
15. Lymphomas and multiple myeloma	1,362	1	4	27	68	184	192	189	66	730
16. Leukemia	919	11	20	47	57	105	113	118	47	518
Other malignant neoplasms	3,316	16	29	74	182	546	512	414	128	1,901
B. Other neoplasms	**556**	**6**	**5**	**11**	**23**	**55**	**65**	**78**	**43**	**286**
C. Diabetes mellitus	**4,192**	**1**	**3**	**43**	**300**	**676**	**465**	**384**	**159**	**2,032**
D. Endocrine disorders	**2,442**	**355**	**46**	**73**	**127**	**190**	**114**	**117**	**69**	**1,090**
E. Neuropsychiatric conditions	**31,230**	**520**	**689**	**4,235**	**3,162**	**1,975**	**1,202**	**1,445**	**1,020**	**14,248**
1. Unipolar depressive disorders	8,408	0	268	873	963	662	259	75	24	3,126
2. Bipolar affective disorder	1,056	0	20	436	69	3	1	0	0	531
3. Schizophrenia	1,115	0	120	401	43	11	4	2	1	582
4. Epilepsy	464	13	31	55	66	47	21	14	5	252
5. Alcohol use disorders	4,171	0	25	1,289	1,269	592	107	38	7	3,328
6. Alzheimer's and other dementias	7,468	22	11	15	15	92	455	957	817	2,384
7. Parkinson's disease	1,086	0	0	0	8	91	159	196	91	546
8. Multiple sclerosis	293	0	6	29	40	34	10	5	1	124
9. Drug use disorders	1,242	0	10	490	336	104	4	0	0	944
10. Post-traumatic stress disorder	369	0	2	39	36	17	1	1	0	96
11. Obsessive-compulsive disorder	399	—	2	91	56	10	3	2	0	164
12. Panic disorder	532	—	8	149	3	14	2	2	0	178
13. Insomnia (primary)	691	—	4	57	77	77	46	26	6	292
14. Migraine	1,129	8	101	162	14	0	0	0	0	285
15. Mental retardation, lead-caused	187	87	1	2	2	2	1	1	0	96
Other neuropsychiatric disorders	2,619	390	78	146	165	218	128	126	67	1,319
F. Sense organ diseases	**7,676**	**0**	**1**	**38**	**577**	**1,100**	**1,024**	**718**	**130**	**3,589**
1. Glaucoma	268	0	0	1	9	41	33	17	6	107
2. Cataracts	493	0	0	4	30	67	61	30	9	201
3. Vision disorders, age-related	1,525	0	1	9	59	212	191	103	34	611
4. Hearing loss, adult onset	5,387	—	—	24	479	779	739	567	81	2,669
Other sense organ disorders	3	0	0	0	0	0	0	0	0	1
G. Cardiovascular diseases	**29,859**	**43**	**22**	**189**	**1,089**	**3,491**	**3,771**	**4,524**	**2,787**	**15,916**
1. Rheumatic heart disease	199	1	0	2	5	15	18	17	8	65
2. Hypertensive heart disease	1,209	0	0	4	39	119	108	135	119	526
3. Ischemic heart disease	12,390	1	3	37	425	1,797	1,879	2,132	1,126	7,400
4. Cerebrovascular disease	9,354	6	4	27	279	937	1,105	1,360	792	4,510
5. Inflammatory heart diseases	982	9	5	34	91	160	135	122	53	610
Other cardiovascular diseases	5,724	26	9	85	251	463	526	758	689	2,806
H. Respiratory diseases	**9,801**	**312**	**236**	**370**	**492**	**1,141**	**950**	**1,151**	**609**	**5,261**
1. Chronic obstructive pulmonary disease	5,282	1	4	48	249	785	614	750	367	2,818
2. Asthma	1,660	121	198	272	101	79	38	38	18	865
Other respiratory diseases	2,859	190	34	50	143	277	298	363	224	1,579

Table 3C.8 Continued

			Female					
0–4	5–14	15–29	30–44	45–59	60–69	70–79	80+	Total
1,992	*1,160*	*5,264*	*6,885*	*11,998*	*10,807*	*14,159*	*12,308*	*64,572*
24	48	159	1,068	3,204	2,886	3,090	1,458	11,939
0	0	2	12	43	33	30	18	139
0	0	0	4	31	38	44	24	142
0	0	7	53	131	139	174	107	611
0	0	8	74	324	357	451	270	1,483
1	1	3	15	65	103	124	49	360
0	0	1	17	115	156	196	92	578
0	0	3	87	466	521	534	181	1,792
0	0	6	27	48	32	32	20	165
0	0	12	371	916	534	456	202	2,492
0	0	11	90	117	50	37	15	319
0	0	4	55	204	152	125	47	586
0	1	10	56	214	170	147	54	651
—	—	—	—	—	—	—	—	—
0	0	0	6	23	36	62	47	174
1	3	18	40	123	155	198	94	632
9	16	29	41	74	77	100	55	401
13	27	47	119	311	334	381	184	1,416
6	**6**	**9**	**20**	**43**	**48**	**78**	**62**	**271**
1	**2**	**28**	**227**	**570**	**467**	**535**	**330**	**2,161**
365	**37**	**101**	**152**	**260**	**122**	**162**	**152**	**1,351**
456	**621**	**4,183**	**2,837**	**2,139**	**1,419**	**2,303**	**3,024**	**16,982**
0	253	1,479	1,654	1,228	411	172	86	5,283
0	16	427	74	4	2	1	1	526
0	61	407	41	12	4	4	2	533
11	30	45	46	35	19	17	9	212
0	8	341	312	143	26	12	2	843
22	11	15	15	117	596	1,679	2,631	5,084
0	0	0	7	68	140	197	129	540
0	7	32	52	48	18	10	3	169
0	6	·151	103	35	2	0	0	297
0	2	108	87	69	3	4	1	273
—	4	120	89	19	3	1	0	235
—	7	301	5	31	4	4	1	354
—	3	63	100	104	69	50	10	398
11	153	585	94	0	0	0	0	844
83	1	1	2	2	1	1	0	91
329	60	110	157	225	121	152	147	1,301
1	**3**	**41**	**556**	**1,179**	**1,217**	**851**	**239**	**4,087**
0	1	2	15	48	51	31	14	161
0	1	4	32	91	87	54	22	292
1	1	10	95	300	246	176	85	915
—	—	24	414	740	832	589	118	2,718
0	0	0	0	0	0	0	0	1
35	**24**	**117**	**566**	**1,602**	**2,212**	**4,337**	**5,048**	**13,943**
0	2	2	6	21	33	43	27	134
0	0	3	20	65	86	186	323	684
1	3	19	121	537	881	1,677	1,751	4,991
5	6	20	215	648	813	1,548	1,591	4,844
10	4	17	40	66	69	93	74	372
20	8	57	164	266	329	791	1,283	2,918
257	**262**	**322**	**576**	**904**	**699**	**861**	**660**	**4,540**
1	1	57	435	656	452	522	341	2,465
90	238	212	42	66	55	55	37	796
166	23	53	99	182	192	283	282	1,280

(Continues on the following page.)

Cause	Total	Male								Total
		0–4	5–14	15–29	30–44	45–59	60–69	70–79	80+	
I. Digestive diseases	**6,536**	**270**	**21**	**98**	**521**	**1,182**	**682**	**532**	**259**	**3,566**
1. Peptic ulcer disease	295	0	1	7	18	43	33	37	22	160
2. Cirrhosis of the liver	2,146	3	2	13	297	657	328	144	27	1,471
3. Appendicitis	35	1	2	4	5	4	2	2	1	20
Other digestive diseases	4,060	267	16	75	202	478	319	350	209	1,916
J. Genitourinary diseases	**2,074**	**23**	**2**	**19**	**53**	**292**	**237**	**276**	**198**	**1,101**
1. Nephritis and nephrosis	929	6	2	10	31	78	95	139	105	467
2. Benign prostatic hypertrophy	342	—	—	0	0	159	90	64	29	342
Other genitourinary system diseases	803	17	1	9	22	55	51	73	64	292
K. Skin diseases	**288**	**2**	**2**	**5**	**11**	**18**	**17**	**28**	**27**	**110**
L. Musculoskeletal diseases	**6,437**	**7**	**18**	**76**	**478**	**776**	**531**	**447**	**113**	**2,447**
1. Rheumatoid arthritis	1,051	1	5	10	45	103	66	51	14	295
2. Osteoarthritis	3,786	0	0	20	188	444	370	320	54	1,397
3. Gout	480	—	0	12	181	145	42	20	8	408
4. Low back pain	246	4	9	18	39	36	14	9	3	132
Other musculoskeletal disorders	875	2	4	16	25	49	39	47	33	215
M. Congenital anomalies	**1,420**	**623**	**17**	**32**	**28**	**24**	**9**	**5**	**2**	**740**
1. Abdominal wall defect	6	3	0	0	0	0	0	0	0	3
2. Anencephaly	18	8	0	0	0	0	0	0	0	8
3. Anorectal atresia	2	1	0	0	0	0	0	0	0	1
4. Cleft lip	6	3	0	0	0	0	0	0	0	3
5. Cleft palate	7	3	0	0	0	0	0	0	0	3
6. Esophageal atresia	3	1	0	0	0	0	0	0	0	1
7. Renal agenesis	15	10	0	0	0	0	0	0	0	10
8. Down syndrome	196	88	1	3	3	8	2	0	0	104
9. Congenital heart anomalies	758	335	8	18	16	10	4	3	1	394
10. Spina bifida	63	26	1	1	1	0	0	0	0	29
Other congenital anomalies	347	144	8	10	8	6	3	2	1	183
N. Oral conditions	**957**	**45**	**70**	**44**	**49**	**115**	**94**	**26**	**5**	**448**
1. Dental caries	462	44	70	39	23	23	17	11	4	230
2. Periodontal disease	28	—	—	3	8	2	1	0	0	14
3. Edentulism	454	—	—	1	18	89	76	14	1	198
Other oral diseases	12	2	0	0	1	1	0	0	0	5
III. Injuries	**11,244**	**234**	**391**	**2,308**	**2,120**	**1,517**	**562**	**376**	**185**	**7,692**
A. Unintentional injuries	**7,876**	**215**	**334**	**1,579**	**1,302**	**928**	**385**	**289**	**158**	**5,189**
1. Road traffic accidents	3,045	38	90	921	571	336	113	67	20	2,157
2. Poisonings	494	3	3	88	162	75	10	5	2	347
3. Falls	1,459	41	57	176	163	159	91	96	72	856
4. Fires	215	15	13	21	31	33	10	8	3	136
5. Drownings	304	23	20	58	45	40	18	13	5	222
6. Other unintentional injuries	2,360	94	151	315	330	285	142	100	55	1,471
B. Intentional injuries	**3,368**	**19**	**57**	**729**	**818**	**588**	**176**	**87**	**27**	**2,503**
1. Self-inflicted injuries	2,581	0	38	441	635	523	165	83	26	1,911
2. Violence	765	19	19	278	175	63	11	4	1	571
3. War	10	0	0	4	4	1	0	0	0	9
Other intentional injuries	12	0	0	5	5	2	0	0	0	12

Table 3C.8 Continued

				Female				
0–4	**5–14**	**15–29**	**30–44**	**45–59**	**60–69**	**70–79**	**80+**	**Total**
204	**25**	**94**	**298**	**681**	**488**	**637**	**542**	**2,969**
0	1	4	10	30	19	34	37	135
1	2	8	117	237	151	123	37	675
0	2	2	3	2	1	2	2	15
203	20	80	168	411	318	478	466	2,145
22	**6**	**22**	**57**	**153**	**157**	**262**	**294**	**973**
5	4	7	20	56	83	142	146	462
—	—	—	—	—	—	—	—	—
17	2	15	37	97	74	121	148	511
3	**3**	**6**	**12**	**20**	**22**	**44**	**70**	**178**
7	**37**	**118**	**443**	**1,092**	**945**	**938**	**411**	**3,990**
3	21	34	121	285	140	102	51	755
0	0	15	187	605	676	688	217	2,389
0	0	4	13	21	15	15	4	72
2	11	12	28	32	14	10	5	114
2	5	52	94	149	100	123	134	660
568	**19**	**23**	**23**	**24**	**10**	**8**	**4**	**679**
2	0	0	0	0	0	0	0	2
9	0	0	0	0	0	0	0	9
1	0	0	0	0	0	0	0	1
3	0	0	0	0	0	0	0	3
4	0	0	0	0	0	0	0	4
1	0	0	0	0	0	0	0	2
5	0	0	0	0	0	0	0	6
74	1	2	3	8	3	0	0	92
311	8	12	13	10	4	4	2	364
30	1	1	1	0	0	0	0	34
129	9	7	6	5	3	3	2	164
43	**67**	**42**	**48**	**126**	**115**	**54**	**15**	**509**
41	66	37	22	23	18	15	9	232
—	0	3	8	2	1	1	0	14
—	—	1	18	100	96	37	4	256
2	0	0	1	1	0	1	1	7
164	*269*	*771*	*770*	*623*	*311*	*347*	*296*	*3,552*
149	237	578	501	413	233	298	279	2,687
30	69	308	195	145	66	57	18	888
2	3	26	63	37	8	5	3	147
29	33	64	56	64	61	129	167	603
10	13	11	14	13	6	7	4	79
13	13	8	9	11	8	13	6	82
65	106	162	163	142	84	87	80	889
15	**32**	**193**	**270**	**211**	**79**	**49**	**17**	**865**
0	20	130	203	185	73	45	15	670
15	12	63	66	26	6	4	1	194
0	0	0	0	0	0	0	0	1
0	0	0	0	0	0	0	0	0

Source: Authors' compilation.

Note: — = an estimate of zero; the number zero in a cell indicates a non-zero estimate of less than 500.

a. Does not include liver cancer and cirrhosis DALYs(3,0) resulting from chronic hepatitis virus infection.

b. This cause category includes "Causes arising in the perinatal period" as defined in the International Classification of Diseases, principally low birthweight, prematurity, birth asphyxia, and birth trauma, and does not include all causes of DALYs(3,0) occurring in the perinatal period.

Table 3C.9 DALYs(3,0) by Cause, Sex, and Age in the World, 2001
(thousands)

| Cause | Total | Male | | | | | | | | |
		0–4	5–14	15–29	30–44	45–59	60–69	70–79	80+	Total[a]
Population (millions)	*6,148*	*317*	*623*	*808*	*653*	*415*	*164*	*88*	*25*	*3,093*
All causes	**1,535,871**	**221,294**	**44,197**	**105,973**	**116,457**	**130,728**	**88,774**	**63,545**	**21,509**	**792,478**
I. Communicable, maternal, perinatal,	*560,937*	*170,202*	*16,479*	*22,918*	*32,862*	*19,064*	*8,386*	*5,140*	*1,890*	*276,941*
and nutritional conditions										
A. **Infectious and parasitic diseases**	**324,038**	**79,163**	**12,459**	**20,598**	**30,632**	**16,275**	**5,573**	**2,727**	**709**	**168,136**
1. **Tuberculosis**	**36,093**	**731**	**616**	**4,401**	**6,990**	**5,969**	**2,799**	**1,195**	**204**	**22,906**
2. **Sexually transmitted diseases**	**9,483**	**1,509**	**19**	**712**	**546**	**506**	**146**	**55**	**16**	**3,509**
excluding HIV/AIDS										
a. Syphilis	4,134	1,009	2	106	268	429	140	53	15	2,021
b. Chlamydia	2,538	36	5	158	36	1	0	—	—	236
c. Gonorrhea	2,578	449	12	445	220	7	1	0	0	1,135
d. Other sexually transmitted	233	15	0	3	22	69	4	2	1	117
diseases										
3. **HIV/AIDS**	**71,461**	**5,324**	**1,571**	**8,918**	**16,879**	**4,616**	**438**	**43**	**1**	**37,790**
4. **Diarrheal diseases**	**59,141**	**27,878**	**705**	**548**	**587**	**482**	**280**	**213**	**121**	**30,814**
5. **Childhood-cluster diseases**	**43,305**	**17,046**	**3,307**	**685**	**279**	**127**	**36**	**13**	**6**	**21,498**
a. Pertussis	11,543	5,691	50	—	—	—	0	—	—	5,741
b. Poliomyelitis[b]	144	15	8	25	17	5	1	1	0	72
c. Diphtheria	164	76	6	1	1	1	0	0	0	86
d. Measles	23,113	8,433	2,717	302	0	0	0	0	—	11,452
e. Tetanus	8,341	2,831	526	356	260	121	34	12	6	4,146
6. **Meningitis**	**5,607**	**1,335**	**477**	**360**	**252**	**214**	**78**	**58**	**15**	**2,788**
7. **Hepatitis B[c]**	**2,167**	**93**	**108**	**226**	**410**	**453**	**121**	**45**	**11**	**1,467**
Hepatitis C[c]	**1,029**	**31**	**44**	**83**	**182**	**235**	**70**	**32**	**7**	**684**
8. **Malaria**	**39,970**	**17,345**	**498**	**455**	**385**	**278**	**125**	**71**	**20**	**19,178**
9. **Tropical-cluster diseases**	**10,312**	**362**	**1,939**	**2,250**	**1,365**	**706**	**162**	**63**	**13**	**6,860**
a. Trypanosomiasis	1,333	67	322	189	149	104	9	3	0	844
b. Chagas' disease	585	0	0	126	62	67	32	12	4	303
c. Schistosomiasis	1,526	88	279	208	144	113	58	25	5	920
d. Leishmaniasis	1,762	89	383	306	171	66	19	6	0	1,039
e. Lymphatic filariasis	4,667	111	935	1,385	769	272	19	6	1	3,497
f. Onchocerciasis	439	7	20	37	71	84	25	10	3	257
10. **Leprosy**	**192**	**7**	**19**	**16**	**23**	**29**	**11**	**8**	**1**	**115**
11. **Dengue**	**529**	**61**	**143**	**12**	**9**	**6**	**3**	**2**	**1**	**238**
12. **Japanese encephalitis**	**604**	**91**	**69**	**47**	**65**	**11**	**3**	**2**	**1**	**288**
13. **Trachoma**	**2,630**	**2**	**2**	**23**	**155**	**213**	**150**	**88**	**21**	**654**
14. **Intestinal nematode infections**	**2,349**	**229**	**914**	**12**	**8**	**10**	**6**	**3**	**1**	**1,183**
a. Ascariasis	1,158	112	463	1	0	0	0	0	0	577
b. Trichuriasis	492	45	206	1	1	1	1	0	0	254
c. Hookworm disease	636	56	238	10	6	8	5	2	1	325
Other intestinal infections	63	16	6	1	1	2	1	0	0	28
Other infectious diseases	39,165	7,118	2,028	1,850	2,498	2,419	1,145	839	270	18,166
B. **Respiratory infections**	**89,184**	**32,372**	**2,521**	**1,104**	**1,417**	**2,019**	**2,487**	**2,185**	**1,094**	**45,200**
1. Lower respiratory infections	85,920	31,687	1,940	1,026	1,330	1,936	2,411	2,137	1,072	43,540
2. Upper respiratory infections	1,740	428	69	67	75	80	74	48	21	862
3. Otitis media	1,525	258	511	11	12	3	2	1	0	798
C. **Maternal conditions**	**26,774**	**—**	**—**	**—**	**—**	**—**	**—**	**—**	**—**	**—**
1. Maternal hemorrhage	3,926	—	—	—	—	—	—	—	—	—
2. Maternal sepsis	5,345	—	—	—	—	—	—	—	—	—
3. Hypertensive disorders	1,894	—	—	—	—	—	—	—	—	—
of pregnancy										
4. Obstructed labor	2,504	—	—	—	—	—	—	—	—	—
5. Abortion	3,506	—	—	—	—	—	—	—	—	—
Other maternal conditions	9,599	—	—	—	—	—	—	—	—	—
D. **Perinatal conditions[d]**	**90,477**	**49,368**	**1**	**1**	**0**	**0**	**0**	**0**	**—**	**49,370**
1. Low birthweight	43,064	23,236	0	—	0	—	0	—	—	23,236
2. Birth asphyxia and birth trauma	31,958	17,938	1	0	0	0	—	—	—	17,939
Other perinatal conditions	15,455	8,195	0	1	0	0	—	0	—	8,196

Table 3C.9 Continued

| | Female | | | | | | | | |
0–4	5–14	15–29	30–44	45–59	60–69	70–79	80+	Total
301	*589*	*774*	*635*	*415*	*180*	*115*	*47*	*3,055*
209,408	**43,382**	**103,829**	**94,055**	**102,675**	**79,356**	**73,462**	**37,225**	**743,392**
161,941	*18,601*	*44,243*	*31,448*	*13,090*	*6,683*	*5,319*	*2,673*	*283,997*
80,936	**13,324**	**23,820**	**20,168**	**10,054**	**4,047**	**2,658**	**894**	**155,902**
655	**663**	**3,393**	**3,760**	**2,606**	**1,318**	**659**	**133**	**13,187**
1,698	**71**	**2,822**	**914**	**306**	**108**	**49**	**6**	**5,974**
1,219	3	407	244	128	65	42	4	2,113
34	50	1,744	325	128	21	0	0	2,302
434	18	661	323	7	2	0	0	1,443
11	0	10	23	44	20	6	2	116
5,144	**1,545**	**12,434**	**11,416**	**2,766**	**316**	**50**	**1**	**33,671**
25,682	**667**	**443**	**420**	**396**	**292**	**257**	**172**	**28,327**
17,204	**3,413**	**708**	**286**	**134**	**39**	**16**	**7**	**21,807**
5,752	50	0	—	0	0	—	—	5,802
15	7	25	17	5	1	1	0	72
61	16	0	0	0	0	0	0	78
8,546	2,799	315	0	0	0	—	0	11,661
2,830	541	368	268	129	38	15	6	4,195
1,497	**602**	**296**	**163**	**128**	**73**	**45**	**14**	**2,818**
163	**50**	**146**	**110**	**130**	**56**	**34**	**12**	**701**
62	**19**	**57**	**51**	**70**	**42**	**33**	**10**	**345**
18,796	**501**	**516**	**400**	**322**	**145**	**87**	**26**	**20,793**
297	959	954	510	550	108	58	17	3,452
37	187	121	79	57	6	2	0	490
0	0	138	46	56	24	13	5	282
59	190	151	92	57	23	24	9	606
115	302	192	58	34	17	4	0	723
78	260	320	184	297	22	8	1	1,169
7	20	32	51	49	15	7	2	183
9	**18**	**13**	**15**	**11**	**7**	**4**	**1**	**77**
70	**176**	**19**	**11**	**7**	**4**	**3**	**1**	**291**
145	**101**	**32**	**24**	**8**	**4**	**2**	**0**	**316**
2	**5**	**51**	**443**	**600**	**470**	**313**	**93**	**1,976**
244	**890**	**10**	**5**	**7**	**5**	**2**	**1**	**1,166**
125	455	0	0	0	0	0	0	581
39	197	1	0	1	0	0	0	238
54	232	8	5	6	4	2	0	311
25	7	1	0	1	1	1	0	36
9,268	3,643	1,925	1,642	2,014	1,059	1,049	400	20,999
30,531	**3,104**	**1,688**	**1,195**	**1,354**	**2,125**	**2,355**	**1,632**	**43,984**
29,804	2,475	1,636	1,158	1,325	2,072	2,316	1,593	42,380
480	162	44	36	27	51	39	39	878
247	467	8	2	2	2	0	0	727
0	**158**	**17,269**	**8,898**	**449**	**0**	**0**	**0**	**26,774**
0	0	1,914	1,860	152	—	—	—	3,926
—	0	3,823	1,439	83	—	—	—	5,345
—	1	1,147	700	46	—	—	0	1,894
—	—	1,751	740	14	—	—	—	2,504
—	155	2,702	647	2	—	—	—	3,506
—	2	5,932	3,512	154	0	0	0	9,599
41,105	**1**	**0**	**0**	**0**	**0**	**0**	**0**	**41,106**
19,828	0	—	—	—	—	—	—	19,828
14,019	0	0	—	0	—	0	0	14,020
7,258	1	0	0	0	0	0	0	7,259

(Continues on the following page.)

Cause	Total		0–4	5–14	15–29	30–44	45–59	60–69	70–79	80+	Total[a]
		Male									
E. Nutritional deficiencies	**30,463**		**9,299**	**1,498**	**1,215**	**812**	**770**	**326**	**227**	**87**	**14,234**
1. Protein-energy malnutrition	15,578		6,926	433	124	68	125	106	80	41	7,903
2. Iodine deficiency	2,876		1,074	352	0	1	2	1	0	0	1,431
3. Vitamin A deficiency	711		233	70	3	6	10	5	2	0	329
4. Iron-deficiency anemia	10,245		899	609	1,064	704	567	174	93	28	4,138
Other nutritional disorders	1,053		166	34	23	34	67	40	52	18	433
II. Noncommunicable diseases	***807,839***		***42,899***	***13,697***	***45,319***	***56,267***	***96,868***	***75,790***	***56,282***	***18,997***	***406,118***
A. Malignant neoplasms	**100,641**		**590**	**812**	**2,086**	**5,229**	**16,460**	**15,681**	**10,393**	**2,630**	**53,882**
1. Mouth and oropharynx cancers	4,654		5	12	119	420	1,243	986	412	86	3,284
2. Esophageal cancer	5,955		1	2	30	326	1,303	1,330	695	119	3,806
3. Stomach cancer	11,244		3	8	127	656	2,353	2,114	1,355	313	6,930
4. Colon and rectal cancers	8,236		1	4	118	437	1,195	1,277	972	293	4,297
5. Liver cancer	9,169		21	16	221	942	2,602	1,619	837	131	6,388
6. Pancreas cancer	2,853		0	2	7	129	530	474	322	82	1,547
7. Trachea, bronchus, and lung cancers	16,099		3	7	68	689	3,545	4,005	2,547	479	11,344
8. Melanoma and other skin cancers	909		1	2	22	74	163	116	84	30	493
9. Breast cancer	8,036		0	0	0	3	11	9	7	2	33
10. Cervix uteri cancer	4,119		—	—	—	—	—	—	—	—	—
11. Corpus uteri cancer	1,494		—	—	—	—	—	—	—	—	—
12. Ovarian cancer	2,139		—	—	—	—	—	—	—	—	—
13. Prostate cancer	2,691		1	1	4	16	276	812	1,101	480	2,691
14. Bladder cancer	2,174		2	2	10	58	331	480	454	157	1,494
15. Lymphomas and multiple myeloma	5,131		67	200	340	436	616	513	360	107	2,639
16. Leukemia	4,883		235	368	683	346	415	327	250	77	2,702
Other malignant neoplasms	10,854		251	190	336	696	1,876	1,618	996	273	6,235
B. Other neoplasms	**2,096**		**74**	**71**	**137**	**140**	**240**	**182**	**155**	**61**	**1,060**
C. Diabetes mellitus	**19,997**		**43**	**73**	**489**	**1,528**	**2,990**	**2,087**	**1,395**	**428**	**9,033**
D. Endocrine disorders	**13,385**		**4,018**	**262**	**378**	**423**	**601**	**306**	**255**	**124**	**6,368**
E. Neuropsychiatric conditions	**168,305**		**10,811**	**6,627**	**28,133**	**16,184**	**9,011**	**3,933**	**3,768**	**1,969**	**80,437**
1. Unipolar depressive disorders	51,835		0	2,720	6,565	5,955	3,739	1,165	255	57	20,457
2. Bipolar affective disorder	9,734		0	267	4,090	523	17	5	0	0	4,903
3. Schizophrenia	11,642		0	901	4,132	611	168	36	16	4	5,869
4. Epilepsy	6,223		514	668	916	657	341	127	62	17	3,301
5. Alcohol use disorders	15,178		2	126	5,319	4,696	2,214	396	100	15	12,868
6. Alzheimer's and other dementias	17,108		203	87	100	84	346	1,243	2,470	1,558	6,092
7. Parkinson's disease	2,325		5	3	10	74	241	299	351	140	1,124
8. Multiple sclerosis	1,209		1	49	194	165	74	21	9	2	515
9. Drug use disorders	5,647		1	79	2,255	1,506	559	31	4	1	4,436
10. Post-traumatic stress disorder	2,382		0	25	308	212	106	3	2	1	658
11. Obsessive-compulsive disorder	3,535		—	160	789	403	114	23	10	1	1,500
12. Panic disorder	4,547		—	78	1,358	19	71	9	6	1	1,540
13. Insomnia (primary)	2,909		—	32	335	375	265	142	58	12	1,218
14. Migraine	5,980		52	613	832	94	6	0	0	0	1,596
15. Mental retardation, lead-caused	8,786		4,406	17	24	9	6	2	1	0	4,466
Other neuropsychiatric disorders	19,263		5,627	802	908	802	745	431	422	160	9,895
F. Sense organ diseases	**79,951**		**30**	**167**	**1,659**	**8,646**	**13,118**	**8,066**	**3,831**	**734**	**36,251**
1. Glaucoma	4,380		7	30	129	356	690	414	207	51	1,883
2. Cataracts	28,643		17	101	610	2,480	4,636	2,734	1,289	290	12,157
3. Vision disorders, age-related	16,889		3	35	314	1,322	2,678	1,790	877	210	7,228
4. Hearing loss, adult onset	29,994		—	—	605	4,486	5,110	3,125	1,454	182	14,962
Other sense organ disorders	45		3	2	3	2	4	3	4	2	22
G. Cardiovascular diseases	**208,787**		**1,460**	**892**	**3,711**	**10,077**	**28,477**	**29,423**	**24,660**	**8,866**	**107,566**
1. Rheumatic heart disease	6,350		231	171	554	458	618	361	221	58	2,672
2. Hypertensive heart disease	11,178		27	21	114	473	1,413	1,516	1,276	524	5,365
3. Ischemic heart disease	84,273		104	219	1,070	4,207	14,072	13,452	10,641	3,396	47,161
4. Cerebrovascular disease	72,024		221	150	590	2,334	8,861	10,972	9,360	2,995	35,482
5. Inflammatory heart diseases	6,793		269	85	423	706	917	684	542	206	3,832
Other cardiovascular diseases	28,170		608	246	959	1,899	2,597	2,436	2,620	1,687	13,054

Table 3C.9 Continued

				Female				
0–4	5–14	15–29	30–44	45–59	60–69	70–79	80+	Total
9,368	**2,013**	**1,467**	**1,186**	**1,232**	**511**	**306**	**146**	**16,230**
6,707	492	54	69	100	109	83	61	7,676
1,101	338	1	1	2	1	1	0	1,445
288	70	9	4	8	3	2	0	383
965	1,067	1,383	1,091	1,075	349	131	48	6,107
309	46	20	21	48	50	90	37	620
40,092	*14,171*	*43,825*	*51,687*	*82,360*	*69,779*	*66,115*	*33,693*	*401,721*
611	**717**	**1,761**	**6,147**	**14,252**	**11,268**	**8,926**	**3,076**	**46,759**
9	6	34	135	458	379	254	95	1,371
1	2	21	131	696	669	485	142	2,148
1	4	104	564	1,192	1,069	1,007	374	4,315
1	3	55	402	1,009	1,029	988	452	3,939
33	20	148	378	805	705	551	141	2,780
0	1	10	88	327	367	371	142	1,306
6	29	32	368	1,401	1,404	1,216	301	4,755
1	3	17	65	116	91	85	38	416
1	2	74	1,540	3,213	1,714	1,080	380	8,004
0	2	352	608	1,564	972	507	113	4,119
2	3	22	217	522	378	268	82	1,494
2	19	100	313	737	518	350	100	2,139
—	—	—	—	—	—	—	—	—
21	7	14	83	132	160	174	91	681
89	175	234	333	520	514	456	171	2,492
247	288	362	345	372	255	221	91	2,181
196	155	183	577	1,187	1,043	915	363	4,618
55	**57**	**79**	**152**	**270**	**168**	**166**	**89**	**1,037**
60	**80**	**428**	**1,458**	**3,193**	**2,781**	**2,195**	**767**	**10,963**
3,720	**250**	**534**	**606**	**786**	**454**	**403**	**263**	**7,017**
10,335	**6,740**	**28,102**	**16,199**	**10,155**	**5,338**	**5,790**	**5,208**	**87,868**
0	2,565	9,300	9,818	6,672	2,226	604	191	31,378
0	229	4,036	536	21	7	1	1	4,831
1	252	4,329	842	253	54	33	9	5,773
426	672	837	483	293	111	74	26	2,922
0	49	1,003	771	386	70	27	4	2,310
184	82	104	89	398	1,746	3,961	4,452	11,016
6	4	7	63	228	305	386	203	1,202
1	63	245	225	105	34	17	5	695
0	48	604	398	148	10	2	1	1,211
0	18	832	578	269	14	10	3	1,724
—	308	889	593	187	40	16	4	2,036
—	78	2,717	30	145	19	15	3	3,007
—	31	367	512	403	237	115	26	1,692
143	1,720	2,006	510	4	0	0	0	4,384
4,265	19	17	10	6	1	1	0	4,320
5,309	599	809	742	635	463	529	283	9,368
31	**117**	**1,309**	**9,039**	**15,393**	**10,710**	**5,686**	**1,415**	**43,700**
5	26	143	415	861	598	340	109	2,496
14	63	564	2,858	6,205	4,110	2,109	563	16,487
9	25	236	1,512	3,392	2,484	1,534	469	9,661
—	—	363	4,252	4,932	3,516	1,698	271	15,032
3	2	4	2	3	3	4	2	23
1,650	**955**	**3,251**	**6,314**	**18,322**	**24,551**	**29,769**	**16,410**	**101,222**
246	249	591	593	829	590	441	140	3,679
24	25	81	328	1,165	1,458	1,688	1,043	5,812
75	170	1,022	2,014	6,735	10,077	11,270	5,749	37,112
161	145	369	1,695	6,784	9,541	11,892	5,957	36,542
213	88	274	362	554	522	612	335	2,961
932	277	914	1,321	2,255	2,365	3,866	3,186	15,116

(Continues on the following page.)

Table 3C.9 Continued

Cause	Total	0–4	5–14	15–29	30–44	45–59	60–69	70–79	80+	Total[a]
					Male					
H. Respiratory diseases	**67,887**	**3,566**	**1,935**	**2,738**	**3,410**	**8,403**	**7,418**	**6,618**	**2,497**	**36,585**
1. Chronic obstructive pulmonary disease	38,736	49	19	168	1,556	6,144	5,776	5,216	1,866	20,795
2. Asthma	13,174	1,134	1,546	2,056	930	793	323	194	54	7,030
Other respiratory diseases	15,977	2,383	370	514	924	1,465	1,319	1,208	578	8,761
I. Digestive diseases	**58,937**	**7,636**	**879**	**2,686**	**5,094**	**8,203**	**4,118**	**2,531**	**830**	**31,977**
1. Peptic ulcer disease	5,096	91	67	401	685	1,009	487	306	96	3,142
2. Cirrhosis of the liver	15,778	259	154	634	2,131	3,828	1,776	818	148	9,749
3. Appendicitis	412	7	30	40	42	58	26	21	7	232
Other digestive diseases	37,651	7,279	628	1,611	2,236	3,307	1,829	1,386	579	18,854
J. Genitourinary diseases	**18,455**	**999**	**347**	**744**	**1,053**	**3,908**	**1,626**	**1,259**	**518**	**10,453**
1. Nephritis and nephrosis	10,005	333	285	593	808	1,182	933	717	285	5,136
2. Benign prostatic hypertrophy	2,955	—	—	0	12	2,277	346	236	84	2,955
Other genitourinary system diseases	5,495	665	63	150	233	449	347	306	148	2,362
K. Skin diseases	**3,985**	**501**	**227**	**306**	**298**	**274**	**147**	**123**	**63**	**1,939**
L. Musculoskeletal diseases	**32,130**	**209**	**450**	**1,369**	**3,786**	**4,338**	**2,120**	**1,136**	**249**	**13,657**
1. Rheumatoid arthritis	4,695	12	80	181	291	411	215	121	28	1,341
2. Osteoarthritis	17,452	0	3	387	1,536	2,414	1,430	723	106	6,600
3. Gout	3,265	0	0	135	1,488	999	188	59	14	2,884
4. Low back pain	1,938	72	176	202	251	220	70	32	8	1,030
Other musculoskeletal disorders	4,780	124	190	464	220	294	217	200	92	1,802
M. Congenital anomalies	**24,952**	**11,975**	**319**	**371**	**95**	**59**	**21**	**12**	**4**	**12,855**
1. Abdominal wall defect	116	63	0	0	0	0	0	0	0	63
2. Anencephaly	563	266	0	0	0	0	0	0	0	267
3. Anorectal atresia	33	21	0	0	0	0	0	0	0	21
4. Cleft lip	122	64	0	0	0	0	0	0	0	64
5. Cleft palate	138	70	0	0	0	0	0	0	0	70
6. Esophageal atresia	49	24	0	0	0	0	0	0	0	24
7. Renal agenesis	68	39	0	1	0	0	0	0	0	41
8. Down syndrome	3,612	1,824	29	60	6	10	2	0	0	1,932
9. Congenital heart anomalies	13,949	6,533	172	219	58	25	9	5	2	7,023
10. Spina bifida	1,551	732	10	5	1	1	0	0	0	750
Other congenital anomalies	4,751	2,340	106	85	29	23	9	6	2	2,599
N. Oral conditions	**8,331**	**988**	**633**	**511**	**305**	**786**	**662**	**147**	**23**	**4,054**
1. Dental caries	5,214	962	628	380	167	274	139	71	19	2,640
2. Periodontal disease	235	—	—	29	55	21	8	4	1	118
3. Edentulism	2,747	—	—	96	77	486	514	71	2	1,245
Other oral diseases	135	25	5	7	6	5	2	1	1	52
III. Injuries	***167,094***	***8,193***	***14,022***	***37,737***	***27,329***	***14,796***	***4,598***	***2,124***	***623***	***109,420***
A. Unintentional injuries	**121,111**	**7,822**	**12,781**	**22,914**	**16,768**	**10,264**	**3,317**	**1,600**	**496**	**75,962**
1. Road traffic accidents	35,063	1,224	3,358	8,492	6,496	3,539	973	429	88	24,598
2. Poisonings	7,608	289	322	1,051	1,429	1,348	378	95	17	4,930
3. Falls	15,041	1,024	1,727	2,336	1,547	1,161	560	456	202	9,013
4. Fires	10,295	938	878	905	769	409	123	63	17	4,103
5. Drownings	9,695	1,034	1,700	1,893	1,103	622	169	75	22	6,618
6. Other unintentional injuries	43,410	3,313	4,795	8,238	5,426	3,184	1,114	481	150	26,700
B. Intentional injuries	**45,983**	**370**	**1,240**	**14,822**	**10,560**	**4,533**	**1,281**	**523**	**127**	**33,457**
1. Self-inflicted injuries	20,255	3	376	4,379	3,689	2,372	811	377	84	12,092
2. Violence	18,897	259	779	7,703	4,535	1,569	302	106	29	15,282
3. War	6,502	91	71	2,632	2,258	563	157	35	12	5,818
Other intentional injuries	329	17	15	109	79	28	11	5	2	265

Table 3C.9 Continued

	Female								
0–4	**5–14**	**15–29**	**30–44**	**45–59**	**60–69**	**70–79**	**80+**	**Total**
2,966	**2,051**	**2,259**	**2,982**	**5,901**	**5,313**	**6,400**	**3,430**	**31,302**
64	22	186	1,704	4,199	4,030	5,140	2,596	17,941
830	1,759	1,561	646	724	319	214	91	6,145
2,072	270	512	632	977	964	1,045	744	7,217
7,276	**1,189**	**2,465**	**3,047**	**5,311**	**3,355**	**2,898**	**1,420**	**26,960**
98	57	198	343	530	318	278	132	1,954
597	301	509	921	1,760	1,065	704	173	6,030
6	23	30	23	37	25	24	10	179
6,575	808	1,728	1,760	2,984	1,947	1,891	1,104	18,797
648	**339**	**742**	**1,072**	**1,838**	**1,436**	**1,261**	**665**	**8,002**
271	279	443	584	1,152	966	805	370	4,869
—	—	—	—	—	—	—	—	—
377	60	299	489	686	470	457	295	3,132
351	**161**	**290**	**307**	**330**	**221**	**223**	**163**	**2,046**
194	**582**	**1,803**	**3,946**	**5,710**	**3,382**	**2,124**	**733**	**18,473**
24	203	510	738	1,043	478	266	92	3,354
0	4	647	2,319	3,738	2,395	1,412	337	10,852
0	0	25	158	105	49	35	9	381
37	213	138	227	187	65	32	10	908
133	161	482	504	637	395	379	286	2,978
11,269	**325**	**292**	**101**	**64**	**23**	**16**	**6**	**12,097**
52	0	0	0	0	0	0	0	53
293	1	1	0	0	0	0	0	295
12	0	0	0	0	0	0	0	12
59	0	0	0	0	0	0	0	59
67	0	0	0	0	0	0	0	67
24	0	0	0	0	0	0	0	24
25	0	0	0	0	0	0	0	27
1,571	31	56	6	12	3	0	0	1,680
6,426	195	186	65	30	10	9	4	6,926
785	8	5	2	1	0	0	0	801
1,955	88	44	27	20	9	6	2	2,152
926	**608**	**511**	**315**	**835**	**777**	**259**	**47**	**4,277**
901	600	364	163	274	153	88	31	2,574
—	0	28	53	21	8	5	2	117
—	—	98	81	534	613	163	13	1,502
25	8	21	18	5	3	2	1	83
7,376	*10,611*	*15,762*	*10,920*	*7,225*	*2,894*	*2,027*	*860*	*57,675*
7,155	9,559	11,043	7,597	5,176	2,228	1,631	759	45,149
1,118	2,411	2,486	2,076	1,519	492	293	70	10,465
207	296	498	600	586	353	111	29	2,679
983	1,455	1,061	624	567	391	574	372	6,027
1,089	1,088	2,077	1,154	485	150	112	37	6,192
775	935	593	337	226	107	77	28	3,077
2,984	3,374	4,329	2,806	1,793	736	464	223	16,710
221	**1,051**	**4,719**	**3,323**	**2,050**	**666**	**396**	**100**	**12,526**
1	429	3,311	2,177	1,398	467	302	79	8,163
202	425	1,267	986	489	152	77	16	3,615
6	191	126	148	151	43	14	5	683
12	7	15	11	12	4	2	1	64

Source: Authors' compilation.

Note: — = an estimate of zero; the number zero in a cell indicates a non-zero estimate of less than 500.

a. World totals for males and females include residual populations not included in the World Bank regions.

b. For East Asia and Pacific, Europe and Central Asia, and Latin America and the Caribbean regions, these figures include late effects of polio cases with onset prior to regional certification of polio eradication in 1994, 2000, and 2002, respectively.

c. Does not include liver cancer and cirrhosis DALYs(3,0) resulting from chronic hepatitis virus infection.

d. This cause category includes "Causes arising in the perinatal period" as defined in the International Classification of Diseases, principally low birthweight, prematurity, birth asphyxia, and birth trauma, and does not include all causes of DALYs(3,0) occurring in the perinatal period.

ACKNOWLEDGMENTS

In writing this chapter we have drawn on documentation prepared by the many people involved in the GBD studies and acknowledged this as far as possible by means of citations. We would especially like to acknowledge the assistance of Doris Ma Fat and Mie Inoue, who compiled comprehensive summaries of mortality data sources for GBD 2001 (Mathers, Lopez, and others 2004), which we have drawn on here, and the assistance of Chalapati Rao, who carried out analyses of the latest mortality data for China, India, Iran, Turkey, and various other countries.

Many people, both inside and outside WHO, contributed to the GBD analyses reported here. Apart from the authors, current and former staff of the former WHO Global Program on Evidence for Health Policy who worked directly on the GBD 2001 include Omar Ahmad, José Ayuso, Prerna Banati, Stephen Begg, Christina Bernard, Cynthia Boschi-Pinto, Marisol Concha, Carmen Dolea, Majid Ezzati, Doris Ma Fat, Brodie Ferguson, Kim Moesgaard Iburg, Mie Inoue, Jeremy Lauer, Matilde Leonardi, Steve Lim, Rafael Lozano, Sue Piccolo, Chalapati Rao, Tanuja Rastogi, Eduardo Sabaté, Joshua Salomon, Toshi Satoh, Kenji Shibuya, Claudia Stein, Lana Tomaskovic, Niels Tomijima, Thomas Truelsen, Bedirhan Ustün, Marie-Claude von Rulach, Sarah Wild, and Hongyi Xu. We also gratefully acknowledge the support of David Evans, director of the Global Program on Evidence for Health Policy.

We also wish to acknowledge the contributions of staff in various WHO programs and of expert groups outside WHO who provided advice and collaborated in the reviews of epidemiological data and in the estimation of the burden of disease. While it is not possible to name all those who contributed to this effort, we would like to note the considerable assistance and inputs provided by Carla AbouZahr, Elisabeth Aahman, Jan Barendregt, Maureen Birmingham, Jennifer Bryce, Mercedes de Onis, Chris Dye, Jacques Ferlay, Anthony Gerbase, Ken Hill, Yvan Hutin, Gareth Jones, Hilary King, Eline Korenromp, Daniel Lavanchy, Silvio Mariotti, Mike McKenna, Catherine Michaud, Chris Nelson, Tomoko Ono, Donatella Pascolini, Margie Peden, Bruce Pfleger, Paola Pisani, Annette Pruss-Ustun, Juergen Rehm, Serge Resnikoff, Sue Robertson, Gojke Roglic, Kate Strong, Deborah Symmonds, Theo Vos, Neff Walker, Catherine Watt, and Lara Wolfson.

We would also like to thank the Child Health Epidemiology Reference Group, chaired by Robert Black, and established to provide technical advice to WHO on the estimation of child mortality and the burden of disease; the Bone and Joint Decade's Bone and Joint Monitor Project coordinated by Anthony Woolf; and the Joint United Nations Programme on HIVAIDS and WHO Working Group on Global HIV/AIDS and STI Surveillance. The authors gratefully acknowledge financial support for this project from the National Institute on Aging (research grant number PO1 AG17625). The authors alone are responsible for the views expressed in this chapter, which do not necessarily reflect the opinions of the WHO or of its member states.

REFERENCES

Abdallah, M. B., and S. Zehani. 2000. *Registre des Cancers Nord-Tunisie 1994*. Tunis, Tunisia:Ministry of Public Health, Salah Azaiz Institute, and National Institute of Public Health.

Ahman, E., C. Dolea, and I. Shah. 2003. "Global Burden of Unsafe Abortion in the Year 2000." GBD 2000 Working Paper, World Health Organization, Geneva. http://www.who.int/evidence/bod.

Alley, W. S., G. J. van Oortmarssen, B. A. Boatin, N. J. Nagelkerke, A. P. Plaisier, J. H. Remme, J. Lazdins, G. J. Borsboom, and J. D. Habb. 2001. "Macrofilaricides and Onchocerciasis Control, Mathematical Modeling of the Prospects for Elimination." *BMC Public Health* 1 (1): 12.

American Psychiatric Association. 1994. *Diagnostic and Statistical Manual on Mental Disorders*, 4th ed. Washington, DC: American Psychiatric Press.

Anand, S., and K. Hanson. 1997. "Disability-Adjusted Life Years: A Critical Review." *Journal of Health Economics* 16 (6): 685–702.

———. 1998. "DALYs: Efficiency Versus Equity." *World Development* 26 (2): 307–10.

Ayuso-Mateos, J. L. 2002a. "Global Burden of Bipolar Disorder in the Year 2000." GBD 2000 Working Paper, World Health Organization, Geneva. http://www.who.int/evidence/bod.

———. 2002b. "Global Burden of Obsessive Compulsive Disorders in the Year 2000." GBD 2000 Working Paper, World Health Organization, Geneva. http://www.who.int/evidence/bod.

———. 2002c. "Global Burden of Post-Traumatic Stress Disorder in the Year 2000: Version 1 Estimates." GBD 2000 Working Paper, World Health Organization, Geneva. http://www.who.int/evidence/bod.

———. 2002d. "Global Burden of Schizophrenia in the Year 2000: Version 1 Estimates." GBD 2000 Working Paper, World Health Organization, Geneva. http://www.who.int/evidence/bod.

Ayuso-Mateos, J. L, J. L. Vazquez-Barquero, C. Dowrick, V. Lehtinen, O. S. Dalgard, P. Casey, C. Wilkinson, L. Lasa, H. Page, G. Dunn, G. Wilkinson, and the ODIN Group. 2001. "Depressive Disorders in Europe: Prevalence Figures from the ODIN Study." *British Journal of Psychiatry* 179 (4): 308–16.

Bannister, J., and K. Hill. 2004. "Mortality in China, 1964–2000." *Population Studies* 58 (1): 55–75.

Barendregt, J., G. J. van Oortmarssen, T. Vos, and C. J. L. Murray. 2003. "A Generic Model for the Assessment of Disease Epidemiology: The Computational Basis of DisMod II." *Population Health Metrics* 1: 4.

Baskent University. 2005. *Burden of Disease Final Report*. Ankara: Turkish Ministry of Health and Baskent University, Refik Saydam Hygiene Presidency, School of Public Health.

Begg, S., N. Tomijima, T. Vos, and C. D. Mathers. 2002. "Global Burden of Injury in the Year 2000: An Overview of Methods." GBD 2000 Working

Paper, World Health Organization, Geneva. http://www.who.int/evidence/bod.

Bern, C. 2004. "Diarrhoeal Diseases." In *The Global Epidemiology of Infectious Diseases*, ed. C. J. L. Murray, A. D. Lopez, and C. D. Mathers, 1–27. Vol. 4 of *Global Burden of Disease and Injury Series*. Geneva: World Health Organization. http://whqlibdoc.who.int/publications/2004/9241592303.pdf.

Boschi-Pinto, C., L. Tomaskovic, E. Gouws, and K Shibuya. Forthcoming. "Estimates of the Distribution of Child Deaths Due to Diarrhea in Developing Regions of the World."

Bradshaw, D., P. Groenewald, R. Laubscher, N. Nannan, B. Nojilana, R. Norman, D. Pieterse, M. Schneider, D. E. Bourne, I. M. Timaeus, R. Dorrington, and L. Johnson. 2003. *Initial Burden of Disease Estimates for South Africa, 2000.* Cape Town: South African Medical Research Council.

Brooker, S., M. Rowlands, L. Haller, L. Savioli, and D. A. P. Bundy. 2000. "Towards an Atlas of Human Helminth Infection in Sub-Saharan Africa: The Use of Geographical Information systems (GIS)." *Parasitology Today* 16 (7): 303–7.

Brooker, S., M. Beasley, M. Ndinaromtan, E. M. Madjiouroum, M. Baboguel, E. Djenguinabe, S. I. Hay, and D. A. Bundy. 2002. "Use of Remote Sensing and a Geographical Information System in a National Helminth Control Programme in Chad." *Bulletin of the World Health Organization* 80 (10): 783–9.

Bundhamcharoen, K., Y. Teerawatananon, T. Vos, and S. Begg. 2002. *Burden of Disease and Injuries in Thailand: Priority Setting for Policy.* Bangkok: Ministry of Public Health.

Bundy, D. A. P., M. S. Chan, G. F. Medley, D. Jamison, and L. Savioli. 2004. "Intestinal Nematode Infections." In *The Global Epidemiology of Infectious Diseases*, ed. C. J. L. Murray, A. D. Lopez, and C. D. Mathers, 243–300. Vol. 4 of *Global Burden of Disease and Injury Series*. Geneva: World Health Organization. http://whqlibdoc.who.int/publications/2004/9241592303.pdf.

Center for Research on the Epidemiology of Disasters. 2001. "EM-DAT: The OFDA/CRED International Disaster Database." Brussels, Belgium: Université Catholique de Louvain. http://www.em-dat.net.

Chan, M. S. 1997. "The Global Burden of Intestinal Nematode Infections: Fifty Years On." *Parasitology Today* 13: 438–43.

Chenet, L., M. McKee, D. Leon, V. Shkolnikov, and S. Vassin. 1998. "Alcohol and Cardiovascular Mortality in Moscow: New Evidence of a Causal Association." *Journal of Epidemiology and Community Health* 52 (12): 772–4.

Chinn, S., P. Burney, D. Jarvis, and C. Luczynska. 1997. "Variation in Bronchial Responsiveness in the European Community Respiratory Health Survey (ECRHS)." *European Respiratory Journal* 10 (11): 2495–2501.

Cooper, R. S., B. Osotimehin, J. S. Kaufman, and T. Forrester. 1998. "Disease Burden in Sub-Saharan Africa: What Should We Conclude in the Absence of Data?" *Lancet* 351 (9097): 208–10.

Corbett, E. L, C. J. Watt, N. Walker, D. Maher, B. G. Williams, M. C. Raviglione, and C. Dye. 2003. "The Growing Burden of Tuberculosis: Global Trends and Interactions with the HIV Epidemic." *Archives of Internal Medicine* 163: 1009–21.

Crowcroft, N. S., C. Stein, P. Duclos, and M. Birmingham. 2003. "How Best to Estimate the Global Burden of Pertussis?" *Lancet Infectious Diseases* 3 (7): 413–8.

Degenhardt, L., W. Hall, M. Warner-Smith, and M. Lynskey. 2003. "Illicit Drugs." In *Comparative Quantification of Health Risks: Global and Regional Burden of Disease Attributable to Selected Major Risk Factors*, ed. M. Ezzati, A. D. Lopez, A. Rodgers, and C. J. L. Murray, 1109–75. Geneva: World Health Organization.

Dempsey, M. 1947. "Decline in Tuberculosis: The Death Rate Fails to Tell the Entire Story." *American Review of Tuberculosis* 56: 143–51.

de Onis, M., and M. Blossner. 2003. "The World Health Organization Global Database on Child Growth and Malnutrition: Methodology and Applications." *International Journal of Epidemiology* 32 (4): 518–26.

de Onis, M., E. A. Frongillo, and M. Blossner. 2000. "Is Malnutrition Declining? An Analysis of Changes in Levels of Child Malnutrition Since 1980." *Bulletin of the World Health Organization* 78 (10): 1222–33.

de Onis, M., M. Blossner, E. Borghi, R. Morris, and E. A. Frongillo. 2004. "Methodology for Estimating Regional and Global Trends of Child Malnutrition." *International Journal of Epidemiology* 33 (6): 1260–70.

de Silva, N. R., S. Brooker, P. J. Hotez, A. Montresor, D. Engels, and L. Savioli. 2003. "Soil-Transmitted Helminth Infections: Updating the Global Picture." *Trends in Parasitology* 19 (12): 547–51.

Dolea, C., and C. AbouZahr. 2003a. "Global Burden of Hypertensive Disorders in Pregnancy in the Year 2000." GBD 2000 Working Paper, World Health Organization, Geneva. http://www.who.int/ evidence/bod.

———. 2003b. "Global Burden of Obstructed Labor in the Year 2000." GBD 2000 Working Paper, World Health Organization, Geneva. http://www.who.int/evidence/bod.

Dolea, C., and C. Stein. 2003. "Global Burden of Maternal Sepsis in the Year 2000." GBD 2000 Working Paper, World Health Organization, Geneva. http://www.who.int/evidence/bod.

Dolea, C., C. AbouZahr, and C. Stein. 2003. "Global Burden of Maternal Hemorrhage in the Year 2000." GBD 2000 Working Paper, World Health Organization, Geneva. http://www.who.int/evidence/bod.

Dolin, P. J., H. Faal, G. J. Johnson, D. Minassian, S. Sowa, S. Day, J. Ajewale, A. A. Mohamed, and A. Foster. 1997. "Reduction of Trachoma in a Sub-Saharan Village in Absence of a Disease Control Programme." *Lancet* 349 (9064): 1511–2.

Doumenge, J. P., K. E. Mott, C. Cheung, D. Villenave, O. Chapuis, M. F. Perrin, and G. Reaud-Thomas. 1987. *CEGET/WHO Atlas de la Répartition Mondiale des Schistosomiases (Atlas of the Global Distribution of Schistosomiasis)*. Bordeaux, France: Presses Universitaires de Bordeaux.

Dye, C., S. Scheele, P. Dolin, V. Pathania, and M. C. Raviglione. 1999. "Global Burden of Tuberculosis: Estimated Incidence, Prevalence, and Mortality by Country." *Journal of the American Medical Association* 282 (7): 677–86.

European Monitoring Centre for Drugs and Drug Addiction. 2002. *Annual Report on the State of the Drug Problem in the European Union and Norway.* Lisbon: European Monitoring Centre for Drugs and Drug Addiction.

Ezzati, M., A. D. Lopez, S. Vander Hoorn, A. Rodgers, C. J. L Murray, and Comparative Risk Assessment Collaborative Group. 2002. "Selected Major Risk Factors and Global and Regional Burden of Disease." *Lancet* 360 (9343): 1347–60.

Ezzati, M., S. Vander Hoorn, A. Rodgers, A. D. Lopez, C. D. Mathers, C. J. L. Murray, and Comparative Risk Factors Collaborating Group. 2003. "Estimates of Global and Regional Potential Health Gains from Reducing Multiple Major Risk Factors." *Lancet* 362 (9380): 271–80.

Ferlay, J., F. Bray, P. Pisani, and D. M. Parkin. 2001. "Globocan 2000: Cancer Incidence, Mortality, and Prevalence Worldwide." Version 1.0. International Agency for Research on Cancer CancerBase No. 5. Lyon, France: International Agency for Research on Cancer Press.

Fewtrell, L. J., A. Pruss-Ustun, P. Landrigan, and J. L Ayuso-Mateos. 2004. "Estimating the Global Burden of Disease of Mild Mental Retardation and Cardiovascular Diseases from Environmental Lead Exposure." *Environmental Research* 94 (2): 120–33.

Field, M. J., and G. M. Gold, eds. 1998. *Summarizing Population Health: Directions for the Development and Application of Population Metrics.* Washington, DC: National Academy Press.

Frick, K., E. Basilion, C. Hanson, and A. Colchero. 2003. "Estimating the Burden and Economic Impact of Trachomatous Visual Loss." *Ophthalmic Epidemiology* 10 (2): 121–32.

Gajalakshmi, V., R. Peto, S. Kanaka, and S. Balasubramian. 2002. "Verbal Autopsy of 48,000 Adult Deaths Attributable to Medical Causes in Chennai (formerly Madras)." *BioMed Central* 16, no. 2(1): 7.

Galazka, A. M., and S. E. Robertson. 2004. "Pertussis." In *The Global Epidemiology of Infectious Diseases*, ed. C. J. L. Murray, A. D. Lopez, and C. D. Mathers, 29–54. Vol. 4 of *Global Burden of Disease and Injury Series*. Geneva: World Health Organization. http://whqlibdoc.who.int/publications/2004/9241592303.pdf.

Gavrilova, N. S., V. G. Semyonova, G. N. Evdokushkina, and L. A. Gavrilov. 2000. "The Response of Violent Mortality to Economic Crisis in Russia." *Population Research and Policy Review* 19 (5): 397–419.

Gerbase, A. C., J. T. Rowley, D. H. L. Heymann, S. F. B. Berkley, and P. Piot. 1998. "Global Prevalence and Incidence Estimates of Selected Curable STDs." *Sexually Transmitted Diseases* 74 (Suppl 1): S12–S16.

Ghana Health Assessment Project Team. 1981. "A Quantitative Method of Assessing the Health Impact of Different Diseases in Less Developed Countries." *International Journal of Epidemiology* 10 (1): 72–80.

Gleditsch, N. P., P. Wallensteen, M. Eriksson, M. Sollenberg, and H. Strand. 2002. "Armed Conflict 1946–2001: A New Dataset." *Journal of Peace Research* 39 (5): 615–37.

Global Burden of Hepatitis C Working Group. 2004. "Global Burden of Disease (GBD) for Hepatitis C." *Journal of Clinical Pharmacology* 44 (1): 20–9.

Handicap International. 2001. *Landmine Victim Assistance: World Report 2001*. Lyon, France: Handicap International.

Hill, K., C. AbouZahr, and T. Wardlaw. 2001. "Estimates of Maternal Mortality for 1995." *Bulletin of the World Health Organization* 79 (3): 182–93.

Horton, R. 2005. "The Ellison Institute: Monitoring Health, Challenging WHO." *Lancet* 366 (9481): 179–81.

Human Rights Watch. 2001. *Landmine Monitor Report: 2001—Toward a Mine-Free World*. New York: Human Rights Watch.

Hyder, A. A., G. Rotllanat, and R. H. Morrow. 1998. "Measuring the Burden of Disease: Healthy Life-Years." *American Journal of Public Health* 88 (2): 196–202.

ISAAC Steering Committee. 1998a. "Worldwide Variation in the Prevalence of Symptoms of Asthma, Allergic Rhinoconjunctivitis, and Atopic Eczema: The International Study of Asthma and Allergies in Childhood (ISAAC)." *Lancet* 351 (9111): 1225–32.

———. 1998b. "Worldwide Variations in the Prevalence of Asthma Symptoms: The International Study of Asthma and Allergies in Childhood (ISAAC)." *European Respiratory Journal* 12 (2): 315–35.

Jamison, D. T. 1996. "Foreword to the *Global Burden of Disease and Injury Series*." In *The Global Burden of Disease: A Comprehensive Assessment of Mortality and Disability from Diseases, Injuries, and Risk Factors in 1990 and Projected to 2020*, ed. C. J. L. Murray and A. D. Lopez, xvi–xxiii. Vol. 1 of *Global Burden of Disease and Injury*. Cambridge, MA: Harvard School of Public Health.

Jamison, D. T., W. H. Mosley, A. R. Measham, and J. L. Bobadilla. 1993. *Disease Control Priorities in Developing Countries*. New York: Oxford University Press.

Jamison, D. T., J.G. Breman, A. R. Measham, G. Alleyne, M. Claeson, D. B. Evans, P. Jha, and P. Mills and P. Mubgrove. 2006. *Disease Control Priorities in Developing Countries*, 2nd ed. New York: Oxford University Press.

Karvonen, M., M. Viik-Kajander, E. Moltchanova, I. Libman, R. LaPorte, and J. Tuomilehto. 2000. "Incidence of Childhood Type 1 Diabetes Worldwide. Diabetes Mondiale (DiaMond) Project Group." *Diabetes Care* 23 (10): 1516–26.

Katz, J., and G. King. 1999. "A Statistical Model for Multiparty Electoral Data." *American Political Science Review* 93 (1): 15–32.

Kauhanen, J., G. A. Kaplan, D. E. Goldberg, and J. T. Salonen. 1997. "Beer Binging and Mortality: Results from the Kuopio Ischaemic Heart Disease Risk Factor Study, A Prospective Population-Based Study." *British Medical Journal* 315 (7112): 846–51.

Korenromp, E. L. 2005. "Malaria Incidence Estimates at Country Level for the Year 2004." Proposed estimates and draft report, World Health Organization, Roll Back Malaria Monitoring and Evaluation Reference Group and Malaria Epidemiology Reference Group Task Force on Malaria Morbidity, Geneva.

Korenromp, E., B. G. Williams, E. Gouws, C. Dye, and R. W. Snow. 2003. "Measurement of Trends in Childhood Malaria Mortality in Africa: An Assessment of Progress Toward Targets Based on Verbal Autopsy." *Lancet Infectious Diseases* 3 (6): 349–58.

Kruijshaar, M., N. Hoeymans, J. Skijker, M. E. A. Stouthard, and M. Essink-Bot. 2005. "Has the Burden of Depression Been Overestimated?" *Bulletin of the World Health Organization* 83 (8): 443–8.

Lavanchy, D. 2004. "Hepatitis B Virus Epidemiology, Disease Burden, Treatment, and Current and Emerging Prevention and Control Measures." *Journal of Viral Hepatitis* 11 (2): 97–107.

Lawn, J. E., S. Cousens, and J. Zupan. 2005. "Four Million Neonatal Deaths: When? Where? Why?" *Lancet* 365 (9462): 891–900.

LeDuc, J. W., K. Esteves, and N. G. Gratz. 2004. "Dengue and Dengue Haemorrhagic Fever." In *The Global Epidemiology of Infectious Diseases*, ed. C. J. L. Murray, A. D. Lopez, and C. D. Mathers, 219–42. Vol. 4 of *Global Burden of Disease and Injury Series*. Geneva: World Health Organization. http://whqlibdoc.who.int/publications/2004/9241592303.pdf.

Leonardi, M., and C. D. Mathers. 2003. "Global Burden of Migraine in the Year 2000: Summary of Methods and Data Sources." GBD 2000 Working Paper, World Health Organization, Geneva. http://www.who.int/evidence/bod.

Lopez, A. D., K. Shibuya, C. Rao, and C. D. Mathers. Forthcoming. "Estimating the Burden of Chronic Obstructive Pulmonary Disease: Methods and Results from the Global Burden of Disease Study." *European Respiratory Journal*.

Lopez, A. D., O. Ahmad, M. Guillot, B. Ferguson, J. Salomon, C. J. L. Murray, and K. H. Hill. 2002. *World Mortality in 2000: Life Tables for 191 Countries*. Geneva: World Health Organization.

Lozano, R., C. J. L. Murray, J. Frenk, and J. Bobadilla. 1995. "Burden of Disease Assessment and Health System Reform: Results of a Study in Mexico." *Journal of International Development* 7 (3): 555–64.

Lozano, R., C. J. L. Murray, A. D. Lopez, and T. Satoh. 2001. "Miscoding and Misclassification of Ischaemic Heart Disease Mortality." Global Program on Evidence for Health Policy Discussion Paper 12, World Health Organization, Geneva. http://www.who.int/evidence.

Mahapatra, P. 2002. *Estimating National Burden of Disease: The Burden of Disease in Andhra Pradesh, 1990's*. Hyderabad, India: Institute of Health Systems.

Mari Bhat, P. N. 2002. "Completeness of India's Sample Registration System: An Assessment Using the General Growth Balance Method." *Population Studies* 56 (2): 119–34.

Marshall, M. G., and T. R. Gurr. 2003. *Peace and Conflict 2003: A Global Survey of Armed Conflicts, Self-Determination Movements, and Democracy*. College Park, MD: Center for International Development and Conflict Management.

Mathers, C. D., and J. L. Ayuso-Mateos. 2003. "Global Burden of Alcohol Use Disorders in the Year 2000: Summary of Methods and Data Sources." GBD 2000 Working Paper, World Health Organization, Geneva. http://www.who.int/evidence/bod.

Mathers, C. D., and A. de Francisco. 2004. "The Global Burden of Disease." In *Monitoring Financial Flows for Health Research*, vol. 2, ed. Global

Forum for Health Research, 55–67. Geneva: Global Forum for Health Research.

Mathers, C. D., and M. Leonardi. 2003. "Global Burden of Dementia in the Year 2000: Summary of Methods and Data Sources." GBD 2000 Working Paper, World Health Organization, Geneva. http://www.who.int/evidence/bod.

Mathers, C. D., C. J. L. Murray, and J. A. Salomon. 2003. "Methods for Measuring Healthy Life Expectancy." In *Health Systems Performance Assessment: Debates, Methods, and Empiricism*, ed. C. J. L. Murray and D. Evans, 437–70. Geneva: World Health Organization.

Mathers, C. D., A. Smith, and M. Concha. 2003. "Global Burden of Hearing Loss in the Year 2000." GBD 2000 Working Paper, World Health Organization, Geneva. http://www.who.int/evidence/bod.

Mathers, C. D., T. Vos, and C. Stevenson. 1999. *The Burden of Disease and Injury in Australia*. Canberra: Australian Institute of Health and Welfare.

Mathers, C. D., J. A. Salomon, C. J. L. Murray, and A. D. Lopez. 2003. "Alternative Summary Measures of Average Population Health." In *Health Systems Performance Assessment: Debates, Methods, and Empiricism*, ed. C. J. L. Murray and D. Evans, 319–34. Geneva: World Health Organization.

Mathers, C. D., T. Truelsen, S. Begg, and T. Satoh. 2004. "Global Burden of Ischaemic Heart Disease in the Year 2000." GBD 2000 Working Paper, World Health Organization, Geneva. http://www.who.int/evidence/bod.

Mathers, C. D., M. Ezzati, A. D. Lopez, C. J. L Murray, and A. Rogers. 2002. "Causal Decomposition of Summary Measures of Population Health." In *Summary Measures of Population Health: Concepts, Ethics, Measurement, and Applications*, ed. C. J. L. Murray, J. A. Salomon, C. D. Mathers, and A. D. Lopez, 273–90. Geneva: World Health Organization. http://www.who.int/pub/smph/en/index.html.

Mathers, C. D., D. Ma Fat, M. Inoue, C. Rao, and A. D. Lopez. 2005. "Counting the Dead and What They Died from: An Assessment of the Global Status of Cause of Death Data." *Bulletin of the World Health Organization* 83 (3): 171–7.

Mathers, C. D., C. J. L. Murray, A. D. Lopez, J. A. Salomon, and R. Sadana. 2003. "Global Patterns of Health Expectancy in the Year 2000." In *Determining Health Expectancies*, ed. J. M. Robine, C. Jagger, C. D. Mathers, E. M. Crimmins, and R. M. Suzman, 335–58. Chichester, U.K.: John Wiley & Sons.

Mathers, C. D., K. Shibuya, C. Boschi-Pinto, A. D. Lopez, and C. J. Murray. 2002. "Global and Regional Estimates of Cancer Mortality and Incidence by Site: I. Application of Regional Cancer Survival Model to Estimate Cancer Mortality Distribution by Site." *BMC Cancer* 2 (1): 36.

Mathers, C. D., A. D. Lopez, C. Stein, D. Ma Fat, C. Rao, M. Inoue, K. Shibuya, N. Tomijima, C. Bernard and H. Xu. 2004. "Deaths and Disease Burden by Cause: Global Burden of Disease Estimates for 2001 by World Bank Country Groups." Working Papers Series 18, Second Project on Disease Control Priorities in Developing Countries, World Health Organization; World Bank; and Fogarty International Center, U.S. National Institutes of Health, Washington, DC.

McDowell, I., and C. Newell. 1996. *Measuring Health. A Guide to Rating Scales and Questionnaires*, 2nd ed. Oxford, U.K.: Oxford University Press.

McKenna, M. T., C. M. Michaud, C. J. L. Murray, and J. S. Marks. 2005. "Assessing the Burden of Disease in the United States Using Disability-Adjusted Life Years." *American Journal of Preventive Medicine* 28 (5): 415–23.

Men, T., P. Brennan, P. Boffetta, and D. Zaridze. 2003. "Russian Mortality Trends for 1991–2001: Analysis by Cause and Region." *British Medical Journal* 327 (7421): 964.

Ministry of Public Health. 2002. *Burden of Disease and Injuries in Thailand: Priority Setting for Policy*. Bangkok: Government of Thailand.

Moncayo, A. 2003. "Chagas' Disease: Current Epidemiological Trends after the Interruption of Vectorial and Transfusional Transmission in the Southern Cone Countries." *Memórias do Instituto Oswaldo Cruz* 98 (5): 577–91.

Moncayo, A., F. Guhl, and C. Stein. 2002. "The Global Burden of Chagas' Disease in the Year 2000." GBD 2000 Working Paper, World Health Organization, Geneva. http://www.who.int/evidence/bod.

Murray, C. J. L. 1996. "Rethinking DALYs." In *The Global Burden of Disease*, ed. C. J. L. Murray and A. D. Lopez, 1–98. Vol. 1 of *Global Burden of Disease and Injury Series*. Cambridge, MA: Harvard University Press.

Murray, C. J. L., and A. K. Acharya. 1997. "Understanding DALYs." *Journal of Health Economics* 16 (6): 703–30.

Murray, C. J. L., and A. D. Lopez. 1996a. "Estimating Causes of Death: New Methods and Global and Regional Applications for 1990." In *The Global Burden of Disease*, ed. C. J. L. Murray and A. D. Lopez, 117–200. Vol. 1 of *Global Burden of Disease and Injury Series*. Cambridge, MA: Harvard University Press.

————. 1996b. "Evidence-Based Health Policy: Lessons from the Global Burden of Disease Study." *Science* 274 (5288):740–3.

————, eds. 1996c. *The Global Burden of Disease: A Comprehensive Assessment of Mortality and Disability from Diseases, Injuries, and Risk Factors in 1990 and Projected to 2020*. Vol. 1 of *Global Burden of Disease and Injury Series*. Cambridge, MA: Harvard University Press.

————. 1996d. *Global Health Statistics*. Vol. 2 of *Global Burden of Disease and Injury Series*. Cambridge, MA: Harvard University Press.

————. 1997a. "Global Mortality, Disability, and the Contribution of Risk Factors: Global Burden of Disease Study." *Lancet* 349 (9063): 1436–42.

————. 1997b. "Mortality by Cause for Eight Regions of the World: Global Burden of Disease Study." *Lancet* 349 (9061): 1269–76.

————, eds. 1998. *Health Dimensions of Sex and Reproduction*. Vol. 3 of *Global Burden of Disease and Injury Series*. Cambridge, MA: Harvard University Press.

————. 2000. "Progress and Directions in Refining the Global Burden of Disease Approach: A Response to Williams." *Health Economics* 9 (1): 69–82.

Murray, C. J. L., A. D. Lopez, and D. T. Jamison. 1994. "The Global Burden of Disease in 1990: Summary Results, Sensitivity Analysis, and Future Directions." *Bulletin of the World Health Organization* 72 (3): 495–509.

Murray, C. J., A. D. Lopez, and S. Wibulpolprasert. 2004. "Monitoring Global Health: Time for New Solutions." *British Medical Journal* 329 (7333): 1096–100.

Murray, C. J. L, C. D. Mathers, and J. A. Salomon. 2003. "Towards Evidence-based Public Health." In *Health Systems Performance Assessment: Debates, Methods, and Empiricism*, ed. C. J. L. Murray and D. Evans, 715–26. Geneva: World Health Organization.

Murray, C. J. L., J. A. Salomon, and C. D. Mathers. 2000. "A Critical Examination of Summary Measures of Population Health." *Bulletin of the World Health Organization* 78 (8): 981–94.

Murray, C. J. L, J. A. Salomon, C. D. Mathers, and A. D. Lopez, eds. 2002a. *Summary Measures of Population Health: Concepts, Ethics, Measurement, and Applications*. Geneva: World Health Organization.

————. 2002b. "Summary Measures of Population Health: Conclusions and Recommendations." In *Summary Measures of Population Health: Concepts, Ethics, Measurement, and Applications*, ed. C. J. L. Murray, J. A. Salomon, C. D. Mathers, and A. D. Lopez, 731–56. Geneva: World Health Organization.

Murray, C. J. L., A. Tandon, J. A. Salomon, and C. D. Mathers. 2002. "New Approaches to Enhance Cross-Population Comparability of Survey Results." In *Summary Measures of Population Health: Concepts, Ethics, Measurement, and Applications*, ed. C. J. L. Murray, J. A. Salomon, C. D. Mathers, and A. D. Lopez, 421–31. Geneva: World Health Organization.

Murray, C. J., G. King, A. D. Lopez, N. Tomijima, and E. G. Krug. 2002. "Armed Conflict as a Public Health Problem." *British Medical Journal* 324 (7333): 346–9.

Murray, C. J. L., B. D. Ferguson, A. D. Lopez, M. Guillot, J. A. Salomon, and O. Ahmad. 2003. "Modified Logit Life Table System: Principles, Empirical Validation, and Application." *Population Studies* 57 (2): 1–18.

Pearce, N., J. Sunyer, S. Cheng, S. Chinn, B. Bjorksten, M. Burr, U. Keil, H. R. Anderson, and P. Burney. 2000. "Comparison of Asthma Prevalence in the ISAAC and the ECRHS. ISAAC Steering Committee and the European Community Respiratory Health Survey. International Study of Asthma and Allergies in Childhood." *European Respiratory Journal* 16 (3): 420–6.

Peto, R., A. D. Lopez, J. Boreham, M. Thun, and C. Heath. 1992. "Mortality from Tobacco in Developed Countries: Indirect Estimation from National Vital Statistics." *Lancet* 339 (8804): 1268–78.

Preston, S. H. 1976. *Mortality Patterns in National Populations.* New York: Academic Press.

Project Ploughshares. 2001. *Armed Conflicts Report 2001.* Waterloo, Canada: Project Ploughshares.

———. 2002. *Armed Conflicts Report 2002.* Waterloo, Canada: Project Ploughshares.

Pruss-Ustun, A., L. J. Fewtrell, P. Landrigan, and J. L Ayuso-Mateos. 2004. "Lead Exposure." In *Comparative Quantification of Health Risks: Global and Regional Burden of Disease Attributable to Selected Major Risk Factors,* ed. M. Ezzati, A. D. Lopez, A. Rodgers, and C. J. L Murray, 1495–592. Geneva: World Health Organization.

Ranson, M. K., and T. G. Evans. 1995. "The Global Burden of Trachomatous Visual Impairment: I. Assessing Prevalence." *International Ophthalmology* 19 (5): 261–70.

Rao, C., D. Bradshaw, and C. D. Mathers. 2004. "Improving Death Registration and Statistics in Developing Countries: Lessons from Sub-Saharan Africa." *Southern African Journal of Demography* 9 (2): 79–97.

Rastogi, T., and C. D. Mathers. 2002a. "Global Burden of Iodine Deficiency Disorders in the Year 2000." GBD 2000 Working Paper, World Health Organization, Geneva. http://www.who.int/evidence/bod.

———. 2002b. "Global Burden of Iron Deficiency Anaemia in the Year 2000." GBD 2000 Working Paper, World Health Organization, Geneva. http://www.who.int/evidence/bod.

———. 2002c. "Global Burden of Vitamin A Deficiency in the Year 2000." GBD 2000 Working Paper, World Health Organization, Geneva. http://www.who.int/evidence/bod.

Rehm, J., R. Room, M. Monteiro, G. Gmel, K. Graham, N. Rehn, C. Sempos, U. Frick, and D. Jernigan. 2004. "Alcohol Use." In *Comparative Quantification of Health Risks: Global and Regional Burden of Disease Attributable to Selected Major Risk Factors,* ed. M. Ezzati, A. D. Lopez, A. Rodgers, and C. J. L Murray, 959–1108. Geneva: World Health Organization.

Resnikoff, S., D. Pascolini, D. Etya'ale, I. Kocur, R. Pararajasegaram, G. P. Pokharel, and S. P. Mariotti. 2004. "Global Data on Visual Impairment in the Year 2002." *Bulletin of the World Health Organization* 82 (11): 844–51.

Richards, F. O., B. Boatin, M. Sauerbrey, and A. Seketeli. 2001. "Control of Onchocerciasis Today: Status and Challenges." *Trends in Parasitology* 17 (12): 558–63.

Ries, L. A. G., M. P. Eisner, C. L. Kosary, B. F. Hankey, B. A. Biller, L. Clegg, B. K. Edwards, eds. 2002. *SEER Cancer Statistics Review, 1973–1999.* Bethesda, MD: National Cancer Institute.

Robine, J. M., C. Jagger, C. D. Mathers, E. M. Crimmins, and R. M. Suzman. 2003. *Determining Health Expectancies.* Chichester, U.K.: John Wiley & Sons.

Roglic, G., N. Unwin, P. H. Bennett, C. D. Mathers, J. Tuomilheto, and H. King. 2005. "The Realistic Burden of Mortality Attributable to Diabetes: Estimates for the Year 2000." *Diabetes Care* 28 (9): 2130–5.

Rowe, A. K., R. W. Steketee, S. Y. Rowe, R. W. Snow, E. Korenromp, J. A. Schellenberg, C. Stein, B. Nahler, J. Bryce, and R. Black. 2004. "Estimates of the Burden of Mortality Directly Attributable to Malaria for Children under Five Years of Age in Africa for the Year 2000." Final report for the Child Health Epidemiology Reference Group. http://www.who.int/child-adolescent-health/New_Publications/ CHILD_HEALTH/EPI/CHERG_Malaria_ Mortality.pdf.

Rudan, I., L. Tomaskovic, C. Boschi-Pinto, and H. Campbell. 2004. "Global Estimate of the Incidence of Clinical Pneumonia among Children under Five Years of Age." *Bulletin of the World Health Organization* 82 (12): 895–903.

Sadana, R. 2002. "Development of Standardized Health State Descriptions." In *Summary Measures of Population Health: Concepts, Ethics, Measurement, and Applications,* ed. C. J. L. Murray, J. A. Salomon, C. D. Mathers, and A. D. Lopez, 315–28. Geneva: World Health Organization.

Sadana, R., C. D. Mathers, A. D. Lopez, C. J. L Murray, and K. Moesgaard-Iburg. 2002. "Comparative Analyses of More Than 50 Household Surveys on Health Status." In *Summary Measures of Population Health: Concepts, Ethics, Measurement, and Applications,* ed. C. J. L. Murray, J. A. Salomon, C. D. Mathers, and A. D. Lopez, 369–86. Geneva: World Health Organization.

Salomon, J. A., and C. J. L. Murray. 2001a. "Compositional Models for Mortality by Age, Sex, and Cause." Global Program on Evidence for Health Policy Discussion Paper 11, World Health Organization, Geneva. http://www.who.int/evidence.

———. 2001b. "Modelling HIV/AIDS Epidemics in Sub-Saharan Africa Using Seroprevalence Data from Antenatal Clinics." *Bulletin of the World Health Organization* 79 (7): 596–607.

———. 2002a. "The Epidemiologic Transition Revisited: Compositional Models for Causes of Death by Age and Sex." *Population and Development Review* 28 (2): 205–28.

———. 2002b. "Estimating Health State Valuations Using a Multiple-Method Protocol." In *Summary Measures of Population Health: Concepts, Ethics, Measurement, and Applications,* ed. C. J. L. Murray, J. A. Salomon, C. D. Mathers, and A. D. Lopez, 487–99. Geneva: World Health Organization.

———. 2004. "A Multimethod Approach to Estimating Health State Valuations." *Health Economics* 13 (3): 281–90

Salomon, J. A., C. J. L. Murray, T. B. Ustun, and S. Chatterji. 2003. "Health State Valuations in Summary Measures of Population Health." In *Health Systems Performance Assessment: Debate, Methods, and Empiricism,* ed. C. J. L. Murray and D. Evans, 409–36. Geneva: World Health Organization.

Salomon, J. A., C. D. Mathers, S. Chatterji, R. Sadana, T. B. Ustun, and C. J. L. Murray. 2003. "Quantifying Individual Levels of Health: Definitions, Concepts, and Measurement Issues." In *Health Systems Performance Assessment: Debate, Methods, and Empiricism,* ed. C. J. L. Murray, and D. Evans, 301–18. Geneva: World Health Organization.

Schwartlander, B., K. A. Stanecki, T. Brown, P. O. Way, R. Monasch, J. Chin, D. Tarantola, and N. Walker. 1999. "Country-Specific Estimates and Models of HIV and AIDS: Methods and Limitations." *AIDS* 13 (17): 2445–58.

Semenova, V. G., N. S. Gavrilova, Y. A. Varavikova, L. A. Gavrilov, and G. N. Yevdokushkina. 2000. "Rise in Violent Death Rates in Russia as a Consequence of the Economic Crisis." *Diseases Prevention and Health Promotion* 4: 3–10.

Setel, P. W., O. Sankoh, C. Rao, V. A. Velkoff, C. D. Mathers, Y. Gonghuan, I. Hemed, P. Jha, and A. D. Lopez. 2005. "Sample Registration of Vital Events with Verbal Autopsy: A Renewed Commitment to Measuring and Monitoring Vital Statistics." *Bulletin of the World Health Organization* 83 (8): 611–17.

Shibuya, K., and M. Ezzati. 2003. "Global Burden of Onchocerciasis in the Year 2000: Summary of Methods and Data Sources." GBD 2000

Working Paper, World Health Organization, Geneva. http://www.who.int/evidence/bod.

Shibuya, K., and C. D. Mathers. 2003. "Global Burden of Trachoma in the Year 2000: Summary of Methods and Data Sources." GBD 2000 Working Paper, World Health Organization, Geneva. http://www.who.int/evidence/bod.

Shibuya, K., C. D. Mathers, C. Boschi-Pinto, A. D. Lopez, and C. J. L. Murray. 2002. "Global and Regional Estimates of Cancer Mortality and Incidence by Site: II. Results for the Global Burden of Disease Study 2000." *BMC Cancer* 2: 37.

Shkolnikov, V., M. McKee, and D. A. Leon. 2001. "Changes in Life Expectancy in Russia in the Mid-1990s." *Lancet* 357 (9260): 917–21.

Single, E., L. Robson, X. Xie, and J. Rehm. 2002. *The Costs of Substance Abuse in Canada*. Ottawa: Canadian Centre on Substance Abuse.

Snow, R. W., M. Craig, U. Deichmann, and K. Marsh. 1999. "Estimating Mortality, Morbidity, and Disability Due to Malaria among Africa's Non-pregnant Population." *Bulletin of the World Health Organization* 77 (8): 624–40.

Stein, C. 2002a. "Global Burden of Leprosy in the Year 2000." GBD 2000 Working Paper, World Health Organization, Geneva. http://www.who.int/evidence/bod.

———. 2002b. "Global Burden of Poliomyelitis in the Year 2000." GBD 2000 Working Paper, World Health Organization, Geneva. http://www.who.int/evidence/bod.

———. 2002c. "Global Burden of Protein-Energy Malnutrition in the Year 2000." GBD 2000 Working Paper, World Health Organization, Geneva. http://www.who.int/evidence/bod.

Stein, C., and M. Robertson. 2002. "Global Burden of Diphtheria in the Year 2000." GBD 2000 Working Paper, World Health Organization, Geneva. http://www.who.int/evidence/bod.

Stouthard, M., M. Essink-Bot, G. Bonsel, J. Barendregt, and P. Kramers. 1997. *Disability Weights for Diseases in the Netherlands*. Rotterdam, Netherlands: Erasmus University, Department of Public Health.

Stover, J., N. Walker, G. P. Garnett, J. A. Salomon, K. A. Stanecki, P. D. Ghys, N. C. Grassly, R. M. Anderson, and B. Schwartlander. 2002. "Can We Reverse the HIV/AIDS Pandemic with an Expanded Response?" *Lancet* 360 (9326): 73–77.

Symmons, D. P., C. D. Mathers, and B. Pfleger. 2002a. "The Global Burden of Osteoarthritis in the Year 2000." GBD 2000 Working Paper, World Health Organization, Geneva. http://www.who.int/evidence/bod.

———. 2002b. "The Global Burden of Rheumatoid Arthritis in the Year 2000." GBD 2000 Working Paper, World Health Organization, Geneva. http://www.who.int/evidence/bod.

Tan-Torres Edejer, T. R. Baltussen, T. Adam, R. Hutubessy, A Acharya, D. B. Evans, and C. J. L. Murray. 2003. *WHO Guide to Cost-Effectiveness Analysis*. Geneva: World Health Organization.

Thylefors, B., A. D. Negrel, R. Pararajasegaram, and K. Y. Dadzie. 1995. "Global Data on Blindness." *Bulletin of the World Health Organization* 73 (1): 115–21.

Truelsen, T., S. Begg, C. D. Mathers, and T. Satoh. 2002. "Global Burden of Cerebrovascular Disease in the Year 2000." GBD 2000 Working Paper, World Health Organization, Geneva. http://www.who.int/evidence/bod.

UNAIDS (Joint United Nations Programme on HIV/AIDS) Reference Group on Estimates Model and Projections. 2002. "Improved Methods and Assumptions for Estimation and Projection of HIV/AIDS Epidemics." *AIDS* 16: 1–16.

UNICEF (United Nations Children's Fund) and WHO (World Health Organization). 2005. *Low Birthweight: Country, Regional, and Global Estimates*. New York: UNICEF.

United Nations Population Division. 2003. *World Population Prospects: The 2002 Revision*. New York: United Nations.

Ustun, T. B., and D. Chisholm. 2001. "Global Burden of Disease Study for Psychiatric Disorders." *Psychiatrisch Prax* 28 (Suppl 1): S7–S11.

Ustun, T. B., J. L. Ayuso-Mateos, S. Chatterji, C. D. Mathers, and C. J. L. Murray. 2005. "Global Burden of Depressive Disorders in the Year 2000." *British Journal of Psychiatry* 184: 386–92.

Ustun, T. B., S. Chatterji, A. Mechbal, C. J. L. Murray, and World Health Survey Collaborating Groups. 2003. "The World Health Surveys." In *Health Systems Performance Assessment: Debates, Methods, and Empiricism*, ed. C. J. L. Murray and D. Evans, 797–808. Geneva: World Health Organization.

Ustun, T. B., S. Chatterji, M. Villanueva, L. Bendib, C. Celik, R. Sadana, N. Valentine, C. Mathers, J. P. Ortiz, A. Tandon, J. Salomon, Y. Cao, X. W. Jun, and C. J. L. Murray. 2003. "The WHO Multicountry Household Survey Study on Health and Responsiveness 2000–2001." In *Health Systems Performance Assessment: Debates, Methods, and Empiricism*, ed. C. J. L. Murray and D. Evans, 761–96. Geneva: World Health Organization.

van der Werf, M. J., and S. J. de Vlas. 2001. *Morbidity and Infection with Schistosomes or Soil-Transmitted Helminths*. Report prepared for the World Health Organization Parasitic Diseases and Vector Control. Rotterdam, Netherlands: Erasmus University.

Vos, T., M. Tobias, H. Gareeboo, F. Roussety, S. Huttley, and C. J. L. Murray. 1995. *Mauritius Health Sector Reform, National Burden of Disease Study, Final Report of Consultancy*. Port Louis, Mauritius: Ministry of Health and Ministry of Economic Planning and Development.

Walker, N., K. A. Stanecki, T. Brown, J. Stover, S. Lazzari, J. M. Garcia-Calleja, B. Schwartlander, and P. D. Ghys. 2003. "Methods and Procedures for Estimating HIV/AIDS and Its Impact: The UNAIDS/WHO Estimates for the End of 2001." *AIDS* 17 (15): 2215–25.

Ware, J. E., and C. D. Sherbourne. 1992. "The MOS 36-Item Short Form Health Survey (SF-36): I. Conceptual Framework and Item Selection." *Medical Care* 30 (6): 473–83.

Warren, S., and K. G. Warren. 2001. *Multiple Sclerosis*. Geneva: World Health Organization.

WHO (World Health Organization). 1977. *Manual of the International Statistical Classification of Diseases, Injuries, and Causes of Death*, 9th rev, vol. 1. Geneva: WHO.

———. 1992. *International Classification of Diseases and Related Health Problems*, 10th rev. Geneva: WHO.

———. 1995. "Onchocerciasis and Its Control: Report of a WHO Expert Committee on Onchocerciasis Control." WHO Technical Report Series 852, World Health Organization, Geneva.

———. 1996. *Investing in Health Research and Development. Report of the Ad Hoc Committee on Health Research Relating to Future Intervention Options*. Geneva: WHO.

———. 2000. *World Health Report 2000. Health Systems: Improving Performance*. Geneva: WHO.

———. 2001a. *Assessment of Iodine Deficiency Disorders and Monitoring their Elimination*. Document WHO/NHD/01.1. Geneva: WHO.

———. 2001b. "Epidemics of Meningococcal Disease, African Meningitis Belt, 2001." *Weekly Epidemiological Record* 76 (37): 281–8.

———. 2001c. *Global Prevalence and Incidence of Selected Curable Sexually Transmitted Infections: Overview and Estimates*. WHO/CDS/CSR/EDC/2001.10. Geneva: WHO.

———. 2001d. *World Health Report 2001: Mental Health—New Understanding, New Hope*. Geneva: WHO.

———. 2002a. "Global Distribution of Hepatitis A, B, and C, 2001." *Weekly Epidemiological Record* 77 (6): 41–8.

———. 2002b. *Hepatitis B*. WHO/CDS/CSR/LYO/2002.2:Hepatitis B. Geneva: WHO, Department of Communicable Diseases Surveillance and Response.

———. 2002c. "Leprosy: Global Situation." *Weekly Epidemiological Record* 77 (1): 1–8.

———. 2002d. *World Health Report 2002. Reducing Risks, Promoting Healthy Life.* Geneva: WHO.

———. 2003a. *Global Tuberculosis Control: Surveillance, Planning, and Financing.* Geneva: WHO.

———. 2003b. *World Health Report 2003: Shaping the Future.* Geneva: WHO.

———. 2004a. *Unsafe Abortion.* Geneva: WHO.

———. 2004b. *World Health Report 2004: Changing History.* Geneva: WHO.

WHO Nutrition Program. 2002a. "Database on Anaemia." Geneva: WHO. http://www.who.int/nut/db_mdis.htm.

———. 2002b. "Database on Vitamin A Deficiency." Geneva: WHO. http://www.who.int/nut/db_mdis.htm.

———. 2005. "Database on Iodine Deficiency Disorders." Geneva: WHO. http://www3.who.int/whosis/micronutrient/.

WHO, UNICEF, and UNFPA (World Health Organization, United Nations Children's Fund, and United Nations Population Fund). 2003. *Maternal Mortality in 2000: Estimates Developed by WHO, UNICEF and UNFPA.* Geneva: WHO.

Wild, S., G. Roglic, A. Green, R. Sicree, and H. King. 2004. "Global Prevalence of Diabetes: Estimates for the Year 2000 and Projections for 2030." *Diabetes Care* 27 (5): 1047–53.

Williams, A. 1997. "Intergenerational Equity: An Exploration of the 'Fair Innings' Argument." *Health Economics* 6 (2): 117–32.

———. 1999. Calculating the Global Burden of Disease: Time for a Strategic Reappraisal. *Health Economics* 8 (1): 1–8.

Williams, B. G., E. Gouws, C. Boschi-Pinto, J. Bryce, and C. Dye. 2002. "Estimates of World-wide Distribution of Child Deaths from Acute Respiratory Infections." *Lancet* 2 (1): 25–32.

Wolfson, M. C. 1999. "Measuring Health: Visions and Practicalities." *Statistical Journal of the United Nations Economic Commission for Europe* 16 (1): 1–17.

World Bank. 1993. *World Development Report 1993. Investing in Health.* New York: Oxford University Press.

———. 2003. *World Development Report 2003: Sustainable Development in a Dynamic World: Transforming Institutions, Growth, and Quality of Life.* New York: Oxford University Press.

Yang, G. H., J. Hu, K. Q. Rao, J. Ma, C. Rao, and A. D. Lopez. 2005. "Mortality Registration and Surveillance in China: History, Current Situation, and Challenges." *Population Health Metrics* 3: 3.

Zatonski, W. 1998. "Alcohol and Health: What Is Good for the French May Not Be for the Russians." *Journal of Epidemiology and Community Health* 52 (12): 766–7.

Zeckhauser, R., and D. Shepard. 1976. "Where Now for Saving Lives?" *Law and Contemporary Problems* 40 (4): 5–45.

Chapter 4

Comparative Quantification of Mortality and Burden of Disease Attributable to Selected Risk Factors

Majid Ezzati, Stephen Vander Hoorn, Alan D. Lopez, Goodarz Danaei, Anthony Rodgers, Colin D. Mathers, and Christopher J. L. Murray

Detailed descriptions of the level and distribution of diseases and injuries and their causes are important inputs into strategies for improving population health. A substantial body of work has focused on quantifying causes of mortality and, more recently, the burden of disease (Murray and Lopez 1997; Preston, 1976; see also chapter 3 in this volume). Data on disease or injury outcomes alone, such as death or hospitalization, tend to focus on the need for curative or palliative services. Reliable and comparable analyses of risks to health are critical for preventing disease and injury. Investigators have frequently analyzed morbidity and mortality due to risk factors in the context of methodological traditions of individual risk factors and for selected populations (Kunzli and others 2000; Leigh and others 1999; McGinnis and Foege 1993; Peto and others 1992; Single and others 1999; Smith 2000; Smith, Corvalan, and Kjellstrom 1999; Willet 2002). As a result, most estimates have been affected by the following shortcomings, which limit comparability:

- The causal attribution of morbidity and mortality due to risk factors has been estimated relative to arbitrary exposure levels without standardizing baseline exposure across risk factors. For example, the implicit baseline for the burden of injuries attributable to occupational factors has been "no work," because estimates have been based on occupational registries intended to register all injuries, regardless of whether they are avoidable (Leigh and others 1999).

- The intermediate stages and interactions in the causal process have not been considered when calculating the disease burden attributable to risk factors. As a result, attributable burden could only be calculated for those risk factor and disease combinations for which epidemiological studies had been conducted.

- The outcomes of analyses have been morbidity or mortality from specific diseases without conversion to a standard unit, making comparisons among different diseases and/or risk factors difficult.

To permit the assessment of risk factors in a unified framework while acknowledging characteristics specific to individual risk factors, the Comparative Risk Assessment (CRA) project initiated a systematic evaluation of the changes in population health that would result from modifying the population distribution of exposure to a risk factor or to a group of risk factors (Murray and others 2003; Murray and Lopez 1999; Ezzati and others 2004). In particular, the CRA framework

- compares the burden of disease due to the observed distribution of exposure in a population with the burden from an alternative distribution consistently defined across risk factors;
- considers multiple stages in the causal network of multiple risk factors and disease outcomes to allow inferences about combinations of risk factors for which epidemiological studies have not been conducted, including the joint effects of changes in multiple risk factors;
- converts the burden of disease and injury into a summary measure of population health that permits comparing fatal and nonfatal outcomes while also taking severity and duration into account (the summary measure used in this chapter is the disability-adjusted life year [DALY], whose definition and calculation are described in chapter 3).

Therefore, even though CRA is similar to other risk assessment exercises in the sense that it applies knowledge about the hazardous effects of risk factors from epidemiological research to data on exposure in the broader population, it creates conceptual and methodological consistency in measuring the impacts of various risk factors on population health. Furthermore, we have attempted to use consistent and comparable criteria for evaluating the scientific evidence on prevalence, causality, and magnitude of hazardous effects across risk factors. As a result, the unified framework for describing population exposure to risk factors and their consequences for population health is an important step in linking the growing interest in the causal determinants of health across a variety of disciplines from natural, physical, and medical sciences to the social sciences and humanities.

We note that risk assessment as defined here is distinct from intervention analysis, whose purpose is to estimate the benefits of a given intervention or group of interventions in a specific population at a particular time. Rather, risk assessment aims at mapping alternative population health scenarios that arise from changes in the distribution of exposure to risk factors, irrespective of whether exposure change is achievable using existing interventions. The alternative visions of population health in turn contribute to identifying those risk factors for which effective or cost-effective interventions should be implemented or new interventions should be developed.

BURDEN OF DISEASE ATTRIBUTABLE TO RISK FACTORS

Mathers and others (2002) describe two traditions for the causal attribution of health outcomes or states: categorical attribution and counterfactual analysis. In categorical attribution, an event such as death is attributed to a single cause, such as a disease or a risk factor, or to a group of causes, according to a defined set of rules such as the International Classification of Diseases (ICD) system (WHO 1992). In counterfactual analysis, the effects of one or a group of diseases or risk factors is estimated by comparing the current or future disease burden with the levels that would be expected under some alternative hypothetical scenario, referred to as the counterfactual, including the absence of or reduction in the diseases or risk factors of interest (see Maldonado and Greenland 2002 for a discussion of the conceptual and methodological issues involved in the use of counterfactuals). In theory, causal attribution of the burden of disease to risk factors can be done using both categorical and counterfactual approaches. For example, researchers have used categorical attribution for attributing diseases and injuries to occupational risk factors in occupational health registries (Leigh and others 1999) and motor vehicle accidents to alcohol use. However, categorical attribution to risk factors overlooks that many diseases have multiple causes (Rothman 1976).

The CRA estimates of the burden of disease and injuries due to risk factors are based on a counterfactual exposure distribution that would result in the lowest population risk, irrespective of whether currently attainable in practice, referred to as the theoretical-minimum-risk exposure distribution (Murray and Lopez 1999). Using the theoretical-minimum-risk exposure distribution as the counterfactual has the advantage of providing an indication of potential gains in population health from reducing the risk from all levels of suboptimal exposure in a consistent way across risk factors.

RISK FACTOR SELECTION

The CRA project included a selected group of risk factors, presented in table 4.1. The criteria for selecting risk factors included the following:

- they were likely to be among the leading causes of the disease burden globally or regionally;
- they were not too specific, for example, every one of the hundreds of air pollutants or fruits and vegetables, or too

Table 4.1 CRA Risk Factors, Exposure Variables, Theoretical-Minimum-Risk Exposure Distributions, and Disease Outcomes

Risk factor	Exposure variable	Theoretical-minimum-risk exposure distribution	Disease outcomes[a]
Childhood and maternal undernutrition			
Childhood underweight	Children < -1 SD weight-for-age compared to the international reference group in 1 SD increments	Same proportion of children below -1 SD weight-for-age as the international reference group	Mortality and acute morbidity from diarrhea, malaria, measles, pneumonia, and selected other Group I (communicable, maternal, perinatal, and nutritional) diseases; *long-term risks of undernutrition*
Iron-deficiency anemia	Hemoglobin concentration distribution, estimated from prevalence of anemia	Hemoglobin distributions that are estimated to occur if all iron deficiency were eliminated[b]	Anemia and its sequelae (including cognitive impairment), maternal and perinatal mortality
Vitamin A deficiency	Prevalence of vitamin A deficiency, estimated as low serum retinol concentrations (< 0.70 μmol/L) among children aged 0–4 years and among pregnant women (aged 15–44 years)	No vitamin A deficiency	Mortality due to diarrhea, measles, malaria, and miscellaneous infectious causes of disease (children under five), morbidity due to malaria (children under five), maternal mortality (pregnant women), vitamin A deficiency and its sequelae (all age groups); *maternal morbidity, low birthweight, and other perinatal conditions*
Zinc deficiency	Less than the U.S. recommended dietary allowances for zinc	The entire population consuming sufficient dietary zinc to meet physiological needs, taking into account routine and illness-related losses and bioavailability	Diarrhea, pneumonia, malaria; *adult and pregnancy outcomes*
Other nutrition-related risk factors and physical activity			
High blood pressure	Usual level of systolic blood pressure	115 SD 6 mmHg	IHD, stroke, hypertensive disease, and selected other cardiovascular diseases; *renal failure*
High cholesterol	Usual level of total blood cholesterol	3.8 SD 0.6 mmol/L	IHD, stroke; *other cardiovascular diseases*
Overweight and obesity (high BMI)	BMI (height/weight squared)	21 SD 1 kg/m^2	IHD, stroke, hypertensive disease, diabetes, osteoarthritis, endometrial and colon cancers, postmenopausal breast cancer; *gallbladder cancer, kidney cancer, breathlessness, back pain, dermatitis, menstrual disorders and infertility, gallstones, psychological effects*
Low fruit and vegetable intake	Daily fruit and vegetable intake	600 SD 50 g intake per day for adults	IHD, stroke, colorectal cancer, gastric cancer, lung cancer, esophageal cancer
Physical inactivity	Three categories of inactive, insufficiently active (< 2.5 hours per week of moderate-intensity activity, or less than 4,000 KJ/week), and sufficiently active. Activity in discretionary-time, work, and transport considered	All having at least 2.5 hours per week of moderate-intensity activity or equivalent (4,000 KJ/week)	IHD, breast cancer, colorectal cancer, diabetes; *falls and osteoporosis, osteoarthritis, lower back pain, prostate cancer*
Addictive substances			
Smoking	Current levels of smoking impact ratio (indirect indicator of accumulated smoking risk based on excess lung cancer mortality)	No smoking	Lung cancer, upper aerodigestive cancer, stomach cancer, liver cancer, pancreas cancer, cervix uteri cancer, bladder cancer, leukemia, COPD, other respiratory diseases, IHD, stroke, selected other cardiovascular diseases except hypertensive heart disease, and selected other medical causes in adults over 30 years of age; *fire injuries, maternal outcomes, and perinatal conditions*[c]
Alcohol use	Current alcohol consumption volumes and patterns	No alcohol use[d]	IHD, stroke, hypertensive disease, diabetes, liver cancer, mouth and oropharynx cancer, breast cancer, esophageal cancer, selected other cancers, cirrhosis of the liver, epilepsy, alcohol use disorders, depression, intentional and unintentional injuries; *selected other cardiovascular diseases and cancers, social consequences*

(Continues on the following page.)

Table 4.1 Continued

Risk factor	Exposure variable	Theoretical-minimum-risk exposure distribution	Disease outcomes[a]
Illicit drug use	Use of amphetamine, cocaine, heroin, or other opioids, and intravenous drug use	No illicit drug use	HIV/AIDS, overdose, drug use disorder, suicide, and trauma; *other neuropsychological diseases, social consequences, hepatitis B and hepatitis C*
Sexual and reproductive health			
Unsafe sex	Sex with an infected partner without any measures to prevent infection	No unsafe sex	HIV/AIDS, sexually transmitted infections, and cervical cancer
Non-use and use of ineffective methods of contraception	Prevalence of traditional methods or non-use of contraception	Use of modern contraceptives for all women who want to space or limit future pregnancies	Maternal mortality and morbidity; *increased perinatal and child mortality with lower birth intervals*
Environmental risks			
Unsafe water, sanitation, and hygiene	Six scenarios, ranging from regulated water and sanitation with hygiene to no improved water supply and no improved sanitation	Absence of transmission of diarrheal disease through water, sanitation, and hygiene	Diarrheal diseases
Urban air pollution	Estimated annual average particulate matter concentration for particles with aerodynamic diameters less than 2.5 or 10 microns ($PM_{2.5}$ or PM_{10})	7.5 $\mu g/m^3$ for $PM_{2.5}$ 15 $\mu g/m^3$ for PM_{10}	Mortality from combined respiratory and selected cardiovascular causes in adults over 30, lung cancer, acute respiratory infection mortality in children under five; *cardiovascular and respiratory morbidity*
Indoor smoke from household use of solid fuels	Household use of solid fuels and ventilation	No household solid fuel use	Acute lower respiratory infections in children under five, COPD, lung cancer (coal);[e] *low birthweight, cataracts, tuberculosis, asthma, lung cancer from biomass*
Other selected risks			
Contaminated injections in health care settings	Exposure to at least one contaminated injection	No contaminated injections	Acute infection with hepatitis B virus (HBV), hepatitis C virus (HCV), and HIV, cirrhosis and liver cancer
Child sexual abuse	Prevalence of noncontact abuse, contact abuse, and intercourse	No abuse	Depression, panic disorder, alcohol abuse/dependence, drug abuse/dependence, post-traumatic stress disorder and suicide in adulthood; *non-mental health outcomes, such as sexually transmitted diseases, unwanted pregnancies, and injuries*

Sources: Table 1 in Ezzati and others 2002, and individual risk factor chapters in Ezzati and others 2004 for data sources.

Note: BMI = body mass index, COPD = chronic obstructive pulmonary disease, IHD = ischemic heart disease, KJ = kilo joules, SD = standard deviation. New disease outcomes are used here when more recent epidemiological analyses enabled improvements over those of the CRA project (for example, multiple cancer sites assessed separately, versus grouped together, for smoking). Several risk factors (lead exposure, global climate change, and selected occupational risks) were included in the CRA project but not in the current analysis because of conceptual and empirical difficulties in converting estimates of exposure and/or hazards from the GBD analysis subregions to the World Bank regions.

a. Outcomes in italic are those that are likely to be causal but not quantified due to lack of sufficient evidence on the magnitude of hazardous effect.

b. The resulting hemoglobin levels vary across regions and age-sex groups because the other risks for anemia (for example, malaria) vary.

c. In estimating years of life lost because of disability (YLD) due to smoking in the CRA project (Ezzati and Lopez 2004), population attributable fractions (PAFs) for disease incidence were assumed to be the same as PAFs for mortality for cancers and COPD, and one-half of PAFs for mortality for all other diseases. In the current analysis, PAFs for disease incidence were assumed to be the same as those for mortality for cancers, COPD, and cardiovascular diseases—for which smoking is expected to increase mortality through increasing incidence—and zero for all other diseases. The estimated total disease burden from smoking is robust to assumptions about the effects of smoking on incidence of diseases other than major chronic diseases (cancers, COPD, and cardiovascular diseases).

d. The theoretical-minimum-risk exposure level for alcohol is zero, the global theoretical minimum. Specific population subgroups or diseases may have a non-zero theoretical-minimum-risk exposure (see figure 4.2) (Rehm and others 2004).

e. In the CRA project, PAFs for indoor smoke from household use of solid fuels were applied to COPD and lung cancer mortality and disease burden after subtracting the smoking-attributable burden (Smith, Mehta, and Maeusezahl-Feuz 2004). This overlooks multi-causality of COPD and lung cancer, which is also illustrated empirically in the analysis of the hazards of smoking in China (Liu and others 1998). Therefore, we applied PAFs to total mortality from COPD and lung cancer.

broad, such as the environment or diet taken as a single exposure;

- the likelihood of causality was high based on collective scientific knowledge;

- reasonably complete data on exposure and risk levels were available or sufficient data were available to extrapolate information when necessary;

- they were potentially modifiable.

The risks to health examined in the CRA project cover many of the important hazards to health addressed in various fields of scientific inquiry. Arguably, hundreds of risk exposures are harmful to health. We selected only a relatively small number of exposures for quantification, largely determined by the availability of data and scientific research about their level and health effects in different parts of the world.

We also had to make choices about the definition of each risk factor. Given the close interrelationships among diet, exercise, and physiological risks on the one hand, or among water, sanitation, and personal hygiene on the other, the exact definition of what a risk factor is requires careful attention. The absence of a particular risk factor like dietary fat intake from table 4.1 does not imply that it is of limited relevance. Similarly, the assessment of unsafe sex separately from that of non-use and use of ineffective methods of contraception does not override their close linkages. Rather, we focused the analysis on risk factors for which we were likely to be able to satisfactorily quantify their population exposure distributions and health effects using existing scientific evidence and available data and for which intervention strategies are available or might be envisioned.

Estimating Population Attributable Fractions

The contribution of a risk factor to disease or mortality is expressed as the fraction of disease or death attributable to the risk factor in a population and is referred to as the population attributable fraction (PAF), and is given by the generalized potential impact fraction in equation 4.1 (Eide and Heuch 2001; Walter 1980).

$$PAF = \frac{\int_{x=0}^{m} RR(x)P(x)dx - \int_{x=0}^{m} RR(x)P'(x)dx}{\int_{x=0}^{m} RR(x)P(x)dx}, \quad (4.1a)$$

where $RR(x)$ is the relative risk at exposure level x, $P(x)$ is the population distribution of exposure, $P'(x)$ is the counterfactual distribution of exposure, and m is the maximum exposure level.

The corresponding relationship when exposure is described as a discrete variable with n levels is given by

$$PAF = \frac{\sum_{i=1}^{n} P_i RR_i - \sum_{i=1}^{n} P'_i RR_i}{\sum_{i=1}^{n} P_i RR_i}. \quad (4.1b)$$

PAFs obtained in this way estimate the proportional reduction in disease or death that would occur if exposure

to the risk factor were reduced to the counterfactual distribution. The alternative (counterfactual) scenario used is the exposure distribution that would result in the lowest population risk, referred to as the theoretical-minimum-risk exposure distribution (Ezzati and others 2002; Murray and Lopez 1999). For risk factors for which the assumption of constant relative risk was not appropriate, we estimated PAFs by accounting for the determinants of hazard heterogeneity. For example, the PAFs for injuries as a result of alcohol use accounted for alcohol drinking patterns (moderate versus binge).

Because most diseases are caused by multiple risk factors, PAFs for individual risk factors for the same disease overlap and can add to more than 100 percent (Murray and Lopez 1999; Rothman 1976). For example, some deaths from childhood pneumonia may have been avoided by preventing exposure to indoor smoke from household use of solid fuels, childhood underweight, and zinc deficiency (which itself affects weight-for-age); and some cardiovascular disease events may be due to a combination of smoking, physical inactivity, and low fruit and vegetable intake. Such cases would be attributed to all these risk factors.

Attributable Mortality and Burden of Disease

For each risk factor and disease pair, we calculated PAFs for each age and sex group, and in each region, using the relationships in equations 4.1a and 4.1b, separately for mortality (PAF_M) and incidence (PAF_I) when the relative risks for mortality and incidence were different. For each of these age, sex, and region groups, we obtained estimates of mortality (AM_{ij}) and the burden of disease (AB_{ij}) from disease j attributable to risk factor i as follows:

$$AM_{ij} = PAF_{M\text{-}ij} \times M_j, \quad (4.2a)$$

$$A\text{-}YLL_{ij} = PAF_{M\text{-}ij} \times YLL_j, \quad (4.2b)$$

$$A\text{-}YLD_{ij} = PAF_{I\text{-}ij} \times YLD_j, \quad (4.2c)$$

$$AB_{ij} = A\text{-}YLL_{ij} + A\text{-}YLD_{ij}, \quad (4.2d)$$

where YLL denotes years of life lost because of premature mortality and YLD denotes years of healthy life lost as a result of disability.

Data on Exposure and Hazard

Between 1999 and 2002, for each risk factor, an expert working group conducted a comprehensive review of the published literature and other sources (government reports, international databases, and so on) to obtain data on the prevalence of risk factor exposure and hazard size (relative risk or absolute hazard size when appropriate, such as the effects of lead on blood pressure) (Ezzati and others 2004). The work included collecting primary data and undertaking a number of reanalyses of original data, systematic reviews, and meta-analyses. To increase comparability while acknowledging the fundamental differences in exposure and hazard quantification across risk factors, the criteria for using the scientific evidence included consistency of exposure variables used in exposure data sources with those used in epidemiological studies on hazard, population representativeness of exposure data, and study design for estimating the magnitude of hazardous effects (including minimizing the effects of confounders).

Data were initially presented separately for males and females and broken down into eight age groups (0–4, 5–14, 15–29, 30–44, 45–59, 60–69, 70–79, and 80 years old and older) and the 14 epidemiological subregions of the Global Burden of Disease (GBD) study (see chapter 3), which are based on a combination of World Health Organization regions and child and adult mortality levels, as described in the annexes of the annual *World Health Report 2002* (WHO 2002). Data sources, models, and assumptions used to extrapolate exposure or relative risk across countries or regions are described in detail in chapters devoted to individual risk factors elsewhere (Ezzati and others 2004). External reviewers anonymously peer reviewed each risk factor chapter, including conducting re-reviews as appropriate.

In this reanalysis, estimates of mortality and disease burden attributable to risk factors were needed in World Bank regions (see map 1 inside the front cover). For six risk factors (childhood underweight, high blood pressure, high cholesterol, overweight and obesity, smoking, and indoor smoke from household use of solid fuels), country-level data were available and allowed reestimating exposure directly for World Bank regions. In such cases, we used newly available data sources on exposure to update CRA project estimations. For seven risk factors (unsafe water, sanitation, and hygiene; zinc deficiency; vitamin A deficiency; iron deficiency anemia; physical inactivity; low fruit and vegetable intake; and child sexual abuse), we estimated exposure in World Bank regions from the 14 GBD subregions using population-weighted averages. For another five risk factors (unsafe sex, urban air pollution, illicit drug use, non-use and use of ineffective methods of contraception,

and contaminated injections in health care settings), where both exposure and hazards change across populations, we converted PAFs from GBD subregions to World Bank regions, with PAFs weighted by age-, sex-, and disease-specific mortality rates. The prevalence of alcohol use was converted from GBD subregions to World Bank regions and was used to estimate exposure and PAFs in World Bank regions for most disease outcomes, because relative risks did not vary across populations. For all injury outcomes, ischemic heart disease, depression, stroke, and diabetes, whose hazards varied across regions, PAFs were converted from GBD subregions to World Bank regions using mortality weighting.

Theoretical-Minimum-Risk Exposure Distributions

The theoretical-minimum-risk exposure distribution was zero for risk factors for which zero exposure could be defined and reflected minimum risk, such as no smoking. For some risk factors, zero exposure was an inappropriate choice, either because it is physiologically impossible, as in the case of body mass index (BMI) or high cholesterol, or because physical lower limits to exposure reduction exist, as for concentrations of ambient particulate matter. For the latter risk factors, we used the lowest levels observed in specific populations and epidemiological studies to choose the theoretical-minimum-risk exposure distribution. For example, counterfactual exposure distributions of 115 mmHg for systolic blood pressure and 3.8 mmol/L for total cholesterol, each with a small standard deviation, are the lowest levels at which meta-analyses of cohort studies have characterized dose-response relationships (Chen and others 1991; Eastern Stroke and Coronary Heart Disease Collaborative Research Group 1998; Law, Wald, and Thompson 1994).

Alcohol has benefits as well as causing harm for different diseases depending on the disease and on patterns of alcohol consumption (Corrao and others 2000; Puddey and others 1999). Rehm and others (2004) chose a counterfactual of zero for alcohol use. This was because despite its benefits for cardiovascular diseases in some populations, the global and regional burden of disease due to alcohol use was dominated by its impacts on neuropsychiatric diseases and injuries that are considerably larger than these benefits.

Finally, for factors with protective effects, namely, fruit and vegetable intake and physical activity, we chose a counterfactual exposure distribution based on a combination of levels observed in high-intake populations and the level to which the benefits may continue given current scientific evidence. Table 4.1 reports the theoretical-minimum-risk exposure distributions for the risk factors.

BURDEN OF DISEASE ATTRIBUTABLE TO INDIVIDUAL RISK FACTORS

Detailed results by risk factor, disease outcome, age, sex, and region are provided in annex 4A. Figure 4.1 shows the contributions of the leading global risk factors to all-cause mortality and burden of disease. The different ordering of risk factors in their contributions to mortality and to the disease burden expressed in DALYs reflects the age profile of mortality, such as the higher contribution to the disease burden from mortality among children as a result of underweight, and of nonfatal outcomes, such as neuropsychiatric diseases caused by alcohol use.

The leading causes of mortality and the disease burden include risk factors for communicable, maternal, perinatal, and nutritional conditions (Group I as defined in chapter 3), such as undernutrition; indoor smoke from household use of solid fuels; unsafe water, sanitation, and hygiene, whose burden is primarily concentrated in low-income regions of South Asia and Sub-Saharan Africa; and unsafe sex. They also include risk factors for noncommunicable diseases and injuries (Groups II and III as defined in chapter 3), such as high blood pressure and cholesterol, smoking, alcohol use, and overweight and obesity, which affect most regions.

Undernutrition is the single leading global cause of health loss, as it was in 1990 (the 2001 results disaggregate undernutrition into underweight and micronutrient deficiencies). Even though the prevalence of underweight has decreased in most regions in the past decade, it has increased in Sub-Saharan Africa (de Onis, Frongilla, and Blossner 2000; de Onis and others 2004), where its effects are disproportionately large because of simultaneous exposure to other risk factors for childhood disease. Three-quarters of the burden of disease attributable to unsafe sex is also in Sub-Saharan Africa, primarily as a result of HIV/AIDS, followed by South Asia (13 percent). The burden of disease attributable to unsafe water, sanitation, and hygiene has declined since 1990, mostly because of a worldwide decline in mortality from diarrheal disease, which is partly a result of improved case management interventions, particularly oral rehydration therapy. The increase in the global burden of disease attributable to smoking since 1990 mostly reflects the increased accumulated hazards of this risk, which is most noticeable in developing countries, but the increase is

also partially due to methodological changes based on new evidence on the magnitude of the hazard after correction for confounding (Ezzati, Henley, Lopez, and others 2005; Ezzati, Henley, Thun, and others 2005; Ezzati and Lopez 2003; Thun, Apicella, and Henley 2000). The large increase in the burden of disease due to high blood pressure is likely to be an outcome of major methodological improvements, that is, relative risks that account for regression dilution bias and choice of theoretical-minimum-risk exposure distribution based on epidemiological evidence versus clinical definitions.

Table 4.2 shows the distributions of mortality and the disease burden attributable to the risk factors by age and sex. The disease burden attributable to underweight and micronutrient deficiencies in children was equally distributed among males and females, but the total all-age disease burden from iron and vitamin A deficiencies was slightly greater among females because of the effects on maternal mortality and morbidity conditions. Other diet-related risks, physical inactivity, environmental risks, and unsafe sex contributed almost equally to the disease burden in males and females. Approximately 77 to 86 percent of the disease burden from addictive substances occured among men, reflecting the social and economic forces that have so far made addictive substances more widely used by men, especially in developing countries. Women suffered an estimated two-thirds of the disease burden from child sexual abuse and all of the burden caused by non-use and use of ineffective methods of contraception.

The estimated disease burdens from childhood undernutrition and unsafe water, sanitation, and hygiene were almost exclusively among children under five years of age. For these risks, more than 90 percent of the total attributable burden occurred in this age group, with the exception of iron deficiency, where adults bore more than 40 percent of burden, especially women of childbearing age. The disease burdens attributable to overweight and obesity and smoking were almost equally distributed among adults below and above the age of 60 years. The disease burdens attributable to other diet-related risks and physical inactivity were higher among those older than 60 (see also chapter 5).

More than 90 percent of the disease burden attributable to non-use and use of ineffective methods of contraception, illicit drug use, and child sexual abuse and more than 75 percent of the disease burden attributable to alcohol use and unsafe sex occurred in adults younger than 60. Most of the risks whose burden is concentrated among younger adults are those with outcomes that include HIV/AIDS,

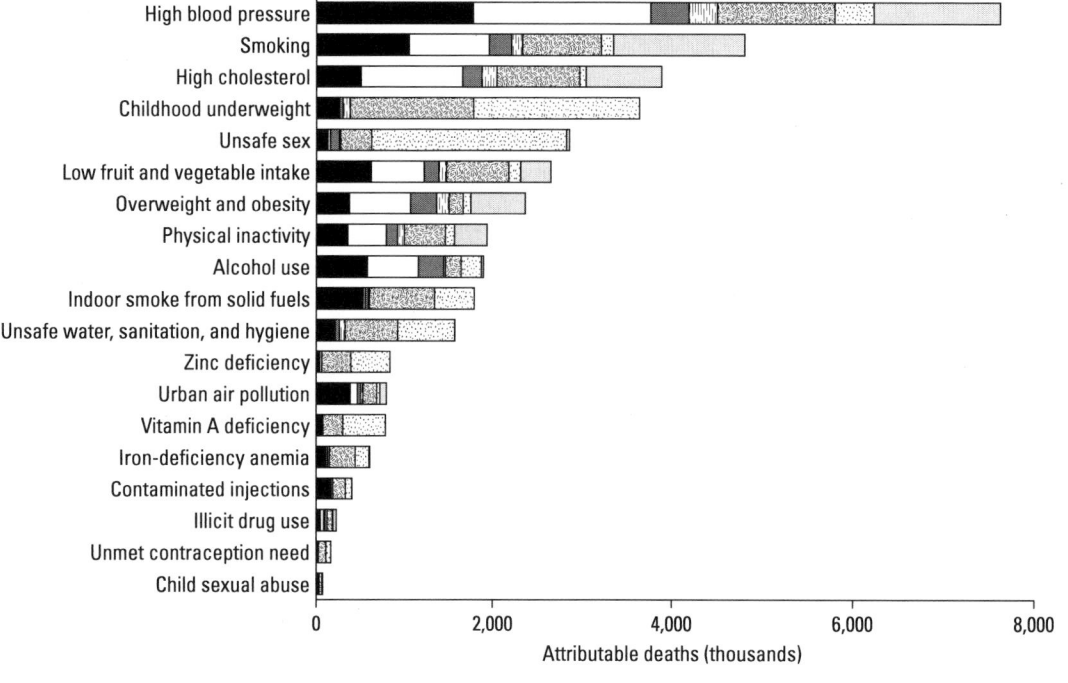

a. Mortality

Attributable deaths (thousands)

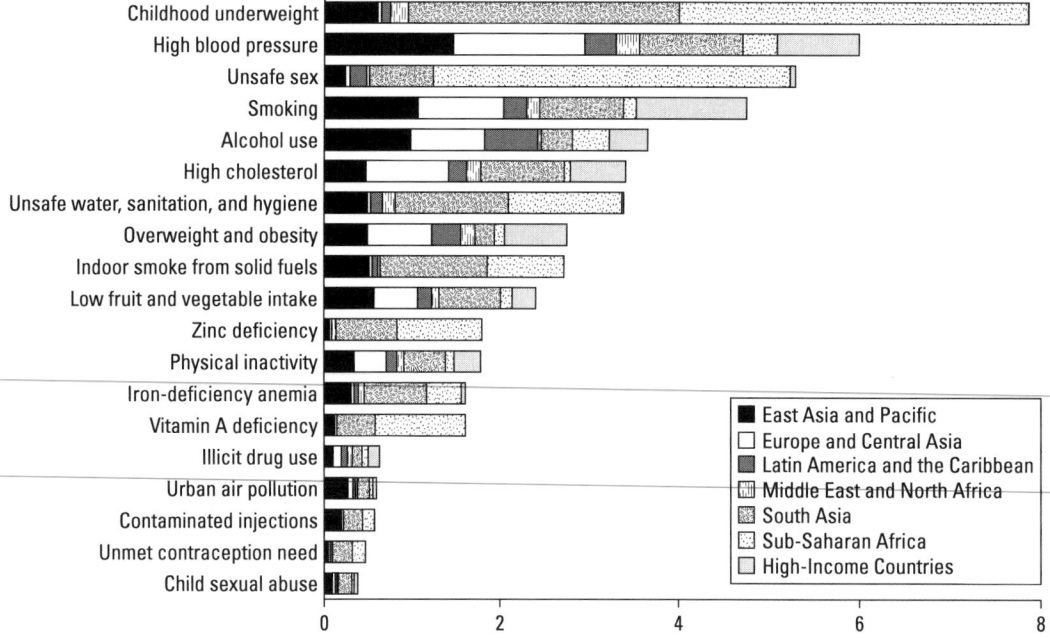

b. Burden of Disease

Legend:
- East Asia and Pacific
- Europe and Central Asia
- Latin America and the Caribbean
- Middle East and North Africa
- South Asia
- Sub-Saharan Africa
- High-Income Countries

Attributable disease burden (% global DALYs; total 1.54 billion)

Source: Authors' calculations.

Note: The figure shows estimated mortality and disease burden attributable to each risk factor considered individually, relative to its own theoretical minimum risk exposure distribution. These risks act in part through, or jointly with, other risks. Consequently, the burden due to groups of risk factors will usually be less than the sum of individual risks. "Unmet contraception need" refers to "Non-use and use of ineffective methods of contraception" in table 4.1.

Figure 4.1 Mortality and the Burden of Disease Attributable to Leading Global Risk Factors, by World Bank Region

Table 4.2 Distribution of Risk Factor-Attributable Mortality and Burden of Disease, by Age and Sex.

	Mortality						Disease burden					
	0–4	5–14	15–59	60+	Males	Females	0–4	5–14	15–59	60+	Males	Females
World												
Childhood and maternal undernutrition												
Childhood underweight	100	0	0	0	50	50	100	0	0	0	50	50
Iron-deficiency anemia	68	1	25	5	43	57	57	7	33	3	44	56
Vitamin A deficiency	93	0	7	0	47	53	94	0	6	0	47	53
Zinc deficiency	100	0	0	0	51	49	100	0	0	0	51	49
Other nutrition-related risk factors and physical inactivity												
High blood pressure	0	0	13	87	47	53	0	0	25	75	50	50
High cholesterol	0	0	23	77	48	52	0	0	40	60	52	48
Overweight and obesity (high BMI)	0	0	27	73	45	55	0	0	47	53	45	55
Low fruit and vegetable consumption	0	0	23	77	53	47	0	0	38	62	55	45
Physical inactivity	0	0	21	79	50	50	0	0	38	62	52	48
Addictive substances												
Smoking	0	0	31	69	76	24	0	0	50	50	77	23
Alcohol use	1	1	65	33	90	10	1	2	82	15	86	14
Illicit drugs use	0	0	99	1	79	21	0	1	98	0	77	23
Sexual and reproductive health												
Unsafe sex	14	4	75	8	48	52	17	4	76	3	47	53
Non-use and use of ineffective methods of contraception	0	0	100	0	0	100	0	0	100	0	0	100
Environmental risk factors												
Unsafe water, sanitation, and hygiene	90	0	3	7	52	48	91	2	5	2	52	48
Urban air pollution	3	0	16	81	52	48	7	0	28	65	53	47
Indoor smoke from household use of solid fuels	52	0	8	40	45	55	71	0	10	18	48	52
Other selected risk factors												
Contaminated injections in health care settings	12	3	52	32	63	37	17	5	60	18	60	40
Child sexual abuse	0	0	80	20	50	50	0	0	93	7	36	64
Low- and middle-income countries												
Childhood and maternal undernutrition												
Childhood underweight	100	0	0	0	50	50	100	0	0	0	50	50
Iron-deficiency anemia	69	1	26	4	43	57	59	7	32	3	44	56
Vitamin A deficiency	93	0	7	0	47	53	94	0	6	0	47	53
Zinc deficiency	100	0	0	0	51	49	100	0	0	0	51	49
Other nutrition-related risk factors and physical inactivity												
High blood pressure	0	0	14	86	47	53	0	0	26	74	49	51
High cholesterol	0	0	26	74	48	52	0	0	42	58	52	48
Overweight and obesity (high BMI)	0	0	30	70	44	56	0	0	49	51	43	57
Low fruit and vegetable consumption	0	0	24	76	53	47	0	0	39	61	54	46
Physical inactivity	0	0	23	77	50	50	0	0	39	61	51	49
Addictive substances												
Smoking	0	0	38	62	82	18	0	0	55	45	82	18
Alcohol use	1	1	59	39	84	16	1	2	79	17	84	16
Illicit drugs use	0	0	98	2	81	19	0	1	98	1	79	21

(Continues on the following page.)

Table 4.2 Continued

	Mortality						Disease burden					
	0–4	5–14	15–59	60+	Males	Females	0–4	5–14	15–59	60+	Males	Females
Low- and middle-income countries (continued)												
Sexual and reproductive health												
Unsafe sex	14	4	75	7	49	51	17	4	76	3	47	53
Non-use and use of ineffective methods of contraception	0	0	100	0	0	100	0	0	100	0	0	100
Environmental risk factors												
Unsafe water, sanitation, and hygiene	90	0	3	7	52	48	91	2	5	2	52	48
Urban air pollution	3	0	17	80	52	48	8	0	28	64	53	47
Indoor smoke from household use of solid fuels	52	0	8	40	45	55	71	0	10	18	48	52
Other selected risk factors												
Contaminated injections in health care settings	12	3	52	32	63	37	17	5	60	18	60	40
Child sexual abuse	100	0	0	0	50	50	100	0	0	0	50	50
High-income countries												
Childhood and maternal undernutrition												
Childhood underweight	100	0	0	0	55	45	100	0	0	0	51	49
Iron-deficiency anemia	13	1	5	82	36	64	9	5	66	20	39	61
Vitamin A deficiency	81	0	19	0	44	56	86	0	14	0	47	53
Zinc deficiency	100	0	0	0	55	45	100	0	0	0	52	48
Other nutrition-related risk factors and physical inactivity												
High blood pressure	0	0	7	93	45	55	0	0	18	82	52	48
High cholesterol	0	0	14	86	49	51	0	0	32	68	57	43
Overweight and obesity (high BMI)	0	0	18	82	49	51	0	0	40	60	50	50
Low fruit and vegetable consumption	0	0	16	84	56	44	0	0	33	67	61	39
Physical inactivity	0	0	14	86	50	50	0	0	32	68	54	46
Addictive substances												
Smoking	0	0	17	83	64	36	0	0	36	64	65	35
Alcohol use[a]	3	4	477	−384	531	−431	1	1	103	−5	96	4
Illicit drugs use	0	0	99	1	68	32	0	1	99	0	68	32
Sexual and reproductive health												
Unsafe sex	0	0	67	33	36	64	2	0	85	13	40	60
Non-use and use of ineffective methods of contraception	0	0	100	0	0	100	0	0	100	0	0	100
Environmental risk factors												
Unsafe water, sanitation, and hygiene	7	1	6	86	39	61	53	6	27	14	50	50
Urban air pollution	0	0	10	90	51	49	0	0	23	77	56	44
Indoor smoke from household use of solid fuels	2	0	8	90	39	61	2	0	56	41	31	69
Other selected risk factors												
Contaminated injections in health care settings	10	2	53	35	63	37	16	3	67	13	61	39
Child sexual abuse	0	0	81	22	48	52	0	0	96	4	36	64

Source: Authors' calculations.

Note: BMI = body mass index. Numbers show percentage of total death or disease burden in each age group or for each sex.

a. The figures are the ratio of deaths in each age group or for each sex to the total alcohol-attributable deaths and disease burden. Because the beneficial effects of alcohol are age dependent (more benefits for cardiovascular diseases in older ages) and because the benefit-harm ratio is larger for women than for men (smaller alcohol-attributable burden from injuries), the ratios in younger ages or for males are larger than 100 percent and those in older ages or for females are negative.

maternal conditions, neuropsychiatric diseases, and injuries. This illustrates the large, and at times neglected, disease burden from risks that affect young adults, especially in low-and-middle-income countries, with important consequences for economic development.

Only a small fraction of the disease burden from the risk factors considered was among those aged 5 to 14 years. This was because some of the leading conditions that affect this age group, such as motor vehicle accidents and other injuries and depression, have complex and heterogeneous causes that could not easily be included in the risk-based framework used. For other leading diseases of this group, such as diarrhea and lower respiratory infections, most epidemiological studies have focused on children younger than five and do not provide estimates of hazardous effects for older children.

Figure 4.2 presents the burden of disease due to the 10 leading risk factors for low- and middle-income countries and for high-income countries by disease or disease group. Leading causes of the burden of disease in low- and middle-income countries include the risk factors affecting the poor and associated with communicable, maternal, perinatal, and nutritional conditions (Group I)—such as childhood

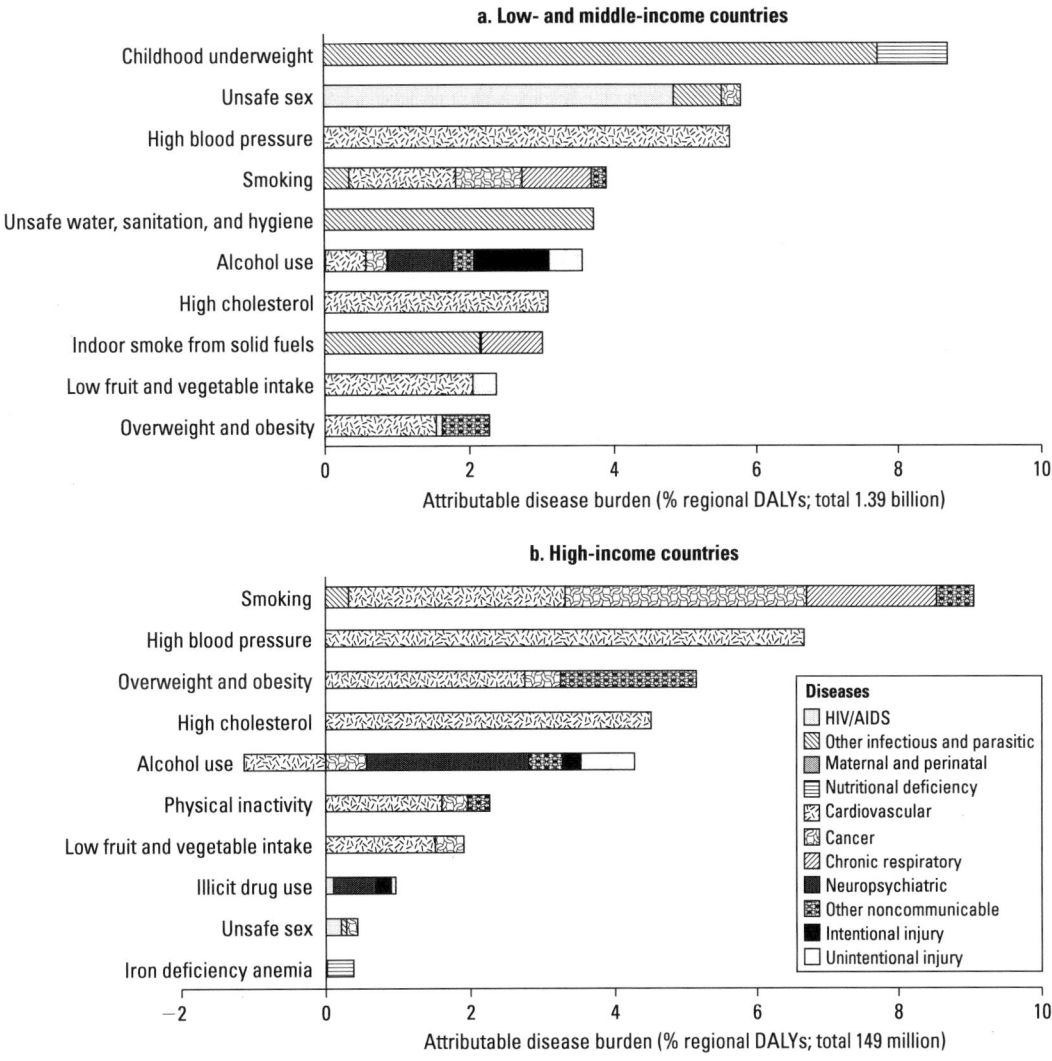

Figure 4.2 Burden of Disease Attributable to 10 Leading Regional Risk Factors, by Disease Type

Source: Authors' calculations.

underweight (8.7 percent); unsafe water, sanitation, and hygiene (3.7 percent); indoor smoke from household use of solid fuels (3.0 percent); and unsafe sex (5.8 percent)—along with risk factors for noncommunicable diseases (Group II), including addictive substances, nutrition related risks, and physical inactivity.

The relative contribution of unsafe sex was disproportionately larger in Sub-Saharan Africa (17.8 percent) than in all other regions, because HIV/AIDS prevalence and mortality are higher in Sub-Saharan Africa than anywhere else. This makes unsafe sex a leading cause of the burden of disease in this region together with childhood underweight (17.1 percent). The outcomes of these two risk factors were mostly communicable, maternal, perinatal, and nutritional conditions, which dominate the disease burden in high-mortality developing regions.

In addition to their relative magnitude, the absolute loss of healthy life years attributed to risk factors in low- and middle-income regions is enormous. In these regions, which account for 85 percent of the global population, childhood underweight and unsafe sex alone contributed more to the loss of healthy life (200 million DALYs[3,0]) than all diseases and injuries in high-income countries (149 million DALYs[3,0]). In high-income countries, smoking (12.9 percent), high blood pressure (9.3 percent), overweight and obesity (7.2 percent), high cholesterol (6.3 percent), and alcohol use (4.4 percent) were the leading causes of loss of healthy life, contributing mainly to noncommunicable diseases and injuries (groups II and III).

JOINT EFFECTS OF MULTIPLE RISK FACTORS

Many users of risk assessment, who may be familiar with categorical attribution systems such as the ICD, desire information characterized by additive decomposition. In other words, they would like to know what fraction of the disease burden is related to a particular risk factor or group of risk factors independent of changes in other risk factors. As Mathers and others (2002) discuss, additive decomposition is not generally a property of counterfactual attribution, because many diseases are caused by the interaction of multiple determinants acting simultaneously (Rothman 1976; Rothman and Greenland 1998; Walter 1980; Yerushalmy and Palmer 1959). Indeed, the sum of PAFs for a single disease due to multiple risk factors is theoretically unbounded.

Although epidemiologically unavoidable and conceptually acceptable, the lack of additivity adds to policy complexity and implies the need for great care when interpreting and communicating estimates of PAF and attributable burden. With multiple attribution, a reduction in one risk factor would seem to make other, equally important, risk factors potentially irrelevant from a perspective with limited scope in relation to interpreting quantitative results. It also necessitates the development of methods to quantify the effects of joint counterfactual distributions for multiple risk factors. Estimating the joint effects of multiple distal and proximal risks is particularly important, because many factors act through other intermediate factors (Murray and Lopez 1999; Yerushalmy and Palmer 1959) or in combination with other factors. For example, education, occupation, and income may affect smoking, physical activity, and diet, which are risk factors for cardiovascular diseases, both directly and through further layers of such intermediate factors as BMI, blood pressure, and high cholesterol. Multicausality also means that a range of interventions can be used for disease prevention, with the specific choices determined by factors such as cost, technology availability, infrastructure, and preferences.

In equations 4.1a and 4.1b, RR, P, and P' may represent joint relative risks and exposure distributions for multiple risk factors, that is, x may be a vector of risk factors, with RR for each risk factor estimated at the appropriate level of the remaining ones (Eide and Heuch 2001). While such data have been gathered for a small number of risk factor combinations, for example, alcohol and smoking for oral cancer (Rothman and Keller 1972) and some cardiovascular risks (Neaton and Wentworth 1992; Yusuf and others 2004), they are generally rare in epidemiological studies. Alternatively, for n biologically independent and uncorrelated risk factors, the joint PAF is given by equation 4.3 (Miettinen 1974; Walter 1976):

$$PAF = 1 - \prod_{i=1}^{n} (1 - PAF_i), \qquad (4.3)$$

where PAF_i shows the PAFs of individual risk factors.

If risk factors are independent and uncorrelated, the proportion of the remaining disease that is attributed to the ith additional risk factor equals PAF_i, and hence $(1 - PAF_i)$ is not attributable to this factor. Therefore, the second term in the right-hand-side of equation 4.3, that is, the product of all $(1 - PAF_i)$ terms, is the fraction of disease not attributable to any of the n risk factors. One minus this term is the fraction attributable to the combined effects of the n risk factors.

Estimating the joint effects of multiple risk factors is, in practice, complex and does not follow the simple, independent, and uncorrelated relationship of equation 4.3 for

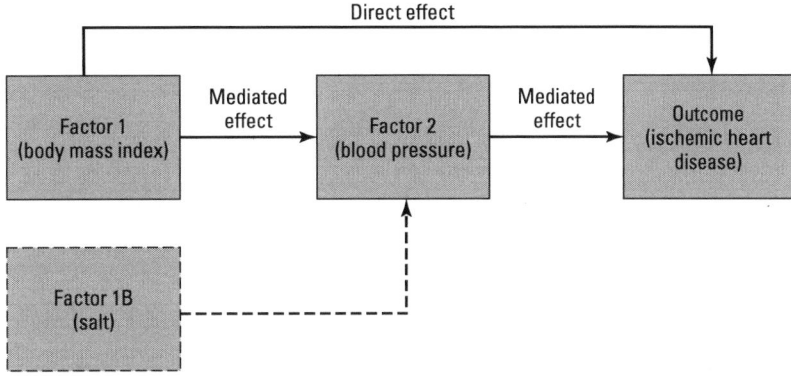

Note: Some of the effects of a risk factor (for example, body mass index–BMI) may be mediated through other factors (for example, blood pressure). When estimating the total effects of individual distal factors on disease, both mediated and direct effects should be considered, because, in the presence of mediated effects, controlling for the intermediated factor would attenuate the effects of the more distal one (Greenland 1987). When estimating the joint effects of the more distal factor (for example, BMI) *and* the intermediate one (for example, blood pressure), the direct and mediated effects must be separated, especially if the intermediate factor is affected by other distal factors (for example, dietary salt).

Figure 4.3 Mediated and Direct Effects of a Risk Factor

several reasons. First, some of the effects of the more distal factors, such as physical inactivity, are mediated through intermediate factors. For instance, a proportion of the hazards of physical inactivity is mediated through overweight and obesity, which is itself mediated through elevated blood pressure (figure 4.3). Estimating the joint effects of distal and intermediate factors requires knowledge of independent hazards of the distal ones (versus individual risk factor effects, which are based on total hazard). Second, the hazard due to a risk factor may depend on the presence of other risk factors (Koopman 1981; Rothman and Greenland 1998) (effect modification).[1] Third, correlation may exist between exposures to multiple risk factors because they are affected by the same distal factors and policies. For example, undernutrition, unsafe water and sanitation, and use of solid fuels are more common among poor rural households in developing countries and smokers generally have higher and more harmful patterns of alcohol consumption and worse diets than nonsmokers.

The epidemiological literature refers to the first and second issues as biological interaction and the third issue as statistical interaction (Miettinen 1974; Rothman and Greenland 1998; Rothman, Greenland, and Walker 1980). This distinction is, however, somewhat arbitrary, and the three scenarios may occur simultaneously. For example, zinc deficiency affects mortality from diarrhea directly as well as by reducing growth (first issue) (Brown and others 2002; Zinc Investigators' Collaborative Group 1999), and may also be correlated with

underweight, other micronutrient deficiencies, and unsafe water and sanitation (third issue). Similarly, alcohol and smoking may not only be correlated (third issue), but also affect each other's hazard for some diseases (second issue) (Rothman and Keller 1972).

Data Sources for Mediated Effects and Effect Modification

Despite the emphasis on removing or minimizing the effects of confounding in epidemiological research, mediated and stratified hazards have received disproportionately little empirical attention. We therefore reviewed the literature and reanalyzed cohort data to strengthen the empirical basis for considering interactions. The sensitivity of estimates to these assumptions were negligible as described in detail elsewhere (Ezzati, Vander Hoorn, and others 2004; Ezzati and others 2003).

Joint Hazards of Cardiovascular Disease Risk Factors. Epidemiological studies of the effects of overweight and obesity, physical inactivity, and low fruit and vegetable intake on cardiovascular diseases have illustrated some attenuation of the effects after adjustment for intermediate factors such as blood pressure or cholesterol (Berlin and Colditz 1990; Blair, Cheng, and Holder 2001; Eaton 1992; Gaziano and others 1995; Jarrett, Shipley, and Rose 1982; Jousilahti and others 1999; Khaw and Barrett-Connor 1987; Liu and others 2000, 2001; Manson and others 1990, 2002;

Rosengren, Wedel, and Wilhelmsen 1999; Tate, Manfreda, and Cuddy 1998). This attenuation confirms that some of the hazard of the more distal factors is mediated through the intermediate ones (figure 4.3). The extent of attenuation has varied from study to study, but has consistently been less than half of the excess risk of the distal factors. We used an estimate of 50 percent as the proportion of the excess risk from these risk factors mediated through intermediate factors that are themselves among the selected risks. To include effect modification, we used deviations from the multiplicative model of 10 percent for ischemic heart disease and 30 percent for ischemic stroke based on existing studies, both submultiplicative (Eastern Stroke and Coronary Heart Disease Collaborative Research Group 1998; Neaton and Wentworth 1992).

Joint Hazards of Smoking and Other Risk Factors. Liu and others (1998, figures 4 and 6) find that in China, the relative risks of mortality from lung and other cancers, respiratory diseases, and vascular diseases are approximately constant in different cities where mortality rates for these diseases among nonsmokers varied by a factor of 4 to 10. Studies that stratified hazards of smoking on serum cholesterol have confirmed this finding (Jee and others 1999).

Joint Hazards of Childhood Undernutrition for Infectious Diseases. Zinc affects growth in children (Brown and others 2002), and some of its effects on infectious diseases may be mediated through reducing growth. Because no published source for such mediated effects existed, data from some of the available zinc trials were reanalyzed (Zinc Investigators' Collaborative Group 1999). We used an upper bound of 50 percent on the proportion of zinc deficiency risk mediated through underweight.

Investigators have found that vitamin A deficiency, which affects some of the same diseases as underweight and zinc deficiency, does not change the hazard size for the other two risk factors based on stratified results from clinical trials and recent reviews of the literature on micronutrient deficiencies (Christian and West 1998; Ramakrishnan, Latham, and Abel 1995; Ramakrishnan and Martorell 1998; West and others 1991).

Joint Hazards of Undernutrition and Environmental Risk Factors in Childhood Diseases. Anthropometric (growth) indicators of childhood nutrition, such as weight-for-age, are aggregate measures of multiple factors that include

nutrition and previous infection (Pelletier, Frongillo, and Habicht 1993; Scrimshaw, Taylor, and Gordon 1968; UNICEF 1990). Therefore, some of the risks from indoor smoke from household use of solid fuels and unsafe water, sanitation, and hygiene, which result in lower respiratory infections and diarrhea respectively, may be mediated through underweight. In a review of the literature, Briend (1990) concludes that attempts to disentangle direct and mediated contributions, especially over the long periods needed to affect population-level anthropometry, have not established diarrhea as a significant cause of underweight. Other works, however, have found evidence that infection, especially diarrhea, could reduce growth and increase the prevalence of underweight (Black 1991; Guerrant and others 1992; Lutter and others 1989, 1992; Martorell, Habicht and others 1975; Martorell, Yarbrough, and others 1975; Stephensen 1999). To account for potential mediated effects, we considered an upper bound of 50 percent on the proportion of the excess risks from indoor smoke from household use of solid fuels and unsafe water, sanitation, and hygiene mediated through underweight in regions where underweight was present.

Risk Factor Correlation

To estimate the joint effects of risk factors with a continuous exposure variable, for instance, blood pressure and cholesterol, each integral in the *PAF* relationship may be replaced with $\int_{x_1=0}^{m_1} \int_{x_2=0}^{m_2} RR_1(x_1)RR_2(x_2)P(x_1, x_2)dx_1\,dx_2$, where subscripts 1 and 2 denote the two risk factors and P is the joint distribution of the two exposures. If joint *RR* were a linear function of exposure levels (x_1 and x_2), then correlation between the two risk factors would not affect total hazard. Because individual *RRs* are nonlinear functions of exposure, for example, in a Cox proportional hazard model, and joint *RRs* are the product of such nonlinear terms, positive correlation between risk factors would, in general, imply a larger PAF than zero correlation,[2] which in turn would be larger than negative correlation. Similarly, for categorical risk factors, positive correlation would in general result in a larger PAF (see also Greenland 1984). For the range of exposures and relative risks in the CRA, this secondary effect of risk factor correlation would be considerably smaller than the joint attributable fraction, as described in detail elsewhere (Ezzati and others 2003).

Table 4.3 Joint Contributions (PAFs) of the Leading Risk Factors to Mortality and Burden of Disease, by Region

Region	Mortality			Burden of disease [DALYs(3,0)]		
	Male	Female	Both	Male	Female	Both
Low- and middle-income countries	46% (25.5)	45% (22.8)	46% (48.3)	37% (715)	35% (671)	36% (1,386)
East Asia and Pacific	39% (6.9)	35% (6.1)	37% (13.1)	29% (181)	24% (165)	27% (346)
Europe and Central Asia	63% (3.0)	61% (2.7)	62% (5.7)	50% (64)	41% (53)	46% (116)
Latin America and the Caribbean	42% (1.8)	40% (1.4)	41% (3.3)	32% (57)	25% (48)	29% (104)
Middle East and North Africa	40% (1.1)	40% (0.8)	40% (1.9)	26% (35)	25% (31)	25% (66)
South Asia	44% (7.1)	40% (6.5)	42% (13.6)	35% (204)	33% (205)	34% (409)
Sub-Saharan Africa	52% (5.6)	56% (5.2)	54% (10.8)	48% (175)	50% (170)	49% (345)
High-income countries	48% (4.0)	40% (3.9)	44% (7.9)	40% (77)	28% (72)	34% (149)
World	46% (29.5)	44% (26.7)	45% (56.2)	38% (792)	34% (743)	36% (1,535)

Source: Authors' calculations.

Note: The risk factors are those listed in table 4.1. Numbers in parentheses show total number of deaths and DALYs(3, 0), in millions.

BURDEN OF DISEASE ATTRIBUTABLE TO MULTIPLE RISK FACTORS

This section presents the disease burden attributable to the joint hazards of the risk factors in table 4.1.

All Selected Risk Factors

Table 4.3 shows the joint contributions of all the risk factors shown in table 4.1 to the total mortality and disease burden in different regions. Globally, an estimated 45 percent of mortality and 36 percent of the disease burden were attributable to the joint effects of the 19 selected risk factors. Sub-Saharan Africa (49 percent of the disease burden) and Europe and Central Asia (46 percent of the disease burden) had the largest regional PAFs, and the Middle East and North Africa (25 percent of the disease burden) and East Asia and the Pacific (27 percent of the disease burden) had the smallest. The regions with large joint PAFs are those where a relatively small number of diseases and their risk factors are responsible for large losses of life, for example, HIV/AIDS and childhood disease risk factors in Sub-Saharan Africa and cardiovascular risks, smoking, and alcohol consumption in Europe and Central Asia. Those with smaller joint PAFs are regions where the causes of health loss are distributed among a larger number of diseases and their risk factors.

Table 4.4 shows the individual and joint contributions of the selected risk factors to the 10 leading diseases in the world and in low- and middle-income and high-income countries. As the table shows, for most diseases the joint effects of these risk factors were substantially less than the crude sum of their individual effects. For example, globally four separate risk factors were each responsible for 88, 50, 20, and 11 percent of the diarrheal disease burden, but with a joint PAF of 92 percent; or seven separate risk factors were each responsible for 45, 46, 18, 28, 21, 17, and 17 percent of ischemic heart disease, but with a joint PAF of 80 percent. This confirms that the joint actions of more than one of these risk factors acting simultaneously or through other factors cause a large proportion of disease.

Globally, large fractions of the burden of HIV/AIDS (96 percent), diarrhea (92 percent), ischemic heart disease (80 percent), lung cancer (74 percent), stroke (65 percent), chronic obstructive pulmonary disease (64 percent), and lower respiratory infections (53 percent) were attributable to the joint effects of the 19 risk factors considered here. The joint PAFs for a number of other important diseases and injuries, such as perinatal and maternal conditions, certain other cancers, and intentional and unintentional injuries, which have more diverse risk factors, were smaller but non-negligible. Even though the fraction of the total malaria burden attributable to childhood undernutrition was relatively large (59 percent), this was because of the contribution of mortality at younger ages to the malaria burden. No adult malaria was attributed to the risk factors in table 4.1, because the epidemiological literature has focused on quantifying increased risk of malaria as a result of childhood undernutrition only. Finally, with the exception of alcohol and drug dependence, which were fully attributable to their namesake risk factors, small or zero fractions of neuropsychiatric conditions, tuberculosis, congenital anomalies, and a number of other diseases were attributed to the risk factors considered here.

Table 4.4 Individual and Joint Contributions of Risk Factors to 10 Leading Diseases and Total Burden of Disease

Disease	Proportion of global disease burden (%) [total: 1.54 billion DALYs(3.0)]	Proportion of global mortality (%) (total: 56.2 million deaths)	World — PAFs for individual risk factors (for disease burden)	Joint PAF – disease burden (%)	Joint PAF – mortality (%)
Lower respiratory infections	5.6	6.7	Childhood underweight (37%); zinc deficiency (15%); indoor smoke from solid fuels (35%); smoking (4%)[a]; urban air pollution (1%)[b]	53	42
Ischemic heart disease	5.5	12.6	High blood pressure (45%); high cholesterol (48%); overweight and obesity (18%); low fruit and vegetable intake (28%); physical inactivity (21%); smoking (17%); alcohol use (2%); urban air pollution (2%)[b]	80	79
Stroke	4.7	9.6	High blood pressure (54%); high cholesterol (16%); overweight and obesity (12%); low fruit and vegetable intake (11%); physical inactivity (7%); smoking (13%); alcohol use (3%); urban air pollution (3%)[b]	65	60
HIV/AIDS	4.7	4.6	Unsafe sex (95%); contaminated injections in health care settings (5%); illicit drug use (3%)	96	96
Diarrheal diseases	3.9	3.2	Childhood underweight (50%); vitamin A deficiency (22%); zinc deficiency (12%); unsafe water, sanitation, and hygiene (88%)	92	93
Unipolar depressive disorders	3.4	0.0	Alcohol use (2%); childhood sexual abuse (5%)	6	NA[c]
Low birthweight	2.8	2.3	Iron-deficiency anemia (14%); alcohol use (0.5%)	16	17
Malaria	2.6	2.1	Childhood underweight (51%); vitamin A deficiency (19%); zinc deficiency (22%)	59	61
Chronic obstructive pulmonary disease	2.5	4.8	Indoor smoke from solid fuels (30%); urban air pollution (2%)[b]; smoking (44%)	64	62
Tuberculosis	2.4	2.9	Smoking (4%)[a]	9	10
Communicable, maternal, perinatal, and nutritional conditions	36.5	32.3	Multiple risks (see annex 4A)	46	47
Noncommunicable diseases	52.6	58.5	Multiple risks (see annex 4A)	33	49
Injuries	10.9	9.2	Multiple risks (see annex 4A)	15	18
All causes	100	100	All 19 selected risks (see annex 4A)	36	46

Low- and middle-income countries

Disease	Proportion of regional disease burden (%) [total: 1.39 billion DALYs(3,0)]	Proportion of regional mortality (%) (total: 48.3 million deaths)	PAFs for individual risk factors (for disease burden)	Joint PAF – disease burden (%)	Joint PAF – mortality (%)
Lower respiratory infections	6.0	7.0	Childhood underweight (38%); zinc deficiency (16%); indoor smoke from solid fuels (36%); smoking (4%)[a]; urban air pollution (4%)[b]	54	44
Ischemic heart disease	5.2	11.8	High blood pressure (44%); high cholesterol (46%); overweight and obesity (16%); low fruit and vegetable intake (30%); physical inactivity (21%); smoking (15%); alcohol use (4%); urban air pollution (2%)[b]	80	78
HIV/AIDS	5.1	5.3	Unsafe sex (95%); contaminated injections in health care settings (5%); illicit drug use (3%)	97	97
Stroke	4.5	9.5	High blood pressure (54%); high cholesterol (15%); overweight and obesity (10%); low fruit and vegetable intake (11%); physical inactivity (6%); smoking (12%); alcohol use (5%); urban air pollution (4%)[b]	64	61
Diarrheal diseases	4.2	3.7	Childhood underweight (56%); vitamin A deficiency (22%); zinc deficiency (12%); unsafe water, sanitation, and hygiene (88%)	93	94
Unipolar major depression	3.1	0.0	Alcohol use (1%); childhood sexual abuse (5%)	6	NA[c]
Low birthweight	3.1	2.7	Iron-deficiency anemia (14%); alcohol use (0.5%)	16	17
Malaria	2.9	2.5	Childhood underweight (51%); vitamin A deficiency (19%); zinc deficiency (22%)	59	61
Tuberculosis	2.6	3.3	Smoking (4%)[c]	9	10
Chronic obstructive pulmonary disease	2.4	4.9	Indoor smoke from solid fuels (35%); urban air pollution (2%)[b]; smoking (40%)	63	60
Communicable, maternal, perinatal, and nutritional conditions	39.8	36.4	Multiple risks (see annex 4A)	47	48
Noncommunicable diseases	48.9	53.8	Multiple risks (see annex 4A)	33	50
Injuries	11.2	9.8	Multiple risks (see annex 4A)	15	18
All causes	100	100	All 19 selected risks (see annex 4A)	36	46

(Continues on the following page.)

Table 4.4 Continued

High-income countries

Disease	Proportion of regional disease burden (%) [total: 149.2 million DALYs(3.0)]	Proportion of regional mortality (%) [total: 7.9 million deaths]	PAFs for individual risk factors (for disease burden)	Joint PAF – disease burden (%)	Joint PAF – mortality (%)
Ischemic heart disease	8.3	17.3	High blood pressure (48%); high cholesterol (57%); overweight and obesity (27%); low fruit and vegetable intake (19%); physical inactivity (21%); smoking (23%); alcohol use (−13%); urban air pollution (1%)[b]	84	80
Stroke	6.3	9.9	High blood pressure (56%); high cholesterol (25%); overweight and obesity (20%); low fruit and vegetable intake (9%); physical inactivity (8%); smoking (21%); alcohol use (−11%); urban air pollution (1%)[b]	68	54
Unipolar depressive disorders	5.6	0.0	Alcohol use (4%); childhood sexual abuse (4%)	7	NA[c]
Dementia and other degenerative and hereditary central nervous system disorders	5.0	2.6	None of the selected risks	NA	NA
Trachea, bronchus, and lung cancers	3.6	5.8	Indoor smoke from solid fuels (coal only) (0%); smoking (84%); low fruit and vegetable intake (9%); urban air pollution (3%)[b]	86	87
Hearing loss	3.6	0.0	None of the selected risks	NA	NA
Chronic obstructive pulmonary disease	3.5	3.8	Indoor smoke from solid fuels (0%); urban air pollution (1%)[b]; smoking (73%)	73	76
Diabetes mellitus	2.8	2.6	Overweight and obesity (76%); physical inactivity (15%); smoking (4%)[a]; alcohol use (−5%)	78	74
Alcohol use disorders	2.8	0.3	Alcohol use (100%); childhood sexual abuse (6%)	100	100
Osteoarthritis	2.7	2.4	Overweight and obesity (20%); smoking (4%)[a]	20	NA[c]
Communicable, maternal, perinatal, and nutritional conditions	5.7	7.0	Multiple risks (see annex 4A)	18	18
Noncommunicable diseases	86.7	87.0	Multiple risks (see annex 4A)	37	48
Injuries	7.5	6.0	Multiple risks (see annex 4A)	21	22
All causes	100	100	All 19 selected risks (see annex 4A)	34	44

Source: Authors' calculations.

Note: NA = not applicable. Risk factors are those listed in table 4.1. These factors also contribute to other diseases that are not among the leading 10.

a. Affected by smoking in the category "other respiratory diseases" or "selected other medical causes" (Ezzati and Lopez 2003, 2004; Peto and others 1992). The PAF has large uncertainty.

b. Affected by urban air pollution in the category "cardiopulmonary diseases." The PAF for individual causes has large uncertainty.

c. The number of deaths coded to "hearing loss," "unipolar depressive disorders," "osteoarthritis," and "dementia and other degenerative and hereditary central nervous system disorders" is zero or very small in the GBD database, making the mortality PAF for these diseases undefined or unstable.

An important finding of this analysis is the key role of nutrition in health worldwide. Approximately 11 percent of the global disease burden was attributable to the joint effects of underweight or micronutrient deficiencies. In addition, almost 16 percent of the burden (28 percent for those aged 30 years and older) can be attributed to risk factors that have substantial dietary determinants (high blood pressure, high cholesterol, overweight and obesity, and low fruit and vegetable intake) and to physical inactivity. These patterns are not uniform within regions, however, and the transition has been healthier in some countries than in others (Lee, Popkin, and Kim 2000; Popkin 2002a, 2002b; Popkin and others 2001). Furthermore, the major nutritional and related risk factors show interregional heterogeneity, for instance, the relative contributions of blood pressure, cholesterol, and BMI differed across regions.

At the same time, the joint contributions of these risk factors left an important part of the global disease burden unexplained, because only a small fraction of some important diseases was attributable to the risk factors considered here. These include diseases whose determinants (a) are diffuse among environmental and behavioral factors, for example, some cancers, perinatal conditions, and neuropsychiatric diseases; (b) have more complex, multifactor etiology and often heterogeneous determinants in different populations, and are therefore difficult to quantify without data on a small scale, such as tuberculosis and injuries; (c) involve long delays between risk factor exposure and disease outcome; or (d) have limited quantitative research at the population level, for instance, neuropsychiatric diseases, often as a result of the previous three factors as well as difficulties in measuring exposure or outcome (Evans 1976, 1978). The mitigation of many such conditions, including malaria, tuberculosis, and injuries, may be better guided by analyses of the effects of interventions tailored to individual settings than by risk factor analysis.

Risk Factor Clusters

In addition to estimating the joint contributions of all the risk factors in table 4.1 to the all-cause mortality and disease burden, we also examined the role of selected clusters of risks that may be of particular interest to disease prevention policies and programs. The risk factor clusters were those affecting cancers (alcohol use, smoking, low fruit and vegetable intake, indoor smoke from household use of solid fuels, urban air pollution, overweight and obesity, physical inactivity, contaminated injections in health care settings, and unsafe sex), cardiovascular diseases (high blood pressure,

high cholesterol, smoking, overweight and obesity, alcohol use, physical inactivity, low fruit and vegetable intake, and urban air pollution), and child mortality (childhood underweight; vitamin A deficiency; zinc deficiency; iron deficiency anemia; unsafe water, sanitation, and hygiene; and indoor smoke from household use of solid fuels). Tables 4.5 through 4.7 show the individual and joint contributions of these risk factors to mortality and to the burden of disease for specific diseases within each cluster.

Globally, the cancers with the largest mortality fraction attributable to the risk factors in table 4.1 were cervix uteri cancer (100 percent); trachea, bronchus, and lung cancers (74 percent); and esophagus cancer (62 percent), and those with the smallest joint PAFs were colon and rectum cancers (13 percent) and leukemia (9 percent) (table 4.5). The largest number of deaths attributable to the joint effects of the risk factors was from trachea, bronchus, and lung cancer (930,000 deaths) and liver cancer (283,000 deaths), which reflects both the relatively large joint PAF and the total number of deaths from these cancers. Except for cervix uteri cancer, which was by definition fully attributable to the risk factor unsafe sex, joint PAFs were larger in high-income countries than in low- and middle-income countries for all cancer sites, mostly because of the higher contribution of smoking and alcohol use. The joint PAFs for all cancers combined, however, were similar for the two groups of countries (34 percent versus 37 percent for the disease burden), because of the distributions of total mortality from various site-specific cancers.

Almost two-thirds of all cardiovascular deaths were attributable to eight of the selected risk factors that affect these outcomes (table 4.6). The joint effects of these risk factors were much lower than the crude sum of individual effects (64 percent versus 126 percent for the disease burden), pointing to the extensive overlap in their hazards for cardiovascular diseases compared with cancers. The overlap is partly because the hazardous effects of some risks are mediated through others and partly because multiple risk factors act in combination. The joint PAF differed little between low- and middle-income and high-income countries, reflecting the high levels of multiple cardiovascular risk factors in many middle-income nations (Ezzati and others 2005). Coupled with substantially more cardiovascular deaths and a larger disease burden in low- and middle-income countries, these risk factors result in a much larger loss of healthy life in these nations.

Worldwide, approximately half of the mortality among children under five years of age (about 5 million deaths) was attributable to six major risk factors, with childhood underweight alone accounting for more than a quarter of all child

Table 4.5 Individual and Joint Contributions of Risk Factors to Mortality and Burden of Disease from Site-Specific Cancers

Cancer type	Deaths	Proportion of global disease burden (%) [total: 1.54 billion DALYs(3.0)]	PAFs for individual risk factors for mortality (first number) and disease burden (second number)	World Joint PAF – mortality (%)	Joint PAF – disease burden (%)
Mouth and oropharynx	311,633	0.30	Alcohol use (16%; 18%), smoking (42%; 42%)	52	54
Esophagus	437,511	0.39	Alcohol use (26%; 27%), smoking (42%; 42%), low fruit and vegetable intake (18%; 19%)	62	63
Stomach	841,693	0.73	Smoking (13%; 13%), low fruit and vegetable intake (18%; 19%)	28	30
Colon and rectal	613,740	0.53	Overweight and obesity (11%; 12%), physical inactivity (15%; 16%), low fruit and vegetable intake (2%; 2%)	13	14
Liver	606,441	0.59	Smoking (14%; 14%), alcohol use (25%; 25%), contaminated injections in health care setting (18%; 19%)	47	47
Pancreas	226,981	0.19	Smoking (22%; 22%)	22	22
Trachea, bronchus, and lung	1,226,574	1.04	Smoking (70%; 67%), low fruit and vegetable intake (11%; 12%), indoor smoke from household use of solid fuels (1%; 1%), urban air pollution (5%; 5%)	76	74
Breast	472,424	0.52	Alcohol use (5%; 5%), overweight and obesity (9%; 8%), physical inactivity (10%; 10%)	21	19
Cervix uteri	234,728	0.27	Smoking (2%; 2%), unsafe sex (100%; 100%)[a]	100	100
Corpus uteri	70,881	0.10	Overweight and obesity (40%; 46%)	40	42
Bladder	175,318	0.14	Smoking (28%; 27%)	28	27
Leukemia	263,169	0.32	Smoking (9%; 6%)	9	6
Selected other neoplasms[b]	145,802	0.14	Alcohol use (6%; 5%)	6	5
All other neoplasms	1,391,507	1.27	None of the selected risk factors	0	0
All cancers	7,018,402	6.53	Alcohol use (5%; 5%), smoking (21%; 21%), low fruit and vegetable intake (5%; 5%), indoor smoke from household use of solid fuels (<0.5%; <0.5%), urban air pollution (1%; 1%), overweight and obesity (2%; 2%), physical inactivity (2%; 2%), contaminated injections in health care setting (2%; 2%), unsafe sex (3%; 4%)	35	34

Low- and middle-income countries

Cancer type	Deaths	Proportion of regional disease burden (%) [total: 1.39 billion DALYs(3,0)]	PAFs for individual risk factors for mortality (first number) and disease burden (second number)	Joint PAF – mortality (%)	Joint PAF – disease burden (%)
Mouth and oropharynx	271,074	0.29	Alcohol use (14%; 15%), smoking (37%; 39%)	48	50
Esophagus	379,760	0.38	Alcohol use (24%; 25%), smoking (37%; 39%), low fruit and vegetable intake (19%; 20%)	58	60
Stomach	695,426	0.69	Smoking (11%; 11%), low fruit and vegetable intake (19%; 20%)	27	29
Colon and rectal	356,949	0.36	Overweight and obesity (9%; 9%), physical inactivity (15%; 16%), low fruit and vegetable intake (2%; 3%)	11	12
Liver	504,407	0.57	Smoking (11%; 12%), alcohol use (23%; 24%), contaminated injections in health care setting (21%; 22%)	45	46
Pancreas	116,827	0.12	Smoking (15%; 16%)	15	16
Trachea, bronchus, and lung	770,938	0.77	Smoking (60%; 59%), low fruit and vegetable intake (13%; 13%), indoor smoke from household use of solid fuels (2%; 2%), urban air pollution (7%; 7%)	69	68
Breast	317,195	0.40	Alcohol use (4%; 4%), overweight and obesity (7%; 7%), physical inactivity (10%; 10%)	18	17
Cervix uteri	218,064	0.27	Smoking (2%; 2%), unsafe sex (100%; 100%)[a]	100	100
Corpus uteri	43,926	0.07	Overweight and obesity (37%; 39%)	37	39
Bladder	116,682	0.11	Smoking (21%; 21%)	21	21
Leukemia	190,059	0.28	Smoking (6%; 4%)	6	4
Selected other neoplasms[b]	88,706	0.11	Alcohol use (4%; 4%)	4	4
All other neoplasms	882,001	0.95	None of the selected risk factors	0	0
All cancers	4,952,014	5.37	Alcohol use (5%; 6%), smoking (18%; 19%), low fruit and vegetable intake (6%; 6%), indoor smoke from household use of solid fuels (<0.5%; <0.5%), urban air pollution (1%; 1%), overweight and obesity (1%; 2%), physical inactivity (2%;.2%), contaminated injections in health care setting (2%; 2%), unsafe sex (4%; 5%)	34	34

(Continues on the following page.)

Table 4.5 Continued

Cancer type	Deaths	Proportion of regional disease burden (%) [total: 149.2 million DALYs(3.0)]	High-income countries		
			PAFs for individual risk factors for mortality (first number) and disease burden (second number)	Joint PAF – mortality (%)	Joint PAF – disease burden (%)
Mouth and oropharynx	40,559	0.39	Alcohol use (33%; 35%), smoking (71%; 71%)	80	80
Esophagus	57,752	0.47	Alcohol use (41%; 43%), smoking (71%; 71%), low fruit and vegetable intake (12%; 13%)	85	86
Stomach	146,267	1.09	Smoking (25%; 25%), low fruit and vegetable intake (12%; 13%)	34	35
Colon and rectal	256,791	2.13	Overweight and obesity (14%; 15%), physical inactivity (14%; 16%), low fruit and vegetable intake (1%; 2%)	15	17
Liver	102,033	0.82	Smoking (29%; 29%), alcohol use (32%; 33%), contaminated injections in health care setting (3%; 4%)	52	54
Pancreas	110,154	0.83	Smoking (30%; 30%)	30	30
Trachea, bronchus, and lung	455,636	3.62	Smoking (86%; 84%), low fruit and vegetable intake (8%; 9%), indoor smoke from household use of solid fuels (0%; 0%), urban air pollution (3%; 3%)	87	86
Breast	155,230	1.68	Alcohol use (9%; 9%), overweight and obesity (13%; 12%), physical inactivity (9%; 10%)	27	26
Cervix uteri	16,663	0.21	Smoking (11%; 10%), unsafe sex (100%; 100%)[a]	100	100
Corpus uteri	26,955	0.39	Overweight and obesity (43%; 46%)	43	46
Bladder	58,636	0.45	Smoking (41%; 41%)	41	41
Leukemia	73,110	0.62	Smoking (17%; 15%)	17	15
Selected other neoplasms[b]	57,095	0.37	Alcohol use (8%; 9%)	8	9
All other neoplasms	509,507	4.28	None of the selected risk factors	0	0
All cancers	2,066,388	17.35	Alcohol use (4%; 5%), smoking (29%; 29%), low fruit and vegetable intake (3%; 3%), indoor smoke from household use of solid fuels (0%; 0%), urban air pollution (1%; 1%), overweight and obesity (3%; 4%), physical inactivity (2%; 3%), contaminated injections in health care setting (<0.5%; <0.5%), unsafe sex (1%; 1%)	37	37

Source: Authors' calculations.

Note: Risk factors are those listed in table 4.1.

a. Currently, a proportion of human papilloma virus (HPV) infections that lead to cervix uteri cancer are transmitted through routes other than sexual contact. The PAF for unsafe sex, as defined in the CRA project (Slaymaker and others 2004), measures the current population-level cervix cancer mortality that would be reduced, had there never been any sexual transmission of infection (that is, the consequences of past and current exposure, as we do for accumulated hazards of smoking). By considering the health consequences of past and current exposure, nearly all sexually transmitted diseases are attributable to unsafe sex. This is because, in the absence of sexual transmission in the past, current infections transmitted through other forms of contact would not occur if the infected hosts acquired their infection sexually (and so on in the sequence of past infected hosts).

b. This category includes neoplasms under the ICD-9 three-digit codes 210–239.

Table 4.6 Individual and Joint Contributions of Risk Factors to Mortality and Burden of Disease from Cardiovascular Diseases

World

Disease	Deaths	Proportion of global disease burden (%) [total: 1.54 billion DALYs(3.0)]	PAFs for individual risk factors for mortality (first number) and disease burden (second number)	Joint PAF – mortality (%)	Joint PAF – disease burden (%)
Ischemic heart disease	7,060,851	5.5	High blood pressure (47%; 45%), high cholesterol (45%; 48%), smoking (12%; 17%), overweight and obesity (15%; 18%), alcohol use (1%; 2%), physical inactivity (19%; 21%), low fruit and vegetable intake (25%; 28%), urban air pollution (3%; 2%)[a]	79	80
Stroke	5,387,500	4.7	High blood pressure (54%; 54%), high cholesterol (13%; 16%), smoking (8%; 13%), overweight and obesity (8%; 12%), alcohol use (2%; 3%), physical inactivity (6%; 7%), low fruit and vegetable intake (9%; 11%), urban air pollution (3%; 2%)[a]	60	65
Hypertensive disease	888,144	0.7	High blood pressure (79%; 75%), overweight and obesity (29%; 33%), alcohol use (15%; 15%), urban air pollution (3%; 2%)[a]	85	83
Selected other cardiovascular diseases[b]	2,335,514	1.8	High blood pressure (28%; 24%), smoking (14%; 12%)	37	33
All cardiovascular diseases	16,386,531	13.5	High blood pressure (46%; 44%), high cholesterol (24%; 25%), smoking (10%; 13%), overweight and obesity (11%; 13%), alcohol use (2%; 3%), physical inactivity (10%; 11%), low fruit and vegetable intake (14%; 15%), urban air pollution (2%; 2%)[a]	63	64

Low- and middle-income countries

Disease	Deaths	Proportion of regional disease burden (%) [total: 1.39 billion DALYs(3.0)]	PAFs for individual risk factors for mortality (first number) and disease burden (second number)	Joint PAF – mortality (%)	Joint PAF – disease burden (%)
Ischemic heart disease	5,696,844	5.2	High blood pressure (47%; 44%), high cholesterol (43%; 46%), smoking (11%; 15%), overweight and obesity (14%; 16%), alcohol use (4%; 4%), physical inactivity (20%; 21%), low fruit and vegetable intake (27%; 30%), urban air pollution (4%; 2%)[a]	78	80
Stroke	4,606,426	4.5	High blood pressure (54%; 54%), high cholesterol (12%; 15%), smoking (8%; 12%), overweight and obesity (7%; 10%), alcohol use (5%; 5%), physical inactivity (6%; 6%), low fruit and vegetable intake (10%; 11%), urban air pollution (4%; 2%)[a]	61	64
Hypertensive disease	759,487	0.7	High blood pressure (79%; 75%), overweight and obesity (28%; 31%), alcohol use (14%; 14%), urban air pollution (4%; 2%)[a]	84	82

(Continues on the following page.)

Table 4.6 Continued

Low- and middle-income countries

Disease	Deaths	Proportion of regional disease burden (%) [total: 1.39 billion DALYs(3,0)]	PAFs for individual risk factors for mortality (first number) and disease burden (second number)	Joint PAF – mortality (%)	Joint PAF – disease burden (%)
Selected other cardiovascular diseases[b]	1,659,570	1.6	High blood pressure (27%; 23%), smoking (9%; 9%)	33	29
All cardiovascular diseases	13,347,471	12.9	High blood pressure (47%; 44%), high cholesterol (23%; 24%), smoking (9%; 11%), overweight and obesity (10%; 12%), alcohol use (4%; 4%), physical inactivity (10%; 11%), low fruit and vegetable intake (15%; 16%), urban air pollution (3%; 2%)[a]	64	63

High-income countries

Disease	Deaths	Proportion of regional disease burden (%) [total; 142.9 million DALYs(3,0)]	PAFs for individual risk factors for mortality (first number) and disease burden (second number)	Joint PAF – mortality (%)	Joint PAF – disease burden (%)
Ischemic heart disease	1,364,007	8.3	High blood pressure (49%; 48%), high cholesterol (52%; 57%), smoking (15%; 23%), overweight and obesity (19%; 27%), alcohol use (−12%; −13%), physical inactivity (19%; 21%), low fruit and vegetable intake (16%; 19%), urban air pollution (2%; 1%)[a]	80	84
Stroke	781,074	6.3	High blood pressure (54%; 56%), high cholesterol (17%; 25%), smoking (10%; 21%), overweight and obesity (12%; 20%), alcohol use (−13%; −11%), physical inactivity (6%; 8%), low fruit and vegetable intake (6%; 9%), urban air pollution (2%; 1%)[a]	54	68
Hypertensive disease	128,657	0.8	High blood pressure (84%; 82%), overweight and obesity (38%; 45%), alcohol use (23%; 24%), urban air pollution (2%; 1%)[a]	91	91
Selected other cardiovascular diseases[b]	675,944	3.8	High blood pressure (29%; 29%), smoking (26%; 25%)	48	46
All cardiovascular diseases	3,039,060	20.0	High blood pressure (46%; 46%), high cholesterol (28%; 32%), smoking (15%; 21%), overweight and obesity (13%; 19%), alcohol use (−8%; −8%), physical inactivity (10%; 11%), low fruit and vegetable intake (9%; 11%), urban air pollution (1%; 1%)[a]	64	69

Source: Authors' calculations.

Note: Risk factors are those listed in table 4.1.

a. Affected by urban air pollution in the category "cardiopulmonary diseases." The PAFs for individual causes have large uncertainty.

b. This category includes ICD-9 three-digit codes 415–417, 423–424, 426–429, 440–448, 451–459.

Table 4.7 Individual and Joint Contributions of Risk Factors to Mortality and Burden of Disease from Major Diseases of Children

World

Disease[a]	Deaths	Proportion of global disease burden (%) [total: 1.54 billion DALYs(3.0)]	PAFs for individual risk factors for mortality (first number) and disease burden (second number)	Joint PAF – mortality (%)	Joint PAF – disease burden (%)
Measles	556,384	1.1	Childhood underweight (44%; 44%), vitamin A deficiency (20%; 20%)	55	55
Diarrheal diseases	1,598,754	3.5	Childhood underweight (61%; 55%), vitamin A deficiency (24%; 22%), zinc deficiency (13%; 12%), unsafe water, sanitation, and hygiene (88%; 88%)	94	93
Lower respiratory infections	1,914,189	4.0	Childhood underweight (54%; 52%), zinc deficiency (21%; 21%), indoor air pollution (49%; 48%)	72	70
Malaria	1,086,298	2.3	Childhood underweight (55%; 51%), vitamin A deficiency (19%; 19%), zinc deficiency (22%; 22%)	68	65
Conditions arising during the perinatal period	2,520,986	5.9	Iron-deficiency anemia (16%; 14%)	16	14
All other childhood diseases	2,921,834	11.2	Partially attributable to childhood underweight and vitamin A deficiency (see annex 4A for details).	Not estimated	Not estimated
All causes	10,598,444	28.0	Childhood underweight (27%; 20%), vitamin A deficiency (7%; 5%), zinc deficiency (8%; 6%), unsafe water, sanitation, and hygiene (13%; 11%), indoor air pollution (9%; 7%), iron-deficiency anemia (4%; 3%)	49	40

Low- and middle-income countries

Disease[a]	Deaths	Proportion of regional disease burden (%) [total: 1.39 billion DALYs(3.0)]	PAFs for individual risk factors for mortality (first number) and disease burden (second number)	Joint PAF – mortality (%)	Joint PAF – disease burden (%)
Measles	556,312	1.2	Childhood underweight (44%; 44%), vitamin A deficiency (20%; 20%)	55	55
Diarrheal diseases	1,598,336	3.8	Childhood underweight (61%; 56%), vitamin A deficiency (24%; 22%), zinc deficiency (13%; 12%), unsafe water, sanitation, and hygiene (88%; 88%)	94	93
Lower respiratory infections	1,912,599	4.4	Childhood underweight (54%; 52%), zinc deficiency (21%; 21%), indoor air pollution (49%; 48%)	72	70
Malaria	1,086,237	2.6	Childhood underweight (55%; 51%), vitamin A deficiency (19%; 19%), zinc deficiency (22%; 22%)	68	65
Conditions arising during the perinatal period	2,488,718	6.4	Iron-deficiency anemia (16%; 14%)	16	14

(Continues on the following page.)

Table 4.7 Continued

Low- and middle-income countries

Disease[a]	Deaths	Proportion of regional disease burden (%) [total: 1.39 billion DALYs(3,0)]	PAFs for individual risk factors for mortality (first number) and disease burden (second number)	Joint PAF—mortality (%)	Joint PAF—disease burden (%)
All other childhood diseases	2,883,496	12.0	Partially attributable to childhood underweight and vitamin A deficiency (see annex 4A for details).	Not estimated	Not estimated
All causes	10,525,699	30.5	Childhood underweight (27%; 21%), vitamin A deficiency (7%; 5%), zinc deficiency (8%; 7%), unsafe water, sanitation, and hygiene (13%; 11%), indoor air pollution (9%; 7%), iron-deficiency anemia (4%; 3%)	49	41

High-income countries

Disease[a]	Deaths	Proportion of regional disease burden (%) [total: 149.2 million DALYs(3,0)]	PAFs for individual risk factors for mortality (first number) and disease burden (second number)	Joint PAF—mortality (%)	Joint PAF—disease burden (%)
Measles	73	0.0	Childhood underweight (0%; 0%), vitamin A deficiency (1%; 0%)	1	0
Diarrheal diseases	418	0.2	Childhood underweight (0%; 0%), vitamin A deficiency (1%; 0%), zinc deficiency (1%; 1%), unsafe water, sanitation, and hygiene (65%; 65%)	66	66
Lower respiratory infections	1,590	0.0	Childhood underweight (0%; 0%), zinc deficiency (3%; 3%), indoor air pollution (0%; 0%)	1	1
Malaria	61	0.0	Childhood underweight (0%; 0%), vitamin A deficiency (1%; 1%), zinc deficiency (3%; 3%)	2	2
Conditions arising during the perinatal period	32,268	0.9	Iron-deficiency anemia (3%; 2%)	3	2
All other childhood diseases	38,337	3.4	Partially attributable to childhood underweight and vitamin A deficiency (see annex 4A for details).	Not estimated	Not estimated
All causes	72,746	4.6	Childhood underweight (0%; 0%), vitamin A deficiency (0%; 0%), zinc deficiency (0%; 0%), unsafe water, sanitation, and hygiene (0%; 2%), indoor air pollution (0%; 0%), iron-deficiency anemia (1%; 0%)	2	4

Source: Authors' calculations.

Note: Risk factors are those listed in table 4.1.

a. By definition, the diseases protein-energy malnutrition (ICD-9 three-digit codes 260–263), iron-deficiency anemia (ICD-9 three-digit codes 280–285), and vitamin A deficiency (ICD-9 three-digit code 264) are 100 percent attributable to their corresponding namesake risk factors. Thus, the PAFs for these diseases are not shown. PAFs, attributable mortality, and attributable disease burden are reported in annex 4A.

deaths. Practically all the mortality and disease burden from childhood diseases attributable to major risk factors occurred in low- and middle-income countries (table 4.7). The reasons for this large disparity in the disease burden attributable to risk factors are higher risk factor exposure coupled with lower access to case management, which affects child mortality together with risk factor exposure.

DIRECTIONS FOR FUTURE RESEARCH

Health research has at times focused on topics that, while scientifically intriguing, have not always taken population health consequences into account when shaping specific research questions (Editorial 2001; Gross, Anserson, and Powe 1999; Horton 2003). The collation of evidence on exposure and hazard for different risks and the existing data gaps revealed the areas where data and monitoring need to be improved for better quantification of important risks and for more effective intervention. This includes the need for more detailed and higher quality data on exposure to most risks using exposure variables that capture the full distribution of hazards in the population. Important examples include detailed data on alcohol consumption volumes and patterns, dietary and biological markers for micronutrients, physical activity, and indoor smoke from household use of solid fuels, all of which were quantified using indirect measures with limited resolution. Furthermore, assumptions and extrapolations were needed in quantifying the relationships between risk factors and disease because of research gaps for some important global risk factors. Examples include limited quantitative assessments of the hazards of specific sexual behaviors for HIV/AIDS and other sexually transmitted diseases (UNAIDS 2001), of alcohol drinking patterns (Puddey and others 1999), or of exposure to indoor smoke from household use of solid fuels (Ezzati and Kammen 2002). Equally important are detailed exposure data for risks that have traditionally been studied in developed countries, but have global importance and require more detailed data and hazard quantification in developing regions, including smoking, body mass index, blood pressure, and cholesterol (Yusuf and others 2004).

The limited evidence on the effects of multiple risk factors and risk factor interactions also points to important gaps in research on multirisk and stratified hazards. Including multiple layers of causality in epidemiological research and risk assessment would allow investigators to estimate the benefits of reducing combinations of distal and proximal exposures using multiple interventions. Examples of such integrated strategies include using education and economic tools to promote physical activity and a healthier diet coupled with screening and lowering cholesterol, and addressing the overall childhood nutrition and physical environment instead of focusing on individual components. In such research, risk factor groups should be selected based on both biological relationships and socioeconomic factors that affect multiple diseases. Examples include those risk factors that are affected by the same policies and distal socioeconomic factors, such as malnutrition; unsafe water, sanitation, and hygiene; indoor smoke from household use of solid fuels; and rural development policies, or affect the same group of diseases, for instance, the previous example for childhood infectious diseases and smoking, diet, physical activity, and blood pressure for vascular diseases. Once risk factors are selected, the emphasis on reducing confounding should be matched by equally important inquiry into independent and mediated hazard sizes that are stratified based on the levels of other risks.

Finally, to inform interventions and policies, similar analyses should take place at smaller scales than global or regional levels, for example, rural and urban areas or different geographical regions of individual countries, and should include micro-level data and possibly a more comprehensive list of both distal and proximal risk factors, such as adverse life events and stress, risk factors for injuries, salt and fat intake, and blood glucose.

DISCUSSION

Despite inherent uncertainties in population health risk assessment, described in chapter 5 and in chapters devoted to individual risk factors elsewhere (Ezzati and others 2004), the quantification of the burden of disease attributable to the individual and joint hazards of selected risk factors illustrates that those risk factors that affect the poorest regions and populations, such as undernutrition; unsafe water, sanitation, and hygiene; and indoor smoke from household use of solid fuels, continue to dominate the loss of health worldwide. These are coupled with hazards such as alcohol use, smoking, high blood pressure, high cholesterol, and overweight and obesity that are globally widespread and have large health effects.

The large remaining burden due to childhood mortality risks such as undernutrition; unsafe water, sanitation, and hygiene; and indoor smoke from household use of solid fuels indicates the persistent need for developing and delivering effective interventions, including lowering the costs of pertinent technological interventions. At the same time, four of the five leading causes of lost healthy life affect adults: high blood pressure, unsafe sex, smoking, and alcohol use (figure 4.1). Risk factors for both adult communicable and noncommunicable diseases already make substantial contributions to the disease burden even in regions with low income and high infant mortality. Therefore, the public health community should continually reassess the need for interventions addressing both childhood disease risk factors and those that affect adult health. Dynamic and systematic policy responses can, to a large extent, mitigate the spread of such risk factors and their more distal causes throughout the development process, for example, through cleaner environmental or healthier nutritional transitions (Arrow and others 1995; Lee, Popkin, and Kim 2000). In addition, as illustrated by the persistence of diseases such as malaria or the large increase in the disease burden due to HIV/AIDS and its risk factors since 1990, as well as the potential for generalized HIV/AIDS epidemics in some Eastern European countries (MacLehose, McKee, and Weinberg 2002) and China (Kaufman and Jing 2002), risk factors for important communicable diseases also require dynamic monitoring and policy responses.

Risk factors that were not among the leading global causes of the disease burden should not be neglected for a number of reasons. First, the analysis could be expanded with other risk factors that are both prevalent and hazardous. Second, although smaller than other risk factors, many make non-negligible contributions to the burden of disease in various populations. For example, in the low- and middle-income countries of East Asia and the Pacific, which is dominated by China in terms of population, urban air pollution from transportation and industrial and household energy use based on coal has health effects comparable to those of micronutrient deficiencies. Similarly, non-use and use of ineffective methods of contraception was associated with a larger disease burden than most chronic disease risk factors among females in South Asia and Sub-Saharan Africa. Third, for other risk factors, such as child sexual abuse, ethical considerations may outweigh direct contribu-

tions to the disease burden in policy debate. Finally, while the burden of disease due to a risk factor may be comparatively small, effective or cost-effective interventions may be known. Examples include reducing the number of unnecessary injections at health facilities coupled with the use of sterile syringes and the reduction in exposure to urban air pollution in industrial countries in the second half of the 20th century, which often also led to benefits such as energy savings.

A small number of risks account for large contributions to the global loss of healthy life. Furthermore, several are relatively prominent in regions at all stages of development. While reducing all the risks discussed to their theoretical minimums may not be possible using current interventions, the results illustrate that preventing disease by addressing known distal and proximal risk factors can provide substantial and underutilized public health gains. Treating established disease will always have a role in public health, especially in the case of diseases such as tuberculosis, where treatment contributes to prevention. At the same time, the current devotion of a disproportionately small share of resources to prevention by reducing major known risk factors through personal and nonpersonal interventions should be reconsidered in a more systematic way in light of the evidence presented here.

The estimates of the joint contributions of 19 selected global risk factors showed that these risks together contributed to a considerable loss of healthy life in different regions of the world. In particular, for some of the leading global diseases, such as lower respiratory infections, diarrhea, HIV/AIDS, lung cancer, ischemic heart disease, and stroke, substantial proportions were attributable to these selected risk factors. This concentration of the disease burden further emphasizes the contribution of leading risks such as undernutrition, unsafe sex, high blood pressure, and smoking and alcohol use to the loss of healthy life globally. The results further emphasize that for more effective and affordable implementation of a prevention paradigm, policies, programs, and scientific research should acknowledge and take advantage of the interactive and correlated role of major risks to health, across and within causality layers.

ANNEX 4A: Population Attributable Fractions, Attributable Deaths, Years of Life Lost Because of Premature Mortality (YLL), and Disability-Adjusted Life Years (DALYs) by Risk Factor, Disease Outcome, Age, Sex, and Region

Table 4A.1

Risk factor: Childhood underweight
Disease: Diarrheal diseases

Region	0–4 years Male	0–4 years Female	5–14 years Male	5–14 years Female	15–29 years Male	15–29 years Female	30–44 years Male	30–44 years Female	45–59 years Male	45–59 years Female	60–69 years Male	60–69 years Female	70–79 years Male	70–79 years Female	80+ years Male	80+ years Female	Total Male	Total Female	All
PAF of Mortality (%)																			
East Asia and Pacific	46	46	NA	NA	NA	NA	NA	NA	NA	NA	NA	NA	NA	NA	NA	NA	41	41	41
Europe and Central Asia	27	27	NA	NA	NA	NA	NA	NA	NA	NA	NA	NA	NA	NA	NA	NA	22	21	22
Latin America and the Caribbean	24	24	NA	NA	NA	NA	NA	NA	NA	NA	NA	NA	NA	NA	NA	NA	21	21	21
Middle East and North Africa	42	42	NA	NA	NA	NA	NA	NA	NA	NA	NA	NA	NA	NA	NA	NA	37	38	38
South Asia	71	71	NA	NA	NA	NA	NA	NA	NA	NA	NA	NA	NA	NA	NA	NA	64	64	64
Sub-Saharan Africa	60	60	NA	NA	NA	NA	NA	NA	NA	NA	NA	NA	NA	NA	NA	NA	54	54	54
Low- and middle-income countries	61	61	NA	NA	NA	NA	NA	NA	NA	NA	NA	NA	NA	NA	NA	NA	54	54	54
High-income countries	0	0	NA	NA	NA	NA	NA	NA	NA	NA	NA	NA	NA	NA	NA	NA	0	0	0
WORLD	60	61	NA	NA	NA	NA	NA	NA	NA	NA	NA	NA	NA	NA	NA	NA	54	54	54
PAF of YLL (%)																			
East Asia and Pacific	46	46	NA	NA	NA	NA	NA	NA	NA	NA	NA	NA	NA	NA	NA	NA	43	44	44
Europe and Central Asia	27	27	NA	NA	NA	NA	NA	NA	NA	NA	NA	NA	NA	NA	NA	NA	24	24	24
Latin America and the Caribbean	24	24	NA	NA	NA	NA	NA	NA	NA	NA	NA	NA	NA	NA	NA	NA	23	23	23
Middle East and North Africa	42	42	NA	NA	NA	NA	NA	NA	NA	NA	NA	NA	NA	NA	NA	NA	40	40	40
South Asia	71	71	NA	NA	NA	NA	NA	NA	NA	NA	NA	NA	NA	NA	NA	NA	68	68	68
Sub-Saharan Africa	60	60	NA	NA	NA	NA	NA	NA	NA	NA	NA	NA	NA	NA	NA	NA	57	58	57
Low- and middle-income countries	61	61	NA	NA	NA	NA	NA	NA	NA	NA	NA	NA	NA	NA	NA	NA	58	58	58
High-income countries	0	0	NA	NA	NA	NA	NA	NA	NA	NA	NA	NA	NA	NA	NA	NA	0	0	0
WORLD	60	61	NA	NA	NA	NA	NA	NA	NA	NA	NA	NA	NA	NA	NA	NA	58	58	58
PAF of DALYs (%)																			
East Asia and Pacific	40	40	NA	NA	NA	NA	NA	NA	NA	NA	NA	NA	NA	NA	NA	NA	32	32	32
Europe and Central Asia	19	18	NA	NA	NA	NA	NA	NA	NA	NA	NA	NA	NA	NA	NA	NA	15	15	15
Latin America and the Caribbean	19	18	NA	NA	NA	NA	NA	NA	NA	NA	NA	NA	NA	NA	NA	NA	15	15	15
Middle East and North Africa	37	37	NA	NA	NA	NA	NA	NA	NA	NA	NA	NA	NA	NA	NA	NA	33	33	33
South Asia	66	66	NA	NA	NA	NA	NA	NA	NA	NA	NA	NA	NA	NA	NA	NA	62	62	62
Sub-Saharan Africa	57	57	NA	NA	NA	NA	NA	NA	NA	NA	NA	NA	NA	NA	NA	NA	54	53	53
Low- and middle-income countries	56	56	NA	NA	NA	NA	NA	NA	NA	NA	NA	NA	NA	NA	NA	NA	50	50	50
High-income countries	0	0	NA	NA	NA	NA	NA	NA	NA	NA	NA	NA	NA	NA	NA	NA	0	0	0
WORLD	55	55	NA	NA	NA	NA	NA	NA	NA	NA	NA	NA	NA	NA	NA	NA	50	50	50
Attributable Mortality (thousands)																			
East Asia and Pacific	48	44	NA	NA	NA	NA	NA	NA	NA	NA	NA	NA	NA	NA	NA	NA	48	44	92
Europe and Central Asia	2	1	NA	NA	NA	NA	NA	NA	NA	NA	NA	NA	NA	NA	NA	NA	2	1	3
Latin America and the Caribbean	6	5	NA	NA	NA	NA	NA	NA	NA	NA	NA	NA	NA	NA	NA	NA	6	5	11
Middle East and North Africa	14	13	NA	NA	NA	NA	NA	NA	NA	NA	NA	NA	NA	NA	NA	NA	14	13	28
South Asia	233	214	NA	NA	NA	NA	NA	NA	NA	NA	NA	NA	NA	NA	NA	NA	233	214	446
Sub-Saharan Africa	203	184	NA	NA	NA	NA	NA	NA	NA	NA	NA	NA	NA	NA	NA	NA	203	184	386
Low- and middle-income countries	506	461	NA	NA	NA	NA	NA	NA	NA	NA	NA	NA	NA	NA	NA	NA	506	461	967
High-income countries	0	0	NA	NA	NA	NA	NA	NA	NA	NA	NA	NA	NA	NA	NA	NA	0	0	0
WORLD	506	461	NA	NA	NA	NA	NA	NA	NA	NA	NA	NA	NA	NA	NA	NA	506	461	967
Attributable YLL (thousands)																			
East Asia and Pacific	1,464	1,338	NA	NA	NA	NA	NA	NA	NA	NA	NA	NA	NA	NA	NA	NA	1,464	1,338	2,802
Europe and Central Asia	51	46	NA	NA	NA	NA	NA	NA	NA	NA	NA	NA	NA	NA	NA	NA	51	46	97
Latin America and the Caribbean	180	164	NA	NA	NA	NA	NA	NA	NA	NA	NA	NA	NA	NA	NA	NA	180	164	344
Middle East and North Africa	439	408	NA	NA	NA	NA	NA	NA	NA	NA	NA	NA	NA	NA	NA	NA	439	408	847
South Asia	7,050	6,510	NA	NA	NA	NA	NA	NA	NA	NA	NA	NA	NA	NA	NA	NA	7,050	6,510	13,560
Sub-Saharan Africa	6,122	5,595	NA	NA	NA	NA	NA	NA	NA	NA	NA	NA	NA	NA	NA	NA	6,122	5,595	11,717
Low- and middle-income countries	15,307	14,061	NA	NA	NA	NA	NA	NA	NA	NA	NA	NA	NA	NA	NA	NA	15,307	14,061	29,367
High-income countries	0	0	NA	NA	NA	NA	NA	NA	NA	NA	NA	NA	NA	NA	NA	NA	0	0	0
WORLD	15,307	14,061	NA	NA	NA	NA	NA	NA	NA	NA	NA	NA	NA	NA	NA	NA	15,307	14,061	29,367
Attributable DALYs (thousands)																			
East Asia and Pacific	1,480	1,354	NA	NA	NA	NA	NA	NA	NA	NA	NA	NA	NA	NA	NA	NA	1,480	1,354	2,834
Europe and Central Asia	52	47	NA	NA	NA	NA	NA	NA	NA	NA	NA	NA	NA	NA	NA	NA	52	47	99
Latin America and the Caribbean	183	166	NA	NA	NA	NA	NA	NA	NA	NA	NA	NA	NA	NA	NA	NA	183	166	349
Middle East and North Africa	444	413	NA	NA	NA	NA	NA	NA	NA	NA	NA	NA	NA	NA	NA	NA	444	413	856
South Asia	7,127	6,582	NA	NA	NA	NA	NA	NA	NA	NA	NA	NA	NA	NA	NA	NA	7,127	6,582	13,709
Sub-Saharan Africa	6,158	5,630	NA	NA	NA	NA	NA	NA	NA	NA	NA	NA	NA	NA	NA	NA	6,158	5,630	11,788
Low- and middle-income countries	15,444	14,192	NA	NA	NA	NA	NA	NA	NA	NA	NA	NA	NA	NA	NA	NA	15,444	14,192	29,636
High-income countries	0	0	NA	NA	NA	NA	NA	NA	NA	NA	NA	NA	NA	NA	NA	NA	0	0	0
WORLD	15,444	14,192	NA	NA	NA	NA	NA	NA	NA	NA	NA	NA	NA	NA	NA	NA	15,444	14,192	29,636

Source: Authors' calculations.
Note: NA = not applicable.

Table 4A.2

Risk factor: Childhood underweight
Disease: Measles

Region	0–4 years Male	Female	5–14 years Male	Female	15–29 years Male	Female	30–44 years Male	Female	45–59 years Male	Female	60–69 years Male	Female	70–79 years Male	Female	80+ years Male	Female	Total Male	Female	All
PAF of Mortality (%)																			
East Asia and Pacific	31	31	NA	NA	NA	NA	NA	NA	NA	NA	NA	NA	NA	NA	NA	NA	18	18	18
Europe and Central Asia	16	16	NA	NA	NA	NA	NA	NA	NA	NA	NA	NA	NA	NA	NA	NA	11	11	11
Latin America and the Caribbean	*	*	NA	NA	NA	NA	NA	NA	NA	NA	NA	NA	NA	NA	NA	NA	*	*	*
Middle East and North Africa	28	28	NA	NA	NA	NA	NA	NA	NA	NA	NA	NA	NA	NA	NA	NA	17	18	18
South Asia	53	53	NA	NA	NA	NA	NA	NA	NA	NA	NA	NA	NA	NA	NA	NA	36	36	36
Sub-Saharan Africa	43	43	NA	NA	NA	NA	NA	NA	NA	NA	NA	NA	NA	NA	NA	NA	34	33	34
Low- and middle-income countries	44	44	NA	NA	NA	NA	NA	NA	NA	NA	NA	NA	NA	NA	NA	NA	32	32	32
High-income countries	0	0	NA	NA	NA	NA	NA	NA	NA	NA	NA	NA	NA	NA	NA	NA	0	0	0
WORLD	44	44	NA	NA	NA	NA	NA	NA	NA	NA	NA	NA	NA	NA	NA	NA	32	32	32
PAF of YLL (%)																			
East Asia and Pacific	31	31	NA	NA	NA	NA	NA	NA	NA	NA	NA	NA	NA	NA	NA	NA	18	18	18
Europe and Central Asia	16	16	NA	NA	NA	NA	NA	NA	NA	NA	NA	NA	NA	NA	NA	NA	11	11	11
Latin America and the Caribbean	*	*	NA	NA	NA	NA	NA	NA	NA	NA	NA	NA	NA	NA	NA	NA	*	*	*
Middle East and North Africa	28	28	NA	NA	NA	NA	NA	NA	NA	NA	NA	NA	NA	NA	NA	NA	17	18	18
South Asia	53	53	NA	NA	NA	NA	NA	NA	NA	NA	NA	NA	NA	NA	NA	NA	36	37	36
Sub-Saharan Africa	43	43	NA	NA	NA	NA	NA	NA	NA	NA	NA	NA	NA	NA	NA	NA	34	34	34
Low- and middle-income countries	44	44	NA	NA	NA	NA	NA	NA	NA	NA	NA	NA	NA	NA	NA	NA	32	32	32
High-income countries	0	0	NA	NA	NA	NA	NA	NA	NA	NA	NA	NA	NA	NA	NA	NA	0	0	0
WORLD	44	44	NA	NA	NA	NA	NA	NA	NA	NA	NA	NA	NA	NA	NA	NA	32	32	32
PAF of DALYs (%)																			
East Asia and Pacific	30	30	NA	NA	NA	NA	NA	NA	NA	NA	NA	NA	NA	NA	NA	NA	18	18	18
Europe and Central Asia	16	16	NA	NA	NA	NA	NA	NA	NA	NA	NA	NA	NA	NA	NA	NA	11	10	11
Latin America and the Caribbean	*	*	NA	NA	NA	NA	NA	NA	NA	NA	NA	NA	NA	NA	NA	NA	*	*	*
Middle East and North Africa	27	27	NA	NA	NA	NA	NA	NA	NA	NA	NA	NA	NA	NA	NA	NA	17	18	17
South Asia	53	53	NA	NA	NA	NA	NA	NA	NA	NA	NA	NA	NA	NA	NA	NA	36	36	36
Sub-Saharan Africa	42	42	NA	NA	NA	NA	NA	NA	NA	NA	NA	NA	NA	NA	NA	NA	34	33	34
Low- and middle-income countries	44	44	NA	NA	NA	NA	NA	NA	NA	NA	NA	NA	NA	NA	NA	NA	32	32	32
High-income countries	0	0	NA	NA	NA	NA	NA	NA	NA	NA	NA	NA	NA	NA	NA	NA	0	0	0
WORLD	44	44	NA	NA	NA	NA	NA	NA	NA	NA	NA	NA	NA	NA	NA	NA	32	32	32
Attributable Mortality (thousands)																			
East Asia and Pacific	7	7	NA	NA	NA	NA	NA	NA	NA	NA	NA	NA	NA	NA	NA	NA	7	7	14
Europe and Central Asia	0	0	NA	NA	NA	NA	NA	NA	NA	NA	NA	NA	NA	NA	NA	NA	0	0	1
Latin America and the Caribbean	0	0	NA	NA	NA	NA	NA	NA	NA	NA	NA	NA	NA	NA	NA	NA	0	0	0
Middle East and North Africa	1	1	NA	NA	NA	NA	NA	NA	NA	NA	NA	NA	NA	NA	NA	NA	1	1	3
South Asia	38	40	NA	NA	NA	NA	NA	NA	NA	NA	NA	NA	NA	NA	NA	NA	38	40	78
Sub-Saharan Africa	75	75	NA	NA	NA	NA	NA	NA	NA	NA	NA	NA	NA	NA	NA	NA	75	75	150
Low- and middle-income countries	122	123	NA	NA	NA	NA	NA	NA	NA	NA	NA	NA	NA	NA	NA	NA	122	123	245
High-income countries	0	0	NA	NA	NA	NA	NA	NA	NA	NA	NA	NA	NA	NA	NA	NA	0	0	0
WORLD	122	123	NA	NA	NA	NA	NA	NA	NA	NA	NA	NA	NA	NA	NA	NA	122	123	245
Attributable YLL (thousands)																			
East Asia and Pacific	205	212	NA	NA	NA	NA	NA	NA	NA	NA	NA	NA	NA	NA	NA	NA	205	212	416
Europe and Central Asia	13	12	NA	NA	NA	NA	NA	NA	NA	NA	NA	NA	NA	NA	NA	NA	13	12	25
Latin America and the Caribbean	0	0	NA	NA	NA	NA	NA	NA	NA	NA	NA	NA	NA	NA	NA	NA	0	0	0
Middle East and North Africa	40	42	NA	NA	NA	NA	NA	NA	NA	NA	NA	NA	NA	NA	NA	NA	40	42	82
South Asia	1,145	1,205	NA	NA	NA	NA	NA	NA	NA	NA	NA	NA	NA	NA	NA	NA	1,145	1,205	2,350
Sub-Saharan Africa	2,275	2,267	NA	NA	NA	NA	NA	NA	NA	NA	NA	NA	NA	NA	NA	NA	2,275	2,267	4,542
Low- and middle-income countries	3,678	3,738	NA	NA	NA	NA	NA	NA	NA	NA	NA	NA	NA	NA	NA	NA	3,678	3,738	7,415
High-income countries	0	0	NA	NA	NA	NA	NA	NA	NA	NA	NA	NA	NA	NA	NA	NA	0	0	0
WORLD	3,678	3,738	NA	NA	NA	NA	NA	NA	NA	NA	NA	NA	NA	NA	NA	NA	3,678	3,738	7,415
Attributable DALYs (thousands)																			
East Asia and Pacific	205	212	NA	NA	NA	NA	NA	NA	NA	NA	NA	NA	NA	NA	NA	NA	205	212	416
Europe and Central Asia	13	12	NA	NA	NA	NA	NA	NA	NA	NA	NA	NA	NA	NA	NA	NA	13	12	25
Latin America and the Caribbean	0	0	NA	NA	NA	NA	NA	NA	NA	NA	NA	NA	NA	NA	NA	NA	0	0	0
Middle East and North Africa	40	42	NA	NA	NA	NA	NA	NA	NA	NA	NA	NA	NA	NA	NA	NA	40	42	82
South Asia	1,145	1,205	NA	NA	NA	NA	NA	NA	NA	NA	NA	NA	NA	NA	NA	NA	1,145	1,205	2,350
Sub-Saharan Africa	2,275	2,267	NA	NA	NA	NA	NA	NA	NA	NA	NA	NA	NA	NA	NA	NA	2,275	2,267	4,542
Low- and middle-income countries	3,678	3,738	NA	NA	NA	NA	NA	NA	NA	NA	NA	NA	NA	NA	NA	NA	3,678	3,738	7,415
High-income countries	0	0	NA	NA	NA	NA	NA	NA	NA	NA	NA	NA	NA	NA	NA	NA	0	0	0
WORLD	3,678	3,738	NA	NA	NA	NA	NA	NA	NA	NA	NA	NA	NA	NA	NA	NA	3,678	3,738	7,415

Source: Authors' calculations.

Note: NA = not applicable.

*The number of deaths (and hence YLL) directly coded to a number of diseases, especially neuropsychiatric and musculoskeletal diseases, is zero or very small. For other diseases, mortality or disease burden may be zero in some region-age-sex groups. In such cases, the population attributable fractions would be undefined or unstable and have not been calculated.

Table 4A.3

Risk factor: Childhood underweight
Disease: Malaria

Region	0–4 years Male	0–4 years Female	5–14 years Male	5–14 years Female	15–29 years Male	15–29 years Female	30–44 years Male	30–44 years Female	45–59 years Male	45–59 years Female	60–69 years Male	60–69 years Female	70–79 years Male	70–79 years Female	80+ years Male	80+ years Female	Total Male	Total Female	Total All
PAF of Mortality (%)																			
East Asia and Pacific	41	41	NA	NA	NA	NA	NA	NA	NA	NA	NA	NA	NA	NA	NA	NA	37	37	37
Europe and Central Asia	23	23	NA	NA	NA	NA	NA	NA	NA	NA	NA	NA	NA	NA	NA	NA	15	16	16
Latin America and the Caribbean	21	21	NA	NA	NA	NA	NA	NA	NA	NA	NA	NA	NA	NA	NA	NA	18	19	19
Middle East and North Africa	38	38	NA	NA	NA	NA	NA	NA	NA	NA	NA	NA	NA	NA	NA	NA	33	34	33
South Asia	66	66	NA	NA	NA	NA	NA	NA	NA	NA	NA	NA	NA	NA	NA	NA	60	60	60
Sub-Saharan Africa	55	55	NA	NA	NA	NA	NA	NA	NA	NA	NA	NA	NA	NA	NA	NA	50	50	50
Low- and middle-income countries	55	55	NA	NA	NA	NA	NA	NA	NA	NA	NA	NA	NA	NA	NA	NA	49	50	50
High-income countries	0	0	NA	NA	NA	NA	NA	NA	NA	NA	NA	NA	NA	NA	NA	NA	0	0	0
WORLD	55	55	NA	NA	NA	NA	NA	NA	NA	NA	NA	NA	NA	NA	NA	NA	49	50	50
PAF of YLL (%)																			
East Asia and Pacific	41	41	NA	NA	NA	NA	NA	NA	NA	NA	NA	NA	NA	NA	NA	NA	39	39	39
Europe and Central Asia	23	23	NA	NA	NA	NA	NA	NA	NA	NA	NA	NA	NA	NA	NA	NA	17	19	18
Latin America and the Caribbean	21	21	NA	NA	NA	NA	NA	NA	NA	NA	NA	NA	NA	NA	NA	NA	19	19	19
Middle East and North Africa	38	38	NA	NA	NA	NA	NA	NA	NA	NA	NA	NA	NA	NA	NA	NA	34	35	35
South Asia	66	66	NA	NA	NA	NA	NA	NA	NA	NA	NA	NA	NA	NA	NA	NA	62	62	62
Sub-Saharan Africa	55	55	NA	NA	NA	NA	NA	NA	NA	NA	NA	NA	NA	NA	NA	NA	51	51	51
Low- and middle-income countries	55	55	NA	NA	NA	NA	NA	NA	NA	NA	NA	NA	NA	NA	NA	NA	51	51	51
High-income countries	0	0	NA	NA	NA	NA	NA	NA	NA	NA	NA	NA	NA	NA	NA	NA	0	0	0
WORLD	55	55	NA	NA	NA	NA	NA	NA	NA	NA	NA	NA	NA	NA	NA	NA	51	51	51
PAF of DALYs (%)																			
East Asia and Pacific	39	37	NA	NA	NA	NA	NA	NA	NA	NA	NA	NA	NA	NA	NA	NA	33	28	31
Europe and Central Asia	6	7	NA	NA	NA	NA	NA	NA	NA	NA	NA	NA	NA	NA	NA	NA	2	2	2
Latin America and the Caribbean	16	14	NA	NA	NA	NA	NA	NA	NA	NA	NA	NA	NA	NA	NA	NA	9	7	8
Middle East and North Africa	35	35	NA	NA	NA	NA	NA	NA	NA	NA	NA	NA	NA	NA	NA	NA	28	30	29
South Asia	59	60	NA	NA	NA	NA	NA	NA	NA	NA	NA	NA	NA	NA	NA	NA	44	46	45
Sub-Saharan Africa	51	51	NA	NA	NA	NA	NA	NA	NA	NA	NA	NA	NA	NA	NA	NA	47	47	47
Low- and middle-income countries	51	51	NA	NA	NA	NA	NA	NA	NA	NA	NA	NA	NA	NA	NA	NA	46	46	46
High-income countries	0	0	NA	NA	NA	NA	NA	NA	NA	NA	NA	NA	NA	NA	NA	NA	0	0	0
WORLD	51	51	NA	NA	NA	NA	NA	NA	NA	NA	NA	NA	NA	NA	NA	NA	46	46	46
Attributable Mortality (thousands)																			
East Asia and Pacific	8	3	NA	NA	NA	NA	NA	NA	NA	NA	NA	NA	NA	NA	NA	NA	8	3	11
Europe and Central Asia	0	0	NA	NA	NA	NA	NA	NA	NA	NA	NA	NA	NA	NA	NA	NA	0	0	0
Latin America and the Caribbean	0	0	NA	NA	NA	NA	NA	NA	NA	NA	NA	NA	NA	NA	NA	NA	0	0	0
Middle East and North Africa	3	3	NA	NA	NA	NA	NA	NA	NA	NA	NA	NA	NA	NA	NA	NA	3	3	6
South Asia	18	20	NA	NA	NA	NA	NA	NA	NA	NA	NA	NA	NA	NA	NA	NA	18	20	38
Sub-Saharan Africa	257	285	NA	NA	NA	NA	NA	NA	NA	NA	NA	NA	NA	NA	NA	NA	257	285	542
Low- and middle-income countries	286	312	NA	NA	NA	NA	NA	NA	NA	NA	NA	NA	NA	NA	NA	NA	286	312	598
High-income countries	0	0	NA	NA	NA	NA	NA	NA	NA	NA	NA	NA	NA	NA	NA	NA	0	0	0
WORLD	286	312	NA	NA	NA	NA	NA	NA	NA	NA	NA	NA	NA	NA	NA	NA	286	312	598
Attributable YLL (thousands)																			
East Asia and Pacific	231	104	NA	NA	NA	NA	NA	NA	NA	NA	NA	NA	NA	NA	NA	NA	231	104	335
Europe and Central Asia	0	0	NA	NA	NA	NA	NA	NA	NA	NA	NA	NA	NA	NA	NA	NA	0	0	0
Latin America and the Caribbean	5	4	NA	NA	NA	NA	NA	NA	NA	NA	NA	NA	NA	NA	NA	NA	5	4	9
Middle East and North Africa	91	102	NA	NA	NA	NA	NA	NA	NA	NA	NA	NA	NA	NA	NA	NA	91	102	193
South Asia	542	606	NA	NA	NA	NA	NA	NA	NA	NA	NA	NA	NA	NA	NA	NA	542	606	1,148
Sub-Saharan Africa	7,770	8,683	NA	NA	NA	NA	NA	NA	NA	NA	NA	NA	NA	NA	NA	NA	7,770	8,683	16,452
Low- and middle-income countries	8,638	9,499	NA	NA	NA	NA	NA	NA	NA	NA	NA	NA	NA	NA	NA	NA	8,638	9,499	18,137
High-income countries	0	0	NA	NA	NA	NA	NA	NA	NA	NA	NA	NA	NA	NA	NA	NA	0	0	0
WORLD	8,638	9,499	NA	NA	NA	NA	NA	NA	NA	NA	NA	NA	NA	NA	NA	NA	8,638	9,499	18,137
Attributable DALYs (thousands)																			
East Asia and Pacific	232	106	NA	NA	NA	NA	NA	NA	NA	NA	NA	NA	NA	NA	NA	NA	232	106	338
Europe and Central Asia	0	0	NA	NA	NA	NA	NA	NA	NA	NA	NA	NA	NA	NA	NA	NA	0	0	0
Latin America and the Caribbean	5	4	NA	NA	NA	NA	NA	NA	NA	NA	NA	NA	NA	NA	NA	NA	5	4	9
Middle East and North Africa	92	103	NA	NA	NA	NA	NA	NA	NA	NA	NA	NA	NA	NA	NA	NA	92	103	195
South Asia	557	620	NA	NA	NA	NA	NA	NA	NA	NA	NA	NA	NA	NA	NA	NA	557	620	1,177
Sub-Saharan Africa	7,876	8,789	NA	NA	NA	NA	NA	NA	NA	NA	NA	NA	NA	NA	NA	NA	7,876	8,789	16,665
Low- and middle-income countries	8,763	9,622	NA	NA	NA	NA	NA	NA	NA	NA	NA	NA	NA	NA	NA	NA	8,763	9,622	18,385
High-income countries	0	0	NA	NA	NA	NA	NA	NA	NA	NA	NA	NA	NA	NA	NA	NA	0	0	0
WORLD	8,763	9,622	NA	NA	NA	NA	NA	NA	NA	NA	NA	NA	NA	NA	NA	NA	8,763	9,622	18,385

Source: Authors' calculations.
Note: NA = not applicable.

Table 4A.4

Risk factor: Childhood underweight
Disease: Lower respiratory infections

Region	0–4 years Male	0–4 years Female	5–14 years Male	5–14 years Female	15–29 years Male	15–29 years Female	30–44 years Male	30–44 years Female	45–59 years Male	45–59 years Female	60–69 years Male	60–69 years Female	70–79 years Male	70–79 years Female	80+ years Male	80+ years Female	Total Male	Total Female	All
PAF of Mortality (%)																			
East Asia and Pacific	39	39	NA	NA	NA	NA	NA	NA	NA	NA	NA	NA	NA	NA	NA	NA	10	15	13
Europe and Central Asia	21	21	NA	NA	NA	NA	NA	NA	NA	NA	NA	NA	NA	NA	NA	NA	6	8	7
Latin America and the Caribbean	20	20	NA	NA	NA	NA	NA	NA	NA	NA	NA	NA	NA	NA	NA	NA	6	5	5
Middle East and North Africa	35	35	NA	NA	NA	NA	NA	NA	NA	NA	NA	NA	NA	NA	NA	NA	24	24	24
South Asia	63	63	NA	NA	NA	NA	NA	NA	NA	NA	NA	NA	NA	NA	NA	NA	37	37	37
Sub-Saharan Africa	52	52	NA	NA	NA	NA	NA	NA	NA	NA	NA	NA	NA	NA	NA	NA	39	33	36
Low- and middle-income countries	54	53	NA	NA	NA	NA	NA	NA	NA	NA	NA	NA	NA	NA	NA	NA	31	29	30
High-income countries	0	0	NA	NA	NA	NA	NA	NA	NA	NA	NA	NA	NA	NA	NA	NA	0	0	0
WORLD	54	53	NA	NA	NA	NA	NA	NA	NA	NA	NA	NA	NA	NA	NA	NA	28	26	27
PAF of YLL (%)																			
East Asia and Pacific	39	39	NA	NA	NA	NA	NA	NA	NA	NA	NA	NA	NA	NA	NA	NA	18	25	22
Europe and Central Asia	21	21	NA	NA	NA	NA	NA	NA	NA	NA	NA	NA	NA	NA	NA	NA	10	12	11
Latin America and the Caribbean	20	20	NA	NA	NA	NA	NA	NA	NA	NA	NA	NA	NA	NA	NA	NA	10	10	10
Middle East and North Africa	35	35	NA	NA	NA	NA	NA	NA	NA	NA	NA	NA	NA	NA	NA	NA	29	29	29
South Asia	63	63	NA	NA	NA	NA	NA	NA	NA	NA	NA	NA	NA	NA	NA	NA	49	48	49
Sub-Saharan Africa	52	52	NA	NA	NA	NA	NA	NA	NA	NA	NA	NA	NA	NA	NA	NA	43	37	40
Low- and middle-income countries	54	53	NA	NA	NA	NA	NA	NA	NA	NA	NA	NA	NA	NA	NA	NA	40	38	39
High-income countries	0	0	NA	NA	NA	NA	NA	NA	NA	NA	NA	NA	NA	NA	NA	NA	0	0	0
WORLD	54	53	NA	NA	NA	NA	NA	NA	NA	NA	NA	NA	NA	NA	NA	NA	39	37	38
PAF of DALYs (%)																			
East Asia and Pacific	35	35	NA	NA	NA	NA	NA	NA	NA	NA	NA	NA	NA	NA	NA	NA	17	23	21
Europe and Central Asia	20	20	NA	NA	NA	NA	NA	NA	NA	NA	NA	NA	NA	NA	NA	NA	9	12	10
Latin America and the Caribbean	16	16	NA	NA	NA	NA	NA	NA	NA	NA	NA	NA	NA	NA	NA	NA	9	9	9
Middle East and North Africa	33	33	NA	NA	NA	NA	NA	NA	NA	NA	NA	NA	NA	NA	NA	NA	27	27	27
South Asia	61	61	NA	NA	NA	NA	NA	NA	NA	NA	NA	NA	NA	NA	NA	NA	47	47	47
Sub-Saharan Africa	51	51	NA	NA	NA	NA	NA	NA	NA	NA	NA	NA	NA	NA	NA	NA	42	36	39
Low- and middle-income countries	52	51	NA	NA	NA	NA	NA	NA	NA	NA	NA	NA	NA	NA	NA	NA	39	37	38
High-income countries	0	0	NA	NA	NA	NA	NA	NA	NA	NA	NA	NA	NA	NA	NA	NA	0	0	0
WORLD	52	51	NA	NA	NA	NA	NA	NA	NA	NA	NA	NA	NA	NA	NA	NA	38	36	37
Attributable Mortality (thousands)																			
East Asia and Pacific	24	47	NA	NA	NA	NA	NA	NA	NA	NA	NA	NA	NA	NA	NA	NA	24	47	71
Europe and Central Asia	4	3	NA	NA	NA	NA	NA	NA	NA	NA	NA	NA	NA	NA	NA	NA	4	3	7
Latin America and the Caribbean	5	4	NA	NA	NA	NA	NA	NA	NA	NA	NA	NA	NA	NA	NA	NA	5	4	8
Middle East and North Africa	14	12	NA	NA	NA	NA	NA	NA	NA	NA	NA	NA	NA	NA	NA	NA	14	12	26
South Asia	259	262	NA	NA	NA	NA	NA	NA	NA	NA	NA	NA	NA	NA	NA	NA	259	262	521
Sub-Saharan Africa	226	165	NA	NA	NA	NA	NA	NA	NA	NA	NA	NA	NA	NA	NA	NA	226	165	391
Low- and middle-income countries	532	493	NA	NA	NA	NA	NA	NA	NA	NA	NA	NA	NA	NA	NA	NA	532	493	1,024
High-income countries	0	0	NA	NA	NA	NA	NA	NA	NA	NA	NA	NA	NA	NA	NA	NA	0	0	0
WORLD	532	493	NA	NA	NA	NA	NA	NA	NA	NA	NA	NA	NA	NA	NA	NA	532	493	1,024
Attributable YLL (thousands)																			
East Asia and Pacific	730	1,430	NA	NA	NA	NA	NA	NA	NA	NA	NA	NA	NA	NA	NA	NA	730	1,430	2,160
Europe and Central Asia	116	98	NA	NA	NA	NA	NA	NA	NA	NA	NA	NA	NA	NA	NA	NA	116	98	214
Latin America and the Caribbean	137	117	NA	NA	NA	NA	NA	NA	NA	NA	NA	NA	NA	NA	NA	NA	137	117	254
Middle East and North Africa	414	379	NA	NA	NA	NA	NA	NA	NA	NA	NA	NA	NA	NA	NA	NA	414	379	793
South Asia	7,838	7,974	NA	NA	NA	NA	NA	NA	NA	NA	NA	NA	NA	NA	NA	NA	7,838	7,974	15,812
Sub-Saharan Africa	6,851	5,016	NA	NA	NA	NA	NA	NA	NA	NA	NA	NA	NA	NA	NA	NA	6,851	5,016	11,867
Low- and middle-income countries	16,086	15,014	NA	NA	NA	NA	NA	NA	NA	NA	NA	NA	NA	NA	NA	NA	16,086	15,014	31,100
High-income countries	0	0	NA	NA	NA	NA	NA	NA	NA	NA	NA	NA	NA	NA	NA	NA	0	0	0
WORLD	16,086	15,014	NA	NA	NA	NA	NA	NA	NA	NA	NA	NA	NA	NA	NA	NA	16,086	15,014	31,100
Attributable DALYs (thousands)																			
East Asia and Pacific	762	1,486	NA	NA	NA	NA	NA	NA	NA	NA	NA	NA	NA	NA	NA	NA	762	1,486	2,248
Europe and Central Asia	117	100	NA	NA	NA	NA	NA	NA	NA	NA	NA	NA	NA	NA	NA	NA	117	100	217
Latin America and the Caribbean	144	124	NA	NA	NA	NA	NA	NA	NA	NA	NA	NA	NA	NA	NA	NA	144	124	269
Middle East and North Africa	424	388	NA	NA	NA	NA	NA	NA	NA	NA	NA	NA	NA	NA	NA	NA	424	388	812
South Asia	8,016	8,147	NA	NA	NA	NA	NA	NA	NA	NA	NA	NA	NA	NA	NA	NA	8,016	8,147	16,162
Sub-Saharan Africa	6,935	5,053	NA	NA	NA	NA	NA	NA	NA	NA	NA	NA	NA	NA	NA	NA	6,935	5,053	11,988
Low- and middle-income countries	16,398	15,298	NA	NA	NA	NA	NA	NA	NA	NA	NA	NA	NA	NA	NA	NA	16,398	15,298	31,696
High-income countries	0	0	NA	NA	NA	NA	NA	NA	NA	NA	NA	NA	NA	NA	NA	NA	0	0	0
WORLD	16,398	15,298	NA	NA	NA	NA	NA	NA	NA	NA	NA	NA	NA	NA	NA	NA	16,398	15,298	31,696

Source: Authors' calculations.
Note: NA = not applicable.

Table 4A.5

Risk factor: Childhood underweight
Disease: Protein-energy malnutrition

Region	0–4 years Male	Female	5–14 years Male	Female	15–29 years Male	Female	30–44 years Male	Female	45–59 years Male	Female	60–69 years Male	Female	70–79 years Male	Female	80+ years Male	Female	Total Male	Female	All
PAF of Mortality (%)																			
East Asia and Pacific	100	100	NA	NA	NA	NA	NA	NA	NA	NA	NA	NA	NA	NA	NA	NA	50	40	45
Europe and Central Asia	100	100	NA	NA	NA	NA	NA	NA	NA	NA	NA	NA	NA	NA	NA	NA	14	14	14
Latin America and the Caribbean	100	100	NA	NA	NA	NA	NA	NA	NA	NA	NA	NA	NA	NA	NA	NA	37	32	35
Middle East and North Africa	100	100	NA	NA	NA	NA	NA	NA	NA	NA	NA	NA	NA	NA	NA	NA	88	85	87
South Asia	100	100	NA	NA	NA	NA	NA	NA	NA	NA	NA	NA	NA	NA	NA	NA	45	52	49
Sub-Saharan Africa	100	100	NA	NA	NA	NA	NA	NA	NA	NA	NA	NA	NA	NA	NA	NA	73	77	74
Low- and middle-income countries	100	100	NA	NA	NA	NA	NA	NA	NA	NA	NA	NA	NA	NA	NA	NA	58	58	58
High-income countries	100	100	NA	NA	NA	NA	NA	NA	NA	NA	NA	NA	NA	NA	NA	NA	2	1	1
WORLD	100	100	NA	NA	NA	NA	NA	NA	NA	NA	NA	NA	NA	NA	NA	NA	56	55	56
PAF of YLL (%)																			
East Asia and Pacific	100	100	NA	NA	NA	NA	NA	NA	NA	NA	NA	NA	NA	NA	NA	NA	62	57	60
Europe and Central Asia	100	100	NA	NA	NA	NA	NA	NA	NA	NA	NA	NA	NA	NA	NA	NA	22	24	23
Latin America and the Caribbean	100	100	NA	NA	NA	NA	NA	NA	NA	NA	NA	NA	NA	NA	NA	NA	61	59	60
Middle East and North Africa	100	100	NA	NA	NA	NA	NA	NA	NA	NA	NA	NA	NA	NA	NA	NA	93	90	92
South Asia	100	100	NA	NA	NA	NA	NA	NA	NA	NA	NA	NA	NA	NA	NA	NA	47	55	52
Sub-Saharan Africa	100	100	NA	NA	NA	NA	NA	NA	NA	NA	NA	NA	NA	NA	NA	NA	84	86	85
Low- and middle-income countries	100	100	NA	NA	NA	NA	NA	NA	NA	NA	NA	NA	NA	NA	NA	NA	69	69	69
High-income countries	100	100	NA	NA	NA	NA	NA	NA	NA	NA	NA	NA	NA	NA	NA	NA	6	4	4
WORLD	100	100	NA	NA	NA	NA	NA	NA	NA	NA	NA	NA	NA	NA	NA	NA	69	68	69
PAF of DALYs (%)																			
East Asia and Pacific	100	100	NA	NA	NA	NA	NA	NA	NA	NA	NA	NA	NA	NA	NA	NA	91	91	91
Europe and Central Asia	100	100	NA	NA	NA	NA	NA	NA	NA	NA	NA	NA	NA	NA	NA	NA	85	86	86
Latin America and the Caribbean	100	100	NA	NA	NA	NA	NA	NA	NA	NA	NA	NA	NA	NA	NA	NA	72	71	72
Middle East and North Africa	100	100	NA	NA	NA	NA	NA	NA	NA	NA	NA	NA	NA	NA	NA	NA	98	96	97
South Asia	100	100	NA	NA	NA	NA	NA	NA	NA	NA	NA	NA	NA	NA	NA	NA	84	83	84
Sub-Saharan Africa	100	100	NA	NA	NA	NA	NA	NA	NA	NA	NA	NA	NA	NA	NA	NA	92	93	92
Low- and middle-income countries	100	100	NA	NA	NA	NA	NA	NA	NA	NA	NA	NA	NA	NA	NA	NA	88	88	88
High-income countries	100	100	NA	NA	NA	NA	NA	NA	NA	NA	NA	NA	NA	NA	NA	NA	57	47	52
WORLD	100	100	NA	NA	NA	NA	NA	NA	NA	NA	NA	NA	NA	NA	NA	NA	88	87	88
Attributable Mortality (thousands)																			
East Asia and Pacific	7	5	NA	NA	NA	NA	NA	NA	NA	NA	NA	NA	NA	NA	NA	NA	7	5	12
Europe and Central Asia	0	0	NA	NA	NA	NA	NA	NA	NA	NA	NA	NA	NA	NA	NA	NA	0	0	0
Latin America and the Caribbean	7	6	NA	NA	NA	NA	NA	NA	NA	NA	NA	NA	NA	NA	NA	NA	7	6	13
Middle East and North Africa	3	4	NA	NA	NA	NA	NA	NA	NA	NA	NA	NA	NA	NA	NA	NA	3	4	7
South Asia	13	20	NA	NA	NA	NA	NA	NA	NA	NA	NA	NA	NA	NA	NA	NA	13	20	33
Sub-Saharan Africa	40	34	NA	NA	NA	NA	NA	NA	NA	NA	NA	NA	NA	NA	NA	NA	40	34	74
Low- and middle-income countries	70	69	NA	NA	NA	NA	NA	NA	NA	NA	NA	NA	NA	NA	NA	NA	70	69	139
High-income countries	0	0	NA	NA	NA	NA	NA	NA	NA	NA	NA	NA	NA	NA	NA	NA	0	0	0
WORLD	70	69	NA	NA	NA	NA	NA	NA	NA	NA	NA	NA	NA	NA	NA	NA	70	69	140
Attributable YLL (thousands)																			
East Asia and Pacific	212	150	NA	NA	NA	NA	NA	NA	NA	NA	NA	NA	NA	NA	NA	NA	212	150	363
Europe and Central Asia	4	4	NA	NA	NA	NA	NA	NA	NA	NA	NA	NA	NA	NA	NA	NA	4	4	7
Latin America and the Caribbean	212	180	NA	NA	NA	NA	NA	NA	NA	NA	NA	NA	NA	NA	NA	NA	212	180	392
Middle East and North Africa	103	119	NA	NA	NA	NA	NA	NA	NA	NA	NA	NA	NA	NA	NA	NA	103	119	221
South Asia	392	608	NA	NA	NA	NA	NA	NA	NA	NA	NA	NA	NA	NA	NA	NA	392	608	1,000
Sub-Saharan Africa	1,202	1,042	NA	NA	NA	NA	NA	NA	NA	NA	NA	NA	NA	NA	NA	NA	1,202	1,042	2,244
Low- and middle-income countries	2,124	2,102	NA	NA	NA	NA	NA	NA	NA	NA	NA	NA	NA	NA	NA	NA	2,124	2,102	4,226
High-income countries	2	1	NA	NA	NA	NA	NA	NA	NA	NA	NA	NA	NA	NA	NA	NA	2	1	3
WORLD	2,126	2,104	NA	NA	NA	NA	NA	NA	NA	NA	NA	NA	NA	NA	NA	NA	2,126	2,104	4,229
Attributable DALYs (thousands)																			
East Asia and Pacific	1,303	1,184	NA	NA	NA	NA	NA	NA	NA	NA	NA	NA	NA	NA	NA	NA	1,303	1,184	2,487
Europe and Central Asia	75	74	NA	NA	NA	NA	NA	NA	NA	NA	NA	NA	NA	NA	NA	NA	75	74	149
Latin America and the Caribbean	345	311	NA	NA	NA	NA	NA	NA	NA	NA	NA	NA	NA	NA	NA	NA	345	311	655
Middle East and North Africa	351	341	NA	NA	NA	NA	NA	NA	NA	NA	NA	NA	NA	NA	NA	NA	351	341	692
South Asia	2,319	2,441	NA	NA	NA	NA	NA	NA	NA	NA	NA	NA	NA	NA	NA	NA	2,319	2,441	4,759
Sub-Saharan Africa	2,497	2,322	NA	NA	NA	NA	NA	NA	NA	NA	NA	NA	NA	NA	NA	NA	2,497	2,322	4,819
Low- and middle-income countries	6,889	6,672	NA	NA	NA	NA	NA	NA	NA	NA	NA	NA	NA	NA	NA	NA	6,889	6,672	13,561
High-income countries	35	33	NA	NA	NA	NA	NA	NA	NA	NA	NA	NA	NA	NA	NA	NA	35	33	67
WORLD	6,924	6,705	NA	NA	NA	NA	NA	NA	NA	NA	NA	NA	NA	NA	NA	NA	6,924	6,705	13,628

Source: Authors' calculations.
Note: NA = not applicable.

Table 4A.6

Risk factor: Childhood underweight
Disease: Selected other Group I diseases

Region	0–4 years Male	0–4 years Female	5–14 years Male	5–14 years Female	15–29 years Male	15–29 years Female	30–44 years Male	30–44 years Female	45–59 years Male	45–59 years Female	60–69 years Male	60–69 years Female	70–79 years Male	70–79 years Female	80+ years Male	80+ years Female	Total Male	Total Female	All
PAF of Mortality (%)																			
East Asia and Pacific	40	40	NA	NA	NA	NA	NA	NA	NA	NA	NA	NA	NA	NA	NA	NA	4	5	4
Europe and Central Asia	22	22	NA	NA	NA	NA	NA	NA	NA	NA	NA	NA	NA	NA	NA	NA	3	6	3
Latin America and the Caribbean	20	20	NA	NA	NA	NA	NA	NA	NA	NA	NA	NA	NA	NA	NA	NA	5	4	4
Middle East and North Africa	36	36	NA	NA	NA	NA	NA	NA	NA	NA	NA	NA	NA	NA	NA	NA	14	13	13
South Asia	64	64	NA	NA	NA	NA	NA	NA	NA	NA	NA	NA	NA	NA	NA	NA	11	17	14
Sub-Saharan Africa	53	53	NA	NA	NA	NA	NA	NA	NA	NA	NA	NA	NA	NA	NA	NA	20	18	19
Low- and middle-income countries	53	55	NA	NA	NA	NA	NA	NA	NA	NA	NA	NA	NA	NA	NA	NA	12	14	13
High-income countries	0	0	NA	NA	NA	NA	NA	NA	NA	NA	NA	NA	NA	NA	NA	NA	0	0	0
WORLD	53	55	NA	NA	NA	NA	NA	NA	NA	NA	NA	NA	NA	NA	NA	NA	12	14	13
PAF of YLL (%)																			
East Asia and Pacific	40	40	NA	NA	NA	NA	NA	NA	NA	NA	NA	NA	NA	NA	NA	NA	6	7	7
Europe and Central Asia	22	22	NA	NA	NA	NA	NA	NA	NA	NA	NA	NA	NA	NA	NA	NA	4	8	5
Latin America and the Caribbean	20	20	NA	NA	NA	NA	NA	NA	NA	NA	NA	NA	NA	NA	NA	NA	7	5	6
Middle East and North Africa	36	36	NA	NA	NA	NA	NA	NA	NA	NA	NA	NA	NA	NA	NA	NA	20	16	18
South Asia	64	64	NA	NA	NA	NA	NA	NA	NA	NA	NA	NA	NA	NA	NA	NA	16	21	19
Sub-Saharan Africa	53	53	NA	NA	NA	NA	NA	NA	NA	NA	NA	NA	NA	NA	NA	NA	24	20	22
Low- and middle-income countries	53	55	NA	NA	NA	NA	NA	NA	NA	NA	NA	NA	NA	NA	NA	NA	17	18	17
High-income countries	0	0	NA	NA	NA	NA	NA	NA	NA	NA	NA	NA	NA	NA	NA	NA	0	0	0
WORLD	53	55	NA	NA	NA	NA	NA	NA	NA	NA	NA	NA	NA	NA	NA	NA	16	18	17
PAF of DALYs (%)																			
East Asia and Pacific	29	27	NA	NA	NA	NA	NA	NA	NA	NA	NA	NA	NA	NA	NA	NA	5	4	5
Europe and Central Asia	17	16	NA	NA	NA	NA	NA	NA	NA	NA	NA	NA	NA	NA	NA	NA	3	3	3
Latin America and the Caribbean	15	14	NA	NA	NA	NA	NA	NA	NA	NA	NA	NA	NA	NA	NA	NA	5	3	4
Middle East and North Africa	30	29	NA	NA	NA	NA	NA	NA	NA	NA	NA	NA	NA	NA	NA	NA	14	8	10
South Asia	52	56	NA	NA	NA	NA	NA	NA	NA	NA	NA	NA	NA	NA	NA	NA	13	15	14
Sub-Saharan Africa	47	47	NA	NA	NA	NA	NA	NA	NA	NA	NA	NA	NA	NA	NA	NA	19	15	17
Low- and middle-income countries	44	47	NA	NA	NA	NA	NA	NA	NA	NA	NA	NA	NA	NA	NA	NA	13	12	13
High-income countries	0	0	NA	NA	NA	NA	NA	NA	NA	NA	NA	NA	NA	NA	NA	NA	0	0	0
WORLD	43	46	NA	NA	NA	NA	NA	NA	NA	NA	NA	NA	NA	NA	NA	NA	13	12	12
Attributable Mortality (thousands)																			
East Asia and Pacific	21	18	NA	NA	NA	NA	NA	NA	NA	NA	NA	NA	NA	NA	NA	NA	21	18	39
Europe and Central Asia	2	2	NA	NA	NA	NA	NA	NA	NA	NA	NA	NA	NA	NA	NA	NA	2	2	4
Latin America and the Caribbean	5	4	NA	NA	NA	NA	NA	NA	NA	NA	NA	NA	NA	NA	NA	NA	5	4	9
Middle East and North Africa	8	8	NA	NA	NA	NA	NA	NA	NA	NA	NA	NA	NA	NA	NA	NA	8	8	16
South Asia	106	173	NA	NA	NA	NA	NA	NA	NA	NA	NA	NA	NA	NA	NA	NA	106	173	279
Sub-Saharan Africa	156	153	NA	NA	NA	NA	NA	NA	NA	NA	NA	NA	NA	NA	NA	NA	156	153	309
Low- and middle-income countries	298	358	NA	NA	NA	NA	NA	NA	NA	NA	NA	NA	NA	NA	NA	NA	298	358	656
High-income countries	0	0	NA	NA	NA	NA	NA	NA	NA	NA	NA	NA	NA	NA	NA	NA	0	0	0
WORLD	298	358	NA	NA	NA	NA	NA	NA	NA	NA	NA	NA	NA	NA	NA	NA	298	358	656
Attributable YLL (thousands)																			
East Asia and Pacific	646	546	NA	NA	NA	NA	NA	NA	NA	NA	NA	NA	NA	NA	NA	NA	646	546	1,193
Europe and Central Asia	61	53	NA	NA	NA	NA	NA	NA	NA	NA	NA	NA	NA	NA	NA	NA	61	53	114
Latin America and the Caribbean	154	109	NA	NA	NA	NA	NA	NA	NA	NA	NA	NA	NA	NA	NA	NA	154	109	263
Middle East and North Africa	247	249	NA	NA	NA	NA	NA	NA	NA	NA	NA	NA	NA	NA	NA	NA	247	249	497
South Asia	3,197	5,265	NA	NA	NA	NA	NA	NA	NA	NA	NA	NA	NA	NA	NA	NA	3,197	5,265	8,462
Sub-Saharan Africa	4,700	4,658	NA	NA	NA	NA	NA	NA	NA	NA	NA	NA	NA	NA	NA	NA	4,700	4,658	9,358
Low- and middle-income countries	9,005	10,881	NA	NA	NA	NA	NA	NA	NA	NA	NA	NA	NA	NA	NA	NA	9,005	10,881	19,887
High-income countries	0	0	NA	NA	NA	NA	NA	NA	NA	NA	NA	NA	NA	NA	NA	NA	0	0	0
WORLD	9,005	10,881	NA	NA	NA	NA	NA	NA	NA	NA	NA	NA	NA	NA	NA	NA	9,005	10,881	19,887
Attributable DALYs (thousands)																			
East Asia and Pacific	646	546	NA	NA	NA	NA	NA	NA	NA	NA	NA	NA	NA	NA	NA	NA	646	546	1,193
Europe and Central Asia	61	53	NA	NA	NA	NA	NA	NA	NA	NA	NA	NA	NA	NA	NA	NA	61	53	114
Latin America and the Caribbean	154	109	NA	NA	NA	NA	NA	NA	NA	NA	NA	NA	NA	NA	NA	NA	154	109	263
Middle East and North Africa	247	249	NA	NA	NA	NA	NA	NA	NA	NA	NA	NA	NA	NA	NA	NA	247	249	497
South Asia	3,197	5,265	NA	NA	NA	NA	NA	NA	NA	NA	NA	NA	NA	NA	NA	NA	3,197	5,265	8,462
Sub-Saharan Africa	4,700	4,658	NA	NA	NA	NA	NA	NA	NA	NA	NA	NA	NA	NA	NA	NA	4,700	4,658	9,358
Low- and middle-income countries	9,005	10,881	NA	NA	NA	NA	NA	NA	NA	NA	NA	NA	NA	NA	NA	NA	9,005	10,881	19,887
High-income countries	0	0	NA	NA	NA	NA	NA	NA	NA	NA	NA	NA	NA	NA	NA	NA	0	0	0
WORLD	9,005	10,881	NA	NA	NA	NA	NA	NA	NA	NA	NA	NA	NA	NA	NA	NA	9,005	10,881	19,887

Source: Authors' calculations.
Note: NA = not applicable.

Table 4A.7

Risk factor: Childhood underweight
Disease: All causes

Region	0–4 years Male	0–4 years Female	5–14 years Male	5–14 years Female	15–29 years Male	15–29 years Female	30–44 years Male	30–44 years Female	45–59 years Male	45–59 years Female	60–69 years Male	60–69 years Female	70–79 years Male	70–79 years Female	80+ years Male	80+ years Female	Total Male	Total Female	All
PAF of Mortality (%)																			
East Asia and Pacific	16	18	NA	NA	NA	NA	NA	NA	NA	NA	NA	NA	NA	NA	NA	NA	2	2	2
Europe and Central Asia	8	9	NA	NA	NA	NA	NA	NA	NA	NA	NA	NA	NA	NA	NA	NA	0	0	0
Latin America and the Caribbean	10	10	NA	NA	NA	NA	NA	NA	NA	NA	NA	NA	NA	NA	NA	NA	1	1	1
Middle East and North Africa	19	21	NA	NA	NA	NA	NA	NA	NA	NA	NA	NA	NA	NA	NA	NA	4	5	5
South Asia	37	40	NA	NA	NA	NA	NA	NA	NA	NA	NA	NA	NA	NA	NA	NA	9	11	10
Sub-Saharan Africa	40	42	NA	NA	NA	NA	NA	NA	NA	NA	NA	NA	NA	NA	NA	NA	17	17	17
Low- and middle-income countries	34	35	NA	NA	NA	NA	NA	NA	NA	NA	NA	NA	NA	NA	NA	NA	7	8	8
High-income countries	0	0	NA	NA	NA	NA	NA	NA	NA	NA	NA	NA	NA	NA	NA	NA	0	0	0
WORLD	33	35	NA	NA	NA	NA	NA	NA	NA	NA	NA	NA	NA	NA	NA	NA	6	7	6
PAF of YLL (%)																			
East Asia and Pacific	16	18	NA	NA	NA	NA	NA	NA	NA	NA	NA	NA	NA	NA	NA	NA	3	4	4
Europe and Central Asia	8	9	NA	NA	NA	NA	NA	NA	NA	NA	NA	NA	NA	NA	NA	NA	1	1	1
Latin America and the Caribbean	10	10	NA	NA	NA	NA	NA	NA	NA	NA	NA	NA	NA	NA	NA	NA	2	3	2
Middle East and North Africa	19	21	NA	NA	NA	NA	NA	NA	NA	NA	NA	NA	NA	NA	NA	NA	7	8	7
South Asia	37	40	NA	NA	NA	NA	NA	NA	NA	NA	NA	NA	NA	NA	NA	NA	14	17	15
Sub-Saharan Africa	40	42	NA	NA	NA	NA	NA	NA	NA	NA	NA	NA	NA	NA	NA	NA	21	21	21
Low- and middle-income countries	34	35	NA	NA	NA	NA	NA	NA	NA	NA	NA	NA	NA	NA	NA	NA	11	13	12
High-income countries	0	0	NA	NA	NA	NA	NA	NA	NA	NA	NA	NA	NA	NA	NA	NA	0	0	0
WORLD	33	35	NA	NA	NA	NA	NA	NA	NA	NA	NA	NA	NA	NA	NA	NA	10	12	11
PAF of DALYs (%)																			
East Asia and Pacific	14	15	NA	NA	NA	NA	NA	NA	NA	NA	NA	NA	NA	NA	NA	NA	3	3	3
Europe and Central Asia	6	7	NA	NA	NA	NA	NA	NA	NA	NA	NA	NA	NA	NA	NA	NA	0	1	1
Latin America and the Caribbean	7	7	NA	NA	NA	NA	NA	NA	NA	NA	NA	NA	NA	NA	NA	NA	1	2	1
Middle East and North Africa	14	16	NA	NA	NA	NA	NA	NA	NA	NA	NA	NA	NA	NA	NA	NA	5	5	5
South Asia	31	34	NA	NA	NA	NA	NA	NA	NA	NA	NA	NA	NA	NA	NA	NA	11	12	11
Sub-Saharan Africa	36	37	NA	NA	NA	NA	NA	NA	NA	NA	NA	NA	NA	NA	NA	NA	17	17	17
Low- and middle-income countries	28	29	NA	NA	NA	NA	NA	NA	NA	NA	NA	NA	NA	NA	NA	NA	8	9	9
High-income countries	1	1	NA	NA	NA	NA	NA	NA	NA	NA	NA	NA	NA	NA	NA	NA	0	0	0
WORLD	27	29	NA	NA	NA	NA	NA	NA	NA	NA	NA	NA	NA	NA	NA	NA	8	8	8
Attributable Mortality (thousands)																			
East Asia and Pacific	115	124	NA	NA	NA	NA	NA	NA	NA	NA	NA	NA	NA	NA	NA	NA	115	124	239
Europe and Central Asia	8	7	NA	NA	NA	NA	NA	NA	NA	NA	NA	NA	NA	NA	NA	NA	8	7	15
Latin America and the Caribbean	23	19	NA	NA	NA	NA	NA	NA	NA	NA	NA	NA	NA	NA	NA	NA	23	19	42
Middle East and North Africa	44	43	NA	NA	NA	NA	NA	NA	NA	NA	NA	NA	NA	NA	NA	NA	44	43	87
South Asia	666	728	NA	NA	NA	NA	NA	NA	NA	NA	NA	NA	NA	NA	NA	NA	666	728	1,394
Sub-Saharan Africa	957	896	NA	NA	NA	NA	NA	NA	NA	NA	NA	NA	NA	NA	NA	NA	957	896	1,853
Low- and middle-income countries	1,814	1,816	NA	NA	NA	NA	NA	NA	NA	NA	NA	NA	NA	NA	NA	NA	1,814	1,816	3,630
High-income countries	0	0	NA	NA	NA	NA	NA	NA	NA	NA	NA	NA	NA	NA	NA	NA	0	0	0
WORLD	1,814	1,816	NA	NA	NA	NA	NA	NA	NA	NA	NA	NA	NA	NA	NA	NA	1,814	1,816	3,630
Attributable YLL (thousands)																			
East Asia and Pacific	3,488	3,781	NA	NA	NA	NA	NA	NA	NA	NA	NA	NA	NA	NA	NA	NA	3,488	3,781	7,269
Europe and Central Asia	245	213	NA	NA	NA	NA	NA	NA	NA	NA	NA	NA	NA	NA	NA	NA	245	213	458
Latin America and the Caribbean	687	573	NA	NA	NA	NA	NA	NA	NA	NA	NA	NA	NA	NA	NA	NA	687	573	1,261
Middle East and North Africa	1,334	1,299	NA	NA	NA	NA	NA	NA	NA	NA	NA	NA	NA	NA	NA	NA	1,334	1,299	2,633
South Asia	20,164	22,167	NA	NA	NA	NA	NA	NA	NA	NA	NA	NA	NA	NA	NA	NA	20,164	22,167	42,331
Sub-Saharan Africa	28,919	27,261	NA	NA	NA	NA	NA	NA	NA	NA	NA	NA	NA	NA	NA	NA	28,919	27,261	56,181
Low- and middle-income countries	54,838	55,295	NA	NA	NA	NA	NA	NA	NA	NA	NA	NA	NA	NA	NA	NA	54,838	55,295	110,132
High-income countries	2	1	NA	NA	NA	NA	NA	NA	NA	NA	NA	NA	NA	NA	NA	NA	2	1	3
WORLD	54,839	55,296	NA	NA	NA	NA	NA	NA	NA	NA	NA	NA	NA	NA	NA	NA	54,839	55,296	110,135
Attributable DALYs (thousands)																			
East Asia and Pacific	4,628	4,887	NA	NA	NA	NA	NA	NA	NA	NA	NA	NA	NA	NA	NA	NA	4,628	4,887	9,516
Europe and Central Asia	319	285	NA	NA	NA	NA	NA	NA	NA	NA	NA	NA	NA	NA	NA	NA	319	285	604
Latin America and the Caribbean	831	714	NA	NA	NA	NA	NA	NA	NA	NA	NA	NA	NA	NA	NA	NA	831	714	1,546
Middle East and North Africa	1,598	1,537	NA	NA	NA	NA	NA	NA	NA	NA	NA	NA	NA	NA	NA	NA	1,598	1,537	3,134
South Asia	22,361	24,259	NA	NA	NA	NA	NA	NA	NA	NA	NA	NA	NA	NA	NA	NA	22,361	24,259	46,620
Sub-Saharan Africa	30,440	28,720	NA	NA	NA	NA	NA	NA	NA	NA	NA	NA	NA	NA	NA	NA	30,440	28,720	59,160
Low- and middle-income countries	60,177	60,403	NA	NA	NA	NA	NA	NA	NA	NA	NA	NA	NA	NA	NA	NA	60,177	60,403	120,579
High-income countries	35	33	NA	NA	NA	NA	NA	NA	NA	NA	NA	NA	NA	NA	NA	NA	35	33	67
WORLD	60,211	60,436	NA	NA	NA	NA	NA	NA	NA	NA	NA	NA	NA	NA	NA	NA	60,211	60,436	120,647

Source: Authors' calculations.
Note: NA = not applicable.

Table 4A.8

Risk factor: Iron-deficiency anemia
Disease: Maternal conditions

Region	0–4 years Male	Female	5–14 years Male	Female	15–29 years Male	Female	30–44 years Male	Female	45–59 years Male	Female	60–69 years Male	Female	70–79 years Male	Female	80+ years Male	Female	Total Male	Female	All
PAF of Mortality (%)																			
East Asia and Pacific	NA	NA	NA	NA	NA	17	NA	17	NA	NA	NA	NA	NA	NA	NA	NA	NA	16	16
Europe and Central Asia	NA	NA	NA	NA	NA	8	NA	8	NA	NA	NA	NA	NA	NA	NA	NA	NA	8	8
Latin America and the Caribbean	NA	NA	NA	NA	NA	7	NA	7	NA	NA	NA	NA	NA	NA	NA	NA	NA	7	7
Middle East and North Africa	NA	NA	NA	NA	NA	14	NA	15	NA	NA	NA	NA	NA	NA	NA	NA	NA	14	14
South Asia	NA	NA	NA	NA	NA	22	NA	23	NA	NA	NA	NA	NA	NA	NA	NA	NA	22	22
Sub-Saharan Africa	NA	NA	NA	NA	NA	14	NA	14	NA	NA	NA	NA	NA	NA	NA	NA	NA	13	13
Low- and middle-income countries	NA	NA	NA	NA	NA	17	NA	18	NA	NA	NA	NA	NA	NA	NA	NA	NA	17	17
High-income countries	NA	NA	NA	NA	NA	4	NA	4	NA	NA	NA	NA	NA	NA	NA	NA	NA	4	4
WORLD	NA	NA	NA	NA	NA	17	NA	18	NA	NA	NA	NA	NA	NA	NA	NA	NA	17	17
PAF of YLL (%)																			
East Asia and Pacific	NA	NA	NA	NA	NA	17	NA	17	NA	NA	NA	NA	NA	NA	NA	NA	NA	16	16
Europe and Central Asia	NA	NA	NA	NA	NA	8	NA	8	NA	NA	NA	NA	NA	NA	NA	NA	NA	8	8
Latin America and the Caribbean	NA	NA	NA	NA	NA	7	NA	7	NA	NA	NA	NA	NA	NA	NA	NA	NA	7	7
Middle East and North Africa	NA	NA	NA	NA	NA	14	NA	15	NA	NA	NA	NA	NA	NA	NA	NA	NA	14	14
South Asia	NA	NA	NA	NA	NA	22	NA	23	NA	NA	NA	NA	NA	NA	NA	NA	NA	22	22
Sub-Saharan Africa	NA	NA	NA	NA	NA	14	NA	14	NA	NA	NA	NA	NA	NA	NA	NA	NA	13	13
Low- and middle-income countries	NA	NA	NA	NA	NA	17	NA	18	NA	NA	NA	NA	NA	NA	NA	NA	NA	17	17
High-income countries	NA	NA	NA	NA	NA	4	NA	4	NA	NA	NA	NA	NA	NA	NA	NA	NA	4	4
WORLD	NA	NA	NA	NA	NA	17	NA	18	NA	NA	NA	NA	NA	NA	NA	NA	NA	17	17
PAF of DALYs (%)																			
East Asia and Pacific	NA	NA	NA	NA	NA	3	NA	8	NA	NA	NA	NA	NA	NA	NA	NA	NA	5	5
Europe and Central Asia	NA	NA	NA	NA	NA	1	NA	1	NA	NA	NA	NA	NA	NA	NA	NA	NA	1	1
Latin America and the Caribbean	NA	NA	NA	NA	NA	2	NA	3	NA	NA	NA	NA	NA	NA	NA	NA	NA	2	2
Middle East and North Africa	NA	NA	NA	NA	NA	3	NA	6	NA	NA	NA	NA	NA	NA	NA	NA	NA	4	4
South Asia	NA	NA	NA	NA	NA	9	NA	16	NA	NA	NA	NA	NA	NA	NA	NA	NA	12	12
Sub-Saharan Africa	NA	NA	NA	NA	NA	8	NA	11	NA	NA	NA	NA	NA	NA	NA	NA	NA	8	8
Low- and middle-income countries	NA	NA	NA	NA	NA	7	NA	12	NA	NA	NA	NA	NA	NA	NA	NA	NA	9	9
High-income countries	NA	NA	NA	NA	NA	0	NA	0	NA	NA	NA	NA	NA	NA	NA	NA	NA	0	0
WORLD	NA	NA	NA	NA	NA	7	NA	12	NA	NA	NA	NA	NA	NA	NA	NA	NA	8	8
Attributable Mortality (thousands)																			
East Asia and Pacific	NA	NA	NA	NA	NA	3	NA	3	NA	NA	NA	NA	NA	NA	NA	NA	NA	6	6
Europe and Central Asia	NA	NA	NA	NA	NA	0	NA	0	NA	NA	NA	NA	NA	NA	NA	NA	NA	0	0
Latin America and the Caribbean	NA	NA	NA	NA	NA	1	NA	0	NA	NA	NA	NA	NA	NA	NA	NA	NA	1	1
Middle East and North Africa	NA	NA	NA	NA	NA	1	NA	1	NA	NA	NA	NA	NA	NA	NA	NA	NA	2	2
South Asia	NA	NA	NA	NA	NA	22	NA	22	NA	NA	NA	NA	NA	NA	NA	NA	NA	44	44
Sub-Saharan Africa	NA	NA	NA	NA	NA	17	NA	13	NA	NA	NA	NA	NA	NA	NA	NA	NA	31	31
Low- and middle-income countries	NA	NA	NA	NA	NA	44	NA	41	NA	NA	NA	NA	NA	NA	NA	NA	NA	85	85
High-income countries	NA	NA	NA	NA	NA	0	NA	0	NA	NA	NA	NA	NA	NA	NA	NA	NA	0	0
WORLD	NA	NA	NA	NA	NA	44	NA	41	NA	NA	NA	NA	NA	NA	NA	NA	NA	85	85
Attributable YLL (thousands)																			
East Asia and Pacific	NA	NA	NA	NA	NA	73	NA	84	NA	NA	NA	NA	NA	NA	NA	NA	NA	158	158
Europe and Central Asia	NA	NA	NA	NA	NA	3	NA	2	NA	NA	NA	NA	NA	NA	NA	NA	NA	5	5
Latin America and the Caribbean	NA	NA	NA	NA	NA	16	NA	12	NA	NA	NA	NA	NA	NA	NA	NA	NA	29	29
Middle East and North Africa	NA	NA	NA	NA	NA	27	NA	28	NA	NA	NA	NA	NA	NA	NA	NA	NA	55	55
South Asia	NA	NA	NA	NA	NA	608	NA	565	NA	NA	NA	NA	NA	NA	NA	NA	NA	1,173	1,173
Sub-Saharan Africa	NA	NA	NA	NA	NA	488	NA	337	NA	NA	NA	NA	NA	NA	NA	NA	NA	826	826
Low- and middle-income countries	NA	NA	NA	NA	NA	1,217	NA	1,029	NA	NA	NA	NA	NA	NA	NA	NA	NA	2,246	2,246
High-income countries	NA	NA	NA	NA	NA	0	NA	1	NA	NA	NA	NA	NA	NA	NA	NA	NA	1	1
WORLD	NA	NA	NA	NA	NA	1,217	NA	1,030	NA	NA	NA	NA	NA	NA	NA	NA	NA	2,247	2,247
Attributable DALYs (thousands)																			
East Asia and Pacific	NA	NA	NA	NA	NA	73	NA	84	NA	NA	NA	NA	NA	NA	NA	NA	NA	158	158
Europe and Central Asia	NA	NA	NA	NA	NA	3	NA	2	NA	NA	NA	NA	NA	NA	NA	NA	NA	5	5
Latin America and the Caribbean	NA	NA	NA	NA	NA	16	NA	12	NA	NA	NA	NA	NA	NA	NA	NA	NA	29	29
Middle East and North Africa	NA	NA	NA	NA	NA	27	NA	28	NA	NA	NA	NA	NA	NA	NA	NA	NA	55	55
South Asia	NA	NA	NA	NA	NA	608	NA	565	NA	NA	NA	NA	NA	NA	NA	NA	NA	1,173	1,173
Sub-Saharan Africa	NA	NA	NA	NA	NA	488	NA	337	NA	NA	NA	NA	NA	NA	NA	NA	NA	826	826
Low- and middle-income countries	NA	NA	NA	NA	NA	1,217	NA	1,029	NA	NA	NA	NA	NA	NA	NA	NA	NA	2,246	2,246
High-income countries	NA	NA	NA	NA	NA	0	NA	1	NA	NA	NA	NA	NA	NA	NA	NA	NA	1	1
WORLD	NA	NA	NA	NA	NA	1,217	NA	1,030	NA	NA	NA	NA	NA	NA	NA	NA	NA	2,247	2,247

Source: Authors' calculations.
Note: NA = not applicable.

Table 4A.9

| Risk factor: | Iron-deficiency anemia |
| Disease: | Perinatal conditions |

Region	0–4 years		5–14 years		15–29 years		30–44 years		45–59 years		60–69 years		70–79 years		80+ years		Total		
	Male	Female	Male	Female	Male	Female	Male	Female	Male	Female	Male	Female	Male	Female	Male	Female	Male	Female	All
PAF of Mortality (%)																			
East Asia and Pacific	13	13	NA	NA	NA	NA	NA	NA	NA	NA	NA	NA	NA	NA	NA	NA	13	13	13
Europe and Central Asia	6	6	NA	NA	NA	NA	NA	NA	NA	NA	NA	NA	NA	NA	NA	NA	6	6	6
Latin America and the Caribbean	5	5	NA	NA	NA	NA	NA	NA	NA	NA	NA	NA	NA	NA	NA	NA	5	5	5
Middle East and North Africa	12	12	NA	NA	NA	NA	NA	NA	NA	NA	NA	NA	NA	NA	NA	NA	12	12	12
South Asia	18	18	NA	NA	NA	NA	NA	NA	NA	NA	NA	NA	NA	NA	NA	NA	18	18	18
Sub-Saharan Africa	20	20	NA	NA	NA	NA	NA	NA	NA	NA	NA	NA	NA	NA	NA	NA	20	20	20
Low- and middle-income countries	16	16	NA	NA	NA	NA	NA	NA	NA	NA	NA	NA	NA	NA	NA	NA	16	16	16
High-income countries	3	3	NA	NA	NA	NA	NA	NA	NA	NA	NA	NA	NA	NA	NA	NA	3	3	3
WORLD	16	16	NA	NA	NA	NA	NA	NA	NA	NA	NA	NA	NA	NA	NA	NA	16	16	16
PAF of YLL (%)																			
East Asia and Pacific	13	13	NA	NA	NA	NA	NA	NA	NA	NA	NA	NA	NA	NA	NA	NA	13	13	13
Europe and Central Asia	6	6	NA	NA	NA	NA	NA	NA	NA	NA	NA	NA	NA	NA	NA	NA	6	6	6
Latin America and the Caribbean	5	5	NA	NA	NA	NA	NA	NA	NA	NA	NA	NA	NA	NA	NA	NA	5	5	5
Middle East and North Africa	12	12	NA	NA	NA	NA	NA	NA	NA	NA	NA	NA	NA	NA	NA	NA	12	12	12
South Asia	18	18	NA	NA	NA	NA	NA	NA	NA	NA	NA	NA	NA	NA	NA	NA	18	18	18
Sub-Saharan Africa	20	20	NA	NA	NA	NA	NA	NA	NA	NA	NA	NA	NA	NA	NA	NA	20	20	20
Low- and middle-income countries	16	16	NA	NA	NA	NA	NA	NA	NA	NA	NA	NA	NA	NA	NA	NA	16	16	16
High-income countries	3	3	NA	NA	NA	NA	NA	NA	NA	NA	NA	NA	NA	NA	NA	NA	3	3	3
WORLD	16	16	NA	NA	NA	NA	NA	NA	NA	NA	NA	NA	NA	NA	NA	NA	16	16	16
PAF of DALYs (%)																			
East Asia and Pacific	11	11	NA	NA	NA	NA	NA	NA	NA	NA	NA	NA	NA	NA	NA	NA	11	11	11
Europe and Central Asia	5	5	NA	NA	NA	NA	NA	NA	NA	NA	NA	NA	NA	NA	NA	NA	5	5	5
Latin America and the Caribbean	4	4	NA	NA	NA	NA	NA	NA	NA	NA	NA	NA	NA	NA	NA	NA	4	4	4
Middle East and North Africa	9	8	NA	NA	NA	NA	NA	NA	NA	NA	NA	NA	NA	NA	NA	NA	9	8	9
South Asia	16	16	NA	NA	NA	NA	NA	NA	NA	NA	NA	NA	NA	NA	NA	NA	16	16	16
Sub-Saharan Africa	18	17	NA	NA	NA	NA	NA	NA	NA	NA	NA	NA	NA	NA	NA	NA	18	17	17
Low- and middle-income countries	14	13	NA	NA	NA	NA	NA	NA	NA	NA	NA	NA	NA	NA	NA	NA	14	13	14
High-income countries	2	2	NA	NA	NA	NA	NA	NA	NA	NA	NA	NA	NA	NA	NA	NA	2	2	2
WORLD	14	13	NA	NA	NA	NA	NA	NA	NA	NA	NA	NA	NA	NA	NA	NA	14	13	14
Attributable Mortality (thousands)																			
East Asia and Pacific	35	32	NA	NA	NA	NA	NA	NA	NA	NA	NA	NA	NA	NA	NA	NA	35	32	66
Europe and Central Asia	2	1	NA	NA	NA	NA	NA	NA	NA	NA	NA	NA	NA	NA	NA	NA	2	1	3
Latin America and the Caribbean	5	4	NA	NA	NA	NA	NA	NA	NA	NA	NA	NA	NA	NA	NA	NA	5	4	9
Middle East and North Africa	7	5	NA	NA	NA	NA	NA	NA	NA	NA	NA	NA	NA	NA	NA	NA	7	5	12
South Asia	108	89	NA	NA	NA	NA	NA	NA	NA	NA	NA	NA	NA	NA	NA	NA	108	89	197
Sub-Saharan Africa	66	48	NA	NA	NA	NA	NA	NA	NA	NA	NA	NA	NA	NA	NA	NA	66	48	114
Low- and middle-income countries	223	179	NA	NA	NA	NA	NA	NA	NA	NA	NA	NA	NA	NA	NA	NA	223	179	402
High-income countries	1	0	NA	NA	NA	NA	NA	NA	NA	NA	NA	NA	NA	NA	NA	NA	1	0	1
WORLD	224	179	NA	NA	NA	NA	NA	NA	NA	NA	NA	NA	NA	NA	NA	NA	224	179	403
Attributable YLL (thousands)																			
East Asia and Pacific	1,047	970	NA	NA	NA	NA	NA	NA	NA	NA	NA	NA	NA	NA	NA	NA	1,047	970	2,016
Europe and Central Asia	61	45	NA	NA	NA	NA	NA	NA	NA	NA	NA	NA	NA	NA	NA	NA	61	45	106
Latin America and the Caribbean	151	117	NA	NA	NA	NA	NA	NA	NA	NA	NA	NA	NA	NA	NA	NA	151	117	268
Middle East and North Africa	225	147	NA	NA	NA	NA	NA	NA	NA	NA	NA	NA	NA	NA	NA	NA	225	147	372
South Asia	3,272	2,704	NA	NA	NA	NA	NA	NA	NA	NA	NA	NA	NA	NA	NA	NA	3,272	2,704	5,976
Sub-Saharan Africa	2,001	1,466	NA	NA	NA	NA	NA	NA	NA	NA	NA	NA	NA	NA	NA	NA	2,001	1,466	3,466
Low- and middle-income countries	6,757	5,448	NA	NA	NA	NA	NA	NA	NA	NA	NA	NA	NA	NA	NA	NA	6,757	5,448	12,205
High-income countries	17	13	NA	NA	NA	NA	NA	NA	NA	NA	NA	NA	NA	NA	NA	NA	17	13	30
WORLD	6,774	5,461	NA	NA	NA	NA	NA	NA	NA	NA	NA	NA	NA	NA	NA	NA	6,774	5,461	12,235
Attributable DALYs (thousands)																			
East Asia and Pacific	1,047	970	NA	NA	NA	NA	NA	NA	NA	NA	NA	NA	NA	NA	NA	NA	1,047	970	2,016
Europe and Central Asia	61	45	NA	NA	NA	NA	NA	NA	NA	NA	NA	NA	NA	NA	NA	NA	61	45	106
Latin America and the Caribbean	151	117	NA	NA	NA	NA	NA	NA	NA	NA	NA	NA	NA	NA	NA	NA	151	117	268
Middle East and North Africa	225	147	NA	NA	NA	NA	NA	NA	NA	NA	NA	NA	NA	NA	NA	NA	225	147	372
South Asia	3,272	2,704	NA	NA	NA	NA	NA	NA	NA	NA	NA	NA	NA	NA	NA	NA	3,272	2,704	5,976
Sub-Saharan Africa	2,001	1,466	NA	NA	NA	NA	NA	NA	NA	NA	NA	NA	NA	NA	NA	NA	2,001	1,466	3,466
Low- and middle-income countries	6,757	5,448	NA	NA	NA	NA	NA	NA	NA	NA	NA	NA	NA	NA	NA	NA	6,757	5,448	12,205
High-income countries	17	13	NA	NA	NA	NA	NA	NA	NA	NA	NA	NA	NA	NA	NA	NA	17	13	30
WORLD	6,774	5,461	NA	NA	NA	NA	NA	NA	NA	NA	NA	NA	NA	NA	NA	NA	6,774	5,461	12,235

Source: Authors' calculations.
Note: NA = not applicable.

Table 4A.10

Risk factor: Iron-deficiency anemia
Disease: Iron-deficiency anemia

Region	0–4 years Male	Female	5–14 years Male	Female	15–29 years Male	Female	30–44 years Male	Female	45–59 years Male	Female	60–69 years Male	Female	70–79 years Male	Female	80+ years Male	Female	Total Male	Female	All
PAF of Mortality (%)																			
East Asia and Pacific	100	100	100	100	100	100	100	100	100	100	100	100	100	100	100	100	100	100	100
Europe and Central Asia	100	100	100	100	100	100	100	100	100	100	100	100	100	100	100	100	100	100	100
Latin America and the Caribbean	100	100	100	100	100	100	100	100	100	100	100	100	100	100	100	100	100	100	100
Middle East and North Africa	100	100	100	100	100	100	100	100	100	100	100	100	100	100	100	100	100	100	100
South Asia	100	100	100	100	100	100	100	100	100	100	100	100	100	100	100	100	100	100	100
Sub-Saharan Africa	100	100	100	100	100	100	100	100	100	100	100	100	100	100	100	100	100	100	100
Low- and middle-income countries	100	100	100	100	100	100	100	100	100	100	100	100	100	100	100	100	100	100	100
High-income countries	100	100	100	100	100	100	100	100	100	100	100	100	100	100	100	100	100	100	100
WORLD	100	100	100	100	100	100	100	100	100	100	100	100	100	100	100	100	100	100	100
PAF of YLL (%)																			
East Asia and Pacific	100	100	100	100	100	100	100	100	100	100	100	100	100	100	100	100	100	100	100
Europe and Central Asia	100	100	100	100	100	100	100	100	100	100	100	100	100	100	100	100	100	100	100
Latin America and the Caribbean	100	100	100	100	100	100	100	100	100	100	100	100	100	100	100	100	100	100	100
Middle East and North Africa	100	100	100	100	100	100	100	100	100	100	100	100	100	100	100	100	100	100	100
South Asia	100	100	100	100	100	100	100	100	100	100	100	100	100	100	100	100	100	100	100
Sub-Saharan Africa	100	100	100	100	100	100	100	100	100	100	100	100	100	100	100	100	100	100	100
Low- and middle-income countries	100	100	100	100	100	100	100	100	100	100	100	100	100	100	100	100	100	100	100
High-income countries	100	100	100	100	100	100	100	100	100	100	100	100	100	100	100	100	100	100	100
WORLD	100	100	100	100	100	100	100	100	100	100	100	100	100	100	100	100	100	100	100
PAF of DALYs (%)																			
East Asia and Pacific	100	100	100	100	100	100	100	100	100	100	100	100	100	100	100	100	100	100	100
Europe and Central Asia	100	100	100	100	100	100	100	100	100	100	100	100	100	100	100	100	100	100	100
Latin America and the Caribbean	100	100	100	100	100	100	100	100	100	100	100	100	100	100	100	100	100	100	100
Middle East and North Africa	100	100	100	100	100	100	100	100	100	100	100	100	100	100	100	100	100	100	100
South Asia	100	100	100	100	100	100	100	100	100	100	100	100	100	100	100	100	100	100	100
Sub-Saharan Africa	100	100	100	100	100	100	100	100	100	100	100	100	100	100	100	100	100	100	100
Low- and middle-income countries	100	100	100	100	100	100	100	100	100	100	100	100	100	100	100	100	100	100	100
High-income countries	100	100	100	100	100	100	100	100	100	100	100	100	100	100	100	100	100	100	100
WORLD	100	100	100	100	100	100	100	100	100	100	100	100	100	100	100	100	100	100	100
Attributable Mortality (thousands)																			
East Asia and Pacific	1	1	0	0	1	2	1	5	2	7	0	3	0	1	0	1	6	19	25
Europe and Central Asia	0	0	0	0	0	0	0	0	0	0	0	0	0	0	0	0	2	2	3
Latin America and the Caribbean	1	1	0	0	1	0	1	0	1	1	1	0	1	1	1	2	6	6	13
Middle East and North Africa	1	1	0	1	0	0	0	0	0	0	0	0	0	1	0	1	2	3	6
South Asia	0	2	2	1	2	2	4	7	11	21	0	7	0	0	0	0	19	42	61
Sub-Saharan Africa	5	7	1	2	0	0	0	0	1	1	1	0	0	0	0	0	8	11	18
Low- and middle-income countries	9	11	3	5	4	5	6	13	15	30	2	12	2	4	2	4	43	83	126
High-income countries	0	0	0	0	0	0	0	0	0	0	0	0	0	1	1	4	2	5	7
WORLD	9	11	3	5	4	5	6	13	15	30	2	12	3	5	3	7	46	88	133
Attributable YLL (thousands)																			
East Asia and Pacific	28	17	10	8	40	43	21	118	35	134	6	45	3	12	1	4	145	381	526
Europe and Central Asia	8	6	3	2	6	3	5	4	4	4	3	4	2	4	1	1	31	29	60
Latin America and the Caribbean	30	18	10	12	19	14	20	11	15	21	8	7	7	12	5	8	114	104	218
Middle East and North Africa	26	21	6	16	3	5	2	4	2	4	3	4	3	7	1	4	47	64	111
South Asia	12	64	47	43	44	70	88	171	215	434	2	122	2	3	0	1	411	908	1,319
Sub-Saharan Africa	159	208	22	60	3	13	7	4	12	12	7	4	2	2	0	0	212	303	515
Low- and middle-income countries	265	334	98	139	114	148	142	312	284	610	29	186	20	40	8	19	960	1,789	2,748
High-income countries	0	0	0	2	0	0	1	1	2	2	2	3	4	7	6	14	17	29	45
WORLD	265	334	98	141	114	148	143	314	287	612	31	189	24	47	14	33	976	1,817	2,794
Attributable DALYs (thousands)																			
East Asia and Pacific	124	116	176	465	325	391	160	275	157	311	50	86	17	29	3	8	1,013	1,682	2,695
Europe and Central Asia	34	32	25	40	24	122	22	31	16	24	21	12	7	8	1	2	149	271	421
Latin America and the Caribbean	62	47	22	40	48	75	25	51	18	28	12	11	9	15	5	9	201	276	477
Middle East and North Africa	56	53	70	144	57	58	32	33	17	27	10	10	7	9	2	4	250	338	587
South Asia	330	374	106	175	318	363	346	479	294	558	31	182	15	36	4	6	1,443	2,172	3,616
Sub-Saharan Africa	273	323	199	173	180	200	88	137	27	41	16	15	6	8	1	1	789	899	1,688
Low- and middle-income countries	879	945	598	1,037	953	1,210	672	1,005	530	989	139	316	60	106	15	30	3,846	5,637	9,483
High-income countries	20	20	11	28	111	173	31	85	37	85	35	33	33	25	13	18	291	467	758
WORLD	899	964	609	1,066	1,064	1,382	703	1,091	567	1,074	174	348	93	131	28	48	4,137	6,104	10,241

Source: Authors' calculations.

Table 4A.11

Risk factor: Iron-deficiency anemia
Disease: All causes

Region	0–4 years Male	0–4 years Female	5–14 years Male	5–14 years Female	15–29 years Male	15–29 years Female	30–44 years Male	30–44 years Female	45–59 years Male	45–59 years Female	60–69 years Male	60–69 years Female	70–79 years Male	70–79 years Female	80+ years Male	80+ years Female	Total Male	Total Female	All
PAF of Mortality (%)																			
East Asia and Pacific	5	5	0	0	0	2	0	2	0	1	0	0	0	0	0	0	1	1	1
Europe and Central Asia	2	2	0	1	0	1	0	0	0	0	0	0	0	0	0	0	0	0	0
Latin America and the Caribbean	3	2	1	2	0	2	0	1	0	1	0	0	0	0	0	0	1	1	1
Middle East and North Africa	4	3	1	2	0	3	0	2	0	0	0	0	0	0	0	1	1	1	1
South Asia	6	5	1	0	0	5	1	6	1	3	0	1	0	0	0	0	2	3	2
Sub-Saharan Africa	3	3	0	1	0	3	0	2	0	0	0	0	0	0	0	0	1	2	2
Low- and middle-income countries	4	4	0	1	0	3	0	3	0	1	0	0	0	0	0	0	1	2	1
High-income countries	1	1	0	1	0	0	0	0	0	0	0	0	0	0	0	0	0	0	0
WORLD	4	4	0	1	0	3	0	3	0	1	0	0	0	0	0	0	1	1	1
PAF of YLL (%)																			
East Asia and Pacific	5	5	0	0	0	2	0	2	0	1	0	0	0	0	0	0	1	2	1
Europe and Central Asia	2	2	0	1	0	1	0	0	0	0	0	0	0	0	0	0	0	0	0
Latin America and the Caribbean	3	2	1	2	0	2	0	1	0	1	0	0	0	0	0	0	1	1	1
Middle East and North Africa	4	3	1	2	0	3	0	2	0	0	0	0	0	0	0	1	1	2	2
South Asia	6	5	1	0	0	5	1	6	1	3	0	1	0	0	0	0	3	4	3
Sub-Saharan Africa	3	3	0	1	0	3	0	2	0	0	0	0	0	0	0	0	2	2	2
Low- and middle-income countries	4	4	0	1	0	3	0	3	0	1	0	0	0	0	0	0	2	2	2
High-income countries	1	1	0	1	0	0	0	0	0	0	0	0	0	0	0	0	0	0	0
WORLD	4	4	0	1	0	3	0	3	0	1	0	0	0	0	0	0	1	2	2
PAF of DALYs (%)																			
East Asia and Pacific	4	3	2	6	1	2	1	2	0	1	0	0	0	0	0	0	1	2	1
Europe and Central Asia	2	2	1	3	0	2	0	1	0	0	0	0	0	0	0	0	0	1	0
Latin America and the Caribbean	2	2	1	1	0	1	0	1	0	0	0	0	0	0	0	0	1	1	1
Middle East and North Africa	3	2	3	6	1	2	1	2	0	1	0	0	0	0	0	0	1	2	2
South Asia	5	4	1	1	1	3	1	4	1	2	0	1	0	0	0	0	2	3	3
Sub-Saharan Africa	3	2	2	1	1	2	0	2	0	0	0	0	0	0	0	0	2	2	2
Low- and middle-income countries	4	3	1	2	1	2	1	2	0	1	0	0	0	0	0	0	1	2	2
High-income countries	1	1	1	2	1	3	0	1	0	1	0	0	0	0	0	0	0	1	1
WORLD	3	3	1	2	1	3	1	2	0	1	0	0	0	0	0	0	1	2	2
Attributable Mortality (thousands)																			
East Asia and Pacific	35	32	0	0	1	4	1	8	2	7	0	3	0	1	0	1	41	56	97
Europe and Central Asia	2	2	0	0	0	0	0	0	0	0	0	0	0	0	0	0	4	3	7
Latin America and the Caribbean	6	4	0	0	1	1	1	1	1	1	1	0	1	1	1	2	11	11	23
Middle East and North Africa	8	6	0	1	0	1	0	1	0	0	0	0	0	1	0	1	10	10	20
South Asia	108	91	2	1	2	24	4	30	11	21	0	7	0	0	0	0	127	175	302
Sub-Saharan Africa	71	55	1	2	0	18	0	14	1	1	1	0	0	0	0	0	74	90	163
Low- and middle-income countries	232	190	3	5	4	49	6	54	15	30	2	12	2	4	2	4	266	346	613
High-income countries	1	0	0	0	0	0	0	0	0	0	0	0	0	1	1	4	3	5	8
WORLD	232	190	3	5	4	49	6	54	15	30	2	12	3	5	3	7	269	351	621
Attributable YLL (thousands)																			
East Asia and Pacific	1,075	987	10	8	40	117	21	202	35	134	6	45	3	12	1	4	1,192	1,509	2,700
Europe and Central Asia	70	51	3	2	6	7	5	6	4	4	3	4	2	4	1	1	92	79	171
Latin America and the Caribbean	182	135	10	12	19	30	20	24	15	21	8	7	7	12	5	8	265	249	515
Middle East and North Africa	251	168	6	16	3	32	2	32	2	4	3	4	3	7	1	4	272	267	538
South Asia	3,284	2,768	47	43	44	678	88	736	215	434	2	122	2	3	0	1	3,683	4,785	8,468
Sub-Saharan Africa	2,160	1,673	22	60	3	501	7	342	12	12	7	4	2	2	0	0	2,213	2,594	4,807
Low- and middle-income countries	7,022	5,782	98	139	114	1,364	142	1,341	284	610	29	186	20	40	8	19	7,717	9,482	17,199
High-income countries	18	13	0	2	0	1	1	2	2	2	2	3	4	7	6	14	34	43	77
WORLD	7,039	5,795	98	141	114	1,365	143	1,343	287	612	31	189	24	47	14	33	7,750	9,525	17,275
Attributable DALYs (thousands)																			
East Asia and Pacific	1,171	1,086	176	465	325	464	160	359	157	311	50	86	17	29	3	8	2,060	2,809	4,869
Europe and Central Asia	95	76	25	40	24	125	22	33	16	24	21	12	7	8	1	2	211	321	532
Latin America and the Caribbean	214	164	22	40	48	91	25	63	18	28	12	11	9	15	5	9	352	421	774
Middle East and North Africa	281	200	70	144	57	85	32	61	17	27	10	10	7	9	2	4	475	540	1,015
South Asia	3,602	3,078	106	175	318	971	346	1,044	294	558	31	182	15	36	4	6	4,715	6,049	10,764
Sub-Saharan Africa	2,273	1,788	199	173	180	689	88	474	27	41	16	15	6	8	1	1	2,790	3,190	5,980
Low- and middle-income countries	7,636	6,393	598	1,037	953	2,426	672	2,034	530	989	139	316	60	106	15	30	10,602	13,331	23,933
High-income countries	37	33	11	28	111	173	31	86	37	85	35	33	33	25	13	18	308	481	789
WORLD	7,673	6,425	609	1,066	1,064	2,599	703	2,120	567	1,074	174	348	93	131	28	48	10,911	13,812	24,722

Source: Authors' calculations.

Table 4A.12

Risk factor: Vitamin A deficiency
Disease: Diarrheal diseases

Region	0–4 years Male	0–4 years Female	5–14 years Male	5–14 years Female	15–29 years Male	15–29 years Female	30–44 years Male	30–44 years Female	45–59 years Male	45–59 years Female	60–69 years Male	60–69 years Female	70–79 years Male	70–79 years Female	80+ years Male	80+ years Female	Total Male	Total Female	All
PAF of Mortality (%)																			
East Asia and Pacific	19	19	NA	NA	NA	NA	NA	NA	NA	NA	NA	NA	NA	NA	NA	NA	17	17	17
Europe and Central Asia	0	0	NA	NA	NA	NA	NA	NA	NA	NA	NA	NA	NA	NA	NA	NA	0	0	0
Latin America and the Caribbean	15	15	NA	NA	NA	NA	NA	NA	NA	NA	NA	NA	NA	NA	NA	NA	13	12	12
Middle East and North Africa	15	15	NA	NA	NA	NA	NA	NA	NA	NA	NA	NA	NA	NA	NA	NA	13	13	13
South Asia	25	25	NA	NA	NA	NA	NA	NA	NA	NA	NA	NA	NA	NA	NA	NA	23	23	23
Sub-Saharan Africa	27	27	NA	NA	NA	NA	NA	NA	NA	NA	NA	NA	NA	NA	NA	NA	24	24	24
Low- and middle-income countries	24	24	NA	NA	NA	NA	NA	NA	NA	NA	NA	NA	NA	NA	NA	NA	22	22	22
High-income countries	1	1	NA	NA	NA	NA	NA	NA	NA	NA	NA	NA	NA	NA	NA	NA	0	0	0
WORLD	24	24	NA	NA	NA	NA	NA	NA	NA	NA	NA	NA	NA	NA	NA	NA	22	22	22
PAF of YLL (%)																			
East Asia and Pacific	19	19	NA	NA	NA	NA	NA	NA	NA	NA	NA	NA	NA	NA	NA	NA	18	18	18
Europe and Central Asia	0	0	NA	NA	NA	NA	NA	NA	NA	NA	NA	NA	NA	NA	NA	NA	0	0	0
Latin America and the Caribbean	15	15	NA	NA	NA	NA	NA	NA	NA	NA	NA	NA	NA	NA	NA	NA	14	14	14
Middle East and North Africa	15	15	NA	NA	NA	NA	NA	NA	NA	NA	NA	NA	NA	NA	NA	NA	14	14	14
South Asia	25	25	NA	NA	NA	NA	NA	NA	NA	NA	NA	NA	NA	NA	NA	NA	24	24	24
Sub-Saharan Africa	27	27	NA	NA	NA	NA	NA	NA	NA	NA	NA	NA	NA	NA	NA	NA	25	26	25
Low- and middle-income countries	24	24	NA	NA	NA	NA	NA	NA	NA	NA	NA	NA	NA	NA	NA	NA	23	23	23
High-income countries	1	1	NA	NA	NA	NA	NA	NA	NA	NA	NA	NA	NA	NA	NA	NA	0	0	0
WORLD	24	24	NA	NA	NA	NA	NA	NA	NA	NA	NA	NA	NA	NA	NA	NA	23	23	23
PAF of DALYs (%)																			
East Asia and Pacific	16	16	NA	NA	NA	NA	NA	NA	NA	NA	NA	NA	NA	NA	NA	NA	13	13	13
Europe and Central Asia	0	0	NA	NA	NA	NA	NA	NA	NA	NA	NA	NA	NA	NA	NA	NA	0	0	0
Latin America and the Caribbean	11	11	NA	NA	NA	NA	NA	NA	NA	NA	NA	NA	NA	NA	NA	NA	9	9	9
Middle East and North Africa	13	13	NA	NA	NA	NA	NA	NA	NA	NA	NA	NA	NA	NA	NA	NA	12	12	12
South Asia	23	23	NA	NA	NA	NA	NA	NA	NA	NA	NA	NA	NA	NA	NA	NA	22	22	22
Sub-Saharan Africa	25	25	NA	NA	NA	NA	NA	NA	NA	NA	NA	NA	NA	NA	NA	NA	24	24	24
Low- and middle-income countries	22	22	NA	NA	NA	NA	NA	NA	NA	NA	NA	NA	NA	NA	NA	NA	20	20	20
High-income countries	0	0	NA	NA	NA	NA	NA	NA	NA	NA	NA	NA	NA	NA	NA	NA	0	0	0
WORLD	22	22	NA	NA	NA	NA	NA	NA	NA	NA	NA	NA	NA	NA	NA	NA	20	20	20
Attributable Mortality (thousands)																			
East Asia and Pacific	20	18	NA	NA	NA	NA	NA	NA	NA	NA	NA	NA	NA	NA	NA	NA	20	18	38
Europe and Central Asia	0	0	NA	NA	NA	NA	NA	NA	NA	NA	NA	NA	NA	NA	NA	NA	0	0	0
Latin America and the Caribbean	4	3	NA	NA	NA	NA	NA	NA	NA	NA	NA	NA	NA	NA	NA	NA	4	3	7
Middle East and North Africa	5	5	NA	NA	NA	NA	NA	NA	NA	NA	NA	NA	NA	NA	NA	NA	5	5	10
South Asia	83	76	NA	NA	NA	NA	NA	NA	NA	NA	NA	NA	NA	NA	NA	NA	83	76	158
Sub-Saharan Africa	90	82	NA	NA	NA	NA	NA	NA	NA	NA	NA	NA	NA	NA	NA	NA	90	82	172
Low- and middle-income countries	201	184	NA	NA	NA	NA	NA	NA	NA	NA	NA	NA	NA	NA	NA	NA	201	184	385
High-income countries	0	0	NA	NA	NA	NA	NA	NA	NA	NA	NA	NA	NA	NA	NA	NA	0	0	0
WORLD	201	184	NA	NA	NA	NA	NA	NA	NA	NA	NA	NA	NA	NA	NA	NA	201	184	385
Attributable YLL (thousands)																			
East Asia and Pacific	599	555	NA	NA	NA	NA	NA	NA	NA	NA	NA	NA	NA	NA	NA	NA	599	555	1,154
Europe and Central Asia	0	0	NA	NA	NA	NA	NA	NA	NA	NA	NA	NA	NA	NA	NA	NA	0	0	1
Latin America and the Caribbean	108	98	NA	NA	NA	NA	NA	NA	NA	NA	NA	NA	NA	NA	NA	NA	108	98	206
Middle East and North Africa	155	144	NA	NA	NA	NA	NA	NA	NA	NA	NA	NA	NA	NA	NA	NA	155	144	299
South Asia	2,500	2,308	NA	NA	NA	NA	NA	NA	NA	NA	NA	NA	NA	NA	NA	NA	2,500	2,308	4,808
Sub-Saharan Africa	2,719	2,486	NA	NA	NA	NA	NA	NA	NA	NA	NA	NA	NA	NA	NA	NA	2,719	2,486	5,205
Low- and middle-income countries	6,081	5,592	NA	NA	NA	NA	NA	NA	NA	NA	NA	NA	NA	NA	NA	NA	6,081	5,592	11,673
High-income countries	0	0	NA	NA	NA	NA	NA	NA	NA	NA	NA	NA	NA	NA	NA	NA	0	0	0
WORLD	6,081	5,592	NA	NA	NA	NA	NA	NA	NA	NA	NA	NA	NA	NA	NA	NA	6,081	5,592	11,673
Attributable DALYs (thousands)																			
East Asia and Pacific	599	555	NA	NA	NA	NA	NA	NA	NA	NA	NA	NA	NA	NA	NA	NA	599	555	1,154
Europe and Central Asia	0	0	NA	NA	NA	NA	NA	NA	NA	NA	NA	NA	NA	NA	NA	NA	0	0	1
Latin America and the Caribbean	108	98	NA	NA	NA	NA	NA	NA	NA	NA	NA	NA	NA	NA	NA	NA	108	98	206
Middle East and North Africa	155	144	NA	NA	NA	NA	NA	NA	NA	NA	NA	NA	NA	NA	NA	NA	155	144	299
South Asia	2,500	2,308	NA	NA	NA	NA	NA	NA	NA	NA	NA	NA	NA	NA	NA	NA	2,500	2,308	4,808
Sub-Saharan Africa	2,719	2,486	NA	NA	NA	NA	NA	NA	NA	NA	NA	NA	NA	NA	NA	NA	2,719	2,486	5,205
Low- and middle-income countries	6,081	5,592	NA	NA	NA	NA	NA	NA	NA	NA	NA	NA	NA	NA	NA	NA	6,081	5,592	11,673
High-income countries	0	0	NA	NA	NA	NA	NA	NA	NA	NA	NA	NA	NA	NA	NA	NA	0	0	0
WORLD	6,081	5,592	NA	NA	NA	NA	NA	NA	NA	NA	NA	NA	NA	NA	NA	NA	6,081	5,592	11,673

Source: Authors' calculations.

Note: NA = not applicable.

Table 4A.13

Risk factor: Vitamin A deficiency
Disease: Measles

Region	0–4 years Male	Female	5–14 years Male	Female	15–29 years Male	Female	30–44 years Male	Female	45–59 years Male	Female	60–69 years Male	Female	70–79 years Male	Female	80+ years Male	Female	Total Male	Female	All
PAF of Mortality (%)																			
East Asia and Pacific	15	15	NA	NA	NA	NA	NA	NA	NA	NA	NA	NA	NA	NA	NA	NA	9	9	9
Europe and Central Asia	0	0	NA	NA	NA	NA	NA	NA	NA	NA	NA	NA	NA	NA	NA	NA	0	0	0
Latin America and the Caribbean	*	*	NA	NA	NA	NA	NA	NA	NA	NA	NA	NA	NA	NA	NA	NA	*	*	*
Middle East and North Africa	12	12	NA	NA	NA	NA	NA	NA	NA	NA	NA	NA	NA	NA	NA	NA	7	8	7
South Asia	20	20	NA	NA	NA	NA	NA	NA	NA	NA	NA	NA	NA	NA	NA	NA	13	14	13
Sub-Saharan Africa	21	21	NA	NA	NA	NA	NA	NA	NA	NA	NA	NA	NA	NA	NA	NA	17	17	17
Low- and middle-income countries	20	20	NA	NA	NA	NA	NA	NA	NA	NA	NA	NA	NA	NA	NA	NA	15	15	15
High-income countries	1	1	NA	NA	NA	NA	NA	NA	NA	NA	NA	NA	NA	NA	NA	NA	0	0	0
WORLD	20	20	NA	NA	NA	NA	NA	NA	NA	NA	NA	NA	NA	NA	NA	NA	15	15	15
PAF of YLL (%)																			
East Asia and Pacific	15	15	NA	NA	NA	NA	NA	NA	NA	NA	NA	NA	NA	NA	NA	NA	9	9	9
Europe and Central Asia	0	0	NA	NA	NA	NA	NA	NA	NA	NA	NA	NA	NA	NA	NA	NA	0	0	0
Latin America and the Caribbean	*	*	NA	NA	NA	NA	NA	NA	NA	NA	NA	NA	NA	NA	NA	NA	*	*	*
Middle East and North Africa	12	12	NA	NA	NA	NA	NA	NA	NA	NA	NA	NA	NA	NA	NA	NA	7	8	7
South Asia	20	20	NA	NA	NA	NA	NA	NA	NA	NA	NA	NA	NA	NA	NA	NA	14	14	14
Sub-Saharan Africa	21	21	NA	NA	NA	NA	NA	NA	NA	NA	NA	NA	NA	NA	NA	NA	17	17	17
Low- and middle-income countries	20	20	NA	NA	NA	NA	NA	NA	NA	NA	NA	NA	NA	NA	NA	NA	15	15	15
High-income countries	1	1	NA	NA	NA	NA	NA	NA	NA	NA	NA	NA	NA	NA	NA	NA	0	0	0
WORLD	20	20	NA	NA	NA	NA	NA	NA	NA	NA	NA	NA	NA	NA	NA	NA	15	15	15
PAF of DALYs (%)																			
East Asia and Pacific	15	15	NA	NA	NA	NA	NA	NA	NA	NA	NA	NA	NA	NA	NA	NA	9	9	9
Europe and Central Asia	0	0	NA	NA	NA	NA	NA	NA	NA	NA	NA	NA	NA	NA	NA	NA	0	0	0
Latin America and the Caribbean	*	*	NA	NA	NA	NA	NA	NA	NA	NA	NA	NA	NA	NA	NA	NA	0	0	0
Middle East and North Africa	11	11	NA	NA	NA	NA	NA	NA	NA	NA	NA	NA	NA	NA	NA	NA	7	7	7
South Asia	20	20	NA	NA	NA	NA	NA	NA	NA	NA	NA	NA	NA	NA	NA	NA	13	14	13
Sub-Saharan Africa	21	21	NA	NA	NA	NA	NA	NA	NA	NA	NA	NA	NA	NA	NA	NA	17	17	17
Low- and middle-income countries	20	20	NA	NA	NA	NA	NA	NA	NA	NA	NA	NA	NA	NA	NA	NA	15	15	15
High-income countries	0	0	NA	NA	NA	NA	NA	NA	NA	NA	NA	NA	NA	NA	NA	NA	0	0	0
WORLD	20	20	NA	NA	NA	NA	NA	NA	NA	NA	NA	NA	NA	NA	NA	NA	15	15	15
Attributable Mortality (thousands)																			
East Asia and Pacific	3	3	NA	NA	NA	NA	NA	NA	NA	NA	NA	NA	NA	NA	NA	NA	3	3	7
Europe and Central Asia	0	0	NA	NA	NA	NA	NA	NA	NA	NA	NA	NA	NA	NA	NA	NA	0	0	0
Latin America and the Caribbean	0	0	NA	NA	NA	NA	NA	NA	NA	NA	NA	NA	NA	NA	NA	NA	0	0	0
Middle East and North Africa	1	1	NA	NA	NA	NA	NA	NA	NA	NA	NA	NA	NA	NA	NA	NA	1	1	1
South Asia	14	15	NA	NA	NA	NA	NA	NA	NA	NA	NA	NA	NA	NA	NA	NA	14	15	29
Sub-Saharan Africa	38	37	NA	NA	NA	NA	NA	NA	NA	NA	NA	NA	NA	NA	NA	NA	38	37	75
Low- and middle-income countries	56	56	NA	NA	NA	NA	NA	NA	NA	NA	NA	NA	NA	NA	NA	NA	56	56	112
High-income countries	0	0	NA	NA	NA	NA	NA	NA	NA	NA	NA	NA	NA	NA	NA	NA	0	0	0
WORLD	56	56	NA	NA	NA	NA	NA	NA	NA	NA	NA	NA	NA	NA	NA	NA	56	56	112
Attributable YLL (thousands)																			
East Asia and Pacific	99	104	NA	NA	NA	NA	NA	NA	NA	NA	NA	NA	NA	NA	NA	NA	99	104	203
Europe and Central Asia	0	0	NA	NA	NA	NA	NA	NA	NA	NA	NA	NA	NA	NA	NA	NA	0	0	0
Latin America and the Caribbean	0	0	NA	NA	NA	NA	NA	NA	NA	NA	NA	NA	NA	NA	NA	NA	0	0	0
Middle East and North Africa	17	18	NA	NA	NA	NA	NA	NA	NA	NA	NA	NA	NA	NA	NA	NA	17	18	34
South Asia	428	451	NA	NA	NA	NA	NA	NA	NA	NA	NA	NA	NA	NA	NA	NA	428	451	879
Sub-Saharan Africa	1,137	1,134	NA	NA	NA	NA	NA	NA	NA	NA	NA	NA	NA	NA	NA	NA	1,137	1,134	2,271
Low- and middle-income countries	1,681	1,706	NA	NA	NA	NA	NA	NA	NA	NA	NA	NA	NA	NA	NA	NA	1,681	1,706	3,388
High-income countries	0	0	NA	NA	NA	NA	NA	NA	NA	NA	NA	NA	NA	NA	NA	NA	0	0	0
WORLD	1,681	1,706	NA	NA	NA	NA	NA	NA	NA	NA	NA	NA	NA	NA	NA	NA	1,681	1,706	3,388
Attributable DALYs (thousands)																			
East Asia and Pacific	99	104	NA	NA	NA	NA	NA	NA	NA	NA	NA	NA	NA	NA	NA	NA	99	104	203
Europe and Central Asia	0	0	NA	NA	NA	NA	NA	NA	NA	NA	NA	NA	NA	NA	NA	NA	0	0	0
Latin America and the Caribbean	0	0	NA	NA	NA	NA	NA	NA	NA	NA	NA	NA	NA	NA	NA	NA	0	0	0
Middle East and North Africa	17	18	NA	NA	NA	NA	NA	NA	NA	NA	NA	NA	NA	NA	NA	NA	17	18	34
South Asia	428	451	NA	NA	NA	NA	NA	NA	NA	NA	NA	NA	NA	NA	NA	NA	428	451	879
Sub-Saharan Africa	1,137	1,134	NA	NA	NA	NA	NA	NA	NA	NA	NA	NA	NA	NA	NA	NA	1,137	1,134	2,271
Low- and middle-income countries	1,681	1,706	NA	NA	NA	NA	NA	NA	NA	NA	NA	NA	NA	NA	NA	NA	1,681	1,706	3,388
High-income countries	0	0	NA	NA	NA	NA	NA	NA	NA	NA	NA	NA	NA	NA	NA	NA	0	0	0
WORLD	1,681	1,706	NA	NA	NA	NA	NA	NA	NA	NA	NA	NA	NA	NA	NA	NA	1,681	1,706	3,388

Source: Authors' calculations.

Note: NA = not applicable.

*The number of deaths (and hence YLL) directly coded to a number of diseases, especially neuropsychiatric and musculoskeletal diseases, is zero or very small. For other diseases, mortality or disease burden may be zero in some region-age-sex groups. In such cases, the population attributable fractions would be undefined or unstable and have not been calculated.

Table 4A.14

Risk factor: Vitamin A deficiency
Disease: Malaria

Region	0–4 years Male	0–4 years Female	5–14 years Male	5–14 years Female	15–29 years Male	15–29 years Female	30–44 years Male	30–44 years Female	45–59 years Male	45–59 years Female	60–69 years Male	60–69 years Female	70–79 years Male	70–79 years Female	80+ years Male	80+ years Female	Total Male	Total Female	All
PAF of Mortality (%)																			
East Asia and Pacific	14	14	NA	NA	NA	NA	NA	NA	NA	NA	NA	NA	NA	NA	NA	NA	12	13	12
Europe and Central Asia	0	0	NA	NA	NA	NA	NA	NA	NA	NA	NA	NA	NA	NA	NA	NA	0	0	0
Latin America and the Caribbean	10	10	NA	NA	NA	NA	NA	NA	NA	NA	NA	NA	NA	NA	NA	NA	9	9	9
Middle East and North Africa	11	11	NA	NA	NA	NA	NA	NA	NA	NA	NA	NA	NA	NA	NA	NA	9	10	9
South Asia	19	19	NA	NA	NA	NA	NA	NA	NA	NA	NA	NA	NA	NA	NA	NA	17	17	17
Sub-Saharan Africa	20	20	NA	NA	NA	NA	NA	NA	NA	NA	NA	NA	NA	NA	NA	NA	18	18	18
Low- and middle-income countries	19	20	NA	NA	NA	NA	NA	NA	NA	NA	NA	NA	NA	NA	NA	NA	17	18	18
High-income countries	1	1	NA	NA	NA	NA	NA	NA	NA	NA	NA	NA	NA	NA	NA	NA	0	0	0
WORLD	19	20	NA	NA	NA	NA	NA	NA	NA	NA	NA	NA	NA	NA	NA	NA	17	18	18
PAF of YLL (%)																			
East Asia and Pacific	14	14	NA	NA	NA	NA	NA	NA	NA	NA	NA	NA	NA	NA	NA	NA	13	13	13
Europe and Central Asia	0	0	NA	NA	NA	NA	NA	NA	NA	NA	NA	NA	NA	NA	NA	NA	0	0	0
Latin America and the Caribbean	10	10	NA	NA	NA	NA	NA	NA	NA	NA	NA	NA	NA	NA	NA	NA	9	10	9
Middle East and North Africa	11	11	NA	NA	NA	NA	NA	NA	NA	NA	NA	NA	NA	NA	NA	NA	10	10	10
South Asia	19	19	NA	NA	NA	NA	NA	NA	NA	NA	NA	NA	NA	NA	NA	NA	17	17	17
Sub-Saharan Africa	20	20	NA	NA	NA	NA	NA	NA	NA	NA	NA	NA	NA	NA	NA	NA	18	18	18
Low- and middle-income countries	19	20	NA	NA	NA	NA	NA	NA	NA	NA	NA	NA	NA	NA	NA	NA	18	18	18
High-income countries	1	1	NA	NA	NA	NA	NA	NA	NA	NA	NA	NA	NA	NA	NA	NA	0	0	0
WORLD	19	20	NA	NA	NA	NA	NA	NA	NA	NA	NA	NA	NA	NA	NA	NA	18	18	18
PAF of DALYs (%)																			
East Asia and Pacific	14	14	NA	NA	NA	NA	NA	NA	NA	NA	NA	NA	NA	NA	NA	NA	11	10	11
Europe and Central Asia	0	0	NA	NA	NA	NA	NA	NA	NA	NA	NA	NA	NA	NA	NA	NA	0	0	0
Latin America and the Caribbean	10	10	NA	NA	NA	NA	NA	NA	NA	NA	NA	NA	NA	NA	NA	NA	6	5	6
Middle East and North Africa	11	11	NA	NA	NA	NA	NA	NA	NA	NA	NA	NA	NA	NA	NA	NA	9	9	9
South Asia	19	19	NA	NA	NA	NA	NA	NA	NA	NA	NA	NA	NA	NA	NA	NA	14	14	14
Sub-Saharan Africa	20	20	NA	NA	NA	NA	NA	NA	NA	NA	NA	NA	NA	NA	NA	NA	18	18	18
Low- and middle-income countries	19	20	NA	NA	NA	NA	NA	NA	NA	NA	NA	NA	NA	NA	NA	NA	18	18	18
High-income countries	1	1	NA	NA	NA	NA	NA	NA	NA	NA	NA	NA	NA	NA	NA	NA	0	0	0
WORLD	19	20	NA	NA	NA	NA	NA	NA	NA	NA	NA	NA	NA	NA	NA	NA	18	18	18
Attributable Mortality (thousands)																			
East Asia and Pacific	3	1	NA	NA	NA	NA	NA	NA	NA	NA	NA	NA	NA	NA	NA	NA	3	1	4
Europe and Central Asia	0	0	NA	NA	NA	NA	NA	NA	NA	NA	NA	NA	NA	NA	NA	NA	0	0	0
Latin America and the Caribbean	0	0	NA	NA	NA	NA	NA	NA	NA	NA	NA	NA	NA	NA	NA	NA	0	0	0
Middle East and North Africa	1	1	NA	NA	NA	NA	NA	NA	NA	NA	NA	NA	NA	NA	NA	NA	1	1	2
South Asia	5	6	NA	NA	NA	NA	NA	NA	NA	NA	NA	NA	NA	NA	NA	NA	5	6	11
Sub-Saharan Africa	92	103	NA	NA	NA	NA	NA	NA	NA	NA	NA	NA	NA	NA	NA	NA	92	103	195
Low- and middle-income countries	101	110	NA	NA	NA	NA	NA	NA	NA	NA	NA	NA	NA	NA	NA	NA	101	110	211
High-income countries	0	0	NA	NA	NA	NA	NA	NA	NA	NA	NA	NA	NA	NA	NA	NA	0	0	0
WORLD	101	110	NA	NA	NA	NA	NA	NA	NA	NA	NA	NA	NA	NA	NA	NA	101	110	211
Attributable YLL (thousands)																			
East Asia and Pacific	76	35	NA	NA	NA	NA	NA	NA	NA	NA	NA	NA	NA	NA	NA	NA	76	35	111
Europe and Central Asia	0	0	NA	NA	NA	NA	NA	NA	NA	NA	NA	NA	NA	NA	NA	NA	0	0	0
Latin America and the Caribbean	3	2	NA	NA	NA	NA	NA	NA	NA	NA	NA	NA	NA	NA	NA	NA	3	2	4
Middle East and North Africa	26	29	NA	NA	NA	NA	NA	NA	NA	NA	NA	NA	NA	NA	NA	NA	26	29	54
South Asia	152	170	NA	NA	NA	NA	NA	NA	NA	NA	NA	NA	NA	NA	NA	NA	152	170	322
Sub-Saharan Africa	2,794	3,125	NA	NA	NA	NA	NA	NA	NA	NA	NA	NA	NA	NA	NA	NA	2,794	3,125	5,919
Low- and middle-income countries	3,050	3,360	NA	NA	NA	NA	NA	NA	NA	NA	NA	NA	NA	NA	NA	NA	3,050	3,360	6,410
High-income countries	0	0	NA	NA	NA	NA	NA	NA	NA	NA	NA	NA	NA	NA	NA	NA	0	0	0
WORLD	3,050	3,360	NA	NA	NA	NA	NA	NA	NA	NA	NA	NA	NA	NA	NA	NA	3,050	3,360	6,410
Attributable DALYs (thousands)																			
East Asia and Pacific	81	40	NA	NA	NA	NA	NA	NA	NA	NA	NA	NA	NA	NA	NA	NA	81	40	121
Europe and Central Asia	0	0	NA	NA	NA	NA	NA	NA	NA	NA	NA	NA	NA	NA	NA	NA	0	0	0
Latin America and the Caribbean	4	3	NA	NA	NA	NA	NA	NA	NA	NA	NA	NA	NA	NA	NA	NA	4	3	6
Middle East and North Africa	28	31	NA	NA	NA	NA	NA	NA	NA	NA	NA	NA	NA	NA	NA	NA	28	31	59
South Asia	176	193	NA	NA	NA	NA	NA	NA	NA	NA	NA	NA	NA	NA	NA	NA	176	193	369
Sub-Saharan Africa	3,069	3,397	NA	NA	NA	NA	NA	NA	NA	NA	NA	NA	NA	NA	NA	NA	3,069	3,397	6,466
Low- and middle-income countries	3,358	3,663	NA	NA	NA	NA	NA	NA	NA	NA	NA	NA	NA	NA	NA	NA	3,358	3,663	7,021
High-income countries	0	0	NA	NA	NA	NA	NA	NA	NA	NA	NA	NA	NA	NA	NA	NA	0	0	0
WORLD	3,358	3,663	NA	NA	NA	NA	NA	NA	NA	NA	NA	NA	NA	NA	NA	NA	3,358	3,663	7,021

Source: Authors' calculations.
Note: NA = not applicable.

Table 4A.15

Risk factor: Vitamin A deficiency
Disease: Other infectious diseases

Region	0–4 years Male	Female	5–14 years Male	Female	15–29 years Male	Female	30–44 years Male	Female	45–59 years Male	Female	60–69 years Male	Female	70–79 years Male	Female	80+ years Male	Female	Total Male	Female	All
PAF of Mortality (%)																			
East Asia and Pacific	3	3	NA	NA	NA	NA	NA	NA	NA	NA	NA	NA	NA	NA	NA	NA	1	1	1
Europe and Central Asia	0	0	NA	NA	NA	NA	NA	NA	NA	NA	NA	NA	NA	NA	NA	NA	0	0	0
Latin America and the Caribbean	2	2	NA	NA	NA	NA	NA	NA	NA	NA	NA	NA	NA	NA	NA	NA	1	0	0
Middle East and North Africa	2	2	NA	NA	NA	NA	NA	NA	NA	NA	NA	NA	NA	NA	NA	NA	1	1	1
South Asia	4	4	NA	NA	NA	NA	NA	NA	NA	NA	NA	NA	NA	NA	NA	NA	1	1	1
Sub-Saharan Africa	4	4	NA	NA	NA	NA	NA	NA	NA	NA	NA	NA	NA	NA	NA	NA	2	2	2
Low- and middle-income countries	3	4	NA	NA	NA	NA	NA	NA	NA	NA	NA	NA	NA	NA	NA	NA	1	1	1
High-income countries	0	0	NA	NA	NA	NA	NA	NA	NA	NA	NA	NA	NA	NA	NA	NA	0	0	0
WORLD	3	4	NA	NA	NA	NA	NA	NA	NA	NA	NA	NA	NA	NA	NA	NA	1	1	1
PAF of YLL (%)																			
East Asia and Pacific	3	3	NA	NA	NA	NA	NA	NA	NA	NA	NA	NA	NA	NA	NA	NA	1	1	1
Europe and Central Asia	0	0	NA	NA	NA	NA	NA	NA	NA	NA	NA	NA	NA	NA	NA	NA	0	0	0
Latin America and the Caribbean	2	2	NA	NA	NA	NA	NA	NA	NA	NA	NA	NA	NA	NA	NA	NA	1	1	1
Middle East and North Africa	2	2	NA	NA	NA	NA	NA	NA	NA	NA	NA	NA	NA	NA	NA	NA	1	1	1
South Asia	4	4	NA	NA	NA	NA	NA	NA	NA	NA	NA	NA	NA	NA	NA	NA	1	2	1
Sub-Saharan Africa	4	4	NA	NA	NA	NA	NA	NA	NA	NA	NA	NA	NA	NA	NA	NA	2	2	2
Low- and middle-income countries	3	4	NA	NA	NA	NA	NA	NA	NA	NA	NA	NA	NA	NA	NA	NA	1	2	1
High-income countries	0	0	NA	NA	NA	NA	NA	NA	NA	NA	NA	NA	NA	NA	NA	NA	0	0	0
WORLD	3	4	NA	NA	NA	NA	NA	NA	NA	NA	NA	NA	NA	NA	NA	NA	1	2	1
PAF of DALYs (%)																			
East Asia and Pacific	2	2	NA	NA	NA	NA	NA	NA	NA	NA	NA	NA	NA	NA	NA	NA	1	1	1
Europe and Central Asia	0	0	NA	NA	NA	NA	NA	NA	NA	NA	NA	NA	NA	NA	NA	NA	0	0	0
Latin America and the Caribbean	2	2	NA	NA	NA	NA	NA	NA	NA	NA	NA	NA	NA	NA	NA	NA	1	1	1
Middle East and North Africa	2	2	NA	NA	NA	NA	NA	NA	NA	NA	NA	NA	NA	NA	NA	NA	1	1	1
South Asia	3	3	NA	NA	NA	NA	NA	NA	NA	NA	NA	NA	NA	NA	NA	NA	1	1	1
Sub-Saharan Africa	4	4	NA	NA	NA	NA	NA	NA	NA	NA	NA	NA	NA	NA	NA	NA	2	2	2
Low- and middle-income countries	3	3	NA	NA	NA	NA	NA	NA	NA	NA	NA	NA	NA	NA	NA	NA	1	1	1
High-income countries	0	0	NA	NA	NA	NA	NA	NA	NA	NA	NA	NA	NA	NA	NA	NA	0	0	0
WORLD	3	3	NA	NA	NA	NA	NA	NA	NA	NA	NA	NA	NA	NA	NA	NA	1	1	1
Attributable Mortality (thousands)																			
East Asia and Pacific	1	0	NA	NA	NA	NA	NA	NA	NA	NA	NA	NA	NA	NA	NA	NA	1	0	1
Europe and Central Asia	0	0	NA	NA	NA	NA	NA	NA	NA	NA	NA	NA	NA	NA	NA	NA	0	0	0
Latin America and the Caribbean	0	0	NA	NA	NA	NA	NA	NA	NA	NA	NA	NA	NA	NA	NA	NA	0	0	0
Middle East and North Africa	0	0	NA	NA	NA	NA	NA	NA	NA	NA	NA	NA	NA	NA	NA	NA	0	0	0
South Asia	2	4	NA	NA	NA	NA	NA	NA	NA	NA	NA	NA	NA	NA	NA	NA	2	4	6
Sub-Saharan Africa	5	5	NA	NA	NA	NA	NA	NA	NA	NA	NA	NA	NA	NA	NA	NA	5	5	9
Low- and middle-income countries	7	10	NA	NA	NA	NA	NA	NA	NA	NA	NA	NA	NA	NA	NA	NA	7	10	17
High-income countries	0	0	NA	NA	NA	NA	NA	NA	NA	NA	NA	NA	NA	NA	NA	NA	0	0	0
WORLD	7	10	NA	NA	NA	NA	NA	NA	NA	NA	NA	NA	NA	NA	NA	NA	7	10	17
Attributable YLL (thousands)																			
East Asia and Pacific	19	14	NA	NA	NA	NA	NA	NA	NA	NA	NA	NA	NA	NA	NA	NA	19	14	33
Europe and Central Asia	0	0	NA	NA	NA	NA	NA	NA	NA	NA	NA	NA	NA	NA	NA	NA	0	0	0
Latin America and the Caribbean	7	5	NA	NA	NA	NA	NA	NA	NA	NA	NA	NA	NA	NA	NA	NA	7	5	12
Middle East and North Africa	6	6	NA	NA	NA	NA	NA	NA	NA	NA	NA	NA	NA	NA	NA	NA	6	6	13
South Asia	47	129	NA	NA	NA	NA	NA	NA	NA	NA	NA	NA	NA	NA	NA	NA	47	129	175
Sub-Saharan Africa	138	144	NA	NA	NA	NA	NA	NA	NA	NA	NA	NA	NA	NA	NA	NA	138	144	282
Low- and middle-income countries	217	297	NA	NA	NA	NA	NA	NA	NA	NA	NA	NA	NA	NA	NA	NA	217	297	515
High-income countries	0	0	NA	NA	NA	NA	NA	NA	NA	NA	NA	NA	NA	NA	NA	NA	0	0	0
WORLD	217	298	NA	NA	NA	NA	NA	NA	NA	NA	NA	NA	NA	NA	NA	NA	217	298	515
Attributable DALYs (thousands)																			
East Asia and Pacific	19	14	NA	NA	NA	NA	NA	NA	NA	NA	NA	NA	NA	NA	NA	NA	19	14	33
Europe and Central Asia	0	0	NA	NA	NA	NA	NA	NA	NA	NA	NA	NA	NA	NA	NA	NA	0	0	0
Latin America and the Caribbean	7	5	NA	NA	NA	NA	NA	NA	NA	NA	NA	NA	NA	NA	NA	NA	7	5	12
Middle East and North Africa	6	6	NA	NA	NA	NA	NA	NA	NA	NA	NA	NA	NA	NA	NA	NA	6	6	13
South Asia	47	129	NA	NA	NA	NA	NA	NA	NA	NA	NA	NA	NA	NA	NA	NA	47	129	175
Sub-Saharan Africa	138	144	NA	NA	NA	NA	NA	NA	NA	NA	NA	NA	NA	NA	NA	NA	138	144	282
Low- and middle-income countries	217	297	NA	NA	NA	NA	NA	NA	NA	NA	NA	NA	NA	NA	NA	NA	217	297	515
High-income countries	0	0	NA	NA	NA	NA	NA	NA	NA	NA	NA	NA	NA	NA	NA	NA	0	0	0
WORLD	217	298	NA	NA	NA	NA	NA	NA	NA	NA	NA	NA	NA	NA	NA	NA	217	298	515

Source: Authors' calculations.
Note: NA = not applicable.

Table 4A.16

Risk factor: Vitamin A deficiency
Disease: Selected maternal conditions

Region	0–4 years Male	Female	5–14 years Male	Female	15–29 years Male	Female	30–44 years Male	Female	45–59 years Male	Female	60–69 years Male	Female	70–79 years Male	Female	80+ years Male	Female	Total Male	Female	All
PAF of Mortality (%)																			
East Asia and Pacific	NA	NA	NA	NA	NA	16	NA	16	NA	NA	NA	NA	NA	NA	NA	NA	NA	16	16
Europe and Central Asia	NA	NA	NA	NA	NA	0	NA	0	NA	NA	NA	NA	NA	NA	NA	NA	NA	0	0
Latin America and the Caribbean	NA	NA	NA	NA	NA	10	NA	10	NA	NA	NA	NA	NA	NA	NA	NA	NA	10	10
Middle East and North Africa	NA	NA	NA	NA	NA	13	NA	14	NA	NA	NA	NA	NA	NA	NA	NA	NA	13	13
South Asia	NA	NA	NA	NA	NA	17	NA	17	NA	NA	NA	NA	NA	NA	NA	NA	NA	17	17
Sub-Saharan Africa	NA	NA	NA	NA	NA	26	NA	26	NA	NA	NA	NA	NA	NA	NA	NA	NA	24	24
Low- and middle-income countries	NA	NA	NA	NA	NA	21	NA	21	NA	NA	NA	NA	NA	NA	NA	NA	NA	20	20
High-income countries	NA	NA	NA	NA	NA	1	NA	1	NA	NA	NA	NA	NA	NA	NA	NA	NA	1	1
WORLD	NA	NA	NA	NA	NA	21	NA	21	NA	NA	NA	NA	NA	NA	NA	NA	NA	20	20
PAF of YLL (%)																			
East Asia and Pacific	NA	NA	NA	NA	NA	16	NA	16	NA	NA	NA	NA	NA	NA	NA	NA	NA	16	16
Europe and Central Asia	NA	NA	NA	NA	NA	0	NA	0	NA	NA	NA	NA	NA	NA	NA	NA	NA	0	0
Latin America and the Caribbean	NA	NA	NA	NA	NA	10	NA	10	NA	NA	NA	NA	NA	NA	NA	NA	NA	10	10
Middle East and North Africa	NA	NA	NA	NA	NA	13	NA	14	NA	NA	NA	NA	NA	NA	NA	NA	NA	13	13
South Asia	NA	NA	NA	NA	NA	17	NA	17	NA	NA	NA	NA	NA	NA	NA	NA	NA	17	17
Sub-Saharan Africa	NA	NA	NA	NA	NA	26	NA	26	NA	NA	NA	NA	NA	NA	NA	NA	NA	24	24
Low- and middle-income countries	NA	NA	NA	NA	NA	21	NA	21	NA	NA	NA	NA	NA	NA	NA	NA	NA	20	20
High-income countries	NA	NA	NA	NA	NA	1	NA	1	NA	NA	NA	NA	NA	NA	NA	NA	NA	1	1
WORLD	NA	NA	NA	NA	NA	21	NA	21	NA	NA	NA	NA	NA	NA	NA	NA	NA	20	20
PAF of DALYs (%)																			
East Asia and Pacific	NA	NA	NA	NA	NA	3	NA	10	NA	NA	NA	NA	NA	NA	NA	NA	NA	5	5
Europe and Central Asia	NA	NA	NA	NA	NA	0	NA	0	NA	NA	NA	NA	NA	NA	NA	NA	NA	0	0
Latin America and the Caribbean	NA	NA	NA	NA	NA	2	NA	5	NA	NA	NA	NA	NA	NA	NA	NA	NA	2	2
Middle East and North Africa	NA	NA	NA	NA	NA	3	NA	7	NA	NA	NA	NA	NA	NA	NA	NA	NA	4	4
South Asia	NA	NA	NA	NA	NA	8	NA	14	NA	NA	NA	NA	NA	NA	NA	NA	NA	10	10
Sub-Saharan Africa	NA	NA	NA	NA	NA	17	NA	22	NA	NA	NA	NA	NA	NA	NA	NA	NA	18	18
Low- and middle-income countries	NA	NA	NA	NA	NA	10	NA	16	NA	NA	NA	NA	NA	NA	NA	NA	NA	12	12
High-income countries	NA	NA	NA	NA	NA	0	NA	0	NA	NA	NA	NA	NA	NA	NA	NA	NA	0	0
WORLD	NA	NA	NA	NA	NA	10	NA	16	NA	NA	NA	NA	NA	NA	NA	NA	NA	12	12
Attributable Mortality (thousands)																			
East Asia and Pacific	NA	NA	NA	NA	NA	1	NA	1	NA	NA	NA	NA	NA	NA	NA	NA	NA	3	3
Europe and Central Asia	NA	NA	NA	NA	NA	0	NA	0	NA	NA	NA	NA	NA	NA	NA	NA	NA	0	0
Latin America and the Caribbean	NA	NA	NA	NA	NA	0	NA	0	NA	NA	NA	NA	NA	NA	NA	NA	NA	0	0
Middle East and North Africa	NA	NA	NA	NA	NA	0	NA	0	NA	NA	NA	NA	NA	NA	NA	NA	NA	1	1
South Asia	NA	NA	NA	NA	NA	9	NA	9	NA	NA	NA	NA	NA	NA	NA	NA	NA	18	18
Sub-Saharan Africa	NA	NA	NA	NA	NA	16	NA	14	NA	NA	NA	NA	NA	NA	NA	NA	NA	30	30
Low- and middle-income countries	NA	NA	NA	NA	NA	27	NA	26	NA	NA	NA	NA	NA	NA	NA	NA	NA	52	52
High-income countries	NA	NA	NA	NA	NA	0	NA	0	NA	NA	NA	NA	NA	NA	NA	NA	NA	0	0
WORLD	NA	NA	NA	NA	NA	27	NA	26	NA	NA	NA	NA	NA	NA	NA	NA	NA	52	52
Attributable YLL (thousands)																			
East Asia and Pacific	NA	NA	NA	NA	NA	35	NA	37	NA	NA	NA	NA	NA	NA	NA	NA	NA	72	72
Europe and Central Asia	NA	NA	NA	NA	NA	0	NA	0	NA	NA	NA	NA	NA	NA	NA	NA	NA	0	0
Latin America and the Caribbean	NA	NA	NA	NA	NA	6	NA	6	NA	NA	NA	NA	NA	NA	NA	NA	NA	12	12
Middle East and North Africa	NA	NA	NA	NA	NA	9	NA	10	NA	NA	NA	NA	NA	NA	NA	NA	NA	19	19
South Asia	NA	NA	NA	NA	NA	249	NA	234	NA	NA	NA	NA	NA	NA	NA	NA	NA	482	482
Sub-Saharan Africa	NA	NA	NA	NA	NA	438	NA	355	NA	NA	NA	NA	NA	NA	NA	NA	NA	794	794
Low- and middle-income countries	NA	NA	NA	NA	NA	737	NA	642	NA	NA	NA	NA	NA	NA	NA	NA	NA	1,379	1,379
High-income countries	NA	NA	NA	NA	NA	0	NA	0	NA	NA	NA	NA	NA	NA	NA	NA	NA	0	0
WORLD	NA	NA	NA	NA	NA	737	NA	642	NA	NA	NA	NA	NA	NA	NA	NA	NA	1,379	1,379
Attributable DALYs (thousands)																			
East Asia and Pacific	NA	NA	NA	NA	NA	35	NA	37	NA	NA	NA	NA	NA	NA	NA	NA	NA	72	72
Europe and Central Asia	NA	NA	NA	NA	NA	0	NA	0	NA	NA	NA	NA	NA	NA	NA	NA	NA	0	0
Latin America and the Caribbean	NA	NA	NA	NA	NA	6	NA	6	NA	NA	NA	NA	NA	NA	NA	NA	NA	12	12
Middle East and North Africa	NA	NA	NA	NA	NA	9	NA	10	NA	NA	NA	NA	NA	NA	NA	NA	NA	19	19
South Asia	NA	NA	NA	NA	NA	249	NA	234	NA	NA	NA	NA	NA	NA	NA	NA	NA	482	482
Sub-Saharan Africa	NA	NA	NA	NA	NA	438	NA	355	NA	NA	NA	NA	NA	NA	NA	NA	NA	794	794
Low- and middle-income countries	NA	NA	NA	NA	NA	737	NA	642	NA	NA	NA	NA	NA	NA	NA	NA	NA	1,379	1,379
High-income countries	NA	NA	NA	NA	NA	0	NA	0	NA	NA	NA	NA	NA	NA	NA	NA	NA	0	0
WORLD	NA	NA	NA	NA	NA	737	NA	642	NA	NA	NA	NA	NA	NA	NA	NA	NA	1,379	1,379

Source: Authors' calculations.
Note: NA = not applicable.

Table 4A.17

Risk factor: Vitamin A deficiency
Disease: Vitamin A deficiency

Region	0–4 years Male	Female	5–14 years Male	Female	15–29 years Male	Female	30–44 years Male	Female	45–59 years Male	Female	60–69 years Male	Female	70–79 years Male	Female	80+ years Male	Female	Total Male	Female	All
PAF of Mortality (%)																			
East Asia and Pacific	100	100	100	100	100	100	100	100	100	100	100	100	100	100	100	100	100	100	100
Europe and Central Asia	100	100	100	100	100	100	100	100	100	100	100	100	100	100	100	100	100	100	100
Latin America and the Caribbean	100	100	100	100	100	100	100	100	100	100	100	100	100	100	100	100	100	100	100
Middle East and North Africa	100	100	100	100	100	100	100	100	100	100	100	100	100	100	100	100	100	100	100
South Asia	100	100	100	100	100	100	100	100	100	100	100	100	100	100	100	100	100	100	100
Sub-Saharan Africa	100	100	100	100	100	100	100	100	100	100	100	100	100	100	100	100	100	100	100
Low- and middle-income countries	100	100	100	100	100	100	100	100	100	100	100	100	100	100	100	100	100	100	100
High-income countries	100	100	100	100	100	100	100	100	100	100	100	100	100	100	100	100	100	100	100
WORLD	100	100	100	100	100	100	100	100	100	100	100	100	100	100	100	100	100	100	100
PAF of YLL (%)																			
East Asia and Pacific	100	100	100	100	100	100	100	100	100	100	100	100	100	100	100	100	100	100	100
Europe and Central Asia	100	100	100	100	100	100	100	100	100	100	100	100	100	100	100	100	100	100	100
Latin America and the Caribbean	100	100	100	100	100	100	100	100	100	100	100	100	100	100	100	100	100	100	100
Middle East and North Africa	100	100	100	100	100	100	100	100	100	100	100	100	100	100	100	100	100	100	100
South Asia	100	100	100	100	100	100	100	100	100	100	100	100	100	100	100	100	100	100	100
Sub-Saharan Africa	100	100	100	100	100	100	100	100	100	100	100	100	100	100	100	100	100	100	100
Low- and middle-income countries	100	100	100	100	100	100	100	100	100	100	100	100	100	100	100	100	100	100	100
High-income countries	100	100	100	100	100	100	100	100	100	100	100	100	100	100	100	100	100	100	100
WORLD	100	100	100	100	100	100	100	100	100	100	100	100	100	100	100	100	100	100	100
PAF of DALYs (%)																			
East Asia and Pacific	100	100	100	100	100	100	100	100	100	100	100	100	100	100	100	100	100	100	100
Europe and Central Asia	100	100	100	100	100	100	100	100	100	100	100	100	100	100	100	100	100	100	100
Latin America and the Caribbean	100	100	100	100	100	100	100	100	100	100	100	100	100	100	100	100	100	100	100
Middle East and North Africa	100	100	100	100	100	100	100	100	100	100	100	100	100	100	100	100	100	100	100
South Asia	100	100	100	100	100	100	100	100	100	100	100	100	100	100	100	100	100	100	100
Sub-Saharan Africa	100	100	100	100	100	100	100	100	100	100	100	100	100	100	100	100	100	100	100
Low- and middle-income countries	100	100	100	100	100	100	100	100	100	100	100	100	100	100	100	100	100	100	100
High-income countries	100	100	100	100	100	100	100	100	100	100	100	100	100	100	100	100	100	100	100
WORLD	100	100	100	100	100	100	100	100	100	100	100	100	100	100	100	100	100	100	100
Attributable Mortality (thousands)																			
East Asia and Pacific	0	0	0	0	0	0	0	0	0	0	0	0	0	0	0	0	0	0	0
Europe and Central Asia	0	0	0	0	0	0	0	0	0	0	0	0	0	0	0	0	0	0	0
Latin America and the Caribbean	0	0	0	0	0	0	0	0	0	0	0	0	0	0	0	0	0	0	0
Middle East and North Africa	0	0	0	0	0	0	0	0	0	0	0	0	0	0	0	0	0	0	0
South Asia	0	1	1	1	0	0	0	0	0	0	0	0	0	0	0	0	2	2	4
Sub-Saharan Africa	7	8	1	1	0	0	0	0	0	0	0	0	0	0	0	0	8	10	18
Low- and middle-income countries	7	9	2	2	0	0	0	0	1	0	0	0	0	0	0	0	11	12	23
High-income countries	0	0	0	0	0	0	0	0	0	0	0	0	0	0	0	0	0	0	0
WORLD	7	9	2	2	0	0	0	0	1	0	0	0	0	0	0	0	11	12	23
Attributable YLL (thousands)																			
East Asia and Pacific	1	0	2	1	0	0	1	0	0	0	0	0	0	0	0	0	5	1	6
Europe and Central Asia	0	0	0	0	0	0	0	0	0	0	0	0	0	0	0	0	0	0	0
Latin America and the Caribbean	0	0	0	0	0	0	0	0	0	0	0	0	0	0	0	0	0	0	1
Middle East and North Africa	0	0	0	0	0	0	0	0	0	0	0	0	0	0	0	0	2	2	4
South Asia	14	37	43	27	0	0	0	0	0	0	0	0	0	0	0	0	57	65	121
Sub-Saharan Africa	196	229	16	33	2	8	5	4	9	8	5	3	1	1	0	0	235	285	520
Low- and middle-income countries	211	267	61	61	3	9	6	4	10	8	5	3	2	2	0	0	298	353	652
High-income countries	0	0	0	0	0	0	0	0	0	0	0	0	0	0	0	0	0	1	1
WORLD	211	267	61	61	3	9	6	4	10	8	5	3	2	2	0	0	298	354	652
Attributable DALYs (thousands)																			
East Asia and Pacific	2	2	3	2	0	0	1	0	0	0	0	0	0	0	0	0	7	3	10
Europe and Central Asia	0	0	0	0	0	0	0	0	0	0	0	0	0	0	0	0	0	1	1
Latin America and the Caribbean	0	0	0	0	0	0	0	0	0	0	0	0	0	0	0	0	0	0	1
Middle East and North Africa	1	1	0	0	0	0	0	0	0	0	0	0	0	0	0	0	3	2	5
South Asia	23	46	46	30	0	0	0	0	0	0	0	0	0	0	0	0	70	77	146
Sub-Saharan Africa	206	238	20	37	2	8	5	4	9	8	5	3	1	1	0	0	249	299	548
Low- and middle-income countries	232	287	70	69	3	9	6	4	10	8	5	3	2	2	0	0	328	382	710
High-income countries	0	0	0	0	0	0	0	0	0	0	0	0	0	0	0	0	0	1	1
WORLD	232	287	70	70	3	9	6	4	10	8	5	3	2	2	0	0	328	382	711

Source: Authors' calculations.

Table 4A.18

Risk factor: Vitamin A deficiency
Disease: All causes

Region	0–4 years Male	0–4 years Female	5–14 years Male	5–14 years Female	15–29 years Male	15–29 years Female	30–44 years Male	30–44 years Female	45–59 years Male	45–59 years Female	60–69 years Male	60–69 years Female	70–79 years Male	70–79 years Female	80+ years Male	80+ years Female	Total Male	Total Female	All
PAF of Mortality (%)																			
East Asia and Pacific	4	3	0	0	0	1	0	0	0	0	0	0	0	0	0	0	0	0	0
Europe and Central Asia	0	0	0	0	0	0	0	0	0	0	0	0	0	0	0	0	0	0	0
Latin America and the Caribbean	2	2	0	0	0	0	0	0	0	0	0	0	0	0	0	0	0	0	0
Middle East and North Africa	3	3	0	0	0	1	0	1	0	0	0	0	0	0	0	0	1	1	1
South Asia	6	6	1	0	0	2	0	2	0	0	0	0	0	0	0	0	1	2	2
Sub-Saharan Africa	10	11	0	0	0	2	0	2	0	0	0	0	0	0	0	0	4	5	5
Low- and middle-income countries	7	7	0	0	0	2	0	1	0	0	0	0	0	0	0	0	1	2	2
High-income countries	0	0	0	0	0	0	0	0	0	0	0	0	0	0	0	0	0	0	0
WORLD	7	7	0	0	0	2	0	1	0	0	0	0	0	0	0	0	1	2	1
PAF of YLL (%)																			
East Asia and Pacific	4	3	0	0	0	1	0	0	0	0	0	0	0	0	0	0	1	1	1
Europe and Central Asia	0	0	0	0	0	0	0	0	0	0	0	0	0	0	0	0	0	0	0
Latin America and the Caribbean	2	2	0	0	0	0	0	0	0	0	0	0	0	0	0	0	0	1	0
Middle East and North Africa	3	3	0	0	0	1	0	1	0	0	0	0	0	0	0	0	1	1	1
South Asia	6	6	0	0	0	2	0	2	0	0	0	0	0	0	0	0	2	3	2
Sub-Saharan Africa	10	11	0	0	0	2	0	2	0	0	0	0	0	0	0	0	5	6	6
Low- and middle-income countries	7	7	0	0	0	2	0	1	0	0	0	0	0	0	0	0	2	3	3
High-income countries	0	0	0	0	0	0	0	0	0	0	0	0	0	0	0	0	0	0	0
WORLD	7	7	0	0	0	2	0	1	0	0	0	0	0	0	0	0	2	3	2
PAF of DALYs (%)																			
East Asia and Pacific	2	2	0	0	0	0	0	0	0	0	0	0	0	0	0	0	0	0	0
Europe and Central Asia	0	0	0	0	0	0	0	0	0	0	0	0	0	0	0	0	0	0	0
Latin America and the Caribbean	1	1	0	0	0	0	0	0	0	0	0	0	0	0	0	0	0	0	0
Middle East and North Africa	2	2	0	0	0	0	0	0	0	0	0	0	0	0	0	0	1	1	1
South Asia	4	4	0	0	0	1	0	1	0	0	0	0	0	0	0	0	2	2	2
Sub-Saharan Africa	9	10	0	0	0	2	0	2	0	0	0	0	0	0	0	0	4	5	5
Low- and middle-income countries	5	6	0	0	0	1	0	1	0	0	0	0	0	0	0	0	2	2	2
High-income countries	0	0	0	0	0	0	0	0	0	0	0	0	0	0	0	0	0	0	0
WORLD	5	6	0	0	0	1	0	1	0	0	0	0	0	0	0	0	1	2	2
Attributable Mortality (thousands)																			
East Asia and Pacific	26	23	NA	0	0	1	0	1	0	0	0	0	0	0	0	0	26	26	52
Europe and Central Asia	0	0	0	0	0	0	0	0	0	0	0	0	0	0	0	0	0	0	0
Latin America and the Caribbean	4	3	0	0	0	0	0	0	0	0	0	0	0	0	0	0	4	4	8
Middle East and North Africa	7	6	0	0	0	0	0	0	0	0	0	0	0	0	0	0	7	7	14
South Asia	104	102	1	1	0	9	0	9	0	0	0	0	0	0	0	0	105	121	226
Sub-Saharan Africa	231	234	1	1	0	16	0	14	0	0	0	0	0	0	0	0	233	266	499
Low- and middle-income countries	372	369	2	2	0	27	0	26	1	0	0	0	0	0	0	0	376	424	800
High-income countries	0	0	0	0	0	0	0	0	0	0	0	0	0	0	0	0	0	0	0
WORLD	372	369	2	2	0	27	0	26	1	0	0	0	0	0	0	0	376	424	800
Attributable YLL (thousands)																			
East Asia and Pacific	794	708	2	1	0	35	1	37	0	0	0	0	0	0	0	0	798	781	1,578
Europe and Central Asia	0	0	0	0	0	0	0	0	0	0	0	0	0	0	0	0	0	0	1
Latin America and the Caribbean	118	105	0	0	0	6	0	6	0	0	0	0	0	0	0	0	118	117	235
Middle East and North Africa	204	197	0	0	0	9	0	10	0	0	0	0	0	0	0	0	206	218	423
South Asia	3,140	3,095	43	27	0	249	0	234	0	0	0	0	0	0	0	0	3,184	3,605	6,788
Sub-Saharan Africa	6,985	7,117	16	33	2	447	5	359	9	8	5	3	1	1	0	0	7,023	7,968	14,991
Low- and middle-income countries	11,241	11,222	61	61	3	746	6	646	10	8	5	3	2	2	0	0	11,329	12,688	24,017
High-income countries	0	0	0	0	0	0	0	0	0	0	0	0	0	0	0	0	0	1	1
WORLD	11,241	11,222	61	61	3	746	6	646	10	8	5	3	2	2	0	0	11,329	12,689	24,017
Attributable DALYs (thousands)																			
East Asia and Pacific	800	714	3	2	0	35	1	37	0	0	0	0	0	0	0	0	805	787	1,592
Europe and Central Asia	1	1	0	0	0	0	0	0	0	0	0	0	0	0	0	0	1	1	2
Latin America and the Caribbean	119	106	0	0	0	6	0	6	0	0	0	0	0	0	0	0	119	118	237
Middle East and North Africa	207	200	0	0	0	9	0	10	0	0	0	0	0	0	0	0	209	221	430
South Asia	3,174	3,127	46	30	0	249	0	234	0	0	0	0	0	0	0	0	3,220	3,640	6,860
Sub-Saharan Africa	7,269	7,399	20	37	2	447	5	359	9	8	5	3	1	1	0	0	7,312	8,253	15,565
Low- and middle-income countries	11,570	11,546	70	69	3	746	6	646	10	8	5	3	2	2	0	0	11,666	13,020	24,686
High-income countries	0	0	0	0	0	0	0	0	0	0	0	0	0	0	0	0	0	1	1
WORLD	11,570	11,546	70	70	3	746	6	646	10	8	5	3	2	2	0	0	11,666	13,020	24,686

Source: Authors' calculations.

Table 4A.19

Risk factor: Zinc deficiency
Disease: Diarrheal diseases

Region	0–4 years		5–14 years		15–29 years		30–44 years		45–59 years		60–69 years		70–79 years		80+ years		Total		
	Male	Female	Male	Female	Male	Female	Male	Female	Male	Female	Male	Female	Male	Female	Male	Female	Male	Female	All
PAF of Mortality (%)																			
East Asia and Pacific	4	4	NA	NA	NA	NA	NA	NA	NA	NA	NA	NA	NA	NA	NA	NA	4	4	4
Europe and Central Asia	3	3	NA	NA	NA	NA	NA	NA	NA	NA	NA	NA	NA	NA	NA	NA	2	2	2
Latin America and the Caribbean	8	8	NA	NA	NA	NA	NA	NA	NA	NA	NA	NA	NA	NA	NA	NA	7	7	7
Middle East and North Africa	10	10	NA	NA	NA	NA	NA	NA	NA	NA	NA	NA	NA	NA	NA	NA	9	9	9
South Asia	16	16	NA	NA	NA	NA	NA	NA	NA	NA	NA	NA	NA	NA	NA	NA	15	15	15
Sub-Saharan Africa	12	12	NA	NA	NA	NA	NA	NA	NA	NA	NA	NA	NA	NA	NA	NA	11	11	11
Low- and middle-income countries	13	13	NA	NA	NA	NA	NA	NA	NA	NA	NA	NA	NA	NA	NA	NA	11	11	11
High-income countries	1	1	NA	NA	NA	NA	NA	NA	NA	NA	NA	NA	NA	NA	NA	NA	0	0	0
WORLD	13	13	NA	NA	NA	NA	NA	NA	NA	NA	NA	NA	NA	NA	NA	NA	11	11	11
PAF of YLL (%)																			
East Asia and Pacific	4	4	NA	NA	NA	NA	NA	NA	NA	NA	NA	NA	NA	NA	NA	NA	4	4	4
Europe and Central Asia	3	3	NA	NA	NA	NA	NA	NA	NA	NA	NA	NA	NA	NA	NA	NA	2	2	2
Latin America and the Caribbean	8	8	NA	NA	NA	NA	NA	NA	NA	NA	NA	NA	NA	NA	NA	NA	8	8	8
Middle East and North Africa	10	10	NA	NA	NA	NA	NA	NA	NA	NA	NA	NA	NA	NA	NA	NA	9	10	9
South Asia	16	16	NA	NA	NA	NA	NA	NA	NA	NA	NA	NA	NA	NA	NA	NA	15	16	16
Sub-Saharan Africa	12	12	NA	NA	NA	NA	NA	NA	NA	NA	NA	NA	NA	NA	NA	NA	12	12	12
Low- and middle-income countries	13	13	NA	NA	NA	NA	NA	NA	NA	NA	NA	NA	NA	NA	NA	NA	12	12	12
High-income countries	1	1	NA	NA	NA	NA	NA	NA	NA	NA	NA	NA	NA	NA	NA	NA	0	0	0
WORLD	13	13	NA	NA	NA	NA	NA	NA	NA	NA	NA	NA	NA	NA	NA	NA	12	12	12
PAF of DALYs (%)																			
East Asia and Pacific	4	4	NA	NA	NA	NA	NA	NA	NA	NA	NA	NA	NA	NA	NA	NA	3	3	3
Europe and Central Asia	3	3	NA	NA	NA	NA	NA	NA	NA	NA	NA	NA	NA	NA	NA	NA	2	2	2
Latin America and the Caribbean	8	8	NA	NA	NA	NA	NA	NA	NA	NA	NA	NA	NA	NA	NA	NA	7	7	7
Middle East and North Africa	10	10	NA	NA	NA	NA	NA	NA	NA	NA	NA	NA	NA	NA	NA	NA	9	9	9
South Asia	16	16	NA	NA	NA	NA	NA	NA	NA	NA	NA	NA	NA	NA	NA	NA	15	15	15
Sub-Saharan Africa	12	12	NA	NA	NA	NA	NA	NA	NA	NA	NA	NA	NA	NA	NA	NA	12	12	12
Low- and middle-income countries	12	12	NA	NA	NA	NA	NA	NA	NA	NA	NA	NA	NA	NA	NA	NA	11	11	11
High-income countries	1	1	NA	NA	NA	NA	NA	NA	NA	NA	NA	NA	NA	NA	NA	NA	1	1	1
WORLD	12	12	NA	NA	NA	NA	NA	NA	NA	NA	NA	NA	NA	NA	NA	NA	11	11	11
Attributable Mortality (thousands)																			
East Asia and Pacific	4	4	NA	NA	NA	NA	NA	NA	NA	NA	NA	NA	NA	NA	NA	NA	4	4	9
Europe and Central Asia	0	0	NA	NA	NA	NA	NA	NA	NA	NA	NA	NA	NA	NA	NA	NA	0	0	0
Latin America and the Caribbean	2	2	NA	NA	NA	NA	NA	NA	NA	NA	NA	NA	NA	NA	NA	NA	2	2	4
Middle East and North Africa	3	3	NA	NA	NA	NA	NA	NA	NA	NA	NA	NA	NA	NA	NA	NA	3	3	7
South Asia	53	49	NA	NA	NA	NA	NA	NA	NA	NA	NA	NA	NA	NA	NA	NA	53	49	102
Sub-Saharan Africa	42	38	NA	NA	NA	NA	NA	NA	NA	NA	NA	NA	NA	NA	NA	NA	42	38	80
Low- and middle-income countries	105	96	NA	NA	NA	NA	NA	NA	NA	NA	NA	NA	NA	NA	NA	NA	105	96	201
High-income countries	0	0	NA	NA	NA	NA	NA	NA	NA	NA	NA	NA	NA	NA	NA	NA	0	0	0
WORLD	105	96	NA	NA	NA	NA	NA	NA	NA	NA	NA	NA	NA	NA	NA	NA	105	96	201
Attributable YLL (thousands)																			
East Asia and Pacific	134	125	NA	NA	NA	NA	NA	NA	NA	NA	NA	NA	NA	NA	NA	NA	134	125	260
Europe and Central Asia	5	5	NA	NA	NA	NA	NA	NA	NA	NA	NA	NA	NA	NA	NA	NA	5	5	10
Latin America and the Caribbean	62	57	NA	NA	NA	NA	NA	NA	NA	NA	NA	NA	NA	NA	NA	NA	62	57	119
Middle East and North Africa	103	96	NA	NA	NA	NA	NA	NA	NA	NA	NA	NA	NA	NA	NA	NA	103	96	199
South Asia	1,610	1,487	NA	NA	NA	NA	NA	NA	NA	NA	NA	NA	NA	NA	NA	NA	1,610	1,487	3,097
Sub-Saharan Africa	1,263	1,156	NA	NA	NA	NA	NA	NA	NA	NA	NA	NA	NA	NA	NA	NA	1,263	1,156	2,419
Low- and middle-income countries	3,179	2,925	NA	NA	NA	NA	NA	NA	NA	NA	NA	NA	NA	NA	NA	NA	3,179	2,925	6,104
High-income countries	0	0	NA	NA	NA	NA	NA	NA	NA	NA	NA	NA	NA	NA	NA	NA	0	0	0
WORLD	3,179	2,925	NA	NA	NA	NA	NA	NA	NA	NA	NA	NA	NA	NA	NA	NA	3,179	2,925	6,104
Attributable DALYs (thousands)																			
East Asia and Pacific	156	146	NA	NA	NA	NA	NA	NA	NA	NA	NA	NA	NA	NA	NA	NA	156	146	301
Europe and Central Asia	7	7	NA	NA	NA	NA	NA	NA	NA	NA	NA	NA	NA	NA	NA	NA	7	7	14
Latin America and the Caribbean	83	77	NA	NA	NA	NA	NA	NA	NA	NA	NA	NA	NA	NA	NA	NA	83	77	160
Middle East and North Africa	120	112	NA	NA	NA	NA	NA	NA	NA	NA	NA	NA	NA	NA	NA	NA	120	112	233
South Asia	1,748	1,616	NA	NA	NA	NA	NA	NA	NA	NA	NA	NA	NA	NA	NA	NA	1,748	1,616	3,364
Sub-Saharan Africa	1,339	1,230	NA	NA	NA	NA	NA	NA	NA	NA	NA	NA	NA	NA	NA	NA	1,339	1,230	2,570
Low- and middle-income countries	3,453	3,188	NA	NA	NA	NA	NA	NA	NA	NA	NA	NA	NA	NA	NA	NA	3,453	3,188	6,641
High-income countries	2	2	NA	NA	NA	NA	NA	NA	NA	NA	NA	NA	NA	NA	NA	NA	2	2	3
WORLD	3,455	3,190	NA	NA	NA	NA	NA	NA	NA	NA	NA	NA	NA	NA	NA	NA	3,455	3,190	6,645

Source: Authors' calculations.
Note: NA = not applicable.

Table 4A.20

Risk factor:　Zinc deficiency
Disease:　Malaria

Region	0–4 years Male	0–4 years Female	5–14 years Male	5–14 years Female	15–29 years Male	15–29 years Female	30–44 years Male	30–44 years Female	45–59 years Male	45–59 years Female	60–69 years Male	60–69 years Female	70–79 years Male	70–79 years Female	80+ years Male	80+ years Female	Total Male	Total Female	All
PAF of Mortality (%)																			
East Asia and Pacific	8	8	NA	NA	NA	NA	NA	NA	NA	NA	NA	NA	NA	NA	NA	NA	7	7	7
Europe and Central Asia	5	5	NA	NA	NA	NA	NA	NA	NA	NA	NA	NA	NA	NA	NA	NA	3	4	4
Latin America and the Caribbean	16	16	NA	NA	NA	NA	NA	NA	NA	NA	NA	NA	NA	NA	NA	NA	14	14	14
Middle East and North Africa	18	18	NA	NA	NA	NA	NA	NA	NA	NA	NA	NA	NA	NA	NA	NA	16	16	16
South Asia	28	28	NA	NA	NA	NA	NA	NA	NA	NA	NA	NA	NA	NA	NA	NA	25	25	25
Sub-Saharan Africa	22	22	NA	NA	NA	NA	NA	NA	NA	NA	NA	NA	NA	NA	NA	NA	20	20	20
Low- and middle-income countries	22	22	NA	NA	NA	NA	NA	NA	NA	NA	NA	NA	NA	NA	NA	NA	20	20	20
High-income countries	3	3	NA	NA	NA	NA	NA	NA	NA	NA	NA	NA	NA	NA	NA	NA	1	1	1
WORLD	22	22	NA	NA	NA	NA	NA	NA	NA	NA	NA	NA	NA	NA	NA	NA	20	20	20
PAF of YLL (%)																			
East Asia and Pacific	8	8	NA	NA	NA	NA	NA	NA	NA	NA	NA	NA	NA	NA	NA	NA	8	8	8
Europe and Central Asia	5	5	NA	NA	NA	NA	NA	NA	NA	NA	NA	NA	NA	NA	NA	NA	4	4	4
Latin America and the Caribbean	16	16	NA	NA	NA	NA	NA	NA	NA	NA	NA	NA	NA	NA	NA	NA	14	14	14
Middle East and North Africa	18	18	NA	NA	NA	NA	NA	NA	NA	NA	NA	NA	NA	NA	NA	NA	17	17	17
South Asia	28	28	NA	NA	NA	NA	NA	NA	NA	NA	NA	NA	NA	NA	NA	NA	26	26	26
Sub-Saharan Africa	22	22	NA	NA	NA	NA	NA	NA	NA	NA	NA	NA	NA	NA	NA	NA	21	20	21
Low- and middle-income countries	22	22	NA	NA	NA	NA	NA	NA	NA	NA	NA	NA	NA	NA	NA	NA	20	21	20
High-income countries	3	3	NA	NA	NA	NA	NA	NA	NA	NA	NA	NA	NA	NA	NA	NA	1	1	1
WORLD	22	22	NA	NA	NA	NA	NA	NA	NA	NA	NA	NA	NA	NA	NA	NA	20	21	20
PAF of DALYs (%)																			
East Asia and Pacific	8	8	NA	NA	NA	NA	NA	NA	NA	NA	NA	NA	NA	NA	NA	NA	7	6	7
Europe and Central Asia	5	5	NA	NA	NA	NA	NA	NA	NA	NA	NA	NA	NA	NA	NA	NA	2	2	2
Latin America and the Caribbean	16	16	NA	NA	NA	NA	NA	NA	NA	NA	NA	NA	NA	NA	NA	NA	9	8	9
Middle East and North Africa	18	18	NA	NA	NA	NA	NA	NA	NA	NA	NA	NA	NA	NA	NA	NA	15	15	15
South Asia	28	28	NA	NA	NA	NA	NA	NA	NA	NA	NA	NA	NA	NA	NA	NA	21	22	21
Sub-Saharan Africa	22	22	NA	NA	NA	NA	NA	NA	NA	NA	NA	NA	NA	NA	NA	NA	20	20	20
Low- and middle-income countries	22	22	NA	NA	NA	NA	NA	NA	NA	NA	NA	NA	NA	NA	NA	NA	20	20	20
High-income countries	3	3	NA	NA	NA	NA	NA	NA	NA	NA	NA	NA	NA	NA	NA	NA	1	1	1
WORLD	22	22	NA	NA	NA	NA	NA	NA	NA	NA	NA	NA	NA	NA	NA	NA	20	20	20
Attributable Mortality (thousands)																			
East Asia and Pacific	1	1	NA	NA	NA	NA	NA	NA	NA	NA	NA	NA	NA	NA	NA	NA	1	1	2
Europe and Central Asia	0	0	NA	NA	NA	NA	NA	NA	NA	NA	NA	NA	NA	NA	NA	NA	0	0	0
Latin America and the Caribbean	0	0	NA	NA	NA	NA	NA	NA	NA	NA	NA	NA	NA	NA	NA	NA	0	0	0
Middle East and North Africa	1	2	NA	NA	NA	NA	NA	NA	NA	NA	NA	NA	NA	NA	NA	NA	1	2	3
South Asia	8	8	NA	NA	NA	NA	NA	NA	NA	NA	NA	NA	NA	NA	NA	NA	8	8	16
Sub-Saharan Africa	103	114	NA	NA	NA	NA	NA	NA	NA	NA	NA	NA	NA	NA	NA	NA	103	114	217
Low- and middle-income countries	114	125	NA	NA	NA	NA	NA	NA	NA	NA	NA	NA	NA	NA	NA	NA	114	125	239
High-income countries	0	0	NA	NA	NA	NA	NA	NA	NA	NA	NA	NA	NA	NA	NA	NA	0	0	0
WORLD	114	125	NA	NA	NA	NA	NA	NA	NA	NA	NA	NA	NA	NA	NA	NA	114	125	239
Attributable YLL (thousands)																			
East Asia and Pacific	45	21	NA	NA	NA	NA	NA	NA	NA	NA	NA	NA	NA	NA	NA	NA	45	21	66
Europe and Central Asia	0	0	NA	NA	NA	NA	NA	NA	NA	NA	NA	NA	NA	NA	NA	NA	0	0	0
Latin America and the Caribbean	4	3	NA	NA	NA	NA	NA	NA	NA	NA	NA	NA	NA	NA	NA	NA	4	3	6
Middle East and North Africa	43	49	NA	NA	NA	NA	NA	NA	NA	NA	NA	NA	NA	NA	NA	NA	43	49	93
South Asia	228	255	NA	NA	NA	NA	NA	NA	NA	NA	NA	NA	NA	NA	NA	NA	228	255	484
Sub-Saharan Africa	3,112	3,480	NA	NA	NA	NA	NA	NA	NA	NA	NA	NA	NA	NA	NA	NA	3,112	3,480	6,592
Low- and middle-income countries	3,432	3,808	NA	NA	NA	NA	NA	NA	NA	NA	NA	NA	NA	NA	NA	NA	3,432	3,808	7,240
High-income countries	0	0	NA	NA	NA	NA	NA	NA	NA	NA	NA	NA	NA	NA	NA	NA	0	0	0
WORLD	3,433	3,808	NA	NA	NA	NA	NA	NA	NA	NA	NA	NA	NA	NA	NA	NA	3,433	3,808	7,241
Attributable DALYs (thousands)																			
East Asia and Pacific	48	24	NA	NA	NA	NA	NA	NA	NA	NA	NA	NA	NA	NA	NA	NA	48	24	72
Europe and Central Asia	0	0	NA	NA	NA	NA	NA	NA	NA	NA	NA	NA	NA	NA	NA	NA	0	0	0
Latin America and the Caribbean	5	4	NA	NA	NA	NA	NA	NA	NA	NA	NA	NA	NA	NA	NA	NA	5	4	9
Middle East and North Africa	48	53	NA	NA	NA	NA	NA	NA	NA	NA	NA	NA	NA	NA	NA	NA	48	53	101
South Asia	264	290	NA	NA	NA	NA	NA	NA	NA	NA	NA	NA	NA	NA	NA	NA	264	290	554
Sub-Saharan Africa	3,417	3,783	NA	NA	NA	NA	NA	NA	NA	NA	NA	NA	NA	NA	NA	NA	3,417	3,783	7,201
Low- and middle-income countries	3,783	4,154	NA	NA	NA	NA	NA	NA	NA	NA	NA	NA	NA	NA	NA	NA	3,783	4,154	7,938
High-income countries	0	0	NA	NA	NA	NA	NA	NA	NA	NA	NA	NA	NA	NA	NA	NA	0	0	0
WORLD	3,783	4,154	NA	NA	NA	NA	NA	NA	NA	NA	NA	NA	NA	NA	NA	NA	3,783	4,154	7,938

Source: Authors' calculations.
Note: NA = not applicable.

Table 4A.21

Risk factor: Zinc deficiency
Disease: Lower respiratory infections

Region	0–4 years Male	0–4 years Female	5–14 years Male	5–14 years Female	15–29 years Male	15–29 years Female	30–44 years Male	30–44 years Female	45–59 years Male	45–59 years Female	60–69 years Male	60–69 years Female	70–79 years Male	70–79 years Female	80+ years Male	80+ years Female	Total Male	Total Female	All
PAF of Mortality (%)																			
East Asia and Pacific	8	8	NA	NA	NA	NA	NA	NA	NA	NA	NA	NA	NA	NA	NA	NA	2	3	3
Europe and Central Asia	5	5	NA	NA	NA	NA	NA	NA	NA	NA	NA	NA	NA	NA	NA	NA	1	2	2
Latin America and the Caribbean	15	15	NA	NA	NA	NA	NA	NA	NA	NA	NA	NA	NA	NA	NA	NA	4	4	4
Middle East and North Africa	17	17	NA	NA	NA	NA	NA	NA	NA	NA	NA	NA	NA	NA	NA	NA	12	12	12
South Asia	26	26	NA	NA	NA	NA	NA	NA	NA	NA	NA	NA	NA	NA	NA	NA	15	16	15
Sub-Saharan Africa	21	21	NA	NA	NA	NA	NA	NA	NA	NA	NA	NA	NA	NA	NA	NA	16	13	15
Low- and middle-income countries	22	21	NA	NA	NA	NA	NA	NA	NA	NA	NA	NA	NA	NA	NA	NA	12	12	12
High-income countries	3	3	NA	NA	NA	NA	NA	NA	NA	NA	NA	NA	NA	NA	NA	NA	0	0	0
WORLD	22	21	NA	NA	NA	NA	NA	NA	NA	NA	NA	NA	NA	NA	NA	NA	11	10	11
PAF of YLL (%)																			
East Asia and Pacific	8	8	NA	NA	NA	NA	NA	NA	NA	NA	NA	NA	NA	NA	NA	NA	4	5	4
Europe and Central Asia	5	5	NA	NA	NA	NA	NA	NA	NA	NA	NA	NA	NA	NA	NA	NA	2	3	2
Latin America and the Caribbean	15	15	NA	NA	NA	NA	NA	NA	NA	NA	NA	NA	NA	NA	NA	NA	7	7	7
Middle East and North Africa	17	17	NA	NA	NA	NA	NA	NA	NA	NA	NA	NA	NA	NA	NA	NA	14	14	14
South Asia	26	26	NA	NA	NA	NA	NA	NA	NA	NA	NA	NA	NA	NA	NA	NA	20	20	20
Sub-Saharan Africa	21	21	NA	NA	NA	NA	NA	NA	NA	NA	NA	NA	NA	NA	NA	NA	17	15	16
Low- and middle-income countries	22	21	NA	NA	NA	NA	NA	NA	NA	NA	NA	NA	NA	NA	NA	NA	16	15	16
High-income countries	3	3	NA	NA	NA	NA	NA	NA	NA	NA	NA	NA	NA	NA	NA	NA	0	0	0
WORLD	22	21	NA	NA	NA	NA	NA	NA	NA	NA	NA	NA	NA	NA	NA	NA	16	15	15
PAF of DALYs (%)																			
East Asia and Pacific	8	8	NA	NA	NA	NA	NA	NA	NA	NA	NA	NA	NA	NA	NA	NA	4	5	5
Europe and Central Asia	5	5	NA	NA	NA	NA	NA	NA	NA	NA	NA	NA	NA	NA	NA	NA	2	3	2
Latin America and the Caribbean	15	15	NA	NA	NA	NA	NA	NA	NA	NA	NA	NA	NA	NA	NA	NA	8	8	8
Middle East and North Africa	17	17	NA	NA	NA	NA	NA	NA	NA	NA	NA	NA	NA	NA	NA	NA	14	14	14
South Asia	26	26	NA	NA	NA	NA	NA	NA	NA	NA	NA	NA	NA	NA	NA	NA	20	20	20
Sub-Saharan Africa	21	21	NA	NA	NA	NA	NA	NA	NA	NA	NA	NA	NA	NA	NA	NA	17	15	16
Low- and middle-income countries	22	21	NA	NA	NA	NA	NA	NA	NA	NA	NA	NA	NA	NA	NA	NA	16	15	16
High-income countries	3	3	NA	NA	NA	NA	NA	NA	NA	NA	NA	NA	NA	NA	NA	NA	0	0	0
WORLD	22	21	NA	NA	NA	NA	NA	NA	NA	NA	NA	NA	NA	NA	NA	NA	16	15	15
Attributable Mortality (thousands)																			
East Asia and Pacific	5	9	NA	NA	NA	NA	NA	NA	NA	NA	NA	NA	NA	NA	NA	NA	5	9	14
Europe and Central Asia	1	1	NA	NA	NA	NA	NA	NA	NA	NA	NA	NA	NA	NA	NA	NA	1	1	2
Latin America and the Caribbean	3	3	NA	NA	NA	NA	NA	NA	NA	NA	NA	NA	NA	NA	NA	NA	3	3	6
Middle East and North Africa	7	6	NA	NA	NA	NA	NA	NA	NA	NA	NA	NA	NA	NA	NA	NA	7	6	13
South Asia	108	109	NA	NA	NA	NA	NA	NA	NA	NA	NA	NA	NA	NA	NA	NA	108	109	218
Sub-Saharan Africa	91	66	NA	NA	NA	NA	NA	NA	NA	NA	NA	NA	NA	NA	NA	NA	91	66	157
Low- and middle-income countries	215	194	NA	NA	NA	NA	NA	NA	NA	NA	NA	NA	NA	NA	NA	NA	215	194	409
High-income countries	0	0	NA	NA	NA	NA	NA	NA	NA	NA	NA	NA	NA	NA	NA	NA	0	0	0
WORLD	215	194	NA	NA	NA	NA	NA	NA	NA	NA	NA	NA	NA	NA	NA	NA	215	194	409
Attributable YLL (thousands)																			
East Asia and Pacific	144	287	NA	NA	NA	NA	NA	NA	NA	NA	NA	NA	NA	NA	NA	NA	144	287	430
Europe and Central Asia	26	22	NA	NA	NA	NA	NA	NA	NA	NA	NA	NA	NA	NA	NA	NA	26	22	49
Latin America and the Caribbean	102	88	NA	NA	NA	NA	NA	NA	NA	NA	NA	NA	NA	NA	NA	NA	102	88	190
Middle East and North Africa	201	184	NA	NA	NA	NA	NA	NA	NA	NA	NA	NA	NA	NA	NA	NA	201	184	385
South Asia	3,279	3,335	NA	NA	NA	NA	NA	NA	NA	NA	NA	NA	NA	NA	NA	NA	3,279	3,335	6,614
Sub-Saharan Africa	2,742	2,009	NA	NA	NA	NA	NA	NA	NA	NA	NA	NA	NA	NA	NA	NA	2,742	2,009	4,751
Low- and middle-income countries	6,495	5,925	NA	NA	NA	NA	NA	NA	NA	NA	NA	NA	NA	NA	NA	NA	6,495	5,925	12,420
High-income countries	1	1	NA	NA	NA	NA	NA	NA	NA	NA	NA	NA	NA	NA	NA	NA	1	1	1
WORLD	6,495	5,926	NA	NA	NA	NA	NA	NA	NA	NA	NA	NA	NA	NA	NA	NA	6,495	5,926	12,421
Attributable DALYs (thousands)																			
East Asia and Pacific	165	325	NA	NA	NA	NA	NA	NA	NA	NA	NA	NA	NA	NA	NA	NA	165	325	490
Europe and Central Asia	28	24	NA	NA	NA	NA	NA	NA	NA	NA	NA	NA	NA	NA	NA	NA	28	24	52
Latin America and the Caribbean	130	114	NA	NA	NA	NA	NA	NA	NA	NA	NA	NA	NA	NA	NA	NA	130	114	244
Middle East and North Africa	219	200	NA	NA	NA	NA	NA	NA	NA	NA	NA	NA	NA	NA	NA	NA	219	200	419
South Asia	3,454	3,506	NA	NA	NA	NA	NA	NA	NA	NA	NA	NA	NA	NA	NA	NA	3,454	3,506	6,960
Sub-Saharan Africa	2,836	2,051	NA	NA	NA	NA	NA	NA	NA	NA	NA	NA	NA	NA	NA	NA	2,836	2,051	4,887
Low- and middle-income countries	6,831	6,220	NA	NA	NA	NA	NA	NA	NA	NA	NA	NA	NA	NA	NA	NA	6,831	6,220	13,052
High-income countries	1	1	NA	NA	NA	NA	NA	NA	NA	NA	NA	NA	NA	NA	NA	NA	1	1	2
WORLD	6,832	6,221	NA	NA	NA	NA	NA	NA	NA	NA	NA	NA	NA	NA	NA	NA	6,832	6,221	13,053

Source: Authors' calculations.
Note: NA = not applicable.

Table 4A.22

Risk factor: Zinc deficiency
Disease: All causes

Region	0–4 years Male	0–4 years Female	5–14 years Male	5–14 years Female	15–29 years Male	15–29 years Female	30–44 years Male	30–44 years Female	45–59 years Male	45–59 years Female	60–69 years Male	60–69 years Female	70–79 years Male	70–79 years Female	80+ years Male	80+ years Female	Total Male	Total Female	All
PAF of Mortality (%)																			
East Asia and Pacific	2	2	NA	NA	NA	NA	NA	NA	NA	NA	NA	NA	NA	NA	NA	NA	0	0	0
Europe and Central Asia	1	1	NA	NA	NA	NA	NA	NA	NA	NA	NA	NA	NA	NA	NA	NA	0	0	0
Latin America and the Caribbean	2	3	NA	NA	NA	NA	NA	NA	NA	NA	NA	NA	NA	NA	NA	NA	0	0	0
Middle East and North Africa	5	5	NA	NA	NA	NA	NA	NA	NA	NA	NA	NA	NA	NA	NA	NA	1	1	1
South Asia	9	9	NA	NA	NA	NA	NA	NA	NA	NA	NA	NA	NA	NA	NA	NA	2	3	2
Sub-Saharan Africa	10	10	NA	NA	NA	NA	NA	NA	NA	NA	NA	NA	NA	NA	NA	NA	4	4	4
Low- and middle-income countries	8	8	NA	NA	NA	NA	NA	NA	NA	NA	NA	NA	NA	NA	NA	NA	2	2	2
High-income countries	0	0	NA	NA	NA	NA	NA	NA	NA	NA	NA	NA	NA	NA	NA	NA	0	0	0
WORLD	8	8	NA	NA	NA	NA	NA	NA	NA	NA	NA	NA	NA	NA	NA	NA	1	2	2
PAF of YLL (%)																			
East Asia and Pacific	2	2	NA	NA	NA	NA	NA	NA	NA	NA	NA	NA	NA	NA	NA	NA	0	0	0
Europe and Central Asia	1	1	NA	NA	NA	NA	NA	NA	NA	NA	NA	NA	NA	NA	NA	NA	0	0	0
Latin America and the Caribbean	2	3	NA	NA	NA	NA	NA	NA	NA	NA	NA	NA	NA	NA	NA	NA	1	1	1
Middle East and North Africa	5	5	NA	NA	NA	NA	NA	NA	NA	NA	NA	NA	NA	NA	NA	NA	2	2	2
South Asia	9	9	NA	NA	NA	NA	NA	NA	NA	NA	NA	NA	NA	NA	NA	NA	4	4	4
Sub-Saharan Africa	10	10	NA	NA	NA	NA	NA	NA	NA	NA	NA	NA	NA	NA	NA	NA	5	5	5
Low- and middle-income countries	8	8	NA	NA	NA	NA	NA	NA	NA	NA	NA	NA	NA	NA	NA	NA	3	3	3
High-income countries	0	0	NA	NA	NA	NA	NA	NA	NA	NA	NA	NA	NA	NA	NA	NA	0	0	0
WORLD	8	8	NA	NA	NA	NA	NA	NA	NA	NA	NA	NA	NA	NA	NA	NA	2	3	3
PAF of DALYs (%)																			
East Asia and Pacific	1	2	NA	NA	NA	NA	NA	NA	NA	NA	NA	NA	NA	NA	NA	NA	0	0	0
Europe and Central Asia	1	1	NA	NA	NA	NA	NA	NA	NA	NA	NA	NA	NA	NA	NA	NA	0	0	0
Latin America and the Caribbean	2	2	NA	NA	NA	NA	NA	NA	NA	NA	NA	NA	NA	NA	NA	NA	0	0	0
Middle East and North Africa	3	4	NA	NA	NA	NA	NA	NA	NA	NA	NA	NA	NA	NA	NA	NA	1	1	1
South Asia	8	8	NA	NA	NA	NA	NA	NA	NA	NA	NA	NA	NA	NA	NA	NA	3	3	3
Sub-Saharan Africa	9	9	NA	NA	NA	NA	NA	NA	NA	NA	NA	NA	NA	NA	NA	NA	4	4	4
Low- and middle-income countries	6	7	NA	NA	NA	NA	NA	NA	NA	NA	NA	NA	NA	NA	NA	NA	2	2	2
High-income countries	0	0	NA	NA	NA	NA	NA	NA	NA	NA	NA	NA	NA	NA	NA	NA	0	0	0
WORLD	6	6	NA	NA	NA	NA	NA	NA	NA	NA	NA	NA	NA	NA	NA	NA	2	2	2
Attributable Mortality (thousands)																			
East Asia and Pacific	11	14	NA	NA	NA	NA	NA	NA	NA	NA	NA	NA	NA	NA	NA	NA	11	14	25
Europe and Central Asia	1	1	NA	NA	NA	NA	NA	NA	NA	NA	NA	NA	NA	NA	NA	NA	1	1	2
Latin America and the Caribbean	6	5	NA	NA	NA	NA	NA	NA	NA	NA	NA	NA	NA	NA	NA	NA	6	5	10
Middle East and North Africa	11	11	NA	NA	NA	NA	NA	NA	NA	NA	NA	NA	NA	NA	NA	NA	11	11	22
South Asia	169	167	NA	NA	NA	NA	NA	NA	NA	NA	NA	NA	NA	NA	NA	NA	169	167	336
Sub-Saharan Africa	235	218	NA	NA	NA	NA	NA	NA	NA	NA	NA	NA	NA	NA	NA	NA	235	218	454
Low- and middle-income countries	433	416	NA	NA	NA	NA	NA	NA	NA	NA	NA	NA	NA	NA	NA	NA	433	416	849
High-income countries	0	0	NA	NA	NA	NA	NA	NA	NA	NA	NA	NA	NA	NA	NA	NA	0	0	0
WORLD	433	416	NA	NA	NA	NA	NA	NA	NA	NA	NA	NA	NA	NA	NA	NA	433	416	849
Attributable YLL (thousands)																			
East Asia and Pacific	323	433	NA	NA	NA	NA	NA	NA	NA	NA	NA	NA	NA	NA	NA	NA	323	433	756
Europe and Central Asia	32	27	NA	NA	NA	NA	NA	NA	NA	NA	NA	NA	NA	NA	NA	NA	32	27	59
Latin America and the Caribbean	169	147	NA	NA	NA	NA	NA	NA	NA	NA	NA	NA	NA	NA	NA	NA	169	147	316
Middle East and North Africa	348	329	NA	NA	NA	NA	NA	NA	NA	NA	NA	NA	NA	NA	NA	NA	348	329	677
South Asia	5,118	5,077	NA	NA	NA	NA	NA	NA	NA	NA	NA	NA	NA	NA	NA	NA	5,118	5,077	10,195
Sub-Saharan Africa	7,117	6,645	NA	NA	NA	NA	NA	NA	NA	NA	NA	NA	NA	NA	NA	NA	7,117	6,645	13,762
Low- and middle-income countries	13,106	12,658	NA	NA	NA	NA	NA	NA	NA	NA	NA	NA	NA	NA	NA	NA	13,106	12,658	25,765
High-income countries	1	1	NA	NA	NA	NA	NA	NA	NA	NA	NA	NA	NA	NA	NA	NA	1	1	2
WORLD	13,107	12,659	NA	NA	NA	NA	NA	NA	NA	NA	NA	NA	NA	NA	NA	NA	13,107	12,659	25,766
Attributable DALYs (thousands)																			
East Asia and Pacific	369	494	NA	NA	NA	NA	NA	NA	NA	NA	NA	NA	NA	NA	NA	NA	369	494	863
Europe and Central Asia	35	31	NA	NA	NA	NA	NA	NA	NA	NA	NA	NA	NA	NA	NA	NA	35	31	66
Latin America and the Caribbean	218	195	NA	NA	NA	NA	NA	NA	NA	NA	NA	NA	NA	NA	NA	NA	218	195	413
Middle East and North Africa	387	366	NA	NA	NA	NA	NA	NA	NA	NA	NA	NA	NA	NA	NA	NA	387	366	752
South Asia	5,467	5,412	NA	NA	NA	NA	NA	NA	NA	NA	NA	NA	NA	NA	NA	NA	5,467	5,412	10,878
Sub-Saharan Africa	7,592	7,065	NA	NA	NA	NA	NA	NA	NA	NA	NA	NA	NA	NA	NA	NA	7,592	7,065	14,657
Low- and middle-income countries	14,068	13,563	NA	NA	NA	NA	NA	NA	NA	NA	NA	NA	NA	NA	NA	NA	14,068	13,563	27,631
High-income countries	3	2	NA	NA	NA	NA	NA	NA	NA	NA	NA	NA	NA	NA	NA	NA	3	2	5
WORLD	14,071	13,565	NA	NA	NA	NA	NA	NA	NA	NA	NA	NA	NA	NA	NA	NA	14,071	13,565	27,636

Source: Authors' calculations.
Note: NA = not applicable.

Table 4A.23

Risk factor: High blood pressure
Disease: Hypertensive heart disease

Region	0–4 years Male	Female	5–14 years Male	Female	15–29 years Male	Female	30–44 years Male	Female	45–59 years Male	Female	60–69 years Male	Female	70–79 years Male	Female	80+ years Male	Female	Total Male	Female	All
PAF of Mortality (%)																			
East Asia and Pacific	NA	NA	NA	NA	NA	NA	24	17	64	69	79	85	80	86	73	81	73	80	76
Europe and Central Asia	NA	NA	NA	NA	NA	NA	63	54	86	90	92	96	92	97	87	94	88	94	91
Latin America and the Caribbean	NA	NA	NA	NA	NA	NA	49	32	76	75	85	88	86	89	79	84	79	82	81
Middle East and North Africa	NA	NA	NA	NA	NA	NA	38	31	72	79	84	91	85	92	79	88	78	86	82
South Asia	NA	NA	NA	NA	NA	NA	29	24	68	62	81	76	82	78	76	71	70	67	69
Sub-Saharan Africa	NA	NA	NA	NA	NA	NA	56	37	73	70	80	82	81	83	75	77	75	76	76
Low- and middle-income countries	NA	NA	NA	NA	NA	NA	37	28	70	72	82	86	83	88	77	83	76	81	79
High-income countries	NA	NA	NA	NA	NA	NA	55	21	75	70	85	87	86	90	82	87	82	86	84
WORLD	NA	NA	NA	NA	NA	NA	38	28	71	72	82	86	83	88	78	84	76	82	79
PAF of YLL (%)																			
East Asia and Pacific	NA	NA	NA	NA	NA	NA	24	17	64	69	79	85	80	86	73	81	69	77	73
Europe and Central Asia	NA	NA	NA	NA	NA	NA	63	54	86	90	92	96	92	97	87	94	86	92	89
Latin America and the Caribbean	NA	NA	NA	NA	NA	NA	49	32	76	75	85	88	86	89	79	84	76	78	77
Middle East and North Africa	NA	NA	NA	NA	NA	NA	38	31	72	79	84	91	85	92	79	88	74	82	78
South Asia	NA	NA	NA	NA	NA	NA	29	24	68	62	81	76	82	78	76	71	63	61	62
Sub-Saharan Africa	NA	NA	NA	NA	NA	NA	56	37	73	70	80	82	81	83	75	77	72	73	72
Low- and middle-income countries	NA	NA	NA	NA	NA	NA	37	28	70	72	82	86	83	88	77	83	71	77	74
High-income countries	NA	NA	NA	NA	NA	NA	55	21	75	70	85	87	86	90	82	87	79	83	81
WORLD	NA	NA	NA	NA	NA	NA	38	28	71	72	82	86	83	88	78	84	72	78	75
PAF of DALYs (%)																			
East Asia and Pacific	NA	NA	NA	NA	NA	NA	24	17	64	69	79	85	80	86	73	81	69	77	73
Europe and Central Asia	NA	NA	NA	NA	NA	NA	63	54	86	90	92	96	92	97	87	94	86	92	89
Latin America and the Caribbean	NA	NA	NA	NA	NA	NA	49	32	76	75	85	88	86	89	79	84	76	78	77
Middle East and North Africa	NA	NA	NA	NA	NA	NA	38	31	72	79	84	91	85	92	79	88	74	82	78
South Asia	NA	NA	NA	NA	NA	NA	29	24	68	62	81	76	82	78	76	71	64	62	63
Sub-Saharan Africa	NA	NA	NA	NA	NA	NA	56	37	73	70	80	82	81	83	75	77	72	73	73
Low- and middle-income countries	NA	NA	NA	NA	NA	NA	37	28	70	72	82	86	83	88	76	83	72	77	75
High-income countries	NA	NA	NA	NA	NA	NA	55	21	75	70	85	87	86	90	82	87	79	84	82
WORLD	NA	NA	NA	NA	NA	NA	38	28	71	72	82	86	83	88	78	84	73	78	75
Attributable Mortality (thousands)																			
East Asia and Pacific	NA	NA	NA	NA	NA	NA	2	1	18	14	37	29	43	49	21	41	120	134	254
Europe and Central Asia	NA	NA	NA	NA	NA	NA	1	1	8	6	12	13	13	22	6	18	41	59	100
Latin America and the Caribbean	NA	NA	NA	NA	NA	NA	1	1	5	4	7	7	10	12	8	16	31	39	71
Middle East and North Africa	NA	NA	NA	NA	NA	NA	1	0	4	4	8	7	11	12	6	8	30	31	61
South Asia	NA	NA	NA	NA	NA	NA	1	0	7	5	10	9	11	9	4	5	33	29	62
Sub-Saharan Africa	NA	NA	NA	NA	NA	NA	1	1	4	5	5	8	5	12	3	7	18	32	50
Low- and middle-income countries	NA	NA	NA	NA	NA	NA	6	3	46	37	79	73	93	116	49	94	273	324	598
High-income countries	NA	NA	NA	NA	NA	NA	1	0	5	2	6	5	12	15	16	47	39	69	109
WORLD	NA	NA	NA	NA	NA	NA	7	4	50	40	85	78	105	131	65	141	313	393	706
Attributable YLL (thousands)																			
East Asia and Pacific	NA	NA	NA	NA	NA	NA	38	17	334	270	494	438	381	503	107	215	1,354	1,443	2,797
Europe and Central Asia	NA	NA	NA	NA	NA	NA	33	15	143	111	168	190	121	228	29	84	493	629	1,121
Latin America and the Caribbean	NA	NA	NA	NA	NA	NA	22	14	94	90	98	109	86	120	39	73	338	406	744
Middle East and North Africa	NA	NA	NA	NA	NA	NA	13	7	83	70	107	107	99	124	28	44	331	351	683
South Asia	NA	NA	NA	NA	NA	NA	23	12	131	108	137	133	94	98	22	26	407	377	785
Sub-Saharan Africa	NA	NA	NA	NA	NA	NA	23	18	72	97	66	126	48	119	14	37	222	397	619
Low- and middle-income countries	NA	NA	NA	NA	NA	NA	151	83	857	747	1,069	1,102	830	1,191	239	479	3,146	3,603	6,749
High-income countries	NA	NA	NA	NA	NA	NA	21	4	86	44	86	71	102	148	67	188	361	456	816
WORLD	NA	NA	NA	NA	NA	NA	172	87	943	792	1,155	1,173	932	1,340	306	668	3,507	4,059	7,566
Attributable DALYs (thousands)																			
East Asia and Pacific	NA	NA	NA	NA	NA	NA	40	18	355	286	532	465	434	552	139	261	1,501	1,581	3,083
Europe and Central Asia	NA	NA	NA	NA	NA	NA	34	16	148	115	176	199	131	246	35	101	524	677	1201
Latin America and the Caribbean	NA	NA	NA	NA	NA	NA	22	14	98	94	104	115	96	131	49	90	369	444	813
Middle East and North Africa	NA	NA	NA	NA	NA	NA	13	7	86	74	112	112	107	132	32	52	350	377	728
South Asia	NA	NA	NA	NA	NA	NA	25	13	142	116	159	151	121	123	36	42	482	444	926
Sub-Saharan Africa	NA	NA	NA	NA	NA	NA	24	19	76	103	71	135	54	133	18	47	243	438	681
Low- and middle-income countries	NA	NA	NA	NA	NA	NA	159	87	905	787	1,153	1,177	943	1,317	309	594	3,470	3,962	7,432
High-income countries	NA	NA	NA	NA	NA	NA	21	4	90	46	92	75	116	166	98	280	418	572	990
WORLD	NA	NA	NA	NA	NA	NA	180	91	995	833	1,245	1,252	1,060	1,483	407	874	3,888	4,534	8,421

Source: Authors' calculations.
Note: NA = not applicable.

Table 4A.24

Risk factor: High blood pressure
Disease: Ischemic heart disease

Region	0–4 years Male	0–4 years Female	5–14 years Male	5–14 years Female	15–29 years Male	15–29 years Female	30–44 years Male	30–44 years Female	45–59 years Male	45–59 years Female	60–69 years Male	60–69 years Female	70–79 years Male	70–79 years Female	80+ years Male	80+ years Female	Total Male	Total Female	All
PAF of Mortality (%)																			
East Asia and Pacific	NA	NA	NA	NA	NA	NA	11	7	34	37	45	51	43	50	35	41	38	44	41
Europe and Central Asia	NA	NA	NA	NA	NA	NA	34	27	55	60	62	72	58	70	50	61	56	65	61
Latin America and the Caribbean	NA	NA	NA	NA	NA	NA	24	15	45	44	52	56	50	55	41	45	46	49	47
Middle East and North Africa	NA	NA	NA	NA	NA	NA	18	15	41	48	51	61	49	59	41	50	44	54	48
South Asia	NA	NA	NA	NA	NA	NA	13	10	36	32	47	43	45	41	37	34	40	37	39
Sub-Saharan Africa	NA	NA	NA	NA	NA	NA	29	17	42	39	47	48	44	47	37	39	43	44	43
Low- and middle-income countries	NA	NA	NA	NA	NA	NA	20	12	42	40	51	53	49	55	41	50	45	49	47
High-income countries	NA	NA	NA	NA	NA	NA	28	9	44	40	53	55	51	56	44	49	47	51	49
WORLD	NA	NA	NA	NA	NA	NA	21	12	42	40	52	53	49	55	42	49	45	50	47
PAF of YLL (%)																			
East Asia and Pacific	NA	NA	NA	NA	NA	NA	11	7	34	37	45	51	43	50	35	41	35	42	39
Europe and Central Asia	NA	NA	NA	NA	NA	NA	34	27	55	60	62	72	58	70	50	61	55	66	60
Latin America and the Caribbean	NA	NA	NA	NA	NA	NA	24	15	45	44	52	56	50	55	41	45	45	48	46
Middle East and North Africa	NA	NA	NA	NA	NA	NA	18	15	41	48	51	61	49	59	41	50	42	52	46
South Asia	NA	NA	NA	NA	NA	NA	13	10	36	32	47	43	45	41	37	34	38	35	37
Sub-Saharan Africa	NA	NA	NA	NA	NA	NA	29	17	42	39	47	48	44	47	37	39	43	43	43
Low- and middle-income countries	NA	NA	NA	NA	NA	NA	20	12	42	40	51	53	49	54	40	49	43	47	45
High-income countries	NA	NA	NA	NA	NA	NA	28	9	44	40	53	55	51	56	44	49	47	51	49
WORLD	NA	NA	NA	NA	NA	NA	21	12	42	40	52	53	49	55	42	49	44	47	45
PAF of DALYs (%)																			
East Asia and Pacific	NA	NA	NA	NA	NA	NA	11	7	34	37	45	51	43	50	35	41	34	41	38
Europe and Central Asia	NA	NA	NA	NA	NA	NA	34	27	55	60	62	72	58	70	50	61	55	66	60
Latin America and the Caribbean	NA	NA	NA	NA	NA	NA	24	15	45	44	52	56	50	55	41	45	44	47	45
Middle East and North Africa	NA	NA	NA	NA	NA	NA	18	15	41	48	51	61	49	59	41	50	41	51	45
South Asia	NA	NA	NA	NA	NA	NA	13	10	36	32	47	43	45	41	37	34	37	34	36
Sub-Saharan Africa	NA	NA	NA	NA	NA	NA	29	17	42	39	47	48	44	47	37	39	42	42	42
Low- and middle-income countries	NA	NA	NA	NA	NA	NA	20	12	42	40	51	53	49	54	40	49	42	46	44
High-income countries	NA	NA	NA	NA	NA	NA	28	9	44	40	53	55	51	56	44	49	47	50	48
WORLD	NA	NA	NA	NA	NA	NA	20	12	42	40	51	53	49	55	42	49	43	46	45
Attributable Mortality (thousands)																			
East Asia and Pacific	NA	NA	NA	NA	NA	NA	3	1	35	21	66	57	81	91	38	77	223	247	471
Europe and Central Asia	NA	NA	NA	NA	NA	NA	13	2	84	26	141	92	155	218	65	227	459	565	1,024
Latin America and the Caribbean	NA	NA	NA	NA	NA	NA	2	1	18	8	25	16	29	24	18	27	93	76	169
Middle East and North Africa	NA	NA	NA	NA	NA	NA	2	1	17	9	25	19	29	28	11	16	83	72	155
South Asia	NA	NA	NA	NA	NA	NA	6	3	89	40	138	99	133	111	50	42	415	296	711
Sub-Saharan Africa	NA	NA	NA	NA	NA	NA	2	1	17	10	24	22	26	26	8	12	77	71	148
Low- and middle-income countries	NA	NA	NA	NA	NA	NA	29	8	258	115	419	307	454	497	190	401	1,350	1,328	2,678
High-income countries	NA	NA	NA	NA	NA	NA	5	0	39	9	69	29	118	88	110	202	340	328	668
WORLD	NA	NA	NA	NA	NA	NA	33	9	297	124	488	336	571	585	300	603	1,690	1,657	3,346
Attributable YLL (thousands)																			
East Asia and Pacific	NA	NA	NA	NA	NA	NA	77	29	652	427	890	859	721	927	186	382	2,527	2,624	5,151
Europe and Central Asia	NA	NA	NA	NA	NA	NA	299	47	1,591	519	1,911	1,388	1,405	2,227	296	1,049	5,502	5,229	10,731
Latin America and the Caribbean	NA	NA	NA	NA	NA	NA	52	14	328	156	342	248	262	250	83	125	1,067	794	1,861
Middle East and North Africa	NA	NA	NA	NA	NA	NA	45	14	312	183	337	291	256	286	53	84	1,003	858	1,861
South Asia	NA	NA	NA	NA	NA	NA	149	83	1,652	797	1,862	1,497	1,193	1,160	244	226	5,100	3,764	8,864
Sub-Saharan Africa	NA	NA	NA	NA	NA	NA	49	13	308	197	332	339	233	269	40	66	962	885	1,846
Low- and middle-income countries	NA	NA	NA	NA	NA	NA	671	200	4,842	2,280	5,673	4,622	4,071	5,120	903	1,933	16,160	14,154	30,315
High-income countries	NA	NA	NA	NA	NA	NA	106	8	723	177	921	432	1,030	876	480	830	3,261	2,324	5,585
WORLD	NA	NA	NA	NA	NA	NA	777	209	5,566	2,457	6,594	5,054	5,101	5,996	1,383	2,763	19,421	16,478	35,899
Attributable DALYs (thousands)																			
East Asia and Pacific	NA	NA	NA	NA	NA	NA	85	32	696	459	934	901	737	945	189	387	2,642	2,723	5,365
Europe and Central Asia	NA	NA	NA	NA	NA	NA	321	53	1,652	557	1,972	1,453	1,429	2,269	300	1,062	5,675	5,395	11,070
Latin America and the Caribbean	NA	NA	NA	NA	NA	NA	59	17	350	170	364	263	270	257	85	128	1,127	835	1,962
Middle East and North Africa	NA	NA	NA	NA	NA	NA	50	16	329	196	353	304	261	290	54	85	1,048	891	1,939
South Asia	NA	NA	NA	NA	NA	NA	170	95	1,753	860	1,960	1,577	1,223	1,186	248	230	5,354	3,948	9,302
Sub-Saharan Africa	NA	NA	NA	NA	NA	NA	54	16	327	210	348	357	239	275	41	67	1,010	924	1,934
Low- and middle-income countries	NA	NA	NA	NA	NA	NA	740	229	5,108	2,451	5,932	4,854	4,159	5,221	917	1,960	16,856	14,716	31,572
High-income countries	NA	NA	NA	NA	NA	NA	121	11	797	213	991	485	1,084	934	497	861	3,490	2,504	5,994
WORLD	NA	NA	NA	NA	NA	NA	861	240	5,905	2,664	6,923	5,339	5,243	6,156	1,414	2,821	20,346	17,220	37,566

Source: Authors' calculations.
Note: NA = not applicable.

Table 4A.25

Risk factor: High blood pressure
Disease: Cerebrovascular disease

Region	0–4 years Male	0–4 years Female	5–14 years Male	5–14 years Female	15–29 years Male	15–29 years Female	30–44 years Male	30–44 years Female	45–59 years Male	45–59 years Female	60–69 years Male	60–69 years Female	70–79 years Male	70–79 years Female	80+ years Male	80+ years Female	Total Male	Total Female	All
PAF of Mortality (%)																			
East Asia and Pacific	NA	NA	NA	NA	NA	NA	15	10	45	49	56	63	53	61	35	41	48	52	50
Europe and Central Asia	NA	NA	NA	NA	NA	NA	45	36	68	73	74	83	70	80	50	61	65	71	69
Latin America and the Caribbean	NA	NA	NA	NA	NA	NA	33	21	57	56	64	68	61	66	41	45	53	54	54
Middle East and North Africa	NA	NA	NA	NA	NA	NA	25	20	52	60	62	73	60	70	41	50	49	59	54
South Asia	NA	NA	NA	NA	NA	NA	18	15	48	43	59	54	56	52	37	34	51	46	49
Sub-Saharan Africa	NA	NA	NA	NA	NA	NA	39	24	54	50	59	60	55	58	37	39	50	51	51
Low- and middle-income countries	NA	NA	NA	NA	NA	NA	27	19	51	52	61	65	58	65	39	47	52	56	54
High-income countries	NA	NA	NA	NA	NA	NA	38	13	57	51	64	67	62	67	44	49	53	54	54
WORLD	NA	NA	NA	NA	NA	NA	28	19	51	52	61	65	58	65	40	48	52	56	54
PAF of YLL (%)																			
East Asia and Pacific	NA	NA	NA	NA	NA	NA	15	10	45	49	56	63	53	61	35	41	47	53	50
Europe and Central Asia	NA	NA	NA	NA	NA	NA	45	36	68	73	74	83	70	80	50	61	66	74	70
Latin America and the Caribbean	NA	NA	NA	NA	NA	NA	33	21	57	56	64	68	61	66	41	45	53	53	53
Middle East and North Africa	NA	NA	NA	NA	NA	NA	25	20	52	60	62	73	60	70	41	50	44	56	50
South Asia	NA	NA	NA	NA	NA	NA	18	15	48	43	59	54	56	52	37	34	50	47	48
Sub-Saharan Africa	NA	NA	NA	NA	NA	NA	39	24	54	50	59	60	55	58	37	39	49	50	49
Low- and middle-income countries	NA	NA	NA	NA	NA	NA	27	19	51	52	61	65	58	64	39	47	52	56	54
High-income countries	NA	NA	NA	NA	NA	NA	38	13	57	51	64	67	62	67	44	49	55	56	56
WORLD	NA	NA	NA	NA	NA	NA	28	19	52	52	61	65	58	65	40	47	52	56	54
PAF of DALYs (%)																			
East Asia and Pacific	NA	NA	NA	NA	NA	NA	15	10	45	49	56	63	53	61	35	41	47	53	50
Europe and Central Asia	NA	NA	NA	NA	NA	NA	45	36	68	73	74	83	70	80	50	61	66	74	71
Latin America and the Caribbean	NA	NA	NA	NA	NA	NA	33	21	57	56	64	68	61	66	41	45	54	54	54
Middle East and North Africa	NA	NA	NA	NA	NA	NA	25	20	52	60	62	73	60	70	41	50	45	57	51
South Asia	NA	NA	NA	NA	NA	NA	18	15	48	43	59	54	56	52	37	34	50	47	49
Sub-Saharan Africa	NA	NA	NA	NA	NA	NA	39	24	54	50	59	60	55	58	37	39	49	50	50
Low- and middle-income countries	NA	NA	NA	NA	NA	NA	26	19	51	52	61	65	58	65	39	47	52	56	54
High-income countries	NA	NA	NA	NA	NA	NA	38	13	57	51	64	67	62	67	44	49	56	56	56
WORLD	NA	NA	NA	NA	NA	NA	28	18	52	52	61	65	58	65	40	47	52	56	54
Attributable Mortality (thousands)																			
East Asia and Pacific	NA	NA	NA	NA	NA	NA	4	2	62	44	139	100	187	211	66	137	458	493	951
Europe and Central Asia	NA	NA	NA	NA	NA	NA	6	3	37	26	81	76	101	180	40	160	264	444	709
Latin America and the Caribbean	NA	NA	NA	NA	NA	NA	2	1	12	10	17	15	23	25	14	24	69	75	144
Middle East and North Africa	NA	NA	NA	NA	NA	NA	1	0	5	4	9	9	13	16	5	9	32	38	71
South Asia	NA	NA	NA	NA	NA	NA	2	1	36	22	82	68	89	90	27	31	237	212	449
Sub-Saharan Africa	NA	NA	NA	NA	NA	NA	4	2	15	18	21	31	24	39	8	16	73	107	179
Low- and middle-income countries	NA	NA	NA	NA	NA	NA	18	9	167	124	350	300	438	560	160	377	1,133	1,369	2,502
High-income countries	NA	NA	NA	NA	NA	NA	2	1	14	8	28	19	63	68	64	151	172	247	418
WORLD	NA	NA	NA	NA	NA	NA	21	9	182	132	378	319	501	628	224	528	1,305	1,616	2,921
Attributable YLL (thousands)																			
East Asia and Pacific	NA	NA	NA	NA	NA	NA	89	39	1,149	871	1,868	1,502	1,665	2,152	330	701	5,100	5,264	10,364
Europe and Central Asia	NA	NA	NA	NA	NA	NA	136	65	698	511	1,088	1,139	911	1,843	182	749	3,015	4,306	7,321
Latin America and the Caribbean	NA	NA	NA	NA	NA	NA	52	33	231	206	233	228	205	250	64	113	785	830	1,615
Middle East and North Africa	NA	NA	NA	NA	NA	NA	15	10	85	89	120	140	118	160	25	46	362	445	808
South Asia	NA	NA	NA	NA	NA	NA	42	21	677	436	1,113	1,022	798	942	134	167	2,762	2,588	5,350
Sub-Saharan Africa	NA	NA	NA	NA	NA	NA	100	48	288	366	282	475	214	402	41	88	926	1,379	2,305
Low- and middle-income countries	NA	NA	NA	NA	NA	NA	433	216	3,128	2,479	4,704	4,506	3,910	5,749	776	1,863	12,951	14,812	27,763
High-income countries	NA	NA	NA	NA	NA	NA	56	14	269	161	379	285	544	675	275	621	1,523	1,756	3,279
WORLD	NA	NA	NA	NA	NA	NA	489	230	3,397	2,640	5,083	4,791	4,454	6,424	1,051	2,484	14,474	16,568	31,042
Attributable DALYs (thousands)																			
East Asia and Pacific	NA	NA	NA	NA	NA	NA	124	55	1,559	1,178	2,451	1,938	1,987	2,532	363	769	6,483	6,471	12,955
Europe and Central Asia	NA	NA	NA	NA	NA	NA	168	89	870	668	1,369	1,466	1,093	2,153	202	817	3,702	5,193	8,895
Latin America and the Caribbean	NA	NA	NA	NA	NA	NA	71	49	321	285	321	308	255	302	72	127	1,041	1,071	2,112
Middle East and North Africa	NA	NA	NA	NA	NA	NA	21	13	113	115	154	173	140	183	28	50	456	534	990
South Asia	NA	NA	NA	NA	NA	NA	52	26	844	538	1,379	1,239	922	1,068	146	182	3,343	3,054	6,397
Sub-Saharan Africa	NA	NA	NA	NA	NA	NA	106	52	321	414	318	536	233	435	43	93	1,021	1,530	2,551
Low- and middle-income countries	NA	NA	NA	NA	NA	NA	542	285	4,027	3,199	5,993	5,660	4,630	6,673	854	2,038	16,046	17,854	33,899
High-income countries	NA	NA	NA	NA	NA	NA	107	28	530	332	712	544	843	1,038	350	782	2,542	2,724	5,265
WORLD	NA	NA	NA	NA	NA	NA	649	312	4,557	3,531	6,705	6,204	5,473	7,711	1,204	2,820	18,587	20,577	39,164

Source: Authors' calculations.
Note: NA = not applicable.

Table 4A.26

Risk factor:	High blood pressure
Disease:	Selected other cardiovascular diseases

Region	0–4 years		5–14 years		15–29 years		30–44 years		45–59 years		60–69 years		70–79 years		80+ years		Total		
	Male	Female	Male	Female	Male	Female	Male	Female	Male	Female	Male	Female	Male	Female	Male	Female	Male	Female	All
PAF of Mortality (%)																			
East Asia and Pacific	NA	NA	NA	NA	NA	NA	7	4	22	24	30	36	24	29	19	23	21	25	23
Europe and Central Asia	NA	NA	NA	NA	NA	NA	24	18	40	45	46	57	37	48	30	39	35	43	39
Latin America and the Caribbean	NA	NA	NA	NA	NA	NA	16	9	31	30	36	40	29	33	23	26	25	28	27
Middle East and North Africa	NA	NA	NA	NA	NA	NA	12	9	27	33	35	45	28	37	23	30	24	28	27
South Asia	NA	NA	NA	NA	NA	NA	8	6	24	20	32	28	25	23	20	18	21	19	20
Sub-Saharan Africa	NA	NA	NA	NA	NA	NA	20	11	29	25	32	33	25	27	20	22	23	23	23
Low- and middle-income countries	NA	NA	NA	NA	NA	NA	15	9	28	27	35	37	28	32	23	28	25	28	27
High-income countries	NA	NA	NA	NA	NA	NA	20	6	30	26	37	39	30	34	25	29	28	30	29
WORLD	NA	NA	NA	NA	NA	NA	16	9	28	27	36	37	29	32	24	29	26	29	28
PAF of YLL (%)																			
East Asia and Pacific	NA	NA	NA	NA	NA	NA	7	4	22	24	30	36	24	29	19	23	19	24	21
Europe and Central Asia	NA	NA	NA	NA	NA	NA	24	18	40	45	46	57	37	48	30	39	34	43	38
Latin America and the Caribbean	NA	NA	NA	NA	NA	NA	16	9	31	30	36	40	29	33	23	26	23	26	25
Middle East and North Africa	NA	NA	NA	NA	NA	NA	12	9	27	33	35	45	28	37	23	30	21	22	21
South Asia	NA	NA	NA	NA	NA	NA	8	6	24	20	32	28	25	23	20	18	18	17	17
Sub-Saharan Africa	NA	NA	NA	NA	NA	NA	20	11	29	25	32	33	25	27	20	22	22	21	21
Low- and middle-income countries	NA	NA	NA	NA	NA	NA	15	9	28	27	35	37	28	32	23	28	23	25	24
High-income countries	NA	NA	NA	NA	NA	NA	20	6	30	26	37	39	30	34	25	29	28	30	29
WORLD	NA	NA	NA	NA	NA	NA	16	9	28	27	36	37	29	32	24	28	24	26	25
PAF of DALYs (%)																			
East Asia and Pacific	NA	NA	NA	NA	NA	NA	7	4	22	24	30	36	24	29	19	23	18	23	20
Europe and Central Asia	NA	NA	NA	NA	NA	NA	24	18	40	45	46	57	37	48	30	39	34	42	38
Latin America and the Caribbean	NA	NA	NA	NA	NA	NA	16	9	31	30	36	40	29	33	23	26	23	25	24
Middle East and North Africa	NA	NA	NA	NA	NA	NA	12	9	27	33	35	45	28	37	23	30	21	21	21
South Asia	NA	NA	NA	NA	NA	NA	8	6	24	20	32	28	25	23	20	18	17	16	17
Sub-Saharan Africa	NA	NA	NA	NA	NA	NA	20	11	29	25	32	33	25	27	20	22	22	20	21
Low- and middle-income countries	NA	NA	NA	NA	NA	NA	14	9	28	27	35	37	28	32	23	28	22	24	23
High-income countries	NA	NA	NA	NA	NA	NA	20	6	30	26	37	39	30	34	25	29	28	29	29
WORLD	NA	NA	NA	NA	NA	NA	15	9	28	26	36	37	29	32	24	29	23	25	24
Attributable Mortality (thousands)																			
East Asia and Pacific	NA	NA	NA	NA	NA	NA	1	0	5	5	10	11	12	21	9	22	37	60	97
Europe and Central Asia	NA	NA	NA	NA	NA	NA	3	1	8	5	14	11	16	30	15	48	56	94	150
Latin America and the Caribbean	NA	NA	NA	NA	NA	NA	1	0	2	2	3	3	5	7	7	12	18	24	43
Middle East and North Africa	NA	NA	NA	NA	NA	NA	0	0	2	2	3	4	4	6	3	5	11	18	29
South Asia	NA	NA	NA	NA	NA	NA	1	1	6	6	10	11	10	17	5	8	33	42	75
Sub-Saharan Africa	NA	NA	NA	NA	NA	NA	2	1	4	4	5	6	6	10	5	9	22	30	52
Low- and middle-income countries	NA	NA	NA	NA	NA	NA	9	3	27	23	44	47	53	91	44	104	177	269	445
High-income countries	NA	NA	NA	NA	NA	NA	2	0	6	3	12	8	22	24	35	84	78	119	197
WORLD	NA	NA	NA	NA	NA	NA	10	4	34	26	57	55	75	115	79	188	254	388	642
Attributable YLL (thousands)																			
East Asia and Pacific	NA	NA	NA	NA	NA	NA	16	9	101	109	130	168	107	212	45	111	399	610	1,009
Europe and Central Asia	NA	NA	NA	NA	NA	NA	82	24	154	96	188	169	141	299	66	216	630	804	1,435
Latin America and the Caribbean	NA	NA	NA	NA	NA	NA	19	8	46	42	47	52	43	67	30	55	185	223	408
Middle East and North Africa	NA	NA	NA	NA	NA	NA	9	5	34	41	37	57	32	64	13	28	124	195	319
South Asia	NA	NA	NA	NA	NA	NA	23	14	118	112	137	167	93	177	27	43	397	512	910
Sub-Saharan Africa	NA	NA	NA	NA	NA	NA	52	22	74	77	64	93	52	104	25	46	267	343	610
Low- and middle-income countries	NA	NA	NA	NA	NA	NA	202	82	527	477	602	706	467	923	205	499	2,003	2,687	4,689
High-income countries	NA	NA	NA	NA	NA	NA	38	6	120	57	166	115	193	241	147	332	663	751	1,414
WORLD	NA	NA	NA	NA	NA	NA	240	89	647	534	768	821	660	1,164	352	830	2,666	3,437	6,103
Attributable DALYs (thousands)																			
East Asia and Pacific	NA	NA	NA	NA	NA	NA	23	12	108	115	133	171	110	216	46	113	419	626	1,045
Europe and Central Asia	NA	NA	NA	NA	NA	NA	91	31	174	104	214	182	166	328	78	242	722	887	1,609
Latin America and the Caribbean	NA	NA	NA	NA	NA	NA	22	9	50	44	52	55	48	71	33	58	205	237	442
Middle East and North Africa	NA	NA	NA	NA	NA	NA	11	6	39	47	43	61	35	68	14	29	141	211	352
South Asia	NA	NA	NA	NA	NA	NA	34	20	147	138	168	188	113	194	32	48	494	588	1,082
Sub-Saharan Africa	NA	NA	NA	NA	NA	NA	57	25	78	79	65	94	53	105	26	46	279	350	630
Low- and middle-income countries	NA	NA	NA	NA	NA	NA	238	104	595	527	674	751	525	982	229	536	2,260	2,901	5,161
High-income countries	NA	NA	NA	NA	NA	NA	49	9	140	70	194	129	227	269	175	375	785	852	1,638
WORLD	NA	NA	NA	NA	NA	NA	287	113	734	597	868	880	752	1,251	404	912	3,045	3,753	6,798

Source: Authors' calculations.
Note: NA = not applicable.

Table 4A.27

Risk factor: High blood pressure
Disease: All causes

Region	0–4 years Male	0–4 years Female	5–14 years Male	5–14 years Female	15–29 years Male	15–29 years Female	30–44 years Male	30–44 years Female	45–59 years Male	45–59 years Female	60–69 years Male	60–69 years Female	70–79 years Male	70–79 years Female	80+ years Male	80+ years Female	Total Male	Total Female	All
PAF of Mortality (%)																			
East Asia and Pacific	NA	NA	NA	NA	NA	NA	1	1	10	11	18	21	20	24	15	19	12	15	14
Europe and Central Asia	NA	NA	NA	NA	NA	NA	7	6	22	24	35	44	40	53	36	50	27	43	35
Latin America and the Caribbean	NA	NA	NA	NA	NA	NA	3	3	13	13	19	20	20	23	16	20	12	15	13
Middle East and North Africa	NA	NA	NA	NA	NA	NA	4	3	17	19	26	32	27	35	23	31	15	19	16
South Asia	NA	NA	NA	NA	NA	NA	1	1	12	10	22	21	22	21	16	15	10	9	10
Sub-Saharan Africa	NA	NA	NA	NA	NA	NA	1	1	6	8	13	20	17	23	14	19	3	5	4
Low- and middle-income countries	NA	NA	NA	NA	NA	NA	2	1	12	12	22	25	24	29	19	26	11	14	13
High-income countries	NA	NA	NA	NA	NA	NA	5	1	12	8	17	15	18	21	18	23	16	20	18
WORLD	NA	NA	NA	NA	NA	NA	2	1	12	11	21	23	23	28	18	25	12	15	14
PAF of YLL (%)																			
East Asia and Pacific	NA	NA	NA	NA	NA	NA	1	1	10	11	18	21	20	24	15	19	8	11	9
Europe and Central Asia	NA	NA	NA	NA	NA	NA	7	6	22	24	35	44	40	53	36	49	21	35	27
Latin America and the Caribbean	NA	NA	NA	NA	NA	NA	3	3	13	13	19	20	20	23	16	20	8	10	9
Middle East and North Africa	NA	NA	NA	NA	NA	NA	4	3	17	19	26	32	27	35	23	31	9	12	10
South Asia	NA	NA	NA	NA	NA	NA	1	1	12	9	22	21	22	21	16	15	6	5	6
Sub-Saharan Africa	NA	NA	NA	NA	NA	NA	1	1	6	8	13	19	17	22	14	19	2	2	2
Low- and middle-income countries	NA	NA	NA	NA	NA	NA	2	1	12	12	22	24	24	29	19	26	7	8	8
High-income countries	NA	NA	NA	NA	NA	NA	5	1	12	8	17	15	18	21	17	22	13	15	14
WORLD	NA	NA	NA	NA	NA	NA	2	1	12	11	21	23	23	28	18	25	8	9	8
PAF of DALYs (%)																			
East Asia and Pacific	NA	NA	NA	NA	NA	NA	1	1	7	7	15	15	18	20	14	16	6	7	6
Europe and Central Asia	NA	NA	NA	NA	NA	NA	5	3	19	16	31	34	35	44	31	42	17	23	20
Latin America and the Caribbean	NA	NA	NA	NA	NA	NA	2	1	9	8	15	14	16	16	14	16	5	5	5
Middle East and North Africa	NA	NA	NA	NA	NA	NA	2	1	11	10	20	22	23	28	20	25	6	6	6
South Asia	NA	NA	NA	NA	NA	NA	1	1	9	6	19	16	20	18	14	13	5	4	4
Sub-Saharan Africa	NA	NA	NA	NA	NA	NA	1	0	5	6	11	15	14	18	12	16	1	2	2
Low- and middle-income countries	NA	NA	NA	NA	NA	NA	2	1	9	8	18	18	21	24	16	21	5	6	6
High-income countries	NA	NA	NA	NA	NA	NA	3	1	9	5	14	11	16	16	15	17	9	9	9
WORLD	NA	NA	NA	NA	NA	NA	2	1	9	7	18	17	20	23	16	20	6	6	6
Attributable Mortality (thousands)																			
East Asia and Pacific	NA	NA	NA	NA	NA	NA	9	4	120	84	252	198	323	371	134	278	838	935	1,773
Europe and Central Asia	NA	NA	NA	NA	NA	NA	23	6	137	62	248	192	286	451	126	452	820	1,163	1,983
Latin America and the Caribbean	NA	NA	NA	NA	NA	NA	6	3	37	25	53	42	67	67	47	78	211	215	426
Middle East and North Africa	NA	NA	NA	NA	NA	NA	3	1	27	19	45	39	56	61	24	38	156	159	315
South Asia	NA	NA	NA	NA	NA	NA	10	5	138	73	240	187	243	227	87	86	718	579	1,297
Sub-Saharan Africa	NA	NA	NA	NA	NA	NA	9	4	40	37	55	68	61	87	24	43	189	240	429
Low- and middle-income countries	NA	NA	NA	NA	NA	NA	62	24	499	300	893	727	1,037	1,264	442	976	2,933	3,290	6,223
High-income countries	NA	NA	NA	NA	NA	NA	9	1	64	22	116	60	214	195	225	485	629	763	1,392
WORLD	NA	NA	NA	NA	NA	NA	71	25	563	322	1,008	787	1,252	1,459	667	1,461	3,561	4,054	7,615
Attributable YLL (thousands)																			
East Asia and Pacific	NA	NA	NA	NA	NA	NA	220	93	2,236	1,677	3,382	2,966	2,874	3,795	668	1,409	9,380	9,940	19,320
Europe and Central Asia	NA	NA	NA	NA	NA	NA	550	150	2,586	1,237	3,354	2,886	2,578	4,596	572	2,098	9,641	10,968	20,608
Latin America and the Caribbean	NA	NA	NA	NA	NA	NA	144	70	699	494	719	637	597	687	215	366	2,375	2,253	4,628
Middle East and North Africa	NA	NA	NA	NA	NA	NA	83	36	513	385	600	594	505	634	119	202	1,820	1,850	3,670
South Asia	NA	NA	NA	NA	NA	NA	237	130	2,578	1,453	3,249	2,819	2,177	2,377	426	463	8,667	7,242	15,909
Sub-Saharan Africa	NA	NA	NA	NA	NA	NA	224	102	742	737	743	1,033	547	894	121	237	2,377	3,004	5,381
Low- and middle-income countries	NA	NA	NA	NA	NA	NA	1,458	581	9,354	5,982	12,048	10,936	9,277	12,983	2,122	4,774	34,260	35,257	69,516
High-income countries	NA	NA	NA	NA	NA	NA	220	32	1,198	440	1,551	902	1,869	1,940	969	1,971	5,808	5,285	11,093
WORLD	NA	NA	NA	NA	NA	NA	1,678	614	10,552	6,422	13,600	11,839	11,146	14,923	3,091	6,745	40,067	40,542	80,610
Attributable DALYs (thousands)																			
East Asia and Pacific	NA	NA	NA	NA	NA	NA	272	117	2,718	2,038	4,049	3,474	3,268	4,244	738	1,530	11,045	11,403	22,447
Europe and Central Asia	NA	NA	NA	NA	NA	NA	614	189	2,844	1,444	3,732	3,301	2,819	4,995	614	2,222	10,623	12,152	22,774
Latin America and the Caribbean	NA	NA	NA	NA	NA	NA	174	89	819	594	841	741	669	761	239	403	2,742	2,587	5,330
Middle East and North Africa	NA	NA	NA	NA	NA	NA	95	42	566	432	663	650	542	674	128	216	1,995	2,014	4,009
South Asia	NA	NA	NA	NA	NA	NA	281	154	2,885	1,652	3,665	3,155	2,380	2,572	462	501	9,673	8,034	17,707
Sub-Saharan Africa	NA	NA	NA	NA	NA	NA	241	113	802	806	802	1,122	579	947	129	254	2,554	3,241	5,795
Low- and middle-income countries	NA	NA	NA	NA	NA	NA	1,678	705	10,635	6,964	13,752	12,442	10,257	14,192	2,309	5,128	38,632	39,431	78,063
High-income countries	NA	NA	NA	NA	NA	NA	298	52	1,556	660	1,989	1,233	2,271	2,408	1,120	2,299	7,234	6,652	13,887
WORLD	NA	NA	NA	NA	NA	NA	1,976	756	12,191	7,625	15,741	13,675	12,528	16,600	3,429	7,427	45,866	46,084	91,950

Source: Authors' calculations.
Note: NA = not applicable.

Table 4A.28

Risk factor: High cholesterol
Disease: Ischemic heart disease

Region	0–4 years Male	0–4 years Female	5–14 years Male	5–14 years Female	15–29 years Male	15–29 years Female	30–44 years Male	30–44 years Female	45–59 years Male	45–59 years Female	60–69 years Male	60–69 years Female	70–79 years Male	70–79 years Female	80+ years Male	80+ years Female	Total Male	Total Female	All
PAF of Mortality (%)																			
East Asia and Pacific	NA	NA	NA	NA	NA	NA	49	41	44	51	29	41	21	35	15	32	27	37	32
Europe and Central Asia	NA	NA	NA	NA	NA	NA	86	83	74	77	54	64	44	55	40	54	54	57	55
Latin America and the Caribbean	NA	NA	NA	NA	NA	NA	84	76	70	69	51	56	41	48	34	42	49	50	49
Middle East and North Africa	NA	NA	NA	NA	NA	NA	75	70	62	67	45	54	36	46	32	43	45	51	47
South Asia	NA	NA	NA	NA	NA	NA	71	76	59	70	41	45	32	38	26	38	42	46	43
Sub-Saharan Africa	NA	NA	NA	NA	NA	NA	10	18	14	36	8	28	2	20	0	18	7	24	15
Low- and middle-income countries	NA	NA	NA	NA	NA	NA	69	65	58	64	41	48	32	43	27	43	41	47	43
High-income countries	NA	NA	NA	NA	NA	NA	89	84	76	76	56	63	45	53	42	52	51	54	52
WORLD	NA	NA	NA	NA	NA	NA	71	66	61	65	43	49	34	45	32	46	43	48	45
PAF of YLL (%)																			
East Asia and Pacific	NA	NA	NA	NA	NA	NA	49	41	44	51	29	41	21	35	15	32	31	39	35
Europe and Central Asia	NA	NA	NA	NA	NA	NA	86	83	74	77	54	64	44	55	40	54	59	60	60
Latin America and the Caribbean	NA	NA	NA	NA	NA	NA	84	76	70	69	51	56	41	48	34	42	55	55	55
Middle East and North Africa	NA	NA	NA	NA	NA	NA	75	70	62	67	45	54	36	46	32	43	49	53	51
South Asia	NA	NA	NA	NA	NA	NA	71	76	59	70	41	45	32	38	26	38	46	48	47
Sub-Saharan Africa	NA	NA	NA	NA	NA	NA	10	18	14	36	8	28	2	20	0	18	8	26	17
Low- and middle-income countries	NA	NA	NA	NA	NA	NA	68	65	59	64	41	48	32	43	27	43	45	48	47
High-income countries	NA	NA	NA	NA	NA	NA	89	84	76	76	56	63	45	53	42	52	57	57	57
WORLD	NA	NA	NA	NA	NA	NA	70	66	61	65	43	49	34	45	32	46	47	50	48
PAF of DALYs (%)																			
East Asia and Pacific	NA	NA	NA	NA	NA	NA	49	41	44	51	29	41	21	35	15	32	31	38	34
Europe and Central Asia	NA	NA	NA	NA	NA	NA	86	83	74	77	54	64	44	55	40	54	59	60	60
Latin America and the Caribbean	NA	NA	NA	NA	NA	NA	84	76	70	69	51	56	41	48	34	42	55	54	55
Middle East and North Africa	NA	NA	NA	NA	NA	NA	75	70	62	67	45	54	36	46	32	43	49	53	51
South Asia	NA	NA	NA	NA	NA	NA	71	76	59	70	41	45	32	38	26	38	46	48	47
Sub-Saharan Africa	NA	NA	NA	NA	NA	NA	10	18	14	36	8	28	2	20	0	18	8	26	17
Low- and middle-income countries	NA	NA	NA	NA	NA	NA	68	65	58	64	41	48	32	43	27	43	45	48	46
High-income countries	NA	NA	NA	NA	NA	NA	89	84	76	76	56	63	45	53	42	52	57	57	57
WORLD	NA	NA	NA	NA	NA	NA	70	66	61	65	43	50	34	45	32	46	47	49	48
Attributable Mortality (thousands)																			
East Asia and Pacific	NA	NA	NA	NA	NA	NA	15	7	46	30	43	46	39	63	16	59	159	205	364
Europe and Central Asia	NA	NA	NA	NA	NA	NA	32	6	113	34	123	83	116	174	53	200	438	497	935
Latin America and the Caribbean	NA	NA	NA	NA	NA	NA	8	3	28	12	25	16	24	21	15	25	99	78	177
Middle East and North Africa	NA	NA	NA	NA	NA	NA	8	3	25	13	22	17	21	22	8	14	85	68	153
South Asia	NA	NA	NA	NA	NA	NA	35	25	144	87	122	105	94	102	35	48	430	367	797
Sub-Saharan Africa	NA	NA	NA	NA	NA	NA	1	1	6	9	4	13	1	11	0	6	12	40	51
Low- and middle-income countries	NA	NA	NA	NA	NA	NA	99	44	362	186	339	280	296	393	128	351	1,223	1,254	2,477
High-income countries	NA	NA	NA	NA	NA	NA	14	3	66	17	73	33	104	84	104	212	361	350	711
WORLD	NA	NA	NA	NA	NA	NA	113	47	428	203	412	313	400	477	232	564	1,585	1,604	3,189
Attributable YLL (thousands)																			
East Asia and Pacific	NA	NA	NA	NA	NA	NA	360	166	858	593	581	690	347	645	79	293	2,225	2,387	4,612
Europe and Central Asia	NA	NA	NA	NA	NA	NA	758	145	2,143	669	1,671	1,245	1,052	1,774	241	927	5,865	4,760	10,624
Latin America and the Caribbean	NA	NA	NA	NA	NA	NA	182	74	515	248	334	247	214	218	69	116	1,313	903	2,216
Middle East and North Africa	NA	NA	NA	NA	NA	NA	191	68	474	259	299	261	187	224	41	73	1,192	885	2,077
South Asia	NA	NA	NA	NA	NA	NA	823	610	2,692	1,736	1,644	1,580	842	1,072	174	256	6,175	5,253	11,428
Sub-Saharan Africa	NA	NA	NA	NA	NA	NA	17	15	105	184	53	194	13	116	0	31	187	539	726
Low- and middle-income countries	NA	NA	NA	NA	NA	NA	2,330	1,077	6,787	3,688	4,581	4,217	2,655	4,048	603	1,695	16,957	14,726	31,683
High-income countries	NA	NA	NA	NA	NA	NA	330	76	1,234	341	979	493	909	842	455	870	3,908	2,623	6,531
WORLD	NA	NA	NA	NA	NA	NA	2,661	1,154	8,021	4,029	5,561	4,709	3,565	4,890	1,058	2,566	20,865	17,348	38,214
Attributable DALYs (thousands)																			
East Asia and Pacific	NA	NA	NA	NA	NA	NA	399	185	916	637	609	724	355	657	80	297	2,359	2,499	4,858
Europe and Central Asia	NA	NA	NA	NA	NA	NA	814	167	2,226	717	1,725	1,304	1,070	1,807	244	940	6,077	4,934	11,011
Latin America and the Caribbean	NA	NA	NA	NA	NA	NA	207	86	550	271	356	262	220	223	70	118	1,402	960	2,362
Middle East and North Africa	NA	NA	NA	NA	NA	NA	212	77	501	276	314	273	191	228	42	74	1,259	927	2,186
South Asia	NA	NA	NA	NA	NA	NA	936	698	2,856	1,871	1,731	1,664	864	1,096	177	260	6,563	5,589	12,152
Sub-Saharan Africa	NA	NA	NA	NA	NA	NA	18	17	111	196	55	205	13	118	0	31	199	567	766
Low- and middle-income countries	NA	NA	NA	NA	NA	NA	2,585	1,229	7,159	3,969	4,789	4,430	2,713	4,129	613	1,719	17,860	15,476	33,336
High-income countries	NA	NA	NA	NA	NA	NA	377	102	1,360	409	1,054	553	956	898	471	903	4,218	2,866	7,084
WORLD	NA	NA	NA	NA	NA	NA	2,963	1,331	8,519	4,378	5,843	4,983	3,669	5,027	1,083	2,622	22,078	18,342	40,420

Source: Authors' calculations.
Note: NA = not applicable.

Table 4A.29

Risk factor: **High cholesterol**
Disease: **Cerebrovascular disease**

Region	0–4 years Male	Female	5–14 years Male	Female	15–29 years Male	Female	30–44 years Male	Female	45–59 years Male	Female	60–69 years Male	Female	70–79 years Male	Female	80+ years Male	Female	Total Male	Female	All
PAF of Mortality (%)																			
East Asia and Pacific	NA	NA	NA	NA	NA	NA	6	5	9	11	8	12	6	11	3	6	6	9	8
Europe and Central Asia	NA	NA	NA	NA	NA	NA	25	23	27	29	23	28	18	24	10	14	19	21	20
Latin America and the Caribbean	NA	NA	NA	NA	NA	NA	22	18	23	23	20	22	16	19	8	10	16	16	16
Middle East and North Africa	NA	NA	NA	NA	NA	NA	18	16	19	22	17	22	14	18	7	10	13	16	15
South Asia	NA	NA	NA	NA	NA	NA	16	18	18	23	16	17	12	14	6	9	13	15	14
Sub-Saharan Africa	NA	NA	NA	NA	NA	NA	2	3	4	10	3	10	1	7	0	4	2	8	5
Low- and middle-income countries	NA	NA	NA	NA	NA	NA	12	12	15	17	13	17	10	15	5	9	11	14	12
High-income countries	NA	NA	NA	NA	NA	NA	27	24	28	28	24	27	19	23	10	13	16	17	17
WORLD	NA	NA	NA	NA	NA	NA	14	13	16	18	14	18	11	16	6	10	11	14	13
PAF of YLL (%)																			
East Asia and Pacific	NA	NA	NA	NA	NA	NA	6	5	9	11	8	12	6	11	3	6	7	10	8
Europe and Central Asia	NA	NA	NA	NA	NA	NA	25	23	27	29	23	28	18	24	10	14	21	23	22
Latin America and the Caribbean	NA	NA	NA	NA	NA	NA	22	18	23	23	20	22	16	19	8	10	18	18	18
Middle East and North Africa	NA	NA	NA	NA	NA	NA	18	16	19	22	17	22	14	18	7	10	13	17	15
South Asia	NA	NA	NA	NA	NA	NA	16	18	18	23	16	17	12	14	6	9	14	16	15
Sub-Saharan Africa	NA	NA	NA	NA	NA	NA	2	3	4	10	3	10	1	7	0	4	2	8	6
Low- and middle-income countries	NA	NA	NA	NA	NA	NA	12	12	15	17	13	17	10	15	5	9	12	15	13
High-income countries	NA	NA	NA	NA	NA	NA	27	24	28	28	24	27	19	23	10	13	20	20	20
WORLD	NA	NA	NA	NA	NA	NA	14	13	16	18	14	18	11	16	6	10	12	15	14
PAF of DALYs (%)																			
East Asia and Pacific	NA	NA	NA	NA	NA	NA	9	7	12	14	10	14	7	12	3	6	9	12	10
Europe and Central Asia	NA	NA	NA	NA	NA	NA	29	28	30	33	26	32	20	26	10	15	24	26	25
Latin America and the Caribbean	NA	NA	NA	NA	NA	NA	27	23	28	27	23	26	17	20	8	10	21	22	22
Middle East and North Africa	NA	NA	NA	NA	NA	NA	22	19	23	25	20	24	15	19	7	10	15	19	17
South Asia	NA	NA	NA	NA	NA	NA	19	21	21	26	17	19	13	15	6	9	16	18	17
Sub-Saharan Africa	NA	NA	NA	NA	NA	NA	2	3	4	11	3	11	1	8	0	4	2	9	6
Low- and middle-income countries	NA	NA	NA	NA	NA	NA	15	15	18	20	15	20	11	16	5	9	14	17	15
High-income countries	NA	NA	NA	NA	NA	NA	36	32	36	36	29	34	21	26	11	14	25	25	25
WORLD	NA	NA	NA	NA	NA	NA	18	17	20	22	17	21	12	18	7	11	15	18	16
Attributable Mortality (thousands)																			
East Asia and Pacific	NA	NA	NA	NA	NA	NA	2	1	13	10	20	19	21	37	5	19	61	85	146
Europe and Central Asia	NA	NA	NA	NA	NA	NA	3	2	15	10	25	26	26	54	8	38	78	130	207
Latin America and the Caribbean	NA	NA	NA	NA	NA	NA	1	1	5	4	5	5	6	7	3	5	20	22	43
Middle East and North Africa	NA	NA	NA	NA	NA	NA	0	0	2	2	2	3	3	4	1	2	8	10	19
South Asia	NA	NA	NA	NA	NA	NA	2	1	14	12	22	22	19	25	4	8	60	67	128
Sub-Saharan Africa	NA	NA	NA	NA	NA	NA	0	0	1	4	1	5	0	5	0	2	3	16	18
Low- and middle-income countries	NA	NA	NA	NA	NA	NA	8	5	49	41	76	79	76	132	20	73	230	331	561
High-income countries	NA	NA	NA	NA	NA	NA	2	1	7	4	10	8	19	23	15	41	53	78	131
WORLD	NA	NA	NA	NA	NA	NA	10	6	56	45	87	87	95	155	35	115	283	409	692
Attributable YLL (thousands)																			
East Asia and Pacific	NA	NA	NA	NA	NA	NA	38	19	236	195	269	280	190	375	24	99	757	968	1,725
Europe and Central Asia	NA	NA	NA	NA	NA	NA	76	41	278	202	342	392	238	552	36	176	971	1,364	2,335
Latin America and the Caribbean	NA	NA	NA	NA	NA	NA	34	29	93	83	73	74	53	71	12	24	265	282	548
Middle East and North Africa	NA	NA	NA	NA	NA	NA	10	7	31	32	33	41	27	42	4	9	106	132	238
South Asia	NA	NA	NA	NA	NA	NA	36	25	256	231	295	325	169	264	20	43	777	887	1,664
Sub-Saharan Africa	NA	NA	NA	NA	NA	NA	4	6	20	74	13	81	3	51	0	9	40	221	261
Low- and middle-income countries	NA	NA	NA	NA	NA	NA	199	129	915	817	1,026	1,193	680	1,356	97	360	2,917	3,855	6,772
High-income countries	NA	NA	NA	NA	NA	NA	39	26	131	88	140	116	165	233	64	169	539	632	1,171
WORLD	NA	NA	NA	NA	NA	NA	238	155	1,046	905	1,166	1,309	845	1,588	161	529	3,456	4,487	7,942
Attributable DALYs (thousands)																			
East Asia and Pacific	NA	NA	NA	NA	NA	NA	76	39	420	344	434	439	253	490	28	115	1,210	1,426	2,637
Europe and Central Asia	NA	NA	NA	NA	NA	NA	107	69	388	302	475	562	305	684	42	197	1,317	1,814	3,131
Latin America and the Caribbean	NA	NA	NA	NA	NA	NA	58	55	155	138	117	116	73	93	14	29	417	430	847
Middle East and North Africa	NA	NA	NA	NA	NA	NA	18	13	49	48	49	57	34	50	5	11	155	179	334
South Asia	NA	NA	NA	NA	NA	NA	53	37	364	324	409	436	209	317	23	48	1,059	1,162	2,221
Sub-Saharan Africa	NA	NA	NA	NA	NA	NA	5	7	24	91	15	97	4	58	0	9	48	262	310
Low- and middle-income countries	NA	NA	NA	NA	NA	NA	317	219	1,400	1,247	1,500	1,707	878	1,692	112	408	4,206	5,273	9,479
High-income countries	NA	NA	NA	NA	NA	NA	100	70	333	235	324	274	291	406	87	228	1,134	1,212	2,347
WORLD	NA	NA	NA	NA	NA	NA	417	289	1,733	1,482	1,823	1,981	1,169	2,098	199	636	5,340	6,486	11,826

Source: Authors' calculations.
Note: NA = not applicable.

Table 4A.30

Risk factor: High cholesterol
Disease: All causes

Region	0–4 years Male	Female	5–14 years Male	Female	15–29 years Male	Female	30–44 years Male	Female	45–59 years Male	Female	60–69 years Male	Female	70–79 years Male	Female	80+ years Male	Female	Total Male	Female	All
PAF of Mortality (%)																			
East Asia and Pacific	NA	NA	NA	NA	NA	NA	3	2	5	5	5	7	4	7	2	5	3	5	4
Europe and Central Asia	NA	NA	NA	NA	NA	NA	11	7	21	17	21	25	20	27	18	26	17	23	20
Latin America and the Caribbean	NA	NA	NA	NA	NA	NA	4	4	11	9	11	10	9	10	6	8	7	7	7
Middle East and North Africa	NA	NA	NA	NA	NA	NA	10	6	17	14	14	16	12	15	9	12	9	9	9
South Asia	NA	NA	NA	NA	NA	NA	5	5	14	13	13	14	10	12	7	9	7	7	7
Sub-Saharan Africa	NA	NA	NA	NA	NA	NA	0	0	1	3	1	5	0	4	0	3	0	1	1
Low- and middle-income countries	NA	NA	NA	NA	NA	NA	4	3	10	9	10	12	9	12	6	11	6	7	6
High-income countries	NA	NA	NA	NA	NA	NA	8	4	14	8	12	10	11	12	9	12	10	11	11
WORLD	NA	NA	NA	NA	NA	NA	4	3	11	9	10	12	9	12	7	12	6	8	7
PAF of YLL (%)																			
East Asia and Pacific	NA	NA	NA	NA	NA	NA	3	2	5	5	5	7	4	7	2	5	3	4	3
Europe and Central Asia	NA	NA	NA	NA	NA	NA	11	7	20	17	21	25	20	27	17	26	15	20	17
Latin America and the Caribbean	NA	NA	NA	NA	NA	NA	4	4	11	9	11	10	9	10	6	8	5	5	5
Middle East and North Africa	NA	NA	NA	NA	NA	NA	10	5	17	14	14	16	12	15	9	12	7	6	6
South Asia	NA	NA	NA	NA	NA	NA	5	5	14	13	13	14	10	12	7	9	5	5	5
Sub-Saharan Africa	NA	NA	NA	NA	NA	NA	0	0	1	3	1	5	0	4	0	3	0	1	0
Low- and middle-income countries	NA	NA	NA	NA	NA	NA	4	3	10	9	10	12	9	12	6	11	4	4	4
High-income countries	NA	NA	NA	NA	NA	NA	8	4	14	8	12	10	10	12	9	12	10	9	10
WORLD	NA	NA	NA	NA	NA	NA	4	3	11	9	10	12	9	12	7	11	5	5	5
PAF of DALYs (%)																			
East Asia and Pacific	NA	NA	NA	NA	NA	NA	2	1	4	3	4	5	3	5	2	4	2	2	2
Europe and Central Asia	NA	NA	NA	NA	NA	NA	8	4	17	11	18	19	17	22	15	21	12	13	12
Latin America and the Caribbean	NA	NA	NA	NA	NA	NA	3	2	8	6	9	7	7	7	5	6	3	3	3
Middle East and North Africa	NA	NA	NA	NA	NA	NA	5	2	11	8	11	11	10	12	7	10	4	4	4
South Asia	NA	NA	NA	NA	NA	NA	4	3	10	9	11	11	9	10	6	8	4	3	4
Sub-Saharan Africa	NA	NA	NA	NA	NA	NA	0	0	1	2	1	4	0	3	0	3	0	0	0
Low- and middle-income countries	NA	NA	NA	NA	NA	NA	3	2	8	6	8	9	7	10	5	9	3	3	3
High-income countries	NA	NA	NA	NA	NA	NA	5	2	10	5	10	7	9	9	7	8	7	6	6
WORLD	NA	NA	NA	NA	NA	NA	3	2	8	6	9	9	8	10	6	9	3	3	3
Attributable Mortality (thousands)																			
East Asia and Pacific	NA	NA	NA	NA	NA	NA	17	8	59	39	63	65	60	100	21	79	220	290	510
Europe and Central Asia	NA	NA	NA	NA	NA	NA	36	8	128	44	149	109	143	228	61	238	516	626	1,142
Latin America and the Caribbean	NA	NA	NA	NA	NA	NA	9	4	33	17	30	21	30	28	18	30	119	100	220
Middle East and North Africa	NA	NA	NA	NA	NA	NA	8	3	27	15	25	20	24	26	9	15	93	79	172
South Asia	NA	NA	NA	NA	NA	NA	37	26	158	99	143	126	113	127	39	56	491	434	925
Sub-Saharan Africa	NA	NA	NA	NA	NA	NA	1	1	7	13	5	18	2	16	0	7	14	56	70
Low- and middle-income countries	NA	NA	NA	NA	NA	NA	107	49	411	227	415	360	372	525	148	425	1,453	1,585	3,038
High-income countries	NA	NA	NA	NA	NA	NA	16	4	73	22	83	41	123	108	119	253	415	428	842
WORLD	NA	NA	NA	NA	NA	NA	123	53	484	248	498	400	495	633	267	678	1,868	2,013	3,880
Attributable YLL (thousands)																			
East Asia and Pacific	NA	NA	NA	NA	NA	NA	398	185	1,094	787	850	970	537	1,020	102	392	2,982	3,354	6,337
Europe and Central Asia	NA	NA	NA	NA	NA	NA	834	186	2,422	871	2,013	1,637	1,290	2,326	277	1,103	6,836	6,124	12,959
Latin America and the Caribbean	NA	NA	NA	NA	NA	NA	216	103	608	331	407	321	267	289	81	140	1,579	1,185	2,764
Middle East and North Africa	NA	NA	NA	NA	NA	NA	201	75	506	291	332	302	214	266	46	82	1,298	1,017	2,315
South Asia	NA	NA	NA	NA	NA	NA	859	635	2,948	1,967	1,940	1,905	1,011	1,335	194	299	6,952	6,140	13,092
Sub-Saharan Africa	NA	NA	NA	NA	NA	NA	21	21	125	258	66	275	16	167	0	40	227	760	988
Low- and middle-income countries	NA	NA	NA	NA	NA	NA	2,529	1,206	7,702	4,505	5,607	5,410	3,335	5,404	700	2,055	19,874	18,581	38,455
High-income countries	NA	NA	NA	NA	NA	NA	369	102	1,365	429	1,119	609	1,074	1,075	519	1,040	4,447	3,254	7,701
WORLD	NA	NA	NA	NA	NA	NA	2,898	1,308	9,067	4,934	6,727	6,019	4,410	6,479	1,219	3,095	24,321	21,835	46,156
Attributable DALYs (thousands)																			
East Asia and Pacific	NA	NA	NA	NA	NA	NA	474	224	1,336	981	1,044	1,163	608	1,147	108	411	3,570	3,925	7,495
Europe and Central Asia	NA	NA	NA	NA	NA	NA	921	235	2,614	1,019	2,200	1,865	1,375	2,491	286	1,137	7,395	6,748	14,142
Latin America and the Caribbean	NA	NA	NA	NA	NA	NA	265	141	705	408	473	378	293	317	84	146	1,819	1,390	3,209
Middle East and North Africa	NA	NA	NA	NA	NA	NA	230	89	550	325	362	330	225	278	47	84	1,414	1,106	2,520
South Asia	NA	NA	NA	NA	NA	NA	989	735	3,220	2,196	2,140	2,100	1,073	1,413	200	309	7,622	6,751	14,373
Sub-Saharan Africa	NA	NA	NA	NA	NA	NA	23	24	135	287	71	302	17	175	0	41	246	829	1,075
Low- and middle-income countries	NA	NA	NA	NA	NA	NA	2,902	1,448	8,559	5,216	6,289	6,137	3,591	5,821	725	2,128	22,066	20,750	42,815
High-income countries	NA	NA	NA	NA	NA	NA	477	172	1,693	644	1,378	827	1,247	1,304	558	1,131	5,353	4,078	9,431
WORLD	NA	NA	NA	NA	NA	NA	3,379	1,620	10,252	5,860	7,667	6,964	4,838	7,125	1,282	3,259	27,419	24,828	52,246

Source: Authors' calculations.
Note: NA = not applicable.

Table 4A.31

Risk factor: Overweight and obesity
Disease: Colon and rectal cancers

Region	0–4 years Male	0–4 years Female	5–14 years Male	5–14 years Female	15–29 years Male	15–29 years Female	30–44 years Male	30–44 years Female	45–59 years Male	45–59 years Female	60–69 years Male	60–69 years Female	70–79 years Male	70–79 years Female	80+ years Male	80+ years Female	Total Male	Total Female	All
PAF of Mortality (%)																			
East Asia and Pacific	NA	NA	NA	NA	NA	NA	6	7	6	8	6	9	5	6	0	1	5	6	6
Europe and Central Asia	NA	NA	NA	NA	NA	NA	12	15	15	20	15	21	13	18	12	14	14	18	16
Latin America and the Caribbean	NA	NA	NA	NA	NA	NA	12	15	13	17	13	17	12	16	9	12	12	15	13
Middle East and North Africa	NA	NA	NA	NA	NA	NA	12	17	13	17	10	14	9	11	7	9	10	13	11
South Asia	NA	NA	NA	NA	NA	NA	2	4	2	5	2	2	1	4	1	0	1	3	2
Sub-Saharan Africa	NA	NA	NA	NA	NA	NA	4	7	5	6	3	5	2	4	1	1	3	5	4
Low- and middle-income countries	NA	NA	NA	NA	NA	NA	7	9	8	11	9	13	8	11	5	6	8	10	9
High-income countries	NA	NA	NA	NA	NA	NA	14	14	16	17	16	18	14	16	11	12	14	15	14
WORLD	NA	NA	NA	NA	NA	NA	8	10	11	13	11	14	11	13	9	10	10	12	11
PAF of YLL (%)																			
East Asia and Pacific	NA	NA	NA	NA	NA	NA	6	7	6	8	6	9	5	6	0	1	5	7	6
Europe and Central Asia	NA	NA	NA	NA	NA	NA	12	15	15	20	15	21	13	18	12	14	14	19	16
Latin America and the Caribbean	NA	NA	NA	NA	NA	NA	12	15	13	17	13	17	12	16	9	12	12	16	14
Middle East and North Africa	NA	NA	NA	NA	NA	NA	12	17	13	17	10	14	9	11	7	9	10	14	12
South Asia	NA	NA	NA	NA	NA	NA	2	4	2	5	2	2	1	4	1	0	2	3	2
Sub-Saharan Africa	NA	NA	NA	NA	NA	NA	4	7	5	6	3	5	2	4	1	1	4	5	4
Low- and middle-income countries	NA	NA	NA	NA	NA	NA	7	9	8	11	9	13	8	11	5	6	8	11	9
High-income countries	NA	NA	NA	NA	NA	NA	14	14	16	17	16	18	14	16	11	12	15	16	15
WORLD	NA	NA	NA	NA	NA	NA	8	10	11	13	11	14	11	13	9	9	10	12	11
PAF of DALYs (%)																			
East Asia and Pacific	NA	NA	NA	NA	NA	NA	6	7	6	8	6	9	5	6	0	1	5	7	6
Europe and Central Asia	NA	NA	NA	NA	NA	NA	12	15	15	20	15	21	13	18	12	14	14	19	16
Latin America and the Caribbean	NA	NA	NA	NA	NA	NA	12	15	13	17	13	17	12	16	9	12	12	16	14
Middle East and North Africa	NA	NA	NA	NA	NA	NA	12	17	13	17	10	14	9	11	7	9	10	14	12
South Asia	NA	NA	NA	NA	NA	NA	2	4	2	5	2	2	1	4	1	0	2	3	2
Sub-Saharan Africa	NA	NA	NA	NA	NA	NA	4	7	5	6	3	5	2	4	1	1	4	5	4
Low- and middle-income countries	NA	NA	NA	NA	NA	NA	7	9	8	11	9	13	8	12	5	6	8	11	9
High-income countries	NA	NA	NA	NA	NA	NA	14	14	16	17	16	18	14	16	11	12	15	16	15
WORLD	NA	NA	NA	NA	NA	NA	8	10	11	13	12	15	11	14	9	10	10	13	12
Attributable Mortality (thousands)																			
East Asia and Pacific	NA	NA	NA	NA	NA	NA	0	0	1	1	1	2	1	1	0	0	4	5	9
Europe and Central Asia	NA	NA	NA	NA	NA	NA	0	0	1	1	2	3	2	3	1	1	6	9	15
Latin America and the Caribbean	NA	NA	NA	NA	NA	NA	0	0	0	1	1	1	1	1	0	1	2	3	5
Middle East and North Africa	NA	NA	NA	NA	NA	NA	0	0	0	0	0	0	0	0	0	0	1	1	1
South Asia	NA	NA	NA	NA	NA	NA	0	0	0	0	0	0	0	0	0	0	0	0	1
Sub-Saharan Africa	NA	NA	NA	NA	NA	NA	0	0	0	0	0	0	0	0	0	0	0	0	1
Low- and middle-income countries	NA	NA	NA	NA	NA	NA	1	1	3	4	5	5	4	6	1	2	14	18	32
High-income countries	NA	NA	NA	NA	NA	NA	0	0	3	2	5	3	7	6	4	6	19	18	37
WORLD	NA	NA	NA	NA	NA	NA	1	1	6	6	10	9	11	12	5	8	33	36	69
Attributable YLL (thousands)																			
East Asia and Pacific	NA	NA	NA	NA	NA	NA	10	11	23	25	20	27	9	12	0	1	63	75	138
Europe and Central Asia	NA	NA	NA	NA	NA	NA	5	6	23	28	30	40	20	35	3	6	81	116	197
Latin America and the Caribbean	NA	NA	NA	NA	NA	NA	3	5	8	11	7	10	6	9	1	3	26	38	63
Middle East and North Africa	NA	NA	NA	NA	NA	NA	2	3	3	3	2	2	1	1	0	0	9	10	18
South Asia	NA	NA	NA	NA	NA	NA	1	1	1	3	1	1	0	1	0	0	4	6	11
Sub-Saharan Africa	NA	NA	NA	NA	NA	NA	1	2	3	3	1	2	0	1	0	0	5	7	12
Low- and middle-income countries	NA	NA	NA	NA	NA	NA	23	27	61	73	62	81	36	59	5	11	188	251	439
High-income countries	NA	NA	NA	NA	NA	NA	10	8	55	43	67	53	59	61	17	28	208	191	399
WORLD	NA	NA	NA	NA	NA	NA	33	35	117	115	129	134	95	120	22	38	396	442	839
Attributable DALYs (thousands)																			
East Asia and Pacific	NA	NA	NA	NA	NA	NA	10	11	25	27	21	28	10	12	0	1	66	79	145
Europe and Central Asia	NA	NA	NA	NA	NA	NA	6	7	25	30	33	43	21	37	3	7	87	124	211
Latin America and the Caribbean	NA	NA	NA	NA	NA	NA	3	5	9	12	8	10	6	9	1	3	27	40	67
Middle East and North Africa	NA	NA	NA	NA	NA	NA	2	3	3	4	2	2	1	1	0	0	9	10	19
South Asia	NA	NA	NA	NA	NA	NA	1	1	1	3	1	1	0	1	0	0	5	6	11
Sub-Saharan Africa	NA	NA	NA	NA	NA	NA	1	2	3	3	1	2	0	1	0	0	6	7	13
Low- and middle-income countries	NA	NA	NA	NA	NA	NA	24	29	65	78	66	86	38	62	5	11	199	266	465
High-income countries	NA	NA	NA	NA	NA	NA	11	10	68	54	81	64	69	73	20	32	251	233	483
WORLD	NA	NA	NA	NA	NA	NA	35	39	134	132	147	150	108	135	26	43	449	499	948

Source: Authors' calculations.
Note: NA = not applicable.

Table 4A.32

Risk factor: Overweight and obesity
Disease: Breast cancer

Region	0–4 years Male	Female	5–14 years Male	Female	15–29 years Male	Female	30–44 years Male	Female	45–59 years Male	Female	60–69 years Male	Female	70–79 years Male	Female	80+ years Male	Female	Total Male	Female	All
PAF of Mortality (%)																			
East Asia and Pacific	NA	NA	NA	NA	NA	NA	NA	NA	NA	5	NA	9	NA	6	NA	1	NA	5	5
Europe and Central Asia	NA	NA	NA	NA	NA	NA	NA	NA	NA	13	NA	21	NA	18	NA	14	NA	15	15
Latin America and the Caribbean	NA	NA	NA	NA	NA	NA	NA	NA	NA	12	NA	17	NA	16	NA	12	NA	12	12
Middle East and North Africa	NA	NA	NA	NA	NA	NA	NA	NA	NA	11	NA	14	NA	11	NA	9	NA	9	9
South Asia	NA	NA	NA	NA	NA	NA	NA	NA	NA	3	NA	2	NA	4	NA	0	NA	2	2
Sub-Saharan Africa	NA	NA	NA	NA	NA	NA	NA	NA	NA	4	NA	5	NA	4	NA	1	NA	4	4
Low- and middle-income countries	NA	NA	NA	NA	NA	NA	NA	NA	NA	7	NA	10	NA	10	NA	5	NA	7	7
High-income countries	NA	NA	NA	NA	NA	NA	NA	NA	NA	11	NA	18	NA	16	NA	12	NA	13	13
WORLD	NA	NA	NA	NA	NA	NA	NA	NA	NA	8	NA	12	NA	12	NA	9	NA	9	9
PAF of YLL (%)																			
East Asia and Pacific	NA	NA	NA	NA	NA	NA	NA	NA	NA	5	NA	9	NA	6	NA	1	NA	5	5
Europe and Central Asia	NA	NA	NA	NA	NA	NA	NA	NA	NA	13	NA	21	NA	18	NA	14	NA	14	14
Latin America and the Caribbean	NA	NA	NA	NA	NA	NA	NA	NA	NA	12	NA	17	NA	16	NA	12	NA	10	10
Middle East and North Africa	NA	NA	NA	NA	NA	NA	NA	NA	NA	11	NA	14	NA	11	NA	9	NA	8	8
South Asia	NA	NA	NA	NA	NA	NA	NA	NA	NA	3	NA	2	NA	4	NA	0	NA	2	2
Sub-Saharan Africa	NA	NA	NA	NA	NA	NA	NA	NA	NA	4	NA	5	NA	4	NA	1	NA	3	3
Low- and middle-income countries	NA	NA	NA	NA	NA	NA	NA	NA	NA	7	NA	10	NA	10	NA	5	NA	7	7
High-income countries	NA	NA	NA	NA	NA	NA	NA	NA	NA	11	NA	18	NA	16	NA	12	NA	12	12
WORLD	NA	NA	NA	NA	NA	NA	NA	NA	NA	8	NA	12	NA	12	NA	9	NA	8	8
PAF of DALYs (%)																			
East Asia and Pacific	NA	NA	NA	NA	NA	NA	NA	NA	NA	5	NA	9	NA	6	NA	1	NA	5	5
Europe and Central Asia	NA	NA	NA	NA	NA	NA	NA	NA	NA	13	NA	21	NA	18	NA	14	NA	14	14
Latin America and the Caribbean	NA	NA	NA	NA	NA	NA	NA	NA	NA	12	NA	17	NA	16	NA	12	NA	10	10
Middle East and North Africa	NA	NA	NA	NA	NA	NA	NA	NA	NA	11	NA	14	NA	11	NA	9	NA	8	8
South Asia	NA	NA	NA	NA	NA	NA	NA	NA	NA	3	NA	2	NA	4	NA	0	NA	2	2
Sub-Saharan Africa	NA	NA	NA	NA	NA	NA	NA	NA	NA	4	NA	5	NA	4	NA	1	NA	3	3
Low- and middle-income countries	NA	NA	NA	NA	NA	NA	NA	NA	NA	7	NA	10	NA	10	NA	5	NA	7	7
High-income countries	NA	NA	NA	NA	NA	NA	NA	NA	NA	11	NA	18	NA	16	NA	12	NA	12	12
WORLD	NA	NA	NA	NA	NA	NA	NA	NA	NA	8	NA	13	NA	13	NA	9	NA	8	8
Attributable Mortality (thousands)																			
East Asia and Pacific	NA	NA	NA	NA	NA	NA	NA	NA	NA	2	NA	2	NA	1	NA	0	NA	5	5
Europe and Central Asia	NA	NA	NA	NA	NA	NA	NA	NA	NA	3	NA	3	NA	3	NA	1	NA	10	10
Latin America and the Caribbean	NA	NA	NA	NA	NA	NA	NA	NA	NA	1	NA	1	NA	1	NA	1	NA	4	4
Middle East and North Africa	NA	NA	NA	NA	NA	NA	NA	NA	NA	1	NA	0	NA	0	NA	0	NA	1	1
South Asia	NA	NA	NA	NA	NA	NA	NA	NA	NA	1	NA	0	NA	1	NA	0	NA	2	2
Sub-Saharan Africa	NA	NA	NA	NA	NA	NA	NA	NA	NA	0	NA	0	NA	0	NA	0	NA	1	1
Low- and middle-income countries	NA	NA	NA	NA	NA	NA	NA	NA	NA	8	NA	8	NA	6	NA	2	NA	23	23
High-income countries	NA	NA	NA	NA	NA	NA	NA	NA	NA	4	NA	5	NA	6	NA	5	NA	20	20
WORLD	NA	NA	NA	NA	NA	NA	NA	NA	NA	12	NA	13	NA	12	NA	6	NA	43	43
Attributable YLL (thousands)																			
East Asia and Pacific	NA	NA	NA	NA	NA	NA	NA	NA	NA	40	NA	27	NA	8	NA	0	NA	75	75
Europe and Central Asia	NA	NA	NA	NA	NA	NA	NA	NA	NA	51	NA	52	NA	29	NA	5	NA	137	137
Latin America and the Caribbean	NA	NA	NA	NA	NA	NA	NA	NA	NA	29	NA	20	NA	11	NA	3	NA	62	62
Middle East and North Africa	NA	NA	NA	NA	NA	NA	NA	NA	NA	12	NA	5	NA	2	NA	0	NA	20	20
South Asia	NA	NA	NA	NA	NA	NA	NA	NA	NA	16	NA	5	NA	6	NA	0	NA	26	26
Sub-Saharan Africa	NA	NA	NA	NA	NA	NA	NA	NA	NA	9	NA	7	NA	3	NA	0	NA	19	19
Low- and middle-income countries	NA	NA	NA	NA	NA	NA	NA	NA	NA	157	NA	116	NA	58	NA	9	NA	339	339
High-income countries	NA	NA	NA	NA	NA	NA	NA	NA	NA	83	NA	82	NA	61	NA	21	NA	247	247
WORLD	NA	NA	NA	NA	NA	NA	NA	NA	NA	239	NA	198	NA	120	NA	29	NA	586	586
Attributable DALYs (thousands)																			
East Asia and Pacific	NA	NA	NA	NA	NA	NA	NA	NA	NA	42	NA	28	NA	8	NA	0	NA	79	79
Europe and Central Asia	NA	NA	NA	NA	NA	NA	NA	NA	NA	55	NA	55	NA	31	NA	5	NA	146	146
Latin America and the Caribbean	NA	NA	NA	NA	NA	NA	NA	NA	NA	31	NA	21	NA	12	NA	3	NA	66	66
Middle East and North Africa	NA	NA	NA	NA	NA	NA	NA	NA	NA	13	NA	5	NA	2	NA	0	NA	21	21
South Asia	NA	NA	NA	NA	NA	NA	NA	NA	NA	16	NA	5	NA	6	NA	0	NA	27	27
Sub-Saharan Africa	NA	NA	NA	NA	NA	NA	NA	NA	NA	9	NA	7	NA	3	NA	0	NA	20	20
Low- and middle-income countries	NA	NA	NA	NA	NA	NA	NA	NA	NA	166	NA	122	NA	62	NA	9	NA	359	359
High-income countries	NA	NA	NA	NA	NA	NA	NA	NA	NA	102	NA	95	NA	73	NA	24	NA	294	294
WORLD	NA	NA	NA	NA	NA	NA	NA	NA	NA	267	NA	217	NA	135	NA	33	NA	653	653

Source: Authors' calculations.
Note: NA = not applicable.

Table 4A.33

Risk factor: **Overweight and obesity**
Disease: **Corpus uteri cancer**

Region	0–4 years Male	0–4 years Female	5–14 years Male	5–14 years Female	15–29 years Male	15–29 years Female	30–44 years Male	30–44 years Female	45–59 years Male	45–59 years Female	60–69 years Male	60–69 years Female	70–79 years Male	70–79 years Female	80+ years Male	80+ years Female	Total Male	Total Female	All
PAF of Mortality (%)																			
East Asia and Pacific	NA	NA	NA	NA	NA	NA	NA	21	NA	24	NA	29	NA	19	NA	3	NA	21	21
Europe and Central Asia	NA	NA	NA	NA	NA	NA	NA	44	NA	54	NA	56	NA	51	NA	41	NA	51	51
Latin America and the Caribbean	NA	NA	NA	NA	NA	NA	NA	44	NA	49	NA	48	NA	46	NA	35	NA	44	44
Middle East and North Africa	NA	NA	NA	NA	NA	NA	NA	49	NA	48	NA	42	NA	34	NA	29	NA	38	38
South Asia	NA	NA	NA	NA	NA	NA	NA	13	NA	18	NA	6	NA	16	NA	0	NA	10	10
Sub-Saharan Africa	NA	NA	NA	NA	NA	NA	NA	23	NA	21	NA	18	NA	15	NA	5	NA	16	16
Low- and middle-income countries	NA	NA	NA	NA	NA	NA	NA	35	NA	41	NA	42	NA	39	NA	25	NA	37	37
High-income countries	NA	NA	NA	NA	NA	NA	NA	41	NA	47	NA	49	NA	46	NA	36	NA	43	43
WORLD	NA	NA	NA	NA	NA	NA	NA	36	NA	43	NA	45	NA	41	NA	31	NA	40	40
PAF of YLL (%)																			
East Asia and Pacific	NA	NA	NA	NA	NA	NA	NA	21	NA	24	NA	29	NA	19	NA	3	NA	23	23
Europe and Central Asia	NA	NA	NA	NA	NA	NA	NA	44	NA	54	NA	56	NA	51	NA	41	NA	52	52
Latin America and the Caribbean	NA	NA	NA	NA	NA	NA	NA	44	NA	49	NA	48	NA	46	NA	35	NA	45	45
Middle East and North Africa	NA	NA	NA	NA	NA	NA	NA	49	NA	48	NA	42	NA	34	NA	29	NA	39	39
South Asia	NA	NA	NA	NA	NA	NA	NA	13	NA	18	NA	6	NA	16	NA	0	NA	11	11
Sub-Saharan Africa	NA	NA	NA	NA	NA	NA	NA	23	NA	21	NA	18	NA	15	NA	5	NA	17	17
Low- and middle-income countries	NA	NA	NA	NA	NA	NA	NA	35	NA	41	NA	42	NA	39	NA	24	NA	39	39
High-income countries	NA	NA	NA	NA	NA	NA	NA	41	NA	47	NA	49	NA	46	NA	36	NA	45	45
WORLD	NA	NA	NA	NA	NA	NA	NA	36	NA	43	NA	45	NA	41	NA	30	NA	41	41
PAF of DALYs (%)																			
East Asia and Pacific	NA	NA	NA	NA	NA	NA	NA	21	NA	24	NA	29	NA	19	NA	3	NA	23	23
Europe and Central Asia	NA	NA	NA	NA	NA	NA	NA	44	NA	54	NA	56	NA	51	NA	41	NA	51	51
Latin America and the Caribbean	NA	NA	NA	NA	NA	NA	NA	44	NA	49	NA	48	NA	46	NA	35	NA	45	45
Middle East and North Africa	NA	NA	NA	NA	NA	NA	NA	49	NA	48	NA	42	NA	34	NA	29	NA	40	40
South Asia	NA	NA	NA	NA	NA	NA	NA	13	NA	18	NA	6	NA	16	NA	0	NA	11	11
Sub-Saharan Africa	NA	NA	NA	NA	NA	NA	NA	23	NA	21	NA	18	NA	15	NA	5	NA	17	17
Low- and middle-income countries	NA	NA	NA	NA	NA	NA	NA	36	NA	43	NA	43	NA	39	NA	24	NA	39	39
High-income countries	NA	NA	NA	NA	NA	NA	NA	41	NA	47	NA	49	NA	46	NA	36	NA	46	46
WORLD	NA	NA	NA	NA	NA	NA	NA	38	NA	44	NA	46	NA	42	NA	31	NA	42	42
Attributable Mortality (thousands)																			
East Asia and Pacific	NA	NA	NA	NA	NA	NA	NA	0	NA	1	NA	1	NA	0	NA	0	NA	2	2
Europe and Central Asia	NA	NA	NA	NA	NA	NA	NA	0	NA	2	NA	3	NA	3	NA	1	NA	8	8
Latin America and the Caribbean	NA	NA	NA	NA	NA	NA	NA	1	NA	1	NA	1	NA	1	NA	1	NA	5	5
Middle East and North Africa	NA	NA	NA	NA	NA	NA	NA	0	NA	0	NA	0	NA	0	NA	0	NA	0	0
South Asia	NA	NA	NA	NA	NA	NA	NA	0	NA	0	NA	0	NA	0	NA	0	NA	0	0
Sub-Saharan Africa	NA	NA	NA	NA	NA	NA	NA	0	NA	0	NA	0	NA	0	NA	0	NA	0	0
Low- and middle-income countries	NA	NA	NA	NA	NA	NA	NA	1	NA	4	NA	5	NA	5	NA	2	NA	16	16
High-income countries	NA	NA	NA	NA	NA	NA	NA	0	NA	2	NA	3	NA	4	NA	3	NA	12	12
WORLD	NA	NA	NA	NA	NA	NA	NA	2	NA	6	NA	8	NA	9	NA	5	NA	28	28
Attributable YLL (thousands)																			
East Asia and Pacific	NA	NA	NA	NA	NA	NA	NA	4	NA	11	NA	9	NA	3	NA	0	NA	28	28
Europe and Central Asia	NA	NA	NA	NA	NA	NA	NA	10	NA	35	NA	42	NA	29	NA	4	NA	120	120
Latin America and the Caribbean	NA	NA	NA	NA	NA	NA	NA	13	NA	28	NA	20	NA	13	NA	3	NA	78	78
Middle East and North Africa	NA	NA	NA	NA	NA	NA	NA	1	NA	2	NA	1	NA	1	NA	0	NA	6	6
South Asia	NA	NA	NA	NA	NA	NA	NA	1	NA	2	NA	1	NA	2	NA	0	NA	6	6
Sub-Saharan Africa	NA	NA	NA	NA	NA	NA	NA	1	NA	2	NA	2	NA	1	NA	0	NA	6	6
Low- and middle-income countries	NA	NA	NA	NA	NA	NA	NA	30	NA	81	NA	75	NA	49	NA	8	NA	243	243
High-income countries	NA	NA	NA	NA	NA	NA	NA	7	NA	35	NA	42	NA	40	NA	14	NA	137	137
WORLD	NA	NA	NA	NA	NA	NA	NA	37	NA	116	NA	116	NA	89	NA	22	NA	380	380
Attributable DALYs (thousands)																			
East Asia and Pacific	NA	NA	NA	NA	NA	NA	NA	8	NA	17	NA	11	NA	3	NA	0	NA	40	40
Europe and Central Asia	NA	NA	NA	NA	NA	NA	NA	21	NA	62	NA	57	NA	33	NA	5	NA	178	178
Latin America and the Caribbean	NA	NA	NA	NA	NA	NA	NA	25	NA	46	NA	25	NA	14	NA	4	NA	115	115
Middle East and North Africa	NA	NA	NA	NA	NA	NA	NA	2	NA	4	NA	2	NA	1	NA	0	NA	9	9
South Asia	NA	NA	NA	NA	NA	NA	NA	1	NA	3	NA	1	NA	2	NA	0	NA	7	7
Sub-Saharan Africa	NA	NA	NA	NA	NA	NA	NA	1	NA	2	NA	2	NA	1	NA	0	NA	7	7
Low- and middle-income countries	NA	NA	NA	NA	NA	NA	NA	59	NA	135	NA	98	NA	56	NA	9	NA	356	356
High-income countries	NA	NA	NA	NA	NA	NA	NA	23	NA	96	NA	75	NA	57	NA	17	NA	267	267
WORLD	NA	NA	NA	NA	NA	NA	NA	82	NA	231	NA	173	NA	113	NA	25	NA	623	623

Source: Authors' calculations.
Note: NA = not applicable.

Table 4A.34

Risk factor: Overweight and obesity
Disease: Diabetes mellitus

Region	0–4 years Male	0–4 years Female	5–14 years Male	5–14 years Female	15–29 years Male	15–29 years Female	30–44 years Male	30–44 years Female	45–59 years Male	45–59 years Female	60–69 years Male	60–69 years Female	70–79 years Male	70–79 years Female	80+ years Male	80+ years Female	Total Male	Total Female	All
PAF of Mortality (%)																			
East Asia and Pacific	NA	NA	NA	NA	NA	NA	54	73	42	63	33	55	38	35	4	7	33	42	38
Europe and Central Asia	NA	NA	NA	NA	NA	NA	80	96	73	95	62	83	73	77	72	67	68	78	74
Latin America and the Caribbean	NA	NA	NA	NA	NA	NA	81	96	71	92	58	76	71	72	60	59	65	74	70
Middle East and North Africa	NA	NA	NA	NA	NA	NA	86	99	70	93	52	72	65	60	55	55	61	69	65
South Asia	NA	NA	NA	NA	NA	NA	30	61	13	56	11	14	8	34	14	0	12	27	19
Sub-Saharan Africa	NA	NA	NA	NA	NA	NA	53	80	43	64	19	36	18	30	10	10	26	39	34
Low- and middle-income countries	NA	NA	NA	NA	NA	NA	57	80	41	70	34	50	38	47	26	29	36	49	43
High-income countries	NA	NA	NA	NA	NA	NA	87	96	77	91	64	78	76	72	69	60	72	68	70
WORLD	NA	NA	NA	NA	NA	NA	61	82	46	72	39	53	47	52	41	43	43	53	49
PAF of YLL (%)																			
East Asia and Pacific	NA	NA	NA	NA	NA	NA	54	73	42	63	33	55	38	35	4	7	36	48	43
Europe and Central Asia	NA	NA	NA	NA	NA	NA	80	96	73	95	62	83	73	77	72	67	66	79	73
Latin America and the Caribbean	NA	NA	NA	NA	NA	NA	81	96	71	92	58	76	71	72	60	59	65	77	72
Middle East and North Africa	NA	NA	NA	NA	NA	NA	86	99	70	93	52	72	65	60	55	55	61	72	67
South Asia	NA	NA	NA	NA	NA	NA	30	61	13	56	11	14	8	34	14	0	12	30	21
Sub-Saharan Africa	NA	NA	NA	NA	NA	NA	53	80	43	64	19	36	18	30	10	10	30	44	39
Low- and middle-income countries	NA	NA	NA	NA	NA	NA	57	80	41	70	34	50	38	47	25	28	37	53	46
High-income countries	NA	NA	NA	NA	NA	NA	87	96	77	91	64	78	76	72	69	60	72	74	73
WORLD	NA	NA	NA	NA	NA	NA	61	82	46	72	39	53	47	52	40	41	43	56	50
PAF of DALYs (%)																			
East Asia and Pacific	NA	NA	NA	NA	NA	NA	54	73	42	63	33	55	38	35	4	7	38	51	45
Europe and Central Asia	NA	NA	NA	NA	NA	NA	80	96	73	95	62	83	73	77	72	67	67	82	76
Latin America and the Caribbean	NA	NA	NA	NA	NA	NA	81	96	71	92	58	76	71	72	60	59	66	79	73
Middle East and North Africa	NA	NA	NA	NA	NA	NA	86	99	70	93	52	72	65	60	55	55	61	74	69
South Asia	NA	NA	NA	NA	NA	NA	30	61	13	56	11	14	8	34	14	0	14	35	24
Sub-Saharan Africa	NA	NA	NA	NA	NA	NA	53	80	43	64	19	36	18	30	10	10	31	46	40
Low- and middle-income countries	NA	NA	NA	NA	NA	NA	54	77	41	71	34	51	39	48	26	29	38	56	48
High-income countries	NA	NA	NA	NA	NA	NA	87	96	77	91	64	78	76	72	69	60	73	78	76
WORLD	NA	NA	NA	NA	NA	NA	61	80	49	75	41	55	49	54	42	43	46	60	54
Attributable Mortality (thousands)																			
East Asia and Pacific	NA	NA	NA	NA	NA	NA	3	3	8	14	10	21	11	16	1	1	32	57	89
Europe and Central Asia	NA	NA	NA	NA	NA	NA	1	1	3	3	4	8	4	9	1	3	14	24	38
Latin America and the Caribbean	NA	NA	NA	NA	NA	NA	3	3	11	15	11	18	14	20	7	13	46	69	114
Middle East and North Africa	NA	NA	NA	NA	NA	NA	1	1	2	3	2	3	3	3	1	1	9	12	20
South Asia	NA	NA	NA	NA	NA	NA	2	2	3	11	3	4	2	9	2	0	12	25	37
Sub-Saharan Africa	NA	NA	NA	NA	NA	NA	1	2	3	8	1	6	1	5	0	1	8	21	28
Low- and middle-income countries	NA	NA	NA	NA	NA	NA	10	11	31	54	31	60	36	63	12	19	121	207	327
High-income countries	NA	NA	NA	NA	NA	NA	3	2	9	7	12	11	23	25	18	32	65	76	142
WORLD	NA	NA	NA	NA	NA	NA	13	13	40	60	43	71	59	87	30	52	186	283	469
Attributable YLL (thousands)																			
East Asia and Pacific	NA	NA	NA	NA	NA	NA	60	82	159	284	131	321	101	170	3	8	454	865	1,319
Europe and Central Asia	NA	NA	NA	NA	NA	NA	33	28	61	69	53	115	38	93	6	16	192	321	512
Latin America and the Caribbean	NA	NA	NA	NA	NA	NA	71	70	201	288	149	271	128	211	32	65	580	906	1,486
Middle East and North Africa	NA	NA	NA	NA	NA	NA	14	15	36	55	29	52	27	36	5	8	111	166	278
South Asia	NA	NA	NA	NA	NA	NA	36	38	62	212	39	60	18	94	11	0	166	404	570
Sub-Saharan Africa	NA	NA	NA	NA	NA	NA	32	46	60	155	20	88	12	47	2	3	126	339	465
Low- and middle-income countries	NA	NA	NA	NA	NA	NA	248	280	579	1,062	421	906	324	652	58	100	1,630	3,001	4,631
High-income countries	NA	NA	NA	NA	NA	NA	63	39	176	133	165	167	201	248	81	144	686	730	1,416
WORLD	NA	NA	NA	NA	NA	NA	310	319	755	1,195	586	1,073	525	900	139	244	2,316	3,731	6,047
Attributable DALYs (thousands)																			
East Asia and Pacific	NA	NA	NA	NA	NA	NA	212	290	293	522	172	402	120	197	3	9	800	1,422	2,221
Europe and Central Asia	NA	NA	NA	NA	NA	NA	87	110	134	205	85	185	57	137	9	28	373	665	1,038
Latin America and the Caribbean	NA	NA	NA	NA	NA	NA	124	153	273	454	176	343	145	253	36	77	754	1,281	2,034
Middle East and North Africa	NA	NA	NA	NA	NA	NA	71	98	78	126	40	71	33	45	6	10	228	350	578
South Asia	NA	NA	NA	NA	NA	NA	119	218	98	371	52	75	22	113	13	0	304	777	1,081
Sub-Saharan Africa	NA	NA	NA	NA	NA	NA	53	80	78	186	23	95	13	50	2	3	170	414	584
Low- and middle-income countries	NA	NA	NA	NA	NA	NA	666	950	954	1,864	548	1,172	391	794	70	128	2,628	4,908	7,536
High-income countries	NA	NA	NA	NA	NA	NA	261	218	521	520	300	364	294	386	109	198	1,484	1,686	3,171
WORLD	NA	NA	NA	NA	NA	NA	927	1,168	1,474	2,384	848	1,536	684	1,181	179	326	4,112	6,595	10,707

Source: Authors' calculations.
Note: NA = not applicable.

Table 4A.35

Risk factor: Overweight and obesity
Disease: Hypertensive heart disease

Region	0–4 years Male	0–4 years Female	5–14 years Male	5–14 years Female	15–29 years Male	15–29 years Female	30–44 years Male	30–44 years Female	45–59 years Male	45–59 years Female	60–69 years Male	60–69 years Female	70–79 years Male	70–79 years Female	80+ years Male	80+ years Female	Total Male	Total Female	All
PAF of Mortality (%)																			
East Asia and Pacific	NA	NA	NA	NA	NA	NA	37	42	32	39	26	39	17	20	1	3	20	21	21
Europe and Central Asia	NA	NA	NA	NA	NA	NA	62	74	61	75	52	68	41	54	28	32	46	53	50
Latin America and the Caribbean	NA	NA	NA	NA	NA	NA	62	74	58	70	48	59	38	49	21	27	40	45	43
Middle East and North Africa	NA	NA	NA	NA	NA	NA	66	81	57	70	42	54	31	37	17	22	36	41	39
South Asia	NA	NA	NA	NA	NA	NA	18	30	9	30	9	9	3	17	4	0	7	15	11
Sub-Saharan Africa	NA	NA	NA	NA	NA	NA	33	47	32	36	14	24	7	16	3	4	15	20	18
Low- and middle-income countries	NA	NA	NA	NA	NA	NA	41	51	37	47	30	41	22	30	10	13	25	30	28
High-income countries	NA	NA	NA	NA	NA	NA	70	72	65	68	54	61	44	49	26	28	42	36	38
WORLD	NA	NA	NA	NA	NA	NA	44	53	40	49	32	42	24	32	14	18	27	31	29
PAF of YLL (%)																			
East Asia and Pacific	NA	NA	NA	NA	NA	NA	37	42	32	39	26	39	17	20	1	3	24	27	26
Europe and Central Asia	NA	NA	NA	NA	NA	NA	62	74	61	75	52	68	41	54	28	32	51	59	55
Latin America and the Caribbean	NA	NA	NA	NA	NA	NA	62	74	58	70	48	59	38	49	21	27	45	53	50
Middle East and North Africa	NA	NA	NA	NA	NA	NA	66	81	57	70	42	54	31	37	17	22	41	47	44
South Asia	NA	NA	NA	NA	NA	NA	18	30	9	30	9	9	3	17	4	0	8	17	12
Sub-Saharan Africa	NA	NA	NA	NA	NA	NA	33	47	32	36	14	24	7	16	3	4	20	25	23
Low- and middle-income countries	NA	NA	NA	NA	NA	NA	41	51	37	47	30	41	22	30	9	12	29	35	32
High-income countries	NA	NA	NA	NA	NA	NA	70	72	65	68	54	61	44	49	26	28	50	45	47
WORLD	NA	NA	NA	NA	NA	NA	43	53	40	49	32	42	24	32	13	17	31	36	34
PAF of DALYs (%)																			
East Asia and Pacific	NA	NA	NA	NA	NA	NA	37	42	32	39	26	39	17	20	1	3	24	27	25
Europe and Central Asia	NA	NA	NA	NA	NA	NA	62	74	61	75	52	68	41	54	28	32	50	59	55
Latin America and the Caribbean	NA	NA	NA	NA	NA	NA	62	74	58	70	48	59	38	49	21	27	45	53	49
Middle East and North Africa	NA	NA	NA	NA	NA	NA	66	81	57	70	42	54	31	37	17	22	41	47	44
South Asia	NA	NA	NA	NA	NA	NA	18	30	9	30	9	9	3	17	4	0	8	17	12
Sub-Saharan Africa	NA	NA	NA	NA	NA	NA	33	47	32	36	14	24	7	16	3	4	19	24	22
Low- and middle-income countries	NA	NA	NA	NA	NA	NA	41	51	37	47	30	40	21	29	9	12	28	34	31
High-income countries	NA	NA	NA	NA	NA	NA	70	72	65	68	54	61	44	49	26	28	48	43	45
WORLD	NA	NA	NA	NA	NA	NA	43	52	39	48	32	42	24	32	13	17	30	35	33
Attributable Mortality (thousands)																			
East Asia and Pacific	NA	NA	NA	NA	NA	NA	2	2	9	8	12	13	9	11	0	1	33	35	68
Europe and Central Asia	NA	NA	NA	NA	NA	NA	1	1	5	5	7	9	6	12	2	6	22	33	55
Latin America and the Caribbean	NA	NA	NA	NA	NA	NA	1	1	4	4	4	5	4	6	2	5	16	22	37
Middle East and North Africa	NA	NA	NA	NA	NA	NA	1	1	4	3	4	4	4	5	1	2	14	15	29
South Asia	NA	NA	NA	NA	NA	NA	1	1	1	3	1	1	0	2	0	0	3	6	10
Sub-Saharan Africa	NA	NA	NA	NA	NA	NA	1	1	2	2	1	2	0	2	0	0	4	8	12
Low- and middle-income countries	NA	NA	NA	NA	NA	NA	7	6	24	25	29	35	24	39	6	15	91	120	211
High-income countries	NA	NA	NA	NA	NA	NA	1	1	4	2	4	3	6	8	5	15	20	29	49
WORLD	NA	NA	NA	NA	NA	NA	8	7	28	27	33	38	30	47	11	30	111	149	260
Attributable YLL (thousands)																			
East Asia and Pacific	NA	NA	NA	NA	NA	NA	59	42	168	152	165	199	80	117	2	7	474	516	990
Europe and Central Asia	NA	NA	NA	NA	NA	NA	32	21	101	93	95	134	54	127	9	29	291	404	695
Latin America and the Caribbean	NA	NA	NA	NA	NA	NA	27	32	71	84	55	73	39	65	10	24	202	278	480
Middle East and North Africa	NA	NA	NA	NA	NA	NA	23	17	66	62	53	63	37	49	6	11	185	202	388
South Asia	NA	NA	NA	NA	NA	NA	15	15	18	53	14	15	3	22	1	0	52	105	157
Sub-Saharan Africa	NA	NA	NA	NA	NA	NA	13	23	31	50	12	37	4	23	1	2	61	135	195
Low- and middle-income countries	NA	NA	NA	NA	NA	NA	169	150	456	495	394	522	217	403	29	72	1,265	1,641	2,906
High-income countries	NA	NA	NA	NA	NA	NA	26	14	74	43	55	50	52	81	21	60	228	248	476
WORLD	NA	NA	NA	NA	NA	NA	195	164	530	537	449	572	268	484	50	132	1,493	1,889	3,382
Attributable DALYs (thousands)																			
East Asia and Pacific	NA	NA	NA	NA	NA	NA	62	44	179	161	178	211	91	128	2	8	513	552	1,065
Europe and Central Asia	NA	NA	NA	NA	NA	NA	33	22	105	97	100	141	58	137	11	35	307	431	738
Latin America and the Caribbean	NA	NA	NA	NA	NA	NA	28	33	74	88	58	77	43	71	13	29	217	299	515
Middle East and North Africa	NA	NA	NA	NA	NA	NA	23	18	68	65	56	66	39	53	7	13	194	215	409
South Asia	NA	NA	NA	NA	NA	NA	16	16	20	57	17	17	4	28	2	0	58	118	176
Sub-Saharan Africa	NA	NA	NA	NA	NA	NA	14	24	33	53	13	40	5	26	1	2	65	145	209
Low- and middle-income countries	NA	NA	NA	NA	NA	NA	177	157	479	520	420	552	241	442	36	87	1,353	1,759	3,112
High-income countries	NA	NA	NA	NA	NA	NA	27	15	78	44	59	53	59	90	32	90	254	292	546
WORLD	NA	NA	NA	NA	NA	NA	204	172	557	564	479	605	300	532	67	177	1,607	2,051	3,658

Source: Authors' calculations.
Note: NA = not applicable.

Table 4A.36

Risk factor:	Overweight and obesity
Disease:	Ischemic heart disease

Region	0–4 years Male	Female	5–14 years Male	Female	15–29 years Male	Female	30–44 years Male	Female	45–59 years Male	Female	60–69 years Male	Female	70–79 years Male	Female	80+ years Male	Female	Total Male	Female	All
PAF of Mortality (%)																			
East Asia and Pacific	NA	NA	NA	NA	NA	NA	23	26	19	23	14	20	7	9	0	1	10	10	10
Europe and Central Asia	NA	NA	NA	NA	NA	NA	42	52	39	51	30	42	20	27	9	10	25	23	24
Latin America and the Caribbean	NA	NA	NA	NA	NA	NA	42	52	36	46	26	34	18	24	6	8	22	23	23
Middle East and North Africa	NA	NA	NA	NA	NA	NA	43	58	35	45	22	29	14	16	5	6	21	22	22
South Asia	NA	NA	NA	NA	NA	NA	10	17	5	16	4	4	1	7	1	0	3	7	5
Sub-Saharan Africa	NA	NA	NA	NA	NA	NA	19	28	17	19	7	12	3	7	1	1	7	9	8
Low- and middle-income countries	NA	NA	NA	NA	NA	NA	26	28	20	27	16	19	10	16	4	6	13	15	14
High-income countries	NA	NA	NA	NA	NA	NA	49	49	43	44	32	36	21	24	8	9	22	16	19
WORLD	NA	NA	NA	NA	NA	NA	28	29	23	28	18	20	12	17	5	7	15	15	15
PAF of YLL (%)																			
East Asia and Pacific	NA	NA	NA	NA	NA	NA	23	26	19	23	14	20	7	9	0	1	13	14	13
Europe and Central Asia	NA	NA	NA	NA	NA	NA	42	52	39	51	30	42	20	27	9	10	30	30	30
Latin America and the Caribbean	NA	NA	NA	NA	NA	NA	42	52	36	46	26	34	18	24	6	8	27	30	28
Middle East and North Africa	NA	NA	NA	NA	NA	NA	43	58	35	45	22	29	14	16	5	6	25	28	26
South Asia	NA	NA	NA	NA	NA	NA	10	17	5	16	4	4	1	7	1	0	4	8	6
Sub-Saharan Africa	NA	NA	NA	NA	NA	NA	19	28	17	19	7	12	3	7	1	1	10	12	11
Low- and middle-income countries	NA	NA	NA	NA	NA	NA	26	28	21	27	16	19	10	15	4	6	16	18	17
High-income countries	NA	NA	NA	NA	NA	NA	49	49	43	44	32	36	21	24	8	9	28	23	26
WORLD	NA	NA	NA	NA	NA	NA	28	29	23	28	18	20	12	17	5	6	18	18	18
PAF of DALYs (%)																			
East Asia and Pacific	NA	NA	NA	NA	NA	NA	23	26	19	23	14	20	7	9	0	1	13	14	13
Europe and Central Asia	NA	NA	NA	NA	NA	NA	42	52	39	51	30	42	20	27	9	10	30	30	30
Latin America and the Caribbean	NA	NA	NA	NA	NA	NA	42	52	36	46	26	34	18	24	6	8	27	30	28
Middle East and North Africa	NA	NA	NA	NA	NA	NA	43	58	35	45	22	29	14	16	5	6	25	28	26
South Asia	NA	NA	NA	NA	NA	NA	10	17	5	16	4	4	1	7	1	0	4	8	6
Sub-Saharan Africa	NA	NA	NA	NA	NA	NA	19	28	17	19	7	12	3	7	1	1	10	12	11
Low- and middle-income countries	NA	NA	NA	NA	NA	NA	26	28	20	27	15	19	10	15	4	6	16	18	16
High-income countries	NA	NA	NA	NA	NA	NA	49	49	43	44	32	36	21	24	8	9	29	23	27
WORLD	NA	NA	NA	NA	NA	NA	28	29	23	28	18	20	12	17	5	6	18	18	18
Attributable Mortality (thousands)																			
East Asia and Pacific	NA	NA	NA	NA	NA	NA	7	4	19	13	20	22	14	16	0	1	60	57	118
Europe and Central Asia	NA	NA	NA	NA	NA	NA	16	4	60	22	68	54	52	86	11	38	207	203	410
Latin America and the Caribbean	NA	NA	NA	NA	NA	NA	4	2	14	8	13	10	11	11	3	5	44	36	81
Middle East and North Africa	NA	NA	NA	NA	NA	NA	5	2	14	9	11	9	8	8	1	2	39	30	69
South Asia	NA	NA	NA	NA	NA	NA	5	6	12	20	12	9	4	18	1	0	34	53	88
Sub-Saharan Africa	NA	NA	NA	NA	NA	NA	1	1	7	5	4	5	2	4	0	0	13	15	29
Low- and middle-income countries	NA	NA	NA	NA	NA	NA	37	19	127	78	127	110	91	142	17	47	399	395	794
High-income countries	NA	NA	NA	NA	NA	NA	8	2	37	10	41	19	50	38	21	36	156	104	261
WORLD	NA	NA	NA	NA	NA	NA	45	21	164	88	168	129	140	180	38	82	555	499	1,055
Attributable YLL (thousands)																			
East Asia and Pacific	NA	NA	NA	NA	NA	NA	165	105	359	262	270	336	124	163	2	7	920	874	1,793
Europe and Central Asia	NA	NA	NA	NA	NA	NA	367	91	1,135	444	917	806	472	873	52	175	2,943	2,388	5,332
Latin America and the Caribbean	NA	NA	NA	NA	NA	NA	90	51	265	166	173	152	97	109	13	23	637	502	1,139
Middle East and North Africa	NA	NA	NA	NA	NA	NA	110	56	271	174	146	140	74	80	7	10	608	460	1,068
South Asia	NA	NA	NA	NA	NA	NA	119	135	228	403	163	139	32	193	6	0	548	870	1,419
Sub-Saharan Africa	NA	NA	NA	NA	NA	NA	32	23	124	99	48	82	15	38	1	2	219	243	462
Low- and middle-income countries	NA	NA	NA	NA	NA	NA	883	461	2,382	1,547	1,717	1,655	814	1,456	80	218	5,875	5,337	11,213
High-income countries	NA	NA	NA	NA	NA	NA	182	45	695	199	552	283	434	377	90	146	1,953	1,050	3,003
WORLD	NA	NA	NA	NA	NA	NA	1,065	506	3,077	1,747	2,268	1,938	1,248	1,833	170	364	7,828	6,387	14,216
Attributable DALYs (thousands)																			
East Asia and Pacific	NA	NA	NA	NA	NA	NA	183	117	383	282	283	353	126	166	2	7	978	925	1,902
Europe and Central Asia	NA	NA	NA	NA	NA	NA	394	104	1,179	476	946	844	480	889	52	178	3,052	2,491	5,543
Latin America and the Caribbean	NA	NA	NA	NA	NA	NA	102	59	283	181	184	161	99	112	13	24	681	538	1,219
Middle East and North Africa	NA	NA	NA	NA	NA	NA	122	64	286	185	153	146	76	81	7	11	644	487	1,131
South Asia	NA	NA	NA	NA	NA	NA	136	155	241	434	172	146	33	198	7	0	588	933	1,521
Sub-Saharan Africa	NA	NA	NA	NA	NA	NA	36	26	132	105	50	86	15	39	1	2	234	258	492
Low- and middle-income countries	NA	NA	NA	NA	NA	NA	972	525	2,505	1,664	1,789	1,737	830	1,484	81	221	6,177	5,631	11,808
High-income countries	NA	NA	NA	NA	NA	NA	208	60	766	239	594	317	456	402	93	152	2,117	1,170	3,287
WORLD	NA	NA	NA	NA	NA	NA	1,180	585	3,270	1,903	2,383	2,055	1,286	1,887	174	372	8,294	6,802	15,096

Source: Authors' calculations.
Note: NA = not applicable.

Table 4A.37

Risk factor:	Overweight and obesity
Disease:	Cerebrovascular disease

Region	0–4 years Male	0–4 years Female	5–14 years Male	5–14 years Female	15–29 years Male	15–29 years Female	30–44 years Male	30–44 years Female	45–59 years Male	45–59 years Female	60–69 years Male	60–69 years Female	70–79 years Male	70–79 years Female	80+ years Male	80+ years Female	Total Male	Total Female	All
PAF of Mortality (%)																			
East Asia and Pacific	NA	NA	NA	NA	NA	NA	7	8	7	9	6	9	4	5	0	0	4	4	4
Europe and Central Asia	NA	NA	NA	NA	NA	NA	21	27	23	30	19	27	14	20	7	8	16	17	16
Latin America and the Caribbean	NA	NA	NA	NA	NA	NA	19	24	20	25	16	21	13	16	5	7	13	15	14
Middle East and North Africa	NA	NA	NA	NA	NA	NA	20	27	19	24	13	18	10	11	4	5	10	12	11
South Asia	NA	NA	NA	NA	NA	NA	5	8	3	9	2	2	1	5	1	0	2	4	3
Sub-Saharan Africa	NA	NA	NA	NA	NA	NA	9	13	9	11	4	7	2	5	1	1	4	6	5
Low- and middle-income countries	NA	NA	NA	NA	NA	NA	11	15	10	14	8	11	6	9	2	4	7	8	7
High-income countries	NA	NA	NA	NA	NA	NA	25	25	25	26	20	23	16	17	7	7	13	11	12
WORLD	NA	NA	NA	NA	NA	NA	13	16	11	15	9	12	7	10	3	5	7	9	8
PAF of YLL (%)																			
East Asia and Pacific	NA	NA	NA	NA	NA	NA	7	8	7	9	6	9	4	5	0	0	5	6	6
Europe and Central Asia	NA	NA	NA	NA	NA	NA	21	27	23	30	19	27	14	20	7	8	17	20	19
Latin America and the Caribbean	NA	NA	NA	NA	NA	NA	19	24	20	25	16	21	13	16	5	7	15	18	16
Middle East and North Africa	NA	NA	NA	NA	NA	NA	20	27	19	24	13	18	10	11	4	5	11	14	13
South Asia	NA	NA	NA	NA	NA	NA	5	8	3	9	2	2	1	5	1	0	2	4	3
Sub-Saharan Africa	NA	NA	NA	NA	NA	NA	9	13	9	11	4	7	2	5	1	1	5	7	6
Low- and middle-income countries	NA	NA	NA	NA	NA	NA	11	15	10	14	8	11	6	9	2	3	7	10	9
High-income countries	NA	NA	NA	NA	NA	NA	25	25	25	26	20	23	16	17	7	7	16	15	16
WORLD	NA	NA	NA	NA	NA	NA	13	16	11	15	9	12	7	10	3	4	8	10	9
PAF of DALYs (%)																			
East Asia and Pacific	NA	NA	NA	NA	NA	NA	10	11	9	11	8	11	5	5	0	1	7	8	7
Europe and Central Asia	NA	NA	NA	NA	NA	NA	25	32	26	34	21	30	15	21	7	9	19	23	21
Latin America and the Caribbean	NA	NA	NA	NA	NA	NA	24	31	23	30	19	24	14	18	5	7	18	22	20
Middle East and North Africa	NA	NA	NA	NA	NA	NA	25	33	22	28	15	20	11	12	4	5	13	17	15
South Asia	NA	NA	NA	NA	NA	NA	6	9	3	10	3	3	1	5	1	0	2	5	4
Sub-Saharan Africa	NA	NA	NA	NA	NA	NA	9	14	10	12	4	8	2	5	1	1	6	8	7
Low- and middle-income countries	NA	NA	NA	NA	NA	NA	14	19	12	17	10	13	6	10	2	3	9	12	10
High-income countries	NA	NA	NA	NA	NA	NA	33	34	32	33	25	29	18	20	7	8	21	20	20
WORLD	NA	NA	NA	NA	NA	NA	16	21	14	18	11	15	8	11	4	5	10	13	12
Attributable Mortality (thousands)																			
East Asia and Pacific	NA	NA	NA	NA	NA	NA	2	1	10	8	15	15	14	17	0	2	42	42	84
Europe and Central Asia	NA	NA	NA	NA	NA	NA	3	2	13	10	21	25	21	44	6	22	63	104	166
Latin America and the Caribbean	NA	NA	NA	NA	NA	NA	1	2	4	5	4	5	5	6	2	3	16	20	37
Middle East and North Africa	NA	NA	NA	NA	NA	NA	1	1	2	2	2	2	2	3	1	1	7	8	15
South Asia	NA	NA	NA	NA	NA	NA	0	0	2	5	3	3	1	8	1	0	8	16	24
Sub-Saharan Africa	NA	NA	NA	NA	NA	NA	1	1	3	4	2	4	1	3	0	0	6	12	18
Low- and middle-income countries	NA	NA	NA	NA	NA	NA	8	7	33	33	48	53	44	81	9	28	142	202	344
High-income countries	NA	NA	NA	NA	NA	NA	2	1	6	4	9	7	16	18	10	22	42	51	94
WORLD	NA	NA	NA	NA	NA	NA	9	8	39	37	57	59	60	99	19	50	184	254	438
Attributable YLL (thousands)																			
East Asia and Pacific	NA	NA	NA	NA	NA	NA	42	30	185	157	207	218	127	171	2	8	563	585	1,148
Europe and Central Asia	NA	NA	NA	NA	NA	NA	65	47	237	210	286	371	186	452	26	104	799	1,183	1,983
Latin America and the Caribbean	NA	NA	NA	NA	NA	NA	30	39	79	92	58	70	42	62	8	17	218	278	496
Middle East and North Africa	NA	NA	NA	NA	NA	NA	12	13	31	36	26	34	19	26	3	5	90	113	203
South Asia	NA	NA	NA	NA	NA	NA	11	11	38	90	47	46	12	86	3	0	111	234	345
Sub-Saharan Africa	NA	NA	NA	NA	NA	NA	23	27	50	72	20	57	8	32	1	2	101	195	296
Low- and middle-income countries	NA	NA	NA	NA	NA	NA	182	167	621	663	644	795	394	829	42	135	1,882	2,589	4,471
High-income countries	NA	NA	NA	NA	NA	NA	36	27	117	81	119	98	136	175	43	90	451	472	923
WORLD	NA	NA	NA	NA	NA	NA	218	194	738	743	763	894	530	1,004	85	225	2,333	3,060	5,394
Attributable DALYs (thousands)																			
East Asia and Pacific	NA	NA	NA	NA	NA	NA	82	61	329	278	333	342	170	223	2	10	917	914	1,831
Europe and Central Asia	NA	NA	NA	NA	NA	NA	91	78	330	313	397	531	239	560	30	116	1,086	1,599	2,685
Latin America and the Caribbean	NA	NA	NA	NA	NA	NA	51	73	132	152	93	108	58	81	9	20	343	433	776
Middle East and North Africa	NA	NA	NA	NA	NA	NA	21	22	48	54	37	47	25	31	3	5	134	159	293
South Asia	NA	NA	NA	NA	NA	NA	16	16	55	127	65	62	15	104	3	0	154	308	462
Sub-Saharan Africa	NA	NA	NA	NA	NA	NA	26	31	59	95	24	68	9	36	1	2	119	233	351
Low- and middle-income countries	NA	NA	NA	NA	NA	NA	287	281	954	1,018	950	1,159	513	1,035	49	153	2,754	3,646	6,399
High-income countries	NA	NA	NA	NA	NA	NA	93	73	297	217	275	232	240	306	58	121	963	949	1,912
WORLD	NA	NA	NA	NA	NA	NA	380	355	1,251	1,235	1,226	1,391	753	1,340	107	274	3,717	4,595	8,311

Source: Authors' calculations.
Note: NA = not applicable.

Table 4A.38

Risk factor: Overweight and obesity
Disease: Osteoarthritis

Region	0–4 years Male	Female	5–14 years Male	Female	15–29 years Male	Female	30–44 years Male	Female	45–59 years Male	Female	60–69 years Male	Female	70–79 years Male	Female	80+ years Male	Female	Total Male	Female	All
PAF of Mortality (%)																			
East Asia and Pacific	NA	NA	NA	NA	NA	NA	8	9	8	10	8	12	6	8	1	1	5	6	6
Europe and Central Asia	NA	NA	NA	NA	NA	NA	16	20	19	26	19	27	17	24	16	18	17	23	21
Latin America and the Caribbean	NA	NA	NA	NA	NA	NA	15	20	17	23	17	22	16	21	12	15	14	17	16
Middle East and North Africa	NA	NA	NA	NA	NA	NA	15	22	17	22	14	18	12	14	9	12	10	16	13
South Asia	NA	NA	NA	NA	NA	NA	3	5	2	7	2	2	1	6	2	0	2	3	3
Sub-Saharan Africa	NA	NA	NA	NA	NA	NA	*	*	7	8	*	7	2	6	2	2	3	5	4
Low- and middle-income countries	NA	NA	NA	NA	NA	NA	12	14	12	16	12	20	10	15	7	12	9	14	12
High-income countries	NA	NA	NA	NA	NA	NA	19	18	21	22	20	23	19	21	15	16	17	17	17
WORLD	NA	NA	NA	NA	NA	NA	15	14	14	18	15	21	14	19	12	15	13	16	15
PAF of YLL (%)																			
East Asia and Pacific	NA	NA	NA	NA	NA	NA	8	9	8	10	8	12	6	8	1	1	7	7	7
Europe and Central Asia	NA	NA	NA	NA	NA	NA	16	20	19	26	19	27	17	24	16	18	16	24	21
Latin America and the Caribbean	NA	NA	NA	NA	NA	NA	15	20	17	23	17	22	16	21	12	15	14	19	17
Middle East and North Africa	NA	NA	NA	NA	NA	NA	15	22	17	22	14	18	12	14	9	12	9	18	13
South Asia	NA	NA	NA	NA	NA	NA	3	5	2	7	2	2	1	6	2	0	2	4	3
Sub-Saharan Africa	NA	NA	NA	NA	NA	NA	*	*	7	8	*	7	2	6	2	2	4	6	6
Low- and middle-income countries	NA	NA	NA	NA	NA	NA	12	14	12	16	12	20	10	15	7	11	10	15	12
High-income countries	NA	NA	NA	NA	NA	NA	19	18	21	22	20	23	19	21	15	16	18	18	18
WORLD	NA	NA	NA	NA	NA	NA	14	14	14	18	15	21	14	18	12	15	13	17	15
PAF of DALYs (%)																			
East Asia and Pacific	NA	NA	NA	NA	NA	NA	8	9	8	10	8	12	6	8	1	1	8	9	9
Europe and Central Asia	NA	NA	NA	NA	NA	NA	16	20	19	26	19	27	17	24	16	18	16	24	21
Latin America and the Caribbean	NA	NA	NA	NA	NA	NA	15	20	17	23	17	22	16	21	12	15	16	21	19
Middle East and North Africa	NA	NA	NA	NA	NA	NA	15	22	17	22	14	18	12	14	9	12	14	18	16
South Asia	NA	NA	NA	NA	NA	NA	3	5	2	7	2	2	1	6	2	0	2	5	4
Sub-Saharan Africa	NA	NA	NA	NA	NA	NA	6	9	7	8	4	7	2	6	2	2	5	7	6
Low- and middle-income countries	NA	NA	NA	NA	NA	NA	9	11	10	14	10	14	9	15	7	10	9	12	11
High-income countries	NA	NA	NA	NA	NA	NA	19	18	21	22	20	23	19	21	15	16	19	21	20
WORLD	NA	NA	NA	NA	NA	NA	10	11	12	15	12	17	13	18	11	14	11	14	13
Attributable Mortality (thousands)																			
East Asia and Pacific	NA	NA	NA	NA	NA	NA	0	0	0	0	0	0	0	0	0	0	0	0	0
Europe and Central Asia	NA	NA	NA	NA	NA	NA	0	0	0	0	0	0	0	0	0	0	0	0	0
Latin America and the Caribbean	NA	NA	NA	NA	NA	NA	0	0	0	0	0	0	0	0	0	0	0	0	0
Middle East and North Africa	NA	NA	NA	NA	NA	NA	0	0	0	0	0	0	0	0	0	0	0	0	0
South Asia	NA	NA	NA	NA	NA	NA	0	0	0	0	0	0	0	0	0	0	0	0	0
Sub-Saharan Africa	NA	NA	NA	NA	NA	NA	0	0	0	0	0	0	0	0	0	0	0	0	0
Low- and middle-income countries	NA	NA	NA	NA	NA	NA	0	0	0	0	0	0	0	0	0	0	0	0	0
High-income countries	NA	NA	NA	NA	NA	NA	0	0	0	0	0	0	0	0	0	0	0	0	1
WORLD	NA	NA	NA	NA	NA	NA	0	0	0	0	0	0	0	0	0	0	0	0	1
Attributable YLL (thousands)																			
East Asia and Pacific	NA	NA	NA	NA	NA	NA	0	0	0	0	0	0	0	0	0	0	0	0	0
Europe and Central Asia	NA	NA	NA	NA	NA	NA	0	0	0	0	0	0	0	0	0	0	0	0	0
Latin America and the Caribbean	NA	NA	NA	NA	NA	NA	0	0	0	0	0	0	0	0	0	0	0	1	1
Middle East and North Africa	NA	NA	NA	NA	NA	NA	0	0	0	0	0	0	0	0	0	0	0	0	0
South Asia	NA	NA	NA	NA	NA	NA	0	0	0	0	0	0	0	0	0	0	0	0	0
Sub-Saharan Africa	NA	NA	NA	NA	NA	NA	0	0	0	0	0	0	0	0	0	0	0	0	0
Low- and middle-income countries	NA	NA	NA	NA	NA	NA	0	0	0	0	0	0	0	0	0	0	1	1	2
High-income countries	NA	NA	NA	NA	NA	NA	0	0	0	0	0	0	0	1	0	1	1	2	3
WORLD	NA	NA	NA	NA	NA	NA	0	0	0	0	0	1	1	1	0	1	2	3	5
Attributable DALYs (thousands)																			
East Asia and Pacific	NA	NA	NA	NA	NA	NA	37	84	76	148	42	78	9	14	0	0	164	325	489
Europe and Central Asia	NA	NA	NA	NA	NA	NA	40	60	53	139	29	93	12	50	1	5	135	348	483
Latin America and the Caribbean	NA	NA	NA	NA	NA	NA	16	19	30	56	20	50	14	34	2	6	81	164	245
Middle East and North Africa	NA	NA	NA	NA	NA	NA	11	22	11	23	4	11	1	3	0	0	27	58	85
South Asia	NA	NA	NA	NA	NA	NA	10	23	7	41	4	7	1	5	0	0	22	76	98
Sub-Saharan Africa	NA	NA	NA	NA	NA	NA	8	21	14	18	3	9	1	3	0	0	27	51	78
Low- and middle-income countries	NA	NA	NA	NA	NA	NA	121	228	191	424	102	248	37	110	3	12	455	1,023	1,478
High-income countries	NA	NA	NA	NA	NA	NA	36	34	93	131	75	156	60	144	8	34	272	500	772
WORLD	NA	NA	NA	NA	NA	NA	157	262	285	556	177	405	97	254	12	46	727	1,523	2,250

Source: Authors' calculations.
Note: NA = not applicable.
*The number of deaths (and hence YLL) directly coded to a number of diseases, especially neuropsychiatric and musculoskeletal diseases, is zero or very small. For other diseases, mortality or disease burden may be zero in some region-age-sex groups. In such cases, the population attributable fractions would be undefined or unstable and have not been calculated.

Table 4A.39

| Risk factor: | Overweight and obesity |
| Disease: | All causes |

Region	0–4 years Male	Female	5–14 years Male	Female	15–29 years Male	Female	30–44 years Male	Female	45–59 years Male	Female	60–69 years Male	Female	70–79 years Male	Female	80+ years Male	Female	Total Male	Female	All
PAF of Mortality (%)																			
East Asia and Pacific	NA	NA	NA	NA	NA	NA	2	3	4	6	4	8	3	4	0	0	2	3	3
Europe and Central Asia	NA	NA	NA	NA	NA	NA	7	8	13	18	14	24	12	19	6	8	10	15	12
Latin America and the Caribbean	NA	NA	NA	NA	NA	NA	4	8	12	19	12	20	10	16	5	7	7	11	9
Middle East and North Africa	NA	NA	NA	NA	NA	NA	8	8	14	17	11	16	9	11	4	5	6	8	7
South Asia	NA	NA	NA	NA	NA	NA	1	2	2	5	2	2	1	4	1	0	1	2	1
Sub-Saharan Africa	NA	NA	NA	NA	NA	NA	1	1	2	4	2	5	1	4	0	1	1	1	1
Low- and middle-income countries	NA	NA	NA	NA	NA	NA	2	2	5	8	6	9	5	8	2	3	3	4	4
High-income countries	NA	NA	NA	NA	NA	NA	7	6	12	11	10	13	9	11	4	6	8	8	8
WORLD	NA	NA	NA	NA	NA	NA	3	3	6	8	7	10	5	8	3	4	4	5	4
PAF of YLL (%)																			
East Asia and Pacific	NA	NA	NA	NA	NA	NA	2	3	4	6	4	8	3	4	0	0	2	3	3
Europe and Central Asia	NA	NA	NA	NA	NA	NA	7	8	13	18	14	24	12	19	6	8	10	15	12
Latin America and the Caribbean	NA	NA	NA	NA	NA	NA	4	8	11	19	12	20	10	16	5	8	5	10	7
Middle East and North Africa	NA	NA	NA	NA	NA	NA	8	8	14	17	11	16	9	11	4	5	5	6	6
South Asia	NA	NA	NA	NA	NA	NA	1	2	2	5	2	2	1	4	1	0	1	1	1
Sub-Saharan Africa	NA	NA	NA	NA	NA	NA	0	1	2	4	2	5	1	4	0	1	0	1	1
Low- and middle-income countries	NA	NA	NA	NA	NA	NA	2	2	5	8	6	9	5	8	2	3	2	3	3
High-income countries	NA	NA	NA	NA	NA	NA	7	6	11	11	10	13	9	11	5	6	8	9	8
WORLD	NA	NA	NA	NA	NA	NA	3	3	6	8	7	10	5	8	3	4	3	4	3
PAF of DALYs (%)																			
East Asia and Pacific	NA	NA	NA	NA	NA	NA	2	3	3	5	4	6	3	4	0	0	2	3	2
Europe and Central Asia	NA	NA	NA	NA	NA	NA	6	7	12	15	13	20	11	17	5	7	8	11	9
Latin America and the Caribbean	NA	NA	NA	NA	NA	NA	4	6	9	14	10	15	9	13	4	6	4	6	5
Middle East and North Africa	NA	NA	NA	NA	NA	NA	6	6	10	11	9	12	8	9	4	5	4	4	4
South Asia	NA	NA	NA	NA	NA	NA	1	2	1	4	2	2	1	3	1	0	1	1	1
Sub-Saharan Africa	NA	NA	NA	NA	NA	NA	1	1	2	3	2	4	1	3	0	1	0	1	1
Low- and middle-income countries	NA	NA	NA	NA	NA	NA	2	3	5	7	5	8	4	7	2	3	2	3	2
High-income countries	NA	NA	NA	NA	NA	NA	6	5	11	11	10	12	8	10	4	5	7	7	7
WORLD	NA	NA	NA	NA	NA	NA	2	3	5	7	6	8	5	8	3	3	2	3	3
Attributable Mortality (thousands)																			
East Asia and Pacific	NA	NA	NA	NA	NA	NA	14	11	48	47	59	76	50	63	2	6	172	202	374
Europe and Central Asia	NA	NA	NA	NA	NA	NA	21	8	82	47	102	104	85	160	21	72	312	391	702
Latin America and the Caribbean	NA	NA	NA	NA	NA	NA	9	9	33	35	33	41	35	47	14	28	124	159	283
Middle East and North Africa	NA	NA	NA	NA	NA	NA	7	4	22	17	19	20	18	19	4	6	69	67	136
South Asia	NA	NA	NA	NA	NA	NA	8	8	19	39	20	18	7	39	4	0	58	104	161
Sub-Saharan Africa	NA	NA	NA	NA	NA	NA	4	5	14	20	7	18	4	14	1	2	31	59	90
Low- and middle-income countries	NA	NA	NA	NA	NA	NA	64	46	218	205	240	275	199	341	46	114	766	981	1,747
High-income countries	NA	NA	NA	NA	NA	NA	13	6	60	31	71	52	101	104	57	119	303	311	614
WORLD	NA	NA	NA	NA	NA	NA	77	51	278	236	311	327	300	445	103	233	1,069	1,292	2,361
Attributable YLL (thousands)																			
East Asia and Pacific	NA	NA	NA	NA	NA	NA	336	274	895	932	793	1,137	441	644	9	31	2,473	3,018	5,491
Europe and Central Asia	NA	NA	NA	NA	NA	NA	502	203	1,558	929	1,381	1,561	770	1,637	96	339	4,306	4,670	8,976
Latin America and the Caribbean	NA	NA	NA	NA	NA	NA	221	209	624	699	442	615	311	480	64	138	1,663	2,142	3,805
Middle East and North Africa	NA	NA	NA	NA	NA	NA	161	106	408	345	256	298	158	195	21	35	1,003	978	1,982
South Asia	NA	NA	NA	NA	NA	NA	182	201	347	778	265	267	66	405	22	0	882	1,651	2,533
Sub-Saharan Africa	NA	NA	NA	NA	NA	NA	102	121	267	395	101	273	39	146	4	9	513	944	1,457
Low- and middle-income countries	NA	NA	NA	NA	NA	NA	1,505	1,114	4,099	4,077	3,238	4,151	1,786	3,508	215	553	10,841	13,403	24,244
High-income countries	NA	NA	NA	NA	NA	NA	317	140	1,118	616	958	774	882	1,044	252	503	3,526	3,077	6,603
WORLD	NA	NA	NA	NA	NA	NA	1,822	1,254	5,217	4,693	4,195	4,925	2,667	4,551	467	1,056	14,368	16,480	30,848
Attributable DALYs (thousands)																			
East Asia and Pacific	NA	NA	NA	NA	NA	NA	586	616	1,285	1,477	1,029	1,454	526	753	10	36	3,437	4,336	7,773
Europe and Central Asia	NA	NA	NA	NA	NA	NA	651	402	1,826	1,377	1,590	1,950	867	1,875	107	378	5,040	5,981	11,022
Latin America and the Caribbean	NA	NA	NA	NA	NA	NA	324	368	801	1,020	539	796	364	586	75	166	2,102	2,935	5,038
Middle East and North Africa	NA	NA	NA	NA	NA	NA	251	228	495	473	292	351	176	217	23	40	1,236	1,308	2,545
South Asia	NA	NA	NA	NA	NA	NA	298	430	422	1,052	311	315	74	456	25	0	1,130	2,253	3,384
Sub-Saharan Africa	NA	NA	NA	NA	NA	NA	139	186	319	471	114	308	43	159	4	10	620	1,134	1,754
Low- and middle-income countries	NA	NA	NA	NA	NA	NA	2,248	2,230	5,148	5,869	3,875	5,174	2,051	4,045	244	630	13,566	17,948	31,515
High-income countries	NA	NA	NA	NA	NA	NA	636	433	1,823	1,403	1,384	1,356	1,178	1,531	321	668	5,341	5,392	10,733
WORLD	NA	NA	NA	NA	NA	NA	2,884	2,663	6,971	7,272	5,259	6,530	3,229	5,577	564	1,298	18,907	23,340	42,248

Source: Authors' calculations.
Note: NA = not applicable.

Table 4A.40

Risk factor: Low fruit and vegetable intake
Disease: Esophageal cancer

Region	0–4 years Male	Female	5–14 years Male	Female	15–29 years Male	Female	30–44 years Male	Female	45–59 years Male	Female	60–69 years Male	Female	70–79 years Male	Female	80+ years Male	Female	Total Male	Female	All
PAF of Mortality (%)																			
East Asia and Pacific	NA	NA	NA	NA	20	22	20	21	19	20	20	22	17	18	13	13	18	19	19
Europe and Central Asia	NA	NA	NA	NA	20	22	21	23	20	22	21	23	16	18	12	13	19	19	19
Latin America and the Caribbean	NA	NA	NA	NA	26	27	27	23	25	26	24	25	18	19	13	13	22	20	21
Middle East and North Africa	NA	NA	NA	NA	22	20	17	18	16	20	15	17	12	14	8	9	14	16	15
South Asia	NA	NA	NA	NA	23	25	23	25	23	25	23	25	18	19	13	14	21	22	21
Sub-Saharan Africa	NA	NA	NA	NA	25	24	19	22	19	24	17	21	12	17	7	11	16	20	17
Low- and middle-income countries	NA	NA	NA	NA	22	24	21	23	20	22	21	23	17	18	12	13	19	20	19
High-income countries	NA	NA	NA	NA	19	20	18	18	16	16	14	14	11	11	8	8	13	11	12
WORLD	NA	NA	NA	NA	22	24	21	23	19	22	20	22	16	18	11	12	18	19	18
PAF of YLL (%)																			
East Asia and Pacific	NA	NA	NA	NA	20	22	20	21	19	20	20	22	17	18	13	13	19	20	19
Europe and Central Asia	NA	NA	NA	NA	20	22	21	23	20	22	21	23	16	18	12	13	20	21	20
Latin America and the Caribbean	NA	NA	NA	NA	26	27	27	23	25	26	24	25	18	19	13	13	23	22	23
Middle East and North Africa	NA	NA	NA	NA	22	20	17	18	16	20	15	17	12	14	8	9	15	17	16
South Asia	NA	NA	NA	NA	23	25	23	25	23	25	23	25	18	19	13	14	22	23	22
Sub-Saharan Africa	NA	NA	NA	NA	25	24	19	22	19	24	17	21	12	17	7	11	17	21	19
Low- and middle-income countries	NA	NA	NA	NA	22	24	21	23	20	22	21	23	17	18	12	13	20	21	20
High-income countries	NA	NA	NA	NA	19	20	18	18	16	16	14	14	11	11	8	8	14	13	14
WORLD	NA	NA	NA	NA	22	24	21	23	19	22	20	22	16	18	11	13	19	20	19
PAF of DALYs (%)																			
East Asia and Pacific	NA	NA	NA	NA	20	22	20	21	19	20	20	22	17	18	13	13	19	20	19
Europe and Central Asia	NA	NA	NA	NA	20	22	21	23	20	22	21	23	16	18	12	13	20	21	20
Latin America and the Caribbean	NA	NA	NA	NA	26	27	27	23	25	26	24	25	18	19	13	13	23	22	23
Middle East and North Africa	NA	NA	NA	NA	22	20	17	18	16	20	15	17	12	14	8	9	15	17	16
South Asia	NA	NA	NA	NA	23	25	23	25	23	25	23	25	18	19	13	14	22	23	22
Sub-Saharan Africa	NA	NA	NA	NA	25	24	19	22	19	24	17	21	12	17	7	11	17	21	19
Low- and middle-income countries	NA	NA	NA	NA	22	24	21	23	20	22	21	23	17	18	12	13	20	21	20
High-income countries	NA	NA	NA	NA	19	20	18	18	16	16	14	14	11	11	8	8	14	13	13
WORLD	NA	NA	NA	NA	22	24	21	23	19	22	20	22	16	18	11	13	19	20	19
Attributable Mortality (thousands)																			
East Asia and Pacific	NA	NA	NA	NA	0	0	2	0	7	4	10	6	7	5	1	2	27	17	44
Europe and Central Asia	NA	NA	NA	NA	0	0	0	0	1	0	1	0	1	0	0	0	3	1	4
Latin America and the Caribbean	NA	NA	NA	NA	0	0	0	0	1	0	1	0	1	0	0	0	3	1	3
Middle East and North Africa	NA	NA	NA	NA	0	0	0	0	0	0	0	0	0	0	0	0	0	0	1
South Asia	NA	NA	NA	NA	0	0	1	1	2	2	4	3	2	2	0	1	9	8	17
Sub-Saharan Africa	NA	NA	NA	NA	0	0	0	0	1	1	1	1	0	0	0	0	2	2	4
Low- and middle-income countries	NA	NA	NA	NA	0	0	3	1	12	7	17	10	10	8	2	3	44	29	73
High-income countries	NA	NA	NA	NA	0	0	0	0	2	0	2	0	1	0	1	0	6	2	7
WORLD	NA	NA	NA	NA	0	0	3	1	13	7	19	10	12	8	3	3	50	30	80
Attributable YLL (thousands)																			
East Asia and Pacific	NA	NA	NA	NA	3	1	37	11	126	81	141	85	63	52	6	9	377	240	616
Europe and Central Asia	NA	NA	NA	NA	0	0	2	1	17	3	16	5	5	4	0	1	42	15	57
Latin America and the Caribbean	NA	NA	NA	NA	0	0	3	1	16	4	11	4	5	2	1	1	36	12	48
Middle East and North Africa	NA	NA	NA	NA	0	0	1	1	2	2	2	1	1	1	0	0	6	5	11
South Asia	NA	NA	NA	NA	2	3	14	12	40	43	55	41	16	16	2	5	130	119	249
Sub-Saharan Africa	NA	NA	NA	NA	1	0	4	3	17	11	10	8	4	4	0	1	36	27	63
Low- and middle-income countries	NA	NA	NA	NA	6	5	62	29	218	145	236	144	94	81	11	16	627	419	1,045
High-income countries	NA	NA	NA	NA	0	0	4	1	30	5	25	5	13	5	2	2	75	18	92
WORLD	NA	NA	NA	NA	7	5	66	29	248	149	260	149	107	85	13	18	702	436	1,138
Attributable DALYs (thousands)																			
East Asia and Pacific	NA	NA	NA	NA	3	1	37	11	128	82	142	86	63	53	6	9	380	242	622
Europe and Central Asia	NA	NA	NA	NA	0	0	2	1	18	3	16	5	6	4	0	1	43	15	57
Latin America and the Caribbean	NA	NA	NA	NA	0	0	3	1	16	4	12	4	5	3	1	1	37	12	49
Middle East and North Africa	NA	NA	NA	NA	0	0	1	1	2	2	2	1	1	1	0	0	6	5	11
South Asia	NA	NA	NA	NA	2	3	14	12	40	43	55	41	17	17	2	5	131	120	250
Sub-Saharan Africa	NA	NA	NA	NA	1	0	4	3	17	12	10	8	4	4	0	1	36	28	64
Low- and middle-income countries	NA	NA	NA	NA	6	5	62	29	220	145	238	145	95	81	11	16	632	421	1,054
High-income countries	NA	NA	NA	NA	0	0	4	1	31	5	25	5	13	5	3	2	77	18	95
WORLD	NA	NA	NA	NA	7	5	67	29	251	150	263	150	108	86	13	18	709	439	1,148

Source: Authors' calculations.
Note: NA = not applicable.

Table 4A.41

Risk factor: Low fruit and vegetable intake
Disease: Stomach cancer

Region	0–4 years Male	Female	5–14 years Male	Female	15–29 years Male	Female	30–44 years Male	Female	45–59 years Male	Female	60–69 years Male	Female	70–79 years Male	Female	80+ years Male	Female	Total Male	Female	All
PAF of Mortality (%)																			
East Asia and Pacific	NA	NA	NA	NA	20	22	20	21	19	20	20	22	17	18	13	13	18	19	18
Europe and Central Asia	NA	NA	NA	NA	20	22	21	23	20	22	21	23	16	18	12	13	19	20	19
Latin America and the Caribbean	NA	NA	NA	NA	26	27	27	23	25	26	24	25	18	19	13	13	21	20	21
Middle East and North Africa	NA	NA	NA	NA	22	20	17	18	16	20	15	17	12	14	8	9	14	16	15
South Asia	NA	NA	NA	NA	23	25	23	25	23	25	23	25	18	19	13	14	20	21	21
Sub-Saharan Africa	NA	NA	NA	NA	25	24	19	22	19	24	17	21	12	17	7	11	15	20	17
Low- and middle-income countries	NA	NA	NA	NA	21	23	21	22	20	21	21	23	17	18	13	13	18	19	19
High-income countries	NA	NA	NA	NA	19	20	18	18	16	16	14	14	11	11	8	8	12	11	12
WORLD	NA	NA	NA	NA	21	23	20	21	19	21	20	22	15	17	11	12	17	18	18
PAF of YLL (%)																			
East Asia and Pacific	NA	NA	NA	NA	20	22	20	21	19	20	20	22	17	18	13	13	19	20	19
Europe and Central Asia	NA	NA	NA	NA	20	22	21	23	20	22	21	23	16	18	12	13	20	21	20
Latin America and the Caribbean	NA	NA	NA	NA	26	27	27	23	25	26	24	25	18	19	13	13	23	22	22
Middle East and North Africa	NA	NA	NA	NA	22	20	17	18	16	20	15	17	12	14	8	9	15	17	16
South Asia	NA	NA	NA	NA	23	25	23	25	23	25	23	25	18	19	13	14	22	23	22
Sub-Saharan Africa	NA	NA	NA	NA	25	24	19	22	19	24	17	21	12	17	7	11	17	21	19
Low- and middle-income countries	NA	NA	NA	NA	21	23	21	22	20	21	21	23	17	18	13	13	19	20	20
High-income countries	NA	NA	NA	NA	19	20	18	18	16	16	14	14	11	11	8	8	13	13	13
WORLD	NA	NA	NA	NA	21	23	20	21	19	21	20	22	15	17	11	12	18	19	19
PAF of DALYs (%)																			
East Asia and Pacific	NA	NA	NA	NA	20	22	20	21	19	20	20	22	17	18	13	13	19	20	19
Europe and Central Asia	NA	NA	NA	NA	20	22	21	23	20	22	21	23	16	18	12	13	20	21	20
Latin America and the Caribbean	NA	NA	NA	NA	26	27	27	23	25	26	24	25	18	19	13	13	23	22	22
Middle East and North Africa	NA	NA	NA	NA	22	20	17	18	16	20	15	17	12	14	8	9	15	17	16
South Asia	NA	NA	NA	NA	23	25	23	25	23	25	23	25	18	19	13	14	22	23	22
Sub-Saharan Africa	NA	NA	NA	NA	25	24	19	22	19	24	17	21	12	17	7	11	17	21	19
Low- and middle-income countries	NA	NA	NA	NA	21	23	21	22	20	21	21	23	17	18	13	13	19	20	20
High-income countries	NA	NA	NA	NA	19	20	18	18	16	16	14	14	11	11	8	8	13	13	13
WORLD	NA	NA	NA	NA	21	23	20	21	19	21	20	22	15	17	11	12	18	19	19
Attributable Mortality (thousands)																			
East Asia and Pacific	NA	NA	NA	NA	1	0	3	3	14	7	17	8	13	9	3	4	51	31	82
Europe and Central Asia	NA	NA	NA	NA	0	0	1	1	3	1	4	2	3	3	0	1	11	8	19
Latin America and the Caribbean	NA	NA	NA	NA	0	0	1	0	2	1	2	1	2	1	1	1	7	5	12
Middle East and North Africa	NA	NA	NA	NA	0	0	0	0	0	0	0	0	0	0	0	0	2	1	3
South Asia	NA	NA	NA	NA	0	0	1	0	1	1	2	1	1	1	0	1	6	4	9
Sub-Saharan Africa	NA	NA	NA	NA	0	0	0	0	1	1	1	1	1	1	0	0	3	3	6
Low- and middle-income countries	NA	NA	NA	NA	1	1	5	4	22	11	27	14	19	15	5	7	79	51	130
High-income countries	NA	NA	NA	NA	0	0	0	0	2	1	3	1	3	2	2	2	11	6	17
WORLD	NA	NA	NA	NA	1	1	6	5	24	12	30	15	23	16	7	8	90	58	147
Attributable YLL (thousands)																			
East Asia and Pacific	NA	NA	NA	NA	15	11	73	68	267	134	231	120	113	92	17	22	716	447	1,163
Europe and Central Asia	NA	NA	NA	NA	2	2	16	14	53	27	59	38	27	28	2	4	158	113	271
Latin America and the Caribbean	NA	NA	NA	NA	3	2	12	10	32	21	29	18	16	13	4	4	95	68	163
Middle East and North Africa	NA	NA	NA	NA	1	1	3	4	7	6	6	4	4	3	0	0	21	18	39
South Asia	NA	NA	NA	NA	4	3	12	7	26	18	30	17	10	7	2	3	84	55	139
Sub-Saharan Africa	NA	NA	NA	NA	2	2	6	6	19	19	10	12	5	6	1	1	43	48	91
Low- and middle-income countries	NA	NA	NA	NA	26	22	122	109	404	225	364	208	175	149	26	35	1,117	748	1,865
High-income countries	NA	NA	NA	NA	1	1	10	9	40	20	41	19	29	19	7	8	129	77	206
WORLD	NA	NA	NA	NA	27	23	133	118	443	245	406	228	204	169	34	43	1,246	825	2,072
Attributable DALYs (thousands)																			
East Asia and Pacific	NA	NA	NA	NA	15	12	74	69	271	135	234	121	115	93	17	23	726	453	1,178
Europe and Central Asia	NA	NA	NA	NA	2	2	16	14	54	27	60	38	27	29	2	4	161	115	275
Latin America and the Caribbean	NA	NA	NA	NA	3	2	12	11	33	21	29	18	16	13	4	4	96	69	165
Middle East and North Africa	NA	NA	NA	NA	1	1	3	4	7	6	6	4	4	3	0	0	22	18	39
South Asia	NA	NA	NA	NA	4	3	12	7	26	18	30	17	11	7	2	3	85	55	140
Sub-Saharan Africa	NA	NA	NA	NA	2	2	6	6	19	20	11	13	5	7	1	1	44	48	92
Low- and middle-income countries	NA	NA	NA	NA	26	22	123	110	409	228	370	211	178	151	27	35	1,132	757	1,889
High-income countries	NA	NA	NA	NA	1	1	10	10	41	20	43	20	30	20	8	9	134	80	214
WORLD	NA	NA	NA	NA	27	23	134	120	450	248	412	231	208	171	35	44	1,266	837	2,103

Source: Authors' calculations.
Note: NA = not applicable.

Table 4A.42

Risk factor: Low fruit and vegetable intake
Disease: Colon and rectal cancers

Region	0–4 years Male	Female	5–14 years Male	Female	15–29 years Male	Female	30–44 years Male	Female	45–59 years Male	Female	60–69 years Male	Female	70–79 years Male	Female	80+ years Male	Female	Total Male	Female	All
PAF of Mortality (%)																			
East Asia and Pacific	NA	NA	NA	NA	3	3	3	3	3	3	3	3	3	3	0	0	2	2	2
Europe and Central Asia	NA	NA	NA	NA	3	3	3	3	3	3	3	3	3	3	0	0	2	3	3
Latin America and the Caribbean	NA	NA	NA	NA	3	4	4	1	3	4	3	3	3	3	0	0	3	2	2
Middle East and North Africa	NA	NA	NA	NA	3	3	2	2	2	3	2	2	2	2	0	0	2	2	2
South Asia	NA	NA	NA	NA	3	3	3	3	3	3	3	3	3	3	0	0	3	3	3
Sub-Saharan Africa	NA	NA	NA	NA	3	3	3	3	2	3	2	3	2	3	0	0	2	3	2
Low- and middle-income countries	NA	NA	NA	NA	3	3	3	3	3	3	3	3	3	3	0	0	2	2	2
High-income countries	NA	NA	NA	NA	3	3	2	2	2	2	2	2	2	2	0	0	1	1	1
WORLD	NA	NA	NA	NA	3	3	3	3	2	3	2	3	2	3	0	0	2	2	2
PAF of YLL (%)																			
East Asia and Pacific	NA	NA	NA	NA	3	3	3	3	3	3	3	3	3	3	0	0	3	3	3
Europe and Central Asia	NA	NA	NA	NA	3	3	3	3	3	3	3	3	3	3	0	0	3	3	3
Latin America and the Caribbean	NA	NA	NA	NA	3	4	4	1	3	4	3	3	3	3	0	0	3	3	3
Middle East and North Africa	NA	NA	NA	NA	3	3	2	2	2	3	2	2	2	2	0	0	2	2	2
South Asia	NA	NA	NA	NA	3	3	3	3	3	3	3	3	3	3	0	0	3	3	3
Sub-Saharan Africa	NA	NA	NA	NA	3	3	3	3	2	3	2	3	2	3	0	0	2	3	3
Low- and middle-income countries	NA	NA	NA	NA	3	3	3	3	3	3	3	3	3	3	0	0	3	3	3
High-income countries	NA	NA	NA	NA	3	3	2	2	2	2	2	2	2	2	0	0	2	2	2
WORLD	NA	NA	NA	NA	3	3	3	3	2	3	2	3	2	3	0	0	2	2	2
PAF of DALYs (%)																			
East Asia and Pacific	NA	NA	NA	NA	3	3	3	3	3	3	3	3	3	3	0	0	3	3	3
Europe and Central Asia	NA	NA	NA	NA	3	3	3	3	3	3	3	3	3	3	0	0	3	3	3
Latin America and the Caribbean	NA	NA	NA	NA	3	4	4	1	3	4	3	3	3	3	0	0	3	3	3
Middle East and North Africa	NA	NA	NA	NA	3	3	2	2	2	3	2	2	2	2	0	0	2	2	2
South Asia	NA	NA	NA	NA	3	3	3	3	3	3	3	3	3	3	0	0	3	3	3
Sub-Saharan Africa	NA	NA	NA	NA	3	3	3	3	2	3	2	3	2	3	0	0	2	3	3
Low- and middle-income countries	NA	NA	NA	NA	3	3	3	3	3	3	3	3	3	3	0	0	3	3	3
High-income countries	NA	NA	NA	NA	3	3	2	2	2	2	2	2	2	2	0	0	2	2	2
WORLD	NA	NA	NA	NA	3	3	3	3	2	3	2	3	2	3	0	0	2	2	2
Attributable Mortality (thousands)																			
East Asia and Pacific	NA	NA	NA	NA	0	0	0	0	0	0	1	1	1	1	0	0	2	2	4
Europe and Central Asia	NA	NA	NA	NA	0	0	0	0	0	0	0	0	0	1	0	0	1	1	2
Latin America and the Caribbean	NA	NA	NA	NA	0	0	0	0	0	0	0	0	0	0	0	0	0	0	1
Middle East and North Africa	NA	NA	NA	NA	0	0	0	0	0	0	0	0	0	0	0	0	0	0	0
South Asia	NA	NA	NA	NA	0	0	0	0	0	0	0	0	0	0	0	0	1	0	1
Sub-Saharan Africa	NA	NA	NA	NA	0	0	0	0	0	0	0	0	0	0	0	0	0	0	0
Low- and middle-income countries	NA	NA	NA	NA	0	0	0	0	1	1	1	1	2	2	0	0	5	4	9
High-income countries	NA	NA	NA	NA	0	0	0	0	0	0	1	0	1	1	0	0	2	1	3
WORLD	NA	NA	NA	NA	0	0	0	0	1	1	2	2	2	2	0	0	6	6	12
Attributable YLL (thousands)																			
East Asia and Pacific	NA	NA	NA	NA	1	1	4	5	9	9	9	9	6	7	0	0	30	29	59
Europe and Central Asia	NA	NA	NA	NA	0	0	1	1	4	4	6	6	4	6	0	0	16	18	33
Latin America and the Caribbean	NA	NA	NA	NA	0	0	1	0	2	2	2	2	1	2	0	0	7	7	13
Middle East and North Africa	NA	NA	NA	NA	0	0	0	0	1	1	0	0	0	0	0	0	2	2	3
South Asia	NA	NA	NA	NA	1	0	2	1	2	2	2	2	1	1	0	0	8	6	15
Sub-Saharan Africa	NA	NA	NA	NA	0	0	1	1	1	1	1	1	1	1	0	0	4	4	7
Low- and middle-income countries	NA	NA	NA	NA	3	1	10	8	19	19	20	20	14	17	0	0	66	65	131
High-income countries	NA	NA	NA	NA	0	0	2	1	7	5	7	5	7	7	0	0	23	19	42
WORLD	NA	NA	NA	NA	3	2	11	10	26	24	27	25	21	24	0	0	89	84	173
Attributable DALYs (thousands)																			
East Asia and Pacific	NA	NA	NA	NA	1	1	5	5	10	9	9	9	6	7	0	0	31	31	62
Europe and Central Asia	NA	NA	NA	NA	0	0	1	1	5	4	6	7	5	6	0	0	17	19	36
Latin America and the Caribbean	NA	NA	NA	NA	0	0	1	0	2	2	2	2	2	2	0	0	7	7	14
Middle East and North Africa	NA	NA	NA	NA	0	0	0	0	1	1	0	0	0	0	0	0	2	2	4
South Asia	NA	NA	NA	NA	1	0	2	1	2	2	2	2	1	1	0	0	9	6	15
Sub-Saharan Africa	NA	NA	NA	NA	0	0	1	1	1	1	1	1	1	1	0	0	4	4	7
Low- and middle-income countries	NA	NA	NA	NA	3	1	10	9	20	20	21	21	14	17	0	0	69	69	138
High-income countries	NA	NA	NA	NA	0	0	2	2	8	6	9	6	8	9	0	0	28	23	51
WORLD	NA	NA	NA	NA	3	2	12	11	29	27	30	27	23	26	0	0	96	92	189

Source: Authors' calculations.
Note: NA = not applicable.

Table 4A.43

Risk factor: Low fruit and vegetable intake
Disease: Trachea, bronchus, and lung cancers

Region	0–4 years Male	0–4 years Female	5–14 years Male	5–14 years Female	15–29 years Male	15–29 years Female	30–44 years Male	30–44 years Female	45–59 years Male	45–59 years Female	60–69 years Male	60–69 years Female	70–79 years Male	70–79 years Female	80+ years Male	80+ years Female	Total Male	Total Female	All
PAF of Mortality (%)																			
East Asia and Pacific	NA	NA	NA	NA	13	14	13	14	12	13	13	15	11	13	10	10	12	13	12
Europe and Central Asia	NA	NA	NA	NA	13	15	14	15	13	14	13	15	11	12	9	10	13	13	13
Latin America and the Caribbean	NA	NA	NA	NA	17	18	17	14	16	17	16	16	12	13	10	10	14	14	14
Middle East and North Africa	NA	NA	NA	NA	14	13	11	12	10	13	9	11	8	10	6	7	9	11	9
South Asia	NA	NA	NA	NA	15	16	15	16	15	17	15	16	12	13	10	11	14	15	14
Sub-Saharan Africa	NA	NA	NA	NA	16	16	12	14	12	16	11	14	8	11	5	8	11	13	11
Low- and middle-income countries	NA	NA	NA	NA	14	15	14	14	13	14	13	15	11	13	10	10	13	13	13
High-income countries	NA	NA	NA	NA	12	13	11	12	10	10	9	9	7	8	6	6	8	8	8
WORLD	NA	NA	NA	NA	14	15	13	14	12	13	12	13	10	10	8	8	11	11	11
PAF of YLL (%)																			
East Asia and Pacific	NA	NA	NA	NA	13	14	13	14	12	13	13	15	11	13	10	10	12	13	13
Europe and Central Asia	NA	NA	NA	NA	13	15	14	15	13	14	13	15	11	12	9	10	13	14	13
Latin America and the Caribbean	NA	NA	NA	NA	17	18	17	14	16	17	16	16	12	13	10	10	15	15	15
Middle East and North Africa	NA	NA	NA	NA	14	13	11	12	10	13	9	11	8	10	6	7	9	11	10
South Asia	NA	NA	NA	NA	15	16	15	16	15	17	15	16	12	13	10	11	14	16	15
Sub-Saharan Africa	NA	NA	NA	NA	16	16	12	14	12	16	11	14	8	11	5	8	11	14	12
Low- and middle-income countries	NA	NA	NA	NA	14	15	14	14	13	14	13	15	11	13	10	10	13	14	13
High-income countries	NA	NA	NA	NA	12	13	11	12	10	10	9	9	7	8	6	6	8	9	9
WORLD	NA	NA	NA	NA	14	15	13	14	12	13	12	13	10	10	8	8	11	12	12
PAF of DALYs (%)																			
East Asia and Pacific	NA	NA	NA	NA	13	14	13	14	12	13	13	15	11	13	10	10	12	13	13
Europe and Central Asia	NA	NA	NA	NA	13	15	14	15	13	14	13	15	11	12	9	10	13	14	13
Latin America and the Caribbean	NA	NA	NA	NA	17	18	17	14	16	17	16	16	12	13	10	10	15	15	15
Middle East and North Africa	NA	NA	NA	NA	14	13	11	12	10	13	9	11	8	10	6	7	9	11	10
South Asia	NA	NA	NA	NA	15	16	15	16	15	17	15	16	12	13	10	11	14	16	15
Sub-Saharan Africa	NA	NA	NA	NA	16	16	12	14	12	16	11	14	8	11	5	8	11	14	12
Low- and middle-income countries	NA	NA	NA	NA	14	15	14	14	13	14	13	15	11	13	10	10	13	14	13
High-income countries	NA	NA	NA	NA	12	13	11	12	10	10	9	9	7	8	6	6	8	9	9
WORLD	NA	NA	NA	NA	14	15	13	14	12	13	12	13	10	10	8	8	11	12	12
Attributable Mortality (thousands)																			
East Asia and Pacific	NA	NA	NA	NA	0	0	1	1	7	4	12	5	9	5	2	1	32	16	48
Europe and Central Asia	NA	NA	NA	NA	0	0	1	0	5	1	7	1	4	1	1	0	17	4	21
Latin America and the Caribbean	NA	NA	NA	NA	0	0	0	0	1	1	2	1	1	1	0	0	5	2	8
Middle East and North Africa	NA	NA	NA	NA	0	0	0	0	0	0	0	0	0	0	0	0	1	0	2
South Asia	NA	NA	NA	NA	0	0	1	0	4	1	6	1	3	1	1	0	15	4	18
Sub-Saharan Africa	NA	NA	NA	NA	0	0	0	0	0	0	0	0	0	0	0	0	1	1	2
Low- and middle-income countries	NA	NA	NA	NA	0	0	3	2	18	6	28	9	18	8	4	2	71	27	98
High-income countries	NA	NA	NA	NA	0	0	1	0	5	2	7	3	8	4	3	2	25	12	36
WORLD	NA	NA	NA	NA	0	0	4	2	23	9	35	12	27	12	7	4	96	39	135
Attributable YLL (thousands)																			
East Asia and Pacific	NA	NA	NA	NA	3	1	35	21	135	72	166	78	80	55	9	7	428	235	664
Europe and Central Asia	NA	NA	NA	NA	1	1	15	5	87	17	97	19	38	13	3	2	241	56	297
Latin America and the Caribbean	NA	NA	NA	NA	1	1	5	4	25	13	24	11	13	6	2	1	71	36	107
Middle East and North Africa	NA	NA	NA	NA	1	0	3	2	7	3	6	2	3	1	0	0	20	8	28
South Asia	NA	NA	NA	NA	3	1	16	7	73	22	76	18	31	8	4	1	203	57	260
Sub-Saharan Africa	NA	NA	NA	NA	0	0	2	1	9	3	6	2	2	1	0	0	18	8	26
Low- and middle-income countries	NA	NA	NA	NA	9	4	76	39	335	130	375	130	167	84	19	12	980	400	1,381
High-income countries	NA	NA	NA	NA	1	0	14	10	93	45	100	46	74	40	15	11	296	151	447
WORLD	NA	NA	NA	NA	9	5	90	49	427	175	474	176	240	124	35	23	1,276	552	1,828
Attributable DALYs (thousands)																			
East Asia and Pacific	NA	NA	NA	NA	3	1	35	21	136	73	168	79	81	56	10	8	433	238	671
Europe and Central Asia	NA	NA	NA	NA	1	1	15	5	88	17	98	19	39	13	3	2	245	56	301
Latin America and the Caribbean	NA	NA	NA	NA	1	1	5	4	25	13	25	11	13	6	3	1	72	36	108
Middle East and North Africa	NA	NA	NA	NA	1	0	3	2	7	3	6	2	3	1	0	0	20	8	28
South Asia	NA	NA	NA	NA	3	1	16	7	73	22	77	18	31	8	4	1	205	57	262
Sub-Saharan Africa	NA	NA	NA	NA	0	0	2	1	9	4	6	2	2	1	0	0	18	9	27
Low- and middle-income countries	NA	NA	NA	NA	9	4	76	40	338	131	379	131	170	86	20	12	992	405	1,397
High-income countries	NA	NA	NA	NA	1	0	14	10	95	46	102	47	76	41	16	11	304	155	460
WORLD	NA	NA	NA	NA	10	5	90	50	433	177	482	179	246	126	36	23	1,297	560	1,856

Source: Authors' calculations.
Note: NA = not applicable.

Table 4A.44

Risk factor:	Low fruit and vegetable intake
Disease:	Ischemic heart disease

Region	0–4 years Male	0–4 years Female	5–14 years Male	5–14 years Female	15–29 years Male	15–29 years Female	30–44 years Male	30–44 years Female	45–59 years Male	45–59 years Female	60–69 years Male	60–69 years Female	70–79 years Male	70–79 years Female	80+ years Male	80+ years Female	Total Male	Total Female	All
PAF of Mortality (%)																			
East Asia and Pacific	NA	NA	NA	NA	31	33	30	32	29	31	31	34	24	26	19	19	26	26	26
Europe and Central Asia	NA	NA	NA	NA	31	34	33	36	31	34	32	35	24	26	17	19	27	25	26
Latin America and the Caribbean	NA	NA	NA	NA	40	40	40	36	38	39	37	38	27	27	20	19	30	28	29
Middle East and North Africa	NA	NA	NA	NA	33	31	27	29	26	31	23	26	18	21	12	14	21	22	21
South Asia	NA	NA	NA	NA	36	38	35	38	35	38	35	37	25	28	19	20	30	31	31
Sub-Saharan Africa	NA	NA	NA	NA	38	37	30	34	29	36	26	33	18	24	11	16	23	27	25
Low- and middle-income countries	NA	NA	NA	NA	34	36	33	35	32	35	32	35	24	26	18	19	27	27	27
High-income countries	NA	NA	NA	NA	30	31	28	28	25	25	22	23	16	17	12	12	17	15	16
WORLD	NA	NA	NA	NA	34	36	32	35	31	35	31	34	22	25	16	17	25	25	25
PAF of YLL (%)																			
East Asia and Pacific	NA	NA	NA	NA	31	33	30	32	29	31	31	34	24	26	19	19	28	29	28
Europe and Central Asia	NA	NA	NA	NA	31	34	33	36	31	34	32	35	24	26	17	19	29	28	28
Latin America and the Caribbean	NA	NA	NA	NA	40	40	40	36	38	39	37	38	27	27	20	19	34	32	33
Middle East and North Africa	NA	NA	NA	NA	33	31	27	29	26	31	23	26	18	21	12	14	23	25	23
South Asia	NA	NA	NA	NA	36	38	35	38	35	38	35	37	25	28	19	20	32	34	33
Sub-Saharan Africa	NA	NA	NA	NA	38	37	30	34	29	36	26	33	18	24	11	16	25	30	27
Low- and middle-income countries	NA	NA	NA	NA	34	36	33	35	32	35	32	35	24	26	18	19	29	30	30
High-income countries	NA	NA	NA	NA	30	31	28	28	25	25	22	23	16	17	12	12	20	17	19
WORLD	NA	NA	NA	NA	34	36	32	35	31	35	31	34	22	25	16	17	28	29	28
PAF of DALYs (%)																			
East Asia and Pacific	NA	NA	NA	NA	31	33	30	32	29	31	31	34	24	26	19	19	28	29	28
Europe and Central Asia	NA	NA	NA	NA	31	34	33	36	31	34	32	35	24	26	17	19	29	28	29
Latin America and the Caribbean	NA	NA	NA	NA	40	40	40	36	38	39	37	38	27	27	20	19	34	32	33
Middle East and North Africa	NA	NA	NA	NA	33	31	27	29	26	31	23	26	18	21	12	14	23	25	24
South Asia	NA	NA	NA	NA	36	38	35	38	35	38	35	37	25	28	19	20	32	34	33
Sub-Saharan Africa	NA	NA	NA	NA	38	37	30	34	29	36	26	33	18	24	11	16	25	30	27
Low- and middle-income countries	NA	NA	NA	NA	34	36	33	35	32	35	32	35	24	26	18	19	29	30	30
High-income countries	NA	NA	NA	NA	30	31	28	28	25	25	22	23	16	17	12	12	20	18	19
WORLD	NA	NA	NA	NA	34	36	32	35	31	35	31	34	22	25	16	17	28	29	28
Attributable Mortality (thousands)																			
East Asia and Pacific	NA	NA	NA	NA	3	2	9	5	30	18	46	38	46	48	20	36	155	147	301
Europe and Central Asia	NA	NA	NA	NA	1	0	12	3	48	15	72	46	63	81	23	73	220	216	436
Latin America and the Caribbean	NA	NA	NA	NA	1	0	4	1	15	7	18	11	16	12	9	11	61	43	105
Middle East and North Africa	NA	NA	NA	NA	1	0	3	1	10	6	11	8	10	10	3	4	39	30	69
South Asia	NA	NA	NA	NA	4	7	17	12	85	47	102	87	76	75	25	25	309	254	563
Sub-Saharan Africa	NA	NA	NA	NA	0	0	2	1	11	9	14	15	11	13	2	5	41	44	85
Low- and middle-income countries	NA	NA	NA	NA	9	10	48	24	200	103	263	205	221	238	83	155	824	735	1,559
High-income countries	NA	NA	NA	NA	0	0	4	1	22	6	29	12	37	27	30	51	123	96	219
WORLD	NA	NA	NA	NA	9	10	52	25	222	108	292	217	259	265	113	206	947	831	1,777
Attributable YLL (thousands)																			
East Asia and Pacific	NA	NA	NA	NA	70	52	221	129	565	358	622	568	408	488	100	179	1,987	1,774	3,761
Europe and Central Asia	NA	NA	NA	NA	25	7	290	62	905	292	980	688	572	821	104	336	2,877	2,207	5,083
Latin America and the Caribbean	NA	NA	NA	NA	16	7	86	36	275	140	241	167	140	125	40	53	798	527	1,325
Middle East and North Africa	NA	NA	NA	NA	22	11	67	28	196	120	153	125	93	101	16	23	548	407	955
South Asia	NA	NA	NA	NA	98	193	406	303	1,587	940	1,380	1,311	677	783	124	137	4,273	3,667	7,940
Sub-Saharan Africa	NA	NA	NA	NA	9	6	51	27	211	185	184	228	96	140	12	27	564	614	1,178
Low- and middle-income countries	NA	NA	NA	NA	242	275	1,122	586	3,739	2,035	3,560	3,087	1,986	2,458	396	755	11,046	9,196	20,242
High-income countries	NA	NA	NA	NA	8	2	104	26	415	110	385	180	325	267	130	208	1,367	793	2,160
WORLD	NA	NA	NA	NA	250	277	1,227	611	4,154	2,145	3,945	3,267	2,311	2,726	527	963	12,413	9,989	22,402
Attributable DALYs (thousands)																			
East Asia and Pacific	NA	NA	NA	NA	101	82	245	144	603	385	652	595	417	498	102	181	2,121	1,885	4,006
Europe and Central Asia	NA	NA	NA	NA	31	11	311	72	939	313	1,012	721	582	837	105	340	2,981	2,294	5,275
Latin America and the Caribbean	NA	NA	NA	NA	28	15	98	41	293	152	257	177	144	128	41	54	861	568	1,429
Middle East and North Africa	NA	NA	NA	NA	30	17	75	32	207	127	160	131	95	103	16	23	584	433	1,016
South Asia	NA	NA	NA	NA	145	230	462	347	1,684	1,013	1,453	1,381	694	800	127	139	4,565	3,911	8,476
Sub-Saharan Africa	NA	NA	NA	NA	16	8	57	32	225	198	193	241	98	142	12	28	601	649	1,250
Low- and middle-income countries	NA	NA	NA	NA	351	364	1,248	667	3,952	2,190	3,728	3,245	2,030	2,508	403	765	11,712	9,739	21,452
High-income countries	NA	NA	NA	NA	11	6	119	34	457	132	414	202	342	285	135	216	1,478	875	2,353
WORLD	NA	NA	NA	NA	363	370	1,367	701	4,409	2,322	4,142	3,447	2,373	2,793	538	981	13,191	10,614	23,805

Source: Authors' calculations.
Note: NA = not applicable.

Table 4A.45

Risk factor: Low fruit and vegetable intake
Disease: Cerebrovascular disease

Region	0–4 years Male	0–4 years Female	5–14 years Male	5–14 years Female	15–29 years Male	15–29 years Female	30–44 years Male	30–44 years Female	45–59 years Male	45–59 years Female	60–69 years Male	60–69 years Female	70–79 years Male	70–79 years Female	80+ years Male	80+ years Female	Total Male	Total Female	All
PAF of Mortality (%)																			
East Asia and Pacific	NA	NA	NA	NA	6	6	6	6	7	7	8	9	8	9	7	7	8	8	8
Europe and Central Asia	NA	NA	NA	NA	10	11	10	11	11	12	12	14	11	12	8	9	11	11	11
Latin America and the Caribbean	NA	NA	NA	NA	11	12	11	10	12	13	13	14	11	12	9	9	11	11	11
Middle East and North Africa	NA	NA	NA	NA	9	9	7	8	8	10	8	9	7	9	6	6	7	8	7
South Asia	NA	NA	NA	NA	10	11	10	11	11	12	12	13	11	12	8	9	11	12	11
Sub-Saharan Africa	NA	NA	NA	NA	11	10	8	10	9	12	9	12	8	10	5	7	8	10	9
Low- and middle-income countries	NA	NA	NA	NA	9	10	8	9	9	10	10	12	9	10	8	8	9	10	10
High-income countries	NA	NA	NA	NA	9	9	8	9	9	8	8	8	7	7	6	6	7	6	6
WORLD	NA	NA	NA	NA	9	10	8	9	9	10	10	12	9	10	7	8	9	9	9
PAF of YLL (%)																			
East Asia and Pacific	NA	NA	NA	NA	6	6	6	6	7	7	8	9	8	9	7	7	8	8	8
Europe and Central Asia	NA	NA	NA	NA	10	11	10	11	11	12	12	14	11	12	8	9	11	12	11
Latin America and the Caribbean	NA	NA	NA	NA	11	12	11	10	12	13	13	14	11	12	9	9	12	12	12
Middle East and North Africa	NA	NA	NA	NA	9	9	7	8	8	10	8	9	7	9	6	6	7	8	7
South Asia	NA	NA	NA	NA	10	11	10	11	11	12	12	13	11	12	8	9	11	12	11
Sub-Saharan Africa	NA	NA	NA	NA	11	10	8	10	9	12	9	12	8	10	5	7	8	11	10
Low- and middle-income countries	NA	NA	NA	NA	9	10	8	9	9	10	10	12	9	10	7	8	9	10	10
High-income countries	NA	NA	NA	NA	9	9	8	9	9	8	8	8	7	7	6	6	7	7	7
WORLD	NA	NA	NA	NA	9	10	8	9	9	10	10	12	9	10	7	8	9	10	9
PAF of DALYs (%)																			
East Asia and Pacific	NA	NA	NA	NA	6	6	8	8	9	9	10	11	9	10	7	8	9	10	9
Europe and Central Asia	NA	NA	NA	NA	10	11	12	14	12	14	14	15	11	12	9	10	12	13	12
Latin America and the Caribbean	NA	NA	NA	NA	11	12	14	13	15	15	15	16	12	12	9	9	14	13	13
Middle East and North Africa	NA	NA	NA	NA	9	9	9	10	10	12	9	10	8	9	6	6	8	9	8
South Asia	NA	NA	NA	NA	10	11	12	12	13	14	14	15	11	12	9	9	12	13	13
Sub-Saharan Africa	NA	NA	NA	NA	11	10	9	10	10	13	10	12	8	11	5	7	9	11	10
Low- and middle-income countries	NA	NA	NA	NA	9	10	10	11	11	12	12	13	10	11	8	9	11	11	11
High-income countries	NA	NA	NA	NA	9	9	11	12	11	11	10	10	8	8	6	6	9	8	9
WORLD	NA	NA	NA	NA	9	10	10	11	11	12	12	13	10	11	7	8	10	11	11
Attributable Mortality (thousands)																			
East Asia and Pacific	NA	NA	NA	NA	0	0	1	1	9	6	21	15	29	31	13	24	74	77	151
Europe and Central Asia	NA	NA	NA	NA	0	0	1	1	6	4	13	13	15	26	7	24	43	68	112
Latin America and the Caribbean	NA	NA	NA	NA	0	0	1	1	3	2	4	3	4	4	3	5	14	15	29
Middle East and North Africa	NA	NA	NA	NA	0	0	0	0	1	1	1	1	2	2	1	1	5	5	10
South Asia	NA	NA	NA	NA	0	0	1	1	9	6	17	17	17	20	6	9	50	53	104
Sub-Saharan Africa	NA	NA	NA	NA	0	0	1	1	3	4	3	6	3	7	1	3	12	21	33
Low- and middle-income countries	NA	NA	NA	NA	2	1	6	4	30	25	60	55	71	91	31	66	198	241	439
High-income countries	NA	NA	NA	NA	0	0	1	0	2	1	4	2	7	8	8	18	21	29	51
WORLD	NA	NA	NA	NA	2	1	6	4	32	26	63	57	78	98	39	83	220	270	489
Attributable YLL (thousands)																			
East Asia and Pacific	NA	NA	NA	NA	9	5	33	22	173	128	280	219	258	317	66	123	819	815	1,634
Europe and Central Asia	NA	NA	NA	NA	8	5	31	20	113	84	181	192	139	265	30	115	503	681	1,184
Latin America and the Caribbean	NA	NA	NA	NA	5	5	18	16	50	48	48	46	38	44	14	21	172	179	352
Middle East and North Africa	NA	NA	NA	NA	6	3	4	4	13	15	15	18	14	20	3	6	57	64	121
South Asia	NA	NA	NA	NA	11	7	22	15	159	127	235	256	152	213	31	45	610	664	1,274
Sub-Saharan Africa	NA	NA	NA	NA	11	9	21	19	50	87	44	93	29	71	5	16	161	296	457
Low- and middle-income countries	NA	NA	NA	NA	50	33	130	97	557	489	805	824	630	931	150	326	2,321	2,700	5,021
High-income countries	NA	NA	NA	NA	2	2	12	9	41	26	47	36	61	75	34	72	198	220	418
WORLD	NA	NA	NA	NA	52	35	142	106	598	515	852	859	691	1,006	184	399	2,519	2,920	5,439
Attributable DALYs (thousands)																			
East Asia and Pacific	NA	NA	NA	NA	9	5	66	45	307	227	451	344	343	414	77	142	1,254	1,178	2,431
Europe and Central Asia	NA	NA	NA	NA	8	5	44	33	157	126	252	275	178	329	35	129	674	896	1,570
Latin America and the Caribbean	NA	NA	NA	NA	5	5	31	30	82	79	77	71	51	57	16	25	263	267	531
Middle East and North Africa	NA	NA	NA	NA	6	3	8	6	20	22	22	24	19	24	4	6	79	86	165
South Asia	NA	NA	NA	NA	11	7	33	22	227	178	326	344	188	256	35	51	818	858	1,677
Sub-Saharan Africa	NA	NA	NA	NA	11	9	24	23	59	107	53	112	33	80	6	18	186	348	534
Low- and middle-income countries	NA	NA	NA	NA	50	33	204	160	853	738	1,182	1,170	812	1,160	172	371	3,275	3,633	6,907
High-income countries	NA	NA	NA	NA	2	2	31	25	103	70	109	84	108	130	47	97	401	409	810
WORLD	NA	NA	NA	NA	53	35	236	185	956	808	1,291	1,255	920	1,290	219	468	3,676	4,042	7,718

Source: Authors' calculations.
Note: NA = not applicable.

Table 4A.46

Risk factor:	Low fruit and vegetable intake
Disease:	All causes

Region	0–4 years Male	0–4 years Female	5–14 years Male	5–14 years Female	15–29 years Male	15–29 years Female	30–44 years Male	30–44 years Female	45–59 years Male	45–59 years Female	60–69 years Male	60–69 years Female	70–79 years Male	70–79 years Female	80+ years Male	80+ years Female	Total Male	Total Female	All
PAF of Mortality (%)																			
East Asia and Pacific	NA	NA	NA	NA	1	1	3	3	6	5	8	8	6	6	4	5	5	5	5
Europe and Central Asia	NA	NA	NA	NA	1	1	5	4	10	8	14	15	12	13	9	11	10	11	10
Latin America and the Caribbean	NA	NA	NA	NA	1	1	3	3	7	6	10	8	7	6	5	4	5	5	5
Middle East and North Africa	NA	NA	NA	NA	1	1	4	3	8	7	8	8	6	7	4	4	4	4	4
South Asia	NA	NA	NA	NA	1	1	3	3	9	8	12	12	9	9	6	6	5	5	5
Sub-Saharan Africa	NA	NA	NA	NA	0	0	0	0	3	3	5	7	4	6	2	4	1	1	1
Low- and middle-income countries	NA	NA	NA	NA	1	1	2	2	7	6	10	10	8	8	5	6	5	5	5
High-income countries	NA	NA	NA	NA	1	1	3	2	6	4	6	5	5	4	3	3	5	4	4
WORLD	NA	NA	NA	NA	1	1	2	2	7	6	9	9	7	8	5	5	5	5	5
PAF of YLL (%)																			
East Asia and Pacific	NA	NA	NA	NA	1	1	3	3	6	5	8	8	6	6	4	4	4	4	4
Europe and Central Asia	NA	NA	NA	NA	1	1	5	4	10	8	14	14	12	13	9	11	9	10	9
Latin America and the Caribbean	NA	NA	NA	NA	1	1	2	3	7	6	10	8	7	6	5	4	4	4	4
Middle East and North Africa	NA	NA	NA	NA	1	1	4	3	8	7	8	8	6	7	4	4	3	3	3
South Asia	NA	NA	NA	NA	1	1	3	3	9	8	12	12	9	9	6	6	4	3	4
Sub-Saharan Africa	NA	NA	NA	NA	0	0	0	0	3	3	5	6	4	6	2	4	1	1	1
Low- and middle-income countries	NA	NA	NA	NA	1	1	2	2	7	6	10	10	8	8	5	6	3	3	3
High-income countries	NA	NA	NA	NA	0	1	3	2	6	4	6	5	5	4	3	3	5	4	4
WORLD	NA	NA	NA	NA	1	1	2	2	7	6	9	9	7	8	5	5	3	3	3
PAF of DALYs (%)																			
East Asia and Pacific	NA	NA	NA	NA	1	1	2	1	4	3	6	5	6	5	4	4	3	2	3
Europe and Central Asia	NA	NA	NA	NA	1	0	3	2	8	5	12	11	10	11	7	9	6	6	6
Latin America and the Caribbean	NA	NA	NA	NA	0	0	2	1	5	4	7	5	6	5	4	3	2	2	2
Middle East and North Africa	NA	NA	NA	NA	1	0	2	1	5	4	6	6	5	6	3	4	2	2	2
South Asia	NA	NA	NA	NA	1	1	2	2	7	5	10	9	8	8	5	5	3	2	3
Sub-Saharan Africa	NA	NA	NA	NA	0	0	0	0	2	3	4	5	4	5	2	3	1	1	1
Low- and middle-income countries	NA	NA	NA	NA	0	0	2	1	5	4	8	7	7	7	5	5	2	2	2
High-income countries	NA	NA	NA	NA	0	0	2	1	4	2	5	3	4	3	3	3	3	2	3
WORLD	NA	NA	NA	NA	0	0	2	1	5	4	7	7	6	6	4	4	3	2	2
Attributable Mortality (thousands)																			
East Asia and Pacific	NA	NA	NA	NA	4	3	17	10	68	39	108	72	104	99	40	67	340	290	630
Europe and Central Asia	NA	NA	NA	NA	1	1	15	4	62	21	99	63	87	111	31	98	295	299	594
Latin America and the Caribbean	NA	NA	NA	NA	1	1	5	3	21	11	26	16	24	19	13	17	91	67	158
Middle East and North Africa	NA	NA	NA	NA	1	1	3	2	12	7	14	10	13	12	4	5	47	37	84
South Asia	NA	NA	NA	NA	4	7	20	14	101	58	131	109	99	98	33	36	389	322	712
Sub-Saharan Africa	NA	NA	NA	NA	1	1	4	2	16	16	19	23	15	22	4	8	59	71	130
Low- and middle-income countries	NA	NA	NA	NA	12	12	65	35	282	153	397	293	342	361	125	232	1,222	1,086	2,308
High-income countries	NA	NA	NA	NA	0	0	6	2	34	11	45	19	58	41	43	73	187	146	333
WORLD	NA	NA	NA	NA	13	13	71	38	315	163	442	313	399	402	168	305	1,408	1,233	2,641
Attributable YLL (thousands)																			
East Asia and Pacific	NA	NA	NA	NA	102	71	405	256	1,276	783	1,448	1,078	927	1,013	199	340	4,355	3,542	7,897
Europe and Central Asia	NA	NA	NA	NA	36	15	356	103	1,179	428	1,339	948	786	1,138	140	457	3,836	3,089	6,925
Latin America and the Caribbean	NA	NA	NA	NA	26	15	125	67	399	227	356	248	213	191	61	80	1,179	829	2,008
Middle East and North Africa	NA	NA	NA	NA	31	15	78	38	226	146	182	149	116	126	21	29	654	504	1,158
South Asia	NA	NA	NA	NA	119	207	474	346	1,886	1,151	1,778	1,645	887	1,029	164	191	5,308	4,568	9,876
Sub-Saharan Africa	NA	NA	NA	NA	23	17	85	58	306	309	256	345	137	224	18	46	825	998	1,822
Low- and middle-income countries	NA	NA	NA	NA	336	341	1,523	868	5,272	3,043	5,359	4,414	3,065	3,720	602	1,143	16,157	13,529	29,686
High-income countries	NA	NA	NA	NA	12	6	146	56	625	211	605	291	509	413	190	301	2,088	1,278	3,366
WORLD	NA	NA	NA	NA	348	347	1,669	924	5,897	3,254	5,965	4,705	3,574	4,133	792	1,444	18,245	14,806	33,051
Attributable DALYs (thousands)																			
East Asia and Pacific	NA	NA	NA	NA	133	102	462	295	1,455	911	1,657	1,234	1,026	1,121	212	363	4,945	4,026	8,970
Europe and Central Asia	NA	NA	NA	NA	42	20	390	126	1,261	491	1,444	1,065	836	1,217	146	476	4,119	3,395	7,514
Latin America and the Caribbean	NA	NA	NA	NA	37	24	150	86	451	272	402	284	231	208	65	85	1,336	959	2,295
Middle East and North Africa	NA	NA	NA	NA	39	21	89	45	244	161	197	162	122	132	21	30	713	551	1,264
South Asia	NA	NA	NA	NA	166	245	540	397	2,052	1,276	1,943	1,803	941	1,090	171	199	5,812	5,008	10,820
Sub-Saharan Africa	NA	NA	NA	NA	29	19	93	65	330	341	274	376	143	235	19	47	888	1,085	1,973
Low- and middle-income countries	NA	NA	NA	NA	446	430	1,725	1,014	5,792	3,453	5,918	4,924	3,299	4,004	633	1,200	17,812	15,024	32,836
High-income countries	NA	NA	NA	NA	16	10	181	81	735	280	703	365	578	490	208	335	2,422	1,561	3,982
WORLD	NA	NA	NA	NA	462	440	1,906	1,095	6,527	3,732	6,620	5,289	3,878	4,493	841	1,535	20,234	16,584	36,819

Source: Authors' calculations.

Note: NA = not applicable.

Table 4A.47

Risk factor: Physical inactivity
Disease: Colon and rectal cancers

Region	0–4 years Male	0–4 years Female	5–14 years Male	5–14 years Female	15–29 years Male	15–29 years Female	30–44 years Male	30–44 years Female	45–59 years Male	45–59 years Female	60–69 years Male	60–69 years Female	70–79 years Male	70–79 years Female	80+ years Male	80+ years Female	Total Male	Total Female	All
PAF of Mortality (%)																			
East Asia and Pacific	NA	NA	NA	NA	14	15	15	16	15	16	16	17	12	13	8	8	14	14	14
Europe and Central Asia	NA	NA	NA	NA	15	16	16	18	17	18	19	22	16	17	11	12	17	17	17
Latin America and the Caribbean	NA	NA	NA	NA	15	17	16	19	16	19	17	23	14	19	10	13	15	18	17
Middle East and North Africa	NA	NA	NA	NA	14	16	16	16	16	16	17	18	13	15	9	10	15	15	15
South Asia	NA	NA	NA	NA	14	15	15	16	15	16	17	17	13	14	8	10	14	14	14
Sub-Saharan Africa	NA	NA	NA	NA	13	14	14	15	15	15	16	16	12	12	8	8	13	13	13
Low- and middle-income countries	NA	NA	NA	NA	14	15	15	16	16	17	17	19	14	15	9	10	15	15	15
High-income countries	NA	NA	NA	NA	16	17	17	18	17	18	18	19	13	15	10	11	14	14	14
WORLD	NA	NA	NA	NA	14	15	16	16	16	17	17	19	14	15	10	10	14	15	15
PAF of YLL (%)																			
East Asia and Pacific	NA	NA	NA	NA	14	15	15	16	15	16	16	17	12	13	8	8	15	15	15
Europe and Central Asia	NA	NA	NA	NA	15	16	16	18	17	18	19	22	16	17	11	12	17	18	18
Latin America and the Caribbean	NA	NA	NA	NA	15	17	16	19	16	19	17	23	14	19	10	13	16	19	18
Middle East and North Africa	NA	NA	NA	NA	14	16	16	16	16	16	17	18	13	15	9	10	15	16	16
South Asia	NA	NA	NA	NA	14	15	15	16	15	16	17	17	13	14	8	10	15	15	15
Sub-Saharan Africa	NA	NA	NA	NA	13	14	14	15	15	15	16	16	12	12	8	8	14	14	14
Low- and middle-income countries	NA	NA	NA	NA	14	15	15	16	16	17	17	19	14	15	9	10	15	16	16
High-income countries	NA	NA	NA	NA	16	17	17	18	17	18	18	19	13	15	10	11	15	16	16
WORLD	NA	NA	NA	NA	14	15	16	16	16	17	17	19	14	15	10	10	15	16	16
PAF of DALYs (%)																			
East Asia and Pacific	NA	NA	NA	NA	14	15	15	16	15	16	16	17	12	13	8	8	15	15	15
Europe and Central Asia	NA	NA	NA	NA	15	16	16	18	17	18	19	22	16	17	11	12	17	18	18
Latin America and the Caribbean	NA	NA	NA	NA	15	17	16	19	16	19	17	23	14	19	10	13	16	19	18
Middle East and North Africa	NA	NA	NA	NA	14	16	16	16	16	16	17	18	13	15	9	10	15	16	16
South Asia	NA	NA	NA	NA	14	15	15	16	15	16	17	17	13	14	8	10	15	15	15
Sub-Saharan Africa	NA	NA	NA	NA	13	14	14	15	15	15	16	16	12	12	8	8	14	14	14
Low- and middle-income countries	NA	NA	NA	NA	14	15	15	16	16	17	17	19	14	15	9	10	15	16	16
High-income countries	NA	NA	NA	NA	16	17	17	18	17	18	18	19	.13	15	10	11	15	16	16
WORLD	NA	NA	NA	NA	14	15	16	17	16	17	17	19	14	15	10	10	15	16	16
Attributable Mortality (thousands)																			
East Asia and Pacific	NA	NA	NA	NA	0	0	1	1	3	3	4	3	3	3	1	1	12	11	22
Europe and Central Asia	NA	NA	NA	NA	0	0	0	0	1	1	3	3	3	3	1	1	8	8	16
Latin America and the Caribbean	NA	NA	NA	NA	0	0	0	0	1	1	1	1	1	1	0	1	3	3	6
Middle East and North Africa	NA	NA	NA	NA	0	0	0	0	0	0	0	0	0	0	0	0	1	1	2
South Asia	NA	NA	NA	NA	0	0	0	0	1	0	1	1	1	0	0	0	3	2	5
Sub-Saharan Africa	NA	NA	NA	NA	0	0	0	0	0	0	0	0	0	0	0	0	1	1	3
Low- and middle-income countries	NA	NA	NA	NA	1	0	2	2	6	5	9	8	7	8	2	3	27	26	54
High-income countries	NA	NA	NA	NA	0	0	0	0	3	2	6	4	6	5	3	6	19	17	36
WORLD	NA	NA	NA	NA	1	0	3	2	9	8	15	12	13	13	5	9	46	44	90
Attributable YLL (thousands)																			
East Asia and Pacific	NA	NA	NA	NA	7	3	25	25	56	50	52	48	24	26	4	6	168	159	326
Europe and Central Asia	NA	NA	NA	NA	1	1	7	7	26	25	40	41	24	33	3	5	101	112	213
Latin America and the Caribbean	NA	NA	NA	NA	1	1	4	6	10	13	10	14	7	10	2	3	34	47	81
Middle East and North Africa	NA	NA	NA	NA	1	1	3	3	4	3	3	3	2	2	0	0	13	11	24
South Asia	NA	NA	NA	NA	4	1	9	6	10	8	13	9	5	5	1	2	43	31	73
Sub-Saharan Africa	NA	NA	NA	NA	1	1	4	3	7	6	5	5	3	3	1	1	22	18	40
Low- and middle-income countries	NA	NA	NA	NA	15	7	54	50	113	106	123	120	64	78	10	18	380	378	758
High-income countries	NA	NA	NA	NA	1	1	12	10	58	45	75	56	55	55	15	25	216	192	408
WORLD	NA	NA	NA	NA	16	8	65	60	172	151	199	176	119	133	25	42	596	570	1,166
Attributable DALYs (thousands)																			
East Asia and Pacific	NA	NA	NA	NA	7	3	26	27	59	54	54	51	25	27	4	6	175	168	343
Europe and Central Asia	NA	NA	NA	NA	1	1	7	8	28	27	43	44	25	34	3	6	108	120	228
Latin America and the Caribbean	NA	NA	NA	NA	1	1	5	6	11	14	11	14	7	11	2	4	36	50	85
Middle East and North Africa	NA	NA	NA	NA	1	1	3	3	4	3	3	3	2	2	0	0	14	12	25
South Asia	NA	NA	NA	NA	4	1	9	6	11	9	13	10	5	5	1	2	43	32	75
Sub-Saharan Africa	NA	NA	NA	NA	1	1	4	3	7	6	6	5	3	3	1	1	22	19	41
Low- and middle-income countries	NA	NA	NA	NA	16	7	55	53	120	113	130	126	67	81	11	18	397	400	797
High-income countries	NA	NA	NA	NA	1	1	13	13	72	57	91	67	65	66	17	29	261	234	494
WORLD	NA	NA	NA	NA	17	9	68	66	192	170	221	194	132	148	28	47	658	633	1,291

Source: Authors' calculations.
Note: NA = not applicable.

Table 4A.48

Risk factor: Physical inactivity
Disease: Breast cancer

Region	0–4 years Male	0–4 years Female	5–14 years Male	5–14 years Female	15–29 years Male	15–29 years Female	30–44 years Male	30–44 years Female	45–59 years Male	45–59 years Female	60–69 years Male	60–69 years Female	70–79 years Male	70–79 years Female	80+ years Male	80+ years Female	Total Male	Total Female	All
PAF of Mortality (%)																			
East Asia and Pacific	NA	NA	NA	NA	NA	8	NA	8	NA	10	NA	10	NA	8	NA	5	NA	9	9
Europe and Central Asia	NA	NA	NA	NA	NA	8	NA	9	NA	11	NA	13	NA	10	NA	7	NA	11	11
Latin America and the Caribbean	NA	NA	NA	NA	NA	9	NA	9	NA	12	NA	14	NA	11	NA	8	NA	11	11
Middle East and North Africa	NA	NA	NA	NA	NA	8	NA	9	NA	10	NA	11	NA	9	NA	6	NA	9	9
South Asia	NA	NA	NA	NA	NA	8	NA	8	NA	10	NA	10	NA	8	NA	6	NA	9	9
Sub-Saharan Africa	NA	NA	NA	NA	NA	8	NA	9	NA	9	NA	10	NA	8	NA	5	NA	9	9
Low- and middle-income countries	NA	NA	NA	NA	NA	8	NA	9	NA	10	NA	11	NA	9	NA	6	NA	10	10
High-income countries	NA	NA	NA	NA	NA	9	NA	10	NA	11	NA	12	NA	9	NA	7	NA	10	9
WORLD	NA	NA	NA	NA	NA	8	NA	9	NA	10	NA	11	NA	9	NA	6	NA	10	10
PAF of YLL (%)																			
East Asia and Pacific	NA	NA	NA	NA	NA	8	NA	8	NA	10	NA	10	NA	8	NA	5	NA	9	9
Europe and Central Asia	NA	NA	NA	NA	NA	8	NA	9	NA	11	NA	13	NA	10	NA	7	NA	11	11
Latin America and the Caribbean	NA	NA	NA	NA	NA	9	NA	9	NA	12	NA	14	NA	11	NA	8	NA	11	11
Middle East and North Africa	NA	NA	NA	NA	NA	8	NA	9	NA	10	NA	11	NA	9	NA	6	NA	10	10
South Asia	NA	NA	NA	NA	NA	8	NA	8	NA	10	NA	10	NA	8	NA	6	NA	9	9
Sub-Saharan Africa	NA	NA	NA	NA	NA	8	NA	9	NA	9	NA	10	NA	8	NA	5	NA	9	9
Low- and middle-income countries	NA	NA	NA	NA	NA	8	NA	9	NA	10	NA	11	NA	9	NA	6	NA	10	10
High-income countries	NA	NA	NA	NA	NA	9	NA	10	NA	11	NA	12	NA	9	NA	7	NA	10	10
WORLD	NA	NA	NA	NA	NA	8	NA	9	NA	10	NA	11	NA	9	NA	6	NA	10	10
PAF of DALYs (%)																			
East Asia and Pacific	NA	NA	NA	NA	NA	8	NA	8	NA	10	NA	10	NA	8	NA	5	NA	9	9
Europe and Central Asia	NA	NA	NA	NA	NA	8	NA	9	NA	11	NA	13	NA	10	NA	7	NA	11	11
Latin America and the Caribbean	NA	NA	NA	NA	NA	9	NA	9	NA	12	NA	14	NA	11	NA	8	NA	11	11
Middle East and North Africa	NA	NA	NA	NA	NA	8	NA	9	NA	10	NA	11	NA	9	NA	6	NA	9	9
South Asia	NA	NA	NA	NA	NA	8	NA	8	NA	10	NA	10	NA	8	NA	6	NA	9	9
Sub-Saharan Africa	NA	NA	NA	NA	NA	8	NA	9	NA	9	NA	10	NA	8	NA	5	NA	9	9
Low- and middle-income countries	NA	NA	NA	NA	NA	8	NA	9	NA	10	NA	11	NA	9	NA	6	NA	10	10
High-income countries	NA	NA	NA	NA	NA	9	NA	10	NA	11	NA	12	NA	9	NA	7	NA	10	10
WORLD	NA	NA	NA	NA	NA	8	NA	9	NA	10	NA	11	NA	9	NA	6	NA	10	10
Attributable Mortality (thousands)																			
East Asia and Pacific	NA	NA	NA	NA	NA	0	NA	1	NA	4	NA	2	NA	1	NA	0	NA	8	8
Europe and Central Asia	NA	NA	NA	NA	NA	0	NA	1	NA	2	NA	2	NA	2	NA	0	NA	7	7
Latin America and the Caribbean	NA	NA	NA	NA	NA	0	NA	0	NA	1	NA	1	NA	1	NA	0	NA	4	4
Middle East and North Africa	NA	NA	NA	NA	NA	0	NA	0	NA	1	NA	0	NA	0	NA	0	NA	1	1
South Asia	NA	NA	NA	NA	NA	0	NA	1	NA	2	NA	2	NA	1	NA	1	NA	7	7
Sub-Saharan Africa	NA	NA	NA	NA	NA	0	NA	0	NA	1	NA	1	NA	1	NA	0	NA	3	3
Low- and middle-income countries	NA	NA	NA	NA	NA	0	NA	4	NA	11	NA	8	NA	5	NA	2	NA	30	30
High-income countries	NA	NA	NA	NA	NA	0	NA	1	NA	4	NA	4	NA	3	NA	3	NA	15	15
WORLD	NA	NA	NA	NA	NA	0	NA	5	NA	15	NA	12	NA	9	NA	4	NA	45	45
Attributable YLL (thousands)																			
East Asia and Pacific	NA	NA	NA	NA	NA	1	NA	33	NA	74	NA	30	NA	11	NA	2	NA	151	151
Europe and Central Asia	NA	NA	NA	NA	NA	1	NA	14	NA	42	NA	32	NA	16	NA	2	NA	107	107
Latin America and the Caribbean	NA	NA	NA	NA	NA	1	NA	12	NA	28	NA	16	NA	8	NA	2	NA	67	67
Middle East and North Africa	NA	NA	NA	NA	NA	0	NA	7	NA	11	NA	4	NA	2	NA	0	NA	24	24
South Asia	NA	NA	NA	NA	NA	1	NA	20	NA	44	NA	31	NA	11	NA	3	NA	111	111
Sub-Saharan Africa	NA	NA	NA	NA	NA	1	NA	9	NA	21	NA	13	NA	6	NA	1	NA	50	50
Low- and middle-income countries	NA	NA	NA	NA	NA	5	NA	93	NA	221	NA	127	NA	54	NA	10	NA	510	510
High-income countries	NA	NA	NA	NA	NA	1	NA	26	NA	82	NA	54	NA	35	NA	11	NA	209	209
WORLD	NA	NA	NA	NA	NA	5	NA	119	NA	303	NA	181	NA	88	NA	22	NA	719	719
Attributable DALYs (thousands)																			
East Asia and Pacific	NA	NA	NA	NA	NA	1	NA	36	NA	78	NA	32	NA	11	NA	2	NA	160	160
Europe and Central Asia	NA	NA	NA	NA	NA	1	NA	15	NA	45	NA	34	NA	17	NA	3	NA	115	115
Latin America and the Caribbean	NA	NA	NA	NA	NA	1	NA	13	NA	30	NA	17	NA	8	NA	2	NA	72	72
Middle East and North Africa	NA	NA	NA	NA	NA	0	NA	7	NA	12	NA	4	NA	2	NA	0	NA	26	26
South Asia	NA	NA	NA	NA	NA	1	NA	21	NA	46	NA	33	NA	12	NA	3	NA	115	115
Sub-Saharan Africa	NA	NA	NA	NA	NA	1	NA	9	NA	22	NA	13	NA	6	NA	1	NA	52	52
Low- and middle-income countries	NA	NA	NA	NA	NA	5	NA	101	NA	233	NA	133	NA	57	NA	11	NA	540	540
High-income countries	NA	NA	NA	NA	NA	1	NA	36	NA	101	NA	63	NA	42	NA	13	NA	256	256
WORLD	NA	NA	NA	NA	NA	6	NA	138	NA	334	NA	196	NA	98	NA	24	NA	796	796

Source: Authors' calculations.
Note: NA = not applicable.

Table 4A.49

Risk factor: Physical inactivity
Disease: Diabetes mellitus

Region	0–4 years Male	0–4 Female	5–14 Male	5–14 Female	15–29 Male	15–29 Female	30–44 Male	30–44 Female	45–59 Male	45–59 Female	60–69 Male	60–69 Female	70–79 Male	70–79 Female	80+ Male	80+ Female	Total Male	Total Female	All
PAF of Mortality (%)																			
East Asia and Pacific	NA	NA	NA	NA	14	14	14	15	14	15	15	15	12	12	8	8	13	13	13
Europe and Central Asia	NA	NA	NA	NA	14	15	15	16	15	16	16	18	13	14	9	10	14	15	15
Latin America and the Caribbean	NA	NA	NA	NA	14	15	15	16	15	16	15	19	12	15	9	11	13	15	14
Middle East and North Africa	NA	NA	NA	NA	14	14	15	15	15	15	15	15	12	13	8	9	13	13	13
South Asia	NA	NA	NA	NA	14	14	14	14	14	14	15	15	11	12	7	8	12	13	13
Sub-Saharan Africa	NA	NA	NA	NA	14	14	15	15	15	15	15	16	12	12	8	8	13	14	13
Low- and middle-income countries	NA	NA	NA	NA	14	14	15	15	14	15	15	16	12	13	8	9	13	14	13
High-income countries	NA	NA	NA	NA	15	16	17	17	16	16	17	17	13	13	9	10	13	12	13
WORLD	NA	NA	NA	NA	14	14	15	15	15	15	15	16	12	13	8	9	13	13	13
PAF of YLL (%)																			
East Asia and Pacific	NA	NA	NA	NA	14	14	14	15	14	15	15	15	12	12	8	8	14	14	14
Europe and Central Asia	NA	NA	NA	NA	14	15	15	16	15	16	16	18	13	14	9	10	15	15	15
Latin America and the Caribbean	NA	NA	NA	NA	14	15	15	16	15	16	15	19	12	15	9	11	14	16	15
Middle East and North Africa	NA	NA	NA	NA	14	14	15	15	15	15	15	15	12	13	8	9	14	14	14
South Asia	NA	NA	NA	NA	14	14	14	14	14	14	15	15	11	12	7	8	13	13	13
Sub-Saharan Africa	NA	NA	NA	NA	14	14	15	15	15	15	15	16	12	12	8	8	14	14	14
Low- and middle-income countries	NA	NA	NA	NA	14	14	15	15	14	15	15	16	12	13	8	9	14	14	14
High-income countries	NA	NA	NA	NA	15	16	17	17	16	16	17	17	13	13	9	10	15	14	14
WORLD	NA	NA	NA	NA	14	14	15	15	15	15	15	16	12	13	8	9	14	14	14
PAF of DALYs (%)																			
East Asia and Pacific	NA	NA	NA	NA	14	14	14	15	14	15	15	15	12	12	8	8	14	14	14
Europe and Central Asia	NA	NA	NA	NA	14	15	15	16	15	16	16	18	13	14	9	10	15	16	15
Latin America and the Caribbean	NA	NA	NA	NA	14	15	15	16	15	16	15	19	12	15	9	11	14	16	15
Middle East and North Africa	NA	NA	NA	NA	14	14	15	15	15	15	15	15	12	13	8	9	14	14	14
South Asia	NA	NA	NA	NA	14	14	14	14	14	14	15	15	11	12	7	8	13	13	13
Sub-Saharan Africa	NA	NA	NA	NA	14	14	15	15	15	15	15	16	12	12	8	8	14	14	14
Low- and middle-income countries	NA	NA	NA	NA	14	14	14	15	14	15	15	16	12	13	8	9	14	14	14
High-income countries	NA	NA	NA	NA	15	16	17	17	16	16	17	17	13	13	9	10	15	15	15
WORLD	NA	NA	NA	NA	14	14	15	15	15	15	16	16	12	13	8	9	14	14	14
Attributable Mortality (thousands)																			
East Asia and Pacific	NA	NA	NA	NA	0	0	1	1	3	3	4	6	4	6	1	2	13	18	30
Europe and Central Asia	NA	NA	NA	NA	0	0	0	0	1	1	1	2	1	2	0	0	3	5	8
Latin America and the Caribbean	NA	NA	NA	NA	0	0	1	0	2	3	3	4	2	4	1	2	9	14	24
Middle East and North Africa	NA	NA	NA	NA	0	0	0	0	0	0	1	1	1	1	0	0	2	2	4
South Asia	NA	NA	NA	NA	0	0	1	0	4	3	4	4	3	3	1	1	13	12	24
Sub-Saharan Africa	NA	NA	NA	NA	0	0	0	0	1	2	1	2	1	2	0	0	4	7	11
Low- and middle-income countries	NA	NA	NA	NA	1	1	3	2	11	11	14	20	11	17	4	6	44	57	101
High-income countries	NA	NA	NA	NA	0	0	1	0	2	1	3	2	4	5	2	5	12	14	26
WORLD	NA	NA	NA	NA	1	1	3	2	13	13	17	22	15	22	6	11	55	71	126
Attributable YLL (thousands)																			
East Asia and Pacific	NA	NA	NA	NA	5	5	16	16	54	66	60	91	31	58	5	10	172	245	417
Europe and Central Asia	NA	NA	NA	NA	3	3	6	5	13	12	14	25	7	17	1	2	43	63	106
Latin America and the Caribbean	NA	NA	NA	NA	3	3	13	11	42	50	40	67	22	45	5	12	125	189	314
Middle East and North Africa	NA	NA	NA	NA	1	1	2	2	8	9	9	11	5	8	1	1	25	32	57
South Asia	NA	NA	NA	NA	12	8	17	9	67	54	52	64	27	33	6	5	181	173	353
Sub-Saharan Africa	NA	NA	NA	NA	3	4	9	9	20	36	16	37	8	19	1	3	58	107	165
Low- and middle-income countries	NA	NA	NA	NA	27	23	63	52	203	226	190	296	100	180	19	32	603	810	1,413
High-income countries	NA	NA	NA	NA	2	1	12	7	38	24	42	37	34	46	11	23	138	138	276
WORLD	NA	NA	NA	NA	29	25	75	59	241	250	233	332	134	226	29	55	741	947	1,689
Attributable DALYs (thousands)																			
East Asia and Pacific	NA	NA	NA	NA	16	15	56	58	101	121	78	114	37	68	6	11	294	386	680
Europe and Central Asia	NA	NA	NA	NA	5	5	16	18	27	34	23	40	10	25	1	4	82	127	209
Latin America and the Caribbean	NA	NA	NA	NA	5	5	23	25	57	79	47	85	25	54	5	14	162	263	425
Middle East and North Africa	NA	NA	NA	NA	4	5	12	15	16	20	12	15	6	10	1	2	52	66	118
South Asia	NA	NA	NA	NA	26	20	56	52	106	94	69	81	32	39	7	6	296	292	589
Sub-Saharan Africa	NA	NA	NA	NA	5	6	15	15	26	43	18	40	9	20	1	3	75	127	202
Low- and middle-income countries	NA	NA	NA	NA	62	56	178	182	334	392	247	376	120	215	22	39	962	1,261	2,223
High-income countries	NA	NA	NA	NA	7	4	50	38	111	94	77	80	49	72	14	31	308	319	628
WORLD	NA	NA	NA	NA	68	61	227	220	445	486	324	456	169	287	36	71	1,270	1,581	2,851

Source: Authors' calculations.
Note: NA = not applicable.

Table 4A.50

Risk factor: Physical inactivity
Disease: Ischemic heart disease

Region	0–4 years Male	Female	5–14 years Male	Female	15–29 years Male	Female	30–44 years Male	Female	45–59 years Male	Female	60–69 years Male	Female	70–79 years Male	Female	80+ years Male	Female	Total Male	Female	All
PAF of Mortality (%)																			
East Asia and Pacific	NA	NA	NA	NA	22	22	22	23	22	23	24	24	19	19	13	12	20	18	19
Europe and Central Asia	NA	NA	NA	NA	22	22	23	24	23	24	25	27	20	21	14	14	21	19	20
Latin America and the Caribbean	NA	NA	NA	NA	22	22	23	24	23	24	24	28	19	23	13	16	20	21	20
Middle East and North Africa	NA	NA	NA	NA	22	22	23	23	23	23	23	23	18	19	12	13	20	20	20
South Asia	NA	NA	NA	NA	22	22	22	22	22	22	23	23	17	18	12	13	19	19	19
Sub-Saharan Africa	NA	NA	NA	NA	22	22	23	24	23	24	24	24	18	19	12	13	20	20	20
Low- and middle-income countries	NA	NA	NA	NA	22	22	22	23	22	23	24	24	19	20	13	14	20	19	20
High-income countries	NA	NA	NA	NA	24	24	26	26	25	25	25	26	20	20	14	15	20	17	19
WORLD	NA	NA	NA	NA	22	22	23	23	23	23	24	24	19	20	13	14	20	19	19
PAF of YLL (%)																			
East Asia and Pacific	NA	NA	NA	NA	22	22	22	23	22	23	24	24	19	19	13	12	21	20	21
Europe and Central Asia	NA	NA	NA	NA	22	22	23	24	23	24	25	27	20	21	14	14	22	21	22
Latin America and the Caribbean	NA	NA	NA	NA	22	22	23	24	23	24	24	28	19	23	13	16	21	23	22
Middle East and North Africa	NA	NA	NA	NA	22	22	23	23	23	23	23	23	18	19	12	13	21	21	21
South Asia	NA	NA	NA	NA	22	22	22	22	22	22	23	23	17	18	12	13	21	21	21
Sub-Saharan Africa	NA	NA	NA	NA	22	22	23	24	23	24	24	24	18	19	12	13	21	21	21
Low- and middle-income countries	NA	NA	NA	NA	22	22	22	23	22	23	24	24	19	20	13	14	21	21	21
High-income countries	NA	NA	NA	NA	24	24	26	26	25	25	25	26	20	20	14	15	22	20	21
WORLD	NA	NA	NA	NA	22	22	23	23	23	23	24	24	19	20	13	14	21	21	21
PAF of DALYs (%)																			
East Asia and Pacific	NA	NA	NA	NA	22	22	22	23	22	23	24	24	19	19	13	12	21	20	21
Europe and Central Asia	NA	NA	NA	NA	22	22	23	24	23	24	25	27	20	21	14	14	22	21	22
Latin America and the Caribbean	NA	NA	NA	NA	22	22	23	24	23	24	24	28	19	23	13	16	21	23	22
Middle East and North Africa	NA	NA	NA	NA	22	22	23	23	23	23	23	23	18	19	12	13	21	21	21
South Asia	NA	NA	NA	NA	22	22	22	22	22	22	23	23	17	18	12	13	21	21	21
Sub-Saharan Africa	NA	NA	NA	NA	22	22	23	24	23	24	24	24	18	19	12	13	21	21	21
Low- and middle-income countries	NA	NA	NA	NA	22	22	22	23	22	23	24	24	19	20	13	14	21	21	21
High-income countries	NA	NA	NA	NA	24	24	26	26	25	25	25	26	20	20	14	15	22	20	21
WORLD	NA	NA	NA	NA	22	22	23	23	23	23	24	24	19	20	13	14	21	21	21
Attributable Mortality (thousands)																			
East Asia and Pacific	NA	NA	NA	NA	2	1	7	4	23	13	35	27	35	34	14	23	116	102	218
Europe and Central Asia	NA	NA	NA	NA	1	0	8	2	35	10	56	34	53	66	18	54	172	166	338
Latin America and the Caribbean	NA	NA	NA	NA	0	0	2	1	9	4	11	8	11	10	6	9	40	33	73
Middle East and North Africa	NA	NA	NA	NA	1	0	2	1	9	4	12	7	10	9	3	4	37	26	64
South Asia	NA	NA	NA	NA	2	4	11	7	54	28	66	53	51	49	16	16	200	157	356
Sub-Saharan Africa	NA	NA	NA	NA	0	0	2	1	9	6	12	11	11	10	3	4	36	33	69
Low- and middle-income countries	NA	NA	NA	NA	6	6	32	15	139	66	193	141	172	178	59	111	601	517	1,118
High-income countries	NA	NA	NA	NA	0	0	4	1	22	6	33	14	46	32	35	60	140	113	253
WORLD	NA	NA	NA	NA	6	6	36	16	161	72	226	154	218	211	94	171	741	630	1,371
Attributable YLL (thousands)																			
East Asia and Pacific	NA	NA	NA	NA	49	34	163	92	433	261	471	399	315	349	68	115	1,499	1,249	2,749
Europe and Central Asia	NA	NA	NA	NA	18	4	199	42	664	208	762	516	481	671	83	250	2,206	1,691	3,897
Latin America and the Caribbean	NA	NA	NA	NA	9	4	50	23	166	87	154	123	99	103	27	43	505	383	889
Middle East and North Africa	NA	NA	NA	NA	15	8	57	22	174	87	155	112	93	94	16	23	511	346	857
South Asia	NA	NA	NA	NA	59	111	256	179	999	549	899	799	458	512	76	85	2,746	2,235	4,981
Sub-Saharan Africa	NA	NA	NA	NA	5	3	39	19	166	120	165	169	95	108	14	22	484	441	925
Low- and middle-income countries	NA	NA	NA	NA	155	164	764	377	2,601	1,312	2,607	2,117	1,541	1,837	283	538	7,952	6,346	14,298
High-income countries	NA	NA	NA	NA	6	2	95	23	414	113	444	204	400	323	151	246	1,511	911	2,422
WORLD	NA	NA	NA	NA	161	166	859	400	3,016	1,425	3,051	2,321	1,942	2,160	435	784	9,464	7,256	16,720
Attributable DALYs (thousands)																			
East Asia and Pacific	NA	NA	NA	NA	71	54	181	102	463	281	494	419	322	355	69	116	1,599	1,326	2,926
Europe and Central Asia	NA	NA	NA	NA	22	7	213	48	689	223	787	540	489	684	84	253	2,284	1,755	4,040
Latin America and the Caribbean	NA	NA	NA	NA	16	8	57	27	177	95	164	130	102	106	27	44	543	411	954
Middle East and North Africa	NA	NA	NA	NA	20	12	64	25	184	93	163	117	95	96	16	23	542	366	908
South Asia	NA	NA	NA	NA	87	132	291	205	1,059	592	946	841	470	524	78	86	2,931	2,380	5,312
Sub-Saharan Africa	NA	NA	NA	NA	9	5	43	22	177	128	173	178	98	110	14	22	514	465	979
Low- and middle-income countries	NA	NA	NA	NA	225	219	849	429	2,749	1,412	2,728	2,225	1,575	1,874	288	545	8,413	6,704	15,117
High-income countries	NA	NA	NA	NA	9	5	109	31	457	136	478	229	421	344	157	256	1,630	999	2,629
WORLD	NA	NA	NA	NA	234	223	958	460	3,205	1,547	3,206	2,454	1,996	2,218	444	801	10,043	7,704	17,747

Source: Authors' calculations.
Note: NA = not applicable.

Table 4A.51

Risk factor	Physical inactivity
Disease:	Cerebrovascular disease

Region	0–4 years		5–14 years		15–29 years		30–44 years		45–59 years		60–69 years		70–79 years		80+ years		Total		
	Male	Female	Male	Female	Male	Female	Male	Female	Male	Female	Male	Female	Male	Female	Male	Female	Male	Female	All
PAF of Mortality (%)																			
East Asia and Pacific	NA	NA	NA	NA	3	3	3	3	4	4	5	5	4	5	3	3	4	4	4
Europe and Central Asia	NA	NA	NA	NA	5	6	6	7	7	8	9	10	8	9	6	6	7	8	8
Latin America and the Caribbean	NA	NA	NA	NA	5	5	5	6	6	8	7	10	7	9	5	7	6	8	7
Middle East and North Africa	NA	NA	NA	NA	4	5	5	5	6	6	7	7	6	7	5	5	6	6	6
South Asia	NA	NA	NA	NA	4	5	5	5	6	6	7	7	6	6	4	5	6	6	6
Sub-Saharan Africa	NA	NA	NA	NA	4	4	4	4	5	5	6	6	5	5	4	4	5	5	5
Low- and middle-income countries	NA	NA	NA	NA	4	4	4	5	5	5	6	7	6	6	4	5	5	6	6
High-income countries	NA	NA	NA	NA	5	6	6	6	7	7	8	8	6	7	5	6	6	6	6
WORLD	NA	NA	NA	NA	4	5	4	5	5	6	6	7	6	6	4	5	5	6	6
PAF of YLL (%)																			
East Asia and Pacific	NA	NA	NA	NA	3	3	3	3	4	4	5	5	4	5	3	3	4	4	4
Europe and Central Asia	NA	NA	NA	NA	5	6	6	7	7	8	9	10	8	9	6	6	8	8	8
Latin America and the Caribbean	NA	NA	NA	NA	5	5	5	6	6	8	7	10	7	9	5	7	6	8	7
Middle East and North Africa	NA	NA	NA	NA	4	5	5	5	6	6	7	7	6	7	5	5	5	6	6
South Asia	NA	NA	NA	NA	4	5	5	5	6	6	7	7	6	6	4	5	5	6	6
Sub-Saharan Africa	NA	NA	NA	NA	4	4	4	4	5	5	6	6	5	5	4	4	5	5	5
Low- and middle-income countries	NA	NA	NA	NA	4	4	4	5	5	5	6	7	6	6	4	5	5	6	6
High-Income Countries	NA	NA	NA	NA	5	6	6	6	7	7	8	8	6	7	5	6	6	7	6
WORLD	NA	NA	NA	NA	4	5	4	5	5	6	6	7	6	6	4	5	5	6	6
PAF of DALYs (%)																			
East Asia and Pacific	NA	NA	NA	NA	3	3	4	5	5	5	6	6	5	5	3	3	5	5	5
Europe and Central Asia	NA	NA	NA	NA	5	6	6	8	8	9	10	11	8	9	6	6	8	9	9
Latin America and the Caribbean	NA	NA	NA	NA	5	5	6	8	7	9	8	12	7	10	5	7	7	9	8
Middle East and North Africa	NA	NA	NA	NA	4	5	6	6	7	7	8	8	7	7	5	5	6	7	6
South Asia	NA	NA	NA	NA	4	5	6	6	6	7	7	8	6	7	4	5	6	7	7
Sub-Saharan Africa	NA	NA	NA	NA	4	4	5	5	5	5	7	7	6	6	4	4	5	6	6
Low- and middle-income countries	NA	NA	NA	NA	4	4	5	6	6	6	7	8	6	7	4	5	6	7	6
High-income countries	NA	NA	NA	NA	5	6	8	8	9	9	9	10	7	8	5	6	8	8	8
WORLD	NA	NA	NA	NA	4	5	6	6	6	7	7	8	6	7	5	5	6	7	7
Attributable Mortality (thousands)																			
East Asia and Pacific	NA	NA	NA	NA	0	0	1	0	5	4	12	8	15	16	6	11	40	39	79
Europe and Central Asia	NA	NA	NA	NA	0	0	1	0	4	3	9	9	11	19	5	17	30	48	79
Latin America and the Caribbean	NA	NA	NA	NA	0	0	0	0	1	1	2	2	3	3	2	4	8	11	19
Middle East and North Africa	NA	NA	NA	NA	0	0	0	0	1	0	1	1	1	2	1	1	4	4	8
South Asia	NA	NA	NA	NA	0	0	0	0	4	3	9	9	9	11	3	4	26	28	54
Sub-Saharan Africa	NA	NA	NA	NA	0	0	0	0	1	2	2	3	2	4	1	2	7	11	18
Low- and middle-income countries	NA	NA	NA	NA	1	1	3	2	17	13	36	32	42	55	17	38	116	141	256
High-income countries	NA	NA	NA	NA	0	0	0	0	2	1	3	2	6	7	7	17	19	28	47
WORLD	NA	NA	NA	NA	1	1	3	2	18	14	39	35	49	62	24	55	135	169	303
Attributable YLL (thousands)																			
East Asia and Pacific	NA	NA	NA	NA	4	2	19	12	100	73	161	121	136	160	31	55	451	424	875
Europe and Central Asia	NA	NA	NA	NA	4	3	17	12	70	53	128	138	103	198	22	78	344	480	824
Latin America and the Caribbean	NA	NA	NA	NA	2	2	8	10	24	28	26	34	23	35	8	17	91	126	217
Middle East and North Africa	NA	NA	NA	NA	3	1	3	2	9	9	13	14	12	16	3	5	44	48	92
South Asia	NA	NA	NA	NA	5	3	11	7	79	59	127	132	81	115	15	24	318	341	658
Sub-Saharan Africa	NA	NA	NA	NA	4	3	11	9	27	37	29	49	21	38	4	9	97	145	242
Low- and middle-income countries	NA	NA	NA	NA	23	15	68	52	309	258	485	488	376	562	83	188	1,344	1,563	2,908
High-income countries	NA	NA	NA	NA	1	1	8	7	32	22	44	35	56	71	31	70	172	206	378
WORLD	NA	NA	NA	NA	24	17	77	59	341	279	529	523	432	633	113	258	1,517	1,769	3,286
Attributable DALYs (thousands)																			
East Asia and Pacific	NA	NA	NA	NA	4	2	37	25	177	128	260	190	182	209	36	64	696	619	1,315
Europe and Central Asia	NA	NA	NA	NA	4	3	24	19	97	78	178	197	133	245	25	87	460	630	1,090
Latin America and the Caribbean	NA	NA	NA	NA	2	2	14	19	40	46	42	53	31	46	9	20	138	186	324
Middle East and North Africa	NA	NA	NA	NA	3	1	5	4	15	13	20	19	15	19	3	5	61	63	124
South Asia	NA	NA	NA	NA	5	3	16	10	113	83	176	178	101	139	17	27	426	439	866
Sub-Saharan Africa	NA	NA	NA	NA	4	3	13	10	32	45	35	59	23	43	5	10	112	170	282
Low- and middle-income countries	NA	NA	NA	NA	23	15	108	88	474	394	711	696	484	700	95	214	1,895	2,107	4,001
High-income countries	NA	NA	NA	NA	1	1	22	18	80	58	102	83	98	125	42	94	346	379	725
WORLD	NA	NA	NA	NA	24	17	130	106	555	452	813	779	583	824	137	308	2,241	2,485	4,726

Source: Authors' calculations.

Note: NA = not applicable.

Table 4A.52

Risk factor: Physical inactivity
Disease: All causes

Region	0–4 years Male	0–4 years Female	5–14 years Male	5–14 years Female	15–29 years Male	15–29 years Female	30–44 years Male	30–44 years Female	45–59 years Male	45–59 years Female	60–69 years Male	60–69 years Female	70–79 years Male	70–79 years Female	80+ years Male	80+ years Female	Total Male	Total Female	All
PAF of Mortality (%)																			
East Asia and Pacific	NA	NA	NA	NA	1	1	2	2	3	4	4	5	4	4	2	3	3	3	3
Europe and Central Asia	NA	NA	NA	NA	1	1	3	3	7	7	10	12	9	11	7	8	7	9	8
Latin America and the Caribbean	NA	NA	NA	NA	0	1	2	2	4	6	6	8	5	7	3	4	3	5	4
Middle East and North Africa	NA	NA	NA	NA	1	1	3	3	7	6	8	8	6	7	4	4	4	4	4
South Asia	NA	NA	NA	NA	1	1	2	2	6	5	7	8	6	6	4	4	3	3	3
Sub-Saharan Africa	NA	NA	NA	NA	0	0	0	0	2	2	4	5	4	4	2	3	1	1	1
Low- and middle-income countries	NA	NA	NA	NA	0	0	1	1	4	4	6	7	5	6	4	4	3	3	3
High-income countries	NA	NA	NA	NA	0	1	3	3	6	5	6	6	5	6	4	4	5	5	5
WORLD	NA	NA	NA	NA	0	0	2	1	4	4	6	7	5	6	4	4	3	4	3
PAF of YLL (%)																			
East Asia and Pacific	NA	NA	NA	NA	1	1	1	2	3	3	4	5	4	4	2	2	2	2	2
Europe and Central Asia	NA	NA	NA	NA	1	1	3	3	7	7	10	11	9	11	7	8	6	8	7
Latin America and the Caribbean	NA	NA	NA	NA	0	1	1	2	4	6	6	8	5	7	3	4	2	4	3
Middle East and North Africa	NA	NA	NA	NA	1	1	3	3	6	6	8	8	6	7	4	4	3	3	3
South Asia	NA	NA	NA	NA	1	1	2	2	5	5	7	8	6	6	4	4	2	2	2
Sub-Saharan Africa	NA	NA	NA	NA	0	0	0	0	2	2	4	5	4	4	2	3	0	1	1
Low- and middle-income countries	NA	NA	NA	NA	0	0	1	1	4	4	6	7	5	6	3	4	2	2	2
High-income countries	NA	NA	NA	NA	0	1	3	3	6	5	6	6	5	6	4	4	5	5	5
WORLD	NA	NA	NA	NA	0	0	2	1	4	4	6	7	5	6	4	4	2	2	2
PAF of DALYs (%)																			
East Asia and Pacific	NA	NA	NA	NA	0	0	1	1	2	2	3	4	3	3	2	2	2	2	2
Europe and Central Asia	NA	NA	NA	NA	0	0	2	2	6	4	9	9	8	9	6	7	5	5	5
Latin America and the Caribbean	NA	NA	NA	NA	0	0	1	1	3	4	5	6	4	5	3	3	2	2	2
Middle East and North Africa	NA	NA	NA	NA	1	0	2	1	4	3	6	5	5	5	3	4	2	2	2
South Asia	NA	NA	NA	NA	0	1	1	1	4	3	6	6	5	5	3	3	2	2	2
Sub-Saharan Africa	NA	NA	NA	NA	0	0	0	0	2	2	3	4	3	4	2	2	0	0	0
Low- and middle-income countries	NA	NA	NA	NA	0	0	1	1	3	3	5	5	5	5	3	3	2	2	2
High-income countries	NA	NA	NA	NA	0	0	2	2	4	3	5	5	4	4	3	3	3	3	3
WORLD	NA	NA	NA	NA	0	0	1	1	3	3	5	5	5	5	3	3	2	2	2
Attributable Mortality (thousands)																			
East Asia and Pacific	NA	NA	NA	NA	2	2	9	7	34	26	55	46	57	59	22	37	180	177	357
Europe and Central Asia	NA	NA	NA	NA	1	0	10	3	41	17	70	50	68	91	24	73	213	235	448
Latin America and the Caribbean	NA	NA	NA	NA	1	0	3	3	13	10	17	17	17	20	9	16	60	66	125
Middle East and North Africa	NA	NA	NA	NA	1	0	3	1	10	6	13	10	12	12	4	5	44	35	78
South Asia	NA	NA	NA	NA	3	4	12	9	62	36	81	69	64	65	20	22	242	205	446
Sub-Saharan Africa	NA	NA	NA	NA	0	0	3	2	12	11	16	18	14	17	4	6	49	55	104
Low- and middle-income countries	NA	NA	NA	NA	8	8	40	26	172	107	252	209	232	263	82	160	787	772	1,559
High-income countries	NA	NA	NA	NA	0	0	5	3	29	14	45	26	62	53	47	90	190	186	376
WORLD	NA	NA	NA	NA	8	8	46	28	201	121	297	235	294	316	130	250	977	958	1,935
Attributable YLL (thousands)																			
East Asia and Pacific	NA	NA	NA	NA	65	45	223	178	643	524	744	690	506	604	108	188	2,290	2,228	4,518
Europe and Central Asia	NA	NA	NA	NA	26	11	229	79	772	339	944	751	615	934	108	338	2,694	2,453	5,147
Latin America and the Caribbean	NA	NA	NA	NA	16	11	76	63	241	206	231	254	151	201	41	77	755	812	1,568
Middle East and North Africa	NA	NA	NA	NA	20	11	66	37	195	120	180	144	111	121	20	30	592	462	1,054
South Asia	NA	NA	NA	NA	79	124	293	220	1,155	715	1,091	1,036	572	676	98	118	3,287	2,890	6,177
Sub-Saharan Africa	NA	NA	NA	NA	14	12	63	48	220	220	216	273	127	174	20	35	660	762	1,423
Low- and middle-income countries	NA	NA	NA	NA	220	214	950	624	3,227	2,124	3,406	3,148	2,082	2,711	394	786	10,279	9,607	19,887
High-income countries	NA	NA	NA	NA	11	6	127	73	542	286	606	385	545	530	207	375	2,038	1,655	3,693
WORLD	NA	NA	NA	NA	231	220	1,077	697	3,769	2,409	4,012	3,534	2,627	3,241	602	1,161	12,318	11,262	23,580
Attributable DALYs (thousands)																			
East Asia and Pacific	NA	NA	NA	NA	98	75	300	247	799	662	887	805	566	670	115	200	2,765	2,659	5,424
Europe and Central Asia	NA	NA	NA	NA	32	17	260	109	842	408	1,029	855	657	1,005	113	353	2,935	2,747	5,681
Latin America and the Caribbean	NA	NA	NA	NA	24	18	98	91	284	264	264	300	165	225	44	84	879	980	1,860
Middle East and North Africa	NA	NA	NA	NA	28	20	84	54	219	142	198	159	118	128	21	31	668	534	1,202
South Asia	NA	NA	NA	NA	122	158	372	293	1,289	824	1,204	1,142	608	718	103	124	3,697	3,259	6,956
Sub-Saharan Africa	NA	NA	NA	NA	20	15	75	59	243	245	233	296	133	182	21	36	723	833	1,556
Low- and middle-income countries	NA	NA	NA	NA	325	303	1,189	853	3,676	2,544	3,815	3,556	2,247	2,928	415	828	11,667	11,012	22,679
High-income countries	NA	NA	NA	NA	18	12	193	137	721	445	748	521	634	648	230	424	2,545	2,187	4,732
WORLD	NA	NA	NA	NA	343	315	1,383	990	4,397	2,989	4,564	4,078	2,881	3,576	645	1,251	14,212	13,199	27,411

Source: Authors' calculations.
Note: NA = not applicable.

Table 4A.53

Risk factor: Unsafe sex
Disease: Sexually transmitted diseases excluding HIV/AIDS

Region	0–4 years Male	0–4 years Female	5–14 years Male	5–14 years Female	15–29 years Male	15–29 years Female	30–44 years Male	30–44 years Female	45–59 years Male	45–59 years Female	60–69 years Male	60–69 years Female	70–79 years Male	70–79 years Female	80+ years Male	80+ years Female	Total Male	Total Female	All
PAF of Mortality (%)																			
East Asia and Pacific	100	100	100	100	100	100	100	100	100	100	100	100	100	100	100	100	100	100	100
Europe and Central Asia	100	100	100	100	100	100	100	100	100	100	100	100	100	100	100	100	100	100	100
Latin America and the Caribbean	100	100	100	100	100	100	100	100	100	100	100	100	100	100	100	100	100	100	100
Middle East and North Africa	100	100	100	100	100	100	100	100	100	100	100	100	100	100	100	100	100	100	100
South Asia	100	100	100	100	100	100	100	100	100	100	100	100	100	100	100	100	100	100	100
Sub-Saharan Africa	100	100	100	100	100	100	100	100	100	100	100	100	100	100	100	100	100	100	100
Low- and middle-income countries	100	100	100	100	100	100	100	100	100	100	100	100	100	100	100	100	100	100	100
High-income countries	100	100	100	100	100	100	100	100	100	100	100	100	100	100	100	100	100	100	100
WORLD	100	100	100	100	100	100	100	100	100	100	100	100	100	100	100	100	100	100	100
PAF of YLL (%)																			
East Asia and Pacific	100	100	100	100	100	100	100	100	100	100	100	100	100	100	100	100	100	100	100
Europe and Central Asia	100	100	100	100	100	100	100	100	100	100	100	100	100	100	100	100	100	100	100
Latin America and the Caribbean	100	100	100	100	100	100	100	100	100	100	100	100	100	100	100	100	100	100	100
Middle East and North Africa	100	100	100	100	100	100	100	100	100	100	100	100	100	100	100	100	100	100	100
South Asia	100	100	100	100	100	100	100	100	100	100	100	100	100	100	100	100	100	100	100
Sub-Saharan Africa	100	100	100	100	100	100	100	100	100	100	100	100	100	100	100	100	100	100	100
Low- and middle-income countries	100	100	100	100	100	100	100	100	100	100	100	100	100	100	100	100	100	100	100
High-income countries	100	100	100	100	100	100	100	100	100	100	100	100	100	100	100	100	100	100	100
WORLD	100	100	100	100	100	100	100	100	100	100	100	100	100	100	100	100	100	100	100
PAF of DALYs (%)																			
East Asia and Pacific	100	100	100	100	100	100	100	100	100	100	100	100	100	100	100	100	100	100	100
Europe and Central Asia	100	100	100	100	100	100	100	100	100	100	100	100	100	100	100	100	100	100	100
Latin America and the Caribbean	100	100	100	100	100	100	100	100	100	100	100	100	100	100	100	100	100	100	100
Middle East and North Africa	100	100	100	100	100	100	100	100	100	100	100	100	100	100	100	100	100	100	100
South Asia	100	100	100	100	100	100	100	100	100	100	100	100	100	100	100	100	100	100	100
Sub-Saharan Africa	100	100	100	100	100	100	100	100	100	100	100	100	100	100	100	100	100	100	100
Low- and middle-income countries	100	100	100	100	100	100	100	100	100	100	100	100	100	100	100	100	100	100	100
High-income countries	100	100	100	100	100	100	100	100	100	100	100	100	100	100	100	100	100	100	100
WORLD	100	100	100	100	100	100	100	100	100	100	100	100	100	100	100	100	100	100	100
Attributable Mortality (thousands)																			
East Asia and Pacific	1	0	0	0	0	0	0	1	1	2	1	1	1	1	1	0	4	4	9
Europe and Central Asia	0	0	0	0	0	0	0	0	0	0	0	0	0	0	0	0	0	0	1
Latin America and the Caribbean	1	0	0	0	0	0	0	0	0	0	0	0	0	0	0	0	1	1	2
Middle East and North Africa	0	0	0	0	0	0	0	0	1	1	0	1	0	0	0	0	2	2	4
South Asia	12	25	0	0	0	0	1	1	7	6	6	4	5	2	2	1	33	38	71
Sub-Saharan Africa	17	12	0	0	1	12	10	8	17	6	3	2	0	1	0	0	48	42	90
Low- and middle-income countries	31	37	0	0	2	13	11	10	26	14	10	7	6	4	3	1	89	87	176
High-income countries	0	0	0	0	0	0	0	0	0	0	0	0	0	0	0	0	0	0	1
WORLD	31	37	0	0	2	13	11	10	26	14	10	7	6	4	3	1	89	88	176
Attributable YLL (thousands)																			
East Asia and Pacific	29	12	0	0	2	2	3	17	18	32	11	12	7	6	3	1	73	81	154
Europe and Central Asia	6	5	0	0	0	1	1	1	1	1	0	0	0	1	0	0	8	9	17
Latin America and the Caribbean	20	5	0	0	1	4	1	4	0	3	0	1	0	1	0	0	24	17	41
Middle East and North Africa	0	2	0	0	2	6	6	6	17	11	7	9	3	3	1	0	35	37	72
South Asia	349	759	0	0	2	3	14	24	128	119	89	52	43	19	12	4	637	981	1,618
Sub-Saharan Africa	525	355	0	0	38	341	229	202	335	128	38	32	0	17	0	0	1,166	1,076	2,241
Low- and middle-income countries	929	1,138	0	1	45	356	254	255	499	293	145	106	55	47	16	5	1,942	2,202	4,143
High-income countries	0	0	0	0	0	0	0	1	0	1	0	1	0	1	0	1	2	5	7
WORLD	929	1,138	0	1	45	356	254	256	500	294	145	106	55	49	16	6	1,943	2,207	4,150
Attributable DALYs (thousands)																			
East Asia and Pacific	78	58	2	9	86	360	46	115	19	34	11	12	7	6	3	1	252	596	848
Europe and Central Asia	8	8	0	2	20	111	13	34	1	2	0	0	0	1	0	0	43	158	200
Latin America and the Caribbean	44	27	1	5	49	205	28	64	1	4	0	1	0	1	0	0	123	306	430
Middle East and North Africa	16	17	1	5	33	161	19	39	17	11	7	9	3	3	1	0	97	245	342
South Asia	581	978	8	26	276	904	146	276	131	124	89	53	43	19	12	4	1,286	2,383	3,669
Sub-Saharan Africa	775	602	6	21	238	1,001	285	359	336	130	38	32	0	17	0	0	1,680	2,163	3,842
Low- and middle-income countries	1,502	1,691	19	69	702	2,741	537	886	504	304	145	107	55	47	16	5	3,481	5,851	9,332
High-income countries	7	6	0	2	9	79	9	27	1	2	0	1	0	1	0	1	26	119	145
WORLD	1,509	1,697	19	71	711	2,820	546	913	505	306	146	108	55	49	16	6	3,507	5,970	9,477

Source: Authors' calculations.

Table 4A.54

Risk factor: Unsafe sex
Disease: HIV/AIDS

Region	0–4 years Male	Female	5–14 years Male	Female	15–29 years Male	Female	30–44 years Male	Female	45–59 years Male	Female	60–69 years Male	Female	70–79 years Male	Female	80+ years Male	Female	Total Male	Female	All
PAF of Mortality (%)																			
East Asia and Pacific	66	66	65	66	66	67	66	66	67	66	67	0	66	0	52	0	66	60	65
Europe and Central Asia	27	30	54	59	28	29	28	29	27	28	28	28	27	27	29	59	28	30	28
Latin America and the Caribbean	90	90	90	90	89	90	89	89	89	89	89	89	89	89	88	88	89	89	89
Middle East and North Africa	94	94	95	90	94	95	95	95	94	95	94	96	95	96	97	97	94	95	94
South Asia	80	80	80	79	79	79	79	79	79	79	79	85	79	85	85	85	79	79	79
Sub-Saharan Africa	100	100	100	100	100	100	100	100	100	100	100	100	100	100	100	100	100	100	100
Low- and middle-income countries	98	98	99	99	93	98	92	97	91	96	94	90	94	87	95	37	93	97	95
High-income countries	62	60	70	66	63	65	67	68	69	70	67	68	68	67	69	68	67	68	67
WORLD	98	98	99	99	93	98	92	97	91	96	93	89	92	87	90	43	93	97	95
PAF of YLL (%)																			
East Asia and Pacific	66	66	65	66	66	67	66	66	67	66	67	0	66	0	52	0	66	63	65
Europe and Central Asia	27	30	54	59	28	29	28	29	27	28	28	28	27	27	29	59	28	30	28
Latin America and the Caribbean	90	90	90	90	89	90	89	89	89	89	89	89	89	89	88	88	89	89	89
Middle East and North Africa	94	94	95	90	94	95	95	95	94	95	94	96	95	96	97	97	94	95	94
South Asia	80	80	80	79	79	79	79	79	79	79	79	85	79	85	85	85	79	79	79
Sub-Saharan Africa	100	100	100	100	100	100	100	100	100	100	100	100	100	100	100	100	100	100	100
Low- and middle-income countries	98	98	99	99	93	98	92	97	91	96	94	90	94	88	94	36	93	98	95
High-income countries	62	60	70	66	63	65	67	68	69	70	67	68	68	67	69	68	67	68	67
WORLD	98	98	99	99	93	98	92	97	91	96	93	89	92	87	89	41	93	97	95
PAF of DALYs (%)																			
East Asia and Pacific	66	66	65	66	66	67	66	66	67	66	67	0	66	0	52	0	66	63	66
Europe and Central Asia	27	30	54	59	28	29	28	29	27	28	28	28	27	27	29	59	28	30	28
Latin America and the Caribbean	90	90	90	90	89	90	89	89	89	89	89	89	89	89	88	88	89	89	89
Middle East and North Africa	94	94	95	90	94	95	95	95	94	95	94	96	95	96	97	97	94	95	94
South Asia	80	80	80	79	79	79	79	79	79	79	79	85	79	85	85	85	79	79	79
Sub-Saharan Africa	100	100	100	100	100	100	100	100	100	100	100	100	100	100	100	100	100	100	100
Low- and middle-income countries	98	98	98	99	91	97	91	97	91	96	94	90	93	88	94	39	93	97	95
High-income countries	62	60	70	66	63	65	67	68	69	70	67	68	68	67	69	68	67	67	67
WORLD	98	98	98	99	91	97	91	97	90	96	93	89	91	87	88	44	92	97	95
Attributable Mortality (thousands)																			
East Asia and Pacific	2	2	0	0	10	3	28	6	11	5	1	0	0	0	0	0	52	16	68
Europe and Central Asia	0	0	0	0	1	0	4	0	2	0	0	0	0	0	0	0	7	1	8
Latin America and the Caribbean	3	3	1	1	10	8	24	11	8	3	1	0	0	0	0	0	48	26	74
Middle East and North Africa	0	0	0	0	1	0	1	0	0	0	0	0	0	0	0	0	2	1	3
South Asia	6	6	1	1	33	15	90	20	33	6	3	0	0	0	0	0	166	49	214
Sub-Saharan Africa	159	153	48	47	185	349	440	374	148	108	23	17	3	4	0	0	1,006	1,051	2,057
Low- and middle-income countries	170	163	51	50	240	376	587	411	201	123	27	17	4	4	0	0	1,281	1,145	2,425
High-income countries	0	0	0	0	1	0	6	2	4	1	1	0	0	0	0	0	11	3	15
WORLD	170	163	51	50	240	377	594	413	205	123	28	18	4	4	0	0	1,292	1,148	2,440
Attributable YLL (thousands)																			
East Asia and Pacific	60	47	7	6	269	86	689	148	213	110	12	0	1	0	0	0	1,251	396	1,647
Europe and Central Asia	2	2	3	3	35	10	89	11	30	4	2	0	0	0	0	0	161	30	190
Latin America and the Caribbean	80	78	36	35	276	223	592	282	163	62	13	4	2	1	0	0	1,162	685	1,847
Middle East and North Africa	8	8	1	1	14	12	21	11	6	3	0	0	0	0	0	0	50	35	85
South Asia	177	169	42	40	882	425	2,181	493	649	133	37	8	4	1	0	0	3,972	1,267	5,239
Sub-Saharan Africa	4,816	4,672	1,420	1,395	4,989	9,577	10,702	9,414	2,903	2,237	317	260	29	41	0	0	25,176	27,596	52,771
Low- and middle-income countries	5,144	4,976	1,510	1,480	6,464	10,332	14,272	10,358	3,963	2,548	383	272	36	42	1	0	31,772	30,008	61,780
High-income countries	1	1	1	1	19	10	147	50	73	18	8	2	2	1	0	0	250	82	332
WORLD	5,144	4,976	1,510	1,481	6,483	10,343	14,419	10,407	4,036	2,566	391	274	37	43	1	0	32,022	30,090	62,112
Attributable DALYs (thousands)																			
East Asia and Pacific	62	48	8	7	437	141	799	171	225	113	14	0	1	0	0	0	1,546	480	2,026
Europe and Central Asia	2	2	4	3	70	26	112	17	33	5	3	0	0	0	0	0	223	53	277
Latin America and the Caribbean	82	80	37	36	385	268	653	300	172	64	14	5	2	1	0	0	1,345	753	2,099
Middle East and North Africa	9	8	1	1	20	15	23	12	7	3	0	0	0	0	0	0	60	39	99
South Asia	181	173	45	43	1,117	568	2,322	544	663	138	39	8	5	1	0	0	4,371	1,475	5,846
Sub-Saharan Africa	4,894	4,748	1,451	1,431	6,041	11,057	11,257	9,961	2,994	2,298	325	266	29	41	0	0	26,992	29,803	56,795
Low- and middle-income countries	5,229	5,059	1,546	1,521	8,070	12,075	15,165	11,006	4,093	2,621	396	280	37	43	1	0	34,537	32,604	67,141
High-income countries	1	1	1	1	53	21	192	59	82	19	9	2	2	1	0	0	341	104	445
WORLD	5,230	5,060	1,547	1,522	8,123	12,095	15,357	11,065	4,176	2,641	406	282	39	43	1	0	34,878	32,708	67,586

Source: Authors' calculations.

Table 4A.55

Risk factor: Unsafe sex
Disease: Cervix uteri cancer

Region	0–4 years Male	Female	5–14 years Male	Female	15–29 years Male	Female	30–44 years Male	Female	45–59 years Male	Female	60–69 years Male	Female	70–79 years Male	Female	80+ years Male	Female	Total Male	Female	All
PAF of Mortality (%)																			
East Asia and Pacific	NA	100	NA	100	NA	100	NA	100	NA	100	NA	100	NA	100	NA	100	NA	100	100
Europe and Central Asia	NA	100	NA	100	NA	100	NA	100	NA	100	NA	100	NA	100	NA	100	NA	100	100
Latin America and the Caribbean	NA	100	NA	100	NA	100	NA	100	NA	100	NA	100	NA	100	NA	100	NA	100	100
Middle East and North Africa	NA	100	NA	100	NA	100	NA	100	NA	100	NA	100	NA	100	NA	100	NA	100	100
South Asia	NA	100	NA	100	NA	100	NA	100	NA	100	NA	100	NA	100	NA	100	NA	100	100
Sub-Saharan Africa	NA	100	NA	100	NA	100	NA	100	NA	100	NA	100	NA	100	NA	100	NA	100	100
Low- and middle-income countries	NA	100	NA	100	NA	100	NA	100	NA	100	NA	100	NA	100	NA	100	NA	100	100
High-income countries	NA	100	NA	100	NA	100	NA	100	NA	100	NA	100	NA	100	NA	100	NA	100	100
WORLD	NA	100	NA	100	NA	100	NA	100	NA	100	NA	100	NA	100	NA	100	NA	100	100
PAF of YLL (%)																			
East Asia and Pacific	NA	100	NA	100	NA	100	NA	100	NA	100	NA	100	NA	100	NA	100	NA	100	100
Europe and Central Asia	NA	100	NA	100	NA	100	NA	100	NA	100	NA	100	NA	100	NA	100	NA	100	100
Latin America and the Caribbean	NA	100	NA	100	NA	100	NA	100	NA	100	NA	100	NA	100	NA	100	NA	100	100
Middle East and North Africa	NA	100	NA	100	NA	100	NA	100	NA	100	NA	100	NA	100	NA	100	NA	100	100
South Asia	NA	100	NA	100	NA	100	NA	100	NA	100	NA	100	NA	100	NA	100	NA	100	100
Sub-Saharan Africa	NA	100	NA	100	NA	100	NA	100	NA	100	NA	100	NA	100	NA	100	NA	100	100
Low- and middle-income countries	NA	100	NA	100	NA	100	NA	100	NA	100	NA	100	NA	100	NA	100	NA	100	100
High-income countries	NA	100	NA	100	NA	100	NA	100	NA	100	NA	100	NA	100	NA	100	NA	100	100
WORLD	NA	100	NA	100	NA	100	NA	100	NA	100	NA	100	NA	100	NA	100	NA	100	100
PAF of DALYs (%)																			
East Asia and Pacific	NA	100	NA	100	NA	100	NA	100	NA	100	NA	100	NA	100	NA	100	NA	100	100
Europe and Central Asia	NA	100	NA	100	NA	100	NA	100	NA	100	NA	100	NA	100	NA	100	NA	100	100
Latin America and the Caribbean	NA	100	NA	100	NA	100	NA	100	NA	100	NA	100	NA	100	NA	100	NA	100	100
Middle East and North Africa	NA	100	NA	100	NA	100	NA	100	NA	100	NA	100	NA	100	NA	100	NA	100	100
South Asia	NA	100	NA	100	NA	100	NA	100	NA	100	NA	100	NA	100	NA	100	NA	100	100
Sub-Saharan Africa	NA	100	NA	100	NA	100	NA	100	NA	100	NA	100	NA	100	NA	100	NA	100	100
Low- and middle-income countries	NA	100	NA	100	NA	100	NA	100	NA	100	NA	100	NA	100	NA	100	NA	100	100
High-income countries	NA	100	NA	100	NA	100	NA	100	NA	100	NA	100	NA	100	NA	100	NA	100	100
WORLD	NA	100	NA	100	NA	100	NA	100	NA	100	NA	100	NA	100	NA	100	NA	100	100
Attributable Mortality (thousands)																			
East Asia and Pacific	NA	0	NA	0	NA	2	NA	3	NA	14	NA	13	NA	11	NA	4	NA	47	47
Europe and Central Asia	NA	0	NA	0	NA	0	NA	3	NA	6	NA	4	NA	4	NA	2	NA	19	19
Latin America and the Caribbean	NA	0	NA	0	NA	1	NA	4	NA	9	NA	5	NA	5	NA	2	NA	26	26
Middle East and North Africa	NA	0	NA	0	NA	0	NA	1	NA	2	NA	1	NA	1	NA	0	NA	5	5
South Asia	NA	0	NA	0	NA	6	NA	5	NA	26	NA	26	NA	14	NA	7	NA	83	83
Sub-Saharan Africa	NA	0	NA	0	NA	1	NA	2	NA	12	NA	10	NA	9	NA	2	NA	38	38
Low- and middle-income countries	NA	0	NA	0	NA	11	NA	19	NA	68	NA	59	NA	44	NA	17	NA	218	218
High-income countries	NA	0	NA	0	NA	0	NA	3	NA	5	NA	3	NA	3	NA	3	NA	17	17
WORLD	NA	0	NA	0	NA	11	NA	22	NA	73	NA	62	NA	47	NA	20	NA	235	235
Attributable YLL (thousands)																			
East Asia and Pacific	NA	0	NA	0	NA	53	NA	82	NA	287	NA	189	NA	117	NA	22	NA	750	750
Europe and Central Asia	NA	0	NA	0	NA	11	NA	79	NA	117	NA	61	NA	45	NA	8	NA	321	321
Latin America and the Caribbean	NA	0	NA	0	NA	27	NA	109	NA	177	NA	80	NA	48	NA	12	NA	454	454
Middle East and North Africa	NA	0	NA	0	NA	10	NA	12	NA	36	NA	18	NA	8	NA	1	NA	86	86
South Asia	NA	0	NA	0	NA	159	NA	123	NA	519	NA	389	NA	145	NA	39	NA	1,375	1,375
Sub-Saharan Africa	NA	0	NA	0	NA	37	NA	62	NA	239	NA	158	NA	96	NA	14	NA	606	606
Low- and middle-income countries	NA	0	NA	1	NA	298	NA	468	NA	1,373	NA	896	NA	459	NA	96	NA	3,592	3,592
High-income countries	NA	0	NA	0	NA	6	NA	66	NA	96	NA	44	NA	34	NA	13	NA	260	260
WORLD	NA	0	NA	1	NA	304	NA	534	NA	1,469	NA	941	NA	494	NA	109	NA	3,852	3,852
Attributable DALYs (thousands)																			
East Asia and Pacific	NA	0	NA	0	NA	65	NA	93	NA	308	NA	196	NA	120	NA	22	NA	805	805
Europe and Central Asia	NA	0	NA	0	NA	15	NA	93	NA	128	NA	64	NA	46	NA	9	NA	356	356
Latin America and the Caribbean	NA	0	NA	0	NA	33	NA	124	NA	191	NA	84	NA	49	NA	13	NA	494	494
Middle East and North Africa	NA	0	NA	0	NA	12	NA	14	NA	38	NA	19	NA	9	NA	1	NA	93	93
South Asia	NA	0	NA	1	NA	175	NA	129	NA	534	NA	397	NA	148	NA	40	NA	1,423	1,423
Sub-Saharan Africa	NA	0	NA	0	NA	41	NA	64	NA	247	NA	162	NA	98	NA	14	NA	627	627
Low- and middle-income countries	NA	0	NA	2	NA	341	NA	517	NA	1,446	NA	922	NA	469	NA	99	NA	3,797	3,797
High-income countries	NA	0	NA	0	NA	11	NA	90	NA	117	NA	50	NA	37	NA	14	NA	319	319
WORLD	NA	0	NA	2	NA	352	NA	607	NA	1,563	NA	972	NA	506	NA	113	NA	4,116	4,116

Source: Authors' calculations.
Note: NA = not applicable.

Table 4A.56

Risk factor: Unsafe sex
Disease: All causes

Region	0–4 years Male	0–4 years Female	5–14 years Male	5–14 years Female	15–29 years Male	15–29 years Female	30–44 years Male	30–44 years Female	45–59 years Male	45–59 years Female	60–69 years Male	60–69 years Female	70–79 years Male	70–79 years Female	80+ years Male	80+ years Female	Total Male	Total Female	All
PAF of Mortality (%)																			
East Asia and Pacific	0	0	0	0	2	2	5	2	1	3	0	1	0	1	0	0	1	1	1
Europe and Central Asia	0	0	1	1	1	2	1	4	0	2	0	1	0	1	0	0	0	1	0
Latin America and the Caribbean	1	2	4	5	6	14	12	15	3	6	0	3	0	2	0	1	3	4	3
Middle East and North Africa	0	0	0	0	1	2	1	2	1	2	0	1	0	1	0	0	0	1	1
South Asia	1	2	1	0	7	4	13	5	4	5	1	3	0	1	0	1	3	3	3
Sub-Saharan Africa	7	8	17	16	35	52	53	57	26	27	6	8	1	4	0	1	19	22	20
Low- and middle-income countries	4	4	7	7	13	25	21	24	6	8	1	3	0	1	0	0	5	6	6
High-income countries	0	0	0	0	1	2	3	5	1	2	0	1	0	0	0	0	0	1	0
WORLD	4	4	7	7	13	25	20	23	5	8	1	3	0	1	0	0	5	6	5
PAF of YLL (%)																			
East Asia and Pacific	0	0	0	0	2	2	5	2	1	3	0	1	0	1	0	0	1	1	1
Europe and Central Asia	0	0	1	1	1	2	1	4	0	2	0	1	0	1	0	0	0	1	1
Latin America and the Caribbean	1	2	4	5	6	14	12	15	3	6	0	3	0	2	0	1	4	5	4
Middle East and North Africa	0	0	0	0	1	2	1	2	1	2	0	1	0	1	0	0	0	1	1
South Asia	1	2	1	0	7	4	13	5	4	5	1	3	0	1	0	1	3	3	3
Sub-Saharan Africa	7	8	17	16	35	52	53	57	27	27	6	8	1	4	0	1	19	23	21
Low- and middle-income countries	4	4	7	7	13	25	22	24	6	8	1	3	0	1	0	1	7	8	8
High-income countries	0	0	0	0	1	2	3	5	1	2	0	1	0	0	0	0	1	1	1
WORLD	4	4	7	7	12	25	21	23	5	8	1	3	0	1	0	0	6	8	7
PAF of DALYs (%)																			
East Asia and Pacific	0	0	0	0	2	3	3	2	1	2	0	1	0	1	0	0	1	1	1
Europe and Central Asia	0	0	0	0	1	3	1	2	0	1	0	1	0	0	0	0	0	1	1
Latin America and the Caribbean	1	1	1	1	4	7	7	7	2	4	0	2	0	1	0	1	3	3	3
Middle East and North Africa	0	0	0	0	1	4	1	2	0	1	0	1	0	0	0	0	0	1	1
South Asia	1	2	0	0	5	5	9	4	3	3	1	2	0	1	0	1	3	3	3
Sub-Saharan Africa	7	7	11	12	27	41	44	46	21	20	5	6	1	3	0	1	16	19	18
Low- and middle-income countries	3	3	4	4	9	16	15	14	4	5	1	2	0	1	0	0	5	6	6
High-income countries	0	0	0	0	1	2	2	2	0	1	0	0	0	0	0	0	0	1	1
WORLD	3	3	4	4	8	15	14	13	4	4	1	2	0	1	0	0	5	6	5
Attributable Mortality (thousands)																			
East Asia and Pacific	3	2	0	0	10	5	29	10	12	21	2	13	1	12	1	4	57	67	124
Europe and Central Asia	0	0	0	0	1	1	4	4	2	6	0	4	0	4	0	2	7	21	28
Latin America and the Caribbean	3	3	1	1	10	9	24	16	8	12	1	6	0	5	0	2	49	53	102
Middle East and North Africa	0	0	0	0	1	1	1	1	1	2	0	2	0	1	0	0	4	8	12
South Asia	17	30	1	1	33	21	91	26	40	38	9	30	5	16	2	8	199	170	369
Sub-Saharan Africa	177	165	48	47	186	362	450	384	165	126	25	29	3	14	0	2	1,054	1,130	2,185
Low- and middle-income countries	201	201	51	50	241	400	598	441	227	205	37	84	10	52	3	18	1,370	1,450	2,819
High-income countries	0	0	0	0	1	1	6	5	4	6	1	3	0	4	0	3	11	21	32
WORLD	201	201	51	50	242	400	604	445	231	210	38	87	10	56	3	21	1,381	1,470	2,851
Attributable YLL (thousands)																			
East Asia and Pacific	89	58	7	6	270	140	692	246	231	429	23	201	9	123	3	23	1,324	1,227	2,551
Europe and Central Asia	7	7	3	3	35	22	89	91	31	121	3	62	0	45	0	9	169	360	529
Latin America and the Caribbean	101	83	36	35	278	253	592	395	163	242	13	86	2	50	0	13	1,186	1,156	2,342
Middle East and North Africa	9	10	1	2	15	28	26	30	23	49	7	27	3	12	1	1	86	159	244
South Asia	525	928	43	41	883	587	2,195	640	777	770	126	449	48	165	12	42	4,609	3,623	8,231
Sub-Saharan Africa	5,341	5,027	1,420	1,396	5,027	9,955	10,931	9,678	3,238	2,603	356	450	29	154	1	14	26,341	29,278	55,619
Low- and middle-income countries	6,072	6,114	1,510	1,482	6,508	10,986	14,526	11,081	4,463	4,215	527	1,274	90	549	17	101	33,714	35,802	69,516
High-income countries	1	1	1	1	19	17	147	116	73	115	8	47	2	36	0	14	252	347	599
WORLD	6,073	6,115	1,511	1,483	6,528	11,002	14,673	11,197	4,536	4,330	536	1,322	92	585	17	116	33,965	36,149	70,115
Attributable DALYs (thousands)																			
East Asia and Pacific	139	107	10	16	523	566	845	379	243	455	25	209	9	126	3	24	1,797	1,881	3,678
Europe and Central Asia	10	10	4	6	90	151	125	144	34	135	3	65	0	47	0	9	266	567	833
Latin America and the Caribbean	126	107	38	41	434	505	681	488	173	259	15	89	2	51	0	13	1,468	1,554	3,022
Middle East and North Africa	25	26	2	6	53	187	43	64	24	52	7	28	3	12	1	1	157	376	534
South Asia	761	1,151	53	70	1,394	1,647	2,468	948	793	795	128	458	48	168	12	43	5,657	5,281	10,938
Sub-Saharan Africa	5,670	5,350	1,458	1,452	6,280	12,100	11,541	10,385	3,330	2,675	363	460	29	156	1	14	28,672	32,593	61,265
Low- and middle-income countries	6,731	6,750	1,565	1,591	8,773	15,157	15,702	12,409	4,598	4,372	542	1,309	92	559	17	104	38,018	42,252	80,270
High-income countries	8	7	1	3	62	111	201	176	83	138	10	53	2	39	0	15	367	542	909
WORLD	6,739	6,757	1,566	1,594	8,834	15,268	15,903	12,586	4,681	4,510	551	1,362	94	598	17	120	38,385	42,794	81,179

Source: Authors' calculations.

Table 4A.57

Risk factor: Alcohol use
Disease: Low birthweight

Region	0–4 years Male	0–4 years Female	5–14 years Male	5–14 years Female	15–29 years Male	15–29 years Female	30–44 years Male	30–44 years Female	45–59 years Male	45–59 years Female	60–69 years Male	60–69 years Female	70–79 years Male	70–79 years Female	80+ years Male	80+ years Female	Total Male	Total Female	All
PAF of Mortality (%)																			
East Asia and Pacific	0	0	NA	NA	NA	NA	NA	NA	NA	NA	NA	NA	NA	NA	NA	NA	0	0	0
Europe and Central Asia	4	4	NA	NA	NA	NA	NA	NA	NA	NA	NA	NA	NA	NA	NA	NA	4	4	4
Latin America and the Caribbean	3	3	NA	NA	NA	NA	NA	NA	NA	NA	NA	NA	NA	NA	NA	NA	3	3	3
Middle East and North Africa	3	3	NA	NA	NA	NA	NA	NA	NA	NA	NA	NA	NA	NA	NA	NA	3	3	3
South Asia	0	0	NA	NA	NA	NA	NA	NA	NA	NA	NA	NA	NA	NA	NA	NA	0	0	0
Sub-Saharan Africa	0	0	NA	NA	NA	NA	NA	NA	NA	NA	NA	NA	NA	NA	NA	NA	0	0	0
Low- and middle-income countries	0	0	NA	NA	NA	NA	NA	NA	NA	NA	NA	NA	NA	NA	NA	NA	0	0	0
High-income countries	2	2	NA	NA	NA	NA	NA	NA	NA	NA	NA	NA	NA	NA	NA	NA	2	2	2
WORLD	0	0	NA	NA	NA	NA	NA	NA	NA	NA	NA	NA	NA	NA	NA	NA	0	0	0
PAF of YLL (%)																			
East Asia and Pacific	0	0	NA	NA	NA	NA	NA	NA	NA	NA	NA	NA	NA	NA	NA	NA	0	0	0
Europe and Central Asia	4	4	NA	NA	NA	NA	NA	NA	NA	NA	NA	NA	NA	NA	NA	NA	4	4	4
Latin America and the Caribbean	3	3	NA	NA	NA	NA	NA	NA	NA	NA	NA	NA	NA	NA	NA	NA	3	3	3
Middle East and North Africa	3	3	NA	NA	NA	NA	NA	NA	NA	NA	NA	NA	NA	NA	NA	NA	3	3	3
South Asia	0	0	NA	NA	NA	NA	NA	NA	NA	NA	NA	NA	NA	NA	NA	NA	0	0	0
Sub-Saharan Africa	0	0	NA	NA	NA	NA	NA	NA	NA	NA	NA	NA	NA	NA	NA	NA	0	0	0
Low- and middle-income countries	0	0	NA	NA	NA	NA	NA	NA	NA	NA	NA	NA	NA	NA	NA	NA	0	0	0
High-income countries	2	2	NA	NA	NA	NA	NA	NA	NA	NA	NA	NA	NA	NA	NA	NA	2	2	2
WORLD	1	0	NA	NA	NA	NA	NA	NA	NA	NA	NA	NA	NA	NA	NA	NA	1	0	0
PAF of DALYs (%)																			
East Asia and Pacific	0	0	NA	NA	NA	NA	NA	NA	NA	NA	NA	NA	NA	NA	NA	NA	0	0	0
Europe and Central Asia	4	4	NA	NA	NA	NA	NA	NA	NA	NA	NA	NA	NA	NA	NA	NA	4	4	4
Latin America and the Caribbean	3	3	NA	NA	NA	NA	NA	NA	NA	NA	NA	NA	NA	NA	NA	NA	3	3	3
Middle East and North Africa	3	3	NA	NA	NA	NA	NA	NA	NA	NA	NA	NA	NA	NA	NA	NA	3	3	3
South Asia	0	0	NA	NA	NA	NA	NA	NA	NA	NA	NA	NA	NA	NA	NA	NA	0	0	0
Sub-Saharan Africa	0	0	NA	NA	NA	NA	NA	NA	NA	NA	NA	NA	NA	NA	NA	NA	0	0	0
Low- and middle-income countries	1	0	NA	NA	NA	NA	NA	NA	NA	NA	NA	NA	NA	NA	NA	NA	1	0	0
High-income countries	2	2	NA	NA	NA	NA	NA	NA	NA	NA	NA	NA	NA	NA	NA	NA	2	2	2
WORLD	1	0	NA	NA	NA	NA	NA	NA	NA	NA	NA	NA	NA	NA	NA	NA	1	0	1
Attributable Mortality (thousands)																			
East Asia and Pacific	0	0	NA	NA	NA	NA	NA	NA	NA	NA	NA	NA	NA	NA	NA	NA	0	0	0
Europe and Central Asia	1	0	NA	NA	NA	NA	NA	NA	NA	NA	NA	NA	NA	NA	NA	NA	1	0	1
Latin America and the Caribbean	0	0	NA	NA	NA	NA	NA	NA	NA	NA	NA	NA	NA	NA	NA	NA	0	0	1
Middle East and North Africa	1	1	NA	NA	NA	NA	NA	NA	NA	NA	NA	NA	NA	NA	NA	NA	1	1	2
South Asia	1	1	NA	NA	NA	NA	NA	NA	NA	NA	NA	NA	NA	NA	NA	NA	1	1	2
Sub-Saharan Africa	0	0	NA	NA	NA	NA	NA	NA	NA	NA	NA	NA	NA	NA	NA	NA	0	0	1
Low- and middle-income countries	3	3	NA	NA	NA	NA	NA	NA	NA	NA	NA	NA	NA	NA	NA	NA	3	3	6
High-income countries	0	0	NA	NA	NA	NA	NA	NA	NA	NA	NA	NA	NA	NA	NA	NA	0	0	0
WORLD	4	3	NA	NA	NA	NA	NA	NA	NA	NA	NA	NA	NA	NA	NA	NA	4	3	6
Attributable YLL (thousands)																			
East Asia and Pacific	3	2	NA	NA	NA	NA	NA	NA	NA	NA	NA	NA	NA	NA	NA	NA	3	2	5
Europe and Central Asia	17	14	NA	NA	NA	NA	NA	NA	NA	NA	NA	NA	NA	NA	NA	NA	17	14	30
Latin America and the Caribbean	12	9	NA	NA	NA	NA	NA	NA	NA	NA	NA	NA	NA	NA	NA	NA	12	9	21
Middle East and North Africa	27	18	NA	NA	NA	NA	NA	NA	NA	NA	NA	NA	NA	NA	NA	NA	27	18	46
South Asia	35	30	NA	NA	NA	NA	NA	NA	NA	NA	NA	NA	NA	NA	NA	NA	35	30	65
Sub-Saharan Africa	12	9	NA	NA	NA	NA	NA	NA	NA	NA	NA	NA	NA	NA	NA	NA	12	9	21
Low- and middle-income countries	105	83	NA	NA	NA	NA	NA	NA	NA	NA	NA	NA	NA	NA	NA	NA	105	83	188
High-income countries	2	2	NA	NA	NA	NA	NA	NA	NA	NA	NA	NA	NA	NA	NA	NA	2	2	4
WORLD	107	85	NA	NA	NA	NA	NA	NA	NA	NA	NA	NA	NA	NA	NA	NA	107	85	192
Attributable DALYs (thousands)																			
East Asia and Pacific	3	3	NA	NA	NA	NA	NA	NA	NA	NA	NA	NA	NA	NA	NA	NA	3	3	5
Europe and Central Asia	19	16	NA	NA	NA	NA	NA	NA	NA	NA	NA	NA	NA	NA	NA	NA	19	16	34
Latin America and the Caribbean	15	13	NA	NA	NA	NA	NA	NA	NA	NA	NA	NA	NA	NA	NA	NA	15	13	28
Middle East and North Africa	30	21	NA	NA	NA	NA	NA	NA	NA	NA	NA	NA	NA	NA	NA	NA	30	21	51
South Asia	37	33	NA	NA	NA	NA	NA	NA	NA	NA	NA	NA	NA	NA	NA	NA	37	33	71
Sub-Saharan Africa	13	10	NA	NA	NA	NA	NA	NA	NA	NA	NA	NA	NA	NA	NA	NA	13	10	22
Low- and middle-income countries	116	95	NA	NA	NA	NA	NA	NA	NA	NA	NA	NA	NA	NA	NA	NA	116	95	211
High-income countries	4	3	NA	NA	NA	NA	NA	NA	NA	NA	NA	NA	NA	NA	NA	NA	4	3	7
WORLD	120	98	NA	NA	NA	NA	NA	NA	NA	NA	NA	NA	NA	NA	NA	NA	120	98	218

Source: Authors' calculations.
Note: NA = not applicable.

Table 4A.58

Risk factor: Alcohol use
Disease: Mouth and oropharynx cancers

Region	0–4 years Male	0–4 years Female	5–14 years Male	5–14 years Female	15–29 years Male	15–29 years Female	30–44 years Male	30–44 years Female	45–59 years Male	45–59 years Female	60–69 years Male	60–69 years Female	70–79 years Male	70–79 years Female	80+ years Male	80+ years Female	Total Male	Total Female	All
PAF of Mortality (%)																			
East Asia and Pacific	NA	NA	NA	NA	30	11	32	11	32	11	29	8	27	4	27	4	30	8	23
Europe and Central Asia	NA	NA	NA	NA	44	31	42	31	43	31	38	26	33	24	32	24	39	26	37
Latin America and the Caribbean	NA	NA	NA	NA	38	29	39	31	39	29	35	26	25	20	25	20	34	24	31
Middle East and North Africa	NA	NA	NA	NA	10	4	9	3	9	3	6	2	4	1	4	2	7	2	5
South Asia	NA	NA	NA	NA	11	4	15	2	8	2	2	0	0	0	0	0	4	1	3
Sub-Saharan Africa	NA	NA	NA	NA	23	12	28	16	27	17	25	14	22	11	22	11	25	13	21
Low- and middle-income countries	NA	NA	NA	NA	19	10	25	9	25	8	15	5	12	5	10	4	18	6	14
High-income countries	NA	NA	NA	NA	41	32	41	31	41	31	35	26	32	23	32	23	36	26	33
WORLD	NA	NA	NA	NA	20	11	27	11	27	10	17	7	15	7	14	8	20	8	16
PAF of YLL (%)																			
East Asia and Pacific	NA	NA	NA	NA	30	11	32	11	32	11	29	8	27	4	27	4	31	9	24
Europe and Central Asia	NA	NA	NA	NA	44	31	42	31	43	31	38	26	33	24	32	24	40	27	38
Latin America and the Caribbean	NA	NA	NA	NA	38	29	39	31	39	29	35	26	25	20	25	20	36	26	33
Middle East and North Africa	NA	NA	NA	NA	10	4	9	3	9	3	6	2	4	1	4	2	7	2	6
South Asia	NA	NA	NA	NA	11	4	15	2	8	2	2	0	0	0	0	0	6	1	4
Sub-Saharan Africa	NA	NA	NA	NA	23	12	28	16	27	17	25	14	22	11	22	11	25	14	22
Low- and middle-income countries	NA	NA	NA	NA	19	10	25	9	25	8	15	5	12	5	10	4	19	6	15
High-income countries	NA	NA	NA	NA	41	32	41	31	41	31	35	26	32	23	32	23	38	27	35
WORLD	NA	NA	NA	NA	20	11	27	11	27	10	17	7	15	7	14	8	22	8	18
PAF of DALYs (%)																			
East Asia and Pacific	NA	NA	NA	NA	30	11	32	11	32	11	29	8	27	4	27	4	31	9	24
Europe and Central Asia	NA	NA	NA	NA	44	31	42	31	43	31	38	26	33	24	32	24	40	27	38
Latin America and the Caribbean	NA	NA	NA	NA	38	29	39	31	39	29	35	26	25	20	25	20	36	25	33
Middle East and North Africa	NA	NA	NA	NA	10	4	9	3	9	3	6	2	4	1	4	2	7	2	6
South Asia	NA	NA	NA	NA	11	4	15	2	8	2	2	0	0	0	0	0	6	1	4
Sub-Saharan Africa	NA	NA	NA	NA	23	12	28	16	27	17	25	14	22	11	22	11	25	14	22
Low- and middle-income countries	NA	NA	NA	NA	19	10	25	9	25	8	15	5	12	5	10	4	19	6	15
High-income countries	NA	NA	NA	NA	41	32	41	31	41	31	35	26	32	23	32	23	38	27	35
WORLD	NA	NA	NA	NA	20	11	27	11	27	10	17	7	15	7	14	8	22	9	18
Attributable Mortality (thousands)																			
East Asia and Pacific	NA	NA	NA	NA	0	0	2	0	5	1	4	0	2	0	1	0	13	2	15
Europe and Central Asia	NA	NA	NA	NA	0	0	1	0	4	0	3	0	1	0	0	0	9	1	10
Latin America and the Caribbean	NA	NA	NA	NA	0	0	0	0	1	0	1	0	1	0	0	0	3	1	4
Middle East and North Africa	NA	NA	NA	NA	0	0	0	0	0	0	0	0	0	0	0	0	0	0	0
South Asia	NA	NA	NA	NA	0	0	1	0	2	0	1	0	0	0	0	0	4	0	4
Sub-Saharan Africa	NA	NA	NA	NA	0	0	0	0	1	0	1	0	1	0	0	0	3	1	4
Low- and middle-income countries	NA	NA	NA	NA	1	0	4	0	13	2	9	1	4	1	1	1	33	5	38
High-income countries	NA	NA	NA	NA	0	0	1	0	4	1	3	1	2	1	1	1	11	3	14
WORLD	NA	NA	NA	NA	1	0	5	1	17	2	12	2	7	2	2	1	44	8	51
Attributable YLL (thousands)																			
East Asia and Pacific	NA	NA	NA	NA	9	1	42	4	97	14	48	6	19	2	3	1	219	28	247
Europe and Central Asia	NA	NA	NA	NA	2	1	14	2	75	7	37	4	10	3	1	1	140	18	158
Latin America and the Caribbean	NA	NA	NA	NA	1	1	7	2	25	4	14	3	5	2	1	1	53	13	65
Middle East and North Africa	NA	NA	NA	NA	0	0	1	0	1	0	1	0	0	0	0	0	4	1	4
South Asia	NA	NA	NA	NA	7	1	24	1	33	3	10	0	0	0	0	0	74	5	79
Sub-Saharan Africa	NA	NA	NA	NA	2	0	7	1	19	5	13	3	6	2	1	0	48	12	60
Low- and middle-income countries	NA	NA	NA	NA	22	3	95	11	252	33	124	17	40	10	6	3	538	76	614
High-income countries	NA	NA	NA	NA	2	1	15	3	75	13	40	8	19	7	5	4	155	35	190
WORLD	NA	NA	NA	NA	23	3	110	14	327	45	163	25	59	17	11	7	693	111	804
Attributable DALYs (thousands)																			
East Asia and Pacific	NA	NA	NA	NA	10	1	43	4	100	14	50	6	19	2	3	1	225	29	253
Europe and Central Asia	NA	NA	NA	NA	2	1	14	2	77	7	38	4	11	3	1	1	144	19	163
Latin America and the Caribbean	NA	NA	NA	NA	1	1	7	2	26	4	14	3	5	2	1	1	54	13	67
Middle East and North Africa	NA	NA	NA	NA	0	0	1	0	1	0	1	0	0	0	0	0	4	1	5
South Asia	NA	NA	NA	NA	7	1	24	1	34	3	11	0	0	0	0	0	76	5	81
Sub-Saharan Africa	NA	NA	NA	NA	2	0	7	2	20	5	13	3	6	2	1	0	49	13	61
Low- and middle-income countries	NA	NA	NA	NA	22	3	96	11	258	34	127	17	41	10	7	3	552	79	631
High-income countries	NA	NA	NA	NA	2	1	16	4	79	13	42	9	21	7	5	4	164	38	202
WORLD	NA	NA	NA	NA	24	4	112	15	337	47	169	26	62	18	12	7	716	117	833

Source: Authors' calculations.
Note: NA = not applicable.

Table 4A.59

Risk factor: Alcohol use
Disease: Esophageal cancer

Region	0–4 years Male	0–4 years Female	5–14 years Male	5–14 years Female	15–29 years Male	15–29 years Female	30–44 years Male	30–44 years Female	45–59 years Male	45–59 years Female	60–69 years Male	60–69 years Female	70–79 years Male	70–79 years Female	80+ years Male	80+ years Female	Total Male	Total Female	All
PAF of Mortality (%)																			
East Asia and Pacific	NA	NA	NA	NA	40	18	42	18	41	19	39	13	36	7	36	7	39	12	29
Europe and Central Asia	NA	NA	NA	NA	49	41	48	40	49	40	45	36	41	34	41	34	45	35	42
Latin America and the Caribbean	NA	NA	NA	NA	44	36	45	37	46	36	43	33	35	29	35	29	41	31	38
Middle East and North Africa	NA	NA	NA	NA	15	6	14	5	13	4	10	3	5	2	6	3	9	3	7
South Asia	NA	NA	NA	NA	18	6	23	3	14	3	4	0	0	0	0	0	6	1	4
Sub-Saharan Africa	NA	NA	NA	NA	33	19	37	22	34	23	32	19	29	16	29	16	32	19	27
Low- and middle-income countries	NA	NA	NA	NA	32	12	37	14	37	16	31	11	30	8	27	8	32	11	24
High-income countries	NA	NA	NA	NA	48	41	48	41	47	40	43	36	41	33	41	33	43	34	41
WORLD	NA	NA	NA	NA	33	12	38	14	38	17	33	13	32	10	31	12	34	13	26
PAF of YLL (%)																			
East Asia and Pacific	NA	NA	NA	NA	40	18	42	18	41	19	39	13	36	7	36	7	39	13	30
Europe and Central Asia	NA	NA	NA	NA	49	41	48	40	49	40	45	36	41	34	41	34	46	36	44
Latin America and the Caribbean	NA	NA	NA	NA	44	36	45	37	46	36	43	33	35	29	35	29	43	33	40
Middle East and North Africa	NA	NA	NA	NA	15	6	14	5	13	4	10	3	5	2	6	3	10	3	7
South Asia	NA	NA	NA	NA	18	6	23	3	14	3	4	0	0	0	0	0	8	1	5
Sub-Saharan Africa	NA	NA	NA	NA	33	19	37	22	34	23	32	19	29	16	29	16	33	20	28
Low- and middle-income countries	NA	NA	NA	NA	32	12	37	14	37	16	31	11	30	8	28	8	33	12	25
High-income countries	NA	NA	NA	NA	48	41	48	41	47	40	43	36	41	33	41	33	44	36	43
WORLD	NA	NA	NA	NA	33	12	38	14	38	17	33	13	32	10	31	12	35	13	27
PAF of DALYs (%)																			
East Asia and Pacific	NA	NA	NA	NA	40	18	42	18	41	19	39	13	36	7	36	7	39	13	30
Europe and Central Asia	NA	NA	NA	NA	49	41	48	40	49	40	45	36	41	34	41	34	46	36	44
Latin America and the Caribbean	NA	NA	NA	NA	44	36	45	37	46	36	43	33	35	29	35	29	43	33	40
Middle East and North Africa	NA	NA	NA	NA	15	6	14	5	13	4	10	3	5	2	6	3	10	3	7
South Asia	NA	NA	NA	NA	18	6	23	3	14	3	4	0	0	0	0	0	8	1	5
Sub-Saharan Africa	NA	NA	NA	NA	33	19	37	22	34	23	32	19	29	16	29	16	33	20	28
Low- and middle-income countries	NA	NA	NA	NA	32	12	37	14	37	16	31	11	30	8	28	8	33	12	25
High-income countries	NA	NA	NA	NA	48	41	48	41	47	40	43	36	41	33	41	33	44	36	43
WORLD	NA	NA	NA	NA	33	12	38	14	38	17	33	13	32	10	31	12	35	13	27
Attributable Mortality (thousands)																			
East Asia and Pacific	NA	NA	NA	NA	0	0	3	0	15	4	20	3	15	2	3	1	57	10	67
Europe and Central Asia	NA	NA	NA	NA	0	0	0	0	2	0	3	1	1	1	0	0	7	2	9
Latin America and the Caribbean	NA	NA	NA	NA	0	0	0	0	2	0	2	0	1	0	1	0	5	1	6
Middle East and North Africa	NA	NA	NA	NA	0	0	0	0	0	0	0	0	0	0	0	0	0	0	0
South Asia	NA	NA	NA	NA	0	0	1	0	1	0	1	0	0	0	0	0	3	0	3
Sub-Saharan Africa	NA	NA	NA	NA	0	0	0	0	2	1	1	0	1	0	0	0	5	2	6
Low- and middle-income countries	NA	NA	NA	NA	0	0	5	1	22	5	26	5	18	3	5	2	76	16	92
High-income countries	NA	NA	NA	NA	0	0	1	0	5	1	6	1	5	1	3	2	19	5	24
WORLD	NA	NA	NA	NA	0	0	5	1	27	6	32	5	24	5	7	3	95	20	116
Attributable YLL (thousands)																			
East Asia and Pacific	NA	NA	NA	NA	6	1	78	10	277	75	270	49	136	20	18	5	785	159	944
Europe and Central Asia	NA	NA	NA	NA	0	0	5	2	42	6	35	8	14	7	1	2	98	26	124
Latin America and the Caribbean	NA	NA	NA	NA	0	0	6	1	29	5	20	5	10	4	3	2	67	17	85
Middle East and North Africa	NA	NA	NA	NA	0	0	1	0	2	0	1	0	0	0	0	0	4	1	5
South Asia	NA	NA	NA	NA	2	1	14	1	24	4	9	0	0	0	0	0	49	7	55
Sub-Saharan Africa	NA	NA	NA	NA	1	0	8	3	31	11	20	7	9	4	2	1	70	26	96
Low- and middle-income countries	NA	NA	NA	NA	9	2	112	17	404	102	355	70	169	35	24	9	1,073	236	1,309
High-income countries	NA	NA	NA	NA	0	0	12	2	91	12	78	13	49	14	12	8	242	49	291
WORLD	NA	NA	NA	NA	10	3	124	19	495	115	433	83	218	49	36	17	1,315	285	1,600
Attributable DALYs (thousands)																			
East Asia and Pacific	NA	NA	NA	NA	6	1	79	10	279	75	273	49	138	20	18	5	793	160	953
Europe and Central Asia	NA	NA	NA	NA	0	0	5	2	43	6	35	8	14	7	2	2	99	26	125
Latin America and the Caribbean	NA	NA	NA	NA	0	0	6	1	29	5	21	5	10	4	3	2	68	18	86
Middle East and North Africa	NA	NA	NA	NA	0	0	1	0	2	0	1	0	0	0	0	0	4	1	5
South Asia	NA	NA	NA	NA	2	1	14	1	24	4	9	0	0	0	0	0	49	7	56
Sub-Saharan Africa	NA	NA	NA	NA	1	0	8	3	31	11	20	7	9	4	2	1	70	26	96
Low- and middle-income countries	NA	NA	NA	NA	10	2	113	17	408	103	359	71	171	35	24	9	1,083	238	1,321
High-income countries	NA	NA	NA	NA	1	0	12	2	93	13	80	13	51	14	13	8	248	50	299
WORLD	NA	NA	NA	NA	10	3	124	19	500	116	439	84	221	50	37	17	1,332	288	1,619

Source: Authors' calculations.
Note: NA = not applicable.

Table 4A.60

Risk factor: Alcohol use
Disease: Liver cancer

Region	0–4 years Male	Female	5–14 years Male	Female	15–29 years Male	Female	30–44 years Male	Female	45–59 years Male	Female	60–69 years Male	Female	70–79 years Male	Female	80+ years Male	Female	Total Male	Female	All
PAF of Mortality (%)																			
East Asia and Pacific	NA	NA	NA	NA	31	12	33	11	32	12	30	8	27	4	27	4	30	8	24
Europe and Central Asia	NA	NA	NA	NA	43	34	41	33	43	34	38	29	32	26	32	26	37	28	34
Latin America and the Caribbean	NA	NA	NA	NA	35	27	36	28	36	27	33	25	25	21	26	21	31	23	27
Middle East and North Africa	NA	NA	NA	NA	10	4	10	3	9	3	7	2	4	1	4	2	7	2	5
South Asia	NA	NA	NA	NA	12	4	16	2	8	2	2	0	0	0	0	0	6	1	4
Sub-Saharan Africa	NA	NA	NA	NA	28	14	33	18	31	18	28	15	24	12	24	12	29	15	24
Low- and middle-income countries	NA	NA	NA	NA	28	10	32	13	31	13	29	11	26	8	25	8	29	10	23
High-income countries	NA	NA	NA	NA	41	34	41	32	40	32	35	28	32	25	32	25	35	26	32
WORLD	NA	NA	NA	NA	28	11	32	13	32	15	30	13	27	12	27	15	30	13	25
PAF of YLL (%)																			
East Asia and Pacific	NA	NA	NA	NA	31	12	33	11	32	12	30	8	27	4	27	4	31	9	25
Europe and Central Asia	NA	NA	NA	NA	43	34	41	33	43	34	38	29	32	26	32	26	39	29	35
Latin America and the Caribbean	NA	NA	NA	NA	35	27	36	28	36	27	33	25	25	21	26	21	32	24	28
Middle East and North Africa	NA	NA	NA	NA	10	4	10	3	9	3	7	2	4	1	4	2	7	3	5
South Asia	NA	NA	NA	NA	12	4	16	2	8	2	2	0	0	0	0	0	7	2	5
Sub-Saharan Africa	NA	NA	NA	NA	28	14	33	18	31	18	28	15	24	12	24	12	29	15	25
Low- and middle-income countries	NA	NA	NA	NA	28	10	32	13	31	13	29	11	26	8	25	8	30	11	24
High-income countries	NA	NA	NA	NA	41	34	41	32	40	32	35	28	32	25	32	25	36	27	33
WORLD	NA	NA	NA	NA	28	11	32	13	32	15	30	13	27	12	27	14	30	13	25
PAF of DALYs (%)																			
East Asia and Pacific	NA	NA	NA	NA	31	12	33	11	32	12	30	8	27	4	27	4	31	9	25
Europe and Central Asia	NA	NA	NA	NA	43	34	41	33	43	34	38	29	32	26	32	26	38	29	35
Latin America and the Caribbean	NA	NA	NA	NA	35	27	36	28	36	27	33	25	25	21	26	21	32	24	28
Middle East and North Africa	NA	NA	NA	NA	10	4	10	3	9	3	7	2	4	1	4	2	7	3	5
South Asia	NA	NA	NA	NA	12	4	16	2	8	2	2	0	0	0	0	0	7	2	5
Sub-Saharan Africa	NA	NA	NA	NA	28	14	33	18	31	18	28	15	24	12	24	12	29	15	25
Low- and middle-income countries	NA	NA	NA	NA	28	10	32	13	31	13	29	11	26	8	25	8	30	11	24
High-income countries	NA	NA	NA	NA	41	34	41	32	40	32	35	28	32	25	32	25	36	27	33
WORLD	NA	NA	NA	NA	28	11	32	13	32	15	30	13	27	12	27	14	30	13	25
Attributable Mortality (thousands)																			
East Asia and Pacific	NA	NA	NA	NA	2	0	9	1	32	3	22	2	14	1	3	0	82	8	90
Europe and Central Asia	NA	NA	NA	NA	0	0	0	0	2	1	2	1	2	1	0	0	6	3	9
Latin America and the Caribbean	NA	NA	NA	NA	0	0	0	0	1	1	1	1	1	1	0	0	3	2	6
Middle East and North Africa	NA	NA	NA	NA	0	0	0	0	0	0	0	0	0	0	0	0	0	0	0
South Asia	NA	NA	NA	NA	0	0	0	0	0	0	0	0	0	0	0	0	1	0	1
Sub-Saharan Africa	NA	NA	NA	NA	0	0	1	0	3	1	2	0	1	0	0	0	9	2	11
Low- and middle-income countries	NA	NA	NA	NA	2	1	12	2	38	5	28	4	18	3	4	1	102	16	117
High-income countries	NA	NA	NA	NA	0	0	1	0	6	1	8	2	7	3	3	3	24	9	33
WORLD	NA	NA	NA	NA	2	1	13	2	44	6	35	6	25	6	7	4	126	25	150
Attributable YLL (thousands)																			
East Asia and Pacific	NA	NA	NA	NA	44	8	223	29	607	59	299	33	128	11	15	2	1,317	142	1,460
Europe and Central Asia	NA	NA	NA	NA	2	1	8	3	32	12	30	14	14	11	2	2	88	43	131
Latin America and the Caribbean	NA	NA	NA	NA	2	1	5	4	16	11	13	9	7	6	2	2	44	33	77
Middle East and North Africa	NA	NA	NA	NA	0	0	1	0	2	1	2	0	1	0	0	0	6	1	7
South Asia	NA	NA	NA	NA	3	2	8	1	7	1	1	0	0	0	0	0	20	3	24
Sub-Saharan Africa	NA	NA	NA	NA	8	3	35	9	62	14	31	7	11	4	2	1	150	38	188
Low- and middle-income countries	NA	NA	NA	NA	59	15	281	45	726	97	376	63	161	34	21	7	1,625	262	1,887
High-income countries	NA	NA	NA	NA	2	1	20	5	104	21	101	28	63	31	14	12	305	97	402
WORLD	NA	NA	NA	NA	62	16	301	50	831	118	477	91	225	64	35	19	1,930	359	2,289
Attributable DALYs (thousands)																			
East Asia and Pacific	NA	NA	NA	NA	45	8	224	29	610	60	301	33	130	11	16	2	1,326	143	1,469
Europe and Central Asia	NA	NA	NA	NA	2	1	8	3	32	12	30	14	14	11	2	2	88	43	132
Latin America and the Caribbean	NA	NA	NA	NA	2	1	5	4	16	11	13	9	7	6	2	2	44	33	78
Middle East and North Africa	NA	NA	NA	NA	0	0	1	0	2	1	2	0	1	0	0	0	6	1	7
South Asia	NA	NA	NA	NA	3	2	8	1	7	1	1	0	0	0	0	0	20	3	24
Sub-Saharan Africa	NA	NA	NA	NA	8	3	35	9	62	14	32	7	12	5	2	1	150	38	189
Low- and middle-income countries	NA	NA	NA	NA	60	15	282	46	730	98	379	63	163	34	21	8	1,635	264	1,898
High-income countries	NA	NA	NA	NA	2	1	20	5	106	21	102	29	65	31	15	12	310	99	409
WORLD	NA	NA	NA	NA	62	16	302	51	836	119	482	92	227	65	36	20	1,945	362	2,307

Source: Authors' calculations.
Note: NA = not applicable.

Table 4A.61

Risk factor: Alcohol use
Disease: Breast cancer

Region	0–4 years Male	Female	5–14 years Male	Female	15–29 years Male	Female	30–44 years Male	Female	45–59 years Male	Female	60–69 years Male	Female	70–79 years Male	Female	80+ years Male	Female	Total Male	Female	All
PAF of Mortality (%)																			
East Asia and Pacific	NA	NA	NA	NA	NA	0	NA	0	NA	4	NA	3	NA	1	NA	1	NA	3	3
Europe and Central Asia	NA	NA	NA	NA	NA	0	NA	0	NA	12	NA	10	NA	9	NA	9	NA	9	9
Latin America and the Caribbean	NA	NA	NA	NA	NA	0	NA	0	NA	9	NA	8	NA	7	NA	7	NA	7	7
Middle East and North Africa	NA	NA	NA	NA	NA	0	NA	0	NA	1	NA	0	NA	0	NA	1	NA	1	1
South Asia	NA	NA	NA	NA	NA	0	NA	0	NA	1	NA	0	NA	0	NA	0	NA	0	0
Sub-Saharan Africa	NA	NA	NA	NA	NA	0	NA	0	NA	6	NA	4	NA	3	NA	3	NA	4	4
Low- and middle-income countries	NA	NA	NA	NA	NA	0	NA	0	NA	5	NA	4	NA	4	NA	4	NA	4	4
High-income countries	NA	NA	NA	NA	NA	0	NA	0	NA	12	NA	10	NA	8	NA	8	NA	9	9
WORLD	NA	NA	NA	NA	NA	0	NA	0	NA	7	NA	6	NA	6	NA	6	NA	5	5
PAF of YLL (%)																			
East Asia and Pacific	NA	NA	NA	NA	NA	0	NA	0	NA	4	NA	3	NA	1	NA	1	NA	3	3
Europe and Central Asia	NA	NA	NA	NA	NA	0	NA	0	NA	12	NA	10	NA	9	NA	9	NA	9	9
Latin America and the Caribbean	NA	NA	NA	NA	NA	0	NA	0	NA	9	NA	8	NA	7	NA	7	NA	7	7
Middle East and North Africa	NA	NA	NA	NA	NA	0	NA	0	NA	1	NA	0	NA	0	NA	1	NA	1	1
South Asia	NA	NA	NA	NA	NA	0	NA	0	NA	1	NA	0	NA	0	NA	0	NA	0	0
Sub-Saharan Africa	NA	NA	NA	NA	NA	0	NA	0	NA	6	NA	4	NA	3	NA	3	NA	4	4
Low- and middle-income countries	NA	NA	NA	NA	NA	0	NA	0	NA	5	NA	4	NA	4	NA	3	NA	4	4
High-income countries	NA	NA	NA	NA	NA	0	NA	0	NA	12	NA	10	NA	8	NA	8	NA	9	9
WORLD	NA	NA	NA	NA	NA	0	NA	0	NA	7	NA	6	NA	6	NA	6	NA	5	5
PAF of DALYs (%)																			
East Asia and Pacific	NA	NA	NA	NA	NA	0	NA	0	NA	4	NA	3	NA	1	NA	1	NA	3	3
Europe and Central Asia	NA	NA	NA	NA	NA	0	NA	0	NA	12	NA	10	NA	9	NA	9	NA	9	9
Latin America and the Caribbean	NA	NA	NA	NA	NA	0	NA	0	NA	9	NA	8	NA	7	NA	7	NA	6	6
Middle East and North Africa	NA	NA	NA	NA	NA	0	NA	0	NA	1	NA	0	NA	0	NA	1	NA	0	0
South Asia	NA	NA	NA	NA	NA	0	NA	0	NA	1	NA	0	NA	0	NA	0	NA	0	0
Sub-Saharan Africa	NA	NA	NA	NA	NA	0	NA	0	NA	6	NA	4	NA	3	NA	3	NA	4	4
Low- and middle-income countries	NA	NA	NA	NA	NA	0	NA	0	NA	5	NA	4	NA	4	NA	3	NA	4	4
High-income countries	NA	NA	NA	NA	NA	0	NA	0	NA	12	NA	10	NA	8	NA	8	NA	9	9
WORLD	NA	NA	NA	NA	NA	0	NA	0	NA	7	NA	6	NA	6	NA	6	NA	5	5
Attributable Mortality (thousands)																			
East Asia and Pacific	NA	NA	NA	NA	NA	0	NA	0	NA	2	NA	1	NA	0	NA	0	NA	2	2
Europe and Central Asia	NA	NA	NA	NA	NA	0	NA	0	NA	2	NA	2	NA	1	NA	1	NA	6	6
Latin America and the Caribbean	NA	NA	NA	NA	NA	0	NA	0	NA	1	NA	1	NA	0	NA	0	NA	3	3
Middle East and North Africa	NA	NA	NA	NA	NA	0	NA	0	NA	0	NA	0	NA	0	NA	0	NA	0	0
South Asia	NA	NA	NA	NA	NA	0	NA	0	NA	0	NA	0	NA	0	NA	0	NA	0	0
Sub-Saharan Africa	NA	NA	NA	NA	NA	0	NA	0	NA	1	NA	0	NA	0	NA	0	NA	1	1
Low- and middle-income countries	NA	NA	NA	NA	NA	0	NA	0	NA	6	NA	3	NA	2	NA	1	NA	12	12
High-income countries	NA	NA	NA	NA	NA	0	NA	0	NA	4	NA	3	NA	3	NA	3	NA	14	14
WORLD	NA	NA	NA	NA	NA	0	NA	0	NA	10	NA	6	NA	5	NA	4	NA	26	26
Attributable YLL (thousands)																			
East Asia and Pacific	NA	NA	NA	NA	NA	0	NA	0	NA	31	NA	8	NA	2	NA	0	NA	42	42
Europe and Central Asia	NA	NA	NA	NA	NA	0	NA	0	NA	46	NA	25	NA	14	NA	3	NA	87	87
Latin America and the Caribbean	NA	NA	NA	NA	NA	0	NA	0	NA	23	NA	10	NA	5	NA	2	NA	39	39
Middle East and North Africa	NA	NA	NA	NA	NA	0	NA	0	NA	1	NA	0	NA	0	NA	0	NA	1	1
South Asia	NA	NA	NA	NA	NA	0	NA	0	NA	3	NA	0	NA	0	NA	0	NA	3	3
Sub-Saharan Africa	NA	NA	NA	NA	NA	0	NA	0	NA	12	NA	6	NA	3	NA	1	NA	21	21
Low- and middle-income countries	NA	NA	NA	NA	NA	0	NA	0	NA	116	NA	49	NA	23	NA	6	NA	193	193
High-income countries	NA	NA	NA	NA	NA	0	NA	0	NA	87	NA	46	NA	32	NA	14	NA	179	179
WORLD	NA	NA	NA	NA	NA	0	NA	0	NA	203	NA	95	NA	55	NA	20	NA	373	373
Attributable DALYs (thousands)																			
East Asia and Pacific	NA	NA	NA	NA	NA	0	NA	0	NA	33	NA	8	NA	2	NA	1	NA	44	44
Europe and Central Asia	NA	NA	NA	NA	NA	0	NA	0	NA	49	NA	27	NA	15	NA	3	NA	93	93
Latin America and the Caribbean	NA	NA	NA	NA	NA	0	NA	0	NA	24	NA	10	NA	5	NA	2	NA	41	41
Middle East and North Africa	NA	NA	NA	NA	NA	0	NA	0	NA	1	NA	0	NA	0	NA	0	NA	1	1
South Asia	NA	NA	NA	NA	NA	0	NA	0	NA	3	NA	0	NA	0	NA	0	NA	3	3
Sub-Saharan Africa	NA	NA	NA	NA	NA	0	NA	0	NA	13	NA	6	NA	3	NA	1	NA	22	22
Low- and middle-income countries	NA	NA	NA	NA	NA	0	NA	0	NA	123	NA	52	NA	24	NA	6	NA	205	205
High-income countries	NA	NA	NA	NA	NA	0	NA	0	NA	107	NA	53	NA	38	NA	17	NA	215	215
WORLD	NA	NA	NA	NA	NA	0	NA	0	NA	230	NA	105	NA	62	NA	23	NA	420	420

Source: Authors' calculations.
Note: NA = not applicable.

Table 4A.62

Risk factor: Alcohol use
Disease: Selected other neoplasms

Region	0–4 years Male	Female	5–14 years Male	Female	15–29 years Male	Female	30–44 years Male	Female	45–59 years Male	Female	60–69 years Male	Female	70–79 years Male	Female	80+ years Male	Female	Total Male	Female	All
PAF of Mortality (%)																			
East Asia and Pacific	NA	NA	NA	NA	9	3	9	3	9	3	8	2	7	1	7	1	8	2	4
Europe and Central Asia	NA	NA	NA	NA	14	9	13	9	14	9	12	8	9	7	9	7	11	8	9
Latin America and the Caribbean	NA	NA	NA	NA	11	8	11	8	11	8	10	7	7	5	7	5	8	6	7
Middle East and North Africa	NA	NA	NA	NA	2	1	2	1	2	1	2	0	1	0	1	0	1	0	1
South Asia	NA	NA	NA	NA	3	1	4	0	2	0	0	0	0	0	0	0	2	0	1
Sub-Saharan Africa	NA	NA	NA	NA	7	3	9	4	8	4	7	3	6	3	6	3	6	3	4
Low- and middle-income countries	NA	NA	NA	NA	5	3	6	3	7	3	6	3	4	2	4	2	5	3	4
High-income countries	NA	NA	NA	NA	13	9	13	9	13	9	10	7	9	7	9	6	10	7	8
WORLD	NA	NA	NA	NA	6	4	7	4	8	4	7	4	7	4	8	5	7	4	6
PAF of YLL (%)																			
East Asia and Pacific	NA	NA	NA	NA	9	3	9	3	9	3	8	2	7	1	7	1	7	2	4
Europe and Central Asia	NA	NA	NA	NA	14	9	13	9	14	9	12	8	9	7	9	7	11	8	10
Latin America and the Caribbean	NA	NA	NA	NA	11	8	11	8	11	8	10	7	7	5	7	5	8	6	7
Middle East and North Africa	NA	NA	NA	NA	2	1	2	1	2	1	2	0	1	0	1	0	2	1	1
South Asia	NA	NA	NA	NA	3	1	4	0	2	0	0	0	0	0	0	0	2	0	1
Sub-Saharan Africa	NA	NA	NA	NA	7	3	9	4	8	4	7	3	6	3	6	3	5	3	4
Low- and middle-income countries	NA	NA	NA	NA	5	3	6	3	7	3	6	3	4	2	4	2	5	2	4
High-income countries	NA	NA	NA	NA	13	9	13	9	13	9	10	7	9	7	9	6	10	7	9
WORLD	NA	NA	NA	NA	6	4	7	4	8	4	7	4	7	4	8	5	6	4	5
PAF of DALYs (%)																			
East Asia and Pacific	NA	NA	NA	NA	9	3	9	3	9	3	8	2	7	1	7	1	7	2	4
Europe and Central Asia	NA	NA	NA	NA	14	9	13	9	14	9	12	8	9	7	9	7	11	8	10
Latin America and the Caribbean	NA	NA	NA	NA	11	8	11	8	11	8	10	7	7	5	7	5	8	6	7
Middle East and North Africa	NA	NA	NA	NA	2	1	2	1	2	1	2	0	1	0	1	0	2	1	1
South Asia	NA	NA	NA	NA	3	1	4	0	2	0	0	0	0	0	0	0	2	0	1
Sub-Saharan Africa	NA	NA	NA	NA	7	3	9	4	8	4	7	3	6	3	6	3	5	3	4
Low- and middle-income countries	NA	NA	NA	NA	5	3	6	3	7	3	6	3	4	2	4	2	5	2	4
High-income countries	NA	NA	NA	NA	13	9	13	9	13	9	10	7	9	7	9	6	10	7	9
WORLD	NA	NA	NA	NA	6	4	7	4	8	4	7	4	7	4	8	5	6	4	5
Attributable Mortality (thousands)																			
East Asia and Pacific	NA	NA	NA	NA	0	0	0	0	0	0	0	0	0	0	0	0	1	0	1
Europe and Central Asia	NA	NA	NA	NA	0	0	0	0	0	0	0	0	0	0	0	0	0	0	1
Latin America and the Caribbean	NA	NA	NA	NA	0	0	0	0	0	0	0	0	0	0	0	0	1	0	1
Middle East and North Africa	NA	NA	NA	NA	0	0	0	0	0	0	0	0	0	0	0	0	0	0	0
South Asia	NA	NA	NA	NA	0	0	0	0	0	0	0	0	0	0	0	0	0	0	0
Sub-Saharan Africa	NA	NA	NA	NA	0	0	0	0	0	0	0	0	0	0	0	0	0	0	0
Low- and middle-income countries	NA	NA	NA	NA	0	0	0	0	1	0	1	0	0	0	0	0	2	1	3
High-income countries	NA	NA	NA	NA	0	0	0	0	0	0	0	0	1	1	1	1	3	2	5
WORLD	NA	NA	NA	NA	0	0	0	0	1	1	1	0	1	1	1	1	5	3	8
Attributable YLL (thousands)																			
East Asia and Pacific	NA	NA	NA	NA	1	0	2	1	5	2	2	1	1	0	0	0	11	4	15
Europe and Central Asia	NA	NA	NA	NA	1	0	1	1	2	2	2	1	1	1	0	0	7	5	12
Latin America and the Caribbean	NA	NA	NA	NA	1	1	2	1	3	2	2	1	1	1	0	0	8	6	14
Middle East and North Africa	NA	NA	NA	NA	0	0	1	0	1	0	1	0	0	0	0	0	3	1	4
South Asia	NA	NA	NA	NA	2	0	1	0	1	0	0	0	0	0	0	0	3	1	4
Sub-Saharan Africa	NA	NA	NA	NA	1	0	1	1	1	1	1	1	0	0	0	0	5	3	8
Low- and middle-income countries	NA	NA	NA	NA	7	2	7	4	13	7	7	3	3	2	1	1	38	19	57
High-income countries	NA	NA	NA	NA	1	1	3	2	7	4	7	4	7	5	4	4	29	19	48
WORLD	NA	NA	NA	NA	8	3	10	6	20	11	13	7	11	7	5	5	67	38	105
Attributable DALYs (thousands)																			
East Asia and Pacific	NA	NA	NA	NA	1	0	2	1	5	2	2	1	1	0	0	0	11	4	15
Europe and Central Asia	NA	NA	NA	NA	1	0	1	1	2	2	2	1	1	1	0	0	7	5	12
Latin America and the Caribbean	NA	NA	NA	NA	1	1	2	1	3	2	2	1	1	1	0	0	8	6	14
Middle East and North Africa	NA	NA	NA	NA	0	0	1	0	1	0	1	0	0	0	0	0	3	1	4
South Asia	NA	NA	NA	NA	2	0	1	0	1	0	0	0	0	0	0	0	3	1	4
Sub-Saharan Africa	NA	NA	NA	NA	1	0	1	1	1	1	1	1	0	0	0	0	5	3	8
Low- and middle-income countries	NA	NA	NA	NA	7	2	7	4	13	7	7	3	3	2	1	1	38	19	57
High-income countries	NA	NA	NA	NA	1	1	3	2	7	4	7	4	7	5	4	4	29	19	48
WORLD	NA	NA	NA	NA	8	3	10	6	20	11	13	7	11	7	5	5	67	38	105

Source: Authors' calculations.
Note: NA = not applicable.

Table 4A.63

| Risk factor: | Alcohol use |
| Disease: | Diabetes mellitus |

Region	0–4 years		5–14 years		15–29 years		30–44 years		45–59 years		60–69 years		70–79 years		80+ years		Total		
	Male	Female	Male	Female	Male	Female	Male	Female	Male	Female	Male	Female	Male	Female	Male	Female	Male	Female	All
PAF of Mortality (%)																			
East Asia and Pacific	NA	NA	NA	NA	0	0	0	0	0	0	0	0	0	0	0	0	0	0	0
Europe and Central Asia	NA	NA	NA	NA	0	0	0	0	0	0	0	0	0	0	−1	−1	0	0	0
Latin America and the Caribbean	NA	NA	NA	NA	0	0	0	1	0	0	0	0	0	0	0	0	0	0	0
Middle East and North Africa	NA	NA	NA	NA	0	0	0	0	0	0	0	0	0	0	0	0	0	0	0
South Asia	NA	NA	NA	NA	0	0	0	0	0	0	0	0	0	0	0	0	0	0	0
Sub-Saharan Africa	NA	NA	NA	NA	0	0	0	0	0	0	0	0	0	0	0	0	0	0	0
Low- and middle-income countries	NA	NA	NA	NA	0	0	0	0	0	0	0	0	0	0	0	0	0	0	0
High-income countries	NA	NA	NA	NA	−7	−5	−7	−6	−6	−5	−4	−4	−3	−4	−3	−5	−4	−5	−4
WORLD	NA	NA	NA	NA	0	0	−1	0	−1	0	−1	0	−1	−1	−1	−2	−1	−1	−1
PAF of YLL (%)																			
East Asia and Pacific	NA	NA	NA	NA	0	0	0	0	0	0	0	0	0	0	0	0	0	0	0
Europe and Central Asia	NA	NA	NA	NA	0	0	0	0	0	0	0	0	0	0	−1	−1	0	0	0
Latin America and the Caribbean	NA	NA	NA	NA	0	0	0	1	0	0	0	0	0	0	0	0	0	0	0
Middle East and North Africa	NA	NA	NA	NA	0	0	0	0	0	0	0	0	0	0	0	0	0	0	0
South Asia	NA	NA	NA	NA	0	0	0	0	0	0	0	0	0	0	0	0	0	0	0
Sub-Saharan Africa	NA	NA	NA	NA	0	0	0	0	0	0	0	0	0	0	0	0	0	0	0
Low- and middle-income countries	NA	NA	NA	NA	0	0	0	0	0	0	0	0	0	0	0	0	0	0	0
High-income countries	NA	NA	NA	NA	−7	−5	−7	−6	−6	−5	−4	−4	−3	−4	−3	−5	−4	−4	−4
WORLD	NA	NA	NA	NA	0	0	−1	0	−1	0	−1	0	−1	−1	−1	−2	−1	−1	−1
PAF of DALYs (%)																			
East Asia and Pacific	NA	NA	NA	NA	0	0	0	0	0	0	0	0	0	0	0	0	0	0	0
Europe and Central Asia	NA	NA	NA	NA	0	0	0	0	0	0	0	0	0	0	−1	−1	0	0	0
Latin America and the Caribbean	NA	NA	NA	NA	0	0	0	1	0	0	0	0	0	0	0	0	0	0	0
Middle East and North Africa	NA	NA	NA	NA	0	0	0	0	0	0	0	0	0	0	0	0	0	0	0
South Asia	NA	NA	NA	NA	0	0	0	0	0	0	0	0	0	0	0	0	0	0	0
Sub-Saharan Africa	NA	NA	NA	NA	0	0	0	0	0	0	0	0	0	0	0	0	0	0	0
Low- and middle-income countries	NA	NA	NA	NA	0	0	0	0	0	0	0	0	0	0	0	0	0	0	0
High-income countries	NA	NA	NA	NA	−7	−5	−7	−6	−6	−5	−4	−4	−3	−4	−3	−5	−5	−5	−5
WORLD	NA	NA	NA	NA	−1	0	−1	−1	−1	−1	−1	−1	−1	−1	−1	−2	−1	−1	−1
Attributable Mortality (thousands)																			
East Asia and Pacific	NA	NA	NA	NA	0	0	0	0	0	0	0	0	0	0	0	0	0	0	0
Europe and Central Asia	NA	NA	NA	NA	0	0	0	0	0	0	0	0	0	0	0	0	0	0	0
Latin America and the Caribbean	NA	NA	NA	NA	0	0	0	0	0	0	0	0	0	0	0	0	0	0	0
Middle East and North Africa	NA	NA	NA	NA	0	0	0	0	0	0	0	0	0	0	0	0	0	0	0
South Asia	NA	NA	NA	NA	0	0	0	0	0	0	0	0	0	0	0	0	0	0	0
Sub-Saharan Africa	NA	NA	NA	NA	0	0	0	0	0	0	0	0	0	0	0	0	0	0	0
Low- and middle-income countries	NA	NA	NA	NA	0	0	0	0	0	0	0	0	0	0	0	0	0	0	0
High-income countries	NA	NA	NA	NA	0	0	0	0	−1	0	−1	−1	−1	−1	−1	−3	−3	−5	−9
WORLD	NA	NA	NA	NA	0	0	0	0	−1	0	−1	−1	−1	−1	−1	−3	−3	−5	−9
Attributable YLL (thousands)																			
East Asia and Pacific	NA	NA	NA	NA	0	0	0	0	0	0	0	0	0	0	0	0	0	0	0
Europe and Central Asia	NA	NA	NA	NA	0	0	0	0	0	0	0	0	0	0	0	0	0	0	0
Latin America and the Caribbean	NA	NA	NA	NA	0	0	0	1	0	0	0	0	0	0	0	0	0	1	1
Middle East and North Africa	NA	NA	NA	NA	0	0	0	0	0	0	0	0	0	0	0	0	0	0	0
South Asia	NA	NA	NA	NA	0	0	0	0	0	0	0	0	0	0	0	0	0	0	0
Sub-Saharan Africa	NA	NA	NA	NA	0	0	0	0	0	0	0	0	0	0	0	0	0	0	0
Low- and middle-income countries	NA	NA	NA	NA	0	0	0	1	0	0	0	0	0	0	0	0	0	0	0
High-income countries	NA	NA	NA	NA	−1	0	−5	−2	−14	−7	−10	−9	−8	−14	−4	−12	−41	−44	−86
WORLD	NA	NA	NA	NA	−1	0	−5	−2	−14	−7	−10	−9	−8	−14	−4	−12	−41	−44	−85
Attributable DALYs (thousands)																			
East Asia and Pacific	NA	NA	NA	NA	0	0	0	0	0	0	0	0	0	0	0	0	0	0	0
Europe and Central Asia	NA	NA	NA	NA	0	0	0	0	0	0	0	0	0	0	0	0	0	0	−1
Latin America and the Caribbean	NA	NA	NA	NA	0	0	0	2	0	0	0	0	0	0	0	0	0	2	2
Middle East and North Africa	NA	NA	NA	NA	0	0	0	0	0	0	0	0	0	0	0	0	0	0	0
South Asia	NA	NA	NA	NA	0	0	0	0	0	0	0	0	0	0	0	0	0	0	0
Sub-Saharan Africa	NA	NA	NA	NA	0	0	0	0	0	0	0	0	0	0	0	0	0	0	0
Low- and middle-income countries	NA	NA	NA	NA	0	0	0	2	0	0	0	0	0	0	0	0	0	1	1
High-income countries	NA	NA	NA	NA	−3	−1	−21	−14	−41	−29	−19	−19	−12	−21	−5	−16	−99	−100	−200
WORLD	NA	NA	NA	NA	−3	−1	−21	−12	−41	−29	−19	−19	−12	−21	−5	−17	−100	−99	−199

Source: Authors' calculations.

Note: NA = not applicable.

Table 4A.64

Risk factor: Alcohol use
Disease: Unipolar depressive disorders

Region	0–4 years Male	Female	5–14 years Male	Female	15–29 years Male	Female	30–44 years Male	Female	45–59 years Male	Female	60–69 years Male	Female	70–79 years Male	Female	80+ years Male	Female	Total Male	Female	All
PAF of Mortality (%)																			
East Asia and Pacific	NA	NA	NA	NA	2	0	2	0	2	0	2	0	2	0	2	0	2	0	1
Europe and Central Asia	NA	NA	NA	NA	6	1	6	1	6	1	6	1	6	1	6	1	6	1	3
Latin America and the Caribbean	NA	NA	NA	NA	7	1	7	1	7	1	7	1	7	1	7	1	7	1	3
Middle East and North Africa	NA	NA	NA	NA	0	0	0	0	0	0	0	0	0	0	0	0	0	0	0
South Asia	NA	NA	NA	NA	*	0	2	0	2	0	2	0	*	0	*	0	2	0	1
Sub-Saharan Africa	NA	NA	NA	NA	*	0	2	*	2	*	*	*	*	*	*	*	2	0	1
Low- and middle-income countries	NA	NA	NA	NA	4	0	2	0	2	0	2	0	6	1	6	1	2	0	1
High-income countries	NA	NA	NA	NA	8	2	8	2	7	2	8	2	8	2	8	2	8	2	4
WORLD	NA	NA	NA	NA	6	1	2	0	2	0	3	0	8	2	8	2	3	1	2
PAF of YLL (%)																			
East Asia and Pacific	NA	NA	NA	NA	2	0	2	0	2	0	2	0	2	0	2	0	2	0	1
Europe and Central Asia	NA	NA	NA	NA	6	1	6	1	6	1	6	1	6	1	6	1	6	1	3
Latin America and the Caribbean	NA	NA	NA	NA	7	1	7	1	7	1	7	1	7	1	7	1	7	1	3
Middle East and North Africa	NA	NA	NA	NA	0	0	0	0	0	0	0	0	0	0	0	0	0	0	0
South Asia	NA	NA	NA	NA	*	0	2	0	2	0	2	0	*	0	*	0	2	0	1
Sub-Saharan Africa	NA	NA	NA	NA	*	0	2	*	2	*	*	*	*	*	*	*	2	0	1
Low- and middle-income countries	NA	NA	NA	NA	4	0	2	0	2	0	2	0	6	1	6	1	2	0	1
High-income countries	NA	NA	NA	NA	8	2	8	2	7	2	8	2	8	2	8	2	8	2	4
WORLD	NA	NA	NA	NA	6	1	2	0	2	0	3	0	8	2	8	2	2	0	1
PAF of DALYs (%)																			
East Asia and Pacific	NA	NA	NA	NA	2	0	2	0	2	0	2	0	2	0	2	0	2	0	1
Europe and Central Asia	NA	NA	NA	NA	6	1	6	1	6	1	6	1	6	1	6	1	5	1	3
Latin America and the Caribbean	NA	NA	NA	NA	7	1	7	1	7	1	7	1	7	1	7	1	6	1	3
Middle East and North Africa	NA	NA	NA	NA	0	0	0	0	0	0	0	0	0	0	0	0	0	0	0
South Asia	NA	NA	NA	NA	2	0	2	0	2	0	2	0	2	0	2	0	2	0	1
Sub-Saharan Africa	NA	NA	NA	NA	2	0	2	0	2	0	2	0	2	0	2	0	2	0	1
Low- and middle-income countries	NA	NA	NA	NA	3	0	3	0	3	0	3	0	3	0	3	0	2	0	1
High-income countries	NA	NA	NA	NA	8	2	8	2	7	2	8	2	8	2	8	2	7	2	4
WORLD	NA	NA	NA	NA	3	1	4	1	4	1	4	1	5	1	5	1	3	0	2
Attributable Mortality (thousands)																			
East Asia and Pacific	NA	NA	NA	NA	0	0	0	0	0	0	0	0	0	0	0	0	0	0	0
Europe and Central Asia	NA	NA	NA	NA	0	0	0	0	0	0	0	0	0	0	0	0	0	0	0
Latin America and the Caribbean	NA	NA	NA	NA	0	0	0	0	0	0	0	0	0	0	0	0	0	0	0
Middle East and North Africa	NA	NA	NA	NA	0	0	0	0	0	0	0	0	0	0	0	0	0	0	0
South Asia	NA	NA	NA	NA	0	0	0	0	0	0	0	0	0	0	0	0	0	0	0
Sub-Saharan Africa	NA	NA	NA	NA	0	0	0	0	0	0	0	0	0	0	0	0	0	0	0
Low- and middle-income countries	NA	NA	NA	NA	0	0	0	0	0	0	0	0	0	0	0	0	0	0	0
High-income countries	NA	NA	NA	NA	0	0	0	0	0	0	0	0	0	0	0	0	0	0	0
WORLD	NA	NA	NA	NA	0	0	0	0	0	0	0	0	0	0	0	0	0	0	0
Attributable YLL (thousands)																			
East Asia and Pacific	NA	NA	NA	NA	0	0	0	0	0	0	0	0	0	0	0	0	0	0	0
Europe and Central Asia	NA	NA	NA	NA	0	0	0	0	0	0	0	0	0	0	0	0	0	0	0
Latin America and the Caribbean	NA	NA	NA	NA	0	0	0	0	0	0	0	0	0	0	0	0	0	0	0
Middle East and North Africa	NA	NA	NA	NA	0	0	0	0	0	0	0	0	0	0	0	0	0	0	0
South Asia	NA	NA	NA	NA	0	0	1	0	1	0	0	0	0	0	0	0	2	0	2
Sub-Saharan Africa	NA	NA	NA	NA	0	0	0	0	0	0	0	0	0	0	0	0	0	0	0
Low- and middle-income countries	NA	NA	NA	NA	0	0	1	0	1	0	0	0	0	0	0	0	2	0	2
High-income countries	NA	NA	NA	NA	0	0	0	0	0	0	0	0	0	0	0	0	1	0	1
WORLD	NA	NA	NA	NA	0	0	1	0	1	0	0	0	0	0	0	0	3	0	3
Attributable DALYs (thousands)																			
East Asia and Pacific	NA	NA	NA	NA	38	0	34	0	24	0	7	0	1	0	0	0	105	0	105
Europe and Central Asia	NA	NA	NA	NA	29	6	27	9	19	6	7	3	2	1	0	0	83	25	109
Latin America and the Caribbean	NA	NA	NA	NA	43	11	41	11	22	6	7	2	1	0	0	0	116	30	146
Middle East and North Africa	NA	NA	NA	NA	0	0	0	0	0	0	0	0	0	0	0	0	0	0	0
South Asia	NA	NA	NA	NA	40	0	33	0	18	0	5	0	1	0	0	0	97	0	97
Sub-Saharan Africa	NA	NA	NA	NA	9	0	7	0	3	0	1	0	0	0	0	0	20	0	20
Low- and middle-income countries	NA	NA	NA	NA	159	18	142	20	88	12	27	5	6	1	1	0	422	56	478
High-income countries	NA	NA	NA	NA	70	30	77	33	46	25	21	8	6	3	2	2	222	101	323
WORLD	NA	NA	NA	NA	229	47	219	53	134	37	47	13	12	5	3	2	644	156	800

Source: Authors' calculations.

Note: NA = not applicable.

*The number of deaths (and hence YLL) directly coded to a number of diseases, especially neuropsychiatric and musculoskeletal diseases, is zero or very small. For other diseases, mortality or disease burden may be zero in some region-age-sex groups. In such cases, the population attributable fractions would be undefined or unstable and have not been calculated.

Table 4A.65

| Risk factor: | Alcohol use |
| Disease: | Epilepsy |

Region	0–4 years Male	0–4 years Female	5–14 years Male	5–14 years Female	15–29 years Male	15–29 years Female	30–44 years Male	30–44 years Female	45–59 years Male	45–59 years Female	60–69 years Male	60–69 years Female	70–79 years Male	70–79 years Female	80+ years Male	80+ years Female	Total Male	Total Female	All
PAF of Mortality (%)																			
East Asia and Pacific	NA	NA	NA	NA	36	8	39	7	41	10	38	6	34	3	34	3	30	6	19
Europe and Central Asia	NA	NA	NA	NA	59	46	57	45	61	48	54	41	42	35	42	35	52	39	48
Latin America and the Caribbean	NA	NA	NA	NA	43	34	46	36	48	37	43	34	30	25	30	25	38	29	34
Middle East and North Africa	NA	NA	NA	NA	13	6	12	5	13	5	10	2	6	2	6	3	9	3	7
South Asia	NA	NA	NA	NA	9	7	18	3	8	3	2	0	0	0	0	0	3	2	2
Sub-Saharan Africa	NA	NA	NA	NA	43	20	50	26	48	29	45	22	38	17	38	17	38	17	30
Low- and middle-income countries	NA	NA	NA	NA	36	15	44	18	45	20	40	16	27	11	27	11	28	11	21
High-income countries	NA	NA	NA	NA	55	44	55	40	55	44	47	37	41	33	41	33	49	35	43
WORLD	NA	NA	NA	NA	37	16	45	20	46	22	41	19	29	15	30	18	30	13	22
PAF of YLL (%)																			
East Asia and Pacific	NA	NA	NA	NA	36	8	39	7	41	10	38	6	34	3	34	3	28	6	18
Europe and Central Asia	NA	NA	NA	NA	59	46	57	45	61	48	54	41	42	35	42	35	51	38	46
Latin America and the Caribbean	NA	NA	NA	NA	43	34	46	36	48	37	43	34	30	25	30	25	37	28	33
Middle East and North Africa	NA	NA	NA	NA	13	6	12	5	13	5	10	2	6	2	6	3	9	3	7
South Asia	NA	NA	NA	NA	9	7	18	3	8	3	2	0	0	0	0	0	2	2	2
Sub-Saharan Africa	NA	NA	NA	NA	43	20	50	26	48	29	45	22	38	17	38	17	36	15	27
Low- and middle-income countries	NA	NA	NA	NA	36	15	44	18	45	20	40	16	27	11	27	11	26	10	19
High-income countries	NA	NA	NA	NA	55	44	55	40	55	44	47	37	41	33	41	33	49	35	44
WORLD	NA	NA	NA	NA	37	16	45	20	46	22	41	19	29	15	30	17	27	11	20
PAF of DALYs (%)																			
East Asia and Pacific	NA	NA	NA	NA	36	8	39	7	41	10	38	6	34	3	34	3	27	5	17
Europe and Central Asia	NA	NA	NA	NA	59	46	57	45	61	48	54	41	42	35	42	35	48	36	43
Latin America and the Caribbean	NA	NA	NA	NA	43	34	46	36	48	37	43	34	30	25	30	25	31	24	28
Middle East and North Africa	NA	NA	NA	NA	13	6	12	5	13	5	10	2	6	2	6	3	8	3	6
South Asia	NA	NA	NA	NA	9	7	18	3	8	3	2	0	0	0	0	0	5	2	3
Sub-Saharan Africa	NA	NA	NA	NA	43	20	50	26	48	29	45	22	38	17	38	17	31	13	23
Low- and middle-income countries	NA	NA	NA	NA	32	16	40	18	41	20	36	16	26	12	26	12	23	10	17
High-income countries	NA	NA	NA	NA	55	44	55	40	55	44	47	37	41	33	41	33	44	33	39
WORLD	NA	NA	NA	NA	34	17	42	20	43	23	38	20	29	17	30	20	24	12	18
Attributable Mortality (thousands)																			
East Asia and Pacific	NA	NA	NA	NA	1	0	2	0	1	0	0	0	0	0	0	0	4	1	5
Europe and Central Asia	NA	NA	NA	NA	1	0	1	0	1	0	0	0	0	0	0	0	3	1	4
Latin America and the Caribbean	NA	NA	NA	NA	1	0	1	0	0	0	0	0	0	0	0	0	2	1	3
Middle East and North Africa	NA	NA	NA	NA	0	0	0	0	0	0	0	0	0	0	0	0	0	0	0
South Asia	NA	NA	NA	NA	0	0	0	0	0	0	0	0	0	0	0	0	0	0	1
Sub-Saharan Africa	NA	NA	NA	NA	2	1	3	1	2	1	1	0	0	0	0	0	9	2	11
Low- and middle-income countries	NA	NA	NA	NA	5	2	6	1	4	1	2	0	1	0	0	0	18	6	24
High-income countries	NA	NA	NA	NA	0	0	1	0	1	0	0	0	0	0	0	0	3	1	4
WORLD	NA	NA	NA	NA	6	2	7	2	5	2	2	1	1	1	1	0	21	7	28
Attributable YLL (thousands)																			
East Asia and Pacific	NA	NA	NA	NA	34	7	40	5	12	3	3	0	1	0	0	0	90	15	106
Europe and Central Asia	NA	NA	NA	NA	21	11	25	10	17	6	3	1	1	1	0	0	67	28	95
Latin America and the Caribbean	NA	NA	NA	NA	15	7	15	7	7	3	2	1	1	0	0	0	40	19	58
Middle East and North Africa	NA	NA	NA	NA	3	1	1	0	1	0	0	0	0	0	0	0	6	2	7
South Asia	NA	NA	NA	NA	5	7	4	1	1	1	0	0	0	0	0	0	10	8	18
Sub-Saharan Africa	NA	NA	NA	NA	65	20	63	13	39	14	15	3	4	2	1	1	188	53	241
Low- and middle-income countries	NA	NA	NA	NA	143	53	148	35	77	26	23	7	7	3	2	1	401	125	526
High-income countries	NA	NA	NA	NA	9	5	18	6	13	6	4	2	2	2	1	1	48	22	71
WORLD	NA	NA	NA	NA	152	58	167	41	90	32	27	9	10	5	3	2	449	147	596
Attributable DALYs (thousands)																			
East Asia and Pacific	NA	NA	NA	NA	71	14	69	10	29	6	9	2	4	0	1	0	184	33	217
Europe and Central Asia	NA	NA	NA	NA	33	20	34	17	23	11	6	4	2	2	0	1	98	55	153
Latin America and the Caribbean	NA	NA	NA	NA	52	37	39	26	21	14	6	5	2	2	0	1	120	84	204
Middle East and North Africa	NA	NA	NA	NA	6	2	3	1	2	1	0	0	0	0	0	0	11	4	15
South Asia	NA	NA	NA	NA	20	17	16	2	3	2	0	0	0	0	0	0	39	22	60
Sub-Saharan Africa	NA	NA	NA	NA	98	36	77	20	43	17	16	4	5	2	1	1	240	79	319
Low- and middle-income countries	NA	NA	NA	NA	279	126	238	77	120	51	38	15	12	7	3	2	692	277	968
High-income countries	NA	NA	NA	NA	30	20	36	18	26	16	10	7	6	6	2	3	110	69	179
WORLD	NA	NA	NA	NA	310	145	274	95	146	66	48	22	18	13	5	5	802	346	1,147

Source: Authors' calculations.
Note: NA = not applicable.

Table 4A.66

Risk factor: Alcohol use
Disease: Alcohol use disorders

Region	0–4 years Male	Female	5–14 years Male	Female	15–29 years Male	Female	30–44 years Male	Female	45–59 years Male	Female	60–69 years Male	Female	70–79 years Male	Female	80+ years Male	Female	Total Male	Female	All
PAF of Mortality (%)																			
East Asia and Pacific	100	100	100	100	100	100	100	100	100	100	100	100	100	100	100	100	100	100	100
Europe and Central Asia	100	100	100	100	100	100	100	100	100	100	100	100	100	100	100	100	100	100	100
Latin America and the Caribbean	100	100	100	100	100	100	100	100	100	100	100	100	100	100	100	100	100	100	100
Middle East and North Africa	100	100	100	100	100	100	100	100	100	100	100	100	100	100	100	100	100	100	100
South Asia	100	100	100	100	100	100	100	100	100	100	100	100	100	100	100	100	100	100	100
Sub-Saharan Africa	100	100	100	100	100	100	100	100	100	100	100	100	100	100	100	100	100	100	100
Low- and middle-income countries	100	100	100	100	100	100	100	100	100	100	100	100	100	100	100	100	100	100	100
High-income countries	100	100	100	100	100	100	100	100	100	100	100	100	100	100	100	100	100	100	100
WORLD	100	100	100	100	100	100	100	100	100	100	100	100	100	100	100	100	100	100	100
PAF of YLL (%)																			
East Asia and Pacific	100	100	100	100	100	100	100	100	100	100	100	100	100	100	100	100	100	100	100
Europe and Central Asia	100	100	100	100	100	100	100	100	100	100	100	100	100	100	100	100	100	100	100
Latin America and the Caribbean	100	100	100	100	100	100	100	100	100	100	100	100	100	100	100	100	100	100	100
Middle East and North Africa	100	100	100	100	100	100	100	100	100	100	100	100	100	100	100	100	100	100	100
South Asia	100	100	100	100	100	100	100	100	100	100	100	100	100	100	100	100	100	100	100
Sub-Saharan Africa	100	100	100	100	100	100	100	100	100	100	100	100	100	100	100	100	100	100	100
Low- and middle-income countries	100	100	100	100	100	100	100	100	100	100	100	100	100	100	100	100	100	100	100
High-income countries	100	100	100	100	100	100	100	100	100	100	100	100	100	100	100	100	100	100	100
WORLD	100	100	100	100	100	100	100	100	100	100	100	100	100	100	100	100	100	100	100
PAF of DALYs (%)																			
East Asia and Pacific	100	100	100	100	100	100	100	100	100	100	100	100	100	100	100	100	100	100	100
Europe and Central Asia	100	100	100	100	100	100	100	100	100	100	100	100	100	100	100	100	100	100	100
Latin America and the Caribbean	100	100	100	100	100	100	100	100	100	100	100	100	100	100	100	100	100	100	100
Middle East and North Africa	100	100	100	100	100	100	100	100	100	100	100	100	100	100	100	100	100	100	100
South Asia	100	100	100	100	100	100	100	100	100	100	100	100	100	100	100	100	100	100	100
Sub-Saharan Africa	100	100	100	100	100	100	100	100	100	100	100	100	100	100	100	100	100	100	100
Low- and middle-income countries	100	100	100	100	100	100	100	100	100	100	100	100	100	100	100	100	100	100	100
High-income countries	100	100	100	100	100	100	100	100	100	100	100	100	100	100	100	100	100	100	100
WORLD	100	100	100	100	100	100	100	100	100	100	100	100	100	100	100	100	100	100	100
Attributable Mortality (thousands)																			
East Asia and Pacific	0	0	0	0	1	0	3	1	4	1	2	0	1	0	0	0	11	2	12
Europe and Central Asia	0	0	0	0	0	0	2	0	3	1	2	0	1	0	0	0	8	2	10
Latin America and the Caribbean	0	0	0	0	1	0	5	0	6	0	2	0	1	0	0	0	15	1	17
Middle East and North Africa	0	0	0	0	1	0	1	0	1	0	0	0	0	0	0	0	3	0	3
South Asia	0	0	0	0	2	0	3	0	4	0	2	0	1	0	0	0	12	1	13
Sub-Saharan Africa	0	0	0	0	0	0	2	1	2	1	1	0	1	0	0	0	5	2	7
Low- and middle-income countries	0	0	0	0	5	0	16	2	19	3	9	2	4	1	1	0	54	8	62
High-income countries	0	0	0	0	0	0	4	1	8	2	4	1	2	1	1	0	18	4	23
WORLD	0	0	0	0	5	0	20	3	27	5	13	2	6	2	2	0	72	12	84
Attributable YLL (thousands)																			
East Asia and Pacific	0	0	0	0	17	4	73	13	80	14	25	3	7	1	1	0	205	35	239
Europe and Central Asia	1	0	1	0	5	1	44	7	66	15	26	7	5	2	0	0	148	32	180
Latin America and the Caribbean	1	0	0	0	27	2	114	10	111	9	31	4	12	1	2	0	297	27	324
Middle East and North Africa	0	0	0	0	22	1	33	2	12	2	2	0	1	0	0	0	70	5	75
South Asia	0	0	0	0	52	0	79	0	68	8	29	6	5	2	1	1	236	16	252
Sub-Saharan Africa	0	0	0	0	6	2	41	13	31	13	9	4	5	5	1	0	92	37	128
Low- and middle-income countries	2	0	1	0	129	10	385	45	369	61	122	23	35	11	5	1	1,048	152	1,200
High-income countries	0	0	0	0	9	2	90	21	146	38	55	13	18	6	3	1	320	81	402
WORLD	2	0	1	0	138	12	475	67	514	98	177	36	53	17	8	2	1,368	233	1,601
Attributable DALYs (thousands)																			
East Asia and Pacific	0	0	33	17	1,475	217	1,510	190	657	75	100	7	18	2	3	0	3,796	507	4,303
Europe and Central Asia	1	0	14	4	620	110	561	100	294	61	56	13	10	3	1	0	1,557	292	1,849
Latin America and the Caribbean	1	0	30	8	1,271	296	590	129	371	77	72	15	18	3	2	1	2,355	528	2,883
Middle East and North Africa	0	0	0	0	23	1	34	2	13	2	2	0	1	0	0	0	73	5	79
South Asia	0	0	15	6	363	13	533	12	189	10	43	6	9	2	2	1	1,153	49	1,202
Sub-Saharan Africa	0	0	10	6	274	25	197	26	97	19	15	4	6	5	1	0	600	85	685
Low- and middle-income countries	2	0	101	41	4,027	661	3,425	460	1,620	243	289	44	62	15	8	2	9,534	1,467	11,001
High-income countries	0	0	25	8	1,289	341	1,269	312	592	143	107	26	38	12	7	2	3,328	843	4,171
WORLD	2	0	126	49	5,316	1,003	4,694	771	2,213	386	396	70	100	27	15	4	12,862	2,310	15,172

Source: Authors' calculations.

Table 4A.67

Risk factor: Alcohol use
Disease: Hypertensive heart disease

Region	0–4 years Male	0–4 years Female	5–14 years Male	5–14 years Female	15–29 years Male	15–29 years Female	30–44 years Male	30–44 years Female	45–59 years Male	45–59 years Female	60–69 years Male	60–69 years Female	70–79 years Male	70–79 years Female	80+ years Male	80+ years Female	Total Male	Total Female	Total All
PAF of Mortality (%)																			
East Asia and Pacific	NA	NA	NA	NA	27	10	29	10	26	10	24	7	22	4	22	4	24	5	14
Europe and Central Asia	NA	NA	NA	NA	39	29	38	28	31	26	28	23	25	21	25	21	28	22	24
Latin America and the Caribbean	NA	NA	NA	NA	33	25	35	27	28	21	26	19	21	17	21	17	24	18	21
Middle East and North Africa	NA	NA	NA	NA	9	3	8	3	7	2	5	1	3	1	3	2	4	1	3
South Asia	NA	NA	NA	NA	10	4	14	1	7	1	2	0	0	0	0	0	3	0	2
Sub-Saharan Africa	NA	NA	NA	NA	22	11	26	14	22	13	20	11	17	9	17	9	20	10	14
Low- and middle-income countries	NA	NA	NA	NA	20	11	26	13	22	11	20	10	17	8	18	9	19	9	14
High-income countries	NA	NA	NA	NA	37	29	37	28	30	25	27	22	25	20	25	20	26	20	23
WORLD	NA	NA	NA	NA	21	12	27	14	22	12	20	10	18	9	20	12	20	11	15
PAF of YLL (%)																			
East Asia and Pacific	NA	NA	NA	NA	27	10	29	10	26	10	24	7	22	4	22	4	24	6	16
Europe and Central Asia	NA	NA	NA	NA	39	29	38	28	31	26	28	23	25	21	25	21	29	23	26
Latin America and the Caribbean	NA	NA	NA	NA	33	25	35	27	28	21	26	19	21	17	21	17	26	19	22
Middle East and North Africa	NA	NA	NA	NA	9	3	8	3	7	2	5	1	3	1	3	2	5	2	3
South Asia	NA	NA	NA	NA	10	4	14	1	7	1	2	0	0	0	0	0	5	1	3
Sub-Saharan Africa	NA	NA	NA	NA	22	11	26	14	22	13	20	11	17	9	17	9	20	11	14
Low- and middle-income countries	NA	NA	NA	NA	20	11	26	13	22	11	20	10	17	8	18	8	20	9	15
High-income countries	NA	NA	NA	NA	37	29	37	28	30	25	27	22	25	20	25	20	28	21	24
WORLD	NA	NA	NA	NA	21	12	27	14	22	12	20	10	18	9	19	11	21	11	16
PAF of DALYs (%)																			
East Asia and Pacific	NA	NA	NA	NA	27	10	29	10	26	10	24	7	22	4	22	4	24	6	15
Europe and Central Asia	NA	NA	NA	NA	39	29	38	28	31	26	28	23	25	21	25	21	29	22	25
Latin America and the Caribbean	NA	NA	NA	NA	33	25	35	27	28	21	26	19	21	17	21	17	26	19	22
Middle East and North Africa	NA	NA	NA	NA	9	3	8	3	7	2	5	1	3	1	3	2	5	2	3
South Asia	NA	NA	NA	NA	10	4	14	1	7	1	2	0	0	0	0	0	5	1	3
Sub-Saharan Africa	NA	NA	NA	NA	22	11	26	14	22	13	20	11	17	9	17	9	20	11	14
Low- and middle-income countries	NA	NA	NA	NA	20	11	26	13	22	11	20	9	17	8	18	8	20	9	14
High-income countries	NA	NA	NA	NA	37	29	37	28	30	25	27	22	25	20	25	20	28	21	24
WORLD	NA	NA	NA	NA	21	12	27	14	22	12	20	10	18	9	19	12	21	11	15
Attributable Mortality (thousands)																			
East Asia and Pacific	NA	NA	NA	NA	0	0	2	0	7	2	11	2	12	2	6	2	39	9	48
Europe and Central Asia	NA	NA	NA	NA	0	0	1	0	3	2	4	3	4	5	2	4	13	14	27
Latin America and the Caribbean	NA	NA	NA	NA	0	0	1	0	2	1	2	2	2	2	2	3	10	9	18
Middle East and North Africa	NA	NA	NA	NA	0	0	0	0	0	0	0	0	0	0	0	0	2	1	2
South Asia	NA	NA	NA	NA	0	0	0	0	1	0	0	0	0	0	0	0	2	0	2
Sub-Saharan Africa	NA	NA	NA	NA	0	0	0	0	1	1	1	1	1	1	1	1	5	4	9
Low- and middle-income countries	NA	NA	NA	NA	1	0	4	2	14	6	19	8	20	10	11	10	70	36	106
High-income countries	NA	NA	NA	NA	0	0	1	0	2	1	2	1	3	3	5	11	13	16	29
WORLD	NA	NA	NA	NA	1	0	5	2	16	7	21	9	23	14	16	21	82	52	135
Attributable YLL (thousands)																			
East Asia and Pacific	NA	NA	NA	NA	8	2	47	10	135	40	151	36	106	21	33	10	479	118	597
Europe and Central Asia	NA	NA	NA	NA	3	1	19	8	52	32	52	45	33	49	8	19	168	154	321
Latin America and the Caribbean	NA	NA	NA	NA	4	3	15	12	34	25	30	23	22	22	10	14	115	99	215
Middle East and North Africa	NA	NA	NA	NA	1	0	3	1	8	2	7	2	3	2	1	1	23	7	30
South Asia	NA	NA	NA	NA	4	1	11	1	14	3	3	0	0	0	0	0	33	4	37
Sub-Saharan Africa	NA	NA	NA	NA	2	1	11	7	21	18	16	17	10	13	3	4	63	60	123
Low- and middle-income countries	NA	NA	NA	NA	21	8	106	38	265	120	259	122	175	106	56	48	881	442	1,323
High-income countries	NA	NA	NA	NA	2	1	14	6	34	16	28	18	30	33	20	43	127	117	244
WORLD	NA	NA	NA	NA	23	9	120	44	299	136	286	140	204	139	76	91	1,009	558	1,567
Attributable DALYs (thousands)																			
East Asia and Pacific	NA	NA	NA	NA	8	2	50	11	144	43	162	38	121	23	42	12	527	127	655
Europe and Central Asia	NA	NA	NA	NA	3	2	20	8	54	33	55	47	36	52	10	22	178	165	342
Latin America and the Caribbean	NA	NA	NA	NA	4	3	16	12	36	26	32	25	24	24	13	18	125	108	232
Middle East and North Africa	NA	NA	NA	NA	1	0	3	1	9	2	7	2	4	2	1	1	24	7	31
South Asia	NA	NA	NA	NA	4	1	12	1	15	3	4	0	0	0	0	0	35	5	40
Sub-Saharan Africa	NA	NA	NA	NA	2	1	11	7	22	19	17	18	12	14	4	5	69	65	134
Low- and middle-income countries	NA	NA	NA	NA	22	9	111	40	280	126	277	129	196	115	71	58	958	477	1,434
High-income countries	NA	NA	NA	NA	2	1	14	6	36	17	30	19	34	37	30	64	145	144	289
WORLD	NA	NA	NA	NA	24	9	126	46	316	142	307	148	230	152	101	122	1,103	620	1,723

Source: Authors' calculations.
Note: NA = not applicable.

Table 4A.68

Risk factor: Alcohol use
Disease: Ischemic heart disease

Region	0–4 years Male	0–4 years Female	5–14 years Male	5–14 years Female	15–29 years Male	15–29 years Female	30–44 years Male	30–44 years Female	45–59 years Male	45–59 years Female	60–69 years Male	60–69 years Female	70–79 years Male	70–79 years Female	80+ years Male	80+ years Female	Total Male	Total Female	All
PAF of Mortality (%)																			
East Asia and Pacific	NA	NA	NA	NA	2	0	3	0	4	0	2	0	1	0	1	0	2	0	1
Europe and Central Asia	NA	NA	NA	NA	13	2	14	2	13	2	13	2	13	2	13	2	13	2	7
Latin America and the Caribbean	NA	NA	NA	NA	14	2	14	2	15	2	15	2	13	1	12	1	14	1	8
Middle East and North Africa	NA	NA	NA	NA	1	0	1	0	1	0	1	0	0	0	0	0	1	0	0
South Asia	NA	NA	NA	NA	5	0	11	0	13	0	3	0	0	0	0	0	4	0	3
Sub-Saharan Africa	NA	NA	NA	NA	5	0	5	0	5	0	5	0	4	0	4	0	5	0	2
Low- and middle-income countries	NA	NA	NA	NA	5	0	9	0	10	0	6	1	5	1	5	1	7	1	4
High-income	NA	NA	NA	NA	−13	−11	−15	−13	−15	−12	−14	−11	−14	−10	−14	−10	−14	−10	−12
WORLD	NA	NA	NA	NA	4	0	7	0	7	0	4	0	1	−1	−1	−3	3	−1	1
PAF of YLL (%)																			
East Asia and Pacific	NA	NA	NA	NA	2	0	3	0	4	0	2	0	1	0	1	0	2	0	1
Europe and Central Asia	NA	NA	NA	NA	13	2	14	2	13	2	13	2	13	2	13	2	13	2	8
Latin America and the Caribbean	NA	NA	NA	NA	14	2	14	2	15	2	15	2	13	1	12	1	14	2	9
Middle East and North Africa	NA	NA	NA	NA	1	0	1	0	1	0	1	0	0	0	0	0	1	0	0
South Asia	NA	NA	NA	NA	5	0	11	0	13	0	3	0	0	0	0	0	6	0	4
Sub-Saharan Africa	NA	NA	NA	NA	5	0	5	0	5	0	5	0	4	0	4	0	5	0	2
Low- and middle-income countries	NA	NA	NA	NA	5	0	9	0	10	0	6	1	5	1	5	1	7	1	4
High-income countries	NA	NA	NA	NA	−13	−11	−15	−13	−15	−12	−14	−11	−14	−10	−14	−10	−14	−10	−13
WORLD	NA	NA	NA	NA	4	0	7	0	7	0	4	0	1	−1	−1	−2	4	−1	2
PAF of DALYs (%)																			
East Asia and Pacific	NA	NA	NA	NA	2	0	3	0	4	0	2	0	1	0	1	0	2	0	1
Europe and Central Asia	NA	NA	NA	NA	13	2	14	2	13	2	13	2	13	2	13	2	13	2	8
Latin America and the Caribbean	NA	NA	NA	NA	14	2	14	2	15	2	15	2	13	1	12	1	14	2	9
Middle East and North Africa	NA	NA	NA	NA	1	0	1	0	1	0	1	0	0	0	0	0	1	0	0
South Asia	NA	NA	NA	NA	5	0	11	0	13	0	3	0	0	0	0	0	6	0	4
Sub-Saharan Africa	NA	NA	NA	NA	5	0	5	0	5	0	5	0	4	0	4	0	5	0	2
Low- and middle-income countries	NA	NA	NA	NA	5	0	9	0	10	0	6	1	5	1	5	1	7	1	4
High-income countries	NA	NA	NA	NA	−13	−11	−15	−13	−15	−12	−14	−11	−14	−10	−14	−10	−14	−10	−13
WORLD	NA	NA	NA	NA	4	0	7	0	7	−1	3	0	1	−1	−1	−2	4	−1	2
Attributable Mortality (thousands)																			
East Asia and Pacific	NA	NA	NA	NA	0	0	1	0	4	0	3	0	2	0	1	0	11	0	11
Europe and Central Asia	NA	NA	NA	NA	0	0	5	0	20	1	29	3	35	6	17	7	107	17	124
Latin America and the Caribbean	NA	NA	NA	NA	0	0	1	0	6	0	7	1	8	0	5	1	28	2	30
Middle East and North Africa	NA	NA	NA	NA	0	0	0	0	0	0	0	0	0	0	0	0	1	0	1
South Asia	NA	NA	NA	NA	1	0	5	0	32	0	9	0	0	0	0	0	46	0	46
Sub-Saharan Africa	NA	NA	NA	NA	0	0	0	0	2	0	3	0	2	0	1	0	8	0	8
Low- and middle-income countries	NA	NA	NA	NA	1	0	13	0	64	1	52	3	46	7	24	8	201	19	220
High-income countries	NA	NA	NA	NA	0	0	−2	0	−13	−3	−18	−6	−32	−16	−35	−41	−101	−66	−167
WORLD	NA	NA	NA	NA	1	0	11	0	51	−1	33	−3	14	−9	−11	−33	100	−46	53
Attributable YLL (thousands)																			
East Asia and Pacific	NA	NA	NA	NA	5	0	22	0	78	0	40	0	17	0	5	0	166	0	166
Europe and Central Asia	NA	NA	NA	NA	11	0	123	4	376	17	399	39	312	64	77	35	1,299	159	1,458
Latin America and the Caribbean	NA	NA	NA	NA	6	0	30	2	110	7	98	9	68	5	24	3	336	26	362
Middle East and North Africa	NA	NA	NA	NA	1	0	3	0	8	0	7	0	0	0	0	0	17	0	17
South Asia	NA	NA	NA	NA	14	0	127	0	590	0	119	0	0	0	0	0	850	0	850
Sub-Saharan Africa	NA	NA	NA	NA	1	0	8	0	36	0	35	0	21	0	4	0	106	0	106
Low- and middle-income countries	NA	NA	NA	NA	36	1	314	5	1,198	24	698	48	419	69	111	37	2,775	184	2,960
High-income countries	NA	NA	NA	NA	−3	−1	−56	−12	−245	−54	−244	−86	−284	−157	−152	−169	−984	−479	−1,463
WORLD	NA	NA	NA	NA	33	0	258	−6	953	−29	453	−39	135	−89	−41	−131	1,791	−295	1,497
Attributable DALYs (thousands)																			
East Asia and Pacific	NA	NA	NA	NA	7	0	24	0	83	0	42	0	17	0	5	0	178	0	178
Europe and Central Asia	NA	NA	NA	NA	13	1	132	4	391	19	412	41	318	65	78	35	1,344	164	1,508
Latin America and the Caribbean	NA	NA	NA	NA	10	1	34	2	117	8	104	9	70	5	25	3	361	28	388
Middle East and North Africa	NA	NA	NA	NA	1	0	3	0	8	0	7	0	0	0	0	0	19	0	19
South Asia	NA	NA	NA	NA	20	0	145	0	626	0	125	0	0	0	0	0	916	0	916
Sub-Saharan Africa	NA	NA	NA	NA	2	0	9	0	39	0	37	0	21	0	4	0	113	0	113
Low- and middle-income countries	NA	NA	NA	NA	52	1	348	6	1,264	26	727	50	427	70	113	38	2,931	192	3,123
High-income countries	NA	NA	NA	NA	−5	−2	−64	−16	−270	−64	−263	−97	−299	−168	−158	−175	−1,057	−522	−1,579
WORLD	NA	NA	NA	NA	48	−1	284	−9	994	−38	464	−47	128	−98	−45	−137	1,873	−330	1,543

Source: Authors' calculations.
Note: NA = not applicable.

Table 4A.69

Risk factor: Alcohol use
Disease: Cerebrovascular disease

Region	0–4 years Male	0–4 Female	5–14 years Male	5–14 Female	15–29 years Male	15–29 Female	30–44 years Male	30–44 Female	45–59 years Male	45–59 Female	60–69 years Male	60–69 Female	70–79 years Male	70–79 Female	80+ years Male	80+ Female	Total Male	Total Female	All
PAF of Mortality (%)																			
East Asia and Pacific	NA	NA	NA	NA	14	1	17	0	15	0	13	0	11	0	10	0	12	0	6
Europe and Central Asia	NA	NA	NA	NA	19	6	19	7	19	6	15	3	10	2	9	1	13	2	7
Latin America and the Caribbean	NA	NA	NA	NA	15	11	17	14	15	10	13	7	7	3	6	2	10	5	7
Middle East and North Africa	NA	NA	NA	NA	3	1	5	1	3	0	2	0	1	0	1	0	2	0	1
South Asia	NA	NA	NA	NA	3	2	6	0	3	0	0	0	0	0	0	0	1	0	0
Sub-Saharan Africa	NA	NA	NA	NA	13	2	16	3	13	5	10	3	8	1	7	1	10	2	5
Low- and middle-income countries	NA	NA	NA	NA	11	3	15	4	12	2	10	1	8	1	7	1	9	1	5
High-income countries	NA	NA	NA	NA	16	−28	16	−32	14	−27	11	−26	7	−25	6	−28	8	−27	−13
WORLD	NA	NA	NA	NA	11	1	15	1	12	1	10	0	8	−2	7	−7	9	−3	2
PAF of YLL (%)																			
East Asia and Pacific	NA	NA	NA	NA	14	1	17	0	15	0	13	0	11	0	10	0	13	0	7
Europe and Central Asia	NA	NA	NA	NA	19	6	19	7	19	6	15	3	10	2	9	1	14	3	8
Latin America and the Caribbean	NA	NA	NA	NA	15	11	17	14	15	10	13	7	7	3	6	2	12	7	9
Middle East and North Africa	NA	NA	NA	NA	3	1	5	1	3	0	2	0	1	0	1	0	2	0	1
South Asia	NA	NA	NA	NA	3	2	6	0	3	0	0	0	0	0	0	0	1	0	1
Sub-Saharan Africa	NA	NA	NA	NA	13	2	16	3	13	5	10	3	8	1	7	1	11	3	6
Low- and middle-income countries	NA	NA	NA	NA	11	3	15	4	12	2	10	1	8	1	7	1	10	1	6
High-income countries	NA	NA	NA	NA	16	−28	16	−32	14	−27	11	−26	7	−25	6	−28	9	−27	−10
WORLD	NA	NA	NA	NA	11	1	15	1	12	1	10	0	8	−2	7	−6	10	−2	4
PAF of DALYs (%)																			
East Asia and Pacific	NA	NA	NA	NA	14	1	14	0	13	0	11	0	10	0	9	0	11	0	6
Europe and Central Asia	NA	NA	NA	NA	19	6	17	5	18	5	14	3	9	2	9	1	13	3	7
Latin America and the Caribbean	NA	NA	NA	NA	15	11	15	11	13	8	11	6	6	3	6	2	10	6	8
Middle East and North Africa	NA	NA	NA	NA	3	1	4	0	3	0	2	0	1	0	1	0	2	0	1
South Asia	NA	NA	NA	NA	3	2	6	0	2	0	0	0	0	0	0	0	1	0	1
Sub-Saharan Africa	NA	NA	NA	NA	13	2	15	3	12	4	10	2	7	1	7	1	10	2	6
Low- and middle-income countries	NA	NA	NA	NA	11	3	13	3	11	2	9	1	7	1	7	1	9	1	5
High-income countries	NA	NA	NA	NA	16	−28	12	−37	10	−32	7	−28	5	−27	5	−29	7	−29	−11
WORLD	NA	NA	NA	NA	11	1	13	−2	11	−1	9	−1	7	−3	6	−7	9	−3	3
Attributable Mortality (thousands)																			
East Asia and Pacific	NA	NA	NA	NA	1	0	4	0	21	0	32	0	37	0	18	0	114	0	114
Europe and Central Asia	NA	NA	NA	NA	1	0	2	0	10	2	16	3	15	5	7	4	52	15	67
Latin America and the Caribbean	NA	NA	NA	NA	0	0	1	1	3	2	3	2	3	1	2	1	13	7	20
Middle East and North Africa	NA	NA	NA	NA	0	0	0	0	0	0	0	0	0	0	0	0	1	0	1
South Asia	NA	NA	NA	NA	0	0	1	0	2	0	1	0	0	0	0	0	3	0	3
Sub-Saharan Africa	NA	NA	NA	NA	0	0	2	0	4	2	4	1	3	1	2	0	14	5	19
Low- and middle-income countries	NA	NA	NA	NA	2	0	10	2	40	6	57	6	58	7	30	5	197	27	224
High-income countries	NA	NA	NA	NA	0	0	1	−1	3	−4	5	−7	7	−25	9	−87	26	−126	−100
WORLD	NA	NA	NA	NA	2	0	11	0	44	2	61	−1	66	−18	39	−82	223	−99	124
Attributable YLL (thousands)																			
East Asia and Pacific	NA	NA	NA	NA	22	1	99	0	394	0	432	0	330	0	92	0	1,369	1	1,370
Europe and Central Asia	NA	NA	NA	NA	15	3	57	12	195	44	222	45	134	56	34	18	656	178	834
Latin America and the Caribbean	NA	NA	NA	NA	7	5	26	23	60	39	46	24	24	12	10	6	174	108	282
Middle East and North Africa	NA	NA	NA	NA	2	0	3	0	6	1	3	1	2	0	0	0	16	2	18
South Asia	NA	NA	NA	NA	4	1	14	0	36	0	9	0	0	0	0	0	62	1	64
Sub-Saharan Africa	NA	NA	NA	NA	12	1	40	7	66	33	49	21	30	8	8	2	206	73	279
Low- and middle-income countries	NA	NA	NA	NA	63	11	239	42	757	117	761	91	520	76	144	26	2,484	363	2,847
High-income countries	NA	NA	NA	NA	4	−5	23	−34	65	−85	62	−109	64	−252	40	−359	259	−845	−586
WORLD	NA	NA	NA	NA	67	5	262	8	822	32	823	−18	584	−177	184	−333	2,743	−482	2,261
Attributable DALYs (thousands)																			
East Asia and Pacific	NA	NA	NA	NA	22	1	119	0	462	0	497	0	357	0	96	0	1,553	1	1,553
Europe and Central Asia	NA	NA	NA	NA	15	3	65	13	225	48	256	48	148	58	36	17	745	188	932
Latin America and the Caribbean	NA	NA	NA	NA	7	5	32	26	73	43	54	26	26	12	10	6	203	119	322
Middle East and North Africa	NA	NA	NA	NA	2	0	3	0	7	1	4	1	2	0	0	0	18	2	20
South Asia	NA	NA	NA	NA	4	1	16	0	39	0	9	0	0	0	0	0	67	1	68
Sub-Saharan Africa	NA	NA	NA	NA	12	1	42	7	71	34	53	22	31	8	8	2	217	75	292
Low- and middle-income countries	NA	NA	NA	NA	63	11	276	47	875	126	873	97	565	79	150	26	2,802	386	3,188
High-income countries	NA	NA	NA	NA	4	−5	33	−79	95	−204	82	−228	75	−411	43	−466	331	−1,394	−1,063
WORLD	NA	NA	NA	NA	67	5	309	−32	970	−78	955	−131	639	−332	194	−440	3,134	−1,008	2,126

Source: Authors' calculations.
Note: NA = not applicable.

Table 4A.70

Risk factor: Alcohol use
Disease: Cirrhosis of the liver

Region	0–4 years Male	Female	5–14 years Male	Female	15–29 years Male	Female	30–44 years Male	Female	45–59 years Male	Female	60–69 years Male	Female	70–79 years Male	Female	80+ years Male	Female	Total Male	Female	All
PAF of Mortality (%)																			
East Asia and Pacific	NA	NA	NA	NA	45	10	49	9	48	9	45	6	40	3	40	3	45	6	31
Europe and Central Asia	NA	NA	NA	NA	69	55	67	54	70	55	62	47	50	40	50	41	64	48	58
Latin America and the Caribbean	NA	NA	NA	NA	56	46	59	49	57	45	51	42	34	30	34	30	52	39	49
Middle East and North Africa	NA	NA	NA	NA	17	8	16	7	16	7	12	3	8	2	8	3	12	4	8
South Asia	NA	NA	NA	NA	12	11	23	4	8	4	2	0	0	0	0	0	7	3	5
Sub-Saharan Africa	NA	NA	NA	NA	50	25	58	33	56	35	53	27	46	20	46	20	53	28	44
Low- and middle-income countries	NA	NA	NA	NA	34	15	49	21	43	22	37	19	29	13	26	11	38	16	30
High-income countries	NA	NA	NA	NA	66	53	65	49	64	51	56	43	49	39	49	39	58	44	54
WORLD	NA	NA	NA	NA	34	15	52	24	46	26	41	22	33	17	31	18	41	20	34
PAF of YLL (%)																			
East Asia and Pacific	NA	NA	NA	NA	45	10	49	9	48	9	45	6	40	3	40	3	45	7	32
Europe and Central Asia	NA	NA	NA	NA	69	55	67	54	70	55	62	47	50	40	50	41	66	50	60
Latin America and the Caribbean	NA	NA	NA	NA	56	46	59	49	57	45	51	42	34	30	34	30	54	42	52
Middle East and North Africa	NA	NA	NA	NA	17	8	16	7	16	7	12	3	8	2	8	3	12	4	9
South Asia	NA	NA	NA	NA	12	11	23	4	8	4	2	0	0	0	0	0	8	3	6
Sub-Saharan Africa	NA	NA	NA	NA	50	25	58	33	56	35	53	27	46	20	46	20	54	29	45
Low- and middle-income countries	NA	NA	NA	NA	34	15	49	21	43	22	37	19	29	13	26	11	39	16	30
High-income countries	NA	NA	NA	NA	66	53	65	49	64	51	56	43	49	39	49	39	60	46	56
WORLD	NA	NA	NA	NA	34	15	52	24	46	26	41	22	33	17	30	17	42	19	34
PAF of DALYs (%)																			
East Asia and Pacific	NA	NA	NA	NA	45	10	49	9	48	9	45	6	40	3	40	3	45	7	32
Europe and Central Asia	NA	NA	NA	NA	69	55	67	54	70	55	62	47	50	40	50	41	66	50	60
Latin America and the Caribbean	NA	NA	NA	NA	56	46	59	49	57	45	51	42	34	30	34	30	55	42	52
Middle East and North Africa	NA	NA	NA	NA	17	8	16	7	16	7	12	3	8	2	8	3	12	4	9
South Asia	NA	NA	NA	NA	12	11	23	4	8	4	2	0	0	0	0	0	8	3	6
Sub-Saharan Africa	NA	NA	NA	NA	50	25	58	33	56	35	53	27	46	20	46	20	54	29	44
Low- and middle-income countries	NA	NA	NA	NA	36	15	49	21	43	22	37	19	29	13	27	11	39	16	30
High-income countries	NA	NA	NA	NA	66	53	65	49	64	51	56	43	49	39	49	39	60	46	56
WORLD	NA	NA	NA	NA	36	16	52	25	46	26	41	22	33	17	31	17	42	19	34
Attributable Mortality (thousands)																			
East Asia and Pacific	NA	NA	NA	NA	2	0	9	1	21	1	13	1	8	0	3	0	56	4	60
Europe and Central Asia	NA	NA	NA	NA	1	0	8	2	17	7	11	5	4	3	1	1	42	19	60
Latin America and the Caribbean	NA	NA	NA	NA	1	0	7	1	12	2	6	2	3	1	1	1	29	7	36
Middle East and North Africa	NA	NA	NA	NA	0	0	0	0	1	0	1	0	0	0	0	0	2	1	3
South Asia	NA	NA	NA	NA	1	1	3	0	3	1	0	0	0	0	0	0	7	2	9
Sub-Saharan Africa	NA	NA	NA	NA	1	0	3	1	7	2	5	2	3	1	1	0	20	6	26
Low- and middle-income countries	NA	NA	NA	NA	6	2	31	5	61	13	35	9	19	6	5	2	157	38	195
High-income countries	NA	NA	NA	NA	0	0	6	2	19	5	12	4	7	4	2	2	47	16	63
WORLD	NA	NA	NA	NA	6	2	37	7	80	18	47	13	26	10	8	5	204	55	258
Attributable YLL (thousands)																			
East Asia and Pacific	NA	NA	NA	NA	50	6	224	15	406	30	173	13	76	5	14	1	943	71	1,014
Europe and Central Asia	NA	NA	NA	NA	32	13	184	58	328	133	145	76	39	35	4	6	732	320	1,052
Latin America and the Caribbean	NA	NA	NA	NA	23	5	168	24	230	44	83	27	23	12	5	3	530	116	646
Middle East and North Africa	NA	NA	NA	NA	3	1	3	1	18	6	10	2	3	1	1	0	39	11	50
South Asia	NA	NA	NA	NA	24	30	69	7	51	13	6	0	0	0	0	0	151	51	202
Sub-Saharan Africa	NA	NA	NA	NA	19	6	81	16	136	46	62	25	31	10	4	1	334	104	438
Low- and middle-income countries	NA	NA	NA	NA	151	60	730	122	1,168	271	480	143	172	62	27	12	2,729	672	3,401
High-income countries	NA	NA	NA	NA	5	2	151	40	362	99	163	55	62	40	11	11	755	247	1,002
WORLD	NA	NA	NA	NA	156	62	881	163	1,531	370	642	198	235	102	38	24	3,483	919	4,403
Attributable DALYs (thousands)																			
East Asia and Pacific	NA	NA	NA	NA	73	8	282	22	476	39	196	16	87	6	16	2	1,131	93	1,224
Europe and Central Asia	NA	NA	NA	NA	45	18	226	80	375	162	160	87	44	40	4	7	853	394	1,247
Latin America and the Caribbean	NA	NA	NA	NA	37	7	208	34	265	55	92	32	26	14	6	4	634	147	781
Middle East and North Africa	NA	NA	NA	NA	4	1	4	2	21	7	11	2	4	1	1	0	46	14	60
South Asia	NA	NA	NA	NA	30	34	84	9	59	15	7	0	0	0	0	0	180	59	240
Sub-Saharan Africa	NA	NA	NA	NA	32	9	101	23	156	56	74	32	36	12	5	2	404	133	537
Low- and middle-income countries	NA	NA	NA	NA	221	78	905	170	1,352	335	541	170	197	73	32	15	3,248	841	4,089
High-income countries	NA	NA	NA	NA	9	4	194	57	421	121	182	65	70	48	13	14	889	310	1,199
WORLD	NA	NA	NA	NA	230	82	1,099	227	1,773	456	723	235	267	121	45	29	4,137	1,150	5,287

Source: Authors' calculations.
Note: NA = not applicable.

Table 4A.71

Risk factor: Alcohol use
Disease: Road traffic accidents

Region	0–4 years Male	Female	5–14 years Male	Female	15–29 years Male	Female	30–44 years Male	Female	45–59 years Male	Female	60–69 years Male	Female	70–79 years Male	Female	80+ years Male	Female	Total Male	Female	All
PAF of Mortality (%)																			
East Asia and Pacific	9	5	9	6	27	7	30	10	13	8	11	6	11	6	11	6	22	8	18
Europe and Central Asia	23	15	26	18	66	23	70	32	47	26	40	19	39	19	36	19	57	23	48
Latin America and the Caribbean	16	11	17	11	54	13	58	19	34	15	28	11	28	11	28	11	45	14	39
Middle East and North Africa	3	2	3	2	8	3	10	4	4	3	3	2	3	2	3	1	6	3	5
South Asia	4	2	4	3	20	3	23	5	10	4	8	3	8	3	8	3	16	3	12
Sub-Saharan Africa	12	8	13	8	38	10	42	14	22	11	18	8	17	8	17	7	25	9	20
Low- and middle-income countries	9	5	10	7	31	8	35	11	18	9	15	7	13	7	13	7	24	8	20
High-income countries	19	12	19	12	40	15	43	20	22	16	18	12	19	13	19	13	32	15	27
WORLD	10	5	11	7	32	9	35	12	18	9	15	8	14	8	14	8	25	9	21
PAF of YLL (%)																			
East Asia and Pacific	9	5	9	6	27	7	30	10	13	8	11	6	11	6	11	6	23	8	19
Europe and Central Asia	23	15	26	18	66	23	70	32	47	26	40	19	39	19	36	19	59	24	50
Latin America and the Caribbean	16	11	17	11	54	13	58	19	34	15	28	11	28	11	28	11	47	14	40
Middle East and North Africa	3	2	3	2	8	3	10	4	4	3	3	2	3	2	3	1	6	3	5
South Asia	4	2	4	3	20	3	23	5	10	4	8	3	8	3	8	3	16	3	13
Sub-Saharan Africa	12	8	13	8	38	10	42	14	22	11	18	8	17	8	17	7	25	9	20
Low- and middle-income countries	9	5	10	7	31	8	35	11	18	9	15	7	13	7	13	7	25	8	21
High-income countries	19	12	19	12	40	15	43	20	22	16	18	12	19	13	19	13	35	16	29
WORLD	10	5	11	7	32	9	35	12	18	9	15	8	14	8	14	8	26	9	21
PAF of DALYs (%)																			
East Asia and Pacific	8	4	8	5	25	6	28	9	13	8	11	6	11	6	11	6	22	7	17
Europe and Central Asia	21	14	23	15	62	21	66	29	45	24	39	18	38	18	35	19	56	22	47
Latin America and the Caribbean	14	9	15	9	50	12	54	17	32	14	27	10	27	10	27	11	43	12	36
Middle East and North Africa	3	2	3	2	7	3	9	4	4	3	3	2	3	2	3	1	6	2	5
South Asia	3	2	4	2	18	3	22	4	10	4	8	3	8	3	8	3	15	3	11
Sub-Saharan Africa	11	7	12	8	35	9	40	13	21	10	17	8	16	8	16	7	24	9	19
Low- and middle-income countries	8	5	9	6	29	7	33	11	17	8	14	7	13	7	13	6	23	7	19
High-income countries	18	11	17	11	38	14	41	18	21	15	18	12	18	12	19	13	33	14	28
WORLD	8	5	9	6	30	8	33	11	17	9	15	7	14	8	14	8	24	8	19
Attributable Mortality (thousands)																			
East Asia and Pacific	0	0	1	0	23	1	21	3	7	2	2	1	1	0	0	0	57	8	64
Europe and Central Asia	0	0	1	0	12	1	13	1	6	1	2	1	1	1	0	0	35	5	40
Latin America and the Caribbean	0	0	1	0	13	1	11	1	4	0	1	0	1	0	0	0	31	3	34
Middle East and North Africa	0	0	0	0	2	0	1	0	0	0	0	0	0	0	0	0	4	1	5
South Asia	0	0	1	0	9	0	12	0	4	1	1	0	1	0	0	0	27	2	30
Sub-Saharan Africa	1	1	5	2	10	1	12	1	4	1	1	0	1	0	0	0	35	6	40
Low- and middle-income countries	3	1	9	3	68	4	70	7	25	5	8	2	5	1	2	1	190	24	213
High-income countries	0	0	0	0	11	1	9	1	3	1	1	0	1	1	1	0	28	5	33
WORLD	3	1	9	3	79	6	79	8	28	6	10	2	6	2	2	1	217	29	246
Attributable YLL (thousands)																			
East Asia and Pacific	12	5	34	13	628	32	521	68	129	39	33	8	13	4	2	1	1,372	172	1,544
Europe and Central Asia	5	3	19	7	329	31	303	32	121	21	31	8	11	5	1	1	820	109	929
Latin America and the Caribbean	8	4	19	7	342	18	267	18	81	9	18	3	8	2	2	0	745	60	805
Middle East and North Africa	5	2	7	2	43	4	35	4	9	2	3	1	1	1	0	0	104	16	119
South Asia	5	4	16	8	242	9	296	12	69	12	12	2	7	1	2	0	650	49	698
Sub-Saharan Africa	42	17	156	58	278	30	281	29	76	15	18	4	6	2	1	0	859	155	1,013
Low- and middle-income countries	76	34	251	95	1,863	124	1,703	163	487	98	116	27	45	15	8	3	4,549	559	5,108
High-income countries	6	3	13	6	312	36	210	31	65	19	19	7	12	7	4	2	639	109	748
WORLD	82	37	264	101	2,175	159	1,913	193	552	116	135	34	57	22	12	5	5,188	668	5,856
Attributable DALYs (thousands)																			
East Asia and Pacific	16	8	44	20	715	43	587	81	141	44	35	9	13	5	2	1	1,554	211	1,765
Europe and Central Asia	6	4	24	10	377	40	338	40	131	25	32	9	11	6	1	1	920	134	1,055
Latin America and the Caribbean	11	6	26	10	408	25	310	23	91	11	20	3	8	2	2	0	876	80	956
Middle East and North Africa	5	2	9	3	54	5	42	5	11	2	3	1	2	1	0	0	126	20	145
South Asia	8	7	25	14	296	12	330	15	77	14	13	3	7	2	2	0	757	67	824
Sub-Saharan Africa	48	23	175	72	336	35	320	34	88	17	20	5	6	2	1	0	993	187	1,181
Low- and middle-income countries	94	49	302	130	2,186	160	1,927	198	539	113	122	29	47	16	8	3	5,226	699	5,924
High-income countries	7	3	16	7	350	43	233	36	71	22	20	8	12	7	4	2	712	128	840
WORLD	101	53	318	138	2,536	203	2,160	234	610	134	142	37	60	23	12	6	5,938	827	6,765

Source: Authors' calculations.

Table 4A.72

Risk factor: Alcohol use
Disease: Poisonings

Region	0–4 years Male	Female	5–14 years Male	Female	15–29 years Male	Female	30–44 years Male	Female	45–59 years Male	Female	60–69 years Male	Female	70–79 years Male	Female	80+ years Male	Female	Total Male	Female	All
PAF of Mortality (%)																			
East Asia and Pacific	NA	NA	NA	NA	20	14	10	9	10	9	10	8	5	4	5	4	10	7	9
Europe and Central Asia	NA	NA	NA	NA	63	40	44	29	44	29	44	29	26	15	25	14	46	28	41
Latin America and the Caribbean	NA	NA	NA	NA	44	23	25	15	24	16	25	15	15	7	15	7	26	11	22
Middle East and North Africa	NA	NA	NA	NA	5	4	3	3	2	2	3	2	1	1	1	1	3	2	3
South Asia	NA	NA	NA	NA	16	7	8	4	8	4	8	4	4	2	4	2	8	4	6
Sub-Saharan Africa	NA	NA	NA	NA	27	17	17	11	16	11	16	10	*	4	*	0	12	8	11
Low- and middle-income countries	NA	NA	NA	NA	34	16	28	13	25	14	24	10	10	5	7	4	24	10	19
High-income countries	NA	NA	NA	NA	32	25	18	16	17	16	17	16	9	8	10	9	20	16	19
WORLD	NA	NA	NA	NA	34	17	27	13	25	14	23	10	10	5	7	5	24	11	19
PAF of YLL (%)																			
East Asia and Pacific	NA	NA	NA	NA	20	14	10	9	10	9	10	8	5	4	5	4	11	7	9
Europe and Central Asia	NA	NA	NA	NA	63	40	44	29	44	29	44	29	26	15	25	14	46	29	42
Latin America and the Caribbean	NA	NA	NA	NA	44	23	25	15	24	16	25	15	15	7	15	7	27	11	22
Middle East and North Africa	NA	NA	NA	NA	5	4	3	3	2	2	3	2	1	1	1	1	3	2	3
South Asia	NA	NA	NA	NA	16	7	8	4	8	4	8	4	4	2	4	2	9	4	6
Sub-Saharan Africa	NA	NA	NA	NA	27	17	17	11	16	11	16	10	*	4	*	0	12	8	10
Low- and middle-income countries	NA	NA	NA	NA	34	16	28	13	25	14	24	10	10	5	7	4	24	10	19
High-income countries	NA	NA	NA	NA	32	25	18	16	17	16	17	16	9	8	10	9	21	17	20
WORLD	NA	NA	NA	NA	34	17	26	13	25	14	23	10	10	5	7	5	24	11	19
PAF of DALYs (%)																			
East Asia and Pacific	NA	NA	NA	NA	20	14	10	9	10	9	10	8	5	4	5	4	10	7	9
Europe and Central Asia	NA	NA	NA	NA	63	40	44	29	44	28	44	29	26	15	25	14	46	28	42
Latin America and the Caribbean	NA	NA	NA	NA	41	19	24	12	23	13	24	13	14	7	14	7	25	10	20
Middle East and North Africa	NA	NA	NA	NA	5	4	3	3	2	2	3	2	1	1	1	1	3	2	3
South Asia	NA	NA	NA	NA	16	7	8	4	8	4	8	4	4	2	4	2	9	4	6
Sub-Saharan Africa	NA	NA	NA	NA	27	17	17	11	16	11	16	10	2	4	2	0	11	8	10
Low- and middle-income countries	NA	NA	NA	NA	34	16	27	13	25	14	23	10	10	5	7	4	24	10	19
High-income countries	NA	NA	NA	NA	31	23	18	15	16	15	16	14	9	8	10	9	21	16	19
WORLD	NA	NA	NA	NA	34	16	26	13	25	14	23	10	10	5	7	5	24	11	19
Attributable Mortality (thousands)																			
East Asia and Pacific	NA	NA	NA	NA	2	1	1	1	1	1	1	0	0	0	0	0	5	2	7
Europe and Central Asia	NA	NA	NA	NA	7	1	12	2	13	3	5	1	1	0	0	0	37	7	44
Latin America and the Caribbean	NA	NA	NA	NA	0	0	0	0	0	0	0	0	0	0	0	0	1	0	1
Middle East and North Africa	NA	NA	NA	NA	0	0	0	0	0	0	0	0	0	0	0	0	0	0	0
South Asia	NA	NA	NA	NA	1	0	1	0	1	0	1	0	0	0	0	0	4	2	6
Sub-Saharan Africa	NA	NA	NA	NA	1	1	1	0	0	0	0	0	0	0	0	0	3	1	4
Low- and middle-income countries	NA	NA	NA	NA	12	3	14	3	16	4	6	2	1	1	0	0	50	12	62
High-income countries	NA	NA	NA	NA	1	0	1	0	1	0	0	0	0	0	0	0	3	1	4
WORLD	NA	NA	NA	NA	13	3	16	3	17	4	6	2	1	1	0	0	53	13	66
Attributable YLL (thousands)																			
East Asia and Pacific	NA	NA	NA	NA	46	17	27	15	25	12	10	5	2	1	0	0	111	51	162
Europe and Central Asia	NA	NA	NA	NA	200	28	275	39	258	52	65	19	6	3	0	0	804	142	946
Latin America and the Caribbean	NA	NA	NA	NA	7	1	4	1	2	0	1	0	0	0	0	0	14	2	16
Middle East and North Africa	NA	NA	NA	NA	2	1	1	0	1	0	0	0	0	0	0	0	3	1	5
South Asia	NA	NA	NA	NA	35	10	14	5	26	7	7	8	1	1	0	0	85	32	116
Sub-Saharan Africa	NA	NA	NA	NA	33	15	24	7	8	3	2	3	0	0	0	0	68	28	97
Low- and middle-income countries	NA	NA	NA	NA	323	73	346	68	319	75	86	34	9	5	1	1	1,085	257	1,342
High-income countries	NA	NA	NA	NA	27	6	29	9	12	5	2	1	0	0	0	0	70	22	92
WORLD	NA	NA	NA	NA	351	79	374	78	331	80	88	35	9	6	1	1	1,155	279	1,434
Attributable DALYs (thousands)																			
East Asia and Pacific	NA	NA	NA	NA	46	17	27	16	25	12	10	5	2	1	0	0	112	52	164
Europe and Central Asia	NA	NA	NA	NA	200	29	275	40	259	53	65	19	6	3	0	0	807	143	950
Latin America and the Caribbean	NA	NA	NA	NA	8	2	4	1	2	0	1	0	0	0	0	0	14	3	17
Middle East and North Africa	NA	NA	NA	NA	2	1	1	0	1	0	0	0	0	0	0	0	3	1	5
South Asia	NA	NA	NA	NA	36	10	15	6	26	8	7	8	1	1	0	0	85	32	117
Sub-Saharan Africa	NA	NA	NA	NA	34	15	25	7	8	3	2	3	0	0	0	0	69	29	97
Low- and middle-income countries	NA	NA	NA	NA	325	74	347	69	322	76	87	34	9	5	1	1	1,090	260	1,350
High-income countries	NA	NA	NA	NA	28	6	29	10	12	6	2	1	0	0	0	0	71	23	94
WORLD	NA	NA	NA	NA	353	80	375	79	334	82	88	35	9	6	1	1	1,161	283	1,444

Source: Authors' calculations.

Note: NA = not applicable.

*The number of deaths (and hence YLL) directly coded to a number of diseases, especially neuropsychiatric and musculoskeletal diseases, is zero or very small. For other diseases, mortality or disease burden may be zero in some region-age-sex groups. In such cases, the population attributable fractions would be undefined or unstable and have not been calculated.

Table 4A.73

Risk factor: Alcohol use
Disease: Falls

Region	0–4 years Male	0–4 years Female	5–14 years Male	5–14 years Female	15–29 years Male	15–29 years Female	30–44 years Male	30–44 years Female	45–59 years Male	45–59 years Female	60–69 years Male	60–69 years Female	70–79 years Male	70–79 years Female	80+ years Male	80+ years Female	Total Male	Total Female	All
PAF of Mortality (%)																			
East Asia and Pacific	NA	NA	NA	NA	15	8	15	8	15	8	11	5	8	2	8	2	12	4	9
Europe and Central Asia	NA	NA	NA	NA	51	26	52	25	51	25	42	17	31	7	28	7	44	12	34
Latin America and the Caribbean	NA	NA	NA	NA	36	14	37	15	37	15	30	10	22	4	22	4	29	6	22
Middle East and North Africa	NA	NA	NA	NA	3	2	4	3	4	2	3	1	2	1	2	1	3	1	2
South Asia	NA	NA	NA	NA	12	4	12	4	12	4	9	2	6	1	6	1	8	2	5
Sub-Saharan Africa	NA	NA	NA	NA	21	8	23	10	23	10	18	6	13	3	12	3	13	4	10
Low- and middle-income countries	NA	NA	NA	NA	18	7	21	9	22	8	16	5	10	2	10	3	15	4	11
High-income countries	NA	NA	NA	NA	23	15	25	16	25	17	20	11	15	5	15	5	18	6	12
WORLD	NA	NA	NA	NA	18	8	22	9	22	9	16	6	11	3	12	4	15	4	11
PAF of YLL (%)																			
East Asia and Pacific	NA	NA	NA	NA	15	8	15	8	15	8	11	5	8	2	8	2	12	5	10
Europe and Central Asia	NA	NA	NA	NA	51	26	52	25	51	25	42	17	31	7	28	7	46	16	39
Latin America and the Caribbean	NA	NA	NA	NA	36	14	37	15	37	15	30	10	22	4	22	4	30	7	25
Middle East and North Africa	NA	NA	NA	NA	3	2	4	3	4	2	3	1	2	1	2	1	2	1	2
South Asia	NA	NA	NA	NA	12	4	12	4	12	4	9	2	6	1	6	1	8	2	6
Sub-Saharan Africa	NA	NA	NA	NA	21	8	23	10	23	10	18	6	13	3	12	3	11	3	9
Low- and middle-income countries	NA	NA	NA	NA	18	7	21	9	22	8	16	5	10	2	9	3	15	4	12
High-income countries	NA	NA	NA	NA	23	15	25	16	25	17	20	11	15	5	15	5	20	8	15
WORLD	NA	NA	NA	NA	18	8	22	9	23	9	17	6	11	3	11	4	16	5	12
PAF of DALYs (%)																			
East Asia and Pacific	NA	NA	NA	NA	10	4	12	6	13	6	10	4	7	2	7	2	8	3	6
Europe and Central Asia	NA	NA	NA	NA	30	14	39	17	43	19	35	12	23	5	22	5	29	10	24
Latin America and the Caribbean	NA	NA	NA	NA	21	7	26	8	30	10	24	6	17	3	18	3	17	4	13
Middle East and North Africa	NA	NA	NA	NA	2	1	3	1	3	1	2	1	2	1	2	0	1	0	1
South Asia	NA	NA	NA	NA	7	3	9	3	10	3	8	2	5	1	6	1	5	1	3
Sub-Saharan Africa	NA	NA	NA	NA	14	5	18	6	20	7	15	5	11	2	9	2	7	2	5
Low- and middle-income countries	NA	NA	NA	NA	12	4	16	6	19	6	14	4	9	2	9	2	10	2	7
High-income countries	NA	NA	NA	NA	13	8	17	9	20	11	16	8	12	3	13	4	14	5	10
WORLD	NA	NA	NA	NA	12	4	16	6	19	7	14	5	9	2	10	3	10	3	7
Attributable Mortality (thousands)																			
East Asia and Pacific	NA	NA	NA	NA	2	0	2	0	2	0	1	0	1	0	1	0	9	2	11
Europe and Central Asia	NA	NA	NA	NA	1	0	3	0	4	0	2	0	1	0	0	0	11	1	12
Latin America and the Caribbean	NA	NA	NA	NA	1	0	1	0	1	0	0	0	0	0	0	0	3	0	3
Middle East and North Africa	NA	NA	NA	NA	0	0	0	0	0	0	0	0	0	0	0	0	0	0	0
South Asia	NA	NA	NA	NA	1	0	1	0	1	0	1	0	1	0	1	0	5	1	6
Sub-Saharan Africa	NA	NA	NA	NA	0	0	0	0	1	0	0	0	0	0	0	0	2	0	2
Low- and middle-income countries	NA	NA	NA	NA	5	1	7	1	8	1	4	1	3	1	2	1	30	5	34
High-income countries	NA	NA	NA	NA	0	0	1	0	1	0	1	0	1	0	2	1	6	2	8
WORLD	NA	NA	NA	NA	5	1	8	1	10	1	5	1	4	1	4	2	36	7	43
Attributable YLL (thousands)																			
East Asia and Pacific	NA	NA	NA	NA	51	7	51	8	47	10	15	4	7	2	3	1	174	32	206
Europe and Central Asia	NA	NA	NA	NA	36	4	66	6	69	7	22	3	7	2	2	1	203	24	226
Latin America and the Caribbean	NA	NA	NA	NA	14	1	17	1	14	1	5	1	2	0	1	0	55	4	58
Middle East and North Africa	NA	NA	NA	NA	1	0	1	0	1	0	0	0	0	0	0	0	4	1	5
South Asia	NA	NA	NA	NA	27	4	24	3	20	5	11	2	8	1	3	0	93	16	109
Sub-Saharan Africa	NA	NA	NA	NA	9	1	9	1	11	1	3	1	2	0	0	0	34	4	38
Low- and middle-income countries	NA	NA	NA	NA	139	18	168	18	163	24	57	10	26	6	10	4	563	80	643
High-income countries	NA	NA	NA	NA	9	1	18	2	24	5	12	3	9	3	8	5	80	19	99
WORLD	NA	NA	NA	NA	148	19	186	21	188	29	68	13	36	9	18	9	643	99	742
Attributable DALYs (thousands)																			
East Asia and Pacific	NA	NA	NA	NA	85	16	67	14	53	13	17	5	8	3	3	2	234	52	286
Europe and Central Asia	NA	NA	NA	NA	79	11	88	9	81	9	27	4	10	3	3	2	287	38	325
Latin America and the Caribbean	NA	NA	NA	NA	32	3	25	2	18	2	6	1	3	1	2	1	86	8	94
Middle East and North Africa	NA	NA	NA	NA	4	1	2	0	1	0	0	0	0	0	0	0	8	2	10
South Asia	NA	NA	NA	NA	48	10	32	5	24	6	12	2	8	1	3	0	127	25	152
Sub-Saharan Africa	NA	NA	NA	NA	15	2	12	1	12	2	4	1	2	0	0	0	45	6	52
Low- and middle-income countries	NA	NA	NA	NA	263	42	226	32	189	32	66	13	31	8	11	4	787	132	919
High-income countries	NA	NA	NA	NA	23	5	28	5	31	7	15	5	12	5	9	6	117	33	150
WORLD	NA	NA	NA	NA	286	47	254	37	220	39	81	18	43	12	21	11	904	165	1,069

Source: Authors' calculations.
Note: NA = not applicable.

Table 4A.74

Risk factor: Alcohol use
Disease: Drownings

Region	0–4 years Male	Female	5–14 years Male	Female	15–29 years Male	Female	30–44 years Male	Female	45–59 years Male	Female	60–69 years Male	Female	70–79 years Male	Female	80+ years Male	Female	Total Male	Female	All
PAF of Mortality (%)																			
East Asia and Pacific	NA	NA	NA	NA	18	15	22	19	21	19	17	15	17	15	17	15	10	8	9
Europe and Central Asia	NA	NA	NA	NA	57	40	64	48	64	47	56	40	54	39	53	40	54	33	50
Latin America and the Caribbean	NA	NA	NA	NA	42	25	48	30	48	30	40	23	39	23	39	24	34	11	30
Middle East and North Africa	NA	NA	NA	NA	5	5	8	9	9	8	8	7	7	4	5	2	4	2	4
South Asia	NA	NA	NA	NA	13	7	17	9	17	9	13	7	14	7	14	7	10	4	8
Sub-Saharan Africa	NA	NA	NA	NA	27	18	33	23	33	23	27	18	27	16	24	3	20	10	18
Low- and middle-income countries	NA	NA	NA	NA	23	14	34	19	34	20	27	15	22	14	18	14	18	8	15
High-income countries	NA	NA	NA	NA	26	23	33	29	33	31	27	25	27	25	26	24	25	21	24
WORLD	NA	NA	NA	NA	23	14	34	19	34	20	27	16	23	16	20	17	18	9	15
PAF of YLL (%)																			
East Asia and Pacific	NA	NA	NA	NA	18	15	22	19	21	19	17	15	17	15	17	15	8	6	8
Europe and Central Asia	NA	NA	NA	NA	57	40	64	48	64	47	56	40	54	39	53	40	52	31	48
Latin America and the Caribbean	NA	NA	NA	NA	42	25	48	30	48	30	40	23	39	23	39	24	32	10	28
Middle East and North Africa	NA	NA	NA	NA	5	5	8	9	9	8	8	7	7	4	5	2	3	2	3
South Asia	NA	NA	NA	NA	13	7	17	9	17	9	13	7	14	7	14	7	9	4	7
Sub-Saharan Africa	NA	NA	NA	NA	27	18	33	23	33	23	27	18	27	16	24	3	18	9	16
Low- and middle-income countries	NA	NA	NA	NA	23	14	34	19	34	20	27	15	22	14	18	14	16	7	13
High-income countries	NA	NA	NA	NA	26	23	33	29	33	31	27	25	27	25	26	24	24	18	22
WORLD	NA	NA	NA	NA	23	14	34	19	34	20	27	16	23	16	20	16	17	7	14
PAF of DALYs (%)																			
East Asia and Pacific	NA	NA	NA	NA	18	15	22	19	21	19	17	15	17	15	17	15	8	6	8
Europe and Central Asia	NA	NA	NA	NA	57	40	64	48	64	47	56	40	54	39	53	40	52	30	48
Latin America and the Caribbean	NA	NA	NA	NA	42	24	48	30	48	30	40	22	39	22	39	24	32	10	28
Middle East and North Africa	NA	NA	NA	NA	5	5	8	9	9	8	8	7	7	4	5	2	3	2	3
South Asia	NA	NA	NA	NA	13	7	17	9	17	9	13	7	14	7	14	7	9	4	7
Sub-Saharan Africa	NA	NA	NA	NA	27	18	33	23	33	23	27	18	25	15	24	3	18	9	16
Low- and middle-income countries	NA	NA	NA	NA	23	14	34	19	34	20	27	15	22	14	18	14	16	7	13
High-income countries	NA	NA	NA	NA	26	22	33	29	33	31	27	24	27	25	26	24	24	18	22
WORLD	NA	NA	NA	NA	23	14	34	19	34	20	27	16	23	16	20	16	17	7	14
Attributable Mortality (thousands)																			
East Asia and Pacific	NA	NA	NA	NA	4	1	2	1	1	1	1	0	0	0	0	0	9	4	13
Europe and Central Asia	NA	NA	NA	NA	4	0	6	1	4	1	1	0	0	0	0	0	15	2	18
Latin America and the Caribbean	NA	NA	NA	NA	2	0	1	0	1	0	0	0	0	0	0	0	5	0	6
Middle East and North Africa	NA	NA	NA	NA	0	0	0	0	0	0	0	0	0	0	0	0	0	0	0
South Asia	NA	NA	NA	NA	2	1	2	0	1	0	0	0	0	0	0	0	6	2	7
Sub-Saharan Africa	NA	NA	NA	NA	3	1	4	0	3	0	0	0	0	0	0	0	10	1	12
Low- and middle-income countries	NA	NA	NA	NA	15	3	15	2	10	2	3	1	2	1	1	1	46	10	55
High-income countries	NA	NA	NA	NA	1	0	1	0	1	0	0	0	0	0	0	0	3	1	4
WORLD	NA	NA	NA	NA	16	3	15	3	11	2	3	1	2	1	1	1	48	11	59
Attributable YLL (thousands)																			
East Asia and Pacific	NA	NA	NA	NA	110	26	49	30	29	17	9	6	4	5	1	2	202	86	288
Europe and Central Asia	NA	NA	NA	NA	105	13	134	14	80	11	20	4	5	2	0	1	344	44	388
Latin America and the Caribbean	NA	NA	NA	NA	67	5	36	2	16	1	4	0	1	0	0	0	125	9	134
Middle East and North Africa	NA	NA	NA	NA	6	1	2	1	1	0	0	0	0	0	0	0	10	2	12
South Asia	NA	NA	NA	NA	59	16	37	9	20	5	5	2	3	2	1	0	124	34	158
Sub-Saharan Africa	NA	NA	NA	NA	79	20	101	6	51	8	4	2	0	0	0	0	234	36	271
Low- and middle-income countries	NA	NA	NA	NA	426	80	358	62	197	43	41	15	14	9	3	3	1,040	211	1,251
High-income countries	NA	NA	NA	NA	15	2	15	3	13	3	5	2	3	3	1	2	52	14	66
WORLD	NA	NA	NA	NA	441	82	373	64	210	46	46	17	17	12	4	5	1,092	226	1,317
Attributable DALYs (thousands)																			
East Asia and Pacific	NA	NA	NA	NA	110	26	49	30	29	17	9	6	4	5	1	2	203	86	289
Europe and Central Asia	NA	NA	NA	NA	106	13	134	14	80	11	20	4	5	2	0	1	344	44	389
Latin America and the Caribbean	NA	NA	NA	NA	67	5	36	2	16	1	4	0	1	0	0	0	125	9	134
Middle East and North Africa	NA	NA	NA	NA	6	1	2	1	1	0	0	0	0	0	0	0	10	2	12
South Asia	NA	NA	NA	NA	59	16	37	9	20	5	5	2	3	2	1	0	124	34	158
Sub-Saharan Africa	NA	NA	NA	NA	79	20	101	6	51	8	4	2	0	0	0	0	235	37	271
Low- and middle-income countries	NA	NA	NA	NA	427	81	359	62	197	43	41	15	14	9	3	3	1,041	212	1,253
High-income countries	NA	NA	NA	NA	15	2	15	3	13	3	5	2	3	3	1	2	52	15	67
WORLD	NA	NA	NA	NA	442	82	374	65	210	46	46	17	17	12	4	5	1,093	227	1,320

Source: Authors' calculations.
Note: NA = not applicable.

Table 4A.75

Risk factor: Alcohol use
Disease: Other unintentional injuries

Region	0–4 years Male	0–4 Female	5–14 Male	5–14 Female	15–29 Male	15–29 Female	30–44 Male	30–44 Female	45–59 Male	45–59 Female	60–69 Male	60–69 Female	70–79 Male	70–79 Female	80+ Male	80+ Female	Total Male	Total Female	All
PAF of Mortality (%)																			
East Asia and Pacific	10	3	10	3	20	13	20	13	17	10	16	11	16	11	16	11	17	9	14
Europe and Central Asia	22	7	23	7	57	34	58	36	53	31	53	32	50	31	47	29	53	30	48
Latin America and the Caribbean	15	5	16	5	45	22	45	23	38	19	38	19	38	19	38	19	37	16	32
Middle East and North Africa	3	1	3	1	6	4	6	5	5	3	5	4	5	3	4	3	5	3	4
South Asia	4	1	4	1	16	7	16	7	13	5	13	5	13	5	13	5	13	5	9
Sub-Saharan Africa	13	4	13	4	30	17	32	18	27	14	25	14	25	12	23	11	25	10	21
Low- and middle-income countries	10	3	9	2	28	11	31	14	29	12	28	13	23	11	22	12	25	9	20
High-income countries	17	5	17	5	31	25	31	25	27	22	27	22	28	22	27	22	28	21	25
WORLD	11	3	9	2	28	12	31	15	29	13	28	14	25	13	24	16	25	10	20
PAF of YLL (%)																			
East Asia and Pacific	10	3	10	3	20	13	20	13	17	10	16	11	16	11	16	11	17	8	14
Europe and Central Asia	22	7	23	7	57	34	58	36	53	31	53	32	50	31	47	29	53	29	48
Latin America and the Caribbean	15	5	16	5	45	22	45	23	38	19	38	19	38	19	38	19	37	14	31
Middle East and North Africa	3	1	3	1	6	4	6	5	5	3	5	4	5	3	4	3	5	2	4
South Asia	4	1	4	1	16	7	16	7	13	5	13	5	13	5	13	5	12	4	9
Sub-Saharan Africa	13	4	13	4	30	17	32	18	27	14	25	14	25	12	23	11	25	9	20
Low- and middle-income countries	10	3	9	2	28	11	30	14	29	12	28	13	24	11	21	11	24	8	19
High-income countries	17	5	17	5	31	25	31	25	27	22	27	22	28	22	27	22	28	20	25
WORLD	11	3	9	2	28	12	30	15	29	13	28	14	25	13	24	15	25	9	19
PAF of DALYs (%)																			
East Asia and Pacific	8	2	6	1	15	8	16	9	13	7	12	8	13	9	14	10	12	6	10
Europe and Central Asia	16	6	13	4	43	23	49	28	47	26	45	27	40	26	34	24	41	21	36
Latin America and the Caribbean	11	4	9	3	32	14	34	15	30	14	30	15	32	17	33	18	25	10	22
Middle East and North Africa	2	0	1	0	4	2	3	3	3	2	4	3	4	2	3	2	3	1	2
South Asia	3	1	3	1	11	5	12	4	10	4	10	4	11	4	11	4	8	3	6
Sub-Saharan Africa	9	3	8	3	23	10	24	12	21	9	19	8	21	9	18	9	17	7	13
Low- and middle-income countries	7	2	5	2	19	7	22	9	22	8	22	9	20	9	18	10	16	6	12
High-income countries	11	3	10	2	20	13	22	14	21	14	22	16	25	19	25	20	20	13	17
WORLD	7	2	6	2	19	7	22	9	22	9	22	10	21	11	21	14	16	6	12
Attributable Mortality (thousands)																			
East Asia and Pacific	1	1	1	0	6	1	6	1	4	1	1	1	1	1	0	1	21	6	27
Europe and Central Asia	1	0	1	0	10	1	14	2	15	2	6	1	2	1	0	1	50	8	58
Latin America and the Caribbean	1	0	1	0	6	1	5	0	4	0	2	0	2	0	1	1	21	3	25
Middle East and North Africa	0	0	0	0	0	0	0	0	0	0	0	0	0	0	0	0	1	0	1
South Asia	0	0	1	0	6	2	5	1	3	1	2	1	1	1	1	0	19	6	25
Sub-Saharan Africa	2	0	1	0	11	1	5	1	2	0	1	0	1	0	0	0	23	3	27
Low- and middle-income countries	5	2	4	1	39	5	37	6	28	5	13	3	7	3	3	3	135	27	162
High-income countries	0	0	0	0	1	0	2	0	2	1	2	1	3	1	3	4	14	7	21
WORLD	5	2	4	1	41	6	39	6	30	6	14	3	9	4	6	6	149	34	183
Attributable YLL (thousands)																			
East Asia and Pacific	37	18	23	4	160	31	158	36	73	19	17	8	7	6	2	3	477	125	602
Europe and Central Asia	18	4	17	2	276	27	346	42	288	47	90	21	21	11	2	3	1,058	156	1,214
Latin America and the Caribbean	27	7	16	3	174	16	131	11	70	8	26	5	14	4	5	4	462	58	520
Middle East and North Africa	4	1	3	1	11	2	4	1	3	1	2	1	1	0	0	0	27	7	34
South Asia	12	6	22	5	167	53	127	28	61	19	23	8	12	6	3	2	427	127	554
Sub-Saharan Africa	59	13	29	10	290	23	126	25	46	10	16	2	8	2	1	1	574	84	658
Low- and middle-income countries	157	49	109	24	1,077	152	891	142	541	103	173	44	63	30	14	13	3,025	557	3,582
High-income countries	7	1	5	1	38	6	51	9	46	11	25	9	22	14	13	15	206	66	272
WORLD	164	50	114	25	1,116	158	942	151	586	114	199	53	85	44	27	27	3,232	623	3,854
Attributable DALYs (thousands)																			
East Asia and Pacific	46	20	45	9	226	72	204	65	91	31	23	13	9	8	3	4	648	221	869
Europe and Central Asia	28	5	42	4	368	45	405	55	320	54	103	25	25	12	3	3	1,294	204	1,497
Latin America and the Caribbean	39	8	41	5	263	30	179	19	90	12	32	6	16	5	6	4	666	88	754
Middle East and North Africa	5	1	7	1	24	7	8	3	5	1	2	1	1	0	0	0	52	14	66
South Asia	23	6	43	14	261	90	176	48	80	25	29	10	14	7	4	2	631	204	835
Sub-Saharan Africa	87	18	75	19	385	57	166	39	61	15	21	3	9	2	1	1	804	155	959
Low- and middle-income countries	229	58	252	52	1,527	301	1,138	231	646	137	211	58	75	35	17	14	4,095	886	4,981
High-income countries	11	2	15	3	63	21	74	23	60	19	31	13	25	16	14	16	291	114	405
WORLD	239	60	267	54	1,590	322	1,211	254	706	157	242	72	100	51	31	30	4,386	1,000	5,386

Source: Authors' calculations.

Table 4A.76

Risk factor: Alcohol use
Disease: Self-inflicted injuries

Region	0–4 years Male	Female	5–14 years Male	Female	15–29 years Male	Female	30–44 years Male	Female	45–59 years Male	Female	60–69 years Male	Female	70–79 years Male	Female	80+ years Male	Female	Total Male	Female	All
PAF of Mortality (%)																			
East Asia and Pacific	NA	NA	NA	NA	10	6	10	6	7	5	7	5	3	3	3	3	8	5	7
Europe and Central Asia	NA	NA	NA	NA	40	17	40	18	32	15	33	16	17	10	16	11	35	15	31
Latin America and the Caribbean	NA	NA	NA	NA	27	10	27	11	21	9	21	9	10	6	10	5	23	9	20
Middle East and North Africa	NA	NA	NA	NA	2	1	2	1	2	1	2	1	1	1	1	1	2	1	2
South Asia	NA	NA	NA	NA	8	3	8	3	6	2	5	2	2	1	2	1	7	3	5
Sub-Saharan Africa	NA	NA	NA	NA	17	6	18	7	13	5	13	6	6	3	6	3	14	6	12
Low- and middle-income countries	NA	NA	NA	NA	15	5	18	6	15	5	14	6	6	4	5	4	15	5	11
High-income countries	NA	NA	NA	NA	17	11	18	11	13	9	13	9	6	6	6	6	14	9	13
WORLD	NA	NA	NA	NA	16	5	18	6	15	6	14	6	6	4	5	4	14	5	11
PAF of YLL (%)																			
East Asia and Pacific	NA	NA	NA	NA	10	6	10	6	7	5	7	5	3	3	3	3	9	5	7
Europe and Central Asia	NA	NA	NA	NA	40	17	40	18	32	15	33	16	17	10	16	11	36	15	33
Latin America and the Caribbean	NA	NA	NA	NA	27	10	27	11	21	9	21	9	10	6	10	5	25	9	21
Middle East and North Africa	NA	NA	NA	NA	2	1	2	1	2	1	2	1	1	1	1	1	2	1	2
South Asia	NA	NA	NA	NA	8	3	8	3	6	2	5	2	2	1	2	1	7	3	5
Sub-Saharan Africa	NA	NA	NA	NA	17	6	18	7	13	5	13	6	6	3	6	3	15	6	13
Low- and middle-income countries	NA	NA	NA	NA	15	5	18	6	15	5	14	6	6	4	5	4	15	5	11
High-income countries	NA	NA	NA	NA	17	11	18	11	13	9	13	9	6	6	6	6	15	10	14
WORLD	NA	NA	NA	NA	16	5	18	6	15	6	14	7	6	4	5	4	15	5	11
PAF of DALYs (%)																			
East Asia and Pacific	NA	NA	NA	NA	10	6	10	6	7	5	7	5	3	3	3	3	8	5	7
Europe and Central Asia	NA	NA	NA	NA	39	16	39	17	32	15	33	16	17	10	16	11	35	15	32
Latin America and the Caribbean	NA	NA	NA	NA	27	9	27	11	21	9	21	9	10	6	10	5	24	8	20
Middle East and North Africa	NA	NA	NA	NA	2	1	2	1	2	1	2	1	1	1	1	1	2	1	1
South Asia	NA	NA	NA	NA	8	3	8	3	6	2	5	2	2	1	2	1	7	2	5
Sub-Saharan Africa	NA	NA	NA	NA	16	5	18	7	13	5	13	6	6	3	6	3	14	5	12
Low- and middle-income countries	NA	NA	NA	NA	15	4	17	6	15	5	14	6	6	4	5	4	15	5	10
High-income countries	NA	NA	NA	NA	17	10	18	10	13	9	13	9	6	6	6	6	15	9	13
WORLD	NA	NA	NA	NA	15	5	17	6	15	6	14	6	6	4	5	4	15	5	11
Attributable Mortality (thousands)																			
East Asia and Pacific	NA	NA	NA	NA	4	2	4	3	2	2	2	1	0	0	0	0	13	8	21
Europe and Central Asia	NA	NA	NA	NA	9	1	12	1	9	1	4	0	1	0	0	0	34	3	38
Latin America and the Caribbean	NA	NA	NA	NA	2	0	2	0	1	0	0	0	0	0	0	0	5	1	6
Middle East and North Africa	NA	NA	NA	NA	0	0	0	0	0	0	0	0	0	0	0	0	0	0	0
South Asia	NA	NA	NA	NA	4	1	3	1	1	0	0	0	0	0	0	0	9	2	12
Sub-Saharan Africa	NA	NA	NA	NA	2	0	1	0	1	0	0	0	0	0	0	0	4	0	4
Low- and middle-income countries	NA	NA	NA	NA	21	5	22	4	14	3	6	2	2	1	1	0	66	15	81
High-income countries	NA	NA	NA	NA	3	0	5	1	3	1	2	0	1	0	0	0	13	3	16
WORLD	NA	NA	NA	NA	24	5	26	5	18	4	8	2	2	1	1	1	79	18	97
Attributable YLL (thousands)																			
East Asia and Pacific	NA	NA	NA	NA	110	59	97	68	46	36	23	14	4	5	1	1	283	182	465
Europe and Central Asia	NA	NA	NA	NA	243	20	281	20	172	15	51	8	10	3	1	1	758	66	824
Latin America and the Caribbean	NA	NA	NA	NA	61	8	41	4	18	2	6	1	1	0	0	0	128	14	142
Middle East and North Africa	NA	NA	NA	NA	2	1	1	0	1	0	0	0	0	0	0	0	4	1	5
South Asia	NA	NA	NA	NA	116	41	75	16	24	6	4	1	1	0	0	0	220	64	284
Sub-Saharan Africa	NA	NA	NA	NA	44	5	31	3	15	2	4	0	1	0	0	0	94	11	105
Low- and middle-income countries	NA	NA	NA	NA	576	133	526	111	275	61	88	23	17	9	3	2	1,486	339	1,825
High-income countries	NA	NA	NA	NA	73	13	110	20	66	16	21	6	5	2	2	1	276	58	335
WORLD	NA	NA	NA	NA	649	146	636	131	342	76	109	29	22	11	4	3	1,762	398	2,160
Attributable DALYs (thousands)																			
East Asia and Pacific	NA	NA	NA	NA	111	60	98	70	47	37	23	14	5	5	1	1	285	187	472
Europe and Central Asia	NA	NA	NA	NA	247	20	284	20	173	15	51	8	10	3	1	1	766	68	834
Latin America and the Caribbean	NA	NA	NA	NA	61	8	42	4	18	2	6	1	1	0	0	0	129	15	144
Middle East and North Africa	NA	NA	NA	NA	2	1	1	0	1	0	0	0	0	0	0	0	4	1	5
South Asia	NA	NA	NA	NA	119	44	76	16	24	6	4	1	1	0	0	0	225	68	292
Sub-Saharan Africa	NA	NA	NA	NA	45	6	31	4	15	2	4	0	1	0	0	0	95	12	107
Low- and middle-income countries	NA	NA	NA	NA	586	140	531	114	277	62	89	24	17	9	3	2	1,504	350	1,854
High-income countries	NA	NA	NA	NA	74	14	112	21	67	16	21	6	5	3	2	1	280	61	341
WORLD	NA	NA	NA	NA	660	154	643	135	344	78	110	30	22	12	4	3	1,784	411	2,195

Source: Authors' calculations.
Note: NA = not applicable.

Table 4A.77

Risk factor: Alcohol use
Disease: Violence

Region	0–4 years Male	0–4 years Female	5–14 years Male	5–14 years Female	15–29 years Male	15–29 years Female	30–44 years Male	30–44 years Female	45–59 years Male	45–59 years Female	60–69 years Male	60–69 years Female	70–79 years Male	70–79 years Female	80+ years Male	80+ years Female	Total Male	Total Female	All
PAF of Mortality (%)																			
East Asia and Pacific	7	7	7	7	18	16	19	16	19	16	19	16	18	16	18	16	18	15	18
Europe and Central Asia	26	25	24	25	59	45	60	46	60	45	60	46	59	46	58	46	59	45	56
Latin America and the Caribbean	14	14	14	14	44	28	44	29	44	28	44	28	43	28	43	29	43	27	42
Middle East and North Africa	3	3	3	4	8	10	8	9	7	7	8	4	9	6	5	8	8	8	8
South Asia	3	3	3	4	14	8	14	8	14	8	14	8	15	8	15	8	13	7	11
Sub-Saharan Africa	11	11	11	11	31	22	32	22	32	21	31	21	30	22	30	23	30	19	28
Low- and middle-income countries	9	9	10	10	33	21	34	22	35	22	34	21	29	23	22	29	32	20	30
High-income countries	15	15	15	15	28	29	29	29	29	30	29	30	29	30	30	31	28	28	28
WORLD	10	9	10	10	33	22	34	23	34	22	34	21	29	23	22	29	32	21	30
PAF of YLL (%)																			
East Asia and Pacific	7	7	7	7	18	16	19	16	19	16	19	16	18	16	18	16	18	15	18
Europe and Central Asia	26	25	24	25	59	45	60	46	60	45	60	46	59	46	58	46	59	45	55
Latin America and the Caribbean	14	14	14	14	44	28	44	29	44	28	44	28	43	28	43	29	43	27	42
Middle East and North Africa	3	3	3	4	8	10	8	9	7	7	8	4	9	6	5	8	8	8	8
South Asia	3	3	3	4	14	8	14	8	14	8	14	8	15	8	15	8	13	7	11
Sub-Saharan Africa	11	11	11	11	31	22	32	22	32	21	31	21	30	22	30	23	30	19	27
Low- and middle-income countries	9	9	10	10	33	21	34	22	35	22	34	21	29	22	22	28	32	20	30
High-income countries	15	15	15	15	28	29	29	29	29	30	29	30	29	30	30	31	28	27	27
WORLD	10	9	10	10	33	22	34	23	35	22	34	21	29	23	22	29	32	20	30
PAF of DALYs (%)																			
East Asia and Pacific	7	7	5	5	16	13	17	14	18	15	18	16	17	16	17	14	16	13	15
Europe and Central Asia	24	24	16	18	46	35	51	38	56	42	57	44	55	43	49	41	50	38	47
Latin America and the Caribbean	12	13	8	10	35	21	35	23	39	25	40	26	38	25	35	24	34	21	33
Middle East and North Africa	3	3	2	3	5	7	6	7	6	6	7	4	8	6	5	7	5	6	6
South Asia	3	3	2	3	12	7	12	7	13	8	13	8	14	8	15	7	11	6	9
Sub-Saharan Africa	9	11	7	10	26	18	28	20	29	20	29	20	26	21	23	22	24	17	23
Low- and middle-income countries	8	8	6	8	27	18	29	20	32	21	32	21	27	22	21	25	27	17	25
High-income countries	15	15	11	12	24	25	25	26	26	28	27	29	26	28	25	26	24	24	24
WORLD	9	9	6	8	27	18	29	20	32	21	32	21	27	22	21	25	27	18	25
Attributable Mortality (thousands)																			
East Asia and Pacific	0	0	0	0	5	1	6	1	3	1	1	0	0	0	0	0	15	3	18
Europe and Central Asia	0	0	0	0	7	1	11	2	8	2	2	1	1	1	0	0	30	8	38
Latin America and the Caribbean	0	0	0	0	28	1	15	1	6	0	2	0	1	0	0	0	52	3	55
Middle East and North Africa	0	0	0	0	0	0	0	0	0	0	0	0	0	0	0	0	1	0	1
South Asia	0	0	0	0	2	0	2	0	1	0	0	0	0	0	0	0	7	2	9
Sub-Saharan Africa	0	0	0	1	17	2	10	2	4	1	1	0	0	0	0	0	33	6	39
Low- and middle-income countries	1	0	1	1	59	6	44	6	23	4	6	2	3	1	1	1	138	22	160
High-income countries	0	0	0	0	2	0	2	1	1	0	0	0	0	0	0	0	5	2	7
WORLD	1	1	1	1	61	7	46	7	23	5	7	2	3	2	1	1	143	24	166
Attributable YLL (thousands)																			
East Asia and Pacific	2	1	3	2	149	20	137	24	55	13	11	4	3	2	1	0	362	67	429
Europe and Central Asia	2	2	3	2	182	40	265	54	164	42	35	15	8	9	1	2	659	166	825
Latin America and the Caribbean	2	2	6	3	760	38	368	24	118	9	21	2	6	1	1	0	1,282	79	1,361
Middle East and North Africa	0	0	0	0	8	2	4	1	2	0	1	0	0	0	0	0	14	4	19
South Asia	1	2	2	2	65	13	50	11	23	10	5	4	4	2	2	0	153	43	196
Sub-Saharan Africa	9	9	13	16	454	57	247	41	84	16	16	4	4	2	0	1	827	144	971
Low- and middle-income countries	17	15	26	25	1,617	170	1,071	156	446	90	89	29	26	15	5	3	3,298	503	3,801
High-income countries	3	2	1	1	56	13	37	15	15	7	3	2	1	1	0	0	116	42	157
WORLD	20	17	28	27	1,673	183	1,108	171	461	96	92	31	27	16	5	4	3,414	545	3,958
Attributable DALYs (thousands)																			
East Asia and Pacific	3	1	5	3	171	24	150	27	57	14	12	4	3	2	1	0	402	75	477
Europe and Central Asia	2	2	5	3	233	51	304	64	173	45	36	16	9	9	1	2	762	192	955
Latin America and the Caribbean	3	2	12	4	972	50	456	31	132	10	23	2	7	1	1	0	1,606	100	1,706
Middle East and North Africa	0	0	0	0	11	3	5	2	2	1	1	0	0	0	0	0	19	6	24
South Asia	1	2	3	3	77	15	57	13	25	10	6	4	4	2	2	0	176	49	225
Sub-Saharan Africa	11	9	23	18	551	69	282	45	91	17	17	4	5	2	1	1	980	163	1,143
Low- and middle-income countries	20	16	48	32	2,015	213	1,254	181	481	96	93	30	28	16	6	4	3,944	586	4,530
High-income countries	3	2	2	2	66	15	43	17	17	7	3	2	1	1	0	0	135	47	181
WORLD	22	18	50	33	2,081	228	1,297	198	497	103	96	32	29	17	6	4	4,079	633	4,711

Source: Authors' calculations.

Table 4A.78

Risk factor: Alcohol use
Disease: Other intentional injuries

Region	0–4 years Male	0–4 years Female	5–14 years Male	5–14 years Female	15–29 years Male	15–29 years Female	30–44 years Male	30–44 years Female	45–59 years Male	45–59 years Female	60–69 years Male	60–69 years Female	70–79 years Male	70–79 years Female	80+ years Male	80+ years Female	Total Male	Total Female	All
PAF of Mortality (%)																			
East Asia and Pacific	NA	NA	NA	NA	13	11	13	10	12	9	12	9	5	4	6	4	12	9	11
Europe and Central Asia	NA	NA	NA	NA	46	31	45	33	44	26	41	35	*	19	33	16	45	28	39
Latin America and the Caribbean	NA	NA	NA	NA	36	22	35	21	35	*	32	22	20	11	18	7	35	16	34
Middle East and North Africa	NA	NA	NA	NA	2	2	3	2	2	2	2	2	1	1	1	1	2	1	2
South Asia	NA	NA	NA	NA	10	5	10	6	10	5	10	6	5	3	5	3	8	4	7
Sub-Saharan Africa	NA	NA	NA	NA	2	2	3	4	3	2	2	5	3	*	1	1	2	2	2
Low- and middle-income countries	NA	NA	NA	NA	15	7	14	12	13	11	10	7	5	3	6	3	12	7	11
High-income countries	NA	NA	NA	NA	21	12	20	20	21	18	21	11	9	6	5	5	20	13	20
WORLD	NA	NA	NA	NA	15	7	14	12	14	11	10	7	5	3	6	3	12	7	11
PAF of YLL (%)																			
East Asia and Pacific	NA	NA	NA	NA	13	11	13	10	12	9	12	9	5	4	6	4	12	9	12
Europe and Central Asia	NA	NA	NA	NA	46	31	45	33	44	26	41	35	*	19	33	16	45	29	39
Latin America and the Caribbean	NA	NA	NA	NA	36	22	35	21	35	*	32	22	20	11	18	7	35	18	35
Middle East and North Africa	NA	NA	NA	NA	2	2	3	2	2	2	2	2	1	1	1	1	2	1	2
South Asia	NA	NA	NA	NA	10	5	10	6	10	5	10	6	5	3	5	3	8	3	7
Sub-Saharan Africa	NA	NA	NA	NA	2	2	3	4	3	2	2	5	3	*	1	1	1	1	1
Low- and middle-income countries	NA	NA	NA	NA	15	7	14	12	13	11	10	7	5	3	6	3	12	7	11
High-income countries	NA	NA	NA	NA	21	12	20	20	21	18	21	11	9	6	5	5	20	13	20
WORLD	NA	NA	NA	NA	15	7	14	12	14	11	10	7	5	3	6	3	12	7	11
PAF of DALYs (%)																			
East Asia and Pacific	NA	NA	NA	NA	12	11	12	10	11	9	12	9	4	4	4	4	11	9	11
Europe and Central Asia	NA	NA	NA	NA	38	30	41	32	42	25	40	35	14	19	14	16	39	22	33
Latin America and the Caribbean	NA	NA	NA	NA	35	22	34	21	35	10	32	22	19	11	17	7	34	18	33
Middle East and North Africa	NA	NA	NA	NA	2	2	3	2	2	2	2	2	1	1	1	1	2	1	2
South Asia	NA	NA	NA	NA	9	5	10	6	10	5	10	6	5	3	4	3	7	3	6
Sub-Saharan Africa	NA	NA	NA	NA	2	2	3	4	3	1	2	5	3	*	1	1	1	1	1
Low- and middle-income countries	NA	NA	NA	NA	14	7	13	12	13	11	10	7	4	3	5	3	11	6	10
High-income countries	NA	NA	NA	NA	19	12	19	20	20	16	20	11	8	6	3	5	19	13	19
WORLD	NA	NA	NA	NA	14	7	14	12	13	11	10	7	4	3	5	3	12	6	11
Attributable Mortality (thousands)																			
East Asia and Pacific	NA	NA	NA	NA	0	0	0	0	0	0	0	0	0	0	0	0	0	0	0
Europe and Central Asia	NA	NA	NA	NA	0	0	0	0	0	0	0	0	0	0	0	0	0	0	0
Latin America and the Caribbean	NA	NA	NA	NA	0	0	0	0	0	0	0	0	0	0	0	0	0	0	0
Middle East and North Africa	NA	NA	NA	NA	0	0	0	0	0	0	0	0	0	0	0	0	0	0	0
South Asia	NA	NA	NA	NA	0	0	0	0	0	0	0	0	0	0	0	0	0	0	0
Sub-Saharan Africa	NA	NA	NA	NA	0	0	0	0	0	0	0	0	0	0	0	0	0	0	0
Low- and middle-income countries	NA	NA	NA	NA	0	0	0	0	0	0	0	0	0	0	0	0	1	0	1
High-income countries	NA	NA	NA	NA	0	0	0	0	0	0	0	0	0	0	0	0	0	0	0
WORLD	NA	NA	NA	NA	1	0	0	0	0	0	0	0	0	0	0	0	1	0	1
Attributable YLL (thousands)																			
East Asia and Pacific	NA	NA	NA	NA	3	0	3	0	1	0	0	0	0	0	0	0	7	1	8
Europe and Central Asia	NA	NA	NA	NA	1	0	2	1	1	1	0	0	0	0	0	0	4	2	6
Latin America and the Caribbean	NA	NA	NA	NA	5	0	1	0	0	0	0	0	0	0	0	0	7	0	7
Middle East and North Africa	NA	NA	NA	NA	0	0	0	0	0	0	0	0	0	0	0	0	1	0	1
South Asia	NA	NA	NA	NA	3	0	3	0	1	0	1	0	0	0	0	0	8	1	9
Sub-Saharan Africa	NA	NA	NA	NA	0	0	0	0	0	0	0	0	0	0	0	0	0	0	0
Low- and middle-income countries	NA	NA	NA	NA	13	1	9	1	3	1	1	0	0	0	0	0	27	4	31
High-income countries	NA	NA	NA	NA	1	0	1	0	0	0	0	0	0	0	0	0	2	0	2
WORLD	NA	NA	NA	NA	14	1	10	1	4	1	1	0	0	0	0	0	29	4	33
Attributable DALYs (thousands)																			
East Asia and Pacific	NA	NA	NA	NA	3	0	3	0	1	0	0	0	0	0	0	0	7	1	8
Europe and Central Asia	NA	NA	NA	NA	1	0	2	1	1	1	0	0	0	0	0	0	5	2	6
Latin America and the Caribbean	NA	NA	NA	NA	6	0	1	0	0	0	0	0	0	0	0	0	7	0	7
Middle East and North Africa	NA	NA	NA	NA	0	0	0	0	0	0	0	0	0	0	0	0	1	0	1
South Asia	NA	NA	NA	NA	4	0	3	0	1	0	1	0	0	0	0	0	8	1	10
Sub-Saharan Africa	NA	NA	NA	NA	0	0	0	0	0	0	0	0	0	0	0	0	0	0	0
Low- and middle-income countries	NA	NA	NA	NA	14	1	10	1	3	1	1	0	0	0	0	0	29	4	33
High-income countries	NA	NA	NA	NA	1	0	1	0	0	0	0	0	0	0	0	0	2	0	2
WORLD	NA	NA	NA	NA	15	1	11	1	4	1	1	0	0	0	0	0	31	4	35

Source: Authors' calculations.

Note: NA = not applicable.

*The number of deaths (and hence YLL) directly coded to a number of diseases, especially neuropsychiatric and musculoskeletal diseases, is zero or very small. For other diseases, mortality or disease burden may be zero in some region-age-sex groups. In such cases, the population attributable fractions would be undefined or unstable and have not been calculated.

Table 4A.79

Risk factor: Alcohol use
Disease: All causes

Region	0–4 years Male	Female	5–14 years Male	Female	15–29 years Male	Female	30–44 years Male	Female	45–59 years Male	Female	60–69 years Male	Female	70–79 years Male	Female	80+ years Male	Female	Total Male	Female	All
PAF of Mortality (%)																			
East Asia and Pacific	0	0	2	1	13	4	13	3	11	3	8	1	6	1	4	0	7	1	4
Europe and Central Asia	1	1	6	3	36	15	28	12	20	10	13	5	10	3	9	2	15	4	10
Latin America and the Caribbean	1	0	5	2	31	6	25	6	17	5	11	4	7	3	5	2	12	3	8
Middle East and North Africa	1	0	1	0	5	1	5	1	3	1	2	0	1	0	1	0	2	0	1
South Asia	0	0	1	0	6	1	6	1	5	1	2	0	0	0	0	0	2	0	1
Sub-Saharan Africa	0	0	2	1	9	1	5	1	6	2	6	2	4	1	3	1	3	1	2
Low- and middle-income countries	0	0	2	1	13	2	11	2	10	3	7	2	5	1	4	1	6	1	4
High-income countries	1	1	6	2	23	9	16	5	9	4	4	0	1	−2	0	−5	3	−3	0
WORLD	0	0	2	1	14	2	12	3	10	3	7	2	4	1	2	−1	6	1	3
PAF of YLL (%)																			
East Asia and Pacific	0	0	2	1	13	4	13	3	11	3	8	1	6	1	4	0	8	1	5
Europe and Central Asia	1	1	6	3	36	15	28	12	20	10	13	5	10	3	9	2	18	6	13
Latin America and the Caribbean	1	0	5	2	31	6	25	6	17	5	11	4	7	3	5	2	14	3	10
Middle East and North Africa	1	0	1	0	5	1	5	1	3	1	2	0	1	0	1	0	2	1	1
South Asia	0	0	1	0	6	1	6	1	5	1	2	0	0	0	0	0	2	0	1
Sub-Saharan Africa	0	0	2	1	9	1	5	1	6	2	6	2	5	1	3	1	3	1	2
Low- and middle-income countries	0	0	2	1	13	2	11	2	10	3	7	2	5	1	4	1	6	1	4
High-income countries	1	1	6	2	23	9	17	5	9	4	4	0	1	−2	0	−5	6	−1	3
WORLD	0	0	2	1	14	2	12	3	10	3	7	2	4	1	2	−1	6	1	4
PAF of DALYs (%)																			
East Asia and Pacific	0	0	2	1	13	3	13	3	9	2	7	1	5	0	4	0	7	1	4
Europe and Central Asia	1	1	4	2	29	7	26	8	18	7	12	4	8	3	7	2	16	4	11
Latin America and the Caribbean	1	0	3	1	28	6	22	5	15	4	9	3	6	2	4	2	13	3	9
Middle East and North Africa	0	0	1	0	3	1	3	0	2	0	1	0	1	0	1	0	1	0	1
South Asia	0	0	1	0	5	1	6	1	4	0	1	0	0	0	0	0	2	0	1
Sub-Saharan Africa	0	0	2	1	8	1	5	1	5	2	5	2	4	1	3	1	3	1	2
Low- and middle-income countries	0	0	2	1	13	2	11	2	8	2	6	1	4	1	3	1	6	1	4
High-income countries	1	0	3	1	25	7	20	5	9	2	3	−1	1	−2	0	−4	8	0	4
WORLD	0	0	2	1	13	2	12	2	9	2	5	1	3	0	2	−1	6	1	4
Attributable Mortality (thousands)																			
East Asia and Pacific	2	1	2	1	53	8	79	14	131	20	116	13	96	8	38	5	517	70	587
Europe and Central Asia	1	1	1	0	54	7	90	13	121	25	92	23	69	27	30	20	459	115	575
Latin America and the Caribbean	2	1	1	0	55	4	52	6	49	10	31	8	23	8	15	8	228	45	273
Middle East and North Africa	1	1	0	0	4	1	4	1	4	1	3	0	2	0	1	0	19	4	22
South Asia	2	1	1	0	30	7	41	4	57	5	19	2	5	2	3	1	157	22	179
Sub-Saharan Africa	4	2	7	3	48	7	46	7	38	11	23	7	16	5	6	2	188	44	232
Low- and middle-income countries	12	6	13	5	244	33	312	44	401	72	284	54	211	50	91	36	1,568	301	1,869
High-income countries	1	0	1	0	21	3	32	5	46	10	27	1	8	−23	−5	−102	130	−106	24
WORLD	12	6	14	5	265	36	344	49	447	83	311	55	219	27	87	−66	1,698	195	1,893
Attributable YLL (thousands)																			
East Asia and Pacific	54	26	60	20	1,454	221	1,893	337	2,497	415	1,563	197	863	88	193	29	8,577	1,333	9,910
Europe and Central Asia	44	23	39	11	1,464	194	2,153	314	2,340	514	1,264	344	630	277	136	94	8,070	1,771	9,841
Latin America and the Caribbean	50	22	41	12	1,515	111	1,254	147	944	201	418	128	204	78	68	38	4,494	738	5,232
Middle East and North Africa	36	22	11	3	107	14	98	13	77	16	39	7	14	5	3	1	384	82	466
South Asia	52	42	39	14	831	189	979	96	1,071	100	256	34	42	16	12	4	3,284	495	3,779
Sub-Saharan Africa	122	47	198	85	1,304	186	1,114	181	733	221	316	109	148	56	29	13	3,963	899	4,862
Low- and middle-income countries	358	182	388	145	6,675	916	7,492	1,088	7,662	1,468	3,855	819	1,901	520	441	180	28,771	5,318	34,090
High-income countries	18	8	19	8	562	82	754	125	880	214	368	13	77	−223	−18	−416	2,660	−188	2,472
WORLD	376	190	406	153	7,237	998	8,246	1,213	8,543	1,682	4,224	832	1,978	297	423	−236	31,432	5,130	36,561
Attributable DALYs (thousands)																			
East Asia and Pacific	68	31	127	50	3,226	511	3,622	580	3,313	515	1,768	215	938	95	213	32	13,276	2,028	15,304
Europe and Central Asia	56	27	84	22	2,374	370	2,925	483	2,754	628	1,391	382	673	298	144	101	10,400	2,311	12,711
Latin America and the Caribbean	69	28	107	27	3,245	485	2,034	332	1,347	312	508	156	227	88	75	44	7,611	1,474	9,085
Middle East and North Africa	40	25	17	4	141	23	115	18	86	20	42	8	15	5	3	2	460	105	565
South Asia	70	47	86	37	1,394	268	1,609	140	1,292	116	292	38	50	17	14	5	4,807	667	5,475
Sub-Saharan Africa	158	60	283	114	1,886	280	1,430	234	870	252	351	122	161	62	32	15	5,171	1,139	6,309
Low- and middle-income countries	462	218	703	255	12,266	1,938	11,734	1,787	9,662	1,843	4,352	921	2,064	565	481	199	41,725	7,724	49,449
High-income countries	24	11	58	20	2,021	495	2,124	444	1,460	262	477	−74	121	−363	1	−499	6,286	294	6,580
WORLD	485	229	761	274	14,287	2,432	13,858	2,230	11,122	2,105	4,829	846	2,185	201	482	−300	48,011	8,018	56,029

Source: Authors' calculations.

Table 4A.80

Risk factor: Illicit drug use
Disease: HIV/AIDS

Region	0–4 years Male	0–4 years Female	5–14 years Male	5–14 years Female	15–29 years Male	15–29 years Female	30–44 years Male	30–44 years Female	45–59 years Male	45–59 years Female	60–69 years Male	60–69 years Female	70–79 years Male	70–79 years Female	80+ years Male	80+ years Female	Total Male	Total Female	All
PAF of Mortality (%)																			
East Asia and Pacific	NA	NA	NA	NA	27	26	27	27	27	27	NA	NA	NA	NA	NA	NA	25	22	24
Europe and Central Asia	NA	NA	NA	NA	74	74	74	74	74	75	NA	NA	NA	NA	NA	NA	71	66	70
Latin America and the Caribbean	NA	NA	NA	NA	9	9	10	10	11	10	NA	NA	NA	NA	NA	NA	9	8	9
Middle East and North Africa	NA	NA	NA	NA	1	0	1	0	1	1	NA	NA	NA	NA	NA	NA	1	0	1
South Asia	NA	NA	NA	NA	2	2	2	2	2	2	NA	NA	NA	NA	NA	NA	2	2	2
Sub-Saharan Africa	NA	NA	NA	NA	0	0	0	0	0	0	NA	NA	NA	NA	NA	NA	0	0	0
Low- and middle-income countries	NA	NA	NA	NA	4	1	4	1	5	2	NA	NA	NA	NA	NA	NA	3	1	2
High-income countries	NA	NA	NA	NA	38	36	35	34	32	32	NA	NA	NA	NA	NA	NA	32	31	32
WORLD	NA	NA	NA	NA	4	1	5	1	5	3	NA	NA	NA	NA	NA	NA	4	1	3
PAF of YLL (%)																			
East Asia and Pacific	NA	NA	NA	NA	27	26	27	27	27	27	NA	NA	NA	NA	NA	NA	25	22	24
Europe and Central Asia	NA	NA	NA	NA	74	74	74	74	74	75	NA	NA	NA	NA	NA	NA	71	65	70
Latin America and the Caribbean	NA	NA	NA	NA	9	9	10	10	11	10	NA	NA	NA	NA	NA	NA	9	8	9
Middle East and North Africa	NA	NA	NA	NA	1	0	1	0	1	1	NA	NA	NA	NA	NA	NA	1	0	1
South Asia	NA	NA	NA	NA	2	2	2	2	2	2	NA	NA	NA	NA	NA	NA	2	2	2
Sub-Saharan Africa	NA	NA	NA	NA	0	0	0	0	0	0	NA	NA	NA	NA	NA	NA	0	0	0
Low- and middle-income countries	NA	NA	NA	NA	4	1	4	1	5	2	NA	NA	NA	NA	NA	NA	3	1	2
High-income countries	NA	NA	NA	NA	38	36	35	34	32	32	NA	NA	NA	NA	NA	NA	33	32	33
WORLD	NA	NA	NA	NA	4	1	5	1	5	3	NA	NA	NA	NA	NA	NA	4	1	2
PAF of DALYs (%)																			
East Asia and Pacific	NA	NA	NA	NA	27	26	27	27	27	27	NA	NA	NA	NA	NA	NA	26	22	25
Europe and Central Asia	NA	NA	NA	NA	74	74	74	74	74	75	NA	NA	NA	NA	NA	NA	72	68	71
Latin America and the Caribbean	NA	NA	NA	NA	9	9	10	10	11	10	NA	NA	NA	NA	NA	NA	9	8	9
Middle East and North Africa	NA	NA	NA	NA	1	0	1	0	1	1	NA	NA	NA	NA	NA	NA	1	0	1
South Asia	NA	NA	NA	NA	2	2	2	2	2	2	NA	NA	NA	NA	NA	NA	2	2	2
Sub-Saharan Africa	NA	NA	NA	NA	0	0	0	0	0	0	NA	NA	NA	NA	NA	NA	0	0	0
Low- and middle-income countries	NA	NA	NA	NA	5	1	5	1	5	3	NA	NA	NA	NA	NA	NA	4	1	3
High-income countries	NA	NA	NA	NA	38	36	35	34	32	32	NA	NA	NA	NA	NA	NA	34	32	33
WORLD	NA	NA	NA	NA	5	1	5	2	6	3	NA	NA	NA	NA	NA	NA	4	1	3
Attributable Mortality (thousands)																			
East Asia and Pacific	NA	NA	NA	NA	4	1	12	2	4	2	NA	NA	NA	NA	NA	NA	20	6	26
Europe and Central Asia	NA	NA	NA	NA	3	1	10	1	4	0	NA	NA	NA	NA	NA	NA	17	3	20
Latin America and the Caribbean	NA	NA	NA	NA	1	1	3	1	1	0	NA	NA	NA	NA	NA	NA	5	2	7
Middle East and North Africa	NA	NA	NA	NA	0	0	0	0	0	0	NA	NA	NA	NA	NA	NA	0	0	0
South Asia	NA	NA	NA	NA	1	0	3	1	1	0	NA	NA	NA	NA	NA	NA	4	1	5
Sub-Saharan Africa	NA	NA	NA	NA	0	0	0	0	0	0	NA	NA	NA	NA	NA	NA	0	0	0
Low- and middle-income countries	NA	NA	NA	NA	10	3	27	5	10	3	NA	NA	NA	NA	NA	NA	47	12	59
High-income countries	NA	NA	NA	NA	0	0	3	1	2	0	NA	NA	NA	NA	NA	NA	5	2	7
WORLD	NA	NA	NA	NA	10	4	30	6	12	4	NA	NA	NA	NA	NA	NA	52	14	65
Attributable YLL (thousands)																			
East Asia and Pacific	NA	NA	NA	NA	111	33	282	60	85	45	NA	NA	NA	NA	NA	NA	478	138	616
Europe and Central Asia	NA	NA	NA	NA	93	27	236	27	81	10	NA	NA	NA	NA	NA	NA	410	64	474
Latin America and the Caribbean	NA	NA	NA	NA	29	23	68	32	20	7	NA	NA	NA	NA	NA	NA	117	63	180
Middle East and North Africa	NA	NA	NA	NA	0	0	0	0	0	0	NA	NA	NA	NA	NA	NA	0	0	0
South Asia	NA	NA	NA	NA	25	11	62	13	18	4	NA	NA	NA	NA	NA	NA	105	28	133
Sub-Saharan Africa	NA	NA	NA	NA	0	0	0	0	0	0	NA	NA	NA	NA	NA	NA	1	1	2
Low- and middle-income countries	NA	NA	NA	NA	258	95	649	133	204	65	NA	NA	NA	NA	NA	NA	1,111	293	1,404
High-income countries	NA	NA	NA	NA	12	6	77	25	34	8	NA	NA	NA	NA	NA	NA	123	39	161
WORLD	NA	NA	NA	NA	270	101	726	158	238	73	NA	NA	NA	NA	NA	NA	1,234	332	1,566
Attributable DALYs (thousands)																			
East Asia and Pacific	NA	NA	NA	NA	180	54	327	70	90	46	NA	NA	NA	NA	NA	NA	597	170	767
Europe and Central Asia	NA	NA	NA	NA	188	67	297	44	90	12	NA	NA	NA	NA	NA	NA	574	123	697
Latin America and the Caribbean	NA	NA	NA	NA	41	28	76	34	21	8	NA	NA	NA	NA	NA	NA	137	70	207
Middle East and North Africa	NA	NA	NA	NA	0	0	0	0	0	0	NA	NA	NA	NA	NA	NA	0	0	1
South Asia	NA	NA	NA	NA	32	15	66	14	18	4	NA	NA	NA	NA	NA	NA	116	33	149
Sub-Saharan Africa	NA	NA	NA	NA	0	0	0	0	0	0	NA	NA	NA	NA	NA	NA	1	1	2
Low- and middle-income countries	NA	NA	NA	NA	440	164	766	163	219	69	NA	NA	NA	NA	NA	NA	1,425	397	1,822
High-income countries	NA	NA	NA	NA	32	12	101	30	39	9	NA	NA	NA	NA	NA	NA	171	50	221
WORLD	NA	NA	NA	NA	472	176	867	193	257	78	NA	NA	NA	NA	NA	NA	1,596	447	2,043

Source: Authors' calculations.
Note: NA = not applicable.

Table 4A.81

Risk factor: Illicit drug use
Disease: Drug use disorders

Region	0–4 years Male	Female	5–14 years Male	Female	15–29 years Male	Female	30–44 years Male	Female	45–59 years Male	Female	60–69 years Male	Female	70–79 years Male	Female	80+ years Male	Female	Total Male	Female	All
PAF of Mortality (%)																			
East Asia and Pacific	100	100	100	100	100	100	100	100	100	100	100	100	100	100	100	100	100	100	100
Europe and Central Asia	100	100	100	100	100	100	100	100	100	100	100	100	100	100	100	100	100	100	100
Latin America and the Caribbean	100	100	100	100	100	100	100	100	100	100	100	100	100	100	100	100	100	100	100
Middle East and North Africa	100	100	100	100	100	100	100	100	100	100	100	100	100	100	100	100	100	100	100
South Asia	100	100	100	100	100	100	100	100	100	100	100	100	100	100	100	100	100	100	100
Sub-Saharan Africa	100	100	100	100	100	100	100	100	100	100	100	100	100	100	100	100	100	100	100
Low- and middle-income countries	100	100	100	100	100	100	100	100	100	100	100	100	100	100	100	100	100	100	100
High-income countries	100	100	100	100	100	100	100	100	100	100	100	100	100	100	100	100	100	100	100
WORLD	100	100	100	100	100	100	100	100	100	100	100	100	100	100	100	100	100	100	100
PAF of YLL (%)																			
East Asia and Pacific	100	100	100	100	100	100	100	100	100	100	100	100	100	100	100	100	100	100	100
Europe and Central Asia	100	100	100	100	100	100	100	100	100	100	100	100	100	100	100	100	100	100	100
Latin America and the Caribbean	100	100	100	100	100	100	100	100	100	100	100	100	100	100	100	100	100	100	100
Middle East and North Africa	100	100	100	100	100	100	100	100	100	100	100	100	100	100	100	100	100	100	100
South Asia	100	100	100	100	100	100	100	100	100	100	100	100	100	100	100	100	100	100	100
Sub-Saharan Africa	100	100	100	100	100	100	100	100	100	100	100	100	100	100	100	100	100	100	100
Low- and middle-income countries	100	100	100	100	100	100	100	100	100	100	100	100	100	100	100	100	100	100	100
High-income countries	100	100	100	100	100	100	100	100	100	100	100	100	100	100	100	100	100	100	100
WORLD	100	100	100	100	100	100	100	100	100	100	100	100	100	100	100	100	100	100	100
PAF of DALYs (%)																			
East Asia and Pacific	100	100	100	100	100	100	100	100	100	100	100	100	100	100	100	100	100	100	100
Europe and Central Asia	100	100	100	100	100	100	100	100	100	100	100	100	100	100	100	100	100	100	100
Latin America and the Caribbean	100	100	100	100	100	100	100	100	100	100	100	100	100	100	100	100	100	100	100
Middle East and North Africa	100	100	100	100	100	100	100	100	100	100	100	100	100	100	100	100	100	100	100
South Asia	100	100	100	100	100	100	100	100	100	100	100	100	100	100	100	100	100	100	100
Sub-Saharan Africa	100	100	100	100	100	100	100	100	100	100	100	100	100	100	100	100	100	100	100
Low- and middle-income countries	100	100	100	100	100	100	100	100	100	100	100	100	100	100	100	100	100	100	100
High-income countries	100	100	100	100	100	100	100	100	100	100	100	100	100	100	100	100	100	100	100
WORLD	100	100	100	100	100	100	100	100	100	100	100	100	100	100	100	100	100	100	100
Attributable Mortality (thousands)																			
East Asia and Pacific	0	0	0	0	1	0	3	1	2	0	0	0	0	0	0	0	6	1	7
Europe and Central Asia	0	0	0	0	2	0	4	1	3	1	1	0	0	0	0	0	9	2	11
Latin America and the Caribbean	0	0	0	0	0	0	1	0	1	0	0	0	0	0	0	0	2	0	2
Middle East and North Africa	0	0	0	0	3	1	7	2	5	1	0	0	0	0	0	0	16	3	19
South Asia	0	0	0	0	4	1	12	2	7	2	1	0	0	0	0	0	24	5	29
Sub-Saharan Africa	0	0	0	0	1	0	1	0	1	0	0	0	0	0	0	0	3	1	4
Low- and middle-income countries	0	0	0	0	11	2	28	6	19	4	2	0	0	0	0	0	60	13	73
High-income countries	0	0	0	0	3	1	5	1	2	1	0	0	0	0	0	0	10	2	13
WORLD	0	0	0	0	13	3	33	7	21	5	2	0	0	0	0	0	70	15	85
Attributable YLL (thousands)																			
East Asia and Pacific	0	0	0	0	30	5	67	17	37	10	2	0	0	0	0	0	136	33	169
Europe and Central Asia	1	0	0	0	41	8	96	22	59	15	8	2	1	1	0	0	206	47	253
Latin America and the Caribbean	0	0	0	0	11	1	23	5	12	3	1	0	0	0	0	0	46	10	56
Middle East and North Africa	0	0	0	0	75	16	176	37	104	23	5	1	1	0	0	0	362	78	440
South Asia	0	0	0	0	118	21	276	58	146	33	7	2	1	1	0	0	550	115	665
Sub-Saharan Africa	0	0	0	0	15	3	34	8	20	5	1	0	0	0	0	0	70	16	86
Low- and middle-income countries	1	0	0	0	290	54	672	148	378	89	23	6	4	2	1	1	1,369	299	1,668
High-income countries	0	0	0	0	72	16	117	29	50	14	1	1	0	0	0	0	240	59	299
WORLD	1	0	1	0	362	70	789	177	427	102	24	7	4	2	1	1	1,609	358	1,968
Attributable DALYs (thousands)																			
East Asia and Pacific	0	0	17	9	172	38	109	27	40	10	2	0	0	0	0	0	340	85	425
Europe and Central Asia	1	0	5	5	188	59	154	42	73	20	9	3	1	1	0	0	431	129	559
Latin America and the Caribbean	0	0	7	7	370	122	152	50	28	9	1	1	0	0	0	0	559	188	746
Middle East and North Africa	0	0	6	5	278	55	241	50	117	26	6	1	1	0	0	0	649	137	786
South Asia	0	0	23	7	285	37	347	65	148	33	7	2	1	1	0	0	812	145	957
Sub-Saharan Africa	0	0	11	9	472	143	165	62	49	16	2	1	0	0	0	0	699	230	929
Low- and middle-income countries	1	0	68	42	1,764	453	1,169	295	455	114	27	8	4	2	1	1	3,489	913	4,402
High-income countries	0	0	10	6	490	151	336	103	104	35	4	2	0	0	0	0	944	297	1,242
WORLD	1	0	79	48	2,254	604	1,505	398	559	148	31	10	4	2	1	1	4,434	1,210	5,644

Source: Authors' calculations.

Table 4A.82

Risk factor: Illicit drug use
Disease: Unintentional injuries

Region	0–4 years Male	Female	5–14 years Male	Female	15–29 years Male	Female	30–44 years Male	Female	45–59 years Male	Female	60–69 years Male	Female	70–79 years Male	Female	80+ years Male	Female	Total Male	Female	All
PAF of Mortality (%)																			
East Asia and Pacific	NA	NA	NA	NA	1	0	3	1	3	0	NA	NA	NA	NA	NA	NA	2	0	1
Europe and Central Asia	NA	NA	NA	NA	0	1	1	4	1	2	NA	NA	NA	NA	NA	NA	0	1	1
Latin America and the Caribbean	NA	NA	NA	NA	1	3	3	11	3	9	NA	NA	NA	NA	NA	NA	1	3	2
Middle East and North Africa	NA	NA	NA	NA	1	1	4	3	3	2	NA	NA	NA	NA	NA	NA	1	1	1
South Asia	NA	NA	NA	NA	1	0	3	1	2	1	NA	NA	NA	NA	NA	NA	1	0	1
Sub-Saharan Africa	NA	NA	NA	NA	1	0	3	1	3	1	NA	NA	NA	NA	NA	NA	1	0	1
Low- and middle-income countries	NA	NA	NA	NA	1	0	3	2	2	1	NA	NA	NA	NA	NA	NA	1	0	1
High-income countries	NA	NA	NA	NA	2	7	7	26	7	18	NA	NA	NA	NA	NA	NA	3	5	4
WORLD	NA	NA	NA	NA	1	1	3	3	3	2	NA	NA	NA	NA	NA	NA	1	1	1
PAF of YLL (%)																			
East Asia and Pacific	NA	NA	NA	NA	1	0	3	1	3	0	NA	NA	NA	NA	NA	NA	2	0	1
Europe and Central Asia	NA	NA	NA	NA	0	1	1	4	1	2	NA	NA	NA	NA	NA	NA	0	2	1
Latin America and the Caribbean	NA	NA	NA	NA	1	3	3	11	3	9	NA	NA	NA	NA	NA	NA	1	3	2
Middle East and North Africa	NA	NA	NA	NA	1	1	4	3	3	2	NA	NA	NA	NA	NA	NA	1	1	1
South Asia	NA	NA	NA	NA	1	0	3	1	2	1	NA	NA	NA	NA	NA	NA	1	0	1
Sub-Saharan Africa	NA	NA	NA	NA	1	0	3	1	3	1	NA	NA	NA	NA	NA	NA	1	0	1
Low- and middle-income countries	NA	NA	NA	NA	1	0	3	2	2	1	NA	NA	NA	NA	NA	NA	1	1	1
High-income countries	NA	NA	NA	NA	2	7	7	26	7	18	NA	NA	NA	NA	NA	NA	4	9	5
WORLD	NA	NA	NA	NA	1	1	3	3	3	2	NA	NA	NA	NA	NA	NA	1	1	1
PAF of DALYs (%)																			
East Asia and Pacific	NA	NA	NA	NA	1	0	3	1	3	0	NA	NA	NA	NA	NA	NA	1	0	1
Europe and Central Asia	NA	NA	NA	NA	0	1	1	4	1	2	NA	NA	NA	NA	NA	NA	0	2	1
Latin America and the Caribbean	NA	NA	NA	NA	1	3	3	11	3	9	NA	NA	NA	NA	NA	NA	1	3	2
Middle East and North Africa	NA	NA	NA	NA	1	1	4	3	3	2	NA	NA	NA	NA	NA	NA	1	1	1
South Asia	NA	NA	NA	NA	1	0	3	1	2	1	NA	NA	NA	NA	NA	NA	1	0	1
Sub-Saharan Africa	NA	NA	NA	NA	1	0	3	1	3	1	NA	NA	NA	NA	NA	NA	1	0	1
Low- and middle-income countries	NA	NA	NA	NA	1	0	3	2	2	1	NA	NA	NA	NA	NA	NA	1	0	1
High-income countries	NA	NA	NA	NA	2	7	7	26	7	18	NA	NA	NA	NA	NA	NA	4	9	5
WORLD	NA	NA	NA	NA	1	1	3	3	3	3	NA	NA	NA	NA	NA	NA	1	1	1
Attributable Mortality (thousands)																			
East Asia and Pacific	NA	NA	NA	NA	1	0	5	0	3	0	NA	NA	NA	NA	NA	NA	9	1	10
Europe and Central Asia	NA	NA	NA	NA	0	0	1	1	1	1	NA	NA	NA	NA	NA	NA	1	1	3
Latin America and the Caribbean	NA	NA	NA	NA	0	0	1	1	1	1	NA	NA	NA	NA	NA	NA	2	1	4
Middle East and North Africa	NA	NA	NA	NA	0	0	1	0	1	0	NA	NA	NA	NA	NA	NA	2	0	2
South Asia	NA	NA	NA	NA	1	0	3	1	2	0	NA	NA	NA	NA	NA	NA	6	1	7
Sub-Saharan Africa	NA	NA	NA	NA	1	0	2	0	1	0	NA	NA	NA	NA	NA	NA	4	0	4
Low- and middle-income countries	NA	NA	NA	NA	4	1	12	3	9	2	NA	NA	NA	NA	NA	NA	25	5	30
High-income countries	NA	NA	NA	NA	1	1	3	3	2	2	NA	NA	NA	NA	NA	NA	6	6	12
WORLD	NA	NA	NA	NA	5	2	15	6	11	4	NA	NA	NA	NA	NA	NA	31	11	42
Attributable YLL (thousands)																			
East Asia and Pacific	NA	NA	NA	NA	41	3	113	8	65	4	NA	NA	NA	NA	NA	NA	218	15	233
Europe and Central Asia	NA	NA	NA	NA	5	5	14	17	10	11	NA	NA	NA	NA	NA	NA	29	33	62
Latin America and the Caribbean	NA	NA	NA	NA	9	6	23	18	17	10	NA	NA	NA	NA	NA	NA	49	34	83
Middle East and North Africa	NA	NA	NA	NA	10	2	22	4	13	2	NA	NA	NA	NA	NA	NA	45	8	53
South Asia	NA	NA	NA	NA	24	6	77	14	42	8	NA	NA	NA	NA	NA	NA	142	27	170
Sub-Saharan Africa	NA	NA	NA	NA	20	3	47	6	21	3	NA	NA	NA	NA	NA	NA	87	12	99
Low- and middle-income countries	NA	NA	NA	NA	109	24	295	68	167	39	NA	NA	NA	NA	NA	NA	570	130	700
High-income countries	NA	NA	NA	NA	23	21	66	73	48	46	NA	NA	NA	NA	NA	NA	137	139	276
WORLD	NA	NA	NA	NA	132	44	360	141	215	84	NA	NA	NA	NA	NA	NA	707	270	976
Attributable DALYs (thousands)																			
East Asia and Pacific	NA	NA	NA	NA	57	6	149	12	80	6	NA	NA	NA	NA	NA	NA	286	24	310
Europe and Central Asia	NA	NA	NA	NA	8	8	17	24	11	13	NA	NA	NA	NA	NA	NA	36	46	82
Latin America and the Caribbean	NA	NA	NA	NA	14	13	33	34	24	17	NA	NA	NA	NA	NA	NA	71	64	134
Middle East and North Africa	NA	NA	NA	NA	18	4	37	9	18	4	NA	NA	NA	NA	NA	NA	73	17	90
South Asia	NA	NA	NA	NA	39	9	106	23	53	11	NA	NA	NA	NA	NA	NA	198	42	240
Sub-Saharan Africa	NA	NA	NA	NA	29	5	60	9	27	5	NA	NA	NA	NA	NA	NA	117	19	135
Low- and middle-income countries	NA	NA	NA	NA	166	44	402	112	212	56	NA	NA	NA	NA	NA	NA	779	212	991
High-income countries	NA	NA	NA	NA	33	39	90	130	64	75	NA	NA	NA	NA	NA	NA	188	244	432
WORLD	NA	NA	NA	NA	199	83	492	242	276	131	NA	NA	NA	NA	NA	NA	967	456	1,423

Source: Authors' calculations.
Note: NA = not applicable.

Table 4A.83

Risk factor: Illicit drug use
Disease: Self-inflicted injuries

Region	0–4 years		5–14 years		15–29 years		30–44 years		45–59 years		60–69 years		70–79 years		80+ years		Total		
	Male	Female	Male	Female	Male	Female	Male	Female	Male	Female	Male	Female	Male	Female	Male	Female	Male	Female	All
PAF of Mortality (%)																			
East Asia and Pacific	NA	NA	NA	NA	1	0	2	0	2	0	NA	NA	NA	NA	NA	NA	1	0	1
Europe and Central Asia	NA	NA	NA	NA	3	6	7	16	5	10	NA	NA	NA	NA	NA	NA	4	7	5
Latin America and the Caribbean	NA	NA	NA	NA	1	2	5	15	5	14	NA	NA	NA	NA	NA	NA	3	7	4
Middle East and North Africa	NA	NA	NA	NA	5	1	20	7	17	7	NA	NA	NA	NA	NA	NA	10	3	7
South Asia	NA	NA	NA	NA	5	1	18	7	21	6	NA	NA	NA	NA	NA	NA	11	3	7
Sub-Saharan Africa	NA	NA	NA	NA	3	1	10	3	8	4	NA	NA	NA	NA	NA	NA	5	2	4
Low- and middle-income countries	NA	NA	NA	NA	3	1	9	3	8	3	NA	NA	NA	NA	NA	NA	5	2	4
High-income countries	NA	NA	NA	NA	3	7	7	12	4	8	NA	NA	NA	NA	NA	NA	4	6	4
WORLD	NA	NA	NA	NA	3	1	9	4	7	4	NA	NA	NA	NA	NA	NA	5	2	4
PAF of YLL (%)																			
East Asia and Pacific	NA	NA	NA	NA	1	0	2	0	2	0	NA	NA	NA	NA	NA	NA	1	0	1
Europe and Central Asia	NA	NA	NA	NA	3	6	7	16	5	10	NA	NA	NA	NA	NA	NA	5	8	5
Latin America and the Caribbean	NA	NA	NA	NA	1	2	5	15	5	14	NA	NA	NA	NA	NA	NA	3	7	4
Middle East and North Africa	NA	NA	NA	NA	5	1	20	7	17	7	NA	NA	NA	NA	NA	NA	10	2	7
South Asia	NA	NA	NA	NA	5	1	18	7	21	6	NA	NA	NA	NA	NA	NA	11	3	7
Sub-Saharan Africa	NA	NA	NA	NA	3	1	10	3	8	4	NA	NA	NA	NA	NA	NA	5	2	4
Low- and middle-income countries	NA	NA	NA	NA	3	1	9	3	8	3	NA	NA	NA	NA	NA	NA	5	2	4
High-income countries	NA	NA	NA	NA	3	7	7	12	4	8	NA	NA	NA	NA	NA	NA	4	7	5
WORLD	NA	NA	NA	NA	3	1	9	4	7	4	NA	NA	NA	NA	NA	NA	5	2	4
PAF of DALYs (%)																			
East Asia and Pacific	NA	NA	NA	NA	1	0	2	0	2	0	NA	NA	NA	NA	NA	NA	1	0	1
Europe and Central Asia	NA	NA	NA	NA	3	6	7	16	5	10	NA	NA	NA	NA	NA	NA	5	8	5
Latin America and the Caribbean	NA	NA	NA	NA	1	2	5	15	5	14	NA	NA	NA	NA	NA	NA	3	6	4
Middle East and North Africa	NA	NA	NA	NA	5	1	20	7	17	7	NA	NA	NA	NA	NA	NA	10	2	7
South Asia	NA	NA	NA	NA	5	1	18	7	21	6	NA	NA	NA	NA	NA	NA	10	3	7
Sub-Saharan Africa	NA	NA	NA	NA	3	1	10	3	8	4	NA	NA	NA	NA	NA	NA	5	2	4
Low- and middle-income countries	NA	NA	NA	NA	3	1	9	3	8	3	NA	NA	NA	NA	NA	NA	5	2	4
High-income countries	NA	NA	NA	NA	3	7	7	12	4	8	NA	NA	NA	NA	NA	NA	4	7	5
WORLD	NA	NA	NA	NA	3	1	9	4	7	4	NA	NA	NA	NA	NA	NA	5	2	4
Attributable Mortality (thousands)																			
East Asia and Pacific	NA	NA	NA	NA	0	0	1	0	1	0	NA	NA	NA	NA	NA	NA	2	0	2
Europe and Central Asia	NA	NA	NA	NA	1	0	2	1	1	0	NA	NA	NA	NA	NA	NA	4	1	6
Latin America and the Caribbean	NA	NA	NA	NA	0	0	0	0	0	0	NA	NA	NA	NA	NA	NA	1	0	1
Middle East and North Africa	NA	NA	NA	NA	0	0	0	0	0	0	NA	NA	NA	NA	NA	NA	1	0	1
South Asia	NA	NA	NA	NA	3	0	7	1	4	1	NA	NA	NA	NA	NA	NA	14	3	17
Sub-Saharan Africa	NA	NA	NA	NA	0	0	1	0	0	0	NA	NA	NA	NA	NA	NA	1	0	2
Low- and middle-income countries	NA	NA	NA	NA	4	1	11	3	7	2	NA	NA	NA	NA	NA	NA	23	5	28
High-income countries	NA	NA	NA	NA	1	0	2	1	1	1	NA	NA	NA	NA	NA	NA	3	2	5
WORLD	NA	NA	NA	NA	5	1	13	3	8	2	NA	NA	NA	NA	NA	NA	26	7	33
Attributable YLL (thousands)																			
East Asia and Pacific	NA	NA	NA	NA	8	1	20	3	11	2	NA	NA	NA	NA	NA	NA	39	5	44
Europe and Central Asia	NA	NA	NA	NA	20	7	49	17	28	10	NA	NA	NA	NA	NA	NA	98	34	132
Latin America and the Caribbean	NA	NA	NA	NA	3	2	8	5	5	3	NA	NA	NA	NA	NA	NA	16	10	26
Middle East and North Africa	NA	NA	NA	NA	5	1	11	2	4	1	NA	NA	NA	NA	NA	NA	21	4	24
South Asia	NA	NA	NA	NA	71	13	167	34	84	18	NA	NA	NA	NA	NA	NA	323	66	389
Sub-Saharan Africa	NA	NA	NA	NA	8	1	16	2	9	1	NA	NA	NA	NA	NA	NA	33	4	37
Low- and middle-income countries	NA	NA	NA	NA	115	25	272	63	142	35	NA	NA	NA	NA	NA	NA	528	123	651
High-income countries	NA	NA	NA	NA	15	8	41	23	23	13	NA	NA	NA	NA	NA	NA	79	44	123
WORLD	NA	NA	NA	NA	130	34	313	86	164	48	NA	NA	NA	NA	NA	NA	607	167	774
Attributable DALYs (thousands)																			
East Asia and Pacific	NA	NA	NA	NA	8	1	21	3	11	2	NA	NA	NA	NA	NA	NA	40	5	45
Europe and Central Asia	NA	NA	NA	NA	21	8	50	18	29	10	NA	NA	NA	NA	NA	NA	100	36	136
Latin America and the Caribbean	NA	NA	NA	NA	3	2	8	6	5	3	NA	NA	NA	NA	NA	NA	16	11	27
Middle East and North Africa	NA	NA	NA	NA	5	1	11	2	4	1	NA	NA	NA	NA	NA	NA	21	4	25
South Asia	NA	NA	NA	NA	77	16	170	36	86	19	NA	NA	NA	NA	NA	NA	333	71	404
Sub-Saharan Africa	NA	NA	NA	NA	8	1	17	2	9	1	NA	NA	NA	NA	NA	NA	34	5	38
Low- and middle-income countries	NA	NA	NA	NA	122	29	277	67	144	36	NA	NA	NA	NA	NA	NA	543	132	675
High-income countries	NA	NA	NA	NA	15	9	43	25	23	14	NA	NA	NA	NA	NA	NA	81	48	130
WORLD	NA	NA	NA	NA	137	39	320	92	167	50	NA	NA	NA	NA	NA	NA	624	180	804

Source: Authors' calculations.
Note: NA = not applicable.

Table 4A.84

Risk factor: Illicit drug use
Disease: All causes

Region	0–4 years Male	0–4 years Female	5–14 years Male	5–14 years Female	15–29 years Male	15–29 years Female	30–44 years Male	30–44 years Female	45–59 years Male	45–59 years Female	60–69 years Male	60–69 years Female	70–79 years Male	70–79 years Female	80+ years Male	80+ years Female	Total Male	Total Female	Total All
PAF of Mortality (%)																			
East Asia and Pacific	0	0	0	0	2	1	3	1	1	0	0	0	0	0	0	0	1	0	0
Europe and Central Asia	0	0	0	0	4	4	5	3	1	1	0	0	0	0	0	0	1	0	1
Latin America and the Caribbean	0	0	0	0	1	2	2	2	1	1	0	0	0	0	0	0	1	0	0
Middle East and North Africa	0	0	0	0	4	2	10	3	4	1	0	0	0	0	0	0	2	0	1
South Asia	0	0	0	0	2	0	4	1	1	0	0	0	0	0	0	0	1	0	0
Sub-Saharan Africa	0	0	0	0	0	0	0	0	0	0	0	0	0	0	0	0	0	0	0
Low- and middle-income countries	0	0	0	0	2	0	3	1	1	0	0	0	0	0	0	0	1	0	0
High-income countries	0	0	0	0	5	5	7	6	2	1	0	0	0	0	0	0	1	0	0
WORLD	0	0	0	0	2	1	3	1	1	1	0	0	0	0	0	0	1	0	0
PAF of YLL (%)																			
East Asia and Pacific	0	0	0	0	2	1	3	1	1	0	0	0	0	0	0	0	1	0	1
Europe and Central Asia	0	0	0	0	4	4	5	3	2	1	0	0	0	0	0	0	2	1	1
Latin America and the Caribbean	0	0	0	0	1	2	2	2	1	1	0	0	0	0	0	0	1	1	1
Middle East and North Africa	0	0	0	0	4	2	10	3	4	1	0	0	0	0	0	0	2	1	1
South Asia	0	0	0	0	2	0	4	1	1	0	0	0	0	0	0	0	1	0	0
Sub-Saharan Africa	0	0	0	0	0	0	0	0	0	0	0	0	0	0	0	0	0	0	0
Low- and middle-income countries	0	0	0	0	2	0	3	1	1	0	0	0	0	0	0	0	1	0	0
High-income countries	0	0	0	0	5	5	7	6	2	1	0	0	0	0	0	0	1	1	1
WORLD	0	0	0	0	2	1	3	1	1	1	0	0	0	0	0	0	1	0	1
PAF of DALYs (%)																			
East Asia and Pacific	0	0	0	0	2	0	2	1	1	0	0	0	0	0	0	0	1	0	0
Europe and Central Asia	0	0	0	0	5	3	5	2	1	1	0	0	0	0	0	0	2	1	1
Latin America and the Caribbean	0	0	0	0	4	2	3	2	1	0	0	0	0	0	0	0	1	1	1
Middle East and North Africa	0	0	0	0	6	1	7	2	3	1	0	0	0	0	0	0	2	1	1
South Asia	0	0	0	0	2	0	3	1	1	0	0	0	0	0	0	0	1	0	0
Sub-Saharan Africa	0	0	0	0	2	1	1	0	1	0	0	0	0	0	0	0	0	0	0
Low- and middle-income countries	0	0	0	0	3	1	2	1	1	0	0	0	0	0	0	0	1	0	1
High-income countries	0	0	1	0	7	3	5	4	1	1	0	0	0	0	0	0	2	1	1
WORLD	0	0	0	0	3	1	3	1	1	0	0	0	0	0	0	0	1	0	1
Attributable Mortality (thousands)																			
East Asia and Pacific	0	0	0	0	7	2	20	4	10	3	0	0	0	0	0	0	37	8	45
Europe and Central Asia	0	0	0	0	6	2	16	3	9	2	1	0	0	0	0	0	32	7	39
Latin America and the Caribbean	0	0	0	0	2	1	5	2	3	1	0	0	0	0	0	0	10	5	14
Middle East and North Africa	0	0	0	0	3	1	9	2	6	1	0	0	0	0	0	0	19	4	22
South Asia	0	0	0	0	9	2	24	5	15	3	1	0	0	0	0	0	48	10	58
Sub-Saharan Africa	0	0	0	0	2	0	4	1	3	0	0	0	0	0	0	0	8	1	10
Low- and middle-income countries	0	0	0	0	28	7	78	17	45	11	2	0	0	0	0	0	154	35	189
High-income countries	0	0	0	0	4	2	13	6	8	4	0	0	0	0	0	0	25	12	37
WORLD	0	0	0	0	33	9	91	23	53	15	2	0	0	0	0	0	179	47	226
Attributable YLL (thousands)																			
East Asia and Pacific	0	0	0	0	190	42	482	88	197	60	2	0	0	0	0	0	871	191	1,061
Europe and Central Asia	1	0	0	0	159	46	395	83	179	45	8	2	1	1	0	0	743	178	921
Latin America and the Caribbean	0	0	0	0	52	33	122	61	53	23	1	0	0	0	0	0	227	117	345
Middle East and North Africa	0	0	0	0	90	19	210	44	121	26	5	1	1	0	0	0	428	90	517
South Asia	0	0	0	0	238	51	582	120	290	63	7	2	1	1	0	0	1,120	236	1,356
Sub-Saharan Africa	0	0	0	0	43	7	98	16	49	10	1	0	0	0	0	0	191	33	223
Low- and middle-income countries	1	0	0	0	772	198	1,888	411	890	227	23	6	4	2	1	1	3,579	845	4,424
High-income countries	0	0	0	0	121	51	301	150	155	80	1	1	0	0	0	0	578	282	860
WORLD	1	0	1	0	893	248	2,189	561	1,044	308	24	7	4	2	1	1	4,157	1,127	5,284
Attributable DALYs (thousands)																			
East Asia and Pacific	0	0	17	9	417	98	606	112	220	64	2	0	0	0	0	0	1,262	284	1,547
Europe and Central Asia	1	0	5	5	404	141	518	128	203	56	9	3	1	1	0	0	1,140	334	1,474
Latin America and the Caribbean	0	0	7	7	427	165	269	123	77	36	1	1	0	0	0	0	782	332	1,114
Middle East and North Africa	0	0	6	5	302	60	290	61	139	30	6	1	1	0	0	0	743	158	901
South Asia	0	0	23	7	432	77	689	139	305	66	7	2	1	1	0	0	1,458	292	1,750
Sub-Saharan Africa	0	0	11	9	509	149	242	73	86	22	2	1	0	0	0	0	851	254	1,104
Low- and middle-income countries	1	0	68	42	2,492	690	2,614	636	1,030	275	27	8	4	2	1	1	6,237	1,653	7,890
High-income countries	0	0	10	6	571	211	570	287	230	132	4	2	0	0	0	0	1,385	640	2,024
WORLD	1	0	79	48	3,062	901	3,184	924	1,260	407	31	10	4	2	1	1	7,621	2,293	9,914

Source: Authors' calculations.

Table 4A.85

Risk factor: Unsafe water, sanitation, and hygiene
Disease: Diarrheal diseases

Region	0–4 years Male	Female	5–14 years Male	Female	15–29 years Male	Female	30–44 years Male	Female	45–59 years Male	Female	60–69 years Male	Female	70–79 years Male	Female	80+ years Male	Female	Total Male	Female	All
PAF of Mortality (%)																			
East Asia and Pacific	88	88	88	88	88	88	88	88	88	88	88	88	88	88	88	88	88	88	88
Europe and Central Asia	86	86	86	86	86	86	86	86	86	86	86	86	86	86	86	85	86	86	86
Latin America and the Caribbean	87	87	87	87	87	87	87	87	87	87	87	87	87	87	86	87	87	87	87
Middle East and North Africa	87	87	87	87	87	87	87	87	87	87	87	87	87	87	87	87	87	87	87
South Asia	88	88	88	88	88	88	88	88	88	88	88	88	88	88	88	88	88	88	88
Sub-Saharan Africa	88	88	88	88	88	88	88	88	88	88	88	88	88	88	88	88	88	88	88
Low- and middle-income countries	88	88	88	88	88	88	88	88	88	88	88	88	88	88	88	88	88	88	88
High-income countries	66	65	66	65	66	66	66	65	64	64	64	64	62	63	61	62	63	62	62
WORLD	88	88	88	88	88	88	88	88	88	88	88	88	87	87	87	86	88	88	88
PAF of YLL (%)																			
East Asia and Pacific	88	88	88	88	88	88	88	88	88	88	88	88	88	88	88	88	88	88	88
Europe and Central Asia	86	86	86	86	86	86	86	86	86	86	86	86	86	86	86	85	86	86	86
Latin America and the Caribbean	87	87	87	87	87	87	87	87	87	87	87	87	87	87	86	87	87	87	87
Middle East and North Africa	87	87	87	87	87	87	87	87	87	87	87	87	87	87	87	87	87	87	87
South Asia	88	88	88	88	88	88	88	88	88	88	88	88	88	88	88	88	88	88	88
Sub-Saharan Africa	88	88	88	88	88	88	88	88	88	88	88	88	88	88	88	88	88	88	88
Low- and middle-income countries	88	88	88	88	88	88	88	88	88	88	88	88	88	88	88	88	88	88	88
High-income countries	66	65	66	65	66	66	66	65	64	64	64	64	62	63	61	62	64	63	63
WORLD	88	88	88	88	88	88	88	88	88	88	88	88	87	87	87	86	88	88	88
PAF of DALYs (%)																			
East Asia and Pacific	88	88	88	88	88	88	88	88	88	88	88	88	88	88	88	88	88	88	88
Europe and Central Asia	86	86	86	86	86	86	86	86	86	86	86	86	86	86	86	85	86	86	86
Latin America and the Caribbean	87	87	87	87	87	87	87	87	87	87	87	87	87	87	86	87	87	87	87
Middle East and North Africa	87	87	87	87	87	87	87	87	87	87	87	87	87	87	87	87	87	87	87
South Asia	88	88	88	88	88	88	88	88	88	88	88	88	88	88	88	88	88	88	88
Sub-Saharan Africa	88	88	88	88	88	88	88	88	88	88	88	88	88	88	88	88	88	88	88
Low- and middle-income countries	88	88	88	88	88	88	88	88	88	88	88	88	88	88	88	88	88	88	88
High-income countries	66	65	66	65	66	66	66	65	64	64	64	64	62	63	61	62	65	65	65
WORLD	88	88	87	87	87	87	87	87	87	87	87	87	87	87	87	86	88	88	88
Attributable Mortality (thousands)																			
East Asia and Pacific	92	84	1	1	1	1	1	1	2	1	2	2	2	2	3	4	104	94	199
Europe and Central Asia	5	5	0	0	0	0	0	0	0	0	0	0	0	0	0	0	7	6	13
Latin America and the Caribbean	21	19	0	0	0	0	0	0	1	0	1	1	1	1	1	1	25	23	47
Middle East and North Africa	30	28	0	0	0	0	0	0	1	0	1	0	1	1	1	1	34	31	64
South Asia	289	265	1	1	2	1	4	1	5	3	5	4	6	6	8	10	319	292	611
Sub-Saharan Africa	297	270	1	1	2	1	4	2	6	4	6	5	7	7	7	10	329	299	629
Low- and middle-income countries	736	670	3	3	5	2	10	4	13	9	13	12	17	17	20	27	818	745	1,563
High-income countries	0	0	0	0	0	0	0	0	0	0	0	0	0	0	1	1	1	2	4
WORLD	736	671	3	3	5	2	10	4	14	9	13	12	17	18	21	28	819	747	1,567
Attributable YLL (thousands)																			
East Asia and Pacific	2,796	2,556	22	19	29	16	35	16	35	25	24	25	19	23	12	17	2,973	2,697	5,670
Europe and Central Asia	166	148	3	3	5	3	6	3	4	3	2	2	1	2	0	1	187	166	353
Latin America and the Caribbean	641	581	4	4	6	3	9	5	10	8	7	8	7	8	5	7	689	623	1,312
Middle East and North Africa	903	840	12	6	7	2	12	4	11	7	7	7	6	7	4	5	962	878	1,840
South Asia	8,757	8,086	24	24	44	18	87	35	88	62	62	66	55	62	38	48	9,155	8,402	17,557
Sub-Saharan Africa	8,990	8,217	25	26	47	20	93	42	104	77	74	78	61	77	34	49	9,429	8,585	18,014
Low- and middle-income countries	22,254	20,428	89	82	137	61	242	105	253	182	177	185	150	178	94	128	23,396	21,350	44,746
High-income countries	5	4	0	0	0	0	1	0	2	1	2	2	3	4	3	6	15	18	33
WORLD	22,259	20,432	89	83	137	61	243	105	255	183	180	187	153	183	97	133	23,412	21,368	44,780
Attributable DALYs (thousands)																			
East Asia and Pacific	3,237	2,967	153	140	197	175	201	174	138	122	64	64	38	46	17	25	4,046	3,713	7,758
Europe and Central Asia	238	217	11	11	13	11	13	11	9	9	5	5	3	5	1	2	292	270	561
Latin America and the Caribbean	855	787	98	94	34	31	29	26	22	20	12	13	9	11	5	8	1,063	990	2,053
Middle East and North Africa	1,051	982	41	34	20	14	19	11	15	11	8	9	7	8	4	6	1,166	1,073	2,238
South Asia	9,505	8,791	162	153	118	86	122	67	109	82	70	74	59	66	39	50	10,183	9,370	19,552
Sub-Saharan Africa	9,530	8,748	141	141	82	55	112	61	114	88	78	82	63	79	35	49	10,156	9,303	19,459
Low- and middle-income countries	24,416	22,491	606	573	464	372	496	350	407	332	237	247	179	214	101	139	26,905	24,717	51,622
High-income countries	79	74	9	8	13	12	15	14	12	12	7	7	6	8	4	8	145	144	289
WORLD	24,495	22,565	615	582	477	384	511	364	419	343	244	254	185	222	105	147	27,050	24,862	51,911

Source: Authors' calculations.

Table 4A.86

Risk factor: Unsafe water, sanitation, and hygiene
Disease: All causes

Region	0–4 years Male	Female	5–14 years Male	Female	15–29 years Male	Female	30–44 years Male	Female	45–59 years Male	Female	60–69 years Male	Female	70–79 years Male	Female	80+ years Male	Female	Total Male	Female	All
PAF of Mortality (%)																			
East Asia and Pacific	13	12	1	1	0	0	0	0	0	0	0	0	0	0	0	0	2	2	2
Europe and Central Asia	6	6	0	1	0	0	0	0	0	0	0	0	0	0	0	0	0	0	0
Latin America and the Caribbean	9	11	0	1	0	0	0	0	0	0	0	0	0	0	0	0	1	2	1
Middle East and North Africa	13	14	1	1	0	0	1	0	0	0	0	0	0	0	1	1	3	4	3
South Asia	16	14	0	0	0	0	1	0	0	0	0	0	1	1	2	2	4	5	5
Sub-Saharan Africa	13	13	0	0	0	0	0	0	1	1	1	1	2	2	4	4	6	6	6
Low- and middle-income countries	14	13	0	0	0	0	0	0	0	0	0	0	0	0	1	1	3	3	3
High-income countries	0	0	0	0	0	0	0	0	0	0	0	0	0	0	0	0	0	0	0
WORLD	14	13	0	0	0	0	0	0	0	0	0	0	0	0	0	0	1	0	3	3	3
PAF of YLL (%)																			
East Asia and Pacific	13	12	1	1	0	0	0	0	0	0	0	0	0	0	0	0	3	3	3
Europe and Central Asia	6	6	0	1	0	0	0	0	0	0	0	0	0	0	0	0	0	1	0
Latin America and the Caribbean	9	11	0	1	0	0	0	0	0	0	0	0	0	0	0	0	2	3	2
Middle East and North Africa	13	14	1	1	0	0	1	0	0	0	0	0	0	0	1	1	5	6	5
South Asia	16	15	0	0	0	0	1	0	0	0	0	0	1	1	1	2	7	6	6
Sub-Saharan Africa	13	13	0	0	0	0	0	0	1	1	1	1	2	2	4	4	7	7	7
Low- and middle-income countries	14	13	0	0	0	0	0	0	0	0	0	0	0	0	1	1	5	5	5
High-income countries	0	0	0	0	0	0	0	0	0	0	0	0	0	0	0	0	0	0	0
WORLD	14	13	0	0	0	0	0	0	0	0	0	0	0	0	0	0	1	0	4	5	5
PAF of DALYs (%)																			
East Asia and Pacific	10	9	2	2	1	1	1	1	0	0	0	0	0	0	0	0	2	2	2
Europe and Central Asia	5	5	1	1	0	0	0	0	0	0	0	0	0	0	0	0	0	1	0
Latin America and the Caribbean	7	7	3	3	0	0	0	0	0	0	0	0	0	0	0	0	2	2	2
Middle East and North Africa	9	10	2	1	0	0	0	0	0	0	0	0	0	0	1	1	3	3	3
South Asia	13	12	1	1	0	0	0	0	0	0	0	0	0	0	1	1	5	5	5
Sub-Saharan Africa	11	11	1	1	0	0	0	0	1	1	1	1	2	2	3	3	6	5	6
Low- and middle-income countries	11	11	1	1	0	0	0	0	0	0	0	0	0	0	1	1	4	4	4
High-income countries	2	2	1	1	0	0	0	0	0	0	0	0	0	0	0	0	0	0	0
WORLD	11	11	1	1	0	0	0	0	0	0	0	0	0	0	0	0	3	3	3
Attributable Mortality (thousands)																			
East Asia and Pacific	92	84	1	1	1	1	1	1	2	1	2	2	2	2	3	4	104	94	199
Europe and Central Asia	5	5	0	0	0	0	0	0	0	0	0	0	0	0	0	0	7	6	13
Latin America and the Caribbean	21	19	0	0	0	0	0	0	1	0	1	1	1	1	1	1	25	23	47
Middle East and North Africa	30	28	0	0	0	0	0	0	1	0	1	0	1	1	1	1	34	31	64
South Asia	289	265	1	1	2	1	4	1	5	3	5	4	6	6	8	10	319	292	611
Sub-Saharan Africa	297	270	1	1	2	1	4	2	6	4	6	5	7	7	7	10	329	299	629
Low- and middle-income countries	736	670	3	3	5	2	10	4	13	9	13	12	17	17	20	27	818	745	1,563
High-income countries	0	0	0	0	0	0	0	0	0	0	0	0	0	0	1	1	1	2	4
WORLD	736	671	3	3	5	2	10	4	14	9	13	12	17	18	21	28	819	747	1,567
Attributable YLL (thousands)																			
East Asia and Pacific	2,796	2,556	22	19	29	16	35	16	35	25	24	25	19	23	12	17	2,973	2,697	5,670
Europe and Central Asia	166	148	3	3	5	3	6	3	4	3	2	2	1	2	0	1	187	166	353
Latin America and the Caribbean	641	581	4	4	6	3	9	5	10	8	7	8	7	8	5	7	689	623	1,312
Middle East and North Africa	903	840	12	6	7	2	12	4	11	7	7	7	6	7	4	5	962	878	1,840
South Asia	8,757	8,086	24	24	44	18	87	35	88	62	62	66	55	62	38	48	9,155	8,402	17,557
Sub-Saharan Africa	8,990	8,217	25	26	47	20	93	42	104	77	74	78	61	77	34	49	9,429	8,585	18,014
Low- and middle-income countries	22,254	20,428	89	82	137	61	242	105	253	182	177	185	150	178	94	128	23,396	21,350	44,746
High-income countries	5	4	0	0	0	0	1	0	2	1	2	2	3	4	3	6	15	18	33
WORLD	22,259	20,432	89	83	137	61	243	105	255	183	180	187	153	183	97	133	23,412	21,368	44,780
Attributable DALYs (thousands)																			
East Asia and Pacific	3,237	2,967	153	140	197	175	201	174	138	122	64	64	38	46	17	25	4,046	3,713	7,758
Europe and Central Asia	238	217	11	11	13	11	13	11	9	9	5	5	3	5	1	2	292	270	561
Latin America and the Caribbean	855	787	98	94	34	31	29	26	22	20	12	13	9	11	5	8	1,063	990	2,053
Middle East and North Africa	1,051	982	41	34	20	14	19	11	15	11	8	9	7	8	4	6	1,166	1,073	2,238
South Asia	9,505	8,791	162	153	118	86	122	67	109	82	70	74	59	66	39	50	10,183	9,370	19,552
Sub-Saharan Africa	9,530	8,748	141	141	82	55	112	61	114	88	78	82	63	79	35	49	10,156	9,303	19,459
Low- and middle-income countries	24,416	22,491	606	573	464	372	496	350	407	332	237	247	179	214	101	139	26,905	24,717	51,622
High-income countries	79	74	9	8	13	12	15	14	12	12	7	7	6	8	4	8	145	144	289
WORLD	24,495	22,565	615	582	477	384	511	364	419	343	244	254	185	222	105	147	27,050	24,862	51,911

Source: Authors' calculations.

Table 4A.87

Risk factor: Child sexual abuse
Disease: Unipolar depressive disorders

Region	0–4 years Male	0–4 years Female	5–14 years Male	5–14 years Female	15–29 years Male	15–29 years Female	30–44 years Male	30–44 years Female	45–59 years Male	45–59 years Female	60–69 years Male	60–69 years Female	70–79 years Male	70–79 years Female	80+ years Male	80+ years Female	Total Male	Total Female	All
PAF of Mortality (%)																			
East Asia and Pacific	NA	NA	NA	NA	3	4	4	5	4	5	4	5	4	5	4	5	4	5	4
Europe and Central Asia	NA	NA	NA	NA	2	5	3	7	3	7	3	7	3	7	3	7	2	6	5
Latin America and the Caribbean	NA	NA	NA	NA	2	2	4	3	4	3	4	3	4	3	4	3	3	3	3
Middle East and North Africa	NA	NA	NA	NA	2	5	3	7	3	7	3	7	3	7	3	7	2	5	4
South Asia	NA	NA	NA	NA	*	9	6	13	6	13	6	13	*	13	*	13	6	13	10
Sub-Saharan Africa	NA	NA	NA	NA	*	6	4	*	4	*	*	*	*	*	*	*	4	6	5
Low- and middle-income countries	NA	NA	NA	NA	2	5	6	11	6	11	6	11	3	5	3	4	6	11	9
High-income countries	NA	NA	NA	NA	1	4	1	6	2	6	1	6	1	6	1	6	1	6	4
WORLD	NA	NA	NA	NA	2	5	6	11	6	11	6	11	2	6	2	6	5	10	8
PAF of YLL (%)																			
East Asia and Pacific	NA	NA	NA	NA	3	4	4	5	4	5	4	5	4	5	4	5	4	5	4
Europe and Central Asia	NA	NA	NA	NA	2	5	3	7	3	7	3	7	3	7	3	7	2	6	5
Latin America and the Caribbean	NA	NA	NA	NA	2	2	4	3	4	3	4	3	4	3	4	3	3	3	3
Middle East and North Africa	NA	NA	NA	NA	2	5	3	7	3	7	3	7	3	7	3	7	2	4	3
South Asia	NA	NA	NA	NA	*	9	6	13	6	13	6	13	*	13	*	13	6	13	10
Sub-Saharan Africa	NA	NA	NA	NA	*	6	4	*	4	*	*	*	*	*	*	*	4	6	5
Low- and middle-income countries	NA	NA	NA	NA	2	5	6	11	6	11	6	11	3	5	3	4	6	11	9
High-income countries	NA	NA	NA	NA	1	4	1	6	2	6	1	6	1	6	1	6	1	6	4
WORLD	NA	NA	NA	NA	2	5	6	11	6	11	6	11	2	6	2	6	6	11	8
PAF of DALYs (%)																			
East Asia and Pacific	NA	NA	NA	NA	3	4	4	5	4	5	4	5	4	5	4	5	3	4	4
Europe and Central Asia	NA	NA	NA	NA	2	5	3	7	3	7	3	7	3	7	3	7	2	6	4
Latin America and the Caribbean	NA	NA	NA	NA	2	2	4	3	4	3	4	3	4	3	4	3	3	2	2
Middle East and North Africa	NA	NA	NA	NA	2	5	3	7	3	7	3	7	3	7	3	7	2	5	4
South Asia	NA	NA	NA	NA	5	9	6	13	6	13	6	13	6	13	6	13	5	10	8
Sub-Saharan Africa	NA	NA	NA	NA	3	6	4	8	4	8	4	8	4	8	4	8	3	6	5
Low- and middle-income countries	NA	NA	NA	NA	3	6	4	8	4	7	4	7	4	7	4	7	3	6	5
High-income countries	NA	NA	NA	NA	1	4	1	6	2	6	1	6	1	6	1	6	1	5	4
WORLD	NA	NA	NA	NA	3	6	4	7	4	7	4	7	3	7	3	6	3	6	5
Attributable Mortality (thousands)																			
East Asia and Pacific	NA	NA	NA	NA	0	0	0	0	0	0	0	0	0	0	0	0	0	0	0
Europe and Central Asia	NA	NA	NA	NA	0	0	0	0	0	0	0	0	0	0	0	0	0	0	0
Latin America and the Caribbean	NA	NA	NA	NA	0	0	0	0	0	0	0	0	0	0	0	0	0	0	0
Middle East and North Africa	NA	NA	NA	NA	0	0	0	0	0	0	0	0	0	0	0	0	0	0	0
South Asia	NA	NA	NA	NA	0	0	0	0	0	0	0	0	0	0	0	0	0	1	1
Sub-Saharan Africa	NA	NA	NA	NA	0	0	0	0	0	0	0	0	0	0	0	0	0	0	0
Low- and middle-income countries	NA	NA	NA	NA	0	0	0	0	0	0	0	0	0	0	0	0	0	1	1
High-income countries	NA	NA	NA	NA	0	0	0	0	0	0	0	0	0	0	0	0	0	0	0
WORLD	NA	NA	NA	NA	0	0	0	0	0	0	0	0	0	0	0	0	0	1	1
Attributable YLL (thousands)																			
East Asia and Pacific	NA	NA	NA	NA	0	0	0	0	0	0	0	0	0	0	0	0	0	1	1
Europe and Central Asia	NA	NA	NA	NA	0	0	0	0	0	0	0	0	0	0	0	0	0	0	0
Latin America and the Caribbean	NA	NA	NA	NA	0	0	0	0	0	0	0	0	0	0	0	0	0	0	0
Middle East and North Africa	NA	NA	NA	NA	0	0	0	0	0	0	0	0	0	0	0	0	0	0	0
South Asia	NA	NA	NA	NA	0	0	3	3	2	6	1	2	0	0	0	0	5	11	17
Sub-Saharan Africa	NA	NA	NA	NA	0	0	0	0	0	0	0	0	0	0	0	0	0	0	0
Low- and middle-income countries	NA	NA	NA	NA	0	0	3	3	2	7	1	2	0	0	0	0	6	12	18
High-income countries	NA	NA	NA	NA	0	0	0	0	0	0	0	0	0	0	0	0	0	1	1
WORLD	NA	NA	NA	NA	0	0	3	3	2	7	1	2	0	0	0	0	6	13	19
Attributable DALYs (thousands)																			
East Asia and Pacific	NA	NA	NA	NA	50	64	61	120	43	108	12	33	2	8	0	2	169	335	504
Europe and Central Asia	NA	NA	NA	NA	9	32	11	58	8	41	3	19	1	6	0	1	32	158	190
Latin America and the Caribbean	NA	NA	NA	NA	15	23	21	31	11	17	3	5	1	1	0	0	51	77	129
Middle East and North Africa	NA	NA	NA	NA	5	19	8	27	4	14	1	4	0	1	0	0	18	65	83
South Asia	NA	NA	NA	NA	92	292	105	348	58	189	17	66	3	13	1	3	275	911	1,186
Sub-Saharan Africa	NA	NA	NA	NA	13	40	14	44	7	23	2	7	0	1	0	0	37	116	153
Low- and middle-income countries	NA	NA	NA	NA	184	470	220	629	132	392	38	133	7	31	1	7	583	1,662	2,245
High-income countries	NA	NA	NA	NA	9	63	14	95	10	71	4	24	1	10	0	5	39	267	305
WORLD	NA	NA	NA	NA	193	532	234	724	142	463	42	157	9	40	2	12	622	1,928	2,550

Source: Authors' calculations.

Note: NA = not applicable.

* The number of deaths (and hence YLL) directly coded to a number of diseases, especially neuropsychiatric and musculoskeletal diseases, is zero or very small. For other diseases, mortality or disease burden may be zero in some region-age-sex groups. In such cases, the population attributable fractions would be undefined or unstable and have not been calculated.

Table 4A.88

Risk factor: Child sexual abuse
Disease: Alcohol use disorders

Region	0–4 years Male	0–4 years Female	5–14 years Male	5–14 years Female	15–29 years Male	15–29 years Female	30–44 years Male	30–44 years Female	45–59 years Male	45–59 years Female	60–69 years Male	60–69 years Female	70–79 years Male	70–79 years Female	80+ years Male	80+ years Female	Total Male	Total Female	All
PAF of Mortality (%)																			
East Asia and Pacific	NA	NA	NA	NA	4	5	6	7	6	7	6	7	6	7	6	7	6	7	6
Europe and Central Asia	NA	NA	NA	NA	3	7	4	10	4	10	4	10	4	10	4	10	4	10	5
Latin America and the Caribbean	NA	NA	NA	NA	4	3	5	4	5	4	5	4	5	4	5	4	5	4	5
Middle East and North Africa	NA	NA	NA	NA	3	7	4	10	4	10	4	10	4	10	4	*	4	9	4
South Asia	NA	NA	NA	NA	7	13	9	17	9	17	9	17	9	17	9	17	9	17	10
Sub-Saharan Africa	NA	NA	NA	NA	5	8	7	11	7	11	7	11	7	11	7	*	7	11	8
Low- and middle-income countries	NA	NA	NA	NA	5	6	6	8	6	10	6	11	6	11	6	11	6	9	6
High-income countries	NA	NA	NA	NA	2	6	2	8	2	8	2	8	2	8	2	8	2	8	3
WORLD	NA	NA	NA	NA	5	6	5	8	5	9	5	10	5	10	5	10	5	9	6
PAF of YLL (%)																			
East Asia and Pacific	NA	NA	NA	NA	4	5	6	7	6	7	6	7	6	7	6	7	5	7	6
Europe and Central Asia	NA	NA	NA	NA	3	7	4	10	4	10	4	10	4	10	4	10	4	9	5
Latin America and the Caribbean	NA	NA	NA	NA	4	3	5	4	5	4	5	4	5	4	5	4	5	4	5
Middle East and North Africa	NA	NA	NA	NA	3	7	4	10	4	10	4	10	4	10	4	*	4	9	4
South Asia	NA	NA	NA	NA	7	13	9	17	9	17	9	17	9	17	9	17	9	17	9
Sub-Saharan Africa	NA	NA	NA	NA	5	8	7	11	7	11	7	11	7	11	7	*	7	11	8
Low- and middle-income countries	NA	NA	NA	NA	5	6	6	8	6	10	6	11	6	11	6	11	6	9	6
High-income countries	NA	NA	NA	NA	2	6	2	8	2	8	2	8	2	8	2	8	2	8	3
WORLD	NA	NA	NA	NA	5	6	5	8	5	9	5	10	5	10	5	10	5	9	6
PAF of DALYs (%)																			
East Asia and Pacific	NA	NA	NA	NA	4	5	6	7	6	7	6	7	6	7	6	7	5	6	5
Europe and Central Asia	NA	NA	NA	NA	3	7	4	10	4	10	4	10	4	10	4	10	3	9	4
Latin America and the Caribbean	NA	NA	NA	NA	4	3	5	4	5	4	5	4	5	4	5	4	4	3	4
Middle East and North Africa	NA	NA	NA	NA	3	7	4	10	4	10	4	10	4	10	4	10	4	9	4
South Asia	NA	NA	NA	NA	7	13	9	17	9	17	9	17	9	17	9	17	9	14	9
Sub-Saharan Africa	NA	NA	NA	NA	5	8	7	11	7	11	7	11	7	11	7	11	6	9	6
Low- and middle-income countries	NA	NA	NA	NA	4	5	6	7	6	8	6	9	6	10	6	10	5	6	5
High-income countries	NA	NA	NA	NA	2	6	2	8	2	8	2	8	2	8	2	8	2	7	3
WORLD	NA	NA	NA	NA	4	5	5	8	5	8	5	9	5	9	4	9	4	7	5
Attributable Mortality (thousands)																			
East Asia and Pacific	NA	NA	NA	NA	0	0	0	0	0	0	0	0	0	0	0	0	1	0	1
Europe and Central Asia	NA	NA	NA	NA	0	0	0	0	0	0	0	0	0	0	0	0	0	0	0
Latin America and the Caribbean	NA	NA	NA	NA	0	0	0	0	0	0	0	0	0	0	0	0	1	0	1
Middle East and North Africa	NA	NA	NA	NA	0	0	0	0	0	0	0	0	0	0	0	0	0	0	0
South Asia	NA	NA	NA	NA	0	0	0	0	0	0	0	0	0	0	0	0	1	0	1
Sub-Saharan Africa	NA	NA	NA	NA	0	0	0	0	0	0	0	0	0	0	0	0	0	0	1
Low- and middle-income countries	NA	NA	NA	NA	0	0	1	0	1	0	1	0	0	0	0	0	3	1	4
High-income countries	NA	NA	NA	NA	0	0	0	0	0	0	0	0	0	0	0	0	0	0	1
WORLD	NA	NA	NA	NA	0	0	1	0	1	0	1	0	0	0	0	0	4	1	5
Attributable YLL (thousands)																			
East Asia and Pacific	NA	NA	NA	NA	1	0	4	1	5	1	1	0	0	0	0	0	11	2	14
Europe and Central Asia	NA	NA	NA	NA	0	0	2	1	3	1	1	1	0	0	0	0	6	3	9
Latin America and the Caribbean	NA	NA	NA	NA	1	0	6	0	6	0	2	0	1	0	0	0	16	1	17
Middle East and North Africa	NA	NA	NA	NA	1	0	1	0	1	0	0	0	0	0	0	0	3	0	3
South Asia	NA	NA	NA	NA	4	0	8	0	6	1	3	1	1	0	0	0	21	3	24
Sub-Saharan Africa	NA	NA	NA	NA	0	0	3	1	2	1	1	0	0	1	0	0	6	4	10
Low- and middle-income countries	NA	NA	NA	NA	6	1	24	4	22	6	7	2	2	1	0	0	62	14	76
High-income countries	NA	NA	NA	NA	0	0	2	2	3	3	1	1	0	1	0	0	7	7	14
WORLD	NA	NA	NA	NA	7	1	26	5	25	9	9	4	3	2	0	0	69	21	90
Attributable DALYs (thousands)																			
East Asia and Pacific	NA	NA	NA	NA	61	11	84	13	37	5	6	0	1	0	0	0	189	31	220
Europe and Central Asia	NA	NA	NA	NA	18	8	22	10	11	6	2	1	0	0	0	0	53	25	78
Latin America and the Caribbean	NA	NA	NA	NA	48	9	32	5	20	3	4	1	1	0	0	0	105	18	123
Middle East and North Africa	NA	NA	NA	NA	1	0	1	0	1	0	0	0	0	0	0	0	3	0	3
South Asia	NA	NA	NA	NA	25	2	51	2	18	2	4	1	1	0	0	0	98	7	105
Sub-Saharan Africa	NA	NA	NA	NA	13	2	13	3	7	2	1	0	0	1	0	0	35	8	43
Low- and middle-income countries	NA	NA	NA	NA	166	32	204	34	93	18	17	4	4	1	1	0	484	89	573
High-income countries	NA	NA	NA	NA	20	21	29	26	14	12	2	2	1	1	0	0	66	63	129
WORLD	NA	NA	NA	NA	186	53	232	60	107	30	19	6	5	2	1	0	550	152	702

Source: Authors' calculations.

Note: NA = not applicable.

* The number of deaths (and hence YLL) directly coded to a number of diseases, especially neuropsychiatric and musculoskeletal diseases, is zero or very small. For other diseases, mortality or disease burden may be zero in some region-age-sex groups. In such cases, the population attributable fractions would be undefined or unstable and have not been calculated.

Table 4A.89

Risk factor: Child sexual abuse
Disease: Drug use disorders

Region	0–4 years Male	0–4 years Female	5–14 years Male	5–14 years Female	15–29 years Male	15–29 years Female	30–44 years Male	30–44 years Female	45–59 years Male	45–59 years Female	60–69 years Male	60–69 years Female	70–79 years Male	70–79 years Female	80+ years Male	80+ years Female	Total Male	Total Female	All
PAF of Mortality (%)																			
East Asia and Pacific	NA	NA	NA	NA	4	6	5	8	5	8	5	8	5	8	5	8	5	8	6
Europe and Central Asia	NA	NA	NA	NA	3	8	4	11	4	11	4	11	4	11	4	11	4	10	5
Latin America and the Caribbean	NA	NA	NA	NA	4	3	6	5	6	5	6	5	6	5	6	5	6	5	5
Middle East and North Africa	NA	NA	NA	NA	4	8	5	11	5	11	5	11	5	11	5	11	5	10	6
South Asia	NA	NA	NA	NA	8	15	11	20	11	20	11	20	10	20	10	20	10	19	12
Sub-Saharan Africa	NA	NA	NA	NA	5	9	7	12	7	12	7	12	7	12	7	12	7	12	8
Low- and middle-income countries	NA	NA	NA	NA	5	10	7	14	7	14	7	13	7	13	7	14	7	13	8
High-income countries	NA	NA	NA	NA	2	7	3	9	3	9	3	9	3	9	3	9	2	9	4
WORLD	NA	NA	NA	NA	5	10	7	13	7	13	6	13	7	13	7	13	6	13	7
PAF of YLL (%)																			
East Asia and Pacific	NA	NA	NA	NA	4	6	5	8	5	8	5	8	5	8	5	8	5	8	6
Europe and Central Asia	NA	NA	NA	NA	3	8	4	11	4	11	4	11	4	11	4	11	4	10	5
Latin America and the Caribbean	NA	NA	NA	NA	4	3	6	5	6	5	6	5	6	5	6	5	5	5	5
Middle East and North Africa	NA	NA	NA	NA	4	8	5	11	5	11	5	11	5	11	5	11	5	10	6
South Asia	NA	NA	NA	NA	8	15	11	20	11	20	11	20	10	20	10	20	10	19	12
Sub-Saharan Africa	NA	NA	NA	NA	5	9	7	12	7	12	7	12	7	12	7	12	7	12	8
Low- and middle-income countries	NA	NA	NA	NA	5	10	7	14	7	14	7	13	7	13	7	14	7	13	8
High-income countries	NA	NA	NA	NA	2	7	3	9	3	9	3	9	3	9	3	9	2	9	4
WORLD	NA	NA	NA	NA	5	10	7	13	7	13	6	13	7	13	7	13	6	12	7
PAF of DALYs (%)																			
East Asia and Pacific	NA	NA	NA	NA	4	6	5	8	5	8	5	8	5	8	5	8	4	6	5
Europe and Central Asia	NA	NA	NA	NA	3	8	4	11	4	11	4	11	4	11	4	11	4	9	5
Latin America and the Caribbean	NA	NA	NA	NA	4	3	6	5	6	5	6	5	6	5	6	5	5	4	4
Middle East and North Africa	NA	NA	NA	NA	4	8	5	11	5	11	5	11	5	11	5	11	4	9	5
South Asia	NA	NA	NA	NA	8	15	11	20	11	20	11	20	10	20	10	20	9	17	11
Sub-Saharan Africa	NA	NA	NA	NA	5	9	7	12	7	12	7	12	7	12	7	12	6	10	7
Low- and middle-income countries	NA	NA	NA	NA	5	7	7	12	7	13	7	12	7	13	7	14	6	9	6
High-income countries	NA	NA	NA	NA	2	7	3	9	3	9	3	9	3	9	3	9	2	8	3
WORLD	NA	NA	NA	NA	4	7	6	11	6	12	6	12	7	13	7	13	5	9	6
Attributable Mortality (thousands)																			
East Asia and Pacific	NA	NA	NA	NA	0	0	0	0	0	0	0	0	0	0	0	0	0	0	0
Europe and Central Asia	NA	NA	NA	NA	0	0	0	0	0	0	0	0	0	0	0	0	0	0	1
Latin America and the Caribbean	NA	NA	NA	NA	0	0	0	0	0	0	0	0	0	0	0	0	0	0	0
Middle East and North Africa	NA	NA	NA	NA	0	0	0	0	0	0	0	0	0	0	0	0	1	0	1
South Asia	NA	NA	NA	NA	0	0	1	0	1	0	0	0	0	0	0	0	2	1	3
Sub-Saharan Africa	NA	NA	NA	NA	0	0	0	0	0	0	0	0	0	0	0	0	0	0	0
Low- and middle-income countries	NA	NA	NA	NA	1	0	2	1	1	1	0	0	0	0	0	0	4	2	6
High-income countries	NA	NA	NA	NA	0	0	0	0	0	0	0	0	0	0	0	0	0	0	0
WORLD	NA	NA	NA	NA	1	0	2	1	1	1	0	0	0	0	0	0	4	2	6
Attributable YLL (thousands)																			
East Asia and Pacific	NA	NA	NA	NA	1	0	4	1	2	1	0	0	0	0	0	0	7	3	9
Europe and Central Asia	NA	NA	NA	NA	1	1	4	2	3	2	0	0	0	0	0	0	9	5	13
Latin America and the Caribbean	NA	NA	NA	NA	0	0	1	0	1	0	0	0	0	0	0	0	3	0	3
Middle East and North Africa	NA	NA	NA	NA	3	1	9	4	5	2	0	0	0	0	0	0	17	8	25
South Asia	NA	NA	NA	NA	9	3	30	12	15	7	1	0	0	0	0	0	55	22	77
Sub-Saharan Africa	NA	NA	NA	NA	1	0	2	1	1	1	0	0	0	0	0	0	5	2	7
Low- and middle-income countries	NA	NA	NA	NA	16	6	50	21	27	12	2	1	0	0	0	0	95	39	134
High-income countries	NA	NA	NA	NA	1	1	3	3	1	1	0	0	0	0	0	0	6	5	11
WORLD	NA	NA	NA	NA	17	7	53	23	29	13	2	1	0	0	0	0	100	44	145
Attributable DALYs (thousands)																			
East Asia and Pacific	NA	NA	NA	NA	7	2	6	2	2	1	0	0	0	0	0	0	15	5	20
Europe and Central Asia	NA	NA	NA	NA	6	5	7	4	3	2	0	0	0	0	0	0	17	12	28
Latin America and the Caribbean	NA	NA	NA	NA	15	4	9	2	2	0	0	0	0	0	0	0	26	7	33
Middle East and North Africa	NA	NA	NA	NA	10	4	12	5	6	3	0	0	0	0	0	0	28	13	41
South Asia	NA	NA	NA	NA	22	5	37	13	16	7	1	0	0	0	0	0	76	25	101
Sub-Saharan Africa	NA	NA	NA	NA	24	13	12	8	4	2	0	0	0	0	0	0	40	22	62
Low- and middle-income countries	NA	NA	NA	NA	85	34	83	35	32	15	2	1	0	0	0	0	201	84	286
High-income countries	NA	NA	NA	NA	9	10	9	9	3	3	0	0	0	0	0	0	20	23	43
WORLD	NA	NA	NA	NA	93	44	91	44	35	18	2	1	0	0	0	0	221	108	329

Source: Authors' calculations.
Note: NA = not applicable.

Table 4A.90

Risk factor: Child sexual abuse
Disease: Post-traumatic stress disorder

Region	0–4 years Male	Female	5–14 years Male	Female	15–29 years Male	Female	30–44 years Male	Female	45–59 years Male	Female	60–69 years Male	Female	70–79 years Male	Female	80+ years Male	Female	Total Male	Female	All
PAF of Mortality (%)																			
East Asia and Pacific	NA	NA	NA	NA	18	*	23	*	23	28	23	28	23	28	24	28	24	28	26
Europe and Central Asia	NA	NA	NA	NA	12	28	16	35	16	35	16	35	16	35	16	35	15	32	28
Latin America and the Caribbean	NA	NA	NA	NA	16	13	22	18	22	18	22	18	22	18	22	18	22	1	20
Middle East and North Africa	NA	NA	NA	NA	14	28	18	35	18	35	18	35	18	35	18	35	14	23	19
South Asia	NA	NA	NA	NA	*	*	34	*	33	52	*	52	*	*	33	*	33	52	40
Sub-Saharan Africa	NA	NA	NA	NA	*	*	*	*	*	*	*	*	*	*	*	*	*	*	*
Low- and middle-income countries	NA	NA	NA	NA	13	28	27	35	24	32	19	31	18	34	24	35	23	30	26
High-income countries	NA	NA	NA	NA	7	25	10	32	10	32	10	32	10	32	10	32	10	32	22
WORLD	NA	NA	NA	NA	9	28	27	35	19	32	16	31	10	32	24	34	18	31	25
PAF of YLL (%)																			
East Asia and Pacific	NA	NA	NA	NA	18	*	23	*	23	28	23	28	23	28	24	28	23	28	26
Europe and Central Asia	NA	NA	NA	NA	12	28	16	35	16	35	16	35	16	35	16	35	14	31	27
Latin America and the Caribbean	NA	NA	NA	NA	16	13	22	18	22	18	22	18	22	18	22	18	22	1	18
Middle East and North Africa	NA	NA	NA	NA	14	28	18	35	18	35	18	35	18	35	18	35	12	18	15
South Asia	NA	NA	NA	NA	*	*	34	*	33	52	*	52	*	*	33	*	33	52	39
Sub-Saharan Africa	NA	NA	NA	NA	*	*	*	*	*	*	*	*	*	*	*	*	*	*	*
Low- and middle-income countries	NA	NA	NA	NA	13	28	27	35	24	32	18	31	18	34	24	35	22	28	25
High-income countries	NA	NA	NA	NA	7	25	10	32	10	32	10	32	10	32	10	32	9	32	20
WORLD	NA	NA	NA	NA	9	28	27	35	18	32	16	31	10	32	24	34	18	29	24
PAF of DALYs (%)																			
East Asia and Pacific	NA	NA	NA	NA	18	22	23	28	23	28	23	28	23	28	24	28	20	25	24
Europe and Central Asia	NA	NA	NA	NA	12	28	16	35	16	35	16	35	16	35	16	35	14	31	26
Latin America and the Caribbean	NA	NA	NA	NA	16	13	22	18	22	18	22	18	22	18	22	18	18	16	16
Middle East and North Africa	NA	NA	NA	NA	14	28	18	35	18	35	18	35	18	35	18	35	15	30	26
South Asia	NA	NA	NA	NA	26	43	34	52	33	52	33	52	33	51	33	52	28	46	41
Sub-Saharan Africa	NA	NA	NA	NA	19	31	26	39	26	39	26	39	26	39	26	40	20	34	30
Low- and middle-income countries	NA	NA	NA	NA	19	30	25	35	25	36	24	33	23	34	25	33	21	32	29
High-income countries	NA	NA	NA	NA	7	25	10	32	10	32	10	32	10	32	10	32	9	29	24
WORLD	NA	NA	NA	NA	18	29	23	34	22	35	19	33	18	33	19	32	19	31	28
Attributable Mortality (thousands)																			
East Asia and Pacific	NA	NA	NA	NA	0	0	0	0	0	0	0	0	0	0	0	0	0	0	0
Europe and Central Asia	NA	NA	NA	NA	0	0	0	0	0	0	0	0	0	0	0	0	0	0	0
Latin America and the Caribbean	NA	NA	NA	NA	0	0	0	0	0	0	0	0	0	0	0	0	0	0	0
Middle East and North Africa	NA	NA	NA	NA	0	0	0	0	0	0	0	0	0	0	0	0	0	0	0
South Asia	NA	NA	NA	NA	0	0	0	0	0	0	0	0	0	0	0	0	0	0	0
Sub-Saharan Africa	NA	NA	NA	NA	0	0	0	0	0	0	0	0	0	0	0	0	0	0	0
Low- and middle-income countries	NA	NA	NA	NA	0	0	0	0	0	0	0	0	0	0	0	0	0	0	0
High-income countries	NA	NA	NA	NA	0	0	0	0	0	0	0	0	0	0	0	0	0	0	0
WORLD	NA	NA	NA	NA	0	0	0	0	0	0	0	0	0	0	0	0	0	0	0
Attributable YLL (thousands)																			
East Asia and Pacific	NA	NA	NA	NA	0	0	0	0	0	0	0	0	0	0	0	0	0	0	0
Europe and Central Asia	NA	NA	NA	NA	0	0	0	0	0	0	0	0	0	0	0	0	0	0	0
Latin America and the Caribbean	NA	NA	NA	NA	0	0	0	0	0	0	0	0	0	0	0	0	0	0	0
Middle East and North Africa	NA	NA	NA	NA	0	0	0	0	0	0	0	0	0	0	0	0	0	0	0
South Asia	NA	NA	NA	NA	0	0	0	0	0	0	0	0	0	0	0	0	0	0	0
Sub-Saharan Africa	NA	NA	NA	NA	0	0	0	0	0	0	0	0	0	0	0	0	0	0	0
Low- and middle-income countries	NA	NA	NA	NA	0	0	0	0	0	0	0	0	0	0	0	0	0	0	0
High-income countries	NA	NA	NA	NA	0	0	0	0	0	0	0	0	0	0	0	0	0	0	0
WORLD	NA	NA	NA	NA	0	0	0	0	0	0	0	0	0	0	0	0	0	0	0
Attributable DALYs (thousands)																			
East Asia and Pacific	NA	NA	NA	NA	15	53	17	58	9	21	0	1	0	1	0	0	42	134	176
Europe and Central Asia	NA	NA	NA	NA	3	19	3	16	2	6	0	1	0	1	0	0	7	43	51
Latin America and the Caribbean	NA	NA	NA	NA	5	7	4	8	2	3	0	0	0	0	0	0	10	19	29
Middle East and North Africa	NA	NA	NA	NA	3	15	2	9	1	3	0	0	0	0	0	0	5	27	33
South Asia	NA	NA	NA	NA	20	89	15	62	7	32	0	1	0	1	0	0	42	184	226
Sub-Saharan Africa	NA	NA	NA	NA	7	30	4	16	2	8	0	0	0	0	0	0	12	55	67
Low- and middle-income countries	NA	NA	NA	NA	53	214	44	170	22	73	1	4	0	2	0	1	120	463	582
High-income countries	NA	NA	NA	NA	3	27	4	27	2	22	0	1	0	1	0	0	8	79	87
WORLD	NA	NA	NA	NA	55	241	48	197	24	95	1	5	0	3	0	1	128	541	670

Source: Authors' calculations.

Note: NA = not applicable.

* The number of deaths (and hence YLL) directly coded to a number of diseases, especially neuropsychiatric and musculoskeletal diseases, is zero or very small. For other diseases, mortality or disease burden may be zero in some region-age-sex groups. In such cases, the population attributable fractions would be undefined or unstable and have not been calculated.

Table 4A.91

Risk factor:	Child sexual abuse
Disease:	Panic disorder

Region	0–4 years Male	0–4 years Female	5–14 years Male	5–14 years Female	15–29 years Male	15–29 years Female	30–44 years Male	30–44 years Female	45–59 years Male	45–59 years Female	60–69 years Male	60–69 years Female	70–79 years Male	70–79 years Female	80+ years Male	80+ years Female	Total Male	Total Female	Total All
PAF of Mortality (%)																			
East Asia and Pacific	NA	NA	NA	NA	*	*	*	*	*	*	*	*	*	*	*	*	*	*	*
Europe and Central Asia	NA	NA	NA	NA	*	*	*	*	*	*	*	*	*	*	*	*	*	*	*
Latin America and the Caribbean	NA	NA	NA	NA	*	*	*	*	*	*	*	*	*	*	*	*	*	*	*
Middle East and North Africa	NA	NA	NA	NA	*	*	*	*	*	*	*	*	*	*	*	*	*	*	*
South Asia	NA	NA	NA	NA	*	*	*	*	*	*	*	*	*	*	*	*	*	*	*
Sub-Saharan Africa	NA	NA	NA	NA	*	*	*	*	*	*	*	*	*	*	*	*	*	*	*
Low- and middle-income countries	NA	NA	NA	NA	*	*	*	*	*	*	*	*	*	*	*	*	*	*	*
High-income countries	NA	NA	NA	NA	*	*	*	*	*	*	*	*	*	*	*	*	*	*	*
WORLD	NA	NA	NA	NA	*	*	*	*	*	*	*	*	*	*	*	*	*	*	*
PAF of YLL (%)																			
East Asia and Pacific	NA	NA	NA	NA	*	*	*	*	*	*	*	*	*	*	*	*	*	*	*
Europe and Central Asia	NA	NA	NA	NA	*	*	*	*	*	*	*	*	*	*	*	*	*	*	*
Latin America and the Caribbean	NA	NA	NA	NA	*	*	*	*	*	*	*	*	*	*	*	*	*	*	*
Middle East and North Africa	NA	NA	NA	NA	*	*	*	*	*	*	*	*	*	*	*	*	*	*	*
South Asia	NA	NA	NA	NA	*	*	*	*	*	*	*	*	*	*	*	*	*	*	*
Sub-Saharan Africa	NA	NA	NA	NA	*	*	*	*	*	*	*	*	*	*	*	*	*	*	*
Low- and middle-income countries	NA	NA	NA	NA	*	*	*	*	*	*	*	*	*	*	*	*	*	*	*
High-income countries	NA	NA	NA	NA	*	*	*	*	*	*	*	*	*	*	*	*	*	*	*
WORLD	NA	NA	NA	NA	*	*	*	*	*	*	*	*	*	*	*	*	*	*	*
PAF of DALYs (%)																			
East Asia and Pacific	NA	NA	NA	NA	6	9	8	11	8	11	8	11	8	11	8	11	6	9	8
Europe and Central Asia	NA	NA	NA	NA	4	11	6	15	6	15	6	15	6	15	6	15	4	11	9
Latin America and the Caribbean	NA	NA	NA	NA	6	5	8	7	8	7	8	7	8	7	8	7	6	5	5
Middle East and North Africa	NA	NA	NA	NA	5	11	7	15	7	15	7	15	7	15	7	15	5	11	9
South Asia	NA	NA	NA	NA	10	20	14	27	14	27	14	27	14	27	13	27	10	20	16
Sub-Saharan Africa	NA	NA	NA	NA	7	13	9	18	9	18	9	18	9	18	9	18	6	13	11
Low- and middle-income countries	NA	NA	NA	NA	7	12	9	16	9	16	9	16	9	15	9	15	7	12	10
High-income countries	NA	NA	NA	NA	2	10	4	13	4	13	4	13	3	13	3	13	2	10	8
WORLD	NA	NA	NA	NA	6	12	8	15	8	15	8	15	7	15	7	14	6	12	10
Attributable Mortality (thousands)																			
East Asia and Pacific	NA	NA	NA	NA	0	0	0	0	0	0	0	0	0	0	0	0	0	0	0
Europe and Central Asia	NA	NA	NA	NA	0	0	0	0	0	0	0	0	0	0	0	0	0	0	0
Latin America and the Caribbean	NA	NA	NA	NA	0	0	0	0	0	0	0	0	0	0	0	0	0	0	0
Middle East and North Africa	NA	NA	NA	NA	0	0	0	0	0	0	0	0	0	0	0	0	0	0	0
South Asia	NA	NA	NA	NA	0	0	0	0	0	0	0	0	0	0	0	0	0	0	0
Sub-Saharan Africa	NA	NA	NA	NA	0	0	0	0	0	0	0	0	0	0	0	0	0	0	0
Low- and middle-income countries	NA	NA	NA	NA	0	0	0	0	0	0	0	0	0	0	0	0	0	0	0
High-income countries	NA	NA	NA	NA	0	0	0	0	0	0	0	0	0	0	0	0	0	0	0
WORLD	NA	NA	NA	NA	0	0	0	0	0	0	0	0	0	0	0	0	0	0	0
Attributable YLL (thousands)																			
East Asia and Pacific	NA	NA	NA	NA	0	0	0	0	0	0	0	0	0	0	0	0	0	0	0
Europe and Central Asia	NA	NA	NA	NA	0	0	0	0	0	0	0	0	0	0	0	0	0	0	0
Latin America and the Caribbean	NA	NA	NA	NA	0	0	0	0	0	0	0	0	0	0	0	0	0	0	0
Middle East and North Africa	NA	NA	NA	NA	0	0	0	0	0	0	0	0	0	0	0	0	0	0	0
South Asia	NA	NA	NA	NA	0	0	0	0	0	0	0	0	0	0	0	0	0	0	0
Sub-Saharan Africa	NA	NA	NA	NA	0	0	0	0	0	0	0	0	0	0	0	0	0	0	0
Low- and middle-income countries	NA	NA	NA	NA	0	0	0	0	0	0	0	0	0	0	0	0	0	0	0
High-income countries	NA	NA	NA	NA	0	0	0	0	0	0	0	0	0	0	0	0	0	0	0
WORLD	NA	NA	NA	NA	0	0	0	0	0	0	0	0	0	0	0	0	0	0	0
Attributable DALYs (thousands)																			
East Asia and Pacific	NA	NA	NA	NA	24	72	0	1	2	5	0	1	0	0	0	0	27	79	106
Europe and Central Asia	NA	NA	NA	NA	4	22	0	0	0	2	0	0	0	0	0	0	5	26	31
Latin America and the Caribbean	NA	NA	NA	NA	7	12	0	0	0	1	0	0	0	0	0	0	7	13	21
Middle East and North Africa	NA	NA	NA	NA	4	18	0	0	0	1	0	0	0	0	0	0	4	19	24
South Asia	NA	NA	NA	NA	35	131	1	2	2	7	0	1	0	1	0	0	37	141	178
Sub-Saharan Africa	NA	NA	NA	NA	10	42	0	1	0	2	0	0	0	0	0	0	11	45	55
Low- and middle-income countries	NA	NA	NA	NA	84	297	1	4	5	18	1	2	0	2	0	0	92	323	415
High-income countries	NA	NA	NA	NA	4	30	0	1	1	4	0	1	0	1	0	0	4	36	40
WORLD	NA	NA	NA	NA	88	327	2	5	6	22	1	3	0	2	0	0	96	359	455

Source: Authors' calculations.

Note: NA = not applicable.

* The number of deaths (and hence YLL) directly coded to a number of diseases, especially neuropsychiatric and musculoskeletal diseases, is zero or very small. For other diseases, mortality or disease burden may be zero in some region-age-sex groups. In such cases, the population attributable fractions would be undefined or unstable and have not been calculated.

Table 4A.92

Risk factor: Child sexual abuse
Disease: Self-inflicted injuries

Region	0–4 years Male	Female	5–14 years Male	Female	15–29 years Male	Female	30–44 years Male	Female	45–59 years Male	Female	60–69 years Male	Female	70–79 years Male	Female	80+ years Male	Female	Total Male	Female	All
PAF of Mortality (%)																			
East Asia and Pacific	NA	NA	NA	NA	4	6	5	7	5	7	5	7	5	7	5	8	5	7	6
Europe and Central Asia	NA	NA	NA	NA	3	7	4	10	4	10	4	10	4	10	4	10	4	9	5
Latin America and the Caribbean	NA	NA	NA	NA	4	3	5	4	5	4	5	4	5	4	5	4	5	4	4
Middle East and North Africa	NA	NA	NA	NA	3	8	4	10	4	10	4	10	4	10	4	10	4	8	6
South Asia	NA	NA	NA	NA	7	14	10	19	10	18	10	18	10	18	9	18	8	15	11
Sub-Saharan Africa	NA	NA	NA	NA	5	8	6	12	6	12	6	12	6	12	7	12	5	10	6
Low- and middle-income countries	NA	NA	NA	NA	5	10	6	11	6	11	5	9	6	9	6	10	6	10	7
High-income countries	NA	NA	NA	NA	2	6	2	9	2	9	2	9	2	9	2	9	2	8	4
WORLD	NA	NA	NA	NA	5	10	6	11	5	10	5	9	5	9	5	9	5	10	7
PAF of YLL (%)																			
East Asia and Pacific	NA	NA	NA	NA	4	6	5	7	5	7	5	7	5	7	5	8	5	7	6
Europe and Central Asia	NA	NA	NA	NA	3	7	4	10	4	10	4	10	4	10	4	10	4	9	5
Latin America and the Caribbean	NA	NA	NA	NA	4	3	5	4	5	4	5	4	5	4	5	4	5	3	4
Middle East and North Africa	NA	NA	NA	NA	3	8	4	10	4	10	4	10	4	10	4	10	4	8	5
South Asia	NA	NA	NA	NA	7	14	10	19	10	18	10	18	10	18	9	18	8	15	11
Sub-Saharan Africa	NA	NA	NA	NA	5	8	6	12	6	12	6	12	6	12	7	12	5	9	6
Low- and middle-income countries	NA	NA	NA	NA	5	10	6	11	6	10	5	9	6	9	6	10	5	10	7
High-income countries	NA	NA	NA	NA	2	6	2	9	2	9	2	9	2	9	2	9	2	8	4
WORLD	NA	NA	NA	NA	5	10	6	11	5	10	5	9	5	9	5	9	5	10	7
PAF of DALYs (%)																			
East Asia and Pacific	NA	NA	NA	NA	4	6	5	7	5	7	5	7	5	7	5	8	4	7	6
Europe and Central Asia	NA	NA	NA	NA	3	7	4	10	4	10	4	10	4	10	4	10	4	9	5
Latin America and the Caribbean	NA	NA	NA	NA	4	3	5	4	5	4	5	4	5	4	5	4	4	3	4
Middle East and North Africa	NA	NA	NA	NA	3	8	4	10	4	10	4	10	4	10	4	10	4	8	5
South Asia	NA	NA	NA	NA	7	14	10	19	10	18	10	18	10	18	9	18	8	14	11
Sub-Saharan Africa	NA	NA	NA	NA	5	8	6	12	6	12	6	12	6	12	7	12	5	9	6
Low- and middle-income countries	NA	NA	NA	NA	5	10	6	11	6	10	5	9	6	9	6	10	5	10	7
High-income countries	NA	NA	NA	NA	2	6	2	9	2	9	2	9	2	9	2	9	2	8	4
WORLD	NA	NA	NA	NA	5	10	6	11	5	10	5	9	5	9	5	9	5	10	7
Attributable Mortality (thousands)																			
East Asia and Pacific	NA	NA	NA	NA	2	2	2	3	2	3	1	1	1	1	0	1	8	11	19
Europe and Central Asia	NA	NA	NA	NA	1	0	1	0	1	0	0	0	0	0	0	0	4	2	6
Latin America and the Caribbean	NA	NA	NA	NA	0	0	0	0	0	0	0	0	0	0	0	0	1	0	1
Middle East and North Africa	NA	NA	NA	NA	0	0	0	0	0	0	0	0	0	0	0	0	0	0	1
South Asia	NA	NA	NA	NA	4	7	4	4	2	3	1	1	1	1	0	0	11	15	26
Sub-Saharan Africa	NA	NA	NA	NA	0	0	0	0	0	0	0	0	0	0	0	0	2	1	2
Low- and middle-income countries	NA	NA	NA	NA	7	10	8	8	5	6	3	2	2	2	1	1	25	29	54
High-income countries	NA	NA	NA	NA	0	0	1	1	1	1	0	0	0	0	0	0	2	3	5
WORLD	NA	NA	NA	NA	7	10	8	9	6	7	3	3	2	3	1	1	27	32	59
Attributable YLL (thousands)																			
East Asia and Pacific	NA	NA	NA	NA	41	54	49	84	34	54	17	20	8	13	2	3	150	228	377
Europe and Central Asia	NA	NA	NA	NA	18	9	28	11	22	10	6	5	2	3	0	1	77	39	115
Latin America and the Caribbean	NA	NA	NA	NA	8	2	8	2	5	1	1	0	1	0	0	0	24	5	29
Middle East and North Africa	NA	NA	NA	NA	3	7	2	3	1	1	0	0	0	0	0	0	8	12	19
South Asia	NA	NA	NA	NA	103	188	92	96	38	54	8	8	5	6	1	2	247	355	602
Sub-Saharan Africa	NA	NA	NA	NA	12	8	11	6	7	4	2	1	1	0	0	0	33	18	51
Low- and middle-income countries	NA	NA	NA	NA	185	268	191	202	106	124	35	35	16	23	3	6	538	657	1,194
High-income countries	NA	NA	NA	NA	7	8	14	16	12	15	4	6	2	3	1	1	39	49	88
WORLD	NA	NA	NA	NA	192	276	205	217	118	139	39	40	18	26	4	7	577	706	1,283
Attributable DALYs (thousands)																			
East Asia and Pacific	NA	NA	NA	NA	42	59	50	88	34	55	17	21	8	13	2	3	153	240	393
Europe and Central Asia	NA	NA	NA	NA	19	9	29	12	22	11	6	5	2	3	0	1	78	41	119
Latin America and the Caribbean	NA	NA	NA	NA	9	3	8	2	5	1	2	0	1	0	0	0	24	6	30
Middle East and North Africa	NA	NA	NA	NA	4	7	3	3	1	1	0	0	0	0	0	0	8	12	20
South Asia	NA	NA	NA	NA	111	233	94	102	39	55	8	8	5	6	1	2	258	407	664
Sub-Saharan Africa	NA	NA	NA	NA	12	9	11	6	7	4	2	1	1	0	0	0	34	20	54
Low- and middle-income countries	NA	NA	NA	NA	196	320	195	212	108	127	35	36	17	24	3	6	555	726	1,280
High-income countries	NA	NA	NA	NA	7	8	15	17	12	16	4	6	2	4	1	1	41	53	94
WORLD	NA	NA	NA	NA	203	329	209	230	120	143	39	42	19	28	4	7	595	779	1,374

Source: Authors' calculations.
Note: NA = not applicable.

Table 4A.93

Risk factor: Child sexual abuse
Disease: All causes

Region	0–4 years Male	0–4 years Female	5–14 years Male	5–14 years Female	15–29 years Male	15–29 years Female	30–44 years Male	30–44 years Female	45–59 years Male	45–59 years Female	60–69 years Male	60–69 years Female	70–79 years Male	70–79 years Female	80+ years Male	80+ years Female	Total Male	Total Female	All
PAF of Mortality (%)																			
East Asia and Pacific	NA	NA	NA	NA	0	1	0	1	0	0	0	0	0	0	0	0	0	0	0
Europe and Central Asia	NA	NA	NA	NA	0	1	0	1	0	0	0	0	0	0	0	0	0	0	0
Latin America and the Caribbean	NA	NA	NA	NA	0	0	0	0	0	0	0	0	0	0	0	0	0	0	0
Middle East and North Africa	NA	NA	NA	NA	0	1	1	1	0	0	0	0	0	0	0	0	0	0	0
South Asia	NA	NA	NA	NA	1	1	1	1	0	0	0	0	0	0	0	0	0	0	0
Sub-Saharan Africa	NA	NA	NA	NA	0	0	0	0	0	0	0	0	0	0	0	0	0	0	0
Low- and middle-income countries	NA	NA	NA	NA	0	1	0	1	0	0	0	0	0	0	0	0	0	0	0
High-income countries	NA	NA	NA	NA	0	1	0	1	0	0	0	0	0	0	0	0	0	0	0
WORLD	NA	NA	NA	NA	0	1	0	1	0	0	0	0	0	0	0	0	0	0	0
PAF of YLL (%)																			
East Asia and Pacific	NA	NA	NA	NA	0	1	0	1	0	0	0	0	0	0	0	0	0	0	0
Europe and Central Asia	NA	NA	NA	NA	0	1	0	1	0	0	0	0	0	0	0	0	0	0	0
Latin America and the Caribbean	NA	NA	NA	NA	0	0	0	0	0	0	0	0	0	0	0	0	0	0	0
Middle East and North Africa	NA	NA	NA	NA	0	1	1	1	0	0	0	0	0	0	0	0	0	0	0
South Asia	NA	NA	NA	NA	1	1	1	1	0	0	0	0	0	0	0	0	0	0	0
Sub-Saharan Africa	NA	NA	NA	NA	0	0	0	0	0	0	0	0	0	0	0	0	0	0	0
Low- and middle-income countries	NA	NA	NA	NA	0	1	0	1	0	0	0	0	0	0	0	0	0	0	0
High-income countries	NA	NA	NA	NA	0	1	0	1	0	0	0	0	0	0	0	0	0	0	0
WORLD	NA	NA	NA	NA	0	1	0	1	0	0	0	0	0	0	0	0	0	0	0
PAF of DALYs (%)																			
East Asia and Pacific	NA	NA	NA	NA	1	1	1	1	0	1	0	0	0	0	0	0	0	0	0
Europe and Central Asia	NA	NA	NA	NA	1	2	1	2	0	1	0	0	0	0	0	0	0	1	0
Latin America and the Caribbean	NA	NA	NA	NA	1	1	1	1	0	0	0	0	0	0	0	0	0	0	0
Middle East and North Africa	NA	NA	NA	NA	1	1	1	1	0	1	0	0	0	0	0	0	0	1	0
South Asia	NA	NA	NA	NA	1	2	1	2	0	1	0	0	0	0	0	0	0	1	1
Sub-Saharan Africa	NA	NA	NA	NA	0	0	0	0	0	0	0	0	0	0	0	0	0	0	0
Low- and middle-income countries	NA	NA	NA	NA	1	1	1	1	0	1	0	0	0	0	0	0	0	0	0
High-income countries	NA	NA	NA	NA	1	2	1	2	0	1	0	0	0	0	0	0	0	1	0
WORLD	NA	NA	NA	NA	1	1	1	1	0	1	0	0	0	0	0	0	0	1	0
Attributable Mortality (thousands)																			
East Asia and Pacific	NA	NA	NA	NA	2	2	2	3	2	3	1	1	1	1	0	1	9	11	20
Europe and Central Asia	NA	NA	NA	NA	1	0	1	1	1	1	1	0	0	0	0	0	4	2	7
Latin America and the Caribbean	NA	NA	NA	NA	0	0	1	0	1	0	0	0	0	0	0	0	2	0	2
Middle East and North Africa	NA	NA	NA	NA	0	0	1	0	0	0	0	0	0	0	0	0	1	1	2
South Asia	NA	NA	NA	NA	4	7	5	4	3	3	1	1	1	1	0	0	15	16	31
Sub-Saharan Africa	NA	NA	NA	NA	0	0	1	0	1	0	0	0	0	0	0	0	2	1	3
Low- and middle-income countries	NA	NA	NA	NA	8	10	11	9	8	7	3	3	2	2	1	1	33	32	65
High-income countries	NA	NA	NA	NA	0	0	1	1	1	1	0	0	0	0	0	0	3	3	6
WORLD	NA	NA	NA	NA	8	10	12	10	9	8	4	3	2	3	1	1	36	36	71
Attributable YLL (thousands)																			
East Asia and Pacific	NA	NA	NA	NA	43	55	57	86	40	56	18	21	8	13	2	3	168	234	402
Europe and Central Asia	NA	NA	NA	NA	19	9	34	14	27	13	8	6	3	3	0	1	91	47	137
Latin America and the Caribbean	NA	NA	NA	NA	10	2	16	2	11	1	3	0	1	0	0	0	42	7	49
Middle East and North Africa	NA	NA	NA	NA	7	9	13	7	7	4	1	1	0	0	0	0	27	20	48
South Asia	NA	NA	NA	NA	116	191	132	111	62	69	12	11	6	7	1	2	329	391	720
Sub-Saharan Africa	NA	NA	NA	NA	13	8	16	8	11	6	2	1	1	1	0	0	44	24	68
Low- and middle-income countries	NA	NA	NA	NA	208	274	267	229	158	149	45	40	19	24	4	6	700	722	1,423
High-income countries	NA	NA	NA	NA	8	9	19	20	17	19	5	7	2	4	1	2	52	61	114
WORLD	NA	NA	NA	NA	216	283	287	249	175	168	50	47	21	29	5	8	753	784	1,536
Attributable DALYs (thousands)																			
East Asia and Pacific	NA	NA	NA	NA	200	261	219	284	127	195	36	56	12	23	2	6	596	824	1,420
Europe and Central Asia	NA	NA	NA	NA	59	95	72	101	47	68	12	27	4	10	0	2	193	303	497
Latin America and the Caribbean	NA	NA	NA	NA	99	58	74	49	40	25	9	7	2	2	1	0	224	141	365
Middle East and North Africa	NA	NA	NA	NA	27	64	25	45	12	21	2	5	0	1	0	0	66	137	203
South Asia	NA	NA	NA	NA	305	752	302	528	138	291	30	77	9	21	2	5	786	1,675	2,461
Sub-Saharan Africa	NA	NA	NA	NA	79	136	55	77	27	41	5	9	2	3	0	0	168	266	434
Low- and middle-income countries	NA	NA	NA	NA	768	1,366	746	1,083	392	643	94	180	29	60	6	14	2,034	3,346	5,381
High-income countries	NA	NA	NA	NA	52	160	70	176	41	127	10	34	4	16	1	7	178	520	699
WORLD	NA	NA	NA	NA	819	1,526	817	1,259	433	770	104	213	33	76	7	21	2,212	3,867	6,079

Source: Authors' calculations.
Note: NA = not applicable.

Table 4A.94

Risk factor: Indoor smoke from household use of solid fuels
Disease: Lower respiratory infections

Region	0–4 years Male	Female	5–14 years Male	Female	15–29 years Male	Female	30–44 years Male	Female	45–59 years Male	Female	60–69 years Male	Female	70–79 years Male	Female	80+ years Male	Female	Total Male	Female	All
PAF of Mortality (%)																			
East Asia and Pacific	41	41	NA	NA	NA	NA	NA	NA	NA	NA	NA	NA	NA	NA	NA	NA	11	16	14
Europe and Central Asia	20	20	NA	NA	NA	NA	NA	NA	NA	NA	NA	NA	NA	NA	NA	NA	6	7	6
Latin America and the Caribbean	28	28	NA	NA	NA	NA	NA	NA	NA	NA	NA	NA	NA	NA	NA	NA	8	7	8
Middle East and North Africa	14	14	NA	NA	NA	NA	NA	NA	NA	NA	NA	NA	NA	NA	NA	NA	10	10	10
South Asia	52	52	NA	NA	NA	NA	NA	NA	NA	NA	NA	NA	NA	NA	NA	NA	30	31	30
Sub-Saharan Africa	53	53	NA	NA	NA	NA	NA	NA	NA	NA	NA	NA	NA	NA	NA	NA	39	34	37
Low- and middle-income countries	49	48	NA	NA	NA	NA	NA	NA	NA	NA	NA	NA	NA	NA	NA	NA	28	27	27
High-income countries	0	0	NA	NA	NA	NA	NA	NA	NA	NA	NA	NA	NA	NA	NA	NA	0	0	0
WORLD	49	48	NA	NA	NA	NA	NA	NA	NA	NA	NA	NA	NA	NA	NA	NA	26	24	25
PAF of YLL (%)																			
East Asia and Pacific	41	41	NA	NA	NA	NA	NA	NA	NA	NA	NA	NA	NA	NA	NA	NA	19	27	24
Europe and Central Asia	20	20	NA	NA	NA	NA	NA	NA	NA	NA	NA	NA	NA	NA	NA	NA	9	11	10
Latin America and the Caribbean	28	28	NA	NA	NA	NA	NA	NA	NA	NA	NA	NA	NA	NA	NA	NA	14	14	14
Middle East and North Africa	14	14	NA	NA	NA	NA	NA	NA	NA	NA	NA	NA	NA	NA	NA	NA	11	11	11
South Asia	52	52	NA	NA	NA	NA	NA	NA	NA	NA	NA	NA	NA	NA	NA	NA	40	40	40
Sub-Saharan Africa	53	53	NA	NA	NA	NA	NA	NA	NA	NA	NA	NA	NA	NA	NA	NA	44	37	41
Low- and middle-income countries	49	48	NA	NA	NA	NA	NA	NA	NA	NA	NA	NA	NA	NA	NA	NA	37	35	36
High-income countries	0	0	NA	NA	NA	NA	NA	NA	NA	NA	NA	NA	NA	NA	NA	NA	0	0	0
WORLD	49	48	NA	NA	NA	NA	NA	NA	NA	NA	NA	NA	NA	NA	NA	NA	36	34	35
PAF of DALYs (%)																			
East Asia and Pacific	41	41	NA	NA	NA	NA	NA	NA	NA	NA	NA	NA	NA	NA	NA	NA	20	27	24
Europe and Central Asia	20	20	NA	NA	NA	NA	NA	NA	NA	NA	NA	NA	NA	NA	NA	NA	9	11	10
Latin America and the Caribbean	28	28	NA	NA	NA	NA	NA	NA	NA	NA	NA	NA	NA	NA	NA	NA	16	16	16
Middle East and North Africa	14	14	NA	NA	NA	NA	NA	NA	NA	NA	NA	NA	NA	NA	NA	NA	12	11	11
South Asia	52	52	NA	NA	NA	NA	NA	NA	NA	NA	NA	NA	NA	NA	NA	NA	40	40	40
Sub-Saharan Africa	53	53	NA	NA	NA	NA	NA	NA	NA	NA	NA	NA	NA	NA	NA	NA	44	37	41
Low- and middle-income countries	49	48	NA	NA	NA	NA	NA	NA	NA	NA	NA	NA	NA	NA	NA	NA	36	35	36
High-income countries	0	0	NA	NA	NA	NA	NA	NA	NA	NA	NA	NA	NA	NA	NA	NA	0	0	0
WORLD	49	48	NA	NA	NA	NA	NA	NA	NA	NA	NA	NA	NA	NA	NA	NA	35	34	35
Attributable Mortality (thousands)																			
East Asia and Pacific	26	50	NA	NA	NA	NA	NA	NA	NA	NA	NA	NA	NA	NA	NA	NA	26	50	76
Europe and Central Asia	4	3	NA	NA	NA	NA	NA	NA	NA	NA	NA	NA	NA	NA	NA	NA	4	3	7
Latin America and the Caribbean	7	6	NA	NA	NA	NA	NA	NA	NA	NA	NA	NA	NA	NA	NA	NA	7	6	12
Middle East and North Africa	5	5	NA	NA	NA	NA	NA	NA	NA	NA	NA	NA	NA	NA	NA	NA	5	5	10
South Asia	213	215	NA	NA	NA	NA	NA	NA	NA	NA	NA	NA	NA	NA	NA	NA	213	215	429
Sub-Saharan Africa	230	167	NA	NA	NA	NA	NA	NA	NA	NA	NA	NA	NA	NA	NA	NA	230	167	397
Low- and middle-income countries	485	447	NA	NA	NA	NA	NA	NA	NA	NA	NA	NA	NA	NA	NA	NA	485	447	931
High-income countries	0	0	NA	NA	NA	NA	NA	NA	NA	NA	NA	NA	NA	NA	NA	NA	0	0	0
WORLD	485	447	NA	NA	NA	NA	NA	NA	NA	NA	NA	NA	NA	NA	NA	NA	485	447	931
Attributable YLL (thousands)																			
East Asia and Pacific	776	1,530	NA	NA	NA	NA	NA	NA	NA	NA	NA	NA	NA	NA	NA	NA	776	1,530	2,306
Europe and Central Asia	110	93	NA	NA	NA	NA	NA	NA	NA	NA	NA	NA	NA	NA	NA	NA	110	93	203
Latin America and the Caribbean	199	170	NA	NA	NA	NA	NA	NA	NA	NA	NA	NA	NA	NA	NA	NA	199	170	370
Middle East and North Africa	164	150	NA	NA	NA	NA	NA	NA	NA	NA	NA	NA	NA	NA	NA	NA	164	150	314
South Asia	6,454	6,566	NA	NA	NA	NA	NA	NA	NA	NA	NA	NA	NA	NA	NA	NA	6,454	6,566	13,020
Sub-Saharan Africa	6,961	5,098	NA	NA	NA	NA	NA	NA	NA	NA	NA	NA	NA	NA	NA	NA	6,961	5,098	12,059
Low- and middle-income countries	14,663	13,608	NA	NA	NA	NA	NA	NA	NA	NA	NA	NA	NA	NA	NA	NA	14,663	13,608	28,271
High-income countries	0	0	NA	NA	NA	NA	NA	NA	NA	NA	NA	NA	NA	NA	NA	NA	0	0	0
WORLD	14,663	13,608	NA	NA	NA	NA	NA	NA	NA	NA	NA	NA	NA	NA	NA	NA	14,663	13,608	28,271
Attributable DALYs (thousands)																			
East Asia and Pacific	892	1,734	NA	NA	NA	NA	NA	NA	NA	NA	NA	NA	NA	NA	NA	NA	892	1,734	2,626
Europe and Central Asia	115	99	NA	NA	NA	NA	NA	NA	NA	NA	NA	NA	NA	NA	NA	NA	115	99	214
Latin America and the Caribbean	252	222	NA	NA	NA	NA	NA	NA	NA	NA	NA	NA	NA	NA	NA	NA	252	222	475
Middle East and North Africa	178	163	NA	NA	NA	NA	NA	NA	NA	NA	NA	NA	NA	NA	NA	NA	178	163	341
South Asia	6,799	6,902	NA	NA	NA	NA	NA	NA	NA	NA	NA	NA	NA	NA	NA	NA	6,799	6,902	13,700
Sub-Saharan Africa	7,199	5,204	NA	NA	NA	NA	NA	NA	NA	NA	NA	NA	NA	NA	NA	NA	7,199	5,204	12,403
Low- and middle-income countries	15,435	14,325	NA	NA	NA	NA	NA	NA	NA	NA	NA	NA	NA	NA	NA	NA	15,435	14,325	29,761
High-income countries	0	0	NA	NA	NA	NA	NA	NA	NA	NA	NA	NA	NA	NA	NA	NA	0	0	0
WORLD	15,436	14,325	NA	NA	NA	NA	NA	NA	NA	NA	NA	NA	NA	NA	NA	NA	15,436	14,325	29,761

Source: Authors' calculations.
Note: NA = not applicable.

Table 4A.95

Risk factor: Indoor smoke from household use of solid fuels
Disease: Trachea, bronchus, and lung cancers

Region	0–4 years Male	0–4 years Female	5–14 years Male	5–14 years Female	15–29 years Male	15–29 years Female	30–44 years Male	30–44 years Female	45–59 years Male	45–59 years Female	60–69 years Male	60–69 years Female	70–79 years Male	70–79 years Female	80+ years Male	80+ years Female	Total Male	Total Female	All
PAF of Mortality (%)																			
East Asia and Pacific	NA	NA	NA	NA	NA	NA	3	5	3	5	3	5	3	5	3	5	3	5	4
Europe and Central Asia	NA	NA	NA	NA	NA	NA	0	0	0	0	0	0	0	0	0	0	0	0	0
Latin America and the Caribbean	NA	NA	NA	NA	NA	NA	0	0	0	0	0	0	0	0	0	0	0	0	0
Middle East and North Africa	NA	NA	NA	NA	NA	NA	0	0	0	0	0	0	0	0	0	0	0	0	0
South Asia	NA	NA	NA	NA	NA	NA	1	2	1	2	1	2	1	2	1	3	1	2	2
Sub-Saharan Africa	NA	NA	NA	NA	NA	NA	0	0	0	0	0	0	0	0	0	0	0	0	0
Low- and middle-income countries	NA	NA	NA	NA	NA	NA	2	3	2	3	2	3	2	4	2	3	2	3	2
High-income countries	NA	NA	NA	NA	NA	NA	0	0	0	0	0	0	0	0	0	0	0	0	0
WORLD	NA	NA	NA	NA	NA	NA	1	2	1	2	1	2	1	2	1	1	1	2	1
PAF of YLL (%)																			
East Asia and Pacific	NA	NA	NA	NA	NA	NA	3	5	3	5	3	5	3	5	3	5	3	5	4
Europe and Central Asia	NA	NA	NA	NA	NA	NA	0	0	0	0	0	0	0	0	0	0	0	0	0
Latin America and the Caribbean	NA	NA	NA	NA	NA	NA	0	0	0	0	0	0	0	0	0	0	0	0	0
Middle East and North Africa	NA	NA	NA	NA	NA	NA	0	0	0	0	0	0	0	0	0	0	0	0	0
South Asia	NA	NA	NA	NA	NA	NA	1	2	1	2	1	2	1	2	1	3	1	2	2
Sub-Saharan Africa	NA	NA	NA	NA	NA	NA	0	0	0	0	0	0	0	0	0	0	0	0	0
Low- and middle-income countries	NA	NA	NA	NA	NA	NA	2	3	2	3	2	3	2	4	2	3	2	3	2
High-income countries	NA	NA	NA	NA	NA	NA	0	0	0	0	0	0	0	0	0	0	0	0	0
WORLD	NA	NA	NA	NA	NA	NA	1	2	1	2	1	2	1	2	1	1	1	2	1
PAF of DALYs (%)																			
East Asia and Pacific	NA	NA	NA	NA	NA	NA	3	5	3	5	3	5	3	5	3	5	3	5	4
Europe and Central Asia	NA	NA	NA	NA	NA	NA	0	0	0	0	0	0	0	0	0	0	0	0	0
Latin America and the Caribbean	NA	NA	NA	NA	NA	NA	0	0	0	0	0	0	0	0	0	0	0	0	0
Middle East and North Africa	NA	NA	NA	NA	NA	NA	0	0	0	0	0	0	0	0	0	0	0	0	0
South Asia	NA	NA	NA	NA	NA	NA	1	2	1	2	1	2	1	2	1	3	1	2	2
Sub-Saharan Africa	NA	NA	NA	NA	NA	NA	0	0	0	0	0	0	0	0	0	0	0	0	0
Low- and middle-income countries	NA	NA	NA	NA	NA	NA	2	3	2	3	2	3	2	4	2	3	2	3	2
High-income countries	NA	NA	NA	NA	NA	NA	0	0	0	0	0	0	0	0	0	0	0	0	0
WORLD	NA	NA	NA	NA	NA	NA	1	2	1	2	1	2	1	2	1	1	1	2	1
Attributable Mortality (thousands)																			
East Asia and Pacific	NA	NA	NA	NA	NA	NA	0	0	2	1	3	2	2	2	1	1	8	6	14
Europe and Central Asia	NA	NA	NA	NA	NA	NA	0	0	0	0	0	0	0	0	0	0	0	0	0
Latin America and the Caribbean	NA	NA	NA	NA	NA	NA	0	0	0	0	0	0	0	0	0	0	0	0	0
Middle East and North Africa	NA	NA	NA	NA	NA	NA	0	0	0	0	0	0	0	0	0	0	0	0	0
South Asia	NA	NA	NA	NA	NA	NA	0	0	0	0	1	0	0	0	0	0	1	1	2
Sub-Saharan Africa	NA	NA	NA	NA	NA	NA	0	0	0	0	0	0	0	0	0	0	0	0	0
Low- and middle-income countries	NA	NA	NA	NA	NA	NA	0	0	2	2	3	2	3	2	1	1	9	7	16
High-income countries	NA	NA	NA	NA	NA	NA	0	0	0	0	0	0	0	0	0	0	0	0	0
WORLD	NA	NA	NA	NA	NA	NA	0	0	2	2	3	2	3	2	1	1	9	7	16
Attributable YLL (thousands)																			
East Asia and Pacific	NA	NA	NA	NA	NA	NA	8	7	32	28	37	26	21	22	3	4	100	88	187
Europe and Central Asia	NA	NA	NA	NA	NA	NA	0	0	0	0	0	0	0	0	0	0	0	0	0
Latin America and the Caribbean	NA	NA	NA	NA	NA	NA	0	0	0	0	0	0	0	0	0	0	0	0	0
Middle East and North Africa	NA	NA	NA	NA	NA	NA	0	0	0	0	0	0	0	0	0	0	0	0	0
South Asia	NA	NA	NA	NA	NA	NA	1	1	7	3	7	3	3	1	1	0	19	9	28
Sub-Saharan Africa	NA	NA	NA	NA	NA	NA	0	0	0	0	0	0	0	0	0	0	0	0	0
Low- and middle-income countries	NA	NA	NA	NA	NA	NA	9	9	39	31	44	29	24	24	3	4	119	96	215
High-income countries	NA	NA	NA	NA	NA	NA	0	0	0	0	0	0	0	0	0	0	0	0	0
WORLD	NA	NA	NA	NA	NA	NA	9	9	39	31	44	29	24	24	3	4	119	96	215
Attributable DALYs (thousands)																			
East Asia and Pacific	NA	NA	NA	NA	NA	NA	8	8	32	28	37	27	21	23	3	4	101	89	190
Europe and Central Asia	NA	NA	NA	NA	NA	NA	0	0	0	0	0	0	0	0	0	0	0	0	0
Latin America and the Caribbean	NA	NA	NA	NA	NA	NA	0	0	0	0	0	0	0	0	0	0	0	0	0
Middle East and North Africa	NA	NA	NA	NA	NA	NA	0	0	0	0	0	0	0	0	0	0	0	0	0
South Asia	NA	NA	NA	NA	NA	NA	1	1	7	3	7	3	4	1	1	0	19	9	28
Sub-Saharan Africa	NA	NA	NA	NA	NA	NA	0	0	0	0	0	0	0	0	0	0	0	0	0
Low- and middle-income countries	NA	NA	NA	NA	NA	NA	9	9	39	31	44	29	24	24	3	4	120	97	218
High-income countries	NA	NA	NA	NA	NA	NA	0	0	0	0	0	0	0	0	0	0	0	0	0
WORLD	NA	NA	NA	NA	NA	NA	9	9	39	31	44	29	24	24	3	4	120	97	218

Source: Authors' calculations.
Note: NA = not applicable.

Table 4A.96

Risk factor: Indoor smoke from household use of solid fuels
Disease: Chronic obstructive pulmonary disease

Region	0–4 years Male	0–4 Female	5–14 years Male	5–14 Female	15–29 years Male	15–29 Female	30–44 years Male	30–44 Female	45–59 years Male	45–59 Female	60–69 years Male	60–69 Female	70–79 years Male	70–79 Female	80+ years Male	80+ Female	Total Male	Total Female	All
PAF of Mortality (%)																			
East Asia and Pacific	NA	NA	NA	NA	NA	NA	21	43	21	42	21	43	20	42	21	41	21	41	32
Europe and Central Asia	NA	NA	NA	NA	NA	NA	10	24	8	20	9	19	8	18	8	18	8	18	12
Latin America and the Caribbean	NA	NA	NA	NA	NA	NA	18	38	18	38	18	37	17	36	17	35	17	35	25
Middle East and North Africa	NA	NA	NA	NA	NA	NA	7	18	6	17	7	17	7	17	7	17	7	17	11
South Asia	NA	NA	NA	NA	NA	NA	40	65	40	64	40	64	40	64	40	64	40	64	51
Sub-Saharan Africa	NA	NA	NA	NA	NA	NA	40	65	40	65	40	65	40	65	40	64	40	63	48
Low- and middle-income countries	NA	NA	NA	NA	NA	NA	31	54	31	55	27	49	24	45	23	42	26	46	35
High-income countries	NA	NA	NA	NA	NA	NA	0	0	0	0	0	0	0	0	0	0	0	0	0
WORLD	NA	NA	NA	NA	NA	NA	30	52	30	53	25	46	21	41	18	36	22	41	32
PAF of YLL (%)																			
East Asia and Pacific	NA	NA	NA	NA	NA	NA	21	43	21	42	21	43	20	42	21	41	21	42	32
Europe and Central Asia	NA	NA	NA	NA	NA	NA	10	24	8	20	9	19	8	18	8	18	8	19	12
Latin America and the Caribbean	NA	NA	NA	NA	NA	NA	18	38	18	38	18	37	17	36	17	35	17	32	24
Middle East and North Africa	NA	NA	NA	NA	NA	NA	7	18	6	17	7	17	7	17	7	17	6	16	11
South Asia	NA	NA	NA	NA	NA	NA	40	65	40	64	40	64	40	64	40	64	40	64	51
Sub-Saharan Africa	NA	NA	NA	NA	NA	NA	40	65	40	65	40	65	40	65	40	64	39	62	47
Low- and middle-income countries	NA	NA	NA	NA	NA	NA	31	54	31	55	27	49	24	45	23	42	27	48	37
High-income countries	NA	NA	NA	NA	NA	NA	0	0	0	0	0	0	0	0	0	0	0	0	0
WORLD	NA	NA	NA	NA	NA	NA	30	52	30	53	25	46	21	41	19	37	24	44	34
PAF of DALYs (%)																			
East Asia and Pacific	NA	NA	NA	NA	NA	NA	21	43	21	42	21	43	20	42	21	41	21	42	31
Europe and Central Asia	NA	NA	NA	NA	NA	NA	10	24	8	20	9	19	8	18	8	18	8	19	13
Latin America and the Caribbean	NA	NA	NA	NA	NA	NA	18	38	18	38	18	37	17	36	17	35	17	34	25
Middle East and North Africa	NA	NA	NA	NA	NA	NA	7	18	6	17	7	17	7	17	7	17	6	16	10
South Asia	NA	NA	NA	NA	NA	NA	40	65	40	64	40	64	40	64	40	64	40	64	51
Sub-Saharan Africa	NA	NA	NA	NA	NA	NA	40	65	40	65	40	65	40	65	40	64	38	62	46
Low- and middle-income countries	NA	NA	NA	NA	NA	NA	26	44	28	53	26	48	24	45	23	42	25	46	35
High-income countries	NA	NA	NA	NA	NA	NA	0	0	0	0	0	0	0	0	0	0	0	0	0
WORLD	NA	NA	NA	NA	NA	NA	22	33	24	45	23	43	20	41	19	37	22	40	30
Attributable Mortality (thousands)																			
East Asia and Pacific	NA	NA	NA	NA	NA	NA	0	1	10	15	28	47	56	118	40	136	135	316	451
Europe and Central Asia	NA	NA	NA	NA	NA	NA	0	0	1	1	2	1	3	3	1	3	7	9	16
Latin America and the Caribbean	NA	NA	NA	NA	NA	NA	0	0	1	1	2	3	3	4	4	6	10	14	24
Middle East and North Africa	NA	NA	NA	NA	NA	NA	0	0	0	0	0	1	1	1	0	1	2	3	4
South Asia	NA	NA	NA	NA	NA	NA	3	4	36	46	39	40	35	51	14	25	126	167	293
Sub-Saharan Africa	NA	NA	NA	NA	NA	NA	1	1	5	4	8	6	10	10	5	6	29	26	56
Low- and middle-income countries	NA	NA	NA	NA	NA	NA	5	7	53	68	80	97	108	186	64	177	309	535	844
High-income countries	NA	NA	NA	NA	NA	NA	0	0	0	0	0	0	0	0	0	0	0	0	0
WORLD	NA	NA	NA	NA	NA	NA	5	7	53	68	80	97	108	186	64	177	309	535	844
Attributable YLL (thousands)																			
East Asia and Pacific	NA	NA	NA	NA	NA	NA	11	33	173	290	374	695	493	1,189	201	686	1,253	2,892	4,145
Europe and Central Asia	NA	NA	NA	NA	NA	NA	5	4	16	12	29	21	24	33	5	15	79	85	164
Latin America and the Caribbean	NA	NA	NA	NA	NA	NA	4	7	15	24	26	38	31	44	16	28	92	142	234
Middle East and North Africa	NA	NA	NA	NA	NA	NA	1	2	3	7	5	9	5	11	2	4	17	34	50
South Asia	NA	NA	NA	NA	NA	NA	64	104	653	909	535	600	314	531	68	136	1,633	2,281	3,914
Sub-Saharan Africa	NA	NA	NA	NA	NA	NA	32	17	95	79	107	95	89	98	24	32	347	322	669
Low- and middle-income countries	NA	NA	NA	NA	NA	NA	118	167	955	1,322	1,077	1,459	956	1,907	315	902	3,421	5,756	9,177
High-income countries	NA	NA	NA	NA	NA	NA	0	0	0	0	0	0	0	0	0	0	0	1	1
WORLD	NA	NA	NA	NA	NA	NA	118	167	955	1,322	1,077	1,459	956	1,907	316	902	3,421	5,756	9,178
Attributable DALYs (thousands)																			
East Asia and Pacific	NA	NA	NA	NA	NA	NA	66	158	483	410	509	845	555	1,315	222	721	1,836	3,448	5,284
Europe and Central Asia	NA	NA	NA	NA	NA	NA	15	51	26	49	37	37	29	39	6	17	113	193	306
Latin America and the Caribbean	NA	NA	NA	NA	NA	NA	23	98	54	84	46	61	39	56	19	32	181	330	512
Middle East and North Africa	NA	NA	NA	NA	NA	NA	12	10	7	11	6	10	6	11	2	4	33	47	80
South Asia	NA	NA	NA	NA	NA	NA	179	225	784	1,227	631	659	337	560	72	143	2,003	2,814	4,817
Sub-Saharan Africa	NA	NA	NA	NA	NA	NA	45	21	118	91	124	102	94	102	25	33	407	349	755
Low- and middle-income countries	NA	NA	NA	NA	NA	NA	340	562	1,474	1,872	1,353	1,714	1,059	2,083	346	950	4,572	7,181	11,753
High-income countries	NA	NA	NA	NA	NA	NA	0	0	0	1	0	0	0	0	0	0	1	2	3
WORLD	NA	NA	NA	NA	NA	NA	340	562	1,474	1,872	1,354	1,715	1,060	2,083	346	950	4,573	7,182	11,755

Source: Authors' calculations.
Note: NA = not applicable.

Table 4A.97

Risk factor: Indoor smoke from household use of solid fuels
Disease: All causes

Region	0–4 years Male	0–4 years Female	5–14 years Male	5–14 years Female	15–29 years Male	15–29 years Female	30–44 years Male	30–44 years Female	45–59 years Male	45–59 years Female	60–69 years Male	60–69 years Female	70–79 years Male	70–79 years Female	80+ years Male	80+ years Female	Total Male	Total Female	All
PAF of Mortality (%)																			
East Asia and Pacific	4	7	NA	NA	NA	NA	0	0	1	2	2	5	4	8	5	9	2	6	4
Europe and Central Asia	4	4	NA	NA	NA	NA	0	0	0	0	0	0	0	0	0	0	0	0	0
Latin America and the Caribbean	3	3	NA	NA	NA	NA	0	0	0	1	1	1	1	1	1	2	1	1	1
Middle East and North Africa	2	2	NA	NA	NA	NA	0	0	0	0	0	1	0	1	0	1	1	1	1
South Asia	12	12	NA	NA	NA	NA	0	1	3	6	4	4	3	5	3	4	5	6	5
Sub-Saharan Africa	10	8	NA	NA	NA	NA	0	0	1	1	2	2	3	3	3	3	5	4	4
Low- and middle-income countries	9	9	NA	NA	NA	NA	0	0	1	3	2	3	3	4	3	5	3	4	4
High-income countries	0	0	NA	NA	NA	NA	0	0	0	0	0	0	0	0	0	0	0	0	0
WORLD	9	9	NA	NA	NA	NA	0	0	1	2	2	3	2	4	2	3	3	4	3
PAF of YLL (%)																			
East Asia and Pacific	4	7	NA	NA	NA	NA	0	0	1	2	2	5	4	8	5	9	2	5	3
Europe and Central Asia	4	4	NA	NA	NA	NA	0	0	0	0	0	0	0	0	0	0	0	1	0
Latin America and the Caribbean	3	3	NA	NA	NA	NA	0	0	0	1	1	1	1	1	1	2	1	1	1
Middle East and North Africa	2	2	NA	NA	NA	NA	0	0	0	0	0	1	0	1	0	1	1	1	1
South Asia	12	12	NA	NA	NA	NA	0	1	3	6	4	4	3	5	3	4	6	7	6
Sub-Saharan Africa	10	8	NA	NA	NA	NA	0	0	1	1	2	2	3	2	3	3	5	4	5
Low- and middle-income countries	9	9	NA	NA	NA	NA	0	0	1	3	2	3	3	4	3	5	4	5	4
High-income countries	0	0	NA	NA	NA	NA	0	0	0	0	0	0	0	0	0	0	0	0	0
WORLD	9	9	NA	NA	NA	NA	0	0	1	2	2	3	2	4	2	3	3	4	4
PAF of DALYs (%)																			
East Asia and Pacific	3	5	NA	NA	NA	NA	0	1	1	1	2	4	3	6	4	8	2	3	2
Europe and Central Asia	2	2	NA	NA	NA	NA	0	1	0	1	0	0	0	0	0	0	0	1	0
Latin America and the Caribbean	2	2	NA	NA	NA	NA	0	1	1	1	1	1	1	1	1	1	1	1	1
Middle East and North Africa	2	2	NA	NA	NA	NA	0	0	0	0	0	0	0	0	0	0	1	1	1
South Asia	10	10	NA	NA	NA	NA	1	1	3	5	3	3	3	4	2	4	4	5	5
Sub-Saharan Africa	9	7	NA	NA	NA	NA	0	0	1	1	2	1	2	2	2	2	4	3	4
Low- and middle-income countries	7	7	NA	NA	NA	NA	0	1	1	2	2	3	2	4	2	4	3	3	3
High-income countries	0	0	NA	NA	NA	NA	0	0	0	0	0	0	0	0	0	0	0	0	0
WORLD	7	7	NA	NA	NA	NA	0	1	1	2	2	2	2	3	2	3	3	3	3
Attributable Mortality (thousands)																			
East Asia and Pacific	26	50	NA	NA	NA	NA	1	2	11	16	31	48	58	120	41	136	168	373	540
Europe and Central Asia	4	3	NA	NA	NA	NA	0	0	1	1	2	1	3	3	1	3	11	12	22
Latin America and the Caribbean	7	6	NA	NA	NA	NA	0	0	1	1	2	3	3	4	4	6	17	20	37
Middle East and North Africa	5	5	NA	NA	NA	NA	0	0	0	0	0	1	1	1	0	1	7	8	15
South Asia	213	215	NA	NA	NA	NA	3	4	36	47	40	40	35	51	14	26	341	383	724
Sub-Saharan Africa	230	167	NA	NA	NA	NA	1	1	5	4	8	6	10	10	5	6	259	194	453
Low- and middle-income countries	485	447	NA	NA	NA	NA	5	7	55	69	83	99	110	189	64	177	802	988	1,791
High-income countries	0	0	NA	NA	NA	NA	0	0	0	0	0	0	0	0	0	0	0	0	0
WORLD	485	447	NA	NA	NA	NA	5	7	55	69	83	99	110	189	64	177	802	989	1,791
Attributable YLL (thousands)																			
East Asia and Pacific	776	1,530	NA	NA	NA	NA	19	40	205	317	411	721	514	1,212	204	690	2,128	4,510	6,638
Europe and Central Asia	110	93	NA	NA	NA	NA	5	4	16	12	29	21	24	33	5	15	189	178	367
Latin America and the Caribbean	199	170	NA	NA	NA	NA	4	7	15	24	26	38	31	44	16	28	291	313	604
Middle East and North Africa	164	150	NA	NA	NA	NA	1	2	3	7	5	9	5	11	2	4	180	184	364
South Asia	6,454	6,566	NA	NA	NA	NA	66	105	659	912	542	603	317	533	68	137	8,106	8,855	16,961
Sub-Saharan Africa	6,961	5,098	NA	NA	NA	NA	32	17	95	79	107	95	89	98	24	32	7,308	5,420	12,729
Low- and middle-income countries	14,663	13,608	NA	NA	NA	NA	127	175	994	1,352	1,120	1,488	980	1,931	319	906	18,203	19,460	37,663
High-income countries	0	0	NA	NA	NA	NA	0	0	0	0	0	0	0	0	0	0	0	1	1
WORLD	14,663	13,608	NA	NA	NA	NA	127	175	994	1,352	1,120	1,488	980	1,931	319	906	18,203	19,461	37,664
Attributable DALYs (thousands)																			
East Asia and Pacific	892	1,734	NA	NA	NA	NA	74	165	516	437	546	871	576	1,338	225	725	2,828	5,271	8,100
Europe and Central Asia	115	99	NA	NA	NA	NA	15	51	26	49	37	37	29	39	6	17	228	292	520
Latin America and the Caribbean	252	222	NA	NA	NA	NA	23	98	54	84	46	61	39	56	19	32	434	553	986
Middle East and North Africa	178	163	NA	NA	NA	NA	12	10	7	11	6	10	6	11	2	4	211	210	421
South Asia	6,799	6,902	NA	NA	NA	NA	180	226	790	1,230	638	662	340	562	73	144	8,821	9,724	18,545
Sub-Saharan Africa	7,199	5,204	NA	NA	NA	NA	45	21	118	91	124	102	94	102	25	33	7,606	5,553	13,159
Low- and middle-income countries	15,435	14,325	NA	NA	NA	NA	349	570	1,513	1,903	1,398	1,744	1,084	2,107	349	954	20,128	21,603	41,731
High-income countries	0	0	NA	NA	NA	NA	0	0	0	1	0	0	0	0	0	0	1	2	2
WORLD	15,436	14,325	NA	NA	NA	NA	349	571	1,513	1,903	1,398	1,744	1,084	2,107	349	954	20,129	21,605	41,734

Source: Authors' calculations.
Note: NA = not applicable.

Table 4A.98

Risk factor: Contaminated injections in health care setting
Disease: HIV/AIDS

Region	0–4 years Male	Female	5–14 years Male	Female	15–29 years Male	Female	30–44 years Male	Female	45–59 years Male	Female	60–69 years Male	Female	70–79 years Male	Female	80+ years Male	Female	Total Male	Female	All
PAF of Mortality (%)																			
East Asia and Pacific	29	30	20	20	5	10	5	9	5	10	5	0	5	0	2	0	6	10	7
Europe and Central Asia	0	0	0	0	0	1	0	2	0	2	0	2	0	2	0	0	0	2	0
Latin America and the Caribbean	4	4	3	4	0	1	0	1	0	1	0	1	0	1	0	1	1	1	1
Middle East and North Africa	5	5	4	4	4	4	3	4	3	4	3	4	3	4	3	3	4	4	4
South Asia	55	56	50	58	14	24	14	23	13	23	14	11	14	11	5	11	15	28	18
Sub-Saharan Africa	9	9	6	8	2	1	2	1	2	1	2	1	2	1	2	1	3	3	3
Low- and middle-income countries	11	11	8	9	4	3	4	3	4	3	3	1	4	1	2	0	5	4	5
High-income countries	0	0	0	0	0	1	0	0	0	0	0	0	0	0	0	0	0	0	0
WORLD	11	11	8	9	4	3	4	3	4	3	3	1	3	1	1	0	5	4	5
PAF of YLL (%)																			
East Asia and Pacific	29	30	20	20	5	10	5	9	5	10	5	0	5	0	2	0	6	11	8
Europe and Central Asia	0	0	0	0	0	1	0	2	0	2	0	2	0	2	0	0	0	2	0
Latin America and the Caribbean	4	4	3	4	0	1	0	1	0	1	0	1	0	1	0	1	1	1	1
Middle East and North Africa	5	5	4	4	4	4	3	4	3	4	3	4	3	4	3	3	4	4	4
South Asia	55	56	50	58	14	24	14	23	13	23	14	11	14	11	5	11	16	29	19
Sub-Saharan Africa	9	9	6	8	2	1	2	1	2	1	2	1	2	1	2	1	3	3	3
Low- and middle-income countries	11	11	8	9	4	3	4	3	4	3	3	1	4	1	2	0	5	4.	5
High-income countries	0	0	0	0	0	1	0	0	0	0	0	0	0	0	0	0	0	0	0
WORLD	11	11	8	9	4	3	4	3	4	3	3	1	3	1	1	0	5	4	5
PAF of DALYs (%)																			
East Asia and Pacific	29	30	20	20	5	10	5	9	5	10	5	0	5	0	2	0	6	11	7
Europe and Central Asia	0	0	0	0	0	1	0	2	0	2	0	2	0	2	0	0	0	2	1
Latin America and the Caribbean	4	4	3	4	0	1	0	1	0	1	0	1	0	1	0	1	1	1	1
Middle East and North Africa	5	5	4	4	4	4	3	4	3	4	3	4	3	4	3	3	4	4	4
South Asia	55	56	50	58	14	24	14	23	13	23	14	11	14	11	5	11	16	28	19
Sub-Saharan Africa	9	9	6	8	2	1	2	1	2	1	2	1	2	1	2	1	3	3	3
Low- and middle-income countries	11	11	8	9	4	3	4	3	4	3	3	1	4	1	2	0	5	4	5
High-income countries	0	0	0	0	0	1	0	0	0	0	0	0	0	0	0	0	0	0	0
WORLD	11	11	8	9	4	3	4	3	4	3	3	1	3	1	1	0	5	4	5
Attributable Mortality (thousands)																			
East Asia and Pacific	1	1	0	0	1	0	2	1	1	1	0	0	0	0	0	0	5	3	8
Europe and Central Asia	0	0	0	0	0	0	0	0	0	0	0	0	0	0	0	0	0	0	0
Latin America and the Caribbean	0	0	0	0	0	0	0	0	0	0	0	0	0	0	0	0	0	0	1
Middle East and North Africa	0	0	0	0	0	0	0	0	0	0	0	0	0	0	0	0	0	0	0
South Asia	4	4	1	1	6	5	16	6	6	2	0	0	0	0	0	0	32	17	49
Sub-Saharan Africa	14	14	3	4	4	5	8	5	3	1	0	0	0	0	0	0	33	28	61
Low- and middle-income countries	19	18	4	5	10	10	26	12	9	4	1	0	0	0	0	0	70	49	119
High-income countries	0	0	0	0	0	0	0	0	0	0	0	0	0	0	0	0	0	0	0
WORLD	19	18	4	5	10	10	26	12	9	4	1	0	0	0	0	0	70	49	119
Attributable YLL (thousands)																			
East Asia and Pacific	27	21	2	2	20	12	51	21	17	16	1	0	0	0	0	0	118	72	190
Europe and Central Asia	0	0	0	0	0	1	1	1	0	0	0	0	0	0	0	0	2	2	3
Latin America and the Caribbean	4	4	1	1	1	2	2	2	1	1	0	0	0	0	0	0	10	10	20
Middle East and North Africa	0	0	0	0	1	1	1	0	0	0	0	0	0	0	0	0	2	2	4
South Asia	122	118	27	29	154	128	378	143	110	39	6	1	1	0	0	0	797	458	1,255
Sub-Saharan Africa	428	415	90	109	96	125	205	123	56	29	6	3	1	1	0	0	881	806	1,687
Low- and middle-income countries	582	558	121	141	271	269	638	291	183	85	14	4	1	1	0	0	1,809	1,349	3,159
High-income countries	0	0	0	0	0	0	0	0	0	0	0	0	0	0	0	0	0	0	1
WORLD	582	558	121	141	272	269	638	291	183	85	14	4	1	1	0	0	1,810	1,350	3,159
Attributable DALYs (thousands)																			
East Asia and Pacific	28	22	2	2	32	20	59	24	18	16	1	0	0	0	0	0	140	85	225
Europe and Central Asia	0	0	0	0	1	1	1	1	0	0	0	0	0	0	0	0	2	3	5
Latin America and the Caribbean	4	4	1	1	2	3	3	3	1	1	0	0	0	0	0	0	10	11	22
Middle East and North Africa	0	0	0	0	1	1	1	1	0	0	0	0	0	0	0	0	2	2	4
South Asia	125	120	28	31	195	171	402	158	112	40	7	1	1	0	0	0	870	522	1,392
Sub-Saharan Africa	435	422	92	112	116	145	215	130	57	30	6	3	1	1	0	0	923	843	1,766
Low- and middle-income countries	592	569	124	147	346	341	682	317	188	88	14	5	1	1	0	0	1,948	1,466	3,414
High-income countries	0	0	0	0	0	0	0	0	0	0	0	0	0	0	0	0	1	1	1
WORLD	592	569	124	147	346	341	682	317	188	88	14	5	1	1	0	0	1,949	1,466	3,415

Source: Authors' calculations.

Table 4A.99

Risk factor: Contaminated injections in health care setting
Disease: Hepatitis B

Region	0–4 years Male	0–4 years Female	5–14 years Male	5–14 years Female	15–29 years Male	15–29 years Female	30–44 years Male	30–44 years Female	45–59 years Male	45–59 years Female	60–69 years Male	60–69 years Female	70–79 years Male	70–79 years Female	80+ years Male	80+ years Female	Total Male	Total Female	All
PAF of Mortality (%)																			
East Asia and Pacific	42	42	25	32	27	34	27	29	29	24	28	24	26	24	29	29	28	29	29
Europe and Central Asia	2	2	2	1	4	3	4	4	4	4	3	3	2	3	2	3	4	3	3
Latin America and the Caribbean	5	4	6	4	6	6	4	4	3	5	5	5	4	5	5	3	5	4	5
Middle East and North Africa	15	39	30	39	43	32	37	33	23	19	21	24	35	48	45	54	27	35	31
South Asia	52	53	52	52	52	52	51	52	52	51	51	50	51	52	52	52	51	52	52
Sub-Saharan Africa	13	12	9	11	12	11	15	14	14	11	10	15	12	38	44	44	12	13	12
Low- and middle-income countries	18	17	10	27	32	33	30	32	34	29	29	29	36	39	41	36	30	29	30
High-income countries	23	37	8	6	11	5	8	4	6	2	6	2	1	0	1	2	5	2	4
WORLD	18	17	10	27	32	33	30	31	32	27	28	25	32	31	36	29	29	27	29
PAF of YLL (%)																			
East Asia and Pacific	42	42	25	32	27	34	27	29	29	24	28	24	26	24	29	29	28	30	29
Europe and Central Asia	2	2	2	1	4	3	4	4	4	4	3	3	2	3	2	3	4	3	3
Latin America and the Caribbean	5	4	6	4	6	6	4	4	3	5	5	5	4	5	5	3	5	5	5
Middle East and North Africa	15	39	30	39	43	32	37	33	23	19	21	24	35	48	45	54	26	33	29
South Asia	52	53	52	52	52	52	51	52	52	51	51	50	51	52	52	52	52	52	52
Sub-Saharan Africa	13	12	9	11	12	11	15	14	14	11	10	15	12	38	44	44	12	12	12
Low- and middle-income countries	18	17	10	27	32	33	30	32	34	29	29	29	36	39	41	36	29	28	29
High-income countries	23	37	8	6	11	5	8	4	6	2	6	2	1	0	1	2	6	2	5
WORLD	18	17	10	27	32	33	29	31	32	28	28	25	32	31	36	30	28	27	28
PAF of DALYs (%)																			
East Asia and Pacific	42	42	25	32	27	34	27	29	29	24	28	24	26	24	29	29	28	30	29
Europe and Central Asia	2	2	2	1	4	3	4	4	4	4	3	3	2	3	2	3	4	3	4
Latin America and the Caribbean	5	4	6	4	6	6	4	4	3	5	5	5	4	5	5	3	5	5	5
Middle East and North Africa	15	39	30	39	43	32	37	33	23	19	21	24	35	48	45	54	26	33	29
South Asia	52	53	52	52	52	52	51	52	52	51	51	50	51	52	52	52	52	52	52
Sub-Saharan Africa	13	12	9	11	12	11	15	14	14	11	10	15	12	38	44	44	12	12	12
Low- and middle-income countries	18	17	10	27	32	33	30	32	34	29	29	29	36	39	41	36	29	28	29
High-income countries	23	37	8	6	11	5	8	4	6	2	6	2	1	0	1	2	6	2	5
WORLD	18	17	10	27	32	33	29	31	32	28	27	25	31	31	35	30	28	27	28
Attributable Mortality (thousands)																			
East Asia and Pacific	0	0	0	0	1	0	2	0	3	0	1	0	0	0	0	0	8	2	9
Europe and Central Asia	0	0	0	0	0	0	0	0	0	0	0	0	0	0	0	0	0	0	0
Latin America and the Caribbean	0	0	0	0	0	0	0	0	0	0	0	0	0	0	0	0	0	0	0
Middle East and North Africa	0	0	0	0	0	0	0	0	0	0	0	0	0	0	0	0	1	1	2
South Asia	0	0	0	0	2	1	2	1	4	1	1	0	1	0	1	0	10	5	15
Sub-Saharan Africa	0	0	0	0	0	0	0	0	0	0	0	0	0	0	0	0	1	1	3
Low- and middle-income countries	1	1	0	0	3	2	5	1	7	2	2	1	1	1	1	1	20	8	28
High-income countries	0	0	0	0	0	0	0	0	0	0	0	0	0	0	0	0	0	0	0
WORLD	1	1	0	0	3	2	5	1	7	2	2	1	1	1	1	1	20	9	29
Attributable YLL (thousands)																			
East Asia and Pacific	7	7	1	1	18	7	48	11	61	6	14	3	2	1	1	1	152	36	188
Europe and Central Asia	0	0	0	0	1	0	0	0	0	0	0	0	0	0	0	0	2	1	3
Latin America and the Caribbean	0	0	0	0	1	0	1	0	0	0	0	0	0	0	0	0	3	2	4
Middle East and North Africa	2	4	1	2	2	1	3	1	4	2	2	2	2	3	0	1	16	16	31
South Asia	1	2	1	8	45	34	54	18	69	24	13	8	8	5	3	1	194	100	293
Sub-Saharan Africa	6	15	8	2	3	4	11	2	6	3	2	1	0	1	0	0	35	28	63
Low- and middle-income countries	16	27	11	13	70	47	117	33	140	35	31	13	13	10	3	3	401	182	583
High-income countries	0	0	0	0	0	0	1	0	1	0	0	0	0	0	0	0	3	1	4
WORLD	17	27	11	13	70	47	117	33	141	35	31	13	13	10	3	3	404	182	586
Attributable DALYs (thousands)																			
East Asia and Pacific	7	7	1	1	19	8	49	11	63	6	15	3	3	1	1	1	157	37	193
Europe and Central Asia	0	0	0	0	1	0	0	0	0	0	0	0	0	0	0	0	2	1	3
Latin America and the Caribbean	0	0	0	0	1	0	1	0	0	0	0	0	0	0	0	0	3	2	5
Middle East and North Africa	2	4	1	2	2	1	3	1	4	2	2	2	2	4	0	1	16	16	32
South Asia	1	2	1	8	47	35	55	19	71	24	14	8	9	5	3	1	199	102	302
Sub-Saharan Africa	6	15	8	2	3	4	11	2	6	3	2	1	0	1	0	0	36	28	64
Low- and middle-income countries	16	27	11	13	72	48	119	34	144	36	32	14	14	10	4	4	413	186	599
High-income countries	0	0	0	0	0	0	1	0	1	0	1	0	0	0	0	0	3	1	4
WORLD	17	27	11	13	72	48	120	34	146	36	33	14	14	10	4	4	416	187	603

Source: Authors' calculations.

Table 4A.100

Risk factor: Contaminated injections in health care setting
Disease: Hepatitis C

Region	0–4 years Male	Female	5–14 years Male	Female	15–29 years Male	Female	30–44 years Male	Female	45–59 years Male	Female	60–69 years Male	Female	70–79 years Male	Female	80+ years Male	Female	Total Male	Female	All
PAF of Mortality (%)																			
East Asia and Pacific	55	55	32	39	34	41	34	36	35	32	35	32	33	33	35	36	35	37	35
Europe and Central Asia	5	5	6	0	11	8	10	13	11	13	7	8	6	6	6	8	9	9	9
Latin America and the Caribbean	7	7	7	6	1	1	2	5	2	3	2	2	1	1	1	1	2	2	2
Middle East and North Africa	70	57	45	56	62	43	64	39	40	27	30	36	54	67	52	77	48	50	49
South Asia	72	73	66	62	60	59	59	61	60	61	61	61	59	63	61	62	60	61	60
Sub-Saharan Africa	20	18	13	17	18	16	22	19	21	17	15	22	18	54	62	63	18	19	18
Low- and middle-income countries	33	25	15	37	41	40	37	40	40	34	35	32	43	47	47	50	37	36	37
High-income countries	35	49	8	21	6	3	2	1	2	0	1	0	0	0	0	0	1	0	1
WORLD	33	25	15	37	40	40	33	35	32	25	25	18	24	19	27	20	30	26	29
PAF of YLL (%)																			
East Asia and Pacific	55	55	32	39	34	41	34	36	35	32	35	32	33	33	35	36	35	38	36
Europe and Central Asia	5	5	6	0	11	8	10	13	11	13	7	8	6	6	6	8	9	9	9
Latin America and the Caribbean	7	7	7	6	1	1	2	5	2	3	2	2	1	1	1	1	2	3	2
Middle East and North Africa	70	57	45	56	62	43	64	39	40	27	30	36	54	67	52	77	50	46	48
South Asia	72	73	66	62	60	59	59	61	60	61	61	61	59	63	61	62	60	61	60
Sub-Saharan Africa	20	18	13	17	18	16	22	19	21	17	15	22	18	54	62	63	18	18	18
Low- and middle-income countries	33	25	15	37	41	40	37	40	40	34	35	32	43	46	47	51	36	35	36
High-income countries	35	49	8	21	6	3	2	1	2	0	1	0	0	0	0	0	2	0	1
WORLD	33	25	15	37	41	40	33	35	32	26	25	18	24	19	27	22	31	28	30
PAF of DALYs (%)																			
East Asia and Pacific	55	55	32	39	34	41	34	36	35	32	35	32	33	33	35	36	35	38	36
Europe and Central Asia	5	5	6	0	11	8	10	13	11	13	7	8	6	6	6	8	9	9	9
Latin America and the Caribbean	7	7	7	6	1	1	2	5	2	3	2	2	1	1	1	1	2	3	2
Middle East and North Africa	70	57	45	56	62	43	64	39	40	27	30	36	54	67	52	77	50	46	48
South Asia	72	73	66	62	60	59	59	61	60	61	61	61	59	63	61	62	60	61	60
Sub-Saharan Africa	20	18	13	17	18	16	22	19	21	17	15	22	18	54	62	63	18	18	18
Low- and middle-income countries	33	25	15	37	41	40	37	40	40	34	35	32	43	47	47	51	36	35	36
High-income countries	35	49	8	21	6	3	2	1	2	0	1	0	0	0	0	0	1	0	1
WORLD	33	25	15	37	40	40	33	35	31	26	24	17	23	18	25	20	31	28	30
Attributable Mortality (thousands)																			
East Asia and Pacific	0	0	0	0	0	0	1	0	2	0	0	0	0	0	0	0	4	1	5
Europe and Central Asia	0	0	0	0	0	0	0	0	0	0	0	0	0	0	0	0	0	0	0
Latin America and the Caribbean	0	0	0	0	0	0	0	0	0	0	0	0	0	0	0	0	0	0	0
Middle East and North Africa	0	0	0	0	0	0	0	0	0	0	0	0	0	0	0	0	1	1	1
South Asia	0	0	0	0	1	1	1	0	2	1	0	0	0	0	0	0	4	2	7
Sub-Saharan Africa	0	0	0	0	0	0	0	0	0	0	0	0	0	0	0	0	1	1	2
Low- and middle-income countries	0	1	0	0	1	1	2	1	4	1	1	0	1	1	0	0	10	4	14
High-income countries	0	0	0	0	0	0	0	0	0	0	0	0	0	0	0	0	0	0	0
WORLD	0	1	0	0	1	1	2	1	4	1	1	0	1	1	0	0	10	4	15
Attributable YLL (thousands)																			
East Asia and Pacific	2	3	0	0	10	4	25	6	31	3	7	1	1	0	0	0	77	18	95
Europe and Central Asia	0	0	0	0	1	0	0	0	0	0	0	0	0	0	0	0	2	1	3
Latin America and the Caribbean	0	0	0	0	0	0	0	0	0	0	0	0	0	0	0	0	0	0	1
Middle East and North Africa	4	3	1	1	1	0	2	1	4	1	1	1	1	2	0	1	14	11	26
South Asia	1	1	1	4	20	15	24	8	31	11	6	4	4	2	1	1	86	47	133
Sub-Saharan Africa	3	9	5	2	2	3	7	1	3	2	1	1	0	0	0	0	22	17	38
Low- and middle-income countries	10	16	7	7	33	22	58	17	70	18	16	7	7	6	2	2	202	94	296
High-income countries	0	0	0	0	0	0	0	0	1	0	0	0	0	0	0	0	2	0	2
WORLD	10	16	7	7	33	22	59	17	71	18	16	7	7	6	2	2	203	94	298
Attributable DALYs (thousands)																			
East Asia and Pacific	2	3	0	0	10	4	26	6	32	3	8	1	1	1	0	0	80	18	98
Europe and Central Asia	0	0	0	0	1	0	0	0	0	0	0	0	0	0	0	0	2	1	3
Latin America and the Caribbean	0	0	0	0	0	0	0	0	0	0	0	0	0	0	0	0	0	0	1
Middle East and North Africa	4	3	1	1	1	0	2	1	4	1	1	2	1	3	0	1	15	12	27
South Asia	1	1	1	4	20	16	24	9	32	11	6	4	4	2	1	1	89	48	137
Sub-Saharan Africa	3	9	5	2	2	3	7	1	4	2	1	1	0	0	0	0	22	17	39
Low- and middle-income countries	10	16	7	7	33	23	60	17	72	18	17	7	7	6	2	2	208	96	304
High-income countries	0	0	0	0	0	0	0	0	1	0	0	0	0	0	0	0	2	0	2
WORLD	10	16	7	7	33	23	60	18	73	18	17	7	7	6	2	2	210	96	306

Source: Authors' calculations.

Table 4A.101

Risk factor:	Contaminated injections in health care setting
Disease:	Liver cancer

Region	0–4 years Male	0–4 years Female	5–14 years Male	5–14 years Female	15–29 years Male	15–29 years Female	30–44 years Male	30–44 years Female	45–59 years Male	45–59 years Female	60–69 years Male	60–69 years Female	70–79 years Male	70–79 years Female	80+ years Male	80+ years Female	Total Male	Total Female	All
PAF of Mortality (%)																			
East Asia and Pacific	37	38	24	25	24	25	24	24	24	24	24	24	24	24	24	24	24	24	24
Europe and Central Asia	6	5	4	2	4	4	5	6	5	6	5	6	5	6	4	6	5	6	5
Latin America and the Caribbean	2	3	3	3	3	3	2	2	2	2	2	2	2	2	2	2	2	2	2
Middle East and North Africa	29	14	26	13	21	22	22	21	22	28	22	23	20	21	19	20	21	23	22
South Asia	42	38	38	35	35	35	36	35	35	36	36	36	36	36	36	35	36	36	36
Sub-Saharan Africa	10	9	9	9	6	8	6	8	7	8	7	8	7	8	7	8	7	8	7
Low- and middle-income countries	29	32	22	24	23	24	22	21	22	21	21	21	21	20	20	19	22	21	21
High-income countries	4	15	3	7	12	11	10	11	5	6	3	4	1	2	1	1	3	3	3
WORLD	27	32	21	24	22	24	22	21	20	20	18	18	16	16	13	12	19	18	18
PAF of YLL (%)																			
East Asia and Pacific	37	38	24	25	24	25	24	24	24	24	24	24	24	24	24	24	24	24	24
Europe and Central Asia	6	5	4	2	4	4	5	6	5	6	5	6	5	6	4	6	5	6	5
Latin America and the Caribbean	2	3	3	3	3	3	2	2	2	2	2	2	2	2	2	2	2	2	2
Middle East and North Africa	29	14	26	13	21	22	22	21	22	28	22	23	20	21	19	20	22	24	22
South Asia	42	38	38	35	35	35	36	35	35	36	36	36	36	36	36	35	36	36	36
Sub-Saharan Africa	10	9	9	9	6	8	6	8	7	8	7	8	7	8	7	8	7	8	7
Low- and middle-income countries	29	32	22	24	23	24	22	22	22	21	21	21	21	20	20	19	22	21	22
High-income countries	4	15	3	7	12	11	10	11	5	6	3	4	1	2	1	1	4	3	4
WORLD	27	32	21	24	22	24	22	21	20	20	18	18	16	16	14	13	19	19	19
PAF of DALYs (%)																			
East Asia and Pacific	37	38	24	25	24	25	24	24	24	24	24	24	24	24	24	24	24	24	24
Europe and Central Asia	6	5	4	2	4	4	5	6	5	6	5	6	5	6	4	6	5	6	5
Latin America and the Caribbean	2	3	3	3	3	3	2	2	2	2	2	2	2	2	2	2	2	2	2
Middle East and North Africa	29	14	26	13	21	22	22	21	22	28	22	23	20	21	19	20	22	24	22
South Asia	42	38	38	35	35	35	36	35	35	36	36	36	36	36	36	35	36	36	36
Sub-Saharan Africa	10	9	9	9	6	8	6	8	7	8	7	8	7	8	7	8	7	8	7
Low- and middle-income countries	29	32	22	24	23	24	22	22	22	21	21	21	21	20	20	19	22	21	22
High-income countries	4	15	3	7	12	11	10	11	5	6	3	4	1	2	1	1	4	3	4
WORLD	27	32	21	24	22	24	22	21	20	20	18	18	16	16	13	13	19	19	19
Attributable Mortality (thousands)																			
East Asia and Pacific	0	0	0	0	1	1	7	2	24	6	18	7	12	7	3	2	65	25	91
Europe and Central Asia	0	0	0	0	0	0	0	0	0	0	0	0	0	0	0	0	1	1	1
Latin America and the Caribbean	0	0	0	0	0	0	0	0	0	0	0	0	0	0	0	0	0	0	0
Middle East and North Africa	0	0	0	0	0	0	0	0	0	0	0	0	0	0	0	0	1	1	2
South Asia	0	0	0	0	0	1	1	0	2	1	2	1	1	1	0	0	6	4	10
Sub-Saharan Africa	0	0	0	0	0	0	0	0	1	0	1	0	0	0	0	0	2	1	3
Low- and middle-income countries	0	0	0	0	2	1	8	3	27	8	21	8	15	8	3	3	76	32	108
High-income countries	0	0	0	0	0	0	0	0	1	0	1	0	0	0	0	0	2	1	3
WORLD	0	0	0	0	2	1	9	3	28	8	21	8	15	8	3	3	78	33	111
Attributable YLL (thousands)																			
East Asia and Pacific	3	7	1	2	35	17	168	61	459	125	242	102	114	69	14	14	1,035	397	1,432
Europe and Central Asia	0	0	0	0	0	0	1	1	4	2	4	3	2	3	0	0	11	9	20
Latin America and the Caribbean	0	0	0	0	0	0	0	0	1	1	1	1	0	1	0	0	3	3	5
Middle East and North Africa	0	0	0	0	1	1	2	2	6	5	5	3	3	2	0	0	18	13	31
South Asia	2	3	1	2	10	15	18	10	29	18	23	11	10	7	2	2	96	68	164
Sub-Saharan Africa	0	0	0	0	2	2	7	4	14	6	8	4	3	3	1	1	36	20	56
Low- and middle-income countries	6	10	3	5	48	35	196	77	513	158	283	124	132	84	17	17	1,198	510	1,708
High-income countries	0	0	0	0	1	0	5	2	14	4	8	4	3	2	0	0	31	12	43
WORLD	6	10	3	5	49	35	201	79	527	161	290	128	135	86	17	18	1,229	523	1,751
Attributable DALYs (thousands)																			
East Asia and Pacific	3	7	1	2	35	17	168	62	462	125	244	103	115	70	14	14	1,041	400	1,441
Europe and Central Asia	0	0	0	0	0	0	1	1	4	2	4	3	2	3	0	1	11	9	20
Latin America and the Caribbean	0	0	0	0	0	0	0	0	1	1	1	1	0	1	0	0	3	3	5
Middle East and North Africa	0	0	0	0	1	1	2	2	6	6	5	3	3	2	0	0	18	13	31
South Asia	2	3	1	2	10	15	18	10	29	18	23	11	10	7	2	2	97	68	165
Sub-Saharan Africa	0	0	0	0	2	2	7	4	15	6	8	4	3	3	1	1	36	20	56
Low- and middle-income countries	6	10	3	5	49	35	197	78	515	159	285	125	134	84	17	18	1,206	513	1,719
High-income countries	0	0	0	0	1	0	5	2	14	4	8	4	3	3	0	0	31	12	44
WORLD	6	11	3	5	49	35	202	80	530	162	292	128	136	87	18	18	1,237	526	1,762

Source: Authors' calculations.

Table 4A.102

Risk factor: Contaminated injections in health care setting
Disease: Cirrhosis of the liver

Region	0–4 years Male	Female	5–14 years Male	Female	15–29 years Male	Female	30–44 years Male	Female	45–59 years Male	Female	60–69 years Male	Female	70–79 years Male	Female	80+ years Male	Female	Total Male	Female	All
PAF of Mortality (%)																			
East Asia and Pacific	32	34	24	28	22	25	21	22	21	21	21	21	22	22	22	22	22	22	22
Europe and Central Asia	7	7	3	1	6	5	7	9	7	9	7	8	6	7	5	6	7	8	7
Latin America and the Caribbean	3	3	3	1	1	2	1	1	1	1	1	2	2	2	2	2	1	2	1
Middle East and North Africa	38	55	36	48	39	41	33	36	39	41	37	39	34	38	32	34	36	39	37
South Asia	39	38	35	35	35	34	34	35	35	36	36	38	37	38	37	37	36	36	36
Sub-Saharan Africa	41	45	25	51	9	13	7	10	10	13	10	10	9	10	9	12	9	12	10
Low- and middle-income countries	37	38	32	34	24	29	16	21	19	22	20	20	21	21	22	21	20	23	21
High-income countries	13	17	7	13	7	5	2	1	1	1	1	1	1	1	1	1	1	1	1
WORLD	37	38	32	34	23	29	14	19	16	19	16	18	17	18	18	17	17	20	18
PAF of YLL (%)																			
East Asia and Pacific	32	34	24	28	22	25	21	22	21	21	21	21	22	22	22	22	22	22	22
Europe and Central Asia	7	7	3	1	6	5	7	9	7	9	7	8	6	7	5	6	7	8	7
Latin America and the Caribbean	3	3	3	1	1	2	1	1	1	1	1	2	2	2	2	2	1	2	1
Middle East and North Africa	38	55	36	48	39	41	33	36	39	41	37	39	34	38	32	34	37	40	38
South Asia	39	38	35	35	35	34	34	35	35	36	36	38	37	38	37	37	36	36	36
Sub-Saharan Africa	41	45	25	51	9	13	7	10	10	13	10	10	9	10	9	12	9	13	11
Low- and middle-income countries	37	38	32	34	24	29	16	21	19	22	20	20	20	21	22	22	20	25	22
High-income countries	13	17	7	13	7	5	2	1	1	1	1	1	1	1	1	1	1	1	1
WORLD	37	38	32	34	23	29	14	19	16	19	16	18	17	18	18	17	17	22	19
PAF of DALYs (%)																			
East Asia and Pacific	32	34	24	28	22	25	21	22	21	21	21	21	22	22	22	22	22	22	22
Europe and Central Asia	7	7	3	1	6	5	7	9	7	9	7	8	6	7	5	6	7	8	7
Latin America and the Caribbean	3	3	3	1	1	2	1	1	1	1	1	2	2	2	2	2	1	2	1
Middle East and North Africa	38	55	36	48	39	41	33	36	39	41	37	39	34	38	32	34	37	40	38
South Asia	39	38	35	35	35	34	34	35	35	36	36	38	37	38	37	37	36	36	36
Sub-Saharan Africa	41	45	25	51	9	13	7	10	10	13	10	10	9	10	9	12	9	13	11
Low- and middle-income countries	37	38	32	34	22	29	16	21	19	22	20	20	21	21	22	22	20	24	22
High-income countries	13	17	7	13	7	5	2	1	1	1	1	1	1	1	1	1	1	1	1
WORLD	37	38	31	34	22	28	14	18	16	19	16	18	17	18	18	17	17	22	19
Attributable Mortality (thousands)																			
East Asia and Pacific	0	1	0	0	1	1	4	2	9	4	6	3	5	4	1	2	27	15	42
Europe and Central Asia	0	0	0	0	0	0	1	0	2	1	1	1	1	1	0	0	4	3	8
Latin America and the Caribbean	0	0	0	0	0	0	0	0	0	0	0	0	0	0	0	0	1	0	1
Middle East and North Africa	0	0	0	0	0	0	0	0	2	2	2	2	2	2	1	1	8	6	14
South Asia	2	5	1	2	2	3	4	3	12	6	8	4	6	4	2	1	38	29	67
Sub-Saharan Africa	0	0	0	0	0	0	0	0	1	1	1	1	1	0	0	0	4	3	6
Low- and middle-income countries	3	6	1	3	4	4	10	5	27	13	18	10	13	10	4	4	82	56	138
High-income countries	0	0	0	0	0	0	0	0	0	0	0	0	0	0	0	0	1	0	1
WORLD	3	6	1	3	4	4	10	5	28	13	19	10	14	10	5	4	82	56	139
Attributable YLL (thousands)																			
East Asia and Pacific	12	18	3	6	24	15	97	38	180	72	83	49	41	37	8	10	447	244	692
Europe and Central Asia	0	0	0	0	3	1	20	10	34	22	15	13	5	6	0	1	77	53	130
Latin America and the Caribbean	0	0	0	0	1	0	3	1	5	1	2	1	1	1	0	0	13	4	17
Middle East and North Africa	5	7	2	3	8	5	7	7	44	35	31	24	15	16	3	4	115	101	216
South Asia	66	167	28	65	68	96	101	66	233	121	110	57	53	38	11	8	669	617	1,286
Sub-Saharan Africa	1	3	0	4	4	3	10	5	24	17	12	10	6	5	1	1	57	47	104
Low- and middle-income countries	84	195	34	77	107	121	239	125	519	269	252	154	121	103	23	23	1,378	1,067	2,445
High-income countries	0	0	0	0	1	0	3	1	6	2	3	2	1	1	0	0	14	7	21
WORLD	84	195	34	78	107	121	242	126	524	271	255	156	122	104	23	24	1,392	1,074	2,466
Attributable DALYs (thousands)																			
East Asia and Pacific	13	19	4	8	36	20	122	54	211	94	94	59	47	45	9	12	536	312	847
Europe and Central Asia	0	0	0	0	4	2	25	13	38	27	17	15	5	7	0	1	89	65	155
Latin America and the Caribbean	0	0	0	0	1	0	4	1	6	2	3	1	1	1	0	0	15	5	21
Middle East and North Africa	7	8	4	4	10	7	9	9	52	46	35	30	17	19	3	5	135	127	262
South Asia	74	194	39	85	83	110	124	83	268	144	123	68	60	45	13	10	785	740	1,524
Sub-Saharan Africa	1	3	1	4	6	4	13	7	27	21	14	12	7	6	1	1	70	59	129
Low- and middle-income countries	95	225	48	101	139	143	296	168	603	333	285	185	138	123	27	29	1,630	1,308	2,938
High-income countries	0	0	0	0	1	0	4	2	7	3	3	2	1	1	0	0	17	9	26
WORLD	95	225	48	102	140	143	300	169	610	336	288	187	140	125	27	30	1,647	1,317	2,964

Source: Authors' calculations.

Table 4A.103

Risk factor: Contaminated injections in health care setting
Disease: All causes

Region	0–4 years Male	Female	5–14 years Male	Female	15–29 years Male	Female	30–44 years Male	Female	45–59 years Male	Female	60–69 years Male	Female	70–79 years Male	Female	80+ years Male	Female	Total Male	Female	All
PAF of Mortality (%)																			
East Asia and Pacific	0	0	0	0	1	1	3	1	3	1	2	1	1	1	0	0	2	1	1
Europe and Central Asia	0	0	0	0	0	0	0	0	0	0	0	0	0	0	0	0	0	0	0
Latin America and the Caribbean	0	0	0	0	0	0	0	0	0	0	0	0	0	0	0	0	0	0	0
Middle East and North Africa	0	0	0	1	1	1	1	1	2	2	2	2	1	1	1	1	1	1	1
South Asia	0	1	1	1	2	2	3	2	2	1	1	1	1	0	1	0	1	1	1
Sub-Saharan Africa	1	1	1	1	1	1	1	1	1	1	1	0	0	0	0	0	1	1	1
Low- and middle-income countries	0	1	1	1	1	1	2	1	2	1	1	1	1	0	0	0	1	1	1
High-income countries	0	0	0	0	0	0	0	0	0	0	0	0	0	0	0	0	0	0	0
WORLD	0	1	1	1	1	1	2	1	2	1	1	1	1	0	0	0	1	1	1
PAF of YLL (%)																			
East Asia and Pacific	0	0	0	0	1	1	3	1	3	1	2	1	1	1	1	0	2	1	1
Europe and Central Asia	0	0	0	0	0	0	0	0	0	0	0	0	0	0	0	0	0	0	0
Latin America and the Caribbean	0	0	0	0	0	0	0	0	0	0	0	0	0	0	0	0	0	0	0
Middle East and North Africa	0	0	0	1	1	1	1	1	2	2	2	2	1	1	1	1	1	1	1
South Asia	0	1	1	1	2	2	3	2	2	1	1	1	1	0	1	0	1	1	1
Sub-Saharan Africa	1	1	1	1	1	1	1	1	1	1	1	0	0	0	0	0	1	1	1
Low- and middle-income countries	0	1	1	1	1	1	2	1	2	1	1	1	1	0	0	0	1	1	1
High-income countries	0	0	0	0	0	0	0	0	0	0	0	0	0	0	0	0	0	0	0
WORLD	0	1	1	1	1	1	2	1	2	1	1	1	1	0	0	0	1	1	1
PAF of DALYs (%)																			
East Asia and Pacific	0	0	0	0	1	0	2	1	2	1	1	1	1	1	0	0	1	1	1
Europe and Central Asia	0	0	0	0	0	0	0	0	0	0	0	0	0	0	0	0	0	0	0
Latin America and the Caribbean	0	0	0	0	0	0	0	0	0	0	0	0	0	0	0	0	0	0	0
Middle East and North Africa	0	0	0	0	0	0	0	0	1	1	1	1	1	1	1	1	1	1	1
South Asia	0	0	1	1	1	1	2	1	2	1	1	0	1	0	1	0	1	1	1
Sub-Saharan Africa	1	1	1	1	1	1	1	1	1	0	0	0	0	0	0	0	1	1	1
Low- and middle-income countries	0	0	0	1	1	1	1	1	1	1	1	0	1	0	0	0	1	1	1
High-income countries	0	0	0	0	0	0	0	0	0	0	0	0	0	0	0	0	0	0	0
WORLD	0	0	0	1	1	1	1	1	1	1	1	0	0	0	0	0	1	0	1
Attributable Mortality (thousands)																			
East Asia and Pacific	2	2	0	0	4	2	16	6	39	11	25	10	18	10	4	4	109	46	154
Europe and Central Asia	0	0	0	0	0	0	1	0	2	1	1	1	1	1	0	0	5	4	9
Latin America and the Caribbean	0	0	0	0	0	0	0	0	0	0	0	0	0	0	0	0	1	1	2
Middle East and North Africa	0	0	0	0	0	0	1	0	3	2	3	2	2	2	1	1	10	9	19
South Asia	6	10	2	4	11	10	24	10	24	10	12	5	8	5	3	2	91	56	147
Sub-Saharan Africa	15	15	4	4	4	5	10	5	5	3	2	1	1	1	0	0	41	34	75
Low- and middle-income countries	23	27	6	8	19	18	52	22	74	28	44	20	30	19	9	8	257	150	407
High-income countries	0	0	0	0	0	0	0	0	1	0	1	0	0	0	0	0	3	1	4
WORLD	23	27	6	8	20	18	53	22	75	28	44	20	31	20	9	8	260	151	412
Attributable YLL (thousands)																			
East Asia and Pacific	51	56	7	11	107	56	388	137	748	221	346	155	159	108	22	25	1,829	767	2,596
Europe and Central Asia	1	0	0	0	4	2	23	11	38	25	19	16	7	9	1	1	93	66	159
Latin America and the Caribbean	4	4	2	2	3	3	7	4	7	3	3	2	2	1	0	0	28	19	48
Middle East and North Africa	12	14	4	6	11	7	16	11	57	44	39	31	21	24	3	6	164	143	307
South Asia	192	290	58	109	297	289	575	246	471	213	158	80	76	51	17	12	1,843	1,290	3,133
Sub-Saharan Africa	438	442	104	117	106	137	239	135	103	57	29	18	11	9	1	2	1,031	917	1,949
Low- and middle-income countries	698	807	175	243	529	493	1,248	544	1,424	564	595	302	274	203	45	46	4,988	3,203	8,191
High-income countries	0	0	0	0	2	1	10	3	22	6	11	5	4	4	1	1	49	20	70
WORLD	699	807	175	244	530	494	1,258	547	1,446	570	605	308	278	206	45	47	5,038	3,223	8,261
Attributable DALYs (thousands)																			
East Asia and Pacific	53	58	8	12	132	69	424	158	786	244	360	166	166	116	24	28	1,954	851	2,805
Europe and Central Asia	1	0	0	0	6	4	28	16	43	30	21	18	7	10	1	2	107	79	186
Latin America and the Caribbean	5	4	2	2	4	3	8	4	8	4	4	2	2	2	0	0	32	21	53
Middle East and North Africa	14	15	6	7	14	9	18	14	66	55	43	36	23	27	4	7	186	170	356
South Asia	202	321	70	132	355	346	623	279	512	239	174	91	84	59	19	14	2,040	1,481	3,521
Sub-Saharan Africa	445	449	107	120	128	158	253	144	108	62	31	21	12	11	2	2	1,087	967	2,054
Low- and middle-income countries	719	847	193	273	639	589	1,353	614	1,523	634	633	335	294	225	49	53	5,404	3,570	8,974
High-income countries	1	0	0	0	2	1	11	4	24	7	11	6	4	4	1	1	54	23	76
WORLD	720	848	194	273	641	590	1,364	618	1,547	640	644	341	299	229	50	53	5,458	3,592	9,050

Source: Authors' calculations.

Table 4A.104

Risk factor: Urban air pollution
Disease: Respiratory infections

Region	0–4 years Male	0–4 years Female	5–14 years Male	5–14 years Female	15–29 years Male	15–29 years Female	30–44 years Male	30–44 years Female	45–59 years Male	45–59 years Female	60–69 years Male	60–69 years Female	70–79 years Male	70–79 years Female	80+ years Male	80+ years Female	Total Male	Total Female	All
PAF of Mortality (%)																			
East Asia and Pacific	2	2	NA	NA	NA	NA	NA	NA	NA	NA	NA	NA	NA	NA	NA	NA	1	1	1
Europe and Central Asia	1	1	NA	NA	NA	NA	NA	NA	NA	NA	NA	NA	NA	NA	NA	NA	0	0	0
Latin America and the Caribbean	1	1	NA	NA	NA	NA	NA	NA	NA	NA	NA	NA	NA	NA	NA	NA	0	0	0
Middle East and North Africa	2	2	NA	NA	NA	NA	NA	NA	NA	NA	NA	NA	NA	NA	NA	NA	1	1	1
South Asia	1	1	NA	NA	NA	NA	NA	NA	NA	NA	NA	NA	NA	NA	NA	NA	1	1	1
Sub-Saharan Africa	1	1	NA	NA	NA	NA	NA	NA	NA	NA	NA	NA	NA	NA	NA	NA	1	1	1
Low- and middle-income countries	1	1	NA	NA	NA	NA	NA	NA	NA	NA	NA	NA	NA	NA	NA	NA	1	1	1
High-income countries	2	2	NA	NA	NA	NA	NA	NA	NA	NA	NA	NA	NA	NA	NA	NA	0	0	0
WORLD	1	1	NA	NA	NA	NA	NA	NA	NA	NA	NA	NA	NA	NA	NA	NA	1	1	1
PAF of YLL (%)																			
East Asia and Pacific	2	2	NA	NA	NA	NA	NA	NA	NA	NA	NA	NA	NA	NA	NA	NA	1	1	1
Europe and Central Asia	1	1	NA	NA	NA	NA	NA	NA	NA	NA	NA	NA	NA	NA	NA	NA	1	1	1
Latin America and the Caribbean	1	1	NA	NA	NA	NA	NA	NA	NA	NA	NA	NA	NA	NA	NA	NA	1	1	1
Middle East and North Africa	2	2	NA	NA	NA	NA	NA	NA	NA	NA	NA	NA	NA	NA	NA	NA	1	1	1
South Asia	1	1	NA	NA	NA	NA	NA	NA	NA	NA	NA	NA	NA	NA	NA	NA	1	1	1
Sub-Saharan Africa	1	1	NA	NA	NA	NA	NA	NA	NA	NA	NA	NA	NA	NA	NA	NA	1	1	1
Low- and middle-income countries	1	1	NA	NA	NA	NA	NA	NA	NA	NA	NA	NA	NA	NA	NA	NA	1	1	1
High-income countries	2	2	NA	NA	NA	NA	NA	NA	NA	NA	NA	NA	NA	NA	NA	NA	0	0	0
WORLD	1	1	NA	NA	NA	NA	NA	NA	NA	NA	NA	NA	NA	NA	NA	NA	1	1	1
PAF of DALYs (%)																			
East Asia and Pacific	2	2	NA	NA	NA	NA	NA	NA	NA	NA	NA	NA	NA	NA	NA	NA	1	1	1
Europe and Central Asia	1	1	NA	NA	NA	NA	NA	NA	NA	NA	NA	NA	NA	NA	NA	NA	1	1	1
Latin America and the Caribbean	1	1	NA	NA	NA	NA	NA	NA	NA	NA	NA	NA	NA	NA	NA	NA	1	1	1
Middle East and North Africa	2	2	NA	NA	NA	NA	NA	NA	NA	NA	NA	NA	NA	NA	NA	NA	1	1	1
South Asia	1	1	NA	NA	NA	NA	NA	NA	NA	NA	NA	NA	NA	NA	NA	NA	1	1	1
Sub-Saharan Africa	1	1	NA	NA	NA	NA	NA	NA	NA	NA	NA	NA	NA	NA	NA	NA	1	1	1
Low- and middle-income countries	1	1	NA	NA	NA	NA	NA	NA	NA	NA	NA	NA	NA	NA	NA	NA	1	1	1
High-income countries	1	1	NA	NA	NA	NA	NA	NA	NA	NA	NA	NA	NA	NA	NA	NA	0	0	0
WORLD	1	1	NA	NA	NA	NA	NA	NA	NA	NA	NA	NA	NA	NA	NA	NA	1	1	1
Attributable Mortality (thousands)																			
East Asia and Pacific	1	3	NA	NA	NA	NA	NA	NA	NA	NA	NA	NA	NA	NA	NA	NA	1	3	4
Europe and Central Asia	0	0	NA	NA	NA	NA	NA	NA	NA	NA	NA	NA	NA	NA	NA	NA	0	0	0
Latin America and the Caribbean	0	0	NA	NA	NA	NA	NA	NA	NA	NA	NA	NA	NA	NA	NA	NA	0	0	1
Middle East and North Africa	1	1	NA	NA	NA	NA	NA	NA	NA	NA	NA	NA	NA	NA	NA	NA	1	1	1
South Asia	5	5	NA	NA	NA	NA	NA	NA	NA	NA	NA	NA	NA	NA	NA	NA	5	5	10
Sub-Saharan Africa	4	3	NA	NA	NA	NA	NA	NA	NA	NA	NA	NA	NA	NA	NA	NA	4	3	6
Low- and middle-income countries	11	11	NA	NA	NA	NA	NA	NA	NA	NA	NA	NA	NA	NA	NA	NA	11	11	23
High-income countries	0	0	NA	NA	NA	NA	NA	NA	NA	NA	NA	NA	NA	NA	NA	NA	0	0	0
WORLD	11	11	NA	NA	NA	NA	NA	NA	NA	NA	NA	NA	NA	NA	NA	NA	11	11	23
Attributable YLL (thousands)																			
East Asia and Pacific	44	83	NA	NA	NA	NA	NA	NA	NA	NA	NA	NA	NA	NA	NA	NA	44	83	127
Europe and Central Asia	7	6	NA	NA	NA	NA	NA	NA	NA	NA	NA	NA	NA	NA	NA	NA	7	6	13
Latin America and the Caribbean	9	8	NA	NA	NA	NA	NA	NA	NA	NA	NA	NA	NA	NA	NA	NA	9	8	17
Middle East and North Africa	20	19	NA	NA	NA	NA	NA	NA	NA	NA	NA	NA	NA	NA	NA	NA	20	19	39
South Asia	152	154	NA	NA	NA	NA	NA	NA	NA	NA	NA	NA	NA	NA	NA	NA	152	154	306
Sub-Saharan Africa	107	79	NA	NA	NA	NA	NA	NA	NA	NA	NA	NA	NA	NA	NA	NA	107	79	186
Low- and middle-income countries	340	349	NA	NA	NA	NA	NA	NA	NA	NA	NA	NA	NA	NA	NA	NA	340	349	688
High-income countries	1	0	NA	NA	NA	NA	NA	NA	NA	NA	NA	NA	NA	NA	NA	NA	1	0	1
WORLD	340	349	NA	NA	NA	NA	NA	NA	NA	NA	NA	NA	NA	NA	NA	NA	340	349	689
Attributable DALYs (thousands)																			
East Asia and Pacific	44	83	NA	NA	NA	NA	NA	NA	NA	NA	NA	NA	NA	NA	NA	NA	44	83	127
Europe and Central Asia	7	6	NA	NA	NA	NA	NA	NA	NA	NA	NA	NA	NA	NA	NA	NA	7	6	13
Latin America and the Caribbean	9	8	NA	NA	NA	NA	NA	NA	NA	NA	NA	NA	NA	NA	NA	NA	9	8	17
Middle East and North Africa	20	19	NA	NA	NA	NA	NA	NA	NA	NA	NA	NA	NA	NA	NA	NA	20	19	39
South Asia	152	154	NA	NA	NA	NA	NA	NA	NA	NA	NA	NA	NA	NA	NA	NA	152	154	306
Sub-Saharan Africa	107	79	NA	NA	NA	NA	NA	NA	NA	NA	NA	NA	NA	NA	NA	NA	107	79	186
Low- and middle-income countries	340	349	NA	NA	NA	NA	NA	NA	NA	NA	NA	NA	NA	NA	NA	NA	340	349	688
High-income countries	1	0	NA	NA	NA	NA	NA	NA	NA	NA	NA	NA	NA	NA	NA	NA	1	0	1
WORLD	340	349	NA	NA	NA	NA	NA	NA	NA	NA	NA	NA	NA	NA	NA	NA	340	349	689

Source: Authors' calculations.
Note: NA = not applicable.

Table 4A.105

Risk factor: Urban air pollution
Disease: Trachea, bronchus, and lung cancers

Region	0–4 years Male	0–4 years Female	5–14 years Male	5–14 years Female	15–29 years Male	15–29 years Female	30–44 years Male	30–44 years Female	45–59 years Male	45–59 years Female	60–69 years Male	60–69 years Female	70–79 years Male	70–79 years Female	80+ years Male	80+ years Female	Total Male	Total Female	All
PAF of Mortality (%)																			
East Asia and Pacific	NA	NA	NA	NA	NA	NA	9	9	9	9	9	9	9	10	9	10	9	9	9
Europe and Central Asia	NA	NA	NA	NA	NA	NA	4	4	4	4	4	4	4	3	4	3	4	4	4
Latin America and the Caribbean	NA	NA	NA	NA	NA	NA	4	4	4	4	4	4	4	4	4	4	4	4	4
Middle East and North Africa	NA	NA	NA	NA	NA	NA	6	6	6	6	6	6	6	6	6	6	6	6	6
South Asia	NA	NA	NA	NA	NA	NA	5	5	5	5	5	5	5	5	5	5	5	5	5
Sub-Saharan Africa	NA	NA	NA	NA	NA	NA	4	3	3	3	3	3	3	3	4	3	3	3	3
Low- and middle-income countries	NA	NA	NA	NA	NA	NA	7	7	6	7	6	7	7	8	7	7	6	7	7
High-income countries	NA	NA	NA	NA	NA	NA	3	3	3	3	3	3	3	3	3	3	3	3	3
WORLD	NA	NA	NA	NA	NA	NA	6	6	5	6	5	6	5	5	4	5	5	5	5
PAF of YLL (%)																			
East Asia and Pacific	NA	NA	NA	NA	NA	NA	9	9	9	9	9	9	9	10	9	10	9	9	9
Europe and Central Asia	NA	NA	NA	NA	NA	NA	4	4	4	4	4	4	4	3	4	3	4	4	4
Latin America and the Caribbean	NA	NA	NA	NA	NA	NA	4	4	4	4	4	4	4	4	4	4	4	4	4
Middle East and North Africa	NA	NA	NA	NA	NA	NA	6	6	6	6	6	6	6	6	6	6	6	5	6
South Asia	NA	NA	NA	NA	NA	NA	5	5	5	5	5	5	5	5	5	5	5	5	5
Sub-Saharan Africa	NA	NA	NA	NA	NA	NA	4	3	3	3	3	3	3	3	4	3	3	3	3
Low- and middle-income countries	NA	NA	NA	NA	NA	NA	7	7	6	7	6	7	7	8	7	7	6	7	7
High-income countries	NA	NA	NA	NA	NA	NA	3	3	3	3	3	3	3	3	3	3	3	3	3
WORLD	NA	NA	NA	NA	NA	NA	6	6	5	6	5	6	5	6	4	5	5	6	5
PAF of DALYs (%)																			
East Asia and Pacific	NA	NA	NA	NA	NA	NA	9	9	9	9	9	9	9	9	9	9	9	9	9
Europe and Central Asia	NA	NA	NA	NA	NA	NA	4	4	4	4	3	4	3	3	3	3	3	4	3
Latin America and the Caribbean	NA	NA	NA	NA	NA	NA	4	4	4	4	4	4	4	4	4	4	4	4	4
Middle East and North Africa	NA	NA	NA	NA	NA	NA	6	6	6	6	6	6	6	6	5	6	6	5	6
South Asia	NA	NA	NA	NA	NA	NA	5	5	5	5	5	5	5	5	5	5	5	5	5
Sub-Saharan Africa	NA	NA	NA	NA	NA	NA	4	3	3	3	3	3	3	3	3	3	3	3	3
Low- and middle-income countries	NA	NA	NA	NA	NA	NA	7	7	6	7	6	7	6	8	6	7	6	7	7
High-income countries	NA	NA	NA	NA	NA	NA	3	3	3	3	3	3	3	3	3	3	3	3	3
WORLD	NA	NA	NA	NA	NA	NA	6	6	5	6	5	6	5	5	4	5	5	6	5
Attributable Mortality (thousands)																			
East Asia and Pacific	NA	NA	NA	NA	NA	NA	1	1	5	3	9	3	7	4	2	1	24	12	36
Europe and Central Asia	NA	NA	NA	NA	NA	NA	0	0	1	0	2	0	1	0	0	0	5	1	6
Latin America and the Caribbean	NA	NA	NA	NA	NA	NA	0	0	0	0	1	0	1	0	0	0	2	1	2
Middle East and North Africa	NA	NA	NA	NA	NA	NA	0	0	0	0	0	0	0	0	0	0	1	0	1
South Asia	NA	NA	NA	NA	NA	NA	0	0	1	0	2	0	1	0	0	0	5	1	6
Sub-Saharan Africa	NA	NA	NA	NA	NA	NA	0	0	0	0	0	0	0	0	0	0	0	0	0
Low- and middle-income countries	NA	NA	NA	NA	NA	NA	2	1	9	3	13	4	11	5	3	2	37	15	52
High-income countries	NA	NA	NA	NA	NA	NA	0	0	1	1	2	1	3	1	1	1	8	4	12
WORLD	NA	NA	NA	NA	NA	NA	2	1	10	4	16	5	14	6	4	2	45	19	64
Attributable YLL (thousands)																			
East Asia and Pacific	NA	NA	NA	NA	NA	NA	25	14	101	52	117	51	65	42	9	7	316	166	482
Europe and Central Asia	NA	NA	NA	NA	NA	NA	4	1	24	4	26	4	12	4	1	1	67	14	81
Latin America and the Caribbean	NA	NA	NA	NA	NA	NA	1	1	7	3	7	3	5	2	1	1	21	10	31
Middle East and North Africa	NA	NA	NA	NA	NA	NA	2	1	4	1	4	1	2	1	0	0	12	4	16
South Asia	NA	NA	NA	NA	NA	NA	5	2	23	6	24	5	12	3	2	0	67	17	84
Sub-Saharan Africa	NA	NA	NA	NA	NA	NA	0	0	2	1	2	1	1	0	0	0	5	2	7
Low- and middle-income countries	NA	NA	NA	NA	NA	NA	38	20	162	68	179	65	96	51	13	9	488	213	701
High-income countries	NA	NA	NA	NA	NA	NA	3	3	24	13	31	14	27	14	7	5	92	49	141
WORLD	NA	NA	NA	NA	NA	NA	41	23	186	81	209	79	123	65	20	14	580	262	842
Attributable DALYs (thousands)																			
East Asia and Pacific	NA	NA	NA	NA	NA	NA	25	14	101	52	117	51	65	42	9	7	316	166	482
Europe and Central Asia	NA	NA	NA	NA	NA	NA	4	1	24	4	26	4	12	4	1	1	67	14	81
Latin America and the Caribbean	NA	NA	NA	NA	NA	NA	1	1	7	3	7	3	5	2	1	1	21	10	31
Middle East and North Africa	NA	NA	NA	NA	NA	NA	2	1	4	1	4	1	2	1	0	0	12	4	16
South Asia	NA	NA	NA	NA	NA	NA	5	2	23	6	24	5	12	3	2	0	67	17	84
Sub-Saharan Africa	NA	NA	NA	NA	NA	NA	0	0	2	1	2	1	1	0	0	0	5	2	7
Low- and middle-income countries	NA	NA	NA	NA	NA	NA	38	20	162	68	179	65	96	51	13	9	488	213	701
High-income countries	NA	NA	NA	NA	NA	NA	3	3	24	13	31	14	27	14	7	5	92	49	141
WORLD	NA	NA	NA	NA	NA	NA	41	23	186	81	209	79	123	65	20	14	580	262	842

Source: Authors' calculations.
Note: NA = not applicable.

Table 4A.106

Risk factor: Urban air pollution
Disease: Selected cardiopulmonary causes

Region	0–4 years Male	0–4 years Female	5–14 years Male	5–14 years Female	15–29 years Male	15–29 years Female	30–44 years Male	30–44 years Female	45–59 years Male	45–59 years Female	60–69 years Male	60–69 years Female	70–79 years Male	70–79 years Female	80+ years Male	80+ years Female	Total Male	Total Female	All
PAF of Mortality (%)																			
East Asia and Pacific	NA	NA	NA	NA	NA	NA	6	6	6	6	6	6	6	6	7	7	6	6	6
Europe and Central Asia	NA	NA	NA	NA	NA	NA	2	3	2	3	3	3	3	2	3	2	2	2	2
Latin America and the Caribbean	NA	NA	NA	NA	NA	NA	3	3	3	3	3	3	3	3	3	3	3	3	3
Middle East and North Africa	NA	NA	NA	NA	NA	NA	4	4	4	5	4	5	4	5	4	4	4	4	4
South Asia	NA	NA	NA	NA	NA	NA	4	3	3	3	3	3	3	3	4	3	3	3	3
Sub-Saharan Africa	NA	NA	NA	NA	NA	NA	2	2	2	2	2	2	3	2	3	2	1	1	1
Low- and middle-income countries	NA	NA	NA	NA	NA	NA	4	4	4	4	4	4	4	4	5	4	4	4	4
High-income countries	NA	NA	NA	NA	NA	NA	2	2	2	2	2	2	2	2	2	2	2	2	2
WORLD	NA	NA	NA	NA	NA	NA	4	4	4	4	4	4	4	4	4	4	3	3	3
PAF of YLL (%)																			
East Asia and Pacific	NA	NA	NA	NA	NA	NA	6	6	6	6	6	6	6	6	7	7	6	5	6
Europe and Central Asia	NA	NA	NA	NA	NA	NA	2	3	2	3	3	3	3	2	3	2	2	2	2
Latin America and the Caribbean	NA	NA	NA	NA	NA	NA	3	3	3	3	3	3	3	3	3	3	3	3	3
Middle East and North Africa	NA	NA	NA	NA	NA	NA	4	4	4	5	4	5	4	5	4	4	3	3	3
South Asia	NA	NA	NA	NA	NA	NA	4	3	3	3	3	3	3	3	4	3	2	2	2
Sub-Saharan Africa	NA	NA	NA	NA	NA	NA	2	2	2	2	2	2	3	2	3	2	1	1	1
Low- and middle-income countries	NA	NA	NA	NA	NA	NA	4	4	4	4	4	4	4	4	5	5	3	3	3
High-income countries	NA	NA	NA	NA	NA	NA	2	2	2	2	2	2	2	2	2	2	2	2	2
WORLD	NA	NA	NA	NA	NA	NA	4	4	4	4	4	4	4	4	4	4	3	3	3
PAF of DALYs (%)																			
East Asia and Pacific	NA	NA	NA	NA	NA	NA	4	4	4	5	5	5	6	6	6	6	4	5	4
Europe and Central Asia	NA	NA	NA	NA	NA	NA	2	2	2	2	2	2	2	2	2	2	2	2	2
Latin America and the Caribbean	NA	NA	NA	NA	NA	NA	2	2	3	2	3	3	3	3	3	3	2	2	2
Middle East and North Africa	NA	NA	NA	NA	NA	NA	3	3	4	4	4	4	4	4	4	4	3	3	3
South Asia	NA	NA	NA	NA	NA	NA	3	3	3	3	3	3	3	3	3	3	2	2	2
Sub-Saharan Africa	NA	NA	NA	NA	NA	NA	2	2	2	2	2	2	2	2	2	2	1	1	1
Low- and middle-income countries	NA	NA	NA	NA	NA	NA	3	3	3	3	4	4	4	4	4	4	2	3	2
High-income countries	NA	NA	NA	NA	NA	NA	1	1	1	1	2	2	2	2	2	2	1	1	1
WORLD	NA	NA	NA	NA	NA	NA	3	3	3	3	3	3	4	4	4	4	2	2	2
Attributable Mortality (thousands)																			
East Asia and Pacific	NA	NA	NA	NA	NA	NA	5	3	23	14	41	29	62	62	40	71	171	179	349
Europe and Central Asia	NA	NA	NA	NA	NA	NA	2	1	6	3	10	6	12	15	6	17	37	41	78
Latin America and the Caribbean	NA	NA	NA	NA	NA	NA	1	1	3	2	4	3	5	4	5	6	18	16	34
Middle East and North Africa	NA	NA	NA	NA	NA	NA	1	0	3	2	4	3	5	5	3	3	15	13	28
South Asia	NA	NA	NA	NA	NA	NA	3	2	16	10	22	18	24	23	11	12	76	65	141
Sub-Saharan Africa	NA	NA	NA	NA	NA	NA	1	1	3	3	4	4	4	5	2	3	15	15	30
Low- and middle-income countries	NA	NA	NA	NA	NA	NA	13	8	54	33	85	62	113	113	67	112	332	329	660
High-income countries	NA	NA	NA	NA	NA	NA	1	0	3	1	5	3	10	8	12	20	31	33	64
WORLD	NA	NA	NA	NA	NA	NA	14	9	57	34	90	65	123	121	79	132	363	362	724
Attributable YLL (thousands)																			
East Asia and Pacific	NA	NA	NA	NA	NA	NA	125	79	421	282	547	431	550	628	198	356	1,842	1,776	3,618
Europe and Central Asia	NA	NA	NA	NA	NA	NA	40	14	121	50	137	97	111	152	29	78	438	391	829
Latin America and the Caribbean	NA	NA	NA	NA	NA	NA	23	16	55	38	51	40	46	45	22	30	197	169	365
Middle East and North Africa	NA	NA	NA	NA	NA	NA	21	12	53	35	53	44	46	47	13	17	186	155	341
South Asia	NA	NA	NA	NA	NA	NA	80	56	294	199	299	268	211	237	55	63	939	824	1,763
Sub-Saharan Africa	NA	NA	NA	NA	NA	NA	31	30	60	55	54	58	39	49	10	15	194	206	401
Low- and middle-income countries	NA	NA	NA	NA	NA	NA	319	207	1,006	658	1,141	939	1,005	1,157	326	560	3,797	3,520	7,317
High-income countries	NA	NA	NA	NA	NA	NA	16	8	59	27	69	43	85	80	53	83	282	240	522
WORLD	NA	NA	NA	NA	NA	NA	336	214	1,065	685	1,209	981	1,090	1,237	379	644	4,079	3,761	7,839
Attributable DALYs (thousands)																			
East Asia and Pacific	NA	NA	NA	NA	NA	NA	125	79	421	282	547	431	550	628	198	356	1,842	1,776	3,618
Europe and Central Asia	NA	NA	NA	NA	NA	NA	40	14	121	50	137	97	111	152	29	78	438	391	829
Latin America and the Caribbean	NA	NA	NA	NA	NA	NA	23	16	55	38	51	40	46	45	22	30	197	169	365
Middle East and North Africa	NA	NA	NA	NA	NA	NA	21	12	53	35	53	44	46	47	13	17	186	155	341
South Asia	NA	NA	NA	NA	NA	NA	80	56	294	199	299	268	211	237	55	63	939	824	1,763
Sub-Saharan Africa	NA	NA	NA	NA	NA	NA	31	30	60	55	54	58	39	49	10	15	194	206	401
Low- and middle-income countries	NA	NA	NA	NA	NA	NA	319	207	1,006	658	1,141	939	1,005	1,157	326	560	3,797	3,520	7,317
High-income countries	NA	NA	NA	NA	NA	NA	16	8	59	27	69	43	85	80	53	83	282	240	522
WORLD	NA	NA	NA	NA	NA	NA	336	214	1,065	685	1,209	981	1,090	1,237	379	644	4,079	3,761	7,839

Source: Authors' calculations.
Note: NA = not applicable.

Table 4A.107

Risk factor: Urban air pollution
Disease: All causes

Region	0–4 years Male	Female	5–14 years Male	Female	15–29 years Male	Female	30–44 years Male	Female	45–59 years Male	Female	60–69 years Male	Female	70–79 years Male	Female	80+ years Male	Female	Total Male	Female	All
PAF of Mortality (%)																			
East Asia and Pacific	0	0	NA	NA	NA	NA	1	1	2	2	4	3	4	4	5	5	3	3	3
Europe and Central Asia	0	0	NA	NA	NA	NA	1	1	1	1	2	2	2	2	2	2	1	2	1
Latin America and the Caribbean	0	0	NA	NA	NA	NA	0	1	1	1	2	1	2	2	2	2	1	1	1
Middle East and North Africa	0	0	NA	NA	NA	NA	1	1	2	2	2	2	3	3	3	3	2	2	2
South Asia	0	0	NA	NA	NA	NA	1	0	2	1	2	2	2	2	2	2	1	1	1
Sub-Saharan Africa	0	0	NA	NA	NA	NA	0	0	1	1	1	1	1	1	1	1	0	0	0
Low- and middle-income countries	0	0	NA	NA	NA	NA	1	1	2	1	2	2	3	3	3	3	1	2	2
High-income countries	0	0	NA	NA	NA	NA	0	0	1	1	1	1	1	1	1	1	1	1	1
WORLD	0	0	NA	NA	NA	NA	1	1	1	1	2	2	2	2	2	2	1	1	1
PAF of YLL (%)																			
East Asia and Pacific	0	0	NA	NA	NA	NA	1	1	2	2	4	3	4	4	5	5	2	2	2
Europe and Central Asia	0	0	NA	NA	NA	NA	1	1	1	1	2	2	2	2	2	2	1	1	1
Latin America and the Caribbean	0	0	NA	NA	NA	NA	0	1	1	1	2	1	2	2	2	2	1	1	1
Middle East and North Africa	0	0	NA	NA	NA	NA	1	1	2	2	2	2	3	3	3	3	1	1	1
South Asia	0	0	NA	NA	NA	NA	1	0	2	1	2	2	2	2	2	2	1	1	1
Sub-Saharan Africa	0	0	NA	NA	NA	NA	0	0	1	1	1	1	1	1	1	1	0	0	0
Low- and middle-income countries	0	0	NA	NA	NA	NA	1	0	2	1	2	2	3	3	3	3	1	1	1
High-income countries	0	0	NA	NA	NA	NA	0	0	1	1	1	1	1	1	1	1	1	1	1
WORLD	0	0	NA	NA	NA	NA	1	0	1	1	2	2	2	2	2	2	1	1	1
PAF of DALYs (%)																			
East Asia and Pacific	0	0	NA	NA	NA	NA	1	0	1	1	2	2	3	3	4	4	1	1	1
Europe and Central Asia	0	0	NA	NA	NA	NA	0	0	1	1	1	1	2	1	2	1	1	1	1
Latin America and the Caribbean	0	0	NA	NA	NA	NA	0	0	1	1	1	1	1	1	1	1	0	0	0
Middle East and North Africa	0	0	NA	NA	NA	NA	1	0	1	1	2	2	2	2	2	2	1	1	1
South Asia	0	0	NA	NA	NA	NA	0	0	1	1	2	1	2	2	2	2	1	0	1
Sub-Saharan Africa	0	0	NA	NA	NA	NA	0	0	0	0	1	1	1	1	1	1	0	0	0
Low- and middle-income countries	0	0	NA	NA	NA	NA	0	0	1	1	2	1	2	2	2	2	1	1	1
High-income countries	0	0	NA	NA	NA	NA	0	0	0	0	1	0	1	1	1	1	0	0	0
WORLD	0	0	NA	NA	NA	NA	0	0	1	1	2	1	2	2	2	2	1	1	1
Attributable Mortality (thousands)																			
East Asia and Pacific	1	3	NA	NA	NA	NA	6	4	28	17	49	32	69	66	42	72	196	193	389
Europe and Central Asia	0	0	NA	NA	NA	NA	2	1	8	3	12	7	14	15	7	17	42	42	84
Latin America and the Caribbean	0	0	NA	NA	NA	NA	1	1	3	2	4	3	6	5	5	7	20	17	37
Middle East and North Africa	1	1	NA	NA	NA	NA	1	1	3	2	4	3	5	5	3	3	17	14	31
South Asia	5	5	NA	NA	NA	NA	4	2	17	10	24	18	25	23	12	12	86	71	157
Sub-Saharan Africa	4	3	NA	NA	NA	NA	1	1	3	3	4	4	4	5	2	3	19	18	37
Low- and middle-income countries	11	11	NA	NA	NA	NA	15	9	63	36	98	67	123	118	69	113	380	355	735
High-income countries	0	0	NA	NA	NA	NA	1	0	4	2	7	4	13	9	14	21	39	37	76
WORLD	11	11	NA	NA	NA	NA	16	10	67	38	105	71	136	127	83	135	419	392	811
Attributable YLL (thousands)																			
East Asia and Pacific	44	83	NA	NA	NA	NA	150	94	522	334	664	482	615	670	207	363	2,202	2,025	4,227
Europe and Central Asia	7	6	NA	NA	NA	NA	44	15	146	54	163	102	123	155	30	79	512	411	923
Latin America and the Caribbean	9	8	NA	NA	NA	NA	24	17	62	41	58	43	51	47	23	31	227	187	414
Middle East and North Africa	20	19	NA	NA	NA	NA	22	13	57	36	57	45	49	48	13	17	218	177	395
South Asia	152	154	NA	NA	NA	NA	86	58	318	205	323	274	223	240	57	64	1,159	995	2,154
Sub-Saharan Africa	107	79	NA	NA	NA	NA	31	30	63	56	55	58	40	49	10	15	307	287	594
Low- and middle-income countries	340	349	NA	NA	NA	NA	357	227	1,167	726	1,320	1,003	1,101	1,209	340	569	4,625	4,082	8,707
High-income countries	1	0	NA	NA	NA	NA	20	10	83	40	99	57	112	94	60	88	374	290	664
WORLD	340	349	NA	NA	NA	NA	377	237	1,251	766	1,419	1,060	1,213	1,302	400	657	4,999	4,372	9,371
Attributable DALYs (thousands)																			
East Asia and Pacific	44	83	NA	NA	NA	NA	150	94	522	334	664	482	615	670	207	363	2,202	2,025	4,227
Europe and Central Asia	7	6	NA	NA	NA	NA	44	15	146	54	163	102	123	155	30	79	512	411	923
Latin America and the Caribbean	9	8	NA	NA	NA	NA	24	17	62	41	58	43	51	47	23	31	227	187	414
Middle East and North Africa	20	19	NA	NA	NA	NA	22	13	57	36	57	45	49	48	13	17	218	177	395
South Asia	152	154	NA	NA	NA	NA	86	58	318	205	323	274	223	240	57	64	1,159	995	2,154
Sub-Saharan Africa	107	79	NA	NA	NA	NA	31	30	63	56	55	58	40	49	10	15	307	287	594
Low- and middle-income countries	340	349	NA	NA	NA	NA	357	227	1,167	726	1,320	1,003	1,101	1,209	340	569	4,625	4,082	8,707
High-income countries	1	0	NA	NA	NA	NA	20	10	83	40	99	57	112	94	60	88	374	290	664
WORLD	340	349	NA	NA	NA	NA	377	237	1,251	766	1,419	1,060	1,213	1,302	400	657	4,999	4,372	9,371

Source: Authors' calculations.
Note: NA = not applicable.

Table 4A.108

Risk factor: Smoking
Disease: Chronic obstructive pulmonary disease

Region	0–4 years Male	0–4 years Female	5–14 years Male	5–14 years Female	15–29 years Male	15–29 years Female	30–44 years Male	30–44 years Female	45–59 years Male	45–59 years Female	60–69 years Male	60–69 years Female	70–79 years Male	70–79 years Female	80+ years Male	80+ years Female	Total Male	Total Female	All
PAF of Mortality (%)																			
East Asia and Pacific	NA	NA	NA	NA	NA	NA	70	42	54	21	48	21	41	17	44	13	44	16	29
Europe and Central Asia	NA	NA	NA	NA	NA	NA	87	44	89	51	86	43	78	45	64	27	79	38	64
Latin America and the Caribbean	NA	NA	NA	NA	NA	NA	52	23	68	45	64	44	59	42	60	47	60	43	53
Middle East and North Africa	NA	NA	NA	NA	NA	NA	69	63	67	38	64	28	59	26	60	11	60	25	45
South Asia	NA	NA	NA	NA	NA	NA	52	0	70	25	66	25	59	9	58	0	64	16	42
Sub-Saharan Africa	NA	NA	NA	NA	NA	NA	23	15	46	22	42	18	35	13	33	13	38	15	29
Low- and middle-income countries	NA	NA	NA	NA	NA	NA	53	18	65	25	58	24	48	17	47	14	53	18	36
High-income countries	NA	NA	NA	NA	NA	NA	71	62	81	69	80	70	79	73	79	74	79	73	76
WORLD	NA	NA	NA	NA	NA	NA	54	19	65	27	59	27	52	22	54	22	56	23	40
PAF of YLL (%)																			
East Asia and Pacific	NA	NA	NA	NA	NA	NA	70	42	54	21	48	21	41	17	44	13	46	18	31
Europe and Central Asia	NA	NA	NA	NA	NA	NA	87	44	89	51	86	43	78	45	64	27	81	41	68
Latin America and the Caribbean	NA	NA	NA	NA	NA	NA	52	23	68	45	64	44	59	42	60	47	59	38	50
Middle East and North Africa	NA	NA	NA	NA	NA	NA	69	63	67	38	64	28	59	26	60	11	59	28	46
South Asia	NA	NA	NA	NA	NA	NA	52	0	70	25	66	25	59	9	58	0	65	19	44
Sub-Saharan Africa	NA	NA	NA	NA	NA	NA	23	15	46	22	42	18	35	13	33	13	38	16	30
Low- and middle-income countries	NA	NA	NA	NA	NA	NA	53	18	65	25	58	24	48	17	47	14	55	20	38
High-income countries	NA	NA	NA	NA	NA	NA	71	62	81	69	80	70	79	73	79	74	79	72	76
WORLD	NA	NA	NA	NA	NA	NA	54	19	65	27	60	27	52	22	53	21	57	24	41
PAF of DALYs (%)																			
East Asia and Pacific	NA	NA	NA	NA	NA	NA	70	42	54	21	48	21	41	17	44	13	48	19	34
Europe and Central Asia	NA	NA	NA	NA	NA	NA	87	44	89	51	86	43	78	45	64	27	81	42	64
Latin America and the Caribbean	NA	NA	NA	NA	NA	NA	52	23	68	45	64	44	59	42	60	47	60	35	48
Middle East and North Africa	NA	NA	NA	NA	NA	NA	69	63	67	38	64	28	59	26	60	11	61	34	52
South Asia	NA	NA	NA	NA	NA	NA	52	0	70	25	66	25	59	9	58	0	65	18	43
Sub-Saharan Africa	NA	NA	NA	NA	NA	NA	23	15	46	22	42	18	35	13	33	13	37	16	30
Low- and middle-income countries	NA	NA	NA	NA	NA	NA	60	27	62	27	58	25	48	18	47	14	55	21	40
High-income countries	NA	NA	NA	NA	NA	NA	71	62	81	69	80	70	79	73	79	74	77	68	73
WORLD	NA	NA	NA	NA	NA	NA	62	36	65	34	60	30	53	23	54	22	58	28	44
Attributable Mortality (thousands)																			
East Asia and Pacific	NA	NA	NA	NA	NA	NA	2	1	25	7	66	23	113	48	83	44	289	123	412
Europe and Central Asia	NA	NA	NA	NA	NA	NA	2	0	9	2	22	3	25	8	9	5	66	18	84
Latin America and the Caribbean	NA	NA	NA	NA	NA	NA	0	0	3	1	7	3	12	5	12	8	35	18	53
Middle East and North Africa	NA	NA	NA	NA	NA	NA	1	0	2	1	4	1	5	2	3	0	14	4	18
South Asia	NA	NA	NA	NA	NA	NA	3	0	63	18	65	15	52	7	20	0	204	40	244
Sub-Saharan Africa	NA	NA	NA	NA	NA	NA	1	0	6	1	8	2	9	2	4	1	28	6	34
Low- and middle-income countries	NA	NA	NA	NA	NA	NA	9	2	108	30	172	48	216	71	131	58	635	210	845
High-income countries	NA	NA	NA	NA	NA	NA	0	0	6	4	20	11	51	30	58	48	135	93	227
WORLD	NA	NA	NA	NA	NA	NA	9	3	114	34	191	58	267	102	188	106	770	302	1,072
Attributable YLL (thousands)																			
East Asia and Pacific	NA	NA	NA	NA	NA	NA	37	31	453	144	874	347	998	483	414	221	2,776	1,226	4,002
Europe and Central Asia	NA	NA	NA	NA	NA	NA	40	7	168	30	294	47	227	80	40	23	769	188	957
Latin America and the Caribbean	NA	NA	NA	NA	NA	NA	11	4	58	29	95	46	105	52	55	38	325	168	493
Middle East and North Africa	NA	NA	NA	NA	NA	NA	12	8	35	16	51	15	47	17	14	3	158	58	216
South Asia	NA	NA	NA	NA	NA	NA	83	0	1,144	350	890	231	465	75	100	0	2,683	657	3,339
Sub-Saharan Africa	NA	NA	NA	NA	NA	NA	18	4	110	27	112	26	78	19	20	7	338	83	420
Low- and middle-income countries	NA	NA	NA	NA	NA	NA	202	55	1,968	596	2,317	712	1,920	726	643	290	7,048	2,380	9,428
High-income countries	NA	NA	NA	NA	NA	NA	11	6	111	71	259	159	446	307	256	213	1,083	756	1,838
WORLD	NA	NA	NA	NA	NA	NA	212	61	2,079	667	2,576	871	2,365	1,033	899	503	8,131	3,136	11,267
Attributable DALYs (thousands)																			
East Asia and Pacific	NA	NA	NA	NA	NA	NA	215	152	1,264	204	1,190	421	1,123	534	457	232	4,250	1,543	5,793
Europe and Central Asia	NA	NA	NA	NA	NA	NA	127	94	277	123	369	83	272	96	47	25	1,093	422	1,514
Latin America and the Caribbean	NA	NA	NA	NA	NA	NA	65	59	206	99	168	73	133	65	64	43	636	339	976
Middle East and North Africa	NA	NA	NA	NA	NA	NA	113	35	85	24	61	17	50	17	14	3	325	96	420
South Asia	NA	NA	NA	NA	NA	NA	232	0	1,375	473	1,050	253	499	79	106	0	3,262	806	4,068
Sub-Saharan Africa	NA	NA	NA	NA	NA	NA	26	5	137	31	129	28	83	20	21	7	395	90	485
Low- and middle-income countries	NA	NA	NA	NA	NA	NA	779	345	3,344	954	2,968	876	2,160	811	710	310	9,961	3,296	13,257
High-income countries	NA	NA	NA	NA	NA	NA	178	268	632	453	491	316	590	383	289	253	2,181	1,673	3,853
WORLD	NA	NA	NA	NA	NA	NA	957	612	3,976	1,407	3,459	1,192	2,750	1,194	1,000	563	12,142	4,968	17,110

Source: Authors' calculations.
Note: NA = not applicable.

Table 4A.109

Risk factor: Smoking
Disease: Trachea, bronchus, and lung cancers

Region	0–4 years Male	0–4 Female	5–14 years Male	5–14 Female	15–29 years Male	15–29 Female	30–44 years Male	30–44 Female	45–59 years Male	45–59 Female	60–69 years Male	60–69 Female	70–79 years Male	70–79 Female	80+ years Male	80+ Female	Total Male	Total Female	All
PAF of Mortality (%)																			
East Asia and Pacific	NA	NA	NA	NA	NA	NA	51	19	52	20	60	25	59	19	60	12	57	20	45
Europe and Central Asia	NA	NA	NA	NA	NA	NA	76	21	93	55	95	54	93	51	83	26	92	48	85
Latin America and the Caribbean	NA	NA	NA	NA	NA	NA	36	10	78	49	85	55	84	49	81	45	80	47	70
Middle East and North Africa	NA	NA	NA	NA	NA	NA	52	36	77	42	85	38	84	33	80	13	79	34	69
South Asia	NA	NA	NA	NA	NA	NA	33	0	79	29	86	34	84	12	80	0	80	22	70
Sub-Saharan Africa	NA	NA	NA	NA	NA	NA	18	10	58	27	69	27	66	20	58	18	61	23	51
Low- and middle-income countries	NA	NA	NA	NA	NA	NA	51	16	71	29	76	33	74	26	71	18	72	27	60
High-income countries	NA	NA	NA	NA	NA	NA	55	33	88	73	92	78	93	78	91	72	91	74	86
WORLD	NA	NA	NA	NA	NA	NA	51	20	75	44	81	50	82	49	83	51	79	47	70
PAF of YLL (%)																			
East Asia and Pacific	NA	NA	NA	NA	NA	NA	51	19	52	20	60	25	59	19	60	12	56	21	44
Europe and Central Asia	NA	NA	NA	NA	NA	NA	76	21	93	55	95	54	93	51	83	26	92	49	85
Latin America and the Caribbean	NA	NA	NA	NA	NA	NA	36	10	78	49	85	55	84	49	81	45	78	45	67
Middle East and North Africa	NA	NA	NA	NA	NA	NA	52	36	77	42	85	38	84	33	80	13	76	35	65
South Asia	NA	NA	NA	NA	NA	NA	33	0	79	29	86	34	84	12	80	0	78	23	67
Sub-Saharan Africa	NA	NA	NA	NA	NA	NA	18	10	58	27	69	27	66	20	58	18	59	23	49
Low- and middle-income countries	NA	NA	NA	NA	NA	NA	51	16	71	29	76	33	74	26	71	17	71	27	59
High-income countries	NA	NA	NA	NA	NA	NA	55	33	88	73	92	78	93	78	91	72	90	74	84
WORLD	NA	NA	NA	NA	NA	NA	51	20	75	43	81	50	82	48	82	50	77	45	67
PAF of DALYs (%)																			
East Asia and Pacific	NA	NA	NA	NA	NA	NA	51	19	52	20	60	25	59	19	60	12	56	21	44
Europe and Central Asia	NA	NA	NA	NA	NA	NA	76	21	93	55	95	54	93	51	83	26	92	49	85
Latin America and the Caribbean	NA	NA	NA	NA	NA	NA	36	10	78	49	85	55	84	49	81	45	78	45	67
Middle East and North Africa	NA	NA	NA	NA	NA	NA	52	36	77	42	85	38	84	33	80	13	76	35	65
South Asia	NA	NA	NA	NA	NA	NA	33	0	79	29	86	34	84	12	80	0	78	23	67
Sub-Saharan Africa	NA	NA	NA	NA	NA	NA	18	10	58	27	69	27	66	20	58	18	59	23	49
Low- and middle-income countries	NA	NA	NA	NA	NA	NA	51	16	71	29	76	33	74	26	71	17	71	27	59
High-income countries	NA	NA	NA	NA	NA	NA	55	33	88	73	92	78	93	78	91	72	90	74	84
WORLD	NA	NA	NA	NA	NA	NA	51	20	75	44	81	50	82	49	82	50	77	45	67
Attributable Mortality (thousands)																			
East Asia and Pacific	NA	NA	NA	NA	NA	NA	6	1	31	6	57	9	45	8	11	2	150	25	176
Europe and Central Asia	NA	NA	NA	NA	NA	NA	4	0	34	3	50	4	34	5	5	1	126	14	140
Latin America and the Caribbean	NA	NA	NA	NA	NA	NA	0	0	6	2	10	3	10	2	4	1	31	8	39
Middle East and North Africa	NA	NA	NA	NA	NA	NA	1	0	3	0	4	0	4	0	1	0	12	1	14
South Asia	NA	NA	NA	NA	NA	NA	2	0	21	2	32	2	23	1	7	0	85	5	90
Sub-Saharan Africa	NA	NA	NA	NA	NA	NA	0	0	2	0	3	0	1	0	0	0	7	1	8
Low- and middle-income countries	NA	NA	NA	NA	NA	NA	12	2	97	13	156	19	117	17	28	4	411	55	466
High-income countries	NA	NA	NA	NA	NA	NA	3	1	44	17	80	26	107	39	49	25	283	108	391
WORLD	NA	NA	NA	NA	NA	NA	15	3	141	30	236	45	225	56	77	29	693	163	856
Attributable YLL (thousands)																			
East Asia and Pacific	NA	NA	NA	NA	NA	NA	139	29	583	112	765	136	410	85	58	9	1,953	371	2,324
Europe and Central Asia	NA	NA	NA	NA	NA	NA	83	7	629	66	688	66	316	53	23	5	1,740	196	1,936
Latin America and the Caribbean	NA	NA	NA	NA	NA	NA	11	3	120	38	133	39	89	23	19	6	373	109	482
Middle East and North Africa	NA	NA	NA	NA	NA	NA	12	5	51	10	55	6	34	4	5	0	158	25	183
South Asia	NA	NA	NA	NA	NA	NA	36	0	389	37	437	38	212	7	35	0	1,109	82	1,191
Sub-Saharan Africa	NA	NA	NA	NA	NA	NA	2	1	42	6	35	5	13	2	2	0	94	14	108
Low- and middle-income countries	NA	NA	NA	NA	NA	NA	284	45	1,814	269	2,114	290	1,073	174	143	20	5,427	797	6,224
High-income countries	NA	NA	NA	NA	NA	NA	67	28	810	331	1,074	396	957	402	233	123	3,141	1,281	4,422
WORLD	NA	NA	NA	NA	NA	NA	351	73	2,624	599	3,187	686	2,030	576	376	144	8,568	2,078	10,646
Attributable DALYs (thousands)																			
East Asia and Pacific	NA	NA	NA	NA	NA	NA	140	30	588	113	774	138	416	86	59	9	1,978	375	2,353
Europe and Central Asia	NA	NA	NA	NA	NA	NA	84	7	636	66	698	67	322	54	24	5	1,764	199	1,963
Latin America and the Caribbean	NA	NA	NA	NA	NA	NA	11	3	122	38	135	39	90	24	20	7	379	110	488
Middle East and North Africa	NA	NA	NA	NA	NA	NA	12	5	52	10	56	6	35	4	6	0	160	25	185
South Asia	NA	NA	NA	NA	NA	NA	36	0	392	37	442	38	215	7	36	0	1,121	83	1,203
Sub-Saharan Africa	NA	NA	NA	NA	NA	NA	2	1	42	6	36	5	13	2	2	0	95	14	109
Low- and middle-income countries	NA	NA	NA	NA	NA	NA	285	45	1,833	271	2,141	292	1,090	176	147	21	5,496	805	6,302
High-income countries	NA	NA	NA	NA	NA	NA	68	29	828	338	1,103	407	991	416	247	129	3,237	1,319	4,556
WORLD	NA	NA	NA	NA	NA	NA	354	74	2,661	609	3,244	699	2,081	592	394	150	8,734	2,124	10,858

Source: Authors' calculations.
Note: NA = not applicable.

Table 4A.110

Risk factor: Smoking
Disease: Liver cancer

Region	0–4 years Male	Female	5–14 years Male	Female	15–29 years Male	Female	30–44 years Male	Female	45–59 years Male	Female	60–69 years Male	Female	70–79 years Male	Female	80+ years Male	Female	Total Male	Female	All
PAF of Mortality (%)																			
East Asia and Pacific	NA	NA	NA	NA	NA	NA	26	4	15	1	12	1	9	1	10	1	14	1	10
Europe and Central Asia	NA	NA	NA	NA	NA	NA	49	4	55	5	47	4	34	4	21	2	43	4	27
Latin America and the Caribbean	NA	NA	NA	NA	NA	NA	14	2	24	4	21	4	18	4	18	5	19	4	12
Middle East and North Africa	NA	NA	NA	NA	NA	NA	25	8	23	3	21	2	18	2	18	1	20	3	13
South Asia	NA	NA	NA	NA	NA	NA	14	0	25	2	22	2	18	1	17	0	19	1	12
Sub-Saharan Africa	NA	NA	NA	NA	NA	NA	4	1	11	1	10	1	8	1	7	1	9	1	6
Low- and middle-income countries	NA	NA	NA	NA	NA	NA	23	3	16	2	15	2	12	2	12	1	15	2	11
High-income countries	NA	NA	NA	NA	NA	NA	27	8	38	11	37	11	35	13	36	14	36	12	29
WORLD	NA	NA	NA	NA	NA	NA	23	3	19	3	19	3	18	4	21	6	19	4	14
PAF of YLL (%)																			
East Asia and Pacific	NA	NA	NA	NA	NA	NA	26	4	15	1	12	1	9	1	10	1	15	2	11
Europe and Central Asia	NA	NA	NA	NA	NA	NA	49	4	55	5	47	4	34	4	21	2	46	4	29
Latin America and the Caribbean	NA	NA	NA	NA	NA	NA	14	2	24	4	21	4	18	4	18	5	19	4	11
Middle East and North Africa	NA	NA	NA	NA	NA	NA	25	8	23	3	21	2	18	2	18	1	20	3	13
South Asia	NA	NA	NA	NA	NA	NA	14	0	25	2	22	2	18	1	17	0	18	1	11
Sub-Saharan Africa	NA	NA	NA	NA	NA	NA	4	1	11	1	10	1	8	1	7	1	8	1	6
Low- and middle-income countries	NA	NA	NA	NA	NA	NA	23	3	16	2	15	2	12	2	12	1	16	2	12
High-income countries	NA	NA	NA	NA	NA	NA	27	8	38	11	37	11	35	13	36	14	36	12	29
WORLD	NA	NA	NA	NA	NA	NA	23	3	19	3	19	3	18	4	20	6	18	3	14
PAF of DALYs (%)																			
East Asia and Pacific	NA	NA	NA	NA	NA	NA	26	4	15	1	12	1	9	1	10	1	15	2	11
Europe and Central Asia	NA	NA	NA	NA	NA	NA	49	4	55	5	47	4	34	4	21	2	45	4	29
Latin America and the Caribbean	NA	NA	NA	NA	NA	NA	14	2	24	4	21	4	18	4	18	5	19	4	11
Middle East and North Africa	NA	NA	NA	NA	NA	NA	25	8	23	3	21	2	18	2	18	1	20	3	13
South Asia	NA	NA	NA	NA	NA	NA	14	0	25	2	22	2	18	1	17	0	18	1	11
Sub-Saharan Africa	NA	NA	NA	NA	NA	NA	4	1	11	1	10	1	8	1	7	1	8	1	6
Low- and middle-income countries	NA	NA	NA	NA	NA	NA	23	3	16	2	15	2	12	2	12	1	16	2	12
High-income countries	NA	NA	NA	NA	NA	NA	27	8	38	11	37	11	35	13	36	14	36	12	29
WORLD	NA	NA	NA	NA	NA	NA	23	3	19	3	19	3	18	4	20	6	18	3	14
Attributable Mortality (thousands)																			
East Asia and Pacific	NA	NA	NA	NA	NA	NA	7	0	15	0	9	0	5	0	1	0	37	2	38
Europe and Central Asia	NA	NA	NA	NA	NA	NA	0	0	2	0	3	0	2	0	0	0	7	0	8
Latin America and the Caribbean	NA	NA	NA	NA	NA	NA	0	0	1	0	1	0	1	0	0	0	2	0	2
Middle East and North Africa	NA	NA	NA	NA	NA	NA	0	0	0	0	0	0	0	0	0	0	1	0	1
South Asia	NA	NA	NA	NA	NA	NA	0	0	1	0	1	0	1	0	0	0	3	0	3
Sub-Saharan Africa	NA	NA	NA	NA	NA	NA	0	0	1	0	1	0	0	0	0	0	3	0	3
Low- and middle-income countries	NA	NA	NA	NA	NA	NA	9	0	20	1	14	1	8	1	2	0	53	3	56
High-income countries	NA	NA	NA	NA	NA	NA	1	0	5	0	8	1	8	2	3	1	25	4	29
WORLD	NA	NA	NA	NA	NA	NA	9	1	25	1	22	1	16	2	5	2	78	7	85
Attributable YLL (thousands)																			
East Asia and Pacific	NA	NA	NA	NA	NA	NA	176	9	280	7	121	6	44	3	6	0	627	26	654
Europe and Central Asia	NA	NA	NA	NA	NA	NA	10	0	41	2	37	2	15	2	1	0	104	6	110
Latin America and the Caribbean	NA	NA	NA	NA	NA	NA	2	0	10	2	8	2	5	1	1	0	26	5	32
Middle East and North Africa	NA	NA	NA	NA	NA	NA	3	1	6	1	5	0	3	0	0	0	16	2	18
South Asia	NA	NA	NA	NA	NA	NA	7	0	21	1	14	1	5	0	1	0	48	2	50
Sub-Saharan Africa	NA	NA	NA	NA	NA	NA	4	0	23	1	11	1	4	0	1	0	42	3	45
Low- and middle-income countries	NA	NA	NA	NA	NA	NA	202	11	381	14	197	11	75	7	10	1	864	44	908
High-income countries	NA	NA	NA	NA	NA	NA	13	1	100	7	107	11	70	16	16	7	306	42	348
WORLD	NA	NA	NA	NA	NA	NA	215	12	481	20	303	22	145	23	26	8	1,170	85	1,256
Attributable DALYs (thousands)																			
East Asia and Pacific	NA	NA	NA	NA	NA	NA	177	9	282	7	122	6	44	3	6	0	631	27	657
Europe and Central Asia	NA	NA	NA	NA	NA	NA	10	0	41	2	38	2	15	2	1	0	104	6	111
Latin America and the Caribbean	NA	NA	NA	NA	NA	NA	2	0	10	2	8	2	5	1	1	0	27	5	32
Middle East and North Africa	NA	NA	NA	NA	NA	NA	3	1	6	1	5	0	3	0	0	0	16	2	18
South Asia	NA	NA	NA	NA	NA	NA	7	0	21	1	15	1	5	0	1	0	49	2	50
Sub-Saharan Africa	NA	NA	NA	NA	NA	NA	4	0	23	1	11	1	4	0	1	0	42	3	45
Low- and middle-income countries	NA	NA	NA	NA	NA	NA	202	11	383	14	198	11	75	7	10	1	869	44	913
High-income countries	NA	NA	NA	NA	NA	NA	13	1	101	7	108	12	72	16	16	7	311	43	354
WORLD	NA	NA	NA	NA	NA	NA	216	12	484	21	306	22	147	23	27	8	1,180	86	1,267

Source: Authors' calculations.
Note: NA = not applicable.

Table 4A.111

Risk factor: Smoking
Disease: Cervix uteri cancer

Region	0–4 years Male	Female	5–14 years Male	Female	15–29 years Male	Female	30–44 years Male	Female	45–59 years Male	Female	60–69 years Male	Female	70–79 years Male	Female	80+ years Male	Female	Total Male	Female	All
PAF of Mortality (%)																			
East Asia and Pacific	NA	NA	NA	NA	NA	NA	NA	4	NA	1	NA	1	NA	1	NA	1	NA	1	1
Europe and Central Asia	NA	NA	NA	NA	NA	NA	NA	4	NA	5	NA	4	NA	4	NA	2	NA	4	4
Latin America and the Caribbean	NA	NA	NA	NA	NA	NA	NA	2	NA	4	NA	4	NA	4	NA	5	NA	4	4
Middle East and North Africa	NA	NA	NA	NA	NA	NA	NA	8	NA	3	NA	2	NA	2	NA	1	NA	3	3
South Asia	NA	NA	NA	NA	NA	NA	NA	0	NA	2	NA	2	NA	1	NA	0	NA	1	1
Sub-Saharan Africa	NA	NA	NA	NA	NA	NA	NA	1	NA	1	NA	1	NA	1	NA	1	NA	1	1
Low- and middle-income countries	NA	NA	NA	NA	NA	NA	NA	2	NA	2	NA	2	NA	1	NA	1	NA	2	2
High-income countries	NA	NA	NA	NA	NA	NA	NA	8	NA	11	NA	11	NA	13	NA	14	NA	11	11
WORLD	NA	NA	NA	NA	NA	NA	NA	3	NA	3	NA	2	NA	2	NA	3	NA	2	2
PAF of YLL (%)																			
East Asia and Pacific	NA	NA	NA	NA	NA	NA	NA	4	NA	1	NA	1	NA	1	NA	1	NA	2	2
Europe and Central Asia	NA	NA	NA	NA	NA	NA	NA	4	NA	5	NA	4	NA	4	NA	2	NA	4	4
Latin America and the Caribbean	NA	NA	NA	NA	NA	NA	NA	2	NA	4	NA	4	NA	4	NA	5	NA	3	3
Middle East and North Africa	NA	NA	NA	NA	NA	NA	NA	8	NA	3	NA	2	NA	2	NA	1	NA	3	3
South Asia	NA	NA	NA	NA	NA	NA	NA	0	NA	2	NA	2	NA	1	NA	0	NA	1	1
Sub-Saharan Africa	NA	NA	NA	NA	NA	NA	NA	1	NA	1	NA	1	NA	1	NA	1	NA	1	1
Low- and middle-income countries	NA	NA	NA	NA	NA	NA	NA	2	NA	2	NA	2	NA	1	NA	1	NA	2	2
High-income countries	NA	NA	NA	NA	NA	NA	NA	8	NA	11	NA	11	NA	13	NA	14	NA	10	10
WORLD	NA	NA	NA	NA	NA	NA	NA	3	NA	3	NA	2	NA	2	NA	3	NA	2	2
PAF of DALYs (%)																			
East Asia and Pacific	NA	NA	NA	NA	NA	NA	NA	4	NA	1	NA	1	NA	1	NA	1	NA	2	2
Europe and Central Asia	NA	NA	NA	NA	NA	NA	NA	4	NA	5	NA	4	NA	4	NA	2	NA	4	4
Latin America and the Caribbean	NA	NA	NA	NA	NA	NA	NA	2	NA	4	NA	4	NA	4	NA	5	NA	3	3
Middle East and North Africa	NA	NA	NA	NA	NA	NA	NA	8	NA	3	NA	2	NA	2	NA	1	NA	3	3
South Asia	NA	NA	NA	NA	NA	NA	NA	0	NA	2	NA	2	NA	1	NA	0	NA	1	1
Sub-Saharan Africa	NA	NA	NA	NA	NA	NA	NA	1	NA	1	NA	1	NA	1	NA	1	NA	1	1
Low- and middle-income countries	NA	NA	NA	NA	NA	NA	NA	2	NA	2	NA	2	NA	1	NA	1	NA	2	2
High-income countries	NA	NA	NA	NA	NA	NA	NA	8	NA	11	NA	11	NA	13	NA	14	NA	10	10
WORLD	NA	NA	NA	NA	NA	NA	NA	3	NA	3	NA	2	NA	2	NA	3	NA	2	2
Attributable Mortality (thousands)																			
East Asia and Pacific	NA	NA	NA	NA	NA	NA	0	0	0	0	0	0	0	0	0	0	0	1	1
Europe and Central Asia	NA	NA	NA	NA	NA	NA	0	0	0	0	0	0	0	0	0	0	0	1	1
Latin America and the Caribbean	NA	NA	NA	NA	NA	NA	0	0	0	0	0	0	0	0	0	0	0	1	1
Middle East and North Africa	NA	NA	NA	NA	NA	NA	0	0	0	0	0	0	0	0	0	0	0	0	0
South Asia	NA	NA	NA	NA	NA	NA	0	0	0	0	0	0	0	0	0	0	0	1	1
Sub-Saharan Africa	NA	NA	NA	NA	NA	NA	0	0	0	0	0	0	0	0	0	0	0	0	0
Low- and middle-income countries	NA	NA	NA	NA	NA	NA	0	0	0	2	0	1	0	1	0	0	0	4	4
High-income countries	NA	NA	NA	NA	NA	NA	0	0	0	1	0	0	0	0	0	0	0	2	2
WORLD	NA	NA	NA	NA	NA	NA	0	1	0	2	0	1	0	1	0	1	0	6	6
Attributable YLL (thousands)																			
East Asia and Pacific	NA	NA	NA	NA	NA	NA	0	3	0	4	0	3	0	1	0	0	0	11	11
Europe and Central Asia	NA	NA	NA	NA	NA	NA	0	3	0	6	0	2	0	2	0	0	0	14	14
Latin America and the Caribbean	NA	NA	NA	NA	NA	NA	0	2	0	7	0	3	0	2	0	1	0	15	15
Middle East and North Africa	NA	NA	NA	NA	NA	NA	0	1	0	1	0	0	0	0	0	0	0	3	3
South Asia	NA	NA	NA	NA	NA	NA	0	0	0	9	0	7	0	1	0	0	0	17	17
Sub-Saharan Africa	NA	NA	NA	NA	NA	NA	0	1	0	4	0	2	0	1	0	0	0	7	7
Low- and middle-income countries	NA	NA	NA	NA	NA	NA	0	10	0	31	0	17	0	7	0	1	0	66	66
High-income countries	NA	NA	NA	NA	NA	NA	0	5	0	10	0	5	0	4	0	2	0	27	27
WORLD	NA	NA	NA	NA	NA	NA	0	15	0	42	0	22	0	11	0	3	0	93	93
Attributable DALYs (thousands)																			
East Asia and Pacific	NA	NA	NA	NA	NA	NA	0	3	0	4	0	3	0	1	0	0	0	12	12
Europe and Central Asia	NA	NA	NA	NA	NA	NA	0	4	0	7	0	3	0	2	0	0	0	15	15
Latin America and the Caribbean	NA	NA	NA	NA	NA	NA	0	2	0	8	0	3	0	2	0	1	0	16	16
Middle East and North Africa	NA	NA	NA	NA	NA	NA	0	1	0	1	0	0	0	0	0	0	0	3	3
South Asia	NA	NA	NA	NA	NA	NA	0	0	0	9	0	7	0	1	0	0	0	17	17
Sub-Saharan Africa	NA	NA	NA	NA	NA	NA	0	1	0	4	0	2	0	1	0	0	0	7	7
Low- and middle-income countries	NA	NA	NA	NA	NA	NA	0	11	0	33	0	18	0	7	0	1	0	70	70
High-income countries	NA	NA	NA	NA	NA	NA	0	7	0	13	0	6	0	5	0	2	0	32	32
WORLD	NA	NA	NA	NA	NA	NA	0	18	0	46	0	24	0	12	0	3	0	102	102

Source: Authors' calculations.
Note: NA = not applicable.

Table 4A.112

Risk factor: Smoking
Disease: Bladder cancer

Region	0–4 years Male	0–4 Female	5–14 Male	5–14 Female	15–29 Male	15–29 Female	30–44 Male	30–44 Female	45–59 Male	45–59 Female	60–69 Male	60–69 Female	70–79 Male	70–79 Female	80+ Male	80+ Female	Total Male	Total Female	All
PAF of Mortality (%)																			
East Asia and Pacific	NA	NA	NA	NA	NA	NA	34	10	21	4	17	4	14	3	15	2	16	3	12
Europe and Central Asia	NA	NA	NA	NA	NA	NA	59	11	64	13	57	10	44	11	28	5	49	10	41
Latin America and the Caribbean	NA	NA	NA	NA	NA	NA	19	4	32	11	29	11	25	10	25	12	26	11	21
Middle East and North Africa	NA	NA	NA	NA	NA	NA	33	20	31	8	28	6	24	5	25	2	28	7	24
South Asia	NA	NA	NA	NA	NA	NA	19	0	34	5	30	5	24	1	24	0	27	2	15
Sub-Saharan Africa	NA	NA	NA	NA	NA	NA	6	3	16	4	14	3	11	2	10	2	12	3	9
Low- and middle-income countries	NA	NA	NA	NA	NA	NA	33	3	35	6	32	6	25	5	21	3	28	4	21
High-income countries	NA	NA	NA	NA	NA	NA	36	19	48	25	47	26	45	29	45	30	46	29	41
WORLD	NA	NA	NA	NA	NA	NA	33	4	38	9	36	10	32	13	33	18	34	13	28
PAF of YLL (%)																			
East Asia and Pacific	NA	NA	NA	NA	NA	NA	34	10	21	4	17	4	14	3	15	2	17	4	13
Europe and Central Asia	NA	NA	NA	NA	NA	NA	59	11	64	13	57	10	44	11	28	5	53	10	45
Latin America and the Caribbean	NA	NA	NA	NA	NA	NA	19	4	32	11	29	11	25	10	25	12	27	10	21
Middle East and North Africa	NA	NA	NA	NA	NA	NA	33	20	31	8	28	6	24	5	25	2	28	9	25
South Asia	NA	NA	NA	NA	NA	NA	19	0	34	5	30	5	24	1	24	0	28	2	13
Sub-Saharan Africa	NA	NA	NA	NA	NA	NA	6	3	16	4	14	3	11	2	10	2	13	3	9
Low- and middle-income countries	NA	NA	NA	NA	NA	NA	33	3	35	6	32	6	25	5	21	3	30	5	21
High-income countries	NA	NA	NA	NA	NA	NA	36	19	48	25	47	26	45	29	45	30	46	28	41
WORLD	NA	NA	NA	NA	NA	NA	33	4	38	9	36	10	32	13	33	17	34	10	26
PAF of DALYs (%)																			
East Asia and Pacific	NA	NA	NA	NA	NA	NA	34	10	21	4	17	4	14	3	15	2	17	4	13
Europe and Central Asia	NA	NA	NA	NA	NA	NA	59	11	64	13	57	10	44	11	28	5	53	10	45
Latin America and the Caribbean	NA	NA	NA	NA	NA	NA	19	4	32	11	29	11	25	10	25	12	27	10	21
Middle East and North Africa	NA	NA	NA	NA	NA	NA	33	20	31	8	28	6	24	5	25	2	28	9	25
South Asia	NA	NA	NA	NA	NA	NA	19	0	34	5	30	5	24	1	24	0	28	2	13
Sub-Saharan Africa	NA	NA	NA	NA	NA	NA	6	3	16	4	14	3	11	2	10	2	13	3	9
Low- and middle-income countries	NA	NA	NA	NA	NA	NA	33	3	36	6	33	6	25	5	21	3	30	5	21
High-income countries	NA	NA	NA	NA	NA	NA	36	19	48	25	47	26	45	29	45	30	46	28	41
WORLD	NA	NA	NA	NA	NA	NA	34	5	39	9	37	10	32	13	34	17	35	11	27
Attributable Mortality (thousands)																			
East Asia and Pacific	NA	NA	NA	NA	NA	NA	0	0	1	0	1	0	1	0	1	0	3	0	4
Europe and Central Asia	NA	NA	NA	NA	NA	NA	0	0	2	0	4	0	3	0	1	0	9	0	10
Latin America and the Caribbean	NA	NA	NA	NA	NA	NA	0	0	0	0	0	0	1	0	0	0	2	0	2
Middle East and North Africa	NA	NA	NA	NA	NA	NA	0	0	1	0	1	0	1	0	0	0	3	0	4
South Asia	NA	NA	NA	NA	NA	NA	0	0	0	0	2	0	1	0	1	0	4	0	5
Sub-Saharan Africa	NA	NA	NA	NA	NA	NA	0	0	0	0	0	0	0	0	0	0	1	0	1
Low- and middle-income countries	NA	NA	NA	NA	NA	NA	1	0	4	0	8	0	7	0	3	0	23	2	24
High-income countries	NA	NA	NA	NA	NA	NA	0	0	2	0	4	1	7	1	7	3	19	5	24
WORLD	NA	NA	NA	NA	NA	NA	1	0	6	1	11	1	14	2	10	3	42	7	48
Attributable YLL (thousands)																			
East Asia and Pacific	NA	NA	NA	NA	NA	NA	2	1	9	1	13	1	11	1	3	0	38	3	42
Europe and Central Asia	NA	NA	NA	NA	NA	NA	5	0	33	1	48	2	28	2	3	0	116	6	122
Latin America and the Caribbean	NA	NA	NA	NA	NA	NA	0	0	4	1	5	1	5	1	2	1	17	3	20
Middle East and North Africa	NA	NA	NA	NA	NA	NA	5	1	18	1	14	1	8	0	2	0	46	3	49
South Asia	NA	NA	NA	NA	NA	NA	1	0	9	2	21	2	12	0	4	0	46	5	51
Sub-Saharan Africa	NA	NA	NA	NA	NA	NA	0	0	4	0	4	0	2	0	1	0	11	1	12
Low- and middle-income countries	NA	NA	NA	NA	NA	NA	13	2	77	6	104	7	65	5	15	1	274	22	296
High-income countries	NA	NA	NA	NA	NA	NA	2	1	29	4	49	8	62	15	29	12	171	40	211
WORLD	NA	NA	NA	NA	NA	NA	16	3	105	10	152	14	128	20	44	13	445	61	507
Attributable DALYs (thousands)																			
East Asia and Pacific	NA	NA	NA	NA	NA	NA	2	1	10	1	14	1	11	1	3	0	41	4	45
Europe and Central Asia	NA	NA	NA	NA	NA	NA	5	0	37	1	52	2	30	2	4	0	128	6	134
Latin America and the Caribbean	NA	NA	NA	NA	NA	NA	1	0	5	1	6	1	5	1	2	1	18	3	21
Middle East and North Africa	NA	NA	NA	NA	NA	NA	6	1	19	1	14	1	8	0	2	0	49	3	53
South Asia	NA	NA	NA	NA	NA	NA	1	0	9	2	22	2	13	0	4	0	49	5	54
Sub-Saharan Africa	NA	NA	NA	NA	NA	NA	0	0	4	1	4	0	2	0	1	0	11	1	13
Low- and middle-income countries	NA	NA	NA	NA	NA	NA	15	3	85	7	112	7	70	5	16	1	297	23	320
High-income countries	NA	NA	NA	NA	NA	NA	4	1	45	6	64	9	78	18	36	14	228	49	276
WORLD	NA	NA	NA	NA	NA	NA	20	4	130	12	176	16	147	23	53	16	525	72	597

Source: Authors' calculations.
Note: NA = not applicable.

Table 4A.113

Risk factor: Smoking
Disease: Pancreas cancer

Region	0–4 years Male	0–4 years Female	5–14 years Male	5–14 years Female	15–29 years Male	15–29 years Female	30–44 years Male	30–44 years Female	45–59 years Male	45–59 years Female	60–69 years Male	60–69 years Female	70–79 years Male	70–79 years Female	80+ years Male	80+ years Female	Total Male	Total Female	All
PAF of Mortality (%)																			
East Asia and Pacific	NA	NA	NA	NA	NA	NA	24	8	14	3	11	3	9	3	9	2	12	3	8
Europe and Central Asia	NA	NA	NA	NA	NA	NA	46	9	52	12	45	9	32	10	19	5	42	9	26
Latin America and the Caribbean	NA	NA	NA	NA	NA	NA	13	4	22	9	19	9	16	9	17	10	18	9	14
Middle East and North Africa	NA	NA	NA	NA	NA	NA	23	18	21	7	19	5	16	4	16	2	19	6	14
South Asia	NA	NA	NA	NA	NA	NA	13	0	24	4	21	4	16	1	16	0	19	2	12
Sub-Saharan Africa	NA	NA	NA	NA	NA	NA	4	2	10	3	9	3	7	2	6	2	8	3	5
Low- and middle-income countries	NA	NA	NA	NA	NA	NA	27	7	27	7	25	6	18	6	14	5	23	6	15
High-income countries	NA	NA	NA	NA	NA	NA	25	17	36	22	35	23	33	26	33	27	34	26	30
WORLD	NA	NA	NA	NA	NA	NA	26	9	30	12	29	13	26	17	27	20	28	16	22
PAF of YLL (%)																			
East Asia and Pacific	NA	NA	NA	NA	NA	NA	24	8	14	3	11	3	9	3	9	2	13	4	9
Europe and Central Asia	NA	NA	NA	NA	NA	NA	46	9	52	12	45	9	32	10	19	5	45	9	29
Latin America and the Caribbean	NA	NA	NA	NA	NA	NA	13	4	22	9	19	9	16	9	17	10	19	9	14
Middle East and North Africa	NA	NA	NA	NA	NA	NA	23	18	21	7	19	5	16	4	16	2	20	7	14
South Asia	NA	NA	NA	NA	NA	NA	13	0	24	4	21	4	16	1	16	0	20	3	12
Sub-Saharan Africa	NA	NA	NA	NA	NA	NA	4	2	10	3	9	3	7	2	6	2	9	3	5
Low- and middle-income countries	NA	NA	NA	NA	NA	NA	27	7	27	7	25	6	18	6	14	5	24	6	16
High-income countries	NA	NA	NA	NA	NA	NA	25	17	36	22	35	23	33	26	33	27	34	24	30
WORLD	NA	NA	NA	NA	NA	NA	26	9	30	12	29	13	26	17	26	19	28	14	22
PAF of DALYs (%)																			
East Asia and Pacific	NA	NA	NA	NA	NA	NA	24	8	14	3	11	3	9	3	9	2	13	4	9
Europe and Central Asia	NA	NA	NA	NA	NA	NA	46	9	52	12	45	9	32	10	19	5	45	9	29
Latin America and the Caribbean	NA	NA	NA	NA	NA	NA	13	4	22	9	19	9	16	9	17	10	19	9	14
Middle East and North Africa	NA	NA	NA	NA	NA	NA	23	18	21	7	19	5	16	4	16	2	20	7	14
South Asia	NA	NA	NA	NA	NA	NA	13	0	24	4	21	4	16	1	16	0	20	3	12
Sub-Saharan Africa	NA	NA	NA	NA	NA	NA	4	2	10	3	9	3	7	2	6	2	9	3	5
Low- and middle-income countries	NA	NA	NA	NA	NA	NA	27	7	27	7	25	6	18	6	14	5	24	6	16
High-income countries	NA	NA	NA	NA	NA	NA	25	17	36	22	35	23	33	26	33	27	34	25	30
WORLD	NA	NA	NA	NA	NA	NA	26	9	30	12	29	14	26	17	27	19	28	14	22
Attributable Mortality (thousands)																			
East Asia and Pacific	NA	NA	NA	NA	NA	NA	0	0	1	0	1	0	0	0	0	0	3	1	3
Europe and Central Asia	NA	NA	NA	NA	NA	NA	1	0	3	0	3	0	2	1	0	0	8	1	9
Latin America and the Caribbean	NA	NA	NA	NA	NA	NA	0	0	0	0	1	0	0	0	0	0	2	1	3
Middle East and North Africa	NA	NA	NA	NA	NA	NA	0	0	0	0	0	0	0	0	0	0	0	0	1
South Asia	NA	NA	NA	NA	NA	NA	0	0	0	0	1	0	0	0	0	0	1	0	2
Sub-Saharan Africa	NA	NA	NA	NA	NA	NA	0	0	0	0	0	0	0	0	0	0	0	0	0
Low- and middle-income countries	NA	NA	NA	NA	NA	NA	1	0	5	1	5	1	3	1	1	0	14	3	18
High-income countries	NA	NA	NA	NA	NA	NA	0	0	4	1	5	2	6	5	4	5	19	14	33
WORLD	NA	NA	NA	NA	NA	NA	1	0	8	2	10	3	9	6	4	6	33	17	50
Attributable YLL (thousands)																			
East Asia and Pacific	NA	NA	NA	NA	NA	NA	9	3	18	2	9	2	4	1	1	0	41	8	50
Europe and Central Asia	NA	NA	NA	NA	NA	NA	13	1	51	6	39	6	14	6	1	1	118	20	138
Latin America and the Caribbean	NA	NA	NA	NA	NA	NA	1	0	8	3	7	4	4	3	1	1	22	11	33
Middle East and North Africa	NA	NA	NA	NA	NA	NA	1	1	2	1	2	0	1	0	0	0	6	2	8
South Asia	NA	NA	NA	NA	NA	NA	2	0	7	1	7	1	3	0	1	0	20	2	22
Sub-Saharan Africa	NA	NA	NA	NA	NA	NA	0	0	2	1	1	0	1	0	0	0	4	2	6
Low- and middle-income countries	NA	NA	NA	NA	NA	NA	26	5	90	14	65	13	27	11	4	2	212	45	256
High-income countries	NA	NA	NA	NA	NA	NA	7	3	67	25	70	35	55	50	17	24	216	138	354
WORLD	NA	NA	NA	NA	NA	NA	34	7	157	39	135	49	82	61	21	26	428	183	611
Attributable DALYs (thousands)																			
East Asia and Pacific	NA	NA	NA	NA	NA	NA	9	3	19	2	9	2	4	1	1	0	42	9	50
Europe and Central Asia	NA	NA	NA	NA	NA	NA	13	1	52	6	39	6	15	6	1	1	120	20	140
Latin America and the Caribbean	NA	NA	NA	NA	NA	NA	1	0	8	3	7	4	4	3	1	1	22	11	34
Middle East and North Africa	NA	NA	NA	NA	NA	NA	1	1	2	1	2	1	1	0	0	0	6	2	8
South Asia	NA	NA	NA	NA	NA	NA	2	0	8	1	7	1	3	0	1	0	20	2	22
Sub-Saharan Africa	NA	NA	NA	NA	NA	NA	0	0	2	1	1	0	1	0	0	0	4	2	6
Low- and middle-income countries	NA	NA	NA	NA	NA	NA	26	5	91	14	66	13	27	11	4	2	214	45	259
High-income countries	NA	NA	NA	NA	NA	NA	8	3	68	26	72	36	57	51	18	25	222	142	364
WORLD	NA	NA	NA	NA	NA	NA	34	8	159	40	138	50	84	62	22	28	436	187	623

Source: Authors' calculations.
Note: NA = not applicable.

Table 4A.114

Risk factor: Smoking
Disease: Stomach cancer

Region	0–4 years Male	0–4 years Female	5–14 years Male	5–14 years Female	15–29 years Male	15–29 years Female	30–44 years Male	30–44 years Female	45–59 years Male	45–59 years Female	60–69 years Male	60–69 years Female	70–79 years Male	70–79 years Female	80+ years Male	80+ years Female	Total Male	Total Female	All
PAF of Mortality (%)																			
East Asia and Pacific	NA	NA	NA	NA	NA	NA	23	4	13	1	11	1	8	1	9	1	11	1	8
Europe and Central Asia	NA	NA	NA	NA	NA	NA	45	4	51	5	44	4	31	4	19	2	40	4	25
Latin America and the Caribbean	NA	NA	NA	NA	NA	NA	12	2	21	4	19	4	16	4	16	5	17	4	12
Middle East and North Africa	NA	NA	NA	NA	NA	NA	23	8	21	3	19	2	16	2	16	1	18	3	12
South Asia	NA	NA	NA	NA	NA	NA	12	0	23	2	20	2	16	1	15	0	18	1	12
Sub-Saharan Africa	NA	NA	NA	NA	NA	NA	4	1	10	1	9	1	7	1	6	1	8	1	5
Low- and middle-income countries	NA	NA	NA	NA	NA	NA	23	3	19	2	17	2	13	2	12	1	16	2	11
High-income countries	NA	NA	NA	NA	NA	NA	24	8	35	11	34	11	32	13	33	13	33	12	25
WORLD	NA	NA	NA	NA	NA	NA	23	4	21	3	20	3	17	4	18	5	19	4	13
PAF of YLL (%)																			
East Asia and Pacific	NA	NA	NA	NA	NA	NA	23	4	13	1	11	1	8	1	9	1	12	2	8
Europe and Central Asia	NA	NA	NA	NA	NA	NA	45	4	51	5	44	4	31	4	19	2	43	4	27
Latin America and the Caribbean	NA	NA	NA	NA	NA	NA	12	2	21	4	19	4	16	4	16	5	18	4	12
Middle East and North Africa	NA	NA	NA	NA	NA	NA	23	8	21	3	19	2	16	2	16	1	18	3	12
South Asia	NA	NA	NA	NA	NA	NA	12	0	23	2	20	2	16	1	15	0	18	1	12
Sub-Saharan Africa	NA	NA	NA	NA	NA	NA	4	1	10	1	9	1	7	1	6	1	8	1	5
Low- and middle-income countries	NA	NA	NA	NA	NA	NA	23	3	19	2	17	2	13	2	12	1	17	2	11
High-income countries	NA	NA	NA	NA	NA	NA	24	8	35	11	34	11	32	13	33	13	33	11	25
WORLD	NA	NA	NA	NA	NA	NA	23	4	21	3	20	3	17	4	18	5	19	3	13
PAF of DALYs (%)																			
East Asia and Pacific	NA	NA	NA	NA	NA	NA	23	4	13	1	11	1	8	1	9	1	12	2	8
Europe and Central Asia	NA	NA	NA	NA	NA	NA	45	4	51	5	44	4	31	4	19	2	43	4	27
Latin America and the Caribbean	NA	NA	NA	NA	NA	NA	12	2	21	4	19	4	16	4	16	5	18	4	12
Middle East and North Africa	NA	NA	NA	NA	NA	NA	23	8	21	3	19	2	16	2	16	1	18	3	12
South Asia	NA	NA	NA	NA	NA	NA	12	0	23	2	20	2	16	1	15	0	18	1	12
Sub-Saharan Africa	NA	NA	NA	NA	NA	NA	4	1	10	1	9	1	7	1	6	1	8	1	5
Low- and middle-income countries	NA	NA	NA	NA	NA	NA	23	3	19	2	17	2	13	2	12	1	17	2	11
High-income countries	NA	NA	NA	NA	NA	NA	24	8	35	11	34	11	32	13	33	13	33	11	25
WORLD	NA	NA	NA	NA	NA	NA	23	4	21	3	20	3	17	4	18	5	19	3	13
Attributable Mortality (thousands)																			
East Asia and Pacific	NA	NA	NA	NA	NA	NA	4	0	10	0	9	1	6	1	2	0	31	2	33
Europe and Central Asia	NA	NA	NA	NA	NA	NA	1	0	7	0	9	0	5	1	1	0	24	2	25
Latin America and the Caribbean	NA	NA	NA	NA	NA	NA	0	0	1	0	2	0	2	0	1	0	6	1	7
Middle East and North Africa	NA	NA	NA	NA	NA	NA	0	0	0	0	1	0	1	0	0	0	2	0	2
South Asia	NA	NA	NA	NA	NA	NA	0	0	1	0	2	0	1	0	1	0	5	0	5
Sub-Saharan Africa	NA	NA	NA	NA	NA	NA	0	0	1	0	0	0	0	0	0	0	1	0	2
Low- and middle-income countries	NA	NA	NA	NA	NA	NA	6	1	21	1	23	1	15	1	5	1	69	5	74
High-income countries	NA	NA	NA	NA	NA	NA	1	0	5	1	8	1	10	2	7	3	29	7	36
WORLD	NA	NA	NA	NA	NA	NA	6	1	26	2	30	2	25	4	11	4	99	12	111
Attributable YLL (thousands)																			
East Asia and Pacific	NA	NA	NA	NA	NA	NA	86	12	186	9	122	8	56	5	12	1	462	35	497
Europe and Central Asia	NA	NA	NA	NA	NA	NA	33	2	134	6	124	6	50	7	4	1	346	22	368
Latin America and the Caribbean	NA	NA	NA	NA	NA	NA	5	1	28	3	22	3	14	2	5	1	74	11	85
Middle East and North Africa	NA	NA	NA	NA	NA	NA	4	2	9	1	8	0	5	0	1	0	27	3	30
South Asia	NA	NA	NA	NA	NA	NA	6	0	26	1	26	1	9	0	3	0	70	3	73
Sub-Saharan Africa	NA	NA	NA	NA	NA	NA	1	0	10	1	5	1	3	0	1	0	20	2	22
Low- and middle-income countries	NA	NA	NA	NA	NA	NA	136	17	393	22	308	19	137	15	24	3	998	77	1,074
High-income countries	NA	NA	NA	NA	NA	NA	14	4	87	13	103	15	87	21	30	13	322	67	389
WORLD	NA	NA	NA	NA	NA	NA	151	21	480	36	411	34	224	37	54	17	1,320	143	1,463
Attributable DALYs (thousands)																			
East Asia and Pacific	NA	NA	NA	NA	NA	NA	87	12	189	9	123	8	57	5	12	1	468	36	503
Europe and Central Asia	NA	NA	NA	NA	NA	NA	34	2	136	6	127	6	51	7	4	1	351	22	374
Latin America and the Caribbean	NA	NA	NA	NA	NA	NA	6	1	28	3	23	3	14	2	5	1	75	11	86
Middle East and North Africa	NA	NA	NA	NA	NA	NA	4	2	9	1	8	0	5	0	1	0	27	3	30
South Asia	NA	NA	NA	NA	NA	NA	6	0	26	1	26	1	9	0	3	0	71	3	73
Sub-Saharan Africa	NA	NA	NA	NA	NA	NA	1	0	10	1	5	1	3	0	1	0	20	3	23
Low- and middle-income countries	NA	NA	NA	NA	NA	NA	137	17	398	22	312	19	140	15	25	3	1,012	77	1,090
High-income countries	NA	NA	NA	NA	NA	NA	14	4	90	14	107	15	91	22	32	14	334	70	404
WORLD	NA	NA	NA	NA	NA	NA	152	21	488	36	419	34	231	38	57	18	1,346	147	1,493

Source: Authors' calculations.
Note: NA = not applicable.

Table 4A.115

Risk factor: Smoking
Disease: Upper aerodigestive cancer

Region	0–4 years Male	0–4 years Female	5–14 years Male	5–14 years Female	15–29 years Male	15–29 years Female	30–44 years Male	30–44 years Female	45–59 years Male	45–59 years Female	60–69 years Male	60–69 years Female	70–79 years Male	70–79 years Female	80+ years Male	80+ years Female	Total Male	Total Female	All
PAF of Mortality (%)																			
East Asia and Pacific	NA	NA	NA	NA	NA	NA	65	28	48	13	42	13	36	10	38	8	43	12	32
Europe and Central Asia	NA	NA	NA	NA	NA	NA	84	30	87	36	83	29	73	30	58	17	81	28	69
Latin America and the Caribbean	NA	NA	NA	NA	NA	NA	46	14	62	30	59	30	54	28	54	32	57	29	49
Middle East and North Africa	NA	NA	NA	NA	NA	NA	64	48	62	25	59	18	53	16	54	6	56	21	43
South Asia	NA	NA	NA	NA	NA	NA	46	0	65	15	61	15	53	5	53	0	57	9	39
Sub-Saharan Africa	NA	NA	NA	NA	NA	NA	19	9	40	13	36	10	30	7	28	8	34	10	25
Low- and middle-income countries	NA	NA	NA	NA	NA	NA	56	15	58	15	53	15	45	10	46	6	51	12	37
High-income countries	NA	NA	NA	NA	NA	NA	66	46	77	55	76	56	74	60	75	61	75	58	71
WORLD	NA	NA	NA	NA	NA	NA	57	17	60	18	56	17	50	15	53	17	55	16	42
PAF of YLL (%)																			
East Asia and Pacific	NA	NA	NA	NA	NA	NA	65	28	48	13	42	13	36	10	38	8	45	13	33
Europe and Central Asia	NA	NA	NA	NA	NA	NA	84	30	87	36	83	29	73	30	58	17	82	30	72
Latin America and the Caribbean	NA	NA	NA	NA	NA	NA	46	14	62	30	59	30	54	28	54	32	57	28	50
Middle East and North Africa	NA	NA	NA	NA	NA	NA	64	48	62	25	59	18	53	16	54	6	55	23	44
South Asia	NA	NA	NA	NA	NA	NA	46	0	65	15	61	15	53	5	53	0	56	11	39
Sub-Saharan Africa	NA	NA	NA	NA	NA	NA	19	9	40	13	36	10	30	7	28	8	34	10	25
Low- and middle-income countries	NA	NA	NA	NA	NA	NA	56	15	58	15	53	15	45	10	46	6	52	13	39
High-income countries	NA	NA	NA	NA	NA	NA	66	46	77	55	76	56	74	60	75	61	75	56	71
WORLD	NA	NA	NA	NA	NA	NA	57	17	61	18	56	17	50	15	52	16	55	16	42
PAF of DALYs (%)																			
East Asia and Pacific	NA	NA	NA	NA	NA	NA	65	28	48	13	42	13	36	10	38	8	45	13	33
Europe and Central Asia	NA	NA	NA	NA	NA	NA	84	30	87	36	83	29	73	30	58	17	82	30	72
Latin America and the Caribbean	NA	NA	NA	NA	NA	NA	46	14	62	30	59	30	54	28	54	32	57	28	50
Middle East and North Africa	NA	NA	NA	NA	NA	NA	64	48	62	25	59	18	53	16	54	6	55	23	44
South Asia	NA	NA	NA	NA	NA	NA	46	0	65	15	61	15	53	5	53	0	56	11	39
Sub-Saharan Africa	NA	NA	NA	NA	NA	NA	19	9	40	13	36	10	30	7	28	8	34	10	25
Low- and middle-income countries	NA	NA	NA	NA	NA	NA	56	15	58	15	53	15	45	10	46	6	52	13	39
High-income countries	NA	NA	NA	NA	NA	NA	66	46	77	55	76	56	74	60	75	61	75	56	71
WORLD	NA	NA	NA	NA	NA	NA	57	17	61	18	56	17	50	15	53	16	55	17	42
Attributable Mortality (thousands)																			
East Asia and Pacific	NA	NA	NA	NA	NA	NA	9	1	25	3	27	4	17	3	4	1	83	13	95
Europe and Central Asia	NA	NA	NA	NA	NA	NA	2	0	12	1	11	1	5	1	1	0	30	3	33
Latin America and the Caribbean	NA	NA	NA	NA	NA	NA	1	0	4	0	4	1	3	1	1	1	13	2	15
Middle East and North Africa	NA	NA	NA	NA	NA	NA	0	0	1	0	1	0	1	0	0	0	4	1	4
South Asia	NA	NA	NA	NA	NA	NA	4	0	19	3	32	4	16	1	6	0	78	8	86
Sub-Saharan Africa	NA	NA	NA	NA	NA	NA	0	0	3	1	3	0	2	0	1	0	9	1	11
Low- and middle-income countries	NA	NA	NA	NA	NA	NA	16	1	65	8	78	9	44	6	14	2	216	28	244
High-income countries	NA	NA	NA	NA	NA	NA	2	0	15	2	16	2	15	4	7	5	56	14	70
WORLD	NA	NA	NA	NA	NA	NA	18	2	80	10	94	12	59	11	21	8	272	42	314
Attributable YLL (thousands)																			
East Asia and Pacific	NA	NA	NA	NA	NA	NA	206	25	470	67	364	58	158	34	23	6	1,222	190	1,412
Europe and Central Asia	NA	NA	NA	NA	NA	NA	38	4	226	13	145	11	48	11	4	2	460	41	501
Latin America and the Caribbean	NA	NA	NA	NA	NA	NA	14	1	80	9	50	9	24	7	7	3	175	29	204
Middle East and North Africa	NA	NA	NA	NA	NA	NA	11	5	18	4	14	2	7	2	1	0	52	13	64
South Asia	NA	NA	NA	NA	NA	NA	102	0	365	57	436	56	147	10	31	0	1,080	123	1,203
Sub-Saharan Africa	NA	NA	NA	NA	NA	NA	8	2	65	10	42	6	17	3	3	1	135	22	158
Low- and middle-income countries	NA	NA	NA	NA	NA	NA	378	36	1,224	160	1,051	142	401	67	69	12	3,124	417	3,541
High-income countries	NA	NA	NA	NA	NA	NA	41	7	287	39	222	38	134	42	34	24	717	150	867
WORLD	NA	NA	NA	NA	NA	NA	419	43	1,511	199	1,274	180	535	109	102	36	3,842	567	4,408
Attributable DALYs (thousands)																			
East Asia and Pacific	NA	NA	NA	NA	NA	NA	208	25	476	67	369	59	160	34	23	6	1,238	193	1,430
Europe and Central Asia	NA	NA	NA	NA	NA	NA	38	4	231	13	148	12	49	11	4	2	471	42	512
Latin America and the Caribbean	NA	NA	NA	NA	NA	NA	14	1	82	9	51	9	25	7	7	3	179	29	208
Middle East and North Africa	NA	NA	NA	NA	NA	NA	11	5	19	4	14	2	8	2	1	0	52	13	65
South Asia	NA	NA	NA	NA	NA	NA	102	0	371	58	444	56	150	10	32	0	1,099	125	1,224
Sub-Saharan Africa	NA	NA	NA	NA	NA	NA	8	2	66	10	42	6	18	3	3	1	137	23	160
Low- and middle-income countries	NA	NA	NA	NA	NA	NA	382	37	1,244	162	1,069	144	409	68	71	12	3,176	424	3,599
High-income countries	NA	NA	NA	NA	NA	NA	42	8	298	41	231	39	141	44	36	26	747	157	904
WORLD	NA	NA	NA	NA	NA	NA	424	45	1,541	203	1,300	183	550	112	108	38	3,923	581	4,504

Source: Authors' calculations.
Note: NA = not applicable.

Table 4A.116

Risk factor: Smoking
Disease: Leukemia

Region	0–4 years Male	Female	5–14 years Male	Female	15–29 years Male	Female	30–44 years Male	Female	45–59 years Male	Female	60–69 years Male	Female	70–79 years Male	Female	80+ years Male	Female	Total Male	Female	All
PAF of Mortality (%)																			
East Asia and Pacific	NA	NA	NA	NA	NA	NA	19	2	10	1	8	1	7	1	7	0	6	1	4
Europe and Central Asia	NA	NA	NA	NA	NA	NA	39	2	45	3	38	2	26	2	15	1	28	2	16
Latin America and the Caribbean	NA	NA	NA	NA	NA	NA	10	1	17	2	15	2	13	2	13	2	8	1	5
Middle East and North Africa	NA	NA	NA	NA	NA	NA	18	4	17	2	15	1	13	1	13	0	9	1	6
South Asia	NA	NA	NA	NA	NA	NA	10	0	19	1	16	1	12	0	12	0	7	0	4
Sub-Saharan Africa	NA	NA	NA	NA	NA	NA	3	0	8	1	7	1	5	0	5	0	4	0	3
Low- and middle-income countries	NA	NA	NA	NA	NA	NA	17	2	18	1	17	1	13	1	11	1	10	1	6
High-income countries	NA	NA	NA	NA	NA	NA	20	4	29	5	28	6	27	7	27	7	25	6	17
WORLD	NA	NA	NA	NA	NA	NA	18	2	21	2	21	2	19	3	21	5	14	2	9
PAF of YLL (%)																			
East Asia and Pacific	NA	NA	NA	NA	NA	NA	19	2	10	1	8	1	7	1	7	0	5	1	3
Europe and Central Asia	NA	NA	NA	NA	NA	NA	39	2	45	3	38	2	26	2	15	1	25	2	15
Latin America and the Caribbean	NA	NA	NA	NA	NA	NA	10	1	17	2	15	2	13	2	13	2	6	1	4
Middle East and North Africa	NA	NA	NA	NA	NA	NA	18	4	17	2	15	1	13	1	13	0	7	1	4
South Asia	NA	NA	NA	NA	NA	NA	10	0	19	1	16	1	12	0	12	0	5	0	3
Sub-Saharan Africa	NA	NA	NA	NA	NA	NA	3	0	8	1	7	1	5	0	5	0	4	0	2
Low- and middle-income countries	NA	NA	NA	NA	NA	NA	17	2	18	1	17	1	13	1	10	1	7	1	4
High-income countries	NA	NA	NA	NA	NA	NA	20	4	29	5	28	6	27	7	27	7	23	5	15
WORLD	NA	NA	NA	NA	NA	NA	18	2	21	2	21	2	19	3	20	4	10	1	6
PAF of DALYs (%)																			
East Asia and Pacific	NA	NA	NA	NA	NA	NA	19	2	10	1	8	1	7	1	7	0	5	1	3
Europe and Central Asia	NA	NA	NA	NA	NA	NA	39	2	45	3	38	2	26	2	15	1	25	2	15
Latin America and the Caribbean	NA	NA	NA	NA	NA	NA	10	1	17	2	15	2	13	2	13	2	6	1	4
Middle East and North Africa	NA	NA	NA	NA	NA	NA	18	4	17	2	15	1	13	1	13	0	7	1	4
South Asia	NA	NA	NA	NA	NA	NA	10	0	19	1	16	1	12	0	12	0	5	0	3
Sub-Saharan Africa	NA	NA	NA	NA	NA	NA	3	0	8	1	7	1	5	0	5	0	4	0	2
Low- and middle-income countries	NA	NA	NA	NA	NA	NA	17	2	18	1	17	1	13	1	10	1	7	1	4
High-income countries	NA	NA	NA	NA	NA	NA	20	4	29	5	28	6	27	7	27	7	23	5	15
WORLD	NA	NA	NA	NA	NA	NA	18	2	21	2	21	2	19	4	21	4	10	1	6
Attributable Mortality (thousands)																			
East Asia and Pacific	NA	NA	NA	NA	NA	NA	1	0	1	0	0	0	0	0	0	0	2	0	3
Europe and Central Asia	NA	NA	NA	NA	NA	NA	1	0	1	0	1	0	1	0	0	0	4	0	4
Latin America and the Caribbean	NA	NA	NA	NA	NA	NA	0	0	0	0	0	0	0	0	0	0	1	0	1
Middle East and North Africa	NA	NA	NA	NA	NA	NA	0	0	0	0	0	0	0	0	0	0	1	0	1
South Asia	NA	NA	NA	NA	NA	NA	0	0	0	0	0	0	0	0	0	0	2	0	2
Sub-Saharan Africa	NA	NA	NA	NA	NA	NA	0	0	0	0	0	0	0	0	0	0	0	0	0
Low- and middle-income countries	NA	NA	NA	NA	NA	NA	2	0	3	0	3	0	2	0	1	0	10	1	11
High-income countries	NA	NA	NA	NA	NA	NA	0	0	2	0	2	0	3	1	3	1	10	2	12
WORLD	NA	NA	NA	NA	NA	NA	3	0	4	0	5	0	5	1	3	1	20	3	23
Attributable YLL (thousands)																			
East Asia and Pacific	NA	NA	NA	NA	NA	NA	20	3	14	1	6	0	3	0	1	0	44	4	49
Europe and Central Asia	NA	NA	NA	NA	NA	NA	15	1	23	1	18	1	8	1	1	0	63	3	66
Latin America and the Caribbean	NA	NA	NA	NA	NA	NA	3	0	5	1	3	0	2	0	1	0	14	2	16
Middle East and North Africa	NA	NA	NA	NA	NA	NA	4	1	3	1	2	0	1	0	0	0	11	1	13
South Asia	NA	NA	NA	NA	NA	NA	6	0	8	0	6	0	2	0	1	0	23	1	24
Sub-Saharan Africa	NA	NA	NA	NA	NA	NA	0	0	2	0	1	0	1	0	0	0	5	0	5
Low- and middle-income countries	NA	NA	NA	NA	NA	NA	50	5	55	3	36	2	16	1	3	0	161	11	172
High-income countries	NA	NA	NA	NA	NA	NA	11	2	29	4	31	4	30	6	12	4	113	19	132
WORLD	NA	NA	NA	NA	NA	NA	61	6	85	7	67	6	46	7	15	4	274	31	304
Attributable DALYs (thousands)																			
East Asia and Pacific	NA	NA	NA	NA	NA	NA	21	3	14	1	7	0	3	0	1	0	45	4	49
Europe and Central Asia	NA	NA	NA	NA	NA	NA	15	1	23	1	18	1	8	1	1	0	64	3	68
Latin America and the Caribbean	NA	NA	NA	NA	NA	NA	3	0	5	1	3	0	2	0	1	0	14	2	16
Middle East and North Africa	NA	NA	NA	NA	NA	NA	4	1	3	0	2	0	1	0	0	0	12	1	13
South Asia	NA	NA	NA	NA	NA	NA	6	0	8	0	6	0	2	0	1	0	24	1	24
Sub-Saharan Africa	NA	NA	NA	NA	NA	NA	0	0	2	0	1	0	1	0	0	0	5	0	5
Low- and middle-income countries	NA	NA	NA	NA	NA	NA	50	5	56	3	37	2	17	1	3	0	163	12	175
High-income countries	NA	NA	NA	NA	NA	NA	11	2	30	4	32	4	32	6	13	4	118	20	139
WORLD	NA	NA	NA	NA	NA	NA	62	6	87	7	69	6	48	8	16	4	282	32	313

Source: Authors' calculations.
Note: NA = not applicable.

Table 4A.117

Risk factor: Smoking
Disease: Ischemic heart disease

Region	0–4 years Male	0–4 years Female	5–14 years Male	5–14 years Female	15–29 years Male	15–29 years Female	30–44 years Male	30–44 years Female	45–59 years Male	45–59 years Female	60–69 years Male	60–69 years Female	70–79 years Male	70–79 years Female	80+ years Male	80+ years Female	Total Male	Total Female	All
PAF of Mortality (%)																			
East Asia and Pacific	NA	NA	NA	NA	NA	NA	54	9	21	7	8	4	3	1	0	1	10	2	6
Europe and Central Asia	NA	NA	NA	NA	NA	NA	76	10	65	23	37	11	13	5	0	1	30	5	17
Latin America and the Caribbean	NA	NA	NA	NA	NA	NA	35	4	32	19	15	11	6	4	0	3	13	7	10
Middle East and North Africa	NA	NA	NA	NA	NA	NA	53	19	32	15	15	6	6	2	0	0	16	5	11
South Asia	NA	NA	NA	NA	NA	NA	35	0	34	9	16	5	6	1	0	0	16	3	10
Sub-Saharan Africa	NA	NA	NA	NA	NA	NA	13	2	16	8	7	3	2	1	0	1	7	3	5
Low- and middle-income countries	NA	NA	NA	NA	NA	NA	50	5	38	12	20	6	7	2	0	1	18	4	11
High-income countries	NA	NA	NA	NA	NA	NA	56	18	49	40	28	27	14	15	0	10	17	13	15
WORLD	NA	NA	NA	NA	NA	NA	50	5	40	14	21	8	9	4	0	4	18	6	12
PAF of YLL (%)																			
East Asia and Pacific	NA	NA	NA	NA	NA	NA	54	9	21	7	8	4	3	1	0	1	14	4	9
Europe and Central Asia	NA	NA	NA	NA	NA	NA	76	10	65	23	37	11	13	5	0	1	40	8	26
Latin America and the Caribbean	NA	NA	NA	NA	NA	NA	35	4	32	19	15	11	6	4	0	3	19	9	15
Middle East and North Africa	NA	NA	NA	NA	NA	NA	53	19	32	15	15	6	6	2	0	0	21	7	15
South Asia	NA	NA	NA	NA	NA	NA	35	0	34	9	16	5	6	1	0	0	21	4	13
Sub-Saharan Africa	NA	NA	NA	NA	NA	NA	13	2	16	8	7	3	2	1	0	1	9	3	6
Low- and middle-income countries	NA	NA	NA	NA	NA	NA	50	5	38	12	20	6	7	2	0	1	24	5	15
High-income countries	NA	NA	NA	NA	NA	NA	56	18	49	40	28	27	14	15	0	10	26	17	22
WORLD	NA	NA	NA	NA	NA	NA	50	5	40	14	21	8	9	4	0	4	24	7	17
PAF of DALYs (%)																			
East Asia and Pacific	NA	NA	NA	NA	NA	NA	54	9	21	7	8	4	3	1	0	1	14	4	9
Europe and Central Asia	NA	NA	NA	NA	NA	NA	76	10	65	23	37	11	13	5	0	1	41	8	26
Latin America and the Caribbean	NA	NA	NA	NA	NA	NA	35	4	32	19	15	11	6	4	0	3	19	9	15
Middle East and North Africa	NA	NA	NA	NA	NA	NA	53	19	32	15	15	6	6	2	0	0	21	7	15
South Asia	NA	NA	NA	NA	NA	NA	35	0	34	9	16	5	6	1	0	0	21	4	13
Sub-Saharan Africa	NA	NA	NA	NA	NA	NA	13	2	16	8	7	3	2	1	0	1	9	3	6
Low- and middle-income countries	NA	NA	NA	NA	NA	NA	50	5	38	12	20	6	7	2	0	1	24	5	15
High-income countries	NA	NA	NA	NA	NA	NA	56	18	49	40	28	27	14	15	0	10	26	18	23
WORLD	NA	NA	NA	NA	NA	NA	50	5	40	14	21	8	9	4	0	4	24	7	17
Attributable Mortality (thousands)																			
East Asia and Pacific	NA	NA	NA	NA	NA	NA	16	1	22	4	12	5	6	2	0	1	56	14	70
Europe and Central Asia	NA	NA	NA	NA	NA	NA	29	1	99	10	84	14	36	15	0	5	248	45	293
Latin America and the Caribbean	NA	NA	NA	NA	NA	NA	3	0	13	3	7	3	4	2	0	2	27	11	38
Middle East and North Africa	NA	NA	NA	NA	NA	NA	6	1	13	3	7	2	4	1	0	0	30	7	36
South Asia	NA	NA	NA	NA	NA	NA	17	0	84	11	47	12	18	2	0	0	166	24	190
Sub-Saharan Africa	NA	NA	NA	NA	NA	NA	1	0	6	2	3	2	1	0	0	0	12	4	16
Low- and middle-income countries	NA	NA	NA	NA	NA	NA	72	3	237	34	161	37	68	22	1	8	539	105	644
High-income countries	NA	NA	NA	NA	NA	NA	9	1	43	9	36	14	33	23	1	40	122	86	208
WORLD	NA	NA	NA	NA	NA	NA	81	4	280	43	197	51	100	45	2	48	661	191	852
Attributable YLL (thousands)																			
East Asia and Pacific	NA	NA	NA	NA	NA	NA	392	36	409	86	165	69	51	23	1	5	1,018	220	1,238
Europe and Central Asia	NA	NA	NA	NA	NA	NA	672	17	1,881	202	1,138	209	323	153	1	24	4,015	605	4,620
Latin America and the Caribbean	NA	NA	NA	NA	NA	NA	75	4	237	69	97	50	32	20	0	9	442	151	594
Middle East and North Africa	NA	NA	NA	NA	NA	NA	134	19	244	59	98	28	32	10	0	1	508	117	625
South Asia	NA	NA	NA	NA	NA	NA	403	0	1,566	223	632	175	159	17	1	0	2,761	415	3,176
Sub-Saharan Africa	NA	NA	NA	NA	NA	NA	22	2	119	39	46	23	13	5	0	1	199	70	269
Low- and middle-income countries	NA	NA	NA	NA	NA	NA	1,698	78	4,455	679	2,177	553	610	229	4	39	8,944	1,578	10,522
High-income countries	NA	NA	NA	NA	NA	NA	207	16	793	179	489	211	286	229	5	162	1,780	798	2,577
WORLD	NA	NA	NA	NA	NA	NA	1,905	94	5,247	858	2,666	764	896	458	9	201	10,724	2,376	13,099
Attributable DALYs (thousands)																			
East Asia and Pacific	NA	NA	NA	NA	NA	NA	434	41	437	92	174	72	52	24	1	5	1,097	234	1,331
Europe and Central Asia	NA	NA	NA	NA	NA	NA	722	20	1,953	217	1,175	219	328	156	1	24	4,179	635	4,815
Latin America and the Caribbean	NA	NA	NA	NA	NA	NA	86	5	253	76	104	53	33	20	0	9	476	162	638
Middle East and North Africa	NA	NA	NA	NA	NA	NA	149	21	257	63	103	29	33	11	0	1	542	124	667
South Asia	NA	NA	NA	NA	NA	NA	458	0	1,661	240	666	184	163	18	1	0	2,949	442	3,391
Sub-Saharan Africa	NA	NA	NA	NA	NA	NA	24	2	126	42	48	24	13	5	0	1	212	74	286
Low- and middle-income countries	NA	NA	NA	NA	NA	NA	1,872	88	4,687	730	2,269	581	622	233	4	40	9,455	1,672	11,127
High-income countries	NA	NA	NA	NA	NA	NA	237	22	873	215	526	237	300	244	6	168	1,942	886	2,829
WORLD	NA	NA	NA	NA	NA	NA	2,109	110	5,561	945	2,795	818	923	478	10	208	11,397	2,559	13,956

Source: Authors' calculations.
Note: NA = not applicable.

Table 4A.118

Risk factor: Smoking

Disease: Selected other cardiovascular diseases

Region	0–4 years Male	0–4 years Female	5–14 years Male	5–14 years Female	15–29 years Male	15–29 years Female	30–44 years Male	30–44 years Female	45–59 years Male	45–59 years Female	60–69 years Male	60–69 years Female	70–79 years Male	70–79 years Female	80+ years Male	80+ years Female	Total Male	Total Female	All
PAF of Mortality (%)																			
East Asia and Pacific	NA	NA	NA	NA	NA	NA	22	7	13	3	10	3	8	2	9	2	10	2	5
Europe and Central Asia	NA	NA	NA	NA	NA	NA	44	7	50	9	43	7	30	8	18	4	32	5	16
Latin America and the Caribbean	NA	NA	NA	NA	NA	NA	12	3	21	8	18	8	15	7	16	8	15	7	11
Middle East and North Africa	NA	NA	NA	NA	NA	NA	22	15	20	6	18	4	15	4	15	1	15	3	8
South Asia	NA	NA	NA	NA	NA	NA	12	0	22	3	19	3	15	1	15	0	15	1	7
Sub-Saharan Africa	NA	NA	NA	NA	NA	NA	4	2	10	3	8	2	6	1	6	2	6	2	4
Low- and middle-income countries	NA	NA	NA	NA	NA	NA	21	4	23	4	21	4	16	3	13	3	16	3	9
High-income countries	NA	NA	NA	NA	NA	NA	24	14	34	19	33	19	31	22	32	23	31	22	26
WORLD	NA	NA	NA	NA	NA	NA	21	5	25	6	24	6	20	7	21	12	21	9	14
PAF of YLL (%)																			
East Asia and Pacific	NA	NA	NA	NA	NA	NA	22	7	13	3	10	3	8	2	9	2	10	2	6
Europe and Central Asia	NA	NA	NA	NA	NA	NA	44	7	50	9	43	7	30	8	18	4	36	6	21
Latin America and the Caribbean	NA	NA	NA	NA	NA	NA	12	3	21	8	18	8	15	7	16	8	14	6	10
Middle East and North Africa	NA	NA	NA	NA	NA	NA	22	15	20	6	18	4	15	4	15	1	14	3	8
South Asia	NA	NA	NA	NA	NA	NA	12	0	22	3	19	3	15	1	15	0	14	1	7
Sub-Saharan Africa	NA	NA	NA	NA	NA	NA	4	2	10	3	8	2	6	1	6	2	6	2	3
Low- and middle-income countries	NA	NA	NA	NA	NA	NA	21	4	23	4	21	4	16	3	13	3	17	3	9
High-income countries	NA	NA	NA	NA	NA	NA	24	14	34	19	33	19	31	22	32	23	30	21	25
WORLD	NA	NA	NA	NA	NA	NA	21	5	25	6	24	6	20	7	20	11	20	6	12
PAF of DALYs (%)																			
East Asia and Pacific	NA	NA	NA	NA	NA	NA	22	7	13	3	10	3	8	2	9	2	10	2	6
Europe and Central Asia	NA	NA	NA	NA	NA	NA	44	7	50	9	43	7	30	8	18	4	36	6	21
Latin America and the Caribbean	NA	NA	NA	NA	NA	NA	12	3	21	8	18	8	15	7	16	8	14	6	10
Middle East and North Africa	NA	NA	NA	NA	NA	NA	22	15	20	6	18	4	15	4	15	1	14	3	8
South Asia	NA	NA	NA	NA	NA	NA	12	0	22	3	19	3	15	1	15	0	13	1	7
Sub-Saharan Africa	NA	NA	NA	NA	NA	NA	4	2	10	3	8	2	6	1	6	2	6	2	3
Low- and middle-income countries	NA	NA	NA	NA	NA	NA	21	4	24	4	22	4	16	3	13	3	16	3	9
High-income countries	NA	NA	NA	NA	NA	NA	24	14	34	19	33	19	31	22	32	23	30	21	25
WORLD	NA	NA	NA	NA	NA	NA	21	5	26	6	24	6	20	7	21	11	19	6	12
Attributable Mortality (thousands)																			
East Asia and Pacific	NA	NA	NA	NA	NA	NA	2	1	3	1	3	1	4	1	4	1	17	5	22
Europe and Central Asia	NA	NA	NA	NA	NA	NA	6	0	10	1	13	1	13	5	9	5	51	12	63
Latin America and the Caribbean	NA	NA	NA	NA	NA	NA	1	0	2	1	2	1	3	1	4	4	11	6	17
Middle East and North Africa	NA	NA	NA	NA	NA	NA	1	0	1	0	1	0	2	1	2	0	7	2	9
South Asia	NA	NA	NA	NA	NA	NA	1	0	6	1	6	1	6	1	4	0	23	3	26
Sub-Saharan Africa	NA	NA	NA	NA	NA	NA	0	0	1	0	1	0	1	1	1	1	6	2	8
Low- and middle-income countries	NA	NA	NA	NA	NA	NA	12	2	23	4	27	5	29	10	25	11	115	30	146
High-income countries	NA	NA	NA	NA	NA	NA	2	1	7	2	11	4	23	16	44	66	87	88	175
WORLD	NA	NA	NA	NA	NA	NA	14	2	30	6	38	9	53	25	69	77	203	119	321
Attributable YLL (thousands)																			
East Asia and Pacific	NA	NA	NA	NA	NA	NA	55	14	59	12	45	13	36	15	21	7	217	61	278
Europe and Central Asia	NA	NA	NA	NA	NA	NA	151	10	192	20	173	21	116	48	40	21	672	120	792
Latin America and the Caribbean	NA	NA	NA	NA	NA	NA	14	3	31	11	23	10	23	14	20	17	111	54	165
Middle East and North Africa	NA	NA	NA	NA	NA	NA	17	8	25	7	19	5	17	6	9	1	87	27	114
South Asia	NA	NA	NA	NA	NA	NA	33	0	110	18	84	19	55	8	20	0	302	45	347
Sub-Saharan Africa	NA	NA	NA	NA	NA	NA	9	4	25	8	16	6	13	6	7	3	71	27	98
Low- and middle-income countries	NA	NA	NA	NA	NA	NA	279	38	443	76	361	74	259	97	116	50	1,458	335	1,794
High-income countries	NA	NA	NA	NA	NA	NA	45	15	134	41	149	56	201	155	184	260	713	527	1,240
WORLD	NA	NA	NA	NA	NA	NA	324	54	577	117	510	131	461	252	300	309	2,171	863	3,034
Attributable DALYs (thousands)																			
East Asia and Pacific	NA	NA	NA	NA	NA	NA	77	19	63	13	46	13	37	15	21	7	244	67	312
Europe and Central Asia	NA	NA	NA	NA	NA	NA	168	13	217	22	197	23	137	53	47	23	765	133	899
Latin America and the Caribbean	NA	NA	NA	NA	NA	NA	16	3	34	11	26	10	25	15	22	19	123	58	181
Middle East and North Africa	NA	NA	NA	NA	NA	NA	20	9	29	8	22	5	19	7	9	1	99	31	130
South Asia	NA	NA	NA	NA	NA	NA	49	0	137	22	103	22	67	9	23	0	380	53	432
Sub-Saharan Africa	NA	NA	NA	NA	NA	NA	10	4	26	9	17	6	13	6	8	3	74	28	102
Low- and middle-income countries	NA	NA	NA	NA	NA	NA	339	48	506	85	411	80	298	104	131	53	1,685	370	2,055
High-income countries	NA	NA	NA	NA	NA	NA	59	23	157	49	174	63	237	174	218	294	845	604	1,448
WORLD	NA	NA	NA	NA	NA	NA	398	72	663	134	585	143	535	278	349	347	2,530	974	3,503

Source: Authors' calculations.

Note: NA = not applicable.

Table 4A.119

Risk factor: Smoking
Disease: Cerebrovascular disease

Region	0–4 years Male	Female	5–14 years Male	Female	15–29 years Male	Female	30–44 years Male	Female	45–59 years Male	Female	60–69 years Male	Female	70–79 years Male	Female	80+ years Male	Female	Total Male	Female	All
PAF of Mortality (%)																			
East Asia and Pacific	NA	NA	NA	NA	NA	NA	35	22	22	9	8	5	3	2	0	0	7	3	5
Europe and Central Asia	NA	NA	NA	NA	NA	NA	60	23	66	28	37	12	12	7	0	0	25	6	14
Latin America and the Caribbean	NA	NA	NA	NA	NA	NA	20	10	33	24	15	13	5	6	0	0	11	7	9
Middle East and North Africa	NA	NA	NA	NA	NA	NA	35	39	32	19	15	7	5	3	0	0	11	6	8
South Asia	NA	NA	NA	NA	NA	NA	20	0	35	11	16	6	5	1	0	0	13	3	8
Sub-Saharan Africa	NA	NA	NA	NA	NA	NA	6	6	17	10	6	4	2	1	0	0	6	3	4
Low- and middle-income countries	NA	NA	NA	NA	NA	NA	32	15	33	14	16	7	5	3	0	0	12	4	8
High-income countries	NA	NA	NA	NA	NA	NA	37	38	49	46	28	30	13	20	0	0	12	8	10
WORLD	NA	NA	NA	NA	NA	NA	32	17	34	16	17	8	6	5	0	0	12	5	8
PAF of YLL (%)																			
East Asia and Pacific	NA	NA	NA	NA	NA	NA	35	22	22	9	8	5	3	2	0	0	10	4	7
Europe and Central Asia	NA	NA	NA	NA	NA	NA	60	23	66	28	37	12	12	7	0	0	34	10	20
Latin America and the Caribbean	NA	NA	NA	NA	NA	NA	20	10	33	24	15	13	5	6	0	0	16	11	13
Middle East and North Africa	NA	NA	NA	NA	NA	NA	35	39	32	19	15	7	5	3	0	0	13	8	11
South Asia	NA	NA	NA	NA	NA	NA	20	0	35	11	16	6	5	1	0	0	16	4	10
Sub-Saharan Africa	NA	NA	NA	NA	NA	NA	6	6	17	10	6	4	2	1	0	0	8	4	6
Low- and middle-income countries	NA	NA	NA	NA	NA	NA	32	15	33	14	16	7	5	3	0	0	16	6	11
High-income countries	NA	NA	NA	NA	NA	NA	37	38	49	46	28	30	13	20	0	0	20	16	18
WORLD	NA	NA	NA	NA	NA	NA	32	17	34	16	17	8	6	5	0	0	17	7	12
PAF of DALYs (%)																			
East Asia and Pacific	NA	NA	NA	NA	NA	NA	35	22	22	9	8	5	3	2	0	0	11	5	8
Europe and Central Asia	NA	NA	NA	NA	NA	NA	60	23	66	28	37	12	12	7	0	0	35	10	21
Latin America and the Caribbean	NA	NA	NA	NA	NA	NA	20	10	33	24	15	13	5	6	0	0	17	12	14
Middle East and North Africa	NA	NA	NA	NA	NA	NA	35	39	32	19	15	7	5	3	0	0	15	9	12
South Asia	NA	NA	NA	NA	NA	NA	20	0	35	11	16	6	5	1	0	0	17	5	11
Sub-Saharan Africa	NA	NA	NA	NA	NA	NA	6	6	17	10	6	4	2	1	0	0	8	5	6
Low- and middle-income countries	NA	NA	NA	NA	NA	NA	32	16	32	14	16	7	5	3	0	0	17	6	12
High-income countries	NA	NA	NA	NA	NA	NA	37	38	49	46	28	30	13	20	0	0	23	19	21
WORLD	NA	NA	NA	NA	NA	NA	33	19	34	17	17	9	6	5	0	0	18	8	13
Attributable Mortality (thousands)																			
East Asia and Pacific	NA	NA	NA	NA	NA	NA	9	3	30	8	20	8	9	6	0	0	68	26	94
Europe and Central Asia	NA	NA	NA	NA	NA	NA	8	2	36	10	40	11	17	16	0	0	101	39	139
Latin America and the Caribbean	NA	NA	NA	NA	NA	NA	1	1	7	4	4	3	2	2	0	0	14	10	25
Middle East and North Africa	NA	NA	NA	NA	NA	NA	1	1	3	1	2	1	1	1	0	0	7	4	11
South Asia	NA	NA	NA	NA	NA	NA	2	0	27	6	22	7	8	2	0	0	59	15	74
Sub-Saharan Africa	NA	NA	NA	NA	NA	NA	1	1	5	4	2	2	1	1	0	0	9	7	16
Low- and middle-income countries	NA	NA	NA	NA	NA	NA	21	7	107	33	90	32	39	27	1	0	258	100	358
High-income countries	NA	NA	NA	NA	NA	NA	2	2	13	7	12	9	13	20	1	0	40	38	78
WORLD	NA	NA	NA	NA	NA	NA	24	9	120	40	102	41	52	48	1	0	298	138	436
Attributable YLL (thousands)																			
East Asia and Pacific	NA	NA	NA	NA	NA	NA	210	81	557	167	270	115	83	64	1	0	1,120	427	1,548
Europe and Central Asia	NA	NA	NA	NA	NA	NA	182	41	673	197	537	172	155	159	1	0	1,547	569	2,116
Latin America and the Caribbean	NA	NA	NA	NA	NA	NA	31	17	133	87	53	44	18	24	0	0	236	171	407
Middle East and North Africa	NA	NA	NA	NA	NA	NA	21	19	52	28	28	13	10	7	0	0	111	67	179
South Asia	NA	NA	NA	NA	NA	NA	46	0	496	115	296	111	75	17	1	0	914	242	1,157
Sub-Saharan Africa	NA	NA	NA	NA	NA	NA	17	13	89	70	31	31	8	9	0	0	144	123	267
Low- and middle-income countries	NA	NA	NA	NA	NA	NA	506	171	2,001	664	1,215	486	350	280	3	0	4,073	1,600	5,674
High-income countries	NA	NA	NA	NA	NA	NA	54	41	235	145	162	129	110	204	3	0	563	519	1,082
WORLD	NA	NA	NA	NA	NA	NA	560	212	2,235	809	1,377	615	460	484	5	0	4,636	2,119	6,755
Attributable DALYs (thousands)																			
East Asia and Pacific	NA	NA	NA	NA	NA	NA	293	114	756	227	354	148	99	76	1	0	1,503	565	2,067
Europe and Central Asia	NA	NA	NA	NA	NA	NA	224	57	838	257	675	222	186	186	1	0	1,924	722	2,646
Latin America and the Caribbean	NA	NA	NA	NA	NA	NA	43	25	185	120	73	59	23	28	0	0	324	232	556
Middle East and North Africa	NA	NA	NA	NA	NA	NA	29	26	69	36	36	16	12	8	0	0	147	86	233
South Asia	NA	NA	NA	NA	NA	NA	57	0	619	142	367	134	87	19	1	0	1,131	295	1,426
Sub-Saharan Africa	NA	NA	NA	NA	NA	NA	18	14	99	79	35	35	9	10	0	0	160	138	298
Low- and middle-income countries	NA	NA	NA	NA	NA	NA	663	236	2,566	861	1,541	615	416	327	3	0	5,188	2,038	7,226
High-income countries	NA	NA	NA	NA	NA	NA	103	82	462	298	305	247	170	313	3	0	1,043	940	1,983
WORLD	NA	NA	NA	NA	NA	NA	766	317	3,028	1,159	1,845	861	586	640	6	0	6,231	2,978	9,209

Source: Authors' calculations.
Note: NA = not applicable.

Table 4A.120

Risk factor: Smoking
Disease: Selected respiratory diseases

Region	0–4 years Male	Female	5–14 years Male	Female	15–29 years Male	Female	30–44 years Male	Female	45–59 years Male	Female	60–69 years Male	Female	70–79 years Male	Female	80+ years Male	Female	Total Male	Female	All
PAF of Mortality (%)																			
East Asia and Pacific	NA	NA	NA	NA	NA	NA	27	8	16	3	8	3	5	2	3	0	9	2	5
Europe and Central Asia	NA	NA	NA	NA	NA	NA	51	9	56	11	36	8	21	6	7	1	33	4	24
Latin America and the Caribbean	NA	NA	NA	NA	NA	NA	15	4	25	9	14	9	10	5	6	3	10	4	7
Middle East and North Africa	NA	NA	NA	NA	NA	NA	26	18	24	7	14	5	10	3	6	0	7	2	5
South Asia	NA	NA	NA	NA	NA	NA	15	0	27	4	15	4	10	1	6	0	9	1	5
Sub-Saharan Africa	NA	NA	NA	NA	NA	NA	4	2	12	3	6	3	4	1	2	1	2	1	2
Low- and middle-income countries	NA	NA	NA	NA	NA	NA	17	4	23	4	13	4	8	2	4	1	8	1	5
High-income countries	NA	NA	NA	NA	NA	NA	29	17	40	22	27	22	22	17	14	9	19	11	15
WORLD	NA	NA	NA	NA	NA	NA	18	4	24	5	14	5	10	4	8	4	9	2	6
PAF of YLL (%)																			
East Asia and Pacific	NA	NA	NA	NA	NA	NA	27	8	16	3	8	3	5	2	3	0	9	2	6
Europe and Central Asia	NA	NA	NA	NA	NA	NA	51	9	56	11	36	8	21	6	7	1	32	4	23
Latin America and the Caribbean	NA	NA	NA	NA	NA	NA	15	4	25	9	14	9	10	5	6	3	9	3	6
Middle East and North Africa	NA	NA	NA	NA	NA	NA	26	18	24	7	14	5	10	3	6	0	5	2	3
South Asia	NA	NA	NA	NA	NA	NA	15	0	27	4	15	4	10	1	6	0	7	1	4
Sub-Saharan Africa	NA	NA	NA	NA	NA	NA	4	2	12	3	6	3	4	1	2	1	2	0	1
Low- and middle-income countries	NA	NA	NA	NA	NA	NA	17	4	23	4	13	4	8	2	4	1	6	1	4
High-income countries	NA	NA	NA	NA	NA	NA	29	17	40	22	27	22	22	17	14	9	22	14	18
WORLD	NA	NA	NA	NA	NA	NA	18	4	24	5	14	5	10	4	7	3	7	1	4
PAF of DALYs (%)																			
East Asia and Pacific	NA	NA	NA	NA	NA	NA	22	7	13	3	7	3	5	1	3	0	8	2	5
Europe and Central Asia	NA	NA	NA	NA	NA	NA	44	7	49	8	29	5	15	4	5	1	26	3	18
Latin America and the Caribbean	NA	NA	NA	NA	NA	NA	13	3	22	8	13	8	9	5	6	3	7	2	5
Middle East and North Africa	NA	NA	NA	NA	NA	NA	20	15	19	6	12	4	9	2	5	0	4	2	3
South Asia	NA	NA	NA	NA	NA	NA	13	0	23	4	14	4	9	1	5	0	6	1	3
Sub-Saharan Africa	NA	NA	NA	NA	NA	NA	4	2	11	3	6	2	4	1	2	0	2	0	1
Low- and middle-income countries	NA	NA	NA	NA	NA	NA	15	3	20	4	11	4	7	1	4	1	6	1	4
High-income countries	NA	NA	NA	NA	NA	NA	14	7	22	11	18	14	18	14	12	8	15	9	12
WORLD	NA	NA	NA	NA	NA	NA	15	3	20	4	12	4	9	3	7	3	6	1	4
Attributable Mortality (thousands)																			
East Asia and Pacific	NA	NA	NA	NA	NA	NA	21	4	18	2	11	2	7	2	3	1	60	10	70
Europe and Central Asia	NA	NA	NA	NA	NA	NA	13	1	21	1	8	1	3	1	1	0	46	3	49
Latin America and the Caribbean	NA	NA	NA	NA	NA	NA	2	0	5	1	3	1	3	1	2	1	15	5	20
Middle East and North Africa	NA	NA	NA	NA	NA	NA	1	1	2	0	1	0	1	0	0	0	6	2	7
South Asia	NA	NA	NA	NA	NA	NA	16	0	38	3	25	4	15	1	4	0	98	8	106
Sub-Saharan Africa	NA	NA	NA	NA	NA	NA	4	1	11	2	4	1	2	0	0	0	21	4	26
Low- and middle-income countries	NA	NA	NA	NA	NA	NA	58	7	95	9	52	9	32	5	10	2	246	32	279
High-income countries	NA	NA	NA	NA	NA	NA	1	0	5	2	7	3	16	8	18	17	48	30	78
WORLD	NA	NA	NA	NA	NA	NA	59	7	101	10	59	12	47	13	29	19	294	62	356
Attributable YLL (thousands)																			
East Asia and Pacific	NA	NA	NA	NA	NA	NA	510	96	341	39	143	34	64	16	15	4	1,073	188	1,261
Europe and Central Asia	NA	NA	NA	NA	NA	NA	301	14	414	19	115	9	29	7	2	1	861	49	911
Latin America and the Caribbean	NA	NA	NA	NA	NA	NA	51	7	97	21	38	17	25	12	9	6	220	64	284
Middle East and North Africa	NA	NA	NA	NA	NA	NA	26	19	32	7	18	4	11	2	2	0	90	33	123
South Asia	NA	NA	NA	NA	NA	NA	389	0	716	57	334	65	138	10	19	0	1,596	133	1,729
Sub-Saharan Africa	NA	NA	NA	NA	NA	NA	105	33	214	32	52	14	16	4	2	1	389	84	473
Low- and middle-income countries	NA	NA	NA	NA	NA	NA	1,382	170	1,815	175	700	144	283	51	50	11	4,229	551	4,780
High-income countries	NA	NA	NA	NA	NA	NA	32	11	100	31	94	44	134	81	76	66	437	233	670
WORLD	NA	NA	NA	NA	NA	NA	1,414	181	1,915	207	794	188	417	132	126	77	4,666	784	5,450
Attributable DALYs (thousands)																			
East Asia and Pacific	NA	NA	NA	NA	NA	NA	510	96	341	39	143	34	64	16	15	4	1,073	188	1,261
Europe and Central Asia	NA	NA	NA	NA	NA	NA	301	14	414	19	115	9	29	7	2	1	861	49	911
Latin America and the Caribbean	NA	NA	NA	NA	NA	NA	51	7	97	21	38	17	25	12	9	6	220	64	284
Middle East and North Africa	NA	NA	NA	NA	NA	NA	26	19	32	7	18	4	11	2	2	0	90	33	123
South Asia	NA	NA	NA	NA	NA	NA	389	0	716	57	334	65	138	10	19	0	1,596	133	1,729
Sub-Saharan Africa	NA	NA	NA	NA	NA	NA	105	33	214	32	52	14	16	4	2	1	389	84	473
Low- and middle-income countries	NA	NA	NA	NA	NA	NA	1,382	170	1,815	175	700	144	283	51	50	11	4,229	551	4,780
High-income countries	NA	NA	NA	NA	NA	NA	32	11	100	31	94	44	134	81	76	66	437	233	670
WORLD	NA	NA	NA	NA	NA	NA	1,414	181	1,915	207	794	188	417	132	126	77	4,666	784	5,450

Source: Authors' calculations.
Note: NA = not applicable.

Table 4A.121

Risk factor: Smoking
Disease: Selected medical conditions

Region	0–4 years Male	Female	5–14 years Male	Female	15–29 years Male	Female	30–44 years Male	Female	45–59 years Male	Female	60–69 years Male	Female	70–79 years Male	Female	80+ years Male	Female	Total Male	Female	All
PAF of Mortality (%)																			
East Asia and Pacific	NA	NA	NA	NA	NA	NA	21	6	12	2	6	2	4	1	2	0	6	2	4
Europe and Central Asia	NA	NA	NA	NA	NA	NA	42	7	48	8	29	6	16	4	5	1	28	5	17
Latin America and the Caribbean	NA	NA	NA	NA	NA	NA	11	3	19	7	11	6	8	4	4	2	9	4	6
Middle East and North Africa	NA	NA	NA	NA	NA	NA	20	13	19	5	11	3	7	2	4	0	10	3	6
South Asia	NA	NA	NA	NA	NA	NA	11	0	21	3	12	3	7	1	4	0	10	1	5
Sub-Saharan Africa	NA	NA	NA	NA	NA	NA	3	2	9	2	5	2	3	1	1	0	3	1	2
Low- and middle-income countries	NA	NA	NA	NA	NA	NA	17	4	19	4	10	3	6	2	3	1	9	2	5
High-income countries	NA	NA	NA	NA	NA	NA	22	13	32	17	21	17	17	13	10	6	17	10	13
WORLD	NA	NA	NA	NA	NA	NA	17	4	20	5	12	5	9	4	6	4	10	4	7
PAF of YLL (%)																			
East Asia and Pacific	NA	NA	NA	NA	NA	NA	21	6	12	2	6	2	4	1	2	0	7	2	4
Europe and Central Asia	NA	NA	NA	NA	NA	NA	42	7	48	8	29	6	16	4	5	1	31	5	19
Latin America and the Caribbean	NA	NA	NA	NA	NA	NA	11	3	19	7	11	6	8	4	4	2	9	4	7
Middle East and North Africa	NA	NA	NA	NA	NA	NA	20	13	19	5	11	3	7	2	4	0	10	3	6
South Asia	NA	NA	NA	NA	NA	NA	11	0	21	3	12	3	7	1	4	0	9	1	5
Sub-Saharan Africa	NA	NA	NA	NA	NA	NA	3	2	9	2	5	2	3	1	1	0	2	1	2
Low- and middle-income countries	NA	NA	NA	NA	NA	NA	17	4	19	4	10	3	6	2	3	1	9	2	5
High-income countries	NA	NA	NA	NA	NA	NA	22	13	32	17	21	17	17	13	10	6	20	12	16
WORLD	NA	NA	NA	NA	NA	NA	17	4	21	5	12	5	9	4	6	3	10	3	6
PAF of DALYs (%)																			
East Asia and Pacific	NA	NA	NA	NA	NA	NA	3	1	2	0	1	0	1	0	1	0	1	0	1
Europe and Central Asia	NA	NA	NA	NA	NA	NA	12	1	12	1	7	1	5	1	2	0	7	1	4
Latin America and the Caribbean	NA	NA	NA	NA	NA	NA	3	1	6	2	4	2	3	1	2	1	3	1	2
Middle East and North Africa	NA	NA	NA	NA	NA	NA	3	1	4	1	4	1	3	1	2	0	2	1	1
South Asia	NA	NA	NA	NA	NA	NA	2	0	5	1	3	1	3	0	2	0	2	0	1
Sub-Saharan Africa	NA	NA	NA	NA	NA	NA	1	0	2	1	2	1	1	0	1	0	1	0	0
Low- and middle-income countries	NA	NA	NA	NA	NA	NA	3	1	4	1	3	1	2	1	2	0	2	0	1
High-income countries	NA	NA	NA	NA	NA	NA	4	2	6	2	5	3	6	4	6	3	5	3	4
WORLD	NA	NA	NA	NA	NA	NA	3	1	4	1	3	1	3	1	3	1	2	1	2
Attributable Mortality (thousands)																			
East Asia and Pacific	NA	NA	NA	NA	NA	NA	8	2	10	2	6	2	4	1	1	0	29	8	37
Europe and Central Asia	NA	NA	NA	NA	NA	NA	7	1	14	1	8	2	4	1	1	0	34	5	39
Latin America and the Caribbean	NA	NA	NA	NA	NA	NA	2	0	8	2	5	3	4	2	2	1	20	9	29
Middle East and North Africa	NA	NA	NA	NA	NA	NA	1	1	4	1	2	1	2	0	0	0	10	3	13
South Asia	NA	NA	NA	NA	NA	NA	4	0	20	3	8	2	5	0	2	0	40	5	45
Sub-Saharan Africa	NA	NA	NA	NA	NA	NA	1	0	3	1	2	1	1	0	0	0	7	3	10
Low- and middle-income countries	NA	NA	NA	NA	NA	NA	23	4	59	10	31	10	21	6	6	2	139	33	173
High-income countries	NA	NA	NA	NA	NA	NA	3	1	13	4	12	7	17	14	13	16	57	42	99
WORLD	NA	NA	NA	NA	NA	NA	26	5	71	15	42	17	38	20	19	18	196	76	272
Attributable YLL (thousands)																			
East Asia and Pacific	NA	NA	NA	NA	NA	NA	198	60	192	37	77	33	34	13	6	2	507	146	653
Europe and Central Asia	NA	NA	NA	NA	NA	NA	169	14	261	30	111	25	39	15	2	1	583	86	668
Latin America and the Caribbean	NA	NA	NA	NA	NA	NA	46	9	143	46	63	42	35	22	9	7	296	125	421
Middle East and North Africa	NA	NA	NA	NA	NA	NA	31	19	67	19	33	11	17	5	2	0	151	54	205
South Asia	NA	NA	NA	NA	NA	NA	98	0	384	54	109	32	49	4	9	0	648	90	738
Sub-Saharan Africa	NA	NA	NA	NA	NA	NA	18	6	61	20	23	14	10	4	1	1	114	45	160
Low- and middle-income countries	NA	NA	NA	NA	NA	NA	561	108	1,109	206	415	157	184	65	30	10	2,299	545	2,845
High-income countries	NA	NA	NA	NA	NA	NA	67	27	236	86	155	105	150	140	55	67	664	424	1,089
WORLD	NA	NA	NA	NA	NA	NA	628	135	1,345	292	571	261	334	205	85	76	2,963	970	3,933
Attributable DALYs (thousands)																			
East Asia and Pacific	NA	NA	NA	NA	NA	NA	198	60	192	37	77	33	34	13	6	2	507	146	653
Europe and Central Asia	NA	NA	NA	NA	NA	NA	169	14	261	30	111	25	39	15	2	1	583	86	668
Latin America and the Caribbean	NA	NA	NA	NA	NA	NA	46	9	143	46	63	42	35	22	9	7	296	125	421
Middle East and North Africa	NA	NA	NA	NA	NA	NA	31	19	67	19	33	11	17	5	2	0	151	54	205
South Asia	NA	NA	NA	NA	NA	NA	98	0	384	54	109	32	49	4	9	0	648	90	738
Sub-Saharan Africa	NA	NA	NA	NA	NA	NA	18	6	61	20	23	14	10	4	1	1	114	45	160
Low- and middle-income countries	NA	NA	NA	NA	NA	NA	561	108	1,109	206	415	157	184	65	30	10	2,299	545	2,845
High-income countries	NA	NA	NA	NA	NA	NA	67	27	236	86	155	105	150	140	55	67	664	424	1,089
WORLD	NA	NA	NA	NA	NA	NA	628	135	1,345	292	571	261	334	205	85	76	2,963	970	3,933

Source: Authors' calculations.
Note: NA = not applicable.

Table 4A.122

Risk factor: Smoking
Disease: All causes

Region	0–4 years Male	Female	5–14 years Male	Female	15–29 years Male	Female	30–44 years Male	Female	45–59 years Male	Female	60–69 years Male	Female	70–79 years Male	Female	80+ years Male	Female	Total Male	Female	All
PAF of Mortality (%)																			
East Asia and Pacific	NA	NA	NA	NA	NA	NA	14	4	16	5	16	6	14	5	12	3	12	4	8
Europe and Central Asia	NA	NA	NA	NA	NA	NA	22	5	40	12	36	9	21	6	8	2	25	5	16
Latin America and the Caribbean	NA	NA	NA	NA	NA	NA	5	2	18	9	16	9	13	6	10	5	10	5	8
Middle East and North Africa	NA	NA	NA	NA	NA	NA	14	8	19	8	15	5	10	3	7	1	9	3	6
South Asia	NA	NA	NA	NA	NA	NA	7	0	25	6	22	5	13	1	8	0	11	2	6
Sub-Saharan Africa	NA	NA	NA	NA	NA	NA	1	0	6	2	7	2	5	1	4	1	2	1	1
Low- and middle-income countries	NA	NA	NA	NA	NA	NA	9	2	21	6	20	6	14	4	10	2	11	3	7
High-income countries	NA	NA	NA	NA	NA	NA	13	7	31	18	32	20	26	18	17	11	23	14	19
WORLD	NA	NA	NA	NA	NA	NA	9	2	22	7	22	8	16	6	12	5	12	4	9
PAF of YLL (%)																			
East Asia and Pacific	NA	NA	NA	NA	NA	NA	14	4	16	5	16	6	14	5	13	3	10	3	7
Europe and Central Asia	NA	NA	NA	NA	NA	NA	22	5	40	12	36	9	21	6	8	2	25	6	17
Latin America and the Caribbean	NA	NA	NA	NA	NA	NA	5	2	17	9	16	9	13	6	10	5	7	4	6
Middle East and North Africa	NA	NA	NA	NA	NA	NA	14	8	19	8	15	5	10	3	7	1	7	3	5
South Asia	NA	NA	NA	NA	NA	NA	7	0	25	6	22	5	13	1	8	0	8	1	5
Sub-Saharan Africa	NA	NA	NA	NA	NA	NA	1	0	6	2	7	2	5	1	4	1	1	0	1
Low- and middle-income countries	NA	NA	NA	NA	NA	NA	9	2	21	6	20	6	14	4	10	2	8	2	5
High-income countries	NA	NA	NA	NA	NA	NA	13	7	31	18	32	20	27	18	17	11	23	15	20
WORLD	NA	NA	NA	NA	NA	NA	9	2	22	7	22	8	16	6	12	5	9	3	6
PAF of DALYs (%)																			
East Asia and Pacific	NA	NA	NA	NA	NA	NA	9	3	12	3	13	4	11	4	11	3	7	2	5
Europe and Central Asia	NA	NA	NA	NA	NA	NA	17	4	33	8	31	7	19	5	7	2	19	4	13
Latin America and the Caribbean	NA	NA	NA	NA	NA	NA	4	2	13	6	13	6	10	4	8	4	5	2	4
Middle East and North Africa	NA	NA	NA	NA	NA	NA	9	4	13	4	11	3	9	2	6	1	5	2	3
South Asia	NA	NA	NA	NA	NA	NA	5	0	19	4	18	4	12	1	7	0	6	1	4
Sub-Saharan Africa	NA	NA	NA	NA	NA	NA	1	0	5	2	6	2	5	1	4	1	1	0	1
Low- and middle-income countries	NA	NA	NA	NA	NA	NA	6	1	16	4	16	4	12	3	9	2	6	1	4
High-income countries	NA	NA	NA	NA	NA	NA	8	6	23	12	24	13	21	13	14	8	16	9	13
WORLD	NA	NA	NA	NA	NA	NA	6	2	17	5	18	6	14	5	10	4	7	2	5
Attributable Mortality (thousands)																			
East Asia and Pacific	NA	NA	NA	NA	NA	NA	86	16	191	35	221	55	219	73	112	50	829	230	1,059
Europe and Central Asia	NA	NA	NA	NA	NA	NA	73	5	249	30	255	39	150	53	27	16	754	143	897
Latin America and the Caribbean	NA	NA	NA	NA	NA	NA	11	2	51	16	44	18	43	18	28	19	177	73	250
Middle East and North Africa	NA	NA	NA	NA	NA	NA	12	4	30	8	26	6	22	5	8	1	97	24	121
South Asia	NA	NA	NA	NA	NA	NA	51	0	282	47	243	49	148	14	45	0	768	110	879
Sub-Saharan Africa	NA	NA	NA	NA	NA	NA	9	3	41	11	28	9	20	5	7	2	105	30	135
Low- and middle-income countries	NA	NA	NA	NA	NA	NA	241	31	844	146	817	175	601	169	226	89	2,730	610	3,340
High-income countries	NA	NA	NA	NA	NA	NA	24	7	162	50	221-	81	309	166	213	230	929	533	1,462
WORLD	NA	NA	NA	NA	NA	NA	265	37	1,006	196	1,038	256	910	335	439	319	3,659	1,143	4,802
Attributable YLL (thousands)																			
East Asia and Pacific	NA	NA	NA	NA	NA	NA	2,041	403	3,573	689	2,975	825	1,950	745	560	256	11,099	2,919	14,018
Europe and Central Asia	NA	NA	NA	NA	NA	NA	1,711	122	4,725	598	3,467	581	1,367	546	124	77	11,394	1,925	13,319
Latin America and the Caribbean	NA	NA	NA	NA	NA	NA	265	51	955	327	600	268	381	183	130	90	2,331	918	3,249
Middle East and North Africa	NA	NA	NA	NA	NA	NA	282	107	563	155	346	86	193	54	38	5	1,421	408	1,829
South Asia	NA	NA	NA	NA	NA	NA	1,211	0	5,243	926	3,294	738	1,330	150	224	0	11,302	1,815	13,117
Sub-Saharan Africa	NA	NA	NA	NA	NA	NA	207	66	765	220	379	129	178	55	37	13	1,566	484	2,050
Low- and middle-income countries	NA	NA	NA	NA	NA	NA	5,716	750	15,824	2,915	11,059	2,627	5,400	1,734	1,113	442	39,113	8,468	47,581
High-income countries	NA	NA	NA	NA	NA	NA	572	168	3,018	987	2,963	1,216	2,723	1,674	949	976	10,225	5,021	15,246
WORLD	NA	NA	NA	NA	NA	NA	6,289	919	18,842	3,902	14,023	3,843	8,123	3,407	2,062	1,418	49,338	13,489	62,827
Attributable DALYs (thousands)																			
East Asia and Pacific	NA	NA	NA	NA	NA	NA	2,370	567	4,632	817	3,403	939	2,104	810	606	268	13,116	3,402	16,518
Europe and Central Asia	NA	NA	NA	NA	NA	NA	1,909	231	5,116	770	3,762	679	1,481	597	140	82	12,408	2,361	14,769
Latin America and the Caribbean	NA	NA	NA	NA	NA	NA	344	114	1,178	439	705	315	419	203	143	97	2,789	1,168	3,957
Middle East and North Africa	NA	NA	NA	NA	NA	NA	410	146	650	176	374	93	203	56	40	5	1,676	476	2,153
South Asia	NA	NA	NA	NA	NA	NA	1,443	0	5,727	1,099	3,591	797	1,400	158	237	0	12,397	2,055	14,452
Sub-Saharan Africa	NA	NA	NA	NA	NA	NA	219	69	813	236	404	136	185	57	39	14	1,659	512	2,171
Low- and middle-income countries	NA	NA	NA	NA	NA	NA	6,695	1,128	18,117	3,538	12,238	2,960	5,791	1,882	1,204	466	44,046	9,973	54,019
High-income countries	NA	NA	NA	NA	NA	NA	837	487	3,920	1,580	3,463	1,539	3,043	1,915	1,047	1,070	12,309	6,590	18,900
WORLD	NA	NA	NA	NA	NA	NA	7,532	1,615	22,037	5,118	15,701	4,499	8,834	3,796	2,251	1,536	56,355	16,564	72,919

Source: Authors' calculations.
Note: NA = not applicable.

Table 4A.123

Risk factor:	Non-use and use of ineffective methods of contraception
Disease:	Abortion

Region	0–4 years Male	Female	5–14 years Male	Female	15–29 years Male	Female	30–44 years Male	Female	45–59 years Male	Female	60–69 years Male	Female	70–79 years Male	Female	80+ years Male	Female	Total Male	Female	All
PAF of Mortality (%)																			
East Asia and Pacific	NA	NA	NA	NA	NA	84	NA	87	NA	NA	NA	NA	NA	NA	NA	NA	NA	84	84
Europe and Central Asia	NA	NA	NA	NA	NA	86	NA	86	NA	NA	NA	NA	NA	NA	NA	NA	NA	85	85
Latin America and the Caribbean	NA	NA	NA	NA	NA	85	NA	88	NA	NA	NA	NA	NA	NA	NA	NA	NA	86	86
Middle East and North Africa	NA	NA	NA	NA	NA	89	NA	89	NA	NA	NA	NA	NA	NA	NA	NA	NA	89	89
South Asia	NA	NA	NA	NA	NA	92	NA	94	NA	NA	NA	NA	NA	NA	NA	NA	NA	93	93
Sub-Saharan Africa	NA	NA	NA	NA	NA	88	NA	89	NA	NA	NA	NA	NA	NA	NA	NA	NA	88	88
Low- and middle-income countries	NA	NA	NA	NA	NA	89	NA	91	NA	NA	NA	NA	NA	NA	NA	NA	NA	90	90
High-income countries	NA	NA	NA	NA	NA	71	NA	74	NA	NA	NA	NA	NA	NA	NA	NA	NA	71	71
WORLD	NA	NA	NA	NA	NA	89	NA	91	NA	NA	NA	NA	NA	NA	NA	NA	NA	90	90
PAF of YLL (%)																			
East Asia and Pacific	NA	NA	NA	NA	NA	84	NA	87	NA	NA	NA	NA	NA	NA	NA	NA	NA	84	84
Europe and Central Asia	NA	NA	NA	NA	NA	86	NA	86	NA	NA	NA	NA	NA	NA	NA	NA	NA	85	85
Latin America and the Caribbean	NA	NA	NA	NA	NA	85	NA	88	NA	NA	NA	NA	NA	NA	NA	NA	NA	86	86
Middle East and North Africa	NA	NA	NA	NA	NA	89	NA	89	NA	NA	NA	NA	NA	NA	NA	NA	NA	89	89
South Asia	NA	NA	NA	NA	NA	92	NA	94	NA	NA	NA	NA	NA	NA	NA	NA	NA	93	93
Sub-Saharan Africa	NA	NA	NA	NA	NA	88	NA	89	NA	NA	NA	NA	NA	NA	NA	NA	NA	88	88
Low- and middle-income countries	NA	NA	NA	NA	NA	89	NA	91	NA	NA	NA	NA	NA	NA	NA	NA	NA	90	90
High-income countries	NA	NA	NA	NA	NA	71	NA	74	NA	NA	NA	NA	NA	NA	NA	NA	NA	71	71
WORLD	NA	NA	NA	NA	NA	89	NA	91	NA	NA	NA	NA	NA	NA	NA	NA	NA	90	90
PAF of DALYs (%)																			
East Asia and Pacific	NA	NA	NA	NA	NA	84	NA	87	NA	NA	NA	NA	NA	NA	NA	NA	NA	82	82
Europe and Central Asia	NA	NA	NA	NA	NA	86	NA	86	NA	NA	NA	NA	NA	NA	NA	NA	NA	82	82
Latin America and the Caribbean	NA	NA	NA	NA	NA	85	NA	88	NA	NA	NA	NA	NA	NA	NA	NA	NA	83	83
Middle East and North Africa	NA	NA	NA	NA	NA	89	NA	89	NA	NA	NA	NA	NA	NA	NA	NA	NA	84	84
South Asia	NA	NA	NA	NA	NA	92	NA	94	NA	NA	NA	NA	NA	NA	NA	NA	NA	88	88
Sub-Saharan Africa	NA	NA	NA	NA	NA	88	NA	89	NA	NA	NA	NA	NA	NA	NA	NA	NA	84	84
Low- and middle-income countries	NA	NA	NA	NA	NA	89	NA	91	NA	NA	NA	NA	NA	NA	NA	NA	NA	86	86
High-income countries	NA	NA	NA	NA	NA	71	NA	74	NA	NA	NA	NA	NA	NA	NA	NA	NA	71	71
WORLD	NA	NA	NA	NA	NA	89	NA	91	NA	NA	NA	NA	NA	NA	NA	NA	NA	86	86
Attributable Mortality (thousands)																			
East Asia and Pacific	NA	NA	NA	NA	NA	2	NA	2	NA	NA	NA	NA	NA	NA	NA	NA	NA	4	4
Europe and Central Asia	NA	NA	NA	NA	NA	0	NA	0	NA	NA	NA	NA	NA	NA	NA	NA	NA	0	0
Latin America and the Caribbean	NA	NA	NA	NA	NA	1	NA	1	NA	NA	NA	NA	NA	NA	NA	NA	NA	2	2
Middle East and North Africa	NA	NA	NA	NA	NA	1	NA	1	NA	NA	NA	NA	NA	NA	NA	NA	NA	1	1
South Asia	NA	NA	NA	NA	NA	15	NA	11	NA	NA	NA	NA	NA	NA	NA	NA	NA	26	26
Sub-Saharan Africa	NA	NA	NA	NA	NA	19	NA	6	NA	NA	NA	NA	NA	NA	NA	NA	NA	25	25
Low- and middle-income countries	NA	NA	NA	NA	NA	39	NA	20	NA	NA	NA	NA	NA	NA	NA	NA	NA	59	59
High-income countries	NA	NA	NA	NA	NA	0	NA	0	NA	NA	NA	NA	NA	NA	NA	NA	NA	0	0
WORLD	NA	NA	NA	NA	NA	39	NA	20	NA	NA	NA	NA	NA	NA	NA	NA	NA	59	59
Attributable YLL (thousands)																			
East Asia and Pacific	NA	NA	NA	NA	NA	61	NA	50	NA	NA	NA	NA	NA	NA	NA	NA	NA	111	111
Europe and Central Asia	NA	NA	NA	NA	NA	3	NA	3	NA	NA	NA	NA	NA	NA	NA	NA	NA	6	6
Latin America and the Caribbean	NA	NA	NA	NA	NA	38	NA	17	NA	NA	NA	NA	NA	NA	NA	NA	NA	55	55
Middle East and North Africa	NA	NA	NA	NA	NA	21	NA	13	NA	NA	NA	NA	NA	NA	NA	NA	NA	35	35
South Asia	NA	NA	NA	NA	NA	424	NA	276	NA	NA	NA	NA	NA	NA	NA	NA	NA	701	701
Sub-Saharan Africa	NA	NA	NA	NA	NA	532	NA	148	NA	NA	NA	NA	NA	NA	NA	NA	NA	680	680
Low- and middle-income countries	NA	NA	NA	NA	NA	1,080	NA	508	NA	NA	NA	NA	NA	NA	NA	NA	NA	1,588	1,588
High-income countries	NA	NA	NA	NA	NA	1	NA	1	NA	NA	NA	NA	NA	NA	NA	NA	NA	2	2
WORLD	NA	NA	NA	NA	NA	1,080	NA	509	NA	NA	NA	NA	NA	NA	NA	NA	NA	1,590	1,590
Attributable DALYs (thousands)																			
East Asia and Pacific	NA	NA	NA	NA	NA	104	NA	53	NA	NA	NA	NA	NA	NA	NA	NA	NA	156	156
Europe and Central Asia	NA	NA	NA	NA	NA	10	NA	3	NA	NA	NA	NA	NA	NA	NA	NA	NA	14	14
Latin America and the Caribbean	NA	NA	NA	NA	NA	77	NA	20	NA	NA	NA	NA	NA	NA	NA	NA	NA	97	97
Middle East and North Africa	NA	NA	NA	NA	NA	108	NA	19	NA	NA	NA	NA	NA	NA	NA	NA	NA	127	127
South Asia	NA	NA	NA	NA	NA	984	NA	310	NA	NA	NA	NA	NA	NA	NA	NA	NA	1,294	1,294
Sub-Saharan Africa	NA	NA	NA	NA	NA	1,127	NA	184	NA	NA	NA	NA	NA	NA	NA	NA	NA	1,311	1,311
Low- and middle-income countries	NA	NA	NA	NA	NA	2,410	NA	589	NA	NA	NA	NA	NA	NA	NA	NA	NA	3,000	3,000
High-income countries	NA	NA	NA	NA	NA	2	NA	1	NA	NA	NA	NA	NA	NA	NA	NA	NA	3	3
WORLD	NA	NA	NA	NA	NA	2,412	NA	590	NA	NA	NA	NA	NA	NA	NA	NA	NA	3,002	3,002

Source: Authors' calculations.
Note: NA = not applicable.

Table 4A.124

Risk factor: Non-use and use of ineffective methods of contraception
Disease: Maternal causes other than abortion

Region	0–4 years Male	Female	5–14 years Male	Female	15–29 years Male	Female	30–44 years Male	Female	45–59 years Male	Female	60–69 years Male	Female	70–79 years Male	Female	80+ years Male	Female	Total Male	Female	All
PAF of Mortality (%)																			
East Asia and Pacific	NA	NA	NA	NA	NA	4	NA	30	NA	NA	NA	NA	NA	NA	NA	NA	NA	19	19
Europe and Central Asia	NA	NA	NA	NA	NA	7	NA	44	NA	NA	NA	NA	NA	NA	NA	NA	NA	19	19
Latin America and the Caribbean	NA	NA	NA	NA	NA	20	NA	51	NA	NA	NA	NA	NA	NA	NA	NA	NA	34	34
Middle East and North Africa	NA	NA	NA	NA	NA	8	NA	40	NA	NA	NA	NA	NA	NA	NA	NA	NA	24	24
South Asia	NA	NA	NA	NA	NA	8	NA	60	NA	NA	NA	NA	NA	NA	NA	NA	NA	34	34
Sub-Saharan Africa	NA	NA	NA	NA	NA	4	NA	28	NA	NA	NA	NA	NA	NA	NA	NA	NA	14	14
Low- and middle-income countries	NA	NA	NA	NA	NA	6	NA	43	NA	NA	NA	NA	NA	NA	NA	NA	NA	23	23
High-income countries	NA	NA	NA	NA	NA	3	NA	9	NA	NA	NA	NA	NA	NA	NA	NA	NA	6	6
WORLD	NA	NA	NA	NA	NA	6	NA	43	NA	NA	NA	NA	NA	NA	NA	NA	NA	23	23
PAF of YLL (%)																			
East Asia and Pacific	NA	NA	NA	NA	NA	4	NA	30	NA	NA	NA	NA	NA	NA	NA	NA	NA	18	18
Europe and Central Asia	NA	NA	NA	NA	NA	7	NA	44	NA	NA	NA	NA	NA	NA	NA	NA	NA	19	19
Latin America and the Caribbean	NA	NA	NA	NA	NA	20	NA	51	NA	NA	NA	NA	NA	NA	NA	NA	NA	33	33
Middle East and North Africa	NA	NA	NA	NA	NA	8	NA	40	NA	NA	NA	NA	NA	NA	NA	NA	NA	24	24
South Asia	NA	NA	NA	NA	NA	8	NA	60	NA	NA	NA	NA	NA	NA	NA	NA	NA	33	33
Sub-Saharan Africa	NA	NA	NA	NA	NA	4	NA	28	NA	NA	NA	NA	NA	NA	NA	NA	NA	14	14
Low- and middle-income countries	NA	NA	NA	NA	NA	6	NA	43	NA	NA	NA	NA	NA	NA	NA	NA	NA	23	23
High-income countries	NA	NA	NA	NA	NA	3	NA	9	NA	NA	NA	NA	NA	NA	NA	NA	NA	6	6
WORLD	NA	NA	NA	NA	NA	6	NA	43	NA	NA	NA	NA	NA	NA	NA	NA	NA	23	23
PAF of DALYs (%)																			
East Asia and Pacific	NA	NA	NA	NA	NA	4	NA	30	NA	NA	NA	NA	NA	NA	NA	NA	NA	12	12
Europe and Central Asia	NA	NA	NA	NA	NA	7	NA	44	NA	NA	NA	NA	NA	NA	NA	NA	NA	17	17
Latin America and the Caribbean	NA	NA	NA	NA	NA	20	NA	51	NA	NA	NA	NA	NA	NA	NA	NA	NA	30	30
Middle East and North Africa	NA	NA	NA	NA	NA	8	NA	40	NA	NA	NA	NA	NA	NA	NA	NA	NA	20	20
South Asia	NA	NA	NA	NA	NA	8	NA	60	NA	NA	NA	NA	NA	NA	NA	NA	NA	27	27
Sub-Saharan Africa	NA	NA	NA	NA	NA	4	NA	28	NA	NA	NA	NA	NA	NA	NA	NA	NA	12	12
Low- and middle-income countries	NA	NA	NA	NA	NA	7	NA	43	NA	NA	NA	NA	NA	NA	NA	NA	NA	19	19
High-income countries	NA	NA	NA	NA	NA	3	NA	9	NA	NA	NA	NA	NA	NA	NA	NA	NA	5	5
WORLD	NA	NA	NA	NA	NA	7	NA	42	NA	NA	NA	NA	NA	NA	NA	NA	NA	19	19
Attributable Mortality (thousands)																			
East Asia and Pacific	NA	NA	NA	NA	NA	1	NA	5	NA	NA	NA	NA	NA	NA	NA	NA	NA	6	6
Europe and Central Asia	NA	NA	NA	NA	NA	0	NA	0	NA	NA	NA	NA	NA	NA	NA	NA	NA	0	0
Latin America and the Caribbean	NA	NA	NA	NA	NA	1	NA	3	NA	NA	NA	NA	NA	NA	NA	NA	NA	5	5
Middle East and North Africa	NA	NA	NA	NA	NA	0	NA	3	NA	NA	NA	NA	NA	NA	NA	NA	NA	3	3
South Asia	NA	NA	NA	NA	NA	6	NA	52	NA	NA	NA	NA	NA	NA	NA	NA	NA	59	59
Sub-Saharan Africa	NA	NA	NA	NA	NA	4	NA	25	NA	NA	NA	NA	NA	NA	NA	NA	NA	29	29
Low- and middle-income countries	NA	NA	NA	NA	NA	13	NA	90	NA	NA	NA	NA	NA	NA	NA	NA	NA	103	103
High-income countries	NA	NA	NA	NA	NA	0	NA	0	NA	NA	NA	NA	NA	NA	NA	NA	NA	0	0
WORLD	NA	NA	NA	NA	NA	13	NA	90	NA	NA	NA	NA	NA	NA	NA	NA	NA	103	103
Attributable YLL (thousands)																			
East Asia and Pacific	NA	NA	NA	NA	NA	15	NA	136	NA	NA	NA	NA	NA	NA	NA	NA	NA	150	150
Europe and Central Asia	NA	NA	NA	NA	NA	3	NA	9	NA	NA	NA	NA	NA	NA	NA	NA	NA	12	12
Latin America and the Caribbean	NA	NA	NA	NA	NA	39	NA	83	NA	NA	NA	NA	NA	NA	NA	NA	NA	122	122
Middle East and North Africa	NA	NA	NA	NA	NA	13	NA	71	NA	NA	NA	NA	NA	NA	NA	NA	NA	84	84
South Asia	NA	NA	NA	NA	NA	179	NA	1,320	NA	NA	NA	NA	NA	NA	NA	NA	NA	1,499	1,499
Sub-Saharan Africa	NA	NA	NA	NA	NA	116	NA	633	NA	NA	NA	NA	NA	NA	NA	NA	NA	749	749
Low- and middle-income countries	NA	NA	NA	NA	NA	365	NA	2,251	NA	NA	NA	NA	NA	NA	NA	NA	NA	2,616	2,616
High-income countries	NA	NA	NA	NA	NA	0	NA	1	NA	NA	NA	NA	NA	NA	NA	NA	NA	2	2
WORLD	NA	NA	NA	NA	NA	365	NA	2,252	NA	NA	NA	NA	NA	NA	NA	NA	NA	2,617	2,617
Attributable DALYs (thousands)																			
East Asia and Pacific	NA	NA	NA	NA	NA	89	NA	317	NA	NA	NA	NA	NA	NA	NA	NA	NA	405	405
Europe and Central Asia	NA	NA	NA	NA	NA	24	NA	54	NA	NA	NA	NA	NA	NA	NA	NA	NA	78	78
Latin America and the Caribbean	NA	NA	NA	NA	NA	160	NA	205	NA	NA	NA	NA	NA	NA	NA	NA	NA	365	365
Middle East and North Africa	NA	NA	NA	NA	NA	54	NA	169	NA	NA	NA	NA	NA	NA	NA	NA	NA	223	223
South Asia	NA	NA	NA	NA	NA	431	NA	1,886	NA	NA	NA	NA	NA	NA	NA	NA	NA	2,318	2,318
Sub-Saharan Africa	NA	NA	NA	NA	NA	196	NA	826	NA	NA	NA	NA	NA	NA	NA	NA	NA	1,021	1,021
Low- and middle-income countries	NA	NA	NA	NA	NA	954	NA	3,457	NA	NA	NA	NA	NA	NA	NA	NA	NA	4,411	4,411
High-income countries	NA	NA	NA	NA	NA	7	NA	13	NA	NA	NA	NA	NA	NA	NA	NA	NA	21	21
WORLD	NA	NA	NA	NA	NA	961	NA	3,471	NA	NA	NA	NA	NA	NA	NA	NA	NA	4,432	4,432

Source: Authors' calculations.
Note: NA = not applicable.

Table 4A.125

Risk factor: Non-use and use of ineffective methods of contraception
Disease: All causes

Region	0–4 years Male	Female	5–14 years Male	Female	15–29 years Male	Female	30–44 years Male	Female	45–59 years Male	Female	60–69 years Male	Female	70–79 years Male	Female	80+ years Male	Female	Total Male	Female	All
PAF of Mortality (%)																			
East Asia and Pacific	NA	NA	NA	NA	NA	1	NA	2	NA	NA	NA	NA	NA	NA	NA	NA	NA	0	0
Europe and Central Asia	NA	NA	NA	NA	NA	0	NA	0	NA	NA	NA	NA	NA	NA	NA	NA	NA	0	0
Latin America and the Caribbean	NA	NA	NA	NA	NA	4	NA	4	NA	NA	NA	NA	NA	NA	NA	NA	NA	0	0
Middle East and North Africa	NA	NA	NA	NA	NA	3	NA	6	NA	NA	NA	NA	NA	NA	NA	NA	NA	1	0
South Asia	NA	NA	NA	NA	NA	4	NA	13	NA	NA	NA	NA	NA	NA	NA	NA	NA	1	1
Sub-Saharan Africa	NA	NA	NA	NA	NA	3	NA	5	NA	NA	NA	NA	NA	NA	NA	NA	NA	1	1
Low- and middle-income countries	NA	NA	NA	NA	NA	3	NA	6	NA	NA	NA	NA	NA	NA	NA	NA	NA	1	0
High-income countries	NA	NA	NA	NA	NA	0	NA	0	NA	NA	NA	NA	NA	NA	NA	NA	NA	0	0
WORLD	NA	NA	NA	NA	NA	3	NA	6	NA	NA	NA	NA	NA	NA	NA	NA	NA	1	0
PAF of YLL (%)																			
East Asia and Pacific	NA	NA	NA	NA	NA	1	NA	2	NA	NA	NA	NA	NA	NA	NA	NA	NA	0	0
Europe and Central Asia	NA	NA	NA	NA	NA	0	NA	0	NA	NA	NA	NA	NA	NA	NA	NA	NA	0	0
Latin America and the Caribbean	NA	NA	NA	NA	NA	4	NA	4	NA	NA	NA	NA	NA	NA	NA	NA	NA	1	0
Middle East and North Africa	NA	NA	NA	NA	NA	3	NA	6	NA	NA	NA	NA	NA	NA	NA	NA	NA	1	0
South Asia	NA	NA	NA	NA	NA	4	NA	13	NA	NA	NA	NA	NA	NA	NA	NA	NA	2	1
Sub-Saharan Africa	NA	NA	NA	NA	NA	3	NA	5	NA	NA	NA	NA	NA	NA	NA	NA	NA	1	1
Low- and middle-income countries	NA	NA	NA	NA	NA	3	NA	6	NA	NA	NA	NA	NA	NA	NA	NA	NA	1	0
High-income countries	NA	NA	NA	NA	NA	0	NA	0	NA	NA	NA	NA	NA	NA	NA	NA	NA	0	0
WORLD	NA	NA	NA	NA	NA	3	NA	6	NA	NA	NA	NA	NA	NA	NA	NA	NA	1	0
PAF of DALYs (%)																			
East Asia and Pacific	NA	NA	NA	NA	NA	1	NA	2	NA	NA	NA	NA	NA	NA	NA	NA	NA	0	0
Europe and Central Asia	NA	NA	NA	NA	NA	1	NA	1	NA	NA	NA	NA	NA	NA	NA	NA	NA	0	0
Latin America and the Caribbean	NA	NA	NA	NA	NA	3	NA	3	NA	NA	NA	NA	NA	NA	NA	NA	NA	1	0
Middle East and North Africa	NA	NA	NA	NA	NA	3	NA	5	NA	NA	NA	NA	NA	NA	NA	NA	NA	1	1
South Asia	NA	NA	NA	NA	NA	5	NA	9	NA	NA	NA	NA	NA	NA	NA	NA	NA	2	1
Sub-Saharan Africa	NA	NA	NA	NA	NA	4	NA	4	NA	NA	NA	NA	NA	NA	NA	NA	NA	1	1
Low- and middle-income countries	NA	NA	NA	NA	NA	3	NA	5	NA	NA	NA	NA	NA	NA	NA	NA	NA	1	1
High-income countries	NA	NA	NA	NA	NA	0	NA	0	NA	NA	NA	NA	NA	NA	NA	NA	NA	0	0
WORLD	NA	NA	NA	NA	NA	3	NA	4	NA	NA	NA	NA	NA	NA	NA	NA	NA	1	0
Attributable Mortality (thousands)																			
East Asia and Pacific	NA	NA	NA	NA	NA	3	NA	7	NA	NA	NA	NA	NA	NA	NA	NA	NA	10	10
Europe and Central Asia	NA	NA	NA	NA	NA	0	NA	0	NA	NA	NA	NA	NA	NA	NA	NA	NA	1	1
Latin America and the Caribbean	NA	NA	NA	NA	NA	3	NA	4	NA	NA	NA	NA	NA	NA	NA	NA	NA	7	7
Middle East and North Africa	NA	NA	NA	NA	NA	1	NA	3	NA	NA	NA	NA	NA	NA	NA	NA	NA	5	5
South Asia	NA	NA	NA	NA	NA	22	NA	63	NA	NA	NA	NA	NA	NA	NA	NA	NA	85	85
Sub-Saharan Africa	NA	NA	NA	NA	NA	23	NA	31	NA	NA	NA	NA	NA	NA	NA	NA	NA	54	54
Low- and middle-income countries	NA	NA	NA	NA	NA	52	NA	110	NA	NA	NA	NA	NA	NA	NA	NA	NA	162	162
High-income countries	NA	NA	NA	NA	NA	0	NA	0	NA	NA	NA	NA	NA	NA	NA	NA	NA	0	0
WORLD	NA	NA	NA	NA	NA	52	NA	110	NA	NA	NA	NA	NA	NA	NA	NA	NA	162	162
Attributable YLL (thousands)																			
East Asia and Pacific	NA	NA	NA	NA	NA	76	NA	186	NA	NA	NA	NA	NA	NA	NA	NA	NA	262	262
Europe and Central Asia	NA	NA	NA	NA	NA	6	NA	12	NA	NA	NA	NA	NA	NA	NA	NA	NA	18	18
Latin America and the Caribbean	NA	NA	NA	NA	NA	77	NA	100	NA	NA	NA	NA	NA	NA	NA	NA	NA	177	177
Middle East and North Africa	NA	NA	NA	NA	NA	34	NA	84	NA	NA	NA	NA	NA	NA	NA	NA	NA	118	118
South Asia	NA	NA	NA	NA	NA	604	NA	1,596	NA	NA	NA	NA	NA	NA	NA	NA	NA	2,200	2,200
Sub-Saharan Africa	NA	NA	NA	NA	NA	648	NA	781	NA	NA	NA	NA	NA	NA	NA	NA	NA	1,429	1,429
Low- and middle-income countries	NA	NA	NA	NA	NA	1,445	NA	2,759	NA	NA	NA	NA	NA	NA	NA	NA	NA	4,203	4,203
High-income countries	NA	NA	NA	NA	NA	1	NA	2	NA	NA	NA	NA	NA	NA	NA	NA	NA	3	3
WORLD	NA	NA	NA	NA	NA	1,446	NA	2,761	NA	NA	NA	NA	NA	NA	NA	NA	NA	4,207	4,207
Attributable DALYs (thousands)																			
East Asia and Pacific	NA	NA	NA	NA	NA	192	NA	370	NA	NA	NA	NA	NA	NA	NA	NA	NA	562	562
Europe and Central Asia	NA	NA	NA	NA	NA	35	NA	58	NA	NA	NA	NA	NA	NA	NA	NA	NA	92	92
Latin America and the Caribbean	NA	NA	NA	NA	NA	237	NA	226	NA	NA	NA	NA	NA	NA	NA	NA	NA	462	462
Middle East and North Africa	NA	NA	NA	NA	NA	163	NA	188	NA	NA	NA	NA	NA	NA	NA	NA	NA	350	350
South Asia	NA	NA	NA	NA	NA	1,415	NA	2,196	NA	NA	NA	NA	NA	NA	NA	NA	NA	3,612	3,612
Sub-Saharan Africa	NA	NA	NA	NA	NA	1,323	NA	1,010	NA	NA	NA	NA	NA	NA	NA	NA	NA	2,332	2,332
Low- and middle-income countries	NA	NA	NA	NA	NA	3,364	NA	4,046	NA	NA	NA	NA	NA	NA	NA	NA	NA	7,411	7,411
High-income countries	NA	NA	NA	NA	NA	9	NA	14	NA	NA	NA	NA	NA	NA	NA	NA	NA	23	23
WORLD	NA	NA	NA	NA	NA	3,373	NA	4,061	NA	NA	NA	NA	NA	NA	NA	NA	NA	7,434	7,434

Source: Authors' calculations.
Note: NA = not applicable.

NOTES

1. Some special cases of effect modification can be identified through the terminology of "sufficient" and "component" causes (Rothman 1976; Rothman and Greenland 1998) with implications for the assessment of joint interventions as follows:

- If two risk factors are sufficient causes for a disease and a fraction of the population is affected by both sufficient causes, then the burden avoidable by reductions in both risk factors is larger than the sum of the burdens avoidable by reduction of each individual risk factor. This is because for those affected by the two risks, removal of both risks is needed to avoid disease (and hence the hazard as measured by the avoidable fraction of disease depends on the presence of the other risk). Consider, for example, the role of clean water and sanitary latrines as risk factors for diarrheal diseases. Improving water quality alone may not have much effect on the prevalence of disease without the introduction of sanitation or hygienic behavior, because fecal-oral transmission may take place through routes other than drinking water (Curtis, Cairncross, and Yonli 2000; Esrey 1996). However, the introduction of both clean water sources and sanitary latrines may reduce disease levels substantially. In the extreme, where every exposed person is affected by both sufficient causes, a change in exposure to a risk factor may result in no change in disease outcome under some circumstances. This phenomenon is known as saturation.

- If two risk factors are component causes of the same sufficient cause, then the burden avoidable by reductions in both risk factors is smaller than the sum of the burdens attributable to each individual risk factor. This is a case of synergy or positive interaction between risk factors, in which the existence of both risk factors has an effect larger than the sum of the effects from the existence of each (Rothman 1976). Synergistic interactions may be complete or partial depending on whether the risk factors are components of a single or multiple sufficient causes. Rothman (1976) uses the inheritance of the phenylketonuria gene and phenylalanine in the diet as an example of synergy.

2. Submultiplicative effect modification could result in a slightly smaller PAF even with positive correlation for some *RR* values.

REFERENCES

Arrow, K., B. Bolin, R. Costanza, P. Dasgupta, C. Folke, C. S. Holling, B.-O. Jansson, S. Levin, K.-G. Maler, C. Perrings, and D. Pimente. 1995. "Economic Growth, Carrying Capacity, and the Environment." *Science* 168 (2): 520–21.

Berlin, J. A., and G. A. Colditz. 1990. "A Meta-analysis of Physical Activity in the Prevention of Coronary Heart Disease." *American Journal of Epidemiology* 132 (4): 612–28.

Black, R. E. 1991. "Would Control of Childhood Infectious Diseases Reduce Malnutrition? *Acta Paediatrica Scandandinavica Supplement* 374: 133–40.

Blair, S. N., Y. Cheng, and J. S. Holder. 2001. "Is Physical Activity or Physical Fitness More Important in Defining Health Benefits?" *Medicine and Science in Sports and Exercise* 33 (6 Suppl): S379–S399.

Briend, A. 1990. "Is Diarrhoea a Major Cause of Malnutrition among the Under-Fives in Developing Countries? A Review of Available Evidence." *European Journal of Clinical Nutrition* 44 (9): 611–28.

Brown, K. H., J. M. Peerson, J. Rivera, and L. H. Allen. 2002. "Effect of Supplemental Zinc on the Growth and Serum Zinc Concentrations of Prepubertal Children: A Meta-analysis of Randomized Controlled Trials." *American Journal of Clinical Nutrition* 75 (6): 1062–71.

Chen, Z., R. Peto, R. Collins, S. MacMahon, J. Lu, and W. Li. 1991. "Serum Cholesterol Concentration and Coronary Heart Disease in Population with Low Cholesterol Concentrations." *British Medical Journal* 303 (6797): 276–82.

Christian, P., and K. P. West, Jr. 1998. "Interactions between Zinc and Vitamin A: An Update." *American Journal of Clinical Nutrition* 68 (2 Suppl): 435S–441S.

Corrao, G., L. Rubbiati, V. Bagnardi, A. Zambon, and K. Poikolainen. 2000. "Alcohol and Coronary Heart Disease: A Meta-analysis." *Addiction* 95 (10): 1505–23.

Curtis, V., S. Cairncross, and R. Yonli. 2000. "Domestic Hygiene and Diarrhoea: Pinpointing the Problem." *Tropical Medicine and International Health* 5 (1): 22–32.

de Onis, M., M. Blossner, E. Borghi, E. A. Frongillo, and R. Morris. 2004. "Estimates of Global Prevalence of Childhood Underweight in 1990 and 2015." *Journal of the American Medical Association* 291 (21): 2600–6.

de Onis, M., E. Frongillo, and M. Blossner. 2000. "Is Malnutrition Declining? An Analysis of Changes in Levels of Child Malnutrition since 1980." *Bulletin of the World Health Organization* 78 (10): 1222–33.

Eastern Stroke and Coronary Heart Disease Collaborative Research Group. 1998. "Blood Pressure, Cholesterol, and Stroke in Eastern Asia." *Lancet* 352 (9143): 1801–7.

Eaton, C.B. 1992. "Relation of Physical Activity and Cardiovascular Fitness to Coronary Heart Disease, Part I: A Meta-analysis of the Independent Relation of Physical Activity and Coronary Heart Disease." *Journal of the American Board of Family Practice* 5 (1): 31–42.

Editorial. 2001. "The Human Genome, in Proportion." *Lancet* 357 (9255): 489.

Eide, G. E., and I. Heuch. 2001. "Attributable Fractions: Fundamental Concepts and Their Visualization." *Statistical Methods in Medical Research* 10 (3): 159–93.

Esrey, S. A. 1996. "Water, Waste, and Well-Being: A Multicountry Study." *American Journal of Epidemiology* 143 (6): 608–23.

Evans, A. S. 1976. "Causation and Disease: The Henle-Koch Postulates Revisited." *Yale Journal of Biology and Medicine* 49 (2): 175–95.

———. 1978. "Causation and Disease: A Chronological Journey." *American Journal of Epidemiology* 108 (4): 249–58.

Ezzati, M., and D. M. Kammen. 2002. "The Health Impacts of Exposure to Indoor Air Pollution from Solid Fuels in Developing Countries: Knowledge, Gaps, and Data Needs." *Environmental Health Perspectives* 110 (11): 1057–68.

Ezzati, M., and A. D. Lopez. 2003. "Estimates of Global Mortality Attributable to Smoking in 2000." *Lancet* 362 (9387): 847–52.

———. 2004. "Smoking and Oral Tobacco Use." In *Comparative Quantification of Health Risks: Global and Regional Burden of Disease Attributable to Selected Major Risk Factors,* ed. M. Ezzati, A. D. Lopez, A. Rodgers, and C. J. L. Murray, 883–956. Geneva: World Health Organization.

Ezzati, M., S. J. Henley, A. D. Lopez, and M. J. Thun. 2005. "The Role of Smoking in Global and Regional Cancer Epidemiology: Current Patterns and Research Needs." *International Journal of Cancer* 116 (6): 963–71.

Ezzati, M., S. J. Henley, M. J. Thun, and A. D. Lopez. 2005. "The Role of Smoking in Global and Regional Cardiovascular Mortality." *Circulation* 112 (4): 489–97.

Ezzati, M., A. D. Lopez, A. Rodgers, and C. J. L. Murray. 2004. *Comparative Quantification of Health Risks: Global and Regional Burden of Disease Attributable to Selected Major Risk Factors.* Geneva: World Health Organization.

Ezzati, M., A. D. Lopez, A. Rodgers, S. Vander Hoorn, C. J. L. Murray, and the Comparative Risk Assessment Collaborative Group. 2002.

"Selected Major Risk Factors and Global and Regional Burden of Disease." *Lancet* 360 (9343): 1347–60.

Ezzati, M., S. Vander Hoorn, A. Rodgers, A. D. Lopez, C. D. Mathers, and C. J. L. Murray. 2004. "Potential Health Gains from Reducing Multiple Risk Factors." In *Comparative Quantification of Health Risks: Global and Regional Burden of Disease Attributable to Selected Major Risk Factors,* ed. M. Ezzati, A. D. Lopez, A. Rodgers, and C. J. L. Murray, 2167–90. Geneva: World Health Organization.

Ezzati, M., S. Vander Hoorn, A. Rodgers, A. D. Lopez, C. D. Mathers, C. J. L. Murray, and the Comparative Risk Assessment Collaborative Group. 2003. "Estimates of Global and Regional Potential Health Gains from Reducing Multiple Major Risk Factors." *Lancet* 362 (9380): 271–80.

Ezzati, M., S. Vander Hoorn, C. M. M. Lawes, R. Leach, W. P. T. James, A. D. Lopez, A. Rodgers, and C. J. L. Murray. 2005. "Rethinking the 'Diseases of Affluence' Paradigm: Global Patterns of Nutritional Risks in Relation to Economic Development." *PLoS Medicine* 2 (5): e133.

Gaziano, J. M., J. E. Manson, L. G. Branch, G. A. Colditz, W. C. Willett, and J. E. Buring. 1995. "A Prospective Study of Consumption of Carotenoids in Fruits and Vegetables and Decreased Cardiovascular Mortality in the Elderly." *Annals of Epidemiology* 5 (4): 255–60.

Greenland, S. 1984. "Bias in Methods for Deriving Standardized Morbidity Ratio and Attributable Fraction Estimates." *Statistics in Medicine* 3: 131–41.

———. 1987. "Quantitative Methods in the Review of Epidemiologic Literature." *Epidemiologic Reviews* 9: 1–30.

Gross, C. P., G. F. Anderson, and N. R. Powe. 1999. "The Relation between Funding by the National Institutes of Health and the Burden of Disease." *New England Journal of Medicine* 340 (24): 1881–7.

Guerrant, R. L., J. B. Schorling, J. F. McAuliffe, and M. A. de Souza. 1992. "Diarrhea as a Cause and an Effect of Malnutrition: Diarrhea Prevents Catch-Up Growth and Malnutrition Increases Diarrhea Frequency and Duration." *American Journal of Tropical Medicine and Hygiene* 47 (1 pt 2): 28–35.

Horton, R. 2003. "Medical Journals: Evidence of Bias against the Diseases of Poverty." *Lancet* 361 (9359): 712–3.

Jarrett, R. J., M. J. Shipley, and G. Rose. 1982. "Weight and Mortality in the Whitehall Study." *British Medical Journal* 285 (6341): 535–7.

Jee, S. H., I. Suh, I. S. Kim, and L. J. Appel. 1999. "Smoking and Atherosclerotic Cardiovascular Disease in Men with Low Levels of Serum Cholesterol: The Korea Medical Insurance Corporation Study." *Journal of the American Medical Association* 282 (22): 2149–55.

Jousilahti, P., E. Vartiainen, J. Tuomilehto, and P. Puska. 1999. "Sex, Age, Cardiovascular Risk Factors, and Coronary Heart Disease: A Prospective Follow-Up Study of 14,786 Middle-Aged Men and Women in Finland." *Circulation* 99 (9): 1165–72.

Kaufman, J., and J. Jing. 2002. "China and AIDS: The Time to Act Is Now." *Science* 296 (5577): 2339–40.

Khaw, K. T., and E. Barrett-Connor. 1987. "Dietary Fiber and Reduced Ischemic Heart Disease Mortality Rates in Men and Women: A 12-Year Prospective Study." *American Journal of Epidemiology* 126 (6): 1093–102.

Koopman, J. S. 1981. "Interaction between Discrete Causes." *American Journal of Epidemiology* 113 (6): 716–24.

Kunzli, N., R. Kaiser, S. Medina, M. Studnicka, O. Chanel, P. Filliger, M. Herry, F. Horak, V. Puybonnieux-Texier, P. Quenel, J. Schneider, R. Seethaler, J. C. Vergnaud, and H. Sommer. 2000. "Public-Health Impact of Outdoor and Traffic-Related Air Pollution: A European Assessment." *Lancet* 356 (9232): 795–801.

Law, M. R., N. J. Wald, and S. G. Thompson. 1994. "By How Much and How Quickly Does Reduction in Serum Cholesterol Concentration Lower Risk of Ischaemic Heart Disease?" *British Medical Journal* 308 (6925): 367–73.

Lee, M.-J., B. M. Popkin, and S. Kim. 2000. "The Unique Aspects of the Nutrition Transition in South Korea: The Retention of Healthful Elements in Their Traditional Diet." *Public Health Nutrition* 5 (14): 197–203.

Leigh, J., P. Macaskill, E. Kuosma, and J. Mandryk. 1999. "Global Burden of Disease and Injury Due to Occupational Factors." *Epidemiology* 10 (5): 626–31.

Liu, B. Q., R. Peto, Z. M. Chen, J. Boreham, Y. P. Wu, J. Y. Li, T. C. Campbell, and J. S. Chen. 1998. "Emerging Tobacco Hazards in China: 1. Retrospective Proportional Mortality Study of One Million Deaths." *British Medical Journal* 317 (7170): 1411–22.

Liu, S., I. M. Lee, U. Ajani, S. R. Cole, J. E. Buring, and J. E. Manson. 2001. "Intake of Vegetables Rich in Carotenoids and Risk of Coronary Heart Disease in Men: The Physicians' Health Study." *International Journal of Epidemiology* 30 (1): 130–5.

Liu, S., J. E. Manson, I. M. Lee, S. R. Cole, C. H. Hennekens, W. C. Willett, and J. E. Buring. 2000. "Fruit and Vegetable Intake and Risk of Cardiovascular Disease: The Women's Health Study." *American Journal of Clinical Nutrition* 72 (4): 922–8.

Lutter, C. K., J. P. Habicht, J. A. Rivera, R. Martorell. 1992. "The Relationship between Energy Intake and Diarrheal Disease in Their Effects on Child Growth: Biological Model, Evidence, and Implications for Public Health Policy." *Food and Nutrition Bulletin* 14: 36–42.

Lutter, C. K., J. O. Mora, J. P. Habicht, K. M. Rasmussen, D. S. Robson, S. G. Sellers, M. G. Perri, D. S. Sheps, M. B. Pettinger, D. S. Siscovick. 1989. "Nutritional Supplementation: Effects on Child Stunting because of Diarrhea." *American Journal of Clinical Nutrition* 50 (1): 1–8.

MacLehose, L., M. McKee, and J. Weinberg. 2002. "Responding to the Challenge of Communicable Disease in Europe." *Science* 295 (5562): 2047–50.

Maldonado, G., and S. Greenland. 2002. "Estimating Causal Effects." *International Journal of Epidemiology* 31 (2): 422–9.

Manson, J. E., G. A. Colditz, M. J. Stampfer, W. C. Willett, B. Rosner, R. R. Monson, F. E. Speizer, and C. H. Hennekens. 1990. "A Prospective Study of Obesity and Risk of Coronary Heart Disease in Women." *New England Journal of Medicine* 322 (13): 882–9.

Manson, J. E., P. Greenland, A. Z. LaCroix, M. L. Stefanick, C. P. Mouton, A. Oberman, M. G. Perri, D. S. Sheps, M. B. Pettinger, D. S. Siscovick. 2002. "Walking Compared with Vigorous Exercise for the Prevention of Cardiovascular Events in Women." *New England Journal of Medicine* 347 (10): 755–56.

Martorell, R., J. P. Habicht, C. Yarbrough, A. Lechtig, R. E. Klein, and K. A. Western. 1975. "Acute Morbidity and Physical Growth in Rural Guatemalan Children." *American Journal of Diseases of Children* 129 (11): 1296–301.

Martorell, R., C. Yarbrough, A. Lechtig, J. P. Habicht, and R. E. Klein. 1975. "Diarrheal Diseases and Growth Retardation in Preschool Guatemalan Children." *American Journal of Physical Anthropology* 43 (3): 341–6.

Mathers, C. D., M. Ezzati, A. D. Lopez, C. J. L. Murray, and A. Rodgers. 2002. "Causal Decomposition of Summary Measures of Population Health." In *Summary Measures of Population Health: Concepts, Ethics, Measurement, and Applications,* ed. C. J. L. Murray, J. Salomon, C. D. Mathers, and A. D. Lopez. 273–290. Geneva: World Health Organization.

McGinnis, J. M., and W. H. Foege. 1993. "Actual Causes of Death in the United States." *Journal of American Medical Association* 270 (18): 2207–12.

Miettinen, O. S. 1974. "Proportion of Disease Caused or Prevented by a Given Exposure, Trait, or Intervention." *American Journal of Epidemiology* 99 (5): 325–32.

Murray, C. J. L., M. Ezzati, A. D. Lopez, A. Rodgers, and S. Vander Hoorn. 2003. "Comparative Quantification of Health Risks: Conceptual Framework and Methodological Issues." *Population Health Metrics* 1 (1): 1.

Murray, C. J. L., and A. D. Lopez. 1997. "Global Mortality, Disability, and the Contribution of Risk Factors: Global Burden of Disease Study." *Lancet* 349 (9063): 1436–42.

———. 1999. "On the Comparable Quantification of Health Risks: Lessons from the Global Burden of Disease." *Epidemiology* 10 (5): 594–605.

Neaton, J. D., and D. Wentworth. 1992. "Serum Cholesterol, Blood Pressure, Cigarette Smoking, and Death from Coronary Heart Disease. Overall Findings and Differences by Age for 316,099 White Men. Multiple Risk Factor Intervention Trial Research Group." *Archives of Internal Medicine* 152 (1): 56–64.

Pelletier, D. L., E. A. Frongillo, Jr., and J. P. Habicht. 1993. "Epidemiologic Evidence for a Potentiating Effect of Malnutrition on Child Mortality." *American Journal of Public Health* 83 (8): 1130–3.

Peto, R., A. D. Lopez, J. Boreham, M. Thun, and C. Heath, Jr. 1992. "Mortality from Tobacco in Developed Countries." *Lancet* 339 (8804): 1268–78.

Popkin, B. M. 2002a. "An Overview on the Nutrition Transition and Its Health Implications: The Bellagio Meeting." *Public Health Nutrition* 5 (1A): 93–103.

———. 2002b. "The Shift in Stages of the Nutrition Transition in the Developing World Differs from Past Experiences." *Public Health Nutrition* 5 (1A): 205–14.

Popkin, B. M., S. Horton, S. Kim, A. Mahal, and J. Shuigao. 2001. "Trends in Diet, Nutritional Status and Diet-Related Noncommunicable Diseases in China and India: The Economic Costs of the Nutrition Transition." *Nutrition Reviews* 59 (12): 379–90.

Preston, S. H. 1976. *Mortality Patterns in National Populations: With Special Reference to Recorded Causes of Death.* New York: Academic Press.

Puddey, I. B., V. Rakic, S. B. Dimmitt, and L. J. Beilin. 1999. "Influence of Pattern of Drinking on Cardiovascular Disease and Cardiovascular Risk Factors: A Review." *Addiction* 94 (5): 649–63.

Ramakrishnan, U., and R. Martorell. 1998. "The Role of Vitamin A in Reducing Child Mortality and Morbidity and Improving Growth." *Salud Publica de Mexico* 40 (2): 189–198.

Ramakrishnan, U., M. C. Latham, and R. Abel. 1995. "Vitamin A Supplementation Does Not Improve Growth of Preschool Children: A Randomized, Double-Blind Field Trial in South India." *Journal of Nutrition* 125 (2): 202–11.

Rehm, J., R. Room, M. Monteiro, G. Gmel, K. Graham, N. Rehn, C. T. Sempas, V. Frick, and D. Jerrigan. 2004. "Alcohol Use." In *Comparative Quantification of Health Risks: Global and Regional Burden of Disease Attributable to Selected Major Risk Factors,* ed. M. Ezzati, A. D. Lopez, C. J. Murray, and A. Rogers, 959–1108. Geneva: World Health Organization.

Rosengren, A., H. Wedel, and L. Wilhelmsen. 1999. "Body Weight and Weight Gain during Adult Life in Men in Relation to Coronary Heart Disease and Mortality: A Prospective Population." *European Health Journal* 20 (4): 269–77.

Rothman, K. J. 1976. "Causes." *American Journal of Epidemiology* 104 (6): 587–92.

Rothman, K. J., and S. Greenland. 1998. *Modern Epidemiology.* Philadelphia: Lippincott-Raven.

Rothman, K. J., and A. Keller. 1972. "The Effect of Joint Exposure to Alcohol and Tobacco on the Risk of Cancer of the Mouth and Pharynx." *Journal of Chronic Disease* 25 (12): 711–6.

Rothman, K. J., S. Greenland, and A. M. Walker. 1980. "Concepts of Interaction." *American Journal of Epidemiology* 112 (4): 467–70.

Scrimshaw, N. S., C. E. Taylor, and J. E. Gordon. 1968. *Interactions of Nutrition and Infection.* World Health Organization Monograph Series 57. Geneva: World Health Organization.

Single, E., L. Robson, J. Rehm, and X. Xie. 1999. "Morbidity and Mortality Attributable to Alcohol, Tobacco, and Illicit Drug Use in Canada." *American Journal of Public Health* 89 (3): 385–90.

Slaymaker, E., N. Walker, B. Zaba, and M. Collumbien. 2004. "Unsafe Sex." In *Comparative Quantification of Health Risks: Global and Regional Burden of Disease Attributable to Selected Major Risk Factors,* ed. M. Ezzati, A. D. Lopez, A. Rodgers, and C. J. L. Murray, 1177–254. Geneva: World Health Organization.

Smith, K. R. 2000. "The National Burden of Disease from Indoor Air Pollution in India." *Proceedings of the National Academy of Sciences* 97 (24): 13286–93.

Smith, K. R., C. F. Corvalan, and T. Kjellstrom. 1999. "How Much Global Ill Health Is Attributable to Environmental Factors." *Epidemiology* 10 (5): 573–84.

Smith, K. R., S. Mehta, and M. Maeusezahl-Feuz. 2004. "Indoor Air Pollution from Household Use of Solid Fuels." In *Comparative Quantification of Health Risks: Global and Regional Burden of Disease Attributable to Selected Major Risk Factors,* ed. M. Ezzati, A. D. Lopez, C. J. Murray, and A. Rogers, 1435–94. Geneva: World Health Organization.

Stephensen, C. B. 1999. "Burden of Infection on Growth Failure." *Journal of Nutrition* 129 (25 Suppl): 534S–538S.

Tate, R. B., J. Manfreda, and T. E. Cuddy. 1998. "The Effect of Age on Risk Factors for Ischemic Heart Disease: The Manitoba Follow-up Study, 1948–1993." *Annals of Epidemiology* 8 (7): 415–21.

Thun, M. J., L. F. Apicella, and S. J. Henley. 2000. "Smoking vs. Other Risk Factors as the Cause of Smoking-Attributable Mortality: Confounding in the Courtroom." *Journal of the American Medical Association* 284 (6): 706–12.

UNAIDS (Joint United Nations Programme on HIV/AIDS). 2001. *Together We Can: Leadership in a World of AIDS.* Geneva: UNAIDS. http://www.unaids.org/UNGASS/leadership/English/leader_en.pdf.

UNICEF (United Nations Children's Fund). 1990. *Strategy to Improve Nutrition of Children and Women in Developing Countries: A UNICEF Policy Review.* New York: UNICEF.

Walter, S. D. 1976. "The Estimation and Interpretation of Attributable Risk in Health Research." *Biometrics* 32 (4): 829–49.

———. 1980. "Prevention of Multifactorial Disease." *American Journal of Epidemiology* 112 (3): 409–16.

West, K. P., Jr, R. P. Pokhrel, J. Katz, S. C. LeClerq, S. K. Khatry, S. R. Shrestha, E. K. Pradhan, J. M. Tielsch, M. R. Pandey, and A. Sommer. 1991. "Efficacy of Vitamin A in Reducing Preschool Child Mortality in Nepal." *Lancet* 338 (8759): 67–71.

WHO (World Health Organization). 1992. *International Statistical Classification of Disease and Related Health Problems,* 10th ed. Geneva: WHO.

WHO (World Health Organization). 2002. *World Health Report 2002: Reducing Risks, Promoting Healthy Life.* Geneva: WHO.

Willet, W. C. 2002. "Balancing Life-Style and Genomics Research for Disease Prevention." *Science* 296 (5568): 695–8.

Yerushalmy, J., and C. E. Palmer. 1959. "On the Methodology of Investigations of Etiologic Factors in Chronic Diseases." *Journal of Chronic Disease* 108 (1): 27–40.

Yusuf, S., S. Hawken, S. Ounpuu, T. Dans, A. Avezum, F. Lanas, M. McQueen, A. Budaj, P. Pais, J. Varigos, L. Lisheng, and the INTER-HEART Study Investigators. 2004. "Effect of Potentially Modifiable Risk Factors Associated with Myocardial Infarction in 52 Countries (the INTERHEART Study): Case-Control Study." *Lancet* 364 (9438): 937–52.

Zinc Investigators' Collaborative Group. 1999. "Prevention of Diarrhea and Pneumonia by Zinc Supplementation in Children in Developing Countries: Pooled Analysis of Randomized Controlled Trials." *Journal of Pediatrics* 135 (6): 689–97.

Part **II**

Sensitivity Analyses

Sensitivity and Uncertainty Analyses for Burden of Disease and Risk Factor Estimates

Colin D. Mathers, Joshua A. Salomon, Majid Ezzati, Stephen Begg, Stephen Vander Hoorn, and Alan D. Lopez

Modern epidemiological studies generally report confidence or uncertainty intervals around their estimates, often based on the variation observed in sample data. Estimates of the burden of disease and of risk factors, which extrapolate from specific data sources and epidemiological studies to population-level measures, are subject to a broader range of uncertainty because of the combination of multiple data sources and value choices. Hence, the reported uncertainty intervals should ideally include all sources of uncertainty, including those arising from measurement error, systematic biases, and modeling and extrapolation to compensate for incomplete data. In contrast to uncertainty analysis, which attempts to formally quantify the limitations of available data, sensitivity analysis examines how key analytic outputs vary when input quantities are systematically varied. Following Murray and Lopez (1996b), this chapter uses sensitivity analysis to examine the specific effects of social values that have been incorporated in the design of the disability-adjusted life year (DALY).

Taking account of uncertainty in such value parameters as the rate of time preference used to discount future outcomes is not common. Even if there is empirical evidence on

population preferences for discount rates and uncertainty in these estimates, investigators have argued that the choice of discount rate for use in analysis is essentially a social value judgment and should not include uncertainty (Morgan and Henrion 1990). Although there is uncertainty about the social value judgment and about its effects on decisions based on the analysis, varying the value deterministically in the analysis and performing a sensitivity analysis to examine the impact on the outcomes of interest is usually preferable to uncertainty analysis. Thus, the 1990 Global Burden of Disease (GBD) study (Murray and Lopez 1996b) examined the sensitivity of the ranking of causes of the burden of disease globally when discount rates and age weights were varied across a range of possible values.

Health state valuations, which link mortality information with information on nonfatal health outcomes in summary measures of population health, fit somewhat more ambiguously within the framework of uncertainty analysis. If we conceptualize a health state in terms of levels in multiple domains of health, health state valuation involves the weighting of these domains to arrive at an overall assessment of the health level associated with the state. These valuations, unlike values such as time preference, do not have any clear normative basis; that is, while we might rely on philosophical arguments about intergenerational equity in choosing a discount rate, no obvious arguments pertain to the relative importance of mobility versus cognition in overall assessments of health levels. The choice of measurement strategies for eliciting health state valuations does sometimes introduce normative questions, but these pertain to additional considerations, such as concern for fair distribution, which are orthogonal to the assessment of the health state itself.

DISCOUNTING AND AGE WEIGHTING IN THE DALY MEASURE

This section briefly reviews the rationale and implementation of discounting and age weights in the standard DALY. To denote different choices for the discount rate and age weights, we use the notation DALYs(r,K), where r is the discount rate in percent (not a fraction as in the GBD 1990 study) and K is the age-weighting modulation factor, a parameter that allows uniform ($K = 0$) or the GBD nonuniform ($K = 1$) age weighting to be used. With this notation, DALYs(3,0) denotes the DALY with a 3 percent discount rate and uniform age weights as used in the Disease Control Priorities Project (DCPP) and DALYs(3,1) denotes the 3 percent discount rate and varying age weights as used in the GBD study. Similarly, we may refer to the DALY components of years of life lost due to premature mortality (YLL) and years of healthy life lost due to disability (YLD) as YLL(r,K) or YLD(r,K) using the same convention.

Discounting

Discounting future benefits is standard practice in economic analysis. Murray (1996) and Murray and Acharya (1997) review the theoretical and empirical arguments for and against discounting with a specific emphasis on health, including the possibility of negative discount rates. In addition to individual discounting and discount rates, policies dealing with risk must address the issue of benefits for different populations across time. As a result, these policies must address ethical and analytical dilemmas related to the valuation of current and future health and welfare in the form of social discount rates (Kneese 1999).

Some have argued that discounting should not be applied to future health gains or losses because health is not commensurable with money and cannot be reinvested elsewhere, but most criticisms of discounting in relation to

the DALY have focused on the functional form and the level chosen (Fox-Rushby 2002). Epidemiologists and demographers, who tend to focus on measuring or estimating years of life or health without "valuing" either, rarely use discounting. Murray and Acharya (1997) conclude that the strongest argument for discounting is the disease eradication and health research paradox. According to this argument, not discounting future health would lead to the conclusion that all of society's health resources should be invested in research programs or programs for disease eradication, which produce an infinite stream of benefits, rather than any programs that improve the health of the current generation. Such an excessive intergenerational "sacrifice" is a particularly powerful argument for discounting future health (Parfit 1984). Note that this argument does not claim that future welfare or health is less valuable than current welfare or health, but rather uses discounting as a tool to avoid excessive sacrifice by the current generation to the point of investing all resources in future health.

Murray and Acharya argue that the social discount rate should be smaller than the return on capital investment, but note that the choice of a discount rate for health benefits, even if technically desirable, may result in morally unacceptable allocations between generations (see also Dasgupta, Mäler, and Barrett 1999). Because of the complexities in the choice of discount rate, the 1990 GBD study published discounted and undiscounted estimates of the global burden of disease (Murray and Lopez 1996a).

The U.S. Panel on Cost-Effectiveness in Health and Medicine has recommended that health economic analyses use a 3 percent real discount rate to adjust both costs and health outcomes (Gold and others 1996), but that analysts should examine the sensitivity of the results to the discount rate. The 1990 GBD study, the updated estimates published in recent World Health Organization (WHO) world health reports, and the DCPP have all used 3 percent discounting for DALYs.

Age Weighting

The 1990 GBD study weighted a year of healthy life lived at young ages and older ages lower than years lived at other ages. This choice was based on a number of studies that indicated a broad social preference to value a year lived by a young adult more highly than a year lived by a young child or an older adult (Murray 1996). Not all such studies agree that the youngest and oldest ages should be given less weight; nor do they agree on the relative magnitude of the differences.

Age weights are perhaps the most controversial value choice built into the DALY. Criticisms of age weights have fallen into five categories:

- Age weighting is unacceptable on equity grounds and every year of life is of equal value (Anand and Hanson 1997).
- Age weights are not empirically based and have not been validated for large populations.
- Age weights do not reflect social values; for example, the DALY values the life of a newborn about equally to that of a 20-year-old, whereas the empirical data suggest a fourfold difference (Bobadilla 1996; see also chapter 6 in this book).
- Age weights result in more YLL for deaths at all ages from birth to 39 compared with discounted YLL not weighted by age (Barendregt, Bonneux, and van der Maas 1996).
- Age weights add an extra level of complexity to burden of disease analysis that obscures the method and makes little overall difference to the rankings of diseases and injuries.

Murray and Acharya (1997) argue that age weights are not in themselves inequitable, because everyone potentially lives through every age, and that they do reflect legitimate societal priorities. As discussed in chapter 3, the DCPP uses uniform age weights and thus values a year of healthy life equally at all ages. Chapter 6 presents an analysis in which a more extreme form of age weighting is applied to the deaths of young children.

Discounting, Age Weights, and the YLL Loss Function

DALYs are calculated as the sum of YLL from a cause and the YLD for incident cases of the health condition (see chapter 3 for more details). Murray (1996) provides general formulas for YLL and YLD that allow the annual discount rate r and the age-weighting parameters (K, C, β) to be varied. When K is set equal to 1, then the DALY includes an age-weighting function of the form $Cxe^{-\beta x}$, where x is the age in years and β and C are constants. For the 1990 GBD study, Murray and Lopez chose $\beta = 0.04$. The value of $\beta = 0.04$ was chosen to give an age pattern similar to that seen in available empirical data. C is a parameter chosen to ensure that the total global DALYs are the same with and without age weighting, estimated at $C = 0.1658$ for the 1990 GBD study. Figure 5.1 illustrates the form of the age-weighting function for $\beta = 0.02$, 0.04, and 0.06. For the other two

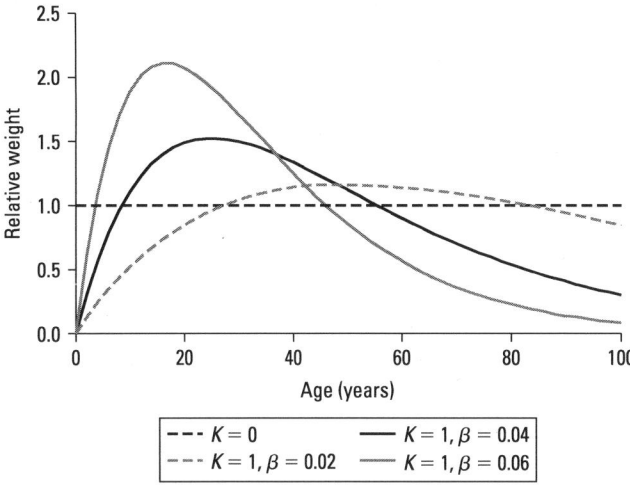

Source: Authors' calculations.

Figure 5.1 Age-Weighting Function Incorporated into the DALY

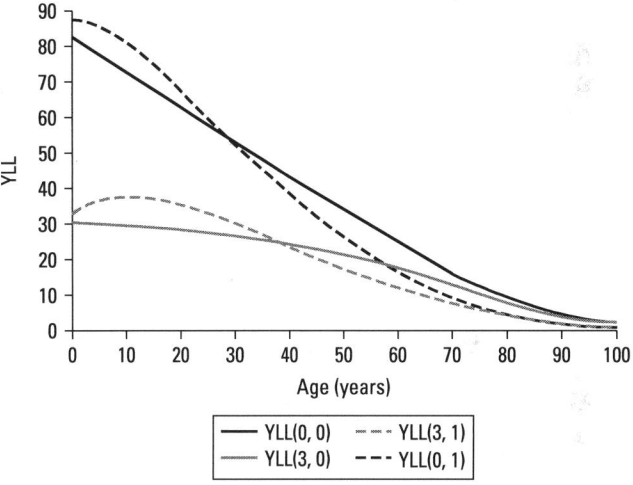

Source: Authors' calculations.

Note: YLL(r, K) denotes YLL calculated with discount rate r (percent) and standard age weighting ($K = 1$) or uniform age weighting ($K = 0$).

Figure 5.2 Effect of Age Weighting and Discounting on the YLL per Death at Various Ages for Females

choices of β (0.02 or 0.06), the value of C was varied to ensure the same area under the curve from age 0 to 100 years.

The age-weighting function specifies the relative value of a year of life lived at different ages either for YLD or YLL estimates. To estimate the total years of life lost due to death at age x, the age-weighting function is integrated over all ages above x. Table 5.1 shows the resulting loss function for selected exact ages, also plotted in figure 5.2 for females. The male-female gap in YLL(0,0), 2.5 years at birth, is reduced to 0.1 years for YLL(3,1) (figure 5.3). Figure 5.4 shows the effect on YLL of varying the parameter β in the age-weighting

Table 5.1 Standard Life Expectancies at Selected Exact Ages and Discounted YLL Due to a Death at Selected Ages

Age	YLL (0,0) per death– standard life expectancy (years)		YLL (3,0) per death– 3% discounting, uniform age weights (years)		YLL (3,1) per death– 3% discounting, standard age weights (years)	
	Males	**Females**	**Males**	**Females**	**Males**	**Females**
0	80.00	82.50	30.31	30.53	33.01	33.13
5	75.38	77.95	29.86	30.12	36.46	36.59
15	65.41	68.02	28.65	29.00	36.80	36.99
30	50.51	53.27	26.01	26.59	29.62	29.92
45	35.77	38.72	21.93	22.90	20.17	20.66
60	21.81	24.83	16.01	17.51	11.48	12.22
70	13.58	16.20	11.15	12.83	6.69	7.48
80	7.45	8.90	6.67	7.81	3.27	3.76
90	3.54	4.25	3.36	3.99	1.30	1.53
100	1.46	2.00	1.43	1.94	0.42	0.57

Source: Authors' calculations.

function. Values of β higher than 0.04 give relatively greater weight to younger ages and less to older ages; values of β lower than 0.04 give relatively lower weight to younger ages and more to older ages.

Table 5.2 further examines the effects of varying the parameter β in the age-weighting function on the weights applicable at different ages. For the standard DALY, $\beta = 0.04$ implies a maximum age weight of 1.52 at age 25, and the age weight is greater than 1 over the range 8.4 to 54.2 years. Compare this with $\beta = 0.03$, which gives a maximum age weight of 1.29 at age 33.3 years with a prime age range (weight greater than 1) of 14.9 to 63.0 years. Note that the choice of $\beta = 0.03$ gives a prime age range that matches fairly typical ages for formal entry and exit from work in many societies (Mahapatra 2001). We do not consider variations in β further here. Sensitivity analyses for GBD 2001 that follow compare standard age weights ($\beta = 0.4$) with uniform age weights.

SENSITIVITY OF BURDEN OF DISEASE AND INJURY RESULTS TO VARIATIONS IN KEY PARAMETER VALUES

This section examines the sensitivity of the DALY estimates for the global burden of disease in 2001 to alternative assumptions about the discount rate and age weighting. As discussed in chapter 3, the DALY measures the future stream

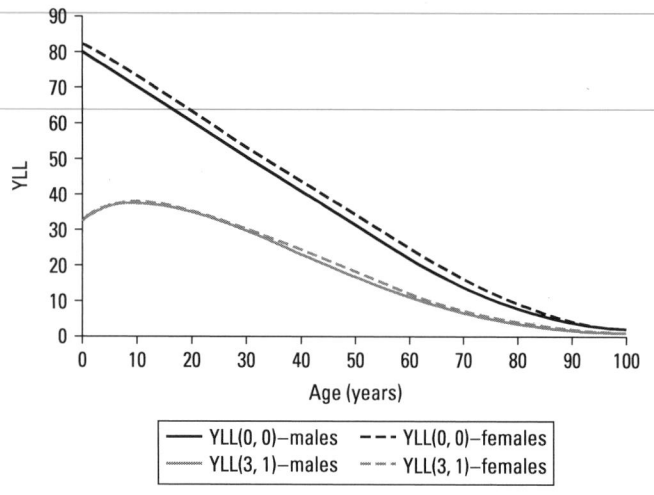

Figure 5.3 Effect of Age Weighting and Discounting on the Male-Female Gap in YLL per Death

Source: Authors' calculations.

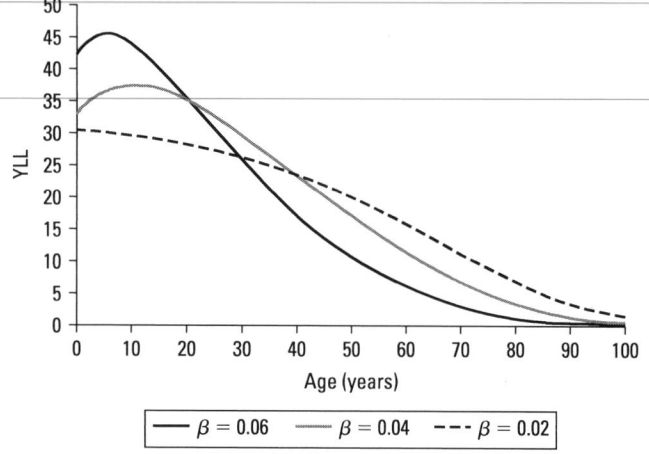

Source: Authors' calculations.

Note: The discount rate is held constant at 3 percent for the examples shown.

Figure 5.4 Effect on YLL per Death of Varying the Parameter β in the DALY Age-Weighting Function

Table 5.2 Implications of Variation in Choice of Age-Weight Parameter β on the Age-Weighting Function

Age-weight parameter β	Age-weight[a] constant C	Maximum age weight	Age of maximum age weight	Age range for which age weight is > 1
0.02	0.0634	1.17	50.0	27.2–83.1
0.03	0.1051	1.29	33.3	14.9–63.0
0.04	0.1658	1.52	25.0	8.4–54.2
0.05	0.2487	1.83	20.0	5.2–50.7
0.06	0.3560	2.18	16.7	3.5–46.9

Source: Authors' calculations.

Note: This form of presentation was suggested by Mahapatra 2001.

a. For values of β other than 0.04, the age-weight constant C was chosen so that total global DALYs(3,1) for 2001 were the same as for $\beta = 0.04$.

of healthy years of life lost due to each incident case of disease or injury. It is thus an incidence-based measure rather than a prevalence-based measure. The GBD study applied a 3 percent time discount rate to years of life lost in the future to estimate the net present value of years of life lost. With this discount rate, a year of healthy life gained in 10 years' time is valued at 24 percent less than one gained now (note that the standard DALY uses an instantaneous 3 percent discount rate, which results in an annual discount factor that is slightly higher).

Table 5.3 summarizes the effects of varying the discount rate and age weights. Changes in the discount rate and age weights have little effect on the proportion of the burden in males and females. However, changes in the discount rate have an important effect on the proportion of the burden due to nonfatal outcomes (YLD), on the age distribution of

the burden, and on the distribution of the burden by broad cause group. When the discount rate is set to zero, the proportion of burden due to YLD is just over a quarter of the total burden. When the discount rate is set to 3 percent, then 36 to 38 percent of the burden is due to YLD, depending on whether age weights are also applied.

Similarly, a nonzero discount rate significantly reduces the importance of the burden of disease or injury in children. This effect is more pronounced in low- and middle-income countries, where children bear a disproportionately large share of the total burden (figure 5.5). Because of the differences in the cause structure of the disease burden by age, these effects also influence the overall distribution of DALYs by broad cause group for low- and middle-income countries. In contrast, for high-income countries, while some changes in the age distribution of the burden are apparent, the choice

Table 5.3 Comparison of the Effects of Changing the Discount Rate (r) and the Age-Weighting Factor (K) on the Composition of DALYs(r,K), 2001

	World			Low- and middle-income countries		
	DALYs(0,0)	DALYs(3,0)	DALYs(3,1)	DALYs(0,0)	DALYs(3,0)	DALYs(3,1)
Total DALYs (millions)	2,645	1,536	1,476	2,447	1,387	1,357
By outcome (%)						
Total YLD	27	36	38	26	34	36
Total YLL	73	64	62	74	66	64
By cause (%)						
Group I	47	37	41	50	40	44
Group II	42	53	47	38	49	43
Group III	12	11	12	12	11	13
By sex (%)						
Male	51	52	52	51	52	52
Female	49	48	48	49	48	48
By age group (%)						
0–4	39	28	30	41	31	32
5–14	6	6	8	7	6	8
15–44	26	27	35	26	28	35
45–59	12	15	14	12	15	13
60+	16	24	15	14	21	13

Source: Authors' calculations.

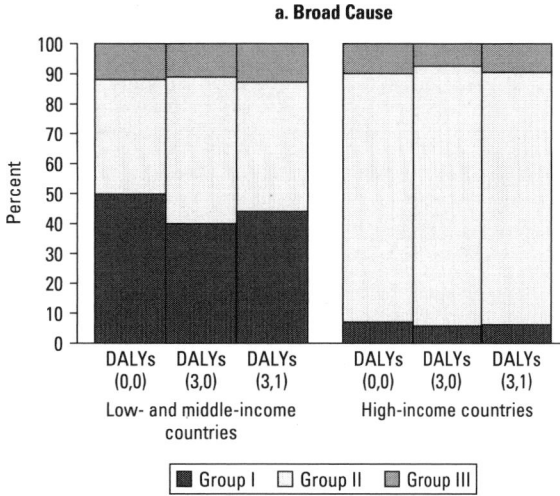

a. Broad Cause

Low- and middle-income countries / High-income countries

DALYs (0,0) · DALYs (3,0) · DALYs (3,1)

■ Group I □ Group II ■ Group III

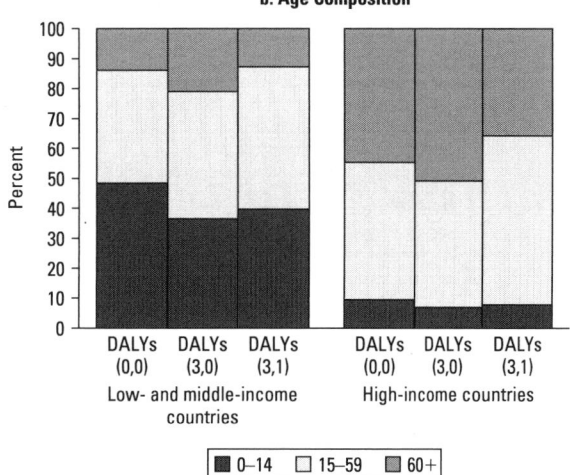

b. Age Composition

Low- and middle-income countries / High-income countries

DALYs (0,0) · DALYs (3,0) · DALYs (3,1)

■ 0–14 □ 15–59 ■ 60+

Source: Authors' calculations.

Note: The notation DALY(*r*, *K*) denotes DALYs calculated with discount rate *r* (percent) or standard or uniform age weighting (*K* = 1 or 0, respectively).

Figure 5.5 Effects of Changing the Discount Rate and Age Weighting on DALYs' Broad Cause and Age Composition, 2001

of discounting (and age weights) has relatively little influence on the broad cause group breakdown of the total burden of disease (figure 5.5).

The effects of introducing nonuniform age weights are generally much smaller than the effects of introducing nonzero discounting. A comparison of the discounted DALYs with and without age weighting in table 5.3 shows that the main effect is on the age distribution of the disease burden. For both high-income and low- and middle-income countries, age weights reduce the importance of the share of the burden borne by older people. In low- and middle-income countries, people aged 60 years and older suffer 21 percent of

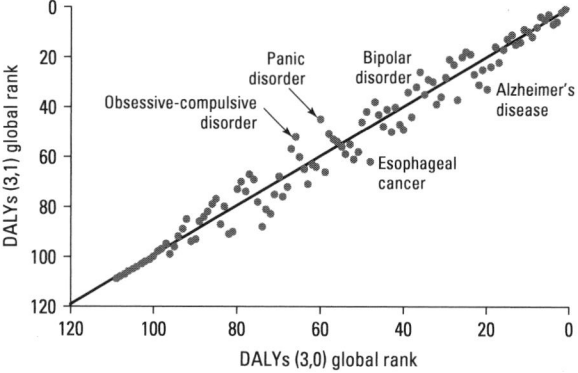

Source: Authors' calculations.
Note: Rank 1 is the largest cause.

Figure 5.6 Relationship between the Rank Order of Causes of the Global Burden Using DALYs(3,1) and DALYs(3,0) in 2001

the total burden of disease and injury. This declines to 13 percent when nonuniform age weights are used. As shown in the second part of figure 5.5, the effects of discounting and age weighting on the age structure of the burden of disease largely offset each other for older ages, so that for DALYs(0,0) and DALYs(3,1) the share of the burden for those aged 60 years and older is quite similar. Overall, the importance of Group I conditions (communicable diseases, maternal and perinatal conditions, and nutritional deficiencies) is also slightly enhanced by age weighting and that of Group II conditions (noncommunicable diseases) is reduced. The effects on Group III (injuries) are relatively minor.

Figure 5.6 compares the rank order of causes contributing to the global burden of disease measured using DALYs(3,1) and DALYs(3,0). The introduction of nonuniform age weights has the most impact on neuropsychiatric disorders, such as bipolar disorder, panic disorder, and obsessive-compulsive disorder, whose prevalence is greatest in younger and middle-aged people. Age-weighted DALYs give less importance to causes whose burden falls predominantly on older ages.

Figure 5.7 compares ranks for causes measured using undiscounted DALYs(0,0) and discounted DALYs(3,0), both with uniform age weights (*K* = 0). A zero discount rate gives greater importance to causes with a larger burden at younger ages, such as whooping cough (pertussis) and meningitis, and lower importance to causes predominantly affecting older ages. However, the different choices of discount rates and age weights do not cause any large changes in the rank ordering of diseases and injuries, which is to a large degree anchored in absolute differences in the burden arising from large differences in prevalence and mortality levels across causes.

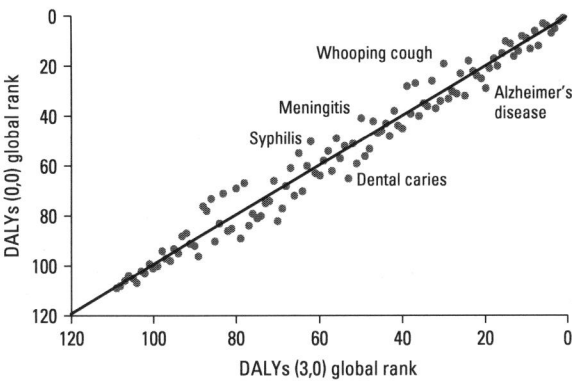

Source: Authors' calculations.

Note: Rank 1 is the largest cause.

Figure 5.7 Relationship between the Rank Order of Causes of the Global Burden of Disease in 2001, Using Uniform Age Weights and 3 Percent Discounting and No Discounting

Table 5.4 compares DALYs(3,0) with DALYs(3,1) and DALYs(0,0) in more detail according to the second level of cause disaggregation within a group. These more detailed results confirm the major conclusions outlined earlier on the impacts of discounting and age weighting. DALYs(0,0) give greater weight to perinatal conditions (the International Classification of Diseases [ICD] category of conditions arising in the perinatal period) and respiratory infections, which primarily affect young children, than either of the discounted forms of DALYs. In contrast, the age-weighted DALYs(3,1) give more weight than DALYs(3,0) to causes that predominantly affect younger adult ages, such as neuropsychiatric conditions and injuries. DALYs(3,0) give greater weight than either DALYs(3,1) or DALYs(0,0) to causes that predominantly affect older people, such as cardiovascular diseases and cancers.

Figure 5.8 summarizes the effects of changing the discount rate and age weighting on the global rankings for the

Table 5.4 Effects of Changing the Discount Rate (*r*) and the Age-Weighting Factor (*K*) on the Second-Level Cause Group Composition of DALYs(*r*,*K*), 2001
(percentages of total DALYs)

Group/cause	Low- and middle-income countries			High-income countries		
	DALYs(0,0)	DALYs(3,0)	DALYs(3,1)	DALYs(0,0)	DALYs(3,0)	DALYs(3,1)
All causes	100.0	100.0	100.0	100.0	100.0	100.0
I. Communicable, maternal, perinatal, and nutritional conditions	49.8	39.8	43.9	6.9	5.7	6.1
A. Infectious and parasitic diseases	28.0	23.1	25.5	2.5	2.3	2.3
B. Respiratory infections	8.2	6.3	6.6	1.6	1.7	1.3
C. Maternal conditions	1.8	1.9	2.2	0.3	0.3	0.4
D. Perinatal conditions	9.4	6.4	7.2	1.9	0.9	1.3
E. Nutritional deficiencies	2.2	2.1	2.3	0.6	0.6	0.8
II. Noncommunicable diseases	38.4	48.9	43.4	83.1	86.6	84.7
A. Malignant neoplasms	4.5	5.4	4.2	17.4	17.3	14.8
B. Other neoplasms	0.1	0.1	0.1	0.4	0.4	0.3
C. Diabetes mellitus	0.9	1.1	0.9	2.7	2.8	2.6
D. Endocrine disorders	0.6	0.8	0.5	1.5	1.6	1.4
E. Neuropsychiatric conditions	7.1	9.9	11.7	18.8	20.9	27.0
F. Sense organ diseases	3.9	5.2	4.6	5.3	5.1	4.8
G. Cardiovascular diseases	10.0	12.9	9.4	18.8	20.0	15.6
H. Respiratory diseases	3.2	4.2	3.4	6.3	6.6	6.5
I. Digestive diseases	3.0	3.8	3.0	4.1	4.4	4.1
J. Genitourinary diseases	1.0	1.2	1.0	1.2	1.4	1.2
K. Skin diseases	0.2	0.3	0.3	0.2	0.2	0.2
L. Musculoskeletal diseases	1.4	1.9	1.8	4.2	4.3	4.1
M. Congenital anomalies	2.2	1.7	2.0	1.7	1.0	1.3
N. Oral conditions	0.3	0.5	0.5	0.6	0.6	0.7
III. Injuries	11.9	11.2	12.7	9.9	7.5	9.3
A. Unintentional injuries	8.7	8.2	9.3	6.9	5.3	6.5
B. Intentional injuries	3.2	3.1	3.5	3.0	2.3	2.8

Source: Authors' calculations.

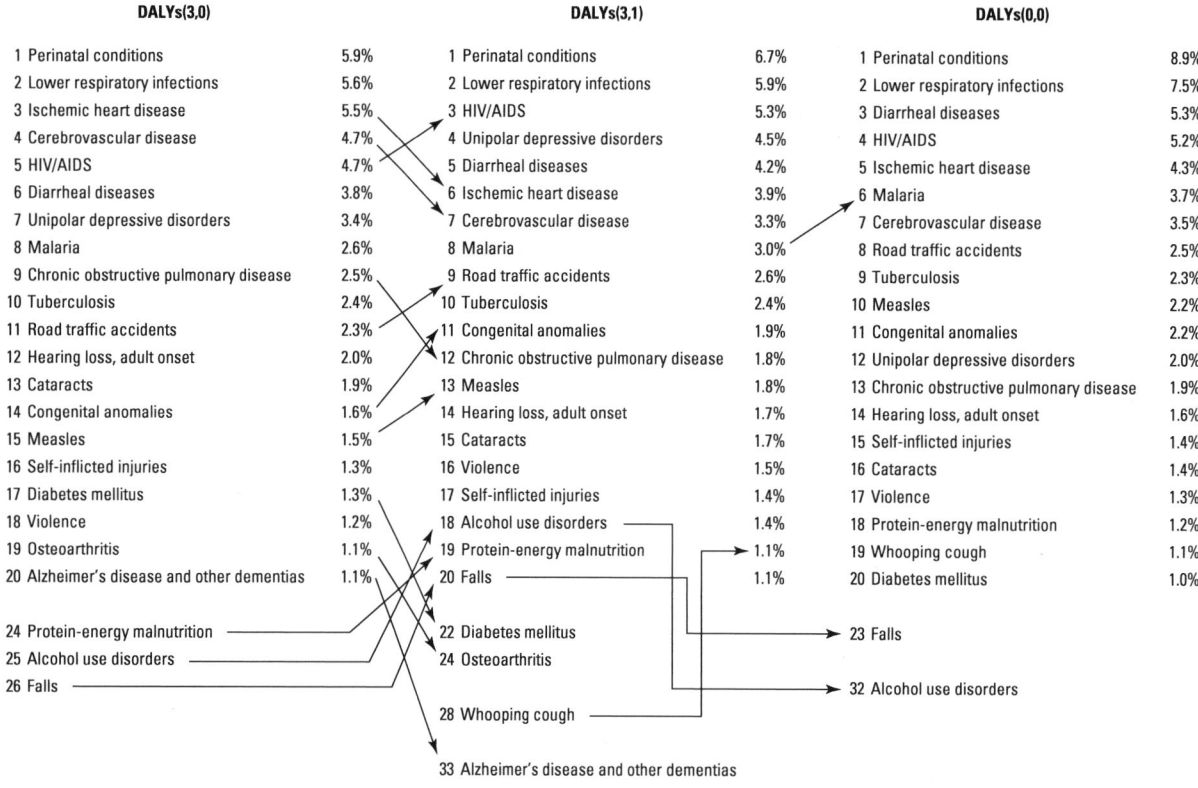

DALYs(3,0)		DALYs(3,1)		DALYs(0,0)	
1 Perinatal conditions	5.9%	1 Perinatal conditions	6.7%	1 Perinatal conditions	8.9%
2 Lower respiratory infections	5.6%	2 Lower respiratory infections	5.9%	2 Lower respiratory infections	7.5%
3 Ischemic heart disease	5.5%	3 HIV/AIDS	5.3%	3 Diarrheal diseases	5.3%
4 Cerebrovascular disease	4.7%	4 Unipolar depressive disorders	4.5%	4 HIV/AIDS	5.2%
5 HIV/AIDS	4.7%	5 Diarrheal diseases	4.2%	5 Ischemic heart disease	4.3%
6 Diarrheal diseases	3.8%	6 Ischemic heart disease	3.9%	6 Malaria	3.7%
7 Unipolar depressive disorders	3.4%	7 Cerebrovascular disease	3.3%	7 Cerebrovascular disease	3.5%
8 Malaria	2.6%	8 Malaria	3.0%	8 Road traffic accidents	2.5%
9 Chronic obstructive pulmonary disease	2.5%	9 Road traffic accidents	2.6%	9 Tuberculosis	2.3%
10 Tuberculosis	2.4%	10 Tuberculosis	2.4%	10 Measles	2.2%
11 Road traffic accidents	2.3%	11 Congenital anomalies	1.9%	11 Congenital anomalies	2.2%
12 Hearing loss, adult onset	2.0%	12 Chronic obstructive pulmonary disease	1.8%	12 Unipolar depressive disorders	2.0%
13 Cataracts	1.9%	13 Measles	1.8%	13 Chronic obstructive pulmonary disease	1.9%
14 Congenital anomalies	1.6%	14 Hearing loss, adult onset	1.7%	14 Hearing loss, adult onset	1.6%
15 Measles	1.5%	15 Cataracts	1.7%	15 Self-inflicted injuries	1.4%
16 Self-inflicted injuries	1.3%	16 Violence	1.5%	16 Cataracts	1.4%
17 Diabetes mellitus	1.3%	17 Self-inflicted injuries	1.4%	17 Violence	1.3%
18 Violence	1.2%	18 Alcohol use disorders	1.4%	18 Protein-energy malnutrition	1.2%
19 Osteoarthritis	1.1%	19 Protein-energy malnutrition	1.1%	19 Whooping cough	1.1%
20 Alzheimer's disease and other dementias	1.1%	20 Falls	1.1%	20 Diabetes mellitus	1.0%
24 Protein-energy malnutrition		22 Diabetes mellitus		23 Falls	
25 Alcohol use disorders		24 Osteoarthritis		32 Alcohol use disorders	
26 Falls		28 Whooping cough			
		33 Alzheimer's disease and other dementias			

Source: Authors' calculations.

Figure 5.8 Effects of Changing the Discount Rate and Age Weighting on Global Rankings for the Top 20 Causes of the Burden of Disease, 2001

top 20 causes of the burden of disease in 2001. The left-hand column shows the rankings for causes measured using DALYs(3,0) as used for the DCPP. The middle column is for DALYs(3,1), as used by WHO to present the GBD analysis. The principal difference is that the use of DALYs(3,0) results in relatively greater importance being placed on chronic diseases of middle and older ages, such as ischemic heart disease and stroke, and somewhat lesser on HIV/AIDS, road traffic accidents, congenital anomalies, and other disorders affecting children and younger adults. Undiscounted DALYs, shown in the right-hand column, give proportionately greater importance to conditions affecting children, such as malaria and measles.

SENSITIVITY OF RISK FACTOR ESTIMATES TO VARIATIONS IN KEY PARAMETER VALUES

Figures 5.9 to 5.11 examine the sensitivity of the burden of disease attributable to each of the 19 risk factors discussed in chapter 4 to key DALY discounting and age-weighting parameters for the world, for low-and-middle-income countries,

and for high-income countries. The figures plot the attributable disease burden estimated by altering one key parameter against the baseline of DALYs(3,0) used in chapter 4. To allow comparability, all burdens attributable to risk factors are shown as a proportion of the total global or regional disease burden, which is itself estimated with the corresponding parameters.

Including age weighting, DALYs(3,1), increases the relative health consequences of risks that affect people in young and middle ages (alcohol use, illicit drug use, and unsafe sex) and lowers the relative contribution of those risks that result in death in older ages (high blood pressure, high cholesterol, low fruit and vegetable intake, overweight and obesity, physical inactivity, and smoking). In addition, the burden of disease attributable to childhood and maternal underweight increases as a proportion of the total global or regional burden of disease. This increase probably reflects a relative reduction in the total burden of those diseases that affect older adults, and hence a relative increase in the total burden of those diseases that affect young children. Because childhood and maternal underweight is a risk factor for this

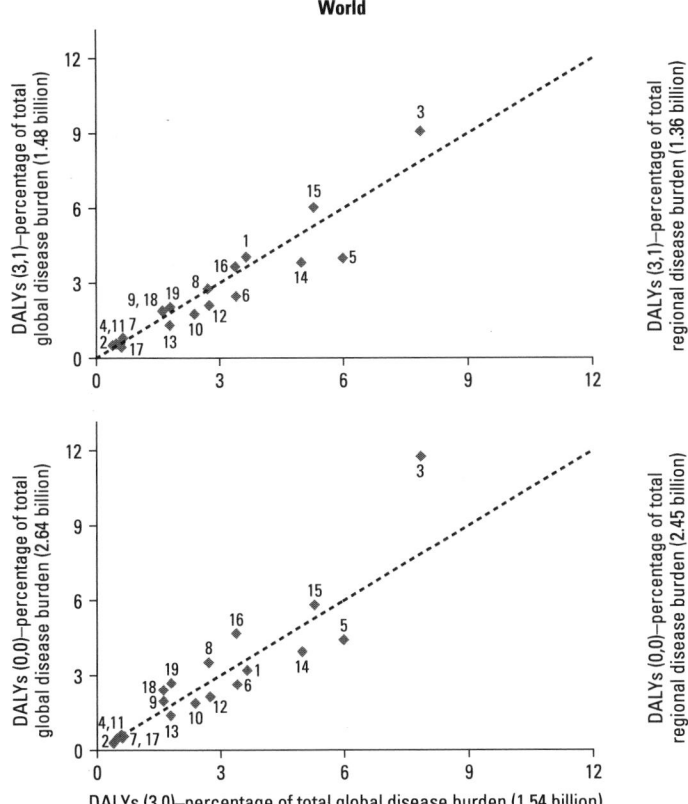

World

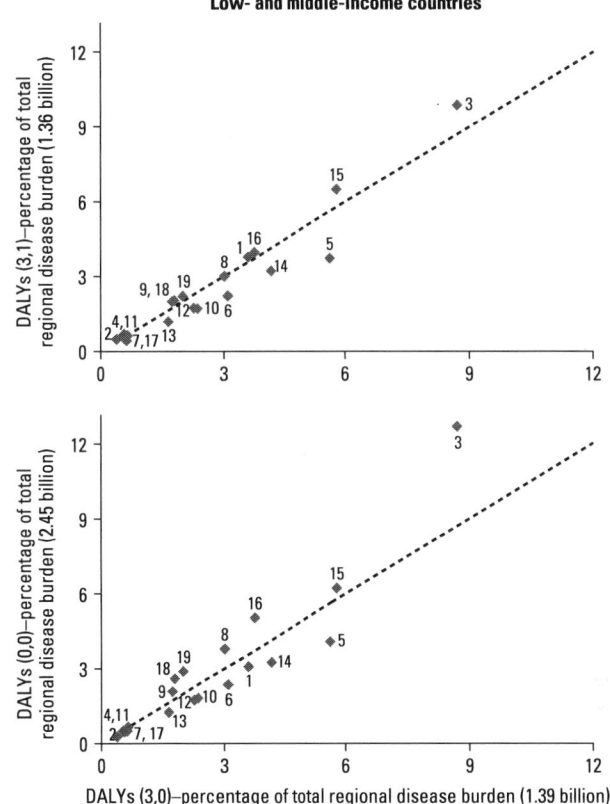

Low- and middle-income countries

Source: Authors' calculations.

Note: Each point corresponds to the proportion of total GBD attributable to one risk factor. (1) alcohol use; (2) child sexual abuse; (3) childhood underweight; (4) contaminated injections in health care setting; (5) high blood pressure; (6) high cholesterol; (7) illicit drug use; (8) indoor smoke from household use of solid fuels; (9) iron deficiency anemia; (10) low fruit and vegetable intake; (11) non-use and use of ineffective methods of contraception; (12) overweight and obesity (high body mass index); (13) physical inactivity; (14) smoking; (15) unsafe sex; (16) unsafe water, sanitation, and hygiene; (17) urban air pollution; (18) vitamin A deficiency; (19) zinc deficiency.

Figure 5.9 Effects of Changes in Key DALY Parameters on Proportion of the Global Disease Burden Attributable to Risk Factors.

Source: Authors' calculations.

Note: Each point corresponds to the proportion of total GBD attributable to one risk factor. (1) alcohol use; (2) child sexual abuse; (3) childhood underweight; (4) contaminated injections in health care setting; (5) high blood pressure; (6) high cholesterol; (7) illicit drug use; (8) indoor smoke from household use of solid fuels; (9) iron deficiency anemia; (10) low fruit and vegetable intake; (11) non-use and use of ineffective methods of contraception; (12) overweight and obesity (high body mass index); (13) physical inactivity; (14) smoking; (15) unsafe sex; (16) unsafe water, sanitation, and hygiene; (17) urban air pollution; (18) vitamin A deficiency; (19) zinc deficiency.

Figure 5.10 Effects of Changes in Key DALY Parameters on Proportion of the Regional Disease Burden Attributable to Risk Factors for Low- and Middle-Income Countries

latter group of diseases, its attributable burden as a share of the total global or regional disease burden increases.

Removing discounting, DALYs(0,0), results in a large relative increase in the disease burden attributable to risk factors that affect young children, including childhood underweight; indoor smoke from household use of solid fuels; unsafe water, sanitation, and hygiene; vitamin A deficiency; and zinc deficiency. This is mirrored by a decrease in the disease burden attributable to the risk factors for diseases that affect adults, because the total burden of the chronic diseases affected by these risks is reduced. This effect is more noticeable in the low- and middle-income countries than in the high-income countries, where childhood mortality is low and the overall share of the disease burden is less sensitive to discounting.

Sensitivity to key DALY parameters differed in the low- and middle-income countries and the high-income countries. The burden of disease attributable to risk factors for chronic diseases in adults (high blood pressure, high cholesterol, low fruit and vegetable intake, overweight and obesity, physical inactivity, and smoking) was more sensitive to these parameters in low- and middle-income countries than in high-income countries because deaths attributable to these risks occurred at younger ages in the former. By contrast, the burden of disease attributable to alcohol was much more sensitive to age-weighting in the high-income countries because many of the hazards of this risk, especially those related to injuries and neuropsychiatric conditions, occur among younger adults in this group of countries.

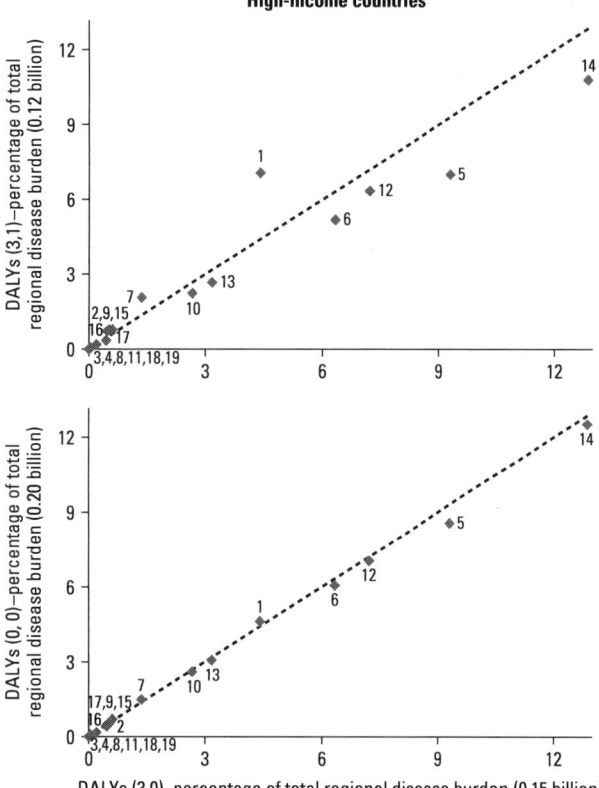

High-income countries

Source: Authors' calculations.

Note: Each point corresponds to the proportion of total GBD attributable to one risk factor. (1) alcohol use; (2) child sexual abuse; (3) childhood underweight; (4) contaminated injections in health care setting; (5) high blood pressure; (6) high cholesterol; (7) illicit drug use; (8) indoor smoke from household use of solid fuels; (9) iron deficiency anemia; (10) low fruit and vegetable intake; (11) non-use and use of ineffective methods of contraception; (12) overweight and obesity (high body mass index); (13) physical inactivity; (14) smoking; (15) unsafe sex; (16) unsafe water, sanitation, and hygiene; (17) urban air pollution; (18) vitamin A deficiency; (19) zinc deficiency.

Figure 5.11 Effects of Changes in Key DALY Parameters on Proportion of the Regional Disease Burden Attributable to Risk Factors for High-Income Countries

UNCERTAINTY ANALYSIS OF THE GLOBAL BURDEN OF DISEASE ESTIMATES

The 2001 GBD study estimated mortality and the burden of disease for a comprehensive set of disease and injury causes and for all regions of the world, including regions with limited, incomplete, and uncertain data. To allow users of the information to assess whether the information uncertainty range is compatible with the purpose at hand, providing some analysis and guidance on levels of uncertainty is important (Murray, Mathers, and Salomon 2003). This is difficult to do, because apart from the large number and disparate nature of the data sources used (see chapter 3), information or knowledge about the quality of and potential biases in the data is often limited. This and the following sections provide an overview of initial efforts to quantify the uncertainty associated with the estimation of deaths by cause, with disability weights, and with epidemiological estimates of incidence and prevalence for GBD 2001.

Sources of Uncertainty

Uncertainty in estimated disease burden may arise from the following sources:

- incomplete information, for example, when estimates for a population are based on observations from a sample;
- potential biases in information, for instance, issues concerning the representativeness for a whole population of estimates from a study of a subgroup or the validity of a survey instrument in addressing the quantity of interest;
- heterogeneity or from disagreements among information sources, as when several studies give different estimates for the same quantity of interest;
- model uncertainty, for example, the variables or functional form specified in a regression model;
- the data generation process itself; for instance, investigators may only infer risks from event counts in a population, which means that they can never know the risks themselves with certainty.

The most familiar and most commonly quantified kind of uncertainty arises from random error in the direct measurement of a quantity. An estimate of an epidemiological quantity for a population will have uncertainty arising from the finite sample used in the study as well as from random measurement error. The standard error of the mean or the confidence interval for such a quantity specifies the distribution of uncertainty in knowledge of the true mean value in the population (assuming no systematic error).

Most measurement involves not only random (stochastic) error, but also systematic error arising from biases in the measurement instrument, for instance, unrepresentativeness of a sampling frame for a survey, or from inaccuracies in the assumptions used to infer the actual quantity from the available data, for example, estimating the prevalence of a disease for a country from studies of representative subpopulations. Examinations of historical measurements reveal a consistent tendency to underestimate systematic error, perhaps because systematic error usually relates to sources of error that are unknown or about which little is known. Ignoring systematic error when estimating uncertainty is common, but this often results in substantial underestimation of the true uncertainty (Morgan and Henrion 1990).

Putting upper and lower bounds on the systematic error component is often possible, for example, where a disease process has biological limits or where evidence from a range of populations provides likely upper and lower limits to an epidemiological parameter such as prevalence or case fatality. In addition, consistency analysis across the various inputs for the DALY calculation (incidence, prevalence, case fatality rates or relative risk of mortality, and remission rates) often helps identify sources of systematic error and provides some basis for quantifying them (Kruijshaar, Barendregt, and Hoeymans 2002; Mathers, Murray, and Lopez 2002). This is discussed further in chapter 3.

Much of the uncertainty in estimates of deaths or DALYs for the 2001 GBD study is associated with the assessment of systematic errors in primary data. Chapter 3 examined primary data sources and their reliability in some detail and provided summary tabulations of the numbers of data sources available across regions and causes. This review clearly indicated that even though most countries have some information about prevalence, incidence, and mortality from some diseases and injuries and about population exposures to risk factors, it is generally fragmented, partial, incomparable, and diagnostically uncertain. One of the explicit aims of the GBD approach is to provide a coherent framework for integrating, validating, analyzing, and disseminating fragmentary information on the health of populations so that it is truly useful for health policy and planning. An important aspect of this framework is to assess the reliability and validity of data, particularly in relation to systematic error, and hence to provide some guide to the uncertainty in the resulting estimates.

Describing and Quantifying Uncertainty

We follow Morgan and Henrion's (1990) approach toward interpreting and using probability to describe and quantify uncertainty. The classical or frequentist view of probability defines the probability of an event occurring in a particular trial or experiment as the frequency with which it would occur during a long sequence of similar experiments. For many quantities of real interest, it is difficult to imagine how to operationalize a long sequence of relevant, similar experiments. An example of such a quantity would be the probability, estimated in late 2005, that avian influenza will cause a major global epidemic with deaths exceeding, say, 1 million in 2006. One approach has been to distinguish events whose probabilities are knowable through a series of experiments

from those whose probabilities are unknowable or uncertain because no unique and operationalizable set of similar experiments exists, but this essentially limits the use of probabilities to games of chance.

Alternatively, a Bayesian view of probability defines it as the degree to which a person believes that an event will occur, or that a parameter has a certain value, given all the relevant information currently known to that person. Because different people have different information, they may legitimately assign different probabilities to the same event. These subjective probabilities must obey all the same axioms and rules as frequentist probabilities. These conceptual distinctions do not usually affect the practice of statistical inference, and essentially the same formal inference models of probability may be applied (King, Tomz, and Wittenberg 2000; Morgan and Henrion 1990). Moreover, when an empirical series of data from trials becomes available, the Bayesian assessment of probability should converge to the frequentist assessment, assuming the Bayesian approach uses the data rationally to update the assessments.

Our general approach to describing and estimating uncertainty in quantities of interest is to express them as probability distributions using a Bayesian interpretation of probability as expressing uncertainty of an observed or hypothetical event given a set of assumptions about the world. Probability distributions can therefore be used to express uncertainty about epidemiological quantities, such as the prevalence of depression in a particular population, the population values reflected in health state valuations, or the underlying risk of mortality due to a specific cause in a specific population.

Advances in computer technology have facilitated analytical methods for dealing with uncertainty enormously. One general approach to combining the uncertainties of multiple inputs into estimates relies on numerical simulation methods. The simulation approach uses multiple samples from probability distributions around uncertain inputs to allow estimates of the probability distributions around quantities of interest that may be complicated functions of these inputs, without the need to solve difficult, or in many cases insoluble, mathematical equations (King, Tomz, and Wittenberg 2000; Vose 2000).

UNCERTAINTY ESTIMATES FOR ALL-CAUSE MORTALITY AND LIFE EXPECTANCIES

Chapters 2 and 3 describe methods for estimating life tables for each of 192 WHO member states. For those countries with vital registration data projected using time series regression models on the parameters of the logit life table system, we accounted for uncertainty around the regression coefficients by taking 1,000 draws of the parameters using the regression estimates and variance-covariance matrix of the estimators. For each of the draws, we calculated a new life table. In cases where additional sources of information provided information on the limits of uncertainty ranges around $_5q_0$ (the mortality risk for children under five years of age) and $_{45}q_{15}$ (the mortality risk for adults between the ages of 15 and 60), the 1,000 draws were constrained so that each life table produced estimates within these specified ranges. The range of 1,000 life tables produced by these multiple draws reflects some of the uncertainty around the projected trends in mortality, notably, the imprecise quantification of systematic changes in the logit parameters over the time period captured in available vital registration data.

For countries that did not have time series data on mortality by age and sex, the following steps were undertaken. First, point estimates and ranges around $_5q_0$ and $_{45}q_{15}$ for males and females were developed on a country-by-country basis as described in chapter 2 and elsewhere (Lopez and others 2002). For countries where the $_5q_0$ estimate for 2001 was based on an analysis of available data sources for earlier years, such as surveys and censuses, the uncertainty range for $_5q_0$ was typically dominated by the uncertainty resulting from the scatter of survey-based direct and indirect estimates of child mortality for earlier years and the uncertainty in extrapolation of the trend to 2001, rather than the sampling error associated with individual estimates. For countries without usable information on levels of adult mortality, $_{45}q_{15}$ was estimated, along with uncertainty ranges, based on regression models of $_{45}q_{15}$ versus $_5q_0$ as observed in a set of almost 2,000 life tables judged to be of good quality. Estimated levels of child and adult mortality were then applied to a modified logit life table model, using a global standard, to estimate the full life table in 2001; HIV/AIDS deaths and war deaths were added to total mortality rates where necessary. Uncertainty ranges for HIV/AIDS were estimated as described elsewhere (Grassly and others 2004). In countries with substantial numbers of war deaths, estimates of their uncertainty range were also incorporated into the life table uncertainty analysis.

Figure 5.12 plots the final estimated uncertainty ranges for $_5q_0$ and $_{45}q_{15}$ for 192 WHO member states for males and females. Using Monte Carlo simulation methods, 1,000 random life tables were generated by drawing samples from normal distributions around these inputs with variances defined in reference to the defined ranges of uncertainty for $_5q_0$ and $_{45}q_{15}$. In countries where uncertainty around $_5q_0$ and

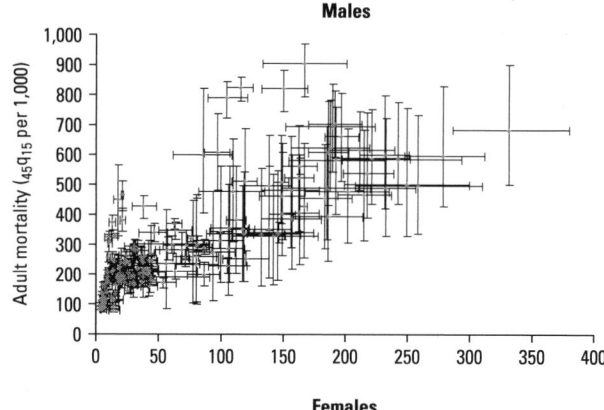

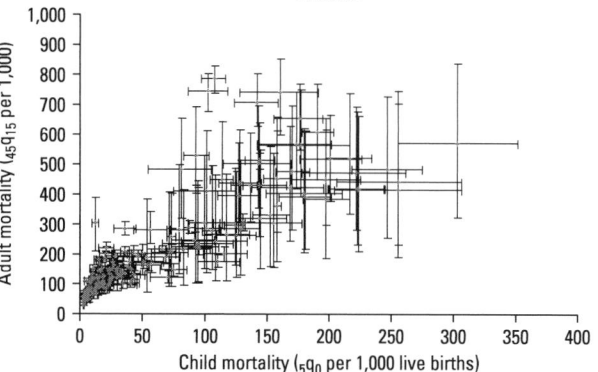

Source: Authors' calculations.

Figure 5.12 Uncertainty Ranges for Child and Adult Mortality for WHO Member States, 2001

$_{45}q_{15}$ was considerable because of a paucity of survey or surveillance information, the samples were drawn from wide distributions, but then constrained within prior specified maximum and minimum possible values for $_5q_0$ and $_{45}q_{15}$. For each country, the results of this analysis were 1,000 different simulated life tables that were then used to describe ranges around key indicators, such as life expectancy at birth and age- and sex-specific mortality rates.

Figure 5.13 illustrates the resulting uncertainty ranges for life expectancy at birth for the World Bank regions (see map 1 inside the book's front cover). For high-income countries, where relatively complete death registration data are available, the uncertainty ranges for life expectancy at birth are around ±0.07 years for females and ±0.16 years for males. For regions such as Latin America and the Caribbean, where death registration data are available for most countries but are often incomplete, the uncertainty ranges are larger, typically around ±0.5 years. For regions with partial data on child mortality only, where adult mortality is predicted from child mortality, the uncertainty ranges are much larger, and

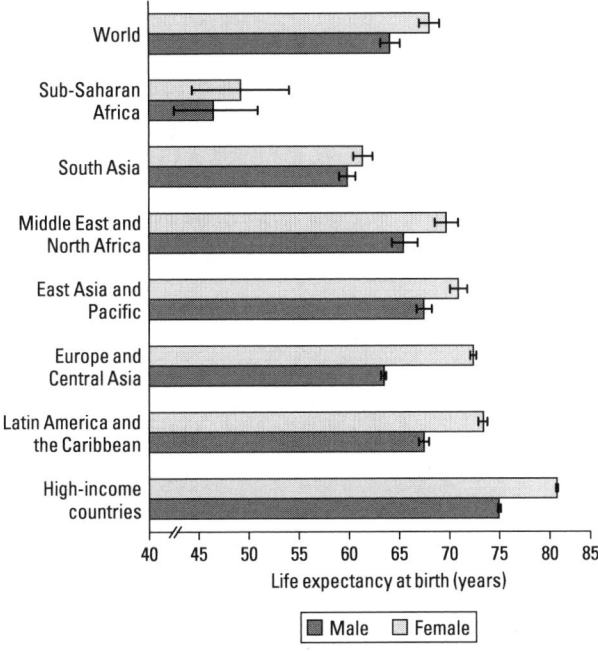

Source: Authors' calculations.

Figure 5.13 Uncertainty in Average Life Expectancy at Birth, by Sex and DCPP Region, 2001

for Sub-Saharan Africa are typically around ±5.0 years. Across the regions, this translates to considerable heterogeneity in uncertainty ranges for life expectancies at birth and for estimates of all-cause mortality levels.

UNCERTAINTY ESTIMATES FOR REGIONAL MORTALITY BY CAUSE

We use a simulation approach to estimate uncertainty ranges for deaths by cause for GBD 2001. These uncertainty ranges take into account uncertainty in the expected number of total deaths (life table uncertainty); uncertainty in the estimated proportions of broad cause Groups I, II, and III (where relevant for countries without vital registration data or with incomplete coverage); uncertainty in the diagnosis of underlying cause; uncertainty arising from the miscoding of underlying cause; and fundamental Poisson uncertainty in the estimated death rate arising from the observation of a finite number of deaths in a fixed time interval. This analysis was carried out by country.

As described in the previous section, a total of 1,000 life tables were developed for each of the 192 WHO member states to quantify the uncertainty distribution of key life

table parameters. We then used the age-specific mortality rates from the 1,000 life tables to estimate the uncertainty distribution for the expected number of total deaths for 2001. Uncertainty in the underlying cause attribution was estimated in terms of the relative uncertainty of the proportion of deaths due to each specific cause. The estimates of cause-specific relative uncertainty were based on advice from nosologists and experts in the area of cross-country mortality analysis on the general levels of uncertainty in the attribution of specific causes within Groups I, II and III, together with detailed advice on particular causes with known higher levels of attribution uncertainty according to the ICD. Information on the latter causes derives from comparative analyses across countries, across time periods, and across ICD revisions, together with information from a variety of country-specific coding quality studies involving recoding or dual coding of deaths and comparisons with the original attributed causes.

Based on this advice, for cause distributions derived from vital registration data coded using ICD-10 (the 10th edition of the ICD), we generally assumed that diagnostic uncertainty and coding uncertainty together resulted in approximate relative 95 percent uncertainty ranges of ±3 percent for Group I causes, ±7 percent for Group II causes, and ±2 percent for Group III causes. Larger uncertainty ranges were assumed for specific causes known to have greater levels of diagnostic or coding error; for WHO member states that have been using ICD-10 coding for less than three years; for member states still using ICD-9 coding (with particular attention to causes where coding rates between ICD-9 and ICD-10 are known to differ); and for member states using other cause coding systems or verbal autopsy methods, or where cause of death models were used to estimate death distributions across Groups I, II, and III. In the latter case, an additional relative uncertainty for the estimation of Group I, II, and III proportions was estimated from the prediction uncertainty ranges associated with the CodMod regression model (see chapter 3).

Uncertainty estimates also took into account the redistribution of general, cancer, cardiovascular, and injury ill-defined cause codes and incomplete coverage of vital registration data. The relative uncertainty range for each cause was then combined with the estimated uncertainty distribution for all-cause mortality to provide estimates of the uncertainty distributions of cause-specific mortality estimates for all ages and both sexes at the country level.

The analysis of uncertainty in cause of death estimates at the country level thus combines quantitative, country-specific information on uncertainty in all-cause mortality and, in some cases, also in major cause group distributions, together with quantified average relative uncertainty ranges for specific cause attributions based on expert advice and adjusted for specific causes and for country-specific information on data sources, type of cause information available, and indicators of data quality. Here we summarize these uncertainty estimates at the regional level to provide some indication of the range of uncertainty for cause-specific mortality estimates across the World Bank regions as reported in chapter 3. This requires some additional assumptions about the cross-country correlations in uncertainty distributions.

At one extreme, if all country-level estimates have uncorrelated uncertainty because they are derived from completely independent data sets, then even with high levels of uncertainty at the country level, there will be considerably less uncertainty at the regional or global level. At the other extreme, if the uncertainty in country-level estimates for a cause derives predominantly from a single source or assumption, for example, about the case fatality rate of malaria, that is applied in deriving each country estimate, then the uncertainty distributions will be highly correlated and the regional uncertainty will be of a similar relative magnitude as each of the country uncertainty ranges.

With respect to cross-country correlations for life table and cause of death estimates based on death registration data, we assumed that even though life table uncertainties would be uncorrelated, relative uncertainties in cause of death attribution for specific causes were likely to be correlated because of systematic errors in ICD coding practices across countries for specific causes. We arbitrarily set this correlation at 25 percent. For life table estimates not based on death registration data, we assumed some correlation in uncertainty because even though estimates of childhood mortality came from independent sources, the method for determining adult mortality was similar across countries. We therefore set this correlation at 50 percent.

We assumed that cross-country correlation for relative cause of death uncertainties in the absence of vital registration data would vary depending on the method of causal attribution. Attributions based on some data and country-level predictions or assumptions were assumed to have less correlation than those based simply on regional patterns. In the case of the latter, we set the correlation at 75 percent; in the former, we set it at 50 percent or 25 percent depending on the degree of independence of the underlying inputs. We assumed greater independence for cancers and maternal conditions and less independence for tuberculosis, HIV/AIDS, sexually transmitted infections, diarrheal diseases, childhood-cluster diseases, meningitis, tropical-cluster diseases, lower respiratory infections, and perinatal conditions. We set cross-country correlations for war and drug use disorders at 25 percent for all countries, including those with vital registration data, to reflect the different methods used to obtain estimates for these causes.

We derived 95 percent uncertainty intervals by cause for World Bank regions in 2001 from the foregoing assumptions using simulation methods. We constructed 1,000 draws with the required correlation structure between countries separately for each cause, and the 2.5th percentile and the 97.5th percentile of expected deaths were taken to be the lower and upper bounds of the corresponding uncertainty interval. Note that these ranges provide guidance on uncertainty in the underlying cause-specific death rates, as expressed in terms of expected deaths in the population in 2001. Uncertainty in population estimates is not included, and the uncertainty ranges relate to underlying death rates, not to the numbers of deaths that actually occurred in 2001.

Table 5.5 summarizes regional uncertainty ranges for total estimated deaths for selected causes for 2001. Uncertainty ranges for estimated all-cause deaths increase from around ±1 percent for high-income countries to (−15 percent, +21 percent) for Sub-Saharan Africa. For specific causes, regional uncertainty ranges are generally higher, except for those causes for which cause-specific mortality estimates were available based on country-specific data from cause-specific surveillance systems (see chapter 3). For example, the uncertainty range for HIV/AIDS deaths in Sub-Saharan Africa is somewhat narrower than the all-cause mortality range, reflecting the substantial database for these estimates from antenatal clinic surveillance data and seroprevalence surveys, albeit still with considerable uncertainty arising from issues around the representativeness of the available data and the assumptions relating to survival and case fatality rates (Grassly and others 2004).

For most other causes, uncertainty ranges are greater than for the all-cause mortality estimates, because additional uncertainty is associated with cause attribution, as described earlier. For example, the relative uncertainty ranges for ischemic heart disease range from around ±12 percent for high-income countries to (−24 percent, +34 percent) for Sub-Saharan Africa (table 5.5). While the uncertainty range for high-income countries may seem surprisingly large, it reflects not only uncertainty in overall mortality levels, but also uncertainty in the attribution of underlying cause and in the attribution of causes coded to cancer, cardiovascular, and injury ill-defined cause codes or to the ICD chapter for symptoms, signs, and ill-defined conditions. The proportion of deaths coded to these two groups of causes is surprisingly large for some high-income countries (Mathers and others 2005).

Figure 5.14 illustrates the relative insensitivity of the regional uncertainty ranges to the assumptions about cross-country correlation of uncertainty. The broad patterns of the uncertainty ranges for causes across regions provide useful additional guidance to policy makers in interpreting regional differences, particularly in judging which policy questions these estimates can help address and for which the uncertainty levels are too great to allow useful inferences.

UNCERTAINTY IN DISABILITY WEIGHTS

Although health state valuations are often treated as value parameters without uncertainty, we argue that unlike social choices such as the discount rate, no clear normative basis is available on which to assign relative values to the different dimensions of health that collectively define the universe of health states. Ideally, these values should be derived from empirical data among representative populations (Salomon and others 2003). Numerous challenges are associated with population-based data collection for the purpose of health state valuations, particularly given the broad scope of valuations required for a comprehensive assessment of disease burden. As a result, the current empirical base for disability weights remains well short of this ideal. Given the

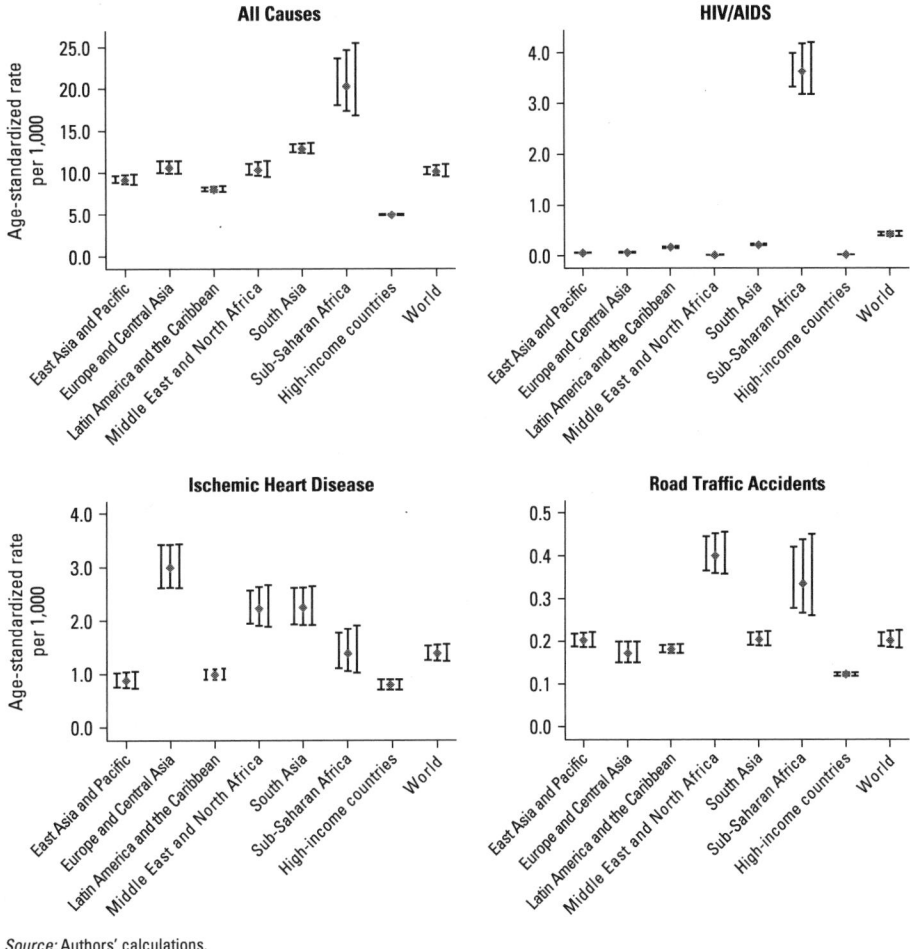

Source: Authors' calculations.

Note: Cross-country correlations in uncertainty distributions for countries without vital registration data were varied from 0 percent (left-hand bar) to 25 percent (middle bar) and 50 percent (right-hand bar) for each region.

Figure 5.14 Sensitivity of Uncertainty Ranges to Changes in Between-Country Correlation Assumptions

Table 5.5 Estimated Total Deaths and 95 Percent Uncertainty Ranges for Selected Causes, by Region, 2001
(thousands)

Cause	East Asia and Pacific		Europe and Central Asia		Latin America and the Caribbean		Middle East and North Africa	
	Deaths	Uncertainty	Deaths	Uncertainty	Deaths	Uncertainty	Deaths	Uncertainty
All causes	13,070	12,379–13,866	5,669	5,334–6,122	3,277	3,166–3,411	1,914	1,790–2,088
Tuberculosis	534	497–578	66	58–76	45	41–50	23	21–26
HIV/AIDS	106	97–116	28	24–35	83	74–94	4	3–4
Diarrheal diseases	226	199–252	15	14–16	55	49–61	74	65–84
Pertussis	3	3–4	0	0–0	6	5–8	8	6–9
Diphtheria	1	1–1	0	0–0	0	0–0	0	0–0
Measles	76	66–85	8	7–8	0	0–0	15	13–18
Tetanus	27	25–30	0	0–0	1	1–1	4	3–5
Meningitis	33	29–39	14	13–15	17	15–20	10	9–11
Hepatitis B	32	29–36	3	3–4	4	4–5	6	5–7
Hepatitis C	13	12–15	1	1–1	2	2–2	3	3–3
Malaria	30	25–36	0	0–0	2	1–2	19	17–22
Schistosomiasis	3	3–4	0	0–0	1	1–1	8	8–9
Lower respiratory infections	544	449–655	104	94–116	157	140–177	108	90–130
Upper respiratory infections	27	25–30	4	4–5	3	2–3	2	2–3
Maternal conditions	37	23–56	3	2–4	16	12–21	15	10–22
Perinatal conditions	502	447–567	57	53–62	164	153–177	106	95–122
Stomach cancer	442	386–504	101	89–114	57	53–61	18	16–20
Colon and rectal cancers	159	142–179	96	87–106	37	34–39	10	9–11
Trachea, bronchus, and lung cancers	387	341–438	165	148–187	55	51–59	20	18–22
Breast cancer	93	83–103	63	59–68	37	34–40	14	13–15
Cervix uteri cancer	47	42–52	19	18–21	26	24–29	5	4–5
Corpus uteri cancer	8	7–9	17	15–18	12	11–12	1	1–1
Prostate cancer	16	14–17	25	23–29	37	34–39	6	5–7
Lymphomas, multiple myeloma	42	37–46	23	21–24	24	22–26	12	11–13
Leukemia	76	68–86	27	25–29	22	21–24	14	13–16
Diabetes mellitus	233	152–326	51	45–59	163	135–197	31	21–44
Alzheimer's and other dementias	58	37–82	10	8–11	14	12–16	3	2–5
Parkinson's disease	26	22–30	4	3–4	5	4–5	3	2–3
Drug use disorders	7	5–11	11	8–15	2	2–3	19	13–26
Ischemic heart disease	1,151	967–1,371	1,685	1,473–1,928	358	322–398	323	276–382
Cerebrovascular disease	1,902	1,606–2,236	1,029	888–1,189	267	240–298	130	111–153
Chronic obstructive pulmonary disease	1,415	1,218–1,634	130	119–143	99	92–109	41	35–47
Asthma	56	41–74	27	21–34	12	10–14	7	5–8
Cirrhosis of the liver	193	166–225	103	94–115	74	69–81	37	33–43
Nephritis and nephrosis	186	160–217	36	33–40	55	50–61	42	37–48
Road traffic accidents	361	334–394	83	73–96	88	83–93	99	88–112
Poisonings	83	78–90	106	90–127	3	3–4	7	7–8
Falls	122	114–132	35	32–40	15	14–16	12	10–13
Fires	36	33–41	20	16–24	5	4–5	13	12–15
Drownings	144	135–156	35	30–41	19	18–20	14	12–16
Other unintentional injuries	189	176–204	121	106–140	78	74–83	36	33–41
Self-inflicted injuries	323	294–356	121	105–141	30	28–32	14	13–17
Violence	103	93–117	68	57–81	130	123–138	10	9–12
War	14	9–20	17	13–23	6	6–7	8	5–12

Source: Authors' calculations.

Table 5.5 Continued

(thousands)

South Asia		Sub-Saharan Africa		High-income countries		World	
Deaths	Uncertainty	Deaths	Uncertainty	Deaths	Uncertainty	Deaths	Uncertainty
13,557	13,053–14,240	10,837	9,267–13,164	7,891	7,830–7,963	56,216	53,387–60,173
604	567–652	317	258–400	16	15–17	1,605	1,476–1,771
272	255–292	2,058	1,802–2,367	22	21–23	2,573	2,325–2,872
695	628–757	712	571–908	6	6–6	1,782	1,557–2,065
108	90–130	176	134–233	0	0–0	301	243–382
3	3–3	1	1–2	0	0–0	6	5–7
216	190–241	447	355–577	1	1–2	762	637–925
140	131–152	121	97–156	0	0–0	293	259–343
71	66–79	23	19–29	4	4–5	173	157–195
28	26–31	21	16–28	5	5–6	100	90–114
11	10–12	8	6–11	12	11–12	51	46–56
63	57–71	1,093	841–1,465	0	0–0	1,207	941–1,596
0	0–0	2	2–3	0	0–0	14	13–16
1,414	1,173–1,698	1,080	833–1,419	345	310–371	3,751	3,181–4,456
20	19–22	13	10–17	4	4–4	73	66–83
199	158–252	237	158–341	1	1–1	508	381–676
1,086	985–1,215	573	462–732	32	31–34	2,521	2,250–2,876
45	40–52	33	28–40	146	135–157	842	773–917
35	31–40	20	17–24	257	238–276	614	579–648
129	113–146	15	13–17	456	421–491	1,227	1,152–1,302
76	67–85	34	28–43	155	144–167	472	444–502
83	73–95	38	32–46	17	15–18	235	215–258
4	4–5	3	2–3	27	25–29	71	67–75
21	18–24	40	33–48	119	110–128	264	248–282
82	72–93	34	28–42	115	106–124	330	309–354
38	33–43	14	11–16	73	67–79	263	247–281
196	127–273	82	54–118	202	172–235	959	744–1,207
81	52–113	7	4–10	207	175–241	380	314–447
9	8–10	5	4–6	45	42–48	95	88–104
29	19–41	4	2–6	13	11–15	85	64–109
1,838	1,567–2,148	343	260–458	1,364	1,203–1,533	7,061	6,328–7,844
923	788–1,078	355	269–474	781	689–874	5,388	4,790–6,067
577	502–662	116	89–153	297	280–317	2,675	2,370–3,030
78	57–101	26	19–35	28	24–32	233	186–287
185	161–214	59	45–79	118	110–126	771	696–863
132	114–152	101	77–135	111	104–119	662	586–758
238	221–258	200	159–261	121	117–125	1,189	1,090–1,317
90	86–96	37	29–50	21	20–22	349	324–381
112	106–119	20	16–26	71	69–74	387	368–412
183	173–194	44	35–58	9	9–10	310	287–339
90	85–96	66	52–86	16	16–17	384	355–424
280	265–298	127	99–168	82	79–85	913	847–1,003
224	206–245	36	29–47	126	121–131	874	816–943
79	74–85	141	114–181	24	23–25	556	504–624
26	15–39	136	54–221	0	0–0	207	114–308

limitations in currently available information, an examination of the contribution of uncertainty around health state valuations to overall uncertainty in burden of disease estimates measured using YLD or DALYs is useful.

Conceptually, the basis for assigning disability weights to specific sequelae requires an understanding of (a) the distribution of health states among those living with the particular sequelae, where a health state is defined by the levels on the various dimensions that constitute health; and (b) a valuation function that provides a systematic way to aggregate across multiple dimensions of health in order to arrive at a single index value that captures the overall level of health associated with a given health state (Salomon and others 2003). While disability weights may vary across regions because of variation in either component, we have proposed elsewhere that for purposes of standardization and global comparisons, computing disability weights based on an average global valuation function is the most appropriate approach (Murray and others 2002). The need to understand variation in the distribution of health states among people living with given sequelae highlights the critical link between the epidemiological inputs of burden and the estimated disability weights.

In this section, we undertake a first analysis of the contribution of uncertainty in disability weights to uncertainty in the GBD DALY estimates. Given that the current set of disability weights reflects the accumulation of a wide array of different empirical inputs rather than the result of the comprehensive and standardized approach defined earlier as the ideal, we operationalize our analysis of uncertainty in terms of error around the disability weights by sequelae rather than in terms of the uncertainty arising from the constituent components, that is, the health state distributions and the valuation function. Based on this approach, the results offer guidance on the sensitivity of burden estimates to a certain degree of uncertainty around disability weights, but do not necessarily capture all sources of uncertainty and their covariance. As noted earlier, certain specific measurement methods for eliciting health state valuations, for example, the person trade-off or standard gamble, may have important normative implications that are orthogonal to the assessment of health levels. However, undertaking a sensitivity analysis that focuses on a specific measurement approach is not appropriate here, because the weights currently used in the GBD estimates have been derived from the synthesis of multiple data sources rather than from a single measurement method.

Because of the natural constraints on the range of values that disability weights may assume, we have incorporated normal distributions with constant variance in the space of the logit of disability weights. The logit transformation is given by $logit(x) = \ln[x/(1-x)]$. By allowing for normally distributed error in logit space, ranges in the natural space of valuations are constrained to fall between 0 and 1. We chose a value of 0.6 for the standard deviation of the logits, based on the standard deviations observed across the mean valuations by country for an array of conditions included in the WHO multicountry survey study from 2000–1 (with valuation modules implemented in 14 countries) (Salomon and others 2003; Ustun and others 2003). Although the variability in country means may reflect a range of different factors, including the possibility of real valuation heterogeneity, we use this value to approximate the average level of uncertainty around the set of disability weights used in the GBD study. A constant value in logit space yields absolute ranges that widen at the midpoint of the interval and narrow as the disability weight approaches 0 or 1 (figure 5.15). In relative terms, the uncertainty is greatest for the smallest disability weights and narrows as more severe weights are attained (figure 5.16).

To trace the implications of this uncertainty through to the calculation of DALYs(3,0) used in the DCPP, we took 100 draws from each of 622 independent normal distributions with a mean of 0 and a standard deviation of 0.6 (for the 622 sequelae included in the calculations). For each of the sequelae we applied a given sampled value as a perturbation of all age, sex, and region estimates of logit-transformed

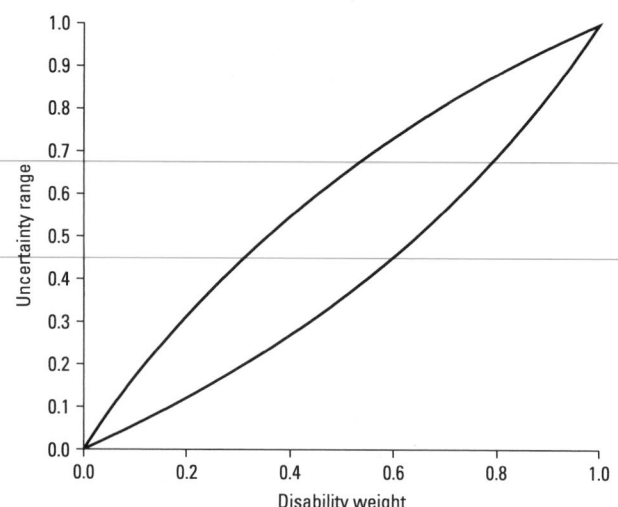

Source: Authors' calculations.

Figure 5.15 Assumed 95 Percent Uncertainty Ranges for Disability Weights Based on Constant Variance Distribution for Logit of Disability Weight

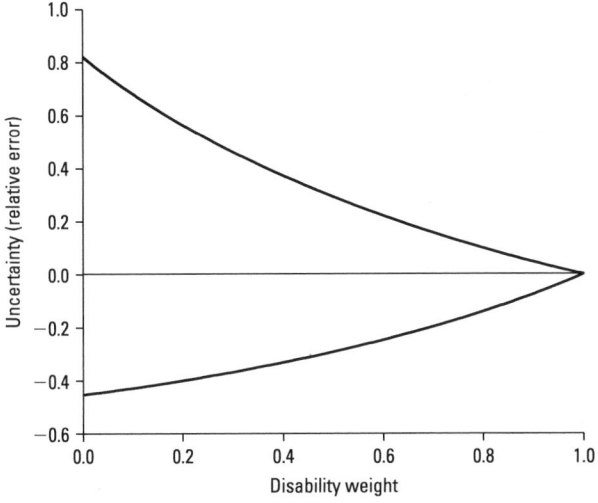

Source: Authors' calculations.

Figure 5.16 Relative 95 Percent Uncertainty Ranges for Disability Weights Based on the Assumption of a Constant Variance Distribution for Logit of Disability Weight across All Disability Weights

disability weights pertaining to that sequela, and recomputed YLD(3,0) based on the disability weight plus the random perturbation (after reversing the transformation for the sum). We estimated uncertainty ranges by taking the 2.5th and 97.5th percentiles across the 100 values of the various quantities of interest based on the random draws of error around the disability weights. This method implies the simplifying assumption that errors are uncorrelated between sequelae but perfectly correlated for all estimates within a sequela. In addition to YLD(3,0) numbers, we recomputed YLD ranks resulting from each set of sampled values, and also calculated DALY numbers and ranks by adding each YLD(3,0) draw to constant YLL(3,0) estimates by sequela. Our intent is only to provide an indication of the sensitivity of the YLD and DALY results to disability weight uncertainty. We did not attempt either to carry out a full empirically based analysis of this issue or to combine this source of uncertainty with mortality uncertainty and uncertainty in epidemiological estimates to give a comprehensive uncertainty analysis for the DALY estimates.

Table 5.6 presents the resulting uncertainty ranges for YLD and DALYs by cause for low- and middle-income countries. As would be expected, DALY uncertainty ranges due to disability weight uncertainty are generally largest for those causes dominated by YLD and smallest for those causes dominated by YLL. Uncertainty ranges are also large for those YLD-dominated causes with high

prevalence and low disability weight (with high relative uncertainty), such as hearing loss and anemia. Figure 5.17 summarizes in graphical form the uncertainty in total DALYs for low- and middle income countries for the 20 highest-ranked causes.

Table 5.7 presents the resulting 95 percent uncertainty ranges for the 40 leading causes of the burden of disease in low- and middle-income countries. Taking into account uncertainty in disability weights does not result in significant uncertainty in the ranking of the top four causes, with only the third (ischemic heart disease) and fourth (HIV/AIDS) possibly changing places. The total estimated DALYs for these two causes differ by less than 2 percent, so this is not surprising. Among the other top 10 causes, the disability weight uncertainty could change the rankings of individual causes by up to two ranks, with the exception of depressive disorders, which could change by up to four ranks. This reflects both the high relative uncertainty in the disability weight for mild depression and the fact that YLD are responsible for almost all depression DALYs. Among conditions ranked 20th to 30th in table 5.7, uncertainty ranges for most ranks are relatively narrow with the exception of nonfatal, high-prevalence conditions such as hearing loss and osteoarthritis, where the uncertainty in rank may be as much as ±15 places.

This analysis confirms the importance of efforts to improve the measurement of disability weights for health states close to full health, that is, with disability weights close to zero, particularly for health states with high prevalence in many populations, such as mild to moderate sense organ impairment or mild to moderate anemia. Unfortunately, most of the available choice-based or trade-off methods involving comparison in some form with death or survival present greater cognitive challenges to respondents when applied to health states close to full health.

UNCERTAINTY ARISING FROM EPIDEMIOLOGICAL ESTIMATES

Uncertainty in YLD estimates is mainly determined by the uncertainty in (a) epidemiological estimates for the prevalence and/or incidence of disability associated with specific causes or cause groups; and (b) disability weights arising from uncertainty in health state valuations and, in some cases, also in the disability severity distribution associated with a condition.

For a subset of the GBD causes, analysts carrying out reviews and analyses for the estimation of YLD also estimated

Table 5.6 Estimated 95 Percent Uncertainty Ranges for YLD and DALYs Arising from Uncertainty in Disability Weights for Selected Causes for Low- and Middle-Income Countries, 2001
(thousands)

Cause	YLD(3,0)	Uncertainty range	DALYs(3,0)	Uncertainty range
Group I				
Tuberculosis	4,134	2,706–6,219	35,882	34,400–37,900
Syphilis	407	310–574	4,122	4,021–4,286
Chlamydia	2,255	1,766–3,073	2,438	1,949–3,256
Gonorrhea	2,530	2,038–3,369	2,550	2,058–3,390
HIV/AIDS	5,973	4,142–8,195	70,857	68,900–73,000
Diarrheal diseases	7,836	4,236–12,900	58,685	55,100–63,800
Pertussis	2,291	1,763–2,986	11,408	10,900–12,100
Poliomyelitis	126	84–170	136	94–180
Diphtheria	0	0–1	164	164–164
Measles	193	113–319	23,097	23,000–23,200
Tetanus	14	10–16	8,337	8,329–8,335
Meningitis	1,131	915–1,416	5,477	5,255–5,756
Hepatitis B	52	28–96	2,082	2,056–2,124
Hepatitis C	21	11–39	844	832–860
Malaria	4,501	3,521–5,672	39,944	39,000–41,100
Trypanosomiasis	72	49–101	1,333	1,310–1,361
Chagas' disease	358	275–501	584	500–727
Schistosomiasis	1,313	727–2,563	1,525	938–2,774
Leishmaniasis	411	291–610	1,757	1,636–1,955
Lymphatic filariasis	4,446	3,365–6,947	4,455	3,374–6,956
Onchocerciasis	439	361–541	439	361–541
Leprosy	93	56–142	191	154–239
Dengue	5	3–10	529	526–533
Japanese encephalitis	231	187–276	598	554–644
Trachoma	2,618	2,023–3,192	2,621	2,025–3,195
Ascariasis	1,311	707–2,190	1,413	808–2,291
Trichuriasis	713	518–1,000	800	604–1,087
Hookworm disease	7	4–13	63	60–69
Lower respiratory infections	4,430	3,128–6,525	83,579	82,300–85,700
Upper respiratory infections	181	108–318	1,680	1,609–1,819
Otitis media	1,336	811–2,136	1,424	899–2,224
Maternal hemorrhage	232	61–162	3,923	3,750–3,851
Maternal sepsis	3,290	827–2,048	5,269	2,804–4,025
Hypertensive disorders	—	0–0	1,890	1,888–1,888
Obstructed labor	1,349	842–1,477	2,495	1,988–2,622
Abortion	1,732	1,034–2,344	3,503	2,803–4,112
Perinatal causes	13,525	10,300–18,100	89,121	85,900–93,800
Protein-energy malnutrition	9,337	6,616–14,300	15,450	12,700–20,400
Iodine deficiency	2,685	1,617–2,206	2,875	1,807–2,396
Vitamin A deficiency	58	34–88	711	685–740
Iron-deficiency anemia	6,736	4,782–10,300	9,488	7,530–13,000
Group II				
Mouth and oropharynx cancers	107	80–127	4,079	4,049–4,097
Esophageal cancer	42	29–56	5,251	5,235–5,262
Stomach cancer	124	95–160	9,613	9,577–9,643
Colon and rectal cancers	241	179–315	5,058	4,993–5,128
Liver cancer	49	37–63	7,943	7,926–7,952
Pancreas cancer	18	16–19	1,621	1,617–1,620
Trachea, bronchus, and lung cancers	137	117–155	10,697	10,700–10,700
Melanoma and other skin cancers	10	6–15	501	497–505
Breast cancer	308	226–386	5,527	5,440–5,600
Cervix uteri cancer	205	140–282	3,800	3,732–3,875
Corpus uteri cancer	276	200–416	908	831–1,046
Ovarian cancer	98	71–138	1,488	1,460–1,527

Table 5.6 Continued

(thousands)

Cause	YLD(3,0)	Uncertainty range	DALYs(3,0)	Uncertainty range
Prostate cancer	91	63–109	1,479	1,448–1,494
Bladder cancer	104	76–134	1,504	1,474–1,532
Lymphomas, multiple myeloma	69	49–98	3,770	3,746–3,795
Leukemia	58	33–86	3,964	3,936–3,989
Diabetes mellitus	5,662	4,229–7,736	15,806	14,400–17,900
Endocrine disorders	7,581	4,447–12,700	10,947	7,814–16,100
Unipolar depressive disorders	43,223	30,400–53,600	43,429	30,600–53,800
Bipolar affective disorder	8,676	5,636–12,100	8,681	5,642–12,100
Schizophrenia	10,156	7,419–12,800	10,530	7,793–13,200
Epilepsy	2,942	1,541–5,758	5,759	4,356–8,573
Alcohol use disorders	9,808	6,086–15,700	11,009	7,286–16,900
Alzheimer's and other dementias	8,172	6,690–9,790	9,641	8,158–11,300
Parkinson's disease	767	513–1,085	1,239	984–1,557
Multiple sclerosis	770	501–1,039	916	647–1,185
Drug use disorders	2,736	1,693–3,825	4,406	3,361–5,493
Post-traumatic stress disorder	2,013	1,217–3,918	2,013	1,218–3,919
Obsessive-compulsive disorder	3,136	1,726–5,532	3,136	1,726–5,532
Panic disorder	4,017	2,530–6,052	4,017	2,530–6,052
Insomnia (primary)	2,219	1,314–3,883	2,219	1,314–3,883
Migraine	4,851	2,720–7,503	4,851	2,720–7,503
Mental retardation, lead-caused	8,474	5,358–12,100	8,601	5,484–12,300
Glaucoma	4,110	2,986–5,393	4,111	2,987–5,395
Cataracts	28,155	21,500–37,100	28,155	21,500–37,100
Vision disorders, age-related	15,360	10,900–19,400	15,360	10,900–19,400
Hearing loss, adult onset	24,610	14,000–43,800	24,610	14,000–43,800
Rheumatic heart disease	607	404–863	6,152	5,945–6,404
Hypertensive heart disease	888	542–1,358	9,969	9,612–10,400
Ischemic heart disease	3,921	2,525–5,369	71,874	70,400–73,300
Cerebrovascular disease	11,096	7,209–17,100	62,652	58,700–68,600
Inflammatory heart diseases	1,309	765–1,908	5,812	5,263–6,406
Chronic obstructive pulmonary disease	8,473	5,670–12,400	33,457	30,600–37,300
Asthma	7,713	4,479–13,600	11,513	8,277–17,400
Peptic ulcer disease	1,154	556–1,737	4,802	4,203–5,383
Cirrhosis of the liver	2,329	1,391–3,289	13,635	12,700–14,600
Appendicitis	60	42–81	377	358–397
Nephritis and nephrosis	546	288–869	9,078	8,811–9,392
Benign prostatic hypertrophy	2,304	1,229–3,999	2,613	1,538–4,308
Skin diseases	2,924	1,764–4,425	3,697	2,535–5,197
Rheumatoid arthritis	3,433	2,132–5,436	3,645	2,344–5,648
Osteoarthritis	13,651	8,636–22,400	13,667	8,652–22,400
Gout	2,768	1,697–4,053	2,785	1,714–4,070
Low back pain	1,676	1,093–2,670	1,692	1,109–2,685
Congenital anomalies	9,295	7,047–11,700	23,538	21,300–26,000
Dental caries	4,752	2,771–8,429	4,752	2,771–8,429
Periodontal disease	206	124–368	207	125–369
Edentulism	2,293	1,349–3,476	2,293	1,349–3,476
Group III				
Road traffic accidents	7,195	6,489–8,063	32,022	31,300–32,900
Poisonings	135	107–170	7,119	7,088–7,151
Falls	8,055	7,035–9,203	13,582	12,600–14,700
Fires	2,719	2,199–3,286	10,081	9,557–10,600
Drownings	37	33–41	9,389	9,379–9,387
Self-inflicted injuries	1,236	1,040–1,489	17,677	17,500–17,900
Violence	5,405	4,734–6,420	18,135	17,500–19,100
War	1,569	1,321–1,887	6,496	6,240–6,806

Source: Authors' calculations.

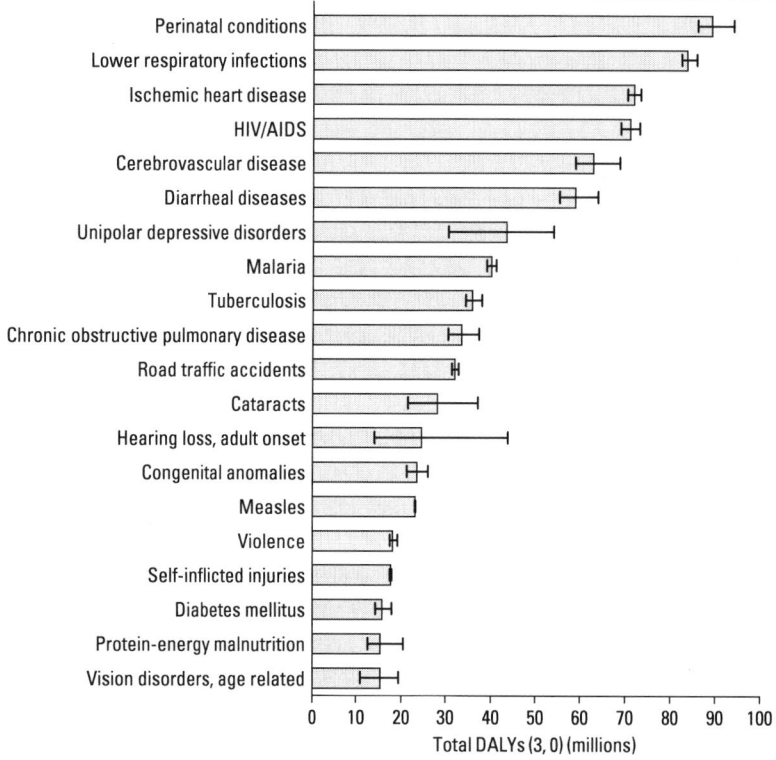

Figure 5.17 Estimated 95 Percent Uncertainty in Total DALYs(3,0) Due to Uncertainty in Estimation of Disability Weights, Top 20 Causes, Low- and Middle-Income Countries

Source: Authors' calculations.

levels of uncertainty in regional prevalences. These assessments took into account not only typical levels of measurement error in the input data sets, but also expert judgment on the degree of uncertainty arising from the lack of representativeness of the available data for each region. The resulting uncertainty ranges vary considerably across causes, ranging from relatively certain estimates for some causes such as polio, for which intensive surveillance systems are in place, to highly uncertain estimates for other causes such as osteoarthritis, where for some regions not a single usable dataset was found, and where for others the latest available data were decades old. The summary tables provided in chapter 3 for numbers of data sources used for YLD estimates by cause and region provide one indication of the relative uncertainty associated with YLD estimates for different causes.

For some causes, such as stroke and ischemic heart disease, YLD estimates were essentially derived from estimates of cause-specific mortality by means of models of regional variations in case fatality rates. In such cases, YLD uncertainty will be significantly higher than the uncertainty associated with cause-specific mortality estimates given the

considerable uncertainty in case fatality rates for most low- and middle-income countries and in models used to infer the burden of nonfatal disease from mortality. YLD uncertainty will generally be greater than YLL uncertainty, and will also vary across causes according to both the typical uncertainty associated with the measurement of incidence or prevalence according to GBD case definitions and with the number and representativeness of available studies. For a subset of 16 major causes of YLD for which analysts estimated indicative uncertainty ranges, the typical uncertainty for regional prevalence estimates ranged from ±10 percent to ±90 percent, with a median value of ±41 percent. Uncertainty ranges were generally higher for low- and middle-income countries than for high-income countries.

UNCERTAINTY IN THE DISEASE BURDEN ATTRIBUTABLE TO RISK FACTORS

The assessments of the disease burden attributable to selected risk factors reported in chapter 4 are affected by

Table 5.7 Estimated 95 Percent Uncertainty Ranges Arising from Uncertainty in Disability Weights for the Top 40 Causes of the Burden of Disease in Low- and Middle-Income Countries, 2001

Rank	Uncertainty range	Cause	DALYs (thousands)	Uncertainty range
1	1–1	Perinatal conditions	89,121	85,900–93,800
2	2–2	Lower respiratory infections	83,579	82,300–85,700
3	3–4	Ischemic heart disease	71,874	70,400–73,300
4	3–4	HIV/AIDS	70,857	68,900–73,000
5	5–6	Cerebrovascular disease	62,652	58,700–68,600
6	5–6	Diarrheal diseases	58,685	55,100–63,800
7	7–11	Unipolar depressive disorders	43,429	30,600–53,800
8	7–9	Malaria	39,944	39,000–41,100
9	8–10	Tuberculosis	35,882	34,400–37,900
10	9–12	Chronic obstructive pulmonary disease	33,457	30,600–37,300
11	10–13	Road traffic accidents	32,022	31,300–32,900
12	9–14	Cataracts	28,155	21,500–37,100
13	8–21	Hearing loss, adult onset	24,610	14,000–43,800
14	12–15	Congenital anomalies	23,538	21,300–26,000
15	13–15	Measles	23,097	23,000–23,200
16	15–18	Violence	18,135	17,500–19,100
17	16–19	Self-inflicted injuries	17,677	17,500–17,900
18	17–22	Diabetes mellitus	15,806	14,400–17,900
19	15–25	Protein-energy malnutrition	15,450	12,700–20,400
20	16–27	Vision disorders, age-related	15,360	10,900–19,400
21	16–36	Osteoarthritis	13,667	8,652–22,400
22	20–25	Cirrhosis of the liver	13,635	12,700–14,600
23	20–24	Falls	13,582	12,600–14,700
24	18–38	Asthma	11,513	8,277–17,400
25	23–29	Pertussis	11,408	10,900–12,100
26	19–40	Alcohol use disorders	11,009	7,286–16,900
27	18–40	Endocrine disorders	10,947	7,814–16,100
28	25–31	Trachea, bronchus, and lung cancers	10,697	10,700–10,700
29	22–39	Schizophrenia	10,530	7,793–13,200
30	27–34	Fires	10,081	9,557–10,600
31	27–34	Hypertensive heart disease	9,969	9,612–10,400
32	26–38	Alzheimer's and other dementias	9,641	8,158–11,300
33	29–36	Stomach cancer	9,613	9,577–9,643
34	25–40	Iron-deficiency anemia	9,488	7,530–13,000
35	31–37	Drownings	9,389	9,379–9,387
36	33–38	Nephritis and nephrosis	9,078	8,811–9,392
37	27–46	Bipolar affective disorder	8,681	5,642–12,100
38	24–47	Mental retardation, lead-caused	8,601	5,484–12,300
39	36–39	Tetanus	8,337	8,329–8,335
40	37–41	Liver cancer	7,943	7,926–7,952

Source: Authors' calculations.

additional sources of uncertainty, beyond the uncertainty in DALY estimates for specific disease and injury outcomes discussed earlier. A full uncertainty analysis of such burden estimates has not yet been carried out, but would involve assessment of the following additional types of uncertainty:

- uncertainty in the estimated distributions of population risk exposure;
- uncertainty in estimates of relative risks for cause-specific mortality and incidence associated with specific expo-

sures, for which a significant source of uncertainty is the extrapolation of relative risks measured at other ages to older age groups;
- uncertainty associated with estimating joint effects of risk factors.

Uncertainty in exposure and in both the existence and magnitude of hazardous effect always affects quantitative risk assessment. In one taxonomy, risk assessment uncertainty can be divided into parameter uncertainty and model uncertainty

(National Research Council 1994). Parameter uncertainty is often quantifiable using random variable methods, for example, uncertainty due to sample size or measurement error. Model uncertainty is due to gaps in scientific theory, measurement technology, and data. It includes uncertainty in causal relationships or the form of the exposure-response relationship (for instance, threshold versus continuous or linear versus nonlinear), the level of bias in measurement, and so on. Defined broadly, model uncertainty also includes extrapolation of exposure or hazard from one population to another. Model uncertainty dominates uncertainty in risk assessment, a result of difficulty in carrying out direct studies on exposure, hazard, and background disease burden. This has motivated innovative assumptions and extrapolations even in the case of the most widely studied risk factors like smoking (Peto and others 1992).

Uncertainty around disease causation (Evans 1978; Hill 1965) was, in practice, secondary to uncertainty around hazard size, for example, relative risk, because when causality was uncertain, the estimates of relative risk needed for risk assessment were also unknown or uncertain. For example, whether the relationships between physical inactivity and lower back pain or between alcohol and violence are causal has equivalent questions on the magnitude of hazard of each risk for the disease outcome. Collective scientific knowledge from disciplines such as social and behavioral sciences, physiology and neuroscience, and epidemiology would confirm the possibility of a causal relationship in the foregoing cases, but would shift the uncertainty to hazard size. As a result, for some risk factors, we could only quantify the contribution to a subset of disease outcomes because epidemiological studies did not provide enough information for all risk factor and disease pairs, even when the causal relationship was believed or suspected.

Estimates of hazard in individual epidemiological studies were adjusted for confounding as much as possible. Extrapolation of hazard from a limited number of studies to other populations has received less attention. While the robustness of proportional measures of risk has been confirmed for more proximal factors in studies across populations (Eastern Stroke and Coronary Heart Disease Collaborative Research Group 1998; Horton 2000; Law, Wald, and Thompson 1994), their extrapolation is an important source of uncertainty for more distal risks (such as childhood sexual abuse) or those whose effects are heterogeneous (for example, alcohol and injuries versus alcohol and cancer).

Direct exposure data for many risk factors are limited both because of measurement difficulties and because of underinvestment in risk factor surveillance. To allow maximum use

of available data, such risk factors were represented using indirect or aggregate indicators, for instance, smoking impact ratio for accumulated hazards of smoking, weight-for-age for childhood undernutrition, and use of solid fuels for indoor air pollution. Furthermore, for some risks multiple data sources allowed limiting the range of exposure estimates. For example, in the absence of alcohol surveys, information on total alcohol production, trade, and unrecorded consumption provided upper bounds on the fraction of the population that would be in the highest consumption category. Finally, some of the risk factors examined in chapter 4 were represented using continuous exposure variables such as high blood pressure. Others used categorical variables, for example, indoor smoke from household use of solid fuels, childhood underweight, and physical inactivity, even though the health effects occur along a continuum. This choice reflected the availability of exposure data and hazard estimates in categories. In such cases, the contribution to disease within the baseline category would not have been captured.

In addition to uncertainty in exposure and hazard, the uncertainty of estimated population attributable fractions (PAFs) is determined by the analytical properties of the PAF relationship. In particular, the PAF relationship is an increasing concave function of relative risk and exposure level, approaching 100 percent asymptotically, that is, the rate of increase declines with increasing relative risk or prevalence (figure 5.18). Therefore, if a risk factor or group of risk factors individually or jointly account for large

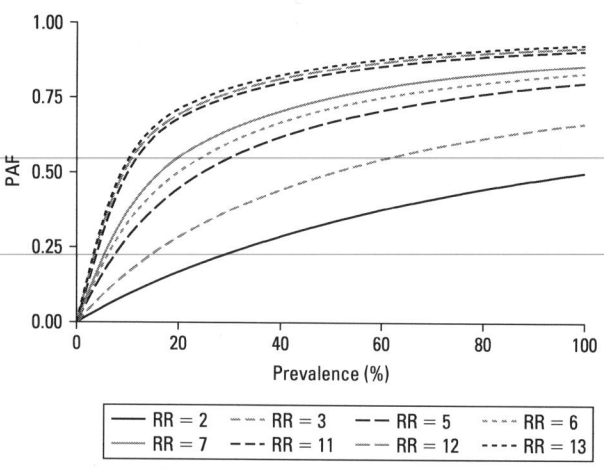

Source: Authors' calculations.

Note: The population attributable fraction (PAF) relationship is an increasing concave function of both prevalence (seen in the shape of each curve) and relative risk, RR (seen in the declining distance between each adjacent pair of curves). This limits the sensitivity of individual or joint PAFs to uncertainty in input parameters, when PAFs are relatively large.

Figure 5.18 PAF Sensitivity to Exposure and Relative Risks

fractions of specific diseases, the PAFs are more robust to uncertainty in inputs. Finally, there is uncertainty in mortality and disease burden estimates to which the estimated PAF are applied (see the previous section).

The findings in chapter 4 should therefore be considered within the context of limited available data and viewed as subject to uncertainty, which varies across risk factors and geographical regions. For further discussion of sources and quantification of uncertainty for specific risk factors see Ezzati and others (2004).

DISCUSSION

As described in chapter 3, the data requirements for adequate measurements of the global burden of disease are substantial and include information about age at death, cause of death, age-specific incidence of diseases and injuries, typical duration of life lived with the sequelae of diseases and injuries, and some quantification of the severity of disability assessed according to a common framework. While the ethical, philosophical, and conceptual issues involved in quantifying states of health other than perfect health are still very much a matter of debate, a substantial body of empirical evidence on the variations across individuals and populations in health state valuations is now available.

We have shown in this chapter that the distribution of the global burden of disease and the overall rankings of various conditions in terms of their contribution to it are largely insensitive to alternative assumptions about the discount rate and age weighting. The major effect of discounting and age weighting is to enhance the importance of neuropsychiatric conditions and sexually transmitted infections. While disease rankings are relatively unaffected, the share of the burden due to disability, the age distribution of the burden, and the distribution of the burden by broad cause group are sensitive to the discount rate but less affected by age weighting.

When compared with the discounted and age-weighted DALY used in the 1990 GBD study and the WHO updates for 2000–2, the DCPP's use of discounted but not age-weighted DALYs results in somewhat more weight being given to the chronic diseases of older ages and somewhat less weight being given to mental disorders and injuries, which affect younger adults disproportionately. Of the value choices incorporated into the standard DALYs(3,1), the nonuniform age weights have been the most controversial. Apart from the DCPP, a number of national burden of disease studies, including those in Australia and Canada (Mathers, Vos, and Stevenson 1999; Public Health Agency of Canada 2005), have chosen not to apply the nonuniform age weights, presumably on equity grounds. In contrast, some investigators concerned with the inequitable health burden of the low- and middle-income countries have argued for ignoring all deaths over a certain age on the grounds that they are not premature—an extreme form of age weighting (Williams 1997). Chapter 6 presents some empirical evidence in making the case for a stronger form of age weighting for infants and younger children, that is, age weights that depart further from unity than the standard age weighting used in the DALY.

Although the choices for discounting and age weighting do affect the cause and age distributions of the burden of disease to some extent, and the results of specific cost-effectiveness studies may be even more sensitive to these choices, we conclude that the uncertainty of the underlying epidemiological choices is vastly more consequential than these social preferences when interpreting the results of burden of disease analysis. The validity and reliability, and hence the utility, of burden of disease studies for public policy depend much more strongly on the quality and availability of the underlying epidemiological data.

The GBD study has been criticized for making estimates of mortality and burden of disease for regions with limited, incomplete, and uncertain data (Cooper and others 1998; Gupta, Sankaranarayanan, and Ferlay 1994). Murray and Lopez describe the GBD approach as a "'meta-synthesis,' or in other words, the construction of a comprehensive and comparable view of health problems using all available sources of information" (Murray and Lopez 1996b, p. 289). The incorporation of many types of information about a comprehensive set of causes of death and disability results in estimates that are much less likely to be biased than those that emerge from an examination of specific health conditions in isolation. It also avoids the tendency to assume that if no data are available or the data are highly uncertain, then there is no disease burden.

We argue that including uncertain results (with quantified uncertainty to the extent possible) is far preferable than leaving blank cells in tables intended to provide policy makers with an overall assessment of the burden of disease in populations. We maintain that providing large volumes of unsynthesized, biased, and incomplete data relating to population health does not generally allow policy makers to make the best use of such information. Unless they have considerable analytic resources of their own, the unsynthesized products of the research enterprise are of little help to decision makers, who will often then resort to decisions on the basis of ideology, of their own beliefs about what is important, or of political imperatives.

The quantities of interest for the GBD study are the underlying rates of incidence, remission, and mortality for defined causes for whole populations for a specified time period, and the assessment of these often requires synthesizing data from multiple studies or making adjustments for biases in relation to population, age groups, or time periods. A major source of uncertainty for the GBD estimates is the uncertainty associated with extrapolating from one or more subgroups to a regional population. For example, how representative of the incidence and prevalence patterns of dementia in Sub-Saharan Africa are two or three population-representative studies of rural or urban populations in specific regions of specific countries? The uncertainty associated with extrapolating from a set of studies in subpopulations to the regional population is related to potential systematic (selection) biases and is much more difficult to quantify than the uncertainty associated with stochastic variation due to sample size or measurement error.

Estimates of deaths from specific causes undergo continual revision as new data and syntheses become available, yet drawing a time cutoff is a necessary (if somewhat arbitrary) condition for preparing any volume such as this which reports comprehensive and consistent global and regional estimates of deaths and burden of disease (see also annex 6C). During 2001 WHO established the Child Health Epidemiology Reference Group (CHERG) to review and synthesise data on cause of deaths under age 5. While early CHERG results contributed substantially to the GBD analyses in this volume, much of their work became available well after the cutoff date for this publication. While CHERG has published revised estimates of the distribution of child deaths by cause (Bryce and others 2005), based on recent comprehensive reviews of epidemiological data, these analyses used cause categories not consistent with the GBD (including use of incompatible cause categories for neonatal and other child deaths), fewer cause categories than the GBD, and left study deaths assigned to ill-defined categories in the 'Other' category. Additionally, at the date of writing, the CHERG evidence has not been brought into the GBD analytic and consistency framework, involving consistent mapping to causal categories and checking of internal consistency between incidence, prevalence and mortality estimates for specific causes.

To the extent that they can be compared with the GBD 2001 estimates, the WHO/CHERG estimates at the global level are differ substantially for tetanus (46% higher), lower respiratory infections (56% higher), and are somewhat lower for measles, malaria, low birthweight and noncommunicable diseases. It is not possible at this stage, to conclude whether or how much the WHO/CHERG analyses would modify the GBD 2001 results reported in this volume, when they are properly brought into the GBD analytic framework. However, they do give some indications that new evidence is becoming available for child deaths, and that uncertainty ranges for GBD estimates of child deaths may be greater for some causes than indicated by the analyses presented in this chapter.

The 1990 GBD study and GBD 2001 were both meta-syntheses of the available data, using the best models and tools available at the time, whose primary aims were to provide a comprehensive assessment of the current burden of disease. The assessment of trends between 1990 and 2001 is a much more difficult task, as discussed in chapter 2. The comparability of best point in time estimates is difficult to assess given changes in both the availability of data and in the methods used to synthesize those data for many of the causes. Murray, Mathers, and Salomon (2003) discuss this issue in more detail and conclude that to assess change or evaluate programs, extrapolating current levels of burden of disease from past measurements is inadequate, and that the assessment must include measurements carried out at both points in time or explicit measurement of the relevant trends or rates of change.

CONCLUSIONS

The 2001 GBD study uses a summary measure of population health, the DALY, that explicitly incorporates several important social values. This has the advantage that the effects of changing preferences can be readily explored through sensitivity analysis, as illustrated in this chapter. Another advantage of the burden of disease approach is that it entails a data audit, whereby the completeness, reliability, and consistency of routinely collected data are assessed and critical gaps in health data collection are identified. One implication is that periodic quality assessments of, say, routine cause of death data are needed to ensure their continued relevance and reliability for public policy (Mathers and others 2005). Another is the need for a more rational assessment of priority data for the health care sector that places greater emphasis on data collection and data linkage to facilitate burden of disease studies rather than on routine collection of statistics of limited relevance to public health. The burden of disease framework, based on the estimated distribution and duration of health states resulting from incident cases, would benefit greatly from wider availability of linked data sets on health outcomes and further longitudinal research into health state transition probabilities following on from specific disease or injury causes (Kelman and Bass 2002).

A major advance with GBD 2001 has been the systematic, though as yet incomplete, attempt to quantify uncertainty in both national and global assessments of the disease burden. This uncertainty must be taken into account when making cross-national comparisons, and needs to be carefully communicated and interpreted by epidemiologists and policy makers alike. Estimates of mortality in countries without functioning vital registration systems for causes of death will always be substantially more uncertain than those derived from systems where all deaths are registered and medically certified. The same may be said for the quantification of disability due to various conditions, where the gaps in data availability across countries are likely to be even more extreme than for mortality.

Despite the progress of the past decade, the incremental gains in advancing knowledge and understanding of global descriptive epidemiology have been modest. A globally coordinated research and development effort is urgently needed to devise and implement cost-effective approaches to data collection and analysis in poor countries that are targeted to their health development needs, and that can routinely yield comparable information of sufficient quality to establish how the disease and risk factor burden is changing in populations (Murray, Lopez, and Wibulpolprasert 2004).

Much can be learned about the health of populations from relatively modest investments in sample registration systems, provided these are designed to reliably measure the causes of death in sample areas and have sufficient resources to do so. China's Disease Surveillance Points system is a good example of what can be done to improve knowledge about disease and injury control priorities in low-income countries at a modest cost (Lopez 1998; Yang and others 2005). Greater investments in getting the descriptive epidemiology of diseases and injuries correct in poor countries will do vastly more to reduce uncertainty in disease burden assessments than philosophical debate about the appropriateness of social value choices. Just as the production of global and regional estimates should not create the impression that the descriptive epidemiology of disease and injury is reliably known, so the uncertainties around these estimates must not create the impression that not enough is known reliably enough to usefully inform health priorities and programs. Health intelligence is an essential ingredient of the health development process. Those engaged in collecting, analyzing, and disseminating population health information have a responsibility to develop this evidence base using novel methods that communicate what we do know, as well, if not more convincingly, than what we do not know.

Information for policy purposes will never be perfect, but good policy makers will want to benefit from all available information to guide priority setting and action. We might well take solace in the comments of a prominent medical statistician who once cautioned that "Making the best the enemy of the good is a sure way to hinder any statistical progress. The scientific purist who will wait for medical statistics until they are nosologically exact is no wiser than Horace's rustic waiting for the river to flow away" (Greenwood 1948, p. 28).

ACKNOWLEDGMENTS

We wish to acknowledge stimulating discussions with and advice from Christopher J. L. Murray in the development of our approach and analytic tools relating to the analysis and estimation of uncertainty in mortality and GBD estimates. We also acknowledge the assistance of staff of the former Global Program on Evidence for Health Policy at WHO, who helped substantially in the analysis of uncertainty, namely: Doris Ma Fat, Brodie Ferguson, Mie Inoue, and Niels Tomijima. Finally, we thank two referees for extremely useful comments and suggestions that have substantially improved this chapter.

REFERENCES

Anand, S., and K. Hanson. 1997. "Disability-Adjusted Life Years: A Critical Review." *Journal of Health Economics* 16 (6): 685–702.

Barendregt, J. J., L. Bonneux, and P. J. van der Maas. 1996. "DALYs: The Age-Weights on Balance." *Bulletin of the World Health Organization* 74 (4): 439–43.

Bobadilla, J. L. 1996. "Priority Setting and Cost Effectiveness." In *Health Policy and Systems Development: An Agenda for Research*, ed. K Janovsky, 43–60. Geneva: World Health Organization.

Bryce, J., C. Boschi-Pinto, K. Shibuya, R. E. Black and the WHO Child Health Epidemiology Reference Group. 2005. "WHO Estimates of the causes of death in children." *Lancet* 365 (9465): 1147–1152.

Cooper, R. S., B. Osotimehin, J. S. Kaufman, and T. Forrester. 1998. "Disease Burden in Sub-Saharan Africa: What Should We Conclude in the Absence of Data?" *Lancet* 351 (9097): 208–10.

Dasgupta, P., K.-G. Mäler, and S. Barrett. 1999. "Intergenerational Equity, Social Discount Rates, and Global Warming." In *Discounting and Intergenerational Equity*, ed. P. R. Portney and J. P. Weyant, 51–77. Washington, DC: Resources for the Future.

Eastern Stroke and Coronary Heart Disease Collaborative Research Group. 1998. "Blood Pressure, Cholesterol, and Stroke in Eastern Asia." *Lancet* 352 (9143): 1801–7.

Evans, A. S. 1978. "Causation and Disease: A Chronological Journey." *American Journal of Epidemiology* 108 (4): 248–55.

Ezzati, M., A. D. Lopez, A. Rodgers, and C. J. L Murray. 2004. *Comparative Quantification of Health Risks: Global and Regional Burden of Disease Attributable to Several Major Risk Factors.* Geneva: World Health Organization.

Fox-Rushby, J. A. 2002. *Disability Adjusted Life Years (DALYS) for Decision-Making? An Overview of the Literature.* London: Office of Health Economics.

Gold, M. R., J. E. Siegel, M. C. Weinstein, and L. B. Russell. 1996. *Cost-Effectiveness in Health and Medicine.* New York: Oxford University Press.

Grassly, N. C., M. Morgan, N. Walker, G. P. Garnett, K. A. Stanecki, J. Stover, T. Brown, and P. D. Ghys. 2004. "Uncertainty in Estimates of HIV/AIDS: The Estimation and Application of Plausibility Bounds." *Sexually Transmitted Infections* 80 (Suppl 1): S31–S38.

Greenwood, M. 1948. "Medical Statistics from Graunt to Farr: The Fitzpatrick Lectures for the Years 1941 and 1943." Cambridge, U.K.: Cambridge University Press.

Gupta, P., R. Sankaranarayanan, and J. Ferlay. 1994. "Cancer Deaths in India: Is the Model-Based Approach Valid?" *Bulletin of the World Health Organization* 72 (6): 943–4.

Hill, A. B. 1965. "The Environment and Disease: Association or Causation?" *Proceedings of the Royal Society of Medicine* 58: 295–300.

Horton, R. 2000. "Common Sense and Figures: The Rhetoric of Validity in Medicine (Bradford Hill Memorial Lecture 1999)." *Statistics in Medicine* 19 (23): 3149–64.

Kelman, C. W., and A. J. Bass. 2002. "Research Use of Linked Health Data: A Best Practice Protocol." *Australian and New Zealand Journal of Public Health* 26 (3): 251–5.

King, G., M. Tomz, and J. Wittenberg. 2000. "Making the Most of Statistical Analyses: Improving Interpretation and Presentation." *American Journal of Political Science* 44 (2): 341–55.

Kneese, A. V. 1999. "The Faustian Bargain." In *The RFF Reader in Environment and Resource Management,* ed. W. D. Oates, 55–60. Washington, DC: Resources for the Future.

Kruijshaar, M., J. Barendregt, and N. Hoeymans. 2002. "The Use of Models in the Estimation of Disease Epidemiology." *Bulletin of the World Health Organization* 80 (8): 622–8.

Law, M. R., N. J. Wald, and S. G. Thompson. 1994. "By How Much and How Quickly Does Reduction in Serum Cholesterol Concentration Lower Risk of Ischaemic Heart Disease?" *British Medical Journal* 308 (6925): 367–73.

Lopez, A. D. 1998. "Counting the Dead in China." *British Medical Journal* 317 (7170): 1399–400.

Lopez, A. D., O. Ahmad, M. Guillot, B. Ferguson, J. Salomon, C. J. L. Murray, and K. H. Hill. 2002. *World Mortality in 2000: Life Tables for 191 Countries.* Geneva: World Health Organization.

Mahapatra, P. 2001. "Local Age Preference, Age Weight, and Discounting Parameters for Computation of DALYs." In *Estimating National Burden of Disease: The Burden of Disease in Andhra Pradesh 1990s,* ed. P. Mahapatra. Hyderabad, India: Institute of Health Systems.

Mathers, C. D., D. Ma Fat, M. Inoue, C. Rao, and A. D. Lopez. 2005. "Counting the Dead and What They Died from: An Assessment of the Global Status of Cause of Death Data." *Bulletin of the World Health Organization* 83 (3): 171–7.

Mathers, C. D., C. J. L Murray, and A. D. Lopez. 2002. "Epidemiological Evidence: Improving Validity through Consistency Analysis." *Bulletin of the World Health Organization* 80 (8): 611.

Mathers, C. D., T. Vos, and C. Stevenson. 1999. *The Burden of Disease and Injury in Australia.* Canberra: Australian Institute of Health and Welfare.

Morgan, M. G., and M. Henrion. 1990. *Uncertainty: A Guide to Dealing with Uncertainty in Quantitative Risk and Policy Analysis.* Cambridge, U.K.: Cambridge University Press.

Murray, C. J. L. 1996. "Rethinking DALYs." In *The Global Burden of Disease,* ed. C. J. L. Murray and A. D. Lopez, 1–98. Vol. 1 of *Global Burden of Disease and Injury Series.* Cambridge, MA: Harvard University Press.

Murray, C. J. L., and A. K. Acharya. 1997. "Understanding DALYs." *Journal of Health Economics* 16 (6): 703–30.

Murray, C. J. L, and A. D. Lopez, eds. 1996a. *The Global Burden of Disease: A Comprehensive Assessment of Mortality and Disability from Diseases, Injuries, and Risk Factors in 1990 and Projected to 2020.* Vol. 1 of *Global Burden of Disease and Injury Series.* Cambridge, MA: Harvard University Press.

———. 1996b. "The Global Burden of Disease in 1990: Final Results and Their Sensitivity to Alternative Epidemiological Perspectives, Discount Rates, Age-Weights, and Disability Weights." In *The Global Burden of Disease,* ed. C. J. L. Murray and A. D. Lopez, 247–93. Vol. 1 of *Global Burden of Disease and Injury Series.* Cambridge, MA: Harvard University Press.

Murray, C. J., A. D. Lopez, and S. Wibulpolprasert. 2004. "Monitoring Global Health: Time for New Solutions." *British Medical Journal* 329 (7333): 1096–100.

Murray, C. J. L, C. D. Mathers, and J. A. Salomon. 2003. "Towards Evidence-Based Public Health." In *Health Systems Performance Assessment: Debates, Methods, and Empiricism,* ed. C. J. L. Murray and D. Evans, 715–26. Geneva: World Health Organization.

Murray, C. J. L, J. A. Salomon, C. D. Mathers, and A. D. Lopez. 2002. "Summary Measures of Population Health: Conclusions and Recommendations." In *Summary Measures of Population Health: Concepts, Ethics, Measurement, and Applications,* ed. C. J. L. Murray, J. A. Salomon, C. D. Mathers, and A. D. Lopez, p. 731–56. Geneva: World Health Organization.

National Research Council. 1994. *Science and Judgment in Risk Assessment.* Washington, DC: National Academy Press.

Parfit, D. 1984. *Reasons and Persons.* Oxford, U.K.: Clarendon Press.

Peto, R., A. D. Lopez, J. Boreham, M. Thun, and C. Heath. 1992. "Mortality from Tobacco in Developed Countries: Indirect Estimation from National Vital Statistics." *Lancet* 339 (8804): 1268–78.

Public Health Agency of Canada. 2005. "Population Health Impact of Disease in Canada." http://www.phac-aspc.gc.ca/phi-isp/summary_measures.html#3.

Salomon, J. A., C. J. L. Murray, T. B. Ustun, and S. Chatterji. 2003. "Health State Valuations in Summary Measures of Population Health." In *Health Systems Performance Assessment: Debate, Methods, and Empiricism,* ed. C. J. L. Murray and D. Evans, 409–36. Geneva: World Health Organization.

Ustun, T. B., S. Chatterji, M. Villanueva, L. Bendib, C. Celik, R. Sadana, N. Valentine, C. Mathers, J. P. Ortiz, A. Tandon, J. Salomon, Y. Cao, X. W. and C. J. L. Murray. 2003. "The WHO Multicountry Household Survey Study on Health and Responsiveness 2000–2001." In *Health Systems Performance Assessment: Debates, Methods, and Empiricism,* ed. C. J. L. Murray and D. Evans, 761–96. Geneva: World Health Organization.

Vose, D. 2000. *Risk Analysis: A Quantitative Guide.* New York: Wiley.

Williams, A. 1997. "Intergenerational Equity: An Exploration of the 'Fair Innings' Argument." *Health Economics* 6 (2): 117–32.

Yang, G. H., J. Hu, K. Q. Rao, J. Ma, C. Rao, and A. D. Lopez. 2005. "Mortality Registration and Surveillance in China: History, Current Situation, and Challenges." *Population Health Metrics* 3: 3.

Chapter **6**

Incorporating Deaths Near the Time of Birth Into Estimates of the Global Burden of Disease

Dean T. Jamison, Sonbol A. Shahid-Salles, Julian Jamison, Joy E. Lawn, and Jelka Zupan

Many countries, including all high-income ones, maintain vital registration systems that provide data on the number of deaths by cause, sex, and age. Some countries also report years of life lost because of premature mortality (YLL) due to each cause, a number that depends on the age of death and on the choice of an algorithm for how YLL should depend on the age of death. The tracking of stillbirths, however, is often incomplete and variable.

As of the early 1990s, no estimates of YLL were available for many developing countries or for regional groupings of such countries. The World Bank (1993), as part of the preparation for its *World Development Report 1993: Investing in Health,* initiated an effort to provide estimates of deaths by age and cause, and hence YLL, for around 100 conditions for eight regional groupings, including all low- and middle-income countries. By adding years of healthy life lost as a result of disability (YLD) to YLL, the World Bank was able to generate estimates of the global burden of disease measured both in deaths by cause and in disability-adjusted life-years (DALYs) (Murray, Lopez, and Jamison 1994; World Bank 1993, appendix B). Murray and Lopez (1997) provide updated and

extended results and a complete description of methods. Global burden of disease estimates have subsequently been used to help guide resource allocation in the health sector and to inform debates about national and international disease control priorities (see chapter 1 in this volume); however, the global burden of disease literature currently provides little insight into the importance of deaths near the time of birth.

The purpose of this chapter is to explore the sensitivity of results within the Global Burden of Disease (GBD) framework to alternative approaches to encompassing the large number of deaths that occur near the time of birth, namely almost 4 million neonatal deaths and 3.3 million stillbirths. The sensitivity analyses in this chapter thus complement those of chapter 5, which explore the effect of variations in discount rates, age weights, and disability weights. Chapter 3 in this volume describes the GBD framework and provides estimates of deaths and DALYs by cause for 2001 using the World Bank regional grouping of countries. (Map 1, inside the front cover of this volume, shows the World Bank regional groupings used throughout this book.) This chapter uses the same framework and numbers to the extent possible, but with the following exceptions:

- We divide the newborn through age 4 category into neonatal (newborn through 27 days), postneonatal (28 days to less than 1 year), and child (1 through 4 years).
- We aggregate the 136 causes noted in chapter 3 into 35 causes.
- We allocate the substantial number of neonatal deaths attributed to pneumonia or sepsis to the chapter 3 category of respiratory infections.
- We explore the sensitivity of the results in chapter 3 to adding stillbirths as a new age category.
- We explore the sensitivity of the results to alternative ways of assigning YLL to deaths under the age of five.

The first section of this chapter deals with mortality: all-cause and cause specific. It uses the results presented in chapter 3, but adds to them estimates of the level of stillbirths and of the level and causes of neonatal mortality. The second section deals with estimation of the burden of disease in DALYs. The inclusion of stillbirths in the analysis highlights the more general issue of how to deal appropriately with deaths at different ages in constructing a measure of YLL.

As emphasized throughout this volume, data on causes of death and disability are fragmentary and are often inconsistent for many regions of the world. This is particularly true for the neonatal period and for stillbirths. One clear implication is the desirability of more and better data. Another implication is that any effort to construct an overall picture of population health must aggregate data of variable, often low, quality and completeness. In some instances this is done essentially as a political process, with various disease advocacy groups advancing their claims to policy makers and in the press. Alternatively, summary measures can be constructed systematically in a way that eliminates internal inconsistencies, describes methods carefully, and imposes the discipline of demographically derived totals into which cause-specific estimates must fit. This is the nature of our work on the global burden of disease.

STILLBIRTHS AND NEONATAL MORTALITY IN THE CONTEXT OF THE GLOBAL BURDEN OF DISEASE

This section first introduces the nomenclature used throughout the chapter. It then provides estimates of deaths and death rates that highlight stillbirths and neonatal deaths and discusses deaths by cause at different ages.

Nomenclature

This chapter follows standard usage where possible, but extends or tightens it as needed. Stillbirth refers to the birth of a dead fetus weighing more than 1,000 grams up to 0.25 years (13 weeks) prior to the expected time of birth (corresponding to 27 weeks of gestational age). Total births are the sum of the number of live births and of stillbirths. Stillbirths are conventionally divided into two categories, antepartum stillbirths, when a fetus dies before the onset of labor, and intrapartum stillbirths, when fetal death occurs during labor. The term fresh stillbirths denotes fetuses born dead but with intact skin, which are assumed to have died less than 12 hours before birth and serve as an observable surrogate measure for intrapartum stillbirths. Individuals younger than 28 days are in the neonatal period and younger than 1 year are infants. The neonatal period is divided into the early neonatal period, which refers to birth to less than 7 days old, and the remaining late neonatal period. The postneonatal period extends from 28 days to under 1 year. Child in this chapter refers to an individual from age one to under age five. (In some other usage, however, child refers to all individuals under age five).

We use standard demographic terminology to indicate death rates at different ages, that is, $_xq_y$ refers to the probability that an individual aged y will die before reaching age y + x and is usually estimated using cross-sectional observations of age-specific mortality rates for individual ages in the age range y to y + x. Using this terminology, the mortality rate for those under one year old (or the infant mortality rate) is $_1q_0$. We extend this terminology to define the complete under one mortality rate as $_{1.25}q_{-.25}$, the child mortality rate as $_4q_1$,[1] the under five mortality rate as $_5q_0$, the stillbirth rate as $_{.25}q_{-.25}$, the neonatal mortality rate as $_{.077}q_0$, and the complete under five mortality rate as $_{5.25}q_{-.25}$. This chapter uses age-specific mortality rates for 2001.

Numbers of Deaths and Death Rates

In 2001, approximately 10.6 million children born alive died before their fifth birthday (8.2 percent of births). Of these deaths, 3.9 million occurred during the neonatal period, that is, under the age of 28 days. Another 3.3 million stillborn children remained outside the vital registration systems of most countries (WHO 2005a). When stillbirths are included among deaths, about half of all deaths of children under five occur under the age of 28 days.

Table 6.1 provides estimates of the numbers of stillbirths in 2001, with numbers broken down by World Bank income categories. The stillbirth numbers in the table come from rates

Table 6.1 Population Totals and Numbers of Births, 2001
thousands

Region	Population (mid-2001)	Live births	Stillbirths	Total births
Low- and middle-income countries	5,221,572	118,505	3,228	121,733
High-income countries	928,660	11,371	45	11,416
World	6,150,233	129,876	3,274	133,150

Sources: Population is calculated from United Nations Population Division 2003, table 1. Live births are calculated from population totals and crude birth rates in World Bank 2003. Stillbirths are calculated from live births, using rates from WHO 2005a.

Table 6.2 Age Distribution of Deaths under Age 5, 2001
thousands

										Deaths under age 5	
	Stillbirths			**Neonatal deaths**			**Deaths ages 28 days to < 1 year**	**Infant deaths (0 ≤ age < 1 year)**	**Child deaths (1 ≤ age < 5 years)**	**After live birth (0 ≤ age < 5 years)**	**Including stillbirth**
	Antepartum	Intrapartum	Total	Early[a]	Late[a]	Total					
Region	a	b	c (a + b)	d	e	f (d + e)	g	h (f + g)	i	j (h + i)	k (j + c)
Low- and middle-income countries	2,152	1,077	3,228	2,889	965	3,854	3,745	7,599	2,935	10,530	13,758
High-income countries	40	5	45	32	9	41	18	59	13	73	119
World	2,192	1,082	3,274	2,921	974	3,896	3,762	7,658	2,948	10,602	13,876

Sources: Columns a, b, c, d, e, and f are calculated from rates provided by WHO 2005a, using live birth totals from table 6.1 of this chapter. Column j is from chapter 3 of this volume. Column h = (infant mortality rate/under-five mortality rate) × total number of deaths from column j. Column i = [(under five mortality rate − infant mortality rate)/under five mortality]; under five mortality rates are from the World Bank (2003, table 2.20). The World Bank under five mortality rates are very close to, but not identical with, those reported in this volume (chapter 2, table 2.3). The World Bank numbers are used because they are accompanied by a consistently generated set of infant mortality rates.
a. The early neonatal period extends from birth to under 7 days of age; the late neonatal period extends from 7 days to under 28 days.

estimated by the World Health Organization (WHO) (WHO 2005a) applied to the birth numbers reported in the table. The table shows that in 2001, the high-income countries (those with a gross national income per capita of more than US $9,076 in 2002) had 11.37 million live births and the low- and middle-income countries had 118.51 million live births.

Table 6.2 provides an age breakdown of deaths among children under five, again with a breakdown by World Bank income category. Early neonatal deaths account for 75 percent of all neonatal deaths. The eight-day period encompassing intrapartum stillbirths and early neonatal deaths accounts for almost 30 percent of the 13.9 million deaths occurring under the age of five. Thus, as shown in figure 6.1 for the low- and middle-income countries, roughly a quarter of the deaths under age five occur in each of the following categories: stillbirths, neonatal deaths, postneonatal infant deaths, and child deaths.

Three recent studies provide extensive literature reviews and model-based estimates of the number of stillbirths and neonatal deaths that extend the WHO estimates used here (WHO 2005a). Lawn, Shibuya, and Stein (2005, tables A–J)

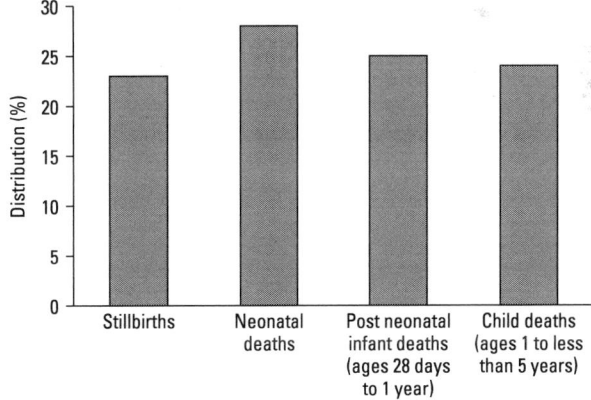

Source: Table 6.2.

Figure 6.1 Age Distribution of Deaths of Children under Five in Low- and Middle-Income Countries, 2001

focus on intrapartum stillbirths and intrapartum-related neonatal deaths. Stanton and others (forthcoming) provide estimates of the number of stillbirths for 190 countries and Hill (forthcoming) provides estimates for neonatal deaths.

Table 6.3 Estimated Death Rates under Age 5, by Country Income Level, 2001
Probability of dying in the x years following age y ($_xq_y$), expressed per thousand live births

Region	Stillbirth rate ($_{0.25}q_{-0.25}$)	Neonatal mortality rate ($_{.077}q_0$)	Under 1 mortality rate ($_1q_0$)	Complete under 1 mortality rate ($_{1.25}q_{-.25}$)	Child mortality rate ($_4q_1$)	Under 5 mortality rate ($_5q_0$)	Complete under 5 mortality rate ($_{5.25}q_{-.25}$)
	a	b	c	d	e	f	g
Low- and middle-income countries	27	33	64	89	25	89	113
High-income countries	4	4	5	9	1	6	10
World	25	30	58	82	23	82	104

Sources: Columns c and f are based on data from the World Bank (2003, table 2.20). Data for columns a, b, d, e, and g are provided by WHO (2005a).
Note: Column a = (total stillbirths)/(total births). Column b = (neonatal deaths)/(live births). Column c = (infant deaths)/(live births). Column d = (infant deaths + stillbirths)/(total births). Column e = (total deaths from ages one to four years)/(live births). Column f = (total deaths under age five)/(live births). Column g = (total deaths under age five including stillbirths)/(total births).

The midpoints of their fairly wide confidence intervals accord with the numbers we use.

Table 6.3 shows death rates, expressed per 1,000 live births, that correspond to the death totals in table 6.2. Column (c), for example, shows an under one or infant mortality rate ($_1q_0$) for low- and middle-income countries of 64 per 1,000. Column (d) shows the effect of including stillbirths to give the complete under one mortality rate ($_{1.25}q_{-.25}$), which is markedly higher at 89 per 1,000 live births. By including stillbirths and providing relatively fine-grained age breakdowns, table 6.3 provides a more comprehensive set of estimates of mortality rates under age five than has hitherto been available. The wide confidence interval that needs to be attached to the estimates (Stanton and others forthcoming) indicates both the need for caution when using these numbers and the importance of further research. Nevertheless, the estimates in table 6.3 are reasonable given currently available information.

Deaths by Cause

Estimates of the total number of deaths in different age groups provide a starting point for breaking those totals down into deaths by cause. This task inevitably involves some degree of arbitrariness because of problems with classifying multiple causes of death or underlying versus proximal causes. That said, available data from vital registration, sentinel surveillance, and verbal autopsy can provide reasonable approximations for most causes. Chapter 3 provides background on how this was done and generates the death by cause estimates used throughout this book.

We use the estimates from chapter 3 for deaths by cause in the newborn through age four age group and aggregate chapter 3 data on age groups over age five into a single category of

deaths for those age five and older. In their preparatory work for chapter 3, its authors estimated cause-specific breakdowns of deaths under age five both for infant deaths and for deaths from age one through age four, that is, deaths occurring at one year of age or older but under age five, and we have used their data in this chapter. Table 6.4 presents this information on deaths by cause aggregated, as previously indicated, into 35 groups of conditions rather than the 136 used in chapter 3.

The aggregate numbers for neonatal deaths and for stillbirths come from WHO (2005a) as reported in table 6.2 (see also WHO 2005b, pp. 170–71). Table 6.4 breaks down neonatal deaths into six causes: diarrheal diseases, tetanus, respiratory infections, low birthweight (essentially preterm birth), birth asphyxia and birth trauma, and congenital anomalies.[2] The estimates by cause were generated for WHO's Child Health Epidemiology Reference Group (CHERG) (see Bryce and others 2005 for a comprehensive presentation of data sources and methods of estimation). WHO (2005b, annex table 4) provides a summary of the numbers.

For the most part, the neonatal death categories used by CHERG align with the categories used by the GBD assessment in chapter 3; however, note the following exceptions:

- CHERG includes a pneumonia and sepsis category, which accounts for 26 percent of neonatal deaths globally and 27 percent in low- and middle-income countries. The GBD categories include respiratory infections (category I.B in our tables), which account for 1.945 million deaths worldwide in the age group 0–4. We allocate all the CHERG-estimated deaths from the combined category sepsis and pneumonia to the neonatal age group's respiratory infections category in order to remain as consistent as possible with the GBD framework in chapter 3. A number of studies have estimated the percentage of the broad category sepsis and pneumonia that is pneumonia with a wide range of findings (see, for example, Bhutta and others 2004 and Bhutta, Ali, and Wajid 2004). Even with blood cultures and chest x-rays, one cannot say for sure if a newborn has sepsis or pneumonia or both, and in any case, the treatment is the same, so one programmatic category is currently appropriate (Lawn, Cousens, and Wilczynska forthcoming).

- CHERG's percentage of neonatal deaths due to tetanus (7 percent) exceeds the GBD estimate for all infant deaths from tetanus but is very close to WHO and GAVI estimates for the year 2000 of 220,000. In keeping with this chapter's spirit of staying as close as possible to GBD estimates from chapter 3, we remain within the GBD envelope for the under-five age group and, as a first approximation, allocate all under one tetanus deaths to the neonatal period. However, while remaining within the under five GBD envelope for tetanus, we have modified, in this case only, the (unpublished) GBD age breakdown between ages 0–1 and 1–4 to allocate 90 percent of under five tetanus deaths to under age one (see table 6.4, note a). The difference between the CHERG and WHO with the GBD estimates for tetanus deaths is substantial and is clearly a priority area for further work.
- The GBD work uses the category low birthweight, which is an outcome of either preterm birth or intrauterine growth retardation. Preterm birth is a major cause of neonatal death. Again in the spirit of remaining within the GBD framework, we allocate preterm births to the low birthweight GBD category. This should not cause confusion as long as it is understood that, for neonatal deaths, low birthweight refers almost entirely to preterm birth. The quantitative importance of preterm birth suggests that this is another category that could be presented separately in the next GBD effort.

We are not aware of any effort to aggregate data on causes of stillbirths that parallels the CHERG effort for neonatal deaths, hence the GBD calculations in this chapter do not attempt to allocate stillbirths by cause. However, even though this chapter does not attempt a review of the CHERG type of the causes of stillbirth, we can advance a few tentative hypotheses. First, an important cause of stillbirth is intrapartum complications. A recent systematic analysis of intrapartum stillbirths gives estimates for 192 countries based on 73 study populations (52 countries, n = 46,779 [73 populations]) suggesting that 1.02 million intrapartum stillbirths (uncertainty 0.66–1.48 million) occur annually, accounting

for 26 percent of global stillbirths. Second, congenital anomalies constitute an important cause of antepartum stillbirth. Third, sexually transmitted diseases and other infections cause antepartum stillbirth, but systematic global estimates are currently limited.

Our categorization of neonatal deaths within the GBD framework has been deliberately conservative in that where interpretation was in any way uncertain, we assigned deaths to the not allocated category. We expect future efforts to be able to substantially reduce the not allocated component for both stillbirths and neonatal deaths, but doing so will require both improved empirical information and modification of the current GBD framework to include classifications important for deaths near the time of birth. Until such improvements are possible, table 6.4 provides a plausible extension of the GBD cause of death framework to include causes of infant and neonatal deaths.

THE BURDEN OF DISEASE RESULTING FROM EVENTS NEAR THE TIME OF BIRTH

This section explains the use of DALYs as a measure of the disease burden and identifies a number of problems associated with the traditional DALY formulation when dealing with events around the time of birth. It proposes a generalized formulation (which annex 6A describes more fully). The chapter then calculates the disease burden using two approaches to explore the sensitivity of GBD estimates to alternative formulations as follows:

- the current DALY formulation extended so as to value the DALY loss from a stillbirth the same as the DALY loss from a death at age 0,
- a generalized DALY formulation allowing the acquisition of life potential (ALP) to be gradual rather than instantaneous.

Defining and Redefining DALYs

The DALY family of indicators measures the disease burden from the age of onset of a condition by summing an indicator of YLL due to the condition and an indicator of disability-adjusted YLD resulting from the condition. While, in principle, the disability weights used in this adjustment could arise from any of the procedures typically used to construct quality-adjusted life years, obtaining disability weights for a large number of causes using any procedure other than the judgments of selected reference groups is currently impractical. Chapter 3 describes the methods currently used.

Table 6.4 Deaths by Age and Cause, 2001 *(thousands)*

	Low- and middle-income countries					
	Deaths under age 5					
	Stillbirth			Neonatal	Deaths aged 28 days to ≤ 1 year	Infant deaths (0 ≤ age < 1 year)
	Antepartum	Intrapartum	Total			
			(a + b)			
	a	b	c	d	e	f
Total deaths	2,152	1,077	3,228	3,854	3,745	7,599
I. Communicable, maternal, perinatal, and nutritional conditions				3,088		6,875
A. Infectious and parasitic diseases				284		2,884
1. Tuberculosis						16
2. Sexually transmitted diseases excluding HIV/AIDS						55
3. HIV/AIDS						202
4. Diarrheal diseases				116	1,105	1,221
5. Childhood-cluster diseases						381
a. Pertussis						96
b. Poliomyelitis						
c. Diphtheria						2
d. Measles[a]						115
e. Tetanus[b]				168		168
6. Meningitis						47
8. Malaria[c]						726
Other[d]						218
B. Respiratory infections[e]				1,002	533	1,535
C. Maternal conditions						
D. Perinatal conditions				1,802		2,384
1. Low birthweight[f]				1,079	136	1,215
2. Birth asphyxia and birth trauma[g]				723		723
3. Other perinatal conditions						446
E. Nutritional deficiencies						96
II. Noncommunicable diseases				308		599
A. Malignant neoplasms						11
C. Diabetes mellitus						2
E. Neuropsychiatric disorders						21
1. Unipolar depressive disorders						
2. Bipolar affective disorder						
3. Schizophrenia						
Other[h]						14
G. Cardiovascular diseases						56
3. Ischemic heart disease						4
4. Cerebrovascular disease						8
Other[i]						42
H. Respiratory diseases						43
I. Digestive diseases						73
M. Congenital anomalies				308	44	352
Other[j]						36
III. Injuries						124
A. Unintentional						121
1. Road traffic accidents						12
Other[k]						109
B. Intentional						5
1. Self-inflicted						
Other[l]						3
IV. Not allocated	2,152	1,077	3,228	458		

Sources: WHO 2005a for columns a–d, unreported estimates undertaken as part of the GBD study, reported in chapter 3 for columns f–g, and chapter 3 of this volume.

Note: The absence of an entry in columns a–d denotes either a value of less than 1,000 deaths or that no estimate was allocated to that entry. For columns f–k, a blank cell indicates that fewer than 1,000 deaths are attributable to the specific cause. Infant and child deaths in columns f and g are based on unreported estimates undertaken as part of the GBD study, reported in chapter 3, of the percentage of under-five deaths that were under age one. Because the sources used for neonatal deaths left a large number unallocated, it is not appropriate to calculate values of column e by subtracting column d from column f except where explicitly noted.

a. WHO 2005b and Bryce and others (2005) estimate that 395,000 deaths occur due to measles. Chapter 3 provides an estimate for measles deaths age zero to four of 763,000.

b. Lawn, Wilczynska, and Cousens (forthcoming) for the CHERG estimate (2005) that 7 percent (260,000) of the 3.854 million global neonatal deaths occur due to tetanus, similar to the WHO and GAVI estimates of 220,000 for the year 2000. Chapter 3 provides an estimate for tetanus deaths ages zero to four of only 187,000. The (unpublished) GBD files used here to allocate deaths under age five to over and under age one allocated 52 percent of tetanus deaths to under age one. The CHERG review (Lawn, Wilczynska, and Cousens forthcoming) suggests this to be a major underestimate, and the 52 percent figure has thus here been revised upward to 90 percent. Consistent with the objectives of this chapter, GBD numbers have been used wherever possible, and the CHERG and WHO estimates are accordingly revised downward by allocating all infant tetanus deaths to the neonatal period.

c. WHO 2005b and Bryce and others (2005) estimate that 853,000 deaths occur due to malaria. Chapter 3 provides an estimate for malaria deaths age zero to four of 1,208,000.

d. Hepatitis, tropical-cluster diseases, leprosy, dengue, Japanese encephalitis, trachoma, intestinal nematode infections, and other infectious diseases.

e. Deaths for respiratory infections in the neonatal age group are those estimated by Lawn, Cousens, and Wilczynska (forthcoming) for their category sepsis or pneumonia. This number was then subtracted from the GBD number of respiratory infections between age zero and one to derive the total in column e.

f. Low-birthweight deaths are those resulting from intrauterine growth retardation or preterm birth. Almost all low-birthweight deaths in the neonatal period result from preterm birth.

Table 6.4 Continued

Low- and middle-income countries				
Deaths under age 5				
Child deaths (1 ≤ age < 5 years)	After live birth	Including stillbirth	Deaths age 5+	Total
(h − f)	(f + g)	(h + c)		(i + j)
g	h	i	j	k
29,345	10,533	13,761	37,843	51,605
2,521	9,396	9,396	8,226	17,622
1,884	4,768	4,768	5,923	10,692
25	40	40	1,550	1,590
13	68	68	108	176
138	340	340	2,214	2,554
378	1,599	1,599	179	1,778
667	1,048	1,048	313	1,363
205	301	301		301
2	5	5	1	6
442	557	557	206	763
19	187	187	106	293
18	64	64	105	169
361	1,087	1,087	58	1,208
299	518	518	1,334	1,854
408	1,943	1,943	1,539	3,483
			507	507
106	2,490	2,490		2,490
76	1,291	1,291		1,291
5	728	728		728
25	471	471		471
99	194	194	257	451
236	835	835	25,202	26,037
26	37	37	4,921	4,957
1	3	3	755	758
23	43	43	605	701
			10	10
			21	21
30	43	43	627	670
26	82	82	13,279	13,362
2	6	6	5,696	5,702
4	12	12	4,598	4,611
22	64	64	2,985	3,049
21	63	63	3,063	3,127
42	115	115	1,487	1,602
69	421	421	56	477
34	71	71	983	1,053
178	302	302	4,415	4,717
170	289	289	2,926	3,216
38	49	49	1,020	1,070
146	240	240	1,903	2,146
8	13	13	1,488	1,501
			749	749
10	13	13	740	753
		3,228		3,228

g. Lawn, Wilczynska, and Cousens (forthcoming) for the CHERG estimate that 23 percent (887,000) of the 4 million global neonatal deaths occur due to birth asphyxia. Chapter 3 of this volume provides an estimate for birth asphyxia and birth trauma deaths ages zero to four of only 739,000 globally, of which 734,000 were estimated to occur under age one. Consistent with the objectives of this chapter, GBD numbers have been used wherever possible, and the CHERG and WHO estimates are accordingly revised downward by allocating all infant birth asphyxia deaths to the neonatal period. Better data in the future will allow for improved estimates.

h. Epilepsy, alcohol use disorders, Alzheimer's disease and other dementias, Parkinson's disease, multiple sclerosis, drug use disorders, post-traumatic stress disorder, obsessive-compulsive disorder, panic disorder, insomnia (primary), migraine, mental retardation attributable to lead exposure, and other neuropsychiatric disorders.

i. Rheumatic heart disease, hypertensive heart disease, inflammatory heart diseases, and other cardiovascular diseases.

j. Other neoplasms, endocrine disorders, sense organ diseases, genitourinary diseases, skin diseases, musculoskeletal diseases, and oral conditions.

k. Poisonings, falls, fires, drownings, and other unintentional injuries.

l. Violence, war, and other intentional injuries.

(Continues on the following page.)

Table 6.4 Continued

	High-income countries					
	Deaths under age 5					
	Stillbirth				Deaths aged 28 days to ≤ 1 year	Infant deaths (0 ≤ age < 1 year)
	Antepartum	Intrapartum	Total	Neonatal		
			(a + b)			
	a	b	c	d	e	f
Total deaths	40	5	45	41	18	59
I. Communicable, maternal, perinatal, and nutritional conditions				16		35
A. Infectious and parasitic diseases				16		2
1. Tuberculosis						
2. Sexually transmitted diseases excluding HIV/AIDS						
3. HIV/AIDS						
4. Diarrheal diseases						
5. Childhood-cluster diseases						
a. Pertussis						
b. Poliomyelitis						
c. Diphtheria						
d. Measles						
e. Tetanus						
6. Meningitis						
8. Malaria						
Other[a]						1
B. Respiratory infections[b]						1
C. Maternal conditions						
D. Perinatal conditions				16		32
1. Low birthweight[c]				10		10
2. Birth asphyxia and birth trauma[d]				6	5	11
3. Other perinatal conditions						12
E. Nutritional deficiencies						
II. Noncommunicable diseases				12		19
A. Malignant neoplasms						
C. Diabetes mellitus						
E. Neuropsychiatric disorders						1
1. Unipolar depressive disorders						
2. Bipolar affective disorder						
3. Schizophrenia						
Other[e]						1
G. Cardiovascular diseases						1
3. Ischemic heart disease						
4. Cerebrovascular disease						
Other[f]						1
H. Respiratory diseases						1
I. Digestive diseases						1
M. Congenital anomalies				12	4	16
Other[g]						1
III. Injuries						2
A. Unintentional						2
1. Road traffic accidents						
Other[h]						1
B. Intentional						1
1. Self-inflicted						
Other[i]						1
IV. Not allocated	40	5	45	13		

Sources: WHO 2005a for columns a–d, unreported estimates undertaken as part of the GBD study, reported in chapter 3 for columns f–g, and chapter 3 of this volume.

Note: The absence of an entry in columns a–d denotes either a value of less than 1,000 deaths or that no estimate was allocated to that entry. For columns f–k, a blank cell indicates that fewer than 1,000 deaths are attributable to the specific cause. Infant and child deaths in columns f and g are based on unreported estimates undertaken as part of the GBD study, reported in chapter 3, of the percentage of under five deaths that were under age one. Because the sources used for neonatal deaths left a large number unallocated, it is not appropriate to calculate values of column e by subtracting column d from column f except where explicitly noted.

a. Hepatitis, tropical-cluster diseases, leprosy, dengue, Japanese encephalitis, trachoma, intestinal nematode infections, and other infectious diseases.

b. This table does not attempt to partition by age the very small number of deaths from respiratory infections under age 5.

c. Low-birthweight deaths are those resulting from intrauterine growth retardation or preterm birth. Almost all low-birthweight deaths in the neonatal period result from preterm birth.

d. The World Health Report 2005 cites that 45 percent (19,000) of the 4 million global neonatal deaths occur due to pre-term birth. Chapter 3 of this volume provides an estimate for low birthweight deaths ages zero to four of only 10,000, of which 10,000 were estimated to occur under age one. Consistent with the objectives of this chapter, GBD numbers have been used wherever possible, and the World Health Report 2005 estimates are accordingly revised downward by allocating all low-birthweight deaths to the neonatal period. Better data in the future will allow for improved estimates.

Table 6.4 Continued

High-income countries				
Deaths under age 5				
Child deaths (1 ≤ age < 5 years)	After live birth	Including stillbirth	Deaths age 5+	Total
(h − f)	(f + g)	(h + c)		(i + j)
g	h	i	j	k
13	73	118	7,864	7,982
2	37	37	515	552
1	3	3	149	152
			16	16
			1	1
			22	22
			5	6
			1	2
			1	1
			1	1
	1	1	3	4
1	2	2	100	101
1	2	2	347	349
			1	1
	32	32		32
	10	39		10
	11	17		11
	12	12		12
			18	18
9	28	28	6,840	6,868
1	2	2	2,065	2,066
			202	202
1	2	2	376	378
			3	3
			2	2
2	2	2	371	373
1	2	2	3,037	3,039
			1,364	1,364
			781	781
1	2	2	892	894
	1	1	476	477
	1	1	334	335
2	18	18	12	30
1	2	2	338	340
5	7	7	464	471
4	6	6	315	321
1	2	2	119	121
3	4	4	196	200
1	1	1	149	151
			126	126
1	1	1	24	25
		45		45

e. Epilepsy, alcohol use disorders, Alzheimer's disease and other dementias, Parkinson's disease, multiple sclerosis, drug use disorders, post-traumatic stress disorder, obsessive-compulsive disorder, panic disorder, insomnia (primary), migraine, mental retardation attributable to lead exposure, and other neuropsychiatric disorders.

f. Rheumatic heart disease, hypertensive heart disease, inflammatory heart diseases, and other cardiovascular diseases.

g. Other neoplasms, endocrine disorders, sense organ diseases, genitourinary diseases, skin diseases, musculoskeletal diseases, and oral conditions.

h. Poisonings, falls, fires, drownings, and other unintentional injuries.

i. Violence, war, and other intentional injuries.

(Continues on the following page.)

Table 6.4 Continued

	World					
	Deaths under age 5					
	Stillbirth					Infant deaths (0 ≤ age < 1 year)
	Antepartum	Intrapartum	Total	Neonatal	Deaths aged 28 days to ≤ 1 year	
			(a + b)			
	a	b	c	d	e	f
Total deaths	2,192	1,082	3,274	3,896	3,762	7,658
I. **Communicable, maternal, perinatal, and nutritional conditions**				3,129		6,910
A. Infectious and parasitic diseases				300		2,886
1. Tuberculosis						16
2. Sexually transmitted diseases excluding HIV/AIDS						55
3. HIV/AIDS						202
4. Diarrheal diseases				116	1,105	1,222
5. Childhood-cluster diseases						381
a. Pertussis						96
b. Poliomyelitis						
c. Diphtheria						2
d. Measles[a]						115
e. Tetanus[b]				168		168
6. Meningitis						47
8. Malaria[c]						726
Other[d]						219
B. Respiratory infections[e]				1,013	523	1,536
C. Maternal conditions						
D. Perinatal conditions				1,832		2,416
1. Low birthweight[f]				1,098	136	1,225
2. Birth asphyxia and birth trauma[g]				734		734
3. Other perinatal conditions						457
E. Nutritional deficiencies						96
II. **Noncommunicable diseases**				321		618
A. Malignant neoplasms						11
C. Diabetes mellitus						2
E. Neuropsychiatric disorders						22
1. Unipolar depressive disorders						
2. Bipolar affective disorder						
3. Schizophrenia						
Other[h]						14
G. Cardiovascular diseases						58
3. Ischemic heart disease						4
4. Cerebrovascular disease						8
Other[i]						43
H. Respiratory diseases						43
I. Digestive diseases						73
M. Congenital anomalies				321	48	368
Other[j]						38
III. **Injuries**						126
A. Unintentional						121
1. Road traffic accidents						12
Other[k]						109
B. Intentional						6
1. Self-inflicted						
Other[l]						4
IV. **Not allocated**	2,192	1,082	3,274	446		

Sources: WHO 2005a for columns a–d, unreported estimates undertaken as part of the GBD study, reported in chapter 3 for columns f–g, and chapter 3 of this volume.

Note: The absence of an entry in columns a–d denotes either a value of less than 1,000 deaths or that no estimate was allocated to that entry. For columns f–k, a blank cell indicates that fewer than 1,000 deaths are attributable to the specific cause. Infant and child deaths in columns f and g are based on unreported estimates undertaken as part of the GBD study, reported in chapter 3, of the percentage of under five deaths that were under age one. Because the sources used for neonatal deaths left a large number unallocated, it is not appropriate to calculate values of column e by subtracting column d from column f except where explicitly noted.

a. WHO 2005b and Bryce and others (2005) estimate that 395,000 deaths occur due to measles. Chapter 3 provides an estimate for measles deaths age zero to four of 763,000.

b. Lawn, Wilczynska, and Cousens (forthcoming) for the CHERG estimate (2005) that 7 percent (260,000) of the 3.854 million global neonatal deaths occur due to tetanus, similar to the WHO and GAVI estimates of 220,000 for the year 2000. Chapter 3 provides an estimate for tetanus deaths ages zero to four of only 187,000. The (unpublished) GBD files used here to allocate deaths under age five to over and under age one allocated 52 percent of tetanus deaths to under age one. The CHERG review (Lawn, Wilczynska, and Cousens forthcoming) suggests this to be a major underestimate, and the 52 percent figure has thus here been revised upward to 90 percent. Consistent with the objectives of this chapter, GBD numbers have been used wherever possible, and the CHERG and WHO estimates are accordingly revised downward by allocating all infant tetanus deaths to the neonatal period.

c. WHO 2005b and Bryce and others (2005) estimate that 853,000 deaths occur due to malaria. Chapter 3 provides an estimate for malaria deaths age zero to four of 1,208,000.

d. Hepatitis, tropical-cluster diseases, leprosy, dengue, Japanese encephalitis, trachoma, intestinal nematode infections, and other infectious diseases.

e. Deaths for respiratory infections in the neonatal age group are those estimated by Lawn, Cousens, and Wilczynska (forthcoming) for their category sepsis or pneumonia. This number was then subtracted from the GBD number of respiratory infections between age zero and one to derive the total in column e.

Table 6.4 Continued

	Deaths under age 5			
World				
Child deaths (1 ≤ age < 5 years)	**After live birth**	**Including stillbirth**	**Deaths age 5+**	**Total**
(h − f)	(f + g)	(h + c)		(i + j)
g	**h**	**i**	**j**	**k**
2,948	**10,606**	**13,880**	**45,662**	**59,542**
2,523	**9,433**	**9,433**	**8,741**	**18,174**
1,886	4,771	4,771	6,072	10,843
25	40	40	1,566	1,606
13	68	68	109	177
138	340	340	2,236	2,576
378	1,600	1,600	184	1,784
668	1,049	1,049	315	1,364
205	301	301		301
			1	1
2	5	5	1	6
442	557	557	206	763
19	187	187	107	293
18	65	65	108	173
361	1,087	1,087	121	1,208
303	522	522	1,434	1,955
409	1,945	1,945	1,886	3,831
			508	508
107	2,522	2,522		2,523
76	1,301	1,301		1,301
5	739	739		739
25	482	482		482
99	194	194	274	469
245	**864**	**864**	**32,042**	**32,905**
27	38	38	6,986	7,024
1	3	3	958	961
24	46	46	1,034	1,079
			13	13
			1	1
			23	23
31	45	45	997	1,043
27	84	84	16,316	16,401
2	6	6	7,060	7,066
4	13	13	5,379	5,392
23	66	66	3,877	3,943
21	64	64	3,540	3,604
42	116	116	1,821	1,936
71	439	439	68	507
35	73	73	1,320	1,393
183	**310**	**310**	**4,879**	**5,188**
175	295	295	3,241	3,536
39	51	51	1,139	1,190
150	244	244	2,102	2,346
8	14	14	1,638	1,652
			875	875
10	14	14	763	777
		3,274		**3,274**

f. Low-birthweight deaths are those resulting from intrauterine growth retardation or preterm birth. Almost all low-birthweight deaths in the neonatal period result from preterm birth.

g. Lawn, Wilczynska, and Cousens (forthcoming) for the CHERG estimate that 23 percent (887,000) of the 4 million global neonatal deaths occur due to birth asphyxia. Chapter 3 of this volume provides an estimate for birth asphyxia and birth trauma deaths ages zero to four of only 739,000 globally, of which 734,000 were estimated to occur under age one. Consistent with the objectives of this chapter, GBD numbers have been used wherever possible, and the CHERG and WHO estimates are accordingly revised downward by allocating all infant birth asphyxia deaths to the neonatal period. Better data in the future will allow for improved estimates.

h. Epilepsy, alcohol use disorders, Alzheimer's disease and other dementias, Parkinson's disease, multiple sclerosis, drug use disorders, post-traumatic stress disorder, obsessive-compulsive disorder, panic disorder, insomnia (primary), migraine, mental retardation attributable to lead exposure, and other neuropsychiatric disorders.

i. Rheumatic heart disease, hypertensive heart disease, inflammatory heart diseases, and other cardiovascular diseases.

j. Other neoplasms, endocrine disorders, sense organ diseases, genitourinary diseases, skin diseases, musculoskeletal diseases, and oral conditions.

k. Poisonings, falls, fires, drownings, and other unintentional injuries.

l. Violence, war, and other intentional injuries.

DALYs generate a measure of the disease burden resulting from premature mortality by integrating a discounted, age-weighted, disability-adjusted stream of life years from the age of death (see equation 6A.2 in annex 6A). The formulation within the family of DALYs previously used to empirically assess the global burden of disease specifies a constant discount rate of 3 percent per year and an age-weighting function that gives low weight to early childhood and older ages and greater weight to middle ages. This volume reports global burden of disease estimates generated using uniform age weights. Chapter 5 provides an extensive exploration of the uncertainty and sensitivity inherent in disease burden assessment, including the results of differing assumptions about age weighting and discount rates.

To be clear about the particular form of DALY being used, the following terminology is employed throughout this volume. DALYs(r,K) are DALYs constructed using a discount rate of r percent per year and an amount of age weighting indexed by a parameter K. Two versions of the DALY are discussed at some length in chapter 5, both using a discount rate of 3 percent per year. DALYs(3,1) are DALYs generated with a discount rate of 3 percent per year and with full age weighting, that is, K = 1. DALYs(3,0) are DALYs generated with a discount rate of 3 percent per year and with no age weighting, that is, K = 0. This volume's results concerning the burden of disease (chapter 3) and of risk (chapter 4) are based on DALYs(3,0). Annex 6B contains tables summarizing alternative calculations of the global burden of disease, and table 6B.4 presents the chapter 3 GBD results based on DALYs(3,0), using this chapter's aggregation of causes, for age groups under five and over five as an aggregate.

This chapter extends the DALY family by modeling a concept of ALP. The intuition behind the ALP concept is that an infant (or fetus) only gradually acquires the full life potential reflected in a stream of life years beginning at birth, that is, ALP can be gradual. The ethical understanding of the concept is based on two judgments: (a) an individual life acquires value only as it acquires self-awareness, and (b) an individual life acquires additional value as it develops bonds with others. (See the discussion in Steinbock 1992, who argues that what we label as life potential is probably acquired some time in the second trimester of pregnancy. Her position is, implicitly, that whenever it occurs, ALP is instantaneous.) To some extent, the age-weighting function of the current DALY formulation attempts to capture these judgments, and in this chapter, gradual acquisition of ALP is modeled as an alternative to age weighting.[3] Mathematically, however, ALP

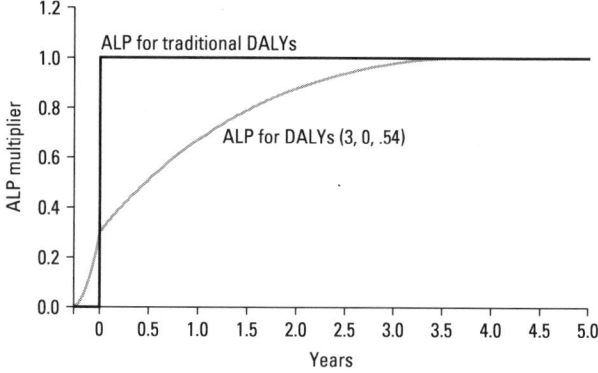

Source: Authors' calculations.

Figure 6.2 ALP, Traditional DALYs, and DALYs (3,0,.54)

and age weighting are independent and can be introduced simultaneously.

Our objective in this chapter is not to provide a detailed philosophical, economic, or medical rationale for gradual ALP, but to generate and apply a straightforward mechanism that allows for it. Annex 6A describes this mechanism, which essentially consists of multiplying the DALYs conventionally generated by a factor that is less than one for younger ages. This factor is zero for an age of −13 weeks (or −0.25 years), rises to a factor value of f^0 at birth, then rises to 1 at time T. Figure 6.2 graphs both the ALP function used later in this chapter and the special case of ALP that jumps from 0 to 1 at age 0 (instantaneous ALP). The ALP implicit in traditional DALYs is instantaneous.

Annex 6A introduces a parameter, A, that indicates the speed of ALP (see equations 6A.3 through 6A.5 for a precise definition of A). A is constructed so that for the fastest possible speed of ALP, namely, instantaneous ALP, A = 1. A is bounded below by 0. This chapter extends the notation DALYs(r,K) used elsewhere in the book in two ways. First, it explicitly indicates the level of A by extending the DALY nomenclature to DALYs(r,K,A). Thus using this nomenclature, DALYs(3,0) become DALYs(3,0,1), because the standard DALY is the special case with instantaneous ALP. Second, when stillbirths are included in the range of events to be measured in the global burden of disease, this is explicitly noted in the DALY nomenclature as DALYs$_{SB}$(r,K,A). Notation around YLL is similarly extended.

Explicit modeling of ALP allows not only the reflection of the ethical judgments just indicated, but also permits three instrumentally useful improvements to the current family of DALYs:

- The DALY loss from a death seconds before birth is, in the current formulation, 0; it jumps to more than 30 years at birth. The ALP formulation allows, but does not require, this discontinuity to be avoided. See column (a) of table 6.5 for values at different ages of the ALP function associated with traditional DALYs and columns (c), (d), and (e) for values of three ALP functions defined in annex 6A.
- The ALP formulation allows, but does not require, a positive DALY loss associated with stillbirths.
- The ratio of the DALY loss from a death at age 20, say, to that at birth is close to 1 for any reasonable set of parameter values in the current DALY formulation. Many people's

ethical judgments would give this ratio a value substantially greater than 1. The ALP formulation allows, but does not require, these judgments. Figure 6.3 shows how this ratio varies as a function of the age-weighting parameter (K) for values of r equal to 3 percent and 10 percent. The ratio rises only to 1.7 with full age weighting and an implausibly high discount rate of 10 percent.

Alternative Calculations of the Burden of Disease

As previously indicated, annex table 6B.4 (based on annex tables 6B.1 to 6B.3) presents the chapter 3 GBD estimates in terms of DALYs(3,0)—or DALYs(3,0,1)—for the under and over five age groups. The DALY(3,0) is the sum of the YLL(3,0,1) and YLD. Annex tables 6B.1, 6B.2, and 6B.3 report deaths by cause, YLL(3,0,1) by cause, and YLD by cause from chapter 3. The numbers in table 6B.4 are the sum of the corresponding numbers in tables 6B.2 and 6B.3.

We generate two alternative assessments of the global burden of disease. Both incorporate stillbirths and the second permits gradual ALP. The YLD numbers that we use come from annex table 6B.3. The YLL differ from YLL(3,0,1) for ages under age five, but are the same for over age five.

Our first alternative is probably the simplest way to incorporate stillbirths. It does so by having an instantaneous ALP function, as with traditional DALYs, but by having that function jump from 0 to 1 at age −13 weeks (−0.25 years) instead of at age 0. Stillbirths are then given the same DALY loss as a death at birth in generating YLL. Column (b) of table 6.5 shows values for this ALP function, which is uniformly 1. We label the YLL generated from this ALP function and a 3 percent discount rate the $YLL_{SB}(3,0,1)$. We label the DALYs based on this YLL as $DALYs_{SB}(3,0,1)$. Table 6.6 shows values of $YLL_{SB}(3,0,1)$ compared with YLL(3,1) and YLL(3,0) for different ages. Annex table 6B.5 shows values for $YLL_{SB}(3,0,1)$ and annex table 6B.6 shows the resulting burden of disease estimates in terms of $DALYs_{SB}(3,0,1)$.

Our second alternative burden of disease assessment is based on gradual ALP. Equation 6A.1 in annex 6A provides our general ALP function and the text describes the meaning of its four parameters. One of the parameters, f^0, is the value of the function at age 0. The intuitive interpretation of f^0 is that it is approximately the ratio of the YLL loss associated with a death at age 0 to that from a death at age 20. Another parameter is T, the age at which the function becomes 1. Annex 6A characterizes three alternative gradual ALPs: f_1, f_2, and f_3. Figure 6.4 shows YLL at different ages for these functions and for YLL(3,0) and YLL(3,1). Table 6.5 shows values for the functions at different ages in

Table 6.5 Values of Selected ALP Functions

(a) t (age)	(b) $f_D(t)^a$	(c) $f_{DSB}(t)^b$	(d) $f_1(t)$	(e) $f_2(t)^c$	(f) $f_3(t)$
−0.25	0.00	1.00	0.00	0.00	0.00
−0.08	0.00	1.00	0.12	0.16	0.30
0.00	1.00	1.00	0.25	0.30	0.50
0.02	1.00	1.00	0.25	0.31	0.52
0.08	1.00	1.00	0.26	0.34	0.59
0.25	1.00	1.00	0.29	0.41	0.74
0.30	1.00	1.00	0.30	0.43	0.78
0.50	1.00	1.00	0.34	0.51	0.88
1.00	1.00	1.00	0.41	0.67	0.98
2.00	1.00	1.00	0.55	0.87	1.00
3.00	1.00	1.00	0.66	0.97	1.00
5.00	1.00	1.00	0.83	1.00	1.00

Source: Authors' calculations.

a. $f_D(t)$ is the traditional DALY formulation that is, stillbirths are not incorporated, and ALP is instantaneous.

b. $f_{DSB}(t)$ is the traditional DALY formulation extended to give equal weight to stillbirths as to deaths at age 0, that is, it leads to $DALYs_{SB}(3,0,1)$.

c. $f_2(t)$ is the ALP function used to generate the $DALY_{SB}(3,0,.54)$ GBD estimates reported in table 6B.8. These are DALYs that incorporate stillbirth and gradual ALP.

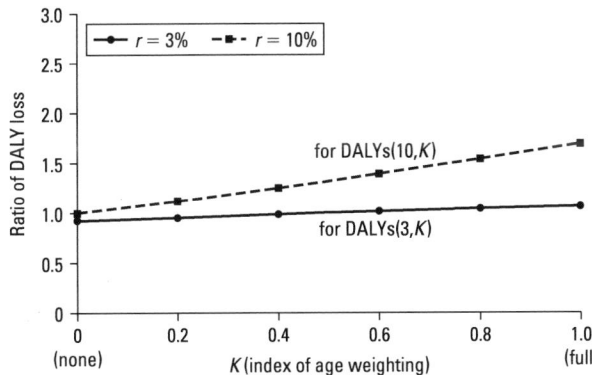

Source: Authors' calculations.

Figure 6.3 Ratio of DALYs Lost at Age 20 to Age 0 as a Function of Age Weighting

Table 6.6 Discounted YLL at Different Ages of Death for Several DALY Formulations

Age group	Representative age of death (years)	YLL(3,1)	YLL(3,0)	YLL$_{SB}$(3,0,1)	YLL$_{SB}$(3,0,.54)
Antepartum	−0.080	0	0	30.42	4.95
Intrapartum	−0.001	0	0	30.42	9.13
Neonatal	0.020	33.09	30.42	30.42	9.40
Infant	0.300	33.36	30.40	30.40	12.95
Postneonatal	0.500	33.56	30.39	30.39	15.42
Child	2.000	34.81	30.28	30.28	26.40

Source: Authors' calculations.

Note: YLL(3,1), YLL(3,0), and YLL$_{SB}$(3,0,1) assume instantaneous ALP (A = 1). YLL(3,1) assumes full age weighting (K = 1); the other three formulations assume uniform age weights (K = 0). YLL$_{SB}$(3,0,.54) assumes gradual acquisition of life potential (A = .54); table 6B.7 reports these YLL and 6B.8 reports the GBD based on their use.

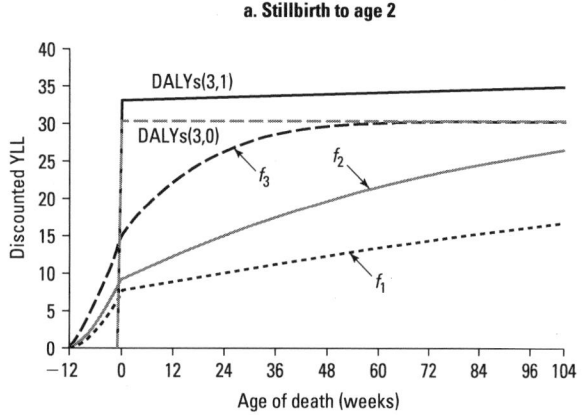

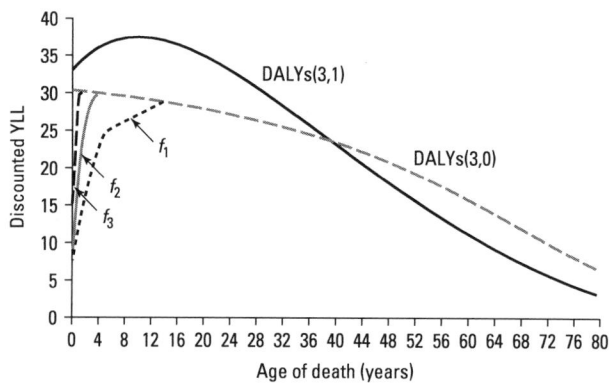

Source: Authors' calculations.

Figure 6.4 YLL for Deaths at Different Ages

columns (c), (d), and (e). We use f$_2$ (with A = .54) to construct the disease burden estimates reported in this chapter and label the resulting YLL and DALYs as YLL$_{SB}$(3,0,.54) and DALYs$_{SB}$(3,0,.54). Table 6.6 shows YLL$_{SB}$(3,0,.54), which are, as intended, markedly lower than YLL$_{SB}$(3,0,1) for very young ages. That is, YLL$_{SB}$(3,0,.54) gives less weight to deaths near the time of birth or to deaths immediately after birth than YLL$_{SB}$(3,0,1).

Only a limited number of empirical studies have attempted to assess directly the views of individuals concerning deaths at different ages. In an important early study, Crawford, Salter, and Jang (1989) relate grief from a death to the concept of reproductive potential in population biology. They conclude that for several diverse human groups the relationship shows grief to be closely related to prehistoric reproductive value. Cropper, Aydede, and Portney (1994) and Johannesson and Johansson (1997) survey members

of populations of high-income countries for trade-offs between deaths in middle and older ages. All three of these studies find that people judge deaths at older middle age as much less important than deaths at younger middle age, but provide no information concerning the trade-off for deaths near the time of birth.

An Institute of Medicine (1985) review of vaccine development priorities uses infant mortality equivalence in cost-effectiveness calculations. The committee members preparing the report collectively judged that the loss from a death at age 20 should be about two times that from an infant death, well above the numbers shown in figure 6.3 for any standard DALY. However, some preliminary trade-off studies by one of the authors of this chapter suggest a value closer to three or four times. What is clear is that no defensible estimate (or even range) is currently available, and hence the numbers we report should be viewed only as perhaps reasonable but only suggestive and as indicating the sensitivity of global burden of disease results from younger ages to better estimates of this parameter.

Annex tables 6B.7 and 6B.8 show $YLL_{SB}(3,0,.54)$ and $DALYs_{SB}(3,0,.54)$. While table 6B.7 only shows the total of DALYs for ages under five, the calculations underlying those totals reflect the age distribution of deaths under age five shown in table 6.4 and the $YLL_{SB}(3,0,.54)$ for deaths at different ages as shown in table 6.6.

Annex tables 6B.1, 6B.6, and 6B.8 provide three alternative assessments of the global burden of disease based on deaths by cause, on $DALYs(3,0)$, $DALYs_{SB}(3,0,1)$, and $DALYs_{SB}(3,0,.54)$. Table 6.4 provides estimates of deaths by cause that include stillbirths (table 6.4, column [k]). We thus have five alternative indicators of the importance of disease at different ages and from different causes. Table 6.7 provides a summary for low- and middle-income countries of the distribution of the disease burden at different ages as assessed by these different measures. $DALYs_{SB}(3,0,1)$ and $DALYs_{SB}(3,0,.54)$ both point to the significance of stillbirths relative to $DALYs(3,0)$, which exclude them altogether, but the gradual ALP approach of $DALYs_{SB}(3,0,.54)$ gives much less importance to stillbirths than $DALYs_{SB}(3,0,1)$ and substantially less importance to the under five burden than $DALYs(3,0)$.

Table 6.8 provides a similar summary of how the assessed burden across groups varies with the measure used. $DALYs_{SB}(3,0,.54)$ give more weight to Group II (noncommunicable diseases) and Group III (injuries) causes than do $DALYs(3,0)$, while $DALYs_{SB}(3,0,1)$ give less weight to these groups than $DALYs(3,0)$. For example, $DALYs_{SB}(3,0,.54)$ give about a 10 percent greater weight to cardiovascular disease than does the DALY (3,0), that is, 14.2 percent versus 12.9 percent.

Table 6.7 Disease Burden at Different Ages Using Different Measures, Low- and Middle-Income Countries, 2001

Age group	Percentage of deaths		Percentage of disease burden		
	Stillbirths excluded	Stillbirths included	DALYs(3,0)	DALYs$_{SB}$(3,0,1)	DALYs$_{SB}$(3,0,.54)
Total deaths or DALYs (millions)	48.4	51.6	1,387.4	1,485.6	1,260.6
Stillbirths	0%	6.3%	0%	6.6%	1.6%
Under age one	15.7	21.0			
Under age five	21.8	26.7	30.6	35.2	23.6
Over age five	78.2	73.3	69.4	64.8	76.4

Source: Authors' calculations.

Note: All three percentage of disease burden formulations assume a 3% discount rate and uniform age weights (that is, $K = 0$). DALYs(3,0) and DALYs$_{SB}$(3,0,1) assume instantaneous ALP ($A = 1$). For DALYs(3,0,.54), $A = .54$.

Table 6.8 Disease Burden from Selected Groups of Causes Using Different Measures, Low- and Middle-Income Countries, 2001

Cause	Percentage of deaths		Percentage of disease burden		
	Stillbirths excluded	Stillbirths included	DALYs(3,0)	DALYs$_{SB}$(3,0,1)	DALYs$_{SB}$(3,0,.54)
Total deaths or DALYs (millions)	48.4	51.6	1,387.4	1,485.6	1,260.6
Group I[a]	36.4%	40.4%	39.8%	43.8%	35.5%
Group II	53.8	50.5	48.9	45.7	52.4
(Of which cardiovascular diseases)	(27.6)	(25.9)	(12.9)	(12.0)	(14.2)
Group III	9.8	9.1	11.2	10.5	12.1

Source: Authors' calculations.

Note: All three percentage of disease burden formulations assume a 3% discount rate and uniform age weights (that is, $K = 0$). DALYs(3,0) and DALYs$_{SB}$(3,0,1) assume instantaneous ALP ($A = 1$). For DALYs(3,0,.54), $A = .54$.

a. The "not allocated" category (from Table 6.4) consists principally of Group I causes and is included with Group I here.

CONCLUSIONS

Previous assessments of the global burden of disease have not included stillbirths or sufficiently emphasized the important causes of neonatal death. This was understandable given the intended focus of these studies. In addition, the inclusion of stillbirths would have highlighted issues about how to weight deaths at different ages that would have been difficult to incorporate into the DALY metrics being used to assess the global burden of disease.

Data on the numbers of stillbirths and neonatal deaths have improved, and a recent major effort by CHERG now provides a much better picture than before of the causes of neonatal death. (Annex C describes the CHERG effort and compares its results with estimates that result from fitting the CHERG estimates into the overall death envelope of chapter 3.) This chapter proposes an approach that incorporates modeling ALP, which allows flexibility in assessing how to weight stillbirths and other early deaths in constructing aggregate measures of the disease burden. This chapter combines new information and new methods into a reassessment of the global burden of disease that is based closely on, but goes beyond, what is reported in chapter 3.

We draw the following conclusions from this exercise:

- The numbers of stillbirths and of neonatal deaths are large. This underscores the importance of implementing tools and policies for addressing them. A number of recent publications point to directions for policy (for example, Darmstadt and others 2005; Institute of Medicine 2003; Lawn and others 2006; Martines and others 2005; Stoll and Measham 2001; Tinker and others 2005; WHO 2005b; Zupan 2005).
- The inclusion of stillbirths within the standard GBD framework is now feasible, and future assessments of the global burden of disease could consider doing so.
- The GBD cause structure would need relatively minor modifications to incorporate deaths at early ages. Birth asphyxia and preterm births could be separate subcategories and sepsis and pneumonia could also be included as a separate category. Rather than reporting a single burden estimate for the under five age group, the more fine-grained age breakdown of table 6.4 could be used.
- The databases on numbers and causes of stillbirths and neonatal deaths require major investments so they can be improved. Undertaking a CHERG type of review of the existing literature to gain a better understanding of the causes of stillbirths is also a priority.

- The selection of a generally appropriate ALP function requires more data on preferences or trade-offs concerning deaths at different ages.

ANNEX 6A: FLEXIBLE FUNCTIONAL FORMS FOR THE ACQUISITION OF LIFE POTENTIAL

This annex provides a technical discussion of issues raised by incorporating late fetal deaths (stillbirths) into the global burden of disease, as measured within the disability-adjusted life year (DALY) framework. One approach is simply to take the DALY loss at birth and discount back to the time of the stillbirth, indicating that there are no life years to lose before birth, but that there are still all the postpartum life years. Essentially this is the standard DALY, but with an age-weighting function equal to 0 before birth. This is feasible, but has several potential drawbacks, in particular, any reasonable discount rate (for example, 3 percent) would thence count all late fetal losses almost the same as a loss at birth. This approach yields the $DALYs_{SB}(3,0,1)$ measure as described in the main text, and table 6B.6 presents global burden of disease estimates using $DALYs_{SB}(3,0,1)$ because these are the simplest extension of $DALYs(3,0)$.

However, as with traditional DALYs, $DALYs_{SB}(3,0,1)$ assume instantaneous acquisition of life potential (ALP), as illustrated in figure 6.2 and discussed in the main text. Whether or not one wishes to include stillbirths in the global burden of disease, this discontinuity (at some given age) is troublesome. The purpose of this annex is to provide a flexible, yet tractable, explicit function that allows for gradual ALP.

One natural approach is to weight the YLL from outside the integral instead of from the inside (as with age weighting), that is, to create a multiplier function (the ALP function), which takes on values between 0 and 1 as a function of age, and use it to ratchet down the YLL function, potentially starting before birth. For convenience and with some regard to the known physiological underpinnings, we take this starting point in time to be the beginning of the third trimester of pregnancy. Roughly speaking, the rate of natural fetal loss becomes noticeable after the beginning of some level of consciousness during the second half of the second trimester. One could force this function to equal 1 at birth, recovering the standard DALYs from that point onward, and this will be a special case of our formulation. However, we have no definitive reason to think that ALP is necessarily complete at birth. Indeed, quite a bit of evidence suggests that in many (if not all) societies worldwide, infants are not given full status, for instance, they are not always named immediately. Thus we wish to allow for continued gradual acquisition after birth and up to some time T that signifies full standing or full ALP. Likewise, starting the acquisition only at birth but proceeding gradually afterward is perfectly possible.

Turning to the specifics, denote the ALP multiplier function by f(t), where t is measured in years and ranges from -0.25 (that is, 13 weeks before birth, the beginning of the third trimester) to T. The function is meaningfully defined for any finite value of T, though it is natural to assume that full life potential is achieved by puberty at the latest. Thus $f(-0.25) = 0$ and $f(T) = 1$. We let $f^0 = f(0)$ be the value at 0. Of course, starting times other than -0.25 are perfectly legitimate as well, but -0.25 is the natural choice given the standard definitions of stillbirth and the gathering and reporting of data using that definition.

We need a functional form that smoothly begins at 0 and rises to f^0, which is at least weakly convex (following the intuition that life potential is acquired increasingly rapidly as birth is approached), and whose curvature is parametrizable. The natural choice is x^γ with $\gamma \geq 1$. This has canonical endpoints of 0 and 1, where x^γ takes on the values 0 and 1, respectively, for any γ, so that as we change the curvature (or skewness), the endpoints remain fixed. Fitting this to our specific domain, we get $x = 4t + 1$ for $-0.25 \leq t < 0$. Finally, if we wish the skewness parameter to lie between 0 and 1 as well (for clarity), we can define g so that $g = 1/(1 - g)$ for $0 \leq g < 1$. This yields $f_-(t) = f^0(4t + 1)^{1/(1-g)}$ for $-0.25 \leq t < 0$. Thus $g = 0$ produces a straight line (zero curvature), while $g = 1$ (defined by fiat) is infinitely skewed: 0 until birth and then jumping to f^0.

For $t \geq 0$, we consider the symmetric version of the same polynomial, that is, $1 - (1 - x)^\beta$. Again we fit this to our domain, namely, from $t = 0$ to $t = T$, and define b so that $b = 1/(1 - b)$ for the skewness. This yields $f_+(t) = 1 - (1 - f^0)[(T - t)/T]^{1/(1-b)}$ for $0 \leq t \leq T$. We check that indeed $f_+(0) = f^0$ and $f_+(T) = 1$ according to this formula for any $0 \leq \beta \leq 1$. If $T = 1$, the formula simplifies to $f_+(t) = 1 - (1 - f^0)(1 - t)^{1/(1-b)}$. This leaves four parameters: f^0, T, g, and b. We can additionally impose $g = b$ if we wish, but this is unnecessary.

Summarizing, the function we use for ALP is

$$f(t) = \begin{cases} f_-(t) = f^0(4t + 1)^{1/(1-g)} \\ \quad (\text{for} \quad -0.25 \leq t < 0) \\ f_+(t) = 1 - (1 - f^0)\,[(T - t)/T]^{1/(1-b)} \\ \quad (\text{for} \quad 0 \leq t \leq T). \end{cases} \tag{6A.1}$$

If $f_D(t)$ is the standard DALY formulation (whether or not age weighting or discounting is used), then $g = b = 1$

(that is, discontinuous jumps around birth from 0 to 1) and $f_D^0 = 1$, so that technically at age 0 the value is already 1 (so the discontinuity is on the left side of age 0 only). Given these parameters, T is immaterial, because the function achieves its maximum immediately. However, the fact that we can replicate the standard DALY means that the gradual acquisition function does indeed generalize it.

Combining these equations with the standard definition of DALYs, the total loss L(a) for a death at age $a \geq -0.25$ is

$$L(a) = f(a) \int_a^\infty Cxe^{-\beta x}e^{-r(x-a)}s_a(x)\,dx, \tag{6A.2}$$

where β is the age-weighting parameter (typically 0.04) if age weighting is used, r is the discount rate (typically 0.03), $s_a(x)$ is the survival probability for reaching age $x \geq a$ conditional on having reached age a, and C is the normalization parameter for the age weights ($C = 0.16243$, see the discussion in chapter 5).

The normalization parameter C in equation (6A.2) was chosen so that the total global burden of disease would be the same with and without age weighting. The index of age weighting referred to in the main text, K, is generated by having a weighted average—with weights of K and $(1 - K)$, where $0 \leq K \leq 1$—of loss functions L(a) that result from equation (6A.2) with the indicated values of β and C and a loss function assuming uniform age weights. That this is at least approximately the case is apparent from figure 6.4b, where the two functions cross at about age 40. Clearly this will not be true when any of the acquisition functions are used, because they reduce the YLL burden at younger ages with no corresponding increase elsewhere, leading to a reduced total burden as measured by absolute DALY levels.

Note, however, that the total burden is no longer the same even for DALYs(3,0) and DALYs(3,1), because the specific value of C was calibrated to 1990 morbidity and mortality statistics. One can readily imagine more neutral (and invariant) normalizations, such as requiring a constant integral over age of death for each of these YLL functions, or perhaps weighting this integral using an idealized survival table. Any variant along these lines would raise the total level of DALYs(3,0,.54) relative to both DALYs(3,0) and DALYs(3,1). Of course, we are for the most part interested only in the relative burden across ages or disease categories, so the absolute totals are of secondary importance.

Finally, to somewhat simplify the number of parameters in the ALP function, we introduce a notion of speed of acquisition, A. Recall that f^0 can be anywhere between 0 and 1, regardless of whether the function f(t) takes on positive values before birth. If $f^0 = 1$ (as in the original DALY), then f = 1 thereafter and the speed A is in some sense as large as possible. To generalize this idea, we look at the total area between the ALP function f(t) and the constant function 1.

Formally, this area is given by the integral of $1 - f(t)$, evaluated from t^0 to T, where t^0 is the first t such that $f(t) > 0$. It is thus typically either -0.25 or 0, depending on whether we are including stillbirths. Call this integral I:

$$I = \int_{t^0}^{T}[1 - f(t)]dt, \qquad (6A.3)$$

Substituting the second part of equation (6A.1), we can evaluate this integral as

$$I = T(1 - f^0)(1 - t^0/T)(1 - b)/(2 - b). \qquad (6A.4)$$

Normalizing so that the speed A lies between 0 and 1 (and higher values denote faster acquisition), we define

$$A = 1/(1 + I). \qquad (6A.5)$$

For example, for $b = 0.7$ (a typical value) and $t^0 = 0$, we obtain a simple formula for the speed parameter A, encapsulating the acquisition function in a single number: $A = 1/[1 + 0.23T(1 - f^0)]$. There is still a trade-off between T and f^0, that is, the relationship between the underlying parameters and A is not one-to-one. A single value for A could have arisen from multiple combinations parameter values, but it still serves as a useful summary statistic. Figure 6A.1 graphs (as a function of T, fixing $b = 0.7$ and $t^0 = 0$) the value of f^0 that yields various specified acquisition speeds A. The analogous figure 6.3 shows less variability in this ratio.

We evaluate three specifications (parameter choices) for the acquisition function. These are, in order of value at birth: f_1, given by ($f_1^0 = 0.25$, $T_1 = 14$, $g_1 = 0.5$, $b_1 = 0.7$); f_2, given by ($f_2^0 = 0.3$, $T_2 = 5$, $g_2 = 0.4$, $b_2 = 0.7$); and f_3, given by ($f_3^0 = 0.5$, $T_3 = 2$, $g_3 = 0.3$, $b_3 = 0.8$). The respective values for A (using $t^0 = -0.25$) are 0.29, 0.54, and 0.84. These three acquisition functions were graphed in figure 6.4. Representative values for specific ages were listed in table 6.5, along with the corresponding values for $f_D(t)$, the traditional formulation for DALYs. Figure 6A.2 shows how the ratio of years of life lost at age 20 to age 0 for these three functions varies with A. We view f_2 (with $T = 5$) as a reasonable

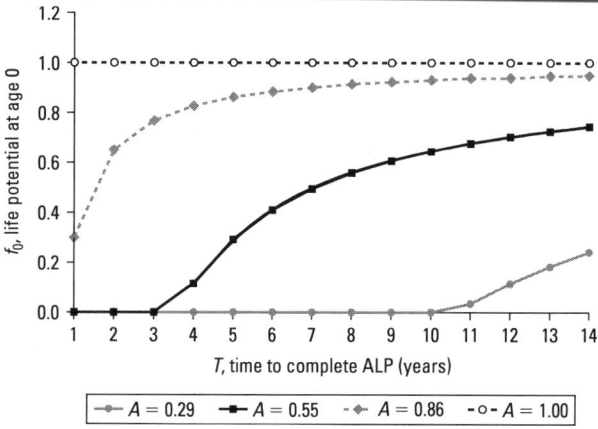

Source: Authors' calculations.
Note: A is rate of ALP.

Figure 6A.1 Relationship between Time to Complete ALP and Life Potential at Age 0 for Several Values of A

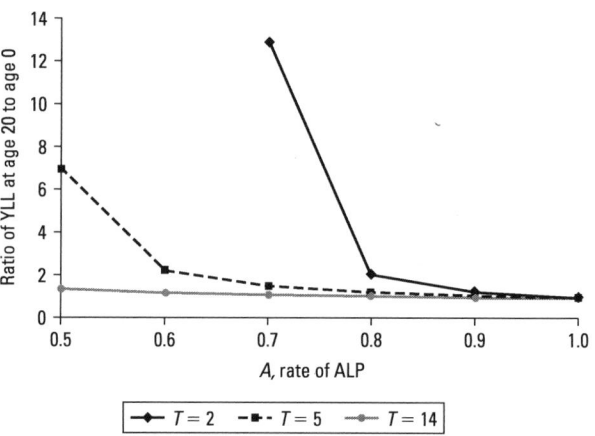

Source: Authors' calculations.
Note: A is rate of ALP. T is the time to complete acquisition of life potential.

Figure 6A.2 Ratio of DALYs Lost at Age 20 to Age 0 as a Function of A

intermediate choice and, with a 3 percent discount rate, have used f_2 to generate what we define as DALYs(3,0,.54). Complete burden of disease calculations are reported using DALYs(3,0,.54) in table 6B.8.

Table 6B.1 Deaths (Excluding Stillbirths) from Selected Causes, by Age, 2001 (thousands)

	Low- and middle-income countries			High-income countries			World		
	Deaths			**Deaths**			**Deaths**		
Cause	**0–4**	**5+**	**Total**	**0–4**	**5+**	**Total**	**0–4**	**5+**	**Total**
Total deaths	**10,533**	**37,843**	**48,377**	**73**	**7,819**	**7,891**	**10,606**	**45,662**	**56,268**
I. Communicable, maternal, perinatal, and nutritional conditions	**9,396**	**8,226**	**17,622**	**37**	**515**	**552**	**9,433**	**8,741**	**18,174**
A. Infectious and parasitic diseases	4,768	5,923	10,692	3	149	152	4,771	6,072	10,843
1. Tuberculosis	40	1,550	1,590		16	16	40	1,566	1,606
2. Sexually transmitted diseases excluding HIV/AIDS	68	108	176		1	1	68	109	177
3. HIV/AIDS	340	2,214	2,554		22	22	340	2,236	2,576
4. Diarrheal diseases	1,599	179	1,778		5	6	1,600	184	1,784
5. Childhood-cluster diseases	1,048	313	1,363		1	2	1,049	315	1,364
a. Pertussis	301		301				301		301
b. Poliomyelitis					1	1		1	1
c. Diphtheria	5	1	6				5	1	6
d. Measles	557	206	763		1	1	557	206	763
e. Tetanus	187	106	293				187	107	293
6. Meningitis	64	105	169	1	3	4	65	108	173
8. Malaria	1,087	58	1,208				1,087	121	1,208
Other I.A. (7, 9–15)[a]	518		1,854	2	100	101	522	1,434	1,955
B. Respiratory infections	1,943	1,539	3,483	2	347	349	1,945	1,886	3,831
C. Maternal conditions		507	507		1	1		508	508
D. Perinatal conditions	2,490		2,490	32		32	2,522		2,523
1. Low birthweight	1,291		1,291	10		10	1,301		1,301
2. Birth asphyxia and birth trauma	728		728	11		11	739		739
3. Other perinatal conditions	471		471	12		12	482		482
E. Nutritional deficiencies	194	257	451		18	18	194	274	469
II. Noncommunicable diseases	**835**	**25,202**	**26,037**	**28**	**6,840**	**6,868**	**864**	**32,042**	**32,905**
A. Malignant neoplasms	37	4,921	4,957	2	2,065	2,066	38	6,986	7,024
C. Diabetes mellitus	3	755	758		202	202	3	958	961
E. Neuropsychiatric disorders	43	605	701	2	376	378	46	1,034	1,079
1. Unipolar depressive disorders		10	10		3	3		13	13
2. Bipolar affective disorder								1	1
3. Schizophrenia		21	21		2	2		23	23
Other II.E. (4–16)[b]		670	670	2	371	373	45	997	1,043
G. Cardiovascular diseases	82	13,279	13,362	2	3,037	3,039	84	16,316	16,401
3. Ischemic heart disease	6	5,696	5,702		1,364	1,364	6	7,060	7,066
4. Cerebrovascular disease	12	4,598	4,611		781	781	13	5,379	5,392
Other II.G. (1, 2, 5, 6)[c]	64		3,049	2	892	894	66	3,877	3,943
H. Respiratory diseases	63	3,063	3,127	1	476	477	64	3,540	3,604
I. Digestive diseases	115	1,487	1,602	1	334	335	116	1,821	1,936
M. Congenital anomalies	421	56	477	18	12	30	439	68	507
Other II. (B, D, F, J, K, L, N)[d]	71		1,053	2	338	340	73	1,320	1,393
III. Injuries	**302**	**4,415**	**4,717**	**7**	**464**	**471**	**310**	**4,879**	**5,188**
A. Unintentional	289	2,926	3,216	6	315	321	295	3,241	3,536
1. Road traffic accidents	49	1,020	1,070	2	119	121	51	1,139	1,190
Other III.A. (2–6)[e]	240		2,146	4	196	200	244	2,102	2,346
B. Intentional	13	1,488	1,501	1	149	151	14	1,638	1,652
1. Self-inflicted		749	749		126	126		875	875
Other III.B. (2–4)[f]	13		753	1	24	25	14	763	777

Source: Chapter 3 of this volume.

Note: A blank cell indicates that fewer than 1,000 deaths are attributable to the specific cause.

a. Hepatitis, tropical-cluster diseases, leprosy, dengue, Japanese encephalitis, trachoma, intestinal nematode infections, and other infectious diseases.

b. Epilepsy, alcohol use disorders, Alzheimer's and other dementias, Parkinson's disease, multiple sclerosis, drug use disorders, post-traumatic stress disorder, obsessive-compulsive disorder, panic disorder, insomnia (primary), migraine, mental retardation attributable to lead exposure, and other neuropsychiatric disorders.

c. Rheumatic heart disease, hypertensive heart disease, inflammatory heart diseases, and other cardiovascular diseases.

d. Other neoplasms, endocrine disorders, sense organ diseases, genitourinary diseases, skin diseases, musculoskeletal diseases, and oral conditions.

e. Poisonings, falls, fires, drownings, and other unintentional injuries.

f. Violence, war, and other intentional injuries.

Table 6B.2 YLL(3,0) from Selected Causes, by Age, 2001 (thousands)

Cause	Low- and middle-income countries YLL 0–4	Low- and middle-income countries YLL 5+	Low- and middle-income countries YLL Total	High-income countries YLL 0–4	High-income countries YLL 5+	High-income countries YLL Total	World YLL 0–4	World YLL 5+	World YLL Total
Total YLL	**319,558**	**590,267**	**909,825**	**2,209**	**75,650**	**77,859**	**321,767**	**665,917**	**987,684**
I. Communicable, maternal, perinatal, and nutritional conditions	**285,058**	**169,531**	**454,589**	**1,133**	**4,258**	**5,391**	**286,191**	**173,789**	**459,980**
A. Infectious and parasitic diseases	144,555	129,584	274,138	96	1,878	1,975	144,651	131,462	276,113
1. Tuberculosis	1,215	30,528	31,743	1	171	172	1,216	30,699	31,915
2. Sexually transmitted diseases excluding HIV/AIDS	2,067	2,079	4,146	1	6	7	2,068	2,085	4,153
3. HIV/AIDS	10,299	54,537	64,836	2	491	493	10,301	55,027	65,328
4. Diarrheal diseases	48,534	2,350	50,884	13	40	53	48,547	2,390	50,937
5. Childhood-cluster diseases	31,751	8,756	40,507	4	30	34	31,755	8,786	40,540
a. Pertussis	9,113		9,113	1		1	9,114		9,114
b. Poliomyelitis	9	1	10		6	6	9	7	16
c. Diphtheria	137	27	164				137	27	164
d. Measles	16,840	6,057	22,897	2	19	21	16,843	6,076	22,918
e. Tetanus	5,652	2,671	8,323	1	5	5	5,653	2,675	8,328
6. Meningitis	1,952	2,391	4,343	23	59	82	1,975	2,450	4,425
8. Malaria	32,981	2,481	35,462	2	2	4	32,982	2,483	35,466
Other I.A. (7, 9–15)[a]	15,705	26,514	42,219	51	1,079	1,130	15,808	36,570	52,378
B. Respiratory infections	58,979	21,810	80,789	52	2,227	2,279	59,031	24,037	83,068
C. Maternal conditions		13,363	13,363		27	27		13,390	13,390
D. Perinatal conditions	75,642		75,643	981	4	984	76,623	4	76,627
1. Low birthweight	39,228		39,228	291		291	39,520		39,520
2. Birth asphyxia and birth trauma	22,118		22,118	336	1	338	22,454	2	22,455
3. Other perinatal conditions	14,296		14,297	353	2	355	14,650	2	14,652
E. Nutritional deficiencies	5,882	4,773	10,656	4	122	126	5,887	4,895	10,782
II. Noncommunicable diseases	**25,345**	**322,376**	**347,721**	**857**	**63,397**	**64,255**	**26,203**	**385,773**	**411,976**
A. Malignant neoplasms	1,110	71,503	72,613	50	23,265	23,315	1,160	94,768	95,928
C. Diabetes mellitus	87	10,054	10,141	1	1,942	1,943	87	11,997	12,084
E. Neuropsychiatric disorders	1,317	10,310	11,626	63	3,259	3,322	1,380	13,569	14,949
1. Unipolar depressive disorders		205	205		21	21	1	226	227
2. Bipolar affective disorder		5	5		4	4		9	9
3. Schizophrenia	1	373	374		24	24	1	397	398
Other II.E. (4–16)[b]	1,314	9,727	11,041	63	3,210	3,273	1,377	12,937	14,314
G. Cardiovascular diseases	2,493	155,750	158,243	63	24,166	24,229	2,557	179,915	182,472
3. Ischemic heart disease	177	67,751	67,928	2	11,483	11,485	179	79,234	79,412
4. Cerebrovascular disease	371	51,170	51,541	11	5,886	5,896	382	57,056	57,438
Other II.G. (1, 2, 5, 6)[c]	1,946	36,828	38,774	50	6,797	6,848	1,996	43,626	45,622
H. Respiratory diseases	1,925	34,570	36,495	30	3,914	3,945	1,955	38,484	40,439
I. Digestive diseases	3,482	23,888	27,370	35	3,680	3,715	3,516	27,568	31,084
M. Congenital anomalies	12,785	1,480	14,265	543	229	771	13,328	1,709	15,037
Other II. (B, D, F, J, K, L, N)[d]	2,147	14,821	16,967	72	2,943	3,015	2,219	17,764	19,983
III. Injuries	**9,155**	**98,361**	**107,516**	**218**	**7,995**	**8,213**	**9,373**	**106,356**	**115,729**
A. Unintentional	8,757	64,384	73,141	186	5,003	5,189	8,943	69,387	78,330
1. Road traffic accidents	1,491	23,331	24,822	52	2,496	2,548	1,543	25,827	27,370
Other III.A. (2–6)[e]	7,266	41,053	48,320	134	2,507	2,640	7,400	43,560	50,960
B. Intentional	398	33,977	34,374	33	2,992	3,024	430	36,969	37,399
1. Self-inflicted	4	16,435	16,439		2,432	2,433	4	18,868	18,871
Other III.B. (2–4)[f]	394	17,542	17,936	32	559	592	426	18,101	18,527

Source: Chapter 3 of this volume.

Note: A blank cell indicates that fewer than 1,000 deaths are attributable to the specific cause.

a. Hepatitis, tropical-cluster diseases, leprosy, dengue, Japanese encephalitis, trachoma, intestinal nematode infections, and other infectious diseases.

b. Epilepsy, alcohol use disorders, Alzheimer's and other dementias, Parkinson's disease, multiple sclerosis, drug use disorders, post-traumatic stress disorder, obsessive-compulsive disorder, panic disorder, insomnia (primary), migraine, mental retardation attributable to lead exposure, and other neuropsychiatric disorders.

c. Rheumatic heart disease, hypertensive heart disease, inflammatory heart diseases, and other cardiovascular diseases.

d. Other neoplasms, endocrine disorders, sense organ diseases, genitourinary diseases, skin diseases, musculoskeletal diseases, and oral conditions.

e. Poisonings, falls, fires, drownings, and other unintentional injuries.

f. Violence, war, and other intentional injuries.

Table 6B.3 YLD from Selected Causes, by Age, 2001 (thousands)

Cause	Low- and middle-income countries YLD 0–4	5+	Total	High-income countries YLD 0–4	5+	Total	World YLD 0–4	5+	Total
Total YLD	**104,557**	**372,465**	**477,022**	**4,592**	**66,717**	**71,309**	**109,148**	**439,182**	**548,330**
I. Communicable, maternal, perinatal,	**45,068**	**52,890**	**97,958**	**1,041**	**2,127**	**3,169**	**46,109**	**55,018**	**101,127**
and nutritional conditions									
A. Infectious and parasitic diseases	15,016	31,552	46,568	467	934	1,401	15,483	32,486	47,969
1. Tuberculosis	170	3,964	4,134	1	46	47	170	47,799	47,969
2. Sexually transmitted diseases excluding HIV/AIDS	1,127	4,065	5,192	12	126	138	1,139	4,190	5,329
3. HIV/AIDS	173	5,802	5,975	1	171	173	175	5,974	6,148
4. Diarrheal diseases	4,814	3,022	7,836	222	170	392	5,036	3,192	8,228
5. Childhood-cluster diseases	2,359	266	2,625	138	4	141	2,496	269	2,766
a. Pertussis	2,192	98	2,290	137	1	138	2,328	100	2,428
b. Poliomyelitis	21	105	126		2	2	21	107	128
c. Diphtheria									
d. Measles	136	58	194	1	1	2	137	58	195
e. Tetanus	9	4	14				9	4	14
6. Meningitis	829	302	1,131	27	22	49	856	324	1,180
8. Malaria	3,158	1,341	4,499		5	5	3,158	1,346	4,504
Other I.A. (7, 9–15)[a]	2,386	12,791	15,177	66	391	457	2,452	13,182	15,634
B. Respiratory infections	3,855	2,095	5,949	46	150	197	3,901	2,245	6,146
C. Maternal conditions					364	364		13,385	13,385
D. Perinatal conditions	13,523		13,523	422		422	13,945		13,945
1. Low birthweight	3,377		3,377	175		175	3,552		3,552
2. Birth asphyxia and birth trauma	9,352		9,352	191		191	9,543		9,543
3. Other perinatal conditions	794		794	56		56	850		850
E. Nutritional deficiencies	12,674	6,223	18,897	107	679	785	12,781	6,902	19,683
II. Noncommunicable diseases	**53,465**	**277,249**	**330,714**	**3,371**	**61,737**	**65,108**	**56,836**	**338,987**	**395,823**
A. Malignant neoplasms	37	2,072	2,109	4	2,566	2,570	41	4,639	4,680
C. Diabetes mellitus	15	5,647	5,662	1	2,249	2,249	16	7,896	7,912
E. Neuropsychiatric disorders	18,854	106,595	125,449	913	26,996	27,909	19,767	133,592	153,358
1. Unipolar depressive disorders		43,222	43,222		8,387	8,387		51,608	51,608
2. Bipolar affective disorder		8,673	8,673		1,052	1,052		9,725	9,725
3. Schizophrenia		10,153	10,153		1,091	1,091		11,244	11,244
Other II.E. (4–16)[b]	18,854	44,548	63,402	913	16,466	17,379	19,767	61,015	80,781
G. Cardiovascular diseases	540	20,091	20,631	15	5,623	5,638	554	25,714	26,268
3. Ischemic heart disease	1	3,923	3,923		908	908	1	4,831	4,831
4. Cerebrovascular disease		11,102	11,102		3,460	3,460		14,562	14,562
Other II.G. (1, 2, 5, 6)[c]	539	5,066	5,605	15	1,255	1,270	554	6,321	6,875
H. Respiratory diseases	4,040	17,546	21,586	539	5,319	5,857	4,578	22,865	27,443
I. Digestive diseases	10,972	14,074	25,045	440	2,382	2,821	11,412	16,455	27,867
M. Congenital anomalies	9,293		9,293	647		647	9,940		9,940
Other II. (B, D, F, J, K, L, N)[d]	9,375	111,564	120,939	813	16,603	17,416	10,528	127,826	138,354
III. Injuries	**6,024**	**42,326**	**48,349**	**180**	**2,852**	**3,032**	**6,203**	**45,178**	**51,381**
A. Unintentional	5,864	34,242	40,106	178	2,510	2,688	6,042	36,752	42,794
1. Road traffic accidents	783	6,413	7,196	16	481	497	798	6,894	7,693
Other III.A. (2–6)[e]	5,082	27,829	32,911	162	2,029	2,191	5,244	29,857	35,101
B. Intentional	159	8,084	8,243	2	342	344	161	8,426	8,587
1. Self-inflicted		1,237	1,237		148	148		1,385	1,385
Other III.B. (2–4)[f]	159	6,847	7,007	2	194	195	161	7,041	7,202

Source: Chapter 3 of this volume.

Note: A blank cell indicates that fewer than 1,000 deaths are attributable to the specific cause.

a. Hepatitis, tropical-cluster diseases, leprosy, dengue, Japanese encephalitis, trachoma, intestinal nematode infections, and other infectious diseases.

b. Epilepsy, alcohol use disorders, Alzheimer's and other dementias, Parkinson's disease, multiple sclerosis, drug use disorders, post-traumatic stress disorder, obsessive-compulsive disorder, panic disorder, insomnia (primary), migraine, mental retardation attributable to lead exposure, and other neuropsychiatric disorders.

c. Rheumatic heart disease, hypertensive heart disease, inflammatory heart diseases, and other cardiovascular diseases.

d. Other neoplasms, endocrine disorders, sense organ diseases, genitourinary diseases, skin diseases, musculoskeletal diseases, and oral conditions.

e. Poisonings, falls, fires, drownings, and other unintentional injuries.

f. Violence, war, and other intentional injuries.

Table 6B.4 The Burden of Disease—DALYs(3,0) from Selected Causes, by Age, 2001 (Excluding Stillbirths) (thousands)

Cause	Low- and middle-income countries DALYs			High-income countries DALYs			World DALYs		
	0–4	5+	Total	0–4	5+	Total	0–4	5+	Total
Total DALYs(3,0)	**424,062**	**963,364**	**1,387,426**	**6,804**	**142,358**	**149,161**	**430,866**	**1,105,721**	**1,536,587**
I. Communicable, maternal, perinatal, and nutritional conditions	**330,086**	**222,553**	**552,639**	**2,177**	**6,384**	**8,561**	**332,263**	**228,937**	**561,200**
A. Infectious and parasitic diseases	159,602	161,226	320,828	563	2,812	3,375	160,165	164,039	324,203
1. Tuberculosis	1,385	34,502	35,887	2	217	219	1,387	34,719	36,106
2. Sexually transmitted diseases excluding HIV/AIDS	3,194	6,149	9,343	13	132	145	3,207	6,280	9,488
3. HIV/AIDS	10,467	60,362	70,830	3	662	665	10,471	61,024	71,495
4. Diarrheal diseases	53,343	5,376	58,719	235	210	444	53,578	5,586	59,164
5. Childhood-cluster diseases	34,124	9,031	43,155	141	33	175	34,266	9,064	43,330
a. Pertussis	11,310	99	11,408	138	2	139	11,448	100	11,548
b. Poliomyelitis	30	106	136		8	8	30	114	144
c. Diphtheria	137	28	164				137	28	164
d. Measles	16,984	6,121	23,106	3	20	23	16,988	6,141	23,129
e. Tetanus	5,663	2,677	8,340	1	5	5	5,664	2,681	8,345
6. Meningitis	2,784	2,695	5,479	50	81	131	2,834	2,776	5,610
8. Malaria	36,159	3,827	39,986	2	7	9	36,161	3,834	39,995
Other I.A. (7, 9–15)[a]	18,144	39,285	57,429	117	1,470	1,587	18,261	40,755	59,016
B. Respiratory infections	62,826	23,926	86,752	98	2,376	2,474	62,924	26,302	89,227
C. Maternal conditions		26,398	26,398		391	391		26,789	26,789
D. Perinatal conditions	89,096		89,096	1,405	4	1,408	90,501	4	90,505
1. Low birthweight	42,606		42,606	467		467	43,072		43,073
2. Birth asphyxia and birth trauma	31,442		31,443	528	1	530	31,971	2	31,972
3. Other perinatal conditions	15,048		15,048	410	2	412	15,458	2	15,460
E. Nutritional deficiencies	18,562	11,002	29,564	111	801	912	18,673	11,803	30,475
II. Noncommunicable diseases	**78,798**	**600,044**	**678,842**	**4,229**	**125,127**	**129,356**	**83,027**	**725,171**	**808,198**
A. Malignant neoplasms	1,148	73,644	74,792	54	25,834	25,888	1,202	99,478	100,680
C. Diabetes mellitus	102	15,715	15,817	1	4,191	4,192	103	19,906	20,009
E. Neuropsychiatric disorders	20,180	116,960	137,140	976	30,254	31,230	21,156	147,214	168,371
1. Unipolar depressive disorders		43,444	43,445		8,408	8,408	1	51,852	51,853
2. Bipolar affective disorder		8,681	8,681		1,056	1,056		9,737	9,737
3. Schizophrenia	1	10,530	10,531		1,115	1,115	1	11,645	11,646
Other II.E. (4–16)[b]	20,178	54,305	74,483	976	19,675	20,651	21,154	73,981	95,134
G. Cardiovascular diseases	3,033	175,983	179,016	78	29,780	29,859	3,111	205,764	208,875
3. Ischemic heart disease	177	71,735	71,913	2	12,388	12,390	180	84,124	84,303
4. Cerebrovascular disease	371	62,326	62,697	11	9,344	9,354	382	71,669	72,051
Other II.G. (1, 2, 5, 6)[c]	2,484	41,922	44,406	65	8,049	8,114	2,550	49,970	52,520
H. Respiratory diseases	5,966	52,146	58,112	569	9,233	9,801	6,535	61,379	67,914
I. Digestive diseases	14,442	37,990	52,433	475	6,061	6,536	14,917	44,051	58,968
M. Congenital anomalies	22,061	1,483	23,544	1,191	228	1,420	23,252	1,712	24,964
Other II. (B, D, F, J, K, L, N)[d]	11,866	126,121	137,987	885	19,546	20,431	12,751	145,667	158,418
III. Injuries	**15,178**	**140,767**	**155,945**	**398**	**10,846**	**11,244**	**15,576**	**151,613**	**167,189**
A. Unintentional	14,621	98,684	1,13,306	364	7,513	7,876	14,985	106,197	121,182
1. Road traffic accidents	2,275	29,766	32,041	68	2,978	3,045	2,343	32,744	35,087
Other III.A. (2–6)[e]	12,346	68,918	81,264	296	4,535	4,831	12,642	73,453	86,095
B. Intentional	557	42,083	42,640	34	3,334	3,368	591	45,416	46,007
1. Self-inflicted	4	17,674	17,678		2,581	2,581	4	20,255	20,259
Other III.B. (2–4)[f]	553	24,409	24,962	34	753	787	587	25,161	25,749

Source: Chapter 3 of this volume.

Note: A blank cell indicates that fewer than 1,000 deaths are attributable to the specific cause.

a. Hepatitis, tropical-cluster diseases, leprosy, dengue, Japanese encephalitis, trachoma, intestinal nematode infections, and other infectious diseases.

b. Epilepsy, alcohol use disorders, Alzheimer's and other dementias, Parkinson's disease, multiple sclerosis, drug use disorders, post-traumatic stress disorder, obsessive-compulsive disorder, panic disorder, insomnia (primary), migraine, mental retardation attributable to lead exposure, and other neuropsychiatric disorders.

c. Rheumatic heart disease, hypertensive heart disease, inflammatory heart diseases, and other cardiovascular diseases.

d. Other neoplasms, endocrine disorders, sense organ diseases, genitourinary diseases, skin diseases, musculoskeletal diseases, and oral conditions.

e. Poisonings, falls, fires, drownings, and other unintentional injuries.

f. Violence, war, and other intentional injuries.

Table 6B.5 YLL$_{SB}$(3,0,1) Calculated to Include Stillbirths (Valued the Same as Newborn Deaths) (thousands)

	Low- and middle-income countries						
	YLL						
	Stillbirth			Under age 5			
Cause	Antepartum	Intrapartum	Total	After live birth	Including stillbirth	age 5+	Total
Total YLL	65,463	32,755	98,198	319,558	417,756	590,267	1,008,023
I. Communicable, maternal, perinatal, and nutritional conditions				285,058	285,058	169,531	454,589
A. Infectious and parasitic diseases				144,555	144,555	129,584	274,138
1. Tuberculosis				1,215	1,215	30,528	31,743
2. Sexually transmitted diseases excluding HIV/AIDS				2,067	2,067	2,079	4,146
3. HIV/AIDS				10,299	10,299	54,537	64,836
4. Diarrheal diseases				48,534	48,534	2,350	50,884
5. Childhood-cluster diseases				31,751	31,751	8,756	40,507
a. Pertussis				9,113	9,113		9,113
b. Poliomyelitis				9	9	1	10
c. Diphtheria				137	137	27	164
d. Measles				16,840	16,840	6,057	22,897
e. Tetanus				5,652	5,652	2,671	8,323
6. Meningitis				1,952	1,952	2,391	4,343
8. Malaria				32,981	32,981	2,481	35,462
Other I.A. (7, 9–15)[a]				15,705	15,705	26,514	42,219
B. Respiratory infections				58,979	58,979	21,810	80,789
C. Maternal conditions						13,363	13,363
D. Perinatal conditions				75,642	75,642		75,643
1. Low birthweight[b]				39,228	39,228		39,228
2. Birth asphyxia and birth trauma				22,118	22,118		22,118
3. Other perinatal conditions				14,296	14,296		14,297
E. Nutritional deficiencies				5,882	5,882	4,773	10,656
II. Noncommunicable diseases				25,345	25,345	322,376	347,721
A. Malignant neoplasms				1,110	1,110	71,503	72,613
C. Diabetes mellitus				87	87	10,054	10,141
E. Neuropsychiatric disorders				1,317	1,317	10,310	11,626
1. Unipolar depressive disorders						205	205
2. Bipolar affective disorder						5	5
3. Schizophrenia				1	1	373	374
Other II.E. (4–16)[c]				1,314	1,314	9,727	11,041
G. Cardiovascular diseases				2,493	2,493	155,750	158,243
3. Ischemic heart disease				177	177	67,751	67,928
4. Cerebrovascular disease				371	371	51,170	51,541
Other II.G. (1, 2, 5, 6)[d]				1,946	1,946	36,828	38,774
H. Respiratory diseases				1,925	1,925	34,570	36,495
I. Digestive diseases				3,482	3,482	23,888	27,370
M. Congenital anomalies				12,785	12,785	1,480	14,265
Other II. (B, D, F, J, K, L, N)[e]				2,147	2,147	14,821	16,967
III. Injuries				9,155	9,155	98,361	107,516
A. Unintentional				8,757	8,757	64,384	73,141
1. Road traffic accidents				1,491	1,491	23,331	24,822
Other III.A. (2–6)[f]				7,266	7,266	41,053	48,320
B. Intentional				398	398	33,977	34,374
1. Self-inflicted				4	4	16,435	16,439
Other III.B. (2–4)[g]				394	394	17,542	17,936
IV. Not allocated	65,463	32,755	98,198		98,198		98,198

Sources: Stillbirth data are from WHO 2005a. Neonatal and perinatal mortality are country, regional, and global estimates. Age 5+ and total data are from table 6.4 for low- and middle-income countries. All other data are from chapter 3 of this volume.

Note: A blank cell indicates that fewer than 1,000 deaths are attributable to the specific cause.

a. Hepatitis, tropical-cluster diseases, leprosy, dengue, Japanese encephalitis, trachoma, intestinal nematode infections, and other infectious diseases.

b. Low birthweight deaths are those resulting from intrauterine growth retardation or preterm birth. Almost all low birthweight deaths in the neonatal period result from preterm birth.

c. Epilepsy, alcohol use disorders, Alzheimer's and other dementias, Parkinson's disease, multiple sclerosis, drug use disorders, post-traumatic stress disorder, obsessive-compulsive disorder, panic disorder, insomnia (primary), migraine, mental retardation attributable to lead exposure, and other neuropsychiatric disorders.

d. Rheumatic heart disease, hypertensive heart disease, inflammatory heart diseases, and other cardiovascular diseases.

e. Other neoplasms, endocrine disorders, sense organ diseases, genitourinary diseases, skin diseases, musculoskeletal diseases, and oral conditions.

f. Poisonings, falls, fires, drownings, and other unintentional injuries.

g. Violence, war, and other intentional injuries.

(Continues on the following page.)

Table 6B.5 Continued

Cause	High-income countries YLL						
	Stillbirth			Under age 5			
	Antepartum	Intrapartum	Total	After live birth	Including stillbirth	age 5+	Total
Total YLL	1,222	153	1,375	2,209	3,583	75,650	79,233
I. Communicable, maternal, perinatal, and nutritional conditions				1,133	1,133	4,258	5,391
A. Infectious and parasitic diseases				96	96	1,878	1,975
1. Tuberculosis				1	1	171	172
2. Sexually transmitted diseases excluding HIV/AIDS				1	1	6	7
3. HIV/AIDS				2	2	491	493
4. Diarrheal diseases				13	13	40	53
5. Childhood-cluster diseases				4	4	30	34
a. Pertussis				1	1		1
b. Poliomyelitis						6	6
c. Diphtheria							
d. Measles				2	2	19	21
e. Tetanus				1	1	5	5
6. Meningitis				23	23	59	82
8. Malaria				2	2	2	4
Other I.A. (7, 9–15)[a]				51	51	1,079	1,130
B. Respiratory infections				52	52	2,227	2,279
C. Maternal conditions						27	27
D. Perinatal conditions				981	981	4	984
1. Low birthweight[b]				291	291		291
2. Birth asphyxia and birth trauma				336	336	1	338
3. Other perinatal conditions				353	353	2	355
E. Nutritional deficiencies				4	4	122	126
II. Noncommunicable diseases				857	857	63,397	64,255
A. Malignant neoplasms				50	50	23,265	23,315
C. Diabetes mellitus				1	1	1,942	1,943
E. Neuropsychiatric disorders				63	63	3,259	3,322
1. Unipolar depressive disorders						21	21
2. Bipolar affective disorder						4	4
3. Schizophrenia						24	24
Other II.E. (4–16)[c]				63	63	3,210	3,273
G. Cardiovascular diseases				63	63	24,166	24,229
3. Ischemic heart disease				2	2	11,483	11,485
4. Cerebrovascular disease				11	11	5,886	5,896
Other II.G. (1, 2, 5, 6)[d]				50	50	6,797	6,848
H. Respiratory diseases				30	30	3,914	3,945
I. Digestive diseases				35	35	3,680	3,715
M. Congenital anomalies				543	543	229	771
Other II. (B, D, F, J, K, L, N)[e]				72	72	2,943	3,015
III. Injuries				218	218	7,995	8,213
A. Unintentional				186	186	5,003	5,189
1. Road traffic accidents				52	52	2,496	2,548
Other III.A. (2–6)[f]				134	134	2,507	2,640
B. Intentional				33	33	2,992	3,024
1. Self-inflicted						2,432	2,433
Other III.B. (2–4)[g]				32	32	559	592
IV. Not allocated	1,222	153	1,375		1,375		1,375

Sources: Stillbirth data are from WHO 2005a. Neonatal and perinatal mortality are country, regional, and global estimates. Age 5+ and total data are from table 6.4 for low- and middle-income countries. All other data are from chapter 3 of this volume.

Note: A blank cell indicates that fewer than 1,000 deaths are attributable to the specific cause.

a. Hepatitis, tropical-cluster diseases, leprosy, dengue, Japanese encephalitis, trachoma, intestinal nematode infections, and other infectious diseases.

b. Low birthweight deaths are those resulting from intrauterine growth retardation or preterm birth. Almost all low birthweight deaths in the neonatal period result from preterm birth.

c. Epilepsy, alcohol use disorders, Alzheimer's and other dementias, Parkinson's disease, multiple sclerosis, drug use disorders, post-traumatic stress disorder, obsessive-compulsive disorder, panic disorder, insomnia (primary), migraine, mental retardation attributable to lead exposure, and other neuropsychiatric disorders.

d. Rheumatic heart disease, hypertensive heart disease, inflammatory heart diseases, and other cardiovascular diseases.

e. Other neoplasms, endocrine disorders, sense organ diseases, genitourinary diseases, skin diseases, musculoskeletal diseases, and oral conditions.

f. Poisonings, falls, fires, drownings, and other unintentional injuries.

g. Violence, war, and other intentional injuries.

Cause	World YLL						
	Stillbirth			Under age 5			
	Antepartum	Intrapartum	Total	After live birth	Including stillbirth	age 5+	Total
Total YLL	66,685	32,907	99,592	321,767	421,360	566,325	987,684
I. Communicable, maternal, perinatal, and nutritional conditions				286,191	286,191	173,789	459,980
A. Infectious and parasitic diseases				144,651	144,651	131,462	276,113
1. Tuberculosis				1,216	1,216	30,699	31,915
2. Sexually transmitted diseases excluding HIV/AIDS				2,068	2,068	2,085	4,153
3. HIV/AIDS				10,301	10,301	55,027	65,328
4. Diarrheal diseases				48,547	48,547	2,390	50,937
5. Childhood-cluster diseases				31,755	31,755	8,786	40,540
a. Pertussis				9,114	9,114		9,114
b. Poliomyelitis				9	9	7	16
c. Diphtheria				137	137	27	164
d. Measles				16,843	16,843	6,076	22,918
e. Tetanus				5,653	5,653	2,675	8,328
6. Meningitis				1,975	1,975	2,450	4,425
8. Malaria				32,982	32,982	2,483	35,466
Other I.A. (7, 9–15)[a]				15,808	15,808	36,570	52,378
B. Respiratory infections				59,031	59,031	24,037	83,068
C. Maternal conditions						13,390	13,390
D. Perinatal conditions				76,623	76,623	4	76,627
1. Low birthweight[b]				39,520	39,520		39,520
2. Birth asphyxia and birth trauma				22,454	22,454	2	22,455
3. Other perinatal conditions				14,650	14,650	2	14,652
E. Nutritional deficiencies				5,887	5,887	4,895	10,782
II. Noncommunicable diseases				26,203	26,203	385,773	411,976
A. Malignant neoplasms				1,160	1,160	94,768	95,928
C. Diabetes mellitus				87	87	11,997	12,084
E. Neuropsychiatric disorders				1,380	1,380	13,569	14,949
1. Unipolar depressive disorders				1	1	226	227
2. Bipolar affective disorder						9	9
3. Schizophrenia				1	1	397	398
Other II.E. (4–16)[c]				1,377	1,377	12,937	14,314
G. Cardiovascular diseases				2,557	2,557	179,915	182,472
3. Ischemic heart disease				179	179	79,234	79,412
4. Cerebrovascular disease				382	382	57,056	57,438
Other II.G. (1, 2, 5, 6)[d]				1,996	1,996	43,626	45,622
H. Respiratory diseases				1,955	1,955	38,484	40,439
I. Digestive diseases				3,516	3,516	27,568	31,084
M. Congenital anomalies				13,328	13,328	1,709	15,037
Other II. (B, D, F, J, K, L, N)[e]				2,219	2,219	17,764	19,983
III. Injuries				9,373	9,373	106,356	115,729
A. Unintentional				8,943	8,943	69,387	78,330
1. Road traffic accidents				1,543	1,543	25,827	27,370
Other III.A. (2–6)[f]				7,400	7,400	43,560	50,960
B. Intentional				430	430	36,969	37,399
1. Self-inflicted				4	4	18,868	18,871
Other III.B. (2–4)[g]				426	426	18,101	18,527
IV. Not allocated	66,685	32,907	99,592		99,592		99,592

Sources: Stillbirth data are from WHO 2005a. Neonatal and perinatal mortality are country, regional, and global estimates. Age 5+ and total data are from table 6.4 for low- and middle-income countries. All other data are from chapter 3 of this volume.

Note: A blank cell indicates that fewer than 1,000 deaths are attributable to the specific cause.

a. Hepatitis, tropical-cluster diseases, leprosy, dengue, Japanese encephalitis, trachoma, intestinal nematode infections, and other infectious diseases.

b. Low birthweight deaths are those resulting from intrauterine growth retardation or preterm birth. Almost all low birthweight deaths in the neonatal period result from preterm birth.

c. Epilepsy, alcohol use disorders, Alzheimer's and other dementias, Parkinson's disease, multiple sclerosis, drug use disorders, post-traumatic stress disorder, obsessive-compulsive disorder, panic disorder, insomnia (primary), migraine, mental retardation attributable to lead exposure, and other neuropsychiatric disorders.

d. Rheumatic heart disease, hypertensive heart disease, inflammatory heart diseases, and other cardiovascular diseases.

e. Other neoplasms, endocrine disorders, sense organ diseases, genitourinary diseases, skin diseases, musculoskeletal diseases, and oral conditions.

f. Poisonings, falls, fires, drownings, and other unintentional injuries.

g. Violence, war, and other intentional injuries.

Table 6B.6 The Burden of Disease—DALYs$_{SB}$(3,0,1). Calculated to Include Stillbirths (Valued the Same as Newborn Deaths) (thousands)

	Low- and middle-income countries						
	DALYs						
	Stillbirth			Under age 5			
Cause	Antepartum	Intrapartum	Total	After live birth	Including stillbirth	age 5+	Total
Total DALYs	65,463	32,755	98,198	424,062	522,260	963,364	1,485,623
I. Communicable, maternal, perinatal, and nutritional conditions				330,086	330,086	222,553	552,639
A. Infectious and parasitic diseases				159,602	159,602	161,226	320,828
1. Tuberculosis				1,385	1,385	34,502	35,887
2. Sexually transmitted diseases excluding HIV/AIDS				3,194	3,194	6,149	9,343
3. HIV/AIDS				10,467	10,467	60,362	70,830
4. Diarrheal diseases				53,343	53,343	5,376	58,719
5. Childhood-cluster diseases				34,124	34,124	9,031	43,155
a. Pertussis				11,310	11,310	99	11,408
b. Poliomyelitis				30	30	106	136
c. Diphtheria				137	137	28	164
d. Measles				16,984	16,984	6,121	23,106
e. Tetanus				5,663	5,663	2,677	8,340
6. Meningitis				2,784	2,784	2,695	5,479
8. Malaria				36,159	36,159	3,827	39,986
Other I.A. (7, 9–15)[a]				18,144	18,144	8	18,152
B. Respiratory infections				62,826	62,826	23,926	86,752
C. Maternal conditions						26,398	26,398
D. Perinatal conditions				89,096	89,096		89,096
1. Low birthweight[b]				42,606	42,606		42,606
2. Birth asphyxia and birth trauma				31,442	31,442		31,443
3. Other perinatal conditions				15,048	15,048		15,048
E. Nutritional deficiencies				18,562	18,562	11,002	29,564
II. Noncommunicable diseases				78,798	78,798	600,044	678,842
A. Malignant neoplasms				1,148	1,148	73,644	74,792
C. Diabetes mellitus				102	102	15,715	15,817
E. Neuropsychiatric disorders				20,180	20,180	116,960	137,140
1. Unipolar depressive disorders						43,444	43,445
2. Bipolar affective disorder						8,681	8,681
3. Schizophrenia				1	1	10,530	10,531
Other II.E. (4–16)[c]				7	7	20	27
G. Cardiovascular diseases				3,033	3,033	175,983	179,016
3. Ischemic heart disease				177	177	71,735	71,913
4. Cerebrovascular disease				371	371	62,326	62,697
Other II.G. (1, 2, 5, 6)[d]				2,484	2,484		2,484
H. Respiratory diseases				5,966	5,966	52,146	58,112
I. Digestive diseases				14,442	14,442	37,990	52,433
M. Congenital anomalies				22,061	22,061	1,483	23,544
Other II. (B, D, F, J, K, L, N)[e]				11,866	11,866	1	11,867
III. Injuries				15,178	15,178	140,767	155,945
A. Unintentional				14,621	14,621	98,684	113,306
1. Road traffic accidents				2,275	2,275	29,766	32,041
Other III.A. (2–6)[f]				12,346	12,346	12	12,358
B. Intentional				557	557	42,083	42,640
1. Self-inflicted				4	4	17,674	17,678
Other III.B. (2–4)[g]				553	553	2	555
IV. Not allocated	65,463	32,755	98,198		98,198		98,198

Sources: Stillbirth data are from WHO 2005a. Neonatal and perinatal mortality are country, regional, and global estimates. Age 5+ and total data are from table 6.4 for low- and middle-income countries. All other data are from chapter 3 of this volume.

Note: A blank cell indicates that fewer than 1,000 deaths are attributable to the specific cause. DALYs used here: DALYs(3,0,1).

a. Hepatitis, tropical-cluster diseases, leprosy, dengue, Japanese encephalitis, trachoma, intestinal nematode infections, and other infectious diseases.

b. Low birthweight deaths are those resulting from intrauterine growth retardation or preterm birth. Almost all low birthweight deaths in the neonatal period result from preterm birth.

c. Epilepsy, alcohol use disorders, Alzheimer's and other dementias, Parkinson's disease, multiple sclerosis, drug use disorders, post-traumatic stress disorder, obsessive-compulsive disorder, panic disorder, insomnia (primary), migraine, mental retardation attributable to lead exposure, and other neuropsychiatric disorders.

d. Rheumatic heart disease, hypertensive heart disease, inflammatory heart diseases, and other cardiovascular diseases.

e. Other neoplasms, endocrine disorders, sense organ diseases, genitourinary diseases, skin diseases, musculoskeletal diseases, and oral conditions.

f. Poisonings, falls, fires, drownings, and other unintentional injuries.

g. Violence, war, and other intentional injuries.

	High-income countries						
	DALYs						
	Stillbirth			**Under age 5**			
Cause	Antepartum	Intrapartum	Total	After live birth	Including stillbirth	age 5+	Total
Total DALYs	**1,222**	**153**	**1,375**	**6,804**	**8,178**	**142,358**	**150,536**
I. Communicable, maternal, perinatal, and nutritional conditions				**2,177**	**2,177**	**6,384**	**8,561**
A. Infectious and parasitic diseases				563	563	2,812	3,375
1. Tuberculosis				2	2	217	219
2. Sexually transmitted diseases excluding HIV/AIDS				13	13	132	145
3. HIV/AIDS				3	3	662	665
4. Diarrheal diseases				235	235	210	444
5. Childhood-cluster diseases				141	141	33	175
a. Pertussis				138	138	2	139
b. Poliomyelitis						8	8
c. Diphtheria							
d. Measles				3	3	20	23
e. Tetanus				1	1	5	5
6. Meningitis				50	50	81	131
8. Malaria				2	2	7	9
Other I.A. (7, 9–15)[a]				117	117	1,470	1,587
B. Respiratory infections				98	98	2,376	2,474
C. Maternal conditions						391	391
D. Perinatal conditions				1,405	1,405	4	1,408
1. Low birthweight[b]				467	467		467
2. Birth asphyxia and birth trauma				528	528	1	530
3. Other perinatal conditions				410	410	2	412
E. Nutritional deficiencies				111	111	801	912
II. Noncommunicable diseases				**4,229**	**4,229**	**125,127**	**129,356**
A. Malignant neoplasms				54	54	25,834	25,888
C. Diabetes mellitus				1	1	4,191	4,192
E. Neuropsychiatric disorders				976	976	30,254	31,230
1. Unipolar depressive disorders						8,408	8,408
2. Bipolar affective disorder						1,056	1,056
3. Schizophrenia						1,115	1,115
Other II.E. (4–16)[c]				976	976	19,675	20,651
G. Cardiovascular diseases				78	78	29,780	29,859
3. Ischemic heart disease				2	2	12,388	12,390
4. Cerebrovascular disease				11	11	9,344	9,354
Other II.G. (1, 2, 5, 6)[d]				65	65	8,049	8,114
H. Respiratory diseases				569	569	9,233	9,801
I. Digestive diseases				475	475	6,061	6,536
M. Congenital anomalies				1,191	1,191	228	1,420
Other II. (B, D, F, J, K, L, N)[e]				885	885	19,546	20,431
III. Injuries				**398**	**398**	**10,846**	**11,244**
A. Unintentional				364	364	7,513	7,876
1. Road traffic accidents				68	68	2,978	3,045
Other III.A. (2–6)[f]				296	296	4,535	4,831
B. Intentional				34	34	3,334	3,368
1. Self-inflicted						2,581	2,581
Other III.B. (2–4)[g]				34	34	753	787
IV. Not allocated	**1,222**	**153**	**1,375**		**1,375**		**1,375**

Sources: Stillbirth data are from WHO 2005a. Neonatal and perinatal mortality are country, regional, and global estimates. Age 5+ and total data are from table 6.4 for low- and middle-income countries. All other data are from chapter 3 of this volume.

Note: A blank cell indicates that fewer than 1,000 deaths are attributable to the specific cause. DALYs used here: DALYs(3,0,1).

a. Hepatitis, tropical-cluster diseases, leprosy, dengue, Japanese encephalitis, trachoma, intestinal nematode infections, and other infectious diseases.

b. Low birthweight deaths are those resulting from intrauterine growth retardation or preterm birth. Almost all low birthweight deaths in the neonatal period result from preterm birth.

c. Epilepsy, alcohol use disorders, Alzheimer's and other dementias, Parkinson's disease, multiple sclerosis, drug use disorders, post-traumatic stress disorder, obsessive-compulsive disorder, panic disorder, insomnia (primary), migraine, mental retardation attributable to lead exposure, and other neuropsychiatric disorders.

d. Rheumatic heart disease, hypertensive heart disease, inflammatory heart diseases, and other cardiovascular diseases.

e. Other neoplasms, endocrine disorders, sense organ diseases, genitourinary diseases, skin diseases, musculoskeletal diseases, and oral conditions.

f. Poisonings, falls, fires, drownings, and other unintentional injuries.

g. Violence, war, and other intentional injuries.

Table 6B.6 Continued

Cause	World DALYs Stillbirth Antepartum	Intrapartum	Total	Under age 5 After live birth	Including stillbirth	age 5+	Total
Total DALYs	66,685	32,907	99,592	430,866	530,458	1,105,721	1,636,179
I. Communicable, maternal, perinatal, and nutritional conditions				332,263	332,263	228,937	561,200
A. Infectious and parasitic diseases				160,165	160,165	164,039	324,203
1. Tuberculosis				1,387	1,387	34,719	36,106
2. Sexually transmitted diseases excluding HIV/AIDS				3,207	3,207	6,280	9,488
3. HIV/AIDS				10,471	10,471	61,024	71,495
4. Diarrheal diseases				53,578	53,578	5,586	59,164
5. Childhood-cluster diseases				34,266	34,266	9,064	43,330
a. Pertussis				11,448	11,448	100	11,548
b. Poliomyelitis				30	30	114	144
c. Diphtheria				137	137	28	164
d. Measles				16,988	16,988	6,141	23,129
e. Tetanus				5,664	5,664	2,681	8,345
6. Meningitis				2,834	2,834	2,776	5,610
8. Malaria				36,161	36,161	3,834	39,995
Other I.A. (7, 9–15)[a]				18,261	18,261	40,755	59,016
B. Respiratory infections				62,924	62,924	26,302	89,227
C. Maternal conditions						26,789	26,789
D. Perinatal conditions				90,501	90,501	4	90,505
1. Low birthweight[b]				43,072	43,072		43,073
2. Birth asphyxia and birth trauma				31,971	31,971	2	31,972
3. Other perinatal conditions				15,458	15,458	2	15,460
E. Nutritional deficiencies				18,673	18,673	11,803	30,475
II. Noncommunicable diseases				83,027	83,027	725,171	808,198
A. Malignant neoplasms				1,202	1,202	99,478	100,680
C. Diabetes mellitus				103	103	19,906	20,009
E. Neuropsychiatric disorders				21,156	21,156	147,214	168,371
1. Unipolar depressive disorders				1	1	51,852	51,853
2. Bipolar affective disorder						9,737	9,737
3. Schizophrenia				1	1	11,645	11,646
Other II.E. (4–16)[c]				21,154	21,154	73,981	95,134
G. Cardiovascular diseases				3,111	3,111	205,764	208,875
3. Ischemic heart disease				180	180	84,124	84,303
4. Cerebrovascular disease				382	382	71,669	72,051
Other II.G. (1, 2, 5, 6)[d]				2,550	2,550	49,970	52,520
H. Respiratory diseases				6,535	6,535	61,379	67,914
I. Digestive diseases				14,917	14,917	44,051	58,968
M. Congenital anomalies				23,252	23,252	1,712	24,964
Other II. (B, D, F, J, K, L, N)[e]				12,751	12,751	145,667	158,418
III. Injuries				15,576	15,576	151,613	167,189
A. Unintentional				14,985	14,985	106,197	121,182
1. Road traffic accidents				2,343	2,343	32,744	35,087
Other III.A. (2–6)[f]				12,642	12,642	73,453	86,095
B. Intentional				591	591	45,416	46,007
1. Self-inflicted				4	4	20,255	20,259
Other III.B. (2–4)[g]				587	587	25,161	25,749
IV. Not allocated	66,685	32,907	99,592		99,592		99,592

Sources: Stillbirth data are from WHO 2005a. Neonatal and perinatal mortality are country, regional, and global estimates. Age 5+ and total data are from table 6.4 for low- and middle-income countries. All other data are from chapter 3 of this volume.

Note: A blank cell indicates that fewer than 1,000 deaths are attributable to the specific cause. DALYs used here: DALYs(3,0,1).

a. Hepatitis, tropical-cluster diseases, leprosy, dengue, Japanese encephalitis, trachoma, intestinal nematode infections, and other infectious diseases.

b. Low birthweight deaths are those resulting from intrauterine growth retardation or preterm birth. Almost all low birthweight deaths in the neonatal period result from preterm birth.

c. Epilepsy, alcohol use disorders, Alzheimer's and other dementias, Parkinson's disease, multiple sclerosis, drug use disorders, post-traumatic stress disorder, obsessive-compulsive disorder, panic disorder, insomnia (primary), migraine, mental retardation attributable to lead exposure, and other neuropsychiatric disorders.

d. Rheumatic heart disease, hypertensive heart disease, inflammatory heart diseases, and other cardiovascular diseases.

e. Other neoplasms, endocrine disorders, sense organ diseases, genitourinary diseases, skin diseases, musculoskeletal diseases, and oral conditions.

f. Poisonings, falls, fires, drownings, and other unintentional injuries.

g. Violence, war, and other intentional injuries.

Table 6B.7 YLL$_{SB}$(3,0,.54) Calculated to Include Stillbirths and Gradual ALP (in thousands)

Cause	Low- and middle-income countries									
	YLL—Stillbirth			YLL 0 ≤ age < 1			YLL under age 5				
	Ante-partum	Intra-partum	Total	Neonatal	YLL aged 28 days to ≤ 1 year	Infant YLL (0 ≤ age < 1 year)	Child YLL (1 ≤ age < 5 years)	After live birth	Including stillbirth	YLL age 5+	Total YLL$_{SB}$ (3,0,.54)
Total YLL	10,652	9,831	20,483	36,232	57,748	98,401	77,480	175,881	196,364	590,267	786,631
I. Communicable, maternal, perinatal, and nutritional conditions				29,027		89,029	66,554	155,583	155,583	169,531	325,113
A. Infectious and parasitic diseases				2,666		37,346	49,747	87,093	87,093	129,584	216,677
1. Tuberculosis						202	648	850	850	30,528	31,378
2. Sexually transmitted diseases excluding HIV/AIDS						710	349	1,059	1,059	2,079	3,138
3. HIV/AIDS						2,615	3,638	6,252	6,252	54,537	60,789
4. Diarrheal diseases				1,087	17,039	15,815	9,983	25,798	25,798	2,350	28,149
5. Childhood-cluster diseases						4,934	17,617	22,551	22,551	8,756	31,307
a. Pertussis						1,247	5,407	6,654	6,654		6,654
b. Poliomyelitis						2	4	6	6	1	7
c. Diphtheria						32	53	85	85	27	113
d. Measles						1,486	11,673	13,158	13,158	6,057	19,215
e. Tetanus				1,579		2,176	502	2,677	2,677	2,671	5,348
6. Meningitis						606	1,235	1,841	1,841	2,391	4,231
8. Malaria						9,404	9,537	18,941	18,941	2,481	21,422
Other I.A. (7, 9–15)[a]						2,826	7,904	10,730	10,730	26,514	37,244
B. Respiratory infections				9,420	8,219	19,880	10,773	30,653	30,653	21,810	52,463
C. Maternal conditions										13,363	13,364
D. Perinatal conditions				16,939		30,871	2,808	33,679	33,679		33,679
1. Low birthweight[b]				10,143	2,097	15,739	2,007	17,746	17,746		17,746
2. Birth asphyxia and birth trauma				6,795		9,361	142	9,503	9,503		9,503
3. Other perinatal conditions						5,769	662	6,432	6,432		6,432
E. Nutritional deficiencies						1,237	2,602	3,840	3,840	4,773	8,613
II. Noncommunicable diseases				2,899		7,755	6,242	13,992	13,992	322,376	336,372
A. Malignant neoplasms						142	679	821	821	71,503	72,324
C. Diabetes mellitus						24	27	51	51	10,054	10,105
E. Neuropsychiatric disorders						271	594	866	866	10,310	11,176
1. Unipolar depressive disorders										205	205
2. Bipolar affective disorder										5	5
3. Schizophrenia								1	1	373	374
Other II.E. (4–16)[c]						176	786	963	963	9,727	10,690
G. Cardiovascular diseases						728	685	1,413	1,413	155,750	157,163
3. Ischemic heart disease						54	44	98	98	67,751	67,849
4. Cerebrovascular disease						102	115	217	217	51,170	51,387
Other II.G. (1, 2, 5, 6)[d]						540	591	1,131	1,131	36,828	37,959
H. Respiratory diseases						552	551	1,103	1,103	34,570	35,673
I. Digestive diseases						939	1,113	2,052	2,052	23,888	25,940
M. Congenital anomalies				2,899		4,559	1,823	6,382	6,382	1,480	7,862
Other II. (B, D, F, J, K, L, N)[e]						471	909	1,380	1,380	14,821	16,201
III. Injuries						1,607	4,706	6,312	6,312	98,361	104,673
A. Unintentional						1,538	4,499	6,037	6,037	64,384	70,421
1. Road traffic accidents						153	990	1,143	1,143	23,331	24,474
Other III.A. (2–6)[f]						1,212	3,863	5,074	5,074	41,053	46,128
B. Intentional						69	206	275	275	33,977	34,252
1. Self-inflicted						1	1	2	2	16,435	16,437
Other III.B. (2–4)[g]						44	254	298	298	17,542	17,840
IV. Not allocated	10,652	9,831	20,483	4,301					20,483		20,483

Sources: Stillbirth data are from WHO 2005a. Neonatal and perinatal mortality are country, regional, and global estimates. Age 5+ and total data are from table 6.4 for low- and middle-income countries. All other data are from chapter 3 of this volume.

Note: A blank cell indicates that fewer than 1,000 deaths are attributable to the specific cause. YLL used here: YLL(3,0,.54).

a. Hepatitis, tropical-cluster diseases, leprosy, dengue, Japanese encephalitis, trachoma, intestinal nematode infections, and other infectious diseases.

b. Low birthweight deaths are those resulting from intrauterine growth retardation or preterm birth. Almost all low birthweight deaths in the neonatal period result from preterm birth.

c. Epilepsy, alcohol use disorders, Alzheimer's and other dementias, Parkinson's disease, multiple sclerosis, drug use disorders, post-traumatic stress disorder, obsessive-compulsive disorder, panic disorder, insomnia (primary), migraine, mental retardation attributable to lead exposure, and other neuropsychiatric disorders.

d. Rheumatic heart disease, hypertensive heart disease, inflammatory heart diseases, and other cardiovascular diseases.

e. Other neoplasms, endocrine disorders, sense organ diseases, genitourinary diseases, skin diseases, musculoskeletal diseases, and oral conditions.

f. Poisonings, falls, fires, drownings, and other unintentional injuries.

g. Violence, war, and other intentional injuries.

(Continues on the following page.)

Table 6B.7 Continued

Cause	YLL—Stillbirth Ante-partum	YLL—Stillbirth Intra-partum	YLL—Stillbirth Total	YLL 0 ≤ age < 1 Neonatal	YLL 0 ≤ age < 1 YLL aged 28 days to ≤ 1 year	YLL 0 ≤ age < 1 Infant YLL (0 ≤ age < 1 year)	YLL under age 5 Child YLL (1 ≤ age < 5 years)	YLL under age 5 After live birth	Including stillbirth	YLL age 5+	Total YLL$_{SB}$ (3,0,.54)
Total YLL	199	46	245	388	278	769	353	1,122	1,366	75,650	77,016
I. Communicable, maternal, perinatal, and nutritional conditions				150		457	53	510	510	4,258	4,768
A. Infectious and parasitic diseases				150		26	30	57	57	1,878	1,935
1. Tuberculosis							1	1	1	171	172
2. Sexually transmitted diseases excluding HIV/AIDS										6	7
3. HIV/AIDS							1	1	1	491	492
4. Diarrheal diseases							2	2	7	40	47
5. Childhood-cluster diseases							2	2	3	30	32
a. Pertussis									1		1
b. Poliomyelitis										6	6
c. Diphtheria											
d. Measles							1	1	1	19	21
e. Tetanus										5	5
6. Meningitis							9	9	9	59	73
8. Malaria										2	3
Other I.A. (7, 9–15)a						10	24	34	34	1,079	1,113
B. Respiratory infections						14	16	30	30	2,227	2,258
C. Maternal conditions										27	27
D. Perinatal conditions				150		415	5	420	420	4	424
1. Low birthweightb				90		124		124	124		124
2. Birth asphyxia and birth trauma				58	77	142	289	431	431	1	146
3. Other perinatal conditions						150	305	455	455	2	153
E. Nutritional deficiencies						1	2	3	3	122	125
II. Noncommunicable diseases				116		251	511	761	761	63,397	63,883
A. Malignant neoplasms						3	7	10	10	23,265	23,305
C. Diabetes mellitus										1,942	1,943
E. Neuropsychiatric disorders						14	26	40	40	3,259	3,299
1. Unipolar depressive disorders										21	21
2. Bipolar affective disorder										4	4
3. Schizophrenia										24	24
Other II.E. (4–16)c						7	19	26	26	3,210	3,236
G. Cardiovascular diseases						18	18	36	36	24,166	24,202
3. Ischemic heart disease						1	1	1	1	11,483	11,484
4. Cerebrovascular disease						3	19	22	22	5,886	5,908
Other II.G. (1, 2, 5, 6)d						12	19	31	31	6,797	6,829
H. Respiratory diseases						8	10	18	18	3,914	3,932
I. Digestive diseases						11	7	19	19	3,680	3,698
M. Congenital anomalies				116	62	208	48	256	256	229	484
Other II. (B, D, F, J, K, L, N)e						17	28	45	45	2,943	2,988
III. Injuries						31	127	158	158	7,995	8,153
A. Unintentional						24	112	137	137	5,003	5,140
1. Road traffic accidents						4	37	41	41	2,496	2,537
Other III.A. (2–6)f						14	87	100	100	2,507	2,607
B. Intentional						7	15	21	21	2,992	3,013
1. Self-inflicted										2,432	2,433
Other III.B. (2–4)g						7	15	21	21	559	581
IV. Not allocated	199	46	245	124					245		245

Sources: Stillbirth data are from WHO 2005a. Neonatal and perinatal mortality are country, regional, and global estimates. Age 5+ and total data are from table 6.4 for low- and middle-income countries. All other data are from chapter 3 of this volume.

Note: A blank cell indicates that fewer than 1,000 deaths are attributable to the specific cause. YLL used here: YLL(3,0,.54).

a. Hepatitis, tropical-cluster diseases, leprosy, dengue, Japanese encephalitis, trachoma, intestinal nematode infections, and other infectious diseases.

b. Low birthweight deaths are those resulting from intrauterine growth retardation or preterm birth. Almost all low birthweight deaths in the neonatal period result from preterm birth.

c. Epilepsy, alcohol use disorders, Alzheimer's and other dementias, Parkinson's disease, multiple sclerosis, drug use disorders, post-traumatic stress disorder, obsessive-compulsive disorder, panic disorder, insomnia (primary), migraine, mental retardation attributable to lead exposure, and other neuropsychiatric disorders.

d. Rheumatic heart disease, hypertensive heart disease, inflammatory heart diseases, and other cardiovascular diseases.

e. Other neoplasms, endocrine disorders, sense organ diseases, genitourinary diseases, skin diseases, musculoskeletal diseases, and oral conditions.

f. Poisonings, falls, fires, drownings, and other unintentional injuries.

g. Violence, war, and other intentional injuries.

Cause	YLL—Stillbirth Ante-partum	Intra-partum	Total	YLL 0 ≤ age < 1 Neonatal	YLL aged 28 days to ≤ 1 year	Infant YLL (0 ≤ age < 1 year)	YLL under age 5 Child YLL (1 ≤ age < 5 years)	After live birth	Including stillbirth	YLL age 5+	Total YLL$_{SB}$ (3,0,.54)
Total YLL	10,851	9,877	20,728	36,620	58,010	99,170	77,833	177,003	197,730	590,267	787,998
I. Communicable, maternal, perinatal, and nutritional conditions				29,413		89,486	66,607	156,092	156,109	169,531	325,623
A. Infectious and parasitic diseases				2,817		37,373	49,777	87,150	88,105	129,584	216,734
1. Tuberculosis						202	649	850	850	30,528	31,379
2. Sexually transmitted diseases excluding HIV/AIDS						711	349	1,059	1,059	2,079	3,138
3. HIV/AIDS						2,615	3,639	6,254	6,254	54,537	60,791
4. Diarrheal diseases				1,087	17,044	15,819	9,986	25,888	25,888	2,350	28,155
5. Childhood-cluster diseases						4,935	17,648	22,580	22,580	8,756	31,335
a. Pertussis						1,248	5,407	6,655	6,655		6,655
b. Poliomyelitis						2	4	6	6	1	7
c. Diphtheria						32	53	85	85	27	113
d. Measles						1,486	11,674	13,160	13,160	6,057	19,217
e. Tetanus				1,579		2,176	489	2,665	2,665	2,671	5,336
6. Meningitis						611	472	1,083	1,083	2,391	3,474
8. Malaria						9,404	9,537	18,942	18,942	2,481	21,423
Other I.A. (7, 9–15)[a]						2,836	7,988	10,825	10,825	26,514	37,338
B. Respiratory infections				9,521	8,065	19,894	10,789	30,683	30,683	21,810	52,493
C. Maternal conditions										13,363	13,364
D. Perinatal conditions				17,221		31,286	2,813	34,099	34,099		34,100
1. Low birthweight[b]				10,320	2,097	15,863	2,007	17,874	17,871		17,871
2. Birth asphyxia and birth trauma				6,898		9,503	145	9,647	9,647		9,648
3. Other perinatal conditions						5,919	664	6,583	6,583		6,583
E. Nutritional deficiencies						1,239	2,604	3,843	3,843	4,773	8,616
II. Noncommunicable diseases				3,015		8,006	6,477	14,482	14,482	322,376	336,858
A. Malignant neoplasms						146	716	861	861	71,503	72,364
C. Diabetes mellitus						24	27	51	51	10,054	10,106
E. Neuropsychiatric disorders						285	621	906	906	10,310	11,216
1. Unipolar depressive disorders										205	205
2. Bipolar affective disorder										5	5
3. Schizophrenia								1	1	373	374
Other II.E. (4–16)[c]						183	827	1,010	1,010	9,727	10,737
G. Cardiovascular diseases						746	704	1,450	1,450	155,750	157,199
3. Ischemic heart disease						54	45	99	99	67,751	67,850
4. Cerebrovascular disease						105	118	223	223	51,170	51,394
Other II.G. (1, 2, 5, 6)[d]						553	609	1,162	1,162	36,828	37,990
H. Respiratory diseases						560	561	1,121	1,121	34,570	35,691
I. Digestive diseases						951	1,120	2,071	2,071	23,888	25,959
M. Congenital anomalies				3,015	740	4,767	1,871	6,638	6,638	1,480	8,118
Other II. (B, D, F, J, K, L, N)[e]						488	937	1,425	1,425	14,821	16,246
III. Injuries						1,638	4,833	6,470	6,470	98,361	104,832
A. Unintentional						1,563	4,611	6,174	6,174	64,384	70,558
1. Road traffic accidents						157	1,027	1,184	1,184	23,331	24,515
Other III.A. (2–6)[f]						1,225	3,951	5,176	5,176	41,053	46,230
B. Intentional						75	221	297	297	33,977	34,053
1. Self-inflicted						1	1	2	2	16,435	16,437
Other III.B. (2–4)[g]						51	269	319	319	17,542	17,861
IV. Not allocated	10,851	9,877	20,728	4,193					20,728		20,728

Sources: Stillbirth data are from WHO 2005a. Neonatal and perinatal mortality are country, regional, and global estimates. Age 5+ and total data are from table 6.4 for low- and middle-income countries. All other data are from chapter 3 of this volume.

Note: A blank cell indicates that fewer than 1,000 deaths are attributable to the specific cause. YLL used here: YLL(3,0,.54).

a. Hepatitis, tropical-cluster diseases, leprosy, dengue, Japanese encephalitis, trachoma, intestinal nematode infections, and other infectious diseases.

b. Low birthweight deaths are those resulting from intrauterine growth retardation or preterm birth. Almost all low birthweight deaths in the neonatal period result from preterm birth.

c. Epilepsy, alcohol use disorders, Alzheimer's and other dementias, Parkinson's disease, multiple sclerosis, drug use disorders, post-traumatic stress disorder, obsessive-compulsive disorder, panic disorder, insomnia (primary), migraine, mental retardation attributable to lead exposure, and other neuropsychiatric disorders.

d. Rheumatic heart disease, hypertensive heart disease, inflammatory heart diseases, and other cardiovascular diseases.

e. Other neoplasms, endocrine disorders, sense organ diseases, genitourinary diseases, skin diseases, musculoskeletal diseases, and oral conditions.

f. Poisonings, falls, fires, drownings, and other unintentional injuries.

g. Violence, war, and other intentional injuries.

Table 6B.8 The Burden of Disease—DALYs$_{SB}$(3,0,.54). Calculated to Include Stillbirths and Gradual ALP (A = .54) (thousands)

	Low- and middle-income countries						
	DALYs						
	Stillbirth			**Under age 5**			**Total DALYs$_{SB}$ (3,0,.54)**
Cause	**Antepartum**	**Intrapartum**	**Total**	**After live birth**	**Including stillbirth**	**age 5+**	
Total DALYs	10,652	9,831	20,483	276,796	297,279	963,364	1,260,643
I. Communicable, maternal, perinatal, and nutritional conditions				201,606	201,606	222,553	424,158
A. Infectious and parasitic diseases				103,064	103,064	161,226	264,291
1. Tuberculosis				1,020	1,020	34,502	35,521
2. Sexually transmitted diseases excluding HIV/AIDS				2,186	2,186	6,149	8,334
3. HIV/AIDS				6,929	6,929	60,362	67,292
4. Diarrheal diseases				27,489	27,489	5,376	32,865
5. Childhood-cluster diseases				21,653	21,653	9,031	30,684
a. Pertussis				8,846	8,846	99	8,945
b. Poliomyelitis				27	27	106	133
c. Diphtheria				86	86	28	113
d. Measles				13,294	13,294	6,121	19,416
e. Tetanus				3,626	3,626	2,677	6,302
6. Meningitis				1,898	1,898	2,695	4,593
8. Malaria				22,099	22,099	3,827	25,926
Other I.A. (7, 9–15)[a]				13,116	13,116	39,285	52,401
B. Respiratory infections				34,508	34,508	23,926	58,434
C. Maternal conditions						26,398	26,398
D. Perinatal conditions				47,202	47,202		47,202
1. Low birthweight[b]				17,624	17,624		17,624
2. Birth asphyxia and birth trauma				18,854	18,854		18,854
3. Other perinatal conditions				7,226	7,226		7,226
E. Nutritional deficiencies				16,514	16,514	11,002	27,516
II. Noncommunicable diseases				**60,277**	**60,277**	**600,044**	**660,320**
A. Malignant neoplasms				858	858	73,644	74,502
C. Diabetes mellitus				65	65	15,715	15,781
E. Neuropsychiatric disorders				19,720	19,720	116,960	136,680
1. Unipolar depressive disorders						43,444	43,444
2. Bipolar affective disorder						8,681	8,681
3. Schizophrenia				1	1	10,530	10,531
Other II.E. (4–16)[c]				19,816	19,816	54,305	74,122
G. Cardiovascular diseases				2,709	2,709	175,983	178,692
3. Ischemic heart disease				99	99	71,735	71,834
4. Cerebrovascular disease				217	217	62,326	62,543
Other II.G. (1, 2, 5, 6)[d]				1,670	1,670	41,922	43,591
H. Respiratory diseases				5,142	5,142	52,146	57,289
I. Digestive diseases				13,024	13,024	37,990	51,015
M. Congenital anomalies				14,689	14,689	1,483	16,172
Other II. (B, D, F, J, K, L, N)[e]				10,755	10,755	126,122	136,876
III. Injuries				**12,177**	**12,177**	**140,767**	**152,944**
A. Unintentional				11,901	11,901	98,684	110,586
1. Road traffic accidents				1,926	1,926	29,766	31,692
Other III.A. (2–6)[f]				10,156	10,156	68,918	79,074
B. Intentional				435	435	42,083	42,517
1. Self-inflicted				2	2	17,674	17,676
Other III.B. (2–4)[g]				457	457	24,409	24,866
IV. Not allocated	10,652	9,831	20,483	2,599	23,082		23,082

Sources: Stillbirth data are from WHO 2005a. Neonatal and perinatal mortality are country, regional, and global estimates. Age 5+ and total data are from table 6.4 for low- and middle-income countries. All other data are from chapter 3 of this volume.

Note: A blank cell indicates that fewer than 1,000 deaths are attributable to the specific cause. DALYs used here: DALYs(3,0,.54).

a. Hepatitis, tropical-cluster diseases, leprosy, dengue, Japanese encephalitis, trachoma, intestinal nematode infections, and other infectious diseases.

b. Low birthweight deaths are those resulting from intrauterine growth retardation or preterm birth. Almost all low birthweight deaths in the neonatal period result from preterm birth.

c. Epilepsy, alcohol use disorders, Alzheimer's and other dementias, Parkinson's disease, multiple sclerosis, drug use disorders, post-traumatic stress disorder, obsessive-compulsive disorder, panic disorder, insomnia (primary), migraine, mental retardation attributable to lead exposure, and other neuropsychiatric disorders.

d. Rheumatic heart disease, hypertensive heart disease, inflammatory heart diseases, and other cardiovascular diseases.

e. Other neoplasms, endocrine disorders, sense organ diseases, genitourinary diseases, skin diseases, musculoskeletal diseases, and oral conditions.

f. Poisonings, falls, fires, drownings, and other unintentional injuries.

g. Violence, war, and other intentional injuries.

| | High-income countries DALYs | | | | | | |
| | Stillbirth | | | Under age 5 | | | Total DALYs$_{SB}$ (3,0,.54) |
Cause	Antepartum	Intrapartum	Total	After live birth	Including stillbirth	age 5+	
Total DALYs	**199**	**46**	**245**	**5,713**	**5,958**	**142,358**	**148,316**
I. Communicable, maternal, perinatal, and nutritional conditions				**1,551**	**1,551**	**6,384**	**7,935**
A. Infectious and parasitic diseases				523	523	2,812	3,335
1. Tuberculosis				1	1	217	219
2. Sexually transmitted diseases excluding HIV/AIDS				12	12	132	144
3. HIV/AIDS				2	2	662	665
4. Diarrheal diseases				224	224	210	438
5. Childhood-cluster diseases				139	139	33	174
a. Pertussis				137	137	2	139
b. Poliomyelitis						8	8
c. Diphtheria							
d. Measles				2	2	20	22
e. Tetanus						5	5
6. Meningitis				36	36	81	122
8. Malaria				1	1	7	8
Other I.A. (7, 9–15)[a]				100	100	1,470	1,570
B. Respiratory infections				76	76	2,376	2,453
C. Maternal conditions						391	391
D. Perinatal conditions				842	842	4	846
1. Low birthweight[b]				299	299		300
2. Birth asphyxia and birth trauma				622	622	1	623
3. Other perinatal conditions				510	510	2	513
E. Nutritional deficiencies				110	110	801	911
II. Noncommunicable diseases				**4,132**	**4,132**	**125,127**	**129,860**
A. Malignant neoplasms				14	14	25,834	25,848
C. Diabetes mellitus				1	1	4,191	4,192
E. Neuropsychiatric disorders				953	953	30,254	31,208
1. Unipolar depressive disorders						8,408	8,408
2. Bipolar affective disorder						1,056	1,056
3. Schizophrenia						1,115	1,115
Other II.E. (4–16)[c]				939	939		20,614
G. Cardiovascular diseases				51	51	29,780	29,832
3. Ischemic heart disease				1	1	12,388	12,390
4. Cerebrovascular disease				22	22	9,344	9,366
Other II.G. (1, 2, 5, 6)[d]				46	46	8,049	8,095
H. Respiratory diseases				557	557	9,233	9,789
I. Digestive diseases				458	458	6,061	6,519
M. Congenital anomalies				903	903	228	1,132
Other II. (B, D, F, J, K, L, N)[e]				858	858	19,546	20,403
III. Injuries				**338**	**338**	**10,846**	**11,184**
A. Unintentional				315	315	7,513	7,827
1. Road traffic accidents				57	57	2,978	3,034
Other III.A. (2–6)[f]				263	263	4,535	4,798
B. Intentional				23	23	3,334	3,357
1. Self-inflicted						2,581	2,581
Other III.B. (2–4)[g]				23	23	753	776
IV. Not allocated	**10,851**	**9,877**	**20,728**		**20,728**		**20,728**

Sources: Stillbirth data are from WHO 2005a. Neonatal and perinatal mortality are country, regional, and global estimates. Age 5+ and total data are from table 6.4 for low- and middle-income countries. All other data are from chapter 3 of this volume.

Note: A blank cell indicates that fewer than 1,000 deaths are attributable to the specific cause. DALYs used here: DALYs(3,0,.54).

a. Hepatitis, tropical-cluster diseases, leprosy, dengue, Japanese encephalitis, trachoma, intestinal nematode infections, and other infectious diseases.

b. Low birthweight deaths are those resulting from intrauterine growth retardation or preterm birth. Almost all low birthweight deaths in the neonatal period result from preterm birth.

c. Epilepsy, alcohol use disorders, Alzheimer's and other dementias, Parkinson's disease, multiple sclerosis, drug use disorders, post-traumatic stress disorder, obsessive-compulsive disorder, panic disorder, insomnia (primary), migraine, mental retardation attributable to lead exposure, and other neuropsychiatric disorders.

d. Rheumatic heart disease, hypertensive heart disease, inflammatory heart disease, and other cardiovascular diseases.

e. Other neoplasms, endocrine disorders, sense organ diseases, genitourinary diseases, skin diseases, musculoskeletal diseases, and oral conditions.

f. Poisonings, falls, fires, drownings, and other unintentional injuries.

g. Violence, war, and other intentional injuries.

(Continues on the following page.)

Table 6B.8 Continued

Cause	World DALYs — Stillbirth — Antepartum	Intrapartum	Total	World DALYs — Under age 5 — After live birth	Including stillbirth	age 5+	Total DALYs$_{SB}$ (3,0,.54)
Total DALYs	**10,851**	**9,877**	**20,728**	**286,151**	**306,879**	**1,105,721**	**1,412,600**
I. Communicable, maternal, perinatal, and nutritional conditions				**202,202**	**202,202**	**228,937**	**431,139**
A. Infectious and parasitic diseases				102,633	102,633	164,039	266,671
1. Tuberculosis				1,021	1,021	34,719	35,740
2. Sexually transmitted diseases excluding HIV/AIDS				2,198	2,198	6,280	8,478
3. HIV/AIDS				6,428	6,428	61,024	67,453
4. Diarrheal diseases				30,841	30,841	5,586	36,427
5. Childhood-cluster diseases				25,076	25,076	9,064	34,140
a. Pertussis				8,983	8,983	100	9,083
b. Poliomyelitis				27	27	114	141
c. Diphtheria				86	86	28	113
d. Measles				13,297	13,297	6,141	19,438
e. Tetanus				2,674	2,674	2,681	5,356
6. Meningitis				1,939	1,939	2,776	4,715
8. Malaria				22,100	22,100	3,834	25,934
Other I.A. (7, 9–15)[a]				13,276	13,276	40,755	54,032
B. Respiratory infections				34,584	34,584	26,302	60,886
C. Maternal conditions						26,789	26,790
D. Perinatal conditions				48,044	48,044	4	48,048
1. Low birthweight[b]				21,422	21,422		21,423
2. Birth asphyxia and birth trauma				19,190	19,190	2	19,192
3. Other perinatal conditions				7,433	7,433	2	7,435
E. Nutritional deficiencies				16,623	16,623	11,803	28,426
II. Noncommunicable diseases				**71,318**	**71,318**	**725,171**	**796,489**
A. Malignant neoplasms				902	902	99,478	100,380
C. Diabetes mellitus				67	67	19,906	19,973
E. Neuropsychiatric disorders				20,673	20,673	147,214	167,887
1. Unipolar depressive disorders						51,852	51,852
2. Bipolar affective disorder						9,737	9,737
3. Schizophrenia				1	1	11,645	11,646
Other II.E. (4–16)[c]				20,777	20,777	73,981	97,757
G. Cardiovascular diseases				2,044	2,044	205,764	207,768
3. Ischemic heart disease				100	100	84,124	84,224
4. Cerebrovascular disease				223	223	71,669	71,893
Other II.G. (1, 2, 5, 6)[d]				1,716	1,716	49,970	51,686
H. Respiratory diseases				5,699	5,699	61,379	67,078
I. Digestive diseases				13,483	13,483	44,051	57,534
M. Congenital anomalies				16,578	16,578	1,712	18,290
Other II. (B, D, F, J, K, L, N)[e]				11,953	11,953	145,667	157,620
III. Injuries				**12,674**	**12,674**	**151,613**	**164,287**
A. Unintentional				12,216	12,216	106,197	118,413
1. Road traffic accidents				1,983	1,983	32,744	34,726
Other III.A. (2–6)[f]				10,420	10,420	73,453	83,874
B. Intentional				237	237	45,416	45,654
1. Self-inflicted				2	2	20,255	20,257
Other III.B. (2–4)[g]				480	480	25,161	25,642
IV. Not allocated	**10,851**	**9,877**	**20,728**		**20,728**		**20,728**

Sources: Stillbirth data are from WHO 2005a. Neonatal and perinatal mortality are country, regional, and global estimates. Age 5+ and total data are from table 6.4 for low- and middle-income countries. All other data are from chapter 3 of this volume.

Note: A blank cell indicates that fewer than 1,000 deaths are attributable to the specific cause. DALYs used here: DALYs(3,0,.54).

a. Hepatitis, tropical-cluster diseases, leprosy, dengue, Japanese encephalitis, trachoma, intestinal nematode infections, and other infectious diseases.

b. Low birthweight deaths are those resulting from intrauterine growth retardation or preterm birth. Almost all low birthweight deaths in the neonatal period result from preterm birth.

c. Epilepsy, alcohol use disorders, Alzheimer's and other dementias, Parkinson's disease, multiple sclerosis, drug use disorders, post-traumatic stress disorder, obsessive-compulsive disorder, panic disorder, insomnia (primary), migraine, mental retardation attributable to lead exposure, and other neuropsychiatric disorders.

d. Rheumatic heart disease, hypertensive heart disease, inflammatory heart diseases, and other cardiovascular diseases.

e. Other neoplasms, endocrine disorders, sense organ diseases, genitourinary diseases, skin diseases, musculoskeletal diseases, and oral conditions.

f. Poisonings, falls, fires, drownings, and other unintentional injuries.

g. Violence, war, and other intentional injuries.

ANNEX C: CAUSES OF NEONATAL MORTALITY: COMPARISON OF NUMBERS FROM THE GLOBAL BURDEN OF DISEASE WITH THOSE FROM THE CHILD HEALTH EPIDEMIOLOGY REFERENCE GROUP

This chapter has examined the consequences of incorporating stillbirths and neonatal deaths (deaths in the 28 days following live birth) into the Global Burden of Disease (GBD) framework. Methods and results of the GBD are presented elsewhere in this book and, in particular, chapter 3 discusses the estimates of deaths by age and cause for 2001 that form the basis for results throughout this book and in this chapter. Estimates of deaths from specific causes undergo continual revision as new data and syntheses become available, yet establishing a time cutoff is a necessary (if somewhat arbitrary) condition for preparing a volume with consistent estimates across chapters. For this volume, the cutoff date for the estimates of deaths by cause in 2001 was late 2003. That date was itself established in response to the need for a separate book—Jamison and others (2006)—to have a consistent set of demographic and epidemiological numbers feeding into its highly diverse chapters.

During 2001, the World Health Organization (WHO) established the Child Health Epidemiology Reference Group (CHERG) to undertake a new synthesis of data on causes of death among children under five. While some early CHERG results influenced the GBD numbers in this volume, for the most part, CHERG's work became available well after the cutoff date for this iteration of the GBD. For this reason, the 2005 WHO estimates (Bryce and others 2005; WHO 2005b) of causes of death among children under five based on CHERG (CHERG/WHO) differ to some extent from the GBD ones used in this volume. Chapter 5 further discusses the two sets of estimates for under-five deaths, and the importance of envelope and epidemiological consistency constraints in generating the GBD numbers. In terms of data sources, the GBD uses epidemiological data together with vital registration data (where available), models extrapolating from vital registration data, and epidemiological consistency checks. CHERG relies relatively more on verbal autopsy based epidemiological data for causes of child death.

The work of CHERG, however, provides a critical input to this chapter not available from the GBD work, that is, a breakdown of the causes of death specifically for the neonatal period. One of the motivations of this chapter is that neonatal deaths account for fully 37 percent of the worldwide total of deaths among children under age five. In preparing this chapter, therefore, we needed to draw fully on

the CHERG analyses of neonatal deaths while—to ensure consistency and comparability with numbers elsewhere in this volume—we use the GBD estimates of total deaths among children under five. This allows estimates of the neonatal burden to be inserted into the larger context of the GBD with its inclusion of 136 causes as well as all age groups older than age five. The specific assumptions we made to reconcile GBD and CHERG numbers are made clear in the text with table 6.4 and in the notes to table 6.4.

The CHERG/WHO results appear as percentages of deaths by one set of causes for neonates and by a mostly different set of causes for children ages 28 days to 5 years. This makes direct comparison with the GBD numbers difficult in the formats in which the two sets of numbers are presented. The difficulty is compounded by occasional differences in the labels (and content) of cause categories and by the fact that the GBD deals with far more causes than CHERG/WHO. Even the truncated GBD cause list used in this chapter uses 35 instead of 136 causes, in contrast to the 10 used by CHERG/WHO. To facilitate comparison of the two sets of findings, annex table 6C.1 uses the 6 of the 10 CHERG/WHO cause categories that are relevant to neonates to compare this chapter's and CHERG's findings for neonatal deaths. To construct table 6C.1 we took proportional allocations of deaths from CHERG/WHO presented in figure 2 of Bryce and others (2005) and applied those proportions to the estimated number of neonatal deaths (3.896 million) used in this chapter. The table is for the world as a whole.

Table 6C.1 Causes of Neonatal Mortality, Worldwide in 2001 *(thousands)*

	Neonatal deaths	
Cause	GBD	CHERG/WHO
Diarrheal disease	116	117
Tetanus[a]	187	273
Respiratory infection[b]	1,013	1,013
Low birthweight[c]	1,098	1,091
Birth asphyxia and birth trauma[d]	739	896
Congenital anomalies	321	312
Other	446	194
TOTAL	**3,896**	**3,896**

Sources: See text.

a. CHERG/WHO conclude that 7 percent (273,000) of global neonatal deaths occur due to tetanus. Chapter 3 of this volume provides an estimate for tetanus deaths for ages zero to four of only 187,000. Consistent with the objectives of this chapter, the GBD numbers are used here, and the CHERG/WHO estimates accordingly revised downward.

b. Deaths for respiratory infections in the neonatal age group are those reported by CHERG/WHO for their category sepsis or pneumonia.

c. Low birthweight deaths are those resulting from intrauterine growth retardation or preterm birth. Almost all low birthweight deaths in the neonatal period result from preterm birth.

d. Chapter 3 provides an estimate for birth asphyxia and birth trauma deaths for ages zero to four of only 739,000 globally. Consistent with the objectives of this chapter, the GBD numbers are used here, and the CHERG/WHO estimates accordingly revised downward.

ACKNOWLEDGMENTS

The authors are indebted to many individuals for valuable inputs, comments, and encouragement. The late José Luis Bobadilla encouraged us concerning the importance of this work and provided guidance to the literature on causes of death among the very young. Kenji Shibuya of WHO provided helpful inputs to an early draft. At an earlier stage of this work, Nancy Hancock and Jia Wang provided valuable inputs for which we are very grateful. Elisabeth Aahman, also of WHO, provided invaluable inputs to the estimates of stillbirth and neonatal mortality rates that this chapter draws on; we owe her particular thanks. Participants at seminars at the Harvard Center for Population and Development and at the Centers for Disease Control and Prevention provided valuable comments, and in particular we would like to thank Sevgi Aral and Lincoln Chen. The editors of this volume and two peer reviewers, Arnab Acharya and Linda Martin, provided detailed and valuable critical reaction. Robert Black provided additional important critical reaction.

NOTES

1. The term child mortality rate is sometimes used to denote what we call the under five mortality rate. We try to avoid confusion by being explicit about the age range covered.

2. Murray and Lopez (1998) and Shibuya and Murray (1998a, 1998b, 1998c) provide an earlier overall assessment of the burden from some of the major causes of neonatal mortality. Low birthweight as a risk factor is further discussed in Fishman and others (2004) and in chapter 4 of this volume.

3. Allowing the use of negative age weights could achieve some of the same effects as gradual ALP.

REFERENCES

Bhutta, Z. A., N. Ali, and A. Wajid. 2004. "Perinatal and Newborn Care in Pakistan: Seeing the Unseen!" In *Maternal and Child Health in Pakistan: Challenges and Opportunities,* ed. Zulfiqar Bhutta, 19–46. Oxford, U.K.: Oxford University Press.

Bhutta, Z. A., F. Raza, A. Hyder, Z. Memon, S. Zaidi, and S. Rasool. 2004. *Final Report: Evaluation of Community-Based Neonatal Mortality in Rural Sindh, Pakistan, Using a Verbal Autopsy Tool.* Geneva: Global Forum for Health Research, Child Health and Nutrition Research Initiative.

Black, R. E., S. S. Morris, and J. Bryce. 2003. "Where and Why Are 10 Million Children Dying Every Year?" *Lancet* 361 (9376): 2226–34.

Bryce, J., C. Boschi-Pinto, K. Shibuya, R. E. Black, and the World Health Organization Child Health Epidemiology Reference Group. 2005. "WHO Estimates of the Causes of Death in Children" *Lancet* 365 (9465): 1147–52.

Crawford, C. B., B. E. Salter, and K. L. Jang. 1989. "Human Grief: Is Its Intensity Related to the Reproductive Value of the Deceased?" *Ethology and Sociobiology* 10 (4): 297–307.

Cropper, M. L., S. L. Aydede, and P. R. Portney. 1994. "Preferences for Life Saving Programs: How the Public Discounts Time and Age." *Journal of Risk and Uncertainty* 8: 243–65.

Darmstadt, G. L., Z. A. Bhutta, S. N. Cousens, T. Adam, N. Walker, and L. de Bernis. 2005. "Evidence-Based, Cost-Effective Interventions: How Many Newborns Can We Save?" *Lancet* 365 (9463): 977–88.

Fishman, S. M., L. E. Caulfied, M. de Onis, M. Blossner, A. A. Hyder, L. Mullany, and R. E. Black. 2004. "Childhood and Maternal Underweight." In *Comparative Quantification of Health Risks: Global and Regional Burden of Disease Attributable to Selected Major Risk Factors,* vol. I, ed. Majid Ezzati, Alan D. Lopez, Anthony Rodgers, and Christopher J. L. Murray, 39–161. Geneva: World Health Organization.

Kill, K. Forthcoming. "Estimates of the Numbers of Neonatal Deaths."

Jamison, D. T., J. G. Breman, A. R. Meashan, G. Alleyne, M. Claeson, D. B. Evans, P. Jha, A. Mills, and P. Musgrove. 2006. *Disease Control Priorities in Developing Countries,* 2nd ed. New York: Oxford University Press.

Johannesson, M., and P. O. Johansson. 1997. "Is the Valuation of a QALY Gained Independent of Age? Some Empirical Evidence." *Journal of Health Economics* 16 (6): 589–99.

Institute of Medicine. 1985. *New Vaccine Development: Establishing Priorities.* Volume 1 of *Diseases of Importance in the United States.* Washington, DC: National Academies Press.

———. 2003. *Improving Birth Outcomes: Meeting the Challenge in the Developing World.* Washington, DC: National Academies Press.

Lawn, J. E., K. Wilczynska, and S. N. Cousens. Forthcoming. *Estimating the Cause of Death for 4 Million Neonates in the Year 2000.*

Lawn, J. E., S. N. Cousens, and J. Zupan. 2005. "Four Million Neonatal Deaths: When? Where? Why?" (*Lancet* Neonatal Series Paper 1.) *Lancet* 365 (9462): 891–900.

Lawn, J. E., K. Shibuya, and C. Stein. 2005. "No Cry at Birth: Global Estimates of Intrapartum Stillbirths and Intrapartum-Related Neonatal Deaths." *Bulletin of the World Health Organization* 83 (6): 409–16.

Lawn, J. E., J. Zupan, G. Begkoyian, and R. Knippenberg. 2006. "Newborn Survival." In *Disease Control Priorities in Developing Countries,* 2nd ed., ed. Dean T. Jamison, Joel G. Breman, A. R. Measham, Mariam Claeson, David B. Evans, Prabhat Jha, A. Mills, and P. Musgrove. New York: Oxford University Press.

Martines, J, V. K. Paul, Z. A. Bhutta, M. Koblinsky, A. Soucat, N. Walker, and R. Bahl. H. Foastad, A. Costello, and the Lancet Neonatal Survival Steering Team. 2005. "Neonatal Survival: A Call for Action." *Lancet* 365 (9465): 1189–97.

Murray, C. J. L., and A. D. Lopez. 1997. "Global Mortality, Disability, and the Contribution of Risk Factors: Global Burden of Disease Study." *Lancet* 349 (9063):1436–42.

———. 1998. "Quantifying the Health Risks of Sex and Reproduction: Implications of Alternative Definitions." In *Health Dimensions of Sex and Reproduction,* ed. C. J. L. Murray and A. D. Lopez, 1–17. Volume 3 of *Global Burden of Disease and Injury Series.* Cambridge, MA: Harvard University Press.

Murray, C. J. L., A. D. Lopez, and D. T. Jamison. 1994. "The Global Burden of Disease in 1990: Summary Results, Sensitivity Analysis, and Future Directions." *Bulletin of the World Health Organization* 72 (3): 495–509.

Shibuya, K., and C. J. L. Murray. 1998a. "Birth Asphyxia." In *Health Dimensions of Sex and Reproduction,* ed. C. J. L. Murray and A. D. Lopez, 429–53. Volume 3 of *Global Burden of Disease and Injury Series.* Cambridge, MA: Harvard University Press.

———. 1998b. "Congenital Anomalies." In *Health Dimensions of Sex and Reproduction,* ed. C. J. L. Murray and A. D. Lopez, 455–512. Volume 3 of *Global Burden of Disease and Injury Series.* Cambridge, MA: Harvard University Press.

———. 1998c. "Low Birth Weight." In *Health Dimensions of Sex and Reproduction,* ed. C. J. L. Murray and A. D. Lopez, 1–17. Volume 3 of

Global Burden of Disease and Injury Series. Cambridge, MA: Harvard University Press.

Stanton, C., J. E. Lawn, H. Rahman, K. Wilczynska-Ketende, and K. Hill. Forthcoming. "Born Dead: Delivering Stillbirth Rate Estimates for 190 Countries."

Steinbock, B. 1992. *Life before Birth, the Moral and Legal Status of Embryos and Fetuses.* New York: Oxford University Press.

Stoll, B. J., and A. R. Measham. 2001. "Children Can't Wait: Improving the Future for the World's Poorest Infants." *Journal of Pediatrics* 139 (5): 729–33.

Tinker, A., P. ten Hoope-Bender, S. Azfar, F. Bustreo, and R. Bell. 2005. "A Continuum of Care to Save Newborn Lives." *Lancet* 365 (9462): 822–25.

United Nations Population Division. 2003. *World Population Prospects: The 2002 Revision.* New York: United Nations.

WHO (World Health Organization). 2005a. "Neonatal and Perinatal Mortality. Country, Regional, and Global Estimates." Draft, WHO, Geneva.

———. 2005b. *World Health Report: Make Every Mother and Child Count.* Geneva: WHO.

World Bank. 1993. *World Development Report 1993: Investing in Health.* New York: Oxford University Press.

———. 2003. *World Development Indicators.* New York: Oxford University Press.

Zupan, J. 2005. "Perinatal Mortality in Developing Countries." *New England Journal of Medicine* 352 (20): 2047–48.

Glossary

Age-standardized rate An age-standardized rate is a weighted average of the age-specific rates, where the weights are the proportions of a standard population in the corresponding age groups (q.v.). The potential confounding effect of age is removed when comparing age-standardized rates computed using the same standard population.

Age weights Factor specifying the relative value of a year of healthy life lived at different ages. The DALY can incorporate non-uniform age weights which give less weight to years of life lived in early childhood and at older ages (see Chapter 5).

AIDS: Acquired Immunodeficiency Syndrome Disease due to infection with the human immunodeficiency virus (HIV).

BMI: Body mass index A measure of underweight and overweight calculated as weight (kg) divided by height squared (m^2).

Case Fatality Rate The proportion of cases of a disease or injury that die as a result of their disease or injury over a specified time period.

CHD: Coronary heart disease Synonymous with ischemic heart disease (q.v.).

Childhood-cluster diseases GBD (q.v.) cause group including the following vaccine-preventable diseases of childhood: pertussis, poliomyelitis, diphtheria, measles and tetanus.

CODMOD: Cause of death model A statistical model for the prediction of the broad distribution of causes of death based on observed historical data on the relationships between cause distributions, and overall levels of mortality and per-capita income (see Chapter 3).

Comorbidity Presence of more than one disease or health condition in an individual at a given time.

COPD: Chronic obstructive pulmonary disease Lung diseases that persistently obstruct bronchial airflow. COPD mainly involves two related diseases—chronic bronchitis and emphysema. COPD is also called chronic obstructive lung disease. Asthma is not included in COPD, as the obstruction to bronchial airflow is usually reversible and between asthma episodes the flow of air through the airways is usually good.

CVD: Cardiovascular disease Cardiovascular disease covers a wide array of disorders, including diseases of the cardiac muscle and of the vascular system supplying the heart, brain, and other vital organs. The most common manifestations of CVD are ischemic heart disease, congestive heart failure, and stroke. CVD is used here as an abbreviation for cardiovascular disease, not cerebrovascular disease (q.v.)

DALY: Disability Adjusted Life Year A measure of the gap in healthy years of life lived by a population as compared with a normative standard. More formally, DALYs are a time based measure which adds together years of life lost due to premature mortality with the equivalent number of years of life lived with disability or illness.

DFLE: Disability-free life expectancy A form of HE (q.v.) which gives a weight of 1 to states of health with no disability above an explicit or implicit threshold and a weight of 0 to states of health with any level of disability above that threshold.

DBP: Diastolic blood pressure

Demography The study of population size, growth and age structure, and of the forces (fertility, mortality, migration) that lead to population change.

Disability Restriction or lack of ability (resulting from an impairment or health condition) to perform an activity in the manner or within the range considered normal. Although the word "disability" is widely used, the ICF (q.v.) uses this term only as a broad umbrella term for capacity and performance in activity/participation domains. The GBD (q.v.) used the term disability, as in the DALY (q.v.), as a synonym for health states (q.v.) less than full health (q.v.). Disability is also commonly used to refer only to long-standing limitations in carrying out activities of daily living.

Disability weight Measure of the relative valuations of a health state on an interval scale. In the GBD (q.v.), health state valuations lie between 0 (full health q.v.) and 1 (states equivalent to death). The disability weight quantifies judgments about overall levels of health associated with different health states (q.v.), not judgments on the relative values of lives lived, persons, or of overall well-being, quality of life or utility. The GBD disability weights are intended to reflect average global valuations.

Discounting Process applied to costs, benefits, and outcomes based on the concept that there is preference for money or health in the present relative to the future.

DisMod An epidemiological disease model linking populations exposed to risk of disease with incident cases, prevalent cases, case fatality and the duration of time lived with a disease or injury, including its sequelae.

DSP Disease Surveillance Points System run by the Chinese Centre for Disease Control and Prevention for the surveillance of mortality and morbidity.

Epidemiological transition The process whereby major communicable diseases and conditions of poverty (e.g. malnutrition) are progressively replaced by non-communicable diseases such as cancers and CVD.

Epidemiology The study of the occurrence and causes of disease and injury in populations.

Full health Health state (q.v.) characterized by optimal levels of functioning or capacity in all the important domains of health, and freedom from any type of illness or disease. The "optimal" levels of functioning are defined as those levels above which further gains would not (in general) be regarded as improvements in health. States of exceptional functioning above these levels are thus considered to be talents or exceptional abilities, not higher states of health.

Garbage codes ICD codes (q.v.) for ill-defined or residual categories of major disease groups (e.g. cardiovascular diseases) that do not provide meaningful information on underlying disease or injury causes of death. Examples include ill-defined primary site of cancer and atherosclerosis.

GBD: Global burden of disease A comprehensive demographic and epidemiological framework to estimate health gaps (q.v.) for an extensive set of disease and injury causes, and for major risk factors, using all available mortality and health data and methods to ensure internal consistency and comparability of estimates. In the first global burden of disease study, Murray and Lopez estimated health gaps using DALYs (q.v.) for eight regions of the world in 1990. This book presents updated estimates for the year 2001 for the world and for World Bank regions.

Group I causes Major disease and injury cause group used in GBD (q.v.). Includes communicable, maternal, perinatal and nutritional conditions. These are causes which are characteristically common in populations who have not yet completed the epidemiological transition (q.v.).

Group II causes Major disease and injury cause group used in GBD (q.v.). Comprises non-communicable diseases, including malignant neoplasms, cardiovascular diseases, chronic respiratory diseases, digestive, musculoskeletal and genitourinary conditions, as well as mental disorders and neurological conditions.

Group III causes Major disease and injury cause group used in GBD (q.v.). Includes unintentional and intentional injuries.

HALE: Health-adjusted life expectancy Any of a number of summary measures which use explicit weights to combine health expectancies for a set of discrete health states into a single indicator of the expectation of equivalent years of good health. Also referred to as 'Healthy life expectancy'.

HE: Health expectancy Generic term for summary measures of population health which estimate the expectation of years of life lived in various health states.

Healthy life expectancy Synonym for HALE (q.v.) or Health-adjusted life expectancy.

Health state Health state refers to an individual's levels of functioning within a set of health domains such as mobility, cognition, pain, emotional functioning, self-care, etc. More specifically, in terms of ICF (q.v.) concepts, health state is defined as the capacities of an individual in all important domains of health, where such domains may include domains of body structure and function, and domains of activities/participation. Health states do not include risk factors, diseases, prognosis or the impact of health states on overall quality of life, well-being or satisfaction.

Health status A general term referring to all aspects of the health of individuals or populations. Usually understood to include mortality risks, diseases, health states (q.v.), impairments and disability. May also include some risk factors or prognosis information.

High income Category in the World Bank income grouping of countries used for countries with Gross National Income (GNI) per capita of US$9,206 or more (exchange rate adjusted currencies) in 2001. See Table 3A-3 for list of countries included.

HIV Acronym for the Human Immunodeficiency Virus, the cause of AIDS (acquired immunodeficiency syndrome).

Ideal health Synonymous with full health (q.v.).

Incidence New cases of disease or injury occurring in a specified population in a given time period.

Incidence rate New cases of disease or injury occurring per unit of population, per unit time.

ICD: International Statistical Classification of Diseases and Related Health Problems A classification of diseases and other causes of mortality prepared by the World Health

Organization since 1948, periodically revised as necessary. The current tenth revision was issued in 1992 to come into effect on 1 January 1993. The ICD is a member of the WHO family of international classifications.

ICF: International Classification of Functioning, Disability and Health A classification of body structures and functions (impairments) and activities/participation domains (performance and capacity). The ICF was endorsed by the WHO World Health Assembly in 2001 as a successor to the 1980 International Classification of Impairment, Disability and Handicap (ICIDH). The ICF is a member of the WHO family of international classifications.

IHD: Ischemic heart disease Any of a number of heart conditions in which heart muscle is damaged or works inefficiently because of an absence or relative deficiency of its blood supply; most often caused by atherosclerosis, it includes angina pectoris, acute myocardial infarction (heart attack), chronic ischemic heart disease and sudden death. The term coronary heart disease is synonymous with IHD.

Life expectancy The average number of years of life expected to be lived by individuals who survive to a specific age. See also: Period life expectancy.

Logit transformation A mathematical function that transforms a variable such as probability of death into another functional form, characterized by asymptotic values.

Low- and middle-income Category in the World Bank income grouping of countries used for countries with Gross National Income (GNI) per capita of less than US$9,206 in 2001 (exchange rate adjusted currencies). See Table 3A-3 for list of countries included.

MONICA Study The MONICA (MONItoring CArdiovascular disease) Study was an international research project coordinated by the World Health Organization from the mid-1980s to the mid-1990s in which teams from 38 populations in 21 countries studied heart disease, stroke and risk factors in their populations.

Neonatal period Persons under the age of 28 days are in the neonatal period. The neonatal period is itself divided into the early neonatal period, age less than 7 days, and the remaining late neonatal period.

PAF: population attributable fraction Proportional reduction in disease or injury that would occur if population exposure to a risk factor or group of risk factors were reduced to an alternative distribution.

Perinatal deaths Includes stillbirths and neonatal deaths from any cause, including tetanus and congenital malformations. The perinatal period includes the period from 27 weeks of gestation to 28 days of life.

Perinatal causes or conditions The cause category *Perinatal causes* refers to the ICD cause group "Conditions arising in the perinatal period". Deaths from these causes (primarily low birth weight and birth trauma/ asphyxia) may occur at any age, but are largely confined to the perinatal period.

Period life expectancy A summary measure of a population's mortality that measures the expectation of years of life lived by a fictitious birth cohort assuming that at each age the cohort experiences the age-specific mortality rates observed in the real population during a specified time period (such as a given calendar year). See also: life expectancy.

Postneonatal period Persons between the age of 28 days and 1 year are in the postneonatal period.

Prevalence Actual number of cases of disease or injury present in a population at any particular moment in time.

Probability of death The chance that an individual, alive at age x, will be dead before his or her $(x + n)^{th}$ birthday, usually written as $_nq_x$. $_5q_0$ denotes the probability that a newborn infant will die before his or her fifth birthday.

PTO: person trade-off A method for valuation of health states that asks respondents to choose between hypothetical interventions that offer health benefits to groups of individuals in different health states.

QALY: Quality-adjusted life year A measure of years of life lived (or gained through an intervention) adjusted for quality of life using health state preferences ranging between 0 (states equivalent to death) through to 1 (full health). QALYs were developed for the assessment of the cost-effectiveness of interventions in health economics. QALYs gained and DALYs averted through an intervention are calculated in very similar ways, and the main differences relate to the interpretation of the weights. Whereas the disability weights in the DALY quantify loss of health, the corresponding QALY weights are often interpreted in terms of well-being, quality of life, or utility.

Risk Factor A risk factor is an attribute or exposure which is causally associated with an increased probability of a disease or injury.

RR: Relative risk Relative risk is a measure of the strength of an association. It is calculated as a ratio of the risk of occurrence of a disease or death among two population groups, such as those exposed to a risk factor and those not exposed.

SD: Standard deviation A measure of the dispersion or spread of values of a variable (e.g. body weight) around a population mean value.

Sensitivity analysis Systematic investigation of the effects on estimates or outcomes of changes in data or parameter inputs or assumptions.

Sequelae The medical conditions that can occur among people who contract a disease or suffer an injury. The GBD (q.v.) focuses on disabling sequelae of diseases and injuries; these may remain present long after the initiating disease episode or injury event.

Standard gamble (SG) A method for valuation of health states based on the axioms of expected utility theory. The standard gamble asks respondents to make choices that weigh improvements in health against mortality risks.

Standard Population A population structure that is used to provide a constant age or covariate distribution, so that the age- and sex-specific rates within different populations can be applied to it and can be compared without confounding by the different age or covariate distributions of the populations.

STD: Sexually transmitted disease See: STI.

STI: Sexually transmitted infection An infection that can be transferred from one person to another through sexual contact. Among the sexually transmitted infections (STIs) are HIV/AIDS, chlamydia, genital herpes, gonorrhea and syphilis. The term "sexually transmitted infection (STI)" corresponds to the older term "sexually transmitted disease (STD)".

SMPH: Summary measures of population health Indicators that summarize the health of a population into a single number. SMPH combine information about mortality and population health states. They may summarize either the average health level or health inequality for a population. The two main classes of summary measures are health expectancies (q.v.) and health gap measures, of which the DALY (q.v.) is the best-known example.

Stillbirth Stillbirth refers to the birth of a dead fetus weighing more than 1,000 grams up to 0.25 years (13 weeks) prior to the expected time of birth (corresponding to 27 weeks of gestational age).

Stroke Stroke is defined as a condition that results in a disruption of blood flow to a region of the brain causing irreversible "death" of brain tissue. There are two main types of stroke: hemorrhagic and ischemic. Stroke is the main cause of mortality and burden for cerebrovascular disease (q.v.).

Sullivan's method A method of calculating health expectancies using data on the current prevalence of health states in a population together with a period life table for the population.

Theoretical-minimum-risk exposure distribution The population distribution of exposure to a risk factor that would result in the lowest population disease burden.

TTO: time trade-off A method for valuation of health states that asks respondents to make hypothetical choices that weigh improvements in health against reduced longevity.

Uncertainty analysis Estimation of range or distribution of uncertainty in estimates based on an assessment of the uncertainty or confidence intervals for all data and parameter inputs. Uncertainty intervals should ideally include all sources of uncertainty, including those arising from systematic biases and measurement error. In contrast, generally reported confidence intervals are based solely on the variation observed in sample data.

Visual analogue scale A method for valuation of health states in which respondents are asked to directly assess health levels associated with different health states. Individuals place these on a 0 to 1 scale representing a continuum from health states considered equivalent to death through to full health (q.v.)

Verbal autopsy A method of inquiry to ascertain the likely cause of death in populations where vital registration of deaths is incomplete and unreliable. Relatives of the deceased are interviewed about symptoms and signs experienced by the deceased prior to death, from which a diagnosis of the probable cause of death is made.

Vital registration A system for the registration of vital events in a population, including births and deaths, with medical certification of the cause of death according to the rules and procedures of the ICD.

YLD: Years Lived With Disability The component of the DALY (q.v.) that measures lost years of healthy life through living in health states of less than full health (q.v.).

YLL: Years of Life Lost The component of the DALY (q.v.) that measures years of life lost due to premature mortality.

Index

The index does not include the data provided in the annexes to the chapters.

Boxes, figures, and tables are indicated by b, f, and t after the page numbers.

Demographic and Health Survey (DHS)
program, 51
demographic trends of major regions
(1990–2001), 18–21, 35, 36–42t
See also mortality rates
distribution by age and location,
19–20, 22f
fertility, 20–21, 20–21t
percentage of regional population
covered by censuses, 18t
population size and growth, 19, 20t
sex ratios, 20, 23f
sources of data and methodology, 18–19
urbanization, 20
dengue, data sources on incidence and
prevalence, 80
depression
alcohol use as risk factor, 332t
child sexual abuse as risk factor, 355t
data sources for incidence and
prevalence, 82
as leading cause of disability, 7, 85
diabetes
alcohol use as risk factor, 331t
as cause of death, 69
incidence and prevalence, data sources
on, 81–82
increasing burden of, 9, 90
obesity as risk factor, 302t
physical inactivity as risk factor, 317t
diarrheal diseases
childhood underweight as risk
factor, 269t
child deaths due to, 31, 33
data sources on
deaths due to, 33, 63
incidence and prevalence, 79
deaths due to, 71, 247
unsafe water, sanitation, and hygiene as
risk factors, 353t
vitamin A deficiency as risk factor, 280t
zinc deficiency as risk factor, 287t
diphtheria, data on deaths due to, 63
disability
See also DALYs (disability-adjusted life
years); years of healthy life lost as
result of disability (YLD)
defined, 51
discounting
in DALY measure, 400, 423
variations in parameter values,
402–406, 403t, 404f, 405f,
405t, 406f
in YLL measure, 401–402, 401f, 402t
Disease Control Priorities Project, regional
reporting categories for, 94t

DisMod, use to ensure consistency in YLD
calculations, 74–75, 75f
drowning, alcohol use as risk factor, 342t
drug abuse
child sexual abuse as risk factor, 357t
data sources on
deaths due to, 64–65
incidence and prevalence, 82
as risk factor, 348–352t
drug resistance, 32

East Asia and Pacific
causes of burden of disease in, 90
DALYs by cause, sex, and age, 186–191t
deaths by cause, sex, and age, 132–137t
mortality rates in, 28
pulmonary disease in, 73
YLL and YLD rates in, 87
economic growth and health, 26–27
edentulism, data sources on incidence and
prevalence, 85
Egypt, death registration and
reporting in, 60
Ellison Institute for Global Health, 93
environmental risk factors and child
undernutrition, 254
epidemiological assessments of cause of
death, 51
epidemiological studies as data source
analysis categories by region, 107t
lack of, 92
for YLD calculations, 76
epilepsy
alcohol use as risk factor, 333t
incidence and prevalence, data sources
on, 82–83
esophageal cancer
alcohol use as risk factor, 327t
low fruit and vegetable intake as risk
factor, 308t
estimates. *See* mortality rates; sensitivity
analysis; uncertainty analysis
Europe and Central Asia
See also specific countries
CVD in, 73
DALYs by cause, sex, and
age, 192–197t
deaths by cause, sex, and
age, 138–143t
demographic structure by age, 19
disease burden in, 9, 91
injuries as cause of burden of disease
in, 91
mortality rates, trends in, 26, 27
sex ratio in, 20, 23f
YLL and YLD rates in, 87

fall-related injuries. *See* injuries
fertility trends, 20–21, 20–21t

gender differences
age weighting and discounting
for YLL, 402f
birth ratio of boys to girls, 20
burden of disease and, 88–89
causes of death, 69, 70t, 126–179t
injuries as cause of health burden,
90, 91–92
mortality rates, 26–27t
uncertainty estimates and, 410, 410f
neuropsychiatric disorders, 85
risk factors and burden of disease for
PAFs, deaths, YLL, and DALYs,
269–393t
traffic accidents, 90, 91
Global Burden of Disease and Risk Factors
(GBD). *See* World Bank
Global Burden of Disease (GBD)
framework, 1–2, 2f, 46–47

Handicap International's annual report on
landmine victims, 65
health expectancies and health
gaps, 47–48, 47f
health facility data as data source for YLD
calculations, 76, 79
health status
how to describe, 50–51
population change and, 17
hearing loss
incidence and prevalence,
data sources on, 83
as leading cause of YLD, 85, 92
heart disease. *See* cardiovascular
disease (CVD)
helminth infections, data sources on
incidence and prevalence, 80
hepatitis B
contaminated injections in health care
setting as risk factor, 367t
incidence and prevalence, data
sources on, 79
hepatitis C
contaminated injections in health care
setting as risk factor, 368t
incidence and prevalence, data sources
on, 79
high-income countries' burden of disease
comparison to low- and middle-income
countries. *See* DALYs (disability-
adjusted life years); years of healthy
life lost as result of disability (YLD)
DALYs by cause, sex, and age, 222–227t

Middle East and North Africa
   DALYs by cause, sex, and age, 204–209t
   deaths by cause, sex, and age, 150–155t
   fertility trends, 20
   injuries as cause of burden of
      disease in, 91
   mortality rates in, 28
   traffic injuries in, 73, 90, 91
migraine, data sources on incidence and
   prevalence, 83
modeling to estimate cause of death for
   countries with poor data, 66–68
Monte Carlo simulation techniques, use in
   cause of death modeling, 67
mortality rates
   See also years of life lost (YLL); *specific*
      disease or condition as cause
   cause of death models, 51
      for countries with poor data, 66–68
   causes of death, 7, 69–72, 70t
      for adults, 71–72, 71t
      for children, 28–32, 69, 71
      in low- and middle-income countries,
         126–131t
      premature death, 73, 73f
      by region, 72–73, 72t
   changes in (1990–2001), 21–28, 32–34
   characteristics by sex and region, 26, 26t
   children. *See* child mortality rates
   death registration information, 5, 22, 51,
      52, 53, 55t, 92
   distribution by major cause group, 68–69,
      68f, 69f
   epidemiological assessments of
      cause of, 51
   estimates of, 19, 21–26, 424
      differences of authors with UN data,
         23–26, 24–25f
   estimating by cause of death, 51–68
      all-cause mortality data, 51–53, 52t
      availability of data from countries, 21,
         54–56, 55t
      classification of causes of disease and
         injury, 53–54
      countries with poor data, modeling for,
         66–68
      data sources and methods for specific
         countries, 59–61, 92, 100–106t
      epidemiological estimates for specific
         causes, 61–66, 62t
      ill-defined causes and "garbage codes,"
         56–59, 57f, 57t, 58t
      risk factors and attributable mortality,
         245, 248f, 249–250t
   traffic accidents as cause of, 69, 71, 73
   trends in, 26–28, 35
   true cause not reported, 54

uncertainty estimates and
      for all-cause mortality, 409–411,
         410f, 411f
      for regions by cause, 411–413, 413f,
         414–415t
MOS (Medical Outcomes Study) Short
   Form 36, 50
mouth cancer, alcohol use as risk factor, 326t
Multiple Indicator Cluster Survey
   program, 51
multiple sclerosis, data sources on incidence
   and prevalence, 82–83

National Cancer Institute's Surveillance,
   Epidemiology, and End Results
   program, 64
neonatal conditions and deaths. *See*
   childbirth conditions; child
   mortality rates
neuropsychiatric disorders
   as cause of health burden, 3–4, 7, 85, 90
   data sources for incidence and
      prevalence, 83
newborn deaths. *See* child mortality rates
Nigeria, neonatal deaths in, 33
noncommunicable diseases
   See also specific diseases
   as cause of health burden, 3–4, 8, 8t, 9,
      89–90, 91
   incidence and prevalence, data sources
      on, 81–85
   risk factors for, 268

obesity as risk factor, 247, 299–307t
onchocerciasis, data sources on incidence
   and prevalence, 80
osteoarthritis
   incidence and prevalence, data sources
      on, 85
   obesity as risk factor, 306t

Pacific region. *See* East Asia and Pacific
PAFs. *See* population attributable fractions
Pakistan, neonatal deaths in, 33
pancreas cancer, smoking as risk factor, 381t
panic disorder, child sexual abuse as risk
   factor, 359t
Parkinson's disease, data sources on
   incidence and prevalence, 83
performance assessment and burden
   of disease as indicator, 4
perinatal conditions
   anemia as risk factor, 277t
   incidence and prevalence, data
      sources on, 81
pertussis, data on deaths due to, 63
physical inactivity as risk factor, 315–320t

pneumonia, 72, 430–431
poisonings, alcohol use as risk factor, 340t
polio, data on deaths due to, 63
population attributable fractions (PAFs),
   245, 269–393t
   uncertainty and, 422–423, 422f
population surveys as data source for YLD
   calculations, 76
population trends. *See* demographic trends
   of major regions (1990–2001)
post-traumatic stress disorder, child sexual
   abuse as risk factor, 358t
premature death, 73, 73f
pulmonary disease, 73
   air pollution as risk factor, 374t
   incidence and prevalence, data sources
      on, 84
   indoor smoke as risk factor, 364t
   smoking as risk factor, 376t

quality-adjusted life year, defined, 47

rectal cancer. *See* colon and rectal cancer
registration of deaths. *See* mortality rates
resource allocation to generate greatest
   reduction in health loss, 5
respiratory infections
   air pollution as risk factor, 372t
   childhood underweight as
      risk factor, 272t
   child deaths due to, 31, 33
   data sources on
      deaths, 63
      incidence and prevalence, 80
   indoor smoke as risk factor, 362t
   smoking as risk factor, 388t
   zinc deficiency as risk factor, 289t
rheumatoid arthritis, data sources
   on incidence and prevalence, 84–85
risk factors, 241–396
   See also Comparative Risk Assessment
      (CRA) project; *specific factors*
      (e.g., alcohol use, malnutrition)
   adult vs. childhood diseases, 268
   air pollution as, 372–375t
   alcohol use as, 325–347t
   anemia as, 276–279t
   as cause of burden of disease, 4, 5, 9–10,
      10t, 242, 247–252, 248f, 249–250t
   expanding analysis to include factors
      not among leading causes, 268
   joint effects of multiple factors,
      255–259, 256–258t
   ordering of, 247, 251–252, 251f, 255t
   as cause of death, 248f, 249–250t
   childhood underweight as, 269–275t
   child sexual abuse as, 355–361t

risk factors *(Continued)*
  cholesterol as, 296–298t
  clusters, 259–267
  contraceptives, non-use or ineffective
    use as, 391–393t
  correlation, 254
  data sources for mediated effects and
    effect modification, 253–254
  drug abuse as, 348–352t
  future research needs, 267
  GBD framework assessing, 6
  high blood pressure as, 291–295t
  indoor smoke as, 362–365t
  injections in health care setting as,
    366–371t
  joint effects of multiple factors,
    252–267, 253f
  low fruit and vegetable intake
    as, 308–314t
  obesity as, 247, 299–307t
  physical inactivity as, 315–320t
  risk assessment, defined, 242
  sanitation and hygiene as, 353–354t
  sensitivity and uncertainty
    analyses, 406–407, 407f
  smoking as, 376–390t
  theoretical-minimum-risk exposure
    distributions, 242, 243–244t,
    246–247
  uncertainty and, 420–423
  unsafe water as, 247, 353–354t
  vitamin A deficiency as, 280–286t
  zinc deficiency as, 287–290t
road accidents. *See* traffic injuries
Russian mortality rate, 26, 27, 87

sanitation and hygiene as risk
  factor, 353–354t
schistosomiasis, data sources on incidence
  and prevalence, 79–80
schizophrenia, data sources on incidence
  and prevalence, 82
sensitivity analysis, 399–407
  age weighting
    in DALY measure, 400–401, 401f, 423
    variations in parameter values,
      402–406, 402f, 403t, 404f, 405f,
      405t, 406f
    in YLL measure, 401–402, 401f, 402f
  discounting
    in DALY measure, 400, 423
    variations in parameter values,
      402–406, 403t, 404f, 405f, 405t, 406f
    in YLL measure, 401–402, 401f
  risk factors, 406–407, 407f
    variations in parameter values, 408f

sepsis and neonatal deaths, 430–431
sexual abuse. *See* child sexual abuse
  as risk factor
sexually transmitted infections
  See also HIV/AIDS
  incidence and prevalence, data
    sources on, 79
  unsafe sex as risk factor, 247, 252,
    321–324t
smoking
  burden of disease attributable to, 247
  joint hazards with other risk factors, 254
  as risk factor, 376–390t
sources of data
  criticism of GBD study based on, 423
  death by cause, 51–68
  demographic trends of major regions
    (1990–2001), 18–19
  lack of, 92–93
  uncertainty and, 408–409
  years of healthy life lost as result
    of disability (YLD), 75–79
South Asia
  See also specific countries
  communicable diseases in, 90
  DALYs by cause, sex, and age, 210–215t
  deaths by cause, sex, and age, 156–161t
  HIV/AIDS in, 72
  noncommunicable diseases in, 90
  sex ratio in, 20, 23f
  suicide in, 73
  YLL and YLD rates in, 87
statistical methods and data, use in cause of
  death modeling, 66–67
stillbirths. *See* child mortality rates
stomach cancer
  as leading cause of cancer deaths, 89
  low fruit and vegetable intake as risk
    factor, 309t
  smoking as risk factor, 382t
strategic health planning, role of, 1
stroke. *See* cerebrovascular disease
Sub-Saharan Africa
  See also specific countries
  child mortality rates in, 26, 32
  communicable diseases in, 72
  DALYs by cause, sex, and age, 216–221t
  data sources on, 92
  deaths by cause, sex, and age,
    162–167t
  fertility trends in, 20
  HIV/AIDS in, 8, 26, 33, 71, 72, 90
  malaria in, 8, 31, 72, 90
  malnutrition in, 247
  mortality rates in, 24–25, 26, 27
  traffic accidents in, 90

unsafe sex in, 247, 252
  YLL and YLD rates in, 87
suicide, 73, 90, 91
surveillance. *See* information
  and surveillance

TB. *See* tuberculosis
tetanus and neonatal deaths, 431
Thailand
  death registration and reporting in, 61
  verbal autopsy study in, 5
theoretical-minimum-risk exposure
  distributions. *See* risk factors
tobacco use. *See* smoking
trachoma, data sources on incidence and
  prevalence, 80
traffic injuries
  alcohol use as risk factor, 339t
  as cause of death, 9, 69, 71, 73
  as cause of health burden, 90, 91
tuberculosis (TB), data sources on
  deaths, 62–63
  incidence and prevalence, 79
Turkey, death registration and
  reporting in, 60–61

uncertainty analysis, 399, 408–409
  criticism of GBD study based on, 423
  cross-national comparisons and, 7, 54
  describing and quantifying uncertainty,
    409
  disability weights and, 413, 416–417, 416f,
    417f, 418–419t, 420f, 421t
  estimates
    for all-cause mortality and life
      expectancies, 409–411, 410f, 411f
    from epidemiological
      estimates, 417, 420
    for regions by cause, 411–413,
      413f, 414–415t
  PAFs and, 422–423, 422f
  risk factors and, 420–423
  sources of uncertainty, 408–409
undernutrition. *See* malnutrition
United Nations Population Division, 18–19,
  23–26, 24–25f
United Nations Programme on
  HIV/AIDS, 63
unsafe sex. *See* sexually transmitted
  infections
unsafe water as risk factor, 247, 353–354t
urbanization trends, 20
uterine cancer, obesity as risk factor, 301t

vaccine-preventable diseases
  See also specific disease

The Developing World by Region

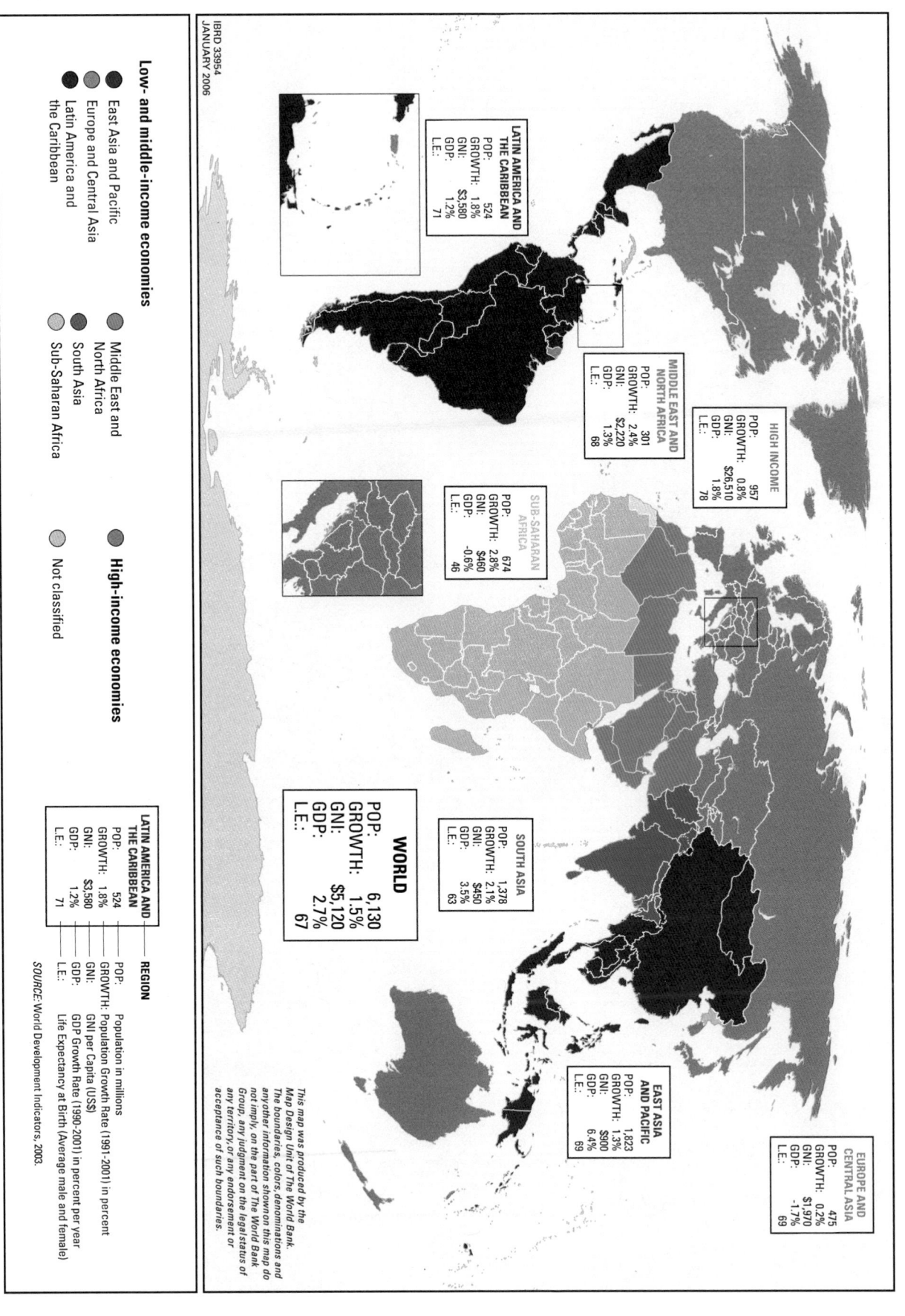

REGION

POP:	Population in millions
GROWTH:	Population Growth Rate (1991-2001) in percent
GNI:	GNI per Capita (US$)
GDP:	GDP Growth Rate (1990-2001) in percent per year
L.E.:	Life Expectancy at Birth (Average male and female)

SOURCE: World Development Indicators, 2003.

LATIN AMERICA AND THE CARIBBEAN

POP:	524
GROWTH:	1.8%
GNI:	$3,580
GDP:	1.2%
L.E.:	71

WORLD

POP:	6,130
GROWTH:	1.5%
GNI:	$5,120
GDP:	2.7%
L.E.:	67

SOUTH ASIA

POP:	1,378
GROWTH:	2.1%
GNI:	$450
GDP:	3.5%
L.E.:	63

EAST ASIA AND PACIFIC

POP:	1,823
GROWTH:	1.3%
GNI:	$900
GDP:	6.4%
L.E.:	69

EUROPE AND CENTRAL ASIA

POP:	475
GROWTH:	0.2%
GNI:	$1,970
GDP:	-1.7%
L.E.:	69

SUB-SAHARAN AFRICA

POP:	674
GROWTH:	2.8%
GNI:	$460
GDP:	-0.6%
L.E.:	46

MIDDLE EAST AND NORTH AFRICA

POP:	301
GROWTH:	2.4%
GNI:	$2,220
GDP:	1.3%
L.E.:	68

HIGH INCOME

POP:	957
GROWTH:	0.8%
GNI:	$26,510
GDP:	1.8%
L.E.:	78

LATIN AMERICA AND THE CARIBBEAN

POP:	524
GROWTH:	1.8%
GNI:	$3,580
GDP:	1.2%
L.E.:	71

Low- and middle-income economies

- East Asia and Pacific
- Europe and Central Asia
- Latin America and the Caribbean
- Middle East and North Africa
- South Asia
- Sub-Saharan Africa

High-income economies

- Not classified

This map was produced by the Map Design Unit of The World Bank. The boundaries, colors, denominations and any other information shown on this map do not imply, on the part of The World Bank Group, any judgment on the legal status of any territory, or any endorsement or acceptance of such boundaries.

IBRD 33954
JANUARY 2006

Rate of Decline in Under-Five Mortality, 1990-2001

Note: Meeting the Millenium Development Goal No.4, to reduce under-5 mortality by 2/3 between 1990 and 2015, requires an average annual rate of decline of 4.3%.

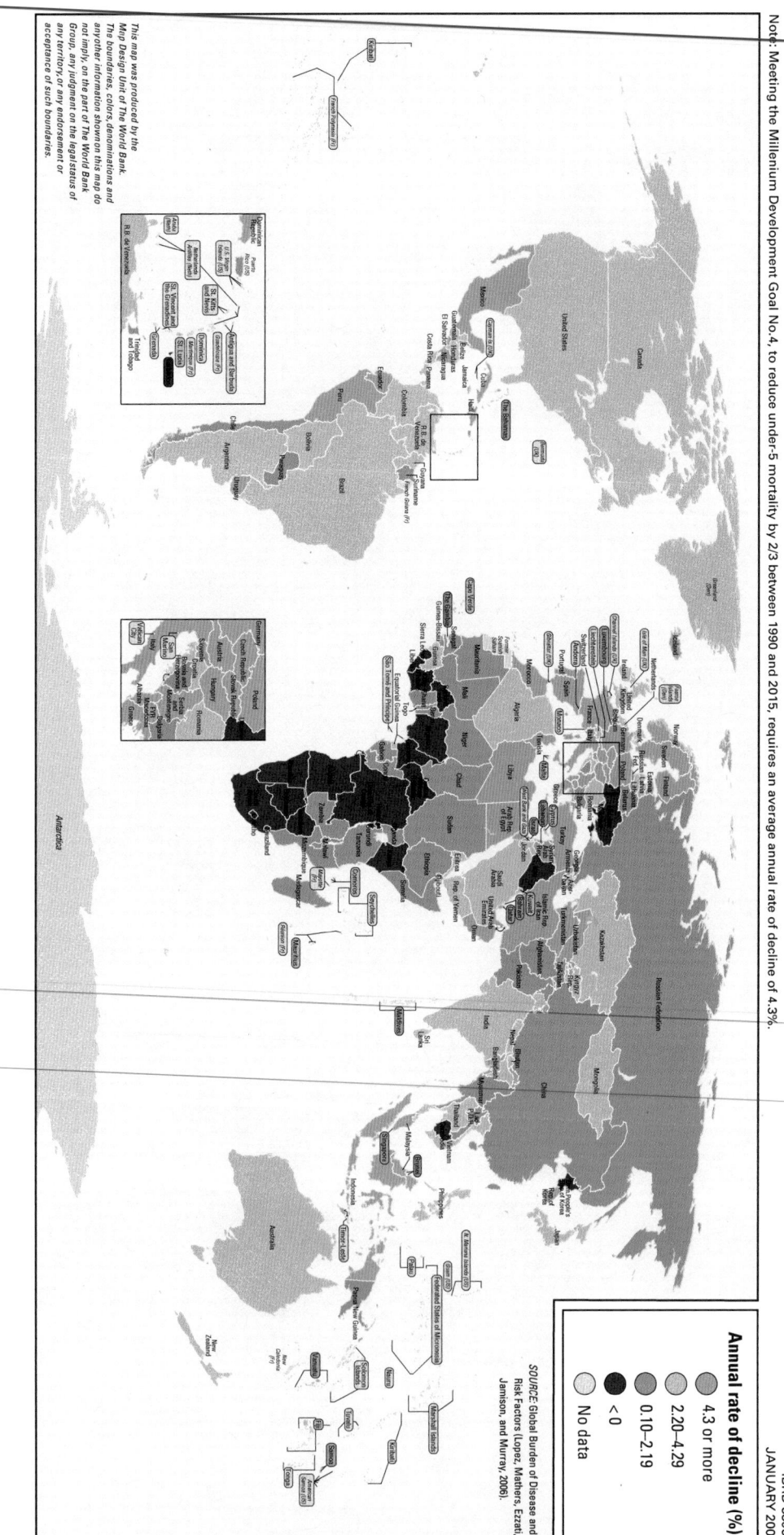

Annual rate of decline (%)

- 4.3 or more
- 2.20–4.29
- 0.10–2.19
- < 0
- No data

SOURCE: Global Burden of Disease and Risk Factors (Lopez, Mathers, Ezzati, Jamison, and Murray, 2006).

IBRD 33953
JANUARY 2006